GMAT®

11TH EDITION

REVIEW

The only study guide with 800 real GMAT® questions —and their answers— by the creators of the test.

The OFFICIAL Guide

THE OFFICIAL GUIDE FOR
GMAT® REVIEW, 11TH EDITION

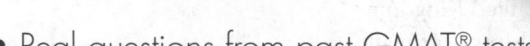

- Real questions from past GMAT® tests
- NEW diagnostic section helps you assess where to focus your test-prep efforts
- NEW organization of questions in order of difficulty saves study time

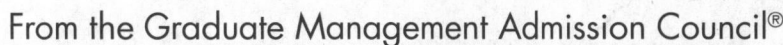

From the Graduate Management Admission Council®

BLACKWELL PUBLISHING
350 Main Street, Malden, MA 02148-5020, USA
9600 Garsington Road, Oxford OX4 2DQ , UK
550 Swanston Street, Carlton, Victoria 3053, Australia

For additional information contact:
Graduate Management Admission Council®
1600 Tysons Blvd., Ste. 1400
McLean VA 22102 USA
www.gmac.com

This eleventh edition first published 2005 by Blackwell Publishing Ltd (except in the United States where published by the Graduate Management Admission Council®)

8 2009

ISBN 978-1-4051-4176-5

A catalogue record for this title is available from the British Library.

Produced by Blanche Brann, LP, Lawrenceville, NJ
Charles Forster, Designer
Mike Wilson, Production Designer

Printed and bound in the United Kingdom
by TJ International Ltd, Padstow, Cornwall

The publisher's policy is to use permanent paper from mills that operate a sustainable forestry policy, and which has been manufactured from pulp processed using acid-free and elementary chlorine-free practices. Furthermore, the publisher ensures that the text paper and cover board used have met acceptable environmental accreditation standards.

For further information on
Blackwell Publishing, visit our website:
www.blackwellpublishing.com

Table of Contents

Dear Future Business Leader,

By using this book to prepare for the GMAT® exam, you are taking a very important step toward gaining admission to a high-quality business or management program and achieving a rewarding career in management. I applaud your decision.

The Graduate Management Admission Council® developed the GMAT® exam more than 50 years ago to help leading graduate schools of business and management choose the applicants who best suit their programs. Today, the test is used by more than 1,800 graduate programs and is given to test takers daily in more than 110 countries around the world. Programs that use GMAT® scores in selective admissions have helped establish the MBA degree as a hallmark of excellence worldwide.

Why do GMAT® scores matter so much? Other admissions factors—such as work experience, grades, admissions essays, and interviews—can say something about who you are and what you have done in your career, but only your GMAT® scores can tell schools how you are likely to perform academically in the business school courses that are fundamental to the MBA degree. In fact, the test has been proven reliable as a predictor of academic performance for more than half a century.

In other words, business schools that require you to take the GMAT® really care about the quality of their student body. And excellent MBA students mean a stronger MBA program, a more enriching learning environment, and a more valuable degree for you to take into the business world. By enrolling in a school that uses the GMAT® test for your graduate business degree, you will maximize the value of your degree, and that value will pay off in many ways, throughout your career.

I wish you great success in preparing for this important next step in your professional education, and I wish you a very rewarding management career.

Sincerely,

David A. Wilson
President and CEO
Graduate Management Admission Council®

1.0 What Is the GMAT®?

1.0 What Is the GMAT®?

The Graduate Management Admission Test® (GMAT®) is a standardized, three-part exam delivered in English. The test was designed to help admissions officers evaluate how suitable individual applicants are for their graduate business and management programs. It measures basic verbal, mathematical, and analytical writing skills that a test taker has developed over a long period of time through education and work.

The GMAT® exam does not a measure a person's knowledge of specific fields of study. Graduate business and management programs enroll people from many different undergraduate and work backgrounds, so rather than test your mastery of any particular subject area, the GMAT® exam will assess your acquired skills. Your GMAT® score will give admissions officers a statistically reliable measure of how well you are likely to perform academically in the core curriculum of a graduate business program.

Of course, there are many other qualifications that can help people succeed in business school and in their careers—for instance, job experience, leadership ability, motivation, and interpersonal skills. The GMAT® exam does not gauge these qualities. That is why your GMAT® score is intended to be used as one standard admissions criterion among other, more subjective, criteria, such as admissions essays and interviews.

1.1 Why Take the GMAT® Test?

GMAT® scores are used by admissions officers in roughly 1,800 graduate business and management programs worldwide. Schools that require prospective students to submit GMAT® scores in the application process are generally interested in admitting the best-qualified applicants for their programs, which means that you may find a more beneficial learning environment at schools that require GMAT® scores as part of your application.

Because the GMAT® test gauges skills that are important to successful study of business and management at the graduate level, your scores will give you a good indication of how well prepared you are to succeed academically in a graduate management program; how well you do on the test may also help you choose the business schools to which you apply. Furthermore, the percentile table you receive with your scores will tell you how your performance on the test compares to the performance of other test takers, giving you one way to gauge your competition for admission to business school.

Myth -vs- FACT

M – If I don't score in the 90th percentile, I won't get into any school I choose.

F – Very few people get super-high scores.

Less than 50 of the more than 200,000 people taking the GMAT® exam each year get a perfect score of 800. Thus, while you may be exceptionally capable, the odds are against your achieving a perfect score. Also, the GMAT® exam is just one piece of your application packet. Admissions officers use GMAT® scores in conjunction with undergraduate record, application essays, interviews, letters of recommendation, and other information when deciding whom to accept into their programs.

Schools consider many different aspects of an application before making an admissions decision, so even if you score well on the GMAT® exam, you should contact the schools that interest you to learn more about them and to ask about how they use GMAT® scores and other admissions criteria (such as your undergraduate grades, essays, and letters of recommendation) to evaluate candidates for admission. School admissions offices, school Web sites, and materials published by the school are the best sources for you to tap when you are doing research about where you might want to go to business school.

For more information about how schools should use GMAT® scores in admissions decisions, please read the Appendix A of this book. For more information on the GMAT®, registering to take the test, sending your scores to schools, and applying to business school, please visit our Web site at www.mba.com.

1.2 GMAT® Test Format

The GMAT® exam consists of four separately timed sections (see the table on the next page). You start the test with two 30-minute Analytical Writing Assessment (AWA) questions that require you to type your responses using the computer keyboard. The writing section is followed by two 75-minute, multiple-choice sections: the Quantitative and Verbal sections of the test.

The GMAT® is a computer-adaptive test (CAT), which means that in the multiple-choice sections of the test, the computer constantly gauges how well you are doing on the test and presents you with questions that are appropriate to your ability level. These questions are drawn from a huge pool of possible test questions. So, although we talk about the GMAT® as one test, the GMAT® exam you take may be completely different from the test the person sitting next to you.

Here's how it works. At the start of each GMAT® multiple-choice section (Verbal and Quantitative), you will be presented with a question of moderate difficulty. The computer uses your response to that first question to determine which question to present next. If you respond correctly, the test usually will give you questions of increasing difficulty. If you respond incorrectly, the next question you see usually will be easier than the one you answered incorrectly. As you continue to respond to the questions presented, the computer will narrow your score to the number that best characterizes your ability. When you complete each section, the computer will have an accurate assessment of your ability.

Myth -vs- FACT

M – Getting an easier question means I answered the last one wrong.

F – Getting an easier question does not necessarily mean you got the previous question wrong.

To ensure that everyone receives the same content, the test selects a specific number of questions of each type. The test may call for your next question to be a relatively hard problem solving item involving arithmetic operations. But, if there are no more relatively difficult problem solving items involving arithmetic, you might be given an easier item.

Most people are not skilled at estimating item difficulty, so don't worry when taking the test or waste valuable time trying to determine the difficulty of the questions you are answering.

Because each question is presented on the basis of your answers to all previous questions, you must answer each question as it appears. You may not skip, return to, or change your responses to previous questions. Random guessing can significantly lower your scores. If you do not know the answer to a question, you should try to eliminate as many choices as possible, then select the answer you think is best. If you answer a question incorrectly by mistake—or correctly by lucky guess—your answers to subsequent questions will lead you back to questions that are at the appropriate level of difficulty for you.

Each multiple-choice question used in the GMAT® exam has been thoroughly reviewed by professional test developers. New multiple-choice questions are tested each time the exam is administered. Answers to trial questions are not counted in the scoring of your test, but the trial questions are not identified and could appear anywhere in the test. Therefore, you should try to do your best on every question.

The test includes the types of questions found in this *Guide*, but the format and presentation of the questions are different on the computer. When you take the exam:

- Only one question at a time is presented on the computer screen.
- The answer choices for the multiple-choice questions will be preceded by circles, rather than by letters.
- Different question types appear in random order in the multiple-choice sections of the test.
- You must select your answer using the computer.
- You must choose an answer and confirm your choice before moving on to the next question.
- You may not go back to change answers to previous questions.

Format of the GMAT®

	Questions	Timing
Analytical Writing Analysis of an Issue Analysis of an Argument	 1 1	 30 min. 30 min.
Optional break		5 min.
Quantitative Problem Solving Data Sufficiency	37	75 min.
Optional break		5 min.
Verbal Reading Comprehension Critical Reasoning Sentence Correction	41	75 min.
	Total Time:	210–220 min.

1.3 What Is the Content of the Test Like?

It is important to recognize that the GMAT® test evaluates skills and abilities developed over a relatively long period of time. Although the sections contain questions that are basically verbal and mathematical, the complete test provides one method of measuring overall ability.

Keep in mind that although the questions in this *Guide* are arranged by question type and ordered from easy to difficult, the test is organized differently. When you take the test, you may see different types of questions in any order.

1.4 Quantitative Section

The GMAT® Quantitative section measures your ability to reason quantitatively, solve quantitative problems, and interpret graphic data.

Two types of multiple-choice questions are used in the Quantitative section:

- Problem solving
- Data sufficiency

Problem solving and data sufficiency questions are intermingled throughout the Quantitative section. Both types of questions require basic knowledge of:

- Arithmetic
- Elementary algebra
- Commonly known concepts of geometry

To review the basic mathematical concepts that will be tested in the GMAT® Quantitative questions, see the math review in chapter 4. For test-taking tips specific to the question types in the Quantitative section of the GMAT® exam, sample questions, and answer explanations, see chapters 5 and 6.

1.5 Verbal Section

The GMAT® Verbal section measures your ability to read and comprehend written material, to reason and evaluate arguments, and to correct written material to conform to standard written English. Because the Verbal section includes reading sections from several different content areas, you may be generally familiar with some of the material; however, neither the reading passages nor the questions assume detailed knowledge of the topics discussed.

Three types of multiple-choice questions are used in the Verbal section:

- Reading comprehension
- Critical reasoning
- Sentence correction

These question types are intermingled throughout the Verbal section.

For test-taking tips specific to each question type in the Verbal section, sample questions, and answer explanations, see chapters 7 through 10.

1.6 What Computer Skills Will I Need?

You only need minimal computer skills to take the GMAT® Computer-Adaptive Test (CAT). You will be required to type your essays on the computer keyboard using standard word–processing keystrokes. In the multiple-choice sections, you will select your responses using either your mouse or the keyboard.

To learn more about the specific skills required to take the GMAT CAT®, download the free test-preparation software available at www.mba.com.

1.7 What Are The Test Centers Like?

The GMAT® test is administered at a test center providing the quiet and privacy of individual computer workstations. You will have the opportunity to take two five-minute breaks—one after completing the essays and another between the Quantitative and Verbal sections. An erasable notepad will be provided for your use during the test.

1.8 How Are Scores Calculated?

Your GMAT® scores are determined by:

- the number of questions you answer
- whether you answer correctly or incorrectly
- the level of difficulty and other statistical characteristics of each question

Your Verbal, Quantitative, and Total GMAT® scores are determined by a complex mathematical procedure that takes into account the difficulty of the questions that were presented to you and how you answered them. When you answer the easier questions correctly, you get a chance to answer harder questions—making it possible to earn a higher score. After you have completed all the questions on the test—or when your time is up—the computer will calculate your scores. Your scores on the Verbal and Quantitative sections are combined to produce your Total score. If you have not responded to all the questions in a section (37 Quantitative questions or 41 Verbal questions), your score is adjusted, using the proportion of questions answered.

Appendix A contains the 2005 percentile ranking tables that explain how your GMAT® scores compare with scores of other 2005 GMAT® test takers.

1.9 Analytical Writing Assessment Scores

The Analytical Writing Assessment consists of two writing tasks: Analysis of an Issue and Analysis of an Argument. The responses to each of these tasks are scored on a 6-point scale, with 6 being the highest score and 1, the lowest. A score of zero (0) is given to responses that are off-topic, are in a foreign language, merely attempt to copy the topic, consist only of keystroke characters, or are blank.

The readers who evaluate the responses are college and university faculty members from various subject matter areas, including management education. These readers read holistically—that is, they respond to the overall quality of your critical thinking and writing. (For details on how readers are qualified, visit www.mba.com.) In addition, responses may be scored by an automated scoring program designed to reflect the judgment of expert readers.

Each response is given two independent ratings. If the ratings differ by more than a point, a third reader adjudicates. (Because of ongoing training and monitoring, discrepant ratings are rare.)

Your final score is the average (rounded to the nearest half point) of the four scores independently assigned to your responses—two scores for the Analysis of an Issue and two for the Analysis of an Argument. For example, if you earned scores of 6 and 5 on the Analysis of an Issue and 4 and 4 on the Analysis of an Argument, your final score would be 5: $(6 + 5 + 4 + 4) \div 4 = 4.75$, which rounds up to 5.

Your Analytical Writing Assessment scores are computed and reported separately from the multiple-choice sections of the test and have no effect on your Verbal, Quantitative, or Total scores. The schools that you have designated to receive your scores may receive your responses to the Analytical Writing Assessment with your score report. Your own copy of your score report will not include copies of your responses.

1.10 Test Development Process

The GMAT® exam is developed by experts who use standardized procedures to ensure high-quality, widely appropriate test material. All questions are subjected to independent reviews and are revised or discarded as necessary. Multiple-choice questions are tested during GMAT® test administrations. Analytical Writing Assessment tasks are tried out on first-year business school students and then assessed for their fairness and reliability. For more information on test development, see www.mba.com.

2.0 How To Prepare

2.0 How To Prepare

2.1 How Can I Best Prepare to Take the Test?

We at the Graduate Management Admission Council® (GMAC®) firmly believe that the test-taking skills you can develop by using this *Guide*—and the Verbal and Quantitative *Guides*, if you want additional practice—are all you need to perform your best when you take the GMAT® test. By answering questions that have appeared on the GMAT® exam before, you will gain experience with the types of questions you may see on the test when you take it. As you practice with this *Guide*, you will develop confidence in your ability to reason through the test questions. No additional techniques or strategies are needed to do well on the standardized test if you develop a practical familiarity with the abilities it requires. Simply by practicing and understanding the concepts that are assessed on the exam, you will learn what you need to know to answer the questions correctly.

2.2 What About Practice Tests?

Because a computer-adaptive test cannot be presented in paper form, we have created GMATPrep® software to help you prepare for the exam. The software is available for download at no charge for those who have created a user profile on www.mba.com. It is also provided on a disk, by request, to anyone who has registered for the GMAT® test. The software includes two practice GMAT® tests plus additional practice questions, information about the test, and tutorials to help you become familiar with how the GMAT® test will appear on the computer screen at the test center.

We recommend that you download the software as you start to prepare for the exam. Take one practice test to better familiarize yourself with the test and to get an idea of how you might score. After you have studied using this book, and as your test date approaches, take the second practice test to determine whether you need to shift your focus to other areas you need to strengthen.

Myth -vs- FACT

M – You need very advanced math skills to get a high GMAT® score.

F – The math skills tested on the GMAT® test are quite basic.

The GMAT® exam only requires basic quantitative analytic skills. You should review the underlying math skills (algebra, geometry, basic arithmetic) presented in this book, but the required skill level is low. The difficulty of GMAT® Quantitative questions stems from the logic and analysis used to solve the problems and not the underlying math skills.

If you complete all the questions in this *Guide* and think you would like additional practice, you may purchase *The Official Guide for GMAT® Verbal Review* or *The Official Guide for GMAT® Quantitative Review* at www.mba.com.

Note: There may be some overlap between this book and the review sections of the GMATPrep® software.

2.3 How Should I Use the Diagnostic Test?

This book contains a Diagnostic Test to help you determine the types of questions that you need to practice most. You should take the Diagnostic Test around the same time that you take the first electronic sample test (using the test-preparation software). The Diagnostic Test will give you a rating—*below average, average, above average,* or *excellent*—of your skills in each type of GMAT® test question. These ratings will help you identify areas to focus on as you prepare for the GMAT® exam.

Use the results of the Diagnostic Test to help you select the right chapter of this book to start with. Next, read the introductory material carefully, and answer the sample questions in that chapter. Make sure you follow the directions for each type of question and try to work as quickly and as efficiently as possible. Then review the explanations for the correct answers, spending as much time as necessary to familiarize yourself with the range of questions or problems presented.

2.4 Where Can I Get Additional Practice?

If you find you would like additional practice with the Verbal section of the test, *The Official Guide for GMAT® Verbal Review* is available for purchase at www.mba.com. If you want more practice with the Quantitative section, *The Official Guide for GMAT® Quantitative Review* is also available for purchase at www.mba.com.

2.5 General Test-Taking Suggestions

Specific test-taking strategies for individual question types are presented later in this book. The following are general suggestions to help you perform your best on the test.

Use your time wisely.

Although the GMAT® exam stresses accuracy more than speed, it is important to use your time wisely. On average, you will have about 1¾ minutes for each verbal question and about 2 minutes for each quantitative question. Once you start the test, an onscreen clock will continuously count the time you have left. You can hide this display if you want, but it is a good idea to check the clock periodically to monitor your progress. The clock will automatically alert you when five minutes remain in the allotted time for the section you are working on.

Answer practice questions ahead of time.

After you become generally familiar with all question types, use the sample questions in this book to prepare for the actual test. It may be useful to time yourself as you answer the practice questions to get an idea of how long you will have for each question during the actual GMAT® test as well as to determine whether you are answering quickly enough to complete the test in the time allotted.

Read all test directions carefully.

The directions explain exactly what is required to answer each question type. If you read hastily, you may miss important instructions and lower your scores. To review directions during the test, click on the Help icon. But be aware that the time you spend reviewing directions will count against the time allotted for that section of the test.

Read each question carefully and thoroughly.
Before you answer a multiple-choice question, determine exactly what is being asked, then eliminate the wrong answers and select the best choice. Never skim a question or the possible answers; skimming may cause you to miss important information or nuances.

Do not spend too much time on any one question.
If you do not know the correct answer, or if the question is too time-consuming, try to eliminate choices you know are wrong, select the best of the remaining answer choices, and move on to the next question. Try not to worry about the impact on your score—guessing may lower your score, but not finishing the section will lower your score more.

Bear in mind that if you do not finish a section in the allotted time, you will still receive a score.

> **Myth -vs- FACT**
>
> **M - It is more important to respond correctly to the test questions than it is to finish the test.**
>
> **F - There is a severe penalty for not completing the GMAT® test.**
>
> If you are stumped by a question, give it your best guess and move on. If you guess incorrectly, the computer program will likely give you an easier question, which you are likely to answer correctly, and the computer will rapidly return to giving you questions matched to your ability. If you don't finish the test, your score will be reduced greatly. Failing to answer five verbal questions, for example, could reduce a person's score from the 91st percentile to the 77th percentile. Pacing is important.

Confirm your answers ONLY when you are ready to move on.
Once you have selected your answer to a multiple-choice question, you will be asked to confirm it. Once you confirm your response, you cannot go back and change it. You may not skip questions, because the computer selects each question on the basis of your responses to preceding questions.

Plan your essay answers before you begin to write.
The best way to approach the two writing tasks that comprise the Analytical Writing Assessment is to read the directions carefully, take a few minutes to think about the question, and plan a response before you begin writing. Take care to organize your ideas and develop them fully, but leave time to reread your response and make any revisions that you think would improve it.

> **Myth -vs- FACT**
>
> **M - The first 10 questions are critical and you should invest the most time on those.**
>
> **F - All questions count.**
>
> It is true that the computer-adaptive testing algorithm uses the first 10 questions to obtain an initial estimate of your ability; however, that is only an *initial* estimate. As you continue to answer questions, the algorithm self-corrects by computing an updated estimate on the basis of all the questions you have taken, and then administers items that are closely matched to this new estimate of your ability. Your final score is based on all your responses and considers the difficulty of all the questions you answered. Taking additional time on the first 10 questions will not game the system and can hurt your ability to finish the test.

3.0 Diagnostic Test

3.0 Diagnostic Test

Like the practice sections later in the book, the Diagnostic Test uses questions from real GMAT® tests. The purpose of the Diagnostic Test is to help you determine how skilled you are in answering each of the five types of questions on the GMAT® exam: data sufficiency, problem solving, reading comprehension, critical reasoning, and sentence correction.

Scores on the Diagnostic Test are designed to help you answer the question, "If all the questions on the GMAT® exam were like the questions in this section, how well would I do?" Your scores are classified as being *excellent, above average, average,* or *below average,* relative to the scores of other test takers. You can use this information to focus your test-preparation activities.

Instructions

1. Take your time answering these questions. The Diagnostic Test is not timed.
2. If you are stumped by a question, you should guess and move on, just like you should do on the real GMAT® exam.
3. You can take one test at a time, if you want. It is better to finish an entire section (Quantitative or Verbal) in one sitting, but this is not a requirement.
4. You can go back and change your answers in the Diagnostic Test.
5. After you take the test, check your answers using the answer key that follows the test. The number of correct answers is your raw score.
6. Convert your raw score, using the table provided.

Note: The Diagnostic Test is designed to give you guidance on how to prepare for the GMAT® exam; however, a strong score on one type of question does not guarantee that you will perform as well on the real GMAT® exam. The statistical reliability of scores on the Diagnostic Test ranges from 0.75 to 0.89, and the subscale classification is about 85%–90% accurate, meaning that your scores on the Diagnostic Test are a good, but not perfect, measure of how you are likely to perform on the real test. Use the tests on the free online software to obtain a good estimate of your expected GMAT® Verbal, Quantitative, and Total Scores.

You should not compare the number of questions you got right in each section. Instead, you should compare how your responses rated in each section.

3.1 Diagnostic Test—Quantitative Sample Questions

Problem Solving

Solve the problem and indicate the best of the answer choices given.
Numbers: All numbers used are real numbers.
Figures: All figures accompanying problem solving questions are intended to provide information useful in solving the problems. Figures are drawn as accurately as possible EXCEPT when it is stated in a specific problem that its figure is not drawn to scale. Straight lines may sometimes appear jagged. All figures lie in a plane unless otherwise indicated.

1. Last month a certain music club offered a discount to preferred customers. After the first compact disc purchased, preferred customers paid \$3.99 for each additional compact disc purchased. If a preferred customer purchased a total of 6 compact discs and paid \$15.95 for the first compact disc, then the dollar amount that the customer paid for the 6 compact discs is equivalent to which of the following?

(A) 5(4.00) + 15.90
(B) 5(4.00) + 15.95
(C) 5(4.00) + 16.00
(D) 5(4.00 – 0.01) + 15.90
(E) 5(4.00 – 0.05) + 15.95

2. The average (arithmetic mean) of the integers from 200 to 400, inclusive, is how much greater than the average of the integers from 50 to 100, inclusive?

(A) 150
(B) 175
(C) 200
(D) 225
(E) 300

3. The sequence $a_1, a_2, a_3, \ldots, a_n, \ldots$ is such that $a_n = \dfrac{a_{n-1} + a_{n-2}}{2}$ for all $n \geq 3$. If $a_3 = 4$ and $a_5 = 20$, what is the value of a_6?

(A) 12
(B) 16
(C) 20
(D) 24
(E) 28

4. Among a group of 2,500 people, 35 percent invest in municipal bonds, 18 percent invest in oil stocks, and 7 percent invest in both municipal bonds and oil stocks. If 1 person is to be randomly selected from the 2,500 people, what is the probability that the person selected will be one who invests in municipal bonds but NOT in oil stocks?

(A) $\frac{9}{50}$
(B) $\frac{7}{25}$
(C) $\frac{7}{20}$
(D) $\frac{21}{50}$
(E) $\frac{27}{50}$

5. A closed cylindrical tank contains 36π cubic feet of water and is filled to half its capacity. When the tank is placed upright on its circular base on level ground, the height of the water in the tank is 4 feet. When the tank is placed on its side on level ground, what is the height, in feet, of the surface of the water above the ground?

(A) 2
(B) 3
(C) 4
(D) 6
(E) 9

6. A marketing firm determined that, of 200 households surveyed, 80 used neither Brand A nor Brand B soap, 60 used only Brand A soap, and for every household that used both brands of soap, 3 used only Brand B soap. How many of the 200 households surveyed used both brands of soap?

(A) 15
(B) 20
(C) 30
(D) 40
(E) 45

7. A certain club has 10 members, including Harry. One of the 10 members is to be chosen at random to be the president, one of the remaining 9 members is to be chosen at random to be the secretary, and one of the remaining 8 members is to be chosen at random to be the treasurer. What is the probability that Harry will be either the member chosen to be the secretary or the member chosen to be the treasurer?

(A) $\frac{1}{720}$
(B) $\frac{1}{80}$
(C) $\frac{1}{10}$
(D) $\frac{1}{9}$
(E) $\frac{1}{5}$

8. If a certain toy store's revenue in November was $\frac{2}{5}$ of its revenue in December and its revenue in January was $\frac{1}{4}$ of its revenue in November, then the store's revenue in December was how many times the average (arithmetic mean) of its revenues in November and January?

(A) $\frac{1}{4}$
(B) $\frac{1}{2}$
(C) $\frac{2}{3}$
(D) 2
(E) 4

9. A researcher computed the mean, the median, and the standard deviation for a set of performance scores. If 5 were to be added to each score, which of these three statistics would change?

(A) The mean only
(B) The median only
(C) The standard deviation only
(D) The mean and the median
(E) The mean and the standard deviation

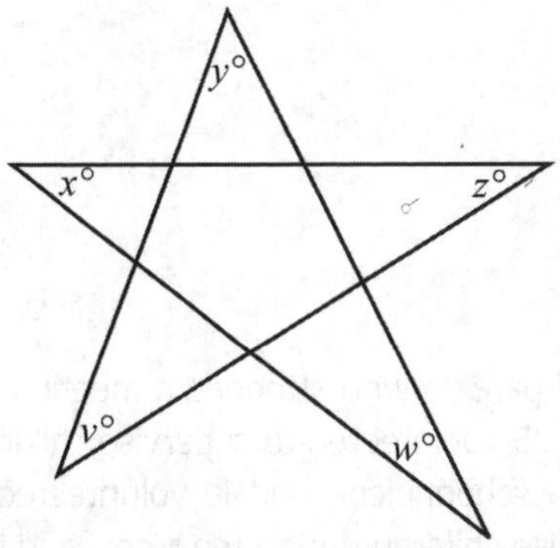

10. In the figure shown, what is the value of $v + x + y + z + w$?

(A) 45
(B) 90
(C) 180
(D) 270
(E) 360

11. Of the three-digit integers greater than 700, how many have two digits that are equal to each other and the remaining digit different from the other two?

(A) 90
(B) 82
(C) 80
(D) 45
(E) 36

12. Positive integer *y* is 50 percent of 50 percent of positive integer *x*, and *y* percent of *x* equals 100. What is the value of *x*?

(A) 50
(B) 100
(C) 200
(D) 1,000
(E) 2,000

13. If *s* and *t* are positive integers such that $\frac{s}{t} = 64.12$, which of the following could be the remainder when *s* is divided by *t*?

(A) 2
(B) 4
(C) 8
(D) 20
(E) 45

14. Of the 84 parents who attended a meeting at a school, 35 volunteered to supervise children during the school picnic and 11 volunteered both to supervise children during the picnic and to bring refreshments to the picnic. If the number of parents who volunteered to bring refreshments was 1.5 times the number of parents who neither volunteered to supervise children during the picnic nor volunteered to bring refreshments, how many of the parents volunteered to bring refreshments?

(A) 25
(B) 36
(C) 38
(D) 42
(E) 45

15. The product of all the prime numbers less than 20 is closest to which of the following powers of 10?

(A) 10^9
(B) 10^8
(C) 10^7
(D) 10^6
(E) 10^5

16. If $\sqrt{3-2x} = \sqrt{2x} + 1$, then $4x^2 =$

(A) 1
(B) 4
(C) $2 - 2x$
(D) $4x - 2$
(E) $6x - 1$

17. If $n = \sqrt{\frac{16}{81}}$, what is the value of $\sqrt{n}$?

(A) $\frac{1}{9}$
(B) $\frac{1}{4}$
(C) $\frac{4}{9}$
(D) $\frac{2}{3}$
(E) $\frac{9}{2}$

18. If *n* is the product of the integers from 1 to 8, inclusive, how many different prime factors greater than 1 does *n* have?

(A) Four
(B) Five
(C) Six
(D) Seven
(E) Eight

19. If *k* is an integer and $2 < k < 7$, for how many different values of *k* is there a triangle with sides of lengths 2, 7, and *k*?

(A) One
(B) Two
(C) Three
(D) Four
(E) Five

20. A right circular cone is inscribed in a hemisphere so that the base of the cone coincides with the base of the hemisphere. What is the ratio of the height of the cone to the radius of the hemisphere?

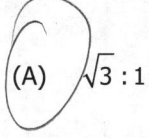

(A) $\sqrt{3}:1$

(B) $1:1$

(C) $\frac{1}{2}:1$

(D) $\sqrt{2}:1$

(E) $2:1$

21. John deposited $10,000 to open a new savings account that earned 4 percent annual interest, compounded quarterly. If there were no other transactions in the account, what was the amount of money in John's account 6 months after the account was opened?

(A) $10,100
(B) $10,101
(C) $10,200
(D) $10,201
(E) $10,400

22. A container in the shape of a right circular cylinder is $\frac{1}{2}$ full of water. If the volume of water in the container is 36 cubic inches and the height of the container is 9 inches, what is the diameter of the base of the cylinder, in inches?

(A) $\frac{16}{9\pi}$

(B) $\frac{4}{\sqrt{\pi}}$

(C) $\frac{12}{\sqrt{\pi}}$

(D) $\sqrt{\frac{2}{\pi}}$

(E) $4\sqrt{\frac{2}{\pi}}$

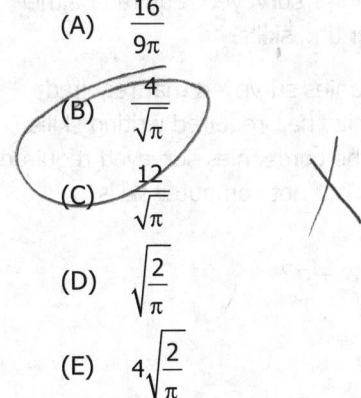

23. If the positive integer x is a multiple of 4 and the positive integer y is a multiple of 6, then xy must be a multiple of which of the following?

I. 8
II. 12
III. 18

(A) II only
(B) I and II only
(C) I and III only
(D) II and III only
(E) I, II, and III

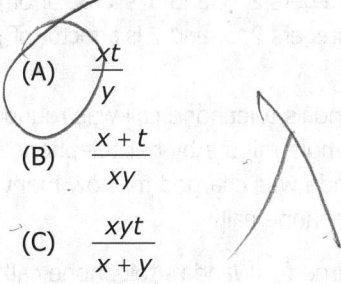

24. Aaron will jog from home at x miles per hour and then walk back home by the same route at y miles per hour. How many miles from home can Aaron jog so that he spends a total of t hours jogging and walking?

(A) $\frac{xt}{y}$

(B) $\frac{x+t}{xy}$

(C) $\frac{xyt}{x+y}$

(D) $\frac{x+y+t}{xy}$

(E) $\frac{y+t}{x}-\frac{t}{y}$

Data Sufficiency

A Statement (1) ALONE is sufficient, but statement (2) alone is not sufficient.
B Statement (2) ALONE is sufficient, but statement (1) alone is not sufficient.
C BOTH statements TOGETHER are sufficient, but NEITHER statement ALONE is sufficient.
D EACH statement ALONE is sufficient.
E Statements (1) and (2) TOGETHER are NOT sufficient.

25. If the units digit of integer n is greater than 2, what is the units digit of n?

    (1) The units digit of n is the same as the units digit of n^2.
    (2) The units digit of n is the same as the units digit of n^3.

26. What is the value of the integer p?

    (1) Each of the integers 2, 3, and 5 is a factor of p.
    (2) Each of the integers 2, 5, and 7 is a factor of p.

27. If the length of Wanda's telephone call was rounded up to the nearest whole minute by her telephone company, then Wanda was charged for how many minutes for her telephone call?

    (1) The total charge for Wanda's telephone call was $6.50.
    (2) Wanda was charged $0.50 more for the first minute of the telephone call than for each minute after the first.

28. What is the perimeter of isosceles triangle MNP?

    (1) $MN = 16$
    (2) $NP = 20$

29. In a survey of retailers, what percent had purchased computers for business purposes?

    (1) 85 percent of the retailers surveyed who owned their own store had purchased computers for business purposes.
    (2) 40 percent of the retailers surveyed owned their own store.

30. The only gift certificates that a certain store sold yesterday were worth either $100 each or $10 each. If the store sold a total of 20 gift certificates yesterday, how many gift certificates worth $10 each did the store sell yesterday?

    (1) The gift certificates sold by the store yesterday were worth a total of between $1,650 and $1,800.
    (2) Yesterday the store sold more than 15 gift certificates worth $100 each.

31. Is the standard deviation of the set of measurements $x_1, x_2, x_3, x_4, \ldots, x_{20}$ less than 3?

    (1) The variance for the set of measurements is 4.
    (2) For each measurement, the difference between the mean and that measurement is 2.

32. Is the range of the integers 6, 3, y, 4, 5, and x greater than 9?

    (1) $y > 3x$
    (2) $y > x > 3$

33. Is $\frac{5^{x+2}}{25} < 1$?

    (1) $5^x < 1$
    (2) $x < 0$

34. Of the companies surveyed about the skills they required in prospective employees, 20 percent required both computer skills and writing skills. What percent of the companies surveyed required neither computer skills nor writing skills?

    (1) Of those companies surveyed that required computer skills, half required writing skills.
    (2) 45 percent of the companies surveyed required writing skills but not computer skills.

35. What is the value of $w + q$?

    (1) $3w = 3 - 3q$
    (2) $5w + 5q = 5$

36. If X and Y are points in a plane and X lies inside the circle C with center O and radius 2, does Y lie inside circle C?

(1) The length of line segment XY is 3.
(2) The length of line segment OY is 1.5.

37. Is $x > y$?

(1) $x = y + 2$
(2) $\frac{x}{2} = y - 1$

38. If Paula drove the distance from her home to her college at an average speed that was greater than 70 kilometers per hour, did it take her less than 3 hours to drive this distance?

(1) The distance that Paula drove from her home to her college was greater than 200 kilometers.
(2) The distance that Paula drove from her home to her college was less than 205 kilometers.

39. In the xy-plane, if line k has negative slope and passes through the point $(-5, r)$, is the x-intercept of line k positive?

(1) The slope of line k is -5.
(2) $r > 0$

40. If \$5,000 invested for one year at p percent simple annual interest yields \$500, what amount must be invested at k percent simple annual interest for one year to yield the same number of dollars?

(1) $k = 0.8p$
(2) $k = 8$

41. If $\frac{x + y}{z} > 0$, is $x < 0$?

(1) $x < y$
(2) $z < 0$

42. Does the integer k have at least three different positive prime factors?

(1) $\frac{k}{15}$ is an integer.
(2) $\frac{k}{10}$ is an integer.

43. In City X last April, was the average (arithmetic mean) daily high temperature greater than the median daily high temperature?

(1) In City X last April, the sum of the 30 daily high temperatures was 2,160°.
(2) In City X last April, 60 percent of the daily high temperatures were less than the average daily high temperature.

44. If m and n are positive integers, is $\left(\sqrt{m}\right)^n$ an integer?

(1) $\left(\sqrt{m}\right)$ is an integer.
(2) $\left(\sqrt{n}\right)$ is an integer.

45. Of the 66 people in a certain auditorium, at most 6 people have their birthdays in any one given month. Does at least one person in the auditorium have a birthday in January?

(1) More of the people in the auditorium have their birthday in February than in March.
(2) Five of the people in the auditorium have their birthday in March.

46. Last year the average (arithmetic mean) salary of the 10 employees of Company X was \$42,800. What is the average salary of the same 10 employees this year?

(1) For 8 of the 10 employees, this year's salary is 15 percent greater than last year's salary.
(2) For 2 of the 10 employees, this year's salary is the same as last year's salary.

47. In a certain classroom, there are 80 books, of which 24 are fiction and 23 are written in Spanish. How many of the fiction books are written in Spanish?

(1) Of the fiction books, there are 6 more that are not written in Spanish than are written in Spanish.
(2) Of the books written in Spanish, there are 5 more nonfiction books than fiction books.

48. If p is the perimeter of rectangle Q, what is the value of p?

(1) Each diagonal of rectangle Q has length 10.
(2) The area of rectangle Q is 48.

3.2 Diagnostic Test—Verbal Sample Questions

Reading Comprehension

The questions in this group are based on the content of a passage. After reading the passage, choose the best answer to each question. Answer all questions following the passage on the basis of what is stated or implied in the passage.

According to economic signaling theory, consumers may perceive the frequency with which an unfamiliar brand is advertised as a cue that the brand is of high quality. The notion that highly advertised brands are associated with high-quality products does have some empirical support. Marquardt and McGann found that heavily advertised products did indeed rank high on certain measures of product quality. **Because large advertising expenditures represent a significant investment on the part of a manufacturer, only companies that expect to recoup these costs in the long run, through consumers' repeat purchases of the product, can afford to spend such amounts.**

However, two studies by Kirmani have found that although consumers initially perceive expensive advertising as a signal of high brand quality, at some level of spending the manufacturer's advertising effort may be perceived as unreasonably high, implying low manufacturer confidence in product quality. If consumers perceive excessive advertising effort as a sign of a manufacturer's desperation, the result may be less favorable brand perceptions. In addition, a third study by Kirmani, of print advertisements, found that the use of color affected consumer perception of brand quality. Because consumers recognize that color advertisements are more expensive than black and white, the point at which repetition of an advertisement is perceived as excessive comes sooner for a color advertisement than for a black-and-white advertisement.

1. Which of the following best describes the purpose of the sentence that is in bold ("Because . . . amounts")?

(A) To show that economic signaling theory fails to explain a finding
(B) To introduce a distinction not accounted for by economic signaling theory
(C) To account for an exception to a generalization suggested by Marquardt and McGann
(D) To explain why Marquardt and McGann's research was conducted
(E) To offer an explanation for an observation reported by Marquardt and McGann

2. The primary purpose of the passage is to:

(A) present findings that contradict one explanation for the effects of a particular advertising practice
(B) argue that theoretical explanations about the effects of a particular advertising practice are of limited value without empirical evidence
(C) discuss how and why particular advertising practices may affect consumers' perceptions
(D) contrast the research methods used in two different studies of a particular advertising practice
(E) explain why a finding about consumer responses to a particular advertising practice was unexpected

3. Kirmani's research, as described in the passage, suggests which of the following regarding consumers' expectations about the quality of advertised products?
   (A) Those expectations are likely to be highest if a manufacturer runs both black-and-white and color advertisements for the same product.
   (B) Those expectations can be shaped by the presence of color in an advertisement as well as by the frequency with which an advertisement appears.
   (C) Those expectations are usually high for frequently advertised new brands but not for frequently advertised familiar brands.
   (D) Those expectations are likely to be higher for products whose black-and-white advertisements are often repeated than for those whose color advertisements are less often repeated.
   (E) Those expectations are less definitively shaped by the manufacturer's advertisements than by information that consumers gather from other sources.

4. Kirmani's third study, as described in the passage, suggests which of the following conclusions about a black-and-white advertisement?
   (A) It can be repeated more frequently than a comparable color advertisement could before consumers begin to suspect low manufacturer confidence in the quality of the advertised product.
   (B) It will have the greatest impact on consumers' perceptions of the quality of the advertised product if it appears during periods when a color version of the same advertisement is also being used.
   (C) It will attract more attention from readers of the print publication in which it appears if it is used only a few times.
   (D) It may be perceived by some consumers as more expensive than a comparable color advertisement.
   (E) It is likely to be perceived by consumers as a sign of higher manufacturer confidence in the quality of the advertised product than a comparable color advertisement would be.

5. The passage suggests that Kirmani would be most likely to agree with which of the following statements about consumers' perceptions of the relationship between the frequency with which a product is advertised and the product's quality?
   (A) Consumers' perceptions about the frequency with which an advertisement appears are their primary consideration when evaluating an advertisement's claims about product quality.
   (B) Because most consumers do not notice the frequency of advertisement, it has little impact on most consumers' expectations regarding product quality.
   (C) Consumers perceive frequency of advertisement as a signal about product quality only when the advertisement is for a product that is newly on the market.
   (D) The frequency of advertisement is not always perceived by consumers to indicate that manufacturers are highly confident about their products' quality.
   (E) Consumers who try a new product that has been frequently advertised are likely to perceive the advertisement's frequency as having been an accurate indicator of the product's quality.

The idea of the brain as an information processor—a machine manipulating blips of energy according to fathomable rules—has come to dominate neuroscience. However, one enemy of the brain-as-computer metaphor is John R. Searle, a philosopher who argues that since computers simply follow algorithms, they cannot deal with important aspects of human thought such as meaning and content. Computers are syntactic, rather than semantic, creatures. People, on the other hand, understand meaning because they have something Searle obscurely calls the causal powers of the brain.

Yet how would a brain work if not by reducing what it learns about the world to information—some kind of code that can be transmitted from neuron to neuron? What else could meaning and content be? If the code can be cracked, a computer should be able to simulate it, at least in principle. But even if a computer could simulate the workings of the mind, Searle would claim that the machine would not really be thinking; it would just be acting as if it were. His argument proceeds thus: if a computer were used to simulate a stomach, with the stomach's churnings faithfully reproduced on a video screen, the machine would not be digesting real food. It would just be blindly manipulating the symbols that generate the visual display.

Suppose, though, that a stomach were simulated using plastic tubes, a motor to do the churning, a supply of digestive juices, and a timing mechanism. If food went in one end of the device, what came out the other end would surely be digested food. Brains, unlike stomachs, are information processors, and if one information processor were made to simulate another information processor, it is hard to see how one and not the other could be said to think. Simulated thoughts and real thoughts are made of the same element: information. The representations of the world that humans carry around in their heads are already simulations. To accept Searle's argument, one would have to deny the most fundamental notion in psychology and neuroscience: that brains work by processing information.

6. The main purpose of the passage is to:

(A) propose an experiment.
(B) analyze a function.
(C) refute an argument.
(D) explain a contradiction.
(E) simulate a process.

7. Which of the following is most consistent with Searle's reasoning as presented in the passage?

(A) Meaning and content cannot be reduced to algorithms.
(B) The process of digestion can be simulated mechanically, but not on a computer.
(C) Simulated thoughts and real thoughts are essentially similar because they are composed primarily of information.
(D) A computer can use "causal powers" similar to those of the human brain when processing information.
(E) Computer simulations of the world can achieve the complexity of the brain's representations of the world.

8. The author of the passage would be most likely to agree with which of the following statements about the simulation of organ functions?

(A) An artificial device that achieves the functions of the stomach could be considered a valid model of the stomach.
(B) Computer simulations of the brain are best used to crack the brain's codes of meaning and content.
(C) Computer simulations of the brain challenge ideas that are fundamental to psychology and neuroscience.
(D) Because the brain and the stomach both act as processors, they can best be simulated by mechanical devices.
(E) The computer's limitations in simulating digestion suggest equal limitations in computer-simulated thinking.

9. It can be inferred that the author of the passage believes that Searle's argument is flawed by its failure to:

   (A) distinguish between syntactic and semantic operations.
   (B) explain adequately how people, unlike computers, are able to understand meaning.
   (C) provide concrete examples illustrating its claims about thinking.
   (D) understand how computers use algorithms to process information.
   (E) decipher the code that is transmitted from neuron to neuron in the brain.

10. From the passage, it can be inferred that the author would agree with Searle on which of the following points?

   (A) Computers operate by following algorithms.
   (B) The human brain can never fully understand its own functions.
   (C) The comparison of the brain to a machine is overly simplistic.
   (D) The most accurate models of physical processes are computer simulations.
   (E) Human thought and computer-simulated thought involve similar processes of representation.

11. Which of the following most accurately represents Searle's criticism of the brain-as-computer metaphor, as that criticism is described in the passage?

   (A) The metaphor is not experimentally verifiable.
   (B) The metaphor does not take into account the unique powers of the brain.
   (C) The metaphor suggests that a brain's functions can be simulated as easily as those of a stomach.
   (D) The metaphor suggests that a computer can simulate the workings of the mind by using the codes of neural transmission.
   (E) The metaphor is unhelpful because both the brain and the computer process information.

Women's grassroots activism and their vision of a new civic consciousness lay at the heart of social reform in the United States throughout the Progressive Era, the period between the depression of 1893 and America's entry into the Second World War. Though largely disenfranchised except for school elections, white middle-class women reformers won a variety of victories, notably in the improvement of working conditions, especially for women and children. Ironically, though, child labor legislation pitted women of different classes against one another. To the reformers, child labor and industrial home work were equally inhumane practices that should be outlawed, but, as a number of women historians have recently observed, working-class mothers did not always share this view. Given the precarious finances of working-class families and the necessity of pooling the wages of as many family members as possible, working-class families viewed the passage and enforcement of stringent child labor statutes as a personal economic disaster and made strenuous efforts to circumvent child labor laws. Yet reformers rarely understood this resistance in terms of the desperate economic situation of working-class families, interpreting it instead as evidence of poor parenting. This is not to dispute women reformers' perception of child labor as a terribly exploitative practice, but their understanding of child labor and their legislative solutions for ending it failed to take account of the economic needs of working-class families.

12. The primary purpose of the passage is to:
    - (A) explain why women reformers of the Progressive Era failed to achieve their goals.
    - (B) discuss the origins of child labor laws in the late nineteenth and early twentieth centuries.
    - (C) compare the living conditions of working-class and middle-class women in the Progressive Era.
    - (D) discuss an oversight on the part of women reformers of the Progressive Era.
    - (E) revise a traditional view of the role played by women reformers in enacting Progressive Era reforms.

13. The "view" mentioned in line 17 of the passage refers to which of the following?
    - (A) Some working-class mothers' resistance to the enforcement of child labor laws
    - (B) Reformers' belief that child labor and industrial home work should be abolished
    - (C) Reformers' opinions about how working-class families raised their children
    - (D) Certain women historians' observation that there was a lack of consensus between women of different classes on the issue of child labor and industrial home work
    - (E) Working-class families' fears about the adverse consequences that child labor laws would have on their ability to earn an adequate living

14. The author of the passage mentions the observations of women historians (lines 15–17) most probably in order to:
    - (A) provide support for an assertion made in the preceding sentence (lines 10–12).
    - (B) raise a question that is answered in the last sentence of the passage (lines 27–32).
    - (C) introduce an opinion that challenges a statement made in the first sentence of the passage.
    - (D) offer an alternative view to the one attributed in the passage to working-class mothers.
    - (E) point out a contradiction inherent in the traditional view of child labor reform as it is presented in the passage.

15. The passage suggests that which of the following was a reason for the difference of opinion between working-class mothers and women reformers on the issue of child labor?

    (A) Reformers' belief that industrial home work was preferable to child labor outside the home
    (B) Reformers' belief that child labor laws should pertain to working conditions but not to pay
    (C) Working-class mothers' resentment at reformers' attempts to interfere with their parenting
    (D) Working-class mothers' belief that child labor was an inhumane practice
    (E) Working-class families' need for every employable member of their families to earn money

16. The author of the passage asserts which of the following about women reformers who tried to abolish child labor?

    (A) They alienated working-class mothers by attempting to enlist them in agitating for progressive causes.
    (B) They underestimated the prevalence of child labor among the working classes.
    (C) They were correct in their conviction that child labor was deplorable but short-sighted about the impact of child labor legislation on working-class families.
    (D) They were aggressive in their attempts to enforce child labor legislation, but were unable to prevent working-class families from circumventing them.
    (E) They were prevented by their nearly total disenfranchisement from making significant progress in child labor reform.

17. According to the passage, one of the most striking achievements of white middle-class women reformers during the Progressive Era was:

    (A) gaining the right to vote in school elections.
    (B) mobilizing working-class women in the fight against child labor.
    (C) uniting women of different classes in grassroots activism.
    (D) improving the economic conditions of working-class families.
    (E) improving women's and children's working conditions.

Critical Reasoning

For these questions, select the best of the answer choices given.

18. Vasquez-Morrell Assurance specializes in insuring manufacturers. Whenever a policyholder makes a claim, a claims adjuster determines the amount that Vasquez-Morrell is obligated to pay. Vasquez-Morrell is cutting its staff of claims adjusters by 15 percent. To ensure that the company's ability to handle claims promptly is affected as little as possible by the staff cuts, consultants recommend that Vasquez-Morrell lay off those adjusters who now take longest, on average, to complete work on claims assigned to them.

    Which of the following, if true, most seriously calls into question the consultants' criterion for selecting the staff to be laid off?

    (A) If the time that Vasquez-Morrell takes to settle claims increases significantly, it could lose business to other insurers.
    (B) Supervisors at Vasquez-Morrell tend to assign the most complex claims to the most capable adjusters.
    (C) At Vasquez-Morrell, no insurance payments are made until a claims adjuster has reached a final determination on the claim.
    (D) There are no positions at Vasquez-Morrell to which staff currently employed as claims adjusters could be reassigned.
    (E) The premiums that Vasquez-Morrell currently charges are no higher than those charged for similar coverage by competitors.

19. Prolonged spells of hot, dry weather at the end of the grape-growing season typically reduce a vineyard's yield, because the grapes stay relatively small. In years with such weather, wine producers can make only a relatively small quantity of wine from a given area of vineyards. Nonetheless, in regions where wine producers generally grow their own grapes, analysts typically expect a long, hot, dry spell late in the growing season to result in increased revenues for local wine producers.

    Which of the following, if true, does most to justify the analysts' expectation?

    (A) The lower a vineyard's yield, the less labor is required to harvest the grapes.
    (B) Long, hot, dry spells at the beginning of the grape-growing season are rare, but they can have a devastating effect on a vineyard's yield.
    (C) Grapes grown for wine production are typically made into wine at or near the vineyard in which they were grown.
    (D) When hot, dry spells are followed by heavy rains, the rains frequently destroy grape crops.
    (E) Grapes that have matured in hot, dry weather make significantly better wine than ordinary grapes.

20. In the past, most children who went sledding in the winter snow in Verland used wooden sleds with runners and steering bars. Ten years ago, smooth plastic sleds became popular; they go faster than wooden sleds but are harder to steer and slow. The concern that plastic sleds are more dangerous is clearly borne out by the fact that the number of children injured while sledding was much higher last winter than it was 10 years ago.

    Which of the following, if true in Verland, most seriously undermines the force of the evidence cited?

(A) A few children still use traditional wooden sleds.
(B) Very few children wear any kind of protective gear, such as helmets, while sledding.
(C) Plastic sleds can be used in a much wider variety of snow conditions than wooden sleds can.
(D) Most sledding injuries occur when a sled collides with a tree, a rock, or another sled.
(E) Because the traditional wooden sleds can carry more than one rider, an accident involving a wooden sled can result in several children being injured.

21. Metal rings recently excavated from seventh-century settlements in the western part of Mexico were made using the same metallurgical techniques as those used by Ecuadorian artisans before and during that period. These techniques are sufficiently complex to make their independent development in both areas unlikely. Since the people of these two areas were in cultural contact, archaeologists hypothesize that the metallurgical techniques used to make the rings found in Mexico were learned by Mexican artisans from Ecuadorian counterparts.

Which of the following would it be most useful to establish in order to evaluate the archaeologists' hypothesis?

(A) Whether metal objects were traded from Ecuador to western Mexico during the seventh century
(B) Whether travel between western Mexico and Ecuador in the seventh century would have been primarily by land or by sea
(C) Whether artisans from western Mexico could have learned complex metallurgical techniques from their Ecuadorian counterparts without actually leaving western Mexico
(D) Whether metal tools were used in the seventh-century settlements in western Mexico
(E) Whether any of the techniques used in the manufacture of the metal rings found in western Mexico are still practiced among artisans in Ecuador today

22. Following several years of declining advertising sales, the *Greenville Times* reorganized its advertising sales force. Before reorganization, the sales force was organized geographically, with some sales representatives concentrating on city-center businesses and others concentrating on different outlying regions. The reorganization attempted to increase the sales representatives' knowledge of clients' businesses by having each sales representative deal with only one type of industry or of retailing. After the reorganization, revenue from advertising sales increased.

In assessing whether the improvement in advertising sales can properly be attributed to the reorganization, it would be most helpful to find out which of the following?

(A) What proportion of the total revenue of the *Greenville Times* is generated by advertising sales?
(B) Has the circulation of the *Greenville Times* increased substantially in the last two years?
(C) Among all the types of industry and retailing that use the *Greenville Times* as an advertising vehicle, which type accounts for the largest proportion of the newspaper's advertising sales?
(D) Do any clients of the sales representatives of the *Greenville Times* have a standing order with the *Times* for a fixed amount of advertising per month?
(E) Among the advertisers in the *Greenville Times*, are there more types of retail business or more types of industrial business?

23. Motorists in a certain country frequently complain that traffic congestion is much worse now than it was 20 years ago. No real measure of how much traffic congestion there was 20 years ago exists, but the motorists' complaints are almost certainly unwarranted. The country's highway capacity has tripled in the last twenty years, thanks to a vigorous highway construction program, whereas the number of automobiles registered in the country has increased by only 75 percent.

Which of the following, if true, most seriously weakens the argument?

(A) Most automobile travel is local, and the networks of roads and streets in the country's settled areas have changed little over the last 20 years.
(B) Gasoline prices are high, and miles traveled per car per year have not changed much over the last 20 years.
(C) The country's urban centers have well-developed public transit systems that carry most of the people who commute into those centers.
(D) The average age of automobiles registered in the country is lower now than it was 20 years ago.
(E) Radio stations have long been broadcasting regular traffic reports that inform motorists about traffic congestion.

24. The percentage of households with an annual income of more than $40,000 is higher in Merton County than in any other county. However, the percentage of households with an annual income of $60,000 or more is higher in Sommer County.

If the statements above are true, which of the following must also be true?

(A) The percentage of households with an annual income of $80,000 is higher in Sommer County than in Merton County.
(B) Merton County has the second highest percentage of households with an annual income of $60,000 or more.
(C) Some households in Merton County have an annual income between $40,000 and $60,000.
(D) The number of households with an annual income of more than $40,000 is greater in Merton County than in Sommer County.
(E) Average annual household income is higher in Sommer County than in Merton County.

25. Tiger beetles are such fast runners that they can capture virtually any nonflying insect. However, when running toward an insect, a tiger beetle will intermittently stop and then, a moment later, resume its attack. Perhaps the beetles cannot maintain their pace and must pause for a moment's rest; but an alternative hypothesis is that while running, tiger beetles are unable to adequately process the resulting rapidly changing visual information and so quickly go blind and stop.

Which of the following, if discovered in experiments using artificially moved prey insects, would support one of the two hypotheses and undermine the other?

(A) When a prey insect is moved directly toward a beetle that has been chasing it, the beetle immediately stops and runs away without its usual intermittent stopping.
(B) In pursuing a swerving insect, a beetle alters its course while running and its pauses become more frequent as the chase progresses.
(C) In pursuing a moving insect, a beetle usually responds immediately to changes in the insect's direction, and it pauses equally frequently whether the chase is up or down an incline.
(D) If, when a beetle pauses, it has not gained on the insect it is pursuing, the beetle generally ends its pursuit.
(E) The faster a beetle pursues an insect fleeing directly away from it, the more frequently the beetle stops.

26. Guillemots are birds of Arctic regions. They feed on fish that gather beneath thin sheets of floating ice, and they nest on nearby land. Guillemots need 80 consecutive snow-free days in a year to raise their chicks, so until average temperatures in the Arctic began to rise recently, the guillemots' range was limited to the southernmost Arctic coast. Therefore, if the warming continues, the guillemots' range will probably be enlarged by being extended northward along the coast.

Which of the following, if true, most seriously weakens the argument?

(A) Even if the warming trend continues, there will still be years in which guillemot chicks are killed by an unusually early snow.
(B) If the Arctic warming continues, guillemots' current predators are likely to succeed in extending their own range farther north.
(C) Guillemots nest in coastal areas, where temperatures are generally higher than in inland areas.
(D) If the Arctic warming continues, much of the thin ice in the southern Arctic will disappear.
(E) The fish that guillemots eat are currently preyed on by a wider variety of predators in the southernmost Arctic regions than they are farther north.

27. Some batches of polio vaccine used around 1960 were contaminated with SV40, a virus that in monkeys causes various cancers. Some researchers now claim that this contamination caused some cases of a certain cancer in humans, mesothelioma. This claim is not undercut by the fact that a very careful survey made in the 1960s of people who had received the contaminated vaccine found no elevated incidence of any cancer, since ________.

(A) most cases of mesothelioma are caused by exposure to asbestos
(B) in some countries, there was no contamination of the vaccine
(C) SV40 is widely used in laboratories to produce cancers in animals
(D) mesotheliomas take several decades to develop
(E) mesothelioma was somewhat less common in 1960 than it is now

28. Gortland has long been narrowly self-sufficient in both grain and meat. However, as per capita income in Gortland has risen toward the world average, per capita consumption of meat has also risen toward the world average, and it takes several pounds of grain to produce one pound of meat. Therefore, since per capita income continues to rise, whereas domestic grain production will not increase, Gortland will soon have to import either grain or meat or both.

Which of the following is an assumption on which the argument depends?

(A) The total acreage devoted to grain production in Gortland will soon decrease.

(B) Importing either grain or meat will not result in a significantly higher percentage of Gortlanders' incomes being spent on food than is currently the case.

(C) The per capita consumption of meat in Gortland is increasing at roughly the same rate across all income levels.

(D) The per capita income of meat producers in Gortland is rising faster than the per capita income of grain producers.

(E) People in Gortland who increase their consumption of meat will not radically decrease their consumption of grain.

29. The Hazelton coal-processing plant is a major employer in the Hazelton area, but national environmental regulations will force it to close if it continues to use old, polluting processing methods. However, to update the plant to use newer, cleaner methods would be so expensive that the plant will close unless it receives the tax break it has requested. In order to prevent a major increase in local unemployment, the Hazelton government is considering granting the plant's request.

Which of the following would be most important for the Hazelton government to determine before deciding whether to grant the plant's request?

(A) Whether the company that owns the plant would open a new plant in another area if the present plant were closed

(B) Whether the plant would employ far fewer workers when updated than it does now

(C) Whether the level of pollutants presently being emitted by the plant is high enough to constitute a health hazard for local residents

(D) Whether the majority of the coal processed by the plant is sold outside the Hazelton area

(E) Whether the plant would be able to process more coal when updated than it does now

30. A physically active lifestyle has been shown to help increase longevity. In the Wistar region of Bellaria, the average age at death is considerably higher than in any other part of the country. Wistar is the only mountainous part of Bellaria. A mountainous terrain makes even such basic activities as walking relatively strenuous; it essentially imposes a physically active lifestyle on people. Clearly, this circumstance explains the long lives of people in Wistar.

Which of the following, if true, most seriously weakens the argument?

(A) In Bellaria all medical expenses are paid by the government, so that personal income does not affect the quality of health care a person receives.

(B) The Wistar region is one of Bellaria's least populated regions.

(C) Many people who live in the Wistar region have moved there in middle age or upon retirement.

(D) The many opportunities for hiking, skiing, and other outdoor activities that Wistar's mountains offer make it a favorite destination for vacationing Bellarians.

(E) Per capita spending on recreational activities is no higher in Wistar than it is in other regions of Bellaria.

31. Cheever College offers several online courses via remote computer connection, in addition to traditional classroom-based courses. A study of student performance at Cheever found that, overall, the average student grade for online courses matched that for classroom-based courses. In this calculation of the average grade, course withdrawals were weighted as equivalent to a course failure, and the rate of withdrawal was much lower for students enrolled in classroom-based courses than for students enrolled in online courses.

If the statements above are true, which of the following must also be true of Cheever College?

(A) Among students who did not withdraw, students enrolled in online courses got higher grades, on average, than students enrolled in classroom-based courses.
(B) The number of students enrolled per course at the start of the school term is much higher, on average, for the online courses than for the classroom-based courses.
(C) There are no students who take both an online and a classroom-based course in the same school term.
(D) Among Cheever College students with the best grades, a significant majority take online, rather than classroom-based, courses.
(E) Courses offered online tend to deal with subject matter that is less challenging than that of classroom-based courses.

32. For years the beautiful Renaissance buildings in Palitito have been damaged by exhaust from the many tour buses that come to the city. There has been little parking space, so most buses have idled at the curb during each stop on their tour, and idling produces as much exhaust as driving. The city has now provided parking that accommodates a third of the tour buses, so damage to Palitito's buildings from the buses' exhaust will diminish significantly.

Which of the following, if true, most strongly supports the argument?

(A) The exhaust from Palitito's few automobiles is not a significant threat to Palitito's buildings.
(B) Palitito's Renaissance buildings are not threatened by pollution other than engine exhaust.
(C) Tour buses typically spend less than one-quarter of the time they are in Palitito transporting passengers from one site to another.
(D) More tourists come to Palitito by tour bus than by any other single means of transportation.
(E) Some of the tour buses that are unable to find parking drive around Palitito while their passengers are visiting a site.

33. During the 1980s and 1990s, the annual number of people who visited the Sordellian Mountains increased continually, and many new ski resorts were built. Over the same period, however, the number of visitors to ski resorts who were caught in avalanches decreased, even though there was no reduction in the annual number of avalanches in the Sordellian Mountains.

Which of the following, if true in the Sordellian Mountains during the 1980s and 1990s, most helps to explain the decrease?

(A) Avalanches were most likely to happen when a large new snowfall covered an older layer of snow.
(B) Avalanches destroyed at least some buildings in the Sordellian Mountains in every year.
(C) People planning new ski slopes and other resort facilities used increasingly accurate information about which locations are likely to be in the path of avalanches.
(D) The average length of stay for people visiting the Sordellian Mountains increased slightly.
(E) Construction of new ski resorts often led to the clearing of wooded areas that had helped to prevent avalanches.

34. A year ago, Dietz Foods launched a yearlong advertising campaign for its canned tuna. Last year Dietz sold 12 million cans of tuna compared to the 10 million sold during the previous year, an increase directly attributable to new customers brought in by the campaign. Profits from the additional sales, however, were substantially less than the cost of the advertising campaign. Clearly, therefore, the campaign did nothing to further Dietz's economic interests.

Which of the following, if true, most seriously weakens the argument?

(A) Sales of canned tuna account for a relatively small percentage of Dietz Foods' profits.
(B) Most of the people who bought Dietz's canned tuna for the first time as a result of the campaign were already loyal customers of other Dietz products.
(C) A less expensive advertising campaign would have brought in significantly fewer new customers for Dietz's canned tuna than did the campaign Dietz Foods launched last year.
(D) Dietz made money on sales of canned tuna last year.
(E) In each of the past five years, there was a steep, industry-wide decline in sales of canned tuna.

Sentence Correction

Each question presents a sentence, part or all of which is underlined. Beneath the sentence you will find five ways of phrasing the underlined part. The first of these repeats the original; the other four are different. If you think the original is best, choose the first answer; otherwise choose one of the others.

These questions test correctness and effectiveness of expression. In choosing your answers, follow the requirements of standard written English; that is, pay attention to grammar, choice of words, and sentence construction. Choose the answer that produces the most effective sentence; this answer should be clear and exact, without awkwardness, ambiguity, redundancy, or grammatical error.

35. Unlike <u>the buildings in Mesopotamian cities, which were arranged haphazardly, the same basic plan was followed for cities of the Indus Valley: with houses</u> laid out on a north-south, east-west grid, and houses and walls were built of standard-size bricks.

(A) the buildings in Mesopotamian cities, which were arranged haphazardly, the same basic plan was followed for all cities of the Indus Valley: with houses
(B) the buildings in Mesopotamian cities, which were haphazard in arrangement, the same basic plan was used in all cities of the Indus Valley: houses were
(C) the arrangement of buildings in Mesopotamian cities, which were haphazard, the cities of the Indus Valley all followed the same basic plan: houses
(D) Mesopotamian cities, in which buildings were arranged haphazardly, the cities of the Indus Valley all followed the same basic plan: houses were
(E) Mesopotamian cities, which had buildings that were arranged haphazardly, the same basic plan was used for all cities in the Indus Valley: houses that were

36. New data from United States Forest Service ecologists show <u>that for every dollar spent on controlled small-scale burning, forest thinning, and the training of fire-management personnel, it saves seven dollars that would not be spent on having to extinguish</u> big fires.

(A) that for every dollar spent on controlled small-scale burning, forest thinning, and the training of fire-management personnel, it saves seven dollars that would not be spent on having to extinguish
(B) that for every dollar spent on controlled small-scale burning, forest thinning, and the training of fire-management personnel, seven dollars are saved that would have been spent on extinguishing
(C) that for every dollar spent on controlled small-scale burning, forest thinning, and the training of fire-management personnel saves seven dollars on not having to extinguish
(D) for every dollar spent on controlled small-scale burning, forest thinning, and the training of fire-management personnel, that it saves seven dollars on not having to extinguish
(E) for every dollar spent on controlled small-scale burning, forest thinning, and the training of fire-management personnel, that seven dollars are saved that would not have been spent on extinguishing

37. Like the grassy fields and old pastures that the upland sandpiper needs for feeding and nesting when it returns in May after wintering in the Argentine Pampas, the sandpipers vanishing in the northeastern United States is a result of residential and industrial development and of changes in farming practices.

(A) the sandpipers vanishing in the northeastern United States is a result of residential and industrial development and of changes in
(B) the bird itself is vanishing in the northeastern United States as a result of residential and industrial development and of changes in
(C) that the birds themselves are vanishing in the northeastern United States is due to residential and industrial development and changes to
(D) in the northeastern United States, sandpipers' vanishing due to residential and industrial development and to changes in
(E) in the northeastern United States, the sandpipers' vanishing, a result of residential and industrial development and changing

38. The results of two recent unrelated studies support the idea that dolphins may share certain cognitive abilities with humans and great apes; the studies indicate dolphins as capable of recognizing themselves in mirrors—an ability that is often considered a sign of self-awareness—and to grasp spontaneously the mood or intention of humans.

(A) dolphins as capable of recognizing themselves in mirrors—an ability that is often considered a sign of self-awareness—and to grasp spontaneously
(B) dolphins' ability to recognize themselves in mirrors—an ability that is often considered as a sign of self-awareness—and of spontaneously grasping
(C) dolphins to be capable of recognizing themselves in mirrors—an ability that is often considered a sign of self-awareness—and to grasp spontaneously
(D) that dolphins have the ability of recognizing themselves in mirrors—an ability that is often considered as a sign of self-awareness—and spontaneously grasping
(E) that dolphins are capable of recognizing themselves in mirrors—an ability that is often considered a sign of self-awareness—and of spontaneously grasping

39. According to scholars, the earliest writing was probably not a direct rendering of speech, but was more likely to begin as a separate and distinct symbolic system of communication, and only later merged with spoken language.

(A) was more likely to begin as
(B) more than likely began as
(C) more than likely beginning from
(D) it was more than likely begun from
(E) it was more likely that it began

40. In 1995 Richard Stallman, a well-known critic of the patent system, testified in Patent Office hearings that, to test the system, a colleague of his had managed to win a patent for one of Kirchhoff's laws, an observation about electric current first made in 1845 and now included in virtually every textbook of elementary physics.

(A) laws, an observation about electric current first made in 1845 and
(B) laws, which was an observation about electric current first made in 1845 and it is
(C) laws, namely, it was an observation about electric current first made in 1845 and
(D) laws, an observation about electric current first made in 1845, it is
(E) laws that was an observation about electric current, first made in 1845, and is

41. Excavators at the Indus Valley site of Harappa in eastern Pakistan say the discovery of inscribed shards dating to circa 2800–2600 BC indicate their development of a Harappan writing system, the use of inscribed seals impressed into clay for marking ownership, and the standardization of weights for trade or taxation occurred many decades, if not centuries, earlier than was previously believed.

(A) indicate their development of a Harappan writing system, the use of
(B) indicate that the development of a Harappan writing system, using
(C) indicates that their development of a Harappan writing system, using
(D) indicates the development of a Harappan writing system, their use of
(E) indicates that the development of a Harappan writing system, the use of

42. The Supreme Court has ruled that public universities may collect student activity fees even with students' objections to particular activities, so long as the groups they give money to will be chosen without regard to their views.

(A) with students' objections to particular activities, as long as the groups they give money to will be
(B) if they have objections to particular activities and the groups that are given the money are
(C) if they object to particular activities, but the groups that the money is given to have to be
(D) from students who object to particular activities, so long as the groups given money are
(E) though students have an objection to particular activities, but the groups that are given the money be

43. Despite the increasing number of women graduating from law school and passing bar examinations, the proportion of judges and partners at major law firms who are women have not risen to a comparable extent.

(A) the proportion of judges and partners at major law firms who are women have not risen to a comparable extent
(B) the proportion of women judges and partners at major law firms have not risen comparably
(C) the proportion of judges and partners at major law firms who are women has not risen comparably
(D) yet the proportion of women judges and partners at major law firms has not risen to a comparable extent
(E) yet the proportion of judges and partners at major law firms who are women has not risen comparably

44. Seldom more than 40 feet wide and 12 feet deep, but it ran 363 miles across the rugged wilderness of upstate New York, the Erie Canal connected the Hudson River at Albany to the Great Lakes at Buffalo, providing the port of New York City with a direct water link to the heartland of the North American continent.

(A) Seldom more than 40 feet wide and 12 feet deep, but it ran 363 miles across the rugged wilderness of upstate New York, the Erie Canal connected
(B) Seldom more than 40 feet wide or 12 feet deep but running 363 miles across the rugged wilderness of upstate New York, the Erie Canal connected
(C) It was seldom more than 40 feet wide and 12 feet deep, and ran 363 miles across the rugged wilderness of upstate New York, but the Erie Canal, connecting
(D) The Erie Canal was seldom more than 40 feet wide or 12 feet deep and it ran 363 miles across the rugged wilderness of upstate New York, which connected
(E) The Erie Canal, seldom more than 40 feet wide and 12 feet deep, but running 363 miles across the rugged wilderness of upstate New York, connecting

45. In 1923, the Supreme Court declared a minimum wage for women and children in the District of Columbia as unconstitutional, and ruling that it was a form of price-fixing and, as such, an abridgment of the right of contract.

(A) the Supreme Court declared a minimum wage for women and children in the District of Columbia as unconstitutional, and
(B) the Supreme Court declared as unconstitutional a minimum wage for women and children in the District of Columbia, and
(C) the Supreme Court declared unconstitutional a minimum wage for women and children in the District of Columbia,
(D) a minimum wage for women and children in the District of Columbia was declared unconstitutional by the Supreme Court,
(E) when the Supreme Court declared a minimum wage for women and children in the District of Columbia as unconstitutional,

46. Researchers have found that individuals who have been blind from birth, and who thus have never seen anyone gesture, nevertheless make hand motions when speaking just as frequently and in virtually the same way as sighted people do, and that they will gesture even when conversing with another blind person.

(A) who thus have never seen anyone gesture, nevertheless make hand motions when speaking just as frequently and in virtually the same way as sighted people do, and that they will gesture
(B) who thus never saw anyone gesturing, nevertheless make hand motions when speaking just as frequent and in virtually the same way as sighted people did, and that they will gesture
(C) who thus have never seen anyone gesture, nevertheless made hand motions when speaking just as frequently and in virtually the same way as sighted people do, as well as gesturing
(D) thus never having seen anyone gesture, nevertheless made hand motions when speaking just as frequent and in virtually the same way as sighted people did, as well as gesturing
(E) thus never having seen anyone gesture, nevertheless to make hand motions when speaking just as frequently and in virtually the same way as sighted people do, and to gesture

47. Like embryonic germ cells, which are cells that develop early in the formation of the fetus and that later generate eggs or sperm, embryonic stem cells have the ability of developing themselves into different kinds of body tissue.

(A) embryonic stem cells have the ability of developing themselves into different kinds of body tissue
(B) embryonic stem cells have the ability to develop into different kinds of body tissue
(C) in embryonic stem cells there is the ability to develop into different kinds of body tissue
(D) the ability to develop themselves into different kinds of body tissue characterizes embryonic stem cells
(E) the ability of developing into different kinds of body tissue characterizes embryonic stem cells

48. Critics contend that the new missile is a weapon whose importance is largely symbolic, more a tool for manipulating people's perceptions than to fulfill a real military need.

(A) for manipulating people's perceptions than to fulfill
(B) for manipulating people's perceptions than for fulfilling
(C) to manipulate people's perceptions rather than that it fulfills
(D) to manipulate people's perceptions rather than fulfilling
(E) to manipulate people's perceptions than for fulfilling

49. As an actress and, more importantly, as a teacher of acting, Stella Adler was one of the most influential artists in the American theater, who trained several generations of actors including Marlon Brando and Robert De Niro.

(A) Stella Adler was one of the most influential artists in the American theater, who trained several generations of actors including
(B) Stella Adler, one of the most influential artists in the American theater, trained several generations of actors who include
(C) Stella Adler was one of the most influential artists in the American theater, training several generations of actors whose ranks included
(D) one of the most influential artists in the American theater was Stella Adler, who trained several generations of actors including
(E) one of the most influential artists in the American theater, Stella Adler, trained several generations of actors whose ranks included

50. By developing the Secure Digital Music Initiative, the recording industry associations of North America, Japan, and Europe hope to create a standardized way of distributing songs and full-length recordings on the Internet that will protect copyright holders and foil the many audio pirates who copy and distribute digital music illegally.

(A) of distributing songs and full-length recordings on the Internet that will protect copyright holders and foil the many audio pirates who copy and distribute
(B) of distributing songs and full-length recordings on the Internet and to protect copyright holders and foiling the many audio pirates copying and distributing
(C) for distributing songs and full-length recordings on the Internet while it protects copyright holders and foils the many audio pirates who copy and distribute
(D) to distribute songs and full-length recordings on the Internet while they will protect copyright holders and foil the many audio pirates copying and distributing
(E) to distribute songs and full-length recordings on the Internet and it will protect copyright holders and foiling the many audio pirates who copy and distribute

51. Whereas a ramjet generally cannot achieve high speeds without the initial assistance of a rocket, high speeds can be attained by scramjets, or supersonic combustion ramjets, in that they reduce airflow compression at the entrance of the engine and letting air pass through at supersonic speeds.

(A) high speeds can be attained by scramjets, or supersonic combustion ramjets, in that they reduce
(B) that high speeds can be attained by scramjets, or supersonic combustion ramjets, is a result of their reducing
(C) the ability of scramjets, or supersonic combustion ramjets, to achieve high speeds is because they reduce
(D) scramjets, or supersonic combustion ramjets, have the ability of attaining high speeds when reducing
(E) scramjets, or supersonic combustion ramjets, can attain high speeds by reducing

52. It will not be possible to implicate melting sea ice in the coastal flooding that many global warming models have projected: just like a glass of water that will not overflow due to melting ice cubes, so melting sea ice does not increase oceanic volume.

(A) like a glass of water that will not overflow due to melting ice cubes
(B) like melting ice cubes that do not cause a glass of water to overflow
(C) a glass of water will not overflow because of melting ice cubes
(D) as melting ice cubes that do not cause a glass of water to overflow
(E) as melting ice cubes do not cause a glass of water to overflow

3.3 Diagnostic Answer Sheet

Quantitative

1.	A	32.	C
2.	D	33.	D
3.	E	34.	C
4.	B	35.	D
5.	B	36.	B
6.	A	37.	A
7.	E	38.	B
8.	E	39.	E
9.	D	40.	D
10.	C	41.	C
11.	C	42.	C
12.	C	43.	B
13.	E	44.	A
14.	B	45.	D
15.	C	46.	E
16.	E	47.	D
17.	D	48.	C
18.	A		
19.	A		
20.	B		
21.	D		
22.	E		
23.	B		
24.	C		
25.	E		
26.	E		
27.	E		
28.	E		
29.	E		
30.	A		
31.	D		

Verbal

1.	E	32.	C
2.	C	33.	C
3.	B	34.	E
4.	A	35.	D
5.	D	36.	B
6.	C	37.	B
7.	A	38.	E
8.	A	39.	B
9.	B	40.	A
10.	A	41.	E
11.	B	42.	D
12.	D	43.	C
13.	B	44.	B
14.	A	45.	C
15.	E	46.	A
16.	C	47.	B
17.	E	48.	B
18.	B	49.	C
19.	E	50.	A
20.	C	51.	E
21.	A	52.	E
22.	B		
23.	A		
24.	C		
25.	B		
26.	D		
27.	D		
28.	E		
29.	B		
30.	C		
31.	A		

3.4 Interpretive Guide

The following table provides a guide for interpreting your score, on the basis of the number of questions you got right.

Interpretive Guide

	Excellent	Above Average	Average	Below Average
Problem Solving	19–24	16–18	10–15	0–9
Data Sufficiency	19–24	16–18	10–15	0–9
Reading Comprehension	16–17	14–15	9–13	0–8
Critical Reasoning	14–17	9–13	6-8	0–5
Sentence Correction	16–18	11–15	8–10	0–7

Remember, you should not compare the number of questions you got right in each section. Instead, you should compare how your response rated in each section.

3.5 Diagnostic Test—Quantitative Answer Explanations

Problem Solving

The following discussion is intended to familiarize you with the most efficient and effective approaches to the kinds of problems common to problem solving questions. The particular questions in this chapter are generally representative of the kinds of quantitative questions you will encounter on the GMAT®. Remember that it is the problem solving strategy that is important, not the specific details of a particular question.

1. Last month a certain music club offered a discount to preferred customers. After the first compact disc purchased, preferred customers paid $3.99 for each additional compact disc purchased. If a preferred customer purchased a total of 6 compact discs and paid $15.95 for the first compact disc, then the dollar amount that the customer paid for the 6 compact discs is equivalent to which of the following?

(A) 5(4.00) + 15.90
(B) 5(4.00) + 15.95
(C) 5(4.00) + 16.00
(D) 5(4.00 – 0.01) + 15.90
(E) 5(4.00 – 0.05) + 15.95

Arithmetic Operations on rational numbers

The cost of the 6 compact discs, with $15.95 for the first one and $3.99 for the other 5 discs, can be expressed as 5(3.99) + 15.95. It is clear from looking at the answer choices that some regrouping of the values is needed because none of the answer choices uses $3.99 in the calculation.

If $4.00 is used instead of $3.99, each one of the 5 additional compact discs is calculated at $0.01 too much, and the total cost is 5(0.01) = $0.05 too high. There is an overage of $0.05 that must be subtracted from the $15.95, or thus $15.95 – $0.05 = $15.90. Therefore, the cost can be expressed as 5(4.00) + 15.90.

The correct answer is A.

2. The average (arithmetic mean) of the integers from 200 to 400, inclusive, is how much greater than the average of the integers from 50 to 100, inclusive?

(A) 150
(B) 175
(C) 200
(D) 225
(E) 300

Arithmetic Statistics

In the list of integers from 200 to 400 inclusive, the middle value is 300. For every integer above 300, there exists an integer below 300 that is the same distance away from 300; thus the average of the integers from 200 to 400, inclusive, will be kept at 300. In the same manner, the average of the integers from 50 to 100, inclusive, is 75.

The difference is 300 – 75 = 225.

The correct answer is D.

3. The sequence $a_1, a_2, a_3, \ldots, a_n, \ldots$ is such that $a_n = \frac{a_{n-1} + a_{n-2}}{2}$ for all $n \geq 3$. If $a_3 = 4$ and $a_5 = 20$, what is the value of a_6 ?

(A) 12
(B) 16
(C) 20
(D) 24
(E) 28

Algebra Applied problems

According to this formula, it is necessary to know the two prior terms in the sequence to determine the value of a term; that is, it is necessary to know both a_{n-1} and a_{n-2} to find a_n. Therefore, to find a_6, the values of a_5 and a_4 must be determined. To find a_4, let $a_n = a_5$, which makes $a_{n-1} = a_4$ and $a_{n-2} = a_3$. Then, by substituting the given values into the formula

$$a_n = \frac{a_{n-1} + a_{n-2}}{2}$$

$$a_5 = \frac{a_4 + a_3}{2}$$

$20 = \frac{a_4 + 4}{2}$ substitute known values

$40 = a_4 + 4$ multiply both sides by 2

$36 = a_4$ subtract 4 from both sides

Then, letting $a_n = a_6$, substitute the known values:

$$a_6 = \frac{a_5 + a_4}{2}$$

$a_6 = \frac{20 + 36}{2}$ substitute known values

$a_6 = \frac{56}{2}$ simplify

$a_6 = 28$

The correct answer is E.

4. Among a group of 2,500 people, 35 percent invest in municipal bonds, 18 percent invest in oil stocks, and 7 percent invest in both municipal bonds and oil stocks. If 1 person is to be randomly selected from the 2,500 people, what is the probability that the person selected will be one who invests in municipal bonds but **NOT** in oil stocks?

(A) $\frac{9}{50}$

(B) $\frac{7}{25}$

(C) $\frac{7}{20}$

(D) $\frac{21}{50}$

(E) $\frac{27}{50}$

Arithmetic Probability

Since there are 2,500 people, 2,500(0.35) = 875 people invest in municipal bonds, and 2,500(0.07) = 175 of those people invest in both municipal bonds and oil stocks. Therefore, there are 875 – 175 = 700 people who invest in municipal bonds but not in oil stocks. Probability of an event =

$$\frac{\text{Number of desired events}}{\text{Total number of events that could occur}}$$

Probability of investing in municipal bonds but not in oil stocks = $\frac{700}{2,500} = \frac{7}{25}$

The correct answer is B.

5. A closed cylindrical tank contains 36π cubic feet of water and is filled to half its capacity. When the tank is placed upright on its circular base on level ground, the height of the water in the tank is 4 feet. When the tank is placed on its side on level ground, what is the height, in feet, of the surface of the water above the ground?

(A) 2
(B) 3
(C) 4
(D) 6
(E) 9

Geometry Volume

Since the cylinder is half full, it will be filled to half its height, whether it is upright or on its side. When the cylinder is on its side, half its height is equal to its radius.

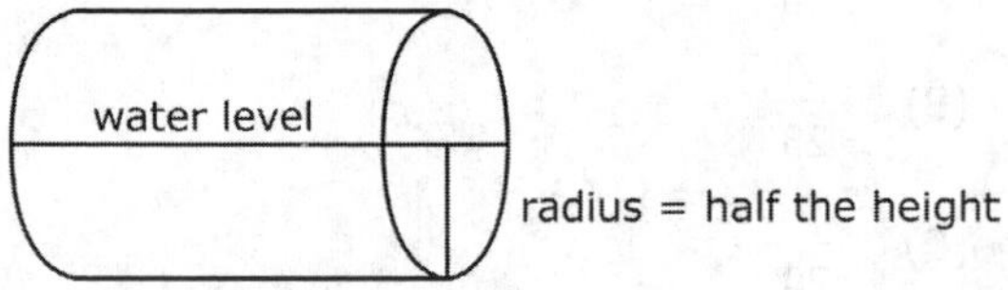

Using the information about the volume of water in the upright cylinder, solve for this radius to determine the height of the water when the cylinder is on its side.

$V = \pi r^2 h$	volume = (π)(radius²)(height)
$36\pi = \pi r^2 h$	known volume of water is 36π
$36 = r^2(4)$	substitute 4 for h; divide both sides by π
$9 = r^2$	solve for r
$3 = r$	radius = height of the water in the cylinder on its side

The correct answer is B.

6. A marketing firm determined that, of 200 households surveyed, 80 used neither Brand A nor Brand B soap, 60 used only Brand A soap, and for every household that used both brands of soap, 3 used only Brand B soap. How many of the 200 households surveyed used both brands of soap?

(A) 15
(B) 20
(C) 30
(D) 40
(E) 45

Arithmetic Operations on rational numbers

Since it is given that 80 households use neither Brand A nor Brand B, then 200 – 80 = 120 must use Brand A, Brand B, or both. It is also given that 60 households use only Brand A and that three times as many households use Brand B exclusively as use both brands. If x is the number of households that use both Brand A and Brand B, then $3x$ use Brand B alone. A Venn diagram can be helpful for visualizing the logic of the given information for this item:

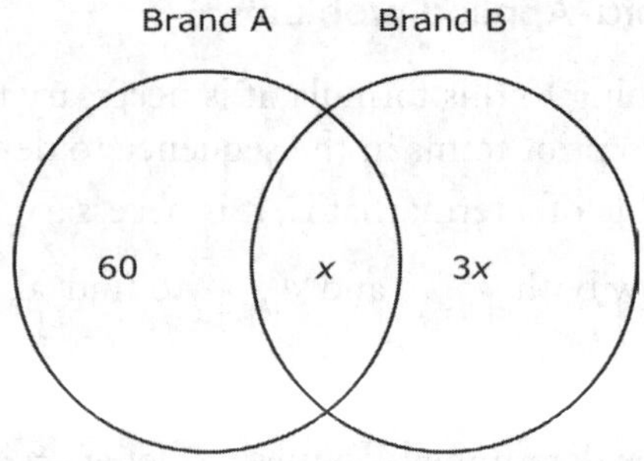

All the sections in the circles can be added up and set equal to 120, and then the equation can be solved for x:

$60 + x + 3x = 120$	
$60 + 4x = 120$	combine like terms
$4x = 60$	subtract 60 from both sides
$x = 15$	divide both sides by 4

The correct answer is A.

7. A certain club has 10 members, including Harry. One of the 10 members is to be chosen at random to be the president, one of the remaining 9 members is to be chosen at random to be the secretary, and one of the remaining 8 members is to be chosen at random to be the treasurer. What is the probability that Harry will be either the member chosen to be the secretary or the member chosen to be the treasurer?

(A) $\frac{1}{720}$
(B) $\frac{1}{80}$
(C) $\frac{1}{10}$
(D) $\frac{1}{9}$
(E) $\frac{1}{5}$

Arithmetic Probability

Two probabilities must be calculated here: (1) the probability of Harry's being chosen for secretary and (2) the probability of Harry's being chosen for treasurer. For any probability, the probability of an event's occurring =

$$\frac{\text{number of ways desired outcome can occur}}{\text{total number of ways the outcome can occur}}.$$

(1) If Harry is to be secretary, he first CANNOT have been chosen for president, and then he must be chosen for secretary. The probability that he will be chosen for president is $\frac{1}{10}$, so the probability of his NOT being chosen for president is $1-\frac{1}{10}=\frac{9}{10}$. Then, the probability of his being chosen for secretary is $\frac{1}{9}$. Once he is chosen, the probability that he will be selected for treasurer is 0, so the probability that he will NOT be selected for treasurer is 1 – 0 = 1. Thus, the probability that Harry will be chosen for secretary is $\left(\frac{9}{10}\right)\left(\frac{1}{9}\right)(1)=\frac{1}{10}$.

(2) If Harry is to be treasurer, he needs to be NOT chosen for president, then NOT chosen for secretary, and then finally chosen for treasurer.

The probability that he will NOT be chosen for president is again $1-\frac{1}{10}=\frac{9}{10}$. The probability of his NOT being chosen for secretary is $1-\frac{1}{9}=\frac{8}{9}$. The probability of his being chosen for treasurer is $\frac{1}{8}$, so the probability that Harry will be chosen for treasurer is $\left(\frac{9}{10}\right)\left(\frac{8}{9}\right)\left(\frac{1}{8}\right)=\frac{1}{10}$.

(3) So, finally, the probability of Harry's being chosen as either secretary or treasurer is thus $\frac{1}{10}+\frac{1}{10}=\frac{2}{10}=\frac{1}{5}$.

The correct answer is E.

8. If a certain toy store's revenue in November was $\frac{2}{5}$ of its revenue in December and its revenue in January was $\frac{1}{4}$ of its revenue in November, then the store's revenue in December was how many times the average (arithmetic mean) of its revenues in November and January?

(A) $\frac{1}{4}$

(B) $\frac{1}{2}$

(C) $\frac{2}{3}$

(D) 2

(E) 4

Arithmetic Statistics

Let n be the store's revenue in November, d be the store's revenue in December, and j be the store's revenue in January. The information from the problem can be expressed as $n=\frac{2}{5}d$ and $j=\frac{1}{4}n$. Substituting $\frac{2}{5}d$ for n in the second equation gives $j=\frac{1}{4}\left(\frac{2}{5}d\right)=\frac{1}{10}d$. Then, the average of the revenues in November and January can be found by using these values in the formula

$$\text{average} = \frac{\text{sum of values}}{\text{number of values}},$$ as follows:

$$\text{average} = \frac{\frac{2}{5}d+\frac{1}{10}d}{2} = \frac{\frac{4}{10}d+\frac{1}{10}d}{2} = \frac{\frac{5}{10}d}{2} = \frac{1}{2}d\left(\frac{1}{2}\right)=\frac{1}{4}d$$

Solve for the store's revenue in December by multiplying both sides of this equation by 4:

$$\text{average} = \frac{1}{4}d$$

$$4(\text{average}) = d$$

Thus, the store's revenue in December was 4 times its average revenue in November and January.

The correct answer is E.

9. A researcher computed the mean, the median, and the standard deviation for a set of performance scores. If 5 were to be added to each score, which of these three statistics would change?

(A) The mean only
(B) The median only
(C) The standard deviation only
(D) The mean and the median
(E) The mean and the standard deviation

Arithmetic Statistics

If 5 were added to each score, the mean would go up by 5, as would the median. However, the spread of the values would remain the same, simply centered around a new value. So, the standard deviation would **NOT** change.

The correct answer is D.

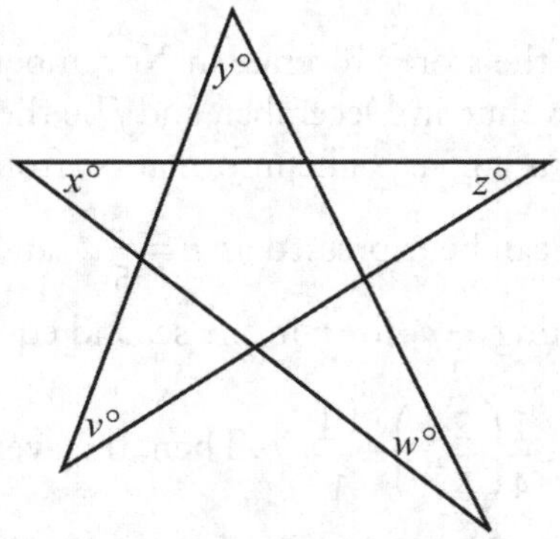

10. In the figure shown, what is the value of $v + x + y + z + w$?

(A) 45
(B) 90
(C) 180
(D) 270
(E) 360

Geometry Angles and their measure

In the following figure, the center section of the star is a pentagon.

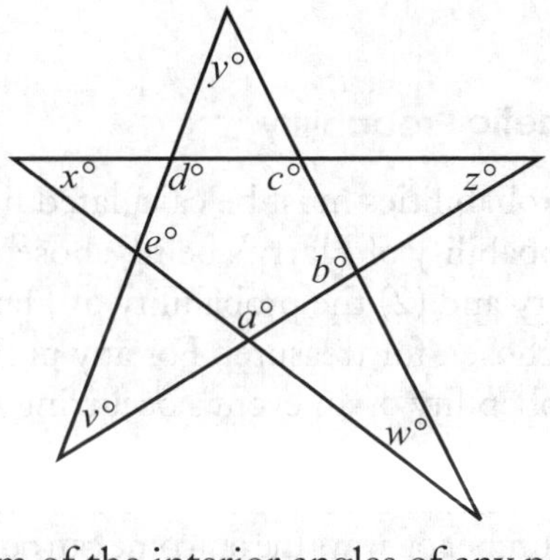

The sum of the interior angles of any polygon is $180(n-2)$, where n is the number of sides. Thus, $a+b+c+d+e=180(5-2)=180(3)=540$. Each of the interior angles of the pentagon defines a triangle with two of the angles at the points of the star. This gives the following five equations:

$a+x+z=180$

$b+v+y=180$

$c+x+w=180$

$d+v+z=180$

$e+y+w=180$

Summing these 5 equations gives:

$a+b+c+d+e+2v+2x+2y+2z+2w=900$

Substituting 540 for $a+b+c+d+e$ gives:

$540+2v+2x+2y+2z+2w=900$

From this:

$2v+2x+2y+2z+2w=360$	subtract 540 from both sides
$2(v+x+y+z+w)=360$	factor out 2 on the left side
$v+x+y+z+w=180$	divide both sides by 2

The correct answer is C.

11. Of the three-digit integers greater than 700, how many have two digits that are equal to each other and the remaining digit different from the other two?

(A) 90
(B) 82
(C) 80
(D) 45
(E) 36

Arithmetic Properties of numbers

In three-digit integers, there are three pairs of digits that can be the same while the other digit is different: tens and ones, hundreds and tens, and hundreds and ones. In each of these pairs, there are 9 options for having the third digit be different from the other two. The single exception to this is in the 700–799 set, where the number 700 cannot be included because the problem calls for integers "greater than 700." So, in the 700–799 set, there are only 8 options for when the tens and ones are the same. This is shown in the table below.

Number of digits available for the third digit when two given digits are the same

Same	701–799	800–899	900–999
tens and ones	8	9	9
hundreds and tens	9	9	9
hundreds and ones	9	9	9

Thus, of the three-digit integers greater than 700, there are 9(9) – 1 = 80 numbers that have two digits that are equal to each other when the remaining digit is different from these two.

The correct answer is C.

12. Positive integer y is 50 percent of 50 percent of positive integer x, and y percent of x equals 100. What is the value of x?

(A) 50
(B) 100
(C) 200
(D) 1,000
(E) 2,000

Arithmetic + Algebra Percents + Simultaneous equations

Because y is a positive integer, y percent is notated as $\frac{y}{100}$. According to the problem,

$$y = 0.50(0.50x)$$

$$\left(\frac{y}{100}\right)x = 100$$

The first equation simplifies to $y = 0.25x$, and multiplying the second equation by 100 gives $xy = 10{,}000$.

Substituting the simplified first equation into this second equation gives:

$x(0.25x) = 10{,}000$

$0.25x^2 = 10{,}000$ simplify left side

$x^2 = 40{,}000$ divide both sides by 0.25

$x = 200$ solve for the value of x

The correct answer is C.

13. If s and t are positive integers such that $\frac{s}{t} = 64.12$, which of the following could be the remainder when s is divided by t?

(A) 2
(B) 4
(C) 8
(D) 20
(E) 45

Arithmetic Operations on rational numbers

By using a long division model, it can be seen that the remainder after dividing s by t is $s - 64t$:

$$\begin{array}{r} 64 \\ t\overline{)\ s\ } \\ \underline{-64t} \\ s - 64t \end{array}$$

Then, the given equation can be written as $64.12t = s$. By splitting portions of t into its integer multiple and its decimal multiple, this becomes $64t + 0.12t = s$, or $0.12t = s - 64t$, which is the remainder. So, $0.12t$ = remainder. Test the answer choices to find the situation in which t is an integer.

A	$0.12t = 2$ or $t = 16.67$	NOT an integer
B	$0.12t = 4$ or $t = 33.33$	NOT an integer
C	$0.12t = 8$ or $t = 66.67$	NOT an integer
D	$0.12t = 20$ or $t = 166.67$	NOT an integer
E	$0.12t = 45$ or $t = 375$	INTEGER

The correct answer is E.

14. Of the 84 parents who attended a meeting at a school, 35 volunteered to supervise children during the school picnic and 11 volunteered both to supervise children during the picnic and to bring refreshments to the picnic. If the number of parents who volunteered to bring refreshments was 1.5 times the number of parents who neither volunteered to supervise children during the picnic nor volunteered to bring refreshments, how many of the parents volunteered to bring refreshments?

(A) 25
(B) 36
(C) 38
(D) 42
(E) 45

Arithmetic Operations on rational numbers

Out of the 35 parents who agreed to supervise children during the school picnic, 11 parents are also bringing refreshments, so 35 – 11 = 24 parents are only supervising children. Let x be the number of parents who volunteered to bring refreshments, and let y be the number of parents who declined to supervise or to bring refreshments. The fact that the number of parents who volunteered to bring refreshments is 1.5 times the number who did not volunteer at all can then be expressed as $x = 1.5y$. A Venn diagram, such as the one below, can be helpful in answering problems of this kind.

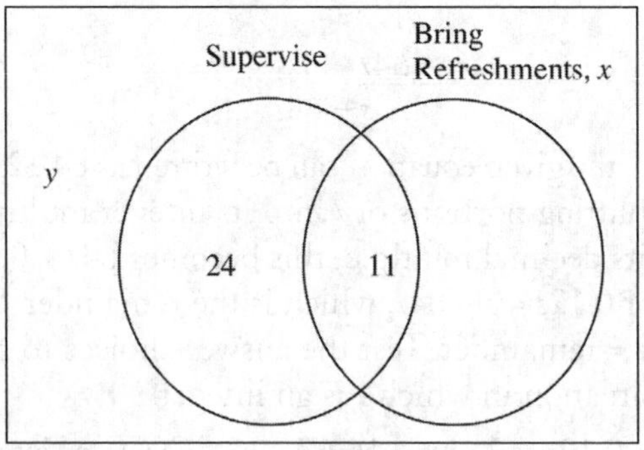

Then, the sum of the sections can be set equal to the total number of parents at the picnic, and the equation can be solved for y:

$y + 24 + x = 84$	sum of sections = total parents at picnic
$y + x = 60$	subtract 24 from each side
$y = 60 - x$	subtract x from each side

Then, substituting the value $60 - x$ for y in the equation $x = 1.5y$ gives the following:

$x = 1.5(60 - x)$	
$x = 90 - 1.5x$	distribute the 1.5
$2.5x = 90$	add $1.5x$ to both sides
$x = 36$	divide both sides by 2.5

The correct answer is B.

15. The product of all the prime numbers less than 20 is closest to which of the following powers of 10?

(A) 10^9
(B) 10^8
(C) 10^7
(D) 10^6
(E) 10^5

Arithmetic Properties of numbers

The prime numbers less than 20 are 2, 3, 5, 7, 11, 13, 17, and 19. Their product is 9,699,690 (arrived at as follows: $2 \times 3 \times 5 \times 7 \times 11 \times 13 \times 17 \times 19 = 9{,}699{,}690$). This is closest to $10{,}000{,}000 = 10^7$ ($10 \times 10 \times 10 \times 10 \times 10 \times 10 \times 10 = 10{,}000{,}000$).

The correct answer is C.

16. If $\sqrt{3 - 2x} = \sqrt{2x} + 1$ then, $4x^2 =$

(A) 1
(B) 4
(C) $2 - 2x$
(D) $4x - 2$
(E) $6x - 1$

Algebra Second-degree equations

Work with the equation to create $4x^2$ on one side.

$\sqrt{3-2x} = \sqrt{2x} + 1$

$\left(\sqrt{3-2x}\right)^2 = \left(\sqrt{2x}+1\right)^2$ square both sides

$3 - 2x = 2x + 2\sqrt{2x} + 1$

$2 - 4x = 2\sqrt{2x}$ move all non–square-root terms to one side (i.e., subtract $2x$ and 1)

$1 - 2x = \sqrt{2x}$ divide both sides by 2

$(1-2x)^2 = \left(\sqrt{2x}\right)^2$ square both sides

$1 - 4x + 4x^2 = 2x$

$4x^2 = 6x - 1$ isolate the $4x^2$ (add $4x$ and subtract 1 from both sides)

The correct answer is E.

17. If $n = \sqrt{\frac{16}{81}}$, what is the value of $\sqrt{n}$?

(A) $\frac{1}{9}$
(B) $\frac{1}{4}$
(C) $\frac{4}{9}$
(D) $\frac{2}{3}$
(E) $\frac{9}{2}$

Arithmetic Operations on radical expressions

Work the problem.

Since $n = \sqrt{\frac{16}{81}} = \frac{4}{9}$, then $\sqrt{n} = \sqrt{\frac{4}{9}} = \frac{2}{3}$.

The correct answer is D.

18. If n is the product of the integers from 1 to 8, inclusive, how many different prime factors greater than 1 does n have?

(A) Four
(B) Five
(C) Six
(D) Seven
(E) Eight

Arithmetic Properties of numbers

If n is the product of the integers from 1 to 8, then its prime factors will be the prime numbers from 1 to 8. There are four prime numbers between 1 and 8: 2, 3, 5, and 7.

The correct answer is A.

19. If k is an integer and $2 < k < 7$, for how many different values of k is there a triangle with sides of lengths 2, 7, and k?

(A) One
(B) Two
(C) Three
(D) Four
(E) Five

Geometry Triangles

In a triangle, the sum of the smaller two sides must be larger than the largest side.

For k values 3, 4, 5, and 6, the only triangle possible is 2, 7, and $k = 6$ because only $2 + 6 > 7$. For k values 3, 4, and 5, the sum of the smaller two sides is not larger than the third side; thus, 6 is the only possible value of k that satisfies the conditions.

The correct answer is A.

20. A right circular cone is inscribed in a hemisphere so that the base of the cone coincides with the base of the hemisphere. What is the ratio of the height of the cone to the radius of the hemisphere?

(A) $\sqrt{3} : 1$

(B) $1 : 1$

(C) $\frac{1}{2} : 1$

(D) $\sqrt{2} : 1$

(E) $2 : 1$

Geometry Volume

As the diagram below shows, the height of the cone will be the radius of the hemisphere, so the ratio is $1 : 1$.

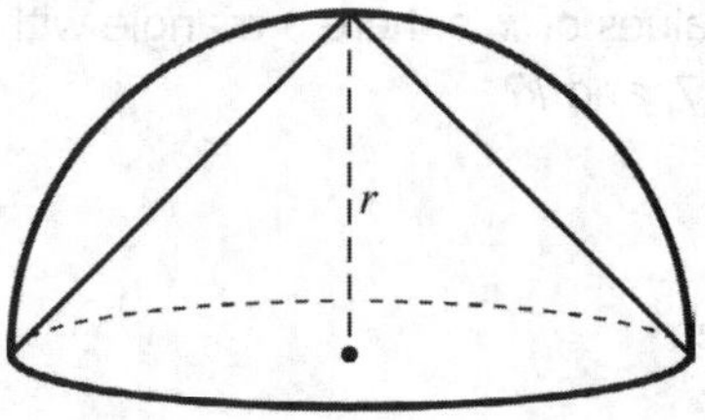

The correct answer is B.

21. John deposited $10,000 to open a new savings account that earned 4 percent annual interest, compounded quarterly. If there were no other transactions in the account, what was the amount of money in John's account 6 months after the account was opened?

(A) $10,100
(B) $10,101
(C) $10,200
(D) $10,201
(E) $10,400

Arithmetic Operations on rational numbers

Since John's account is compounded quarterly, he receives $\frac{1}{4}$ of his annual interest, or 1%, every three months. This is added to the amount already in the account to accrue interest for the next quarter. After 6 months, this process will have occurred twice, so the amount in John's account will then be

$$(\$10,000)(1.01)(1.01) = \$10,000(1.01)^2 = \$10,201$$

The correct answer is D.

22. A container in the shape of a right circular cylinder is $\frac{1}{2}$ full of water. If the volume of water in the container is 36 cubic inches and the height of the container is 9 inches, what is the diameter of the base of the cylinder, in inches?

(A) $\frac{16}{9\pi}$

(B) $\frac{4}{\sqrt{\pi}}$

(C) $\frac{12}{\sqrt{\pi}}$

(D) $\sqrt{\frac{2}{\pi}}$

(E) $4\sqrt{\frac{2}{\pi}}$

Geometry Volume

For a right cylinder, volume = π(radius)^2(height). Since the volume of water is 36 cubic inches and since this represents $\frac{1}{2}$ the container, the water is occupying $\frac{1}{2}$ the container's height, or $9(\frac{1}{2}) =$ 4.5 inches. Let r be the radius of the cylinder.

$36 = \pi r^2(4.5)$

$8 = \pi r^2$ — divide both sides by 4.5

$\frac{8}{\pi} = r^2$ — divide both sides by π

$\sqrt{\frac{8}{\pi}} = r$ — take the square root of both sides

$\frac{2\sqrt{2}}{\sqrt{\pi}} = r$ — simplify the $\sqrt{8}$ to get the radius

Then, since the diameter is twice the length of the radius, the diameter equals $2\left(\frac{2\sqrt{2}}{\sqrt{\pi}}\right) = 4\frac{\sqrt{2}}{\sqrt{\pi}} = 4\sqrt{\frac{2}{\pi}}$.

The correct answer is E.

23. If the positive integer x is a multiple of 4 and the positive integer y is a multiple of 6, then xy must be a multiple of which of the following?

I. 8
II. 12
III. 18

(A) II only
(B) I and II only
(C) I and III only
(D) II and III only
(E) I, II, and III

Arithmetic Properties of numbers

The product xy must be a multiple of 4(6) = 24 and any of its factors. Test each alternative.

I.	$\frac{24}{8} = 3$	8 is a factor of 24 MUST be a multiple of 8
II.	$\frac{24}{12} = 2$	12 is a factor of 24 MUST be a multiple of 12
III.	$\frac{24}{18} = 1\frac{1}{3}$	18 is NOT a factor of 24 NEED NOT be a multiple of 18

The correct answer is B.

24. Aaron will jog from home at x miles per hour and then walk back home by the same route at y miles per hour. How many miles from home can Aaron jog so that he spends a total of t hours jogging and walking?

(A) $\frac{xt}{y}$

(B) $\frac{x+t}{xy}$

(C) $\frac{xyt}{x+y}$

(D) $\frac{x+y+t}{xy}$

(E) $\frac{y+t}{x} - \frac{t}{y}$

Algebra Simplifying algebraic expressions

Let j be the number of hours Aaron spends jogging; then let $t - j$ be the total number of hours he spends walking. It can be stated that Aaron jogs a distance of xj miles and walks a distance of $y(t - j)$ miles. Because Aaron travels the same route, the miles jogged must equal the miles walked, and they can be set equal.

$xj = y(t - j)$	set number of miles equal to each other
$xj = yt - jy$	distribute the y
$xj + jy = yt$	add jy to both sides to get all terms with j to one side
$j(x + y) = yt$	factor out the j
$j = \frac{yt}{x+y}$	divide both sides by $x + y$

So, the number of hours Aaron spends jogging is $j = \frac{yt}{x+y}$.

The number of miles he can jog is xj or, by substitution of this value of j, $x\left(\frac{yt}{x+y}\right) = \frac{xyt}{x+y}$.

The correct answer is C.

Data Sufficiency

The following section on data sufficiency is intended to familiarize you with the most efficient and effective approaches to the kinds of problems common to data sufficiency. The particular questions in this chapter are generally representative of the kinds of data sufficiency questions you will encounter on the GMAT®. Remember that it is the problem solving strategy that is important, not the specific details of a particular question.

25. If the units digit of integer n is greater than 2, what is the units digit of n?

(1) The units digit of n is the same as the units digit of n^2.

(2) The units digit of n is the same as the units digit of n^3.

Arithmetic Arithmetic operations

If the units digit of n is greater than 2, then it can only be the digits 3, 4, 5, 6, 7, 8, or 9.

(1) To solve this problem, it is necessary to find a digit that is the same as the units digit of its square. For example, both 43 squared (1,849) and 303 squared (91,809) have a units digit of 9, which is different from the units digits of 43 and 303. However, 25 squared (625) and 385 squared (148,225) both have a units digit of 5, and 16 and 226 both have a units digit of 6 and their squares (256 and 51,076, respectively) do, too. However, there is no further information to choose between 5 or 6; NOT sufficient.

(2) Once again, 5 and 6 are the only numbers which, when cubed, will both have a 5 or 6 respectively in their units digits. However, the information given does not distinguish between them; NOT sufficient.

Since (1) and (2) together yield the same information but with no direction as to which to choose, there is not enough information to determine the answer.

The correct answer is E;
both statements together are still not sufficient.

26. What is the value of the integer p?

(1) Each of the integers 2, 3, and 5 is a factor of p.

(2) Each of the integers 2, 5, and 7 is a factor of p.

Arithmetic Properties of numbers

(1) These are factors of p, but it is not clear that they are the only factors of p; NOT sufficient.

(2) These are factors of p, but it is not clear that they are the only factors of p; NOT sufficient.

Taken together, (1) and (2) overlap, but again there is no clear indication that these are the only factors of p.

The correct answer is E;
both statements together are still not sufficient.

27. If the length of Wanda's telephone call was rounded up to the nearest whole minute by her telephone company, then Wanda was charged for how many minutes for her telephone call?

(1) The total charge for Wanda's telephone call was $6.50.

(2) Wanda was charged $0.50 more for the first minute of the telephone call than for each minute after the first.

Arithmetic Arithmetic operations

(1) This does not give any information as to the call's cost per minute; NOT sufficient.

(2) From this, it can be determined only that the call was longer than one minute and that the charge for the first minute was $0.50 more than the charge for each succeeding minute; NOT sufficient.

Taking (1) and (2) together, the number of minutes cannot be determined as long as the cost of each minute after the first is unknown. For example, if the cost of each minute after the first minute were

\$0.40, then the cost of the first minute would be \$0.90. Then the total cost of the other minutes would be \$6.50 – \$0.90 = \$5.60, and \$5.60 ÷ \$0.40 would yield 14. In this case, the time of the call would be 1 + 14 = 15 minutes. If, however, the cost of each minute after the first minute were \$0.15, then the cost of the first minute would be \$0.65. Then \$6.50 – \$0.65 would be \$5.85, and this in turn, when divided by \$0.15, would yield 39 minutes, for a total call length of 40 minutes. More information on the cost of each minute after the first minute is still needed.

The correct answer is E;
both statements together are still not sufficient.

28. What is the perimeter of isosceles triangle *MNP*?

(1) *MN* = 16
(2) *NP* = 20

Geometry Triangles

The perimeter of a triangle is the sum of all three sides. In the case of an isosceles triangle, two of the sides are equal. To determine the perimeter of this triangle, it is necessary to know both the length of an equal side and the length of the base of the triangle.

(1) Only gives the length of one side; NOT sufficient.

(2) Only gives the length of one side; NOT sufficient.

Since it is unclear whether *MN* or *NP* is one of the equal sides, it is not possible to determine the length of the third side or the perimeter of the triangle. The perimeter could be either ((2)(16)) + 20 = 52 or ((2)(20)) + 16 = 56.

The correct answer is E;
both statements together are still not sufficient.

29. In a survey of retailers, what percent had purchased computers for business purposes?

(1) 85 percent of the retailers surveyed who owned their own store had purchased computers for business purposes.
(2) 40 percent of the retailers surveyed owned their own store.

Arithmetic Percents

(1) With only this, it cannot be known what percent of the retailers not owning their own store had purchased computers, and so it cannot be known how many retailers purchased computers overall; NOT sufficient.

(2) While this permits the percent of owners and non-owners in the survey to be deduced, the overall percent of retailers who had purchased computers cannot be determined; NOT sufficient.

Using the information from both (1) and (2), the percent of surveyed owner-retailers who had purchased computers can be deduced, and the percent of nonowner-retailers can also be deduced. However, the information that would permit a determination of either the percent of nonowner-retailers who had purchased computers or the overall percent of all retailers (both owners and nonowners) who had purchased computers is still not provided.

The correct answer is E;
both statements together are still not sufficient.

30. The only gift certificates that a certain store sold yesterday were worth either \$100 each or \$10 each. If the store sold a total of 20 gift certificates yesterday, how many gift certificates worth \$10 each did the store sell yesterday?

(1) The gift certificates sold by the store yesterday were worth a total of between \$1,650 and \$1,800.
(2) Yesterday the store sold more than 15 gift certificates worth \$100 each.

Algebra Applied problem + Simultaneous equations + Inequalities

Let x represent the number of \$100 certificates sold, and let y represent the number of \$10 certificates sold. Then the given information can be expressed as $x + y = 20$ or thus $y = 20 - x$. The value of the \$100 certificates sold is $100x$, and the value of the \$10 certificates sold is $10y$.

(1) From this, it is known that $100x + 10y > 1{,}650$. Since $y = 20 - x$, this value can be substituted for y, and the inequality can be solved for x:

$$100x + 10y > 1{,}650$$

$$100x + 10(20 - x) > 1{,}650 \quad \text{substitute for } y$$

$$100x + 200 - 10x > 1{,}650 \quad \text{distribute}$$

$$90x + 200 > 1{,}650 \quad \text{simplify}$$

$$90x > 1{,}450 \quad \text{subtract 200 from both sides}$$

$$x > 16.1$$

Thus, more than 16 of the \$100 certificates were sold. If 17 \$100 certificates were sold, then it must be that 3 \$10 certificates were also sold for a total of \$1,730, which satisfies the condition of being between \$1,650 and \$1,800. If, however, 18 \$100 certificates were sold, then it must be that 2 \$10 certificates were sold, and this totals \$1,820, which is more than \$1,800 and fails to satisfy the condition. Therefore, 3 of the \$10 certificates were sold; SUFFICIENT.

(2) From this it can be known only that the number of \$10 certificates sold was 4 or fewer; NOT sufficient.

The correct answer is A;
statement 1 alone is sufficient.

31. Is the standard deviation of the set of measurements $x_1, x_2, x_3, x_4, \ldots, x_{20}$ less than 3?

(1) The variance for the set of measurements is 4.
(2) For each measurement, the difference between the mean and that measurement is 2.

Arithmetic Statistics

In determining the standard deviation, the difference between each measurement and the mean is squared (the variance), and then the differences are added and divided by the number of measurements. The positive square root of this number is the standard deviation.

(1) If each variance is 4, then the sum of all the variances is 4×20 or 80.

Then $\sqrt{\frac{80}{20}} = \sqrt{4} = 2$, which is less than 3;

SUFFICIENT.

(2) For each measurement, the difference between the mean and that measurement is 2. Therefore, the square of each difference is 4, and the sum of all the squares is $4 \times 20 = 80$. The calculations then proceed as above; SUFFICIENT.

The correct answer is D;
each statement alone is sufficient.

32. Is the range of the integers 6, 3, y, 4, 5, and x greater than 9?

(1) $y > 3x$
(2) $y > x > 3$

Arithmetic Statistics

The range of a set of integers is equal to the difference between the largest integer and the smallest integer. The range of the set of integers 3, 4, 5, and 6 is 3, which is derived from $6 - 3$.

(1) Although it is known that $y > 3x$, the value of x is unknown. If, for example, $x = 1$, then the value of y would be greater than 3. However, if $x = 2$, then the value of y would be greater than 6, and, since 6 would no longer be the largest integer, the range would be affected. Because the actual values of x and y are unknown, the value of the range is also unknown; NOT sufficient.

(2) If $x > 3$, and $y > x$, then x could be 4 and y could be 5. Then the range of the 6 integers would still be $6 - 3$ or 3. However, if x were 4 and y were 15, then the range of the 6 integers would be $15 - 3$, or 12. There is no means to establish the values of x and y, beyond the fact that they both are greater than 3; NOT sufficient.

Taking (1) and (2) together, it is known that $x > 3$ and that $y > 3x$. Since the smallest integer that x could be is thus 4, then $y > 3(4)$ or $y > 12$. Therefore, the integer y must be 13 or larger. When y is equal to 13, the range of the 6 integers is $13 - 3 = 10$, which is larger than 9. As y increases in value, the value of the range will also increase.

The correct answer is C;
both statements together are sufficient.

33. Is $\frac{5^{x+2}}{25} < 1$?

(1) $5^x < 1$
(2) $x < 0$

Algebra Inequalities

Note that $x^{r+s} = (x^r)(x^s)$. Also, note that $x^{-r} = \frac{1}{x^r}$.

(1) The given inequality can be written $\frac{(5^x)(5^2)}{25} < 1$. Since $5^2 = 25$, the equation simplifies to $5^x < 1$; SUFFICIENT.

(2) From this, since $x < 0$, letting $x = -1$, the inequality becomes $\frac{5^{(-1+2)}}{25} < 1$ or $\frac{5^1}{25} < 1$. This yields $\frac{5}{25} < 1$ or $\frac{1}{5} < 1$. If $x = -2$, then the inequality becomes $\frac{5^0}{25} < 1$ or $\frac{1}{25} < 1$, which again is less than 1. As the value of x decreases, the fraction only becomes smaller and thus remains less than one; SUFFICIENT.

The correct answer is D;
each statement alone is sufficient.

34. Of the companies surveyed about the skills they required in prospective employees, 20 percent required both computer skills and writing skills. What percent of the companies surveyed required neither computer skills nor writing skills?

(1) Of those companies surveyed that required computer skills, half required writing skills.
(2) Forty-five percent of the companies surveyed required writing skills but not computer skills.

Arithmetic Percents

The surveyed companies' prospective employees could be placed into one of the following four categories:

1. Having computer skills and having writing skills
2. Having computer skills but not having writing skills
3. Not having computer skills but having writing skills
4. Not having either computer skills or writing skills

It is given that 20 percent of prospective employees fell into category 1. It is necessary to determine what percent of the prospective employees fell into category 4.

(1) This helps identify the percentage in category 2. Since $\frac{1}{2}$ the employees who had to have computer skills also needed to have writing skills (i.e., those in category 1), then the other $\frac{1}{2}$ of the employees who needed computer skills did not need to have writing skills (thus category 2 = category 1). However, this information only establishes that 20 percent need computer skills, but not writing skills; NOT sufficient.

(2) While this establishes category 3, that is, that 45 percent need writing skills but do not need computer skills, no further information is available; NOT sufficient.

Taking (1) and (2) together, the first three categories add up to 85 percent (20 + 20 + 45). Therefore, category 4 would be equal to 100 – 85 = 15 percent of prospective employees not required to have computer skills or writing skills.

The correct answer is C;
both statements together are sufficient.

35. What is the value of $w + q$?

(1) $3w = 3 - 3q$
(2) $5w + 5q = 5$

Algebra First- and second-degree equations

(1) If $3q$ is added to both sides of this equation, it can be rewritten as $3w + 3q = 3$. When each term is then divided by 3, it yields $w + q = 1$; SUFFICIENT.

(2) When each term in this equation is divided by 5, it becomes $w + q = 1$; SUFFICIENT.

The correct answer is D;
each statement alone is sufficient.

36. If X and Y are points in a plane and X lies inside the circle C with center O and radius 2, does Y lie inside circle C?

(1) The length of line segment XY is 3.
(2) The length of line segment OY is 1.5.

Geometry Circles

(1) The maximum distance between two points that lie on a circle is equal to the diameter, or 2 times the radius. Since the radius of circle C is 2, the diameter in this case is 4. It cannot be assumed, however, that X and Y are points on the diameter; X can lie anywhere within the circle. When the distance between X and Y is 3, it is still possible either that Y is within the circle or that Y is outside the circle; NOT sufficient.

(2) If the length of the line segment OY is 1.5 and the circle has a radius of 2, then the distance from the center O to point Y is less than the radius, and point Y must therefore lie within the circle; SUFFICIENT.

The correct answer is B;
statement 2 alone is sufficient.

37. Is $x > y$?

(1) $x = y + 2$
(2) $\frac{x}{2} = y - 1$

Algebra First- and second-degree equations

(1) Since 2 has to be added to y in order to make it equal to x, it can be reasoned that $x > y$; SUFFICIENT.

(2) Multiplying both sides of this equation by 2 results in $x = 2(y - 1)$ or $x = 2y - 2$. If y were 0, then x would be -2, and y would be greater than x. If y were a negative number like -2, then $x = 2(-2) - 2 = -6$, and again y would be greater than x. However, if y were a positive number such as 4, then $x = 2(4) - 2 = 6$, and $x > y$. Since there is no other information concerning the value of y, it cannot be determined if $x > y$; NOT sufficient.

The correct answer is A;
statement 1 alone is sufficient.

38. If Paula drove the distance from her home to her college at an average speed that was greater than 70 kilometers per hour, did it take her less than 3 hours to drive this distance?

(1) The distance that Paula drove from her home to her college was greater than 200 kilometers.
(2) The distance that Paula drove from her home to her college was less than 205 kilometers.

Arithmetic Distance problem

A distance problem uses the formula distance = rate × time. To find the time, the formula would be rearranged as $\text{time} = \frac{\text{distance}}{\text{rate}}$. To solve this problem, it is necessary to know the rate (given here as 70 kilometers per hour) and the distance.

(1) If the distance was *less than* 210 kilometers, then Paula drove for *less than* 3 hours $\left(\frac{209}{70}\right)$. However, if the distance was 210 kilometers *or greater*, Paula drove 3 hours *or more* $\left(\frac{210}{70}\right)$. However, there is no way to know if the distance was more or less than 210 kilometers; NOT sufficient.

(2) From this, the most time that Paula drove would have been $\frac{205}{70}$ or approximately 2.93 hours; SUFFICIENT.

The correct answer is B;
statement 2 alone is sufficient.

39. In the xy-plane, if line k has negative slope and passes through the point $(-5,r)$, is the x-intercept of line k positive?

(1) The slope of line k is -5
(2) $r > 0$

Geometry Coordinate geometry

The x-intercept is the x-coordinate of the point in which the line k crosses the x-axis and would have the coordinates $(x, 0)$.

(1) Knowing the slope of the line does not help in determining the x-intercept, since from point $(-5, r)$ the line k extends in both directions. Without knowing the value of r, the x-intercept could be -5 if r were 0, or it could be other numbers, both positive and negative, depending on the value of r; NOT sufficient.

(2) Knowing that $r > 0$, suggests that the x-intercept is not -5; the point $(-5, r)$, where r is a positive number, does lie in quadrant II. It could, however, be any point with an x-coordinate of -5 in that quadrant and line k could have any negative slope, and so the line k would vary with the value of r. Therefore, the x-intercept of line k cannot be determined; NOT sufficient.

Using (1) and (2) together does not help in the determination of the x-intercept, since the point $(-5,r)$ could have any positive y coordinate and thus line k could cross the x-axis at many different places.

The correct answer is E;
both statements together are still not sufficient.

40. If \$5,000 invested for one year at p percent simple annual interest yields \$500, what amount must be invested at k percent simple annual interest for one year to yield the same number of dollars?

(1) $k = 0.8p$
(2) $k = 8$

Arithmetic Interest problem

With simple annual interest, the formula to use is interest = principal × rate × time. It is given that \$500 = \$5,000 × rate × 1 (year), where the rate p = 10 percent interest.

(1) If p is 10 percent, then $k = 0.8p$ is 0.08. Using the same formula, the time is again 1 year; the interest is the same amount; and the rate is 0.08, or 8 percent. Thus, \$500 = principal × 0.08 × 1, or principal = \$6,250; SUFFICIENT.

(2) If $k = 8$, then the rate is 8 percent, and the same formula and procedure as above are employed again; SUFFICIENT.

The correct answer is D;
each statement alone is sufficient.

41. If $\frac{x+y}{z} > 0$, is $x < 0$?

(1) $x < y$
(2) $z < 0$

Algebra Inequalities

If $\frac{x+y}{z} > 0$, then either one of two cases holds true. Either $(x + y) > 0$ **and** $z > 0$, or $(x + y) < 0$ **and** $z < 0$. In other words, in order for the term to be greater than zero, it must be true that either 1) both the numerator and denominator are greater than 0 or 2) both the numerator and denominator are less than 0.

(1) Regardless of whether $(x + y)$ is positive or negative, the positive or negative value of z must be in agreement with the sign of $(x + y)$ in order for $\frac{x+y}{z} > 0$. However, there is no information about z here; NOT sufficient.

(2) If $z < 0$, then $(x + y)$ must be less than 0. However, this statement gives no information about $(x + y)$; NOT sufficient.

This can be solved using (1) and (2) together. From (2), it is known that $z < 0$, and, going back to the original analysis, for the term to be greater than zero, $(x + y)$ must also be less than 0. Now, if $y > 0$, then x must be less than $y(-1)$ or $x < -y$, thereby confirming that $x < 0$. If instead $y < 0$, since $x < y$, x is also less than 0. Finally, if $y = 0$, then by substitution, $x < 0$.

The correct answer is C;
both statements together are sufficient.

42. Does the integer k have at least three different positive prime factors?

(1) $\frac{k}{15}$ is an integer.

(2) $\frac{k}{10}$ is an integer.

Arithmetic Properties of numbers

(1) The prime factors of 15 are 3 and 5. So in this case, k has at least 2 different positive prime factors, but it is unknown if there are more positive prime factors; NOT sufficient.

(2) The prime factors of 10 are 2 and 5, showing that k has at least these 2 different positive prime factors, but k might also have more; NOT sufficient.

Taking (1) and (2) together, since k is divisible by both 10 and 15, it must be divisible by their different positive prime factors of 2, 3, and 5. Thus k has at least 3 different positive prime factors.

The correct answer is C;
both statements together are sufficient.

43. In City X last April, was the average (arithmetic mean) daily high temperature greater than the median daily high temperature?

(1) In City X last April, the sum of the 30 daily high temperatures was 2,160°.

(2) In City X last April, 60 percent of the daily high temperatures were less than the average daily high temperature.

Arithmetic Statistics

The formula for calculating the arithmetic mean, or the average, is as follows:

$$\text{Average} = \frac{\text{sum of } v \text{ values}}{v}$$

(1) These data will produce an average of $\frac{2160}{30}$ = 72° for last April in City X. However, there is no information regarding the median for comparison; NOT sufficient.

(2) The median is the middle temperature of the data. As such, 50 percent of the daily high temperatures will be above the median, and 50 percent will be below the median. If 60 percent of the daily high temperatures were less than the average daily high temperature, then the average of the daily highs must be greater than the median; SUFFICIENT.

The correct answer is B;
statement 2 alone is sufficient.

44. If m and n are positive integers, is $\left(\sqrt{m}\right)^n$ an integer?

(1) $\left(\sqrt{m}\right)$ is an integer.

(2) $\left(\sqrt{n}\right)$ is an integer.

Arithmetic Properties of numbers

(1) Since m is an integer, $\left(\sqrt{m}\right)^n$ where n is an even number will yield an integer. The information in this statement covers the cases where n is an odd number. Because $\left(\sqrt{m}\right)$ is an integer, these cases will also yield an integer; SUFFICIENT.

(2) The information that $\left(\sqrt{n}\right)$ is an integer is not completely helpful in answering the question. For example, if $\left(\sqrt{m}\right) = \frac{1}{4}$, then $\left(\frac{1}{4}\right)^n$ will also yield a fraction. However, there is no way of knowing if $\left(\sqrt{m}\right)$ is a fraction, a decimal, or an integer; NOT sufficient.

The correct answer is A;
statement 1 alone is sufficient.

45. Of the 66 people in a certain auditorium, at most 6 people have birthdays in any one given month. Does at least one person in the auditorium have a birthday in January?

(1) More of the people in the auditorium have birthdays in February than in March.

(2) Five of the people in the auditorium have birthdays in March.

Algebra Sets and functions

Because it is given that 6 is the greatest number of individuals who can have birthdays in any particular month, these 66 people could be evenly distributed across 11 of the 12 months of the year. That is to say, it could be possible for the distribution to be $11 \times 6 = 66$, and thus any given month, such as January, would not have a person with a birthday. Assume that January has no people with birthdays, and see if this assumption is disproved.

(1) The information that more people have February birthdays than March birthdays indicates that the distribution is not even. Therefore, March is underrepresented and must thus have fewer than 6 birthdays. Since no month can have more than 6 people with birthdays, and every month but January already has as many people with birthdays as it can have, January has to have at least 1 person with a birthday; SUFFICIENT.

(2) Again, March is underrepresented with only 5 birthdays, and none of the other months can have more than 6 birthdays. Therefore, the extra birthday (from March) must occur in January; SUFFICIENT.

The correct answer is D;
each statement alone is sufficient.

46. Last year the average (arithmetic mean) salary of the 10 employees of Company X was $42,800. What is the average salary of the same 10 employees this year?

(1) For 8 of the 10 employees, this year's salary is 15 percent greater than last year's salary.

(2) For 2 of the 10 employees, this year's salary is the same as last year's salary.

Arithmetic Statistics

(1) Since all 10 employees did not receive the same 15 percent increase, it cannot be assumed that the mean this year is 15 percent higher than last year. It remains unknown whether these 8 salaries were the top 8 salaries, the bottom 8 salaries, or somewhere in-between. Without this type of information from last year, the mean for this year cannot be determined; NOT sufficient.

(2) If 2 salaries remained the same as last year, then 8 salaries changed. Without further information about the changes, the mean for this year cannot be determined; NOT sufficient.

Even taking (1) and (2) together, it remains impossible to tell the mean salary for this year without additional data.

The correct answer is E;
both statements together are still not sufficient.

47. In a certain classroom, there are 80 books, of which 24 are fiction and 23 are written in Spanish. How many of the fiction books are written in Spanish?

(1) Of the fiction books, there are 6 more that are not written in Spanish than are written in Spanish.

(2) Of the books written in Spanish, there are 5 more nonfiction books than fiction books.

Algebra Sets and functions

Let x represent the fiction books that are written in Spanish. A table could be set up like the one below, filling in the information that is known or able to be known:

	Spanish	Non-Spanish	Total
Fiction	x		24
Nonfiction			56
Total	23	57	80

(1) If x represents the fiction books written in Spanish, then $x + 6$ can now be used to represent the fiction books that are not written in Spanish. From the table above, it can be seen then that $x + x + 6 = 24$, or $2x = 18$. Therefore, x, or the number of fiction books written in Spanish, is 9; SUFFICIENT.

(2) If x represents the fiction books written in Spanish, then $x + 5$ can now be used to represent the nonfiction books written in Spanish. From the table, it can be said that $x + x + 5 = 23$, or $2x = 18$. Therefore, x, or the number of fiction books written in Spanish, is 9; SUFFICIENT.

The correct answer is D;
each statement alone is sufficient.

48. If p is the perimeter of rectangle Q, what is the value of p?

(1) Each diagonal of rectangle Q has length 10.
(2) The area of rectangle Q is 48.

Geometry Rectangles + Perimeter + Area

The perimeter of a rectangle is equal to 2 times the rectangle's length plus 2 times the rectangle's width, or $p = 2l + 2w$. The diagonals of a rectangle are equal. In a rectangle, because a diagonal forms a right triangle, the length of a diagonal is equal to the square root of the length squared plus the width squared, or $d = \sqrt{l^2 + w^2}$.

(1) If a diagonal = 10, then $10 = \sqrt{l^2 + w^2}$, or, by squaring both sides, $100 = l^2 + w^2$. Without knowing the value or the relationship between the other two sides of the right triangle, it is impossible to solve for l or w, and thus for the perimeter of the rectangle; NOT sufficient.

(2) If the area of the rectangle is 48, then it can be stated that $lw = 48$. However, without further information, the perimeter cannot be determined. For example, l could be 6 and w could be 8, and the perimeter would then be $12 + 16 = 28$. However, it could also be that l is 4 and w is 12, and in that case the perimeter would be $8 + 24 = 32$; NOT sufficient.

Using (1) and (2) together, it is possible to solve this problem. Since from (2) $lw = 48$, then $w = \frac{48}{l}$. Substituting this into $100 = l^2 + w^2$ from (1) the equation can be solved as follows:

$100 = l^2 + \left(\frac{48}{l}\right)^2$	substitution
$100l^2 = l^4 + 2304$	multiply both sides by l^2
$l^4 - 100l^2 + 2304 = 0$	move all terms to one side
$(l^2 - 64)(l^2 - 36) = 0$	factor like a quadratic
$l^2 = 64, l^2 = 36$	solve for l^2

Since l is a length, it must be positive, so l is either 8 or 6. When $l = 8$, $w = \frac{48}{8} = 6$, and when $l = 6$, $w = \frac{48}{6} = 8$, both of which give the same perimeter.

The correct answer is C;
both statements together are sufficient.

3.6 Diagnostic Test—Verbal Answer Explanations

Reading Comprehension

The following discussion is intended to familiarize you with the most efficient and effective approaches to the kinds of problems common to reading comprehension. The particular questions in this chapter are generally representative of the kinds of reading comprehension questions you will encounter on the GMAT®. Remember that it is the problem solving strategy that is important, not the specific details of a particular question.

Questions 1–5 refer to the passage on page 26.

1. Which of the following best describes the purpose of the sentence that is in bold ("Because . . . amounts")?

(A) To show that economic signaling theory fails to explain a finding
(B) To introduce a distinction not accounted for by economic signaling theory
(C) To account for an exception to a generalization suggested by Marquardt and McGann
(D) To explain why Marquardt and McGann's research was conducted
(E) To offer an explanation for an observation reported by Marquardt and McGann

Logical structure

Marquardt and McGann found a correlation between highly advertised products and high-quality products. The connection can be explained by understanding that companies may invest heavily in such advertising, anticipating that recurring purchases of high-quality products will eventually recover these advertising costs. The consumers will continue to buy these products over time because of loyalty to their high quality. The statement in bold provides this explanation for the correlation noted by Marquardt and McGann.

A The shaded sentence does not explain a failure of the economic signaling theory.

B Economic signaling theory is about perceptions of quality, but this explanation is about actual quality and its correlation with advertising.

C No exception is mentioned in Marquardt and McGann's work.

D The statement does not examine why or how the research was undertaken.

E **Correct.** This statement provides an explanation of why highly advertised products *did indeed rank high on certain measures of product quality.*

The correct answer is E.

2. The primary purpose of the passage is to:

(A) present findings that contradict one explanation for the effects of a particular advertising practice.
(B) argue that theoretical explanations about the effects of a particular advertising practice are of limited value without empirical evidence.
(C) discuss how and why particular advertising practices may affect consumers' perceptions.
(D) contrast the research methods used in two different studies of a particular advertising practice.
(E) explain why a finding about consumer responses to a particular advertising practice was unexpected.

Main idea

The primary purpose can be determined only by evaluating the whole passage. The first paragraph discusses consumers' perceptions of quality based on frequency of advertising. The second paragraph discusses three studies that show how consumers base their evaluations of products on the kinds of advertising they see. Therefore, the purpose of the whole passage is to show how consumers' perceptions of products are shaped by certain advertising practices.

A The passage shows that expensive advertising works to a certain point, but not after it; this method examines a continuum, not a contradiction.

B Most of the passage is devoted to empirical evidence.

C **Correct.** The passage shows how the frequency and the kind of advertising influence consumers' perceptions about the quality of the products advertised.

D The passage reports the findings of four studies but does not mention research methods.

E The passage does not indicate that any of the findings were unexpected.

The correct answer is C.

3. Kirmani's research, as described in the passage, suggests which of the following regarding consumers' expectations about the quality of advertised products?

(A) Those expectations are likely to be highest if a manufacturer runs both black-and-white and color advertisements for the same product.

(B) Those expectations can be shaped by the presence of color in an advertisement as well as by the frequency with which an advertisement appears.

(C) Those expectations are usually high for frequently advertised new brands but not for frequently advertised familiar brands.

(D) Those expectations are likely to be higher for products whose black-and-white advertisements are often repeated than for those whose color advertisements are less often repeated.

(E) Those expectations are less definitively shaped by the manufacturer's advertisements than by information that consumers gather from other sources.

Inference

The question's use of the word *suggests* means that the answer depends on making an inference. This research is discussed in the second paragraph. Kirmani found that too much advertising tended to make the consumers believe that manufacturers were desperate. The use of color was also found to affect consumers' perceptions of brand quality. Realizing that color advertising is more expensive than black-and-white, consumers react more quickly to what they perceive to be its overuse than they do to a repetition of black-and-white advertisements.

A This situation is not discussed in the research, at least as it is reported in this passage.

B **Correct.** It can be inferred that consumers' perceptions of product quality are influenced by the use of color in an advertisement and by the frequency of the advertisement's appearance.

C The research does not make a distinction between new and familiar brands.

D The research indicates only that consumers can tolerate black-and-white advertisements for a longer time than color advertisements before dismissing them as excessive.

E There is no discussion of what consumers learn from other sources.

The correct answer is B.

4. Kirmani's third study, as described in the passage, suggests which of the following conclusions about a black-and-white advertisement?

(A) It can be repeated more frequently than a comparable color advertisement could before consumers begin to suspect low manufacturer confidence in the quality of the advertised product.
(B) It will have the greatest impact on consumers' perceptions of the quality of the advertised product if it appears during periods when a color version of the same advertisement is also being used.
(C) It will attract more attention from readers of the print publication in which it appears if it is used only a few times.
(D) It may be perceived by some consumers as more expensive than a comparable color advertisement.
(E) It is likely to be perceived by consumers as a sign of higher manufacturer confidence in the quality of the advertised product than a comparable color advertisement would be.

Inference

Kirmani's third study is discussed in the final two sentences. Consumers suspect expensive advertising results from a manufacturer's lack of confidence in the quality of the product. Consumers reach the point at which they find advertising *excessive* more quickly with color advertising than with black-and-white advertising because they understand that the addition of color increases advertising expenses. It is reasonable to infer that the reverse is also true and thus that consumers will tolerate lengthier repetitions of black-and-white advertising without becoming suspicious of product quality.

A **Correct.** Consumers find color advertising excessive more quickly and thus can be expected to find black-and-white advertising excessive less quickly.

B The study does not discuss concurrent appearances of color and black-and-white advertisements for the same product.

C The sole conclusion about frequency is that consumers can tolerate a greater frequency of black-and-white advertisements than color advertisements.

D It is stated that consumers understand that color advertisements are more expensive.

E The research certainly does not report this finding.

The correct answer is A.

5. The passage suggests that Kirmani would be most likely to agree with which of the following statements about consumers' perceptions of the relationship between the frequency with which a product is advertised and the product's quality?

(A) Consumers' perceptions about the frequency with which an advertisement appears are their primary consideration when evaluating an advertisement's claims about product quality.
(B) Because most consumers do not notice the frequency of advertisement, it has little impact on most consumers' expectations regarding product quality.
(C) Consumers perceive frequency of advertisement as a signal about product quality only when the advertisement is for a product that is newly on the market.
(D) The frequency of advertisement is not always perceived by consumers to indicate that manufacturers are highly confident about their products' quality.
(E) Consumers who try a new product that has been frequently advertised are likely to perceive the advertisement's frequency as having been an accurate indicator of the product's quality.

Inference

The first sentence of the second paragraph provides the answer to this question: *at some level of spending the manufacturer's advertising effort may be perceived as unreasonably high, implying low manufacturer confidence in product quality*. Thus, it is logical to assume that if a product is advertised too frequently, consumers may believe that the manufacturer is spending excessive amounts on advertising because that manufacturer is not confident of the product's quality.

A Kirmani's research, as reported here, does not support this claim.

B Kirmani's research examines how consumers respond to the frequency of advertising; the research does not indicate that consumers do not notice frequency.

C The research does not distinguish between new and familiar products.

D Correct. Excessive advertising may lead consumers to believe that the manufacturer lacks confidence in the quality of the product.

E Kirmani's research does not specifically address new products.

The correct answer is D.

Questions 6–11 refer to the passage on page 28.

6. The main purpose of the passage is to

(A) propose an experiment.
(B) analyze a function.
(C) refute an argument.
(D) explain a contradiction.
(E) simulate a process.

Main idea

Determining the main purpose comes from considering the passage as a whole. The first paragraph begins by noting that *the idea of the brain as an information processor* is generally accepted by neuroscientists. The author then presents Searle as an *enemy* of this position and explains Searle's belief that human thought is more than information processing. The second paragraph questions Searle's position, and the third asserts that the brain is an information processor, refuting Searle's argument.

A The author uses the idea of a mechanical simulation of a stomach as a metaphor for a computer's simulation of thought; this is not a proposal for an experiment.

B The author analyzes Searle's position, but no function is analyzed.

C Correct. The author explains Searle's argument in order to refute it.

D The author points out a weakness in Searle's thinking, but not a contradiction.

E The simulation of a process is included as a metaphor, but it is not essential to the passage.

The correct answer is C.

7. Which of the following is most consistent with Searle's reasoning as presented in the passage?

(A) Meaning and content cannot be reduced to algorithms.
(B) The process of digestion can be simulated mechanically, but not on a computer.
(C) Simulated thoughts and real thoughts are essentially similar because they are composed primarily of information.
(D) A computer can use "causal powers" similar to those of the human brain when processing information.
(E) Computer simulations of the world can achieve the complexity of the brain's representations of the world.

Evaluation

Searle's position is stated in the first paragraph: because computers merely follow algorithms, *they cannot deal with important aspects of human thought such as meaning and content.* Thus, Searle believes that meaning and content cannot be reduced to algorithms.

A Correct. Searle believes that meaning and content cannot be reduced to algorithms.

B The author argues for the mechanical simulation, but offers no evidence that Searle would agree.

C This statement reflects the author's position, but it is the opposite of Searle's.

D Searle asserts that only people, not computers, have *the causal powers of the brain.*

E The passage does not discuss computer simulations of the world.

The correct answer is A.

8. The author of the passage would be most likely to agree with which of the following statements about the simulation of organ functions?

(A) An artificial device that achieves the functions of the stomach could be considered a valid model of the stomach.
(B) Computer simulations of the brain are best used to crack the brain's codes of meaning and content.
(C) Computer simulations of the brain challenge ideas that are fundamental to psychology and neuroscience.
(D) Because the brain and the stomach both act as processors, they can best be simulated by mechanical devices.
(E) The computer's limitations in simulating digestion suggest equal limitations in computer-simulated thinking.

Application

To answer this question, think about how the author would respond to each statement. Anticipating the author's response depends on understanding the author's point of view. In this passage, the author is arguing against Searle's view of the brain and in favor of the brain as information processor. The author believes that the computer can be a model of the brain and uses the example of the mechanical stomach to support his position on simulations.

A Correct. The first two sentences of the third paragraph imply that a mechanical device is a valid model.

B The author believes a computer can simulate the brain but does not comment on how these simulations should be used. There is no way to predict the author's reaction to this statement.

C The author would reject this statement since neuroscience and psychology do in fact see the brain as an information processor.

D The author agrees that both the brain and the stomach act as processors, believes that the computer, a nonmechanical device, can simulate the brain, and offers a way that a mechanical device could simulate the stomach. The author does not suggest that mechanical devices are the best way to simulate both their processes.

E This statement reflects Searle's viewpoint, which the author rejects.

The correct answer is A.

9. It can be inferred that the author of the passage believes that Searle's argument is flawed by its failure to:

(A) distinguish between syntactic and semantic operations.
(B) explain adequately how people, unlike computers, are able to understand meaning.
(C) provide concrete examples illustrating its claims about thinking.
(D) understand how computers use algorithms to process information.
(E) decipher the code that is transmitted from neuron to neuron in the brain.

Inference

The author's attitude toward Searle's argument is apparent in the first paragraph, which ends with the author's summary of what Searle is saying. Computers understand structures, Searle argues, but only people understand meaning. How do people understand meaning? The author notes that Searle is not able to answer this question and is able only to assert that people have *causal powers of the brain.*

A The author makes it clear in the first paragraph that Searle does distinguish between the two. In Searle's view computers are syntactic, interpreting structure or arrangement, rather than semantic, understanding meaning.

B Correct. The first paragraph ends with the contrast between people and computers, "*People, on the other hand, understand meaning because they have something Searle obscurely calls the causal powers of the brain.*" By calling Searle's explanation obscure, the author implies that Searle has not adequately clarified how people understand meaning.

C Nothing in the passage criticizes Searle for not providing concrete examples. Indeed, in the second paragraph, the author anticipates how Searle would react to one concrete example, the computer simulation of the stomach.

D In the first paragraph, the author says that Searle argues that *computers simply follow algorithms*; whether or not Searle understands how they use algorithms is irrelevant.

E Since, as the author suggests in the first paragraph, Searle does not believe information could be a code transmitted from neuron to neuron, he cannot be expected to decipher that code.

The correct answer is B.

10. From the passage, it can be inferred that the author would agree with Searle on which of the following points?

(A) Computers operate by following algorithms.
(B) The human brain can never fully understand its own functions.
(C) The comparison of the brain to a machine is overly simplistic.
(D) The most accurate models of physical processes are computer simulations.
(E) Human thought and computer-simulated thought involve similar processes of representation.

Inference

An inference requires going beyond the material explicitly stated in the passage to the author's ideas that underlie that material. The author and Searle take opposite points of view on the brain as information processor. Their area of agreement is narrow. However, they do both agree that computers work by following algorithms.

A **Correct.** The first paragraph explains that Searle dismisses computers because they *simply follow algorithms*; while the author disagrees with Searle on virtually every other point, no disagreement is voiced here.

B The first paragraph shows this to be Searle's position, but not the author's.

C The first paragraph shows this to be Searle's position, but not the author's.

D The second paragraph explains Searle's rejection of this position.

E The final paragraph establishes this as the author's position, but not Searle's.

The correct answer is A.

11. Which of the following most accurately represents Searle's criticism of the brain-as-computer metaphor, as that criticism is described in the passage?

(A) The metaphor is not experimentally verifiable.
(B) The metaphor does not take into account the unique powers of the brain.
(C) The metaphor suggests that a brain's functions can be simulated as easily as those of a stomach.
(D) The metaphor suggests that a computer can simulate the workings of the mind by using the codes of neural transmission.
(E) The metaphor is unhelpful because both the brain and the computer process information.

Inference

Searle's criticism of the brain-as-computer metaphor is discussed in the first paragraph. Computers are merely machines; only people are endowed with *causal powers of the brain* that allow them to understand meaning and content.

A Searle does not believe in the value of the metaphor, so its verification is beside the point.

B **Correct.** Searle believes that people have something computers do not, *causal powers of the brain* for understanding *important aspects of human thought*.

C Comparing the brain to a computer, the metaphor does not make this suggestion.

D In the second paragraph, the author says, *but even if a computer could simulate the workings of the mind*, making it clear that presently it cannot; this statement does not reflect why Searle rejects the metaphor.

E This is not the basis of Searle's objection since he does not accept the premise that the brain is an information processor.

The correct answer is B.

Questions 12–17 refer to the passage on page 30.

12. The primary purpose of the passage is to:

(A) explain why women reformers of the Progressive Era failed to achieve their goals.
(B) discuss the origins of child labor laws in the late nineteenth and early twentieth centuries.
(C) compare the living conditions of working-class and middle-class women in the Progressive Era.
(D) discuss an oversight on the part of women reformers of the Progressive Era.
(E) revise a traditional view of the role played by women reformers in enacting Progressive Era reforms.

Main idea

Understanding the author's purpose comes only from reflecting on the passage as a whole. The beginning of the passage notes the success of middle-class women reformers in improving working conditions for women and children. The middle discusses the position of working-class mothers, who were more concerned with the economic survival of their families than with labor reform and consequently tried to circumvent the laws. The close of the passage observes that, although middle-class reformers were right to point out exploitation of children, they failed to understand the economic plight of working-class families, who needed the income earned by every possible member. The purpose of this passage is to show the failure of middle-class reformers to understand the economic position of working-class families.

A Lines 6-10 emphasize the victories of the reformers.

B The passage discusses the effects, rather than the origins, of child labor laws.

C Living conditions of middle-class and working-class women are not compared.

D **Correct.** As is made clear, especially in the final sentence of the passage, women reformers failed to understand the economic needs of working-class families.

E A traditional view is not compared with a newer, revised view of the reformers.

The correct answer is D.

13. The "view" mentioned in line 17 of the passage refers to which of the following?

(A) Some working-class mothers' resistance to the enforcement of child labor laws
(B) Reformers' belief that child labor and industrial home work should be abolished
(C) Reformers' opinions about how working-class families raised their children
(D) Certain women historians' observation that there was a lack of consensus between women of different classes on the issue of child labor and industrial home work
(E) Working-class families' fears about the adverse consequences that child labor laws would have on their ability to earn an adequate living

Inference

To find what this appearance of *view* refers to, it is necessary to look back to the beginning of the sentence. *This view*, not shared by working-class mothers, refers to the reformers' conviction that *child labor and industrial home work were equally inhumane practices that should be outlawed.*

A *This view* must refer back to a point already stated; resistance to child labor laws is not discussed until the following sentence.

B **Correct.** *This view* refers to the position of reformers stated earlier in the same sentence: that *child labor and industrial home work...should be outlawed.*

C *This view* must refer back to a point already stated; the reformers' belief that resistance to child labor laws was due to poor parenting is discussed later in the passage.

D A number of women historians have said that working-class mothers did not always share the *view* of middle-class women reformers about child labor.

E *This view* must refer back to a point already stated; the fears of working-class families are examined in the following sentence.

The correct answer is B.

14. The author of the passage mentions the observations of women historians (line 15–17) most probably in order to:

(A) provide support for an assertion made in the preceding sentence (lines 10–12).
(B) raise a question that is answered in the last sentence of the passage (lines 27–32).
(C) introduce an opinion that challenges a statement made in the first sentence of the passage.
(D) offer an alternative view to the one attributed in the passage to working-class mothers.
(E) point out a contradiction inherent in the traditional view of child labor reform as it is presented in the passage.

Evaluation

In lines 10–12, the author asserts that child labor laws *pitted women of different classes against one another*. The view of the middle-class women reformers is stated, and then, to show that working-class mothers did not hold the same opinion, the author turns to the recent work of women historians to support this statement.

A **Correct.** The author uses the recent work of women historians to support the statement that women of different social classes were pitted against one another.

B The women historians *have recently observed*; the verb *observed* introduces a statement rather than a question.

C The reference to women historians has to do with working-class mothers; it does not challenge women's activism and role in social reform.

D The passage supports what the women historians say about working-class mothers.

E The author does not define or present the *traditional* view of child labor reform, nor is any inherent contradiction pointed out.

The correct answer is A.

15. The passage suggests that which of the following was a reason for the difference of opinion between working-class mothers and women reformers on the issue of child labor?

(A) Reformers' belief that industrial home work was preferable to child labor outside the home
(B) Reformers' belief that child labor laws should pertain to working conditions but not to pay
(C) Working-class mothers' resentment at reformers' attempts to interfere with their parenting
(D) Working-class mothers' belief that child labor was an inhumane practice
(E) Working-class families' need for every employable member of their families to earn money

Inference

The question's use of the word *suggests* means that the answer depends on making an inference. Lines 12–23 examine the different views of middle-class reformers and working-class mothers on child labor laws. While the reformers saw child labor as an *inhumane* practice that should be *outlawed*, working class mothers understood *the necessity of pooling the wages of as many family members as possible* and viewed child labor legislation as *a personal economic disaster*.

A Lines 12–14 show that reformers regarded both kinds of work as *equally inhumane practices that should be outlawed.*

B Pay is not specifically discussed in the passage.

C Lines 24–27 indicate that the reformers believed working-class resistance to child labor laws was a sign of poor parenting, but nothing is said about the working-class response to this view.

D Lines 12–17 say that the reformers held this position, but *working class mothers did not always share this view.*

E **Correct.** Lines 17–23 explain that working class families needed *the wages of as many family members as possible.*

The correct answer is E.

16. The author of the passage asserts which of the following about women reformers who tried to abolish child labor?

(A) They alienated working-class mothers by attempting to enlist them in agitating for progressive causes.
(B) They underestimated the prevalence of child labor among the working classes.
(C) They were correct in their conviction that child labor was deplorable but short-sighted about the impact of child labor legislation on working-class families.
(D) They were aggressive in their attempts to enforce child labor legislation, but were unable to prevent working-class families from circumventing them.
(E) They were prevented by their nearly total disenfranchisement from making significant progress in child labor reform.

Supporting ideas

This question is based on information explicitly stated in the final sentence of the passage. Women reformers viewed *child labor as a terribly exploitative practice* but they *failed to take account of the economic needs of working-class families.*

A The passage does not say that reformers tried to enlist working-class mothers in progressive causes.

B No evidence is offered to support such a statement.

C **Correct.** The final sentence makes clear that the reformers recognized child labor as *exploitative* but did not understand *the economic needs of working-class families.*

D The reformers' activities involved promoting legislation; there is no evidence in the passage that the reformers themselves attempted to enforce these laws.

E Lines 6–10 show that the reformers improved working conditions for women and children, despite their disenfranchisement.

The correct answer is C.

17. According to the passage, one of the most striking achievements of white middle-class women reformers during the Progressive Era was:

(A) gaining the right to vote in school elections.
(B) mobilizing working-class women in the fight against child labor.
(C) uniting women of different classes in grassroots activism.
(D) improving the economic conditions of working-class families.
(E) improving women's and children's working conditions.

Supporting ideas

The phrase "according to the passage" indicates that the answer can be found through careful reading of the passage. This question is based on information explicitly stated in lines 7–10, which state that *white middle-class women reformers won a variety of victories, notably in the improvement of working conditions, especially for women and children.*

A Lines 6–7 show that women already had the right to vote in school elections.

B Lines 20–24 show that working-class families *tried to circumvent child labor laws.*

C Lines 11–12 say that one product of grassroots activism, child labor legislation, *pitted women of different classes against one another.*

D Lines 31–32 say that the reformers *failed to take account of the economic needs of working-class families.*

E **Correct.** The passage states that reformers improved the working conditions of women and children.

The correct answer is E.

Critical Reasoning

The following discussion is intended to familiarize you with the most efficient and effective approaches to critical reasoning questions. The particular questions in this chapter are generally representative of the kinds of critical reasoning questions you will encounter on the GMAT®. Remember that it is the problem solving strategy that is important, not the specific details of a particular question.

18. Vasquez-Morrell Assurance specializes in insuring manufacturers. Whenever a policyholder makes a claim, a claims adjuster determines the amount that Vasquez-Morrell is obligated to pay. Vasquez-Morrell is cutting its staff of claims adjusters by 15 percent. To ensure that the company's ability to handle claims promptly is affected as little as possible by the staff cuts, consultants recommend that Vasquez-Morrell lay off those adjusters who now take longest, on average, to complete work on claims assigned to them.

Which of the following, if true, most seriously calls into question the consultants' criterion for selecting the staff to be laid off?

(A) If the time that Vasquez-Morrell takes to settle claims increases significantly, it could lose business to other insurers.

(B) Supervisors at Vasquez-Morrell tend to assign the most complex claims to the most capable adjusters.

(C) At Vasquez-Morrell, no insurance payments are made until a claims adjuster has reached a final determination on the claim.

(D) There are no positions at Vasquez-Morrell to which staff currently employed as claims adjusters could be reassigned.

(E) The premiums that Vasquez-Morrell currently charges are no higher than those charged for similar coverage by competitors.

Evaluation of a Plan

Situation An insurance company must reduce its staff of claims adjusters. To ensure continuing promptness in handling claims, consultants advise the company to lay off those adjusters who take the longest to complete claims.

Reasoning *What problem could there be with the criterion?* The consultants' criterion is the time an adjuster takes to settle a claim. However, some claims are naturally more complicated and require more time. If it is true that the company now assigns these time-consuming cases to its most capable adjusters, then these adjusters would be likely to be the ones who take longest to complete their cases. Laying off the adjusters who take the longest would thus mean laying off the company's most capable staff, which could very well decrease its ability to handle claims promptly.

A The consultants' advice makes sense if increased time to handle claims causes the company to lose business.

B Correct. This statement properly identifies the problem with the consultants' criterion.

C This statement merely describes the process of handling a claim; it does not provide any information about the criterion for layoffs.

D The consultants make no recommendations for reassigning staff, so indicating that there are no positions available does not call their advice into question.

E The consultants do not recommend a change in premiums; noting that they are similar to competitors' premiums does not undermine the plan that the consultants recommend.

The correct answer is B.

19. Prolonged spells of hot, dry weather at the end of the grape-growing season typically reduce a vineyard's yield, because the grapes stay relatively small. In years with such weather, wine producers can make only a relatively small quantity of wine from a given area of vineyards. Nonetheless, in regions where wine producers generally grow their own grapes, analysts typically expect a long, hot, dry spell late in the growing season to result in increased revenues for local wine producers.

Which of the following, if true, does most to justify the analysts' expectation?

(A) The lower a vineyard's yield, the less labor is required to harvest the grapes.

(B) Long, hot, dry spells at the beginning of the grape-growing season are rare, but they can have a devastating effect on a vineyard's yield.

(C) Grapes grown for wine production are typically made into wine at or near the vineyard in which they were grown.

(D) When hot, dry spells are followed by heavy rains, the rains frequently destroy grape crops.

(E) Grapes that have matured in hot, dry weather make significantly better wine than ordinary grapes.

Argument Construction

Situation Hot, dry weather at the end of the grape-growing season reduces yield, so winemakers can only produce a small quantity of wine. However, analysts expect that this weather will increase winemakers' revenues.

Reasoning *What additional piece of information explains the analysts' expectations?* The same conditions that lead to low quantity also lead to something that increases revenues. What could this be? If these weather conditions lead to higher-quality wine that will sell for higher prices, the analysts' expectations for increased revenues are justified.

A Lower labor costs mean less expenditure for the winemakers; this does not explain how revenues would increase.

B This statement about low yields does not explain an increase in revenues.

C The proximity of production to the vineyard is irrelevant to the question of how hot, dry weather can be responsible for decreased yield and increased revenues.

D This statement gives another example of weather's effect on grape crops, but it does not explain how revenues are increased.

E **Correct.** This statement properly provides the explanation that the weather conditions will lead to better wines. With better wines typically commanding higher prices, the winemakers will gain the increased revenues that the analysts anticipate.

The correct answer is E.

20. In the past, most children who went sledding in the winter snow in Verland used wooden sleds with runners and steering bars. Ten years ago, smooth plastic sleds became popular; they go faster than wooden sleds but are harder to steer and slow. The concern that plastic sleds are more dangerous is clearly borne out by the fact that the number of children injured while sledding was much higher last winter than it was 10 years ago.

Which of the following, if true in Verland, most seriously undermines the force of the evidence cited?

(A) A few children still use traditional wooden sleds.

(B) Very few children wear any kind of protective gear, such as helmets, while sledding.

(C) Plastic sleds can be used in a much wider variety of snow conditions than wooden sleds can.

(D) Most sledding injuries occur when a sled collides with a tree, a rock, or another sled.

(E) Because the traditional wooden sleds can carry more than one rider, an accident involving a wooden sled can result in several children being injured.

Argument Evaluation

Situation Ten years ago, wooden sleds began to be replaced by plastic sleds that go faster but are harder to control. Plastic sleds are more dangerous than wooden sleds because more children suffered injuries last year than they did 10 years ago.

Reasoning *What weakens this argument?* This argument depends on a comparison of two kinds of sleds. Any evidence that would either strengthen or weaken the argument must indicate a comparison. Evidence that applies only to one kind of sled or to both kinds of sleds equally cannot weaken this argument. Consider the implications of the evidence presented in the answer choices. If plastic sleds can be used in a wider variety of conditions than wooden sleds can, then plastic sleds can be used more frequently. It is possible that more frequent use, rather than the sleds themselves, has led to more accidents.

A The limited use of some wooden sleds does not weaken the argument.

B The absence of protective gear would affect accidents with both kinds of sleds.

C **Correct.** This statement weakens the argument by providing an alternate explanation for the increased accidents.

D This statement is true of accidents with both kinds of sleds.

E This explains why wooden sleds may be dangerous but does not weaken the argument that plastic sleds are even more dangerous.

The correct answer is C.

21. Metal rings recently excavated from seventh-century settlements in the western part of Mexico were made using the same metallurgical techniques as those used by Ecuadorian artisans before and during that period. These techniques are sufficiently complex to make their independent development in both areas unlikely. Since the people of these two areas were in cultural contact, archaeologists hypothesize that the metallurgical techniques used to make the rings found in Mexico were learned by Mexican artisans from Ecuadorian counterparts.

Which of the following would it be most useful to establish in order to evaluate the archaeologists' hypothesis?

(A) Whether metal objects were traded from Ecuador to western Mexico during the seventh century
(B) Whether travel between western Mexico and Ecuador in the seventh century would have been primarily by land or by sea
(C) Whether artisans from western Mexico could have learned complex metallurgical techniques from their Ecuadorian counterparts without actually leaving western Mexico
(D) Whether metal tools were used in the seventh-century settlements in western Mexico
(E) Whether any of the techniques used in the manufacture of the metal rings found in western Mexico are still practiced among artisans in Ecuador today

Argument Evaluation

Situation Metal rings excavated from seventh-century settlements in western Mexico were made with the same complex techniques used in Ecuador before and during a period when the two cultures were known to be in contact. Mexican artisans are thought to have learned the techniques from Ecuadorian artisans.

Reasoning *What point could best be applied in evaluating this hypothesis?* Consider what specific information would help to assess the archaeologists' theory. It is given that the two areas had some cultural contact. If it were determined that metal objects were traded from one culture to the other, it could be possible that the metalworking techniques were passed along as well. Such evidence would be relevant to the hypothesis that Mexican artisans saw the work of their Ecuadorian counterparts and, from this exchange, learned the techniques to make the metal rings.

A **Correct.** This statement properly identifies information that would be useful in the evaluation of the archaeologists' hypothesis.
B The means of travel is irrelevant to the hypothesis about the source of the techniques.
C The hypothesis is not about where Mexican artisans learned the techniques, but whether they learned them from the Ecuadorians.
D The existence of metal tools provides no helpful information in establishing whether the Ecuadorians were the source of the metallurgical techniques.
E The comparison to the present day is irrelevant to the hypothesis.

The correct answer is A.

22. Following several years of declining advertising sales, the *Greenville Times* reorganized its advertising sales force. Before reorganization, the sales force was organized geographically, with some sales representatives concentrating on city-center businesses and others concentrating on different outlying regions. The reorganization attempted to increase the sales representatives' knowledge of clients' businesses by having each sales representative deal with only one type of industry or of retailing. After the reorganization, revenue from advertising sales increased.

In assessing whether the improvement in advertising sales can properly be attributed to the reorganization, it would be most helpful to find out which of the following?

(A) What proportion of the total revenue of the *Greenville Times* is generated by advertising sales?

(B) Has the circulation of the *Greenville Times* increased substantially in the last two years?

(C) Among all the types of industry and retailing that use the *Greenville Times* as an advertising vehicle, which type accounts for the largest proportion of the newspaper's advertising sales?

(D) Do any clients of the sales representatives of the *Greenville Times* have a standing order with the *Times* for a fixed amount of advertising per month?

(E) Among the advertisers in the *Greenville Times*, are there more types of retail business or more types of industrial business?

Evaluation of a Plan

Situation In the face of declining advertising sales, a newspaper reorganizes its sales force so that sales representatives have a better understanding of businesses. Revenue from advertising sales increased after the reorganization.

Reasoning *What additional evidence would help determine the source of the increased revenue?* In order to attribute the increased revenue to the reorganization of the sales force, other possible causes must be eliminated. Newspaper advertising rates are linked to circulation; when circulation increases, higher rates can be charged and revenues will increase. An alternative explanation might be a significant rise in circulation, so it would be particularly helpful to know if circulation had increased.

A The question concerns only increased revenue from advertising sales; the proportion of advertising revenue to total revenue is outside the scope of the question.

B Correct. This statement provides another possible explanation for increased revenue of advertising sales, and so the answer to this question would help to clarify the reason for the increased revenue.

C Knowing how the advertising sales break down by type of business might be useful for other purposes, but it does not help to show the cause of the increase.

D A fixed amount of advertising would not explain increased revenue, so the answer to this question would be irrelevant.

E Distinguishing between the types of businesses will not contribute to determining whether the reorganization was responsible for the increased revenue.

The correct answer is B.

23. Motorists in a certain country frequently complain that traffic congestion is much worse now than it was twenty years ago. No real measure of how much traffic congestion there was twenty years ago exists, but the motorists' complaints are almost certainly unwarranted. The country's highway capacity has tripled in the last twenty years, thanks to a vigorous highway construction program, whereas the number of automobiles registered in the country has increased by only 75 percent.

Which of the following, if true, most seriously weakens the argument?

(A) Most automobile travel is local, and the networks of roads and streets in the country's settled areas have changed little over the last twenty years.

(B) Gasoline prices are high, and miles traveled per car per year have not changed much over the last 20 years.

(C) The country's urban centers have well-developed public transit systems that carry most of the people who commute into those centers.

(D) The average age of automobiles registered in the country is lower now than it was 20 years ago.

(E) Radio stations have long been broadcasting regular traffic reports that inform motorists about traffic congestion.

Argument Evaluation

Situation Motorists complain that traffic congestion in their country is much worse than it was twenty years ago. But these complaints have no basis since the highway capacity in this country has tripled in the same period, whereas the number of cars registered has risen by only 75 percent.

Reasoning *Which point most undermines the argument that the complaints are unwarranted?* Consider that the response to the generalized complaints about congestion discusses only the topic of highway capacity. What if the congestion that motorists are complaining about is not on highways but on local roads? Discovering that travel tends to be local in this country and that the local roads have not been improved in the last twenty years would seriously weaken the argument.

A **Correct.** This statement properly identifies a weakness in the argument: the response to the broad complaint addresses a different subject, highway capacity, not the issue of traffic congestion encountered by most motorists.

B If high gas prices actually prevented motorists from driving, and if motorists' driving habits were the same as they were twenty years ago, then these points should strengthen the argument that there is no basis for their complaints.

C The number of commuters who use public transit does not affect the argument that the motorists' complaints have no basis.

D The age of registered cars is irrelevant to the argument.

E The radio broadcasts attest to the existence of traffic, but not to its increase, so they do not affect the argument.

The correct answer is A.

24. The percentage of households with an annual income of more than $40,000 is higher in Merton County than in any other county. However, the percentage of households with an annual income of $60,000 or more is higher in Sommer County.

If the statements above are true, which of the following must also be true?

(A) The percentage of households with an annual income of $80,000 is higher in Sommer County than in Merton County.

(B) Merton County has the second highest percentage of households with an annual income of $60,000 or more.

(C) Some households in Merton County have an annual income between $40,000 and $60,000.

(D) The number of households with an annual income of more than $40,000 is greater in Merton County than in Sommer County.

(E) Average annual household income is higher in Sommer County than in Merton County.

Argument Construction

Situation The percentage of households with annual incomes of more than $40,000 is higher in Merton County than in any other county; the percentage of households with annual incomes of $60,000 or more is higher in Sommer County.

Reasoning *On the basis of this information, what point must be true?* The given information makes clear that Merton County has some households that exceed $40,000 in annual income. Sommer County has a higher percentage of households with annual incomes at or above $60,000. A higher percentage of the Merton County households must in turn have annual incomes of $60,000 or less. Thus, the annual income of some households in Merton County is between $40,000 and $60,000.

A Since it is possible that there are no households with an annual income of $80,000 in Sommer County, this statement does not follow from the situation.

B It is not possible to make this determination on the basis of the available evidence; Merton County may have no households at all with an income of more than $60,000.

C **Correct.** This statement properly identifies a conclusion that can be drawn from the given information: in order for the percentage of $40,000-plus incomes to be higher in Merton county than any other county while Sommer has the highest percentage of $60,000-plus incomes, there must be some households in Merton County that bring in between $40,000 and $60,000 annually.

D On the basis of information about the *percentages* of households, it is not possible to arrive at this conclusion about the *number* of households.

E From the given information, it is not possible to determine where the average income is greater. It is entirely possible that the number of $60,000-plus incomes in Sommer County is quite small and that the number of $40,000-plus incomes in Merton County is substantial.

The correct answer is C.

25. Tiger beetles are such fast runners that they can capture virtually any nonflying insect. However, when running toward an insect, a tiger beetle will intermittently stop and then, a moment later, resume its attack. Perhaps the beetles cannot maintain their pace and must pause for a moment's rest; but an alternative hypothesis is that while running, tiger beetles are unable to adequately process the resulting rapidly changing visual information and so quickly go blind and stop.

Which of the following, if discovered in experiments using artificially moved prey insects, would support one of the two hypotheses and undermine the other?

(A) When a prey insect is moved directly toward a beetle that has been chasing it, the beetle immediately stops and runs away without its usual intermittent stopping.

(B) In pursuing a swerving insect, a beetle alters its course while running and its pauses become more frequent as the chase progresses.

(C) In pursuing a moving insect, a beetle usually responds immediately to changes in the insect's direction, and it pauses equally frequently whether the chase is up or down an incline.

(D) If, when a beetle pauses, it has not gained on the insect it is pursuing, the beetle generally ends its pursuit.

(E) The faster a beetle pursues an insect fleeing directly away from it, the more frequently the beetle stops.

Argument Evaluation

Situation Two hypotheses are offered to explain the sudden stop that tiger beetles make while pursuing their prey: (1) they cannot maintain the rapid pace and must rest, and (2) they run too quickly to process visual information and so temporarily go blind.

Reasoning *What point would strengthen one of the two hypotheses and weaken the other?* Consider the information provided in each answer choice, remembering that information that supports one hypothesis must necessarily detract from the other. Any information that is not about pursuit or that affects the two hypotheses equally may be dismissed from consideration. If the frequency of stopping increases when the beetle follows a swerving insect and must constantly change its course, then the second hypothesis is strengthened; the beetle's pauses increase as the variety of visual information that it needs to deal with increases.

A The hypotheses concern ongoing pursuit; since this information is not about the beetle's continuing pursuit of prey, it neither strengthens nor weakens either hypothesis.

B **Correct.** This statement provides information that strengthens the second hypothesis: the swerving pursuit and the resulting continual course adjustments appear to be forcing the beetle to stop with increasing frequency to sort out the erratic visual information.

C In this experiment, since neither vision nor tiredness appears to be problematic, the beetle could be stopping for either reason; this information neither strengthens nor weakens either hypothesis.

D This information is irrelevant since both the hypotheses are about mid-pursuit behaviors.

E The correlation of frequency of stops with speed affects both hypotheses equally; the pauses could be equally due to an inability to maintain the pace or due to a need to process the visual information.

The correct answer is B.

26. Guillemots are birds of Arctic regions. They feed on fish that gather beneath thin sheets of floating ice, and they nest on nearby land. Guillemots need 80 consecutive snow-free days in a year to raise their chicks, so until average temperatures in the Arctic began to rise recently, the guillemots' range was limited to the southernmost Arctic coast. Therefore, if the warming continues, the guillemots' range will probably be enlarged by being extended northward along the coast.

Which of the following, if true, most seriously weakens the argument?

(A) Even if the warming trend continues, there will still be years in which guillemot chicks are killed by an unusually early snow.

(B) If the Arctic warming continues, guillemots' current predators are likely to succeed in extending their own range farther north.

(C) Guillemots nest in coastal areas, where temperatures are generally higher than in inland areas.

(D) If the Arctic warming continues, much of the thin ice in the southern Arctic will disappear.

(E) The fish that guillemots eat are currently preyed on by a wider variety of predators in the southernmost Arctic regions than they are farther north.

Argument Evaluation

Situation In the southern Arctic, guillemots find their prey beneath thin sheets of ice, nest nearby, and require 80 snow-free days to raise their young. A warming trend means that their range may be enlarged by extending northward along the coast.

Reasoning *Which point weakens the argument about the enlargement of the guillemots' range?* How could the birds move northward and simultaneously not enlarge their range? Consider the assumption implied by the idea of *enlargement*. If the guillemots lost their southern habitat, then their northward move would be a displacement rather than an enlargement. If their source of food was no longer available to them in the southern Arctic, then they would abandon that area as part of their range.

A An exceptional year is not an argument against an enlarged range because *an unusually early snow* could happen in the southern Arctic as well.

B If their current predators also migrate northward, then the guillemots' situation has not changed, so this is not an argument against their enlarged range.

C The argument suggests that they will move not inland, but *northward along the coast*.

D **Correct.** This statement properly identifies a factor that weakens the argument: the guillemots' move northward would not enlarge their range if they lost their food source, fish found under thin ice, in the southern Arctic.

E The possibility that they may find prey more easily in the north does not mean that they would abandon the southern Arctic, and so this point does not weaken the argument.

The correct answer is D.

27. Some batches of polio vaccine used around 1960 were contaminated with SV40, a virus that in monkeys causes various cancers. Some researchers now claim that this contamination caused some cases of a certain cancer in humans, mesothelioma. This claim is not undercut by the fact that a very careful survey made in the 1960s of people who had received the contaminated vaccine found no elevated incidence of any cancer, since __________.

(A) most cases of mesothelioma are caused by exposure to asbestos

(B) in some countries, there was no contamination of the vaccine

(C) SV40 is widely used in laboratories to produce cancers in animals

(D) mesotheliomas take several decades to develop

(E) mesothelioma was somewhat less common in 1960 than it is now

Argument Construction

Situation Researchers claim that contaminated polio vaccine administered in 1960 caused some cases of mesothelioma, a type of cancer. Their claim is not undermined by the results of a 1960s survey showing that those who received the contaminated vaccine had no elevated incidence of cancer.

Reasoning *Why did the survey results not challenge the researchers' claim?* The survey did not reveal a higher incidence of mesothelioma. This question then requires completing a sentence that establishes cause. What could be the reason that the people surveyed in the 1960s showed no signs of the disease? If the disease takes decades to develop, then those people surveyed would not yet have shown any signs of it; less than a decade had passed between their exposure to the vaccine and the survey.

A The contaminated vaccine is said to have caused *some* cases, not *most*; the question remains why the survey results pose no obstacle to the researchers' claim.

B The claim is only about contaminated vaccine, not uncontaminated vaccine.

C That the virus can cause cancers in laboratory animals had already been provided as a given; this additional information is irrelevant to the survey of people who received contaminated vaccine.

D Correct. This statement properly identifies the reason that the survey does not call into question the researchers' claim: the people surveyed in the 1960s showed no signs of disease because the cancer takes decades to develop.

E The frequency of mesothelioma in the general population is not related to the claim that contaminated vaccine caused the disease in a specific population.

The correct answer is D.

28. Gortland has long been narrowly self-sufficient in both grain and meat. However, as per capita income in Gortland has risen toward the world average, per capita consumption of meat has also risen toward the world average, and it takes several pounds of grain to produce one pound of meat. Therefore, since per capita income continues to rise, whereas domestic grain production will not increase, Gortland will soon have to import either grain or meat or both.

Which of the following is an assumption on which the argument depends?

(A) The total acreage devoted to grain production in Gortland will soon decrease.

(B) Importing either grain or meat will not result in a significantly higher percentage of Gortlanders' incomes being spent on food than is currently the case.

(C) The per capita consumption of meat in Gortland is increasing at roughly the same rate across all income levels.

(D) The per capita income of meat producers in Gortland is rising faster than the per capita income of grain producers.

(E) People in Gortland who increase their consumption of meat will not radically decrease their consumption of grain.

Argument Construction

Situation A country previously self-sufficient in grain and meat will soon have to import one or the other or both. Consumption of meat has risen as per capita income has risen, and it takes several pounds of grain to produce one pound of meat.

Reasoning *What conditions must be true for the conclusion to be true?* Meat consumption is rising. What about grain consumption? A sharp reduction in the amount of grain consumed could compensate for increased meat consumption, making the conclusion false. If people did radically decrease their grain consumption, it might not be necessary to import grain or meat or both. Since the argument concludes that the imports are necessary, it assumes grain consumption will not plunge.

A The argument makes no assumptions about the acreage devoted to grain; it assumes only that the demand for grain will rise.

B The argument does not discuss the percentage of their income that Gortlanders spend on food, so an assumption about this topic is not needed.

C The argument involves only meat consumption in general, not its distribution by income level.

D Since the argument does not refer to the incomes of meat producers and grain producers, it cannot depend on an assumption about them.

E **Correct.** This statement properly identifies the assumption that there will be no great decrease in grain consumption.

The correct answer is E.

29. The Hazelton coal-processing plant is a major employer in the Hazelton area, but national environmental regulations will force it to close if it continues to use old, polluting processing methods. However, to update the plant to use newer, cleaner methods would be so expensive that the plant will close unless it receives the tax break it has requested. In order to prevent a major increase in local unemployment, the Hazelton government is considering granting the plant's request.

Which of the following would be most important for the Hazelton government to determine before deciding whether to grant the plant's request?

(A) Whether the company that owns the plant would open a new plant in another area if the present plant were closed
(B) Whether the plant would employ far fewer workers when updated than it does now
(C) Whether the level of pollutants presently being emitted by the plant is high enough to constitute a health hazard for local residents
(D) Whether the majority of the coal processed by the plant is sold outside the Hazelton area
(E) Whether the plant would be able to process more coal when updated than it does now

Evaluation of a Plan

Situation Because of the expenses of mandatory updating, a plant that is a major employer in the local area will close unless it receives the tax break it has requested from the local government.

Reasoning *What point is most critical to the evaluation of the request?* Consider the information provided in the answer choices. The plant is important to the local government primarily because it is a major employer of local residents. What if updating the plant changed that by significantly reducing the number of employees needed? It is crucial for the local government to determine whether the plant will continue to employ the same number of people once it has updated.

A The local government is concerned only with the local area, so a new site outside that area is irrelevant.

B Correct. This statement properly identifies a factor that is critical to the plant's argument and the local government's decision.

C Updating is mandatory under national environmental regulations, whether the local residents are affected by the plant's pollutants or not.

D At issue is the plant's role as a major employer; where its product is sold is irrelevant.

E The amount of coal processed by the updated plant is irrelevant to the critical issue of the number of people employed to process that coal.

The correct answer is B.

30. A physically active lifestyle has been shown to help increase longevity. In the Wistar region of Bellaria, the average age at death is considerably higher than in any other part of the country. Wistar is the only mountainous part of Bellaria. A mountainous terrain makes even such basic activities as walking relatively strenuous; it essentially imposes a physically active lifestyle on people. Clearly, this circumstance explains the long lives of people in Wistar.

Which of the following, if true, most seriously weakens the argument?

(A) In Bellaria all medical expenses are paid by the government, so that personal income does not affect the quality of health care a person receives.

(B) The Wistar region is one of Bellaria's least populated regions.

(C) Many people who live in the Wistar region have moved there in middle age or upon retirement.

(D) The many opportunities for hiking, skiing, and other outdoor activities that Wistar's mountains offer make it a favorite destination for vacationing Bellarians.

(E) Per capita spending on recreational activities is no higher in Wistar than it is in other regions of Bellaria.

Argument Evaluation

Situation People in one region of a country live longer than people in other areas. The higher average age at time of death is attributed to the healthy lifestyle of the people in this region, where the mountainous terrain demands a physically active life.

Reasoning *What point weakens the argument?* Consider what assumption underlies the argument that the physically active lifestyle required of living in Wistar is responsible for its residents' relative longevity. The mountainous environment necessitates lifelong levels of rigorous physical activity that build a more robust population. What if a significant portion of the population has not been conditioned since childhood to the demands of the terrain? It is assumed here that the healthy lifestyle imposed by the terrain has shaped residents from birth and accounts for their longer life span. If many residents only moved there later in life, the argument is weakened.

A The argument is not about the quality of health care throughout the country, but the length of the residents' lives in a particular region.

B The rate of population density does not affect the argument.

C **Correct.** This statement properly identifies a point that weakens the argument.

D The area's popularity as a vacation destination does not affect the longevity of the local residents.

E The argument establishes that merely living in the region is strenuous; the spending on recreational activities is irrelevant.

The correct answer is C.

31. Cheever College offers several online courses via remote computer connection, in addition to traditional classroom-based courses. A study of student performance at Cheever found that, overall, the average student grade for online courses matched that for classroom-based courses. In this calculation of the average grade, course withdrawals were weighted as equivalent to a course failure, and the rate of withdrawal was much lower for students enrolled in classroom-based courses than for students enrolled in online courses.

If the statements above are true, which of the following must also be true of Cheever College?

(A) Among students who did not withdraw, students enrolled in online courses got higher grades, on average, than students enrolled in classroom-based courses.
(B) The number of students enrolled per course at the start of the school term is much higher, on average, for the online courses than for the classroom-based courses.
(C) There are no students who take both an online and a classroom-based course in the same school term.
(D) Among Cheever College students with the best grades, a significant majority take online, rather than classroom-based, courses.
(E) Courses offered online tend to deal with subject matter that is less challenging than that of classroom-based courses.

Argument Construction

Situation A comparison of online and classroom courses showed similar average grades. In determining average grades, a course withdrawal was weighted as a course failure. The rate of withdrawal was higher from online than from classroom courses.

Reasoning *What conclusion about the courses can be derived from this comparison?* Consider the ramifications of the methodology used to calculate the grade averages for the two types of courses. Because of course withdrawals, the online courses experienced a higher rate of failure, but the average grade for these courses still matched the average grade for classroom courses. From this it is logical to conclude that, for the two averages to match, the students who remained in the online courses must have had higher initial average grades than those in classroom courses.

A **Correct.** This statement properly identifies the logical conclusion that the higher percentage of withdrawals from online classes requires higher grades, on average, to compensate for the higher rate of failure.

B A number of students cannot be derived from a discussion of average grades and rates of withdrawal.

C This conclusion cannot be determined on the basis of the information provided.

D The information is about average grades; the argument does not provide any basis for a conclusion about best grades.

E It is impossible to determine the difficulty of subject matter from this information.

The correct answer is A.

32. For years the beautiful Renaissance buildings in Palitito have been damaged by exhaust from the many tour buses that come to the city. There has been little parking space, so most buses have idled at the curb during each stop on their tour, and idling produces as much exhaust as driving. The city has now provided parking that accommodates a third of the tour buses, so damage to Palitito's buildings from the buses' exhaust will diminish significantly.

Which of the following, if true, most strongly supports the argument?

(A) The exhaust from Palitito's few automobiles is not a significant threat to Palitito's buildings.

(B) Palitito's Renaissance buildings are not threatened by pollution other than engine exhaust.

(C) Tour buses typically spend less than one-quarter of the time they are in Palitito transporting passengers from one site to another.

(D) More tourists come to Palitito by tour bus than by any other single means of transportation.

(E) Some of the tour buses that are unable to find parking drive around Palitito while their passengers are visiting a site.

Argument Evaluation

Situation Tour buses have damaged Renaissance buildings with their exhaust fumes because lack of parking has kept the buses idling at curbs. Providing new parking for a third of the buses should significantly reduce the damage caused by the exhaust.

Reasoning *What point strengthens the argument?* The argument for reduced damage relies on the reduction of the vehicles' exhaust fumes. Any additional evidence regarding the extent to which the vehicular emissions are likely to be reduced also supports the argument for the benefits of the new parking space. Learning that tour buses spend not just a few minutes but most of their time idling at the curb strengthens the argument. The new parking spaces will allow a third of the tour buses to spend 75 percent of their time with their engines off, causing no damage at all.

A If automobile exhaust is not a threat, the argument is not affected.

B This statement does not address the question of whether the new parking will reduce the damage caused by engine exhaust from the buses.

C **Correct.** This statement properly cites a factor that supports the argument: since most of the buses' time has been spent producing damaging exhaust, the new parking should reduce the damage significantly.

D This statement about tourists' chosen means of transportation is irrelevant to the issue of what the buses do while in the city.

E It is given that the new parking will only provide space for a third of the buses, and thus some buses will continue to idle and some to drive around, continuing to contribute equally to the building damage. This statement does not strengthen the argument.

The correct answer is C.

33. During the 1980s and 1990s, the annual number of people who visited the Sordellian Mountains increased continually, and many new ski resorts were built. Over the same period, however, the number of visitors to ski resorts who were caught in avalanches decreased, even though there was no reduction in the annual number of avalanches in the Sordellian Mountains.

Which of the following, if true in the Sordellian Mountains during the 1980s and 1990s, most helps to explain the decrease?

(A) Avalanches were most likely to happen when a large new snowfall covered an older layer of snow.

(B) Avalanches destroyed at least some buildings in the Sordellian Mountains in every year.

(C) People planning new ski slopes and other resort facilities used increasingly accurate information about which locations are likely to be in the path of avalanches.

(D) The average length of stay for people visiting the Sordellian Mountains increased slightly.

(E) Construction of new ski resorts often led to the clearing of wooded areas that had helped prevent avalanches.

Argument Construction

Situation Over a certain period, new ski resorts accommodated an increasing number of visitors at the same time that fewer visitors were caught in avalanches. Yet there were no fewer avalanches than usual during this period.

Reasoning *What explains the apparent contradiction of increased visitors but fewer visitors caught in avalanches?* More resort visitors would imply more avalanche-related accidents, but the average has shifted so that fewer visitors are being caught in the avalanches. It must be that fewer visitors are exposed to this danger; consider the answer choices to identify a logical reason for this improvement in their exposure. If the likely paths of avalanches had become better understood, that information would have been applied to identify safer locations for new ski slopes and ski resorts. The facilities would thus have been built well out of the way of avalanches, resulting in fewer visitors trapped in avalanches.

A This likelihood would remain true from year to year; it does not explain the decrease.

B This point does not explain why fewer visitors were caught in these avalanches.

C **Correct.** This statement properly identifies a factor that explains the decreased number of accidents.

D The greater length of stay would seem to expose visitors to greater danger.

E This information points to an expected increase, rather than decrease, in visitors who might be caught by avalanches.

The correct answer is C.

34. A year ago, Dietz Foods launched a yearlong advertising campaign for its canned tuna. Last year Dietz sold 12 million cans of tuna compared to the 10 million sold during the previous year, an increase directly attributable to new customers brought in by the campaign. Profits from the additional sales, however, were substantially less than the cost of the advertising campaign. Clearly, therefore, the campaign did nothing to further Dietz's economic interests.

Which of the following, if true, most seriously weakens the argument?

(A) Sales of canned tuna account for a relatively small percentage of Dietz Foods' profits.

(B) Most of the people who bought Dietz's canned tuna for the first time as a result of the campaign were already loyal customers of other Dietz products.

(C) A less expensive advertising campaign would have brought in significantly fewer new customers for Dietz's canned tuna than did the campaign Dietz Foods launched last year.

(D) Dietz made money on sales of canned tuna last year.

(E) In each of the past five years, there was a steep, industry-wide decline in sales of canned tuna.

Argument Evaluation

Situation An advertising campaign was responsible for increased sales of canned tuna. Since the profits from the increased sales were less than the costs of the campaign, the campaign did not contribute to the company's economic interests.

Reasoning *Which point weakens the argument?* Consider the basis of the argument: if profits are lower than costs, the campaign made no contribution to the company's financial well-being. In what case might this be untrue? What if the advertising campaign reversed an industry-wide trend of declining sales? If Dietz experienced increasing sales, while other companies experienced decreased sales, then the campaign did contribute to the economic interests of the company, and the argument is considerably weakened.

A The issue is not the percentage of profits that canned tuna contributes, but the success of the advertising campaign.

B If the customers bought the tuna because of the campaign, it is irrelevant to the argument that they also bought other Dietz products.

C This information neither strengthens nor weakens the argument.

D The argument is not about profits only, but about whether the advertising campaign contributed to the economic interests of the company.

E **Correct.** This statement properly identifies a factor that weakens the argument: the campaign secured the benefits of increased sales at a time when the entire industry was experiencing a decline in sales.

The correct answer is E.

Sentence Correction

The following discussion is intended to familiarize you with the most efficient and effective approaches to sentence correction questions. The particular questions in this chapter are generally representative of the kinds of sentence correction questions you will encounter on the GMAT®. Remember that it is the problem solving strategy that is important, not the specific details of a particular question.

35. Unlike the buildings in Mesopotamian cities, which were arranged haphazardly, the same basic plan was followed for cities of the Indus Valley: with houses laid out on a north-south, east-west grid, and houses and walls were built of standard-size bricks.

(A) the buildings in Mesopotamian cities, which were arranged haphazardly, the same basic plan was followed for all cities of the Indus Valley: with houses
(B) the buildings in Mesopotamian cities, which were haphazard in arrangement, the same basic plan was used in all cities of the Indus Valley: houses were
(C) the arrangement of buildings in Mesopotamian cities, which were haphazard, the cities of the Indus Valley all followed the same basic plan: houses
(D) Mesopotamian cities, in which buildings were arranged haphazardly, the cities of the Indus Valley all followed the same basic plan: houses were
(E) Mesopotamian cities, which had buildings that were arranged haphazardly, the same basic plan was used for all cities in the Indus Valley: houses that were

Comparison-contrast + Modifying clause

The contrast introduced by *unlike* must be logical and clear. Contrasting *the buildings in Mesopotamian cities* with *the same basic plan* does not make sense; *Mesopotamian cities* should be contrasted with *the cities of the Indus Valley*. Also, it needs to be clear that it was the *buildings* in the cities that *were arranged haphazardly* rather than the *cities*. The second half of the sentence needs *houses were laid out* to be parallel in structure to *and houses and walls were built.*

A Illogically contrasts *the buildings in Mesopotamian cities* with *the same basic plan*; not clear whether *which were arranged haphazardly* modifies *cities* or *buildings*; *with houses* lacks parallelism and is confusing.

B Illogically contrasts *the buildings in Mesopotamian cities* with *the same basic plan*; does not clarify what *which were haphazard in arrangement* modifies.

C Illogically contrasts *the arrangement of buildings* with *the cities of the Indus Valley*; not clear whether *which were haphazard* modifies *buildings* or *cities*; *houses* not followed by a verb.

D Correct. In this sentence, *Mesopotamian cities* are properly contrasted with *the cities of the Indus Valley*; *in which buildings were arranged haphazardly* expresses the idea clearly; and *houses* is followed by *were* as required.

E Illogically contrasts *Mesopotamian cities* with *the same basic plan; houses that were* lacks parallelism and is confusing.

The correct answer is D.

36. New data from United States Forest Service ecologists show that for every dollar spent on controlled small-scale burning, forest thinning, and the training of fire-management personnel, it saves seven dollars that would not be spent on having to extinguish big fires.

(A) that for every dollar spent on controlled small-scale burning, forest thinning, and the training of fire-management personnel, it saves seven dollars that would not be spent on having to extinguish

(B) that for every dollar spent on controlled small-scale burning, forest thinning, and the training of fire-management personnel, seven dollars are saved that would have been spent on extinguishing
(C) that for every dollar spent on controlled small-scale burning, forest thinning, and the training of fire-management personnel saves seven dollars on not having to extinguish
(D) for every dollar spent on controlled small-scale burning, forest thinning, and the training of fire-management personnel, that it saves seven dollars on not having to extinguish
(E) for every dollar spent on controlled small-scale burning, forest thinning, and the training of fire-management personnel, that seven dollars are saved that would not have been spent on extinguishing

Logical predication + Rhetorical construction

The pronoun *it* (*it saves seven dollars*) has no referent. Making *seven dollars* the subject of the clause eliminates this problem, and it also fulfills a reader's expectation that after the phrase beginning *for every dollar* another specific amount will be given to balance it. This change in structure also allows the awkward and wordy clause *that would not be spent on having to extinguish* to be rewritten so that *spent* balances *saved*: *seven dollars are saved that would have been spent on extinguishing,* and the unnecessary *having to* is omitted.

A *It* has no referent; *not be spent* is awkward; *on having to extinguish* is wordy.

B Correct. This sentence properly uses *seven dollars* as the subject of the clause to balance *every dollar* in the introductory phrase; the phrasing is concise and parallel.

C *Saves* does not have a subject; construction is not a complete sentence; *not having to extinguish* is wordy and awkward.

D *That* introduces a subordinate rather than main clause, making a sentence fragment; *it* has no referent; *not having to extinguish* is wordy and awkward.

E Introductory *that* makes a sentence fragment; *that would not have been spent on extinguishing* is awkward and illogical.

The correct answer is B.

37. Like the grassy fields and old pastures that the upland sandpiper needs for feeding and nesting when it returns in May after wintering in the Argentine Pampas, the sandpipers vanishing in the northeastern United States is a result of residential and industrial development and of changes in farming practices.

(A) the sandpipers vanishing in the northeastern United States is a result of residential and industrial development and of changes in
(B) the bird itself is vanishing in the northeastern United States as a result of residential and industrial development and of changes in
(C) that the birds themselves are vanishing in the northeastern United States is due to residential and industrial development and changes to
(D) in the northeastern United States, sandpipers' vanishing due to residential and industrial development and to changes in
(E) in the northeastern United States, the sandpipers' vanishing, a result of residential and industrial development and changing

Comparison + Sentence structure

The comparison introduced by *like* must be logical and clear; the point of this comparison is that both the habitat and the bird are disappearing for similar reasons. The comparison must use comparable grammatical components; *the bird itself* is a noun phrase and matches the noun phrases *grassy fields* and *old pastures*.

A Illogically compares *the sandpipers vanishing* to *grassy fields and old pastures*; omits apostrophe in *sandpipers' vanishing*; wordy.

B Correct. This sentence properly compares *the bird itself* to *grassy fields and old pastures*; *is vanishing* as the verb strengthens the sentence by making the comparison clearer.

C Does not finish the comparison begun with *like* but instead substitutes a clause (*that the birds themselves are vanishing*).

D Illogically compares *the sandpipers' vanishing* to *grassy fields and old pastures;* creates a sentence fragment.

E Illogically compares *the sandpipers' vanishing* to *grassy fields and old pastures*; creates a sentence fragment.

The correct answer is B.

38. The results of two recent unrelated studies support the idea that dolphins may share certain cognitive abilities with humans and great apes; the studies indicate <u>dolphins as capable of recognizing themselves in mirrors—an ability that is often considered a sign of self-awareness—and to grasp spontaneously</u> the mood or intention of humans.

(A) dolphins as capable of recognizing themselves in mirrors—an ability that is often considered a sign of self-awareness—and to grasp spontaneously
(B) dolphins' ability to recognize themselves in mirrors—an ability that is often considered as a sign of self-awareness—and of spontaneously grasping
(C) dolphins to be capable of recognizing themselves in mirrors—an ability that is often considered a sign of self-awareness—and to grasp spontaneously
(D) that dolphins have the ability of recognizing themselves in mirrors—an ability that is often considered as a sign of self-awareness—and spontaneously grasping
(E) that dolphins are capable of recognizing themselves in mirrors—an ability that is often considered a sign of self-awareness—and of spontaneously grasping

Grammatical construction + Parallelism

In the context of this sentence, *the studies indicate* must introduce a clause; the clause must begin with *that* and have a subject, *dolphins*, and a verb, *are* (the complete verb phrase would be *are capable of*). The two capabilities should be parallel: *capable of recognizing...and of spontaneously grasping*.

A Context requires a clause, but this construction is not a clause; *capable of recognizing* is not parallel to *to grasp spontaneously*.

B Construction is not a clause, and a clause is required; *dolphins' ability to recognize* is not parallel to *of spontaneously grasping*.

C A clause is required following *the studies indicate*; *to be capable of recognizing* is not parallel to *to grasp spontaneously*.

D *Have the ability of* is wordy and unidiomatic; *of recognizing* and *spontaneously grasping* are not parallel.

E **Correct.** *That* introduces the subordinate clause necessary to complete this sentence properly; *of recognizing* and *of spontaneously grasping* are parallel.

The correct answer is E.

39. According to scholars, the earliest writing was probably not a direct rendering of speech, but <u>was more likely to begin as</u> a separate and distinct symbolic system of communication, and only later merged with spoken language.

(A) was more likely to begin as
(B) more than likely began as
(C) more than likely beginning from
(D) it was more than likely begun from
(E) it was more likely that it began

Idiom + Verb form

This sentence is a comparison in which *probably not x* is balanced by *but more than likely y*. When *more* is used in the comparative form of an adjective (*more difficult*) or adverb (*more likely*), it is followed by *than*. The words used to show the comparison between *x* and *y*, *but more than likely*, must also introduce the correct verb form, allowing *y* to fit grammatically into the rest of the sentence. The subject of the sentence has three verbs, all of which should be parallel: *the earliest writing was...began...merged. Was...to begin* is not parallel and results in a construction that is not grammatically correct.

A In this context, *more likely* is not a complete idiomatic expression; *was...to begin* is not parallel to *was* and *merged.*

B Correct. In this sentence, *more than likely* is the correct comparative construction; the simple past tense *began*, parallel to *was* and *merged*, fits grammatically into the sentence.

C Subject should be followed by three verbs; *beginning from* is not a verb.

D Use of the pronoun *it* makes this construction a main clause, in which case the comma after *communication* must be omitted and *began* must used to be parallel to *merged*; *was...begun* is not the correct tense.

E In this awkward, unclear, and wordy construction, the first *it* must be followed by *is*, not *was*, because the theory is current; the second *it* acts as the subject of the subordinate clause, and this usage requires the omission of the comma after *communication.*

The correct answer is B.

40. In 1995 Richard Stallman, a well-known critic of the patent system, testified in Patent Office hearings that, to test the system, a colleague of his had managed to win a patent for one of Kirchhoff's laws, an observation about electric current first made in 1845 and now included in virtually every textbook of elementary physics.

(A) laws, an observation about electric current first made in 1845 and
(B) laws, which was an observation about electric current first made in 1845 and it is
(C) laws, namely, it was an observation about electric current first made in 1845 and
(D) laws, an observation about electric current first made in 1845, it is
(E) laws that was an observation about electric current, first made in 1845, and is

Logical predication + Parallelism

The function of the entire long phrase (*observation...physics*) that follows *one of Kirchhoff's laws* is to describe that law. It is a noun phrase in apposition, which means that it has the same syntactic relation to all the other parts of the sentence that the noun phrase *one of Kirchhoff's laws* does. Within the long modifying phrase, parallelism is maintained by balancing *an observation...first made* with *and now included.*

A Correct. In this sentence, the noun phrase in apposition properly identifies and explains the law, using parallel structure and concise expression.

B *Which* is ambiguous because it could refer to *one* or to *laws*; *it is* violates the parallelism of *first made* and *now included.*

C *It* is ambiguous; the introduction of *it was* does not allow this construction to fit grammatically into the sentence.

D The referent of *it* is unclear; *it is* creates a run-on sentence and violates the parallelism of *first made* and *now included.*

E *That* appears to refer to *laws* rather than *one*, but the verb is singular; setting the phrase *first made in 1845* off in commas distorts meaning; *is* violates parallelism.

The correct answer is A.

41. Excavators at the Indus Valley site of Harappa in eastern Pakistan say the discovery of inscribed shards dating to circa 2800–2600 BC indicate their development of a Harappan writing system, the use of inscribed seals impressed into clay for marking ownership, and the standardization of weights for trade or taxation occurred many decades, if not centuries, earlier than was previously believed.

(A) indicate their development of a Harappan writing system, the use of
(B) indicate that the development of a Harappan writing system, using
(C) indicates that their development of a Harappan writing system, using
(D) indicates the development of a Harappan writing system, their use of
(E) indicates that the development of a Harappan writing system, the use of

Agreement + Idiom + Parallelism

In long sentences such as this one, the relationship between parts of the sentence may be difficult to see. Here, the main clause of the sentence is *excavators...say* and the logical sequence that follows is *the discovery...indicates that.* The subject of this first subordinate clause is the singular noun *discovery*, which should be followed by the singular verb *indicates* rather than by the plural *indicate*, as is done in the original sentence. *Their*, used with either *development* or *use*, has no clear or logical referent in any of the alternatives. The subject of the following subordinate (*that*) clause, which has *occurred* as its verb, is a series of three phrases, which must be parallel, especially in a sentence of this length and complexity: *the development of..., the use of..., and the standardization of....*

A *Indicate* does not agree with *discovery*; the pronoun *their* has no logical referent, and *their development* is not parallel to *the use* and *the standardization.*

B *Indicate* does not agree with *discovery*; *using* is not parallel to *the development* and *the standardization.*

C *Their* has no logical referent; the series of three elements should be parallel, but here all are different.

D The pronoun *their* has no logical referent, and *their use* is not parallel to *the development* and *the standardization*; the preferred sentence structure would have *indicates* followed by *that* when introducing a clause.

E **Correct.** In this sentence, *indicates* agrees with *discovery* and is followed by *that* to introduce a clause; the three parallel phrases begin with an article (*the*), a noun, and the preposition *of.*

The correct answer is E.

42. The Supreme Court has ruled that public universities can collect student activity fees even with students' objections to particular activities, so long as the groups they give money to will be chosen without regard to their views.

(A) with students' objections to particular activities, as long as the groups they give money to will be
(B) if they have objections to particular activities and the groups that are given the money are
(C) if they object to particular activities, but the groups that the money is given to have to be
(D) from students who object to particular activities, so long as the groups given money are
(E) though students have an objection to particular activities, but the groups that are given the money be

Logical predication + Rhetorical construction

The underlined portion of the sentence fails to establish a clear relationship among *universities*, *students*, and *groups.* To which of these three does *they* refer? It would appear that the *universities* must give the money, but *they* does not have a referent. Furthermore, *they* is followed by *their views*, and in this case *their* must refer to *groups.* Wordy and awkward phrasing as well as an unnecessary shift in verb tense (*will be chosen*) compound the difficulty of understanding this sentence in its original form.

A *With students' objections...*is awkward and dense; *they* does not have a referent; the future *will be* is incorrect since the Supreme Court *has* already *ruled.*

B Referent for *they* is *student activity fees*, which cannot possibly *have objections...*; the use of *and* is illogical.

C *They* refers to student *activity fees* rather than *students*; *but* does not have the sense of *with the provision that* required here; *have to be* is wordy.

D Correct. In this sentence, *from students who object* is clear and idiomatic; *so long as* is used appropriately; *groups given money* eliminates the problem of a pronoun without a referent; *are* is the proper tense.

E *Have an objection* is an unnecessarily wordy way to say *object*; the verb *be* does not complete the latter part of the sentence.

The correct answer is D.

43. Despite the increasing number of women graduating from law school and passing bar examinations, <u>the proportion of judges and partners at major law firms who are women have not risen to a comparable extent</u>.

(A) the proportion of judges and partners at major law firms who are women have not risen to a comparable extent
(B) the proportion of women judges and partners at major law firms have not risen comparably
(C) the proportion of judges and partners at major law firms who are women has not risen comparably
(D) yet the proportion of women judges and partners at major law firms has not risen to a comparable extent
(E) yet the proportion of judges and partners at major law firms who are women has not risen comparably

Agreement + Rhetorical construction

When a number of plural nouns appear in phrases between a singular subject and the verb, it can be easy to overlook the true subject of the verb. Here, *judges*, *partners*, *firms*, and *women* all occur between the singular subject, *proportion*, and the verb, which should also be singular, *has risen*. Concise expression is particularly important in a long construction; *to a comparable extent* may be more concisely expressed as *comparably*.

A Plural verb, *have risen*, does not agree with the singular subject, *proportion*.

B *Have risen* does not agree with *proportion*; here, *women* applies only to *judges*, not to *partners at major law firms*.

C Correct. In this sentence, *has risen* agrees with *proportion*, and *comparably* is more concise than *to a comparable extent*. The modifying clause *who are women* follows (1) *judges* and (2) *partners at major law firms* as closely as is possible given the content of the sentence; this positioning has the virtue of being clear in its meaning.

D The contrast has already been introduced by *despite*, so the addition of *yet* is illogical and ungrammatical; *to a comparable extent* is wordy.

E *Despite* introduces the contrast; adding *yet* is illogical and results in an ungrammatical construction.

The correct answer is C.

44. <u>Seldom more than 40 feet wide and 12 feet deep, but it ran 363 miles across the rugged wilderness of upstate New York, the Erie Canal connected</u> the Hudson River at Albany to the Great Lakes at Buffalo, providing the port of New York City with a direct water link to the heartland of the North American continent.

(A) Seldom more than 40 feet wide and 12 feet deep, but it ran 363 miles across the rugged wilderness of upstate New York, the Erie Canal connected
(B) Seldom more than 40 feet wide or 12 feet deep but running 363 miles across the rugged wilderness of upstate New York, the Erie Canal connected

(C) It was seldom more than 40 feet wide and 12 feet deep, and ran 363 miles across the rugged wilderness of upstate New York, but the Erie Canal, connecting

(D) The Erie Canal was seldom more than 40 feet wide or 12 feet deep and it ran 363 miles across the rugged wilderness of upstate New York, which connected

(E) The Erie Canal, seldom more than 40 feet wide and 12 feet deep, but running 363 miles across the rugged wilderness of upstate New York, connecting

Logical predication + Grammatical construction

The phrase *seldom...deep* is the first half of a modifier that describes *the Erie Canal*. However, because a comma incorrectly follows *deep*, this phrase appears to be the entire modifier, which must agree with the noun or pronoun that immediately follows it. It cannot modify the conjunction *but*, and *it* has no referent; *but it ran* is not a logical or grammatical construction following the modifying phrase. Substituting *running* for *ran* creates a phrase parallel to the first one. To contrast the small size reported in the first phrase with the great distance reported in the second, the two phrases may be joined with *but*; together they create a single modifier correctly modifying *the Erie Canal*. *The Erie Canal* is then the subject of the sentence and requires the verb *connected* to provide a logical statement.

A *But it ran* cannot logically or grammatically follow the modifying phrase.

B Correct. This sentence properly has the single modifier consisting of two contrasting parts.

C Neither *and* nor *but* acts as a logical connector; the use of *connecting* results in a sentence fragment.

D The paired concepts of width and depth should be joined by *and*, not *or*; this construction calls for two main clauses to be separated by a comma after *deep*; *which* is ambiguous.

E The two halves of the modifier should not be separated by a comma after *deep*; the subject is awkwardly and confusingly placed at a great distance from the predicate; the use of *connecting* rather than *connected* creates a sentence fragment.

The correct answer is B.

45. In 1923, <u>the Supreme Court declared a minimum wage for women and children in the District of Columbia as unconstitutional, and</u> ruling that it was a form of price-fixing and, as such, an abridgment of the right of contract.

(A) the Supreme Court declared a minimum wage for women and children in the District of Columbia as unconstitutional, and

(B) the Supreme Court declared as unconstitutional a minimum wage for women and children in the District of Columbia, and

(C) the Supreme Court declared unconstitutional a minimum wage for women and children in the District of Columbia,

(D) a minimum wage for women and children in the District of Columbia was declared unconstitutional by the Supreme Court,

(E) when the Supreme Court declared a minimum wage for women and children in the District of Columbia as unconstitutional,

Idiom + Grammatical construction

This sentence depends on the correct use of an idiom: *the court declares x unconstitutional.* The inverted form should be used here because of the long phrases involved: *the court declares unconstitutional x. The Supreme Court* is the subject of the sentence; *declared* is the verb. *Ruling... contract* acts a modifier describing the action of the main clause; because the modifier is subordinate to the main clause, the conjunction *and* must be omitted. *And* is used to join two independent clauses, not a clause and its modifier.

A *Declared...as unconstitutional* is not the correct idiom; the use of *and* creates an ungrammatical construction.

B *Declared as unconstitutional* is not the correct idiom; the use of *and* creates an ungrammatical construction.

C **Correct.** In this sentence, the correct idiom is used, and the modifier is grammatically and logically attached to the main clause.

D Passive voice construction is weak and wordy; its use causes the modifier to be misplaced and ambiguous.

E *Declared… as unconstitutional* is not the correct idiom; *when* transforms the main clause into a subordinate clause, resulting in a sentence fragment.

The correct answer is C.

46. Researchers have found that individuals who have been blind from birth, and who thus have never seen anyone gesture, nevertheless make hand motions when speaking just as frequently and in virtually the same way as sighted people do, and that they will gesture even when conversing with another blind person.

(A) who thus have never seen anyone gesture, nevertheless make hand motions when speaking just as frequently and in virtually the same way as sighted people do, and that they will gesture

(B) who thus never saw anyone gesturing, nevertheless make hand motions when speaking just as frequent and in virtually the same way as sighted people did, and that they will gesture

(C) who thus have never seen anyone gesture, nevertheless made hand motions when speaking just as frequently and in virtually the same way as sighted people do, as well as gesturing

(D) thus never having seen anyone gesture, nevertheless made hand motions when speaking just as frequent and in virtually the same way as sighted people did, as well as gesturing

(E) thus never having seen anyone gesture, nevertheless to make hand motions when speaking just as frequently and in virtually the same way as sighted people do, and to gesture

Parallelism + Verb form + Diction

The researchers have found (1) *that individuals… make hand motions…as sighted people do* and (2) *that they will gesture…with another blind person.* In the original sentence, the two findings are reported in two parallel subordinate clauses introduced by *that*. The verb tenses are logical and parallel: *who have been blind* and *who have never seen* indicate a condition that began in the past and continues in the present; *make* and *do* refer to present actions. The verb *make* (*hand motions*) is correctly modified by the adverb *frequently* to show how the action of the verb is carried out. The emphatic future *will gesture* is properly used here with *even* to emphasize the extreme or the unexpected.

A **Correct.** Although the original sentence is complicated, the parallelism of its structure and phrasing allows its meaning to be clear and its expression effective.

B Verbs *saw* and *did* indicate action completed in the past; the simple past tense is not appropriate in either case; the adjective *frequent* cannot modify the verb; awkward and muddy.

C *Made* indicates past action, but the present tense is logically required; *as well as gesturing* violates the parallelism of the two subordinate (*that*) clauses; choppy and unclear.

D *Having seen* is not parallel to *have been*; *made* and *did* do not show ongoing action; *frequent* incorrectly modifies the verb; *as well as gesturing* destroys the parallelism of the two subordinate (*that*) clauses; awkward and unclear.

E Replacing the verb *make* with the infinitive *to make* results in an ungrammatical construction that fails to complete the sentence.

The correct answer is A.

47. Like embryonic germ cells, which are cells that develop early in the formation of the fetus and that later generate eggs or sperm, embryonic stem cells have the ability of developing themselves into different kinds of body tissue.

(A) embryonic stem cells have the ability of developing themselves into different kinds of body tissue
(B) embryonic stem cells have the ability to develop into different kinds of body tissue
(C) in embryonic stem cells there is the ability to develop into different kinds of body tissue
(D) the ability to develop themselves into different kinds of body tissue characterizes embryonic stem cells
(E) the ability of developing into different kinds of body tissue characterizes embryonic stem cells

Idiom + Grammatical construction

Two constructions create problems in the original sentence. The first is the unidiomatic construction *have the ability of developing*; *ability* must be followed by an infinitive, *to develop*, not a phrase. The second problematic construction is *to develop themselves into*. In this biological context, the verb *develop* means to progress from an earlier to a later stage; it is used intransitively, which means that it cannot take an object. The pronoun *themselves* acts as an object, creating a construction that is not grammatical or logical. Omitting the pronoun removes the problem.

A *Ability* is incorrectly followed by *of developing*; a pronoun cannot follow *develop*, when it is used, as it is here, in its intransitive sense.

B **Correct.** *Ability* is properly followed by the infinitive in this sentence, and the pronoun *themselves* is omitted.

C This awkward and wordy construction violates the parallelism of *like embryonic germ cells…embryonic stem cells….*

D The two parts of the comparison must be parallel; *like embryonic germ cells* must be followed by *embryonic stem cells*, not *the ability to develop.*

E *Ability* is followed by the unidiomatic *of developing* rather than *to develop*; the main clause must begin with *embryonic stem cells* to balance and complete *like embryonic germ cells.*

The correct answer is B.

48. Critics contend that the new missile is a weapon whose importance is largely symbolic, more a tool for manipulating people's perceptions than to fulfill a real military need.

(A) for manipulating people's perceptions than to fulfill
(B) for manipulating people's perceptions than for fulfilling
(C) to manipulate people's perceptions rather than that it fulfills
(D) to manipulate people's perceptions rather than fulfilling
(E) to manipulate people's perceptions than for fulfilling

Parallelism

This sentence uses the comparative construction *more x than y* where *x* and *y* must be parallel. Here, *x* is *a tool for manipulating people's perceptions*, and *y* is *to fulfill a real military need. A tool* does not need to be repeated in the second half of the comparison because it is understood, but the wording of the two phrases does need to match. There are two acceptable solutions: (1) *for manipulating* can be followed by *for fulfilling* or (2) *to manipulate* can be followed by *to fulfill.*

A *For manipulating* is not parallel to *to fulfill.*

B **Correct.** *For manipulating* and *for fulfilling* are parallel in this sentence.

C *To manipulate* is not parallel to *that it fulfills.*

D *To manipulate* is not parallel to *fulfilling.*

E *To manipulate* is not parallel to *for fulfilling.*

The correct answer is B.

49. As an actress and, more importantly, as a teacher of acting, Stella Adler was one of the most influential artists in the American theater, who trained several generations of actors including Marlon Brando and Robert De Niro.

(A) Stella Adler was one of the most influential artists in the American theater, who trained several generations of actors including
(B) Stella Adler, one of the most influential artists in the American theater, trained several generations of actors who include
(C) Stella Adler was one of the most influential artists in the American theater, training several generations of actors whose ranks included
(D) one of the most influential artists in the American theater was Stella Adler, who trained several generations of actors including
(E) one of the most influential artists in the American theater, Stella Adler, trained several generations of actors whose ranks included

Logical predication

The original sentence contains a number of modifiers, but not all of them are correctly expressed. The clause *who trained*... describes *Stella Adler*, yet a relative clause such as this one must be placed immediately after the noun or pronoun it modifies, and this clause follows *theater* rather than *Adler*. Replacing *who trained* with *training* corrects the error because the phrase *training*... modifies the whole preceding clause rather than the single preceding noun. *Several generations of actors including* shows the same error in reverse; *including* modifies the whole phrase, but the two actors named are not *generations of actors*. The more limiting clause *whose ranks included* (referring to *actors*) is appropriate here.

A Relative (*who*) clause follows *theater* rather than *Adler*; *including* refers to *generations of actors*, when the reference should be to *actors* only.

B This construction, in which the subject is both preceded and followed by modifiers, is awkward; the verbs should be consistently in the past tense, but *include* is present tense.

C **Correct.** In this sentence, substituting *training* for *who trained* and *whose ranks included* for *including* eliminates the modification errors.

D Introductory modifier must be immediately followed by *Stella Adler*, not *one*...; *including* refers to *generations of actors* rather than to *actors* only.

E Introductory modifier must be immediately followed by *Stella Adler*, not *one*.

The correct answer is C.

50. By developing the Secure Digital Music Initiative, the recording industry associations of North America, Japan, and Europe hope to create a standardized way of distributing songs and full-length recordings on the Internet that will protect copyright holders and foil the many audio pirates who copy and distribute digital music illegally.

(A) of distributing songs and full-length recordings on the Internet that will protect copyright holders and foil the many audio pirates who copy and distribute
(B) of distributing songs and full-length recordings on the Internet and to protect copyright holders and foiling the many audio pirates copying and distributing
(C) for distributing songs and full-length recordings on the Internet while it protects copyright holders and foils the many audio pirates who copy and distribute
(D) to distribute songs and full-length recordings on the Internet while they will protect copyright holders and foil the many audio pirates copying and distributing
(E) to distribute songs and full-length recordings on the Internet and it will protect copyright holders and foiling the many audio pirates who copy and distribute

Parallelism

The original sentence depends on the parallelism of its verbs to make its point clearly and effectively. *A standardized way...will protect* and (*will* understood) *foil*; *pirates...copy and distribute.* In the first pair of parallel verbs, *will* does not need to be repeated because it is understood.

A **Correct.** The verbs *will protect* and (*will*) *foil* are parallel in this sentence, as are the verbs *copy* and *distribute.*

B *And to protect* distorts meaning, suggesting that protection comes in addition to *the standardized way*; *foiling* is not parallel to *to protect.*

C *Way for* should instead be *way of*; the pronoun reference in *while it protects* is ambiguous; construction suggests that protection comes from something other than the *standardized way.*

D Pronoun *they* has no referent; use of *while* suggests that protection comes from something other than the *standardized way* of distribution.

E *And it will protect* distorts meaning, suggesting that protection comes in addition to *the standardized way*; *will protect* and *foiling* are not parallel.

The correct answer is A.

51. Whereas a ramjet generally cannot achieve high speeds without the initial assistance of a rocket, <u>high speeds can be attained by scramjets, or supersonic combustion ramjets, in that they reduce</u> airflow compression at the entrance of the engine and letting air pass through at supersonic speeds.

(A) high speeds can be attained by scramjets, or supersonic combustion ramjets, in that they reduce
(B) that high speeds can be attained by scramjets, or supersonic combustion ramjets, is a result of their reducing
(C) the ability of scramjets, or supersonic combustion ramjets, to achieve high speeds is because they reduce
(D) scramjets, or supersonic combustion ramjets, have the ability of attaining high speeds when reducing
(E) scramjets, or supersonic combustion ramjets, can attain high speeds by reducing

Rhetorical construction

The underlined portion of the original sentence is wordy and ineffective. Transforming it from passive (*high speeds can be attained by scramjets*) to active voice (*scramjets can attain high speeds*) eliminates much of the problem. As the subject of the main clause, *scramjets* correctly parallels *a ramjet*, the subject of the subordinate clause; the contrast is thus clearly and effectively drawn. *In that they reduce* is wordy and awkward; it can be replaced by the more concise phrase *by reducing.*

A Passive voice contributes to a wordy, awkward, and ineffective construction; *in that they reduce* is also wordy and awkward.

B Passive voice and subordinate (*that*) clause constructions are wordy, awkward, and ineffective.

C *The ability...is because* is not a grammatical construction; *scramjets*, not *the ability*, should be parallel to *a ramjet.*

D *Have the ability of attaining* is wordy; *when* does not indicate the cause-and-effect relationship.

E **Correct.** *Scramjets* parallels *a ramjet* for an effective contrast in this sentence; the active voice is clear and concise; *by reducing* shows how scramjets attain high speeds.

The correct answer is E.

52. It will not be possible to implicate melting sea ice in the coastal flooding that many global warming models have projected: just like a glass of water that will not overflow due to melting ice cubes, so melting sea ice does not increase oceanic volume.

(A) like a glass of water that will not overflow due to melting ice cubes
(B) like melting ice cubes that do not cause a glass of water to overflow
(C) a glass of water will not overflow because of melting ice cubes
(D) as melting ice cubes that do not cause a glass of water to overflow
(E) as melting ice cubes do not cause a glass of water to overflow

Diction + Parallelism

The preposition *like* introduces phrases; the conjunction *as* may introduce a clause, so *as* is required here. The comparative construction used here is *just as x so y*; *x* and *y* must be parallel. The *y* clause is written in effective subject-verb-object order: *melting sea ice does not increase oceanic volume.* The original wordy, awkward *x* clause is not parallel. To make it parallel, *melting ice cubes* should be the subject of the clause, *do not cause…to overflow* the verb phrase, and *a glass of water* the object.

A *Like* is used in place of *as*; the two elements of comparison are not parallel.

B *Like* is used in place of *as*; *that* violates parallelism.

C *As* or *just as* is needed to introduce the clause; the two clauses are not parallel.

D *That* violates the parallelism of the two clauses and creates an ungrammatical construction.

E **Correct.** This sentence has *just as* properly introducing the first clause, and the two clauses are parallel.

The correct answer is E.

4.0 Math Review

4.0 Math Review

Although this chapter provides a review of some of the mathematical concepts of arithmetic, algebra, and geometry, it is not intended to be a textbook. You should use this chapter to familiarize yourself with the kinds of topics that are tested in the GMAT® exam. You may wish to consult an arithmetic, algebra, or geometry book for a more detailed discussion of some of the topics.

The topics that are covered in section 4.1, "Arithmetic," include the following:

1. Properties of Integers
2. Fractions
3. Decimals
4. Real Numbers
5. Ratio and Proportion
6. Percents
7. Powers and Roots of Numbers
8. Descriptive Statistics
9. Sets
10. Counting Methods
11. Discrete Probability

The content of section 4.2, "Algebra," does not extend beyond what is usually covered in a first-year high school algebra course. The topics included are as follows:

1. Simplifying Algebraic Expressions
2. Equations
3. Solving Linear Equations with One Unknown
4. Solving Two Linear Equations with Two Unknowns
5. Solving Equations by Factoring
6. Solving Quadratic Equations
7. Exponents
8. Inequalities
9. Absolute Value
10. Functions

Section 4.3, "Geometry," is limited primarily to measurement and intuitive geometry or spatial visualization. Extensive knowledge of theorems and the ability to construct proofs, skills that are usually developed in a formal geometry course, are not tested. The topics included in this section are the following:

1. Lines
2. Intersecting Lines and Angles
3. Perpendicular Lines
4. Parallel Lines
5. Polygons (Convex)
6. Triangles
7. Quadrilaterals
8. Circles
9. Rectangular Solids and Cylinders
10. Coordinate Geometry

Section 4.4, "Word Problems," presents examples of and solutions to the following types of word problems:

1. Rate Problems
2. Work Problems
3. Mixture Problems
4. Interest Problems
5. Discount
6. Profit
7. Sets
8. Geometry Problems
9. Measurement Problems
10. Data Interpretation

4.1 Arithmetic

1. Properties of Integers

An *integer* is any number in the set {. . . −3, −2, −1, 0, 1, 2, 3, . . .}. If x and y are integers and $x \neq 0$, then x is a *divisor* (*factor*) of y provided that $y = xn$ for some integer n. In this case, y is also said to be *divisible* by x or to be a *multiple* of x. For example, 7 is a divisor or factor of 28 since 28 = (7)(4), but 8 is not a divisor of 28 since there is no integer n such that $28 = 8n$.

If x and y are positive integers, there exist unique integers q and r, called the *quotient* and *remainder*, respectively, such that $y = xq + r$ and $0 \leq r < x$. For example, when 28 is divided by 8, the quotient is 3 and the remainder is 4 since 28 = (8)(3) + 4. Note that y is divisible by x if and only if the remainder r is 0; for example, 32 has a remainder of 0 when divided by 8 because 32 is divisible by 8. Also, note that when a smaller integer is divided by a larger integer, the quotient is 0 and the remainder is the smaller integer. For example, 5 divided by 7 has the quotient 0 and the remainder 5 since 5 = (7)(0) + 5.

Any integer that is divisible by 2 is an *even integer*; the set of even integers is {. . . −4, −2, 0, 2, 4, 6, 8, . . .}. Integers that are not divisible by 2 are *odd integers*; {. . . −3, −1, 1, 3, 5, . . .} is the set of odd integers.

If at least one factor of a product of integers is even, then the product is even; otherwise the product is odd. If two integers are both even or both odd, then their sum and their difference are even. Otherwise, their sum and their difference are odd.

A *prime* number is a positive integer that has exactly two different positive divisors, 1 and itself. For example, 2, 3, 5, 7, 11, and 13 are prime numbers, but 15 is not, since 15 has four different positive divisors, 1, 3, 5, and 15. The number 1 is not a prime number since it has only one positive divisor. Every integer greater than 1 either is prime or can be uniquely expressed as a product of prime factors. For example,
14 = (2)(7), 81 = (3)(3)(3)(3), and 484 = (2)(2)(11)(11).

The numbers −2, −1, 0, 1, 2, 3, 4, 5 are *consecutive integers*. Consecutive integers can be represented by $n, n + 1, n + 2, n + 3, \ldots$, where n is an integer. The numbers 0, 2, 4, 6, 8 are *consecutive even integers*, and 1, 3, 5, 7, 9 are *consecutive odd integers*. Consecutive even integers can be represented by $2n, 2n + 2, 2n + 4, \ldots$, and consecutive odd integers can be represented by $2n + 1, 2n + 3, 2n + 5, \ldots$, where n is an integer.

Properties of the integer 1. If n is any number, then $1 \cdot n = n$, and for any number $n \neq 0$, $n \cdot \frac{1}{n} = 1$.
The number 1 can be expressed in many ways; for example, $\frac{n}{n} = 1$ for any number $n \neq 0$. Multiplying or dividing an expression by 1, in any form, does not change the value of that expression.

Properties of the integer 0. The integer 0 is neither positive nor negative. If n is any number, then $n + 0 = n$ and $n \cdot 0 = 0$. Division by 0 is not defined.

2. Fractions

In a fraction $\frac{n}{d}$, n is the *numerator* and d is the *denominator*. The denominator of a fraction can never be 0, because division by 0 is not defined.

Two fractions are said to be *equivalent* if they represent the same number. For example, $\frac{8}{36}$ and $\frac{14}{63}$ are equivalent since they both represent the number $\frac{2}{9}$. In each case, the fraction is reduced to lowest terms by dividing both numerator and denominator by their *greatest common divisor* (gcd). The gcd of 8 and 36 is 4 and the gcd of 14 and 63 is 7.

Addition and subtraction of fractions.

Two fractions with the same denominator can be added or subtracted by performing the required operation with the numerators, leaving the denominators the same. For example, $\frac{3}{5} + \frac{4}{5} = \frac{3+4}{5} = \frac{7}{5}$, and $\frac{5}{7} - \frac{2}{7} = \frac{5-2}{7} = \frac{3}{7}$. If two fractions do not have the same denominator, express them as equivalent fractions with the same denominator. For example, to add $\frac{3}{5}$ and $\frac{4}{7}$, multiply the numerator and denominator of the first fraction by 7 and the numerator and denominator of the second fraction by 5, obtaining $\frac{21}{35}$ and $\frac{20}{35}$, respectively; $\frac{21}{35} + \frac{20}{35} = \frac{41}{35}$.

For the new denominator, choosing the *least common multiple* (lcm) of the denominators usually lessens the work. For $\frac{2}{3} + \frac{1}{6}$, the lcm of 3 and 6 is 6 (not 3 × 6 = 18), so

$$\frac{2}{3} + \frac{1}{6} = \frac{2}{3} \times \frac{2}{2} + \frac{1}{6} = \frac{4}{6} + \frac{1}{6} = \frac{5}{6}.$$

Multiplication and division of fractions.

To multiply two fractions, simply multiply the two numerators and multiply the two denominators. For example, $\frac{2}{3} \times \frac{4}{7} = \frac{2\times 4}{3\times 7} = \frac{8}{21}$.

To divide by a fraction, invert the divisor (that is, find its *reciprocal*) and multiply. For example

$$\frac{2}{3} \div \frac{4}{7} = \frac{2}{3} \times \frac{7}{4} = \frac{14}{12} = \frac{7}{6}.$$

In the problem above, the reciprocal of $\frac{4}{7}$ is $\frac{7}{4}$. In general, the reciprocal of a fraction $\frac{n}{d}$ is $\frac{d}{n}$ where n and d are not zero.

Mixed numbers.

A number that consists of a whole number and a fraction, for example, $7\frac{2}{3}$, is a mixed number: $7\frac{2}{3}$ means $7 + \frac{2}{3}$.

To change a mixed number into a fraction, multiply the whole number by the denominator of the fraction and add this number to the numerator of the fraction; then put the result over the denominator of the fraction. For example, $7\frac{2}{3} = \frac{(3 \times 7) + 2}{3} = \frac{23}{3}$.

3. Decimals

In the decimal system, the position of the period or *decimal point* determines the place value of the digits. For example, the digits in the number 7,654.321 have the following place values:

Thousands		Hundreds	Tens	Ones or units		Tenths	Hundredths	Thousandths
7	,	6	5	4	.	3	2	1

Some examples of decimals follow.

$$0.321 = \frac{3}{10} + \frac{2}{100} + \frac{1}{1{,}000} = \frac{321}{1{,}000}$$

$$0.0321 = \frac{0}{10} + \frac{3}{100} + \frac{2}{1{,}000} + \frac{1}{10{,}000} = \frac{321}{10{,}000}$$

$$1.56 = 1 + \frac{5}{10} + \frac{6}{100} = \frac{156}{100}$$

Sometimes decimals are expressed as the product of a number with only one digit to the left of the decimal point and a power of 10. This is called *scientific notation*. For example, 231 can be written as 2.31×10^2 and 0.0231 can be written as 2.31×10^{-2}. When a number is expressed in scientific notation, the exponent of the 10 indicates the number of places that the decimal point is to be moved in the number that is to be multiplied by a power of 10 in order to obtain the product. The decimal point is moved to the right if the exponent is positive and to the left if the exponent is negative. For example, 20.13×10^3 is equal to 20,130 and 1.91×10^{-4} is equal to 0.000191.

Addition and subtraction of decimals.

To add or subtract two decimals, the decimal points of both numbers should be lined up. If one of the numbers has fewer digits to the right of the decimal point than the other, zeros may be inserted to the right of the last digit. For example, to add 17.6512 and 653.27, set up the numbers in a column and add:

$$\begin{array}{r} 17.6512 \\ \underline{+\ 653.2700} \\ 670.9212 \end{array}$$

Likewise for 653.27 minus 17.6512:

$$\begin{array}{r} 653.2700 \\ \underline{-\ 17.6512} \\ 635.6188 \end{array}$$

Multiplication of decimals.

To multiply decimals, multiply the numbers as if they were whole numbers and then insert the decimal point in the product so that the number of digits to the right of the decimal point is equal to the sum of the numbers of digits to the right of the decimal points in the numbers being multiplied. For example:

$$\begin{array}{rl} 2.09 & \text{(2 digits to the right)} \\ \underline{\times\ 1.3} & \text{(1 digit to the right)} \\ 627 & \\ \underline{209} & \\ 2.717 & (2 + 1 = 3 \text{ digits to the right}) \end{array}$$

Division of decimals.

To divide a number (the dividend) by a decimal (the divisor), move the decimal point of the divisor to the right until the divisor is a whole number. Then move the decimal point of the dividend the same number of places to the right, and divide as you would by a whole number. The decimal point in the quotient will be directly above the decimal point in the new dividend. For example, to divide 698.12 by 12.4:

$$12.4\overline{)698.12}$$

will be replaced by:

$$124\overline{)6981.2}$$

and the division would proceed as follows:

$$\begin{array}{r} 56.3 \\ 124\overline{)6981.2} \\ \underline{620} \\ 781 \\ \underline{744} \\ 372 \\ \underline{372} \\ 0 \end{array}$$

4. Real Numbers

All *real* numbers correspond to points on the number line and all points on the number line correspond to real numbers. All real numbers except zero are either positive or negative.

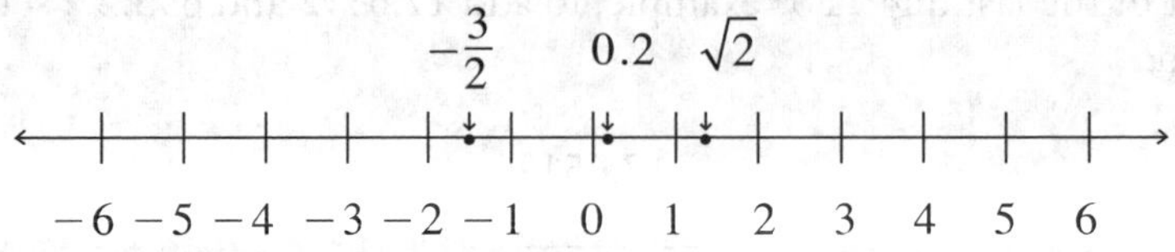

On a number line, numbers corresponding to points to the left of zero are negative and numbers corresponding to points to the right of zero are positive. For any two numbers on the number line, the number to the left is less than the number to the right; for example,
$-4 < -3 < -\frac{3}{2} < -1$, and $1 < \sqrt{2} < 2$.

To say that the number n is between 1 and 4 on the number line means that $n > 1$ and $n < 4$, that is, $1 < n < 4$. If n is "between 1 and 4, inclusive," then $1 \le n \le 4$.

The distance between a number and zero on the number line is called the *absolute value* of the number. Thus 3 and −3 have the same absolute value, 3, since they are both three units from zero. The absolute value of 3 is denoted $|3|$. Examples of absolute values of numbers are

$$|-5| = |5| = 5, \left|-\frac{7}{2}\right| = \frac{7}{2}, \text{ and } |0| = 0$$

Note that the absolute value of any nonzero number is positive.

Here are some properties of real numbers that are used frequently. If x, y, and z are real numbers, then

(1) $x + y = y + x$ and $xy = yx$.
For example, $8 + 3 = 3 + 8 = 11$, and $(17)(5) = (5)(17) = 85$.

(2) $(x + y) + z = x + (y + z)$ and $(xy)z = x(yz)$.
For example, $(7 + 5) + 2 = 7 + (5 + 2) = 7 + (7) = 14$, and
$(5\sqrt{3})(\sqrt{3}) = (5\sqrt{3}\sqrt{3}) = (5)(3) = 15$.

(3) $x(y + z) = xy + xz$.
For example, $718(36) + 718(64) = 718(36 + 64) = 718(100) = 71{,}800$.

(4) If x and y are both positive, then $x + y$ and xy are positive.

(5) If x and y are both negative, then $x + y$ is negative and xy is positive.

(6) If x is positive and y is negative, then xy is negative.

(7) If $xy = 0$, then $x = 0$ or $y = 0$. For example, $3y = 0$ implies $y = 0$.

(8) $|x + y| \le |x| + |y|$. For example, if $x = 10$ and $y = 2$, then $|x + y| = |12| = 12 = |x| + |y|$; and if $x = 10$ and $y = -2$, then $|x + y| = |8| = 8 < 12 = |x| + |y|$.

5. Ratio and Proportion

The *ratio* of the number a to the number b ($b \neq 0$) is $\frac{a}{b}$.

A ratio may be expressed or represented in several ways. For example, the ratio of 2 to 3 can be written as 2 to 3, 2:3, or $\frac{2}{3}$. The order of the terms of a ratio is important. For example, the ratio of the number of months with exactly 30 days to the number with exactly 31 days is $\frac{4}{7}$, not $\frac{7}{4}$.

A *proportion* is a statement that two ratios are equal; for example, $\frac{2}{3} = \frac{8}{12}$ is a proportion. One way to solve a proportion involving an unknown is to cross multiply, obtaining a new equality. For example, to solve for n in the proportion $\frac{2}{3} = \frac{n}{12}$, cross multiply, obtaining $24 = 3n$; then divide both sides by 3, to get $n = 8$.

6. Percents

Percent means *per hundred* or *number out of 100.* A percent can be represented as a fraction with a denominator of 100, or as a decimal. For example, $37\% = \frac{37}{100} = 0.37$.

To find a certain percent of a number, multiply the number by the percent expressed as a decimal or fraction. For example:

$$20\% \text{ of } 90 = 0.2 \times 90 = 18$$

or

$$20\% \text{ of } 90 = \frac{20}{100} \times 90 = \frac{1}{5} \times 90 = 18.$$

Percents greater than 100%.

Percents greater than 100% are represented by numbers greater than 1. For example:

$$300\% = \frac{300}{100} = 3$$

$$250\% \text{ of } 80 = 2.5 \times 80 = 200.$$

Percents less than 1%.

The percent 0.5 % means $\frac{1}{2}$ of 1 percent. For example, 0.5 % of 12 is equal to $0.005 \times 12 = 0.06$.

Percent change.

Often a problem will ask for the percent increase or decrease from one quantity to another quantity. For example, "If the price of an item increases from \$24 to \$30, what is the percent increase in price?" To find the percent increase, first find the amount of the increase; then divide this increase by the original amount, and express this quotient as a percent. In the example above, the percent increase would be found in the following way: the amount of the increase is $(30 - 24) = 6$. Therefore, the percent increase is $\frac{6}{24} = 0.25 = 25\%$.

Likewise, to find the percent decrease (for example, the price of an item is reduced from \$30 to \$24), first find the amount of the decrease; then divide this decrease by the original amount, and express this quotient as a percent. In the example above, the amount of decrease is $(30 - 24) = 6$. Therefore, the percent decrease is $\frac{6}{30} = 0.20 = 20\%$.

Note that the percent increase from 24 to 30 is not the same as the percent decrease from 30 to 24.

In the following example, the increase is greater than 100 percent: If the cost of a certain house in 1983 was 300 percent of its cost in 1970, by what percent did the cost increase?

If n is the cost in 1970, then the percent increase is equal to $\frac{3n - n}{n} = \frac{2n}{n} = 2$, or 200%.

7. Powers and Roots of Numbers

When a number k is to be used n times as a factor in a product, it can be expressed as k^n, which means the nth power of k. For example, $2^2 = 2 \times 2 = 4$ and $2^3 = 2 \times 2 \times 2 = 8$ are powers of 2.

Squaring a number that is greater than 1, or raising it to a higher power, results in a larger number; squaring a number between 0 and 1 results in a smaller number. For example:

$$3^2 = 9 \qquad (9 > 3)$$
$$\left(\frac{1}{3}\right)^2 = \frac{1}{9} \qquad \left(\frac{1}{9} < \frac{1}{3}\right)$$
$$(0.1)^2 = 0.01 \qquad (0.01 < 0.1)$$

A *square root* of a number n is a number that, when squared, is equal to n. The square root of a negative number is not a real number. Every positive number n has two square roots, one positive and the other negative, but $\sqrt{n}$ denotes the positive number whose square is n. For example, $\sqrt{9}$ denotes 3. The two square roots of 9 are $\sqrt{9} = 3$ and $-\sqrt{9} = -3$.

Every real number r has exactly one real *cube root*, which is the number s such that $s^3 = r$. The real cube root of r is denoted by $\sqrt[3]{r}$. Since $2^3 = 8$, $\sqrt[3]{8} = 2$. Similarly, $\sqrt[3]{-8} = -2$, because $(-2)^3 = -8$.

8. Descriptive Statistics

A list of numbers, or numerical data, can be described by various statistical measures. One of the most common of these measures is the *average*, or *(arithmetic) mean*, which locates a type of "center" for the data. The average of n numbers is defined as the sum of the n numbers divided by n. For example, the average of 6, 4, 7, 10, and 4 is $\frac{6+4+7+10+4}{5} = \frac{31}{5} = 6.2$.

The *median* is another type of center for a list of numbers. To calculate the median of n numbers, first order the numbers from least to greatest; if n is odd, the median is defined as the middle number, whereas if n is even, the median is defined as the average of the two middle numbers. In the example above, the numbers, in order, are 4, 4, 6, 7, 10, and the median is 6, the middle number.

For the numbers 4, 6, 6, 8, 9, 12, the median is $\frac{6+8}{2}$ = 7. Note that the mean of these numbers is 7.5. The median of a set of data can be less than, equal to, or greater than the mean. Note that for a large set of data (for example, the salaries of 800 company employees), it is often true that about half of the data is less than the median and about half of the data is greater than the median; but this is not always the case, as the following data show.

3, 5, 7, 7, 7, 7, 7, 7, 8, 9, 9, 9, 9, 10, 10

Here the median is 7, but only $\frac{2}{15}$ of the data is less than the median.

The *mode* of a list of numbers is the number that occurs most frequently in the list. For example, the mode of 1, 3, 6, 4, 3, 5 is 3. A list of numbers may have more than one mode. For example, the list 1, 2, 3, 3, 3, 5, 7, 10, 10, 10, 20 has two modes, 3 and 10.

The degree to which numerical data are spread out or dispersed can be measured in many ways. The simplest measure of dispersion is the *range*, which is defined as the greatest value in the numerical data minus the least value. For example, the range of 11, 10, 5, 13, 21 is 21 – 5 = 16. Note how the range depends on only two values in the data.

One of the most common measures of dispersion is the *standard deviation*. Generally speaking, the more the data are spread away from the mean, the greater the standard deviation. The standard deviation of n numbers can be calculated as follows: (1) find the arithmetic mean, (2) find the differences between the mean and each of the n numbers, (3) square each of the differences, (4) find the average of the squared differences, and (5) take the nonnegative square root of this average. Shown below is this calculation for the data 0, 7, 8, 10, 10, which have arithmetic mean 7.

x	$x - 7$	$(x - 7)^2$
0	-7	49
7	0	0
8	1	1
10	3	9
10	3	9
	Total	68

Standard deviation $\sqrt{\frac{68}{5}} \approx 3.7$

Notice that the standard deviation depends on every data value, although it depends most on values that are farthest from the mean. This is why a distribution with data grouped closely around the mean will have a smaller standard deviation than will data spread far from the mean. To illustrate this, compare the data 6, 6, 6.5, 7.5, 9, which also have mean 7. Note that the numbers in the second set of data seem to be grouped more closely around the mean of 7 than the numbers in the first set. This is reflected in the standard deviation, which is less for the second set (approximately 1.1) than for the first set (approximately 3.7).

There are many ways to display numerical data that show how the data are distributed. One simple way is with a *frequency distribution*, which is useful for data that have values occurring with varying frequencies. For example, the 20 numbers

−4	0	0	−3	−2	−1	−1	0	−1	−4
−1	−5	0	−2	0	−5	−2	0	0	−1

are displayed on the next page in a frequency distribution by listing each different value x and the frequency f with which x occurs.

Data Value x	Frequency f
-5	2
-4	2
-3	1
-2	3
-1	5
0	7
Total	20

From the frequency distribution, one can readily compute descriptive statistics:

Mean: $\frac{(-5)(2)+(-4)(2)+(-3)(1)+(-2)(3)+(-1)(5)+(0)(7)}{20} = -1.6$

Median: −1 (the average of the 10th and 11th numbers)

Mode: 0 (the number that occurs most frequently)

Range: $0 - (-5) = 5$

Standard deviation: $\sqrt{\frac{(-5+1.6)^2(2)+(-4+1.6)^2(2)+\ldots+(0+1.6)^2(7)}{20}} \approx 1.7$

9. Sets

In mathematics a *set* is a collection of numbers or other objects. The objects are called the *elements* of the set. If S is a set having a finite number of elements, then the number of elements is denoted by $|S|$. Such a set is often defined by listing its elements; for example, $S = \{-5,0,1\}$ is a set with $|S| = 3$. The order in which the elements are listed in a set does not matter; thus $\{-5, 0, 1\} = \{0, 1, -5\}$. If all the elements of a set S are also elements of a set T, then S is a *subset* of T; for example, $S = \{-5, 0, 1\}$ is a subset of $T = \{-5, 0, 1, 4, 10\}$.

For any two sets A and B, the *union* of A and B is the set of all elements that are in A *or* in B *or* in both. The *intersection* of A and B is the set of all elements that are both in A *and* in B. The union is denoted by $A \cup B$ and the intersection is denoted by $A \cap B$. As an example, if $A = \{3, 4\}$ and $B = \{4, 5, 6\}$, then $A \cup B = \{3, 4, 5, 6\}$ and $A \cap B = \{4\}$. Two sets that have no elements in common are said to be *disjoint* or *mutually exclusive*.

The relationship between sets is often illustrated with a *Venn diagram* in which sets are represented by regions in a plane. For two sets S and T that are not disjoint and neither is a subset of the other, the intersection $S \cap T$ is represented by the shaded region of the diagram below.

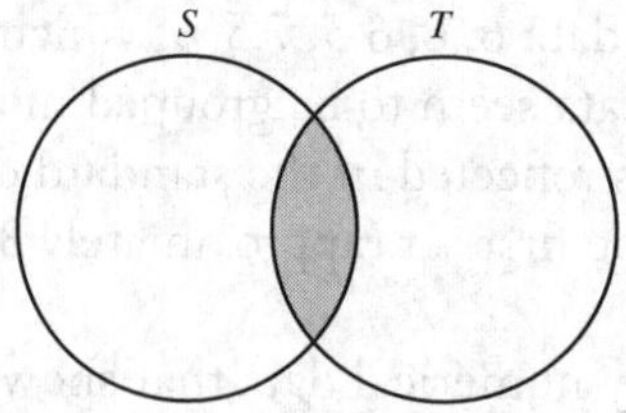

This diagram illustrates a fact about any two finite sets S and T: the number of elements in their union equals the sum of their individual numbers of elements minus the number of elements in their intersection (because the latter are counted twice in the sum); more concisely,

$$|S \cup T| = |S| + |T| - |S \cap T|.$$

This counting method is called the general addition rule for two sets. As a special case, if S and T are disjoint, then

$$|S \cup T| = |S| + |T|$$

since $|S \cap T| = 0$.

10. Counting Methods

There are some useful methods for counting objects and sets of objects without actually listing the elements to be counted. The following principle of multiplication is fundamental to these methods.

If an object is to be chosen from a set of m objects and a second object is to be chosen from a different set of n objects, then there are mn ways of choosing both objects simultaneously.

As an example, suppose the objects are items on a menu. If a meal consists of one entree and one dessert and there are 5 entrees and 3 desserts on the menu, then there are $5 \times 3 = 15$ different meals that can be ordered from the menu. As another example, each time a coin is flipped, there are two possible outcomes, heads and tails. If an experiment consists of 8 consecutive coin flips, then the experiment has 2^8 possible outcomes, where each of these outcomes is a list of heads and tails in some order.

A symbol that is often used with the multiplication principle is the *factorial*. If n is an integer greater than 1, then n factorial, denoted by the symbol $n!$, is defined as the product of all the integers from 1 to n. Therefore,

$$2! = (1)(2) = 2,$$
$$3! = (1)(2)(3) = 6,$$
$$4! = (1)(2)(3)(4) = 24, \text{ etc.}$$

Also, by definition, $0! = 1! = 1$.

The factorial is useful for counting the number of ways that a set of objects can be ordered. If a set of n objects is to be ordered from 1st to nth, then there are n choices for the 1st object, $n - 1$ choices for the 2nd object, $n - 2$ choices for the 3rd object, and so on, until there is only 1 choice for the nth object. Thus, by the multiplication principle, the number of ways of ordering the n objects is

$$n(n-1)(n-2)\cdots(3)(2)(1) = n!.$$

For example, the number of ways of ordering the letters A, B, and C is 3!, or 6:

ABC, ACB, BAC, BCA, CAB, and CBA.

These orderings are called the *permutations* of the letters A, B, and C.

A permutation can be thought of as a selection process in which objects are selected one by one in a certain order. If the order of selection is not relevant and only k objects are to be selected from a larger set of n objects, a different counting method is employed.

Specifically, consider a set of n objects from which a complete selection of k objects is to be made without regard to order, where $0 \le k \le n$. Then the number of possible complete selections of k objects is called the number of *combinations* of n objects taken k at a time and is denoted by $\binom{n}{k}$.

The value of $\binom{n}{k}$ is given by $\binom{n}{k} = \frac{n!}{k!(n-k)!}$.

Note that $\binom{n}{k}$ is the number of k-element subsets of a set with n elements. For example, if $S = \{A, B, C, D, E\}$, then the number of 2-element subsets of S, or the number of combinations of 5 letters taken 2 at a time, is $\binom{5}{2} = \frac{5!}{2!3!} = \frac{120}{(2)(6)} = 10$.

The subsets are {A, B}, {A, C}, {A, D}, {A, E}, {B, C}, {B, D}, {B, E}, {C, D}, {C, E,}, and {D, E}. Note that $\binom{5}{2} = 10 = \binom{5}{3}$ because every 2-element subset chosen from a set of 5 elements corresponds to a unique 3-element subset consisting of the elements *not* chosen.

In general, $\binom{n}{k} = \binom{n}{n-k}$.

11. Discrete Probability

Many of the ideas discussed in the preceding three topics are important to the study of discrete probability. Discrete probability is concerned with *experiments* that have a finite number of *outcomes*. Given such an experiment, an *event* is a particular set of outcomes. For example, rolling a number cube with faces numbered 1 to 6 (similar to a 6-sided die) is an experiment with 6 possible outcomes: 1, 2, 3, 4, 5, or 6. One event in this experiment is that the outcome is 4, denoted {4}; another event is that the outcome is an odd number: {1, 3, 5}.

The probability than an event E occurs, denoted by $P(E)$, is a number between 0 and 1, inclusive. If E has no outcomes, then E is *impossible* and $P(E) = 0$; if E is the set of all possible outcomes of the experiment, then E is *certain* to occur and $P(E) = 1$. Otherwise, E is possible but uncertain, and $0 < P(E) < 1$. If F is a subset of E, then $P(F) \le P(E)$. In the example above, if the probability of each of the 6 outcomes is the same, then the probability of each outcome is $\frac{1}{6}$, and the outcomes are said to be *equally likely*. For experiments in which all the individual outcomes are equally likely, the probability of an event E is

$$P(E) = \frac{\text{The number of outcomes in } E}{\text{The total number of possible outcomes}}.$$

In the example, the probability that the outcome is an odd number is

$$P(\{1,3,5\}) = \frac{|\{1,3,5\}|}{6} = \frac{3}{6}.$$

Given an experiment with events E and F, the following events are defined:
"*not E*" is the set of outcomes that are not outcomes in E;
"*E or F*" is the set of outcomes in E or F or both, that is, $E \cup F$;
"*E and F*" is the set of outcomes in both E and F, that is, $E \cap F$.

The probability that E does not occur is $P(\text{not } E) = 1 - P(E)$. The probability that "$E$ or F" occurs is $P(E \text{ or } F) = P(E) + P(F) - P(E \text{ and } F)$, using the general addition rule at the end of section 4.1.9 ("Sets"). For the number cube, if E is the event that the outcome is an odd number, $\{1, 3, 5\}$, and F is the event that the outcome is a prime number, $\{2, 3, 5\}$, then $P(E \text{ and } F) = P(\{3,5\}) = \frac{2}{6}$ and so $P(E \text{ or } F) = P(E) + P(F) - P(E \text{ and } F) = \frac{3}{6} + \frac{3}{6} - \frac{2}{6} = \frac{4}{6}$.

Note that the event "E or F" is $E \cup F = \{1, 2, 3, 5\}$, and hence $P(E \text{ or } F) = \frac{|\{1,2,3,5\}|}{6} = \frac{4}{6}$.

If the event "E and F" is impossible (that is, $E \cap F$ has no outcomes), then E and F are said to be *mutually exclusive* events, and $P(E \text{ and } F) = 0$. Then the general addition rule is reduced to $P(E \text{ or } F) = P(E) + P(F)$.

This is the special addition rule for the probability of two mutually exclusive events.

Two events A and B are said to be *independent* if the occurrence of either event does not alter the probability that the other event occurs. For one roll of the number cube, let $A = \{2, 4, 6\}$ and let $B = \{5, 6\}$. Then the probability that A occurs is $P(A) = \frac{|A|}{6} = \frac{3}{6} = \frac{1}{2}$, while, *presuming B occurs*, the probability that A occurs is

$$\frac{|A \cap B|}{|B|} = \frac{|\{6\}|}{|\{5,6\}|} = \frac{1}{2}.$$

Similarly, the probability that B occurs is $P(B) = \frac{|B|}{6} = \frac{2}{6} = \frac{1}{3}$, while, *presuming A occurs*, the probability that B occurs is

$$\frac{|B \cap A|}{|A|} = \frac{|\{6\}|}{|\{2,4,6\}|} = \frac{1}{3}.$$

Thus, the occurrence of either event does not affect the probability that the other event occurs. Therefore, A and B are independent.

The following multiplication rule holds for any independent events E and F: $P(E \text{ and } F) = P(E)P(F)$.

For the independent events A and B above, $P(A \text{ and } B) = P(A)P(B) = \left(\frac{1}{2}\right)\left(\frac{1}{3}\right) = \left(\frac{1}{6}\right)$.

Note that the event "A and B" is $A \cap B = \{6\}$, and hence $P(A \text{ and } B) = P(\{6\}) = \frac{1}{6}$. It follows from the general addition rule and the multiplication rule above that if E and F are independent, then

$$P(E \text{ or } F) = P(E) + P(F) - P(E)P(F).$$

For a final example of some of these rules, consider an experiment with events A, B, and C for which $P(A) = 0.23$, $P(B) = 0.40$, and $P(C) = 0.85$. Also, suppose that events A and B are mutually exclusive and events B and C are independent. Then

$$
\begin{aligned}
P(A \text{ or } B) &= P(A) + P(B) \quad \text{(since } A \text{ and } B \text{ are mutually exclusive)} \\
&= 0.23 + 0.40 \\
&= 0.63 \\
P(B \text{ or } C) &= P(B) + P(C) - P(B)P(C) \quad \text{(by independence)} \\
&= 0.40 + 0.85 - (0.40)(0.85) \\
&= 0.91
\end{aligned}
$$

Note that $P(A \text{ or } C)$ and $P(A \text{ and } C)$ cannot be determined using the information given. But it can be determined that A and C are *not* mutually exclusive since $P(A) + P(C) = 1.08$, which is greater than 1, and therefore cannot equal $P(A \text{ or } C)$; from this it follows that $P(A \text{ and } C) \geq 0.08$. One can also deduce that $P(A \text{ and } C) \leq P(A) = 0.23$, since $A \cap C$ is a subset of A, and that $P(A \text{ and } C) \leq P(C) = 0.85$ since C is a subset of $A \cup C$. Thus, one can conclude that $0.85 \leq P(A \text{ or } C) \leq 1$ and $0.85 \leq P(A \text{ or } C) \leq 0.23$.

4.2 Algebra

Algebra is based on the operations of arithmetic and on the concept of an *unknown quantity,* or *variable.* Letters such as x or n are used to represent unknown quantities. For example, suppose Pam has 5 more pencils than Fred. If F represents the number of pencils that Fred has, then the number of pencils that Pam has is $F + 5$. As another example, if Jim's present salary S is increased by 7%, then his new salary is $1.07S$. A combination of letters and arithmetic operations, such as $F + 5$, $\frac{3x^2}{2x-5}$, and $19x^2 - 6x + 3$, is called an *algebraic expression.*

The expression $19x^2 - 6x + 3$ consists of the *terms* $19x^2$, $-6x$, and 3, where 19 is the *coefficient* of x^2, -6 is the coefficient of x^1, and 3 is a *constant term* (or coefficient of $x^0 = 1$). Such an expression is called a *second degree* (or *quadratic*) *polynomial in x* since the highest power of x is 2. The expression $F + 5$ is a *first degree* (or *linear*) *polynomial in F* since the highest power of F is 1. The expression $\frac{3x^2}{2x-5}$ is not a polynomial because it is not a sum of terms that are each powers of x multiplied by coefficients.

1. Simplifying Algebraic Expressions

Often when working with algebraic expressions, it is necessary to simplify them by factoring or combining *like* terms. For example, the expression $6x + 5x$ is equivalent to $(6 + 5)x$, or $11x$. In the expression $9x - 3y$, 3 is a factor common to both terms: $9x - 3y = 3(3x - y)$. In the expression $5x^2 + 6y$, there are no like terms and no common factors.

If there are common factors in the numerator and denominator of an expression, they can be divided out, provided that they are not equal to zero.

For example, if $x \neq 3$, then $\dfrac{x-3}{x-3}$ is equal to 1; therefore,

$$\begin{aligned}\frac{3xy-9y}{x-3} &= \frac{3y(x-3)}{x-3}\\ &= (3y)(1)\\ &= 3y.\end{aligned}$$

To multiply two algebraic expressions, each term of one expression is multiplied by each term of the other expression. For example:

$$\begin{aligned}(3x-4)(9y+x) &= 3x(9y+x) - 4(9y+x)\\ &= (3x)(9y) + (3x)(x) + (-4)(9y) + (-4)(x)\\ &= 27xy + 3x^2 - 36y - 4x\end{aligned}$$

An algebraic expression can be evaluated by substituting values of the unknowns in the expression. For example, if $x = 3$ and $y = -2$, then $3xy - x^2 + y$ can be evaluated as

$$3(3)(-2) - (3)^2 + (-2) = -18 - 9 - 2 = -29$$

2. Equations

A major focus of algebra is to solve equations involving algebraic expressions. Some examples of such equations are

$5x - 2 = 9 - x$ (a linear equation with one unknown)

$3x + 1 = y - 2$ (a linear equation with two unknowns)

$5x^2 + 3x - 2 = 7x$ (a quadratic equation with one unknown)

$\dfrac{x(x-3)(x^2+5)}{x-4} = 0$ (an equation that is factored on one side with 0 on the other)

The *solutions* of an equation with one or more unknowns are those values that make the equation true, or "satisfy the equation," when they are substituted for the unknowns of the equation. An equation may have no solution or one or more solutions. If two or more equations are to be solved together, the solutions must satisfy all the equations simultaneously.

Two equations having the same solution(s) are *equivalent equations*. For example, the equations

$$\begin{aligned}2 + x &= 3\\ 4 + 2x &= 6\end{aligned}$$

each have the unique solution $x = 1$. Note that the second equation is the first equation multiplied by 2. Similarly, the equations

$$\begin{aligned}3x - y &= 6\\ 6x - 2y &= 12\end{aligned}$$

have the same solutions, although in this case each equation has infinitely many solutions. If any value is assigned to x, then $3x - 6$ is a corresponding value for y that will satisfy both equations; for example, $x = 2$ and $y = 0$ is a solution to both equations, as is $x = 5$ and $y = 9$.

3. Solving Linear Equations with One Unknown

To solve a linear equation with one unknown (that is, to find the value of the unknown that satisfies the equation), the unknown should be isolated on one side of the equation. This can be done by performing the same mathematical operations on both sides of the equation. Remember that if the same number is added to or subtracted from both sides of the equation, this does not change the equality; likewise, multiplying or dividing both sides by the same nonzero number does not change the equality. For example, to solve the equation $\frac{5x-6}{3} = 4$ for x, the variable x can be isolated using the following steps:

$$5x - 6 = 12 \quad \text{(multiplying by 3)}$$
$$5x = 12 + 6 = 18 \quad \text{(adding 6)}$$
$$x = \frac{18}{5} \quad \text{(dividing by 5)}$$

The solution, $\frac{18}{5}$, can be checked by substituting it for x in the original equation to determine whether it satisfies that equation:

$$\frac{5\left(\frac{18}{5}\right)-6}{3} = \frac{18-6}{3} = \frac{12}{3} = 4.$$

Therefore, $x = \frac{18}{5}$ is the solution.

4. Solving Two Linear Equations with Two Unknowns

For two linear equations with two unknowns, if the equations are equivalent, then there are infinitely many solutions to the equations, as illustrated at the end of section 4.2.2 ("Equations"). If the equations are not equivalent, then they have either one unique solution or no solution. The latter case is illustrated by the two equations:

$$3x + 4y = 17$$
$$6x + 8y = 35$$

Note that $3x + 4y = 17$ implies $6x + 8y = 34$, which contradicts the second equation. Thus, no values of x and y can simultaneously satisfy both equations.

There are several methods of solving two linear equations with two unknowns. With any method, if a contradiction is reached, then the equations have no solution; if a trivial equation such as $0 = 0$ is reached, then the equations are equivalent and have infinitely many solutions. Otherwise, a unique solution can be found.

One way to solve for the two unknowns is to express one of the unknowns in terms of the other using one of the equations, and then substitute the expression into the remaining equation to obtain an equation with one unknown. This equation can be solved and the value of the unknown substituted into either of the original equations to find the value of the other unknown. For example, the following two equations can be solved for x and y.

$$(1)\ 3x + 2y = 11$$
$$(2)\quad x - y = 2$$

In equation (2), $x = 2 + y$. Substitute $2 + y$ in equation (1) for x:

$$3(2 + y) + 2y = 11$$
$$6 + 3y + 2y = 11$$
$$6 + 5y = 11$$
$$5y = 5$$
$$y = 1$$

If $y = 1$, then $x = 2 + 1 = 3$.

There is another way to solve for x and y by eliminating one of the unknowns. This can be done by making the coefficients of one of the unknowns the same (disregarding the sign) in both equations and either adding the equations or subtracting one equation from the other. For example, to solve the equations

$$(1)\ 6x + 5y = 29$$
$$(2)\ 4x - 3y = -6$$

by this method, multiply equation (1) by 3 and equation (2) by 5 to get

$$18x + 15y = 87$$
$$20x - 15y = -30$$

Adding the two equations eliminates y, yielding $38x = 57$, or $x = \frac{3}{2}$. Finally, substituting $\frac{3}{2}$ for x in one of the equations gives $y = 4$. These answers can be checked by substituting both values into both of the original equations.

5. Solving Equations by Factoring

Some equations can be solved by factoring. To do this, first add or subtract expressions to bring all the expressions to one side of the equation, with 0 on the other side. Then try to factor the nonzero side into a product of expressions. If this is possible, then using property (7) in section 4.1.4 ("Real Numbers") each of the factors can be set equal to 0, yielding several simpler equations that possibly can be solved. The solutions of the simpler equations will be solutions of the factored equation. As an example, consider the equation $x^3 - 2x^2 + x = -5(x-1)^2$:

$$x^3 - 2x^2 + x + 5(x-1)^2 = 0$$
$$x(x^2 + 2x + 1) + 5(x-1)^2 = 0$$
$$x(x-1)^2 + 5(x-1)^2 = 0$$
$$(x+5)(x-1)^2 = 0$$
$$x + 5 = 0 \text{ or } (x-1)^2 = 0$$
$$x = -5 \text{ or } x = 1.$$

For another example, consider $\frac{x(x-3)(x^2+5)}{x-4} = 0$. A fraction equals 0 if and only if its numerator equals 0. Thus, $x(x-3)(x^2+5) = 0$:

$$x = 0 \text{ or } x-3 = 0 \text{ or } x^2 + 5 = 0$$
$$x = 0 \text{ or } x = 3 \text{ or } x^2 + 5 = 0.$$

But $x^2 + 5 = 0$ has no real solution because $x^2 + 5 > 0$ for every real number. Thus, the solutions are 0 and 3.

The solutions of an equation are also called the *roots* of the equation. These roots can be checked by substituting them into the original equation to determine whether they satisfy the equation.

6. Solving Quadratic Equations

The standard form for a *quadratic equation* is

$$ax^2 + bx + c = 0,$$

where a, b, and c are real numbers and $a \neq 0$; for example:

$$x^2 + 6x + 5 = 0,$$
$$3x^2 - 2x = 0, \text{ and}$$
$$x^2 + 4 = 0.$$

Some quadratic equations can easily be solved by factoring. For example:

(1) $$x^2 + 6x + 5 = 0$$
$$(x+5)(x+1) = 0$$
$$x+5 = 0 \quad \text{or} \quad x+1 = 0$$
$$x = -5 \quad \text{or} \quad x = -1$$

(2) $$3x^2 - 3 = 8x$$
$$3x^2 - 8x - 3 = 0$$
$$(3x+1)(x-3) = 0$$
$$3x+1 = 0 \quad \text{or} \quad x-3 = 0$$
$$x = -\frac{1}{3} \quad \text{or} \quad x = 3$$

A quadratic equation has at most two real roots and may have just one or even no real root. For example, the equation $x^2 - 6x + 9 = 0$ can be expressed as $(x-3)^2 = 0$, or $(x-3)(x-3) = 0$; thus the only root is 3. The equation $x^2 + 4 = 0$ has no real root; since the square of any real number is greater than or equal to zero, $x^2 + 4$ must be greater than zero.

An expression of the form $a^2 - b^2$ can be factored as $(a - b)(a + b)$.

For example, the quadratic equation $9x^2 - 25 = 0$ can be solved as follows.

$$(3x-5)(3x+5) = 0$$
$$3x-5 = 0 \text{ or } 3x+5 = 0$$
$$x = \frac{5}{3} \text{ or } x = -\frac{5}{3}$$

If a quadratic expression is not easily factored, then its roots can always be found using the *quadratic formula*: If $ax^2 + bx + c = 0$ $(a \neq 0)$, then the roots are

$$x = \frac{-b + \sqrt{b^2 - 4ac}}{2a} \text{ and } x = \frac{-b - \sqrt{b^2 - 4ac}}{2a}.$$

These are two distinct real numbers unless $b^2 - 4ac \leq 0$. If $b^2 - 4ac = 0$, then these two expressions for x are equal to $-\dfrac{b}{2a}$, and the equation has only one root. If $b^2 - 4ac < 0$, then $\sqrt{b^2 - 4ac}$ is not a real number and the equation has no real roots.

7. Exponents

A positive integer exponent of a number or a variable indicates a product, and the positive integer is the number of times that the number or variable is a factor in the product. For example, x^5 means $(x)(x)(x)(x)(x)$; that is, x is a factor in the product 5 times.

Some rules about exponents follow.

Let x and y be any positive numbers, and let r and s be any positive integers.

(1) $(x^r)(x^s) = x^{(r+s)}$; for example $(2^2)(2^3) = 2^{(2+3)} = 2^5 = 32$.

(2) $\dfrac{x^r}{x^s} = x^{r-s}$; for example, $\dfrac{4^5}{4^2} = 4^{5-2} = 4^3 = 64$.

(3) $(x^r)(y^r) = (xy)^r$; for example, $(3^3)(4^3) = 12^3 = 1{,}728$.

(4) $\left(\dfrac{x}{y}\right)^r = \dfrac{x^r}{y^r}$; for example, $\left(\dfrac{2}{3}\right)^3 = \dfrac{2^3}{3^3} = \dfrac{8}{27}$.

(5) $(x^r)^s = x^{rs} = (x^s)^r$; for example, $(x^3)^4 = x^{12} = (x^4)^3$.

(6) $x^{-r} = \dfrac{1}{x^r}$; for example, $3^{-2} = \dfrac{1}{3^2} = \dfrac{1}{9}$.

(7) $x^0 = 1$; for example, $6^0 = 1$.

(8) $x^{\frac{r}{s}} = \left(x^{\frac{1}{s}}\right)^r = \left(x^r\right)^{\frac{1}{s}} = \sqrt[s]{x^r}$; for example, $8^{\frac{2}{3}} = \left(8^{\frac{1}{3}}\right)^2 = \left(8^2\right)^{\frac{1}{3}} = \sqrt[3]{8^2} = \sqrt[3]{64} = 4$

and $9^{\frac{1}{2}} = \sqrt{9} = 3$.

It can be shown that rules 1–6 also apply when r and s are not integers and are not positive, that is, when r and s are any real numbers.

8. Inequalities

An *inequality* is a statement that uses one of the following symbols:

$\neq$ not equal to
$>$ greater than
$\geq$ greater than or equal to
$<$ less than
$\leq$ less than or equal to

Some examples of inequalities are $5x - 3 < 9$, $6x \geq y$, and $\frac{1}{2} < \frac{3}{4}$. Solving a linear inequality with one unknown is similar to solving an equation; the unknown is isolated on one side of the inequality. As in solving an equation, the same number can be added to or subtracted from both sides of the inequality, or both sides of an inequality can be multiplied or divided by a positive number without changing the truth of the inequality. However, multiplying or dividing an inequality by a negative number reverses the order of the inequality. For example, $6 > 2$, but $(-1)(6) < (-1)(2)$.

To solve the inequality $3x - 2 > 5$ for x, isolate x by using the following steps:

$$3x - 2 > 5$$
$$3x > 7 \text{ (adding 2 to both sides)}$$
$$x > \frac{7}{3} \text{ (dividing both sides by 3)}$$

To solve the inequality $\frac{5x-1}{-2} < 3$ for x, isolate x by using the following steps:

$$\frac{5x-1}{-2} < 3$$
$$5x - 1 > -6 \text{ (multiplying both sides by } -2\text{)}$$
$$5x > -5 \text{ (adding 1 to both sides)}$$
$$x > -1 \text{ (dividing both sides by 5)}$$

9. Absolute Value

The absolute value of x, denoted $|x|$, is defined to be x if $x \geq 0$ and $-x$ if $x < 0$. Note the $\sqrt{x^2}$ denotes that nonnegative square root of x^2, and so $\sqrt{x^2} = |x|$.

10. Functions

An algebraic expression in one variable can be used to define a *function* of that variable. A function is denoted by a letter such as f or g along with the variable in the expression. For example, the expression $x^3 - 5x^2 + 2$ defines a function f that can be denoted by

$$f(x) = x^3 - 5x^2 + 2.$$

The expression $\frac{2z+7}{\sqrt{z+1}}$ defines a function g that can be denoted by

$$g(z) = \frac{2z+7}{\sqrt{z+1}}$$

The symbols "$f(x)$" or "$g(z)$" do not represent products; each is merely the symbol for an expression, and is read "f of x" or "g of z."

Function notation provides a short way of writing the result of substituting a value for a variable. If $x = 1$ is substituted in the first expression, the result can be written $f(1) = -2$, and $f(1)$ is called the "value of f at $x = 1$." Similarly, if $z = 0$ is substituted in the second expression, then the value of g at $z = 0$ is $g(0) = 7$.

Once a function $f(x)$ is defined, it is useful to think of the variable x as an input and $f(x)$ as the corresponding output. In any function there can be no more than one output for any given input. However, more that one input can give the same output; for example, if $h(x) = |x+3|$, then $h(-4) = 1 = h(-2)$.

The set of all allowable inputs for a function is called the *domain* of the function. For f and g defined above, the domain of f is the set of all real numbers and the domain of g is the set of all numbers greater than -1. The domain of any function can be arbitrarily specified, as in the function defined by "$h(x) = 9x - 5$ for $0 \le x \le 10$." Without such a restriction, the domain is assumed to be all values of x that result in a real number when substituted into the function.

The domain of a function can consist of only the positive integers and possibly 0. For example, $a(n) = n^2 + \frac{n}{5}$ for $n = 0, 1, 2, 3, \ldots$.

Such a function is called a *sequence* and $a(n)$ is denoted by a_n. The value of the sequence a_n at $n = 3$ is $a_3 = 3^2 + \frac{3}{5} = 9.60$. As another example, consider the sequence defined by $b_n = (-1)^n (n!)$ for $n = 1, 2, 3, \ldots$. A sequence like this is often indicated by listing its values in the order $b_1, b_2, b_3, \ldots, b_n, \ldots$ as follows:
$-1, 2, -6, \ldots, (-1)^n(n!), \ldots$, and $(-1)^n(n!)$ is called the nth term of the sequence.

4.3 Geometry

1. Lines

In geometry, the word "line" refers to a straight line that extends without end in both directions.

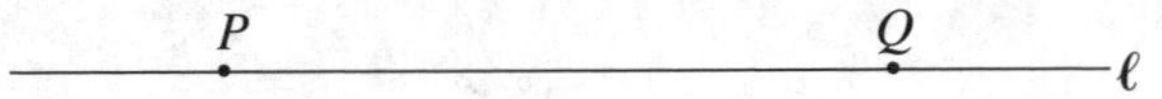

The line above can be referred to as line PQ or line ℓ. The part of the line from P to Q is called a *line segment.* P and Q are the *endpoints* of the segment. The notation PQ is used to denote both the segment and the length of the segment. The intention of the notation can be determined from the context.

2. Intersecting Lines and Angles

If two lines intersect, the opposite angles are called *vertical angles* and have the same measure. In the figure

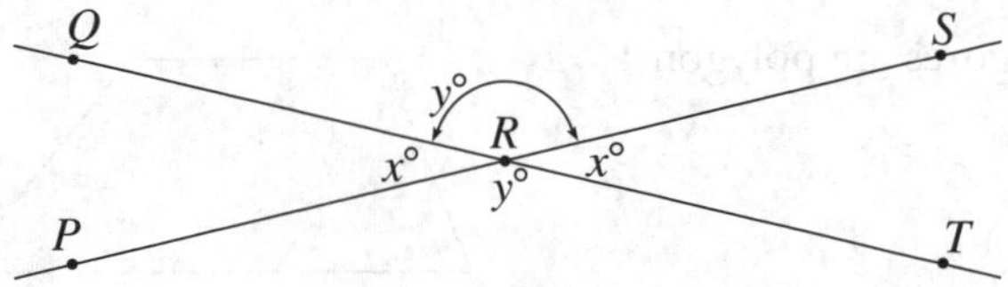

$\angle PRQ$ and $\angle SRT$ are vertical angles and $\angle QRS$ and $\angle PRT$ are vertical angles. Also, $x + y = 180$ since PRS is a straight line.

3. Perpendicular Lines

An angle that has a measure of 90° is a *right angle.* If two lines intersect at right angles, the lines are *perpendicular*. For example:

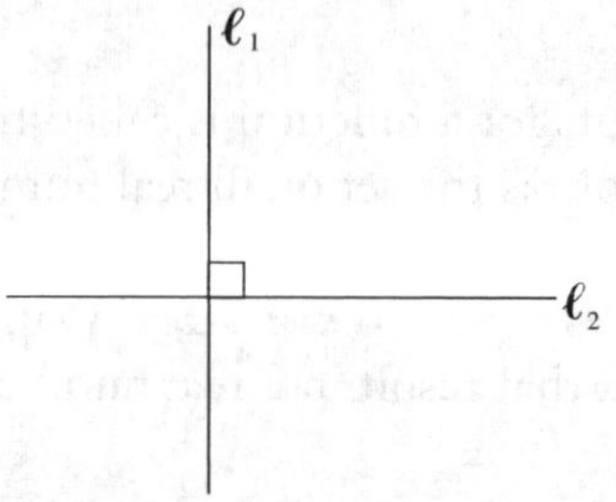

ℓ_1 and ℓ_2 above are perpendicular, denoted by $\ell_1 \perp \ell_2$. A right angle symbol in an angle of intersection indicates that the lines are perpendicular.

4. Parallel Lines

If two lines that are in the same plane do not intersect, the two lines are *parallel.* In the figure

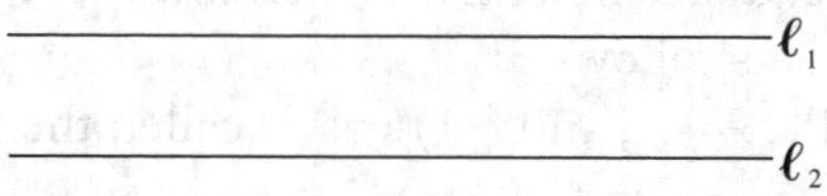

lines ℓ_1 and ℓ_2 are parallel, denoted by $\ell_1 \parallel \ell_2$. If two parallel lines are intersected by a third line, as shown below, then the angle measures are related as indicated, where $x + y = 180$.

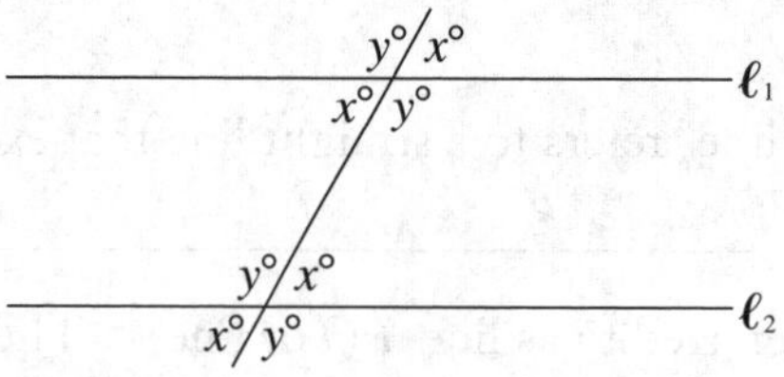

5. Polygons (Convex)

A *polygon* is a closed plane figure formed by three or more line segments, called the *sides* of the polygon. Each side intersects exactly two other sides at their endpoints. The points of intersection of the sides are *vertices*. The term "polygon" will be used to mean a convex polygon, that is, a polygon in which each interior angle has a measure of less than 180°.

The following figures are polygons:

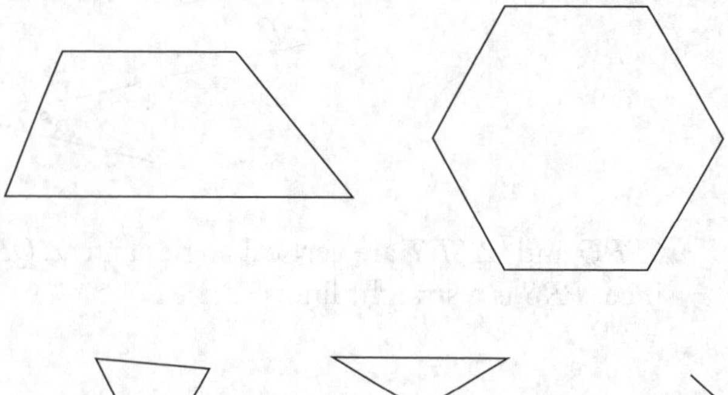

The following figures are not polygons:

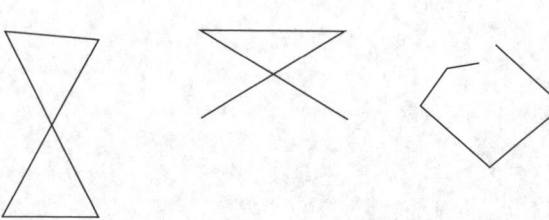

A polygon with three sides is a *triangle*; with four sides, a *quadrilateral*; with five sides, a *pentagon*; and with six sides, a *hexagon*.

The sum of the interior angle measures of a triangle is 180°. In general, the sum of the interior angle measures of a polygon with n sides is equal to $(n-2)180°$. For example, this sum for a pentagon is $(5-2)180 = (3)180 = 540$ degrees.

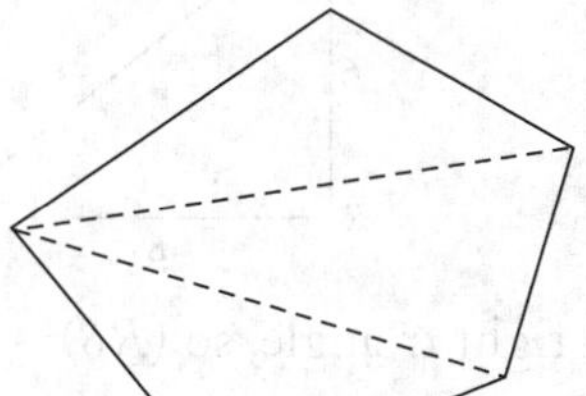

Note that a pentagon can be partitioned into three triangles and therefore the sum of the angle measures can be found by adding the sum of the angle measures of three triangles.

The *perimeter* of a polygon is the sum of the lengths of its sides.

The commonly used phrase "area of a triangle" (or any other plane figure) is used to mean the area of the region enclosed by that figure.

6. Triangles

There are several special types of triangles with important properties. But one property that all triangles share is that the sum of the lengths of any two of the sides is greater than the length of the third side, as illustrated below.

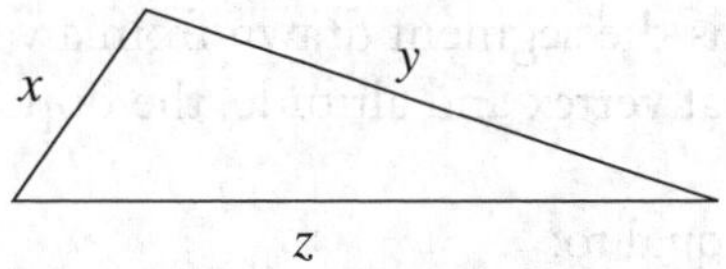

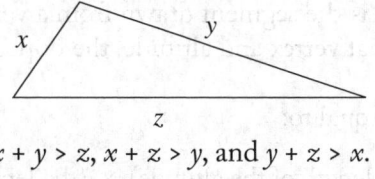

$x + y > z$, $x + z > y$, and $y + z > x$.

An *equilateral* triangle has all sides of equal length. All angles of an equilateral triangle have equal measure. An *isosceles* triangle has at least two sides of the same length. If two sides of a triangle have the same length, then the two angles opposite those sides have the same measure. Conversely, if two angles of a triangle have the same measure, then the sides opposite those angles have the same length. In isosceles triangle PQR below, $x = y$ since $PQ = QR$.

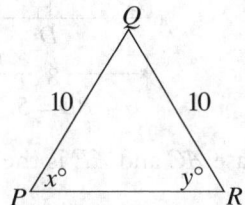

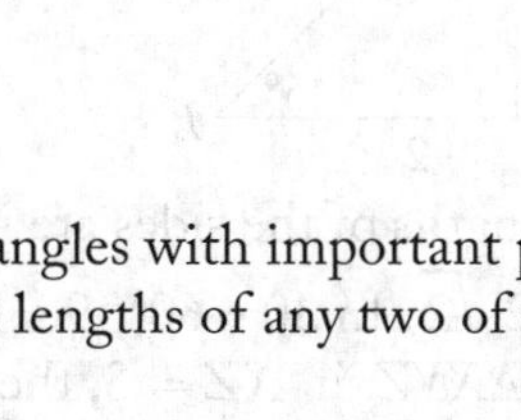

A triangle that has a right angle is a *right* triangle. In a right triangle, the side opposite the right angle is the *hypotenuse*, and the other two sides are the *legs*. An important theorem concerning right triangles is the *Pythagorean theorem*, which states: In a right triangle, the square of the length of the hypotenuse is equal to the sum of the squares of the lengths of the legs.

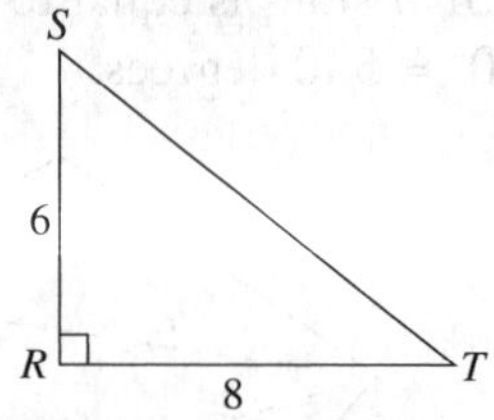

In the figure above, ΔRST is a right triangle, so $(RS)^2 + (RT)^2 = (ST)^2$. Here, $RS = 6$ and $RT = 8$, so $ST = 10$, since $6^2 + 8^2 = 36 + 64 = 100 = (ST)^2$ and $ST = \sqrt{100}$. Any triangle in which the lengths of the sides are in the ratio 3:4:5 is a right triangle. In general, if a, b, and c are the lengths of the sides of a triangle and $a^2 + b^2 = c^2$, then the triangle is a right triangle.

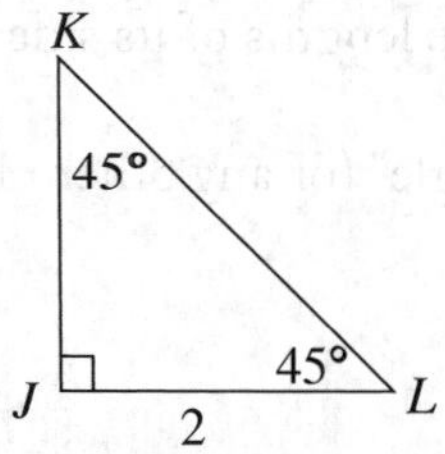

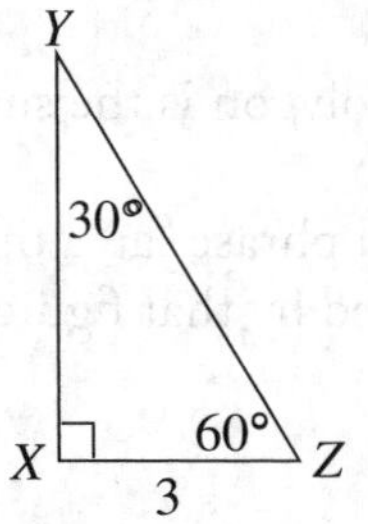

In 45° -45° -90° triangles, the lengths of the sides are in the ratio $1:1:\sqrt{2}$. For example, in ΔJKL, if $JL = 2$, then $JK = 2$ and $KL = 2\sqrt{2}$. In 30° -60° -90° triangles, the lengths of the sides are in the ratio $1:\sqrt{3}:2$. For example, in ΔXYZ, if $XZ = 3$, then $XY = 3\sqrt{3}$ and $YZ = 6$.

The *altitude* of a triangle is the segment drawn from a vertex perpendicular to the side opposite that vertex. Relative to that vertex and altitude, the opposite side is called the *base*.

The area of a triangle is equal to:

$$\frac{(\text{the length of the altitude}) \times (\text{the length of the base})}{2}$$

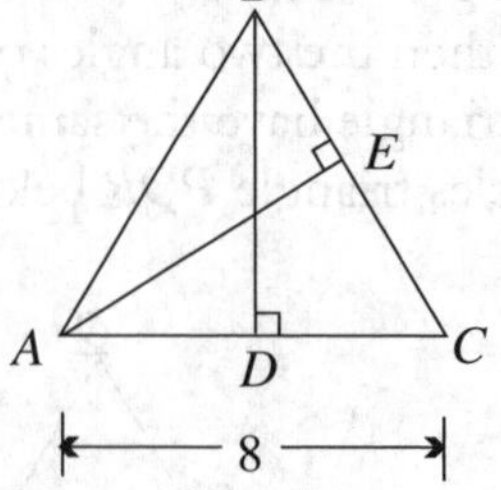

$BD = 5$

In ΔABC, BD is the altitude to base AC and AE is the altitude to base BC. The area of ΔABC is equal to

$$\frac{BD \times AC}{2} = \frac{5 \times 8}{2} = 20.$$

The area is also equal to $\frac{AE \times BC}{2}$. If ΔABC above is isosceles and $AB = BC$, then altitude BD bisects the base; that is, $AD = DC = 4$. Similarly, any altitude of an equilateral triangle bisects the side to which it is drawn.

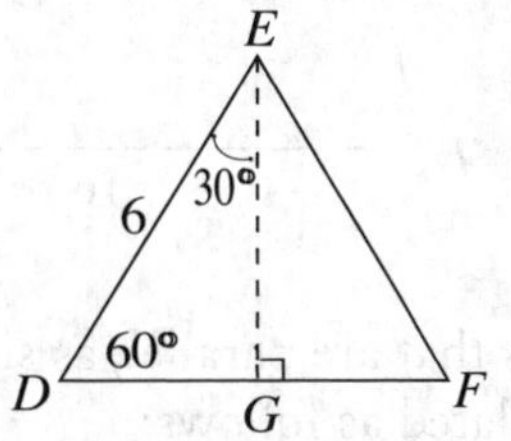

In equilateral triangle DEF, if $DE = 6$, then $DG = 3$ and $EG = 3\sqrt{3}$. The area of ΔDEF is equal to $\frac{3\sqrt{3} \times 6}{2} = 9\sqrt{3}$.

7. Quadrilaterals

A polygon with four sides is a *quadrilateral.* A quadrilateral in which both pairs of opposite sides are parallel is a *parallelogram*. The opposite sides of a parallelogram also have equal length.

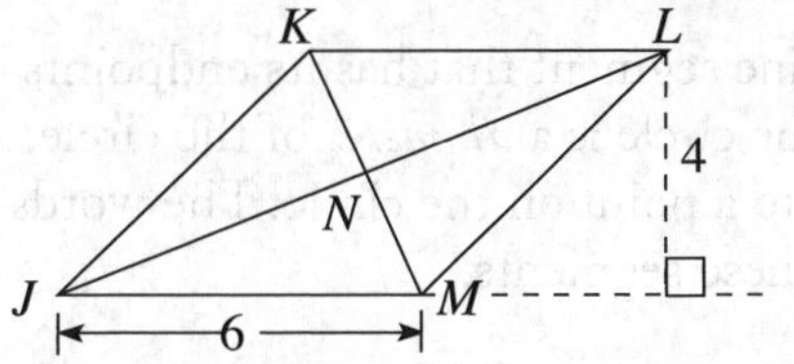

In parallelogram $JKLM$, $JK \parallel LM$ and $JK = LM$; $KL \parallel JM$ and $KL = JM$.

The diagonals of a parallelogram bisect each other (that is, $KN = NM$ and $JN = NL$).

The area of a parallelogram is equal to

(the length of the altitude) × (the length of the base).

The area of $JKLM$ is equal to $4 \times 6 = 24$.

A parallelogram with right angles is a *rectangle,* and a rectangle with all sides of equal length is a *square.*

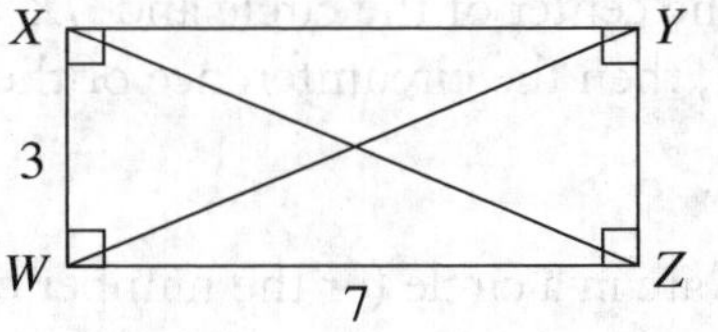

The perimeter of $WXYZ = 2(3) + 2(7) = 20$ and the area of $WXYZ$ is equal to $3 \times 7 = 21$. The diagonals of a rectangle are equal; therefore $WY = XZ = \sqrt{9+49} = \sqrt{58}$.

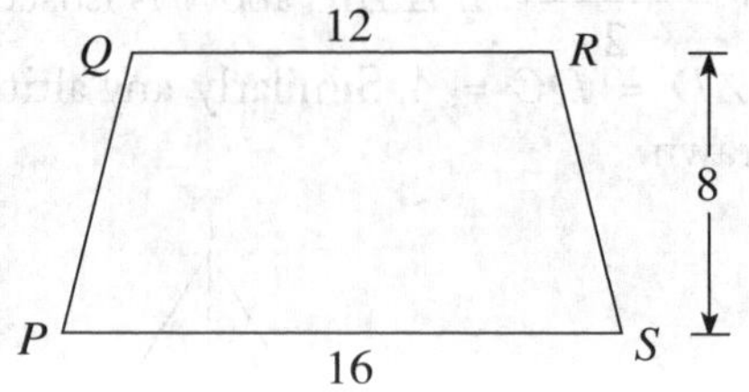

A quadrilateral with two sides that are parallel, as shown above, is a *trapezoid*. The area of trapezoid *PQRS* may be calculated as follows:

$$\frac{1}{2}(\text{sum of bases})(\text{height}) = \frac{1}{2}(QR + PS)(8) = \frac{1}{2}(28 \times 8) = 112.$$

8. Circles

A *circle* is a set of points in a plane that are all located the same distance from a fixed point (the *center* of the circle).

A *chord* of a circle is a line segment that has its endpoints on the circle. A chord that passes through the center of the circle is a *diameter* of the circle. A *radius* of a circle is a segment from the center of the circle to a point on the circle. The words "diameter" and "radius" are also used to refer to the lengths of these segments.

The *circumference* of a circle is the distance around the circle. If r is the radius of the circle, then the circumference is equal to $2\pi r$, where π is approximately $\frac{22}{7}$ or 3.14. The *area* of a circle of radius r is equal to πr^2.

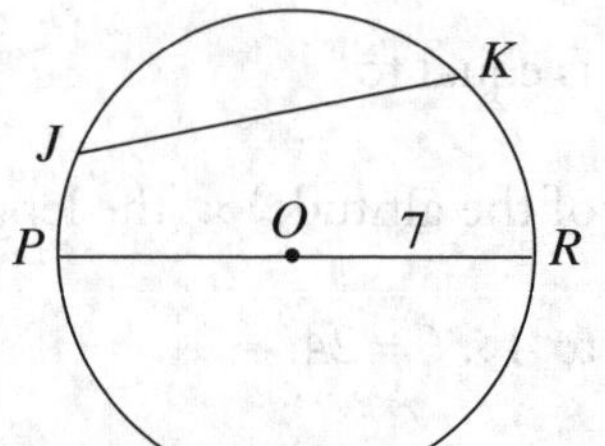

In the circle above, O is the center of the circle and JK and PR are chords. PR is a diameter and OR is a radius. If $OR = 7$, then the circumference of the circle is $2\pi(7) = 14\pi$ and the area of the circle is $\pi(7)^2 = 49\pi$.

The number of degrees of arc in a circle (or the number of degrees in a complete revolution) is 360.

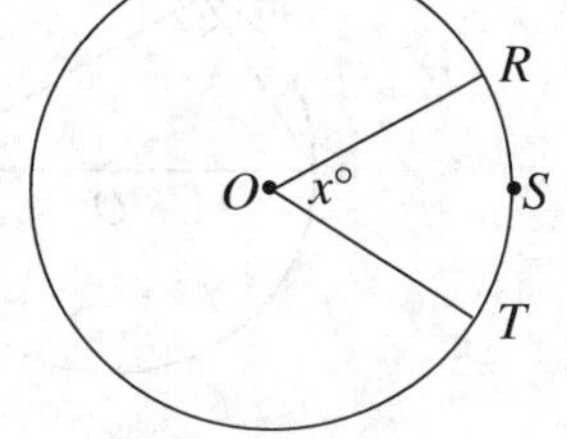

In the circle with center O above, the length of arc RST is $\frac{x}{360}$ of the circumference of the circle; for example, if $x = 60$, then arc RST has length $\frac{1}{6}$ of the circumference of the circle.

A line that has exactly one point in common with a circle is said to be *tangent* to the circle, and that common point is called the *point of tangency*. A radius or diameter with an endpoint at the point of tangency is perpendicular to the tangent line, and, conversely, a line that is perpendicular to a diameter at one of its endpoints is tangent to the circle at that endpoint.

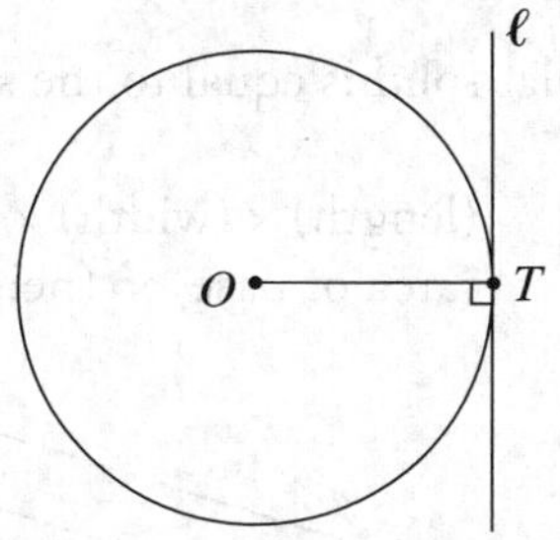

The line ℓ above is tangent to the circle and radius OT is perpendicular to ℓ.

If each vertex of a polygon lies on a circle, then the polygon is *inscribed* in the circle and the circle is *circumscribed* about the polygon. If each side of a polygon is tangent to a circle, then the polygon is *circumscribed* about the circle and the circle is *inscribed* in the polygon.

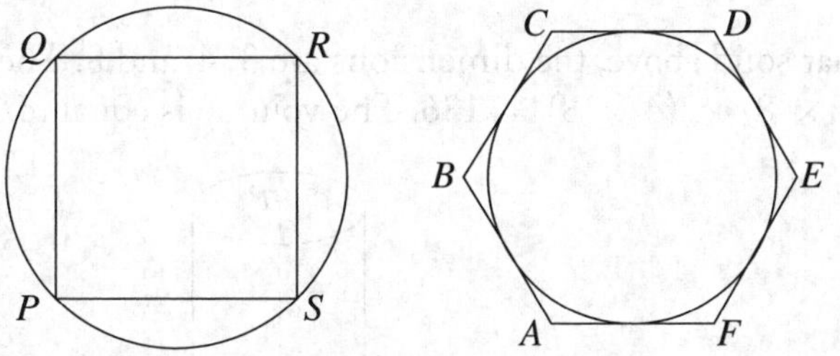

In the figure above, quadrilateral $PQRS$ is inscribed in a circle and hexagon $ABCDEF$ is circumscribed about a circle.

If a triangle is inscribed in a circle so that one of its sides is a diameter of the circle, then the triangle is a right triangle.

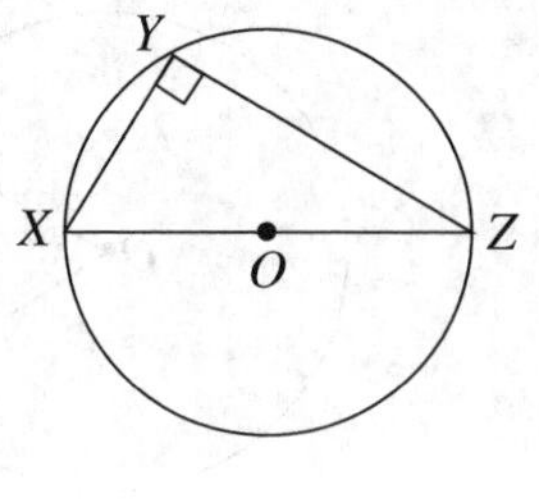

In the circle above, XZ is a diameter and the measure of $\angle XYZ$ is $90°$.

9. Rectangular Solids and Cylinders

A *rectangular solid* is a three-dimensional figure formed by six rectangular surfaces, as shown below. Each rectangular surface is a *face*. Each solid or dotted line segment is an *edge*, and each point at which the edges meet is a *vertex*. A rectangular solid has six faces, twelve edges, and eight vertices. Opposite faces are parallel rectangles that have the same dimensions. A rectangular solid in which all edges are of equal length is a *cube*.

The *surface area* of a rectangular solid is equal to the sum of the areas of all the faces. The *volume* is equal to

$$(\text{length}) \times (\text{width}) \times (\text{height});$$

in other words, $(\text{area of base}) \times (\text{height})$.

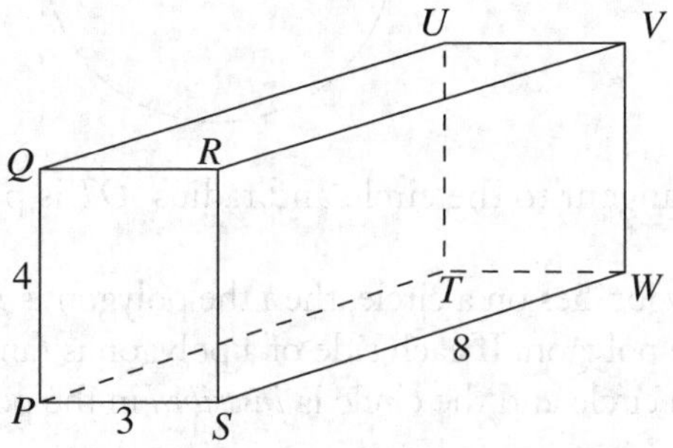

In the rectangular solid above, the dimensions are 3, 4, and 8. The surface area is equal to $2(3 \times 4) + 2(3 \times 8) + 2(4 \times 8) = 136$. The volume is equal to $3 \times 4 \times 8 = 96$.

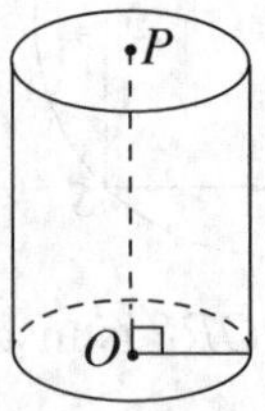

The figure above is a right circular *cylinder*. The two bases are circles of the same size with centers O and P, respectively, and altitude (height) OP is perpendicular to the bases. The surface area of a right circular cylinder with a base of radius r and height h is equal to $2(\pi r^2) + 2\pi rh$ (the sum of the areas of the two bases plus the area of the curved surface).

The volume of a cylinder is equal to $\pi r^2 h$, that is,

$$(\text{area of base}) \times (\text{height}).$$

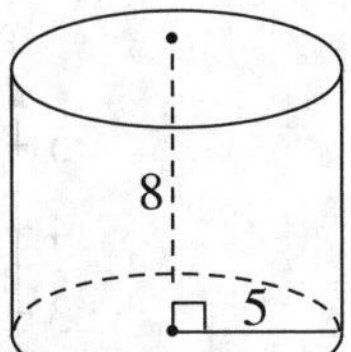

In the cylinder above, the surface area is equal to

$$2(25\pi) + 2\pi(5)(8) = 130\pi,$$

and the volume is equal to

$$25\pi(8) = 200\pi.$$

10. Coordinate Geometry

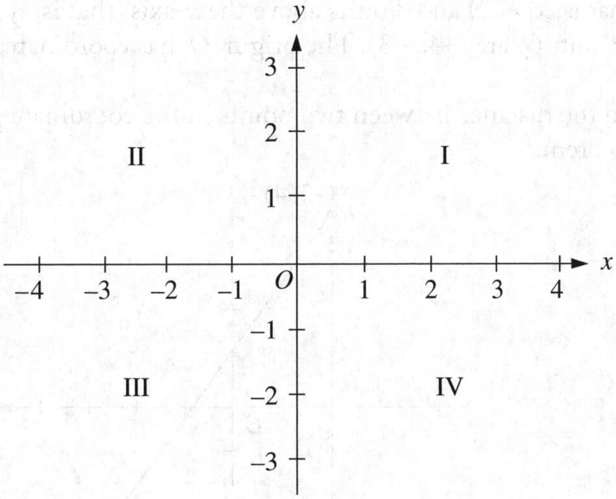

The figure above shows the (rectangular) *coordinate plane*. The horizontal line is called the *x-axis* and the perpendicular vertical line is called the *y-axis*. The point at which these two axes intersect, designated O, is called the *origin*. The axes divide the plane into four quadrants, I, II, III, and IV, as shown.

Each point in the plane has an *x-coordinate* and a *y-coordinate*. A point is identified by an ordered pair (x, y) of numbers in which the x-coordinate is the first number and the y-coordinate is the second number.

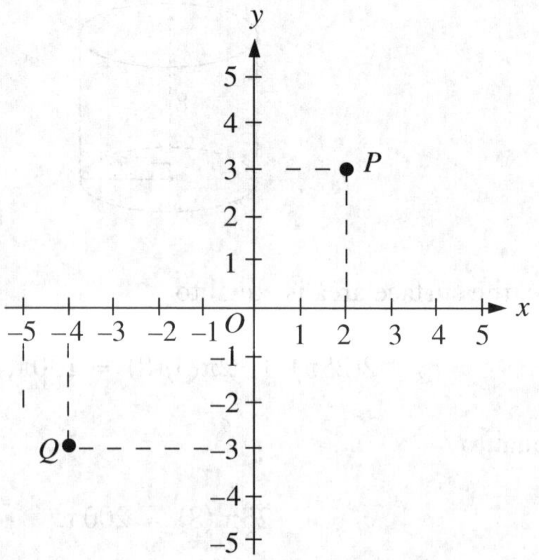

In the graph above, the (x, y) coordinates of point P are (2, 3) since P is 2 units to the right of the y-axis (that is, $x = 2$) and 3 units above the x-axis (that is, $y = 3$). Similarly, the (x, y) coordinates of point Q are (–4, –3). The origin O has coordinates (0, 0).

One way to find the distance between two points in the coordinate plane is to use the Pythagorean theorem.

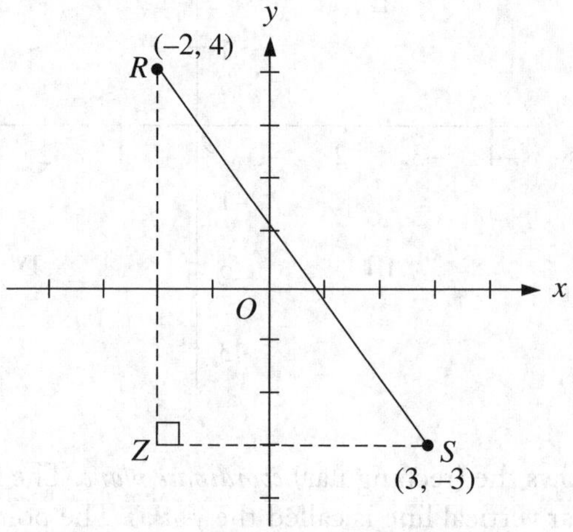

To find the distance between points R and S using the Pythagorean theorem, draw the triangle as shown. Note that Z has (x, y) coordinates (–2, –3), $RZ = 7$, and $ZS = 5$. Therefore, the distance between R and S is equal to

$$\sqrt{7^2 + 5^2} = \sqrt{74}$$

For a line in the coordinate plane, the coordinates of each point on the line satisfy a linear equation of the form $y = mx + b$ (or the form $x = a$ if the line is vertical). For example, each point on the line on the next page satisfies the equation $y = -\frac{1}{2}x + 1$. One can verify this for the points (–2,2), (2,0), and (0,1) by substituting the respective coordinates for x and y in the equation.

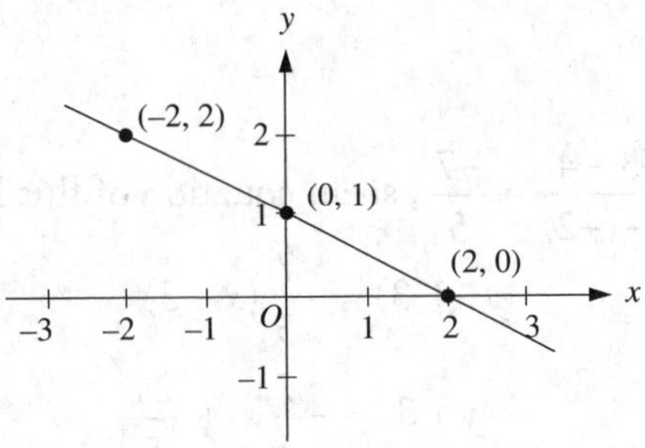

In the equation $y = mx + b$ of a line, the coefficient m is the *slope* of the line and the constant term b is the *y-intercept* of the line. For any two points on the line, the slope is defined to be the ratio of the difference in the y-coordinates to the difference in the x-coordinates. Using (–2,2) and (2,0) above, the slope is

$$\frac{\text{The difference in the } y\text{-coordinates}}{\text{The difference in the } x\text{-coordinates}} = \frac{0-2}{2-(-2)} = \frac{-2}{4} = -\frac{1}{2}.$$

The y-intercept is the y-coordinate of the point at which the line intersects the y-axis. For the line above, the y-intercept is 1, and this is the resulting value of y when x is set equal to 0 in the equation m $y = -\frac{1}{2}x = 1$. The *x-intercept* is the x-coordinate of the point at which the line intersects the x-axis. The x-intercept can be found by setting $y = 0$ and solving for x. For the line $y = -\frac{1}{2}x + 1$, this gives

$$-\frac{1}{2}x + 1 = 0$$

$$-\frac{1}{2}x = -1$$

$$x = 2.$$

Thus, the x-intercept is 2.

Given any two points (x_1, y_1) and (x_2, y_2) with $x_1 \neq x_2$, the equation of the line passing through these points can be found by applying the definition of slope. Since the slope is $m = \frac{y_2 - y_1}{x_2 - x_1}$, then using a point known to be on the line, say (x_1, y_1), any point (x, y) on the line must satisfy $\frac{y - y_1}{x - x_1} = m$, or $y - y_1 = m(x - x_1)$. (Using (x_2, y_2) as the known point would yield an equivalent equation.) For example, consider the points (–2, 4) and (3, –3) on the line below.

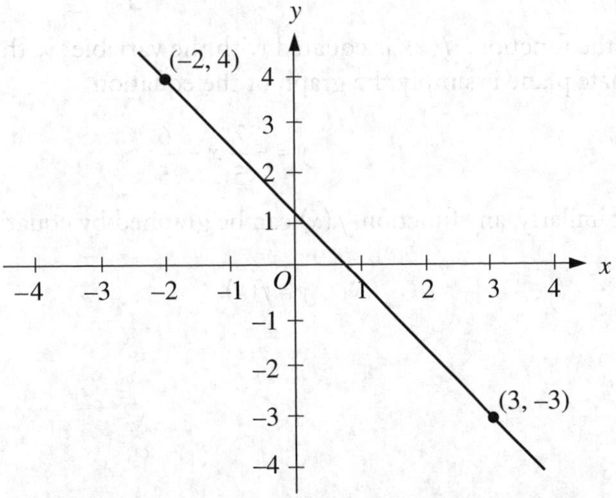

The slope of this line is $\frac{-3-4}{3-(-2)} = \frac{-7}{5}$, so an equation of this line can be found using the point (3, −3) as follows:

$$y-(-3) = -\frac{7}{5}(x-3)$$

$$y+3 = -\frac{7}{5}x + \frac{21}{5}$$

$$y = -\frac{7}{5}x + \frac{6}{5}.$$

The *y*-intercept is $\frac{6}{5}$. The *x-intercept* can be found as follows:

$$0 = -\frac{7}{5}x + \frac{6}{5}$$

$$\frac{7}{5}x = \frac{6}{5}$$

$$x = \frac{6}{7}$$

Both of these intercepts can be seen on the graph.

If the slope of a line is negative, the line slants downward from left to right; if the slope is positive, the line slants upward. If the slope is 0, the line is horizontal; the equation of such a line is of the form $y = b$ since $m = 0$. For a vertical line, slope is not defined, and the equation is of the form $x = a$, where a is the x-intercept.

There is a connection between graphs of lines in the coordinate plane and solutions of two linear equations with two unknowns. If two linear equations with unknowns x and y have a unique solution, then the graphs of the equations are two lines that intersect in one point, which is the solution. If the equations are equivalent, then they represent the same line with infinitely many points or solutions. If the equations have no solution, then they represent parallel lines, which do not intersect.

There is also a connection between functions (see section 4.2.10) and the coordinate plane. If a function is graphed in the coordinate plane, the function can be understood in different and useful ways. Consider the function defined by

$$f(x) = -\frac{7}{5}x + \frac{6}{5}.$$

If the value of the function, $f(x)$, is equated with the variable y, then the graph of the function in the xy-coordinate plane is simply the graph of the equation

$$y = -\frac{7}{5}x + \frac{6}{5}.$$

shown above. Similarly, any function $f(x)$ can be graphed by equating y with the value of the function:

$$y = f(x).$$

So for any x in the domain of the function f, the point with coordinates $(x, f(x))$ is on the graph of f, and the graph consists entirely of these points.

As another example, consider a quadratic polynomial function defined by $f(x) = x^2 - 1$. One can plot several points $(x, f(x))$ on the graph to understand the connection between a function and its graph:

x	$f(x)$
−2	3
−1	0
0	−1
1	0
2	3

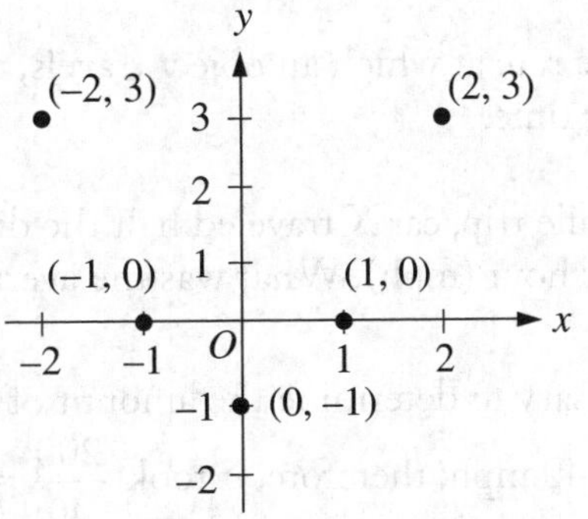

If all the points were graphed for $-2 \le x \le 2$, then the graph would appear as follows.

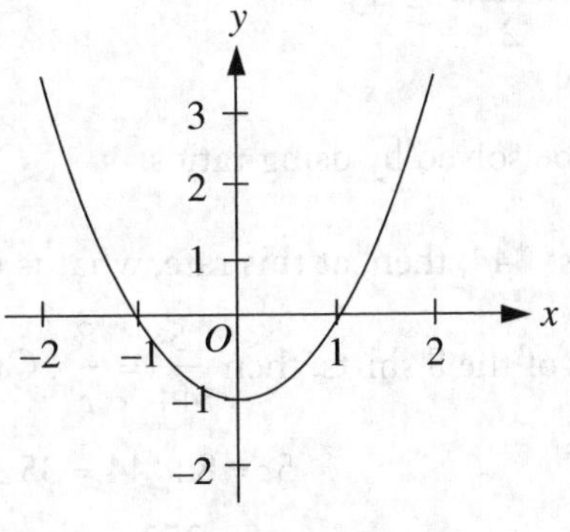

The graph of a quadratic function is called a *parabola* and always has the shape of the curve above, although it may be upside down or have a greater or lesser width. Note that the roots of the equation $f(x) = x^2 - 1 = 0$ are $x = 1$ and $x = -1$; these coincide with the x-intercepts since x-intercepts are found by setting $y = 0$ and solving for x. Also, the y-intercept is $f(0) = -1$ because this is the value of y corresponding to $x = 0$. For any function f, the x-intercepts are the solutions of the equation $f(x) = 0$ and the y-intercept is the value $f(0)$.

4.4 Word Problems

Many of the principles discussed in this chapter are used to solve word problems. The following discussion of word problems illustrates some of the techniques and concepts used in solving such problems.

1. Rate Problems

The distance that an object travels is equal to the product of the average speed at which it travels and the amount of time it takes to travel that distance, that is,

$$\text{Rate} \times \text{Time} = \text{Distance}.$$

Example 1: If a car travels at an average speed of 70 kilometers per hour for 4 hours, how many kilometers does it travel?

Solution: Since rate × time = distance, simply multiply 70 km/hour × 4 hours. Thus, the car travels 280 kilometers in 4 hours.

To determine the average rate at which an object travels, divide the total distance traveled by the total amount of traveling time.

Example 2: On a 400-mile trip, car X traveled half the distance at 40 miles per hour and the other half at 50 miles per hour (mph). What was the average speed of car X?

Solution: First it is necessary to determine the amount of traveling time. During the first 200 miles, the car traveled at 40 mph; therefore, it took $\frac{200}{40} = 5$ hours to travel the first 200 miles. During the second 200 miles, the car traveled at 50 mph; therefore, it took $\frac{200}{50} = 4$ hours to travel the second 200 miles. Thus, the average speed of car X was $\frac{400}{9} = 44\frac{4}{9}$ mph. Note that the average speed is *not* $\frac{40+50}{2} = 45$.

Some rate problems can be solved by using ratios.

Example 3: If 5 shirts cost \$44, then, at this rate, what is the cost of 8 shirts?

Solution: If c is the cost of the 8 shirts, then $\frac{5}{44} = \frac{8}{c}$. Cross multiplication results in the equation

$$5c = 8 \times 44 = 352$$

$$c = \frac{352}{5} = 70.40$$

The 8 shirts cost \$70.40.

2. Work Problems

In a work problem, the rates at which certain persons or machines work alone are usually given, and it is necessary to compute the rate at which they work together (or vice versa).

The basic formula for solving work problems is $\frac{1}{r} + \frac{1}{s} = \frac{1}{h}$, where r and s are, for example, the number of hours it takes Rae and Sam, respectively, to complete a job when working alone, and h is the number of hours it takes Rae and Sam to do the job when working together. The reasoning is that in 1 hour Rae does $\frac{1}{r}$ of the job, Sam does $\frac{1}{s}$ of the job, and Rae and Sam together do $\frac{1}{h}$ of the job.

Example 1: If machine X can produce 1,000 bolts in 4 hours and machine Y can produce 1,000 bolts in 5 hours, in how many hours can machines X and Y, working together at these constant rates, produce 1,000 bolts?

Solution:

$$\frac{1}{4} + \frac{1}{5} = \frac{1}{h}$$

$$\frac{5}{20} + \frac{4}{20} = \frac{1}{h}$$

$$\frac{9}{20} = \frac{1}{h}$$

$$9h = 20$$

$$h = \frac{20}{9} = 2\frac{2}{9}$$

Working together, machines X and Y can produce 1,000 bolts in $2\frac{2}{9}$ hours.

Example 2: If Art and Rita can do a job in 4 hours when working together at their respective constant rates and Art can do the job alone in 6 hours, in how many hours can Rita do the job alone?

Solution:

$$\frac{1}{6} + \frac{1}{R} = \frac{1}{4}$$

$$\frac{R+6}{6R} = \frac{1}{4}$$

$$4R + 24 = 6R$$

$$24 = 2R$$

$$12 = R$$

Working alone, Rita can do the job in 12 hours.

3. Mixture Problems

In mixture problems, substances with different characteristics are combined, and it is necessary to determine the characteristics of the resulting mixture.

Example 1: If 6 pounds of nuts that cost \$1.20 per pound are mixed with 2 pounds of nuts that cost \$1.60 per pound, what is the cost per pound of the mixture?

Solution: The total cost of the 8 pounds of nuts is

$$6(\$1.20) + 2(\$1.60) = \$10.40.$$

The cost per pound is $\frac{\$10.40}{8} = \$1.30.$

Example 2: How many liters of a solution that is 15 percent salt must be added to 5 liters of a solution that is 8 percent salt so that the resulting solution is 10 percent salt?

Solution: Let n represent the number of liters of the 15% solution. The amount of salt in the 15% solution $[0.15n]$ plus the amount of salt in the 8% solution $[(0.08)(5)]$ must be equal to the amount of salt in the 10% mixture $[0.10(n + 5)]$. Therefore,

$$\begin{aligned} 0.15n + 0.08(5) &= 0.10(n + 5) \\ 15n + 40 &= 10n + 50 \\ 5n &= 10 \\ n &= 2 \text{ liters} \end{aligned}$$

Two liters of the 15% salt solution must be added to the 8% solution to obtain the 10% solution.

4. Interest Problems

Interest can be computed in two basic ways. With simple annual interest, the interest is computed on the principal only and is equal to (principal) × (interest rate) × (time). If interest is compounded, then interest is computed on the principal as well as on any interest already earned.

Example 1: If \$8,000 is invested at 6 percent simple annual interest, how much interest is earned after 3 months?

Solution: Since the annual interest rate is 6%, the interest for 1 year is

$$(0.06)(\$8,000) = \$480.$$

The interest earned in 3 months is $\frac{3}{12}(\$480) = \$120.$

Example 2: If \$10,000 is invested at 10 percent annual interest, compounded semiannually, what is the balance after 1 year?

Solution: The balance after the first 6 months would be

$$10000 + (10000)(0.05) = \$10500.$$

The balance after one year would be $10500 + (10500)(0.05) = \$11025.$

Note that the interest rate for each 6-month period is 5%, which is half of the 10% annual rate. The balance after one year can also be expressed as

$$10{,}000\left(1+\frac{0.10}{2}\right)^2 \text{ dollars.}$$

5. Discount

If a price is discounted by n percent, then the price becomes $(100 - n)$ percent of the original price.

Example 1: A certain customer paid \$24 for a dress. If that price represented a 25 percent discount on the original price of the dress, what was the original price of the dress?

Solution: If p is the original price of the dress, then $0.75p$ is the discounted price and $0.75p = \$24$, or $p = \$32$. The original price of the dress was \$32.

Example 2: The price of an item is discounted by 20 percent and then this reduced price is discounted by an additional 30 percent. These two discounts are equal to an overall discount of what percent?

Solution: If p is the original price of the item, then $0.8p$ is the price after the first discount. The price after the second discount is $(0.7)(0.8)p = 0.56p$. This represents an overall discount of 44 percent (100% – 56%).

6. Profit

Gross profit is equal to revenues minus expenses, or selling price minus cost.

Example: A certain appliance costs a merchant \$30. At what price should the merchant sell the appliance in order to make a gross profit of 50 percent of the cost of the appliance?

Solution: If s is the selling price of the appliance, then $s - 30 = (0.5)(30)$, or $s = \$45$. The merchant should sell the appliance for \$45.

7. Sets

If S is the set of numbers 1, 2, 3, and 4, you can write $S = \{1,2,3,4\}$. Sets can also be represented by Venn diagrams. That is, the relationship among the members of sets can be represented by circles.

Example 1: Each of 25 people is enrolled in history, mathematics, or both. If 20 are enrolled in history and 18 are enrolled in mathematics, how many are enrolled in both history and mathematics?

Solution: The 25 people can be divided into three sets: those who study history only, those who study mathematics only, and those who study history and mathematics. Thus a Venn diagram may be drawn as follows, where n is the number of people enrolled in both courses, $20 - n$ is the number enrolled in history only, and $18 - n$ is the number enrolled in mathematics only.

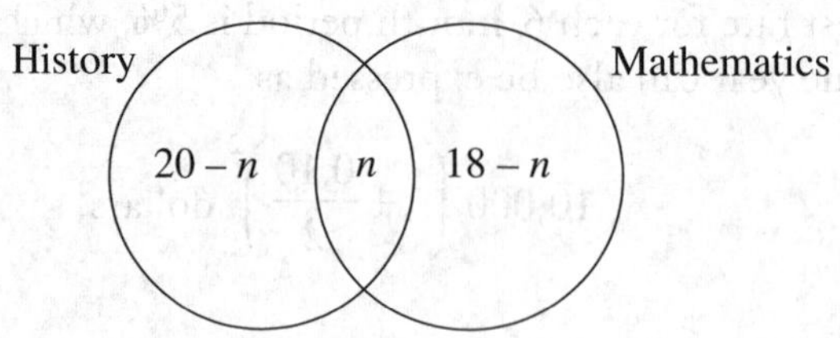

Since there is a total of 25 people, $(20 - n) + n + (18 - n) = 25$, or $n = 13$. Thirteen people are enrolled in both history and mathematics. Note that $20 + 18 - 13 = 25$, which is the general addition rule for two sets (see section 4.1.9).

Example 2: In a certain production lot, 40 percent of the toys are red and the remaining toys are green. Half of the toys are small and half are large. If 10 percent of the toys are red and small, and 40 toys are green and large, how many of the toys are red and large?

Solution: For this kind of problem, it is helpful to organize the information in a table:

	Red	Green	Total
Small	10%		50%
Large			50%
Total	40%	60%	100%

The numbers in the table are the percents given. The following percents can be computed on the basis of what is given:

	Red	Green	Total
Small	10%	40%	50%
Large	30%	20%	50%
Total	40%	60%	100%

Since 20% of the number of toys (n) are green and large, $0.20n = 40$ (40 toys are green and large), or $n = 200$. Therefore, 30% of the 200 toys, or $(0.3)(200) = 60$, are red and large.

8. Geometry Problems

The following is an example of a word problem involving geometry.
Example:

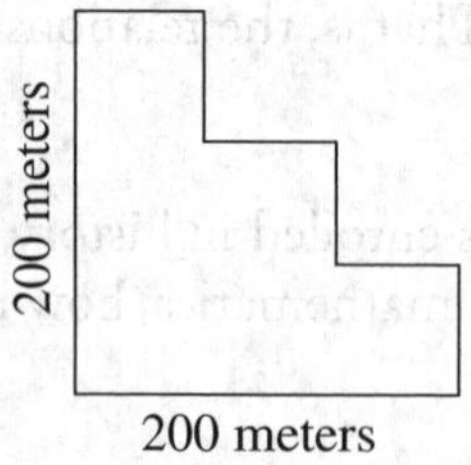

The figure above shows an aerial view of a piece of land. If all angles shown are right angles, what is the perimeter of the piece of land?

Solution: For reference, label the figure as

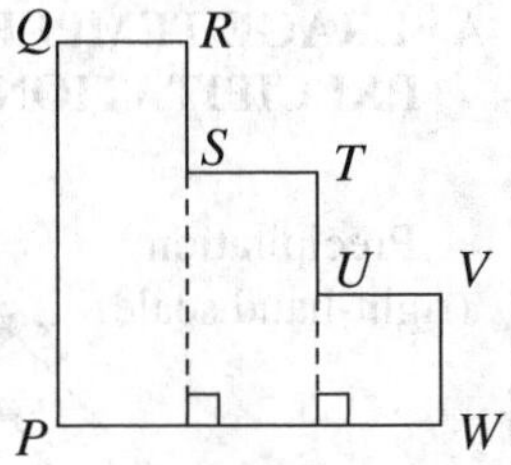

If all the angles are right angles, then $QR + ST + UV = PW$, and $RS + TU + VW = PQ$. Hence, the perimeter of the land is $2PW + 2PQ = 2 \times 200 + 2 \times 200 = 800$ meters.

9. Measurement Problems

Some questions on the GMAT® involve metric units of measure, whereas others involve English units of measure. However, except for units of time, if a question requires conversion from one unit of measure to another, the relationship between those units will be given.

Example: A train travels at a constant rate of 25 meters per second. How many kilometers does it travel in 5 minutes? (1 kilometer = 1,000 meters)

Solution: In 1 minute the train travels (25)(60) = 1,500 meters, so in 5 minutes it travels 7,500 meters. Since 1 kilometer = 1,000 meters, it follows that 7,500 meters equals $\frac{7{,}500}{1{,}000}$, or 7.5 kilometers.

10. Data Interpretation

Occasionally a question or set of questions will be based on data provided in a table or graph. Some examples of tables and graphs are given below.

Example 1:

Population by Age Group
(in thousands)

Age	Population
17 years and under	63,376
18–44 years	86,738
45–64 years	43,845
65 years and over	24,054

How many people are 44 years old or younger?

Solution: The figures in the table are given in thousands. The answer in thousands can be obtained by adding 63,376 thousand and 86,738 thousand. The result is 150,114 thousand, which is 150,114,000.

Example 2:

AVERAGE TEMPERATURE AND PRECIPITATION IN CITY *X*

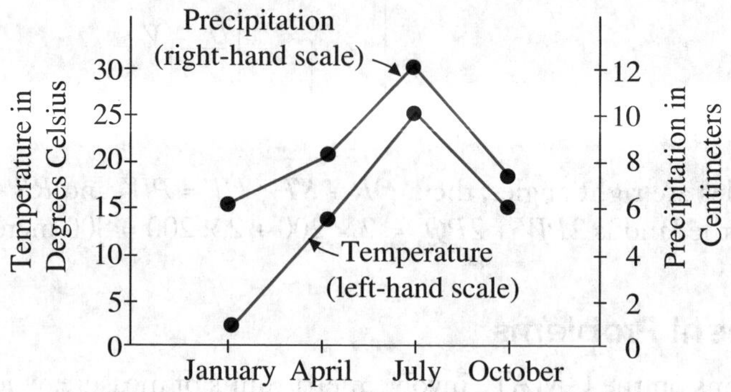

What are the average temperature and precipitation in City X during April?

Solution: Note that the scale on the left applies to the temperature line graph and the one on the right applies to the precipitation line graph. According to the graph, during April the average temperature is approximately 14° Celsius and the average precipitation is 8 centimeters.

Example 3:

DISTRIBUTION OF AL'S WEEKLY NET SALARY

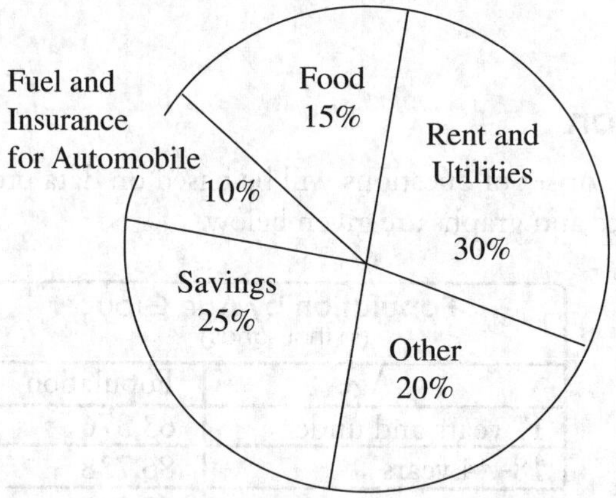

Al's weekly net salary is \$350. To how many of the categories listed was at least \$80 of Al's weekly net salary allocated?

Solution: In the circle graph, the relative sizes of the sectors are proportional to their corresponding values and the sum of the percents given is 100%. Note that $\frac{80}{350}$ is approximately 23%, so at least \$80 was allocated to each of 2 categories—Rent and Utilities, and Savings—since their allocations are each greater than 23%.

5.0 Problem Solving

5.0 Problem Solving

The Quantitative section of the GMAT® test uses problem solving and data sufficiency questions to gauge your skill level. This chapter focuses on problem solving questions. Remember that quantitative questions require knowledge of the following:

- Arithmetic
- Elementary algebra
- Commonly known concepts of geometry

Problem solving questions are designed to test your basic mathematical skills and understanding of elementary mathematical concepts, as well as your ability to reason quantitatively, solve quantitative problems, and interpret graphic data. The mathematics knowledge required to answer the questions is no more advanced than what is generally taught in secondary school (or high school) mathematics classes.

In these questions, you are asked to solve each problem and select the best of the five answer choices given. Begin by reading the question thoroughly to determine exactly what information is given and to make sure you understand what is being asked. Scan the answer choices to understand your options. If the problem seems simple, take a few moments to see whether you can determine the answer. Then check your answer against the choices provided.

If you do not see your answer among the choices, or if the problem is complicated, take a closer look at the answer choices and think again about what the problem is asking. See whether you can eliminate some of the answer choices and narrow down your options. If you are still unable to narrow the answer down to a single choice, reread the question. Keep in mind that the answer will be based solely on the information provided in the question—don't allow your own experience and assumptions to interfere with your ability to find the correct answer to the question.

If you find yourself stuck on a question or unable to select the single correct answer, keep in mind that you have about two minutes to answer each quantitative question. You may run out of time if you take too long to answer any one question, so you may simply need to pick the answer that seems to make the most sense. Although guessing is generally not the best way to achieve a high GMAT® score, making an educated guess is a good strategy for answering questions you are unsure of. Even if your answer to a particular question is incorrect, your answers to other questions will allow the test to accurately gauge your ability level.

The following pages include the directions that will precede questions of this type, test-taking strategies, sample questions, and explanations for all the problems. These explanations present problem solving strategies that could be helpful in answering the questions.

5.1 Test-Taking Strategies for Problem Solving Questions

1. **Pace yourself.**
   Consult the on-screen timer periodically. Work as carefully as possible, but do not spend valuable time checking answers or pondering problems that you find difficult.

2. **Use the erasable notepad provided.**
   Working a problem out may help you avoid errors in solving the problem. If diagrams or figures are not presented, it may help if you draw your own.

3. **Read each question carefully to determine what is being asked.**
   For word problems, take one step at a time, reading each sentence carefully and translating the information into equations or other useful mathematical representations.

4. **Scan the answer choices before attempting to answer a question.**
   Scanning the answers can prevent you from putting answers in a form that is not given (e.g., finding the answer in decimal form, such as 0.25, when the choices are given in fractional form, such as 1/4). Also, if the question requires approximations, a shortcut could serve well (e.g., you may be able to approximate 48 percent of a number by using half).

5. **Don't waste time trying to solve a problem that is too difficult for you.**
   Make your best guess and move on to the next question.

5.2 The Directions

These directions are very similar to those you will see for problem solving questions when you take the GMAT® test. If you read them carefully and understand them clearly before sitting for the GMAT® exam, you will not need to spend too much time reviewing them once the test begins.

Solve the problem and indicate the best of the answer choices given.

Numbers: All numbers used are real numbers.

Figures: A figure accompanying a problem solving question is intended to provide information useful in solving the problem. Figures are drawn as accurately as possible EXCEPT when it is stated in a specific problem that its figure is not drawn to scale. Straight lines may sometimes appear jagged. All figures lie in a plane unless otherwise indicated.

5.3 Problem Solving Sample Questions

Solve the problem and indicate the best of the answer choices given.
Numbers: All numbers used are real numbers.
Figures: A figure accompanying a problem solving question is intended to provide information useful in solving the problem. Figures are drawn as accurately as possible EXCEPT when it is stated in a specific problem that its figure is not drawn to scale. Straight lines may sometimes appear jagged. All figures lie in a plane unless otherwise indicated.

1. A project scheduled to be carried out over a single fiscal year has a budget of $12,600, divided into 12 equal monthly allocations. At the end of the fourth month of that fiscal year, the total amount actually spent on the project was $4,580. By how much was the project over its budget?

(A) $ 380
(B) $ 540
(C) $1,050
(D) $1,380
(E) $1,430

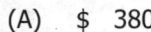

2. For which of the following values of n is $\frac{100+n}{n}$ NOT an integer?

(A) 1
(B) 2
(C) 3
(D) 4
(E) 5

3. Rectangular floors X and Y have equal area. If floor X is 12 feet by 18 feet and floor Y is 9 feet wide, what is the length of floor Y, in feet?

(A) $13\frac{1}{2}$
(B) 18
(C) $18\frac{3}{4}$
(D) 21
(E) 24

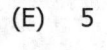

4. A case contains c cartons. Each carton contains b boxes, and each box contains 100 paper clips. How many paper clips are contained in 2 cases?

(A) $100bc$
(B) $\frac{100b}{c}$
(C) $200bc$
(D) $\frac{200b}{c}$
(E) $\frac{200}{bc}$

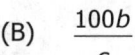

5. The sum of prime numbers that are greater than 60 but less than 70 is

(A) 67
(B) 128
(C) 191
(D) 197
(E) 260

6. A rainstorm increased the amount of water stored in State J reservoirs from 124 billion gallons to 138 billion gallons. If the storm increased the amount of water in the reservoirs to 82 percent of total capacity, approximately how many billion gallons of water were the reservoirs short of total capacity prior to the storm?

(A) 9
(B) 14
(C) 25
(D) 30
(E) 44

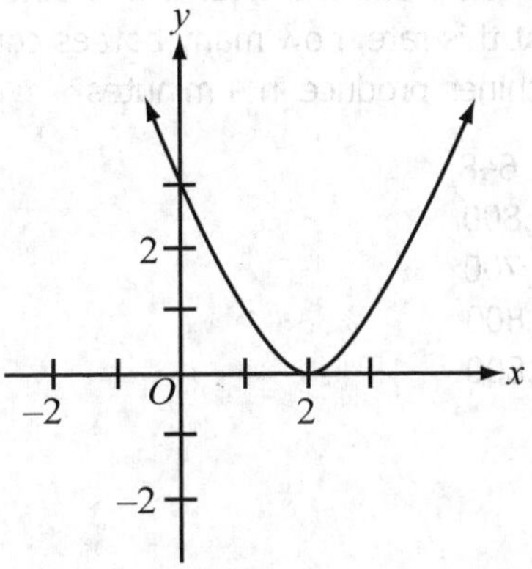

7. On the graph above, when $x = \frac{1}{2}$, $y = 2$; and when $x = 1$, $y = 1$. The graph is symmetric with respect to the vertical line at $x = 2$. According to the graph, when $x = 3$, $y =$

(A) -1
(B) $-\frac{1}{2}$
(C) 0
(D) $\frac{1}{2}$
(E) 1

8. When $\frac{1}{10}$ percent of 5,000 is subtracted from $\frac{1}{10}$ of 5,000, the difference is

(A) 0
(B) 50
(C) 450
(D) 495
(E) 500

9. Which of the following is the value of $\sqrt{\sqrt[3]{0.000064}}$?

(A) 0.004
(B) 0.008
(C) 0.02
(D) 0.04
(E) 0.2

10. Raffle tickets numbered consecutively from 101 through 350 are placed in a box. What is the probability that a ticket selected at random will have a number with a hundreds digit of 2?

(A) $\frac{2}{5}$
(B) $\frac{2}{7}$
(C) $\frac{33}{83}$
(D) $\frac{99}{250}$
(E) $\frac{100}{249}$

11. On Monday, a person mailed 8 packages weighing an average (arithmetic mean) of $12\frac{3}{8}$ pounds, and on Tuesday, 4 packages weighing an average of $15\frac{1}{4}$ pounds. What was the average weight, in pounds, of all the packages the person mailed on both days?

(A) $13\frac{1}{3}$
(B) $13\frac{13}{16}$
(C) $15\frac{1}{2}$
(D) $15\frac{15}{16}$
(E) $16\frac{1}{2}$

12. $0.1 + (0.1)^2 + (0.1)^3 =$

(A) 0.1
(B) 0.111
(C) 0.1211
(D) 0.2341
(E) 0.3

13. A carpenter constructed a rectangular sandbox with a capacity of 10 cubic feet. If the carpenter were to make a similar sandbox twice as long, twice as wide, and twice as high as the first sandbox, what would be the capacity, in cubic feet, of the second sandbox?

(A) 20
(B) 40
(C) 60
(D) 80
(E) 100

14. Which of the following CANNOT be a value of $\frac{1}{x-1}$?

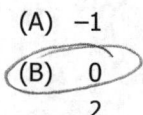

(A) -1
(B) 0
(C) $\frac{2}{3}$
(D) 1
(E) 2

15. A bakery opened yesterday with its daily supply of 40 dozen rolls. Half of the rolls were sold by noon, and 80 percent of the remaining rolls were sold between noon and closing time. How many dozen rolls had not been sold when the bakery closed yesterday?

(A) 1
(B) 2
(C) 3
(D) 4
(E) 5

16. What is the combined area, in square inches, of the front and back of a rectangular sheet of paper measuring $8\frac{1}{2}$ inches by 11 inches?

(A) 38
(B) 44
(C) 88
(D) 176
(E) 187

17. 150 is what percent of 30?

(A) 5%
(B) 20%
(C) 50%
(D) 200%
(E) 500%

18. The ratio 2 to $\frac{1}{3}$ is equal to the ratio

(A) 6 to 1
(B) 5 to 1
(C) 3 to 2
(D) 2 to 3
(E) 1 to 6

19. Running at the same constant rate, 6 identical machines can produce a total of 270 bottles per minute. At this rate, how many bottles could 10 such machines produce in 4 minutes?

(A) 648
(B) 1,800
(C) 2,700
(D) 10,800
(E) 64,800

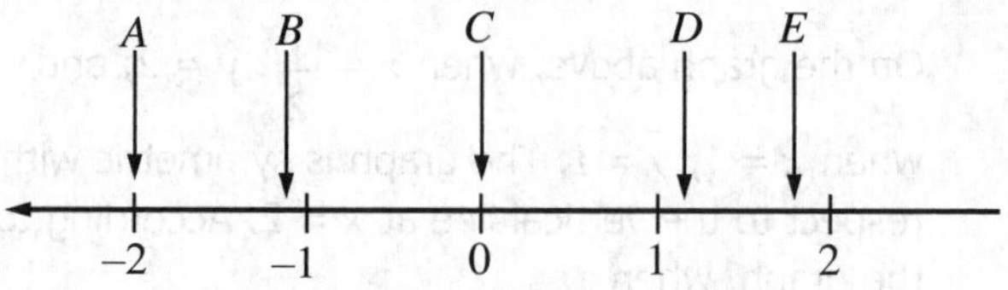

20. Of the five coordinates associated with points *A*, *B*, *C*, *D*, and *E* on the number line above, which has the greatest absolute value?

(A) *A*
(B) *B*
(C) *C*
(D) *D*
(E) *E*

21. If x and y are prime numbers, which of the following CANNOT be the sum of x and y?

(A) 5
(B) 9
(C) 13
(D) 16
(E) 23

22. If each of the following fractions were written as a repeating decimal, which would have the longest sequence of different digits?

(A) $\frac{2}{11}$

(B) $\frac{1}{3}$

(C) $\frac{41}{99}$

(D) $\frac{2}{3}$

(E) $\frac{23}{37}$

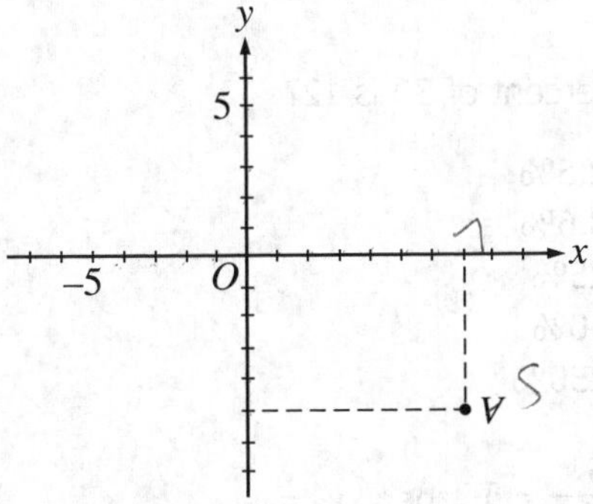

23. In the figure above, the coordinates of point V are

(A) (−7, 5)
(B) (−5, 7)
(C) (5, 7)
(D) (7, 5)
(E) (7,−5)

24. A rope 40 feet long is cut into two pieces. If one piece is 18 feet longer than the other, what is the length, in feet, of the shorter piece?

(A) 9
(B) 11
(C) 18
(D) 22
(E) 29

25. The Earth travels around the Sun at a speed of approximately 18.5 miles per second. This approximate speed is how many miles per hour?

(A) 1,080
(B) 1,160
(C) 64,800
(D) 66,600
(E) 3,996,000

26. If the quotient $\frac{a}{b}$ is positive, which of the following must be true?

(A) $a > 0$
(B) $b > 0$
(C) $ab > 0$
(D) $a - b > 0$
(E) $a + b > 0$

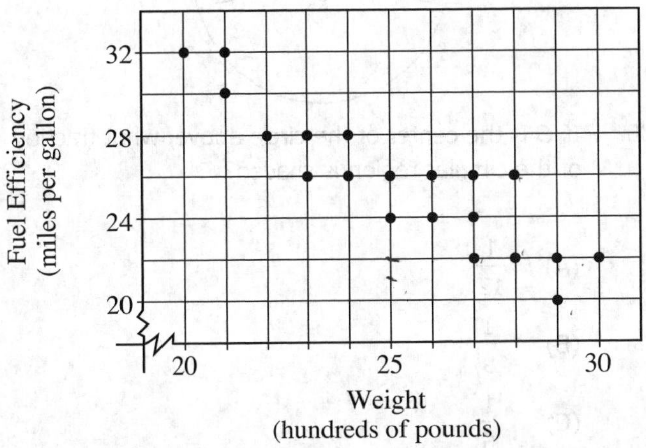

27. The dots on the graph above indicate the weights and fuel efficiency ratings for 20 cars. How many of the cars weigh more than 2,500 pounds and also get more than 22 miles per gallon?

(A) 3
(B) 5
(C) 8
(D) 10
(E) 11

28. How many minutes does it take John to type y words if he types at the rate of x words per minute?

(A) $\frac{x}{y}$

(B) $\frac{y}{x}$

(C) xy

(D) $\frac{60x}{y}$

(E) $\frac{y}{60x}$

29. $\sqrt{(16)(20)+(8)(32)} =$

(A) $4\sqrt{20}$
(B) 24
(C) 25
(D) $4\sqrt{20}+8\sqrt{2}$
(E) 32

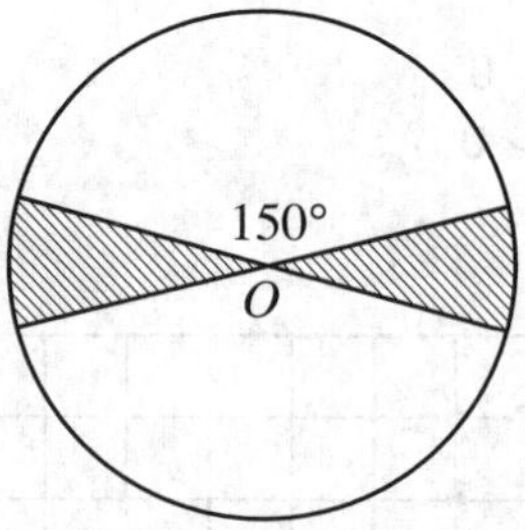

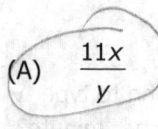

30. If O is the center of the circle above, what fraction of the circular region is shaded?

(A) $\frac{1}{12}$
(B) $\frac{1}{9}$
(C) $\frac{1}{6}$
(D) $\frac{1}{4}$
(E) $\frac{1}{3}$

31. If Juan takes 11 seconds to run y yards, how many seconds will it take him to run x yards at the same rate?

(A) $\frac{11x}{y}$
(B) $\frac{11y}{x}$
(C) $\frac{x}{11y}$
(D) $\frac{11}{xy}$
(E) $\frac{xy}{11}$

32. John has 10 pairs of matched socks. If he loses 7 individual socks, what is the greatest number of pairs of matched socks he can have left?

(A) 7
(B) 6
(C) 5
(D) 4
(E) 3

33. What is the lowest positive integer that is divisible by each of the integers 1 through 7, inclusive?

(A) 420
(B) 840
(C) 1,260
(D) 2,520
(E) 5,040

34. What percent of 30 is 12?

(A) 2.5%
(B) 3.6%
(C) 25%
(D) 40%
(E) 250%

35. If $\frac{1.5}{0.2+x} = 5$, then $x =$

(A) − 3.7
(B) 0.1
(C) 0.3
(D) 0.5
(E) 2.8

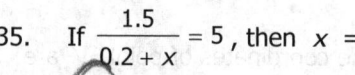

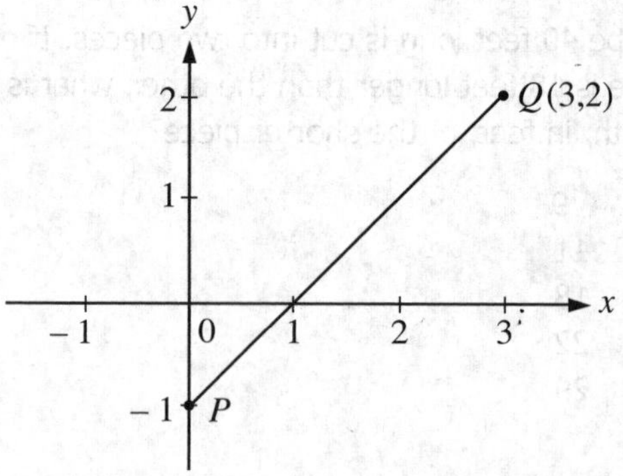

36. In the figure above, the point on segment PQ that is twice as far from P as from Q is

(A) (3, 1)
(B) (2, 1)
(C) (2, – 1)
(D) (1.5, 0.5)
(E) (1, 0)

37. If a positive integer n is divisible by both 5 and 7, then n must also be divisible by which of the following?

I. 12
II. 35
III. 70

(A) None
(B) I only
(C) II only
(D) I and II
(E) II and III

38. If 4 is one solution of the equation $x^2 + 3x + k = 10$, where k is a constant, what is the other solution?

(A) – 7
(B) – 4
(C) – 3
(D) 1
(E) 6

39. If $x = -3$, what is the value of $-3x^2$?

(A) –27
(B) –18
(C) 18
(D) 27
(E) 81

40. $\frac{29^2 + 29}{29} =$

(A) 870
(B) 841
(C) 58
(D) 31
(E) 30

41. If $x = 1 - 3t$ and $y = 2t - 1$, then for what value of t does $x = y$?

(A) $\frac{5}{2}$
(B) $\frac{3}{2}$
(C) $\frac{2}{3}$
(D) $\frac{2}{5}$
(E) 0

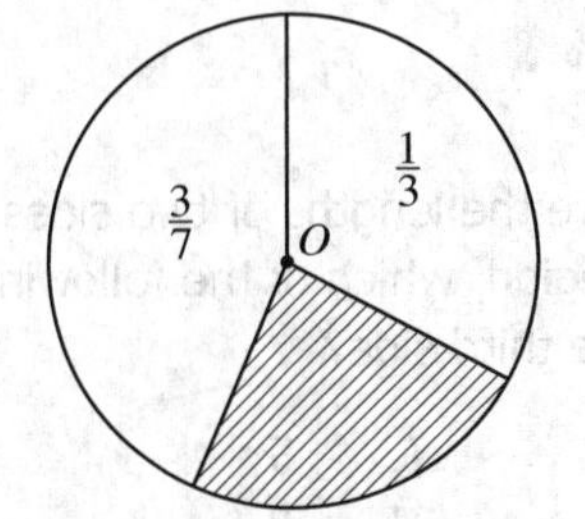

42. In the circular region with center O, shown above, the two unshaded sections constitute $\frac{3}{7}$ and $\frac{1}{3}$ of the area of the circular region. The shaded section constitutes what fractional part of the area of the circular region?

(A) $\frac{3}{5}$
(B) $\frac{6}{7}$
(C) $\frac{2}{21}$
(D) $\frac{5}{21}$
(E) $\frac{16}{21}$

43. $\frac{(0.3)^5}{(0.3)^3} =$

(A) 0.001
(B) 0.01
(C) 0.09
(D) 0.9
(E) 1.0

44. In a horticultural experiment, 200 seeds were planted in plot I and 300 were planted in plot II. If 57 percent of the seeds in plot I germinated and 42 percent of the seeds in plot II germinated, what percent of the total number of planted seeds germinated?

(A) 45.5%
(B) 46.5%
(C) 48.0%
(D) 49.5%
(E) 51.0%

45. If 3 and 8 are the lengths of two sides of a triangular region, which of the following can be the length of the third side?

I. 5
II. 8
III. 11

(A) II only
(B) III only
(C) I and II only
(D) II and III only
(E) I, II, and III

46. How many integers n are there such that $1 < 5n + 5 < 25$?

(A) Five
(B) Four
(C) Three
(D) Two
(E) One

47. A car dealer sold x used cars and y new cars during May. If the number of used cars sold was 10 greater than the number of new cars sold, which of the following expresses this relationship?

(A) $x > 10y$
(B) $x > y + 10$
(C) $x > y - 10$
(D) $x = y + 10$
(E) $x = y - 10$

48. If a 10 percent deposit that has been paid toward the purchase of a certain product is \$110, how much more remains to be paid?

(A) \$880
(B) \$990
(C) \$1,000
(D) \$1,100
(E) \$1,210

49. $\left(\sqrt{7} + \sqrt{7}\right)^2$

(A) 98
(B) 49
(C) 28
(D) 21
(E) 14

50. In a certain population, there are 3 times as many people aged 21 or under as there are people over 21. The ratio of those 21 or under to the total population is

(A) 1 to 2
(B) 1 to 3
(C) 1 to 4
(D) 2 to 3
(E) 3 to 4

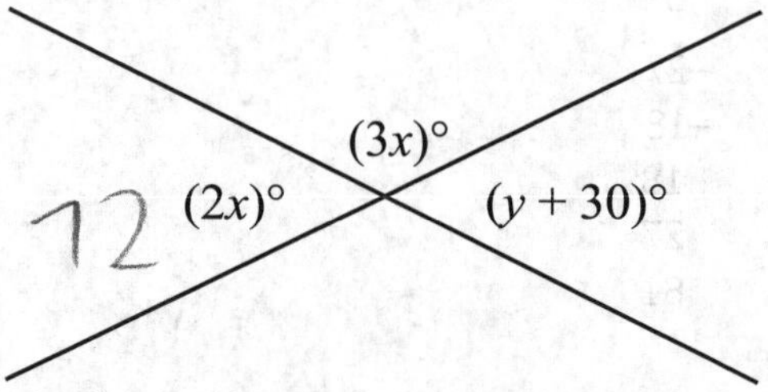

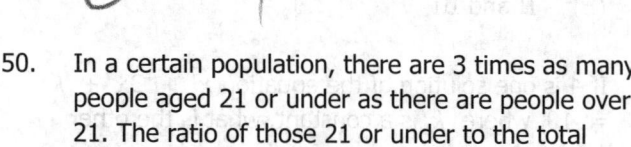

51. In the figure above, the value of y is

(A) 6
(B) 12
(C) 24
(D) 36
(E) 42

52. Kelly and Chris packed several boxes with books. If Chris packed 60 percent of the total number of boxes, what was the ratio of the number of boxes Kelly packed to the number of boxes Chris packed?

(A) 1 to 6
(B) 1 to 4
(C) 2 to 5
(D) 3 to 5
(E) 2 to 3

53. Of the following, which is the closest approximation of $\frac{50.2 \times 0.49}{199.8}$?

(A) $\frac{1}{10}$

(B) $\frac{1}{8}$

(C) $\frac{1}{4}$

(D) $\frac{5}{4}$

(E) $\frac{25}{2}$

54. The average (arithmetic mean) of 10, 30, and 50 is 5 more than the average of 20, 40, and

(A) 15
(B) 25
(C) 35
(D) 45
(E) 55

55. If $y = 4 + (x - 3)^2$, then y is lowest when $x =$

(A) 14
(B) 13
(C) 0
(D) 3
(E) 4

56. Which of the following is NOT equal to the square of an integer?

(A) $\sqrt{\sqrt{1}}$

(B) $\sqrt{4}$

(C) $\frac{18}{2}$

(D) $41 - 25$

(E) 36

57. Fermat primes are prime numbers that can be written in the form $2^k + 1$, where k is an integer and a power of 2. Which of the following is NOT a Fermat prime?

(A) 3
(B) 5
(C) 17
(D) 31
(E) 257

58. If $x^2 = 2y^3$ and $2y = 4$, what is the value of $x^2 + y$?

(A) −14
(B) −2
(C) 3
(D) 6
(E) 18

59. A glucose solution contains 15 grams of glucose per 100 cubic centimeters of solution. If 45 cubic centimeters of the solution were poured into an empty container, how many grams of glucose would be in the container?

(A) 3.00
(B) 5.00
(C) 5.50
(D) 6.50
(E) 6.75

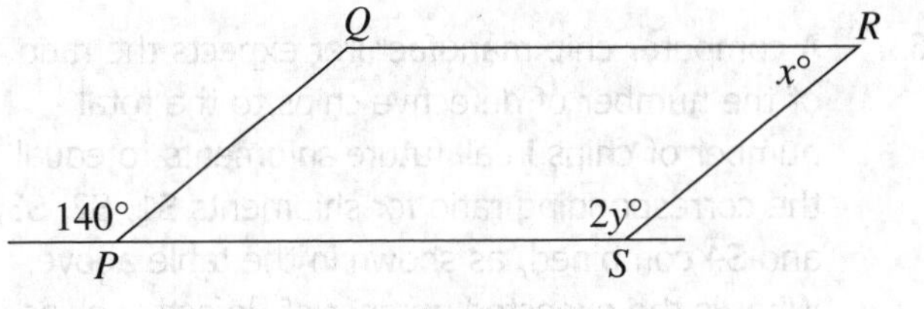

60. In the figure above, if $PQRS$ is a parallelogram, then $y - x =$

(A) 30
(B) 35
(C) 40
(D) 70
(E) 100

61. If 1 kilometer is approximately 0.60 mile, which of the following best approximates the number of kilometers in 2 miles?

(A) $\frac{10}{3}$

(B) 3

(C) $\frac{6}{5}$

(D) $\frac{1}{3}$

(E) $\frac{3}{10}$

62. Lucy invested $10,000 in a new mutual fund account exactly three years ago. The value of the account increased by 10 percent during the first year, increased by 5 percent during the second year, and decreased by 10 percent during the third year. What is the value of the account today?

(A) $10,350
(B) $10,395
(C) $10,500
(D) $11,500
(E) $12,705

Shipment	Number of defective chips in the shipment	Total Number of chips in the shipment
S1	2	5,000
S2	5	12,000
S3	6	18,000
S4	4	16,000

63. A computer chip manufacturer expects the ratio of the number of defective chips to the total number of chips in all future shipments to equal the corresponding ratio for shipments S1, S2, S3, and S4 combined, as shown in the table above. What is the expected number of defective chips in a shipment of 60,000 chips?

(A) 14
(B) 20
(C) 22
(D) 24
(E) 25

A = {2, 3, 4, 5}
B = {4, 5, 6, 7, 8}

64. Two integers will be randomly selected from the sets above, one integer from set *A* and one integer from set *B*. What is the probability that the sum of the two integers will equal 9?

(A) 0.15
(B) 0.20
(C) 0.25
(D) 0.30
(E) 0.33

2, 4, 6, 8, n, 3, 5, 7, 9

65. In the list above, if *n* is an integer between 1 and 10, inclusive, then the median must be

(A) either 4 or 5
(B) either 5 or 6
(C) either 6 or 7
(D) *n*
(E) 5.50

$$\begin{array}{r} 4\ u\ 7 \\ n\ 2\ 3 \\ +\ 1\ 6\ 2 \\ \hline 1,\ 2\ 2\ 2 \end{array}$$

66. If *n* and *u* represent single digits in the correctly worked computation above, what is the value of *n* + *u*?

(A) 7
(B) 9
(C) 10
(D) 11
(E) 13

$$r = 400\left(\frac{D + S - P}{P}\right)$$

67. If stock is sold three months after it is purchased, the formula above relates *P*, *D*, *S*, and *r*, where *P* is the purchase price of the stock, *D* is the amount of any dividend received, *S* is the selling price of the stock, and *r* is the yield of the investment as a percent. If Rose purchased $400 worth of stock, received a dividend of $5, and sold the stock for $420 three months after purchasing it, what was the yield of her investment according to the formula? (Assume that she paid no commissions.)

(A) 1.25%
(B) 5%
(C) 6.25%
(D) 20%
(E) 25%

68. The temperatures in degrees Celsius recorded at 6 in the morning in various parts of a certain country were 10°, 5°, -2°, -1°, -5°, and 15°. What is the median of these temperatures?

(A) −2°C
(B) −1°C
(C) 2°C
(D) 3°C
(E) 5°C

69. If $y\left(\frac{3x-5}{2}\right) = y$ and $y \neq 0$, then $x =$

(A) $\frac{2}{3}$
(B) $\frac{5}{3}$
(C) $\frac{7}{3}$
(D) 1
(E) 4

70. If $x + 5 > 2$ and $x - 3 < 7$, the value of x must be between which of the following pairs of numbers?

(A) −3 and 10
(B) −3 and 4
(C) 2 and 7
(D) 3 and 4
(E) 3 and 10

71. A gym class can be divided into 8 teams with an equal number of players on each team or into 12 teams with an equal number of players on each team. What is the lowest possible number of students in the class?

(A) 20
(B) 24
(C) 36
(D) 48
(E) 96

72. At least $\frac{2}{3}$ of the 40 members of a committee must vote in favor of a resolution for it to pass. What is the greatest number of members who could vote against the resolution and still have it pass?

(A) 19
(B) 17
(C) 16
(D) 14
(E) 13

73. In the Johnsons' monthly budget, the dollar amounts allocated to household expenses, food, and miscellaneous items are in the ratio 5:2:1, respectively. If the total amount allocated to these three categories is $1,800, what is the amount allocated to food?

(A) $900
(B) $720
(C) $675
(D) $450
(E) $225

74. There are 4 more women than men on Centerville's board of education. If there are 10 members on the board, how many are women?

(A) 3
(B) 4
(C) 6
(D) 7
(E) 8

75. Leona bought a 1-year, $10,000 certificate of deposit that paid interest at an annual rate of 8 percent compounded semiannually. What was the total amount of interest paid on this certificate at maturity?

(A) $10,464
(B) $864
(C) $816
(D) $800
(E) $480

76. Which of the following ratios is most nearly equal to the ratio $1 + \sqrt{5}$ to 2?

(A) 8 to 5
(B) 6 to 5
(C) 5 to 4
(D) 2 to 1
(E) 1 to 1

77. $\dfrac{\frac{7}{1}}{5} + \dfrac{\frac{5}{1}}{7} =$

(A) $\dfrac{35}{74}$
(B) $\dfrac{74}{35}$
(C) 35
(D) 70
(E) 74

78. From January 1, 1991, to January 1, 1993, the number of people enrolled in health maintenance organizations increased by 15 percent. The enrollment on January 1, 1993, was 45 million. How many million people, to the nearest million, were enrolled in health maintenance organizations on January 1, 1991?

(A) 38
(B) 39
(C) 40
(D) 41
(E) 42

79. *R* is the set of positive odd integers less than 50, and *S* is the set of the squares of the integers in *R*. How many elements does the intersection of *R* and *S* contain?

(A) None
(B) Two
(C) Four
(D) Five
(E) Seven

80. A retail appliance store priced a video recorder at 20 percent above the wholesale cost of \$200. If a store employee applied the 10 percent employee discount to the retail price to buy the recorder, how much did the employee pay for the recorder?

(A) \$198
(B) \$216
(C) \$220
(D) \$230
(E) \$240

$$y = 248 - 398x$$

81. Which of the following values of *x* gives the greatest value of *y* in the equation above?

(A) 200
(B) 100
(C) 0.5
(D) 0
(E) −1

82. Machine A produces bolts at a uniform rate of 120 every 40 seconds, and machine B produces bolts at a uniform rate of 100 every 20 seconds. If the two machines run simultaneously, how many seconds will it take for them to produce a total of 200 bolts?

(A) 22
(B) 25
(C) 28
(D) 32
(E) 56

83. What is the decimal equivalent of $\left(\frac{1}{5}\right)^5$?

(A) 0.00032
(B) 0.0016
(C) 0.00625
(D) 0.008
(E) 0.03125

84. $\dfrac{90 - 8(20 \div 4)}{\frac{1}{2}} =$

(A) 25
(B) 50
(C) 100
(D) 116
(E) 170

85. A dealer originally bought 100 identical batteries at a total cost of q dollars. If each battery was sold at 50 percent above the original cost per battery, then, in terms of q, for how many dollars was each battery sold?

(A) $\frac{3q}{200}$

(B) $\frac{3q}{2}$

(C) $150q$

(D) $\frac{q}{100} + 50$

(E) $\frac{150}{q}$

86. In an increasing sequence of 10 consecutive integers, the sum of the first 5 integers is 560. What is the sum of the last 5 integers in the sequence?

(A) 585
(B) 580
(C) 575
(D) 570
(E) 565

87. Machine A produces 100 parts twice as fast as machine B does. Machine B produces 100 parts in 40 minutes. If each machine produces parts at a constant rate, how many parts does machine A produce in 6 minutes?

(A) 30
(B) 25
(C) 20
(D) 15
(E) 7.5

88. A necklace is made by stringing N individual beads together in the repeating pattern red bead, green bead, white bead, blue bead, and yellow bead. If the necklace design begins with a red bead and ends with a white bead, then N could equal

(A) 16
(B) 32
(C) 41
(D) 54
(E) 68

89. In the xy-coordinate system, if (a,b) and $(a + 3, b + k)$ are two points on the line defined by the equation $x = 3y - 7$, then $k =$

(A) 9

(B) 3

(C) $\frac{7}{3}$

(D) 1

(E) $\frac{1}{3}$

90. At the rate of m meters per s seconds, how many meters does a cyclist travel in x minutes?

(A) $\frac{m}{sx}$

(B) $\frac{mx}{s}$

(C) $\frac{60m}{sx}$

(D) $\frac{60ms}{x}$

(E) $\frac{60mx}{s}$

91. If Sam were twice as old as he is, he would be 40 years older than Jim. If Jim is 10 years younger than Sam, how old is Sam?

(A) 20
(B) 30
(C) 40
(D) 50
(E) 60

92. In a certain furniture store, each week Nancy earns a salary of \$240 plus 5 percent of the amount of her total sales that exceeds \$800 for the week. If Nancy earned a total of \$450 one week, what were her total sales that week?

(A) \$2,200
(B) \$3,450
(C) \$4,200
(D) \$4,250
(E) \$5,000

List I: 3, 6, 8, 19
List II: x, 3, 6, 8, 19

93. If the median of the numbers in list I above is equal to the median of the numbers in list II above, what is the value of x?

(A) 6
(B) 7
(C) 8
(D) 9
(E) 10

94. In a certain city, 60 percent of the registered voters are Democrats and the rest are Republicans. In a mayoral race, if 75 percent of the registered voters who are Democrats and 20 percent of the registered voters who are Republicans are expected to vote for Candidate A, what percent of the registered voters are expected to vote for Candidate A?

(A) 50%
(B) 53%
(C) 54%
(D) 55%
(E) 57%

95. A certain company retirement plan has a "rule of 70" provision that allows an employee to retire when the employee's age plus years of employment with the company total at least 70. In what year could a female employee hired in 1986 on her 32nd birthday first be eligible to retire under this provision?

(A) 2003
(B) 2004
(C) 2005
(D) 2006
(E) 2007

96. $\frac{1}{2}+\left[\left(\frac{2}{3}\times\frac{3}{8}\right)\div 4\right]-\frac{9}{16}=$

(A) $\frac{29}{16}$
(B) $\frac{19}{16}$
(C) $\frac{15}{16}$
(D) $\frac{9}{13}$
(E) 0

97. Water consists of hydrogen and oxygen, and the approximate ratio, by mass, of hydrogen to oxygen is 2 : 16. Approximately how many grams of oxygen are there in 144 grams of water?

(A) 16
(B) 72
(C) 112
(D) 128
(E) 142

98. If $x(2x + 1) = 0$ and $\left(x+\frac{1}{2}\right)(2x-3) = 0$, then $x =$

(A) -3
(B) $-\frac{1}{2}$
(C) 0
(D) $\frac{1}{2}$
(E) $\frac{3}{2}$

99. On a scale that measures the intensity of a certain phenomenon, a reading of $n + 1$ corresponds to an intensity that is 10 times the intensity corresponding to a reading of n. On that scale, the intensity corresponding to a reading of 8 is how many times as great as the intensity corresponding to a reading of 3?

(A) 5
(B) 50
(C) 10^5
(D) 5^{10}
(E) $8^{10} - 3^{10}$

SOURCES OF FUNDS FOR HIGHWAY MAINTENANCE IN STATE X IN 1983

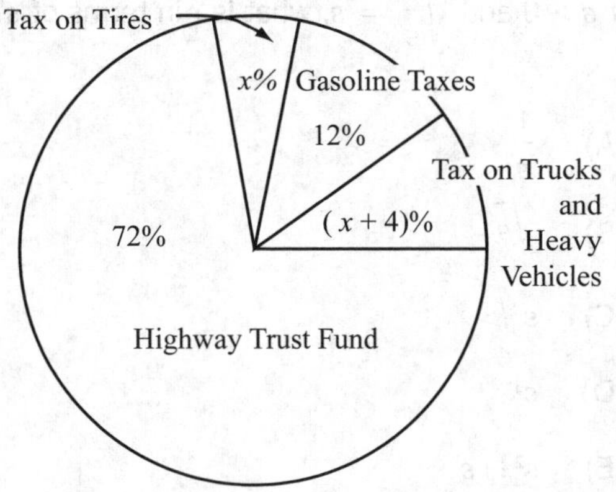

100. According to the graph above, what percent of the funds for highway maintenance came from the tax on tires?

(A) 3%
(B) 6%
(C) 8%
(D) 10%
(E) 16%

101. A poll reveals that the average (arithmetic mean) income of 10 households is \$25,000. If 6 of the households have incomes of \$30,000 each, what is the average income of the other 4 households?

(A) \$21,500
(B) \$20,000
(C) \$17,500
(D) \$7,500
(E) \$7,000

102. If $T = \frac{5}{9}(K - 32)$, and if $T = 290$, then $K =$

(A) $\frac{1,738}{9}$
(B) 322
(C) 490
(D) 554
(E) $\frac{2,898}{5}$

103. The water from one outlet, flowing at a constant rate, can fill a swimming pool in 9 hours. The water from a second outlet, flowing at a constant rate, can fill the same pool in 5 hours. If both outlets are used at the same time, approximately what is the number of hours required to fill the pool?

(A) 0.22
(B) 0.31
(C) 2.50
(D) 3.21
(E) 4.56

104. Diana bought a stereo for \$530, which was the retail price plus a 6 percent sales tax. How much money could she have saved if she had bought the stereo at the same retail price in a neighboring state where she would have paid a sales tax of 5 percent?

(A) \$1.00
(B) \$2.65
(C) \$4.30
(D) \$5.00
(E) \$5.30

105. If a square mirror has a 20-inch diagonal, what is the approximate perimeter of the mirror, in inches?

(A) 40
(B) 60
(C) 80
(D) 100
(E) 120

106. The present ratio of students to teachers at a certain school is 30 to 1. If the student enrollment were to increase by 50 students and the number of teachers were to increase by 5, the ratio of students to teachers would then be 25 to 1. What is the present number of teachers?

(A) 5
(B) 8
(C) 10
(D) 12
(E) 15

107. What is the smallest integer n for which $25^n > 5^{12}$?

(A) 6
(B) 7
(C) 8
(D) 9
(E) 10

108. If x and y are different prime numbers, each greater than 2, which of the following must be true?

I. $x + y \neq 91$
II. $x - y$ is an even integer.
III. $\frac{x}{y}$ is not an integer.

(A) II only
(B) I and II only
(C) I and III only
(D) II and III only
(E) I, II, and III

109. All the following have the same value EXCEPT

(A) $\frac{1+2+3+4+5}{3}$

(B) $\frac{1}{3}(1+1+1+1+1)$

(C) $\frac{1}{3}+\frac{1}{3}+\frac{1}{3}+\frac{1}{3}+\frac{1}{3}$

(D) $\frac{2}{3}\left(\frac{1}{2}+\frac{1}{2}+\frac{1}{2}+\frac{1}{2}+\frac{1}{2}\right)$

(E) $\frac{1}{3}+\frac{2}{6}+\frac{3}{9}+\frac{4}{12}+\frac{5}{15}$

110. If candy bars that regularly sell for $0.40 each are on sale at two for $0.75, what is the percent reduction in the price of two such candy bars purchased at the sale price?

(A) $2\frac{1}{2}\%$

(B) $6\frac{1}{4}\%$

(C) $6\frac{2}{3}\%$

(D) 8%

(E) $12\frac{1}{2}\%$

111. If $s > 0$ and $\sqrt{\frac{r}{s}} = s$, what is r in terms of s?

(A) $\frac{1}{s}$

(B) $\sqrt{s}$

(C) $s\sqrt{s}$

(D) s^3

(E) $s^2 - s$

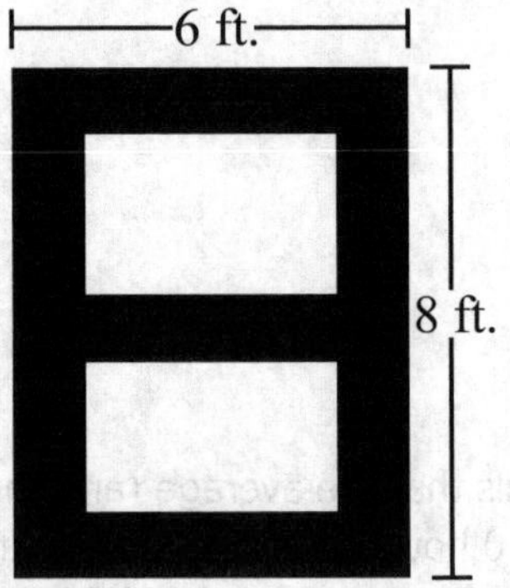

112. The front of a 6-foot-by-8-foot rectangular door has brass rectangular trim, as indicated by the shading in the figure above. If the trim is uniformly 1 foot wide, what fraction of the door's front surface is covered by the trim?

(A) $\frac{13}{48}$

(B) $\frac{5}{12}$

(C) $\frac{1}{2}$

(D) $\frac{7}{12}$

(E) $\frac{5}{8}$

113. If $a = -0.3$, which of the following is true?

(A) $a < a^2 < a^3$
(B) $a < a^3 < a^2$
(C) $a^2 < a < a^3$
(D) $a^2 < a^3 < a$
(E) $a^3 < a < a^2$

114. Which of the following is the product of two integers whose sum is 11?

(A) −42
(B) −28
(C) 12
(D) 26
(E) 32

115. Mary's income is 60 percent more than Tim's income, and Tim's income is 40 percent less than Juan's income. What percent of Juan's income is Mary's income?

(A) 124%
(B) 120%
(C) 96%
(D) 80%
(E) 64%

	City A	City B	City C	City D	City E
City A		•	•	•	•
City B			•	•	•
City C				•	•
City D					•
City E					

116. Each • in the mileage table above represents an entry indicating the distance between a pair of the five cities. If the table were extended to represent the distances between all pairs of 30 cities and each distance were to be represented by only one entry, how many entries would the table then have?

(A) 60
(B) 435
(C) 450
(D) 465
(E) 900

117. Which of the following has a value less than 1?

(A) $2\left(\frac{7}{13}\right)$

(B) $\frac{\sqrt{10}}{2}$

(C) $\frac{2}{\sqrt{2}}$

(D) $\frac{1}{\frac{1}{2}}$

(E) $\left(\frac{9}{10}\right)^2$

118. The ratio of the length to the width of a rectangular advertising display is approximately 3.3 to 2. If the width of the display is 8 meters, what is the approximate length of the display, in meters?

(A) 7
(B) 11
(C) 13
(D) 16
(E) 26

119. The average (arithmetic mean) salary of 15 people in the shipping department at a certain firm is \$20,000. The salary of 5 of the employees is \$25,000 each and the salary of 4 of the employees is \$16,000 each. What is the average salary of the remaining employees?

(A) \$19,250
(B) \$18,500
(C) \$18,000
(D) \$15,850
(E) \$12,300

120. David has d books, which is 3 times as many as Jeff and $\frac{1}{2}$ as many as Paula. How many books do the three of them have altogether, in terms of d?

(A) $\frac{5}{6}d$
(B) $\frac{7}{3}d$
(C) $\frac{10}{3}d$
(D) $\frac{7}{2}d$
(E) $\frac{9}{2}d$

121. There are 8 teams in a certain league and each team plays each of the other teams exactly once. If each game is played by 2 teams, what is the total number of games played?

(A) 15
(B) 16
(C) 28
(D) 56
(E) 64

122. An operation θ is defined by the equation $a \theta b = \frac{a-b}{a+b}$, for all numbers a and b such that $a \neq -b$. If $a \neq -c$ and $a \theta c = 0$, then $c =$

(A) $-a$
(B) $-\frac{1}{a}$
(C) 0
(D) $\frac{1}{a}$
(E) a

123. The price of lunch for 15 people was \$207.00, including a 15 percent gratuity for service. What was the average price per person, EXCLUDING the gratuity?

(A) \$11.73
(B) \$12.00
(C) \$13.80
(D) \$14.00
(E) \$15.87

124. According to a car dealer's sales report, $\frac{1}{3}$ of the cars sold during a certain period were sedans and $\frac{1}{5}$ of the other cars sold were station wagons. If N station wagons were sold during that period, how many sedans, in terms of N, were sold?

(A) $\frac{2}{15}N$
(B) $\frac{3}{5}N$
(C) $\frac{5}{3}N$
(D) $\frac{5}{2}N$
(E) $\frac{15}{2}N$

125. If $\frac{p}{q} < 1$, and p and q are positive integers, which of the following must be greater than 1?

(A) $\sqrt{\frac{p}{q}}$

(B) $\frac{p}{q^2}$

(C) $\frac{p}{2q}$

(D) $\frac{q}{p^2}$

(E) $\frac{q}{p}$

126. It would take one machine 4 hours to complete a large production order and another machine 3 hours to complete the same order. How many hours would it take both machines, working simultaneously at their respective constant rates, to complete the order?

(A) $\frac{7}{12}$

(B) $1\frac{1}{2}$

(C) $1\frac{5}{7}$

(D) $3\frac{1}{2}$

(E) 7

127. To mail a package, the rate is x cents for the first pound and y cents for each additional pound, where $x > y$. Two packages weighing 3 pounds and 5 pounds, respectively, can be mailed separately or combined as one package. Which method is cheaper, and how much money is saved?

(A) Combined, with a saving of $x - y$ cents
(B) Combined, with a saving of $y - x$ cents
(C) Combined, with a saving of x cents
(D) Separately, with a saving of $x - y$ cents
(E) Separately, with a saving of y cents

128. If money is invested at r percent interest, compounded annually, the amount of the investment will double in approximately $\frac{70}{r}$ years. If Pat's parents invested \$5,000 in a long-term bond that pays 8 percent interest, compounded annually, what will be the approximate total amount of the investment 18 years later, when Pat is ready for college?

(A) \$20,000
(B) \$15,000
(C) \$12,000
(D) \$10,000
(E) \$9,000

129. On a recent trip, Cindy drove her car 290 miles, rounded to the nearest 10 miles, and used 12 gallons of gasoline, rounded to the nearest gallon. The actual number of miles per gallon that Cindy's car got on this trip must have been between

(A) $\frac{290}{12.5}$ and $\frac{290}{11.4}$

(B) $\frac{295}{12}$ and $\frac{284}{11.4}$

(C) $\frac{284}{12}$ and $\frac{295}{12}$

(D) $\frac{284}{12.5}$ and $\frac{295}{11.4}$

(E) $\frac{295}{12.5}$ and $\frac{284}{11.4}$

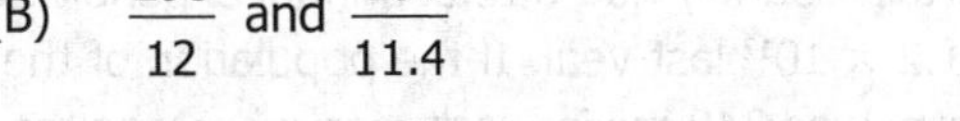

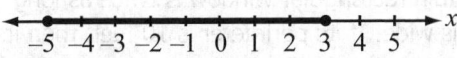

130. Which of the following inequalities is an algebraic expression for the shaded part of the number line above?

(A) $|x| \le 3$

(B) $|x| \le 5$

(C) $|x - 2| \le 3$

(D) $|x - 1| \le 4$

(E) $|x + 1| \le 4$

131. A factory has 500 workers, 15 percent of whom are women. If 50 additional workers are to be hired and all of the present workers remain, how many of the additional workers must be women in order to raise the percent of women employees to 20 percent?

(A) 3
(B) 10
(C) 25
(D) 30
(E) 35

132. In a small snack shop, the average (arithmetic mean) revenue was \$400 per day over a 10-day period. During this period, if the average daily revenue was \$360 for the first 6 days, what was the average daily revenue for the last 4 days?

(A) \$420
(B) \$440
(C) \$450
(D) \$460
(E) \$480

133. A certain country had a total annual expenditure of $\$1.2 \times 10^{12}$ last year. If the population of the country was 240 million last year, what was the per capita expenditure?

(A) \$500
(B) \$1,000
(C) \$2,000
(D) \$3,000
(E) \$5,000

134. A certain rectangular window is twice as long as it is wide. If its perimeter is 10 feet, then its dimensions in feet are

(A) $\frac{3}{2}$ by $\frac{7}{2}$

(B) $\frac{5}{3}$ by $\frac{10}{3}$

(C) 2 by 4

(D) 3 by 6

(E) $\frac{10}{3}$ by $\frac{20}{3}$

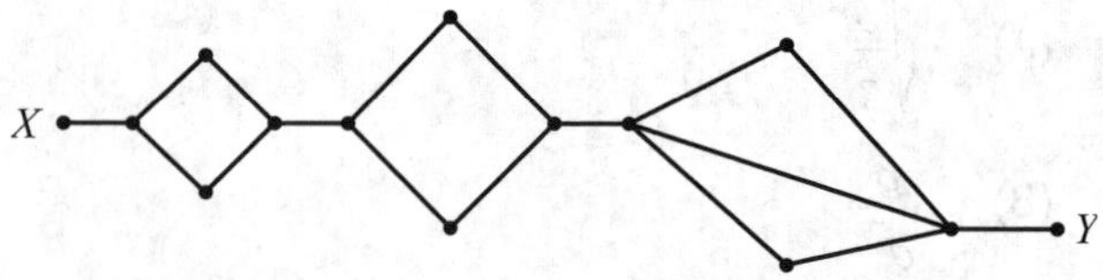

135. The diagram above shows the various paths along which a mouse can travel from point X, where it is released, to point Y, where it is rewarded with a food pellet. How many different paths from X to Y can the mouse take if it goes directly from X to Y without retracing any point along a path?

(A) 6
(B) 7
(C) 12
(D) 14
(E) 17

136. If the operation $\odot$ is defined by $x \odot y = \sqrt{xy}$ for all positive numbers x and y, then $(5 \odot 45) \odot 60 =$

(A) 30
(B) 60
(C) 90
(D) $30\sqrt{15}$
(E) $60\sqrt{15}$

137. A bar over a sequence of digits in a decimal indicates that the sequence repeats indefinitely. What is the value of $(10^4 - 10^2)(0.00\overline{12})$?

(A) 0
(B) $0.\overline{12}$
(C) 1.2
(D) 10
(E) 12

138. At a loading dock, each worker on the night crew loaded $\frac{3}{4}$ as many boxes as each worker on the day crew. If the night crew has $\frac{4}{5}$ as many workers as the day crew, what fraction of all the boxes loaded by the two crews did the day crew load?

(A) $\frac{1}{2}$

(B) $\frac{2}{5}$

(C) $\frac{3}{5}$

(D) $\frac{4}{5}$

(E) $\frac{5}{8}$

139. A restaurant meal cost \$35.50 and there was no tax. If the tip was more than 10 percent but less than 15 percent of the cost of the meal, then the total amount paid must have been between

(A) \$40 and \$42
(B) \$39 and \$41
(C) \$38 and \$40
(D) \$37 and \$39
(E) \$36 and \$37

140. In a weight-lifting competition, the total weight of Joe's two lifts was 750 pounds. If twice the weight of his first lift was 300 pounds more than the weight of his second lift, what was the weight, in pounds, of his first lift?

(A) 225
(B) 275
(C) 325
(D) 350
(E) 400

141. A club collected exactly \$599 from its members. If each member contributed at least \$12, what is the greatest number of members the club could have?

(A) 43
(B) 44
(C) 49
(D) 50
(E) 51

142. Of the 3,600 employees of Company X, $\frac{1}{3}$ are clerical. If the clerical staff were to be reduced by $\frac{1}{3}$, what percent of the total number of the remaining employees would then be clerical?

(A) 25%
(B) 22.2%
(C) 20%
(D) 12.5%
(E) 11.1%

143. $\frac{3.003}{2.002} =$

(A) 1.05
(B) 1.50015
(C) 1.501
(D) 1.5015
(E) 1.5

144. If $\frac{4-x}{2+x} = x$, what is the value of $x^2 + 3x - 4$?

(A) −4
(B) −1
(C) 0
(D) 1
(E) 2

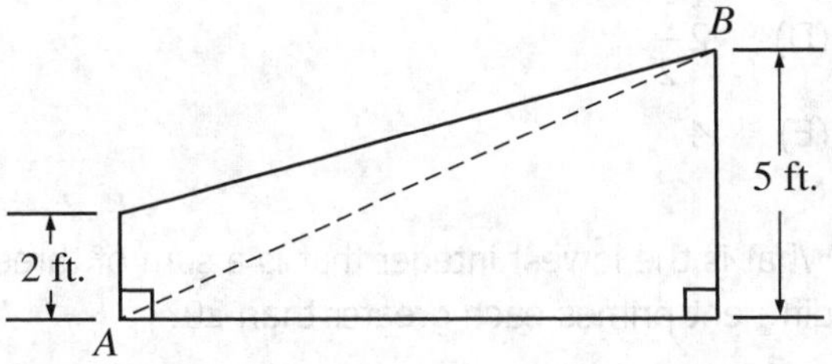

145. The trapezoid shown in the figure above represents a cross section of the rudder of a ship. If the distance from A to B is 13 feet, what is the area of the cross section of the rudder in square feet?

(A) 39
(B) 40
(C) 42
(D) 45
(E) 46.5

146. If $0 \le x \le 4$ and $y < 12$, which of the following CANNOT be the value of xy?

(A) −2
(B) 0
(C) 6
(D) 24
(E) 48

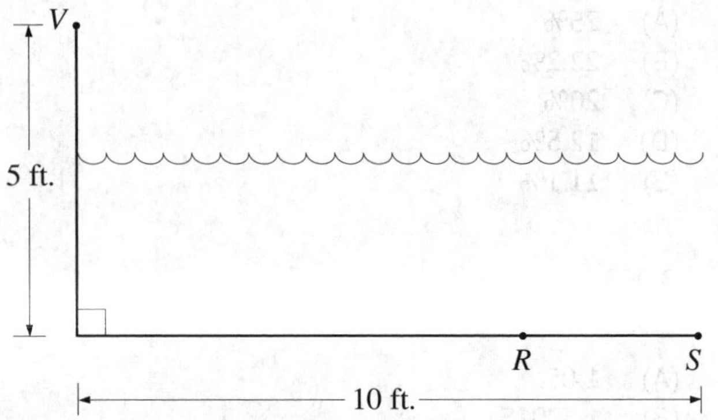

147. In the figure above, V represents an observation point at one end of a pool. From V, an object that is actually located on the bottom of the pool at point R appears to be at point S. If $VR = 10$ feet, what is the distance RS, in feet, between the actual position and the perceived position of the object?

(A) $10 - 5\sqrt{3}$

(B) $10 - 5\sqrt{2}$

(C) 2

(D) $2\frac{1}{2}$

(E) 4

148. What is the lowest integer that is a sum of three different primes each greater than 20?

(A) 69
(B) 73
(C) 75
(D) 79
(E) 83

149. The average (arithmetic mean) of 6, 8, and 10 equals the average of 7, 9, and

(A) 5
(B) 7
(C) 8
(D) 9
(E) 11

150. If $x = -1$, then $\frac{x^4 - x^3 + x^2}{x - 1} =$

(A) $-\frac{3}{2}$

(B) $-\frac{1}{2}$

(C) 0

(D) $\frac{1}{2}$

(E) $\frac{3}{2}$

151. A toy store regularly sells all stock at a discount of 20 percent to 40 percent. If an additional 25 percent were deducted from the discount price during a special sale, what would be the lowest possible price of a toy costing $16 before any discount?

(A) $5.60
(B) $7.20
(C) $8.80
(D) $9.60
(E) $15.20

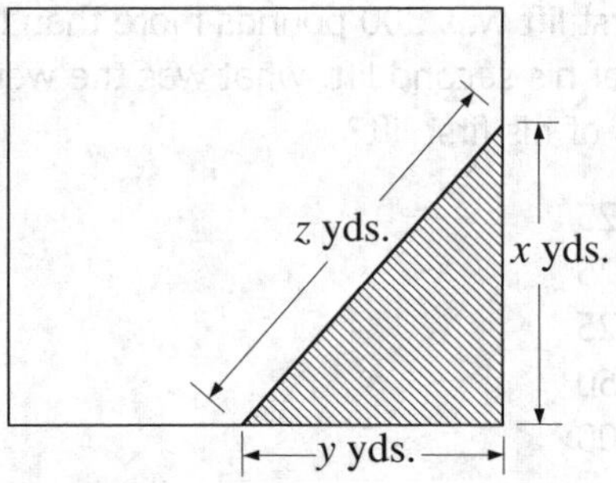

152. The shaded portion of the rectangular lot shown above represents a flower bed. If the area of the bed is 24 square yards and $x = y + 2$, then z equals

(A) $\sqrt{13}$

(B) $2\sqrt{13}$

(C) 6

(D) 8

(E) 10

153. Jack is now 14 years older than Bill. If in 10 years Jack will be twice as old as Bill, how old will Jack be in 5 years?

(A) 9
(B) 19
(C) 21
(D) 23
(E) 33

154. An empty pool being filled with water at a constant rate takes 8 hours to fill to $\frac{3}{5}$ of its capacity. How much more time will it take to finish filling the pool?

(A) 5 hrs. 30 mins.
(B) 5 hrs. 20 mins.
(C) 4 hrs. 48 mins.
(D) 3 hrs. 12 mins.
(E) 2 hrs. 40 mins.

155. A positive number x is multiplied by 2, and this product is then divided by 3. If the positive square root of the result of these two operations equals x, what is the value of x?

(A) $\frac{9}{4}$
(B) $\frac{3}{2}$
(C) $\frac{4}{3}$
(D) $\frac{2}{3}$
(E) $\frac{1}{2}$

156. A tank contains 10,000 gallons of a solution that is 5 percent sodium chloride by volume. If 2,500 gallons of water evaporate from the tank, the remaining solution will be approximately what percent sodium chloride?

(A) 1.25%
(B) 3.75%
(C) 6.25%
(D) 6.67%
(E) 11.7%

157. If $x + 5y = 16$ and $x = -3y$, then $y =$

(A) -24
(B) -8
(C) -2
(D) 2
(E) 8

158. A committee is composed of w women and m men. If 3 women and 2 men are added to the committee, and if one person is selected at random from the enlarged committee, then the probability that a woman is selected can be represented by

(A) $\frac{w}{m}$
(B) $\frac{w}{w+m}$
(C) $\frac{w+3}{m+2}$
(D) $\frac{w+3}{w+m+3}$
(E) $\frac{w+3}{w+m+5}$

159. If the product of the integers w, x, y, and z is 770, and if $1 < w < x < y < z$, what is the value of $w + z$?

(A) 10
(B) 13
(C) 16
(D) 18
(E) 21

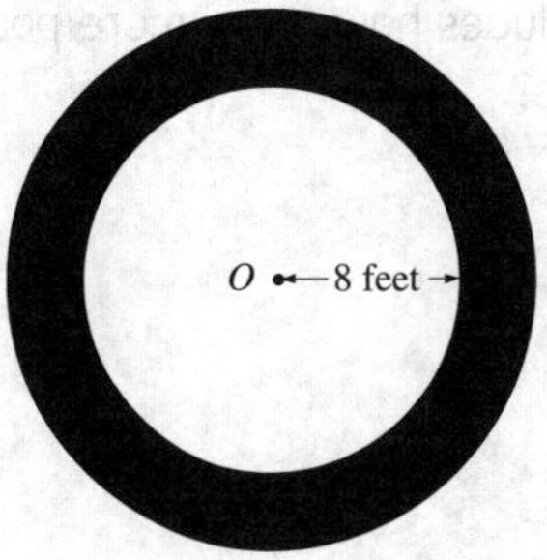

160. The figure above shows a circular flower bed, with its center at O, surrounded by a circular path that is 3 feet wide. What is the area of the path, in square feet?

(A) 25π
(B) 38π
(C) 55π
(D) 57π
(E) 64π

161. The positive integer n is divisible by 25. If $\sqrt{n}$ is greater than 25, which of the following could be the value of $\frac{n}{25}$?

(A) 22
(B) 23
(C) 24
(D) 25
(E) 26

162. $\dfrac{1}{1+\dfrac{1}{2+\dfrac{1}{3}}} =$

(A) $\frac{3}{10}$

(B) $\frac{7}{10}$

(C) $\frac{6}{7}$

(D) $\frac{10}{7}$

(E) $\frac{10}{3}$

163. A fruit-salad mixture consists of apples, peaches, and grapes in the ratio 6 : 5 : 2, respectively, by weight. If 39 pounds of the mixture is prepared, the mixture includes how many more pounds of apples than grapes?

(A) 15
(B) 12
(C) 9
(D) 6
(E) 4

164. Lois has x dollars more than Jim has, and together they have a total of y dollars. Which of the following represents the number of dollars that Jim has?

(A) $\frac{y-x}{2}$

(B) $y-\frac{x}{2}$

(C) $\frac{y}{2}-x$

(D) $2y-x$

(E) $y-2x$

165. During a certain season, a team won 80 percent of its first 100 games and 50 percent of its remaining games. If the team won 70 percent of its games for the entire season, what was the total number of games that the team played?

(A) 180
(B) 170
(C) 156
(D) 150
(E) 105

166. Of 30 applicants for a job, 14 had at least 4 years' experience, 18 had degrees, and 3 had less than 4 years' experience and did not have a degree. How many of the applicants had at least 4 years' experience and a degree?

(A) 14
(B) 13
(C) 9
(D) 7
(E) 5

167. If $1+\frac{1}{x}=2-\frac{2}{x}$, then $x =$

(A) -1

(B) $\frac{1}{3}$

(C) $\frac{2}{3}$

(D) 2

(E) 3

168. Last year, for every 100 million vehicles that traveled on a certain highway, 96 vehicles were involved in accidents. If 3 billion vehicles traveled on the highway last year, how many of those vehicles were involved in accidents? (1 billion = 1,000,000,000)

(A) 288
(B) 320
(C) 2,880
(D) 3,200
(E) 28,800

169. Thirty percent of the members of a swim club have passed the lifesaving test. Among the members who have *not* passed the test, 12 have taken the preparatory course and 30 have not taken the course. How many members are there in the swim club?

(A) 60
(B) 80
(C) 100
(D) 120
(E) 140

170. In a certain company, the ratio of the number of managers to the number of production-line workers is 5 to 72. If 8 additional production-line workers were to be hired, the ratio of the number of managers to the number of production-line workers would be 5 to 74. How many managers does the company have?

(A) 5
(B) 10
(C) 15
(D) 20
(E) 25

171. If $(x-1)^2 = 400$, which of the following could be the value of $x-5$?

(A) 15
(B) 14
(C) −24
(D) −25
(E) −26

172. Which of the following describes all values of x for which $1 - x^2 \geq 0$?

(A) $x \geq 1$
(B) $x \leq -1$
(C) $0 \leq x \leq 1$
(D) $x \leq -1$ or $x \geq 1$
(E) $-1 \leq x \leq 1$

173. The probability is $\frac{1}{2}$ that a certain coin will turn up heads on any given toss. If the coin is to be tossed three times, what is the probability that on at least one of the tosses the coin will turn up tails?

(A) $\frac{1}{8}$
(B) $\frac{1}{2}$
(C) $\frac{3}{4}$
(D) $\frac{7}{8}$
(E) $\frac{15}{16}$

174. Of the final grades received by the students in a certain math course, $\frac{1}{5}$ are A's, $\frac{1}{4}$ are B's, $\frac{1}{2}$ are C's, and the remaining 10 grades are D's. What is the number of students in the course?

(A) 80
(B) 110
(C) 160
(D) 200
(E) 400

175. As x increases from 165 to 166, which of the following must increase?

I. $2x - 5$

II. $1 - \frac{1}{x}$

III. $\frac{1}{x^2 - x}$

(A) I only
(B) III only
(C) I and II
(D) I and III
(E) II and III

176. A rectangular box is 10 inches wide, 10 inches long, and 5 inches high. What is the greatest possible (straight-line) distance, in inches, between any two points on the box?

(A) 15
(B) 20
(C) 25
(D) $10\sqrt{2}$
(E) $10\sqrt{3}$

177. A company accountant estimates that airfares next year for business trips of a thousand miles or less will increase by 20 percent and airfares for all other business trips will increase by 10 percent. This year total airfares for business trips of a thousand miles or less were $9,900 and airfares for all other business trips were $13,000. According to the accountant's estimate, if the same number of business trips will be made next year as this year, how much will be spent for airfares next year?

(A) $22,930
(B) $26,180
(C) $26,330
(D) $26,490
(E) $29,770

178. If $x * y = xy - 2(x + y)$ for all integers x and y, then $2 * (-3) =$

(A) −16
(B) −11
(C) −4
(D) 4
(E) 16

Club	Number of students
Chess	40
Drama	30
Math	25

179. The table above shows the number of students in three clubs at McAuliffe School. Although no student is in all three clubs, 10 students are in both Chess and Drama, 5 students are in both Chess and Math, and 6 students are in both Drama and Math. How many different students are in the three clubs?

(A) 68
(B) 69
(C) 74
(D) 79
(E) 84

180. In a nationwide poll, N people were interviewed. If $\frac{1}{4}$ of them answered "yes" to question 1, and of those, $\frac{1}{3}$ answered "yes" to question 2, which of the following expressions represents the number of people interviewed who did not answer "yes" to both questions?

(A) $\frac{N}{7}$
(B) $\frac{6N}{7}$
(C) $\frac{5N}{12}$
(D) $\frac{7N}{12}$
(E) $\frac{11N}{12}$

181. The ratio of two quantities is 3 to 4. If each of the quantities is increased by 5, what is the ratio of these two new quantities?

(A) $\frac{3}{4}$

(B) $\frac{8}{9}$

(C) $\frac{18}{19}$

(D) $\frac{23}{24}$

(E) It cannot be determined from the information given.

182. If the average (arithmetic mean) of x and y is 60 and the average (arithmetic mean) of y and z is 80, what is the value of $z - x$?

(A) 70
(B) 40
(C) 20
(D) 10
(E) It cannot be determined from the information given.

183. If $\frac{1}{2}$ of the air in a tank is removed with each stroke of a vacuum pump, what fraction of the original amount of air has been removed after 4 strokes?

(A) $\frac{15}{16}$

(B) $\frac{7}{8}$

(C) $\frac{1}{4}$

(D) $\frac{1}{8}$

(E) $\frac{1}{16}$

184. If the two-digit integers M and N are positive and have the same digits, but in reverse order, which of the following CANNOT be the sum of M and N?

(A) 181
(B) 165
(C) 121
(D) 99
(E) 44

185. Car X and car Y traveled the same 80-mile route. If car X took 2 hours and car Y traveled at an average speed that was 50 percent faster than the average speed of car X, how many hours did it take car Y to travel the route?

(A) $\frac{2}{3}$

(B) 1

(C) $1\frac{1}{3}$

(D) $1\frac{3}{5}$

(E) 3

186. If the average (arithmetic mean) of the four numbers K, $2K + 3$, $3K - 5$, and $5K + 1$ is 63, what is the value of K?

(A) 11

(B) $15\frac{3}{4}$

(C) 22

(D) 23

(E) $25\frac{3}{10}$

187. If p is an even integer and q is an odd integer, which of the following must be an odd integer?

(A) $\frac{p}{q}$

(B) pq

(C) $2p + q$

(D) $2(p + q)$

(E) $\frac{3p}{q}$

188. Drum X is $\frac{1}{2}$ full of oil and drum Y, which has twice the capacity of drum *X*, is $\frac{2}{3}$ full of oil. If all of the oil in drum X is poured into drum Y, then drum Y will be filled to what fraction of its capacity?

(A) $\frac{3}{4}$
(B) $\frac{5}{6}$
(C) $\frac{11}{12}$
(D) $\frac{7}{6}$
(E) $\frac{11}{6}$

189. If $x > 0$, $\frac{x}{50} + \frac{x}{25}$ is what percent of x ?

(A) 6%
(B) 25%
(C) 37%
(D) 60%
(E) 75%

190. If the operation ⊛ is defined for all *a* and *b* by the equation $a ⊛ b = \frac{a^2b}{3}$, then $2 ⊛ (3 ⊛ -1) =$

(A) 4
(B) 2
(C) $-\frac{4}{3}$
(D) −2
(E) −4

191. The inside dimensions of a rectangular wooden box are 6 inches by 8 inches by 10 inches. A cylindrical canister is to be placed inside the box so that it stands upright when the closed box rests on one of its six faces. Of all such canisters that could be used, what is the radius, in inches, of the one that has maximum volume?

(A) 3
(B) 4
(C) 5
(D) 6
(E) 8

192. $(\sqrt{2}+1)(\sqrt{2}-1)(\sqrt{3}+1)(\sqrt{3}-1) =$

(A) 2
(B) 3
(C) $2\sqrt{6}$
(D) 5
(E) 6

193. In a certain calculus class, the ratio of the number of mathematics majors to the number of students who are not mathematics majors is 2 to 5. If 2 more mathematics majors were to enter the class, the ratio would be 1 to 2. How many students are in the class?

(A) 10
(B) 12
(C) 21
(D) 28
(E) 35

194. What is the units digit of $(13)^4(17)^2(29)^3$?

(A) 9
(B) 7
(C) 5
(D) 3
(E) 1

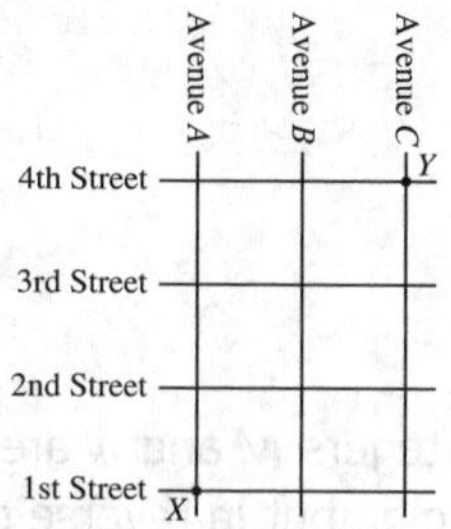

195. Pat will walk from intersection *X* to intersection *Y* along a route that is confined to the square grid of four streets and three avenues shown in the map above. How many routes from *X* to *Y* can Pat take that have the minimum possible length?

(A) 6
(B) 8
(C) 10
(D) 14
(E) 16

196. The ratio, by volume, of soap to alcohol to water in a certain solution is 2:50:100. The solution will be altered so that the ratio of soap to alcohol is doubled while the ratio of soap to water is halved. If the altered solution will contain 100 cubic centimeters of alcohol, how many cubic centimeters of water will it contain?

(A) 50
(B) 200
(C) 400
(D) 625
(E) 800

197. If 75 percent of a class answered the first question on a certain test correctly, 55 percent answered the second question on the test correctly, and 20 percent answered neither of the questions correctly, what percent answered both correctly?

(A) 10%
(B) 20%
(C) 30%
(D) 50%
(E) 65%

198. If $\frac{1}{2}+\frac{1}{3}+\frac{1}{4}=\frac{13}{x}$, which of the following must be an integer?

I. $\frac{x}{8}$

II. $\frac{x}{12}$

III. $\frac{x}{24}$

(A) I only
(B) II only
(C) I and III only
(D) II and III only
(E) I, II, and III

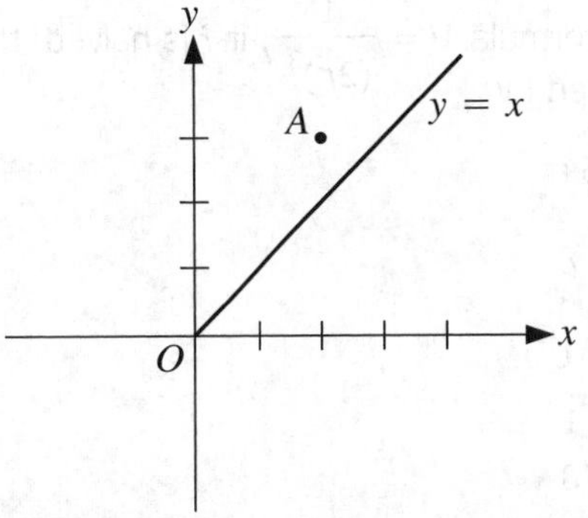

199. In the rectangular coordinate system above, the line $y = x$ is the perpendicular bisector of segment AB (not shown), and the x-axis is the perpendicular bisector of segment BC (not shown). If the coordinates of point A are (2, 3), what are the coordinates of point C?

(A) (−3, −2)
(B) (−3, 2)
(C) (2, −3)
(D) (3, −2)
(E) (2, 3)

200. A store currently charges the same price for each towel that it sells. If the current price of each towel were to be increased by \$1, 10 fewer of the towels could be bought for \$120, excluding sales tax. What is the current price of each towel?

(A) \$1
(B) \$2
(C) \$3
(D) \$4
(E) \$12

201. If the sum of n consecutive integers is 0, which of the following must be true?

I. n is an even number.
II. n is an odd number.
III. The average (arithmetic mean) of the n integers is 0.

(A) I only
(B) II only
(C) III only
(D) I and III
(E) II and III

202. In the formula $V = \frac{1}{(2r)^3}$, if r is halved, then V is multiplied by

(A) 64

(B) 8

(C) 1

(D) $\frac{1}{8}$

(E) $\frac{1}{64}$

203. A certain bakery has 6 employees. It pays annual salaries of $14,000 to each of 2 employees, $16,000 to 1 employee, and $17,000 to each of the remaining 3 employees. The average (arithmetic mean) annual salary of these employees is closest to which of the following?

(A) $15,200
(B) $15,500
(C) $15,800
(D) $16,000
(E) $16,400

204. If x is equal to the sum of the even integers from 40 to 60, inclusive, and y is the number of even integers from 40 to 60, inclusive, what is the value of $x + y$?

(A) 550
(B) 551
(C) 560
(D) 561
(E) 572

Number of Solid-Colored Marbles in Three Jars

Jar	Number of red marbles	Number of green marbles	Total number of red and green marbles
P	x	y	80
Q	y	z	120
R	x	z	160

205. In the table above, what is the number of green marbles in jar R ?

(A) 70
(B) 80
(C) 90
(D) 100
(E) 110

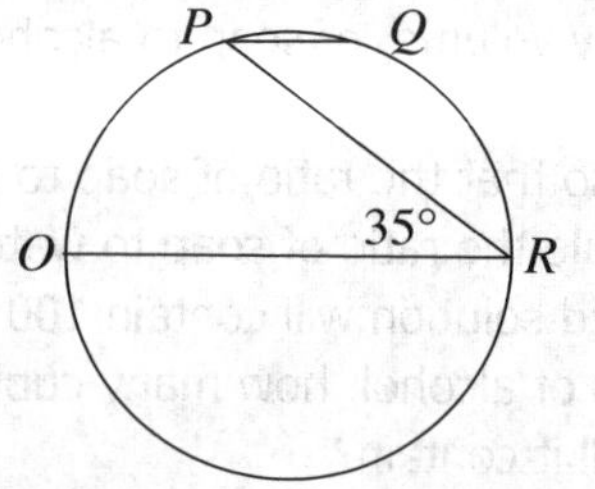

206. In the circle above, PQ is parallel to diameter OR, and OR has length 18. What is the length of minor arc PQ?

(A) 2π

(B) $\frac{9\pi}{4}$

(C) $\frac{7\pi}{2}$

(D) $\frac{9\pi}{2}$

(E) 3π

207. If $n = 4p$, where p is a prime number greater than 2, how many different positive even divisors does n have, including n ?

(A) 2
(B) 3
(C) 4
(D) 6
(E) 8

208. S is a set containing 9 different numbers. T is a set containing 8 different numbers, all of which are members of S. Which of the following statements CANNOT be true?

(A) The mean of S is equal to the mean of T.
(B) The median of S is equal to the median of T.
(C) The range of S is equal to the range of T.
(D) The mean of S is greater than the mean of T.
(E) The range of S is less than the range of T.

209. How many different positive integers are factors of 441?

(A) 4
(B) 6
(C) 7
(D) 9
(E) 11

210. A television manufacturer produces 600 units of a certain model each month at a cost to the manufacturer of \$90 per unit and all of the produced units are sold each month. What is the minimum selling price per unit that will ensure that the monthly profit (revenue from sales minus the manufacturer's cost to produce) on the sales of these units will be at least \$42,000?

(A) \$110
(B) \$120
(C) \$140
(D) \$160
(E) \$180

211. If $4x + 3y = -2$ and $3x + 6 = 0$, what is the value of y?

(A) $-3\frac{1}{3}$

(B) -2

(C) $-\frac{2}{3}$

(D) $\frac{2}{3}$

(E) 2

I. 72, 73, 74, 75, 76
II. 74, 74, 74, 74, 74
III. 62, 74, 74, 74, 89

212. The data sets I, II, and III above are ordered from greatest standard deviation to least standard deviation in which of the following?

(A) I, II, III
(B) I, III, II
(C) II, III, I
(D) III, I, II
(E) III, II, I

213. Which of the following is the lowest positive integer that is divisible by 2, 3, 4, 5, 6, 7, 8, and 9?

(A) 15,120
(B) 3,024
(C) 2,520
(D) 1,890
(E) 1,680

214. Of the 50 researchers in a workgroup, 40 percent will be assigned to team A and the remaining 60 percent to team B. However, 70 percent of the researchers prefer team A and 30 percent prefer team B. What is the lowest possible number of researchers who will NOT be assigned to the team they prefer?

(A) 15
(B) 17
(C) 20
(D) 25
(E) 30

215. If m is the average (arithmetic mean) of the first 10 positive multiples of 5 and if M is the median of the first 10 positive multiples of 5, what is the value of $M - m$?

(A) -5
(B) 0
(C) 5
(D) 25
(E) 27.5

216. If $m > 0$ and x is m percent of y, then, in terms of m, y is what percent of x?

(A) $100m$

(B) $\frac{1}{100m}$

(C) $\frac{1}{m}$

(D) $\frac{10}{m}$

(E) $\frac{10,000}{m}$

217. A certain junior class has 1,000 students and a certain senior class has 800 students. Among these students, there are 60 sibling pairs, each consisting of 1 junior and 1 senior. If 1 student is to be selected at random from each class, what is the probability that the 2 students selected will be a sibling pair?

(A) $\frac{3}{40,000}$

(B) $\frac{1}{3,600}$

(C) $\frac{9}{2,000}$

(D) $\frac{1}{60}$

(E) $\frac{1}{15}$

218. Which of the following CANNOT be the median of the three ordered positive integers x, y, and z?

(A) x

(B) z

(C) $x + z$

(D) $\frac{x+z}{2}$

(E) $\frac{x+z}{3}$

219. What is the 25th digit to the right of the decimal point in the decimal form of $\frac{6}{11}$?

(A) 3
(B) 4
(C) 5
(D) 6
(E) 7

220. John and Mary were each paid x dollars in advance to do a certain job together. John worked on the job for 10 hours and Mary worked 2 hours less than John. If Mary gave John y dollars of her payment so that they would have received the same hourly wage, what was the dollar amount, in terms of y, that John was paid in advance?

(A) $4y$
(B) $5y$
(C) $6y$
(D) $8y$
(E) $9y$

221. $1 + \cfrac{1}{1 + \cfrac{1}{1 + \cfrac{1}{3}}} =$

(A) $\frac{4}{7}$

(B) $\frac{4}{3}$

(C) $\frac{11}{8}$

(D) $\frac{11}{7}$

(E) $\frac{7}{4}$

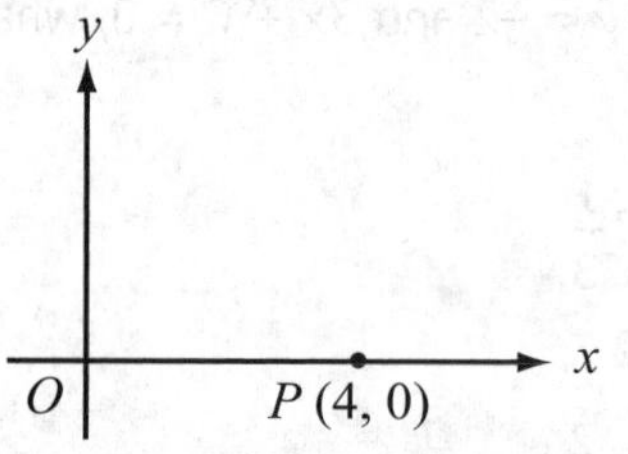

222. In the rectangular coordinate system above, if point R (not shown) lies on the positive y-axis and the area of triangle ORP is 12, what is the y-coordinate of point R?

(A) 3
(B) 6
(C) 9
(D) 12
(E) 24

223. Car A is 20 miles behind car B, which is traveling in the same direction along the same route as car A. Car A is traveling at a constant speed of 58 miles per hour and car B is traveling at a constant speed of 50 miles per hour. How many hours will it take for car A to overtake and drive 8 miles ahead of car B?

(A) 1.5
(B) 2.0
(C) 2.5
(D) 3.0
(E) 3.5

224. For the past n days, the average (arithmetic mean) daily production at a company was 50 units. If today's production of 90 units raises the average to 55 units per day, what is the value of n?

(A) 30
(B) 18
(C) 10
(D) 9
(E) 7

$$\left(\frac{x+1}{x-1}\right)^2$$

225. If $x \neq 0$ and $x \neq 1$, and if x is replaced by $\frac{1}{x}$ everywhere in the expression above, then the resulting expression is equivalent to

(A) $\left(\frac{x+1}{x-1}\right)^2$

(B) $\left(\frac{x-1}{x+1}\right)^2$

(C) $\frac{x^2+1}{1-x^2}$

(D) $\frac{x^2-1}{x^2+1}$

(E) $-\left(\frac{x-1}{x+1}\right)^2$

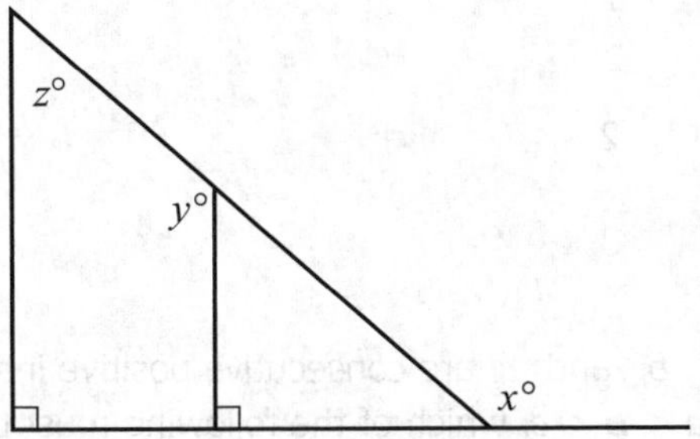

226. In the figure above, if $z = 50$, then $x + y =$

(A) 230
(B) 250
(C) 260
(D) 270
(E) 290

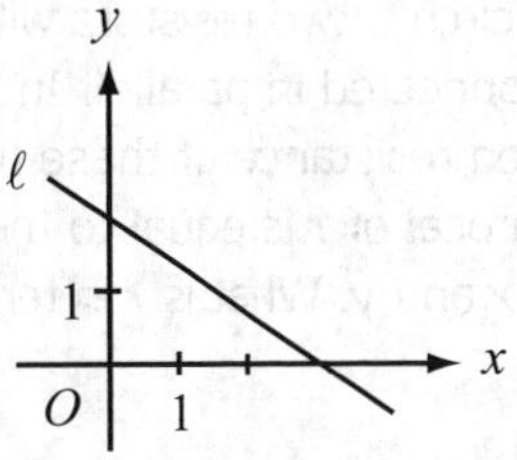

227. In the coordinate system above, which of the following is the equation of line ℓ?

(A) $2x - 3y = 6$
(B) $2x + 3y = 6$
(C) $3x + 2y = 6$
(D) $2x - 3y = -6$
(E) $3x - 2y = -6$

228. If a two-digit positive integer has its digits reversed, the resulting integer differs from the original by 27. By how much do the two digits differ?

(A) 3
(B) 4
(C) 5
(D) 6
(E) 7

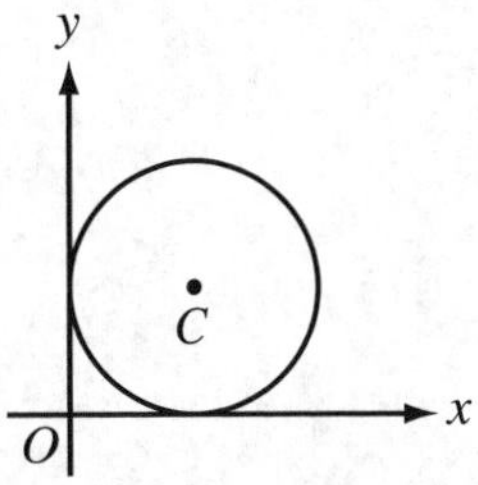

229. The circle with center C shown above is tangent to both axes. If the distance from O to C is equal to k, what is the radius of the circle, in terms of k?

(A) k

(B) $\frac{k}{\sqrt{2}}$

(C) $\frac{k}{\sqrt{3}}$

(D) $\frac{k}{2}$

(E) $\frac{k}{3}$

230. In an electric circuit, two resistors with resistances x and y are connected in parallel. In this case, if r is the combined resistance of these two resistors, then the reciprocal of r is equal to the sum of the reciprocals of x and y. What is r in terms of x and y?

(A) xy

(B) $x + y$

(C) $\frac{1}{x + y}$

(D) $\frac{xy}{x + y}$

(E) $\frac{x + y}{xy}$

231. Xavier, Yvonne, and Zelda each try independently to solve a problem. If their individual probabilities for success are $\frac{1}{4}$, $\frac{1}{2}$, and $\frac{5}{8}$, respectively, what is the probability that Xavier and Yvonne, but not Zelda, will solve the problem?

(A) $\frac{11}{8}$

(B) $\frac{7}{8}$

(C) $\frac{9}{64}$

(D) $\frac{5}{64}$

(E) $\frac{3}{64}$

232. If $\frac{1}{x} - \frac{1}{x+1} = \frac{1}{x+4}$, then x could be

(A) 0
(B) −1
(C) −2
(D) −3
(E) −4

233. $\left(\frac{1}{2}\right)^{-3}\left(\frac{1}{4}\right)^{-2}\left(\frac{1}{16}\right)^{-1} =$

(A) $\left(\frac{1}{2}\right)^{-48}$

(B) $\left(\frac{1}{2}\right)^{-11}$

(C) $\left(\frac{1}{2}\right)^{-6}$

(D) $\left(\frac{1}{8}\right)^{-11}$

(E) $\left(\frac{1}{8}\right)^{-6}$

234. In a certain game, a large container is filled with red, yellow, green, and blue beads worth, respectively, 7, 5, 3, and 2 points each. A number of beads are then removed from the container. If the product of the point values of the removed beads is 147,000, how many red beads were removed?

(A) 5
(B) 4
(C) 3
(D) 2
(E) 0

235. If $\frac{2}{1 + \frac{2}{y}} = 1$, then $y =$

(A) -2

(B) $-\frac{1}{2}$

(C) $\frac{1}{2}$

(D) 2

(E) 3

236. If a, b, and c are consecutive positive integers and $a < b < c$, which of the following must be true?

I. $c - a = 2$
II. abc is an even integer.
III. $\frac{a + b + c}{3}$ is an integer.

(A) I only
(B) II only
(C) I and II only
(D) II and III only
(E) I, II, and III

237. A part-time employee whose hourly wage was increased by 25 percent decided to reduce the number of hours worked per week so that the employee's total weekly income would remain unchanged. By what percent should the number of hours worked be reduced?

(A) 12.5%
(B) 20%
(C) 25%
(D) 50%
(E) 75%

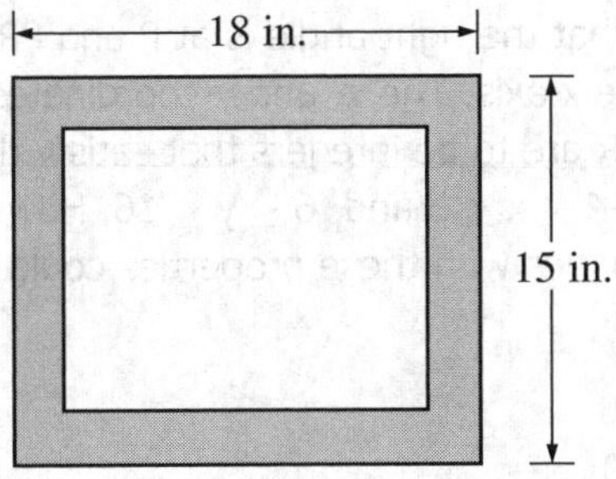

Note: Figure not drawn to scale.

238. The shaded region in the figure above represents a rectangular frame with length 18 inches and width 15 inches. The frame encloses a rectangular picture that has the same area as the frame itself. If the length and width of the picture have the same ratio as the length and width of the frame, what is the length of the picture, in inches?

(A) $9\sqrt{2}$
(B) $\frac{3}{2}$
(C) $\frac{9}{\sqrt{2}}$
(D) $15\left(1-\frac{1}{\sqrt{2}}\right)$
(E) $\frac{9}{2}$

239. Of the 200 students at College T majoring in one or more of the sciences, 130 are majoring in chemistry and 150 are majoring in biology. If at least 30 of the students are not majoring in either chemistry or biology, then the number of students majoring in *both* chemistry and biology could be any number from

(A) 20 to 50
(B) 40 to 70
(C) 50 to 130
(D) 110 to 130
(E) 110 to 150

240. Seed mixture X is 40 percent ryegrass and 60 percent bluegrass by weight; seed mixture Y is 25 percent ryegrass and 75 percent fescue. If a mixture of X and Y contains 30 percent ryegrass, what percent of the weight of the mixture is X?

(A) 10%
(B) $33\frac{1}{3}$%
(C) 40%
(D) 50%
(E) $66\frac{2}{3}$%

241. If the integer n has exactly three positive divisors, including 1 and n, how many positive divisors does n^2 have?

(A) 4
(B) 5
(C) 6
(D) 8
(E) 9

242. If n is a positive integer, then $n(n+1)(n+2)$ is

(A) even only when n is even
(B) even only when n is odd
(C) odd whenever n is odd
(D) divisible by 3 only when n is odd
(E) divisible by 4 whenever n is even

243. A straight pipe 1 yard in length was marked off in fourths and also in thirds. If the pipe was then cut into separate pieces at each of these markings, which of the following gives all the different lengths of the pieces, in fractions of a yard?

(A) $\frac{1}{6}$ and $\frac{1}{4}$ only
(B) $\frac{1}{4}$ and $\frac{1}{3}$ only
(C) $\frac{1}{6}$, $\frac{1}{4}$, and $\frac{1}{3}$
(D) $\frac{1}{12}$, $\frac{1}{6}$, and $\frac{1}{4}$
(E) $\frac{1}{12}$, $\frac{1}{6}$, and $\frac{1}{3}$

244. If $\frac{0.0015 \times 10^m}{0.03 \times 10^k} = 5 \times 10^7$, then $m - k =$

(A) 9
(B) 8
(C) 7
(D) 6
(E) 5

245. If $x + y = a$ and $x - y = b$, then $2xy =$

(A) $\frac{a^2 - b^2}{2}$
(B) $\frac{b^2 - a^2}{2}$
(C) $\frac{a - b}{2}$
(D) $\frac{ab}{2}$
(E) $\frac{a^2 + b^2}{2}$

246. A rectangular circuit board is designed to have width w inches, perimeter p inches, and area k square inches. Which of the following equations must be true?

(A) $w^2 + pw + k = 0$
(B) $w^2 - pw = 2k = 0$
(C) $2w^2 + pw + 2k = 0$
(D) $2w^2 - pw - 2k = 0$
(E) $2w^2 - pw + 2k = 0$

p, r, s, t, u

247. An arithmetic sequence is a sequence in which each term after the first is equal to the sum of the preceding term and a constant. If the list of numbers shown above is an arithmetic sequence, which of the following must also be an arithmetic sequence?

I. $2p, 2r, 2s, 2t, 2u$
II. $p - 3, r - 3, s - 3, t - 3, u - 3$
III. p^2, r^2, s^2, t^2, u^2

(A) I only
(B) II only
(C) III only
(D) I and II
(E) II and III

248. Right triangle PQR is to be constructed in the xy-plane so that the right angle is at P and PR is parallel to the x-axis. The x- and y-coordinates of P, Q, and R are to be integers that satisfy the inequalities $-4 \le x \le 5$ and $6 \le y \le 16$. How many different triangles with these properties could be constructed?

(A) 110
(B) 1,100
(C) 9,900
(D) 10,000
(E) 12,100

249. If n is a positive integer less than 200 and $\frac{14n}{60}$ is an integer, then n has how many different positive prime factors?

(A) 2
(B) 3
(C) 5
(D) 6
(E) 8

5.4 Problem Solving Answer Key

1. A
2. C
3. E
4. C
5. B
6. E
7. E
8. D
9. E
10. A
11. A
12. B
13. D
14. B
15. D
16. E
17. E
18. A
19. B
20. A
21. E
22. E
23. E
24. B
25. D
26. C
27. B
28. B
29. B
30. C
31. A
32. B
33. A
34. D
35. B
36. B
37. C
38. A
39. A
40. E
41. D
42. D
43. C
44. C
45. A
46. B
47. D
48. B
49. C
50. E
51. E
52. E
53. B
54. A
55. D
56. B
57. D
58. E
59. E
60. A
61. A
62. B
63. B
64. B
65. B
66. B
67. E
68. C
69. C
70. A
71. B
72. E
73. D
74. D
75. C
76. A
77. D
78. B
79. C
80. B
81. E
82. B
83. A
84. C
85. A
86. A
87. A
88. E
89. D
90. E
91. B
92. E
93. B
94. B
95. C
96. E
97. D
98. B
99. C
100. B
101. C
102. D
103. D
104. D
105. B
106. E
107. B
108. E
109. A
110. B
111. D
112. D
113. B
114. A
115. C
116. B
117. E
118. C
119. B
120. C
121. C
122. E
123. B
124. D

125. E
126. C
127. A
128. A
129. D
130. E
131. E
132. D
133. E
134. B
135. C
136. A
137. E
138. E
139. B
140. D
141. C
142. A
143. E
144. C
145. C
146. E
147. A
148. E
149. C
150. A
151. B
152. E
153. D
154. B
155. D
156. D
157. E
158. E
159. B
160. D
161. E
162. B
163. B
164. A
165. D
166. E
167. E
168. C
169. A
170. D
171. C
172. E
173. D
174. D
175. C
176. A
177. B
178. C
179. C
180. E
181. E
182. B
183. A
184. A
185. C
186. D
187. C
188. C
189. A
190. E
191. B
192. A
193. D
194. E
195. C
196. E
197. D
198. B
199. D
200. C
201. E
202. B
203. C
204. D
205. D
206. A
207. C
208. E
209. D
210. D
211. E
212. D
213. C
214. A
215. B
216. E
217. A
218. C
219. C
220. E
221. D
222. B
223. E
224. E
225. A
226. D
227. B
228. A
229. B
230. D
231. E
232. C
233. B
234. D
235. D
236. E
237. B
238. A
239. D
240. B
241. B
242. E
243. D
244. A
245. A
246. E
247. D
248. C
249. B

5.5 Problem Solving Answer Explanations

The following discussion is intended to familiarize you with the most efficient and effective approaches to the kinds of problems common to problem solving questions. The particular questions in this chapter are generally representative of the kinds of problem solving questions you will encounter on the GMAT®. Remember that it is the problem solving strategy that is important, not the specific details of a particular question.

1. A project scheduled to be carried out over a single fiscal year has a budget of $12,600, divided into 12 equal monthly allocations. At the end of the fourth month of that fiscal year, the total amount actually spent on the project was $4,580. By how much was the project over its budget?

(A) $ 380
(B) $ 540
(C) $1,050
(D) $1,380
(E) $1,430

Arithmetic Operations with rational numbers

The budget for four months is $\frac{\$12,600}{12} \times 4 = \$4,200$. Thus, the project was $\$4,580 - \$4,200 = \$380$ over budget for the first four months.

The correct answer is A.

2. For which of the following values of n is $\frac{100 + n}{n}$ NOT an integer?

(A) 1
(B) 2
(C) 3
(D) 4
(E) 5

Arithmetic Properties of numbers

Substitute the value for n given in each answer choice into the expression, and then simplify to determine whether that value results in an integer.

A	$\frac{100+1}{1} = \frac{101}{1} = 101$	Integer
B	$\frac{100+2}{2} = \frac{102}{2} = 51$	Integer
C	$\frac{100+3}{3} = \frac{103}{3} = 34.333\ldots$	NOT an integer
D	$\frac{100+4}{4} = \frac{104}{4} = 26$	Integer
E	$\frac{100+5}{5} = \frac{105}{5} = 21$	Integer

The correct answer is C.

3. Rectangular floors X and Y have equal area. If floor X is 12 feet by 18 feet and floor Y is 9 feet wide, what is the length of floor Y, in feet?

(A) $13\frac{1}{2}$
(B) 18
(C) $18\frac{3}{4}$
(D) 21
(E) 24

Geometry Area

Since for a rectangle, area = (width)(length), the area of floor X = 12(18) = 216. It is given that this is also the area of floor Y, so the length of floor Y can be determined by using the same area in a formula solved for length, or $\frac{\text{area}}{\text{width}} = \text{length}$.

Thus, $\frac{216}{9} = 24$ = length of floor Y.

The correct answer is E.

4. A case contains c cartons. Each carton contains b boxes, and each box contains 100 paper clips. How many paper clips are contained in 2 cases?

(A) $100bc$

(B) $\frac{100b}{c}$

(C) $200bc$

(D) $\frac{200b}{c}$

(E) $\frac{200}{bc}$

Algebra Simplifying algebraic expressions

Each case has bc boxes, each of which has 100 paper clips. The total number of paper clips in 2 cases is thus $2(bc)(100) = 200bc$.

The correct answer is C.

5. The sum of prime numbers that are greater than 60 but less than 70 is

(A) 67
(B) 128
(C) 191
(D) 197
(E) 260

Arithmetic Properties of numbers

A prime number is a positive integer divisible by exactly two different positive divisors, 1 and itself. Note that 62, 64, 66, and 68 are also divisible by 2; 63, 66, and 69 are also divisible by 3; and 65 is also divisible by 5. The only prime numbers between 60 and 70 are 61 and 67, and 61 + 67 = 128.

The correct answer is B.

6. A rainstorm increased the amount of water stored in State J reservoirs from 124 billion gallons to 138 billion gallons. If the storm increased the amount of water in the reservoirs to 82 percent of total capacity, approximately how many billion gallons of water were the reservoirs short of total capacity prior to the storm?

(A) 9
(B) 14
(C) 25
(D) 30
(E) 44

Algebra Applied problems

Letting t be the total capacity of the reservoirs in billions of gallons, the information that the post-storm water amount of 138 billion gallons represented 82% of total capacity can be expressed as $0.82t = 138$, and thus $t = \frac{138}{0.82} = 168.3$. Thus, the amount the reservoirs were short of total capacity prior to the storm was 168.3 – 124 = 44.3 billion gallons.

The correct answer is E.

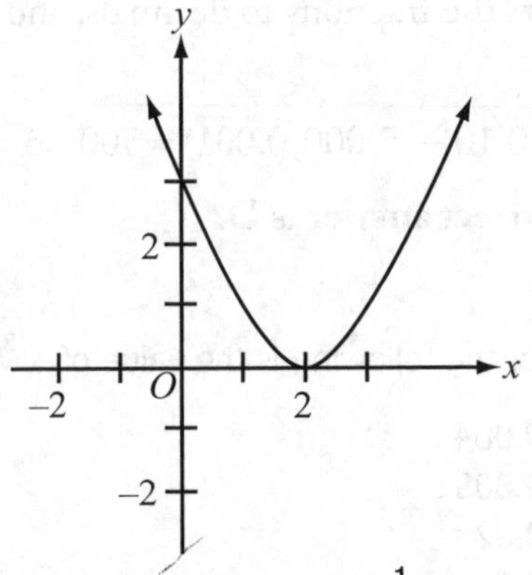

7. On the graph above, when $x = \frac{1}{2}$, $y = 2$; and when $x = 1$, $y = 1$. The graph is symmetrical with respect to the vertical line at $x = 2$. According to the graph, when $x = 3$, $y =$

(A) -1

(B) $-\frac{1}{2}$

(C) 0

(D) $\frac{1}{2}$

(E) 1

Arithmetic + Algebra Interpretation of graphs + Second-degree equations

Since the graph is symmetric with respect to $x = 2$, the y value when $x = 3$ will be the same as the y value when $x = 1$, which is 1.

The correct answer is E.

8. When $\frac{1}{10}$ percent of 5,000 is subtracted from $\frac{1}{10}$ of 5,000, the difference is

(A) 0
(B) 50
(C) 450
(D) 495
(E) 500

Arithmetic Percents

Convert the fractions to decimals, and work the problem.

$$5{,}000(0.10) - 5{,}000(0.001) = 500 - 5 = 495$$

The correct answer is D.

9. Which of the following is the value of $\sqrt{\sqrt[3]{0.000064}}$?

(A) 0.004
(B) 0.008
(C) 0.02
(D) 0.04
(E) 0.2

Arithmetic Operations on radical expressions

Calculate the value of the expression by first finding the cube root and then finding its square root.

$$\sqrt{\sqrt[3]{0.000064}} = \sqrt{0.04} = 0.2$$

The correct answer is E.

10. Raffle tickets numbered consecutively from 101 through 350 are placed in a box. What is the probability that a ticket selected at random will have a number with a hundreds digit of 2?

(A) $\frac{2}{5}$
(B) $\frac{2}{7}$
(C) $\frac{33}{83}$
(D) $\frac{99}{250}$
(E) $\frac{100}{249}$

Arithmetic Probability

There are 250 integers from 101 to 350 inclusive, 100 of which (that is, 200 through 299) have a hundreds digit of 2. Therefore, the probability that a ticket selected from the box at random will have a hundreds digit of 2 can be expressed as $\frac{100}{250} = \frac{2}{5}$.

The correct answer is A.

11. On Monday, a person mailed 8 packages, weighing an average (arithmetic mean) of $12\frac{3}{8}$ pounds, and on Tuesday, 4 packages weighing an average of $15\frac{1}{4}$ pounds. What was the average weight, in pounds, of all the packages the person mailed on both days?

(A) $13\frac{1}{3}$
(B) $13\frac{13}{16}$
(C) $15\frac{1}{2}$
(D) $15\frac{15}{16}$
(E) $16\frac{1}{2}$

Arithmetic Statistics

Since average $= \dfrac{\text{sum of values}}{\text{number of values}}$, the information about the two shipments of packages can be expressed as

$$\text{average} = \frac{8(12\frac{3}{8}) + 4(15\frac{1}{4})}{12} = \frac{8(\frac{99}{8}) + 4(\frac{61}{4})}{12}$$

$$= \frac{99+61}{12} = \frac{160}{12} = 13\frac{1}{3}.$$

The correct answer is A.

12. $0.1 + (0.1)^2 + (0.1)^3 =$

(A) 0.1
(B) 0.111
(C) 0.1211
(D) 0.2341
(E) 0.3

Arithmetic Operations on rational numbers

Calculate the squared and the cubed term, and then add the three terms.

$0.1 + (0.1)^2 + (0.1)^3 = 0.1 + 0.01 + 0.001 = 0.111$

The correct answer is B.

13. A carpenter constructed a rectangular sandbox with a capacity of 10 cubic feet. If the carpenter were to make a similar sandbox twice as long, twice as wide, and twice as high as the first sandbox, what would be the capacity, in cubic feet, of the second sandbox?

(A) 20
(B) 40
(C) 60
(D) 80
(E) 100

Geometry Volume

When all the dimensions of a three-dimensional object are changed by a factor of 2, the capacity, or volume, changes by a factor of $(2)(2)(2) = 2^3 = 8$. Thus the capacity of the second sandbox is $10(8) = 80$ cubic feet.

The correct answer is D.

14. Which of the following CANNOT be a value of $\dfrac{1}{x-1}$?

(A) -1
(B) 0
(C) $\dfrac{2}{3}$
(D) 1
(E) 2

Arithmetic Properties of numbers

Since 1 divided by any number can never equal zero, $\dfrac{1}{x-1} \neq 0$.

The correct answer is B.

15. A bakery opened yesterday with its daily supply of 40 dozen rolls. Half of the rolls were sold by noon, and 80 percent of the remaining rolls were sold between noon and closing time. How many dozen rolls had not been sold when the bakery closed yesterday?

(A) 1
(B) 2
(C) 3
(D) 4
(E) 5

Arithmetic Operations on rational numbers + Percents

Since half of the 40 dozen rolls were sold by noon, then $\frac{1}{2}(40) = 20$ dozen rolls were left to be sold after noon. Because 80 percent of those 20 were sold, $100 - 80 = 20$ percent of them or $20(0.20) = 4$ dozen rolls had not been sold when the bakery closed.

The correct answer is D.

16. What is the combined area, in square inches, of the front and back of a rectangular sheet of paper measuring $8\frac{1}{2}$ inches by 11 inches?

(A) 38
(B) 44
(C) 88
(D) 176
(E) 187

Geometry Area

Since for a rectangle (width)(length) = area, the combined area of the two sides of the sheet is 2(8.5)(11) = 17(11) = 187 square inches.

The correct answer is E.

17. 150 is what percent of 30?

(A) 5%
(B) 20%
(C) 50%
(D) 200%
(E) 500%

Arithmetic Percents

Let x be the percent missing in the problem. The given information can be expressed in the following equation, which can be solved for x.

$150 = (x)(30)$

$5 = x$ divide both sides by 30

Then, 5 expressed as a percent is 500%.

The correct answer is E.

18. The ratio 2 to $\frac{1}{3}$ is equal to the ratio

(A) 6 to 1
(B) 5 to 1
(C) 3 to 2
(D) 2 to 3
(E) 1 to 6

Arithmetic Operations on rational numbers

The ratio 2 to $\frac{1}{3}$ is the same as $\frac{2}{\frac{1}{3}} = 2\left(\frac{3}{1}\right) = 6$, which is the same as a ratio of 6 to 1.

The correct answer is A.

19. Running at the same constant rate, 6 identical machines can produce a total of 270 bottles per minute. At this rate, how many bottles could 10 such machines produce in 4 minutes?

(A) 648
(B) 1,800
(C) 2,700
(D) 10,800
(E) 64,800

Arithmetic Operations on rational numbers

Since there are 6 machines, each machine does $\frac{1}{6}$ of the work. Each machine can produce $270\left(\frac{1}{6}\right) = 45$ bottles per minute, so 10 machines can produce 45(10) = 450 bottles per minute. Therefore, the 10 machines can produce 450(4) = 1,800 bottles in 4 minutes.

The correct answer is B.

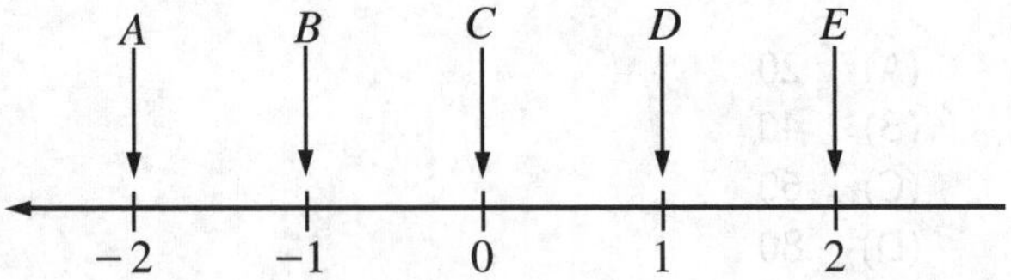

20. Of the five coordinates associated with points *A*, *B*, *C*, *D*, and *E* on the number line above, which has the greatest absolute value?

(A) *A*
(B) *B*
(C) *C*
(D) *D*
(E) *E*

Arithmetic Properties of numbers

The absolute value of a number x is the distance between x and 0 on the number line. The coordinate of point A is farthest from 0 and thus has the greatest absolute value.

The correct answer is A.

21. If x and y are prime numbers, which of the following CANNOT be the sum of x and y?

(A) 5
(B) 9
(C) 13
(D) 16
(E) 23

Arithmetic Properties of numbers

Using known prime numbers, attempt to write each answer choice as the sum of two prime numbers.

A	5 = 2 + 3	sum of two prime numbers
B	9 = 2 + 7	sum of two prime numbers
C	13 = 2 + 11	sum of two prime numbers
D	16 = 3 + 13	sum of two prime numbers
E	23 = 2 + 21	NOT the sum of two prime numbers

Answer choice E is an odd number, which means either x or y, but not both, must be an even number, since even + odd = odd, even + even = even, and odd + odd = even. The only even prime number is 2, and 23 = 2 + 21. Since 21 is not a prime number, 23 CANNOT be expressed as the sum of two prime numbers.

The correct answer is E.

22. If each of the following fractions were written as a repeating decimal, which would have the longest sequence of different digits?

(A) $\frac{2}{11}$
(B) $\frac{1}{3}$
(C) $\frac{41}{99}$
(D) $\frac{2}{3}$
(E) $\frac{23}{37}$

Arithmetic Properties of numbers; Operations on numbers

Compute each fraction's equivalent decimal to determine which one has the longest string of different digits.

A	$\frac{2}{11} = 0.181818\ldots$	2-digit sequence
B	$\frac{1}{3} = 0.333\ldots$	single digit
C	$\frac{41}{99} = 0.414141\ldots$	2-digit sequence
D	$\frac{2}{3} = 0.666\ldots$	single digit
E	$\frac{23}{37} = 0.621621621\ldots$	3-digit sequence

The correct answer is E.

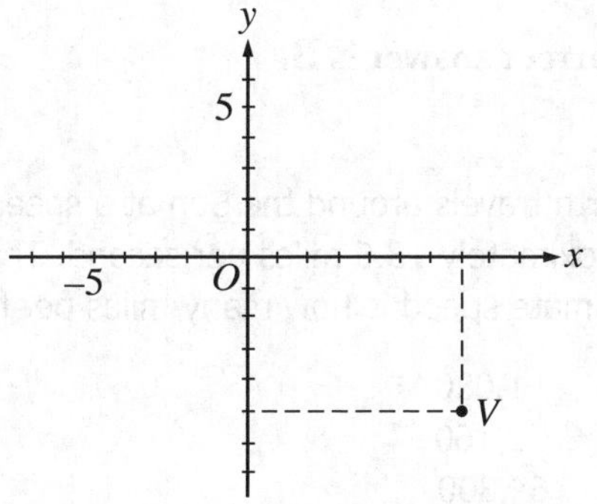

23. In the figure above, the coordinates of point V are

(A) (–7, 5)
(B) (–5, 7)
(C) (5, 7)
(D) (7, 5)
(E) (7,–5)

Geometry Coordinate geometry

The x-coordinate of V is 7, and the y-coordinate of V is –5. Thus, the coordinates, (x, y), of V are $(7, -5)$.

The correct answer is E.

24. A rope 40 feet long is cut into two pieces. If one piece is 18 feet longer than the other, what is the length, in feet, of the shorter piece?

(A) 9
(B) 11
(C) 18
(D) 22
(E) 29

Algebra First-degree equations

Build an equation to express the given information and solve for the answer.

Let x = length of the shorter piece of rope in feet.

Then $x + 18$ = length of the longer piece of rope in feet.

Thus $x + (x + 18) = 40$ is the entire length of the rope in feet.

$2x + 18 = 40$	combine like terms
$2x = 22$	subtract 18 from both sides
$x = 11$	divide both sides by 2

The correct answer is B.

25. The Earth travels around the Sun at a speed of approximately 18.5 miles per second. This approximate speed is how many miles per hour?

(A) 1,080
(B) 1,160
(C) 64,800
(D) 66,600
(E) 3,996,000

Arithmetic Operations on rational numbers

Calculate the equivalent per-hour speed, given that there are 60 seconds in one minute and 60 minutes in one hour.

$$\frac{18.5 \text{ miles}}{1 \cancel{\text{ second}}} \times \frac{60 \cancel{\text{ seconds}}}{1 \cancel{\text{ minute}}} \times \frac{60 \cancel{\text{ minutes}}}{1 \text{ hour}} = \frac{66{,}600 \text{ miles}}{1 \text{ hour}}$$

The correct answer is D.

26. If the quotient $\frac{a}{b}$ is positive, which of the following must be true?

(A) $a > 0$
(B) $b > 0$
(C) $ab > 0$
(D) $a - b > 0$
(E) $a + b > 0$

Arithmetic Properties of numbers

If the quotient $\frac{a}{b}$ is positive, then either a and b are both positive, or a and b are both negative.

A a can be negative as long as b is negative
NEED NOT BE TRUE that $a > 0$

B b can be negative as long as a is negative
NEED NOT BE TRUE that $b > 0$

C (positive)(positive) = positive, and (negative)(negative) = positive
MUST BE TRUE

When deciding whether something must be true, test the case with values known to be true. It takes only one counterexample to prove it false.

D If $a = 4$ and $b = 8$, $a - b = -4$
NEED NOT BE TRUE that $a - b > 0$

E If $a = -4$ and $b = -8$, $a + b = -12$
NEED NOT BE TRUE that $a + b > 0$

The correct answer is C.

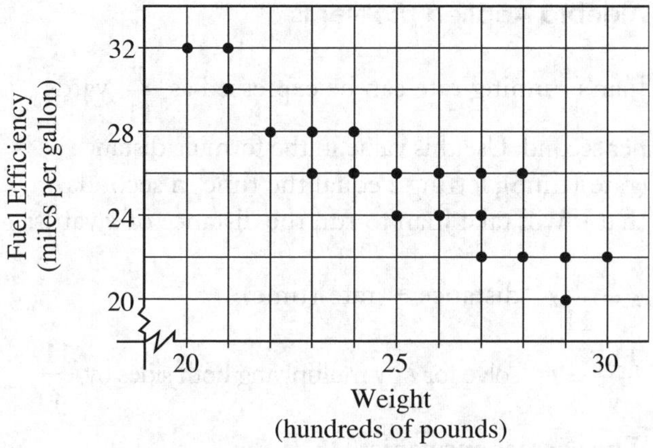

27. The dots on the graph above indicate the weights and fuel efficiency ratings for 20 cars. How many of the cars weigh more than 2,500 pounds and also get more than 22 miles per gallon?

(A) 3
(B) 5
(C) 8
(D) 10
(E) 11

Arithmetic Interpretation of graphs and tables

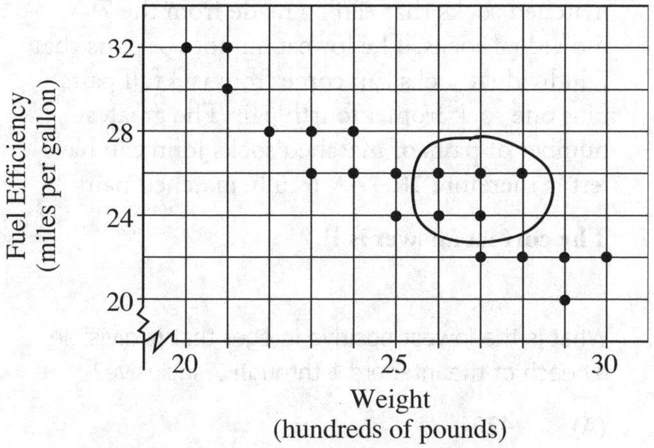

The only dots on the graph that meet the conditions of the problem are those to the right of 25 (that is, the car has a weight in excess of 2,500 pounds) and above 22 (that is, the car has a fuel efficiency over 22 miles per gallon) as shown.

The correct answer is B.

28. How many minutes does it take John to type y words if he types at the rate of x words per minute?

(A) $\frac{x}{y}$

(B) $\frac{y}{x}$

(C) xy

(D) $\frac{60x}{y}$

(E) $\frac{y}{60x}$

Algebra First-degree equation

Let m represent the number of minutes it takes John to type y words. In this rate problem, the number of words typed = (typing rate)(time). Thus, $y = xm$, or $m = \frac{y}{x}$.

The correct answer is B.

29. $\sqrt{(16)(20)+(8)(32)} =$

(A) $4\sqrt{20}$
(B) 24
(C) 25
(D) $4\sqrt{20} + 8\sqrt{2}$
(E) 32

Arithmetic Operations on radical expressions

Work the problem.

$$\sqrt{(16)(20)+(8)(32)} = \sqrt{320+256} = \sqrt{576} = 24$$

The correct answer is B.

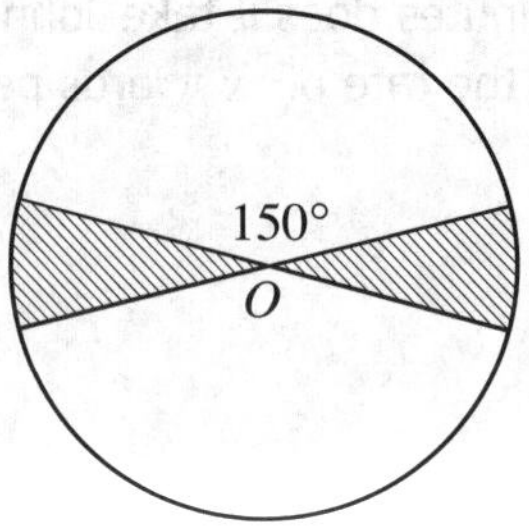

30. If O is the center of the circle above, what fraction of the circular region is shaded?

(A) $\frac{1}{12}$

(B) $\frac{1}{9}$

(C) $\frac{1}{6}$

(D) $\frac{1}{4}$

(E) $\frac{1}{3}$

Geometry Circles and area

Vertical angles are congruent, so 150° + 150° = 300° of the circle is not shaded. Since there are 360° in a circle, this makes 360° – 300° = 60° of the circle shaded. The fraction of the circular region that is shaded is thus $\frac{60}{360} = \frac{1}{6}$.

The correct answer is C.

31. If Juan takes 11 seconds to run y yards, how many seconds will it take him to run x yards at the same rate?

(A) $\frac{11x}{y}$

(B) $\frac{11y}{x}$

(C) $\frac{x}{11y}$

(D) $\frac{11}{xy}$

(E) $\frac{xy}{11}$

Algebra Applied problems

Juan's running rate can be expressed as $\frac{y}{11}$ yards per second. Use this value in the formula distance = (rate)(time), letting t equal the time in seconds that it will take Juan to run the distance of x yards:

$x = \frac{y}{11}t$ distance = (rate)(time)

$\frac{11x}{y} = t$ solve for t by multiplying both sides by $\frac{11}{y}$

The correct answer is A.

32. John has 10 pairs of matched socks. If he loses 7 individual socks, what is the greatest number of pairs of matched socks he can have left?

(A) 7
(B) 6
(C) 5
(D) 4
(E) 3

Arithmetic Operations on rational numbers

Determine first the lowest number of pairs of matched socks that can be made from the 7 individual socks. The lowest number of pairs that 7 individual socks can come from is 3 full pairs plus one sock from a fourth pair. The greatest number of pairs of matched socks John can have left is therefore 10 – 4 = 6 fully matched pairs.

The correct answer is B.

33. What is the lowest positive integer that is divisible by each of the integers 1 through 7, inclusive?

(A) 420
(B) 840
(C) 1,260
(D) 2,520
(E) 5,040

Arithmetic Operations on rational numbers

A number that is divisible by the integers from 1 through 7 inclusive must have 2, 3, 4, 5, 6, and 7 as factors. The lowest positive integer will have no duplication of factors. The lowest common multiple of 2, 3, 4, and 6 is 12, and 5 and 7 are prime, so the lowest positive integer that is divisible by each of the integers 1 through 7 inclusive is 12(5)(7) = 420.

The correct answer is A.

34. What percent of 30 is 12?

(A) 2.5%
(B) 3.6%
(C) 25%
(D) 40%
(E) 250%

Arithmetic Percent

Work the problem.

$$\frac{12}{30} = \frac{2}{5} = \frac{40}{100} = 40\%$$

The correct answer is D.

35. If $\frac{1.5}{0.2 + x} = 5$, then $x =$

(A) − 3.7
(B) 0.1
(C) 0.3
(D) 0.5
(E) 2.8

Algebra First-degree equations

Work the problem to solve for x.

$$\frac{1.5}{0.2 + x} = 5$$

$1.5 = 1 + 5x$	multiply both sides by $0.2 + x$
$0.5 = 5x$	subtract 1 from both sides
$0.1 = x$	divide both sides by 5

The correct answer is B.

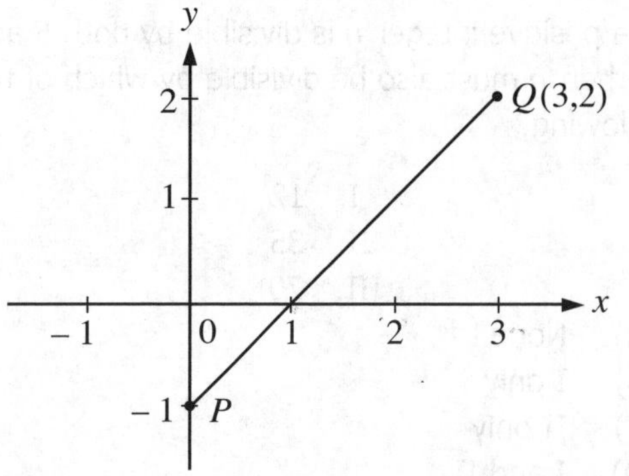

36. In the figure above, the point on segment *PQ* that is twice as far from *P* as from *Q* is

(A) (3, 1)
(B) (2, 1)
(C) (2, – 1)
(D) (1.5, 0.5)
(E) (1, 0)

Geometry Coordinate geometry

On a segment, a point that is twice as far from one end as the other is $\frac{1}{3}$ the distance from one end. The points (0, −1), (1, 0), (2, 1), and (3, 2) are on segment *PQ*, and they divide the segment into three intervals of equal length as shown in the figure below.

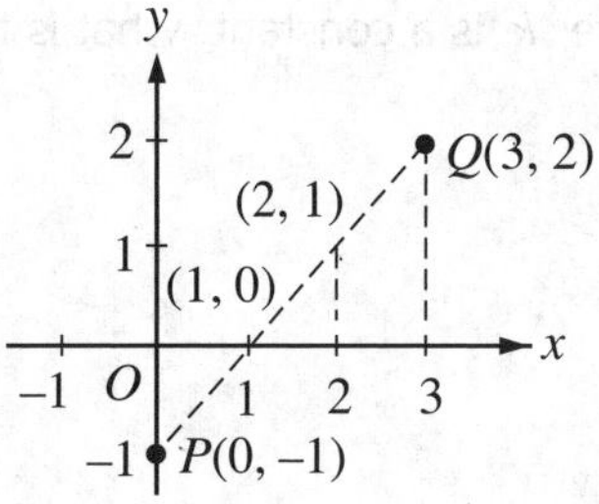

Note that the point (2, 1) is twice as far from $P(0, -1)$ as from $Q(3, 2)$ and also that it is $\frac{1}{3}$ the distance from Q.

The correct answer is B.

37. If a positive integer n is divisible by both 5 and 7, then n must also be divisible by which of the following?

I. 12
II. 35
III. 70

(A) None
(B) I only
(C) II only
(D) I and II
(E) II and III

Arithmetic Properties of numbers

Since 5 and 7 are prime numbers, if n is divisible by both, then n must also be divisible by 5(7) = 35.

I. 12 is not a factor of 35	Need NOT be divisible
II. 35 = 35(1)	MUST be divisible
III. 70 is a multiple of 35, not a factor	Need NOT be divisible

The correct answer is C.

38. If 4 is one solution of the equation $x^2 + 3x + k = 10$, where k is a constant, what is the other solution?

(A) −7
(B) −4
(C) −3
(D) 1
(E) 6

Algebra Second-degree equations

If 4 is one solution of the equation, then substitute 4 for x and solve for k.

$x^2 + 3x + k = 10$	
$(4)^2 + 3(4) + k = 10$	substitute 4 for x
$16 + 12 + k = 10$	simplify
$28 + k = 10$	add terms
$k = -18$	subtract 28 from both sides

Then, substitute −18 for k and solve for x.

$x^2 + 3x - 18 = 10$	substitute 8 for k
$x^2 + 3x - 28 = 0$	subtract 10 from both sides
$(x+7)(x-4) = 0$	factor the equation
$x = -7, x = 4$	solve for x

The correct answer is A.

39. If $x = -3$, what is the value of $-3x^2$?

(A) −27
(B) −18
(C) 18
(D) 27
(E) 81

Algebra Simplifying algebraic expressions

Since $x = -3$, the value of $-3x^2 = -3(-3)^2 = (-3)(-3)(-3) = -27$.

The correct answer is A.

40. $\frac{29^2 + 29}{29} =$

(A) 870
(B) 841
(C) 58
(D) 31
(E) 30

Arithmetic Operations on rational numbers

Work the problem.

$$\frac{29^2 + 29}{29} = \frac{29(29+1)}{29} = \frac{29(30)}{29} = 30$$

The correct answer is E.

41. If $x = 1 - 3t$ and $y = 2t - 1$, then for what value of t does $x = y$?

(A) $\frac{5}{2}$

(B) $\frac{3}{2}$

(C) $\frac{2}{3}$

(D) $\frac{2}{5}$

(E) 0

Algebra Simultaneous equations

Since it is given that $x = y$, set the expressions for x and y equal to each other and solve for t.

$1 - 3t = 2t - 1$

$2 = 5t$ add $3t$ and 1 to both sides, then divide both sides by 5

$\frac{2}{5} = t$

The correct answer is D.

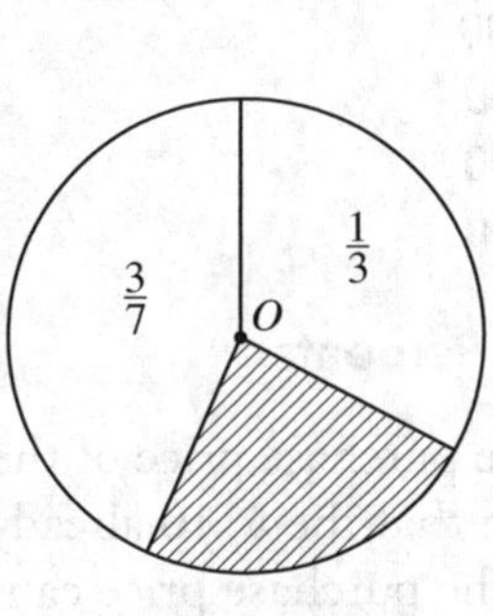

42. In the circular region with center O, shown above, the two unshaded sections constitute $\frac{3}{7}$ and $\frac{1}{3}$ of the area of the circular region. The shaded section constitutes what fractional part of the area of the circular region?

(A) $\frac{3}{5}$

(B) $\frac{6}{7}$

(C) $\frac{2}{21}$

(D) $\frac{5}{21}$

(E) $\frac{16}{21}$

Arithmetic Operations on rational numbers

The two unshaded sections constitute

$\frac{3}{7} + \frac{1}{3} = \frac{9}{21} + \frac{7}{21} = \frac{16}{21}$ of the area of the circular region. Thus, the shaded section constitutes

$1 - \frac{16}{21} = \frac{5}{21}$ of the circular region.

The correct answer is D.

43. $\frac{(0.3)^5}{(0.3)^3} =$

(A) 0.001
(B) 0.01
(C) 0.09
(D) 0.9
(E) 1.0

Arithmetic Operations on rational numbers

Work the problem.

$\frac{(0.3)^5}{(0.3)^3} = (0.3)^{5-3} = (0.3)^2 = 0.09$

The correct answer is C.

44. In a horticultural experiment, 200 seeds were planted in plot I and 300 were planted in plot II. If 57 percent of the seeds in plot I germinated and 42 percent of the seeds in plot II germinated, what percent of the total number of planted seeds germinated?

(A) 45.5%
(B) 46.5%
(C) 48.0%
(D) 49.5%
(E) 51.0%

Arithmetic Percents

The total number of seeds that germinated was $200(0.57) + 300(0.42) = 114 + 126 = 240$. Because this was out of 500 seeds planted, the percent of the total planted that germinated was $\frac{240}{500} = 0.48$, or 48.0%.

The correct answer is C.

45. If 3 and 8 are the lengths of two sides of a triangular region, which of the following can be the length of the third side?

I. 5
II. 8
III. 11

(A) II only
(B) III only
(C) I and II only
(D) II and III only
(E) I, II, and III

Geometry Triangles

In a triangle, the length of the longest side must be smaller than the sum of the lengths of the two other sides. Applying this, test each of these lengths with the lengths of the two sides given to determine which can be possible for the third side of the triangle:

I. $8 = 3 + 5$ CANNOT be a triangle

II. $8 < 3 + 8$ CAN be a triangle

III. $11 = 3 + 8$ CANNOT be a triangle

The correct answer is A.

46. How many integers n are there such that $1 < 5n + 5 < 25$?

(A) Five
(B) Four
(C) Three
(D) Two
(E) One

Algebra Inequalities

Isolate the variable in the inequalities to determine the range within which n lies.

$1 < 5n + 5 < 25$

$-4 < 5n < 20$ subtract 5 from all three values

$-\frac{4}{5} < n < 4$ divide all three values by 5

There are four integers between $-\frac{4}{5}$ and 4, namely 0, 1, 2, and 3.

The correct answer is B.

47. A car dealer sold x used cars and y new cars during May. If the number of used cars sold was 10 greater than the number of new cars sold, which of the following expresses this relationship?

(A) $x > t10y$
(B) $x > y + 10$
(C) $x > y - 10$
(D) $x = y + 10$
(E) $x = y - 10$

Algebra Applied problems

According to the given information, if x is 10 more than y, $x = y + 10$.

The correct answer is D.

48. If a 10 percent deposit that has been paid toward the purchase of a certain product is $110, how much more remains to be paid?

(A) $880
(B) $990
(C) $1,000
(D) $1,100
(E) $1,210

Arithmetic Percents

Let x be the purchase price of the product. The information that the $110 already paid is 10 percent of the purchase price can be expressed as $\$110 = (0.10)x$. From this, $\frac{\$110}{0.10} = x$, or $\$1{,}100 = x$. Subtracting the deposit from this purchase price yields $1,100 – $110 = $990 still remaining to be paid.

The correct answer is B.

49. $\left(\sqrt{7} + \sqrt{7}\right)^2$

(A) 98
(B) 49
(C) 28
(D) 21
(E) 14

Arithmetic Operations with radical expressions

Simplify the expression.

$$\left(\sqrt{7}+\sqrt{7}\right)^2=\left(2\sqrt{7}\right)^2=(2)^2\times\left(\sqrt{7}\right)^2=4\times 7=28.$$

The correct answer is C.

50. In a certain population, there are 3 times as many people aged 21 or under as there are people over 21. The ratio of those 21 or under to the total population is

(A) 1 to 2
(B) 1 to 3
(C) 1 to 4
(D) 2 to 3
(E) 3 to 4

Algebra Applied problems

Let x represent the people over 21. Then $3x$ represents the number of people 21 or under, and $x + 3x = 4x$ represents the total population. Thus, the ratio of those 21 or under to the total population is $\frac{3x}{4x}=\frac{3}{4}$, or 3 to 4.

The correct answer is E.

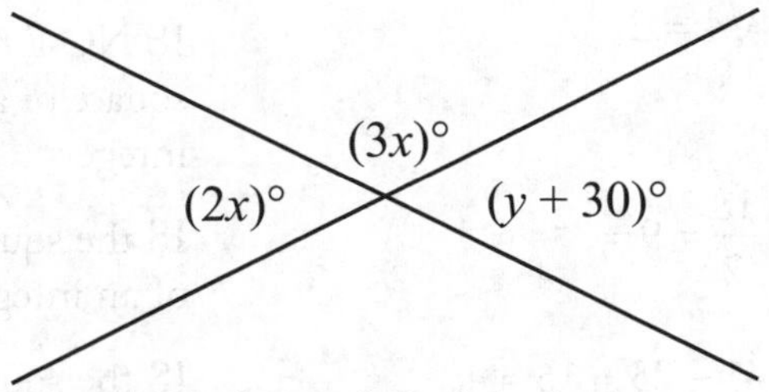

51. In the figure above, the value of y is

(A) 6
(B) 12
(C) 24
(D) 36
(E) 42

Geometry Angle measure in degrees

The sum of the measures of angles that form a straight line equals 180. From this, $2x + 3x = 180$ so $5x = 180$ and thus $x = 36$. Then, because vertical angles are congruent, the measure in degrees of angle $2x$ equals the measure in degrees of angle $(y + 30)$. This can be expressed in the following equation and solved for y:

$2x = y + 30$

$2(36) = y + 30$ — substitute 36 for x

$72 = y + 30$ — simplify

$42 = y$ — subtract 30 from both sides

The correct answer is E.

52. Kelly and Chris packed several boxes with books. If Chris packed 60 percent of the total number of boxes, what was the ratio of the number of boxes Kelly packed to the number of boxes Chris packed?

(A) 1 to 6
(B) 1 to 4
(C) 2 to 5
(D) 3 to 5
(E) 2 to 3

Arithmetic Percent

If Chris packed 60 percent of the boxes, then Kelly packed $100 - 60 = 40$ percent of the boxes. The ratio of the number of boxes Kelly packed to the number Chris packed is $\frac{40\%}{60\%}=\frac{2}{3}$.

The correct answer is E.

53. Of the following, which is the closest approximation of $\frac{50.2 \times 0.49}{199.8}$?

(A) $\frac{1}{10}$

(B) $\frac{1}{8}$

(C) $\frac{1}{4}$

(D) $\frac{5}{4}$

(E) $\frac{25}{2}$

Arithmetic Estimation

Simplify the expression using approximations.

$$\frac{50.2\times 0.49}{199.8}\approx\frac{50\times 0.5}{200}=\frac{25}{200}=\frac{1}{8}$$

The correct answer is B.

54. The average (arithmetic mean) of 10, 30, and 50 is 5 more than the average of 20, 40, and

(A) 15
(B) 25
(C) 35
(D) 45
(E) 55

Arithmetic Statistics

Using the formula $\frac{\text{sum of } n \text{ values}}{n} = \text{average}$, the given information about the first set of numbers can be expressed in the equation $\frac{10+30+50}{3}=30$. From the given information then, the average of the second set of numbers is 30 – 5 = 25. Letting x represent the missing number, set up the equation for calculating the average for the second set of numbers, and solve for x.

$\frac{20+40+x}{3}=25$

$\frac{60+x}{3}=25$ simplify

$60+x=75$ multiply both sides by 3

$x=15$ subtract 15 from both sides

The correct answer is A.

55. If $y = 4 + (x - 3)^2$, then y is lowest when x =

(A) 14
(B) 13
(C) 0
(D) 3
(E) 4

Algebra Second-degree equations

The value of y is lowest when $(x-3)^2$ is least, and that is when $(x-3)^2=0$. Solving this equation for x yields

$(x-3)^2=0$

$x-3=0$ take the square root of both sides

$x=3$ add 3 to both sides

The correct answer is D.

56. Which of the following is NOT equal to the square of an integer?

(A) $\sqrt{\sqrt{1}}$
(B) $\sqrt{4}$
(C) $\frac{18}{2}$
(D) 41 – 25
(E) 36

Arithmetic Properties of numbers

Consider each answer choice.

A $\sqrt{\sqrt{1}}=1=1^2$ IS the square of an integer

B $\sqrt{4}=2$ IS NOT the square of an integer

C $\frac{18}{2}=9=3^2$ IS the square of an integer

D $41-25=16=4^2$ IS the square of an integer

E $36=6^2$ IS the square of an integer.

The correct answer is B.

57. Fermat primes are prime numbers that can be written in the form $2^k + 1$, where k is an integer and a power of 2. Which of the following is NOT a Fermat prime?

(A) 3
(B) 5
(C) 17
(D) 31
(E) 257

Arithmetic Properties of numbers

Consider whether each answer choice can be written in the form $2^k + 1$.

A	$3 = 2^1 + 1$	where $k = 1 = 2^0$
B	$5 = 2^2 + 1$	where $k = 2 = 2^1$
C	$17 = 2^4 + 1$	where $k = 4 = 2^2$
D	$31 = 30 + 1$	30 CANNOT be expressed as an integer power of 2
E	$257 = 2^8 + 1$	where $k = 8 = 2^3$

The correct answer is D.

58. If $x^2 = 2y^3$ and $2y = 4$, what is the value of $x^2 + y$?

(A) −14
(B) −2
(C) 3
(D) 6
(E) 18

Algebra Simplifying algebraic expressions

Solve the given equations for the values of x^2 and y. First, solve for y. Since $2y = 4$, $y = 2$.

Then, substitute 2 for y and solve for x^2:

$x^2 = 2y^3$

$x^2 = 2(2)^3$

$x^2 = 16$

Therefore, by substitution,
$x^2 + y = 16 + 2 = 18$.

The correct answer is E.

59. A glucose solution contains 15 grams of glucose per 100 cubic centimeters of solution. If 45 cubic centimeters of the solution were poured into an empty container, how many grams of glucose would be in the container?

(A) 3.00
(B) 5.00
(C) 5.50
(D) 6.50
(E) 6.75

Algebra Applied problems

Let x be the number of grams of glucose in the 45 cubic centimeters of solution. The proportion comparing the glucose in the 45 cubic centimeters to the given information about the 15 grams of glucose in the entire 100 cubic centimeters of solution can be expressed as $\frac{x}{45} = \frac{15}{100}$, and thus $100x = 675$ or $x = 6.75$.

The correct answer is E.

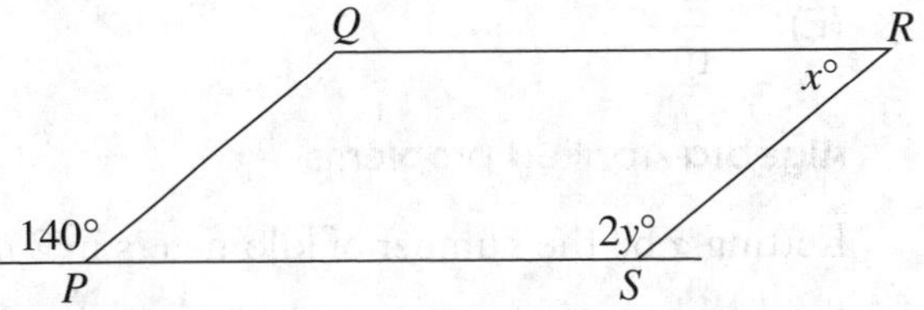

60. In the figure above, if $PQRS$ is a parallelogram, then $y - x =$

(A) 30
(B) 35
(C) 40
(D) 70
(E) 100

Geometry Polygons

Since $PQRS$ is a parallelogram, the following must be true:

$140 = 2y$	corresponding angles are congruent
$2y + x = 180$	consecutive angles are supplementary (sum = 180°)

Solving the first equation for y gives $y = 70$. Substituting this into the second equation gives

$2(70) + x = 180$

$140 + x = 180$

$x = 40$

Thus, $y - x = 70 - 40 = 30$.

The correct answer is A.

61. If 1 kilometer is approximately 0.6 mile, which of the following best approximates the number of kilometers in 2 miles?

(A) $\frac{10}{3}$
(B) 3
(C) $\frac{6}{5}$
(D) $\frac{1}{3}$
(E) $\frac{3}{10}$

Algebra Applied problems

Letting x be the number of kilometers in 2 miles, the problem can be expressed as $\frac{1}{0.6} = \frac{x}{2}$ and solved for x.

$\frac{1}{0.6} = \frac{x}{2}$

$2 = 0.6x$ cross multiply

$\frac{10}{3} = x$ divide both sides by 0.6

The correct answer is A.

62. Lucy invested \$10,000 in a new mutual fund account exactly three years ago. The value of the account increased by 10 percent during the first year, increased by 5 percent during the second year, and decreased by 10 percent during the third year. What is the value of the account today?

(A) \$10,350
(B) \$10,395
(C) \$10,500
(D) \$11,500
(E) \$12,705

Arithmetic Percents

The first year's increase of 10 percent can be expressed as 1.10; the second year's increase of 5 percent can be expressed as 1.05; and the third year's decrease of 10 percent can be expressed as 0.90. Multiply the original value of the account by each of these yearly changes.

$$10,000(1.10)(1.05)(0.90) = 10,395$$

The correct answer is B.

Shipment	Number of defective chips in the shipment	Total number of chips in the shipment
S1	2	5,000
S2	5	12,000
S3	6	18,000
S4	4	16,000

63. A computer chip manufacturer expects the ratio of the number of defective chips to the total number of chips in all future shipments to equal the corresponding ratio for shipments S1, S2, S3, and S4 combined, as shown in the table above. What is the expected number of defective chips in a shipment of 60,000 chips?

(A) 14
(B) 20
(C) 22
(D) 24
(E) 25

Arithmetic + Algebra Interpretation of tables + Applied problems

Let n be the expected number of defective chips in a shipment of 60,000 chips. The proportion comparing the number of defective chips to the total number of chips shipped can be expressed in the following equation and solved for n:

$$\frac{2+5+6+4}{5{,}000+12{,}000+18{,}000+16{,}000}=\frac{n}{60{,}000}$$

$$\frac{17}{51{,}000}=\frac{n}{60{,}000}$$

$$51{,}000n=1{,}020{,}000$$

$$n=20.$$

The correct answer is B.

A = {2, 3, 4, 5}
B = {4, 5, 6, 7, 8}

64. Two integers will be randomly selected from the sets above, one integer from set *A* and one integer from set *B*. What is the probability that the sum of the two integers will equal 9?

(A) 0.15
(B) 0.20
(C) 0.25
(D) 0.30
(E) 0.33

Arithmetic + Algebra Probability + Concepts of sets

The total number of different pairs of numbers, one from set A and one from set B is (4)(5) = 20. Of these 20 pairs of numbers, there are 4 possible pairs that sum to 9: 2 and 7, 3 and 6, 4 and 5, and 5 and 4. Thus, the probability that the sum of the two integers will be 9 is equal to $\frac{4}{20}=0.20$.

The correct answer is B.

2, 4, 6, 8, n, 3, 5, 7, 9

65. In the list above, if *n* is an integer between 1 and 10, inclusive, then the median must be

(A) either 4 or 5
(B) either 5 or 6
(C) either 6 or 7
(D) *n*
(E) 5.50

Arithmetic Statistics

Since the list has an odd number of values, the median will be the middle number when the values are written in ascending order. The given numbers in ascending order are 2, 3, 4, 5, 6, 7, 8, and 9.

If n is 1, 2, 3, 4, or 5, the median will be 5 because that will be the middle number in the list. If n is 6, 7, 8, 9, or 10, the median will be 6 because that will become the middle number in the list.

The correct answer is B.

$$\begin{array}{r} 4\ u\ 7 \\ n\ 2\ 3 \\ +\ 1\ 6\ 2 \\ \hline 1,\ 2\ 2\ 2 \end{array}$$

66. If *n* and *u* represent single digits in the correctly worked computation above, what is the value of *n* + *u*?

(A) 7
(B) 9
(C) 10
(D) 11
(E) 13

Arithmetic Operations on rational numbers

Since the sum of the units digits is 7 + 3 + 2 = 12, the sum of the tens digits must be 1 + u + 2 + 6 = 12 because 1 is carried from the sum of the units digits. Solving this equation for u gives u = 3, and 1 is then carried to the hundreds column, making 1 + 4 + n + 1 = 12. Solving this equation for n gives n = 6. Thus, n + u = 6 + 3 = 9.

The correct answer is B.

$$r = 400\left(\frac{D+S-P}{P}\right)$$

67. If stock is sold three months after it is purchased, the formula above relates P, D, S, and r, where P is the purchase price of the stock, D is the amount of any dividend received, S is the selling price of the stock, and r is the yield of the investment as a percent. If Rose purchased $400 worth of stock, received a dividend of $5, and sold the stock for $420 three months after purchasing it, what was the yield of her investment according to the formula? (Assume that she paid no commissions.)

(A) 1.25%
(B) 5%
(C) 6.25%
(D) 20%
(E) 25%

Algebra First-degree equations

Substitute the values given for D, S, and P into the formula, and solve for r.

$$r = 400\left(\frac{5+420-400}{400}\right)$$

$$r = 25$$

The correct answer is E.

68. The temperatures in degrees Celsius recorded at 6 in the morning in various parts of a certain country were 10º, 5º, -2º, -1º, -5º, and 15º. What is the median of these temperatures?

(A) −2ºC
(B) −1ºC
(C) 2ºC
(D) 3ºC
(E) 5ºC

Arithmetic Statistics

To find the median, the values first must be listed in ascending order:

$-5°, -2°, -1°, 5°, 10°, 15°$

When the number of values in a list is even, the median is the average of the middle two values in the list, and so here, $\frac{-1+5}{2} = \frac{4}{2} = 2$.

The correct answer is C.

69. If $y\left(\frac{3x-5}{2}\right) = y$ and $y \neq 0$, then $x =$

(A) $\frac{2}{3}$
(B) $\frac{5}{3}$
(C) $\frac{7}{3}$
(D) 1
(E) 4

Algebra First-degree equations

Since $y \neq 0$, it is possible to simplify this equation and solve for x as follows:

$$y\left(\frac{3x-5}{2}\right) = y$$

$$\frac{3x-5}{2} = 1 \quad \text{divide both sides by } y$$

$$3x - 5 = 2 \quad \text{multiply both sides by 2}$$

$$3x = 7 \quad \text{solve for } x$$

$$x = \frac{7}{3}$$

The correct answer is C.

70. If $x + 5 > 2$ and $x - 3 < 7$, the value of x must be between which of the following pairs of numbers?

(A) −3 and 10
(B) −3 and 4
(C) 2 and 7
(D) 3 and 4
(E) 3 and 10

Algebra Inequalities

Isolate x in each given inequality. Since $x + 5 > 2$, then $x > -3$. Since $x - 3 < 7$, then $x < 10$. Thus, $-3 < x < 10$, which means the value of x must be between −3 and 10.

The correct answer is A.

71. A gym class can be divided into 8 teams with an equal number of players on each team or into 12 teams with an equal number of players on each team. What is the lowest possible number of students in the class?

(A) 20
(B) 24
(C) 36
(D) 48
(E) 96

Arithmetic Properties of numbers

The lowest value that can be divided evenly by 8 and 12 is their least common multiple (LCM). Since $8 = 2^3$ and $12 = 2^2(3)$, the LCM is $2^3(3) = 24$.

The correct answer is B.

72. At least $\frac{2}{3}$ of the 40 members of a committee must vote in favor of a resolution for it to pass. What is the greatest number of members who could vote against the resolution and still have it pass?

(A) 19
(B) 17
(C) 16
(D) 14
(E) 13

Arithmetic Operations on rational numbers

If at least $\frac{2}{3}$ of the members must vote in favor of a resolution, then no more than $\frac{1}{3}$ of the members can be voting against it. On this 40-member committee, $\frac{1}{3}(40) = 13\frac{1}{3}$, which means that no more than 13 members can vote against the resolution and still have it pass.

The correct answer is E.

73. In the Johnsons' monthly budget, the dollar amounts allocated to household expenses, food, and miscellaneous items are in the ratio 5:2:1, respectively. If the total amount allocated to these three categories is $1,800, what is the amount allocated to food?

(A) $900
(B) $720
(C) $675
(D) $450
(E) $225

Algebra Applied problems

Since the ratio is 5:2:1, let $5x$ be the money allocated to household expenses, $2x$ be the money allocated to food, and $1x$ be the money allocated to miscellaneous items. The given information can then be expressed in the following equation and solved for x.

$5x + 2x + 1x = \$1,800$	
$8x = \$1,800$	combine like terms
$x = \$225$	divide both sides by 8

The money allocated to food is $2x = 2(\$225) = \$450$.

The correct answer is D.

74. There are 4 more women than men on Centerville's board of education. If there are 10 members on the board, how many are women?

(A) 3
(B) 4
(C) 6
(D) 7
(E) 8

Algebra Simultaneous equations + Applied problems

Let m be the number of men on the board and w be the number of women on the board. According to the problem,

$w = m + 4$	4 more women than men
$w + m = 10$	women members plus men members = 10

Substituting $m + 4$ for w in the second equation gives

$m + m + 4 = 10$	
$2m + 4 = 10$	combine like terms
$2m = 6$	subtract 4 from both sides
$m = 3$	divide both sides by 2

Using the first equation, $w = m + 4 = 3 + 4 = 7$ women on the board.

The correct answer is D.

75. Leona bought a 1-year, \$10,000 certificate of deposit that paid interest at an annual rate of 8 percent compounded semiannually. What was the total amount of interest paid on this certificate at maturity?

(A) \$10,464
(B) \$864
(C) \$816
(D) \$800
(E) \$480

Arithmetic Operations with rational numbers

Using the formula $A = P(1+\frac{r}{n})^{nt}$, where A is the amount of money after t (1 year), P is the principal amount invested (\$10,000), r is the annual interest rate (0.08), and n is the number of times compounding occurs annually (2), the given information can be expressed as follows and solved for A:

$$A = (10{,}000)\left(1+\frac{0.08}{2}\right)^{(2)(1)}$$

$$A = (10{,}000)(1.04)^2$$

$$A = (10{,}000)(1.0816)$$

$$A = 10{,}816$$

Thus, since A is the final value of the certificate, the amount of interest paid at maturity is \$10,816 – \$10,000 = \$816.

The correct answer is C.

76. Which of the following ratios is most nearly equal to the ratio $1 + \sqrt{5}$ to 2?

(A) 8 to 5
(B) 6 to 5
(C) 5 to 4
(D) 2 to 1
(E) 1 to 1

Arithmetic Operations on radical expressions

Since $\sqrt{5} \approx 2.2$, $\frac{1+\sqrt{5}}{2} \approx \frac{1+2.2}{2} = \frac{3.2}{2} = 1.6 = \frac{8}{5}$

The correct answer is A.

77. $\dfrac{7}{\frac{1}{5}} + \dfrac{5}{\frac{1}{7}} =$

(A) $\frac{35}{74}$
(B) $\frac{74}{35}$
(C) 35
(D) 70
(E) 74

Arithmetic Operations on rational numbers

Simplify the expression by inverting the fractions in the denominators and multiplying them by their respective numerators, as follows:

$$\frac{7}{\frac{1}{5}} + \frac{5}{\frac{1}{7}} = 7\left(\frac{5}{1}\right) + 5\left(\frac{7}{1}\right) = 7(5) + 5(7) = 35 + 35 = 70$$

The correct answer is D.

78. From January 1, 1991, to January 1, 1993, the number of people enrolled in health maintenance organizations increased by 15 percent. The enrollment on January 1, 1993, was 45 million. How many million people, to the nearest million, were enrolled in health maintenance organizations on January 1, 1991?

(A) 38
(B) 39
(C) 40
(D) 41
(E) 42

Arithmetic + Algebra Percents + Applied problems

Let x be the number of people, in millions, enrolled in health maintenance organizations on January 1, 1991. The information that this enrollment had increased by 15% to 45 million can be expressed as follows, and solved for x.

$x(1.15) = 45$
$x = 39.13$

Thus, to the nearest million, 39 million people were enrolled in health maintenance organizations on January 1, 1991.

The correct answer is B.

79. *R* is the set of positive odd integers less than 50, and *S* is the set of the squares of the integers in *R*. How many elements does the intersection of *R* and *S* contain?

(A) None
(B) Two
(C) Four
(D) Five
(E) Seven

Algebra Concepts of sets

There are 25 positive odd integers less than 50. Of these 25 integers in set R, only the four integers, 1, 9, 25, and 49, ($1^2 = 1,\ 3^2 = 9,\ 5^2 = 25,$ and $7^2 = 49$) are also the squares of integers.

The correct answer is C.

80. A retail appliance store priced a video recorder at 20 percent above the wholesale cost of $200. If a store employee applied the 10 percent employee discount to the retail price to buy the recorder, how much did the employee pay for the recorder?

(A) $198
(B) $216
(C) $220
(D) $230
(E) $240

Arithmetic Percents

From the given information it can be stated that the retail price of the video recorder is 1.20($200) = $240. The employee received a 10 percent discount from this price, which means the employee paid 100 – 10 = 90 percent of the retail price or (0.90)$240 = $216.

The correct answer is B.

$$y = 248 - 398x$$

81. Which of the following values of x gives the greatest value of y in the equation above?

(A) 200
(B) 100
(C) 0.5
(D) 0
(E) –1

Algebra Applied problems

The equation given is linear. Thus, since lines continue in two directions indefinitely, it has no greatest value. So, the solution must be selected from the answer choices offered. The x term is being subtracted; therefore, the larger the x value, the smaller the y value. Conversely, the smaller the x value, the greater the y value. The smallest x value among the answer choices is –1.

The correct answer is E.

82. Machine A produces bolts at a uniform rate of 120 every 40 seconds, and machine B produces bolts at a uniform rate of 100 every 20 seconds. If the two machines run simultaneously, how many seconds will it take for them to produce a total of 200 bolts?

(A) 22
(B) 25
(C) 28
(D) 32
(E) 56

Algebra Applied problems

Determine the production rates for each machine separately, and then calculate their production rate together.

Rate of machine A = $\frac{120}{40} = 3$ bolts per second

Rate of machine B = $\frac{100}{20} = 5$ bolts per second

Combined rate $= 3 + 5 = 8$ bolts per second

Build an equation with s = the number of seconds it takes to produce 200 bolts.

$8s = 200$ (rate)(time) = amount produced

$s = 25$ solve for s

The correct answer is B.

83. What is the decimal equivalent of $\left(\frac{1}{5}\right)^5$?

(A) 0.00032
(B) 0.0016
(C) 0.00625
(D) 0.008
(E) 0.03125

Arithmetic Operations on rational numbers

Convert the fraction to a decimal and work the problem.

$\left(\frac{1}{5}\right)^5 = (0.2)^5 = (0.2)(0.2)(0.2)(0.2)(0.2)$

$= 0.00032$

The correct answer is A.

84. $\dfrac{90 - 8(20 \div 4)}{\frac{1}{2}} =$

(A) 25
(B) 50
(C) 100
(D) 116
(E) 170

Arithmetic Operations on rational numbers

Work the problem.

$\dfrac{90 - 8(20 \div 4)}{\frac{1}{2}} = \dfrac{90 - 8(5)}{\frac{1}{2}} = \dfrac{90 - 40}{\frac{1}{2}} = \dfrac{50}{\frac{1}{2}} =$

$50(2) = 100$

The correct answer is C.

85. A dealer originally bought 100 identical batteries at a total cost of q dollars. If each battery was sold at 50 percent above the original cost per battery, then, in terms of q, for how many dollars was each battery sold?

(A) $\frac{3q}{200}$
(B) $\frac{3q}{2}$
(C) $150q$
(D) $\frac{q}{100} + 50$
(E) $\frac{150}{q}$

Algebra Factoring and simplifying algebraic expressions

Let the original cost per individual battery equal $\frac{q}{100}$ since 100 batteries cost q dollars. Then, since the selling price is 50% above the original cost per battery, the selling price of each battery can be expressed as $\frac{q}{100}(1.50) = \frac{q}{100}\left(\frac{3}{2}\right) = \frac{3q}{200}$.

The correct answer is A.

86. In an increasing sequence of 10 consecutive integers, the sum of the first 5 integers is 560. What is the sum of the last 5 integers in the sequence?

(A) 585
(B) 580
(C) 575
(D) 570
(E) 565

Algebra First-degree equations

Let the first five consecutive integers be represented by x, $x + 1$, $x + 2$, $x + 3$, and $x + 4$. Then, since the sum of the integers is 560, $x+x+1+x+2+x+3+x+4=560$. Thus

$5x+10=560$	simplify
$5x=550$	subtract 10 from both sides
$x=110$	divide both sides by 5

The first integer in the sequence is 110, so the next integers are 111, 112, 113, and 114. From this, the last five integers in the sequence, and thus their sum, can be determined. The sum of the 6th, 7th, 8th, 9th, and 10th integers is 115 + 116 + 117 + 118 + 119 = 585.

The correct answer is A.

87. Machine A produces 100 parts twice as fast as machine B does. Machine B produces 100 parts in 40 minutes. If each machine produces parts at a constant rate, how many parts does machine A produce in 6 minutes?

(A) 30
(B) 25
(C) 20
(D) 15
(E) 7.5

Arithmetic Operations on rational numbers

If machine A produces the parts twice as fast as machine B does, then machine A requires half as much time as machine B does to produce 100 parts. So, if machine B takes 40 minutes for the job, machine A takes 20 minutes for the job. This is a rate of $\frac{100\text{ parts}}{20\text{ minutes}}=5\text{ parts per minute}$. At this rate, in 6 minutes machine A will produce 5(6) = 30 parts.

The correct answer is A.

88. A necklace is made by stringing N individual beads together in the repeating pattern red bead, green bead, white bead, blue bead, and yellow bead. If the necklace design begins with a red bead and ends with a white bead, then N could equal

(A) 16
(B) 32
(C) 41
(D) 54
(E) 68

Algebra Applied problems

The bead pattern repeats after every fifth bead. Since the first bead in this design (or the first in the pattern) is red and the last bead in this design (or third in the pattern) is white, the number of beads in this design is 3 more than some multiple of 5. This can be expressed as $5n + 3$, where n is an integer. Test each of the answer choices to determine which is a multiple of 5 plus a value of 3. Of the options, only 68 = 5(13) + 3 can be written in the form $5n + 3$.

The correct answer is E.

89. In the xy-coordinate system, if (a,b) and $(a + 3, b + k)$ are two points on the line defined by the equation $x = 3y - 7$, then $k =$

(A) 9
(B) 3
(C) $\frac{7}{3}$
(D) 1
(E) $\frac{1}{3}$

Geometry Simple coordinate geometry

Substituting the given coordinates for x and y in the equation $x = 3y - 7$ yields

$a = 3b - 7$

$a + 3 = 3(b + k) - 7$

Then substitute $3b - 7$ for a in second equation, and solve for k

$3b - 7 + 3 = 3b + 3k - 7$	
$3b - 4 = 3b + 3k - 7$	combine like terms
$3 = 3k$	subtract $3b$ from and add 7 to both sides
$1 = k$	divide both sides by 3

The correct answer is D.

90. At the rate of m meters per s seconds, how many meters does a cyclist travel in x minutes?

(A) $\frac{m}{sx}$
(B) $\frac{mx}{s}$
(C) $\frac{60m}{sx}$
(D) $\frac{60ms}{x}$
(E) $\frac{60mx}{s}$

Algebra Simplifying algebraic expressions

Since the cyclist travels at a rate of $\frac{m}{s}$ meters per second, the cyclist travels $60\left(\frac{m}{s}\right) = \frac{60m}{s}$ meters per minute. Thus, in x minutes the cyclist will travel $x\left(\frac{60m}{s}\right) = \frac{60mx}{s}$ meters.

The correct answer is E.

91. If Sam were twice as old as he is, he would be 40 years older than Jim. If Jim is 10 years younger than Sam, how old is Sam?

(A) 20
(B) 30
(C) 40
(D) 50
(E) 60

Algebra Applied problems + Simultaneous equations

Let S be Sam's current age, and let J be Jim's current age. The information in the problem can be expressed in the two equations:

$2S = J + 40$

$J = S - 10$

Substitute this value of J into the first equation, and solve for S:

$2S = (S - 10) + 40$	
$2S = S + 30$	combine like terms
$S = 30$	subtract S from both sides

The correct answer is B.

92. In a certain furniture store, each week Nancy earns a salary of \$240 plus 5 percent of the amount of her total sales that exceeds \$800 for the week. If Nancy earned a total of \$450 one week, what were her total sales that week?

(A) \$2,200
(B) \$3,450
(C) \$4,200
(D) \$4,250
(E) \$5,000

Algebra Applied problems

Let x represent Nancy's total sales for the week. Then, 5% of her total sales over \$800 $(x - 800)$ can be expressed as $0.05(x - 800)$. Her earnings for the week can be expressed in the following equation, which can be solved for x.

$450 = 240 + 0.05(x - 800)$	earnings = \$240 + 5% of sales over \$800
$210 = 0.05x - 40$	subtract 240 from each side and simplify
$250 = 0.05x$	add 40 to each side
$5{,}000 = x$	divide both sides by 0.05

The correct answer is E.

List I: 3, 6, 8, 19
List II: x, 3, 6, 8, 19

93. If the median of the numbers in list I above is equal to the median of the numbers in list II above, what is the value of x?

(A) 6
(B) 7
(C) 8
(D) 9
(E) 10

Arithmetic Statistics

Since list I has an even number of numbers, the median of list I is the average of the middle two numbers, so $\frac{6+8}{2}=7$ is the median of list I. Since list II has an odd number of numbers, the median of list II will be the middle number when the five numbers are put in ascending order. Since the median of list II must be 7 (the median of list I) and since 7 is not in list II, then $x = 7$.

The correct answer is B.

94. In a certain city, 60 percent of the registered voters are Democrats and the rest are Republicans. In a mayoral race, if 75 percent of the registered voters who are Democrats and 20 percent of the registered voters who are Republicans are expected to vote for Candidate A, what percent of the registered voters are expected to vote for Candidate A?

(A) 50%
(B) 53%
(C) 54%
(D) 55%
(E) 57%

Arithmetic + Algebra Percents + Applied problems

Letting v be the number of registered voters in the city, then the information that 60% of the registered voters are Democrats can be expressed as $0.60v$. From this, it can be stated that $1.00v - 0.60v = 0.40v$ are Republicans. The percentage of Democrats and the percentage of Republicans who are expected to vote for candidate A can then be expressed as $(0.75)(0.60v) + (0.20)(0.40v)$. Simplify the expression to determine the total percentage of voters expected to vote for candidate A.

$(0.75)(0.60v) + (0.20)(0.40v)$

$0.45v + 0.08v$

$0.53v$

The correct answer is B.

95. A certain company retirement plan has a "rule of 70" provision that allows an employee to retire when the employee's age plus years of employment with the company total at least 70. In what year could a female employee hired in 1986 on her 32nd birthday first be eligible to retire under this provision?

(A) 2003
(B) 2004
(C) 2005
(D) 2006
(E) 2007

Algebra Applied problems

Construct a table with the data for the first few years after the employee was hired; the pattern of the plan can then be identified from the table.

Year	Number of years after hire	Age	"Rule of 70" value
1986	0	32	32 + 0 = 32
1987	1	33	33 + 1 = 34
1988	2	34	34 + 2 = 36
1989	3	35	35 + 3 = 38

It becomes clear from the table that, for each year of service, the employee makes 2 years of progress toward her "rule of 70" retirement eligibility. Letting y be the number of years after the employee's hire, the following equation can be set up to determine how many years after her hiring this employee will have the 70 combined years needed to be eligible to retire under the "rule of 70" provision.

$32 + 2y = 70$

$2y = 38$

$y = 19$

From this, the employee will reach "rule of 70" eligibility 19 years after she is hired, or 1986 + 19 = 2005.

The correct answer is C.

96. $\frac{1}{2}+\left[\left(\frac{2}{3}\times\frac{3}{8}\right)\div 4\right]-\frac{9}{16}=$

(A) $\frac{29}{16}$

(B) $\frac{19}{16}$

(C) $\frac{15}{16}$

(D) $\frac{9}{13}$

(E) 0

Arithmetic Operations on rational numbers

Simplify by using least common denominators when adding or subtracting fractions, and work the problem.

$$\frac{1}{2}+\left[\left(\frac{2}{3}\times\frac{3}{8}\right)\div 4\right]-\frac{9}{16}=$$

$$\frac{1}{2}+\left[\left(\frac{6}{24}\right)\div 4\right]-\frac{9}{16}=$$

$$\frac{1}{2}+\left[\left(\frac{1}{4}\right)\div 4\right]-\frac{9}{16}=$$

$$\frac{1}{2}+\frac{1}{16}-\frac{9}{16}=$$

$$\frac{8}{16}+\frac{1}{16}-\frac{9}{16}=$$

$$\frac{9}{16}-\frac{9}{16}=0$$

The correct answer is E.

97. Water consists of hydrogen and oxygen, and the approximate ratio, by mass, of hydrogen to oxygen is 2 : 16. Approximately how many grams of oxygen are there in 144 grams of water?

(A) 16

(B) 72

(C) 112

(D) 128

(E) 142

Algebra Applied problems

From this, the ratio of oxygen to water's hydrogen and oxygen combination is known to be $\frac{16}{2+16}$. Letting x be the number of grams of oxygen in 144 grams of water, the proportion comparing oxygen to water's hydrogen and oxygen combination can be expressed as $\frac{16}{2+16}=\frac{x}{144}$ and solved for x as follows:

$\frac{16}{2+16}=\frac{x}{144}$	
$\frac{16}{18}=\frac{x}{144}$	simplify
$\frac{8}{9}=\frac{x}{144}$	simplify again
$9x=1{,}152$	cross multiply
$x=128$	divide both sides by 9

The correct answer is D.

98. If $x(2x+1)=0$ and $\left(x+\frac{1}{2}\right)(2x-3)=0$, then $x=$

(A) -3

(B) $-\frac{1}{2}$

(C) 0

(D) $\frac{1}{2}$

(E) $\frac{3}{2}$

Algebra Second-degree equations + Simultaneous equations

Distributing in both given equations gives:

$$2x^2 + x = 0$$

$$2x^2 - 2x - \frac{3}{2} = 0$$

Then, subtracting the second equation from the first gives

$$3x + \frac{3}{2} = 0$$

$$3x = -\frac{3}{2} \quad \text{solve for } x$$

$$x = -\frac{1}{2}$$

The correct answer is B.

99. On a scale that measures the intensity of a certain phenomenon, a reading of $n + 1$ corresponds to an intensity that is 10 times the intensity corresponding to a reading of n. On that scale, the intensity corresponding to a reading of 8 is how many times as great as the intensity corresponding to a reading of 3?

(A) 5
(B) 50
(C) 10^5
(D) 5^{10}
(E) $8^{10} - 3^{10}$

Arithmetic Operations on rational numbers

Since each increase of 1 in the scale creates an intensity increase of a factor of 10, the intensity of a reading of 8 is $\frac{10^8}{10^3} = 10^{8} - 10^{3} = 10^5$ times an intensity reading of 3.

The correct answer is C.

SOURCES OF FUNDS FOR HIGHWAY MAINTENANCE IN STATE X IN 1983

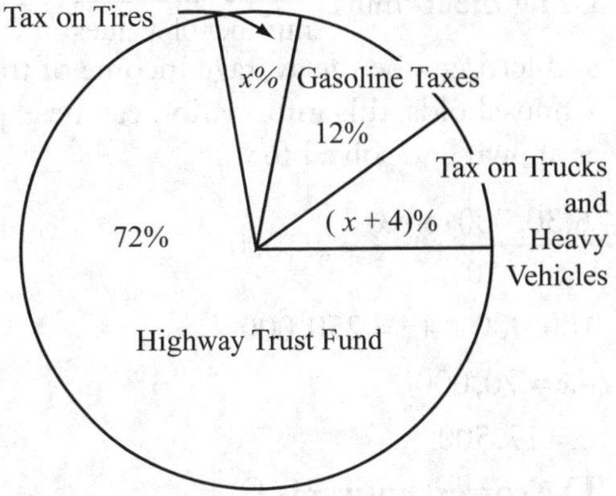

100. According to the graph above, what percent of the funds for highway maintenance came from the tax on tires?

(A) 3%
(B) 6%
(C) 8%
(D) 10%
(E) 16%

Arithmetic Interpretation of graphs

Since all the percentages have to add to 100%, the combined sources of funding can be expressed in the following equation, which can be solved for x, the tax on tires.

$$72 + x + 12 + x + 4 = 100$$

$$88 + 2x = 100$$

$$2x = 12 \quad \text{solve for } x$$

$$x = 6$$

The correct answer is B.

101. A poll reveals that the average (arithmetic mean) income of 10 households is \$25,000. If 6 of the households have incomes of \$30,000 each, what is the average income of the other 4 households?

(A) \$21,500
(B) \$20,000
(C) \$17,500
(D) \$7,500
(E) \$7,000

Arithmetic Statistics

Using the formula $\frac{\text{sum of values}}{\text{number of values}}$ = average, and letting x be the average income of the other 4 households, this information can be expressed as shown and solved for x.

$$\frac{6(30,000)+4x}{10}=25,000$$

$$180,000+4x=250,000$$

$$4x=70,000$$

$$x=17,500$$

The correct answer is C.

102. If $T=\frac{5}{9}(K-32)$, and if $T=290$, then $K=$

(A) $\frac{1,738}{9}$
(B) 322
(C) 490
(D) 554
(E) $\frac{2,898}{5}$

Algebra First-degree equations

Substitute 290 for T in the equation, and solve for K.

$T=\frac{5}{9}(K-32)$

$290=\frac{5}{9}(K-32)$ substitute 290 for T

$\frac{2610}{5}=K-32$ multiply both sides by $\frac{9}{5}$

$522=K-32$ simplify

$554=K$ add 32 to both sides

The correct answer is D.

103. The water from one outlet, flowing at a constant rate, can fill a swimming pool in 9 hours. The water from a second outlet, flowing at a constant rate, can fill the same pool in 5 hours. If both outlets are used at the same time, approximately what is the number of hours required to fill the pool?

(A) 0.22
(B) 0.31
(C) 2.50
(D) 3.21
(E) 4.56

Arithmetic Operations on rational numbers

The first outlet can fill the pool at a rate of $\frac{1}{9}$ of the pool per hour, and the second can fill the pool at a rate of $\frac{1}{5}$ of the pool per hour. Together, they can fill the pool at a rate of $\frac{1}{9}+\frac{1}{5}=\frac{5}{45}+\frac{9}{45}=\frac{14}{45}$ of the pool per hour. Thus, when both outlets are used at the same time, they fill the pool in $\frac{45}{14}=3.21$ hours.

The correct answer is D.

104. Diana bought a stereo for $530, which was the retail price plus a 6 percent sales tax. How much money could she have saved if she had bought the stereo at the same retail price in a neighboring state where she would have paid a sales tax of 5 percent?

(A) $1.00
(B) $2.65
(C) $4.30
(D) $5.00
(E) $5.30

Algebra Applied problems

Letting r be the retail price of the stereo, the information about the total purchase price given the 6% sales tax can be expressed as $530 = 1.06r$, and solved for r.

$$530=1.06r$$

$$500=r$$

In the neighboring state, the stereo would then have cost $500(1.05) = $525. Thus, the amount saved by reducing the sales tax would have been $530 – $525 = $5.

The correct answer is D.

105. If a square mirror has a 20-inch diagonal, what is the approximate perimeter of the mirror, in inches?

(A) 40
(B) 60
(C) 80
(D) 100
(E) 120

Geometry Perimeter + Pythagorean theorem

Let x be the length of one of the sides of the square mirror.

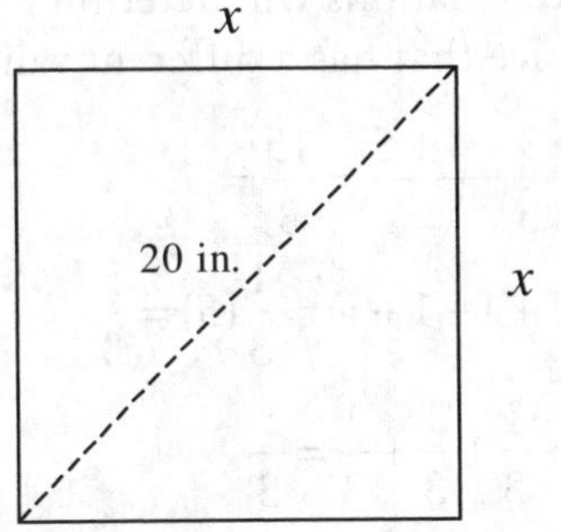

The triangles created by the diagonal are isosceles right triangles for which the Pythagorean theorem yields the following equation that can be solved for x:

$$x^2 + x^2 = 20^2$$

$$2x^2 = 400$$

$$x^2 = 200$$

$$x = 14.14$$

Thus, the perimeter of the square mirror would be $4(14.14) = 56.56 \approx 60$.

The correct answer is B.

106. The present ratio of students to teachers at a certain school is 30 to 1. If the student enrollment were to increase by 50 students and the number of teachers were to increase by 5, the ratio of students to teachers would then be 25 to 1. What is the present number of teachers?

(A) 5
(B) 8
(C) 10
(D) 12
(E) 15

Algebra Applied problems

Let s be the present number of students, and let t be the present number of teachers. According to the problem, the following two equations apply:

$\frac{30}{1} = \frac{s}{t}$ Current student to teacher ratio

$\frac{s+50}{t+5} = \frac{25}{1}$ Future student to teacher ratio

Solving the first equation for s gives $s = 30t$. Substitute this value of s into the second equation, and solve for t.

$$\frac{30t+50}{t+5} = \frac{25}{1}$$

$30t + 50 = 25t + 125$ multiply both sides by $t + 5$

$5t = 75$ simplify by subtraction

$t = 15$

The correct answer is E.

107. What is the smallest integer n for which $25^n > 5^{12}$?

(A) 6
(B) 7
(C) 8
(D) 9
(E) 10

Arithmetic Operations with rational numbers

Since it can be stated that $25 = 5^2$, then it can be stated that $5^{12} = (5^2)^6 = 25^6$. Thus, n must be greater than 6, and the smallest integer for which the inequality holds true is therefore 7.

The correct answer is B.

108. If x and y are different prime numbers, each greater than 2, which of the following must be true?

I. $x + y \neq 91$

II. $x - y$ is an even integer.

III. $\frac{x}{y}$ is not an integer.

(A) II only
(B) I and II only
(C) I and III only
(D) II and III only
(E) I, II, and III

Arithmetic Properties of numbers

Consider each answer choice to determine which conditions are true.

Since all prime numbers greater than 2 are odd, x and y must both be odd.

I. Odd + odd = even; $x + y$ cannot be an odd number; MUST be true

II. Odd – odd = even; $x - y$ must be an even number; MUST be true

Since x and y are primes, it is impossible for one number to be a factor of the other.

III. For $\frac{x}{y}$ to be an integer, y must be a factor of x; MUST be true

The correct answer is E.

109. All the following have the same value EXCEPT

(A) $\frac{1+2+3+4+5}{3}$

(B) $\frac{1}{3}(1+1+1+1+1)$

(C) $\frac{1}{3}+\frac{1}{3}+\frac{1}{3}+\frac{1}{3}+\frac{1}{3}$

(D) $\frac{2}{3}\left(\frac{1}{2}+\frac{1}{2}+\frac{1}{2}+\frac{1}{2}+\frac{1}{2}\right)$

(E) $\frac{1}{3}+\frac{2}{6}+\frac{3}{9}+\frac{4}{12}+\frac{5}{15}$

Arithmetic Operations on rational numbers

Simplifying each answer choice will show which one has a different value from the rest. Starting with A, $\frac{1+2+3+4+5}{3}=\frac{15}{3}=5$.

Notice that by looking over the other four answer choices quickly, it is possible to observe that not one of them can have a value close to 5. Before putting time into doing calculations, it can be beneficial to see whether the problem can be solved simply by observation. In this case, the following calculations will determine the one answer choice that has a different value.

A $\frac{1+2+3+4+5}{3}=\frac{15}{3}=5$

B $\frac{1}{3}(1+1+1+1+1)=\frac{1}{3}(5)=\frac{5}{3}$

C $\frac{1}{3}+\frac{1}{3}+\frac{1}{3}+\frac{1}{3}+\frac{1}{3}=\frac{5}{3}$

D $\frac{2}{3}\left(\frac{1}{2}+\frac{1}{2}+\frac{1}{2}+\frac{1}{2}+\frac{1}{2}\right)=\frac{2}{3}\left(\frac{5}{2}\right)=\frac{5}{3}$

E $\frac{1}{3}+\frac{2}{6}+\frac{3}{9}+\frac{4}{12}+\frac{5}{15}=\frac{1}{3}+\frac{1}{3}+\frac{1}{3}+\frac{1}{3}+\frac{1}{3}=\frac{5}{3}$

The correct answer is A.

110. If candy bars that regularly sell for \$0.40 each are on sale at two for \$0.75, what is the percent reduction in the price of two such candy bars purchased at the sale price?

(A) $2\frac{1}{2}\%$

(B) $6\frac{1}{4}\%$

(C) $6\frac{2}{3}\%$

(D) 8%

(E) $12\frac{1}{2}\%$

Arithmetic Percents

Two candy bars at the regular price cost $2 \times \$0.40 = \$0.80$. The two candy bars at the sale price cost $0.80 – $0.75 = $0.05 less. The percent of the reduction from the regular price can therefore be established as $\frac{\$0.05}{\$0.80} = 0.0625 = 6.25\% = 6\frac{1}{4}\%$.

The correct answer is B.

111. If $s > 0$ and $\sqrt{\frac{r}{s}} = s$, what is r in terms of s?

(A) $\frac{1}{s}$
(B) $\sqrt{s}$
(C) $s\sqrt{s}$
(D) s^3
(E) $s^2 - s$

Algebra Equations

Solve the equation for r as follows:

$\sqrt{\frac{r}{s}} = s$

$\frac{r}{s} = s^2$ square both sides of the equation

$r = s^3$ multiply both sides by s

The correct answer is D.

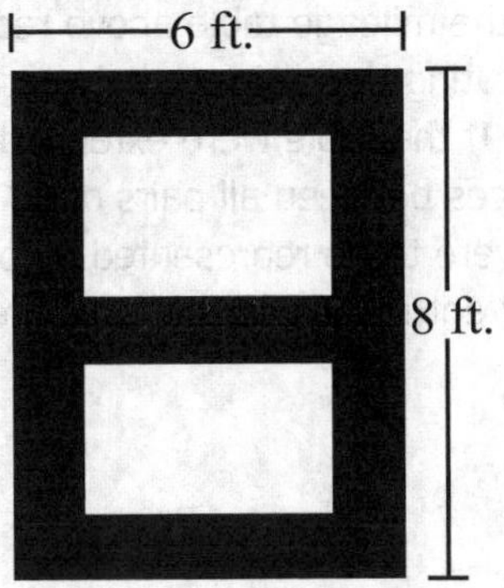

112. The front of a 6-foot-by-8-foot rectangular door has brass rectangular trim, as indicated by the shading in the figure above. If the trim is uniformly 1 foot wide, what fraction of the door's front surface is covered by the trim?

(A) $\frac{13}{48}$
(B) $\frac{5}{12}$
(C) $\frac{1}{2}$
(D) $\frac{7}{12}$
(E) $\frac{5}{8}$

Geometry Area

To determine the area of the trim, find the area of the unshaded portions of the door and subtract this from the door's total area. The width of each unshaded rectangle is the width of the door minus two trim strips, or 6 – 2 = 4 feet. The amount of height available for both unshaded rectangles is the height of the door minus three trim strips, or 8 – 3 = 5 feet. Thus, the area of the unshaded portions is 4 × 5 = 20 square feet. The area of the entire door is 6 × 8 = 48 square feet, so the area of the trim is 48 – 20 = 28 square feet. Therefore, the fraction of the door's front surface that is covered by the trim is $\frac{28}{48} = \frac{7}{12}$.

The correct answer is D.

113. If $a = -0.3$, which of the following is true?

(A) $a < a^2 < a^3$
(B) $a < a^3 < a^2$
(C) $a^2 < a < a^3$
(D) $a^2 < a^3 < a$
(E) $a^3 < a < a^2$

Arithmetic Operations on rational numbers

First, determine the relative values of a, a^2, and a^3, remembering that (negative)(negative) = positive. If $a = -0.3$ then $a^2 = (-0.3)^2 = (-0.3)(-0.3) = 0.09$, and $a^3 = (-0.3)^3 = (-0.3)(-0.3)(-0.3) = -0.027$. Since $-0.3 < -0.027 < 0.09$, then $a < a^3 < a^2$.

The correct answer is B.

114. Which of the following is the product of two integers whose sum is 11?

(A) – 42
(B) – 28
(C) 12
(D) 26
(E) 32

Arithmetic + Algebra Operations on rational numbers + Simultaneous equations + Second-degree equations

For this problem, start by factoring answer choice A, and continue until you find a number with two factors that sum to 11. When A is factored, it can be seen that $-42 = -(2)(3)(7)$, and these three factors are the equivalent of the two factors 14 and -3. This pair of integers yields the product $(14)(-3) = -42$ and the sum $14 + (-3) = 11$ that satisfy the condition of the problem.

Alternatively, this problem can be solved using simultaneous equations. Let x be the first factor and y be the second factor. Then set up two equations for each answer choice and determine whether they can be solved for integer values of x and y. For answer choice A, the equations are

$-42 = xy$

$11 = x + y$

Solving the second equation for x gives $11 - y = x$. Substituting this value of x into the first equation gives

$-42 = (11 - y)y$

$-42 = 11y - y^2$ distribute the y

$y^2 - 11y - 42 = 0$ move all terms to the left side

$(y - 14)(y + 3) = 0$ factor the quadratic

$y - 14 = 0$ $y + 3 = 0$ set each factor equal to zero

$y = 14$ $y = -3$ solve for the variable

Either value will produce the other value for x using either equation.

The correct answer is A.

115. Mary's income is 60 percent more than Tim's income, and Tim's income is 40 percent less than Juan's income. What percent of Juan's income is Mary's income?

(A) 124%
(B) 120%
(C) 96%
(D) 80%
(E) 64%

Algebra + Arithmetic Applied problems + Percents

Let M be Mary's income, T be Tim's income, and J be Juan's income. Mary's income is 60 percent more than Tim's, so $M = T + 0.60T = 1.60T$. Since Tim's income is 40 percent less than Juan's income, Tim's income equals $100 - 40 = 60$ percent of Juan's income, or $T = 0.6J$. Substituting $0.6J$ for T in the first equation gives $M = 1.6(0.6J)$ or $M = 0.96J$. Thus Mary's income is 96% of Juan's income.

The correct answer is C.

	City A	City B	City C	City D	City E
City A		•	•	•	•
City B			•	•	•
City C				•	•
City D					•
City E					

116. Each • in the mileage table above represents an entry indicating the distance between a pair of the five cities. If the table were extended to represent the distances between all pairs of 30 cities and each distance were to be represented by only one entry, how many entries would the table then have?

(A) 60
(B) 435
(C) 450
(D) 465
(E) 900

Arithmetic Interpretation of tables

In a table with 30 cities, there are 30(30) = 900 boxes for entries. However, since a city does not need to have any entry for a distance to and from itself, 30 entries are not needed on the diagonal through the table. Thus, the necessary number of entries is reduced to 900 – 30 = 870 entries. Then, it is given that each pair of cities only needs one table entry, not two as the table allows; therefore, the table only needs to have $\frac{870}{2} = 435$ entries.

The correct answer is B.

117. Which of the following has a value less than 1?

(A) $2\left(\frac{7}{13}\right)$

(B) $\frac{\sqrt{10}}{2}$

(C) $\frac{2}{\sqrt{2}}$

(D) $\frac{1}{\frac{1}{2}}$

(E) $\left(\frac{9}{10}\right)^2$

Arithmetic Operations on radical expressions + Operations on rational numbers

Notice that by looking over the five answer choices quickly, it is possible to observe that the only answer choice that is clearly less than 1 is E, since squaring a fraction that is less than 1 makes an even smaller fraction. Before putting time into doing calculations, it can be beneficial to see whether the problem can be solved simply by observation. In this case, merely simplifying the answer choices will determine the correct one.

A $2\left(\frac{7}{13}\right)=\frac{2}{1}\left(\frac{7}{13}\right)=\frac{14}{13}>1$

B $\frac{\sqrt{10}}{2}\approx\frac{3.16}{2}=1.58>1$

C $\frac{2}{\sqrt{2}}=\sqrt{2}\approx 1.41>1$

D $\frac{1}{\frac{1}{2}}=1\left(\frac{2}{1}\right)=2>1$

E $\left(\frac{9}{10}\right)^2=\frac{81}{100}<1$

The correct answer is E.

118. The ratio of length to the width of a rectangular advertising display is approximately 3.3 to 2. If the width of the display is 8 meters, what is the approximate length of the display, in meters?

(A) 7
(B) 11
(C) 13
(D) 16
(E) 26

Algebra Applied problems

Letting l be the length of the advertising display, the proportion for the ratio of the length to the width can be expressed in the following equation, which can be solved for l:

$\frac{3.3}{2}=\frac{l}{8}$

$13.2 = l$ multiply both sides by 8

The correct answer is C.

119. The average (arithmetic mean) salary of 15 people in the shipping department at a certain firm is \$20,000. The salary of 5 of the employees is \$25,000 each and the salary of 4 of the employees is \$16,000 each. What is the average salary of the remaining employees?

(A) \$19,250
(B) \$18,500
(C) \$18,000
(D) \$15,850
(E) \$12,300

Arithmetic Statistics

The salaries of 15 – 9 = 6 employees are unknown. Let x be the average salary of these 6 employees. Since average = $\frac{\text{sum of values}}{\text{number of value}}$, the following equation can be used to express the information in the problem. Solve for x.

$20{,}000 = \frac{5(25{,}000)+4(16{,}000)+6x}{15}$

$20{,}000 = \frac{125{,}000+64{,}000+6x}{15}$ — multiply the values in the numerator

$300{,}000 = 189{,}000 + 6x$ — multiply both sides by 15; simplify right side

$111{,}000 = 6x$ — subtract 189,000 from both sides

$18{,}500 = x$ — divide both sides by 6

The correct answer is B.

120. David has d books, which is 3 times as many as Jeff and $\frac{1}{2}$ as many as Paula. How many books do the three of them have altogether, in terms of d?

(A) $\frac{5}{6}d$

(B) $\frac{7}{3}d$

(C) $\frac{10}{3}d$

(D) $\frac{7}{2}d$

(E) $\frac{9}{2}d$

Algebra Applied problems + Simultaneous equations

Let J be the number of books that Jeff has, and let P be the number of books Paula has. Then, the given information about David's books can be expressed as $d = 3J$ and $d = \frac{1}{2}P$. Solving these two equations for J and P gives $\frac{d}{3} = J$ and $2d = P$.

Thus, $d + J + P = d + \frac{d}{3} + 2d = 3\frac{1}{3}d = \frac{10}{3}d$.

The correct answer is C.

121. There are 8 teams in a certain league and each team plays each of the other teams exactly once. If each game is played by 2 teams, what is the total number of games played?

(A) 15
(B) 16
(C) 28
(D) 56
(E) 64

Arithmetic Operations on rational numbers

Since no team needs to play itself, each team needs to play 7 other teams. In addition, each game needs to be counted only once, rather than once for each team that plays that game. Since two teams play each game, $\frac{8\times 7}{2} = 28$ games are needed.

The correct answer is C.

122. An operation θ is defined by the equation $a\theta b = \frac{a-b}{a+b}$, for all numbers a and b such that $a \neq -b$. If $a \neq -c$ and $a\theta c = 0$, then $c =$

(A) $-a$

(B) $-\frac{1}{a}$

(C) 0

(D) $\frac{1}{a}$

(E) a

Algebra Simplifying algebraic expressions

Substitute c for b and 0 for $a\theta c$ in the given equation, and solve for c.

$0 = \frac{a-c}{a+c}$

$0 = a - c$ multiply both sides by $a + c$

$c = a$ add c to both sides

The correct answer is E.

123. The price of lunch for 15 people was $207.00, including a 15 percent gratuity for service. What was the average price per person, EXCLUDING the gratuity?

(A) $11.73
(B) $12.00
(C) $13.80
(D) $14.00
(E) $15.87

Arithmetic + Algebra Statistics + Applied problems

Let c be the total price of lunch for everyone excluding the gratuity. Since $207.00 is given as the total price including the 15% gratuity, the total price for the group lunch excluding the gratuity can be expressed as $\$207 = 1.15c$, or $\frac{\$207}{1.15} = \$180 = c$. The average price per person, or $\frac{\text{sum of } v \text{ values}}{v} = \text{average}$, was thus $\frac{\$180}{15} = \$12.00$ for each of the 15 individuals.

The correct answer is B.

124. According to a car dealer's sales report, $\frac{1}{3}$ of the cars sold during a certain period were sedans and $\frac{1}{5}$ of the other cars sold were station wagons. If N station wagons were sold during that period, how many sedans, in terms of N, were sold?

(A) $\frac{2}{15}N$

(B) $\frac{3}{5}N$

(C) $\frac{5}{3}N$

(D) $\frac{5}{2}N$

(E) $\frac{15}{2}N$

Algebra Applied problems + Simultaneous equations

Let c be the total number of cars sold, and let s be the number of sedans sold. If $\frac{1}{3}$ of the cars sold were sedans, then $\frac{2}{3}$ of the cars remained from which the N station wagons could be selected. According to the problem,

$\frac{1}{3}c = s$

$\frac{1}{5}\left(\frac{2}{3}c\right) = N$

Solving the second equation for c gives

$\frac{2}{15}c = N$ multiply fractions

$c = \frac{15}{2}N$ multiply both sides by $\frac{15}{2}$

Substituting this value of c into the first equation gives

$\frac{1}{3}\left(\frac{15}{2}N\right) = s$

$\frac{5}{2}N = s$ multiply and simplify fractions

The correct answer is D.

125. If $\frac{p}{q} < 1$, and p and q are positive integers, which of the following must be greater than 1?

(A) $\sqrt{\frac{p}{q}}$

(B) $\frac{p}{q^2}$

(C) $\frac{p}{2q}$

(D) $\frac{q}{p^2}$

(E) $\frac{q}{p}$

Arithmetic Properties of numbers

Since p and q are positive integers, $0 < \frac{p}{q} < 1$.

A Since $\frac{p}{q} < 1$, then $q > p$. Taking the square root of both sides of the inequality gives $\sqrt{q} > \sqrt{p}$. Then, $\sqrt{\frac{p}{q}} = \frac{\sqrt{p}}{\sqrt{q}}$, so here the denominator will still be larger than the numerator. CANNOT be greater than 1

B Squaring the denominator increases the denominator, which decreases the value of the fraction. CANNOT be greater than 1

C Multiplying the denominator by 2 increases the denominator, which decreases the value of the fraction. CANNOT be greater than 1

D Since $\frac{p}{q} < 1$, then $q > p$. When $p^2 < q$, this expression will be greater than 1, but p^2 need not be less than q. For example, if $p = 2$ and $q = 100$, $\frac{p}{q} = \frac{2}{100}$ and $\frac{q}{p^2} = \frac{100}{2^2} = \frac{100}{4} = 25 > 1$. However, if $p = 3$ and $q = 4$, then $\frac{p}{q} = \frac{3}{4}$ and $\frac{q}{p^2} = \frac{4}{3^2} = \frac{4}{9} < 1$. NEED NOT be greater than 1

E Again, since $\frac{p}{q} < 1$, then $q > p$. Thus, the reciprocal, $\frac{q}{p}$, always has a value greater than 1 because the numerator will always be a larger positive integer than the denominator. MUST be greater than 1

The correct answer is E.

126. It would take one machine 4 hours to complete a large production order and another machine 3 hours to complete the same order. How many hours would it take both machines, working simultaneously at their respective constant rates, to complete the order?

(A) $\frac{7}{12}$

(B) $1\frac{1}{2}$

(C) $1\frac{5}{7}$

(D) $3\frac{1}{2}$

(E) 7

Arithmetic Operations on rational numbers

The first machine can complete $\frac{1}{4}$ of the production order in one hour, and the second machine can complete $\frac{1}{3}$ of the same order in one hour. Thus, working together they can complete $\frac{1}{4} + \frac{1}{3} = \frac{3}{12} + \frac{4}{12} = \frac{7}{12}$ of the order in one hour. Therefore, it will take $\frac{12}{7} = 1\frac{5}{7}$ hours for the two machines working simultaneously to complete the production order.

The correct answer is C.

127. To mail a package, the rate is x cents for the first pound and y cents for each additional pound, where $x > y$. Two packages weighing 3 pounds and 5 pounds, respectively, can be mailed separately or combined as one package. Which method is cheaper, and how much money is saved?

(A) Combined, with a saving of $x - y$ cents
(B) Combined, with a saving of $y - x$ cents
(C) Combined, with a saving of x cents
(D) Separately, with a saving of $x - y$ cents
(E) Separately, with a saving of y cents

Algebra Applied problems

Shipping the two packages separately would cost $1x + 2y$ for the 3-pound package and $1x + 4y$ for the 5-pound package. Shipping them together (as a single 8-pound package) would cost $1x + 7y$. By calculating the sum of the costs for shipping the two packages separately minus the cost for shipping the one combined package, it is possible to determine the difference in cost, as shown.

$((1x+2y)+(1x+4y))-(1x+7y)$	(cost for 3 lb. +cost for 5 lb.) – cost for 8 lb.
$(2x+6y)-(1x+7y)$	combine like terms
$2x+6y-1x-7y$	distribute the negative
$x-y$	combine like terms

Since $x > y$, this value is positive, which means it costs more to ship two packages separately. Thus it is cheaper to mail one combined package at a cost savings of $x - y$ cents.

The correct answer is A.

128. If money is invested at *r* percent interest, compounded annually, the amount of the investment will double in approximately $\frac{70}{r}$ years. If Pat's parents invested \$5,000 in a long-term bond that pays 8 percent interest, compounded annually, what will be the approximate total amount of the investment 18 years later, when Pat is ready for college?

(A) \$20,000
(B) \$15,000
(C) \$12,000
(D) \$10,000
(E) \$9,000

Algebra Applied problems

Since the investment will double in approximately $\frac{70}{r} = \frac{70}{8} = 8.75 \approx 9$ years, it will double every 9 years. The value of the investment over the 18 years will thus be doubled twice. Therefore, its approximate value will be $\$5{,}000(2)(2) = \$20{,}000$.

The correct answer is A.

129. On a recent trip, Cindy drove her car 290 miles, rounded to the nearest 10 miles, and used 12 gallons of gasoline, rounded to the nearest gallon. The actual number of miles per gallon that Cindy's car got on this trip must have been between

(A) $\frac{290}{12.5}$ and $\frac{290}{11.4}$
(B) $\frac{295}{12}$ and $\frac{284}{11.4}$
(C) $\frac{284}{12}$ and $\frac{295}{12}$
(D) $\frac{284}{12.5}$ and $\frac{295}{11.4}$
(E) $\frac{295}{12.5}$ and $\frac{284}{11.4}$

Arithmetic Estimation

The lowest number of miles per gallon can be calculated using the lowest possible miles and the highest amount of gasoline. Conversely, the highest number of miles per gallon can be calculated using the highest possible miles and the lowest amount of gasoline.

Since the miles are rounded to the nearest 10 miles, they can range anywhere from 284 miles to 295 miles. Since the gallons of gasoline are rounded to the nearest gallon, they can range anywhere from 11.4 gallons to 12.5 gallons. Therefore, the following calculations can be set up.

Lowest number of miles per gallon $= \frac{284}{12.5}$

Highest number of miles per gallon $= \frac{295}{11.4}$

The correct answer is D.

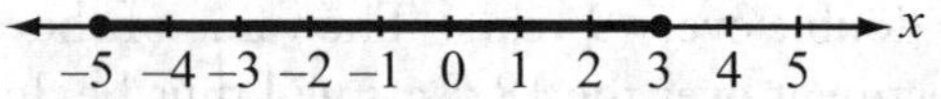

130. Which of the following inequalities is an algebraic expression for the shaded part of the number line above?

(A) $|x| \le 3$

(B) $|x| \le 5$

(C) $|x-2| \le 3$

(D) $|x-1| \le 4$

(E) $|x+1| \le 4$

Algebra Inequalities

The number line above shows $-5 \le x \le 3$. To turn this into absolute value notation, as all the choices are written, the numbers need to be opposite signs of the same value.

Since the distance between −5 and 3 is 8 (3 − (−5) = 8), that distance needs to be split in half with −4 to one side and 4 to the other. Each of these two values is 1 more than the values in the inequality above, so adding 1 to all terms in the inequality gives $-4 \le x+1 \le 4$, which is the same as $|x+1| \le 4$

The correct answer is E.

131. A factory has 500 workers, 15 percent of whom are women. If 50 additional workers are to be hired and all of the present workers remain, how many of the additional workers must be women in order to raise the percent of women employees to 20 percent?

(A) 3
(B) 10
(C) 25
(D) 30
(E) 35

Arithmetic + Algebra Percents + Applied problems

Let w be the number of additional workers who must be women to satisfy the problem. It can be stated that, initially, 500(0.15) = 75 of the workers were women. Since 50 more workers are to be hired, the total workforce will increase to 500 + 50 = 550 employees. The information that the percentage of women employees will be 20 percent after this increase can be expressed in the following equation and solved for w.

$\frac{75+w}{550} = 0.20$

$75+w = 110$ multiply both sides by 550

$w = 35$ subtract 75 from both sides

The correct answer is E.

132. In a small snack shop, the average (arithmetic mean) revenue was \$400 per day over a 10-day period. During this period, if the average daily revenue was \$360 for the first 6 days, what was the average daily revenue for the last 4 days?

(A) \$420
(B) \$440
(C) \$450
(D) \$460
(E) \$480

Arithmetic + Algebra Statistics + Applied problems

Let x be the average daily revenue for the last 4 days. Using the formula $\text{average} = \frac{\text{sum of values}}{\text{number of values}}$, the information regarding the average revenues for the 10-day and 6-day periods can be expressed as follows and solved for x:

$\$400 = \frac{6(\$360)+4x}{10}$

$\$4,000 = \$2,160 + 4x$ multiply both sides by 10

$\$1,840 = 4x$ subtract \$2,160 from both sides

$\$460 = x$ divide both sides by 4

The correct answer is D.

133. A certain country had a total annual expenditure of $\$1.2 \times 10^{12}$ last year. If the population of the country was 240 million last year, what was the per capita expenditure?

(A) \$500
(B) \$1,000
(C) \$2,000
(D) \$3,000
(E) \$5,000

Arithmetic Operations on rational numbers

In scientific notation, 240 million is 2.4×10^8. So, the per capita expenditure was

$$\frac{\$1.2\times10^{12}}{2.4\times10^{8}}=\frac{\$1.2}{2.4}\times10^{12-8}=\$0.5\times10^{4}=\$5{,}000$$

The correct answer is E.

134. A certain rectangular window is twice as long as it is wide. If its perimeter is 10 feet, then its dimensions in feet are

(A) $\frac{3}{2}$ by $\frac{7}{2}$

(B) $\frac{5}{3}$ by $\frac{10}{3}$

(C) 2 by 4

(D) 3 by 6

(E) $\frac{10}{3}$ by $\frac{20}{3}$

Geometry Perimeter

Letting l be the length of the window and w be the width of the window, the information from the problem can be expressed in the following two equations:

$l = 2w$

$2l + 2w = 10$ 2(length) + 2(width) = perimeter

Substitute $2w$ for l in the second equation, and solve for w.

$2(2w) + 2w = 10$

$4w + 2w = 10$ simplify the left side

$6w = 10$ combine like terms

$w = \frac{10}{6} = \frac{5}{3}$ divide both sides by 6 and simplify the fraction

Substitute this value of w in the first equation, and solve for l.

Thus, $l = 2\left(\frac{5}{3}\right) = \frac{10}{3}$.

The correct answer is B.

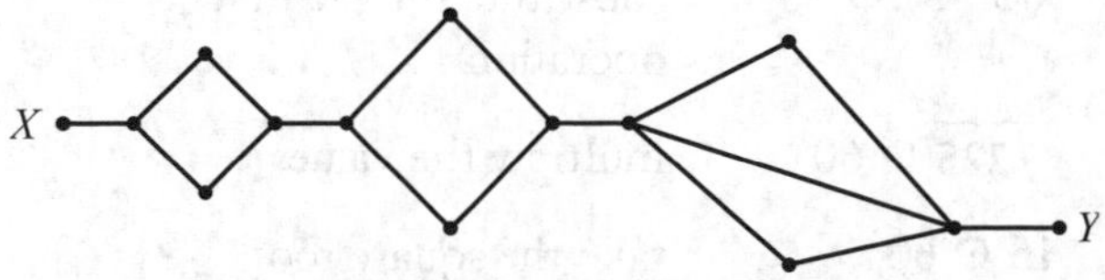

135. The diagram above shows the various paths along which a mouse can travel from point X, where it is released, to point Y, where it is rewarded with a food pellet. How many different paths from X to Y can the mouse take if it goes directly from X to Y without retracing any point along a path?

(A) 6
(B) 7
(C) 12
(D) 14
(E) 17

Arithmetic Elementary combinatorics

The total number of different paths can be found by multiplying the number of possible routes that can be taken from each intersection point of the paths to their next point of intersection. Refer to the figure below.

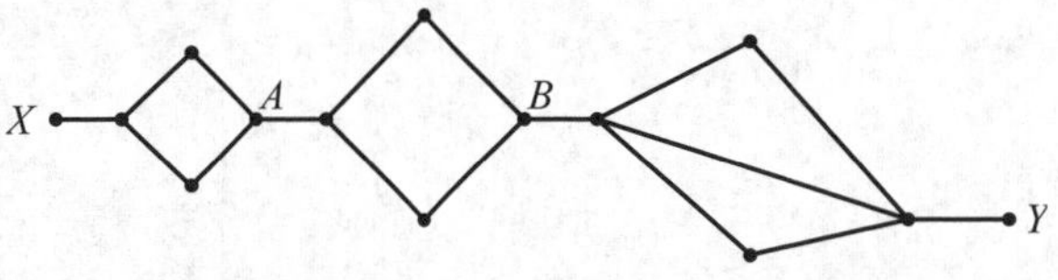

The total number of ways to get from X to A is 2, since there are only 2 paths to choose from. There are also only 2 ways to get from A to B. To get from B to Y, there are 3 possible choices. Thus, the total number of different paths is (2)(2)(3) = 12.

The correct answer is C.

136. If the operation ⊙ is defined by $x \odot y = \sqrt{xy}$ for all positive numbers x and y, then (5 ⊙ 45) ⊙ 60 =

(A) 30
(B) 60
(C) 90
(D) $30\sqrt{15}$
(E) $60\sqrt{15}$

Arithmetic Operations on rational numbers

Substitute the values into the formula and simplify:

(5 ⊙ 45) ⊙ 60

$\sqrt{5(45)} \odot 60$	substitute for the first operation
$\sqrt{225} \odot 60$	multiply the values
15 ⊙ 60	take the square root
$\sqrt{15(60)}$	substitute for the second operation
$\sqrt{900}$	multiply the values
30	take the square root

The correct answer is A.

137. A bar over a sequence of digits in a decimal indicates that the sequence repeats indefinitely. What is the value of $(10^4 - 10^2)(0.00\overline{12})$?

(A) 0
(B) $0.\overline{12}$
(C) 1.2
(D) 10
(E) 12

Arithmetic Operations on rational numbers

Distribute and simplify.

$(10^4 - 10^2)(0.00\overline{12})$

$10^4(0.00\overline{12}) - 10^2(0.00\overline{12})$	distribute the $(0.00\overline{12})$
$10{,}000(0.00\overline{12}) - 100(0.00\overline{12})$	$10^4 = 10{,}000$, and $10^2 = 100$
$12.\overline{12} - 0.\overline{12}$	multiply by multiples of 10 to move the decimals
12	

The correct answer is E.

138. At a loading dock, each worker on the night crew loaded $\frac{3}{4}$ as many boxes as each worker on the day crew. If the night crew has $\frac{4}{5}$ as many workers as the day crew, what fraction of all the boxes loaded by the two crews did the day crew load?

(A) $\frac{1}{2}$
(B) $\frac{2}{5}$
(C) $\frac{3}{5}$
(D) $\frac{4}{5}$
(E) $\frac{5}{8}$

Arithmetic Operations on rational numbers

From this, the workers on the night crew will load $\frac{3}{4}\left(\frac{4}{5}\right)=\frac{3}{5}$ as many boxes as the day crew. The total loaded by both the day and night crews is thus $1+\frac{3}{5}=\frac{5}{5}+\frac{3}{5}=\frac{8}{5}$ of the day crew's work. Therefore, the fraction of all the boxes loaded by the two crews that was done by the day crew was $\frac{1}{\frac{8}{5}}=1\left(\frac{5}{8}\right)=\frac{5}{8}$.

The correct answer is E.

139. A restaurant meal cost $35.50 and there was no tax. If the tip was more than 10 percent but less than 15 percent of the cost of the meal, then the total amount paid must have been between

(A) $40 and $42
(B) $39 and $41
(C) $38 and $40
(D) $37 and $39
(E) $36 and $37

Arithmetic Estimation and percent

First calculate the actual total amount for the meal with a 10% tip and a 15% tip. To calculate each, multiply the cost of the meal by (1 + the percent as a decimal).

10% tip:	15% tip:
$35.50(1.10)	$35.50(1.15)
$39.05	$40.825

The only answer choice that includes all values between $39.05 and $40.83 is B.

The correct answer is B.

140. In a weight-lifting competition, the total weight of Joe's two lifts was 750 pounds. If twice the weight of his first lift was 300 pounds more than the weight of his second lift, what was the weight, in pounds, of his first lift?

(A) 225
(B) 275
(C) 325
(D) 350
(E) 400

Algebra Applied problems

Let F and S be the weights, in pounds, of Joe's first and second lifts, respectively. Use these variables to set up two equations and then solve them.

$F + S = 750$	weight of two lifts was 750 pounds
$2F = S + 300$	twice the weight of first lift was 300 pounds more than the weight of second
$F = 750 - S$	solve the first equation for F
$2(750 - S) = S + 300$	substitute $750 - S$ for F in the second equation
$1{,}500 - 2S = S + 300$	
$1{,}200 = 3S$	solve for S
$400 = S$	

Substituting this value of S back into the first equation gives $F + 400 = 750$, or $F = 350$.

The correct answer is D.

141. A club collected exactly $599 from its members. If each member contributed at least $12, what is the greatest number of members the club could have?

(A) 43
(B) 44
(C) 49
(D) 50
(E) 51

Algebra Applied problems

To determine the greatest possible number of members, first recognize that each member had to contribute the lowest amount given. Build an inequality for the individual contributions and the total amount collected, with n = the number of members in the club, and solve for n.

$12n \leq 599$	(least individual contribution)(number of members) ≤ total collected
$n \leq 49\frac{11}{12}$	solve for n

Since n represents individual people, it must be a whole number; the greatest possible value of n is thus 49.

The correct answer is C.

142. Of the 3,600 employees of Company X, $\frac{1}{3}$ are clerical. If the clerical staff were to be reduced by $\frac{1}{3}$, what percent of the total number of the remaining employees would then be clerical?

(A) 25%
(B) 22.2%
(C) 20%
(D) 12.5%
(E) 11.1%

Arithmetic Percents

First calculate the size of the clerical staff. Then calculate the changes to the clerical staff and the total company staff because of the reduction.

Clerical staff = $3{,}600\left(\frac{1}{3}\right) = 1{,}200$

Clerical staff lost = $1{,}200\left(\frac{1}{3}\right) = 400$

Remaining clerical staff = $1{,}200 - 400 = 800$

Remaining company employees =

$3{,}600 - 400 = 3{,}200$

Percent of remaining employees who are clerical staff = $\frac{800}{3{,}200} = \frac{1}{4} = 25\%$

The correct answer is A.

143. $\frac{3.003}{2.002} =$

(A) 1.05
(B) 1.50015
(C) 1.501
(D) 1.5015
(E) 1.5

Arithmetic Operations on rational numbers

Simplify the expression as follows.

$$\frac{3.003}{2.002} = \frac{3(1.001)}{2(1.001)} = \frac{3}{2} = 1.5$$

The correct answer is E.

144. If $\frac{4 - x}{2 + x} = x$, what is the value of $x^2 + 3x - 4$?

(A) −4
(B) −1
(C) 0
(D) 1
(E) 2

Algebra Second-degree equations

Work the problem.

$$\frac{4 - x}{2 + x} = x$$

$4 - x = x(2 + x)$	multiply both sides by $(2 + x)$
$4 - x = 2x + x^2$	distribute the x
$0 = x^2 + 3x - 4$	move all terms to right side

The correct answer is C.

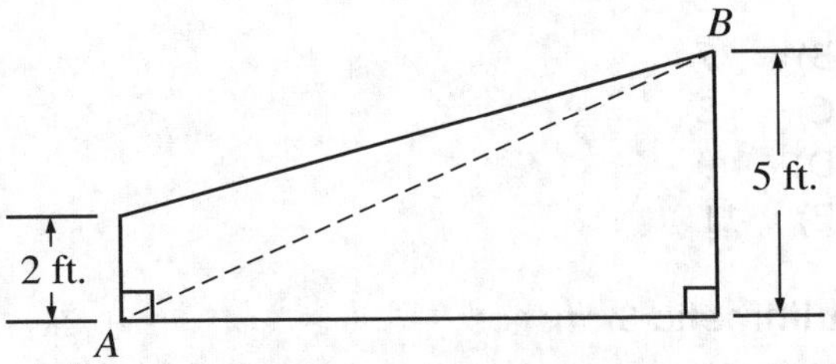

145. The trapezoid shown in the figure above represents a cross section of the rudder of a ship. If the distance from A to B is 13 feet, what is the area of the cross section of the rudder in square feet?

(A) 39
(B) 40
(C) 42
(D) 45
(E) 46.5

Geometry Triangles and the Pythagorean theorem

The formula for calculating the area of a trapezoid is

Area = $\frac{1}{2}$(base 1 + base 2)(height).

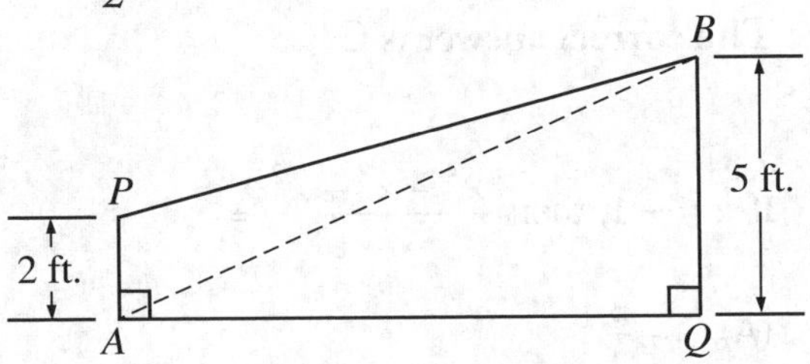

The bases of the trapezoid are given as 2 feet and 5 feet, so only the height (AQ) needs to be found. Since the dashed line AB = 13 feet, and triangle BQA is a right triangle, use the Pythagorean theorem to calculate AQ. Thus,

$AQ = \sqrt{13^2 - 5^2} = \sqrt{144}$, or $AQ = 12$ feet.

Substituting the values into the formula for calculating the area of a trapezoid:

Area = $\frac{1}{2}(2 + 5)(12)$

Area = 42 square feet.

The correct answer is C.

146. If $0 \le x \le 4$ and $y < 12$, which of the following CANNOT be the value of xy?

(A) −2
(B) 0
(C) 6
(D) 24
(E) 48

Arithmetic Operations on rational numbers

If it can be shown by example that an answer choice can be the value of xy, then it is not the correct answer. Find valid values of x and y that yield the products in the answer choices.

A	$x = 1, y = -2, xy = -2$	can be the value of xy (when $x = 1$, $xy = y$; here $y < 12$)
B	$x = 1, y = 0, xy = 0$	can be the value of xy (when $x = 1$, $xy = y$; here $y < 12$)
C	$x = 1, y = 6, xy = 6$	can be the value of xy (when $x = 1$, $xy = y$; here $y < 12$)
D	$x = 4, y = 6, xy = 24$	can be the value of xy (as could $x = 3$, $y = 8$)
E	$x = 4, y < 12, xy < 48$	cannot be the value of xy

In answer choice E, the values of x and y cannot be great enough so that $xy = 48$. Because the maximum value for x is 4, to have the product 48, y must be at least 12, which it cannot be.

The correct answer is E.

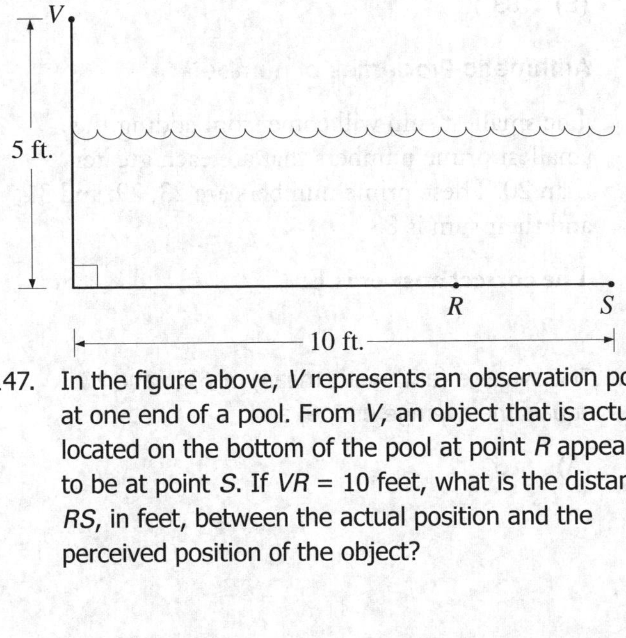

147. In the figure above, V represents an observation point at one end of a pool. From V, an object that is actually located on the bottom of the pool at point R appears to be at point S. If VR = 10 feet, what is the distance RS, in feet, between the actual position and the perceived position of the object?

(A) $10-5\sqrt{3}$
(B) $10-5\sqrt{2}$
(C) 2
(D) $2\frac{1}{2}$
(E) 4

Geometry Pythagorean theorem

Let P be the point 5 feet directly below V. ΔVPR is thus a right triangle.

$VP^2+PR^2=VR^2$	Pythagorean theorem applied to ΔVPR.
$5^2+PR^2=10^2$	substitute known quantities
$25+PR^2=100$	solve for PR
$PR^2=75$	
$PR=5\sqrt{3}$	

Note that $\sqrt{75}=\sqrt{25\cdot 3}=\sqrt{25}\sqrt{3}=5\sqrt{3}$; thus, $RS = PS - PR = 10-5\sqrt{3}$.

The correct answer is A.

148. What is the lowest integer that is a sum of three different primes each greater than 20?

(A) 69
(B) 73
(C) 75
(D) 79
(E) 83

Arithmetic Properties of numbers

The smallest sum will come from adding the smallest prime numbers that are each greater than 20. These prime numbers are 23, 29, and 31, and their sum is 83.

The correct answer is E.

149. The average (arithmetic mean) of 6, 8, and 10 equals the average of 7, 9, and

(A) 5
(B) 7
(C) 8
(D) 9
(E) 11

Arithmetic Statistics

An average, or arithmetic mean, always equals the sum of the values divided by the number of values: $\text{Average}=\frac{\text{sum of } v \text{ values}}{v}$

First, determine the average in the original case:

$$\frac{6+8+10}{3}=\frac{24}{3}=8$$

Then, using the known average, build an equation for the second average with x as the value of the unknown number:

$$\frac{7+9+x}{3}=8$$

$16+x=24$	solve for x
$x=8$	

The correct answer is C.

150. If $x=-1$, then $\frac{x^4-x^3+x^2}{x-1}=$

(A) $-\frac{3}{2}$
(B) $-\frac{1}{2}$
(C) 0
(D) $\frac{1}{2}$
(E) $\frac{3}{2}$

Arithmetic Operations on rational numbers

Substituting the value of -1 for x in the expression results in

$$\frac{(-1)^4-(-1)^3+(-1)^2}{(-1)-1}=\frac{1-(-1)+1}{-2}=-\frac{3}{2}$$

The correct answer is A.

151. A toy store regularly sells all stock at a discount of 20 percent to 40 percent. If an additional 25 percent were deducted from the discount price during a special sale, what would be the lowest possible price of a toy costing $16 before any discount?

(A) $5.60
(B) $7.20
(C) $8.80
(D) $9.60
(E) $15.20

Arithmetic Percents

The lowest possible price is paid when the maximum initial discount of 40% is received.

$16(0.6) = $9.60	calculate the first 40% discount
$9.60(0.75) = $7.20	calculate the second 25% discount

The correct answer is B.

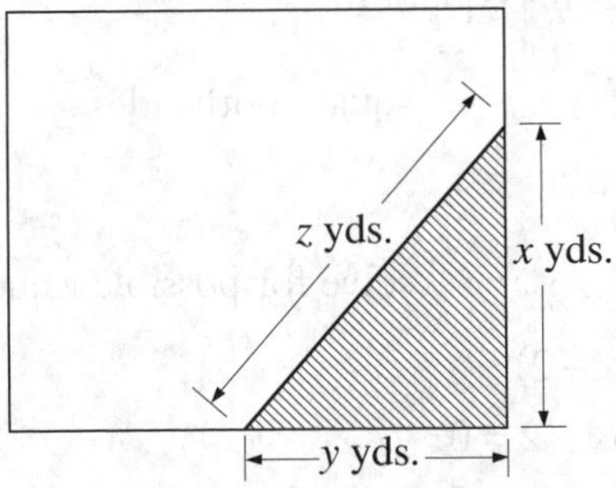

152. The shaded portion of the rectangular lot shown above represents a flower bed. If the area of the bed is 24 square yards and $x = y + 2$, then z equals

(A) $\sqrt{13}$
(B) $2\sqrt{13}$
(C) 6
(D) 8
(E) 10

Geometry Area and the Pythagorean theorem

Using the known area of the triangular flower bed and the known length of side x of the triangle, determine the length of side z of the triangle by applying the formula for calculating the area of a triangle: Area of a triangle = $\frac{1}{2}$(base)(height)

$A = \frac{1}{2}xy$

$24 = \frac{1}{2}(y+2)(y)$	substitute 24 for area and $y + 2$ for x
$48 = y^2 + 2y$	solve for y
$0 = y^2 + 2y - 48$	
$0 = (y+8)(y-6)$	
$y + 8 = 0 \quad y - 6 = 0$	
$y = -8 \quad y = 6$	eliminate $y = -8$ since it has to be a positive length

$x = 6 + 2 = 8$

Since the legs y and x of the right triangle are 6 and 8 yards long, respectively, the hypotenuse, z, must be 10 yards because 6-8-10 is a Pythagorean triple. Alternatively, the Pythagorean theorem can also be used to solve for z, where $x^2 + y^2 = z^2$. Thus, $8^2 + 6^2 = 64 + 36 = 100 = z^2$, and $\sqrt{100} = 10$.

The correct answer is E.

153. Jack is now 14 years older than Bill. If in 10 years Jack will be twice as old as Bill, how old will Jack be in 5 years?

(A) 9
(B) 19
(C) 21
(D) 23
(E) 33

Algebra Applied problems

Letting j and b be Jack's and Bill's current ages, first build equations to express the given information.

$j = b + 14 \qquad j + 10 = 2(b + 10)$

Calculate Bill's current age by solving for b:

$(b + 14) + 10 = 2(b + 10)$ substitute $b + 14$ for j

$b + 24 = 2b + 20$ solve for b

$4 = b$

Then, since the value of b is now known, calculate Jack's current age by substituting 4 for b in the original equation: $j = 4 + 14 = 18$.

Finally, compute Jack's age in 5 years: 18 + 5 = 23.

The correct answer is D.

154. An empty pool being filled with water at a constant rate takes 8 hours to fill to $\frac{3}{5}$ of its capacity. How much more time will it take to finish filling the pool?

(A) 5 hrs. 30 mins.
(B) 5 hrs. 20 mins.
(C) 4 hrs. 48 mins.
(D) 3 hrs. 12 mins.
(E) 2 hrs. 40 mins.

Algebra Applied problems

Build an equation to express the given information and solve for the answer.

Let t = the total time needed to fill the pool.

Since it is given that it takes 8 hours to fill $\frac{3}{5}$ of the pool:

$\frac{3}{5}t = 8$

$t = \frac{40}{3}$ solve for t

$t = 13\frac{1}{3}$

Thus, to calculate the time it will take to finish filling the pool:

$13\frac{1}{3} - 8 = 5\frac{1}{3}$ hours, or 5 hours 20 minutes.

The correct answer is B.

155. A positive number x is multiplied by 2, and this product is then divided by 3. If the positive square root of the result of these two operations equals x, what is the value of x?

(A) $\frac{9}{4}$

(B) $\frac{3}{2}$

(C) $\frac{4}{3}$

(D) $\frac{2}{3}$

(E) $\frac{1}{2}$

Algebra Second-degree equations

Set up an equation according to the given information, and then solve for x.

First, multiply x by 2, divide that by 3, and set the square root of that equal to x:

$$\sqrt{\frac{2x}{3}} = x$$

To solve this equation:

$\frac{2x}{3} = x^2$ square both sides

$2x = 3x^2$

$0 = 3x^2 - 2x$ solve for possible values of x

$0 = x(3x - 2)$

$x = 0,\ 3x - 2 = 0$

since $x > 0$, use $3x - 2 = 0$ to solve for x:

$3x - 2 = 0$

$3x = 2$

$x = \frac{2}{3}$

The correct answer is D.

156. A tank contains 10,000 gallons of a solution that is 5 percent sodium chloride by volume. If 2,500 gallons of water evaporate from the tank, the remaining solution will be approximately what percent sodium chloride?

(A) 1.25%
(B) 3.75%
(C) 6.25%
(D) 6.67%
(E) 11.7%

Arithmetic Operations on rational numbers + Percents

Before the evaporation occurs, the tank contains 10,000 (0.05) = 500 gallons of sodium chloride. After the evaporation occurs, the tank contains 10,000 – 2,500 = 7,500 gallons of solution, of which 500 gallons are known to be sodium chloride. Calculate the percentage based on these postevaporation amounts:

$$\frac{500}{7,500} = 0.0667 = 6.67\%$$

The correct answer is D.

157. If $x + 5y = 16$ and $x = -3y$, then $y =$

(A) – 24
(B) – 8
(C) – 2
(D) 2
(E) 8

Algebra Simultaneous equations

Work the problem.

$x + 5y = 16$ and $x = -3y$

$(-3y) + 5y = 16$	substitute $-3y$ for x in first equation
$2y = 16$	solve for y
$y = 8$	

The correct answer is E.

158. A committee is composed of w women and m men. If 3 women and 2 men are added to the committee, and if one person is selected at random from the enlarged committee, then the probability that a woman is selected can be represented by

(A) $\frac{w}{m}$
(B) $\frac{w}{w+m}$
(C) $\frac{w+3}{m+2}$
(D) $\frac{w+3}{w+m+3}$
(E) $\frac{w+3}{w+m+5}$

Arithmetic Probability

Set up an equation according to the given information regarding the values of w and m. The total number of women on the enlarged committee can be expressed as $w + 3$. The total number of members on the enlarged committee can be expressed as $w + m + 3 + 2$ or thus $w + m + 5$. Then, the probability that the one person selected at random from the enlarged committee is a woman is equal to

$$\frac{\text{the number of women}}{\text{the total number of members}} = \frac{w+3}{w+m+5}.$$

The correct answer is E.

159. If the product of the integers w, x, y, and z is 770, and if $1 < w < x < y < z$, what is the value of $w + z$?

(A) 10
(B) 13
(C) 16
(D) 18
(E) 21

Arithmetic Properties of numbers

Since $1 < w < x < y < z$, none of the four integers w, x, y, and z can be of the same value. The prime factorization of 770 is (2)(5)(7)(11), which is the same number of values as is needed in the problem, so it must be that $w = 2$, $x = 5$, $y = 7$, and $z = 11$. This makes $w + z = 2 + 11 = 13$.

The correct answer is B.

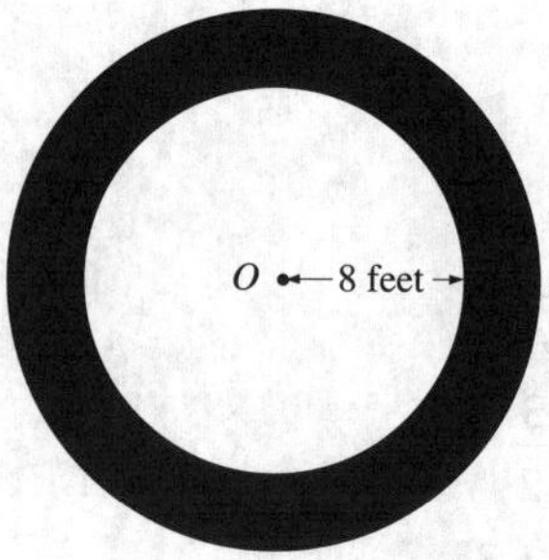

160. The figure above shows a circular flower bed, with its center at *O*, surrounded by a circular path that is 3 feet wide. What is the area of the path, in square feet?

(A) 25π
(B) 38π
(C) 55π
(D) 57π
(E) 64π

Geometry Area (Circles)

The flower bed and the path form two concentric circles. Since the path is 3 feet wide, the radius of the outer circle is 8 feet + 3 feet = 11 feet. The area of a circle can be determined using the formula: area $= \pi(\text{radius})^2$.

The area of the path can thus be found by subtracting the area of the inner circle, A_1, from the area of the outer circle, A_2.

$$A_2 - A_1 = \pi(11)^2 - \pi(8)^2 = 121\pi - 64\pi = 57\pi$$

The correct answer is D.

161. The positive integer *n* is divisible by 25. If $\sqrt{n}$ is greater than 25, which of the following could be the value of $\frac{n}{25}$?

(A) 22
(B) 23
(C) 24
(D) 25
(E) 26

Arithmetic Operations on radical expressions

If $\sqrt{n} > 25$, then $n > 25^2$, or $n > 625$. From this, $\frac{n}{25} > \frac{625}{25}$, or $\frac{n}{25} > 25$.

The correct answer is E.

162. $\dfrac{1}{1+\dfrac{1}{2+\dfrac{1}{3}}} =$

(A) $\frac{3}{10}$
(B) $\frac{7}{10}$
(C) $\frac{6}{7}$
(D) $\frac{10}{7}$
(E) $\frac{10}{3}$

Arithmetic Operations on rational numbers

Work the problem.

$$\frac{1}{1+\frac{1}{2+\frac{1}{3}}} = \frac{1}{1+\frac{1}{\frac{6}{3}+\frac{1}{3}}} = \frac{1}{1+\frac{1}{\frac{7}{3}}} = \frac{1}{1+\frac{3}{7}} = \frac{1}{\frac{7}{7}+\frac{3}{7}} =$$

$$\frac{1}{\frac{10}{7}} = \frac{7}{10}$$

The correct answer is B.

163. A fruit-salad mixture consists of apples, peaches, and grapes in the ratio 6 : 5 : 2, respectively, by weight. If 39 pounds of the mixture is prepared, the mixture includes how many more pounds of apples than grapes?

(A) 15
(B) 12
(C) 9
(D) 6
(E) 4

Algebra Applied problems

Using the given ratios, the information about the fruits in the mixture can be expressed as $6x + 5x + 2x = 39$, or $13x = 39$ and thus $x = 3$. There are $6x$ or $6(3) = 18$ pounds of apples and $2x$ or $2(3) = 6$ pounds of grapes. Therefore, there are $18 - 6 = 12$ more pounds of apples than pounds of grapes in 39 pounds of the mixture.

The correct answer is B.

164. Lois has x dollars more than Jim has, and together they have a total of y dollars. Which of the following represents the number of dollars that Jim has?

(A) $\frac{y-x}{2}$

(B) $y-\frac{x}{2}$

(C) $\frac{y}{2}-x$

(D) $2y-x$

(E) $y-2x$

Algebra Simplifying algebraic expressions

Let J be the number of dollars that Jim has. Then, the amount that Lois has can be expressed as $J + x$ dollars. If Lois and Jim together have a total of y dollars, then:

$y = J + (J + x)$ total dollars = Jim's dollars + Lois's dollars

Solve this for J to determine the number of dollars that Jim has:

$$y = 2J + x$$

$$y - x = 2J$$

$$\frac{y-x}{2} = J$$

The correct answer is A.

165. During a certain season, a team won 80 percent of its first 100 games and 50 percent of its remaining games. If the team won 70 percent of its games for the entire season, what was the total number of games that the team played?

(A) 180
(B) 170
(C) 156
(D) 150
(E) 105

Arithmetic + Algebra Percent + Applied problems

Let G equal the number of games played by the team this season. The given information can be expressed as $(0.80)(100) + 0.50(G - 100) = 0.70G$, that is, 80% of the first 100 games plus 50% of the remaining games equals 70% of the total number of games played. This equation can be solved for G to determine the answer to the problem:

$(0.80)(100) + 0.50(G - 100) = 0.70G$

$80 + 0.50G - 50 = 0.70G$ simplify and distribute

$30 = 0.20G$ simplify and subtract $0.05G$ from both sides

$150 = G$ divide both sides by 0.20

The correct answer is D.

166. Of 30 applicants for a job, 14 had at least 4 years' experience, 18 had degrees, and 3 had less than 4 years' experience and did not have a degree. How many of the applicants had at least 4 years' experience and a degree?

(A) 14
(B) 13
(C) 9
(D) 7
(E) 5

Arithmetic Operations on rational numbers

The problem classified the job applicants in two categories: whether they had more or less than 4 years' experience, and whether they had a degree. The given information can be summarized in the following table:

	At least 4 years' experience	Less than 4 years' experience	Total
Degree			18
No degree		3	
Total	14		30

Thus, according to the given information, 30 – 14 = 16 applicants had less than 4 years' experience. Then, of those applicants with less than 4 years' experience, it is given that 3 applicants did not have a degree, so 16 – 3 = 13 applicants had less than 4 years' experience and had a degree. Therefore, out of the given 18 applicants that had degrees, 13 applicants had less than 4 years' experience, so 18 – 13 = 5 applicants had at least 4 years' experience with a degree. These results are shown in the following table.

	At least 4 years' experience	Less than 4 years' experience	Total
Degree	5	13	18
No degree		3	
Total	14	16	30

The correct answer is E.

167. If $1+\frac{1}{x}=2-\frac{2}{x}$, then $x=$

(A) -1

(B) $\frac{1}{3}$

(C) $\frac{2}{3}$

(D) 2

(E) 3

Algebra First-degree equations

Work the problem to solve the equation for x.

$1+\frac{1}{x}=2-\frac{2}{x}$

$x+1=2x-2$ multiply through by x

$3=x$ solve for x by adding 2 to and subtracting x from both sides

The correct answer is E.

168. Last year, for every 100 million vehicles that traveled on a certain highway, 96 vehicles were involved in accidents. If 3 billion vehicles traveled on the highway last year, how many of those vehicles were involved in accidents? (1 billion = 1,000,000,000)

(A) 288
(B) 320
(C) 2,880
(D) 3,200
(E) 28,800

Arithmetic Operations on rational numbers

According to the given information, 96 out of every 100 million vehicles were in an accident last year. Thus, of the 3 billion vehicles on the highway last year, the number of vehicles involved in accidents was:

$$\frac{96}{100,000,000}\times 3,000,000,000=$$

$$\frac{96}{100}\times 3,000=96\times 30=2,880 \text{ vehicles}$$

The correct answer is C.

169. Thirty percent of the members of a swim club have passed the lifesaving test. Among the members who have *not* passed the test, 12 have taken the preparatory course and 30 have not taken the course. How many members are there in the swim club?

(A) 60
(B) 80
(C) 100
(D) 120
(E) 140

Algebra Applied problems

If 30 percent of the club members have passed the test, then 70 percent have not. Among the members who have not passed the test, 12 have taken the course and 30 have not, for a total of 12 + 30 = 42 members who have not passed the test. Letting x represent the total number of members in the swim club, this information can be expressed as $0.70x = 42$, and so $x = 60$.

The correct answer is A.

170. In a certain company, the ratio of the number of managers to the number of production-line workers is 5 to 72. If 8 additional production-line workers were to be hired, the ratio of the number of managers to the number of production-line workers would be 5 to 74. How many managers does the company have?

(A) 5
(B) 10
(C) 15
(D) 20
(E) 25

Algebra Applied problems

Letting m represent the number of managers and p represent the number of production-line workers, the given information can be expressed as follows:

$\frac{m}{p} = \frac{5}{72}$ original proportion

$\frac{m}{p+8} = \frac{5}{74}$ new proportion with added workers

Since the product of the means equals the product of the extremes for both equations:

$72m = 5p$

$74m = 5p + 40$

Subtract the first equation from the second equation and solve for m:

$2m = 40$

$m = 20$

The correct answer is D.

171. If $(x-1)^2 = 400$, which of the following could be the value of $x - 5$?

(A) 15
(B) 14
(C) −24
(D) −25
(E) −26

Algebra Second-degree equations

Work the problem by taking the square root of both sides and solving for x.

$(x-1)^2 = 400$

$x - 1 = \pm 20$

$x - 1 = -20$, or $x - 1 = 20$

$x = -19$, or $x = 21$

Thus, $x - 5 = -24$ or 16.

The correct answer is C.

172. Which of the following describes all values of x for which $1 - x^2 \geq 0$?

(A) $x \geq 1$
(B) $x \leq -1$
(C) $0 \leq x \leq 1$
(D) $x \leq -1$ or $x \geq 1$
(E) $-1 \leq x \leq 1$

Algebra Inequalities

To solve a quadratic inequality, find the values of the quadratic that equal zero, and then test values to either side of and in between those values to determine which section is correct.

$1 - x^2 \geq 0$

$(1-x)(1+x) \geq 0$

Set the quadratic equal to 0 and solve for x:

$(1-x)(1+x) = 0$

$1 - x = 0, 1 + x = 0$

$1 = x, x = -1$

Test the values:

$x = -2$ $\quad 1 - x^2 \geq 0$

$1 - (-2)^2 \geq 0$

$1 - 4 \geq 0$

$-3 \geq 0$ FALSE

$x = 0$ $\quad 1 - x^2 \geq 0$

$1 - 0^2 \geq 0$

$1 \geq 0$ TRUE

$x = 2$ $\quad 1 - x^2 \geq 0$

$1 - 2^2 \geq 0$

$1 - 4 \geq 0$

$-3 \geq 0$ FALSE

Only the test value between −1 and 1 creates a true statement.

The correct answer is E.

173. The probability is $\frac{1}{2}$ that a certain coin will turn up heads on any given toss. If the coin is tossed three times, what is the probability that on at least one of the tosses the coin will turn up tails?

(A) $\frac{1}{8}$

(B) $\frac{1}{2}$

(C) $\frac{3}{4}$

(D) $\frac{7}{8}$

(E) $\frac{15}{16}$

Arithmetic Probability

Another way of stating that a coin toss will turn up tails at least once is to say that it will not turn up heads every time. The probability that on at least one of the tosses the coin will not turn up heads is 1 minus the probability that the coin will turn up heads on all three tosses. Each toss is an independent event, and so the probability of getting heads all three times is $\left(\frac{1}{2}\right)^3 = \frac{1}{8}$.

Thus, the probability of not getting heads all three times (that is, getting tails at least once) is $1 - \frac{1}{8} = \frac{7}{8}$.

The correct answer is D.

174. Of the final grades received by the students in a certain math course, $\frac{1}{5}$ are A's, $\frac{1}{4}$ are B's, $\frac{1}{2}$ are C's, and the remaining 10 grades are D's. What is the number of students in the course?

(A) 80
(B) 110
(C) 160
(D) 200
(E) 400

Algebra Applied problems

Let x be the number of students in the course. Then $\left(\frac{1}{5}+\frac{1}{4}+\frac{1}{2}\right)x$ or $\left(\frac{4}{20}+\frac{5}{20}+\frac{10}{20}\right)x$ or $\left(\frac{19}{20}\right)x$ of the students received grades of A, B, or C. This means the 10 remaining grades represent $\frac{1}{20}$ of the students in the course.

Thus, $\frac{1}{20}x = 10$, and $x = 200$.

The correct answer is D.

175. As x increases from 165 to 166, which of the following must increase?

I. $2x - 5$

II. $1 - \frac{1}{x}$

III. $\frac{1}{x^2 - x}$

(A) I only
(B) III only
(C) I and II
(D) I and III
(E) II and III

Algebra Simplifying algebraic expressions

Consider the action of each answer choice.

I. This is linear with a positive slope, which is to say, as x increases, $2x$ clearly also increases, and thus the value of the expression must increase.

II. As x increases, the value of the reciprocal $\left(\frac{1}{x}\right)$ decreases. Since the ever-smaller reciprocal is being subtracted, the value of the expression must increase.

III. As x increases, the value of x^2 increases more rapidly than the value of x. Thus, the value of $\frac{1}{x^2 - x}$ will grow the same way as the value of $\frac{1}{x^2}$ will grow. As the value of x increases, the value of $\frac{1}{x^2}$ decreases, so the expression must decrease.

The correct answer is C.

176. A rectangular box is 10 inches wide, 10 inches long, and 5 inches high. What is the greatest possible (straight-line) distance, in inches, between any two points on the box?

(A) 15
(B) 20
(C) 25
(D) $10\sqrt{2}$
(E) $10\sqrt{3}$

Geometry Pythagorean theorem

The greatest possible distance between any two points in a rectangular solid is the space diagonal (AD) of the rectangular solid as shown below.

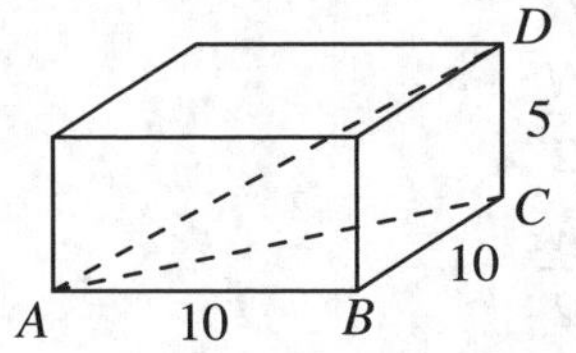

To compute the length of AD, the Pythagorean theorem must be used twice as follows:

Triangle ABC: $AC^2 = AB^2 + BC^2$

$AC^2 = 10^2 + 10^2$

$AC^2 = 200$

$AC = 10\sqrt{2}$

Triangle ACD: $AD^2 = AC^2 + CD^2$

$AD^2 = \left(10\sqrt{2}\right)^2 + 5^2$

$AD^2 = 200 + 25$

$AD^2 = 225$

$AD = 15$

The correct answer is A.

177. A company accountant estimates that airfares next year for business trips of a thousand miles or less will increase by 20 percent and airfares for all other business trips will increase by 10 percent. This year total airfares for business trips of a thousand miles or less were $9,900 and airfares for all other business trips were $13,000. According to the accountant's estimate, if the same number of business trips will be made next year as this year, how much will be spent for airfares next year?

(A) $22,930
(B) $26,180
(C) $26,330
(D) $26,490
(E) $29,770

Arithmetic Percents

Since the airfare for business trips of a thousand miles or less will increase by 20 percent next year, the amount spent will be (1.20)($9,900) = $11,880. Since the airfares for all other business trips will increase by 10 percent next year, the amount spent will be (1.10)($13,000) = $14,300. Thus, according to the accountant's estimate, the total amount spent for airfares next year will be $11,880 + $14,300 = $26,180.

The correct answer is B.

178. If $x * y = xy - 2(x + y)$ for all integers x and y, then $2 * (-3) =$

(A) −16
(B) −11
(C) − 4
(D) 4
(E) 16

Arithmetic Operations on rational numbers

Substitute $2 * (-3)$ for $x * y$ in the given equation, and work the problem.

$x * y = xy - 2(x + y)$

$2 * (-3) = 2(-3) - 2(2 + (-3))$

$2 * (-3) = -6 - 2(-1)$

$2 * (-3) = -6 + 2$

$2 * (-3) = -4$

The correct answer is C.

Club	Number of students
Chess	40
Drama	30
Math	25

179. The table above shows the number of students in three clubs at McAuliffe School. Although no student is in all three clubs, 10 students are in both Chess and Drama, 5 students are in both Chess and Math, and 6 students are in both Drama and Math. How many different students are in the three clubs?

(A) 68
(B) 69
(C) 74
(D) 79
(E) 84

Arithmetic Interpretation of graphs and tables

A good way to solve this problem is to create a Venn diagram. To determine how many students to put in each section, begin by putting the given shared-student data in the overlapping sections. Put 0 in the intersection of all three clubs, 10 in the Chess and Drama intersection, 5 in the Chess and Math intersection, and 6 in the Drama and Math intersection, as shown in the Venn diagram below.

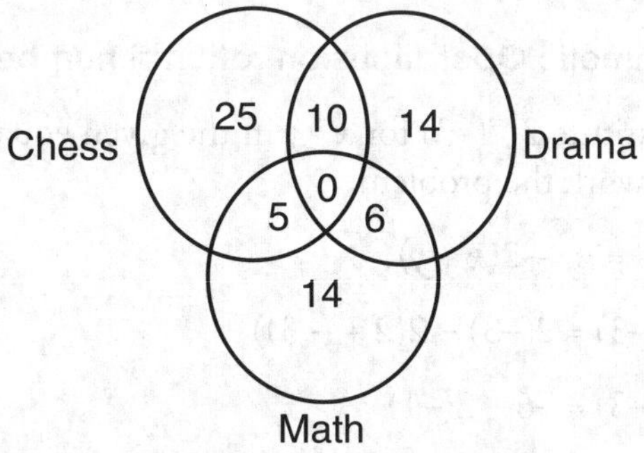

Subtracting the shared students from the totals in each club that are listed in the table establishes the members who belong only to that club. Through this process, it can be determined that the Chess club has 25 such members (40 – 10 – 5 = 25), the Drama club has 14 such members (30 – 10 – 6 = 14), and the Math club has 14 such members (25 – 5 – 6 = 14). Putting the number of unshared club members into the Venn diagram and then adding up all the sections of the diagram gives 25 + 14 + 14 + 10 + 5 + 6 = 74 students.

The correct answer is C.

180. In a nationwide poll, N people were interviewed. If $\frac{1}{4}$ of them answered "yes" to question 1, and of those, $\frac{1}{3}$ answered "yes" to question 2, which of the following expressions represents the number of people interviewed who did not answer "yes" to both questions?

(A) $\frac{N}{7}$
(B) $\frac{6N}{7}$
(C) $\frac{5N}{12}$
(D) $\frac{7N}{12}$
(E) $\frac{11N}{12}$

Algebra Simplifying algebraic expressions

According to the given information, $\left(\frac{1}{4}N\right)$ answered "yes" to question 1, and of those, $\frac{1}{3}$ answered "yes" to question 2; thus $\frac{1}{3}\left(\frac{1}{4}N\right)=\frac{N}{12}$ people answered "yes" to both questions. Thus, $N-\frac{N}{12}=\frac{11N}{12}$ people did not answer "yes" to both questions.

The correct answer is E.

181. The ratio of two quantities is 3 to 4. If each of the quantities is increased by 5, what is the ratio of these two new quantities?

(A) $\frac{3}{4}$
(B) $\frac{8}{9}$
(C) $\frac{18}{19}$

(D) $\frac{23}{24}$

(E) It cannot be determined from the information given.

Algebra Applied problems

Let x and y be the two quantities such that $\frac{x}{y} = \frac{3}{4}$. There is no algebraic operation that can be used to increase x and y each by 5 and determine what happens to the ratio $\frac{3}{4}$. For example, if $x = 3$ and $y = 4$, then $\frac{x+5}{y+5} = \frac{3+5}{4+5} = \frac{8}{9}$.

If $x = 6$ and $y = 8$ (which would still set $\frac{x}{y} = \frac{3}{4}$), then $\frac{x+5}{y+5} = \frac{6+5}{8+5} = \frac{11}{13}$. The ratio of the two new quantities cannot be uniquely determined from the information given.

The correct answer is E.

182. If the average (arithmetic mean) of x and y is 60 and the average (arithmetic mean) of y and z is 80, what is the value of $z - x$?

(A) 70
(B) 40
(C) 20
(D) 10
(E) It cannot be determined from the information given.

Arithmetic + Algebra Statistics + Applied problems

From the given information:

$\frac{x+y}{2} = 60$ average of x and y

$\frac{y+z}{2} = 80$ average of y and z

Solving the first equation for x gives $x = 120 - y$, and solving the second for z gives $z = 160 - y$. Substituting these values into the equation $z - x$ yields

$$z - x = (160 - y) - (120 - y)$$
$$z - x = 160 - y - 120 + y$$
$$z - x = 40$$

The correct answer is B.

183. If $\frac{1}{2}$ of the air in a tank is removed with each stroke of a vacuum pump, what fraction of the original amount of air has been removed after 4 strokes?

(A) $\frac{15}{16}$

(B) $\frac{7}{8}$

(C) $\frac{1}{4}$

(D) $\frac{1}{8}$

(E) $\frac{1}{16}$

Arithmetic Operations on rational numbers

With each stroke's removal of $\frac{1}{2}$ of the tank's air, the amount of air being removed from the tank on that stroke is equal to the amount of air remaining in the tank after that stroke. With the first stroke of the pump, $\frac{1}{2}$ of the air is removed; with the second stroke, $\frac{1}{2} \times \frac{1}{2} = \frac{1}{4}$ of the air is removed, leaving $\frac{1}{4}$ of the air. With the third stroke, $\frac{1}{2} \times \frac{1}{4} = \frac{1}{8}$ of the air is removed, leaving $\frac{1}{8}$ of the air, and with the fourth stroke, $\frac{1}{2} \times \frac{1}{8} = \frac{1}{16}$ of the air is removed. Therefore, with four strokes, $\frac{1}{2} + \frac{1}{4} + \frac{1}{8} + \frac{1}{16} = \frac{8}{16} + \frac{4}{16} + \frac{2}{16} + \frac{1}{16} = \frac{15}{16}$ of the air has been removed.

The correct answer is A.

184. If the two-digit integers M and N are positive and have the same digits, but in reverse order, which of the following CANNOT be the sum of M and N?

(A) 181
(B) 165
(C) 121
(D) 99
(E) 44

Algebra Applied problems

It is given that M and N have the same digits in reverse order. Let $M = 10t + u$ and $N = 10u + t$, where t and u are two digits. Then, $M + N = (10t + u) + (10u + t) = 11t + 11u = 11(t + u)$. This means that any sum of the two integers M and N must also be a multiple of 11. Of the answer choices, only 181 is not a multiple of 11 and thus cannot be the sum of M and N.

The correct answer is A.

185. Car X and car Y traveled the same 80-mile route. If car X took 2 hours and car Y traveled at an average speed that was 50 percent faster than the average speed of car X, how many hours did it take car Y to travel the route?

(A) $\frac{2}{3}$
(B) 1
(C) $1\frac{1}{3}$
(D) $1\frac{3}{5}$
(E) 3

Arithmetic Operations on rational numbers

Substituting the given information in the formula $\text{rate} = \frac{\text{distance}}{\text{time}}$, it can be determined that car X traveled at a rate of $\frac{80 \text{ miles}}{2 \text{ hours}}$, or 40 miles per hour. Thus, car Y traveled at 1.50(40) = 60 miles per hour. At this speed, car Y would travel the 80-mile route in $\frac{80}{60} = \frac{4}{3} = 1\frac{1}{3}$ hours.

The correct answer is C.

186. If the average (arithmetic mean) of the four numbers K, $2K + 3$, $3K - 5$, and $5K + 1$ is 63, what is the value of K?

(A) 11
(B) $15\frac{3}{4}$
(C) 22
(D) 23
(E) $25\frac{3}{10}$

Arithmetic Statistics

Using the formula $\frac{\text{sum of } n \text{ values}}{n} = \text{average}$, the given information can be expressed in the following equation and solved for K.

$$\frac{K + (2K + 3) + (3K - 5) + (5K + 1)}{4} = 63$$

$$\frac{K + 2K + 3K + 5K + 3 - 5 + 1}{4} = 63$$

$$\frac{11K - 1}{4} = 63$$

$$11K - 1 = 252$$

$$11K = 253$$

$$K = 23$$

The correct answer is D.

187. If p is an even integer and q is an odd integer, which of the following must be an odd integer?

(A) $\frac{p}{q}$
(B) pq
(C) $2p + q$
(D) $2(p + q)$
(E) $\frac{3p}{q}$

Arithmetic Properties of numbers

Since it is given that p is even and q is odd, use these properties to test the outcome of each answer choice to determine which one must be odd.

A $\frac{\text{even}}{\text{odd}} = \text{even}$ must be even

B $(\text{even})(\text{odd}) = \text{even}$ must be even

C $2(\text{even}) + \text{odd}$
$= \text{even} + \text{odd} = \text{odd}$ must be odd

D $2(\text{even}) + \text{odd}$
$= 2(\text{odd}) = \text{even}$ must be even

E $\frac{3(\text{even})}{\text{odd}} = \frac{\text{even}}{\text{odd}} = \text{even}$ must be even

The correct answer is C.

188. Drum X is $\frac{1}{2}$ full of oil and drum Y, which has twice the capacity of drum *X*, is $\frac{2}{3}$ full of oil. If all of the oil in drum X is poured into drum Y, then drum Y will be filled to what fraction of its capacity?

(A) $\frac{3}{4}$

(B) $\frac{5}{6}$

(C) $\frac{11}{12}$

(D) $\frac{7}{6}$

(E) $\frac{11}{6}$

Algebra Applied problems

Let y represent the capacity of drum Y. Since Y has twice the capacity of drum X, drum X has half the capacity of drum Y, and thus the capacity of drum X can be expressed as $\frac{1}{2}y$. Since drum X is half full, the amount of oil in drum X is equal to $\frac{1}{2}\left(\frac{1}{2}y\right) = \frac{1}{4}y$. According to the given information, the initial amount of oil in drum Y is $\frac{2}{3}y$. When the oil in drum X is poured into drum Y, drum Y thus contains $\frac{1}{4}y + \frac{2}{3}y = \frac{3}{12}y + \frac{8}{12}y = \frac{11}{12}y$, which is $\frac{11}{12}$ of its capacity.

The correct answer is C.

189. If $x > 0$, $\frac{x}{50} + \frac{x}{25}$ is what percent of x ?

(A) 6%
(B) 25%
(C) 37%
(D) 60%
(E) 75%

Algebra + Arithmetic Simplifying algebraic expressions + Percents

Simplify the expression by using a common denominator for the fractions and solve for x.

If $x > 0$, $\frac{x}{50} + \frac{x}{25} = \frac{x}{50} + \frac{2x}{50} = \frac{3x}{50} = \frac{6x}{100}$ or 6% of x.

The correct answer is A.

190. If the operation ⊛ is defined for all *a* and *b* by the equation $a \circledast b = \frac{a^2b}{3}$, then $2 \circledast (3 \circledast -1) =$

(A) 4
(B) 2
(C) $-\frac{4}{3}$
(D) −2
(E) −4

Arithmetic Operations on rational numbers

The result of the operation $a \circledast b$ can be used wherever the operation $a \circledast b$ occurs. Solve the equation $2 \circledast (3 \circledast -1)$ by calculating each occurrence of the operation ⊛ separately.

First calculate the value of 3 ⊛ −1:

$\frac{3^2(-1)}{3}$

$\frac{9(-1)}{3}$

$\frac{-9}{3}$

−3

Then substitute this calculated value of 3 ⊛ −1 in the expression to find the value of 2 ⊛ −3:

$\frac{2^2(-3)}{3}$

$\frac{4(-3)}{3}$

$\frac{-12}{3}$

−4

The correct answer is E.

191. The inside dimensions of a rectangular wooden box are 6 inches by 8 inches by 10 inches. A cylindrical canister is to be placed inside the box so that it stands upright when the closed box rests on one of its six faces. Of all such canisters that could be used, what is the radius, in inches, of the one that has maximum volume?

(A) 3
(B) 4
(C) 5
(D) 6
(E) 8

Geometry Volume

The largest cylinder that can fit in a rectangular box will have the same height as the box and a diameter equal to the smaller dimension of the top of the box. By definition, the diameter of the canister is twice its radius. One *possible* canister placement in the box is illustrated below.

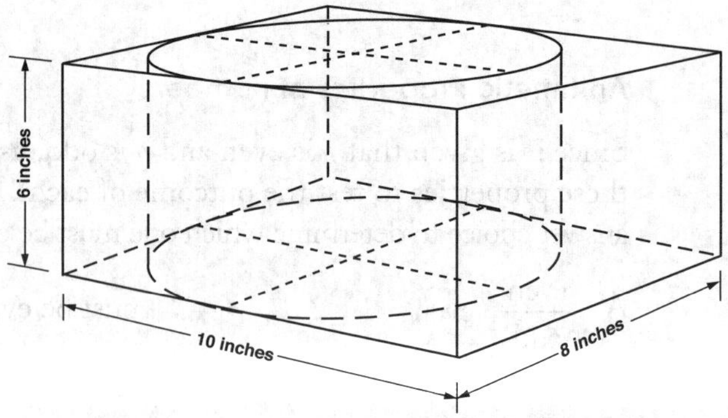

However, since the box can rest on any of three differently sized faces, it is necessary to consider the volume of each possibility. The formula for calculating volume is volume = π(radius)²(height), or $v = \pi r^2 h$; the possible volumes for the canister are those shown in the following table:

Dimensions of the box top	r	h	v
6 by 8	3	10	90π
6 by 10	3	8	72π
8 by 10	4	6	96π

Thus, the radius, in inches, of the canister having the maximum volume is 4.

The correct answer is B.

192. $(\sqrt{2}+1)(\sqrt{2}-1)(\sqrt{3}+1)(\sqrt{3}-1) =$

(A) 2
(B) 3
(C) $2\sqrt{6}$
(D) 5
(E) 6

Arithmetic Operations on radical expressions

Simplify the expression by first recognizing and then multiplying each pair of binomials.

$(\sqrt{2}+1)(\sqrt{2}-1)(\sqrt{3}+1)(\sqrt{3}-1)$

$(\sqrt{2}+1)(\sqrt{2}-1)\times(\sqrt{3}+1)(\sqrt{3}-1)$

$(2+\sqrt{2}-\sqrt{2}-1)(3+\sqrt{3}-\sqrt{3}-1)$

$(2-1)(3-1)$

$(1)(2)$

2

The correct answer is A.

193. In a certain calculus class, the ratio of the number of mathematics majors to the number of students who are not mathematics majors is 2 to 5. If 2 more mathematics majors were to enter the class, the ratio would be 1 to 2. How many students are in the class?

(A) 10
(B) 12
(C) 21
(D) 28
(E) 35

Algebra Simultaneous equations + Applied problems

Letting m represent the number of mathematics majors and n represent the number of non-mathematics majors in the class, the information given about the current student ratio can be expressed as $\frac{m}{n}=\frac{2}{5}$. The information about the ratio of students after adding 2 more mathematics majors can be expressed as $\frac{m+2}{n}=\frac{1}{2}$. Using these two relationships, solve the first equation for m by multiplying and simplifying: $\frac{m}{n}=\frac{2}{5}$ or $5m = 2n$ or $m = 0.4n$. Then, substitute $0.4n$ for m in the second equation, and solve for n by multiplying and simplifying as follows:

$$\frac{0.4n+2}{n}=\frac{1}{2}$$
$$0.8n+4=n$$
$$4=0.2n$$
$$20=n$$

Finally, substitute 20 for n in the equation $\frac{m}{n}=\frac{2}{5}$, and solve for m:

$$\frac{m}{20}=\frac{2}{5}$$
$$5m=40$$
$$m=8$$

Therefore, it can be determined that there are 20 + 8 = 28 students in the class.

The correct answer is D.

194. What is the units digit of $(13)^4(17)^2(29)^3$?

(A) 9
(B) 7
(C) 5
(D) 3
(E) 1

Arithmetic Operations on rational numbers

The units digit of 13^4 is 1, since $3 \times 3 \times 3 \times 3 = 81$; the units digit of 17^2 is 9, since $7 \times 7 = 49$; and the units digit of 29^3 is 9, since $9 \times 9 \times 9 = 729$. Therefore, the units digit of $(13)^4(17)^2(29)^3$ is 1, since $1 \times 9 \times 9 = 81$.

The correct answer is E.

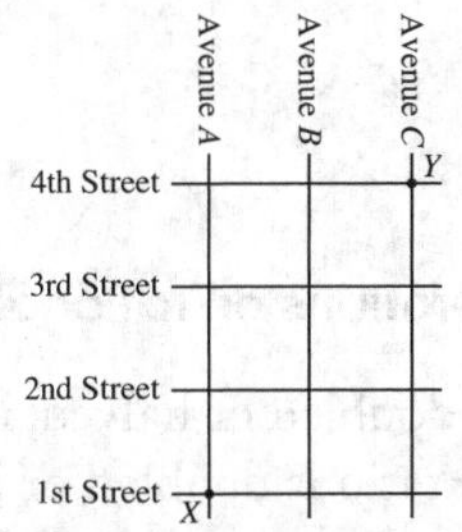

195. Pat will walk from intersection X to intersection Y along a route that is confined to the square grid of four streets and three avenues shown in the preceding map. How many routes from X to Y can Pat take that have the minimum possible length?

(A) 6
(B) 8
(C) 10
(D) 14
(E) 16

Arithmetic Elementary combinatorics

In order to walk from intersection X to intersection Y by one of the routes of minimum possible length, Pat must travel only upward or rightward between the intersections on the map. Let U represent upward movements and R represent rightward movements. It takes 3 upward and 2 rightward movements to complete the route.

The following 10 routes are possible:

UUURR	*URRUU*
UURUR	*RRUUU*
UURRU	*RUUUR*
URUUR	*RUURU*
URURU	*RURUU*

The correct answer is C.

196. The ratio, by volume, of soap to alcohol to water in a certain solution is 2:50:100. The solution will be altered so that the ratio of soap to alcohol is doubled while the ratio of soap to water is halved. If the altered solution will contain 100 cubic centimeters of alcohol, how many cubic centimeters of water will it contain?

(A) 50
(B) 200
(C) 400
(D) 625
(E) 800

Arithmetic Operations on rational numbers

When a ratio is doubled or halved, it means the first value of the ratio is doubled or halved. Thus, when the soap to alcohol ratio of 2:50 is doubled, the new ratio of soap to alcohol is 4:50. When the soap to water ratio of 2:100 is halved, the new ratio of soap to water is 1:100.

Originally the ratio of soap to alcohol to water was 2:50:100. Since soap is now represented by 4, it is necessary to change 1:100 to 4:400 to incorporate all the ratios together. The new solution ratio of soap to alcohol to water is thus 4:50:400.

Since 100 cubic centimeters represents the 50 parts of alcohol in the new solution, 800 cubic centimeters will represent the 400 parts of water in the solution.

The correct answer is E.

197. If 75 percent of a class answered the first question on a certain test correctly, 55 percent answered the second question on the test correctly, and 20 percent answered neither of the questions correctly, what percent answered both correctly?

(A) 10%
(B) 20%
(C) 30%
(D) 50%
(E) 65%

Arithmetic Percents

For questions of this type, it is convenient to draw a Venn diagram to represent the conditions in the problem. For example, the given information can be depicted:

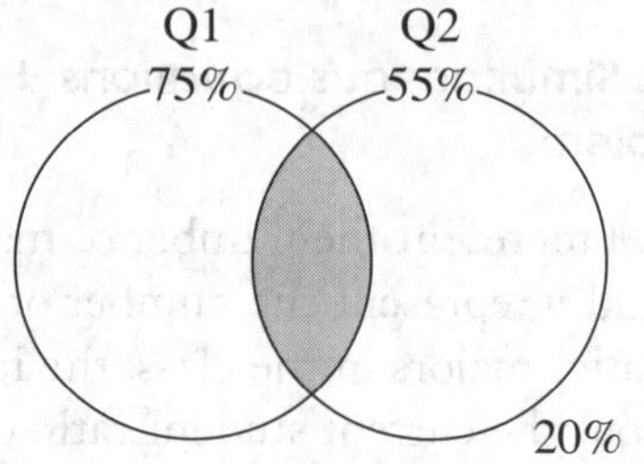

In the diagram it can be seen that the 80% of the class answering a question correctly is represented by the two circles. Let x represent the percent of the class that answered both questions correctly, that is, the shaded region above. Since the sum of the circles minus their overlap equals 80% of the class, the information given in the problem can then be expressed as $75\% + 55\% - x = 80\%$. This equation can be solved for x as follows:

$75\% + 55\% - x = 80\%$
$130\% - x = 80\%$
$-x = -50\%$
$x = 50\%$

The correct answer is D.

198. If $\frac{1}{2} + \frac{1}{3} + \frac{1}{4} = \frac{13}{x}$, which of the following must be an integer?

I. $\frac{x}{8}$

II. $\frac{x}{12}$

III. $\frac{x}{24}$

(A) I only
(B) II only
(C) I and III only
(D) II and III only
(E) I, II, and III

Algebra First-degree equations

First, using the common denominator of the fractions, solve the equation for x.

$\frac{1}{2}+\frac{1}{3}+\frac{1}{4}=\frac{13}{x}$

$\frac{6}{12}+\frac{4}{12}+\frac{3}{12}=\frac{13}{x}$

$\frac{13}{12}=\frac{13}{x}$

$x=12$

Then, consider this value of x in each of the answer choices:

I. $\frac{x}{8}=\frac{12}{8}=1.5$ NOT an integer

II. $\frac{x}{12}=\frac{12}{12}=1$ Integer

III. $\frac{x}{24}=\frac{12}{24}=0.5$ NOT an integer

The correct answer is B.

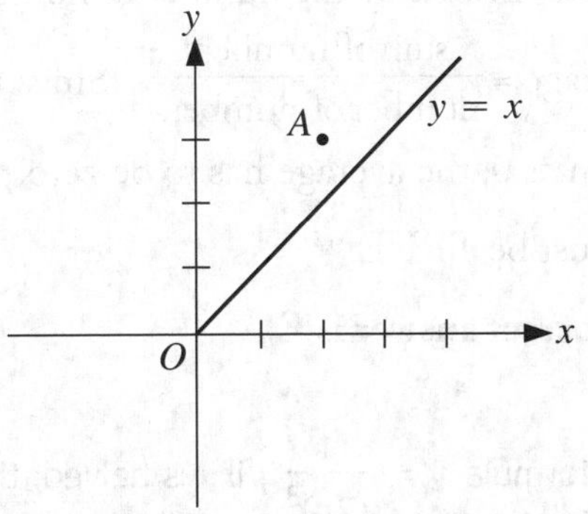

199. In the rectangular coordinate system above, the line $y = x$ is the perpendicular bisector of segment *AB* (not shown), and the *x*-axis is the perpendicular bisector of segment *BC* (not shown). If the coordinates of point *A* are (2, 3), what are the coordinates of point *C*?

(A) (−3, −2)
(B) (−3, 2)
(C) (2, −3)
(D) (3, −2)
(E) (2, 3)

Geometry Simple coordinate geometry

Since the line $y = x$ is the perpendicular bisector of AB, B is the reflection of A through this line. In any reflection through the line $y = x$, the x-coordinate and the y-coordinate of a point become interchanged. Thus, if the coordinates of A are (2, 3), the coordinates of B are (3, 2).

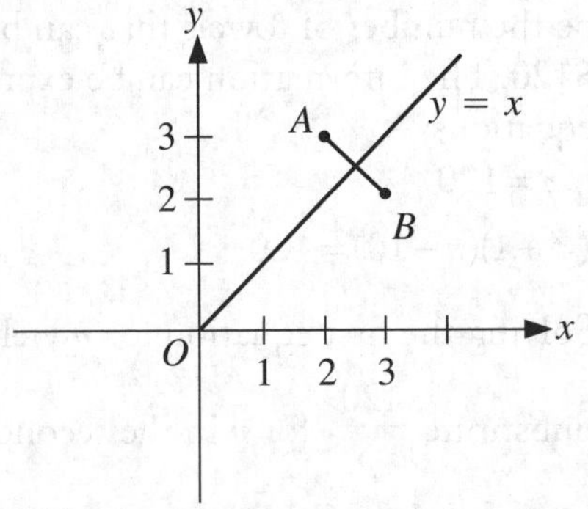

Since the x-axis is the perpendicular bisector of BC, C is the reflection of B through the x-axis. In any reflection through the x-axis, the x-coordinate remains the same, and the sign of the y-coordinate changes.

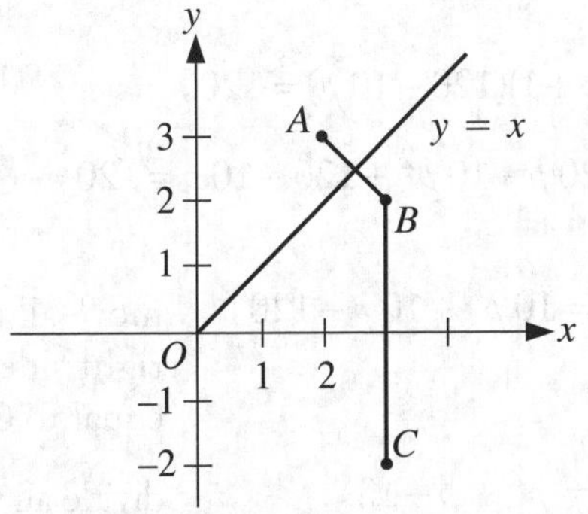

Since the coordinates of B are (3, 2), the coordinates of C are therefore (3, −2).

The correct answer is D.

200. A store currently charges the same price for each towel that it sells. If the current price of each towel were to be increased by $1, 10 fewer of the towels could be bought for $120, excluding sales tax. What is the current price of each towel?

(A) $1
(B) $2
(C) $3
(D) $4
(E) $12

Algebra Applied problems

Let p be the current price per towel, and let n be the number of towels that can be bought for $120. The information can be expressed in the equations:

$pn = 120$

$(p+1)(n-10) = 120$

Solving the first equation for n yields $n = \frac{120}{p}$.

Substitute $\frac{120}{p}$ for n in the second equation, and solve for p as follows:

$(p+1)(\frac{120}{p} - 10) = 120$

$(p+1)(\frac{120}{p} - 10)p = 120p$ — multiply both sides by p

$(p+1)(120 - 10p) = 120p$ — distribute the p

$120p - 10p^2 + 120 - 10p = 120p$ — multiply the binomials

$0 = 10p^2 + 10p - 120$ — move all terms to right side, setting equal to 0

$0 = p^2 + p - 12$ — divide all terms by 10

$0 = (p+4)(p-3)$ — solve for p

$p = -4, p = 3$

Since p needs to be a price, it cannot be -4; it must be 3.

The correct answer is C.

201. If the sum of n consecutive integers is 0, which of the following must be true?

I. n is an even number.
II. n is an odd number.
III. The average (arithmetic mean) of the n integers is 0.

(A) I only
(B) II only
(C) III only
(D) I and III
(E) II and III

Arithmetic Properties of numbers

Consider each answer choice to determine which must be true.

For the sum of n consecutive integers to be 0, there must be an equal number of consecutive integers to the left of 0 and to the right of 0 to balance each other (that is, to cancel each other out) in the addition process. Therefore, because in this case the sum of n consecutive integers will always consist of the single number 0 plus these pairs of negative and positive integers, the sum of n consecutive integers has to be an odd number.

I. Must be FALSE

II. Must be TRUE

The average of a set of numbers is the sum of the numbers divided by the number of numbers, that is, average $= \frac{\text{sum of numbers}}{\text{number of numbers}}$. Since the sum is given as 0, the average has to be zero.

III. Must be TRUE

The correct answer is E.

202. In the formula $V = \frac{1}{(2r)^3}$, if r is halved, then V is multiplied by

(A) 64
(B) 8
(C) 1
(D) $\frac{1}{8}$
(E) $\frac{1}{64}$

Algebra Simplifying algebraic expressions

If r is halved, then it is possible to substitute $\frac{1}{2}r$ for r in the formula and simplify:

$$\frac{1}{(2(\frac{1}{2}r))^3} = \frac{1}{8(\frac{1}{8}r^3)} = \frac{1}{r^3}$$

Compared to the original, where

$V = \frac{1}{(2r)^3} = \frac{1}{8r^3}$, the new value of V is $\frac{1}{r^3}$ or

$8\left(\frac{1}{8r^3}\right) = 8V$. When r is halved, V is multiplied by 8.

The correct answer is B.

203. A certain bakery has 6 employees. It pays annual salaries of \$14,000 to each of 2 employees, \$16,000 to 1 employee, and \$17,000 to each of the remaining 3 employees. The average (arithmetic mean) annual salary of these employees is closest to which of the following?

(A) \$15,200
(B) \$15,500
(C) \$15,800
(D) \$16,000
(E) \$16,400

Arithmetic Statistics

The given information can be expressed as follows, using the formula $\frac{\text{sum of n values}}{\text{n}} = \text{average}$, and then simplified:

$$\frac{2(14{,}000)+16{,}000+3(17{,}000)}{6} = \frac{95{,}000}{6} = 15{,}833$$

The correct answer is C.

204. If x is equal to the sum of the even integers from 40 to 60, inclusive, and y is the number of even integers from 40 to 60, inclusive, what is the value of $x + y$?

(A) 550
(B) 551
(C) 560
(D) 561
(E) 572

Arithmetic Properties of numbers

There are 21 integers between 40 and 60, inclusive, of which 11 are even. Thus, the value of y is 11.

Since the 11 integers are consecutive even integers, the sum of the even integers can be found by taking the sum of the first integer and the last integer and then multiplying that sum by the number of even integers divided by 2. Therefore, the value of x can be calculated as $x = \frac{11(40+60)}{2} = \frac{1100}{2} = 550$.

Thus, the value of $x + y = 550 + 11 = 561$.

The correct answer is D.

Number of Solid-Colored Marbles in Three Jars			
Jar	Number of red marbles	Number of green marbles	Total number of red and green marbles
P	x	y	80
Q	y	z	120
R	x	z	160

205. In the table above, what is the number of green marbles in jar R?

(A) 70
(B) 80
(C) 90
(D) 100
(E) 110

Arithmetic + Algebra Interpretation of tables + Applied problems

First, set up an equation to find the total number of marbles in the three jars as follows:

$x + y + y + z + x + z = 80 + 120 + 160$

$2x + 2y + 2z = 360$ combine the like terms

$x + y + z = 180$ divide both sides by 2

Then, since it can be seen from the table that the number of green marbles in jar R is z, solve for z to answer the problem. To do this most efficiently, use the information from the table for jar P, which is that $x + y = 80$.

$x + y + z = 180$

$80 + z = 180$ substitute 80 for $x + y$

$z = 100$

The correct answer is D.

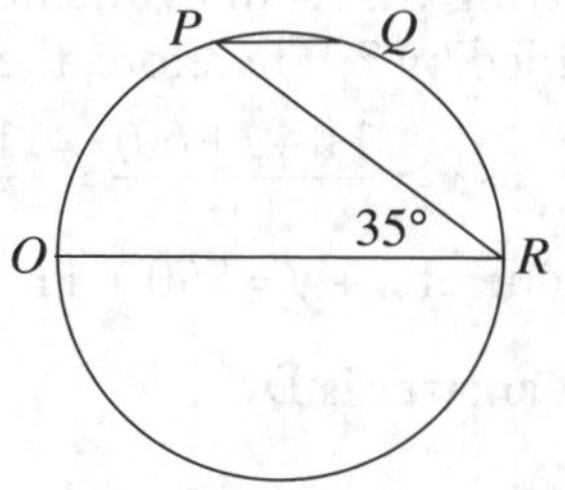

206. In the circle above, *PQ* is parallel to diameter *OR*, and *OR* has length 18. What is the length of minor arc *PQ*?

(A) 2π

(B) $\frac{9\pi}{4}$

(C) $\frac{7\pi}{2}$

(D) $\frac{9\pi}{2}$

(E) 3π

Geometry Circles + Area

Minor arcs always have twice the measure of their inscribed angles. Since the measure of inscribed angle *PRO* is 35°, the measure of minor arc *OP* is 70°. Since *PQ* is parallel to *OR*, angles *PRO* and *QPR* are congruent alternate interior angles. This makes the measure of inscribed angle *QPR* = 35° and the measure of minor arc *QR* = 70°.

Thus, the measure of minor arc *PQ* is 180° – 70° – 70° = 40°, and the length of minor arc *PQ* is $\frac{40}{360} = \frac{1}{9}$ of the length of the circumference of the circle.

Then, since a circumference $C = \pi(\text{diameter})$ and since diameter *OR* has length 18:

$C = \pi d$

$C = \pi(18)$

$C = 18\pi$

Therefore, the length of minor arc $PQ = \frac{1}{9}(18\pi) = 2\pi$.

The correct answer is A.

207. If $n = 4p$, where p is a prime number greater than 2, how many different positive even divisors does n have, including n?

(A) 2
(B) 3
(C) 4
(D) 6
(E) 8

Arithmetic Properties of numbers

Since p is a prime greater than 2, p must be odd. Therefore, the possible even divisors of $n = 4p$ are 2, 4, $2p$, and $4p$.

The correct answer is C.

208. *S* is a set containing 9 different numbers. *T* is a set containing 8 different numbers, all of which are members of *S*. Which of the following statements cannot be true?

(A) The mean of *S* is equal to the mean of *T*.
(B) The median of *S* is equal to the median of *T*.
(C) The range of *S* is equal to the range of *T*.
(D) The mean of *S* is greater than the mean of *T*.
(E) The range of *S* is less than the range of *T*.

Algebra Concepts of Sets

According to the problem, there is only one number, n, that is in *S* that is not in *T*. It is necessary only to show that there is or is not a value of n that makes the statement true. The statement does not always have to be true.

For A through C, let *S* be the integers from 1 to 9, and let *T* be the same integers except for 5.

A Both means = 5 CAN be true

B Both medians = 5 CAN be true

C Both ranges = 9 – 1 = 8 CAN be true

D Let *S* be the integers from 1 though 9, and let *T* be the integers from 1 through 8; the mean of *S* = 5, and the mean of *T* = 4.5. CAN be true

E If *n* is the maximum or minimum value of *S*, it would be removed from *T*, and the range of *T* would thus be less than the range of *S*. If, on the other hand, *n* is not the maximum or minimum value of *S*, the range of *S* would be equal to the range of *T*. The range of *S* cannot be less than the range of *T*. CANNOT be true

The correct answer is E.

209. How many different positive integers are factors of 441 ?

(A) 4
(B) 6
(C) 7
(D) 9
(E) 11

Arithmetic Properties of numbers

Recognize that 441 = (9)(49) = $(3^2)(7^2)$.

Listing all combinations of the factors of 441 gives $1, 3, 7, 3^2, (3)(7), 7^2, (3^2)(7), (3)(7^2)$, and 441, and thus, the following nine different positive integers:

1, 3, 7, 9, 21, 49, 63, 147, and 441.

The correct answer is D.

210. A television manufacturer produces 600 units of a certain model each month at a cost to the manufacturer of $90 per unit and all of the produced units are sold each month. What is the minimum selling price per unit that will ensure that the monthly profit (revenue from sales minus the manufacturer's cost to produce) on the sales of these units will be at least $42,000?

(A) $110
(B) $120
(C) $140
(D) $160
(E) $180

Algebra Inequalities

Letting *x* be the amount the manufacturer sells each unit for in dollars, the profit per unit can be expressed as *x* – 90. Then, the information that the profit on 600 units is at least (greater than or equal to) $42,000 can be expressed in the following inequality, which can be solved for *x*.

$600(x-90) \geq 42{,}000$

$x-90 \geq 70$

$x \geq 160$

The correct answer is D.

211. If 4*x* + 3*y* = –2 and 3*x* + 6 = 0, what is the value of *y*?

(A) $-3\frac{1}{3}$
(B) -2
(C) $-\frac{2}{3}$
(D) $\frac{2}{3}$
(E) 2

Algebra Simultaneous equations

Solve the second equation for *x*. Then, substitute the calculated value of *x* for *x* where it appears in the first equation, and solve for *y*.

$4x+3y=-2$

$3x+6=0$

$3x=-6$ solve second equation for *x*

$x=-2$

$4(-2)+3y=-2$ substitute –2 for *x* in first equation

$-8+3y=-2$

$3y=6$ solve for *y*

$y=2$

The correct answer is E.

I. 72, 73, 74, 75, 76
II. 74, 74, 74, 74, 74
III. 62, 74, 74, 74, 89

212. The data sets I, II, and III above are ordered from greatest standard deviation to least standard deviation in which of the following?

(A) I, II, III
(B) I, III, II
(C) II, III, I
(D) III, I, II
(E) III, II, I

Arithmetic Statistics

To have a large standard deviation means the values are spread far apart with significant variation. Data set II has no variation, so the standard deviation is 0. Data set I has only small variations, so it will have some standard deviation. Data set III has the extreme values 62 and 89, making its standard deviation the largest. The order of the data sets from largest to smallest standard deviation is therefore III, I, II.

The correct answer is D.

213. Which of the following is the lowest positive integer that is divisible by 2, 3, 4, 5, 6, 7, 8, and 9?

(A) 15,120
(B) 3,024
(C) 2,520
(D) 1,890
(E) 1,680

Arithmetic Properties of numbers

The lowest common multiple of 2, 3, 4, 5, 6, 7, 8, and 9 will be the value that has the same prime factors as these numbers and also has them occur the maximum number of times that each particular prime occurs as a factor in any of the 8 numbers.

So, consider the prime factors of these numbers, as well as the maximum occurrences of each prime in any one of the numbers in the list (designated here by the symbol *):

$2 = 2^1$
$3 = 3^1$
$4 = 2^2$
$5 = 5^1$ *
$6 = 2^1 3^1$
$7 = 7^1$ *
$8 = 2^3$ *
$9 = 3^2$ *

Thus, the least common multiple is $2^3 \times 3^2 \times 5^1 \times 7^1 = 2{,}520$.

The correct answer is C.

214. Of the 50 researchers in a workgroup, 40 percent will be assigned to team A and the remaining 60 percent to team B. However, 70 percent of the researchers prefer team A and 30 percent prefer team B. What is the lowest possible number of researchers who will not be assigned to the team they prefer?

(A) 15
(B) 17
(C) 20
(D) 25
(E) 30

Arithmetic Percents

The number of researchers assigned to team A will be (0.40)(50) = 20, and so 30 will be assigned to team B. The number of researchers who prefer team A is (0.70)(50) = 35, and the rest, 15, prefer team B.

If all 15 who prefer team B are assigned to team B, which is to have 30 researchers, then 15 who prefer team A will need to be assigned to team B. Alternatively, since there are only 20 spots on team A, 35 – 20 = 15 who prefer team A but will have to go to team B instead.

The correct answer is A.

215. If m is the average (arithmetic mean) of the first 10 positive multiples of 5 and if M is the median of the first 10 positive multiples of 5, what is the value of $M - m$?

(A) −5
(B) 0
(C) 5
(D) 25
(E) 27.5

Arithmetic Statistics

The first 10 positive multiples of 5 are 5, 10, 15, 20, 25, 30, 35, 40, 45, and 50. From this, the average of the 10 multiples, that is, $\frac{\text{sum of values}}{\text{number of values}}$, can be calculated:

$$m = \frac{5+10+15+20+25+30+35+40+45+50}{10}$$
$$= \frac{275}{10} = 27.5$$

Since there is an even number of multiples, the median, M, is the average of the middle two numbers, 25 and 30:

$$M = \frac{25+30}{2} = 27.5.$$

Therefore, the median minus the average is

$$M - m = 27.5 - 27.5 = 0.$$

The correct answer is B.

216. If $m > 0$ and x is m percent of y, then, in terms of m, y is what percent of x?

(A) $100m$

(B) $\frac{1}{100m}$

(C) $\frac{1}{m}$

(D) $\frac{10}{m}$

(E) $\frac{10{,}000}{m}$

Arithmetic Percents

The information that x is m percent of y can be expressed as $x = \frac{m}{100}y$ and solved for y as follows:

$$x = \frac{m}{100}y$$

$$\frac{100}{m}x = y$$

Then, to convert the fraction $\frac{100}{m}$ to an equivalent percent, multiply by 100, thus obtaining the value of $\frac{10{,}000}{m}$.

The correct answer is E.

217. A certain junior class has 1,000 students and a certain senior class has 800 students. Among these students, there are 60 sibling pairs, each consisting of 1 junior and 1 senior. If 1 student is to be selected at random from each class, what is the probability that the 2 students selected will be a sibling pair?

(A) $\frac{3}{40{,}000}$

(B) $\frac{1}{3{,}600}$

(C) $\frac{9}{2{,}000}$

(D) $\frac{1}{60}$

(E) $\frac{1}{15}$

Arithmetic Probability

The probability of selecting a student from the 1,000 juniors who is a member of a sibling pair is $\frac{60}{1{,}000}$. Then, the probability of selecting the 1 student among the 800 seniors who is the other member of that pair is $\frac{1}{800}$. Therefore, the probability that the 2 students selected will be a sibling pair is $\left(\frac{60}{1{,}000}\right)\left(\frac{1}{800}\right) = \frac{3}{40{,}000}$.

The correct answer is A.

218. Which of the following CANNOT be the median of the three ordered positive integers x, y, and z?

(A) x

(B) z

(C) $x + z$

(D) $\frac{x + z}{2}$

(E) $\frac{x + z}{3}$

Arithmetic Statistics

Since there is an odd number of numbers, the median is the middle number in the list.

A Any one of x, y, or z could be the median value.
B Any one of x, y, or z could be the median value.
C The sum of any two numbers would be greater than the median value, and thus $x + z$ CANNOT be the median.
D $\frac{x+z}{2}$ could be the median if x, y, and z were 2, 4, and 6, respectively.

E $\frac{x+z}{3}$ could be the median if x, y, and z were 2, 4, and 10, respectively.

The correct answer is C.

219. What is the 25th digit to the right of the decimal point in the decimal form of $\frac{6}{11}$?

(A) 3
(B) 4
(C) 5
(D) 6
(E) 7

Arithmetic Properties of numbers

The fraction in its decimal form is $\frac{6}{11} = 0.545454\ldots$. Every odd-numbered digit to the right of the decimal point is 5, so the 25th digit must be 5.

The correct answer is C.

220. John and Mary were each paid x dollars in advance to do a certain job together. John worked on the job for 10 hours and Mary worked 2 hours less than John. If Mary gave John y dollars of her payment so that they would have received the same hourly wage, what was the dollar amount, in terms of y, that John was paid in advance?

(A) $4y$
(B) $5y$
(C) $6y$
(D) $8y$
(E) $9y$

Algebra Applied problems

Let w be the amount of Mary and John's same hourly wage. To set their hourly pay equal, John, who worked 10 hours, needs to be paid $10w$, and Mary, who worked 8 hours, needs to be paid $8w$. Since Mary gave John y dollars, Mary now has $x - y$ dollars and John now has $x + y$ dollars. Their pay can thus be expressed as follows:

$x - y = 8w$	Mary's pay
$x + y = 10w$	John's pay

Subtract the first equation from the second and solve for w.

$2y = 2w$

$y = w$

Substitute y for w in the second equation, and solve for x, the amount each was paid in advance.

$x + y = 10y$

$x = 9y$

The correct answer is E.

221. $1 + \cfrac{1}{1 + \cfrac{1}{1 + \cfrac{1}{3}}} =$

(A) $\frac{4}{7}$
(B) $\frac{4}{3}$
(C) $\frac{11}{8}$
(D) $\frac{11}{7}$
(E) $\frac{7}{4}$

Arithmetic Operations on rational numbers

Work the problem.

$$1+\cfrac{1}{1+\cfrac{1}{1+\cfrac{1}{3}}}=1+\cfrac{1}{1+\cfrac{1}{\frac{4}{3}}}=1+\cfrac{1}{1+\cfrac{3}{4}}$$

$$=1+\cfrac{1}{\frac{7}{4}}=1+\frac{4}{7}=\frac{11}{7}$$

The correct answer is D.

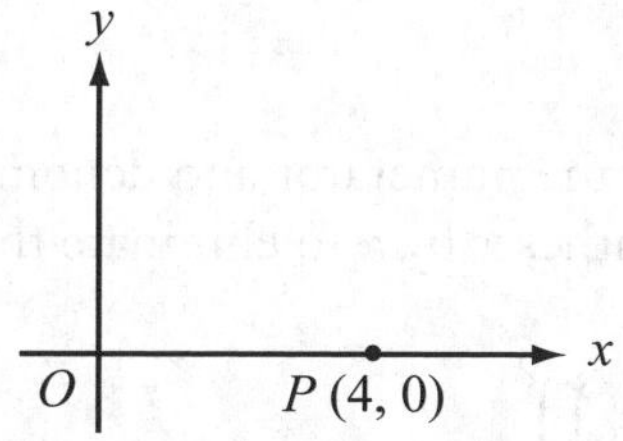

222. In the rectangular coordinate system above, if point *R* (not shown) lies on the positive *y*-axis and the area of triangle *ORP* is 12, what is the *y*-coordinate of point *R*?

(A) 3
(B) 6
(C) 9
(D) 12
(E) 24

Geometry Simple coordinate geometry + Area

Since *O* and *P* of triangle *ORP* are already drawn and *R* has to be on the positive *y*-axis, the triangle is a right triangle with its base length the distance from the origin *O* (0,0) to *P* (4,0), which is 4.

Since the area of a triangle $=\frac{\text{(base)(height)}}{2}$, the information about the area and base can be expressed as follows and solved for the height of triangle *OPR*:

$12=\frac{(4)(\text{height})}{2}$

$12 = 2(\text{height})$ — simplify the right side

$6 = \text{height}$ — solve for the height

On the *y*-axis, the *x*-coordinate is 0 and the *y* coordinate is the distance up the axis that the point is located. In this case, the *y*-coordinate is the height of the triangle.

The correct answer is B.

223. Car A is 20 miles behind car B, which is traveling in the same direction along the same route as car A. Car A is traveling at a constant speed of 58 miles per hour and car B is traveling at a constant speed of 50 miles per hour. How many hours will it take for car A to overtake and drive 8 miles ahead of car B?

(A) 1.5
(B) 2.0
(C) 2.5
(D) 3.0
(E) 3.5

Arithmetic Operations on rational numbers

Understand that car A first has to travel 20 miles to catch up to car B and then has to travel an additional 8 miles ahead of car B, for a total of 28 extra miles to travel relative to car B. It can be stated that car A is traveling 58 −50 = 8 miles per hour faster than car B. Solving the distance = (rate)(time) formula for time yields $\frac{\text{distance}}{\text{rate}} = \text{time}$.

By substitution into this formula, it will take car A $\frac{28 \text{ miles}}{8 \text{ miles per hour}} = 3.5$ hours to overtake and drive 8 miles ahead of car B.

The correct answer is E.

224. For the past n days, the average (arithmetic mean) daily production at a company was 50 units. If today's production of 90 units raises the average to 55 units per day, what is the value of n?

(A) 30
(B) 18
(C) 10
(D) 9
(E) 7

Arithmetic + Algebra Statistics + Applied problems + Simultaneous equations

Let x be the total production of the past n days.

Using the formula average$=\frac{\text{sum of values}}{\text{number of values}}$, the information in the problem can be expressed in the following two equations:

$50 = \frac{x}{n}$ daily average of 50 units over the past n days

$55 = \frac{x+90}{n+1}$ increased daily average when including today's 90 units

Solving the first equation for x gives $x = 50n$. Then substituting $50n$ for x in the second equation gives the following that can be solved for n:

$55 = \frac{50n+90}{n+1}$

$55(n+1) = 50n+90$ multiply both sides by $(n + 1)$

$55n+55 = 50n+90$ distribute the 55

$5n = 35$ subtract $50n$ and 55 from both sides

$n = 7$ divide both sides by 5

The correct answer is E.

$$\left(\frac{x+1}{x-1}\right)^2$$

225. If $x \neq 0$ and $x \neq 1$, and if x is replaced by $\frac{1}{x}$ everywhere in the expression above, then the resulting expression is equivalent to

(A) $\left(\frac{x+1}{x-1}\right)^2$

(B) $\left(\frac{x-1}{x+1}\right)^2$

(C) $\frac{x^2+1}{1-x^2}$

(D) $\frac{x^2-1}{x^2+1}$

(E) $-\left(\frac{x-1}{x+1}\right)^2$

Algebra Simplifying algebraic expressions

Substitute $\frac{1}{x}$ for x in the expression and simplify.

$$\left(\frac{\frac{1}{x}+1}{\frac{1}{x}-1}\right)^2$$

Multiply the numerator and denominator inside the parentheses by x to eliminate the compound fractions.

$$\left(\frac{x\left(\frac{1}{x}+1\right)}{x\left(\frac{1}{x}-1\right)}\right)^2$$

Distribute the x's.

$$\left(\frac{1+x}{1-x}\right)^2$$

Since this is not one of the answer choices, it is necessary to simplify further. With the knowledge that $1 + x = x + 1$ and $1 - x = -(x - 1)$, it can be stated that

$$\left(\frac{1+x}{1-x}\right)^2 = \left(\frac{x+1}{-(x-1)}\right)^2 = \left(-\frac{x+1}{(x-1)}\right)^2 = \left(\frac{x+1}{x-1}\right)^2$$

because the negative, when squared, is positive.

The correct answer is A.

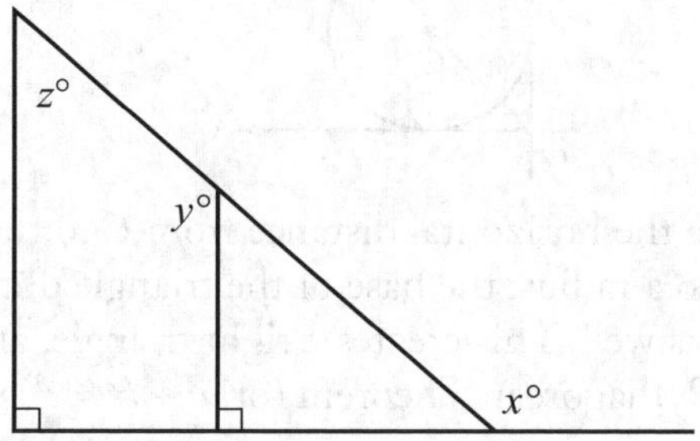

226. In the figure above, if $z = 50$, then $x + y =$

(A) 230
(B) 250
(C) 260
(D) 270
(E) 290

Geometry Angles + Measures of angles

Refer to the figure below.

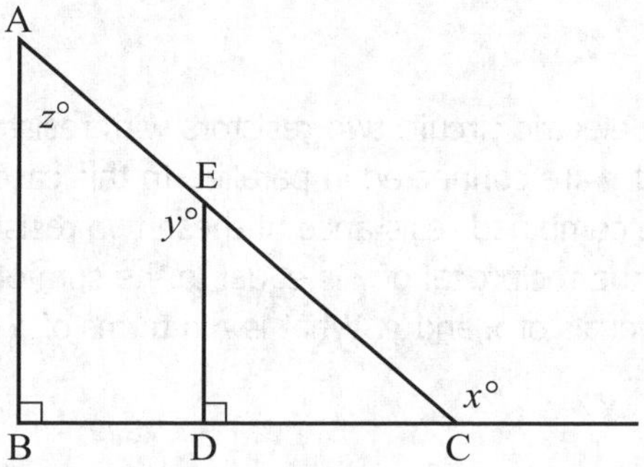

Triangle *ABC* is a right triangle, and segment $\overline{AB}$ is parallel to segment $\overline{ED}$ since they are both perpendicular to the same segment ($\overline{BC}$). Therefore, $m\angle DEC = m\angle BAC = z° = 50°$. So, since $\angle DEC$ and $\angle AED$ form a straight line at *E*, $y + 50 = 180$, or $y = 130$.

The measure of an exterior angle of a triangle is the sum of the measures of the nonadjacent interior angles. Thus,

$m\angle x = m\angle z + 90°$, or

$m\angle x = 50° + 90° = 140°$

Thus, $x + y = 140 + 130 = 270$.

The correct answer is D.

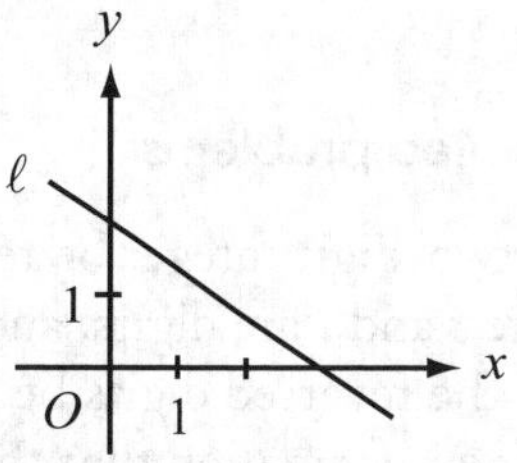

227. In the coordinate system above, which of the following is the equation of line ℓ?

(A) $2x - 3y = 6$
(B) $2x + 3y = 6$
(C) $3x + 2y = 6$
(D) $2x - 3y = -6$
(E) $3x - 2y = -6$

Geometry Simple coordinate geometry

The line is shown going through the points (0, 2) and (3, 0). The slope of the line can be found with the formula $\text{slope} = \frac{\text{change in } y}{\text{change in } x} = \frac{y_2 - y_1}{x_2 - x_1}$, for two points (x_1, y_1) and (x_2, y_2). Thus, the slope of this line equals $\frac{0-2}{3-0} = -\frac{2}{3}$. Using the formula for a line of $y = mx + b$, where *m* is the slope and *b* is the *y*-intercept (in this case, 2), an equation for this line is $y = -\frac{2}{3}x + 2$.

Since this equation must be compared to the available answer choices, the following further steps should be taken:

$y = -\frac{2}{3}x + 2$

$3y = -2x + 6$ multiply both sides by 3

$2x + 3y = 6$ add $2x$ to both sides

The correct answer is B.

228. If a two-digit positive integer has its digits reversed, the resulting integer differs from the original by 27. By how much do the two digits differ?

(A) 3
(B) 4
(C) 5
(D) 6
(E) 7

Algebra Applied problems

Let the one two-digit integer be represented by $10t + s$, where s and t are digits, and let the other integer with the reversed digits be represented by $10s + t$. The information that the difference between the integers is 27 can be expressed in the following equation, which can be solved for the answer.

$(10s+t)-(10t+s)=27$	
$10s+t-10t-s=27$	distribute the negative
$9s-9t=27$	combine like terms
$s-t=3$	divide both sides by 9

Thus, it is seen that the two digits s and t differ by 3.

The correct answer is A.

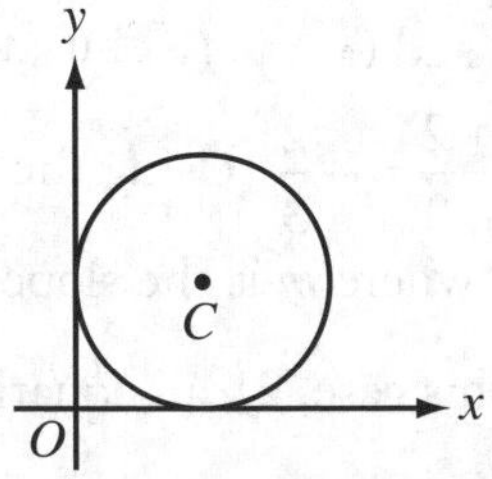

229. The circle with center C shown above is tangent to both axes. If the distance from O to C is equal to k, what is the radius of the circle, in terms of k?

(A) k

(B) $\frac{k}{\sqrt{2}}$

(C) $\frac{k}{\sqrt{3}}$

(D) $\frac{k}{2}$

(E) $\frac{k}{3}$

Geometry Circles + Simple coordinate geometry

In a circle, all distances from the edge of the circle to the center are the same and called the radius, r.

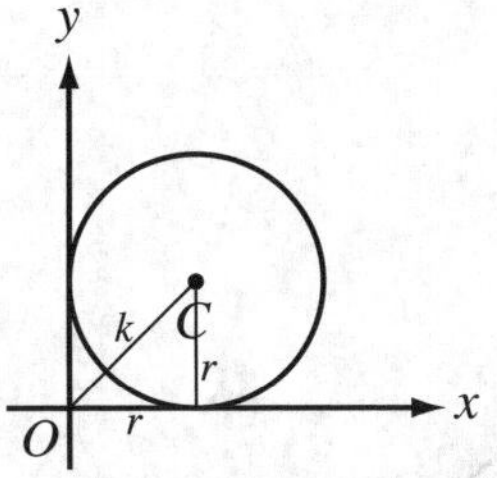

Since the horizontal distance from C to the y-axis is also a radius, the base of the triangle drawn will be r as well. This creates a right triangle, and so the Pythagorean Theorem (or $a^2 + b^2 = c^2$) applies.

$r^2+r^2=k^2$	substitute values into Pythagorean theorem;
$2r^2=k^2$	combine like terms
$r^2=\frac{k^2}{2}$	divide both sides by 2
$r=\sqrt{\frac{k^2}{2}}$	take the square root of both sides
$r=\frac{k}{\sqrt{2}}$	simplify the square root

The correct answer is B.

230. In an electric circuit, two resistors with resistances x and y are connected in parallel. In this case, if r is the combined resistance of these two resistors, then the reciprocal of r is equal to the sum of the reciprocals of x and y. What is r in terms of x and y?

(A) xy

(B) $x + y$

(C) $\frac{1}{x+y}$

(D) $\frac{xy}{x+y}$

(E) $\frac{x+y}{xy}$

Algebra Applied problems

Note that two numbers are reciprocals of each other if and only if their product is 1. Thus the reciprocals of r, x, and y are $\frac{1}{r}, \frac{1}{x}$, and $\frac{1}{y}$ respectively. So, according to the problem, $\frac{1}{r}=\frac{1}{x}+\frac{1}{y}$. To solve this equation for r, begin by creating a common denominator on the right side by multiplying the first fraction by $\frac{y}{y}$ and the second fraction by $\frac{x}{x}$:

$$\frac{1}{r} = \frac{1}{x} + \frac{1}{y}$$

$$\frac{1}{r} = \frac{y}{xy} + \frac{x}{xy}$$

$$\frac{1}{r} = \frac{x+y}{xy}$$ combine the fractions on the right side

$$r = \frac{xy}{x+y}$$ invert the fractions on both sides

The correct answer is D.

231. Xavier, Yvonne, and Zelda each try independently to solve a problem. If their individual probabilities for success are $\frac{1}{4}$, $\frac{1}{2}$, and $\frac{5}{8}$, respectively, what is the probability that Xavier and Yvonne, but not Zelda, will solve the problem?

(A) $\frac{11}{8}$

(B) $\frac{7}{8}$

(C) $\frac{9}{64}$

(D) $\frac{5}{64}$

(E) $\frac{3}{64}$

Arithmetic Probability

Since the individuals' probabilities are independent, they can be multiplied to figure out the combined probability. The probability of Xavier's success is given as $\frac{1}{4}$, and the probability of Yvonne's success is given as $\frac{1}{2}$. Since the probability of Zelda's success is given as $\frac{5}{8}$, then the probability of her NOT solving the problem is $1 - \frac{5}{8} = \frac{3}{8}$. Thus, the combined probability is $\left(\frac{1}{4}\right)\left(\frac{1}{2}\right)\left(\frac{3}{8}\right) = \frac{3}{64}$.

The correct answer is E.

232. If $\frac{1}{x} - \frac{1}{x+1} = \frac{1}{x+4}$, then x could be

(A) 0

(B) −1

(C) −2

(D) −3

(E) −4

Algebra Second-degree equations

Solve the equation for x. Begin by multiplying all the terms by $x(x + 1)(x + 4)$ to eliminate the denominators.

$$\frac{1}{x} - \frac{1}{x+1} = \frac{1}{x+4}$$

$$(x+1)(x+4) - x(x+4) = x(x+1)$$

$$(x+4)(x+1-x) = x(x+1)$$ factor the $(x + 4)$ out front on the left side

$$(x+4)(1) = x(x+1)$$ simplify

$$x+4 = x^2 + x$$ distribute the x on the right side

$$4 = x^2$$ subtract x from both sides

$$\pm 2 = x$$ take the square root of both sides

Both −2 and 2 are square roots of 4 since $(-2)^2 = 4$ and $(2)^2 = 4$. Thus, x could be −2.

The correct answer is C.

233. $\left(\frac{1}{2}\right)^{-3}\left(\frac{1}{4}\right)^{-2}\left(\frac{1}{16}\right)^{-1} =$

(A) $\left(\frac{1}{2}\right)^{-48}$

(B) $\left(\frac{1}{2}\right)^{-11}$

(C) $\left(\frac{1}{2}\right)^{-6}$

(D) $\left(\frac{1}{8}\right)^{-11}$

(E) $\left(\frac{1}{8}\right)^{-6}$

Arithmetic Operations on rational numbers

It is clear from the answer choices that all three factors need to be written with a common denominator, and they thus become

$$\left(\frac{1}{2}\right)^{-3} = \left(\frac{1}{2}\right)^{-3}$$

$$\left(\frac{1}{4}\right)^{-2} = \left(\left(\frac{1}{2}\right)^{2}\right)^{-2} = \left(\frac{1}{2}\right)^{-4}$$

$$\left(\frac{1}{16}\right)^{-1} = \left(\left(\frac{1}{2}\right)^{4}\right)^{-1} = \left(\frac{1}{2}\right)^{-4}$$

So, $\left(\frac{1}{2}\right)^{-3}\left(\frac{1}{4}\right)^{-2}\left(\frac{1}{16}\right)^{-1} =$

$$\left(\frac{1}{2}\right)^{-3}\left(\frac{1}{2}\right)^{-4}\left(\frac{1}{2}\right)^{-4} = \left(\frac{1}{2}\right)^{-3-4-4} = \left(\frac{1}{2}\right)^{-11}.$$

The correct answer is B.

234. In a certain game, a large container is filled with red, yellow, green, and blue beads worth, respectively, 7, 5, 3, and 2 points each. A number of beads are then removed from the container. If the product of the point values of the removed beads is 147,000, how many red beads were removed?

(A) 5
(B) 4
(C) 3
(D) 2
(E) 0

Arithmetic Properties of numbers

From this, the red beads represent factors of 7 in the total point value of 147,000. Since 147,000 = 147(1,000), and 1,000 = 10^3, then 147 is all that needs to be factored to determine the factors of 7. Factoring 147 yields 147 = (3)(49) = (3)(7^2). This means there are 2 factors of 7, or 2 red beads.

The correct answer is D.

235. If $\dfrac{2}{1+\dfrac{2}{y}} = 1$, then $y =$

(A) -2
(B) $-\dfrac{1}{2}$
(C) $\dfrac{1}{2}$
(D) 2
(E) 3

Algebra First-degree equations

Solve for y.

$$\frac{2}{1+\frac{2}{y}} = 1$$

$1+\frac{2}{y} = 2$ — the product of the means equals the product of the extremes

$\frac{2}{y} = 1$ — subtract 1 from each side

$y = 2$ — solve for y

The correct answer is D.

236. If a, b, and c are consecutive positive integers and $a < b < c$, which of the following must be true?

I. $c - a = 2$
II. abc is an even integer.
III. $\dfrac{a+b+c}{3}$ is an integer.

(A) I only
(B) II only
(C) I and II only
(D) II and III only
(E) I, II, and III

Arithmetic Properties of numbers

Since a, b, and c are consecutive positive integers and $a < b < c$, then $b = a + 1$ and $c = a + 2$.

I. $c - a = (a + 2) - a = 2$ MUST be true

II. (odd)(even)(odd) = even MUST be true

(even)(odd)(even) = even MUST be true

III.

$$\frac{a+b+c}{3} = \frac{a+(a+1)+(a+2)}{3} = \frac{3a+3}{3} = a+1 = b$$

b is an integer MUST be true

The correct answer is E.

237. A part-time employee whose hourly wage was increased by 25 percent decided to reduce the number of hours worked per week so that the employee's total weekly income would remain unchanged. By what percent should the number of hours worked be reduced?

(A) 12.5%
(B) 20%
(C) 25%
(D) 50%
(E) 75%

Algebra Applied problems

Let w represent the original hourly wage. Letting h be the original number of hours the employee worked per week, the original weekly income can be expressed as wh. Given a 25% increase in hourly wage, the employee's new wage is thus $1.25w$. Letting H be the reduced number of hours, the problem can then be expressed as:

$1.25wH = wh$ (new wage)(new hours) = (original wage)(original hours)

By dividing both sides by w, this equation can be solved for H:

$1.25H = h$

$H = 0.8h$

Since the new hours should be 0.8 = 80% of the original hours, the number of hours worked should be reduced by 20%.

The correct answer is B.

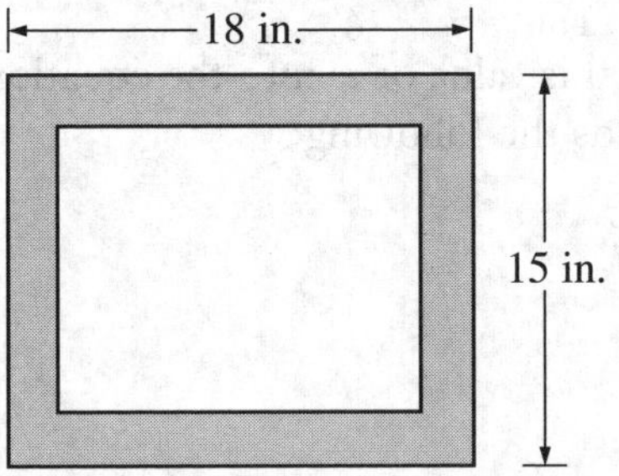

Note: Figure not drawn to scale.

238. The shaded region in the figure above represents a rectangular frame with length 18 inches and width 15 inches. The frame encloses a rectangular picture that has the same area as the frame itself. If the length and width of the picture have the same ratio as the length and width of the frame, what is the length of the picture, in inches?

(A) $9\sqrt{2}$
(B) $\frac{3}{2}$
(C) $\frac{9}{\sqrt{2}}$
(D) $15\left(1-\frac{1}{\sqrt{2}}\right)$
(E) $\frac{9}{2}$

Geometry Area

Let l and w represent the length and width in inches, respectively, of the picture. Since the formula for the area of a rectangle is area = (length)(width), the area of the picture can be expressed as lw, and the area of the frame can be expressed as (18)(15) – lw or 270 – lw. Since it is given that these two areas are equal, then $lw = 270 - lw$, and thus $2lw = 270$ or $lw = 135$.

Additionally, it is given that the length and width of the picture have the same ratio as the length and width of the frame, and so $\frac{l}{w} = \frac{18}{15}$. Thus, $15l = 18w$ or $\frac{15}{18}l = w$ or $\frac{5}{6}l = w$.

Substituting this value of w into the equation $lw = 135$ yields the following:

$$l\left(\frac{5}{6}l\right) = 135$$

$$\frac{5}{6}l^2 = 135$$

$$l^2 = 162$$

$$l = \sqrt{162}$$

$$l = \sqrt{81 \cdot 2}$$

$$l = 9\sqrt{2}$$

The correct answer is A.

239. Of the 200 students at College T majoring in one or more of the sciences, 130 are majoring in chemistry and 150 are majoring in biology. If at least 30 of the students are not majoring in either chemistry or biology, then the number of students majoring in both chemistry and biology could be any number from

(A) 20 to 50
(B) 40 to 70
(C) 50 to 130
(D) 110 to 130
(E) 110 to 150

Arithmetic Operations on rational numbers

A Venn diagram will help with this problem. There are two extremes that need to be considered: (1) having the least number of students majoring in both chemistry and biology and (2) having the greatest number of students majoring in both chemistry and biology.

(1) If at least 30 science majors are not majoring in either chemistry or biology, then at most 200 – 30 = 170 students can be majoring in either or both. Since there are 130 + 150 = 280 biology and chemistry majors (some of whom are individual students majoring in both areas), then there are at least 280 – 170 = 110 majoring in both. The diagram following shows this relationship.

170 TOTAL STUDENTS
FOR CHEMISTRY AND BIOLOGY MAJORS

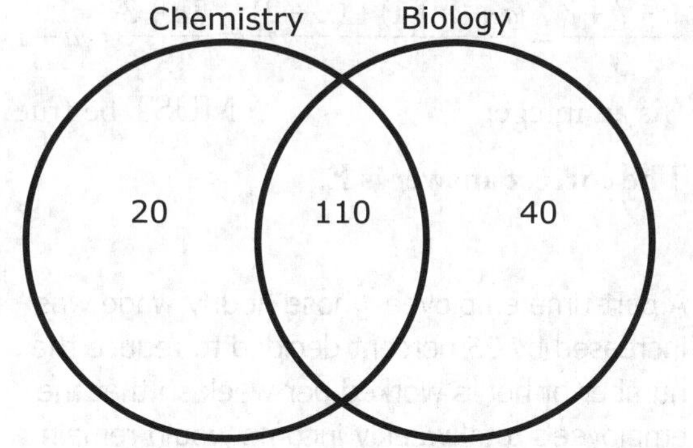

(2) The maximum number of students who can be majoring in both chemistry and biology is 130, since 130 is the number given as majoring in chemistry, the smaller of the two subject areas. Logically, there cannot be more double majors than there are majors in the smaller field. The diagram below shows this relationship in terms of the given numbers of majors in each subject area.

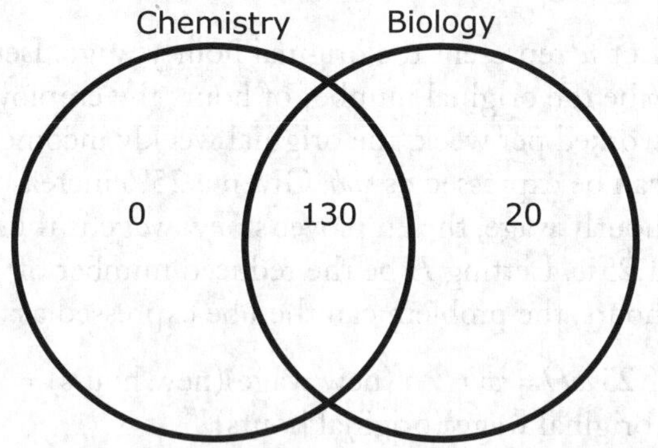

Additionally, from this diagram it can be seen that the total number of students who are majoring in chemistry, or in biology, or in both = 130 + 20 = 150. Thus, there are 200 – 150 = 50 students who are neither chemistry nor biology majors. This number is not in conflict with the condition that 30 is the minimum number of non-chemistry and non-biology majors.

Thus, the number of students majoring in both chemistry and biology could be any number from a minimum of 110 to a maximum of 130.

The correct answer is D.

240. Seed mixture X is 40 percent ryegrass and 60 percent bluegrass by weight; seed mixture Y is 25 percent ryegrass and 75 percent fescue. If a mixture of X and Y contains 30 percent ryegrass, what percent of the weight of the mixture is X?

(A) 10%

(B) $33\frac{1}{3}$ %

(C) 40%

(D) 50%

(E) $66\frac{2}{3}$ %

Algebra Applied problems

Let X be the amount of seed mixture X in the final mixture, and let Y be the amount of seed mixture Y in the final mixture. The final mixture of X and Y needs to contain 30 percent ryegrass seed, so any other kinds of grass seed are irrelevant to the solution to this problem. The information about the ryegrass percentages for X, Y, and the final mixture can be expressed in the following equation and solved for X.

$0.40X + 0.25Y = 0.30(X + Y)$

$0.40X + 0.25Y = 0.30X + 0.30Y$ distribute the 0.30 on the right side

$0.10X = 0.05Y$ subtract $0.30X$ and $0.25Y$ from both sides

$X = 0.5Y$ divide both sides by 0.10

Using this, the percent of the weight of the combined mixture $(X + Y)$ that is X is

$$\frac{X}{X+Y} = \frac{0.5Y}{0.5Y+Y} = \frac{0.5Y}{1.5Y} = \frac{0.5}{1.5} = 0.33\bar{3} = 33\frac{1}{3}\%$$

The correct answer is B.

241. If the integer n has exactly three positive divisors, including 1 and n, how many positive divisors does n^2 have?

(A) 4
(B) 5
(C) 6
(D) 8
(E) 9

Arithmetic + Algebra Properties of numbers + Simplifying algebraic expressions

Most integers have even numbers of factors. For example, 12 has 1, 2, 3, 4, 6, and 12 as factors, and these factors pair up and are multiplied to equal the integer. Even prime numbers have two factors, 1 and themselves. For any integer to have exactly three positive divisors, or factors, it must be the perfect square of a prime number. (Remember, a perfect square is a positive integer that has an integer as its square root.) Thus, the integer would have 1, itself, and the prime number that is its square root as its three factors. Since here the integer is n, then its three factors are 1, $\sqrt{n}$, and n, recognizing that $\sqrt{n}$ is an integer as well.

Then, the factors of n^2 can be any integer factor of $n^2 = n \cdot n = 1 \cdot \sqrt{n} \cdot \sqrt{n} \cdot \sqrt{n} \cdot \sqrt{n}$. Thus, there are 5 positive divisors of n^2: 1, $\sqrt{n}$, $\sqrt{n}\sqrt{n} = n$, $\sqrt{n}\sqrt{n}\sqrt{n} = n\sqrt{n}$, and $\sqrt{n}\sqrt{n}\sqrt{n}\sqrt{n} = n^2$.

The correct answer is B.

242. If n is a positive integer, then $n(n + 1)(n + 2)$ is

(A) even only when n is even
(B) even only when n is odd
(C) odd whenever n is odd
(D) divisible by 3 only when n is odd
(E) divisible by 4 whenever n is even

Arithmetic Properties of numbers

The numbers n, $n + 1$, and $n + 2$ are consecutive integers. Therefore, they are either (odd)(even)(odd) = even, or they are (even)(odd)(even) = even. In either case, the product of $(n + 1)(n + 2)$ is even. Thus, each of answer choices A, B, and C is false.

A statement is false if a counterexample can be shown. Test the statement using an even multiple of 3 as the value of n in the equation. When $n = 6$, $n(n + 1)(n + 2) = 6(7)(8) = 336$. Since in this counterexample n is even but 336 is still divisible by 3, answer choice D is shown to be false. When n is even (meaning divisible by 2), $n + 2$ is also even (and also divisible by 2). So $n(n + 1)(n + 2)$ is always divisible by 4.

The correct answer is E.

243. A straight pipe 1 yard in length was marked off in fourths and also in thirds. If the pipe was then cut into separate pieces at each of these markings, which of the following gives all the different lengths of the pieces, in fractions of a yard?

(A) $\frac{1}{6}$ and $\frac{1}{4}$ only

(B) $\frac{1}{4}$ and $\frac{1}{3}$ only

(C) $\frac{1}{6}$, $\frac{1}{4}$, and $\frac{1}{3}$

(D) $\frac{1}{12}$, $\frac{1}{6}$, and $\frac{1}{4}$

(E) $\frac{1}{12}$, $\frac{1}{6}$, and $\frac{1}{3}$

Arithmetic Operations on rational numbers

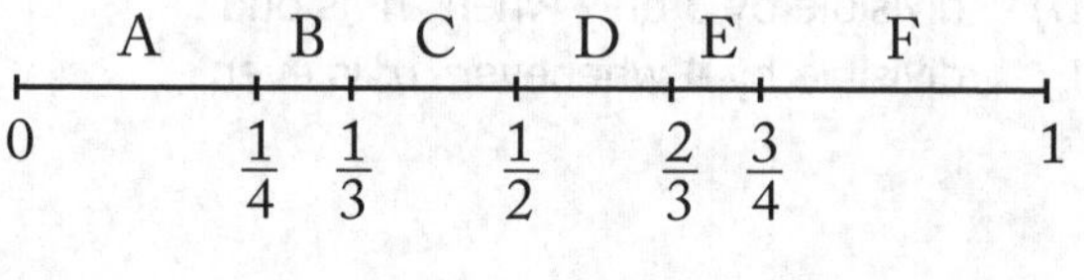

The number line above illustrates the markings on the pipe. Since the pipe is cut at the five markings, six pieces of pipe are produced. The length of each piece, in fractions of a yard, is given in the following table.

Pipe piece	Length
A	$\frac{1}{4} - 0 = \frac{1}{4}$
B	$\frac{1}{3} - \frac{1}{4} = \frac{1}{12}$
C	$\frac{1}{2} - \frac{1}{3} = \frac{1}{6}$
D	$\frac{2}{3} - \frac{1}{2} = \frac{1}{6}$
E	$\frac{3}{4} - \frac{2}{3} = \frac{1}{12}$
F	$1 - \frac{3}{4} = \frac{1}{4}$

The correct answer is D.

244. If $\frac{0.0015 \times 10^m}{0.03 \times 10^k} = 5 \times 10^7$, then $m - k =$

(A) 9
(B) 8
(C) 7
(D) 6
(E) 5

Arithmetic Operations on rational numbers

Work the problem.

$$\frac{0.0015 \times 10^m}{0.03 \times 10^k} = 5 \times 10^7$$

$$\frac{0.0015}{0.03} \times 10^{m-k} = 5 \times 10^7$$

$$0.05 \times 10^{m-k} = 5 \times 10^7$$

$$5 \times 10^{-2} \times 10^{m-k} = 5 \times 10^7$$

$$5 \times 10^{m-k-2} = 5 \times 10^7$$

$$10^{m-k-2} = 10^7$$

Setting the exponents equal gives $m - k - 2 = 7$, so $m - k = 9$.

The correct answer is A.

245. If $x + y = a$ and $x - y = b$, then $2xy =$

(A) $\frac{a^2 - b^2}{2}$

(B) $\frac{b^2 - a^2}{2}$

(C) $\frac{a - b}{2}$

(D) $\frac{ab}{2}$

(E) $\frac{a^2 + b^2}{2}$

Algebra Simplifying algebraic expressions

Begin by adding the two given equations to establish a value for x. Adding $x + y = a$ and $x - y = b$ gives $2x = a + b$ and thus $x = \frac{a+b}{2}$. Then, substitute this value of x into the first equation and solve for y:

$$\frac{a+b}{2} + y = a$$

$y = a - \frac{a+b}{2}$ subtract $\frac{a+b}{2}$ from both sides

$y = \frac{2a}{2} - \frac{a+b}{2}$ create common denominator

$y = \frac{2a-a-b}{2}$ combine fractions

$y = \frac{a-b}{2}$ simplify fraction

Finally, solve the equation, substituting the values now established for x and y:

$$2xy = 2\left(\frac{a+b}{2}\right)\left(\frac{a-b}{2}\right)$$

$$2xy = \frac{2(a+b)(a-b)}{4}$$

$$2xy = \frac{a^2 - b^2}{2}$$

The correct answer is A.

246. A rectangular circuit board is designed to have width w inches, perimeter p inches, and area k square inches. Which of the following equations must be true?

(A) $w^2 + pw + k = 0$
(B) $w^2 - pw = 2k = 0$
(C) $2w^2 + pw + 2k = 0$
(D) $2w^2 - pw - 2k = 0$
(E) $2w^2 - pw + 2k = 0$

Algebra Applied problems

Since there are squared terms in all the choices, the solution will most likely come from the area formula of a rectangle. The area, k, of a rectangle equals its length, l, times its width, w. First, the unknown length of the rectangle needs to be determined from the perimeter. The formula for a perimeter p is $2l + 2w = p$, and thus $2l = p - 2w$, and $l = \frac{p-2w}{2}$. Substituting this into the formula area = (length)(width) or $k = lw$ gives:

$$k = \left(\frac{p-2w}{2}\right)w$$

$k = \frac{pw - 2w^2}{2}$ distribute the w

$2k = pw - 2w^2$ multiply both sides by 2

$2w^2 - pw + 2k = 0$ set equal to 0 by moving all terms to the left side

The correct answer is E.

p, r, s, t, u

247. An arithmetic sequence is a sequence in which each term after the first is equal to the sum of the preceding term and a constant. If the list of numbers shown above is an arithmetic sequence, which of the following must also be an arithmetic sequence?

I. $2p, 2r, 2s, 2t, 2u$
II. $p - 3, r - 3, s - 3, t - 3, u - 3$
III. p^2, r^2, s^2, t^2, u^2

(A) I only
(B) II only
(C) III only
(D) I and II
(E) II and III

Algebra Concepts of sets + Functions

It follows from the definition of arithmetic sequence given in the first sentence that there is a constant c such that $r - p = s - r = t - s = u - t = c$.

To test a sequence to determine whether it is arithmetic, calculate the difference of each pair of consecutive terms in that sequence to see if a constant difference is found.

I. $2r - 2p = 2(r - p) = 2c$
$2s - 2r = 2(s - r) = 2c$
$2t - 2s = 2(t - s) = 2c$
$2u - 2t = 2(u - t) = 2c$ MUST be arithmetic

II. $(r - 3) - (p - 3) = r - p = c$ MUST be arithmetic

Since all values are just three less than the original, the same common difference applies.

III. $r^2 - p^2 = (r - p)(r + p) = c(r + p)$
$s^2 - r^2 = (s - r)(s + r) = c(s + r)$ NEED NOT be arithmetic

Since p, r, s, t, and u are an arithmetic sequence, $r + p \neq s + r$, because $p \neq s$ unless $c = 0$.

The correct answer is D.

248. Right triangle PQR is to be constructed in the xy-plane so that the right angle is at P and PR is parallel to the x-axis. The x- and y-coordinates of P, Q, and R are to be integers that satisfy the inequalities $-4 \leq x \leq 5$ and $6 \leq y \leq 16$. How many different triangles with these properties could be constructed?

(A) 110
(B) 1,100
(C) 9,900
(D) 10,000
(E) 12,100

Geometry + Arithmetic Simple coordinate geometry + Elementary combinatorics

In the xy-plane, right triangle PQR is located in the rectangular area determined by $-4 \leq x \leq 5$ and $6 \leq y \leq 16$ (see following illustration).

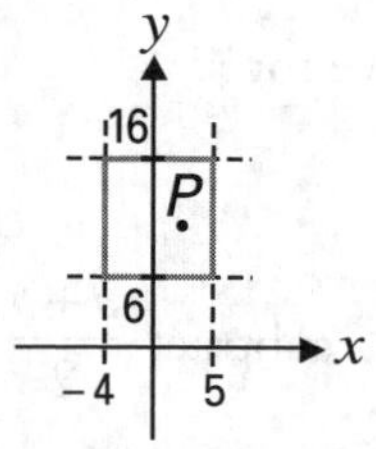

Since the coordinates of points P, Q, and R are integers, there are 10 possible x values and 11 possible y values, so point P can be any one of $10(11) = 110$ points in the rectangular area.

Since R has to be horizontal with respect to P, it has the same y value as P and can have 9 other x values. Q has to be vertical with respect to R, so it has the same x value as R and can have 10 other y values. This gives $110(9)(10) = 9{,}900$ possible triangles.

The correct answer is C.

249. If n is a positive integer less than 200 and $\frac{14n}{60}$ is an integer, then n has how many different positive prime factors?

(A) 2
(B) 3
(C) 5
(D) 6
(E) 8

Arithmetic Properties of numbers

Since $\frac{14n}{60} = \frac{7n}{30}$ is an integer and n is an integer, it follows that n is divisible by 30. The possible values of n that are less than 200 are therefore 30, 60, 90, 120, 150, and 180. Determining the positive prime factors of these 6 numbers will thus identify how many different prime factors n has.

$30 = (2)(3)(5)$

$60 = (2^2)(3)(5)$

$90 = (2)(3^2)(5)$

$120 = (2^3)(3)(5)$

$150 = (2)(3)(5^2)$

$180 = (2^2)(3^2)(5)$

The positive prime factors of n are thus 2, 3, and 5.

The correct answer is B.

6.0 Data Sufficiency

6.0 Data Sufficiency

Data sufficiency questions appear in the Quantitative section of the GMAT® exam. Multiple-choice Data sufficiency questions are intermingled with problem solving questions throughout the section. You will have 75 minutes to complete the Quantitative section of the GMAT® exam, or about 2 minutes to answer each question. These questions require knowledge of the following topics:

- Arithmetic
- Elementary algebra
- Commonly known concepts of geometry

Data sufficiency questions are designed to measure your ability to analyze a quantitative problem, recognize which given information is relevant, and determine at what point there is sufficient information to solve a problem. In these questions, you are to classify each problem according to the five fixed answer choices, rather than find a solution to the problem.

Each Data sufficiency question consists of a question, often accompanied by some initial information, and two statements, labeled (1) and (2), which contain additional information. You must decide whether the information in each statement is sufficient to answer the question or—if neither statement provides enough information—whether the information in the two statements together is sufficient. It is also possible that the statements in combination do not give enough information to answer the question.

Begin by reading the initial information and the question carefully. Next, consider the first statement. Does the information provided by the first statement enable you to answer the question? Go on to the second statement. Try to ignore the information given in the first statement when you consider whether the second statement provides information that, by itself, allows you to answer the question. Now you should be able to say, for each statement, whether it is sufficient to determine the answer.

Next, consider the two statements in tandem. Do they, together, enable you to answer the question?

Look again at your answer choices. Select the one that most accurately reflects whether the statements provide the information required to answer the question.

6.1 Test-Taking Strategies for Data Sufficiency Questions

1. **Do not waste valuable time solving a problem.**
   You only need to determine whether sufficient information is given to solve it.
2. **Consider each statement separately first.**
   Then you can decide whether each alone gives sufficient information to solve the problem. Be sure to disregard the information given in statement (1) when you evaluate the information given in statement (2). If either, or both, of the statements give(s) sufficient information to solve the problem, select the answer corresponding to the description of which statement(s) give(s) sufficient information to solve the problem.
3. **Judge the statements in tandem if neither statement is sufficient by itself.**
   It is possible that the two statements together do not provide sufficient information. Once you decide, select the answer corresponding to the description of whether the statements together give sufficient information to solve the problem.
4. **Answer the question asked.**
   For example, if the question asks, "What is the value of y?" for an answer statement to be sufficient, you must be able to find one and only one value for y. Being able to determine minimum or maximum values for an answer (e.g., $y = x + 2$) is not sufficient, because such answers constitute a range of values rather than the specific value of y.
5. **Be very careful not to make unwarranted assumptions based on the images represented.**
   Figures are not necessarily drawn to scale; they are generalized figures showing little more than intersecting line segments and the relationships of points, angles, and regions. So, for example, if a figure described as a rectangle looks like a square, do *not* conclude that it is, in fact, a square just by looking at the figure.

If statement 1 is sufficient, then the answer must be **A or D.**

If statement 2 is not sufficient, then the answer must be **A.**

If statement 2 is sufficient, then the answer must be **D.**

If statement 1 is not sufficient, then the answer must be **B, C, or E.**

If statement 2 is sufficient, then the answer must be **B.**

If statement 2 is not sufficient, then the answer must be **C or E.**

If both statements together are sufficient, then the answer must be **C.**

If both statements together are still not sufficient, then the answer must be **E.**

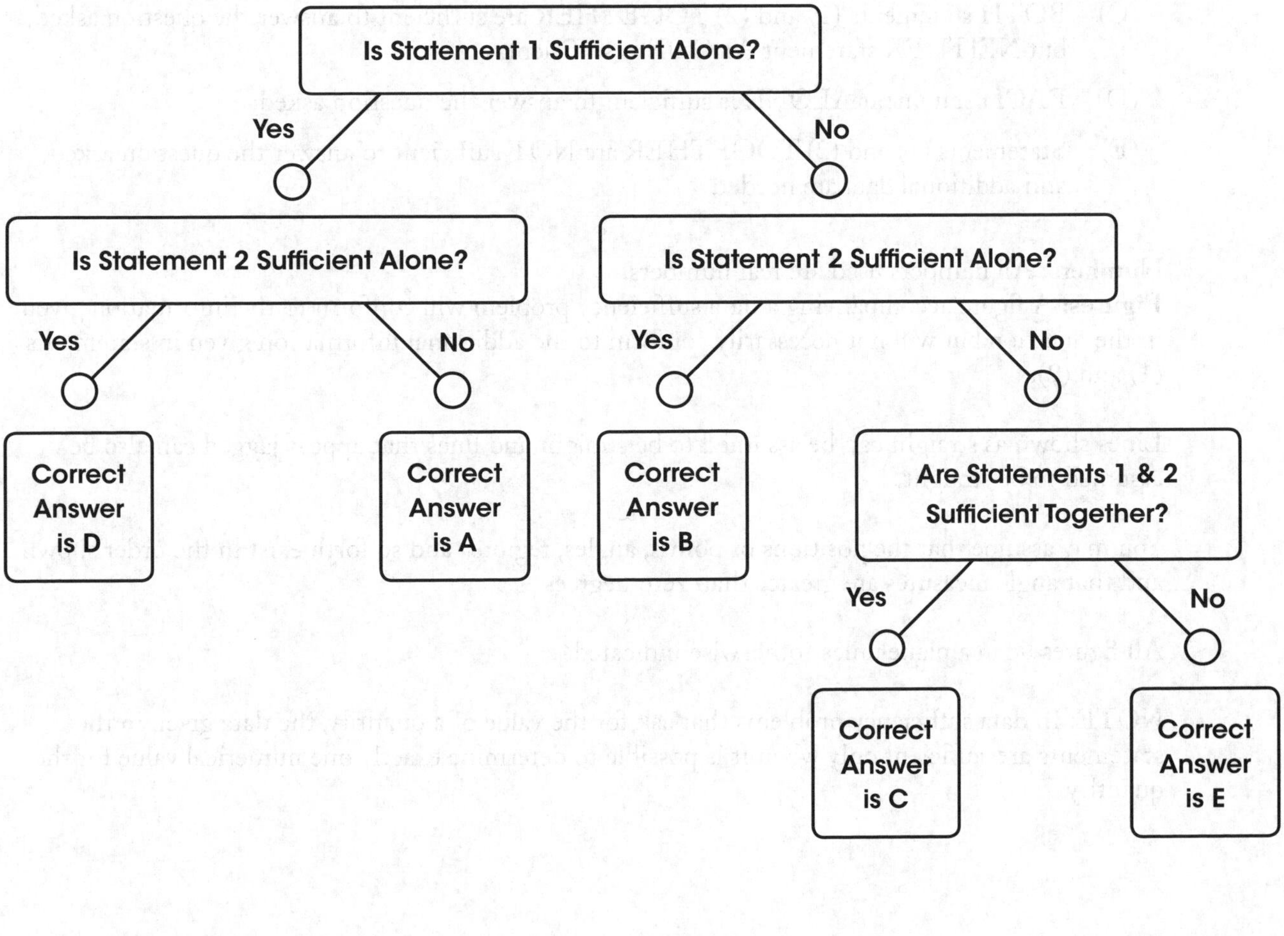

6.2 The Directions

These directions are very similar to those you will see for data sufficiency questions when you take the GMAT® test. If you read the directions carefully and understand them clearly before going to sit for the exam, you will not need to spend too much time reviewing them when you take the GMAT® exam.

Each data sufficiency problem consists of a question and two statements, labeled (1) and (2), that give data. You have to decide whether the data given in the statements are *sufficient* for answering the question. Using the data given in the statements *plus* your knowledge of mathematics and everyday facts (such as the number of days in July or the meaning of *counterclockwise*), you must indicate whether the data given in the statements are sufficient for answering the questions and then indicate one of the following answer choices:

(A) Statement (1) ALONE is sufficient, but statement (2) alone is not sufficient to answer the question asked;

(B) Statement (2) ALONE is sufficient, but statement (1) alone is not sufficient to answer the question asked;

(C) BOTH statements (1) and (2) TOGETHER are sufficient to answer the question asked, but NEITHER statement ALONE is sufficient;

(D) EACH statement ALONE is sufficient to answer the question asked;

(E) Statements (1) and (2) TOGETHER are NOT sufficient to answer the question asked, and additional data are needed.

Numbers: All numbers used are real numbers.
Figures: A figure accompanying a data sufficiency problem will conform to the information given in the question but will not necessarily conform to the additional information given in statements (1) and (2).

Lines shown as straight can be assumed to be straight and lines that appear jagged can also be assumed to be straight.

You may assume that the positions of points, angles, regions, and so forth exist in the order shown and that angle measures are greater than zero degrees.

All figures lie in a plane unless otherwise indicated.

NOTE: In data sufficiency problems that ask for the value of a quantity, the data given in the statements are sufficient only when it is possible to determine exactly one numerical value for the quantity.

6.3 Data Sufficiency Sample Questions

A Statement (1) ALONE is sufficient, but statement (2) alone is not sufficient.
B Statement (2) ALONE is sufficient, but statement (1) alone is not sufficient.
C BOTH statements TOGETHER are sufficient, but NEITHER statement ALONE is sufficient.
D EACH statement ALONE is sufficient.
E Statements (1) and (2) TOGETHER are NOT sufficient to answer the question asked, and additional data are needed.

1. How much is 20 percent of a certain number?

   (1) 10 percent of the number is 5.
   (2) 40 percent of twice the number is 40.

2. A thoroughly blended biscuit mix includes only flour and baking powder. What is the ratio of the number of grams of baking powder to the number of grams of flour in the mix?

   (1) Exactly 9.9 grams of flour is contained in 10 grams of the mix.
   (2) Exactly 0.3 gram of baking powder is contained in 30 grams of the mix.

3. What is the value of $|x|$?

   (1) $x = -|x|$
   (2) $x^2 = 4$

4. Is r greater than 0.27?

   (1) r is greater than $\frac{1}{4}$.
   (2) r is equal to $\frac{3}{10}$.

5. What is the value of the sum of a list of n odd integers?

   (1) $n = 8$
   (2) The square of the number of integers on the list is 64.

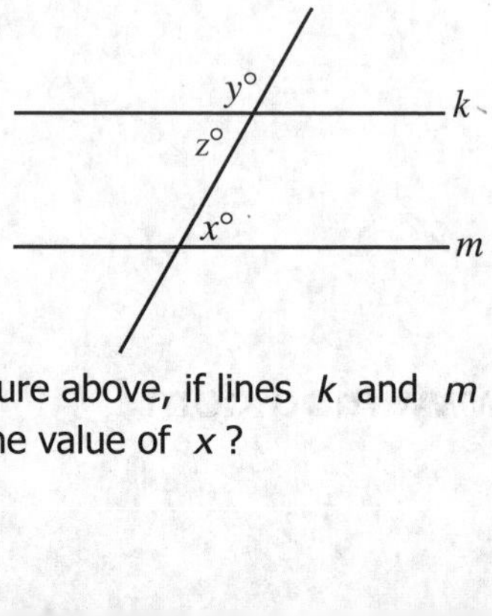

6. In the figure above, if lines k and m are parallel, what is the value of x?

   (1) $y = 120$
   (2) $z = 60$

7. What percent of a group of people are women with red hair?

   (1) Of the women in the group, 5 percent have red hair.
   (2) Of the men in the group, 10 percent have red hair.

8. If r and s are positive integers, r is what percent of s?

   (1) $r = \frac{3}{4}s$
   (2) $r \div s = \frac{75}{100}$

9. Is it true that $a > b$?

   (1) $2a > 2b$
   (2) $a + c > b + c$

10. In a certain class, one student is to be selected at random to read. What is the probability that a boy will read?

    (1) Two-thirds of the students in the class are boys.
    (2) Ten of the students in the class are girls.

11. If $5x + 3y = 17$, what is the value of x?

    (1) x is a positive integer.
    (2) $y = 4x$

12. Does the product $jkmn$ equal 1?

    (1) $\frac{jk}{mn} = 1$
    (2) $j = \frac{1}{k}$ and $m = \frac{1}{n}$

13. A certain expressway has exits J, K, L, and M, in that order. What is the road distance from exit K to exit L?

(1) The road distance from exit J to exit L is 21 kilometers.
(2) The road distance from exit K to exit M is 26 kilometers.

14. Is the integer k a prime number?

(1) $2k = 6$
(2) $1 < k < 6$

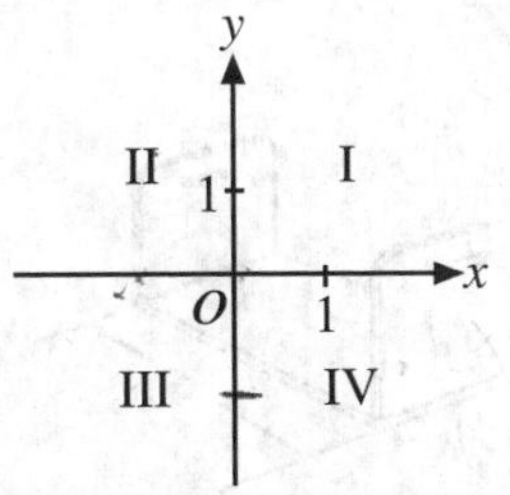

15. If $ab \neq 0$, in what quadrant of the coordinate system above does point (a, b) lie?

(1) (b, a) lies in quadrant IV.
(2) $(a, -b)$ lies in quadrant III.

16. Is x greater than 1.8?

(1) $x > 1.7$
(2) $x > 1.9$

17. If n is an integer, is $n + 1$ odd?

(1) $n + 2$ is an even integer.
(2) $n - 1$ is an odd integer.

18. Is $1 < x < 2$?

(1) $0 < x$
(2) $x < 3$

19. Water is pumped into a partially filled tank at a constant rate through an inlet pipe. At the same time, water is pumped out of the tank at a constant rate through an outlet pipe. At what rate, in gallons per minute, is the amount of water in the tank increasing?

(1) The amount of water initially in the tank is 200 gallons.
(2) Water is pumped into the tank at a rate of 10 gallons per minute and out of the tank at a rate of 10 gallons every $2\frac{1}{2}$ minutes.

20. Is x a negative number?

(1) $9x > 10x$
(2) $x + 3$ is positive.

21. Does $2m - 3n = 0$?

(1) $m \neq 0$
(2) $6m = 9n$

22. What is the value of the integer x?

(1) x is a prime number.
(2) $31 \leq x \leq 37$

23. If P, Q, and R are three distinct points, do line segments PQ and PR have the same length?

(1) P is the midpoint of line segment QR.
(2) Q and R lie on the same circle with center P.

24. Is the number x between 0.2 and 0.7?

(1) $560x < 280$
(2) $700x > 280$

25. If i and j are integers, is $i + j$ an even integer?

(1) $i < 10$
(2) $i = j$

26. If $n + k = m$, what is the value of k?

(1) $n = 10$
(2) $m + 10 = n$

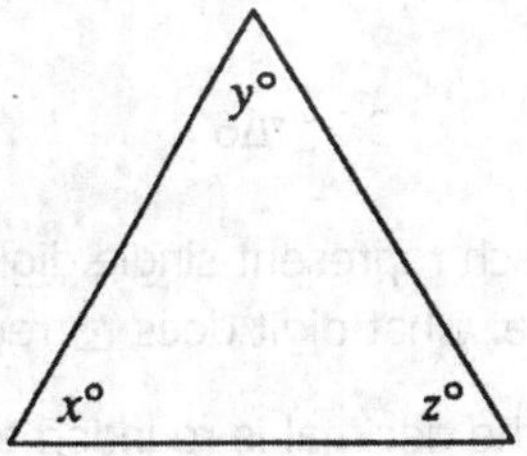

27. Is the triangle above equilateral?

(1) $x = y$
(2) $z = 60$

28. Is x an integer?

(1) $\frac{x}{2}$ is an integer.

(2) $2x$ is an integer.

29. What is the value of x?

(1) $2x + 1 = 0$

(2) $(x + 1)^2 = x^2$

30. What is the value of $\frac{1}{k} + \frac{1}{r}$?

(1) $k + r = 20$

(2) $kr = 64$

31. If x is equal to one of the numbers $\frac{1}{4}$, $\frac{3}{8}$, or $\frac{2}{5}$, what is the value of x?

(1) $\frac{1}{4} < x < \frac{1}{2}$

(2) $\frac{1}{3} < x < \frac{3}{5}$

32. In ΔPQR, if $PQ = x$, $QR = x + 2$, and $PR = y$, which of the three angles of ΔPQR has the greatest degree measure?

(1) $y = x + 3$

(2) $x = 2$

33. What distance did Jane travel?

(1) Bill traveled 40 miles in 40 minutes.

(2) Jane traveled at the same average rate as Bill.

34. What number is 15 percent of x?

(1) 18 is 6 percent of x.

(2) $\frac{2}{3}$ of x is 200.

3.2□Δ6

35. If □ and Δ each represent single digits in the decimal above, what digit does □ represent?

(1) When the decimal is rounded to the nearest tenth, 3.2 is the result.

(2) When the decimal is rounded to the nearest hundredth, 3.24 is the result.

36. The profit from the sale of a certain appliance increases, though not proportionally, with the number of units sold. Did the profit exceed $4 million on sales of 380,000 units?

(1) The profit exceeded $2 million on sales of 200,000 units.

(2) The profit exceeded $5 million on sales of 350,000 units.

37. What is the value of $xy - yz$?

(1) $y = 2$

(2) $x - z = 5$

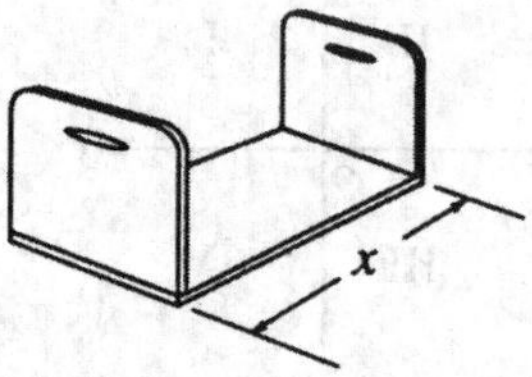

38. Will the first 10 volumes of a 20-volume encyclopedia fit upright in the book rack shown above?

(1) $x = 50$ centimeters

(2) Twelve of the volumes have an average (arithmetic mean) thickness of 5 centimeters.

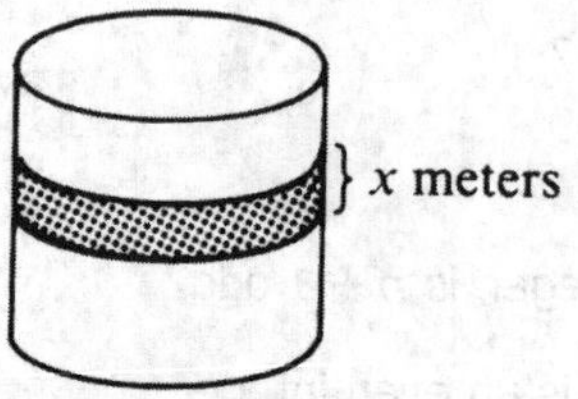

39. A circular tub has a band painted around its circumference, as shown above. What is the surface area of this painted band?

(1) $x = 0.5$

(2) The height of the tub is 1 meter.

40. What is the value of integer n?

(1) $n(n+1) = 6$

(2) $2^{2n} = 16$

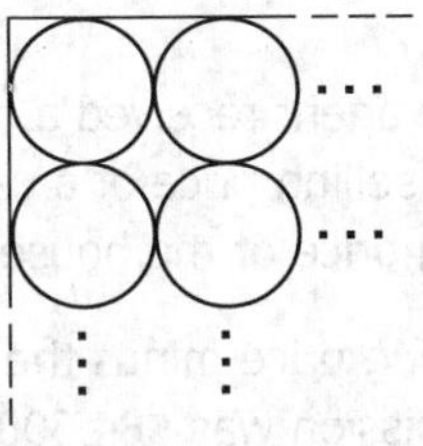

41. The inside of a rectangular carton is 48 centimeters long, 32 centimeters wide, and 15 centimeters high. The carton is filled to capacity with k identical cylindrical cans of fruit that stand upright in rows and columns, as indicated in the figure above. If the cans are 15 centimeters high, what is the value of k?

(1) Each of the cans has a radius of 4 centimeters.
(2) Six of the cans fit exactly along the length of the carton.

$$\begin{cases} x - 4 = z \\ y - x = 8 \\ 8 - z = t \end{cases}$$

42. For the system of equations given, what is the value of z?

(1) $x = 7$
(2) $t = 5$

43. Is x equal to 5?

(1) $x \geq 5$
(2) $x \leq 5$

	R	S	T	U
R	0	y	x	62
S	y	0	56	75
T	x	56	0	69
U	62	75	69	0

44. The table above shows the distance, in kilometers, by the most direct route, between any two of the four cities, R, S, T, and U. For example, the distance between City R and City U is 62 kilometers. What is the value of x?

(1) By the most direct route, the distance between S and T is twice the distance between S and R.
(2) By the most direct route, the distance between T and U is 1.5 times the distance between R and T.

45. What is the value of the two-digit integer x?

(1) The sum of the two digits is 3.
(2) x is divisible by 3.

46. What is the tenths digit in the decimal representation of a certain number?

(1) The number is less than $\frac{1}{3}$.
(2) The number is greater than $\frac{1}{4}$.

47. If the two floors in a certain building are 9 feet apart, how many steps are there in a set of stairs that extends from the first floor to the second floor of the building?

(1) Each step is $\frac{3}{4}$ foot high.
(2) Each step is 1 foot wide.

48. If $xy \neq 0$, is $\frac{x}{y} < 0$?

(1) $x = -y$
(2) $-x = -(-y)$

49. How many people are directors of both Company K and Company R?

(1) There were 17 directors present at a joint meeting of the directors of Company K and Company R, and no directors were absent.
(2) Company K has 12 directors and Company R has 8 directors.

50. If x and y are positive, is $\frac{x}{y}$ greater than 1?

(1) $xy > 1$
(2) $x - y > 0$

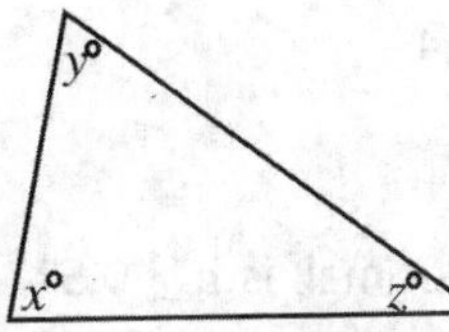

51. What is the value of z in the triangle above?

(1) $x + y = 139$
(2) $y + z = 108$

52. If x, y, and z are nonzero numbers, is $xz = 12$?

(1) $x^2yz = 12xy$

(2) $\frac{z}{4} = \frac{3}{x}$

53. A certain company currently has how many employees?

(1) If 3 additional employees are hired by the company and all of the present employees remain, there will be at least 20 employees in the company.

(2) If no additional employees are hired by the company and 3 of the present employees resign, there will be fewer than 15 employees in the company.

54. What is the value of n in the equation $-25 + 19 + n = s$?

(1) $s = 2$

(2) $\frac{n}{s} = 4$

55. At a certain picnic, each of the guests was served either a single scoop or a double scoop of ice cream. How many of the guests were served a double scoop of ice cream?

(1) At the picnic, 60 percent of the guests were served a double scoop of ice cream.

(2) A total of 120 scoops of ice cream were served to all the guests at the picnic.

56. What is the value of xy?

(1) $y = x + 1$

(2) $y = x^2 + 1$

57. What is the value of $\frac{1}{x} + \frac{1}{y}$?

(1) $x + y = 14$

(2) $xy = 24$

58. If d denotes a decimal, is $d \geq 0.5$?

(1) When d is rounded to the nearest tenth, the result is 0.5.

(2) When d is rounded to the nearest integer, the result is 1.

59. If a real estate agent received a commission of 6 percent of the selling price of a certain house, what was the selling price of the house?

(1) The selling price minus the real estate agent's commission was $84,600.

(2) The selling price was 250 percent of the original purchase price of $36,000.

60. If $\frac{\sqrt{x}}{y} = n$, what is the value of x?

(1) $yn = 10$

(2) $y = 40$ and $n = \frac{1}{4}$

61. How many integers are there between, but not including, integers r and s?

(1) $s - r = 10$

(2) There are 9 integers between, but not including, $r + 1$ and $s + 1$.

62. What is the number of members of Club X who are at least 35 years of age?

(1) Exactly $\frac{3}{4}$ of the members of Club X are under 35 years of age.

(2) The 64 women in Club X constitute 40 percent of the club's membership.

63. Carlotta can drive from her home to her office by one of two possible routes. If she must also return by one of these routes, what is the distance of the shorter route?

(1) When she drives from her home to her office by the shorter route and returns by the longer route, she drives a total of 42 kilometers.

(2) When she drives both ways, from her home to her office and back, by the longer route, she drives a total of 46 kilometers.

64. Is $x > y$?

(1) $x = y + 2$

(2) $\frac{x}{2} = y - 1$

65. If m is an integer, is m odd?

(1) $\frac{m}{2}$ is NOT an even integer.
(2) $m - 3$ is an even integer.

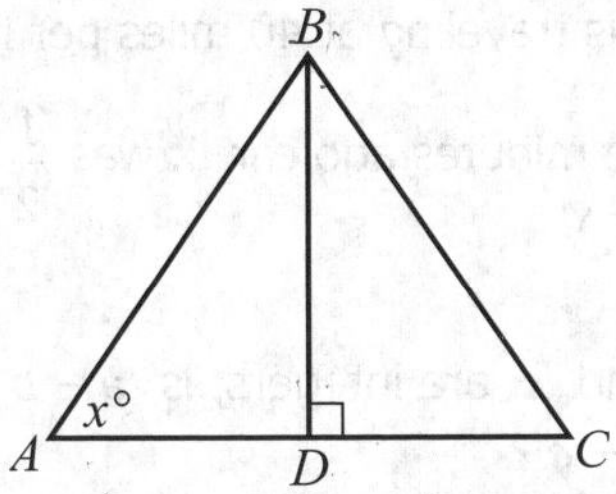

66. What is the area of triangular region ABC above?

(1) The product of BD and AC is 20.
(2) $x = 45$

67. What is the value of $b + c$?

(1) $ab + cd + ac + bd = 6$
(2) $a + d = 4$

68. What is the average (arithmetic mean) of j and k?

(1) The average (arithmetic mean) of $j + 2$ and $k + 4$ is 11.
(2) The average (arithmetic mean) of j, k, and 14 is 10.

69. Paula and Sandy were among those people who sold raffle tickets to raise money for Club X. If Paula and Sandy sold a total of 100 of the tickets, how many of the tickets did Paula sell?

(1) Sandy sold $\frac{2}{3}$ as many of the raffle tickets as Paula did.
(2) Sandy sold 8 percent of all the raffle tickets sold for Club X.

70. Is $ax = 3 - bx$?

(1) $x(a + b) = 3$
(2) $a = b = 1.5$ and $x = 1$.

71. A number of people each wrote down one of the first 30 positive integers. Were any of the integers written down by more than one of the people?

(1) The number of people who wrote down an integer was greater than 40.
(2) The number of people who wrote down an integer was less than 70.

72. In the figure above, is $CD > BC$?

(1) $AD = 20$
(2) $AB = CD$

73. How much did a certain telephone call cost?

(1) The call lasted 53 minutes.
(2) The cost for the first 3 minutes was 5 times the cost for each additional minute.

74. In a certain office, 50 percent of the employees are college graduates and 60 percent of the employees are over forty years old. If 30 percent of those over forty have master's degrees, how many of the employees over forty have master's degrees?

(1) Exactly 100 of the employees are college graduates.
(2) Of the employees 40 years old or less, 25 percent have master's degrees.

75. Is $rst = 1$?

(1) $rs = 1$
(2) $st = 1$

TOTAL EXPENSES FOR THE
FIVE DIVISIONS OF COMPANY *H*

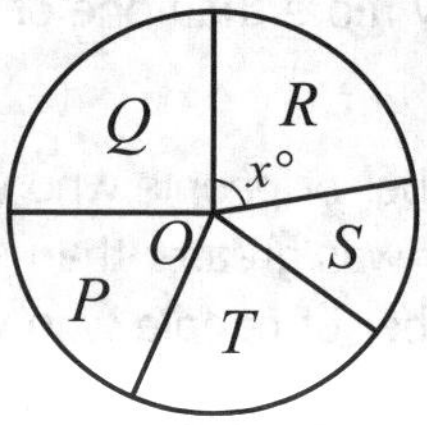

76. The figure above represents a circle graph of Company H's total expenses broken down by the expenses for each of its five divisions. If O is the center of the circle and if Company H's total expenses are $5,400,000, what are the expenses for division R?

(1) x = 94
(2) The total expenses for divisions S and T are twice as much as the expenses for division R.

77. If Ms. Smith's income was 20 percent more for 1991 than it was for 1990, how much was her income for 1991?

(1) Ms. Smith's income for the first 6 months of 1990 was $17,500 and her income for the last 6 months of 1990 was $20,000.
(2) Ms. Smith's income for 1991 was $7,500 greater than her income for 1990.

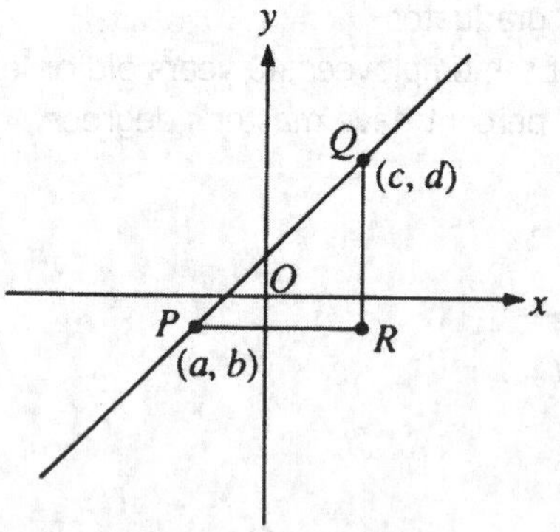

78. In the figure above, segments *PR* and *QR* are each parallel to one of the rectangular coordinate axes. Is the ratio of the length of *QR* to the length of *PR* equal to 1?

(1) $c = 3$ and $d = 4$.
(2) $a = -2$ and $b = -1$.

79. While on a straight road, car X and car Y are traveling at different constant rates. If car X is now 1 mile ahead of car Y, how many minutes from now will car X be 2 miles ahead of car Y?

(1) Car X is traveling at 50 miles per hour and car Y is traveling at 40 miles per hour.
(2) Three minutes ago car X was $\frac{1}{2}$ mile ahead of car Y.

80. If *a*, *b*, and *c* are integers, is $a - b + c$ greater than $a + b - c$?

(1) *b* is negative.
(2) *c* is positive.

81. If a certain animated cartoon consists of a total of 17,280 frames on film, how many minutes will it take to run the cartoon?

(1) The cartoon runs without interruption at the rate of 24 frames per second.
(2) It takes 6 times as long to run the cartoon as it takes to rewind the film, and it takes a total of 14 minutes to do both.

82. A box contains only red chips, white chips, and blue chips. If a chip is randomly selected from the box, what is the probability that the chip will be either white or blue?

(1) The probability that the chip will be blue is $\frac{1}{5}$.
(2) The probability that the chip will be red is $\frac{1}{3}$.

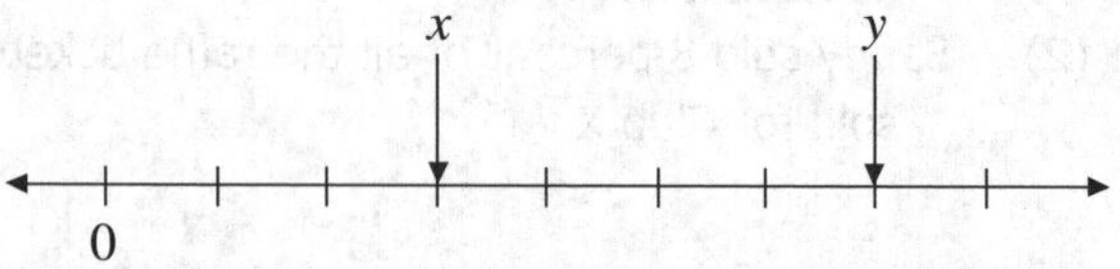

83. If the successive tick marks shown on the number line above are equally spaced and if *x* and *y* are the numbers designating the end points of intervals as shown, what is the value of *y*?

(1) $x = \frac{1}{2}$
(2) $y - x = \frac{2}{3}$

84. On a company-sponsored cruise, $\frac{2}{3}$ of the passengers were company employees and the remaining passengers were their guests. If $\frac{3}{4}$ of the company-employee passengers were managers, what was the number of company-employee passengers who were NOT managers?

(1) There were 690 passengers on the cruise.
(2) There were 230 passengers who were guests of the company employees.

85. In the *xy*-plane, does the point (4, 12) lie on line *k*?

(1) The point (1, 7) lies on line *k*.
(2) The point (–2, 2) lies on line *k*.

86. The length of the edging that surrounds circular garden *K* is $\frac{1}{2}$ the length of the edging that surrounds circular garden *G*. What is the area of garden *K*? (Assume that the edging has negligible width.)

(1) The area of *G* is 25π square meters.
(2) The edging around *G* is 10π meters long.

87. An employee is paid 1.5 times the regular hourly rate for each hour worked in excess of 40 hours per week, excluding Sunday, and 2 times the regular hourly rate for each hour worked on Sunday. How much was the employee paid last week?

(1) The employee's regular hourly rate is $10.
(2) Last week the employee worked a total of 54 hours but did not work more than 8 hours on any day.

88. What was the revenue that a theater received from the sale of 400 tickets, some of which were sold at the full price and the remainder of which were sold at a reduced price?

(1) The number of tickets sold at the full price was $\frac{1}{4}$ of the total number of tickets sold.
(2) The full price of a ticket was $25.

89. If $\circ$ represents one of the operations $+$, $-$, and $\times$, is $k \circ (\ell + m) = (k \circ \ell) + (k \circ m)$ for all numbers k, ℓ, and m?

(1) $k \circ 1$ is not equal to $1 \circ k$ for some numbers k.
(2) $\circ$ represents subtraction.

90. How many of the 60 cars sold last month by a certain dealer had neither power windows nor a stereo?

(1) Of the 60 cars sold, 20 had a stereo but not power windows.
(2) Of the 60 cars sold, 30 had both power windows and a stereo.

91. By what percent did the median household income in Country Y decrease from 1970 to 1980?

(1) In 1970 the median household income in Country Y was $\frac{2}{3}$ of the median household income in Country *X*.
(2) In 1980 the median household income in Country Y was $\frac{1}{2}$ of the median household income in Country X.

92. A certain group of car dealerships agreed to donate *x* dollars to a Red Cross chapter for each car sold during a 30-day period. What was the total amount that was expected to be donated?

(1) A total of 500 cars were expected to be sold.
(2) Sixty more cars were sold than expected, so that the total amount actually donated was $28,000.

93. While driving on the expressway, did Robin ever exceed the 55-mile-per-hour speed limit?

(1) Robin drove 100 miles on the expressway.
(2) Robin drove for 2 hours on the expressway.

94. In Jefferson School, 300 students study French or Spanish or both. If 100 of these students do not study French, how many of these students study both French and Spanish?

(1) Of the 300 students, 60 do not study Spanish.
(2) A total of 240 of the students study Spanish.

95. A certain salesperson's weekly salary is equal to a fixed base salary plus a commission that is directly proportional to the number of items sold during the week. If 50 items are sold this week, what will be the salesperson's salary for this week?

(1) Last week 45 items were sold.
(2) Last week's salary was $405.

96. If Juan had a doctor's appointment on a certain day, was the appointment on a Wednesday?

(1) Exactly 60 hours before the appointment, it was Monday.
(2) The appointment was between 1:00 p.m. and 9:00 p.m.

97. What is the value of $5x^2 + 4x - 1$?

(1) $x(x + 2) = 0$
(2) $x = 0$

98. At Larry's Auto Supply Store, Brand X antifreeze is sold by the gallon and Brand Y motor oil is sold by the quart. Excluding sales tax, what is the total cost for 1 gallon of Brand X antifreeze and 1 quart of Brand Y motor oil?

(1) Excluding sales tax, the total cost for 6 gallons of Brand X antifreeze and 10 quarts of Brand Y motor oil is $58. (There is no quantity discount.)
(2) Excluding sales tax, the total cost for 4 gallons of Brand X antifreeze and 12 quarts of Brand Y motor oil is $44. (There is no quantity discount.)

99. Is $m \neq n$?

(1) $m + n < 0$
(2) $mn < 0$

100. When a player in a certain game tossed a coin a number of times, 4 more heads than tails resulted. Heads or tails resulted each time the player tossed the coin. How many times did heads result?

(1) The player tossed the coin 24 times.
(2) The player received 3 points each time heads resulted and 1 point each time tails resulted, for a total of 52 points.

101. If S is the infinite sequence $S_1 = 9$, $S_2 = 99$, $S_3 = 999$, . . . , $S_k = 10^k - 1$, . . . , is every term in S divisible by the prime number p?

(1) p is greater than 2.
(2) At least one term in sequence S is divisible by p.

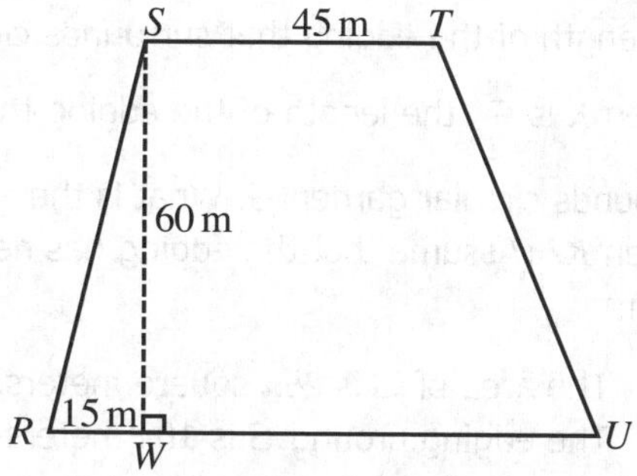

102. Quadrilateral $RSTU$ shown above is a site plan for a parking lot in which side RU is parallel to side ST and RU is longer than ST. What is the area of the parking lot?

(1) RU = 80 meters
(2) $TU = 20\sqrt{10}$ meters

103. If n and k are greater than zero, is $\frac{n}{k}$ an integer?

(1) n and k are both integers.
(2) n^2 and k^2 are both integers.

104. If the average (arithmetic mean) of six numbers is 75, how many of the numbers are equal to 75?

(1) None of the six numbers is less than 75.
(2) None of the six numbers is greater than 75.

105. Is $|x| = y - z$?

(1) $x + y = z$
(2) $x < 0$

106. What was the total amount of revenue that a theater received from the sale of 400 tickets, some of which were sold at x percent of full price and the rest of which were sold at full price?

(1) $x = 50$
(2) Full-price tickets sold for $20 each.

107. Any decimal that has only a finite number of nonzero digits is a terminating decimal. For example, 24, 0.82, and 5.096 are three terminating decimals. If r and s are positive integers and the ratio $\frac{r}{s}$ is expressed as a decimal, is $\frac{r}{s}$ a terminating decimal?

(1) $90 < r < 100$
(2) $s = 4$

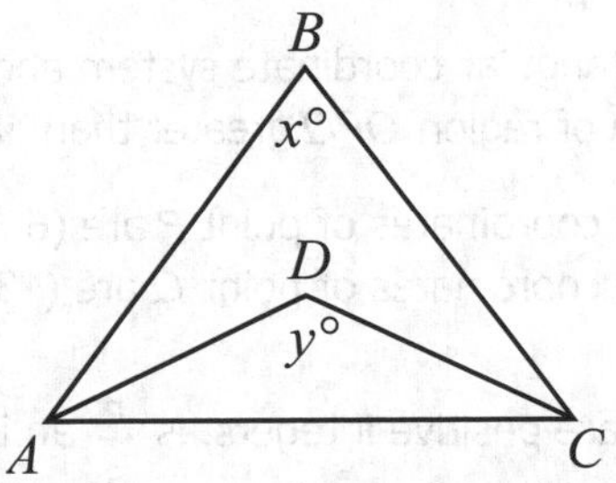

108. In the figure above, what is the value of $x + y$?

(1) $x = 70$
(2) ΔABC and ΔADC are both isosceles triangles.

109. Are positive integers p and q both greater than n?

(1) $p - q$ is greater than n.
(2) $q > p$

110. Whenever Martin has a restaurant bill with an amount between $10 and $99, he calculates the dollar amount of the tip as 2 times the tens digit of the amount of his bill. If the amount of Martin's most recent restaurant bill was between $10 and $99, was the tip calculated by Martin on this bill greater than 15 percent of the amount of the bill?

(1) The amount of the bill was between $15 and $50.
(2) The tip calculated by Martin was $8.

111. The price per share of stock X increased by 10 percent over the same time period that the price per share of stock Y decreased by 10 percent. The reduced price per share of stock Y was what percent of the original price per share of stock X?

(1) The increased price per share of stock X was equal to the original price per share of stock Y.

(2) The increase in the price per share of stock X was $\frac{10}{11}$ the decrease in the price per share of stock Y.

112. Is k greater than t?

(1) $kt = 24$
(2) $k^2 > t^2$

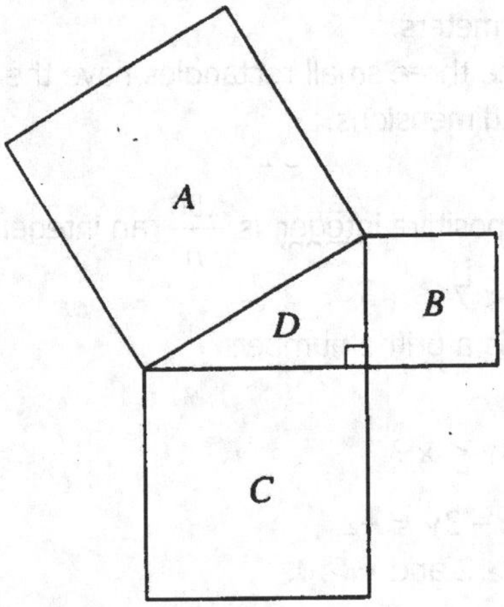

113. In the figure above, if the area of triangular region D is 4, what is the length of a side of square region A?

(1) The area of square region B is 9.
(2) The area of square region C is $\frac{64}{9}$.

114. If x is to be selected at random from set T, what is the probability that $\frac{1}{4}x - 5 \leq 0$?

(1) T is a set of 8 integers.
(2) T is contained in the set of integers from 1 to 25, inclusive.

115. If Sara's age is exactly twice Bill's age, what is Sara's age?

(1) Four years ago, Sara's age was exactly 3 times Bill's age.
(2) Eight years from now, Sara's age will be exactly 1.5 times Bill's age.

116. What is the value of $(a + b)^2$?
(1) $ab = 0$
(2) $(a - b)^2 = 36$

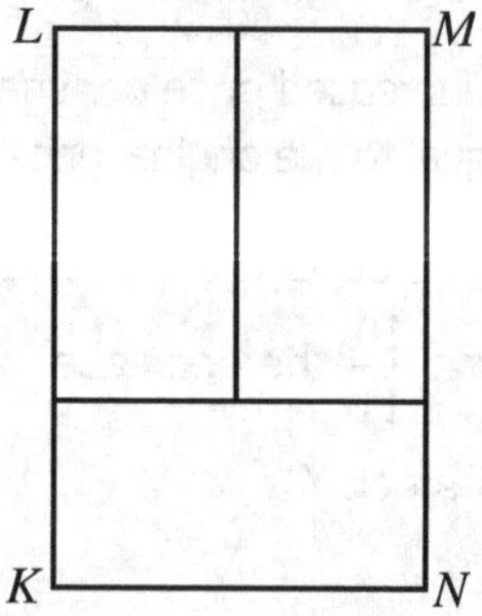

117. In the figure above, what is the ratio $\frac{KN}{MN}$?
(1) The perimeter of rectangle $KLMN$ is 30 meters.
(2) The three small rectangles have the same dimensions.

118. If n is a positive integer, is $\frac{150}{n}$ an integer?
(1) $n < 7$
(2) n is a prime number.

119. Is $2x - 3y < x^2$?
(1) $2x - 3y = -2$
(2) $x > 2$ and $y > 0$.

120. A report consisting of 2,600 words is divided into 23 paragraphs. A 2-paragraph preface is then added to the report. Is the average (arithmetic mean) number of words per paragraph for all 25 paragraphs less than 120?
(1) Each paragraph of the preface has more than 100 words.
(2) Each paragraph of the preface has fewer than 150 words.

121. If $\frac{x}{2} = \frac{3}{y}$, is x less than y?
(1) $y \geq 3$
(2) $y \leq 4$

122. If v and w are different integers, does $v = 0$?
(1) $vw = v^2$
(2) $w = 2$

123. What is the value of $36,500(1.05)^n$?
(1) $n^2 - 5n + 6 = 0$
(2) $n - 2 \neq 0$

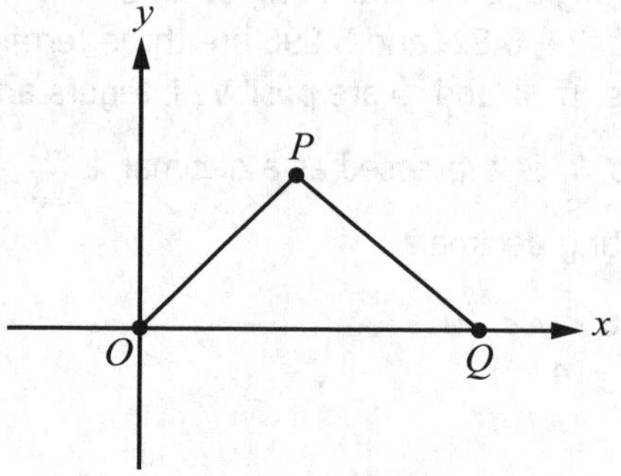

124. In the rectangular coordinate system above, if $OP < PQ$, is the area of region OPQ greater than 48?
(1) The coordinates of point P are (6, 8).
(2) The coordinates of point Q are (13, 0).

125. If r and s are positive integers, is $\frac{r}{s}$ an integer?
(1) Every factor of s is also a factor of r.
(2) Every prime factor of s is also a prime factor of r.

126. If $z^n = 1$, what is the value of z?
(1) n is a nonzero integer.
(2) $z > 0$

$$S = \frac{\frac{2}{n}}{\frac{1}{x} + \frac{2}{3x}}$$

127. In the expression above, if $xn \neq 0$, what is the value of S?
(1) $x = 2n$
(2) $n = \frac{1}{2}$

128. If x is an integer, is $x|x| < 2^x$?
(1) $x < 0$
(2) $x = -10$

129. If n is a positive integer, is the value of $b - a$ at least twice the value of $3^n - 2^n$?

(1) $a = 2^{n+1}$ and $b = 3^{n+1}$
(2) $n = 3$

130. The inflation index for the year 1989 relative to the year 1970 was 3.56, indicating that, on the average, for each dollar spent in 1970 for goods, \$3.56 had to be spent for the same goods in 1989. If the price of a Model K mixer increased precisely according to the inflation index, what was the price of the mixer in 1970?

(1) The price of the Model K mixer was \$102.40 more in 1989 than in 1970.
(2) The price of the Model K mixer was \$142.40 in 1989.

131. Is 5^k less than 1,000?

(1) $5^{k+1} > 3{,}000$
(2) $5^{k-1} = 5^k - 500$

132. If the integer n is greater than 1, is n equal to 2?

(1) n has exactly two positive factors.
(2) The difference of any two distinct positive factors of n is odd.

133. Every member of a certain club volunteers to contribute equally to the purchase of a \$60 gift certificate. How many members does the club have?

(1) Each member's contribution is to be \$4.
(2) If 5 club members fail to contribute, the share of each contributing member will increase by \$2.

134. If m and n are positive integers, is $\sqrt{n-m}$ an integer?

(1) $n > m + 15$
(2) $n = m(m + 1)$

135. If $x < 0$, is $y > 0$?

(1) $\frac{x}{y} < 0$
(2) $y - x > 0$

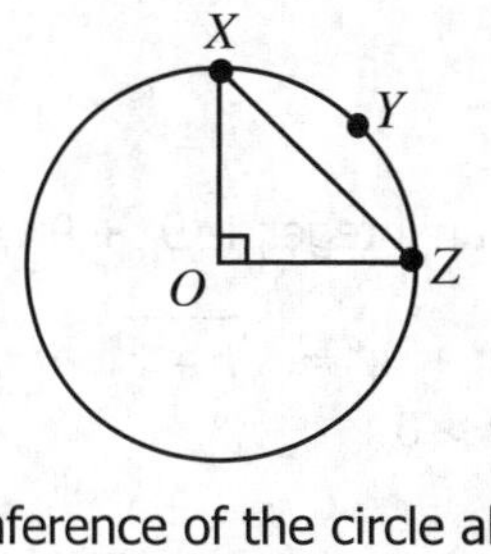

136. What is the circumference of the circle above with center O?

(1) The perimeter of ΔOXZ is $20 + 10\sqrt{2}$.
(2) The length of arc XYZ is 5π.

137. What is the value of $a^4 - b^4$?

(1) $a^2 - b^2 = 16$
(2) $a + b = 8$

138. In a certain business, production index p is directly proportional to efficiency index e, which is in turn directly proportional to investment index i. What is p if $i = 70$?

(1) $e = 0.5$ whenever $i = 60$.
(2) $p = 2.0$ whenever $i = 50$.

139. If $x \neq -y$, is $\frac{x-y}{x+y} > 1$?

(1) $x > 0$
(2) $y < 0$

140. In the rectangular coordinate system, are the points (r, s) and (u, v) equidistant from the origin?

(1) $r + s = 1$
(2) $u = 1 - r$ and $v = 1 - s$.

141. On Jane's credit card account, the average daily balance for a 30-day billing cycle is the average (arithmetic mean) of the daily balances at the end of each of the 30 days. At the beginning of a certain 30-day billing cycle, Jane's credit card account had a balance of \$600. Jane made a payment of \$300 on the account during the billing cycle. If no other amounts were added to or subtracted from the account during the billing cycle, what was the average daily balance on Jane's account for the billing cycle?

(1) Jane's payment was credited on the 21st day of the billing cycle.
(2) The average daily balance through the 25th day of the billing cycle was \$540.

142. If x is an integer, is $9^x + 9^{-x} = b$?

(1) $3^x + 3^{-x} = \sqrt{b+2}$
(2) $x > 0$

143. If $m > 0$ and $n > 0$, is $\frac{m+x}{n+x} > \frac{m}{n}$?

(1) $m < n$
(2) $x > 0$

144. If n is a positive integer, is $\left(\frac{1}{10}\right)^n < 0.01$?

(1) $n > 2$
(2) $\left(\frac{1}{10}\right)^{n-1} < 0.1$

145. Is $\frac{1}{p} > \frac{r}{r^2+2}$?

(1) $p = r$
(2) $r > 0$

146. Is n an integer?

(1) n^2 is an integer.
(2) $\sqrt{n}$ is an integer.

147. If n is a positive integer, is $n^3 - n$ divisible by 4?

(1) $n = 2k + 1$, where k is an integer.
(2) $n^2 + n$ is divisible by 6.

148. What is the tens digit of positive integer x?

(1) x divided by 100 has a remainder of 30.
(2) x divided by 110 has a remainder of 30.

149. If x, y, and z are positive integers, is $x - y$ odd?

(1) $x = z^2$
(2) $y = (z-1)^2$

150. Henry purchased 3 items during a sale. He received a 20 percent discount off the regular price of the most expensive item and a 10 percent discount off the regular price of each of the other 2 items. Was the total amount of the 3 discounts greater than 15 percent of the sum of the regular prices of the 3 items?

(1) The regular price of the most expensive item was \$50, and the regular price of the next most expensive item was \$20.
(2) The regular price of the least expensive item was \$15.

151. If x and y are positive, is the ratio of x to y greater than 3?

(1) x is 2 more than 3 times y.
(2) The ratio of $2x$ to $3y$ is greater than 2.

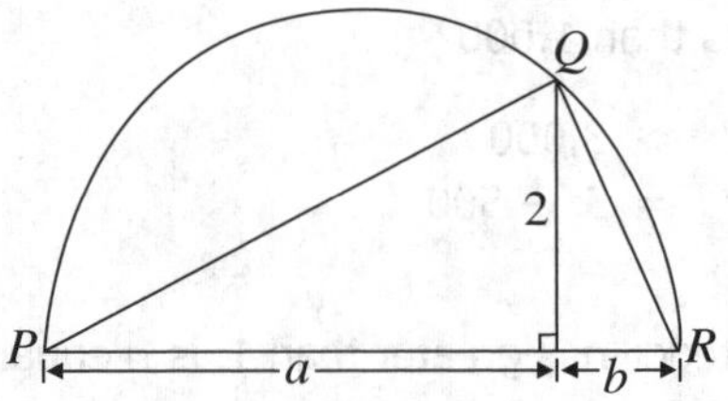

152. If arc PQR above is a semicircle, what is the length of diameter PR?

(1) $a = 4$
(2) $b = 1$

153. Does the integer k have a factor p such that $1 < p < k$?

(1) $k > 4!$
(2) $13! + 2 \le k \le 13! + 13$

154. Is x negative?

(1) $x^3(1 - x^2) < 0$
(2) $x^2 - 1 < 0$

155. Marcia's bucket can hold a maximum of how many liters of water?

(1) The bucket currently contains 9 liters of water.
(2) If 3 liters of water are added to the bucket when it is half full of water, the amount of water in the bucket will increase by $\frac{1}{3}$.

6.4 Data Sufficiency Answer Key

1. D	32. A	63. C	94. D	125. A
2. D	33. E	64. A	95. E	126. C
3. B	34. D	65. B	96. C	127. A
4. B	35. E	66. A	97. B	128. D
5. E	36. B	67. C	98. C	129. A
6. D	37. C	68. D	99. B	130. D
7. E	38. E	69. A	100. D	131. B
8. D	39. E	70. D	101. E	132. B
9. D	40. B	71. A	102. D	133. D
10. A	41. D	72. E	103. E	134. B
11. B	42. D	73. E	104. D	135. A
12. B	43. C	74. A	105. C	136. D
13. E	44. B	75. E	106. E	137. C
14. A	45. E	76. A	107. B	138. B
15. D	46. E	77. D	108. E	139. E
16. B	47. A	78. C	109. C	140. C
17. D	48. D	79. D	110. B	141. D
18. E	49. C	80. C	111. D	142. A
19. B	50. B	81. D	112. E	143. C
20. A	51. A	82. B	113. D	144. D
21. B	52. D	83. D	114. E	145. C
22. E	53. C	84. D	115. D	146. B
23. D	54. D	85. C	116. C	147. A
24. C	55. C	86. D	117. B	148. A
25. B	56. E	87. E	118. C	149. C
26. B	57. C	88. E	119. D	150. A
27. C	58. B	89. D	120. B	151. D
28. A	59. D	90. E	121. A	152. D
29. D	60. D	91. E	122. A	153. B
30. C	61. D	92. C	123. C	154. C
31. E	62. C	93. E	124. A	155. B

6.5 Data Sufficiency Answer Explanations

The following discussion of data sufficiency is intended to familiarize you with the most efficient and effective aproaches to the kinds of problems common to data sufficiency. The particular questions in this chapter are generally representative of the kinds of data sufficiency questions you will encounter on the GMAT®. Remember that it is the problem solving strategy that is important, not the specific details of a particular question.

1. How much is 20 percent of a certain number?

(1) 10 percent of the number is 5.
(2) 40 percent of twice the number is 40.

Arithmetic + Algebra Percents + Applied problem

Let x represent the number.

(1) If 10 percent of the number is 5, then $0.1x = 5$. If both sides of the equation are multiplied by 2, then 20 percent (0.2) of the same number would be $0.2x = 10$. When both sides of this equation are then divided by 0.2, it yields $x = 50$; SUFFICIENT.

(2) This can be rephrased as $0.4(2x) = 40$. Then, if both sides of the equation are divided by 0.4, it yields $2x = 100$, or $x = 50$; SUFFICIENT.

The correct answer is D;
each statement alone is sufficient.

2. A thoroughly blended biscuit mix includes only flour and baking powder. What is the ratio of the number of grams of baking powder to the number of grams of flour in the mix?

(1) Exactly 9.9 grams of flour is contained in 10 grams of the mix.
(2) Exactly 0.3 gram of baking powder is contained in 30 grams of the mix.

Arithmetic Ratios and proportions

Since the mix is thoroughly blended, any amount of the mix will have the ingredients in the same ratio. In any amount of the mix, the ratio of the ingredients can be determined once the amounts of both ingredients are known.

(1) Both the amount of one ingredient and the total amount of mix are known, and thus, by subtraction, the amount of the second ingredient can be determined; SUFFICIENT.

(2) Both the amount of one ingredient and the total amount of mix are known, and thus, by subtraction, the amount of the second ingredient can be determined; SUFFICIENT.

The correct answer is D;
each statement alone is sufficient.

3. What is the value of $|x|$?

(1) $x = -|x|$
(2) $x^2 = 4$

Arithmetic Absolute value

(1) The absolute value of x, $|x|$, is always positive or 0, so this only determines that x is negative or 0; NOT sufficient.

(2) The value of x can be determined ($x = \pm 2$), which leads to finding $|x|$; SUFFICIENT.

The correct answer is B;
statement 2 alone is sufficient.

4. Is r greater than 0.27?

(1) r is greater than $\frac{1}{4}$.

(2) r is equal to $\frac{3}{10}$.

Arithmetic Properties of numbers

(1) If $r > \frac{1}{4}$, then $r > 0.25$. However, since r could be 0.26, or 0.262, for example, both of which are less than 0.27, more information is needed to pinpoint the value of r; NOT sufficient.

(2) If $r = \frac{3}{10}$, then $r = 0.30$, which is greater than 0.27. Therefore, $r > 0.27$; SUFFICIENT.

The correct answer is B;
statement 2 alone is sufficient.

5. What is the value of the sum of a list of n odd integers?

(1) $n = 8$
(2) The square of the number of integers on the list is 64.

Arithmetic Properties of numbers

Some information about the value of the integers themselves is required to determine the value of their sum.

(1) Only the number of integers in the list (n) is given, without any clues as to the identity of the integers; NOT sufficient.

(2) Only information about the number of integers in the list is given, without any clues as to the identity of the integers; NOT sufficient.

With (1) and (2) taken together, the information is still about the number of integers in the list, without any clues as to the identity of the integers.

The correct answer is E;
both statements together are still not sufficient.

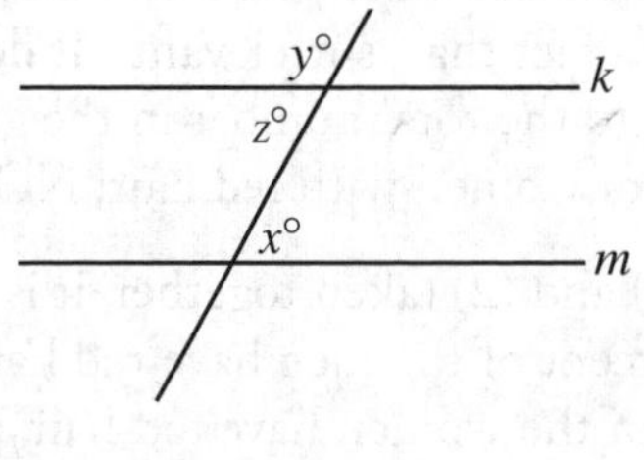

6. In the figure above, if lines k and m are parallel, what is the value of x?

(1) $y = 120$
(2) $z = 60$

Geometry Parallel lines

In the diagram above, y and z are the degree measures of supplementary angles ($y + z = 180$), and z and x are the degree measures of alternate interior angles ($z = x$).

(1) Since y and z are the degree measures of supplementary angles, $y + z = 180$ and thus $z = 180 - y = 180 - 120 = 60$. Since z and x are the degree measures of alternate interior angles, $z = x$, and therefore, $x = 60$; SUFFICIENT.

(2) Since z and x are the degree measures of alternate interior angles, $z = x$, and therefore, $x = 60$; SUFFICIENT.

The correct answer is D;
each statement alone is sufficient.

7. What percent of a group of people are women with red hair?

(1) Of the women in the group, 5 percent have red hair.
(2) Of the men in the group, 10 percent have red hair.

Arithmetic Percents

In order to solve this problem, it is necessary to know the total number of people in the group and the number of women with red hair.

(1) This indicates that 5 percent of the women have red hair, but neither the total number of women nor the total number of people in the group is known. Therefore, further information is needed; NOT sufficient.

(2) This indicates the percent of men who have red hair, a fact that is irrelevant. It does not give a clue as to the total number in the group or the number of women with red hair; NOT sufficient.

With (1) and (2) taken together, it is known what percent of the men have red hair and what percent of the women have red hair, but not what percent of the group are women with red hair.

The correct answer is E;
both statements together are still not sufficient.

8. If r and s are positive integers, r is what percent of s?

(1) $r = \frac{3}{4}s$

(2) $r \div s = \frac{75}{100}$

Arithmetic Percent

To determine r as a percent of s, it suffices to know the ratio of r to s, since any ratio can be converted to a percent.

(1) The ratio of r to s can be determined $\frac{r}{s} = \frac{3}{4}$; SUFFICIENT.

(2) The ratio of r to s can be determined $\frac{r}{s} = \frac{75}{100}$; SUFFICIENT.

The correct answer is D;
each statement alone is sufficient.

9. Is it true that $a > b$?

(1) $2a > 2b$
(2) $a + c > b + c$

Algebra Inequalities

(1) When both sides of $2a > 2b$ are divided by 2, the result is $a > b$; SUFFICIENT.

(2) When c is subtracted from both sides of $a + c > b + c$, the result is $a > b$; SUFFICIENT.

The correct answer is D;
each statement alone is sufficient.

10. In a certain class, one student is to be selected at random to read. What is the probability that a boy will read?

(1) Two-thirds of the students in the class are boys.
(2) Ten of the students in the class are girls.

Arithmetic Probability

(1) Since $\frac{2}{3}$ of the students in the class are boys, the probability that one student selected at random would be a boy is $\frac{2}{3}$; SUFFICIENT.

(2) Although it is known that 10 of the students are girls, the total number of students in the class is unknown, as is the number of boys in the class. From this, it is not possible to determine the probability that a boy would be picked at random; NOT sufficient.

The correct answer is A;
statement 1 alone is sufficient.

11. If $5x + 3y = 17$, what is the value of x?

(1) x is a positive integer.
(2) $y = 4x$

Algebra First- and second-degree equations

(1) This gives no information about the value of x, other than it is positive, which could be an infinite number of possibilities; NOT sufficient.

(2) Substituting $4x$ for y in the given equation yields $5x + 3(4x) = 17$, which can be solved for x; SUFFICIENT.

The correct answer is B;
statement 2 alone is sufficient.

12. Does the product $jkmn$ equal 1?

(1) $\frac{jk}{mn} = 1$

(2) $j = \frac{1}{k}$ and $m = \frac{1}{n}$

Arithmetic Properties of numbers

(1) It can only be determined that $jk = mn$, and there are infinite combinations of numbers that satisfy this equation; NOT sufficient.

(2) It can be determined that $jk = 1$ and that $mn = 1$, and thus that $jkmn = 1$ as well; SUFFICIENT.

The correct answer is B;
statement 2 alone is sufficient.

13. A certain expressway has exits J, K, L, and M, in that order. What is the road distance from exit K to exit L?

(1) The road distance from exit J to exit L is 21 kilometers.
(2) The road distance from exit K to exit M is 26 kilometers.

Geometry Lines

Let JK, KL, and LM be the distances between adjacent exits.

(1) It can only be determined that $KL = 21 - JK$; NOT sufficient.

(2) It can only be determined that $KL = 26 - LM$; NOT sufficient.

Statements (1) and (2) taken together do not provide any of the distances JK, LM, or JM, which would have given the needed information to find KL.

The correct answer is E;
both statements together are still not sufficient.

14. Is the integer k a prime number?

(1) $2k = 6$
(2) $1 < k < 6$

Arithmetic Properties of numbers

(1) Since $2k = 6$, $k = 3$, which is a prime number; SUFFICIENT.

(2) If $1 < k < 6$, then k could be 2, 3, 4, or 5. Of these, 2, 3, and 5 are prime numbers. However, 4 is not a prime number and there is no further information that would eliminate 4 as the value of k; NOT sufficient.

The correct answer is A;
statement 1 alone is sufficient.

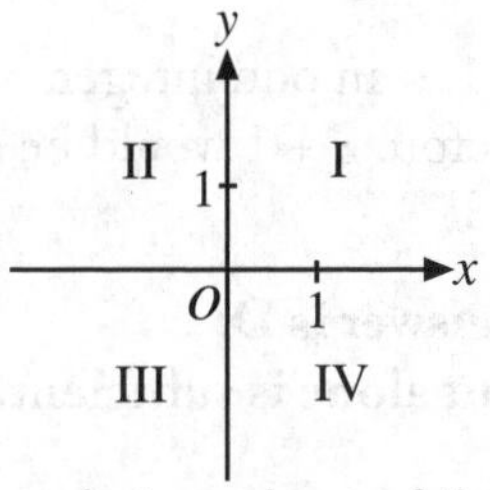

15. If $ab \neq 0$, in what quadrant of the coordinate system above does point (a, b) lie?

(1) (b, a) lies in quadrant IV.
(2) $(a, -b)$ lies in quadrant III.

Geometry Coordinate geometry

(1) If point (b, a) lies in quadrant IV, then $b > 0$ and $a < 0$. Therefore, point (a, b) lies in quadrant II; SUFFICIENT.

(2) If point $(a, -b)$ lies in quadrant III, then $a < 0$, $-b < 0$. It thus follows that $b > 0$. Again, $a < 0$ and $b > 0$ indicate that point (a, b) lies in quadrant II; SUFFICIENT.

The correct answer is D;
each statement alone is sufficient.

16. Is x greater than 1.8?

(1) $x > 1.7$
(2) $x > 1.9$

Arithmetic Properties of numbers

(1) This reveals that while x *could* be greater than 1.8, x could also be a number between 1.7 and 1.8; NOT sufficient.

(2) Since $x > 1.9 > 1.8$, then $x > 1.8$; SUFFICIENT.

The correct answer is B;
statement 2 alone is sufficient.

17. If n is an integer, is $n + 1$ odd?

(1) $n + 2$ is an even integer.
(2) $n - 1$ is an odd integer.

Arithmetic Properties of numbers

(1) Since $n + 2$ is even, n is an even integer, and therefore $n + 1$ would be an odd integer; SUFFICIENT.

(2) Since $n - 1$ is an odd integer, n is an even integer. Therefore $n + 1$ would be an odd integer; SUFFICIENT.

The correct answer is D;
each statement alone is sufficient.

18. Is $1 < x < 2$?

(1) $0 < x$
(2) $x < 3$

Algebra Inequalities

(1) If $x > 0$, x may be between 0 and 1. Also, this does not give an upper limit for x, so that x could, for example, be 3 or 20; NOT sufficient.

(2) If $x < 3$, there are possible values for x between 2 and 3, and this does not define a lower limit for x, so x could, for example, be –1 or –9; NOT sufficient.

Taking (1) and (2) together gives values for x between 0 and 3, or $0 < x < 3$, but does not confine x to $1 < x < 2$.

The correct answer is E;
both statements together are still not sufficient.

19. Water is pumped into a partially filled tank at a constant rate through an inlet pipe. At the same time, water is pumped out of the tank at a constant rate through an outlet pipe. At what rate, in gallons per minute, is the amount of water in the tank increasing?

(1) The amount of water initially in the tank is 200 gallons.
(2) Water is pumped into the tank at a rate of 10 gallons per minute and out of the tank at a rate of 10 gallons every $2\frac{1}{2}$ minutes.

Arithmetic Work Problem

In order to solve this problem, the rate of the water pumping into the tank and the rate of the water pumping out of the tank must both be known.

(1) This only gives the amount of water in the tank initially; NOT sufficient.

(2) This information provides both the needed rates. Since the water is being pumped out of the tank at the rate of 10 gallons every $2\frac{1}{2}$ minutes, that is, 4 gallons every minute, and since 10 gallons are pumped into the tank every minute, the rate at which the water is increasing in the tank is $10 - 4 = 6$ gallons per minute; SUFFICIENT.

The correct answer is B;
statement 2 alone is sufficient.

20. Is x a negative number?

(1) $9x > 10x$
(2) $x + 3$ is positive.

Arithmetic Properties of numbers

(1) If x is a positive number, then $9x$ cannot be greater than $10x$. If $x = 0$, then this equation becomes $0 > 0$, which is not true. Therefore x must be a negative number; SUFFICIENT.

(2) If $x + 3$ is positive, then x must be greater than –3. This would include negative values of x such as –2 and –1, as well as all positive values of x, and it is not possible to determine which is the case here; NOT sufficient.

The correct answer is A;
statement 1 alone is sufficient.

21. Does $2m - 3n = 0$?

(1) $m \neq 0$
(2) $6m = 9n$

Algebra First- and second-degree equations

The question "Does $2m - 3n = 0$?" is equivalent to the simpler question "Does $2m = 3n$?"

(1) This leaves an infinite range of possible values for m, and, since the value(s) for n are not addressed, there is no way to determine the relationship between m and n; NOT sufficient.

(2) Since $6m = 9n$ is equivalent to $3(2m = 3n)$, it can therefore be determined that $2m = 3n$; SUFFICIENT.

The correct answer is B;
statement 2 alone is sufficient.

22. What is the value of the integer x?

(1) x is a prime number.
(2) $31 \le x \le 37$

Arithmetic Properties of numbers

(1) This allows the integer x to be *any* prime, so the value of x cannot be determined; NOT sufficient.

(2) This narrows the definition of the integer x to 31, 32, 33, 34, 35, 36, or 37 but still does not adequately define the value of x; NOT sufficient.

There are two integers that satisfy both (1) and (2): 31 and 37 are prime numbers within the given range. However, there is no further information to choose either one as the single numerical value of x.

The correct answer is E;
both statements together are still not sufficient.

23. If P, Q, and R are three distinct points, do line segments PQ and PR have the same length?

(1) P is the midpoint of line segment QR.
(2) Q and R lie on the same circle with center P.

Geometry Lines + Circles

(1) If P is the midpoint of QR, then by definition, $PQ = PR$; SUFFICIENT.

(2) If Q and R lie on the same circle, of which P is the center point, then any line drawn from P to a point on the circle is a radius. Therefore, PQ and PR are radii, and all radii of a circle are equal; SUFFICIENT.

The correct answer is D;
each statement alone is sufficient.

24. Is the number x between 0.2 and 0.7?

(1) $560x < 280$
(2) $700x > 280$

Algebra Inequalities

(1) It can be determined that $x < 0.5$ by dividing both sides of the inequality by 560. However, it cannot be determined whether x is greater than 0.2; NOT sufficient.

(2) It can be determined that x is greater than 0.4 by dividing both sides of the inequality by 700. However, it cannot be determined whether x is less than 0.7; NOT sufficient.

Taking (1) and (2) together implies that $0.4 < x < 0.5$, which means that x is between 0.2 and 0.7.

The correct answer is C;
both statements together are sufficient.

25. If i and j are integers, is $i + j$ an even integer?

(1) $i < 10$
(2) $i = j$

Arithmetic Properties of numbers

(1) Although $i < 10$, i could be an even number or an odd number less than 10. There is no information about j, so j could be an even number or an odd number. If i and j are both even integers, then $i + j$ is an even integer, and if i and j are both odd integers, then $i + j$ is an even integer. If, however, either i or j is an even integer and the other is an odd integer, then $i + j$ is an odd integer; NOT sufficient.

(2) If $i = j$, then $i + j$ can also be represented as $i + i$ when i is substituted for j in the expression. This can be simplified as $2i$, and since 2 times any integer produces an even integer, then $i + j$ must be an even integer; SUFFICIENT.

The correct answer is B;
statement 2 alone is sufficient.

26. If $n + k = m$, what is the value of k?

(1) $n = 10$
(2) $m + 10 = n$

Algebra First- and second-degree equations

It is given that $n + k = m$, so $k = m - n$. Thus, determining the value of $m - n$ is enough to determine the value of k.

(1) While information is given about the value of n, no information involving m is given. The equation $k = m - n$ or $k = m - 10$ cannot be solved for k; NOT sufficient.

(2) The statement $m + 10 = n$ can be expressed as $m = n - 10$ or, by subtracting n from both sides, $m - n = -10$. The value of $m - n$ and thus the value of k can be determined; SUFFICIENT.

The correct answer is B;
statement 2 alone is sufficient.

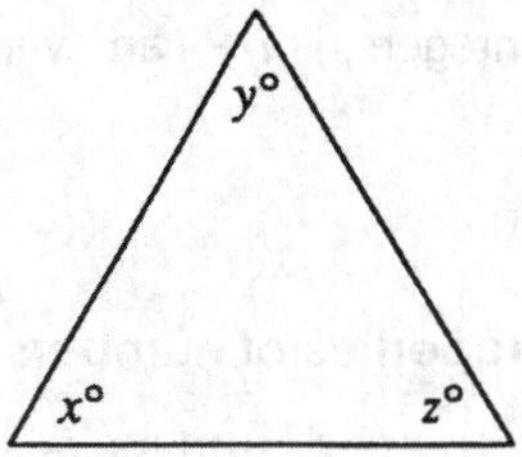

27. Is the triangle above equilateral?

(1) $x = y$
(2) $z = 60$

Geometry Triangles

The sum of the angles of any triangle is 180°. For a triangle to be equilateral, it must be true that all the angles of the triangle are equal. In this case, $x = y = z = 60$ must be true.

(1) Although x and y are equal, they are not necessarily equal to 60°. They could, for example, be 40° and 40°; NOT sufficient.

(2) If $z = 60$, $x + y$ must be 120°. However, x and y are not necessarily 60° and 60°. They could be unequal, for example, 80° and 40°; NOT sufficient.

Taking (1) and (2) together, $z = 60$ means that $x + y = 120$, and $x = y$ is then sufficient to show that $x = y = z = 60$.

The correct answer is C;
both statements together are sufficient.

28. Is x an integer?

(1) $\frac{x}{2}$ is an integer.
(2) $2x$ is an integer.

Arithmetic Properties of numbers

(1) If $\frac{x}{2}$ is an integer, it means that x can be divided by 2 without a remainder. This implies that x is an even integer; SUFFICIENT.

(2) If $2x$ is an integer, then x could also be an integer. However, x could also be an odd number divided by 2, such as $\frac{1}{2}$ or $-\frac{1}{2}$ or $\frac{3}{2}$, none of which is an integer; NOT sufficient.

The correct answer is A;
statement 1 alone is sufficient.

29. What is the value of x?

(1) $2x + 1 = 0$
(2) $(x + 1)^2 = x^2$

Algebra First- and second-degree equations

(1) The value of x can be determined from $2x + 1 = 0$ by subtracting 1 from both sides to get $2x = -1$ and thus $x = -\frac{1}{2}$; SUFFICIENT.

(2) This equation can be expanded to $x^2 + 2x + 1 = x^2$, and thus, by subtracting x^2 from both sides, $2x + 1 = 0$. This is the same equation given and considered in (1); SUFFICIENT.

The correct answer is D;
each statement alone is sufficient.

30. What is the value of $\frac{1}{k} + \frac{1}{r}$?
(1) $k + r = 20$
(2) $kr = 64$

Algebra First- and second-degree equations

The expression $\frac{1}{k} + \frac{1}{r}$ is equivalent to $\frac{r}{kr} + \frac{k}{kr}$ or $\frac{r+k}{kr}$.

(1) If 20 is substituted for $r + k$ in the expression $\frac{r+k}{kr}$, it yields $\frac{20}{kr}$. This cannot be resolved any further; NOT sufficient.

(2) If 64 is substituted for kr in the expression $\frac{r+k}{kr}$, it gives $\frac{r+k}{64}$. Without additional information, this cannot be solved any further; NOT sufficient.

Taking (1) and (2) together, the values can be substituted in the expression $\frac{r+k}{kr}$, giving a value of $\frac{20}{64} = \frac{5}{16}$.

The correct answer is C;
both statements together are sufficient.

31. If x is equal to one of the numbers $\frac{1}{4}$, $\frac{3}{8}$, or $\frac{2}{5}$, what is the value of x?
(1) $\frac{1}{4} < x < \frac{1}{2}$
(2) $\frac{1}{3} < x < \frac{3}{5}$

Algebra Inequalities

In decimal form, $\frac{1}{4} = 0.25$, $\frac{3}{8} = 0.375$, and $\frac{2}{5} = 0.4$.

(1) This can be written as $0.25 < x < 0.5$, so that both $\frac{3}{8}$ and $\frac{2}{5}$ fall within the range and are possible values of x; NOT sufficient.

(2) This can be written as $0.333... < x < 0.6$, so that both $\frac{3}{8}$ and $\frac{2}{5}$ fall within the range and are possible values of x; NOT sufficient.

When both (1) and (2) are taken into consideration and the range is reduced to $0.333... < x < 0.5$, both $\frac{3}{8}$ and $\frac{2}{5}$ still fall within the range and are still possible values of x.

The correct answer is E;
both statements together are still not sufficient.

32. In ΔPQR, if $PQ = x$, $QR = x + 2$, and $PR = y$, which of the three angles of ΔPQR has the greatest degree measure?
(1) $y = x + 3$
(2) $x = 2$

Geometry Triangles

In any triangle, the largest angle is opposite the longest side.

(1) Since $x + 2 > x$, the longest side is either $x + 2$ or y; therefore, it is sufficient to determine whether $y > x + 2$. If $y = x + 3$ and since $x + 3 > x + 2$, it follows by substitution that $y > x + 2$; SUFFICIENT.

(2) Substituting 2 for x yields that $PQ = 2$ and $QR = 4$, but no information is given as to the relationship of these sides with the value of y given for side PR; NOT sufficient.

The correct answer is A;
statement 1 alone is sufficient.

33. What distance did Jane travel?
(1) Bill traveled 40 miles in 40 minutes.
(2) Jane traveled at the same average rate as Bill.

Arithmetic Distance problem

In order to solve distance problems, the formula d = rate × time is used, where d is the distance traveled. Both rate and time must be known in order to find the distance.

(1) If Bill traveled 40 miles in 40 minutes, then his rate of travel was 60 miles per hour. However, this gives no information as to Jane's rate of travel or the length of time that she traveled; NOT sufficient.

(2) It is known that Jane's rate of travel was the same as Bill's, but no information is given as to Bill's rate of travel; NOT sufficient.

Taking (1) and (2) together, it can be determined that Jane's rate of travel was the same as Bill's, or 60 miles per hour. However, it is not known how long Jane traveled, and the distance cannot be found.

The correct answer is E;
both statements together are still not sufficient.

34. What number is 15 percent of x?

(1) 18 is 6 percent of x.

(2) $\frac{2}{3}$ of x is 200.

Arithmetic Percents and fractions

The question can be answered if the value of x is known.

(1) From this, $18 = 0.06x$, which can be solved for x; SUFFICIENT.

(2) This can be expressed as $\frac{2}{3}x = 200$, which can be solved for x; SUFFICIENT.

The correct answer is D;
each statement alone is sufficient.

3.2□Δ6

35. If □ and Δ each represent single digits in the decimal above, what digit does □ represent?

(1) When the decimal is rounded to the nearest tenth, 3.2 is the result.

(2) When the decimal is rounded to the nearest hundredth, 3.24 is the result.

Arithmetic Estimation

(1) Since the tenths digit is 2 in both 3.2□Δ6 and 3.2, the decimal must have been rounded down. Therefore, □ can represent 0, 1, 2, 3, or 4; NOT sufficient.

(2) If the value of Δ is 5, 6, 7, 8, or 9, □ can represent 3, and the decimal must have been rounded up. If the value of Δ is 0, 1, 2, 3, or 4, □ can represent 4, and the decimal must have been rounded down; NOT sufficient.

A variety of numbers, for example 3.2376 and 3.2416, could still satisfy both (1) and (2).

The correct answer is E;
both statements together are still not sufficient.

36. The profit from the sale of a certain appliance increases, though not proportionally, with the number of units sold. Did the profit exceed \$4 million on sales of 380,000 units?

(1) The profit exceeded \$2 million on sales of 200,000 units.

(2) The profit exceeded \$5 million on sales of 350,000 units.

Arithmetic Arithmetic operations + Proportions

(1) If the profits did increase proportionally, it might be reasonable to expect a profit of \$4 million on sales of 400,000 units. However, it is given that the profits do not increase proportionally. Without knowing how the profits increase, it is impossible to tell the profits on sales of 380,000 units; NOT sufficient.

(2) It is given that the profits do increase with the number of units sold. Therefore, since the profit on sales of just 350,000 units well exceeded \$4 million, then sales of 350,000 + 30,000 = 380,000 units would also have a profit exceeding \$4 million; SUFFICIENT.

The correct answer is B;
statement 2 alone is sufficient.

37. What is the value of $xy - yz$?

(1) $y = 2$
(2) $x - z = 5$

Algebra Evaluating expressions

The expression $xy - yz$ can be simplified as $y(x - z)$.

(1) When 2 is substituted for y in $y(x - z)$, it yields $2(x - z)$, and this cannot be evaluated further without additional information; NOT sufficient.

(2) When 5 is substituted for $x - z$ in $y(x - z)$, it yields $5y$, and this cannot be evaluated further without additional information; NOT sufficient.

Together, $y = 2$ from (1) and $x - z = 5$ from (2) can be substituted in $y(x - z)$ to find a value of $2(5) = 10$.

The correct answer is C;
both statements together are sufficient.

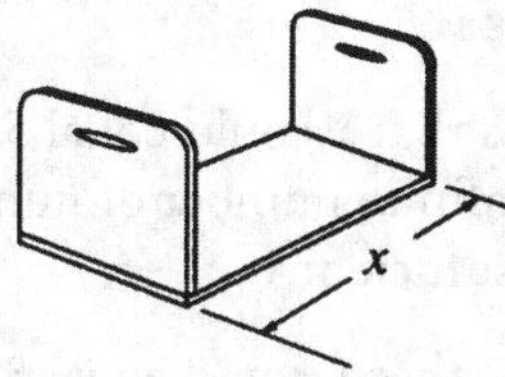

38. Will the first 10 volumes of a 20-volume encyclopedia fit upright in the book rack shown above?

(1) $x = 50$ centimeters
(2) Twelve of the volumes have an average (arithmetic mean) thickness of 5 centimeters.

Arithmetic Measurement

(1) This establishes the length of the book rack but does not give any information about the thickness of the volumes; NOT sufficient.

(2) This establishes the average thickness of 12 of the volumes, but does not give any information about the average thickness of the first 10 volumes; NOT sufficient.

By the same reasoning used in (2), (1) and (2) taken together are not sufficient to answer the question.

The correct answer is E;
both statements together are still not sufficient.

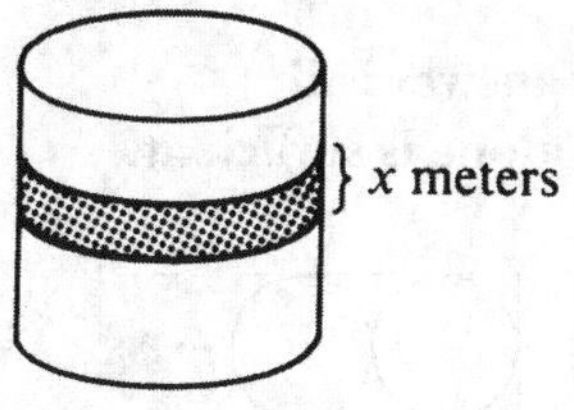

39. A circular tub has a band painted around its circumference, as shown above. What is the surface area of this painted band?

(1) $x = 0.5$
(2) The height of the tub is 1 meter.

Geometry Volume

The surface area of the band is the product of the circumference of the tub and the height of the band. So, both factors must be known for the answer to be determined.

(1) Only one factor, the height of the band, is known; NOT sufficient.

(2) The circumference or the means to find the circumference is not known; NOT sufficient.

With (1) and (2) taken together, there is still no information about the circumference of the tub.

The correct answer is E;
both statements together are still not sufficient.

40. What is the value of integer n?

(1) $n(n+1) = 6$
(2) $2^{2n} = 16$

Arithmetic + Algebra Arithmetic operations + First- and second-degree equations

(1) If $(n+1)$ is multiplied by n, the result is $n^2 + n = 6$. If 6 is subtracted from both sides, the equation becomes $n^2 + n - 6 = 0$. This in turn can be factored as $(n + 3)(n - 2) = 0$. Therefore, n could be either -3 or 2, but there is no further information for deciding between these two values; NOT sufficient.

(2) From $2^{2n} = 16$, 2^{2n} must equal 2^4 (since $2 \times 2 \times 2 \times 2 = 16$). Therefore, $2n = 4$ and $n = 2$; SUFFICIENT.

The correct answer is B;
statement 2 alone is sufficient.

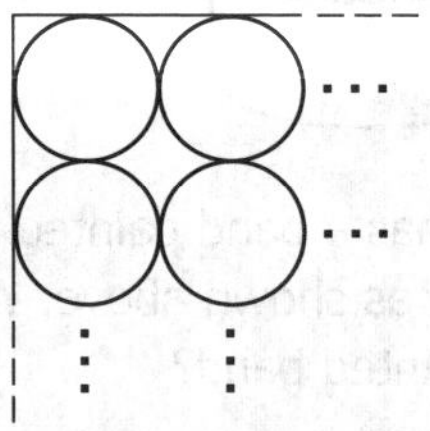

41. The inside of a rectangular carton is 48 centimeters long, 32 centimeters wide, and 15 centimeters high. The carton is filled to capacity with k identical cylindrical cans of fruit that stand upright in rows and columns, as indicated in the figure above. If the cans are 15 centimeters high, what is the value of k?

(1) Each of the cans has a radius of 4 centimeters.
(2) Six of the cans fit exactly along the length of the carton.

Geometry Circles

(1) If the radius of each can is 4 centimeters, the diameter of each can is 8 centimeters. Along the 48-centimeter length of the carton, 6 cans ($48 \div 8$) can be placed; along the 32-centimeter width of the carton, 4 cans ($32 \div 8$) can be placed. Hence, $k = 6 \times 4 = 24$; SUFFICIENT.

(2) If 6 cans fit along the 48-centimeter length of the carton, this implies that the diameter of each can is 8 centimeters ($48 \div 6$). Along the 32-centimeter width, 4 cans can be placed, and again $k = 6 \times 4 = 24$; SUFFICIENT.

The correct answer is D;
each statement alone is sufficient.

$$\begin{cases} x - 4 = z \\ y - x = 8 \\ 8 - z = t \end{cases}$$

42. For the system of equations given, what is the value of z?

(1) $x = 7$
(2) $t = 5$

Algebra First- and second-degree equations

(1) Since $x = 7$, then 7 can be substituted for x in the equation $x - 4 = z$, yielding $z = 3$; SUFFICIENT.

(2) If $t = 5$, then the equation $8 - z = t$ can be used to solve this question:

$8 - z = 5$	substitute for t
$3 - z = 0$	subtract 5 from both sides
$3 = z$	add z to both sides; SUFFICIENT.

The correct answer is D;
each statement alone is sufficient.

43. Is x equal to 5?

(1) $x \geq 5$
(2) $x \leq 5$

Arithmetic + Algebra Properties of numbers + Inequalities

(1) This means that x could equal 5, but it could also equal an infinite number of numbers greater than 5; NOT sufficient.

(2) This means that x could equal 5, but it could also equal an infinite number of numbers less than 5; NOT sufficient.

Taken together, (1) and (2) form the inequality $5 \leq x \leq 5$. This inequality can be true only if $x = 5$.

The correct answer is C;
both statements together are sufficient.

	R	S	T	U
R	0	y	x	62
S	y	0	56	75
T	x	56	0	69
U	62	75	69	0

44. The table above shows the distance, in kilometers, by the most direct route, between any two of the four cities, R, S, T, and U. For example, the distance between City R and City U is 62 kilometers. What is the value of x?

(1) By the most direct route, the distance between S and T is twice the distance between S and R.

(2) By the most direct route, the distance between T and U is 1.5 times the distance between R and T.

Arithmetic + Algebra Tables + First-degree equations

The value of x is the distance between city R and city T; the value of y is the distance between city R and city S.

(1) From this, it can be determined only that $56 = 2y$. No information is given about x; NOT sufficient.

(2) This statement yields the equation $1.5x = 69$, which can be solved for x; SUFFICIENT.

The correct answer is B; statement 2 alone is sufficient.

45. What is the value of the two-digit integer x?

(1) The sum of the two digits is 3.
(2) x is divisible by 3.

Arithmetic Properties of numbers

In a problem of this kind, digits are the integers from 0 through 9, inclusive.

(1) From this, the two-digit integer must be 12, 21, or 30. However, a single numerical value of x cannot be determined; NOT sufficient.

(2) Since there are many two-digit integers divisible by 3, for example, 15, 24, and 27, once again a single numerical value of x cannot be determined; NOT sufficient.

Since all three numbers from (1) are also divisible by 3, (1) and (2) taken together do not provide sufficient information to identify the value of x.

The correct answer is E; both statements together are still not sufficient.

46. What is the tenths digit in the decimal representation of a certain number?

(1) The number is less than $\frac{1}{3}$.
(2) The number is greater than $\frac{1}{4}$.

Arithmetic Properties of numbers

(1) Since the number is less than $\frac{1}{3}$, it is less than 0.333.... However, there is no further information to pinpoint the number among the many numbers less than 0.333...; NOT sufficient.

(2) Since the number is greater than $\frac{1}{4}$, it is greater than 0.25. However, there is no further information to pinpoint the number among the many numbers greater than 0.25; NOT sufficient.From (1) and (2) taken together, the number, n, is greater than 0.25 but less than 0.333..., or $0.25 < n < 0.333...$. Even within this narrower range, there is no way to pinpoint the number or the tenths digit.

The correct answer is E; both statements together are still not sufficient.

47. If the two floors in a certain building are 9 feet apart, how many steps are there in a set of stairs that extends from the first floor to the second floor of the building?

(1) Each step is $\frac{3}{4}$ foot high.
(2) Each step is 1 foot wide.

Arithmetic Arithmetic operations

(1) If each step in the set of stairs is $\frac{3}{4}$ foot high and the set of stairs rises 9 feet from the first floor to the second, the number of steps must be $9 \div \frac{3}{4}$, or $\frac{9}{1} \times \frac{4}{3} = \frac{36}{3} = 12$; SUFFICIENT.

(2) This provides no information regarding the height of the steps, and so the question cannot be answered; NOT sufficient.

The correct answer is A; statement 1 alone is sufficient.

48. If $xy \neq 0$, is $\frac{x}{y} < 0$?

(1) $x = -y$
(2) $-x = -(-y)$

Arithmetic Properties of numbers

(1) Dividing both sides of this equation by y yields $\frac{x}{y} = -1$; thus $\frac{x}{y} < 0$; SUFFICIENT.

(2) If each side of this equation is divided by −1, the result will be the same as (1); SUFFICIENT.

The correct answer is D;
each statement alone is sufficient.

49. How many people are directors of both company K and company R?

(1) There were 17 directors present at a joint meeting of the directors of company K and company R, and no directors were absent.

(2) Company K has 12 directors and company R has 8 directors.

Algebra Sets

(1) This clarifies that company K and company R together have 17 individuals serving as directors. However, there is no information as to the distribution of the company K directors, the company R directors, and the joint directors; NOT sufficient.

(2) This gives the number of directors in each company but no information as to the number of joint directors; NOT sufficient.

Taking (1) and (2) together, it is known from (2) that there are 20 directorships in all. If at a joint meeting, there are only 17 people present, then 20 – 17 = 3 people must be joint directors.

The correct answer is C;
both statements together are sufficient.

50. If x and y are positive, is $\frac{x}{y}$ greater than 1?

(1) $xy > 1$

(2) $x - y > 0$

Algebra Inequalities

Since, being positive, $y > 0$, it follows that $\frac{x}{y} > 1$ if and only if $x > y$.

(1) There are innumerable pairs of different numbers x and y whose product xy is greater than 1. The larger number in each pair can be either x or y; NOT sufficient.

(2) $x - y > 0$ is equivalent to $x > y$; SUFFICIENT.

The correct answer is B;
statement 2 alone is sufficient.

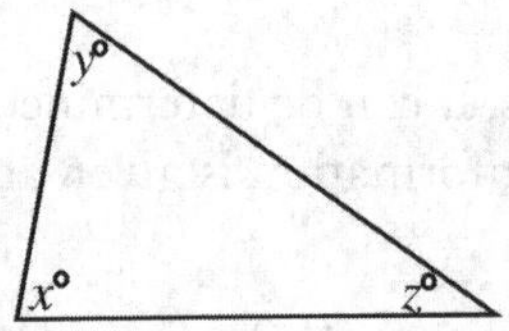

51. What is the value of z in the triangle above?

(1) $x + y = 139$

(2) $y + z = 108$

Geometry Triangles

In any triangle the sum of the interior angles is 180°; here, $x + y + z = 180$.

(1) Since the sum of $x + y$ is known, the value of z can be determined by substituting 139 for $x + y$ in $x + y + z = 180$; SUFFICIENT.

(2) Since the sum of $y + z$ is known, the value of x can be determined by substitution, but there is no way to determine the value of z in the sum $y + z$; NOT sufficient.

The correct answer is A;
statement 1 alone is sufficient.

52. If x, y, and z are nonzero numbers, is $xz = 12$?

(1) $x^2yz = 12xy$

(2) $\frac{z}{4} = \frac{3}{x}$

Algebra First- and second-degree equations

(1) If both sides of the equation $x^2yz = 12xy$ are divided by xy, then the equation becomes $xz = 12$; SUFFICIENT.

(2) When this equation is cross-multiplied, the result is $xz = 12$; SUFFICIENT.

The correct answer is D;
each statement alone is sufficient.

53. A certain company currently has how many employees?

(1) If 3 additional employees are hired by the company and all of the present employees remain, there will be at least 20 employees in the company.

(2) If no additional employees are hired by the company and 3 of the present employees resign, there will be fewer than 15 employees in the company.

Algebra Inequalities

Let n be the current number of employees in the company.

(1) This can be expressed as $n + 3 \geq 20$, and thus $n \geq 17$, which gives a range of possible values of n; NOT sufficient.

(2) This can be expressed as $n - 3 < 15$, and thus $n < 18$, which also gives a range of possible values of n; NOT sufficient.

From (1) and (2) together, the ranges are limited to $n \geq 17$ and $n < 18$, and the value of n can be determined to be 17.

The correct answer is C;
both statements together are sufficient.

54. What is the value of n in the equation $-25 + 19 + n = s$?

(1) $s = 2$

(2) $\frac{n}{s} = 4$

Algebra First- and second-degree equations

(1) If $s = 2$, then the equation becomes $-25 + 19 + n = 2$ or $-6 + n = 2$ or $n = 8$; SUFFICIENT.

(2) If $\frac{n}{s} = 4$, then $n = 4s$. By substituting this value of n in the given equation and simplifying, the equation becomes: $-25 + 19 + 4s = s$ or $-6 + 3s = 0$ or $s = 2$. Once s is found to be 2, the original equation can be solved as above; SUFFICIENT.

The correct answer is D;
each statement alone is sufficient.

55. At a certain picnic, each of the guests was served either a single scoop or a double scoop of ice cream. How many of the guests were served a double scoop of ice cream?

(1) At the picnic, 60 percent of the guests were served a double scoop of ice cream.

(2) A total of 120 scoops of ice cream were served to all the guests at the picnic.

Arithmetic Percent

(1) The total number of guests is unknown, and thus 60% of the total is also unknown; NOT sufficient.

(2) The total number of scoops served is known, but the ratio between single scoops and double scoops is unknown; NOT sufficient.

Using both statements, the ratio of the number of single scoops served to the number of double scoops served can be determined (1) and used with the total number of scoops served (2) to determine the total number of guests who were served a double scoop.

The correct answer is C;
both statements together are sufficient.

56. What is the value of xy?

(1) $y = x + 1$

(2) $y = x^2 + 1$

Algebra First- and second-degree equations

(1) Although it is known that $y = x + 1$, the value of xy cannot be determined; NOT sufficient.

(2) From this it is known that $y = x^2 + 1$, but again the value of xy cannot be determined; NOT sufficient.

Both (1) and (2) taken together imply that $x + 1 = x^2 + 1$, or $x = x^2$. Therefore, either $x = 1$ or $x = 0$. If x equals 1, then $y = 2$, and $xy = 2$. But if $x = 0$, then $y = 1$, and $xy = 0$. So, the value of xy cannot be determined.

The correct answer is E;
both statements together are still not sufficient.

57. What is the value of $\frac{1}{x} + \frac{1}{y}$?

(1) $x + y = 14$

(2) $xy = 24$

Algebra Simplifying expressions

Note that $\frac{1}{x} + \frac{1}{y} = \frac{y}{xy} + \frac{x}{xy}$. This in turn can be simplified to $\frac{x+y}{xy}$.

(1) If $x + y = 14$, then the expression becomes $\frac{14}{xy}$. However, this cannot be solved until the value of xy is known; NOT sufficient.

(2) If $xy = 24$, then the expression becomes $\frac{x+y}{24}$. This cannot be solved until the value of $x + y$ is known; NOT sufficient.

When the values from (1) and (2) are substituted for $\frac{x+y}{xy}$, the expression becomes $\frac{14}{24}$, which can be simplified.

The correct answer is C;
both statements together are sufficient.

58. If d denotes a decimal, is $d \geq 0.5$?

(1) When d is rounded to the nearest tenth, the result is 0.5.

(2) When d is rounded to the nearest integer, the result is 1.

Arithmetic Rounding + Estimating

(1) In this case, for example, the value of d could range from the decimal 0.45 to 0.54. Some of these, such as 0.51 or 0.52, are greater than or equal to 0.5, and others, such as 0.47 or 0.48, are less than 0.5; NOT sufficient.

(2) When the result of rounding d to the nearest integer is 1, d could range in value from the decimal 0.50 to 1.49, which are greater than or equal to 0.5; SUFFICIENT.

The correct answer is B;
statement 2 alone is sufficient.

59. If a real estate agent received a commission of 6 percent of the selling price of a certain house, what was the selling price of the house?

(1) The selling price minus the real estate agent's commission was \$84,600.

(2) The selling price was 250 percent of the original purchase price of \$36,000.

Arithmetic Percent

(1) \$84,600 (selling price – commission) represents 94% (100% – commission of 6%) of the selling price. The selling price can be found by means of the ratio: $\frac{\$84{,}600}{\text{selling price}} = \frac{94}{100}$; SUFFICIENT.

(2) The selling price is equal to 250% of \$36,000 and thus can be calculated; SUFFICIENT.

The correct answer is D;
each statement alone is sufficient.

60. If $\frac{\sqrt{x}}{y} = n$, what is the value of x?

(1) $yn = 10$

(2) $y = 40$ and $n = \frac{1}{4}$

Algebra First- and second-degree equations

$\frac{\sqrt{x}}{y} = n$ is equivalent to $\sqrt{x} = yn$ (if $y \neq 0$). In (1) y cannot equal 0 (since the product of any number and 0 is 0), and in (2) it is given that $y = 40$.

(1) By substitution, $\sqrt{x} = yn = 10$, and x can be determined; SUFFICIENT.

(2) From this, $yn = (40)(1/4) = 10$; and so, by substitution, $\sqrt{x} = yn = 10$, and x can be determined; SUFFICIENT.

The correct answer is D;
each statement alone is sufficient.

61. How many integers are there between, but not including, integers r and s?

(1) $s - r = 10$

(2) There are 9 integers between, but not including, $r + 1$ and $s + 1$.

Arithmetic Properties of numbers

(1) Although the difference between s and r is 10, there are not 10 integers between them. For example, if s is 24 and r is 14, their difference is 10, but there are only 9 integers between them: 15, 16, 17, 18, 19, 20, 21, 22, and 23. This holds true for any two integers whose difference is 10; SUFFICIENT.

(2) Since r and s are the same distance apart as $r+1$ and $s+1$, there would still be 9 integers between r and s in this case, although the integers themselves would change; SUFFICIENT.

The correct answer is D;
each statement alone is sufficient.

62. What is the number of members of Club X who are at least 35 years of age?

(1) Exactly $\frac{3}{4}$ of the members of Club X are under 35 years of age.

(2) The 64 women in Club X constitute 40 percent of the club's membership.

Arithmetic Arithmetic operations

(1) If $\frac{3}{4}$ of the members are less than 35 years old, then $\frac{1}{4}$ of the members are at least 35 years old. However, without any information about the total number of members or the number of members less than 35 years old, the number of members at least 35 years old cannot be determined; NOT sufficient.

(2) Let m = total membership. Since 64 women constitute 40 percent of the membership, $(0.4)(m) = 64$ and thus $m = 160$, so the total membership is 160. However, there is no mention of age, so the number of members at least 35 years old cannot be determined; NOT sufficient.

From (1) and (2) together, $\frac{1}{4}$ of the total membership of 160 are at least 35 years old, so $\frac{1}{4}(160) = 40$.

The correct answer is C;
both statements together are sufficient.

63. Carlotta can drive from her home to her office by one of two possible routes. If she must also return by one of these routes, what is the distance of the shorter route?

(1) When she drives from her home to her office by the shorter route and returns by the longer route, she drives a total of 42 kilometers.

(2) When she drives both ways, from her home to her office and back, by the longer route, she drives a total of 46 kilometers.

Arithmetic Arithmetic operations

(1) Only the sum of the distances of the two routes (42 kilometers) is given and there are infinitely many pairs of numbers with a given sum; NOT sufficient.

(2) The distance of the longer route can be expressed as $\frac{46}{2}$ kilometers, but there is no information about the relationship between the two routes; NOT sufficient.

Using both statements together, the distance of the shorter route can be determined by subtracting the known distance of the longer route (2) from the known sum of the distances of the two routes (1). The distance of the shorter route is thus $42 - \frac{46}{2}$.

The correct answer is C;
both statements together are sufficient.

64. Is $x > y$?

(1) $x = y + 2$

(2) $\frac{x}{2} = y - 1$

Algebra Inequalities

(1) This shows that x is 2 greater than y; SUFFICIENT.

(2) This equation is equivalent to $x = 2y - 2$; thus, by substitution, $x > y$ if and only if $2y - 2 > y$. Since solving this inequality for y yields $2y > y + 2$ or $y > 2$, then $x > y$ if and only if $y > 2$. However, it cannot be determined from this information whether or not $y > 2$; NOT sufficient.

The correct answer is A;
statement 1 alone is sufficient.

65. If m is an integer, is m odd?

(1) $\frac{m}{2}$ is NOT an even integer.
(2) $m - 3$ is an even integer.

Algebra Properties of numbers

(1) Since m could be either the odd integer 3 or the even integer 10 and still satisfy this condition, there is no information to definitively show whether m is odd or even; NOT sufficient.

(2) An odd integer minus an odd integer is always even (e.g., $9 - 3 = 6$); whereas, an even integer minus an odd integer is always odd (e.g., $8 - 3 = 5$). From this, m is odd; SUFFICIENT.

The correct answer is B;
statement 2 alone is sufficient.

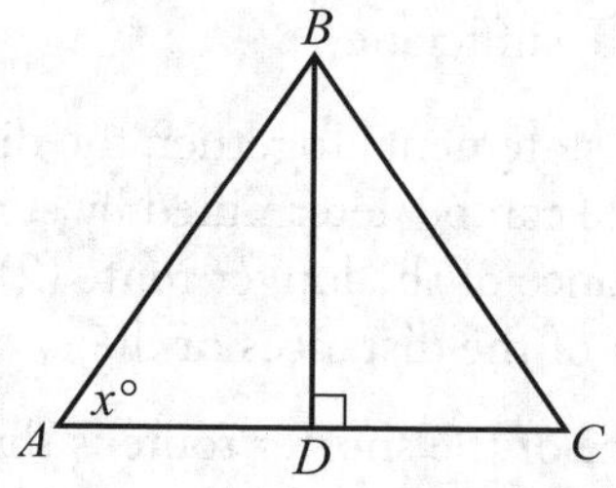

66. What is the area of triangular region ABC above?

(1) The product of BD and AC is 20.
(2) $x = 45$

Geometry Triangles + Area

The area of $\Delta ABC = \frac{BD \times AC}{2}$.

(1) The product of BD and AC is given as 20, so the area of ΔABC is $\frac{20}{2}$ or 10; SUFFICIENT.

(2) With the measurement of x being 45, it is concluded that ΔABD is a 45-45-90 right triangle, where the length of side BD is equal to the length of side AD. However, with no lengths of any side known, there is not enough information to calculate the area; NOT sufficient.

The correct answer is A;
statement 1 alone is sufficient.

67. What is the value of $b + c$?

(1) $ab + cd + ac + bd = 6$
(2) $a + d = 4$

Algebra First- and second-degree equations

(1) The equation $ab + cd + ac + bd = 6$ can be simplified to isolate $b + c$ by regrouping and then factoring as follows:

$(ab + bd) + (ac + cd) = 6$

$b(a + d) + c(a + d) = 6$

$(a + d)(b + c) = 6$

The value of $b + c$, however, cannot be determined unless the value of $a + d$ is known; NOT sufficient.

(2) This provides no information about b and c; NOT sufficient.

Since (2) provides the missing information about the needed value of $a + d$ in (1), the value of $b + c$ can be found when both (1) and (2) are used to complete the equation.

The correct answer is C;
both statements together are sufficient.

68. What is the average (arithmetic mean) of j and k?

(1) The average (arithmetic mean) of $j + 2$ and $k + 4$ is 11.
(2) The average (arithmetic mean) of j, k, and 14 is 10.

Arithmetic Statistics

The average (arithmetic mean) of n numbers is defined as the sum of the n numbers divided by n, or expressed as the average $= \frac{\text{sum of } n \text{ numbers}}{n}$.

The average (arithmetic mean) of $j + k$ can thus be expressed as $\frac{j+k}{2}$.

(1) The information that the average of $j + 2$ and $k + 4$ is 11 can be expressed as $\frac{(j+2)+(k+4)}{2} = 11$. By simplification, $\frac{j+k+6}{2} = 11$. By separating the fraction into its components, $\frac{j+k}{2} + \frac{6}{2} = 11$, and by subtracting 3 from both sides, $\frac{j+k}{2} = 8$; SUFFICIENT.

(2) The information that the mean of j, k, and 14 is 10 can be expressed as $\frac{j+k+14}{3} = 10$. Both sides of this equation can be multiplied by 3 to get $j + k + 14 = 30$, and thus, by subtracting 14 from both sides, $j + k = 16$. Since this establishes the sum of the two numbers j and k, the average of j and k can be determined from this statement; SUFFICIENT.

The correct answer is D; each statement alone is sufficient.

69. Paula and Sandy were among those people who sold raffle tickets to raise money for Club X. If Paula and Sandy sold a total of 100 of the tickets, how many of the tickets did Paula sell?

(1) Sandy sold $\frac{2}{3}$ as many of the raffle tickets as Paula did.

(2) Sandy sold 8 percent of all the raffle tickets sold for Club X.

Algebra Simultaneous equations

If Paula sold p tickets and Sandy sold s tickets, then $p + s = 100$.

(1) Since Sandy sold $\frac{2}{3}$ as many tickets as Paula, $s = \frac{2}{3}p$. The value of p can be determined by solving the two equations simultaneously; SUFFICIENT.

(2) Since the total number of the raffle tickets sold is unknown, the number of tickets that Sandy or Paula sold cannot be determined; NOT sufficient.

The correct answer is A; statement 1 alone is sufficient.

70. Is $ax = 3 - bx$?

(1) $x(a + b) = 3$

(2) $a = b = 1.5$ and $x = 1$.

Algebra First- and second-degree equations

(1) From this:

$x(a + b) = 3$	
$ax + bx = 3$	distributive property
$ax = 3 - bx$	subtract bx from both sides

Thus this statement does show that ax does equal $3 - bx$; SUFFICIENT.

(2) Substituting these values into $ax = 3 - bx$, it can be seen that:

$1.5(1) = 3 - (1.5)(1)$

$1.5 = 3 - 1.5$

The equation $ax = 3 - bx$ is true for the given values; SUFFICIENT.

The correct answer is D; each statement alone is sufficient.

71. A number of people each wrote down one of the first 30 positive integers. Were any of the integers written down by more than one of the people?

(1) The number of people who wrote down an integer was greater than 40.

(2) The number of people who wrote down an integer was less than 70.

Algebra Sets and functions

When the number of integers to choose from is smaller than the number of people making the choice, then at least one of the integers has to be written down by more than one person. When the number of integers to be chosen is the same as or greater than the number of people making the choice, it is very possible that no integer will be written down more than once.

(1) Because the number of people was greater than 30, at least one integer had to be written down by more than one person; SUFFICIENT.

(2) It is not helpful just to know that the number of people was less than 70. If, for instance, the number of people was 35, then at least one of the 30 integers had to be written down by more than one person. If the number of people was instead 25, it was possible that no two people wrote down the same integer; NOT sufficient.

The correct answer is A;
statement 1 alone is sufficient.

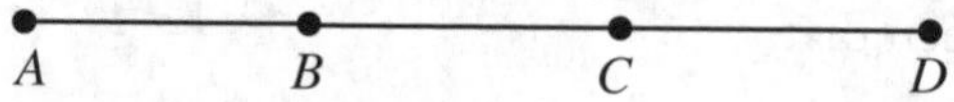

72. In the figure above, is $CD > BC$?

(1) AD = 20
(2) AB = CD

Geometry Lines

(1) Information is given about the total length of the segment shown, which has no bearing on the relative sizes of *CD* and *BC*; NOT sufficient.

(2) Here, *AB* and *CD* are equal, which also has no bearing on the relative sizes of *BC* and *CD*; NOT sufficient.

It cannot be assumed that the figure is drawn to scale. Considering (1) and (2) together, if lengths *AB* and *CD* were each a little larger than pictured, for example,

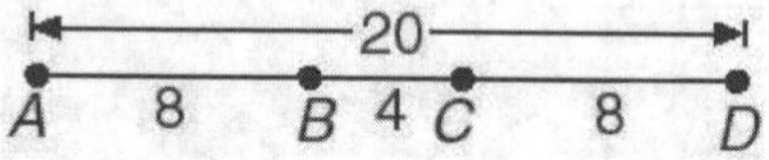

then $BC < CD$. But if the reverse were true, and lengths *AB* and *CD* were instead a little smaller than pictured, then *BC* could be greater than *CD*.

The correct answer is E;
both statements together are still not sufficient.

73. How much did a certain telephone call cost?

(1) The call lasted 53 minutes.
(2) The cost for the first 3 minutes was 5 times the cost for each additional minute.

Algebra Rate problem

The cost of the call depends on the length of the call and the per-minute rates.

(1) This statement only provides information about the length of the call; NOT sufficient.

(2) This statement does not provide actual rates for the telephone call. Relative rates are given, but no information is provided about the length of the call; NOT sufficient.

Let c be the cost of the first 3 minutes. From (2) it can be determined that the cost of each additional minute is $\frac{c}{5}$. The information from (1) and (2) regarding the length of the call and the rate structure can then be expressed in the equation:

Cost of a 53-minute telephone call = $c + \frac{c}{5}(50)$

However, the cost of the 53-minute telephone call cannot be determined because the actual rate per minute is still an unknown quantity.

The correct answer is E;
both statements together are still not sufficient.

74. In a certain office, 50 percent of the employees are college graduates and 60 percent of the employees are over 40 years old. If 30 percent of those over 40 have master's degrees, how many of the employees over 40 have master's degrees?

(1) Exactly 100 of the employees are college graduates.

(2) Of the employees 40 years old or less, 25 percent have master's degrees.

Arithmetic Percents

(1) It is given that 50 percent of the employees are college graduates. Here, it is now known that exactly 100 of the employees are college graduates. Thus, the total number of employees in the company is 200. It is also given that 60 percent of the employees are over 40 years old, which would be (0.60)(200), or 120 employees. Since it is given that 30 percent of those over 40 have master's degrees, then (0.30)(120), or 36 employees are over 40 and have master's degrees; SUFFICIENT.

(2) There is no information regarding *how many* employees fall into any of the categories, and it thus cannot be determined how many employees there are in any category; NOT sufficient.

The correct answer is A;
statement 1 alone is sufficient.

75. Is $rst = 1$?

(1) $rs = 1$
(2) $st = 1$

Arithmetic Properties of numbers

(1) This establishes that $rs = 1$, but since the value of t is unavailable, it is unknown if $rst = 1$; NOT sufficient.

(2) Similarly, this establishes the value of st but the value of r is unknown; NOT sufficient.

Both (1) and (2) taken together are still not sufficient to determine whether or not $rst = 1$. For example, it is true that if $r = s = t = 1$, then $rs = 1$, $st = 1$, and $rst = 1$. However, if $r = t = 5$, and $s = \frac{1}{5}$, then $rs = 1$, $st = 1$, but $rst = 5$.

The correct answer is E;
both statements together are still not sufficient.

TOTAL EXPENSES FOR THE FIVE DIVISIONS OF COMPANY *H*

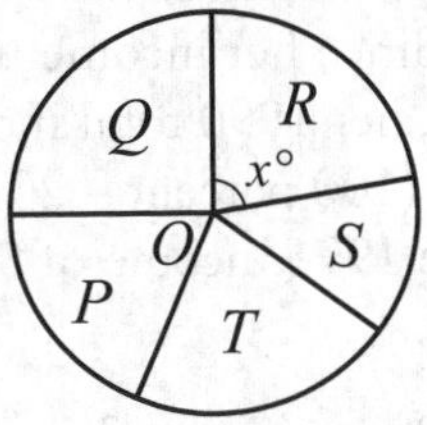

76. The figure above represents a circle graph of Company H's total expenses broken down by the expenses for each of its five divisions. If O is the center of the circle and if Company H's total expenses are \$5,400,000, what are the expenses for division R?

(1) $x = 94$
(2) The total expenses for division S and T are twice as much as the expenses for division R.

Geometry Circles

In this circle, the expenses of division R are equal to the measurement of $\frac{x}{360}$ multiplied by \$5,400,000, or \$15,000x. Therefore, it is necessary to know the measurement of x in order to solve this problem.

(1) The measurement of x is given as 94, so the expenses of R are \$15,000(94) or \$1,410,000; SUFFICIENT.

(2) This gives a comparison among some of the divisions, but the question of the measurement of x is not addressed; NOT sufficient.

The correct answer is A;
statement 1 alone is sufficient.

77. If Ms. Smith's income was 20 percent more for 1991 than it was for 1990, how much was her income for 1991?

(1) Ms. Smith's income for the first 6 months of 1990 was \$17,500 and her income for the last 6 months of 1990 was \$20,000.
(2) Ms. Smith's income for 1991 was \$7,500 greater than her income for 1990.

Arithmetic Arithmetic operations

(1) From this, Ms. Smith's total income for 1990 was \$37,500. Since her income was 20 percent higher in 1991, her 1990 total income multiplied by 120 percent (100 percent + 20 percent) would yield the 1991 income of \$45,000; SUFFICIENT.

(2) Since \$7,500 represents 20 percent of the 1990 income, then the total 1990 income can be represented by \$7,500 × 5 = \$37,500. Since the 1991 income is \$7,500 more than the 1990 income, the 1991 income can be found by adding \$37,500 + \$7,500; SUFFICIENT.

The correct answer is D;
each statement alone is sufficient.

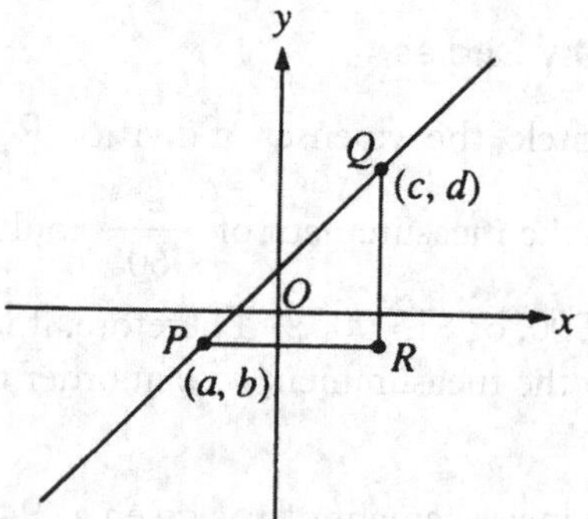

78. In the figure above, segments PR and QR are each parallel to one of the rectangular coordinate axes. Is the ratio of the length of QR to the length of PR equal to 1?

(1) $c = 3$ and $d = 4$.
(2) $a = -2$ and $b = -1$.

Geometry Coordinate geometry

Note that the ratio of QR to PR is the slope (that is, the ratio of the change in the y values to the change in the x values) of the line of which QP is a segment. Two points on a line are necessary to determine the slope of a line.

(1) Only the location of one point (c, d) is given; NOT sufficient.

(2) Only the location of one point (a, b) is given; NOT sufficient.

Together (1) and (2) provide two points on the line, which is sufficient to determine whether the ratio of QR to PR (or the slope) is equal to 1.

The correct answer is C;
both statements together are sufficient.

79. While on a straight road, car X and car Y are traveling at different constant rates. If car X is now 1 mile ahead of car Y, how many minutes from now will car X be 2 miles ahead of car Y?

(1) Car X is traveling at 50 miles per hour and car Y is traveling at 40 miles per hour.

(2) Three minutes ago car X was $\frac{1}{2}$ mile ahead of car Y.

Arithmetic Rate problem

Simply stated, the question is how long will it take car X to get one mile further ahead of car Y than it is now.

(1) At their constant rates, car X would increase its distance from car Y by 10 miles every hour or, equivalently, 1 mile every 6 minutes; SUFFICIENT.

(2) This states that car X increases its distance from car Y by 0.5 mile every 3 minutes, or alternately 1 mile every 6 minutes; SUFFICIENT.

The correct answer is D;
each statement alone is sufficient.

80. If a, b, and c are integers, is $a - b + c$ greater than $a + b - c$?

(1) b is negative.
(2) c is positive.

Algebra Inequalities

Essentially, it is necessary to determine whether the inequality $a - b + c > a + b - c$ is true. This inequality can be simplified as $-b + c > b - c$, which is equivalent to $2c > 2b$, or $c > b$. If it can be determined that the simpler inequality $c > b$ is true, then it follows that $a - b + c > a + b - c$ is also true.

(1) Despite the information that $0 > b$, it cannot be determined whether $c > b$, because c is still unknown; NOT sufficient.

(2) Despite the information that $c > 0$, it cannot be determined whether $c > b$, because b is still unknown; NOT sufficient.

Using (1) and (2) together, it follows that $c > 0 > b$ and $c > b$. Therefore, it can be determined that $a - b + c > a + b - c$ is also true.

The correct answer is C;
both statements together are sufficient.

81. If a certain animated cartoon consists of a total of 17,280 frames on film, how many minutes will it take to run the cartoon?

(1) The cartoon runs without interruption at the rate of 24 frames per second.

(2) It takes 6 times as long to run the cartoon as it takes to rewind the film, and it takes a total of 14 minutes to do both.

Arithmetic Arithmetic operations

(1) Given the frames-per-second speed, it can be determined that it takes $\frac{17,280}{24 \times 60}$ minutes to run the cartoon; SUFFICIENT.

(2) It is given both that it takes 14 minutes to run the cartoon and rewind the film and that, with the ratio 6:1 expressed as a fraction, the cartoon runs $\frac{6}{7}$ of the total time. Thus, it can be determined that running the cartoon takes $\frac{6}{7}$ of the 14 minutes; SUFFICIENT.

The correct answer is D;
each statement alone is sufficient.

82. A box contains only red chips, white chips, and blue chips. If a chip is randomly selected from the box, what is the probability that the chip will be either white or blue?

(1) The probability that the chip will be blue is $\frac{1}{5}$.

(2) The probability that the chip will be red is $\frac{1}{3}$.

Arithmetic Probability

(1) Since the probability of drawing a blue chip is known, the probability of drawing a chip that is not blue (in other words, a red or white chip) can also be found. However, the probability of drawing a white or blue chip cannot be determined from this information; NOT sufficient.

(2) The probability that the chip will be either white or blue is the same as the probability that it will NOT be red. Thus, the probability is $1 - \frac{1}{3} = \frac{2}{3}$; SUFFICIENT.

The correct answer is B;
statement 2 alone is sufficient.

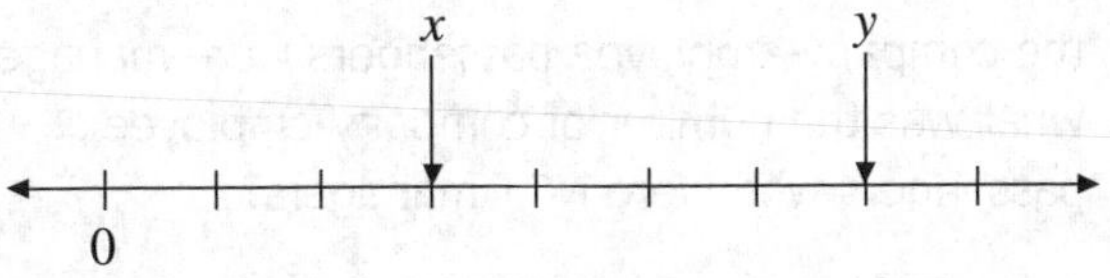

83. If the successive tick marks shown on the number line above are equally spaced and if x and y are the numbers designating the end points of intervals as shown, what is the value of y?

(1) $x = \frac{1}{2}$

(2) $y - x = \frac{2}{3}$

Arithmetic Properties of numbers

(1) If 3 tick marks represent a value of $\frac{1}{2}$, then 6 tick marks would represent a value of 1. From this it can be established that each subdivision of the line represents $\frac{1}{6}$, so the value of y is $\frac{7}{6}$; SUFFICIENT.

(2) From this, the four equal subdivisions between y and x represent a total distance of $\frac{2}{3}$. This implies that each subdivision of the number line has the length $\frac{1}{4}\left(\frac{2}{3}\right)=\frac{1}{6}$, enabling the value of y to be found; SUFFICIENT.

The correct answer is D; each statement alone is sufficient.

84. On a company-sponsored cruise, $\frac{2}{3}$ of the passengers were company employees and the remaining passengers were their guests. If $\frac{3}{4}$ of the company-employee passengers were managers, what was the number of company-employee passengers who were NOT managers?

(1) There was a total of 690 passengers on the cruise.
(2) There was a total of 230 passengers who were guests of the company employees.

Arithmetic Arithmetic operations

(1) From this, since $\frac{2}{3}$ of the passengers were company employees, then $\frac{2}{3} \times 690 = 460$ passengers were company employees. Then, since $\frac{3}{4}$ of the company employees were managers, so $1 - \frac{3}{4} = \frac{1}{4}$ of the company-employee passengers were not managers. Therefore $\frac{1}{4} \times 460 = 115$ company employees who were not managers; SUFFICIENT.

(2) If 230 of the passengers were guests, then this represents $1 - \frac{2}{3} = \frac{1}{3}$ of the cruise passengers. Therefore, there were $230 \times 3 = 690$ passengers all together, $690 - 230 = 460$ of whom were company employees. Since $1 - \frac{3}{4} = \frac{1}{4}$ of the company employees were not managers, $\frac{1}{4} \times 460 = 115$ of the passengers who were company employees were not managers; SUFFICIENT.

The correct answer is D; each statement alone is sufficient.

85. In the *xy*-plane, does the point (4, 12) lie on line *k*?

(1) The point (1, 7) lies on line *k*.
(2) The point (−2, 2) lies on line *k*.

Geometry Coordinate geometry

(1) While many lines could pass through the point (1, 7), only one of these lines would also pass through the point (4, 12). Without further information, it cannot be determined whether line *k* passes through both these points; NOT sufficient.

(2) There are also many lines that could pass through the point (−2, 2), and only one of these lines would also pass through the point (4, 12). From this information, it cannot be determined whether (4, 12) lies on line *k*; NOT sufficient.

Since both points from (1) and (2) lie on line *k*, it can be determined whether the point (4, 12) also lies on line *k*. It does so if the slope of the line that passes through (4, 12) and (1, 7) is the same as the slope of the line that passes through (4, 12) and (−2, 2). The formula for the slope m is $m=\frac{y_2-y_1}{x_2-x_1}$. The calculation of the slope for points (1, 7) and (4, 12) is $m=\frac{12-7}{4-1}=\frac{5}{3}$, and for points (−2, 2) and (4, 12) is $m=\frac{12-2}{4-(-2)}=\frac{10}{6}=\frac{5}{3}$.

Since the slopes for the two lines are the same, it can be concluded that point (4, 12) does indeed lie on the same line *k* as points (1, 7) and (−2, 2).

The correct answer is C; both statements together are sufficient.

86. The length of the edging that surrounds circular garden *K* is $\frac{1}{2}$ the length of the edging that surrounds circular garden *G*. What is the area of garden *K*? (Assume that the edging has negligible width.)

(1) The area of *G* is 25π square meters.
(2) The edging around *G* is 10π meters long.

Geometry Circles + Area

Note that the length of the edging around a circular garden is equal to the circumference of the circle. The formula for the circumference of a circle, where C is the circumference and d is the length of the diameter is $C = \pi d$. The formula for the area of a circle, where A is the area and r is the length of the radius, is $A = \pi r^2$. In any circle, r is equal to $\frac{1}{2}d$. If the length of the edging around K is equal to $\frac{1}{2}$ the length of the edging around G, then the circumference of K is equal to $\frac{1}{2}$ the circumference of G.

(1) Since the area of G is 25π square meters, and since $A = 25\pi$, by substitution and simplification, $25\pi = \pi r^2$ or $25 = r^2$ and $5 = r$. So, if the radius of G is 5, the diameter is 10, and the circumference of G is equal to $C = \pi d$ or $C = 10\pi$. Since the circumference of K is $\frac{1}{2}$ that of G, then the circumference of K is 5π, so the diameter of K is 5. If the diameter of K is 5, the radius of K is 2.5, and the area of K is $A = \pi r^2$, or $A = \pi(2.5)^2$ or 6.25π; SUFFICIENT.

(2) If the edging around G is 10π meters long, then the circumference of G is 10π. The area of K can then by found by proceeding as in (1); SUFFICIENT.

The correct answer is D;
each statement alone is sufficient.

87. An employee is paid 1.5 times the regular hourly rate for each hour worked in excess of 40 hours per week, excluding Sunday, and 2 times the regular hourly rate for each hour worked on Sunday. How much was the employee paid last week?

(1) The employee's regular hourly rate is \$10.
(2) Last week the employee worked a total of 54 hours but did not work more than 8 hours on any day.

Arithmetic Arithmetic operations

The employee's pay consists of at most 40 hours at the regular hourly rate, plus any overtime pay at either 1.5 or 2 times the regular hourly rate.

(1) From this, the employee's regular pay for a 40-hour week is \$400. However, there is no information about overtime, and so the employee's total pay cannot be calculated; NOT sufficient.

(2) From this, the employee worked a total of $54 - 40 = 14$ hours. However, there is no indication of how many hours were worked on Sunday (at 2 times the regular hourly rate) or another day (at 1.5 times the regular hourly rate, or of an hourly rate); NOT sufficient.

With (1) and (2) taken together, there is still no way to calculate the amount of overtime pay.

The correct answer is E;
both statements together are still not sufficient.

88. What was the revenue that a theater received from the sale of 400 tickets, some of which were sold at the full price and the remainder of which were sold at a reduced price?

(1) The number of tickets sold at the full price was $\frac{1}{4}$ of the total number of tickets sold.
(2) The full price of a ticket was \$25.

Arithmetic Arithmetic operations

(1) Since $\frac{1}{4}$ of the tickets were sold at full price, $\frac{3}{4} \times 400 = 300$ tickets were sold at a reduced price. However, the revenue cannot be determined from this information; NOT sufficient.

(2) Although a full-priced ticket cost \$25, the revenue cannot be determined without additional information; NOT sufficient.

When both (1) and (2) are taken together, the revenue from full-priced tickets was 100 × \$25 = \$2,500, but the cost of a reduced-priced ticket is still unknown, and the theater's revenues cannot be calculated.

The correct answer is E; both statements together are still not sufficient.

89. If ° represents one of the operations +, –, and ×, is $k \circ (\ell + m) = (k \circ \ell) + (k \circ m)$ for all numbers k, ℓ, and m?

(1) $k \circ 1$ is not equal to $1 \circ k$ for some numbers k.
(2) ° represents subtraction.

Arithmetic Properties of numbers

(1) For operations + and –, $k \circ 1$ is equal to $1 \circ k$ since both $k + 1 = 1 + k$, and also $k \times 1 = 1 \times k$. Therefore, the operation represented must be subtraction. From this, it is possible to determine whether $k - (\ell + m) = (k - \ell) + (k - m)$ holds for all numbers k, ℓ, and m; SUFFICIENT.

(2) The information is given directly that the operation represented is subtraction. Once again, it can be determined whether $k - (\ell + m) = (k - \ell) + (k - m)$ holds for all numbers k, ℓ, and m; SUFFICIENT.

The correct answer is D;
each statement alone is sufficient.

90. How many of the 60 cars sold last month by a certain dealer had neither power windows nor a stereo?

(1) Of the 60 cars sold, 20 had a stereo but not power windows.
(2) Of the 60 cars sold, 30 had both power windows and a stereo.

Algebra Sets

(1) With this information, there are three other categories of cars that are unknown: those equipped with both a stereo and power windows, with power windows but with no stereo, and with neither power windows nor a stereo; NOT sufficient.

(2) Again there are three other categories that are unknown: those with a stereo but no power windows, with power windows with no stereo, and with neither power windows nor a stereo; NOT sufficient.

From (1) and (2) together, it can be deduced that there were 60 – 50 = 10 cars sold that did not have a stereo. However, it is unknown and cannot be concluded from this information how many of these cars did not have a stereo but did have power windows or did not have either a stereo or power windows.

The correct answer is E;
both statements together are still not sufficient.

91. By what percent did the median household income in Country Y decrease from 1970 to 1980?

(1) In 1970 the median household income in Country Y was $\frac{2}{3}$ of the median household income in Country X.
(2) In 1980 the median household income in Country Y was $\frac{1}{2}$ of the median household income in Country X.

Arithmetic Percents

In order to answer this question, it is necessary to have the data on the median household income in Country Y for both 1970 and 1980.

(1) This offers no information about the actual income in Country X, so the 1970 data for Country Y cannot be determined, and there are no data for Country Y for 1980; NOT sufficient.

(2) This provides no facts about the income of Country X in 1980, and there are no data for Country Y for 1970; NOT sufficient.

Both (1) and (2) together compare the median household income of Country Y to that of Country X for the pertinent dates. However, without any concrete data about Country X, the comparisons are not helpful in calculating the percent decrease in Country Y from 1970 to 1980.

The correct answer is E;
both statements together are still not sufficient.

92. A certain group of car dealerships agreed to donate x dollars to a Red Cross chapter for each car sold during a 30-day period. What was the total amount that was expected to be donated?

(1) A total of 500 cars were expected to be sold.
(2) Sixty more cars were sold than expected, so that the total amount actually donated was \$28,000.

Algebra Applied problem

(1) It is known that 500 cars were expected to be sold, so $500x$ represents the total amount of the expected donation. However, x is unknown so $500x$ cannot be determined; NOT sufficient.

(2) Since $60x$ represents the extra amount donated beyond the expectation, the total amount that it was expected would be donated would be \$28,000 minus $60x$. Again, x is unknown, so the total amount expected to be donated cannot be found; NOT sufficient.

If the information in (1) and (2) is used together, then $500x = \$28{,}000 - 60x$, from which the value of x can be determined. Thus, the total amount expected to be donated can also be determined ($500x$).

The correct answer is C;
both statements together are sufficient.

93. While driving on the expressway, did Robin ever exceed the 55-miles-per-hour speed limit?

(1) Robin drove 100 miles on the expressway.
(2) Robin drove for 2 hours on the expressway.

Arithmetic Distance problem + Statistics

The formula for a distance problem is distance = rate × time. To determine whether Robin ever exceeded the 55-miles-per-hour speed limit,

it is necessary to determine the rate, or rate = $\frac{\text{distance}}{\text{time}}$.

Therefore, it is necessary to know the distance Robin traveled and the time it took Robin to travel that distance.

(1) This gives only the distance that Robin traveled and not the time; NOT sufficient.

(2) This gives only the time that Robin traveled and not the distance; NOT sufficient.

Using the information from (1) and (2), the rate at which Robin traveled is equal to the $\frac{\text{distance}}{\text{time}}$ or $\frac{100}{2}$, for an average speed of 50 miles per hour. However, because this is only Robin's *average* speed, there is no way of knowing whether Robin at some point exceeded the speed limit and then, at another point, traveled under 50 mph.

The correct answer is E;
both statements together are still not sufficient.

94. In Jefferson School, 300 students study French or Spanish or both. If 100 of these students do not study French, how many of these students study both French and Spanish?

(1) Of the 300 students, 60 do not study Spanish.
(2) A total of 240 of the students study Spanish.

Algebra Sets (Venn diagrams)

One way to solve a problem of this kind is to represent the data regarding the 300 students by a Venn diagram. Let x be the number of students who study both French and Spanish, and let y be the number who do not study Spanish (i.e., those who study only French). It is given that there are 100 students who do not study French (i.e., those who study only Spanish). This information can be represented by the Venn diagram below, where $300 = x + y + 100$:

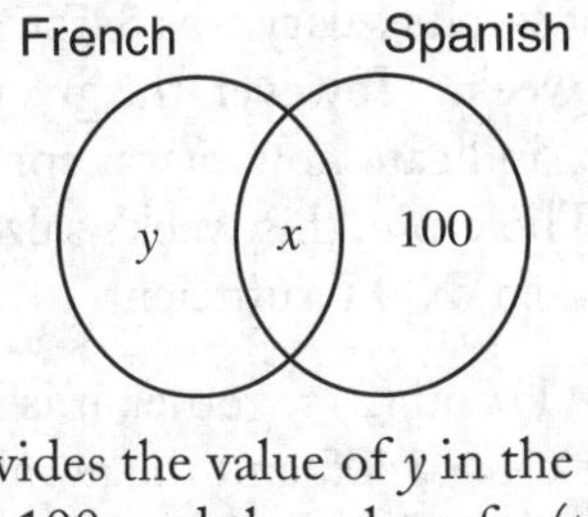

(1) This provides the value of y in the equation $300 = x + y + 100$, and the value of x (the number who study both languages) can thus be determined; SUFFICIENT.

(2) Referring to the Venn diagram above, this provides the information that 240 is the sum of $x + 100$, the number of students who study Spanish. That is, 240 is equal to the number who study both French and Spanish (x) plus the number who study only Spanish (100). Since $240 = x + 100$, the value of x and thus the number who study both languages can be determined; SUFFICIENT.

The correct answer is D;
each statement alone is sufficient.

95. A certain salesperson's weekly salary is equal to a fixed base salary plus a commission that is directly proportional to the number of items sold during the week. If 50 items are sold this week, what will be the salesperson's salary for this week?

(1) Last week 45 items were sold.
(2) Last week's salary was \$405.

Algebra Applied problem

The employee's weekly salary w is equal to the fixed base salary s plus a commission c or $w = s + c$. The commission, in turn, is directly proportional to the number of items sold during the week. Therefore, in order to solve this problem, both the fixed base salary and the commission must be known, as well as the means to calculate the commission based on the number of items sold.

(1) The number of items sold last week does not give any indication as to the fixed base salary or provide a way to calculate the commission; NOT sufficient.

(2) Last week's salary was \$405, so w was \$405 for last week. However, the given information does not indicate how w was spread among s and c. Therefore, this week's salary cannot be determined; NOT sufficient.

Taking (1) and (2) together, it is known that for last week w = \$405 and the number of items sold was 45. This does not provide any clues as to determining this week's salary. For example, s could be \$315, and then the commission based on \$2 per item sold would be \$90. Based on that analysis, for this week, w = \$315 + \$100 = \$415. However if s was \$180 and each item sold merited a commission of \$5, then this week's salary would be w = \$180 + \$250 = \$430.

The correct answer is E;
both statements together are still not sufficient.

96. If Juan had a doctor's appointment on a certain day, was the appointment on a Wednesday?

(1) Exactly 60 hours before the appointment, it was Monday.
(2) The appointment was between 1:00 p.m. and 9:00 p.m.

Arithmetic Arithmetic operations

(1) From this, it is not known at what point on Monday it was 60 hours before the appointment, and the day of the appointment cannot be known. If, for example, the specific point on Monday was 9:00 a.m., 60 hours later it would be 9:00 p.m. Wednesday, and the appointment would thus be on a Wednesday. If the specific point on Monday was instead 9:00 p.m., 60 hours later it would be 9:00 a.m. Thursday, and the appointment would instead fall on a Thursday rather than Wednesday; NOT sufficient.

(2) No information is given about the day of the appointment; NOT sufficient.

Using (1) and (2) together, it can be determined that the point 60 hours before any time from 1:00 p.m. to 9:00 p.m. on any particular day, as given in (2), is a time between 1:00 a.m. and 9:00 a.m. two days earlier. If 60 hours before an appointment in this 1:00 p.m.—9:00 p.m. time frame it was Monday as given in (1), then the appointment had to be on a Wednesday.

The correct answer is C;
both statements together are sufficient.

97. What is the value of $5x^2 + 4x - 1$?

(1) $x(x + 2) = 0$
(2) $x = 0$

Algebra First- and second-degree equations

(1) Since $x(x + 2) = 0$, either $x = 0$ or $x = -2$. However, each of these two values of x yields a different value for $5x^2 + 4x - 1$; NOT sufficient.

(2) Since $x = 0$, the value of the expression can be determined; SUFFICIENT.

The correct answer is B;
statement 2 alone is sufficient.

98. At Larry's Auto Supply Store, Brand X antifreeze is sold by the gallon and Brand Y motor oil is sold by the quart. Excluding sales tax, what is the total cost for 1 gallon of Brand X antifreeze and 1 quart of Brand Y motor oil?

(1) Excluding sales tax, the total cost for 6 gallons of Brand X antifreeze and 10 quarts of Brand Y motor oil is 58. (There is no quantity discount.)

(2) Excluding sales tax, the total cost for 4 gallons of Brand X antifreeze and 12 quarts of Brand Y motor oil is 44. (There is no quantity discount.)

Algebra Applied problem + Simultaneous equations

Let the cost of Brand X be represented by x and the cost of Brand Y be represented by y.

(1) This can be represented by the equation $6x + 10y = 58$. However, since the cost of neither brand is known, the problem cannot be solved; NOT sufficient.

(2) This can be represented by the equation $4x + 12y = 44$. Once again, since the cost of neither brand is known, the answer is still unknown; NOT sufficient.

Taken together, the equations from (1) and (2) can be solved simultaneously:

$6x + 10y = 58$

$4x + 12y = 44$

Solving the second equation for x:

$4(x + 3y) = 44$	distributive property
$x + 3y = 11$	divide both sides by 4
$x = 11 - 3y$	subtract $3y$ from both sides

Substituting this value into the first equation:

$6(11 - 3y) + 10y = 58$	substitute for x
$66 - 18y + 10y = 58$	distributive property
$-8y = -8$	simplify and subtract 66 from both sides
$y = 1$	divide both sides by -8

Substituting this value into the second equation:

$4x + 12y = 44$	
$4x + 12(1) = 44$	substitute for y
$4x = 32$	subtract 12 from both sides
$x = 8$	divide both sides by 4

The cost of Brand X is \$8 and the cost of Brand Y is \$1. The total cost of 1 gallon of Brand X and 1 quart of Brand Y is thus \$9.

The correct answer is C;
both statements together are sufficient.

99. Is $m \neq n$?

(1) $m + n < 0$

(2) $mn < 0$

Algebra Inequalities

(1) If $m + n < 0$, it is possible that $m = n$, for example, $m = -2$, $n = -2$. It is also possible that $m \neq n$, for example, $m = -2$, $n = -3$; NOT sufficient.

(2) Since mn is negative, one of the two numbers must be negative and the other positive, which clearly means that m cannot equal n; SUFFICIENT.

The correct answer is B;
statement 2 alone is sufficient.

100. When a player in a certain game tossed a coin a number of times, 4 more heads than tails resulted. Heads or tails resulted each time the player tossed the coin. How many times did heads result?

(1) The player tossed the coin 24 times.
(2) The player received 3 points each time heads resulted and 1 point each time tails resulted, for a total of 52 points.

Arithmetic + Algebra Probability + Applied problem + Simultaneous equations

The probability of either heads or tails in a non-weighted coin toss is $\frac{1}{2}$. This means that approximately $\frac{1}{2}$ of the time the result will be heads, and approximately $\frac{1}{2}$ of the time the result will be tails. Therefore, it is expected that the number of heads will equal the number of tails. However, in any given series of coin tosses, the outcome may vary slightly, as in this game. In the coin tosses in this problem, there were 4 more heads than tails or, letting h represent heads and t represent tails, $h = t + 4$.

(1) If the coin was tossed 24 times, then the number of heads and the number of tails is equal to 24, or $h + t = 24$. The previous equation and the equation from this statement can be solved simultaneously:

$h + t = 24$

$h = t + 4$

$t + 4 + t = 24$	substitute for h
$2t + 4 = 24$	simplify
$2t = 20$	subtract 4 from both sides
$t = 10$	divide both sides by 2

If tails was the result 10 times, then heads must have been the result 14 times (24 – 10 = 14); SUFFICIENT.

(2) This can be represented by the equation $3h + 1t = 52$ and solved simultaneously with the given equation:

$h = t + 4$

$3h + 1t = 52$

$3(t + 4) + t = 52$	substitute for h
$3t + 12 + t = 52$	distributive property
$4t + 12 = 52$	simplify
$4t = 40$	subtract 12 from both sides
$t = 10$	divide both sides by 4

If tails was the result 10 times, then heads must have been the result 14 times; SUFFICIENT.

The correct answer is D;
each statement alone is sufficient.

101. If S is the infinite sequence $S_1 = 9$, $S_2 = 99$, $S_3 = 999, \ldots, S_k = 10^k - 1, \ldots$, is every term in S divisible by the prime number p?

(1) p is greater than 2.
(2) At least one term in sequence S is divisible by p.

Arithmetic Properties of numbers

To know whether every term in S is divisible by p, it is necessary to establish the value of p. Examine various prime numbers along with the constraints imposed by (1) and (2).

(1) From this, p could be any of the prime numbers 3, 5, 7, 11, etc. While each of the numbers 9, 99, 999, and so forth, is divisible by 3, none of them is divisible by 5. It follows that this information is not enough to determine the value of p; NOT sufficient.

(2) It can be seen that the second term, 99, is divisible by the two primes 3 and 11; the first term, 9, is divisible by 3 only. Thus the value of prime number p still cannot be ascertained; NOT sufficient.

Since the two prime numbers considered in (2), namely, 3 and 11, also satisfy statement (1), it follows that the value of p cannot be determined from these statements.

The correct answer is E;
both statements together are still not sufficient.

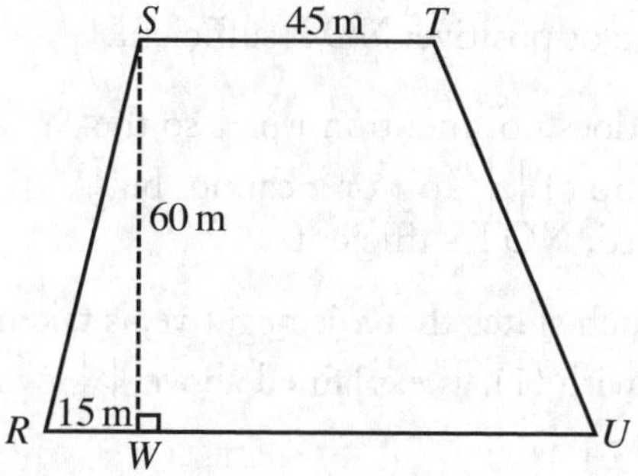

102. Quadrilateral *RSTU* shown above is a site plan for a parking lot in which side *RU* is parallel to side *ST* and *RU* is longer than *ST*. What is the area of the parking lot?

(1) *RU* = 80 meters
(2) $TU = 20\sqrt{10}$ meters

Geometry Area

The area of a quadrilateral region that has parallel sides of lengths a and b and altitude h is $\frac{1}{2}(a+b)h$. Therefore, it is necessary to know the lengths of the two parallel sides and the altitude in order to find the area. The altitude is shown to be 60 m and the length of one of the parallel sides is 45 m.

(1) The length of the base of the quadrilateral lot, that is, the second parallel side, is given. Thus, the area of the lot, in square meters, is $\frac{(45+80)}{2}(60)$; SUFFICIENT.
(Alternatively, if the formula is unfamiliar, drawing the altitude from *T*, as shown in the figure below, can be helpful.)

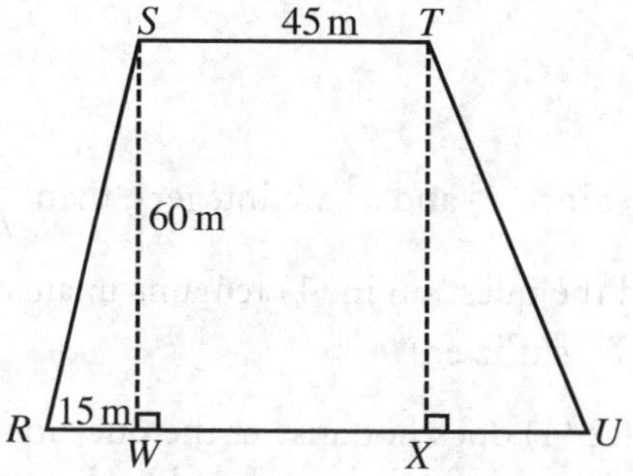

Since $ST = WX$ or 45 m, it can be seen that, in meters, $RU = 15 + 45 + XU$. Since $RU = 80$, then $80 = 15 + 45 + XU$, or $XU = 20$. The area of *RSTU* is the sum of the areas (1/2 bh) of the two triangles ($\triangle SRW = 450\text{ m}^2$ and $\triangle TUX = 600\text{ m}^2$) and the area ($l \times w$) of the rectangle *STWX* (2700 m^2). Thus the same conclusion can be drawn.

(2) Continue to refer to the supplemental figure showing the altitude drawn from *T*. Although the length of the base of the quadrilateral lot is not fully known, parts of the base (*RW* as well as *ST* = *WX*) are known. The only missing information is the length of *XU*. This can be found using the Pythagorean theorem with triangle *TUX*. Since *ST* and *RU* are parallel, $TX = SW = 60$ m. It is given that $TU = 20\sqrt{10}$ m. Using the Pythagorean theorem, where $a^2 + b^2 = c^2$, yields $60^2 + XU^2 = \left(20\sqrt{10}\right)^2$ and by simplification, $3600 + XU^2 = 4000$, and thus $XU^2 = 4000$ and $XU = 20$. Then, the length of *RU*, in meters, is $15 + 45 + 20 = 80$. Since this is the information given in (1), it can similarly be used to find the area of *RSTU*; SUFFICIENT.

The correct answer is D;
each statement alone is sufficient.

103. If n and k are greater than zero, is $\frac{n}{k}$ an integer?

(1) n and k are both integers.
(2) n^2 and k^2 are both integers.

Arithmetic Properties of numbers

(1) While n and k might both be integers, $\frac{n}{k}$ will only be an integer if k is a factor of n. For example, if $n = 8$ and $k = 4$, then $\frac{n}{k}$ is an integer. However, if $n = 10$ and $k = 4$, then $\frac{n}{k}$ is not an integer; NOT sufficient.

(2) Since n^2 and k^2 are integers, then $\frac{n^2}{k^2} = \left(\frac{n}{k}\right)^2$, and the question in (1) remains unanswered; NOT sufficient.

Since (1) does not answer the question, and since (2) can ultimately be reduced to the same form, taking both together does not provide any new information to determine the answer.

The correct answer is E;
both statements together are still not sufficient.

104. If the average (arithmetic mean) of six numbers is 75, how many of the numbers are equal to 75?

(1) None of the six numbers is less than 75.
(2) None of the six numbers is greater than 75.

Arithmetic Statistics

If the average or arithmetic mean of the six numbers is 75, then, since $\frac{450}{6} = 75$, the sum of the six numbers is 450.

(1) From this, if even one of the numbers had a value greater than 75, for example, 76, the sum of the 6 numbers would be 451. Therefore, all 6 numbers have to be 75; SUFFICIENT.

(2) From this, if only one of the numbers had a value less than 75, for example, 74, then the sum of the 6 numbers would be 449. Therefore, once again, it is found that all 6 numbers have to be 75; SUFFICIENT.

The correct answer is D;
each statement alone is sufficient.

105. Is $|x| = y - z$?

(1) $x + y = z$
(2) $x < 0$

Arithmetic + Algebra Arithmetic operations + First- and second-degree equations

(1) If $x + y = z$, then $x = z - y$. In the case where x is positive, then $|x| = x$, and so $|x| = z - y$. In the case where x is negative, then $|x| = -x$, and so $|x| = -(z - y)$, or $|x| = y - z$. Thus $|x|$ could be equal to $y - z$ or $z - y$ depending on whether x is negative or positive; NOT sufficient.

(2) This does not mention y or z so the relationship of $|x|$ to y or z cannot be determined; NOT sufficient.

If (2), which states that x is negative, is taken together with (1), as explained above, $|x|$ would equal $y - z$.

The correct answer is C; both statements together are sufficient.

106. What was the total amount of revenue that a theater received from the sale of 400 tickets, some of which were sold at x percent of full price and the rest of which were sold at full price?

(1) $x = 50$
(2) Full-price tickets sold for $20 each.

Arithmetic Percents

(1) While this reveals that *some* of the 400 tickets were sold at 50 percent of full price and *some* were sold at full price, there is no information as to the amounts in either category, nor is there any information as to the cost of a full-price ticket; NOT sufficient.

(2) Although this specifies the price of the full-price tickets, it is still unknown how many tickets were sold at full price or at a discount. Moreover, the percent of the discount is not disclosed; NOT sufficient.

While (1) and (2) together show that full-price tickets were $20 and discount tickets were 50 percent of that or $10, the number or percentage of tickets sold at either price, and thus the theater's revenue, cannot be determined.

The correct answer is E;
both statements together are still not sufficient.

107. Any decimal that has only a finite number of nonzero digits is a terminating decimal. For example, 24, 0.82, and 5.096 are three terminating decimals. If r and s are positive integers and the ratio $\frac{r}{s}$ is expressed as a decimal, is $\frac{r}{s}$ a terminating decimal?

(1) $90 < r < 100$
(2) $s = 4$

Arithmetic Properties of numbers

(1) This provides no information about the value of s. For example, $\frac{92}{5} = 18.4$, which terminates, but $\frac{92}{3} = 30.666\ldots$, which does not terminate; NOT sufficient.

(2) Division by the number 4 must terminate: the remainder when dividing by 4 must be 0, 1, 2, or 3, so the quotient must end with .0, .25, .5, or .75, respectively; SUFFICIENT.

The correct answer is B; statement 2 alone is sufficient.

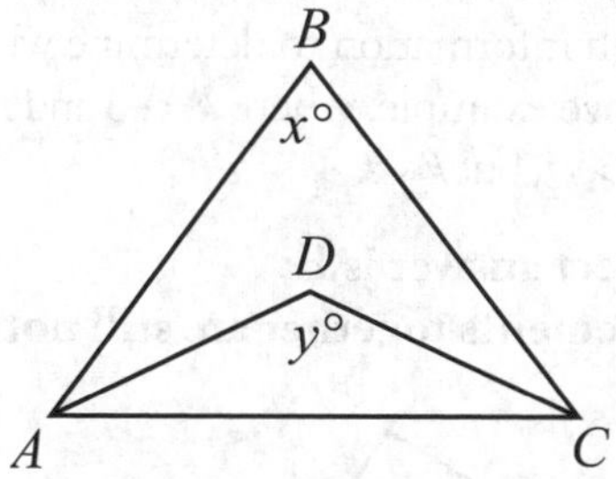

108. In the figure above, what is the value of $x + y$?

(1) $x = 70$
(2) ΔABC and ΔADC are both isosceles triangles.

Geometry Triangles

(1) With only the information that $x = 70$, there is no way to determine the measure of y so that the expression $x + y$ could be evaluated; NOT sufficient.

(2) If ΔABC and ΔADC are isosceles triangles, then two angles are congruent in each triangle. However, since no values are given for any of the angles, there is no way to evaluate $x + y$; NOT sufficient.

Taking (1) and (2) together, since the sum of the angles of a triangle equals 180, if $x = 70$, then $\angle BAC$ and $\angle BCA$ would each equal 55. That information would still not provide a value for any angles in ΔADC. The values of y and thus $x + y$ still remain to be determined.

The correct answer is E; both statements together are still not sufficient.

109. Are positive integers p and q both greater than n?

(1) $p - q$ is greater than n.
(2) $q > p$

Algebra Inequalities

(1) If $p - q > n$, then, when q is added to both sides of the inequality, $p > n + q$. Since q is positive, p must be greater than n, but there is not enough information to determine whether q is greater than n; NOT sufficient.

(2) This does not mention n at all, so the relationship of n to either p or q is unknown; NOT sufficient.

Since (1) establishes that $p > n$, and statement (2) says that $q > p$, the two statements together are sufficient to show that $q > p > n$ and thus that p and q are both greater than n.

The correct answer is C; both statements together are sufficient.

110. Whenever Martin has a restaurant bill with an amount between \$10 and \$99, he calculates the dollar amount of the tip as 2 times the tens digit of the amount of his bill. If the amount of Martin's most recent restaurant bill was between \$10 and \$99, was the tip calculated by Martin on this bill greater than 15 percent of the amount of the bill?

(1) The amount of the bill was between \$15 and \$50.
(2) The tip calculated by Martin was \$8.

Arithmetic Percents

(1) From this, if the amount of the bill was \$20, for example, the tip would have been \$4, which is $\frac{4}{20}$, or 20%. However, for a bill of \$19, the tip would be \$2, which is $\frac{2}{19}$, or approximately 10.5% and thus less than 15%; NOT sufficient.

(2) If the tip was calculated at \$8, that means that the bill was at most \$49.99. Thus the tip was *at least* $\frac{8}{49.99}$, or 16%, of the bill; SUFFICIENT.

The correct answer is B; statement 2 alone is sufficient.

111. The price per share of stock X increased by 10 percent over the same time period that the price per share of stock Y decreased by 10 percent. The reduced price per share of stock Y was what percent of the original price per share of stock X?

(1) The increased price per share of stock X was equal to the original price per share of stock Y.

(2) The increase in the price per share of stock X was $\frac{10}{11}$ the decrease in the price per share of stock Y.

Arithmetic + Algebra Percents + Applied problems + Equations

The amount that stock X increased per share can be represented by $0.1x$, where x represents the original price per share of stock X. The amount that stock Y decreased per share can be represented by $0.1y$, where y represents the original price per share of stock Y. The reduced price per share of stock Y as a percent of the original price per share of stock X can be determined if the relationship between x and y is known.

(1) The increased price per share of stock X is $1.1x$, and that is here given as equal to y, or thus $1.1x = y$. A relationship is shown between x and y; SUFFICIENT.

(2) This establishes that $0.1x = \frac{10}{11} \times 0.1y$, and again a relationship is shown between x and y; SUFFICIENT.

The correct answer is D; each statement alone is sufficient.

112. Is k greater than t?

(1) $kt = 24$

(2) $k^2 > t^2$

Arithmetic + Algebra Arithmetic operations + Inequalities

(1) If it is known that $kt = 24$, it is still unknown whether k is greater than t. For instance, if $k = 6$ and $t = 4$, then $k > t$. However, if $k = 4$, $t = 6$, and then $k < t$; NOT sufficient.

(2) When $k^2 > t^2$, if k and t are both positive, then $k > t$. However, if both k and t are negative, then there can be instances where $k^2 > t^2$ but $k < t$. For instance, if $k^2 = 36$ and $t^2 = 16$, then $k > t$ if $k = 6$ and $t = 4$. However, if $k = -6$ and $t = -4$, then $k < t$; NOT sufficient.

When (1) and (2) are taken together, there is still not enough information to determine whether $k > t$. In the above example, where $k = -6$ and $t = -4$, $kt = 24$ and $k^2 > t^2$, but $k < t$.

The correct answer is E; both statements together are still not sufficient.

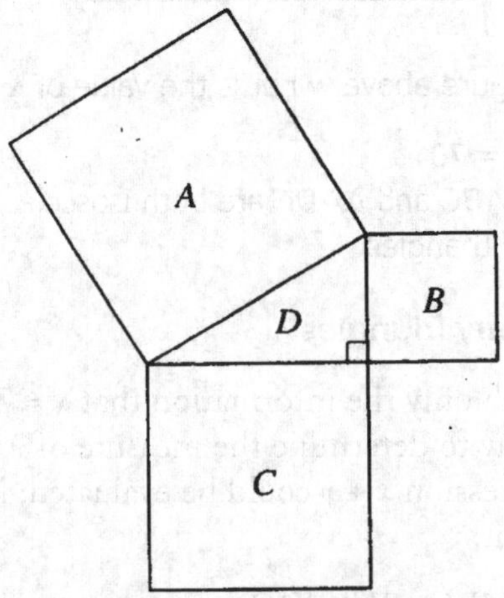

113. In the figure above, if the area of triangular region D is 4, what is the length of a side of square region A?

(1) The area of square region B is 9.

(2) The area of square region C is $\frac{64}{9}$.

Geometry Area

The area of the triangular region D can be represented by $\frac{1}{2}(bh)$, where b is the base of the triangle and is equal to the length of a side of the square region C and h is the height of the triangle and is equal to the length of a side of the square region B. The area of any square is equal to the length of a side squared. The Pythagorean theorem is used to find the length of a side of a right triangle, when the length of the other 2 sides of the triangle are known and is represented by $a^2 + b^2 = c^2$, where a and b are 2 legs of the triangle and c is the hypotenuse.

(1) If the area of B is 9, then the length of each side is 3. Therefore, $h = 3$. Then, b can be determined, since the area of the triangle is by substitution $4 = \frac{1}{2}(3b)$ or $8 = 3b$ or $\frac{8}{3} = b$. Once b is known, the Pythagorean theorem can be used: $\left(\frac{8}{3}\right)^2 + 3^2 = c^2$ or $\frac{64}{9} + 9 = c^2$ or $\frac{145}{9} = c^2$. The length of a side of A is thus $\sqrt{\frac{145}{9}}$; SUFFICIENT.

(2) If the area of C is $\frac{64}{9}$, then the length of each side is $\frac{8}{3}$. Therefore, $b = \frac{8}{3}$. The area of the triangle is $A = \frac{1}{2}(bh)$ or $4 = \frac{1}{2}\left(\frac{8}{3}h\right)$ or $8 = \frac{8}{3}h$ or $3 = h$. Once h is known, the Pythagorean theorem can be used as above; SUFFICIENT.

The correct answer is D;
each statement alone is sufficient.

114. If x is to be selected at random from set T, what is the probability that $\frac{1}{4}x - 5 \le 0$?

(1) T is a set of 8 integers.
(2) T is contained in the set of integers from 1 to 25, inclusive.

Arithmetic + Algebra Probability + Inequalities + Sets

The inequality $\frac{1}{4}x - 5 \le 0$ can be simplified to $\frac{1}{4}x \le 5$ and thus to $x \le 20$, so the question could be stated: "What is the probability that $x \le 20$?"

(1) While there are 8 integers in T, without knowing what integers are in T, the probability that $x \le 20$ cannot be determined; NOT sufficient.

(2) While T is a subset of the integers from 1 to 25, inclusive, the particular integers that are in T are not given. Therefore, the probability that $x \le 20$ cannot be determined; NOT sufficient.

Even both (1) and (2) together are not sufficient because the number of integers in T that are less than or equal to 20 is still unknown.

The correct answer is E;
both statements together are still not sufficient.

115. If Sara's age is exactly twice Bill's age, what is Sara's age?

(1) Four years ago, Sara's age was exactly 3 times Bill's age.
(2) Eight years from now, Sara's age will be exactly 1.5 times Bill's age.

Algebra Applied problems

If s and b represent Sara's and Bill's ages in years, respectively, then $s = 2b$, or $b = \frac{s}{2}$.

(1) This can be written algebraically as $s - 4 = 3(b - 4)$. Substituting $\frac{s}{2}$ for b in this equation gives $s - 4 = 3(\frac{s}{2} - 4)$, which can be simplified and solved for s as follows:

$s - 4 = \frac{3s}{2} - 12$	distribute property
$s + 8 = \frac{3s}{2}$	add 12 to both sides
$2s + 16 = 3s$	multiply by 2
$16 = s$	subtract $2s$ from both sides
	SUFFICIENT.

(2) This can be written algebraically as $s + 8 = 1.5(b + 8)$. Substituting $\frac{s}{2}$ for b in this equation yields $s + 8 = 1.5(\frac{s}{2} + 8)$, which can be simplified and solved for s as follows:

$s + 8 = 0.75s + 12$	distribute property
$0.25s + 8 = 12$	subtract $0.75s$ from both sides
$0.25s = 4$	subtract 8 from both sides
$s = 16$	divide both sides by 0.25 SUFFICIENT.

The correct answer is D;
each statement alone is sufficient.

116. What is the value of $(a + b)^2$?

(1) $ab = 0$
(2) $(a - b)^2 = 36$

Arithmetic + Algebra Arithmetic operations + Simplifying expressions

Recognize that $(a + b)^2$ is equivalent to $a^2 + 2ab + b^2$.

(1) When 0 is substituted for ab in the above, the expression becomes $a^2 + b^2$, which cannot be evaluated without further information; NOT sufficient.

(2) From this, $(a - b)^2$ is equivalent to $a^2 - 2ab + b^2 = 36$. So $a^2 + b^2 = 36 + 2ab$. This cannot be evaluated without further information; NOT sufficient.

Taking the values from (1) and (2) together and substituting into the expression, the value of the expression can be determined.

$(a + b)^2 = a^2 + 2ab + b^2$	
$(a + b)^2 = a^2 + b^2 + 2ab$	regroup
$(a + b)^2 = 36 + 2ab + 2ab$	substitute $36 + 2ab$ for $a^2 + b^2$
$(a + b)^2 = 36 + 4ab$	simplify
$(a + b)^2 = 36$	substitute 0 for ab

The correct answer is C;
both statements together are sufficient.

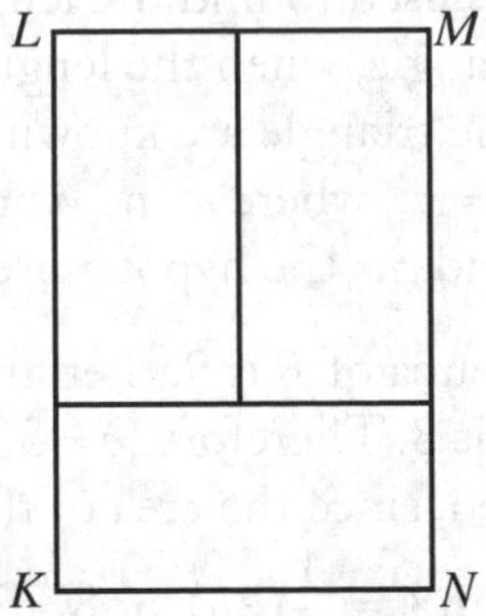

117. In the figure above, what is the ratio $\frac{KN}{MN}$?

(1) The perimeter of rectangle $KLMN$ is 30 meters.
(2) The three small rectangles have the same dimensions.

Geometry Rectangles

(1) It is given that $KLMN$ is a rectangle and that it has a perimeter of 30 meters, so $2(KN) + 2(MN) = 30$, but there is no information about the relative sizes of KN and MN; NOT sufficient.

(2) Since the three small rectangles have the same dimensions, their shorter dimensions are equal to $\frac{s}{2}KN$, and their longer dimensions are equal to KN. Therefore, $MN = KN + \frac{1}{2}KN$, or $\frac{3}{2}KN$, and the ratio $\frac{KN}{MN}$ is equal to $\frac{KN}{\frac{3}{2}KN}$, or $\frac{2}{3}$; SUFFICIENT.

The correct answer is B;
statement 2 alone is sufficient

118. If n is a positive integer, is $\frac{150}{n}$ an integer?

(1) $n < 7$
(2) n is a prime number.

Arithmetic Properties of numbers

(1) If $n < 7$ and is a positive integer, then n could be 1, 2, 3, 4, 5, and 6. If n is 4, then $\frac{150}{n}$ is not an integer, but if n is any of the other possible integers, $\frac{150}{n}$ is an integer. However, there is no information ruling out $n = 4$; NOT sufficient.

(2) If n is a prime number, some values of n (3, 5) will determine that $\frac{150}{n}$ is an integer, where as other values of n (11, 13) will not determine $\frac{150}{n}$ is an integer; NOT sufficient.

Taking (1) and (2) together, n could only be 1, 2, 3, and 5, all of which will yield an integer in the expression $\frac{150}{n}$.

The correct answer is C;
both statements together are sufficient.

119. Is $2x - 3y < x^2$?

(1) $2x - 3y = -2$
(2) $x > 2$ and $y > 0$.

Algebra Inequalities

Whatever the value of x is, the value of x^2 must by definition be at least 0.

(1) Since $2x-3y = -2$ and x^2 must be at least 0, $2x-3y$ will always be less than x^2.

(2) Because $x > 2$, it follows that $x^2 > 2x$. Since $y > 0$, it follows that the term $-3y$ is negative. Since $-3y < 0$, it follows that $-3y$ is also less than x^2. Therefore, $2x - 3y$ must be less than x^2; SUFFICIENT.

The correct answer is D;
each statement alone is sufficient.

120. A report consisting of 2,600 words is divided into 23 paragraphs. A 2-paragraph preface is then added to the report. Is the average (arithmetic mean) number of words per paragraph for all 25 paragraphs less than 120?

(1) Each paragraph of the preface has more than 100 words.
(2) Each paragraph of the preface has fewer than 150 words.

Arithmetic Statistics

When the report has 2,600 words and 23 paragraphs, the average number of words per paragraph (113.04) is less than 120.

(1) When 2 paragraphs are added with more than 100 words each, the average number of words per paragraph will change. How much the average will change is unknown. For instance, if the length of each of the paragraphs in the preface is under 120 words, the average of the report will remain under 120 words per paragraph. If the average number of words in each of the paragraphs in the preface is 300, then the total number of words in the report is 3,200, and the average number of words per paragraph is instead 128 (3,200 ÷ 25); NOT sufficient.

(2) If each paragraph in the preface has *at most* 149 words, then the total number of words in the entire report would be 2,600 + 149 + 149 = 2,898 at most. The average number of words then would be 2,898 ÷ 25, or 115.92; SUFFICIENT.

The correct answer is B;
statement 2 alone is sufficient.

121. If $\frac{x}{2} = \frac{3}{y}$, is x less than y?

(1) $y \geq 3$
(2) $y \leq 4$

Algebra First- and second-degree equations + Inequalities

The equation $\frac{x}{2} = \frac{3}{y}$ can be written as $xy = 6$ or $x = \frac{6}{y}$.

(1) If $y \geq 3$, then $x \leq 2$ in order for $xy = 6$; thus $x < y$; SUFFICIENT.

(2) If $y \le 4$, then x might or might not be less than y. For example, if $y = 2$, then $x = 3$, but if $y = 3$, then $x = 2$; NOT sufficient.

The correct answer is A;
statement 1 alone is sufficient.

122. If v and w are different integers, does $v = 0$?

(1) $vw = v^2$
(2) $w = 2$

Algebra First- and second-degree equations

(1) If v were not zero, then the equation $vw = v^2$ would be equivalent to $w = v$, which is not possible because it is given that w and v are different integers. Therefore, v must be equal to 0; SUFFICIENT.

(2) If $w = 2$, v could be 0, but v could also be any other integer except 2; NOT sufficient.

The correct answer is A;
statement 1 alone is sufficient.

123. What is the value of $36{,}500(1.05)^n$?

(1) $n^2 - 5n + 6 = 0$
(2) $n - 2 \neq 0$

Arithmetic + Algebra Arithmetic operations + First- and second-degree equations

As long as there is a definite value for n, this expression can be evaluated.

(1) The equation $n^2 - 5n + 6 = 0$ can be factored to $(n - 3)(n - 2) = 0$. This in turn would yield values of 2 or 3 for n. However, there is no further information to distinguish which value of n is desired here; NOT sufficient.

(2) If $n - 2 \neq 0$, then n cannot be equal to 2, but n could be any other number, with no way to tell what is required here; NOT sufficient.

When both (1) and (2) are analyzed, because n is not 2, n must therefore be 3.

The correct answer is C;
both statements together are sufficient.

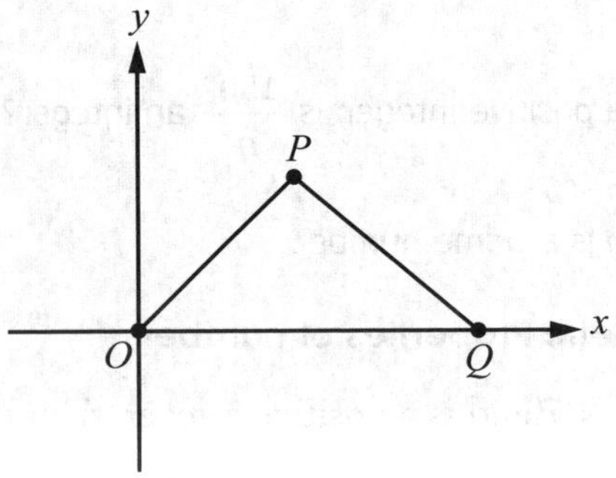

124. In the rectangular coordinate system above, if $OP < PQ$, is the area of region OPQ greater than 48?

(1) The coordinates of point P are (6, 8).
(2) The coordinates of point Q are (13, 0).

Geometry Coordinate Geometry + Triangles

The area of a triangle with base b and altitude h can be determined through the formula $\frac{bh}{2}$. The altitude of a triangle is the line segment drawn from a vertex perpendicular to the side opposite that vertex. In a right triangle the Pythagorean theorem states that the square of the length of the hypotenuse is equal to the sum of the squares of the length of the legs of the triangle.

(1) From this, $h = 8$ in ΔOPQ because the y coordinate of P is 8. Then, knowing h and applying the formula for the area of a triangle, it can be seen that, when the base *is equal to* 12, the area of ΔOPQ is equal to 48, since $\frac{hb}{2} = \frac{(8)(12)}{2} = 48$. Thus, for the area of ΔOPQ to be greater than 48, the base *must be greater than* 12. The x coordinate gives the length of only part of the base of ΔOPQ, as shown in the figure below.

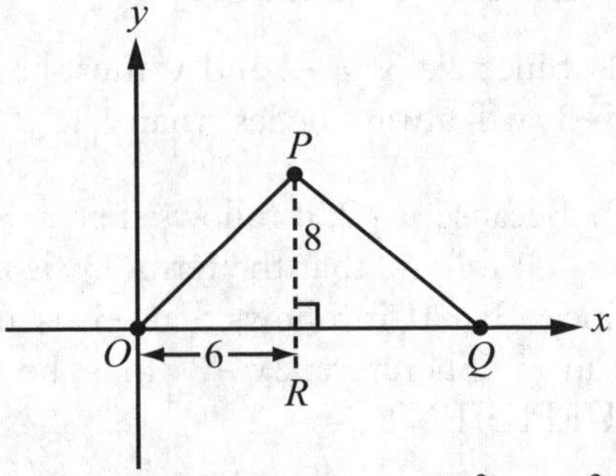

From the Pythagorean theorem, $PR^2 + OR^2 = OP^2$ and thus $64 + 36 = OP^2$ or $OP = 10$. From the given $OP < PQ$, then $10 < PQ$. So, from this determination that PQ is greater than 10, it follows that $RQ > 6$ in order to satisfy the Pythagorean theorem. Since $OR = 6$ and $RQ > 6$, the length of the base OQ is thus greater than 12; SUFFICIENT.

(2) Looking at the x coordinate of Q, it can be concluded that the length of OQ is 13 units; however, since no information is given about the altitude PR, the area cannot be determined; NOT sufficient.

The correct answer is A;
statement 1 alone is sufficient.

125. If r and s are positive integers, is $\frac{r}{s}$ an integer?

(1) Every factor of s is also a factor of r.
(2) Every prime factor of s is also a prime factor of r.

Arithmetic Properties of numbers

(1) The integer s is by definition a factor of itself. From this, every factor of s is also a factor of r. Therefore, $\frac{r}{s}$ must be an integer; SUFFICIENT.

(2) From this, by example, if $r = 18$ and $s = 6$, then 6 has the prime factors 2 and 3, each of which is also a factor of 18, and $\frac{r}{s} = \frac{18}{6}$, which is an integer. However, if $r = 18$ and $s = 8$, then r has the prime factors 2 and 3, and s has a prime factor 2, which satisfies this condition. Even though in this case the prime factor of s is a prime factor of r, $\frac{r}{s} = \frac{18}{8}$, which is not an integer; NOT sufficient.

The correct answer is A;
statement 1 alone is sufficient.

126. If $z^n = 1$, what is the value of z?

(1) n is a nonzero integer.
(2) $z > 0$

Arithmetic Arithmetic operations

(1) From this it is known that n is a nonzero integer, and since $z^n = 1$, it follows that z is either 1 or −1. Because (positive)(positive)(positive) = positive and (negative)(negative)(negative) = negative, if n is odd, then it follows from $z^n = 1$ that $z = 1$. However, if n were even, then because (positive)(positive) = positive and (negative)(negative) = positive, z could be 1 or −1; NOT sufficient.

(2) While it is known from this that z is positive, if n were 0, any positive value of z would satisfy $z^n = 1$; NOT sufficient.

Both (1) and (2) taken together are sufficient because (1) limits z to 1 or −1 and (2) eliminates −1.

The correct answer is C;
both statements together are sufficient.

$$S = \frac{\frac{2}{n}}{\frac{1}{x} + \frac{2}{3x}}$$

127. In the expression above, if $xn \neq 0$, what is the value of S?

(1) $x = 2n$
(2) $n = \frac{1}{2}$

Algebra First- and second-degree equations

It may be helpful first to simplify the given equation:

$$S = \frac{\frac{2}{n}}{\frac{1}{x} + \frac{2}{3x}} = \frac{\frac{2}{n}}{\frac{3}{3x} + \frac{2}{3x}} = \frac{\frac{2}{n}}{\frac{5}{3x}} = \frac{2}{n}\left(\frac{3x}{5}\right) = \frac{6x}{5n}$$

(1) Substituting $x = 2n$ in the simplified equation yields $S = \frac{6(2n)}{5n} = \frac{12}{5}$; SUFFICIENT.

(2) Substituting $n = \frac{1}{2}$ in the simplified equation yields $S = \frac{6x}{5\left(\frac{1}{2}\right)}$. The value of S cannot be determined unless the value of x is known; NOT sufficient.

The correct answer is A;
statement 1 alone is sufficient.

128. If x is an integer, is $x|x| < 2^x$?

(1) $x < 0$
(2) $x = -10$

Arithmetic Properties of numbers

Note that x^{-r} is equivalent to $\frac{1}{x^r}$; for example, $2^{-2} = \frac{1}{2^2} = \frac{1}{4}$.

(1) If $x < 0$, then x is a negative integer. The absolute value of x would be a positive integer, and the product of $x|x|$ would be a negative integer. When x is a negative number, the term 2^x is a positive fraction. Therefore, the statement $x|x| < 2^x$ would be true, since a negative integer would be less than a positive fraction; SUFFICIENT.

(2) The fact that $x = -10$ is a specific case of the argument in (1); SUFFICIENT.

The correct answer is D;
each statement alone is sufficient.

129. If n is a positive integer, is the value of $b - a$ at least twice the value of $3^n - 2^n$?

(1) $a = 2^{n+1}$ and $b = 3^{n+1}$
(2) $n = 3$

Arithmetic Arithmetic operations

If x is any positive number and r and s are any positive integers, then $x^{r+s} = (x^r)(x^s)$. Therefore, $2^{n+1} = 2^n(2^1)$. It is also a property of exponents that $2^1 = 2$.

(1) From this, applying the properties of exponents:

$b - a = 3^{n+1} - 2^{n+1}$
$b - a = 3(3^n) - 2(2^n)$

Twice the value of the given expression $3^n - 2^n$ is equal to $2(3^n - 2^n)$ or $2(3^n) - 2(2^n)$. It is known that $b - a = 3(3^n) - 2(2^n)$, which is greater than $2(3^n) - 2(2^n)$. Thus, $b - a$ is at least twice the value of $3^n - 2^n$; SUFFICIENT.

(2) This statement gives no information about $b - a$; NOT sufficient.

The correct answer is A;
statement 1 alone is sufficient.

130. The inflation index for the year 1989 relative to the year 1970 was 3.56, indicating that, on the average, for each dollar spent in 1970 for goods, \$3.56 had to be spent for the same goods in 1989. If the price of a Model K mixer increased precisely according to the inflation index, what was the price of the mixer in 1970?

(1) The price of the Model K mixer was \$102.40 more in 1989 than in 1970.
(2) The price of the Model K mixer was \$142.40 in 1989.

Arithmetic Proportions

The ratio of 1970 goods to 1989 goods is 1:3.56 or $\frac{1}{3.56}$. This ratio can be used to set up a proportion between 1970 goods and 1989 goods. Let x represent the 1970 price of the mixer.

(1) From this, the 1989 price of the mixer can be expressed as x + \$102.40. Therefore a proportion can be set up and solved for x:

$$\frac{1}{3.56} = \frac{x}{x + \$102.40}$$

$x + \$102.40 = 3.56x$	cross multiply
$\$102.40 = 2.56x$	subtract x from both sides
$\$40 = x$	divide both sides by 2.56

The price of the mixer in 1970 was \$40; SUFFICIENT.

(2) The following proportion can be set up using the information that the 1989 price of the mixer was \$142.40:

$\frac{1}{3.56} = \frac{x}{\$142.40}$

$3.56x = \$142.40$ cross multiply

$x = \$40$ divide both sides by 3.56

The price of the mixer in 1970 was $40; SUFFICIENT.

The correct answer is D;
each statement alone is sufficient.

131. Is 5^k less than 1,000?

(1) $5^{k+1} > 3{,}000$
(2) $5^{k-1} = 5^k - 500$

Arithmetic Arithmetic operations

If x is any positive number and r and s are any positive integers, then $x^{-r} = \frac{1}{x^r}$ and $x^{r+s} = (x^r)(x^s)$. Therefore, $5^{k+1} = 5^k(5^1)$. When both sides of this equation are divided by 5^1 (which equals 5), the resultant equation is $\frac{5^{k+1}}{5} = 5^k$.

(1) If both sides of this given inequality are divided by 5, it yields $\frac{5^{k+1}}{5} > \frac{3{,}000}{5}$ or $5^k > 600$. Although it is known that $5^k > 600$, it is unknown if 5^k is less than 1,000; NOT sufficient.

(2) It is given that $5^{k-1} = 5^k - 500$, thus:

$5^k - 5^{k-1} = 500$ subtract 5^k from both sides; divide all terms by −1

$5^k - 5^k(5^{-1}) = 500$ property of exponents

$5^k - 5^k\left(\frac{1}{5}\right) = 500$ substitute for 5^{-1}

$5^k\left(1-\frac{1}{5}\right) = 500$ factor out 5^k

$5^k\left(\frac{4}{5}\right) = 500$ simplify

$5^k = 500\left(\frac{5}{4}\right)$ multiply both sides by $\left(\frac{5}{4}\right)$

$5^k = 625$, which is less than 1,000; SUFFICIENT.

The correct answer is B;
statement 2 alone is sufficient.

132. If the integer n is greater than 1, is n equal to 2?

(1) n has exactly two positive factors.
(2) The difference of any two distinct positive factors of n is odd.

Arithmetic Properties of numbers

(1) If n has exactly 2 positive factors, then n is a prime number, since each prime number p has only the factors p and 1. However, n could be any prime number; NOT sufficient.

(2) Note that if $n > 2$ and n is odd, then 1 and n are factors of n, and their difference is even. Also, if $n > 2$ and n is even, then 2 and n are factors of n, and their difference is even.

Thus, no integer greater than 2 satisfies this statement. However, $n = 2$ does satisfy this statement since 1 and 2 are the only positive factors of 2 and their difference is odd; SUFFICIENT.

The correct answer is B;
statement 2 alone is sufficient.

133. Every member of a certain club volunteers to contribute equally to the purchase of a $60 gift certificate. How many members does the club have?

(1) Each member's contribution is to be $4.
(2) If 5 club members fail to contribute, the share of each contributing member will increase by $2.

Arithmetic + Algebra Arithmetic operations + Simultaneous equations

(1) If each member's contribution is to be $4 and the total amount to be collected is $60, then $60 \div 4 = 15$ members in the club; SUFFICIENT.

(2) Let c represent each person's contribution, and let x represent the number of members in the club. From the given information, it is known that $\frac{60}{x}=c$. From this, it is also known that

$\frac{60}{(x-5)}=c+2$.

These two equations can be solved simultaneously for x:

$\frac{60}{x-5}=\frac{60}{x}+2$	substitute for c
$\frac{60}{x-5}=\frac{60+2x}{x}$	add fraction and whole number
$60x=(x-5)(60+2x)$	cross multiply
$60x=2x^2-10x+60x-300$	multiply
$0=2x^2-10x-300$	subtract $60x$ from both sides
$0=2(x-15)(x+10)$	factor

Therefore, x could be 15 or -10. Since there cannot be -10 members, x must be 15; so there are 15 members in the club; SUFFICIENT.

The correct answer is D;
each statement alone is sufficient.

134. If m and n are positive integers, is $\sqrt{n-m}$ an integer?

(1) $n > m + 15$
(2) $n = m(m + 1)$

Arithmetic + Algebra Arithmetic operations + Inequalities

(1) Since $n > m + 15$, it follows that $n - m > 15$. If $n - m = 16$, then $\sqrt{n-m}=4$, which is an integer; however, if $n - m = 17$, then $\sqrt{n-m}=\sqrt{17}$, which is not an integer; NOT sufficient.

(2) If $n = m(m + 1)$, then $n = m^2 + m$. Therefore, $n - m = m^2$. Thus, $\sqrt{n-m}=\sqrt{m^2}=m$, an integer; SUFFICIENT.

The correct answer is B;
statement 2 alone is sufficient.

135. If $x < 0$, is $y > 0$?

(1) $\frac{x}{y}<0$

(2) $y - x > 0$

Algebra Inequalities

(1) In order for $x < 0$ and $\frac{x}{y}<0$ to be true, y must be greater than 0. If $y = 0$, then $\frac{x}{y}$ would be undefined. If $y < 0$, then $\frac{x}{y}$ would be a positive number; SUFFICIENT.

(2) Here, if $x < 0$, then y could be 0. For example, if y was 0 and x was -3, then $y - x > 0$ would be $0 - (-3) > 0$ or $3 > 0$. The statement would also be true if y were less than 0 but greater than x. For example, if $y = -2$ and $x = -7$, then $-2 - (-7) > 0$ or $5 > 0$. Finally, this statement would also be true if $y > 0$. Without any further information, it is impossible to tell whether $y > 0$; NOT sufficient.

The correct answer is A;
statement 1 alone is sufficient.

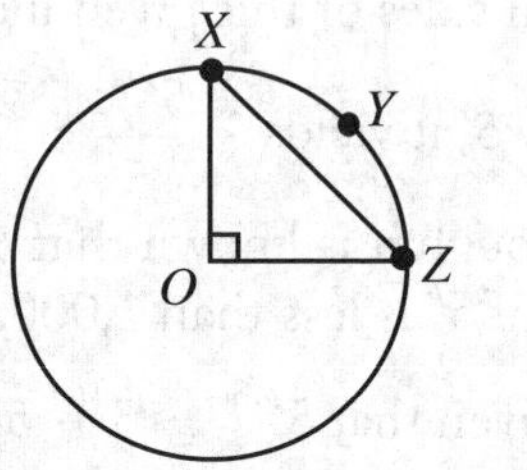

136. What is the circumference of the circle above with center O?

(1) The perimeter of ΔOXZ is $20 + 10\sqrt{2}$.
(2) The length of arc XYZ is 5π.

Geometry Circles

The circumference of the circle can be found if the radius r is known. ΔOXZ is a right triangle with $OX = OZ = r$ (since O is the center). The perimeter of ΔOXZ is the sum of OX (or r) + OZ (or r) + XZ, or the perimeter = $2r + XZ$. From the Pythagorean theorem,

$$XZ^2 = OX^2 + OZ^2$$
$$XZ^2 = r^2 + r^2$$
$$XZ = \sqrt{r^2 + r^2}$$
$$XZ = \sqrt{2r^2}$$
$$XZ = r\sqrt{2}$$

The perimeter of ΔOXZ is then $2r + r\sqrt{2}$.

(1) The perimeter of ΔOXZ is $20 + 10\sqrt{2}$. Thus, $2r + r\sqrt{2} = 20 + 10\sqrt{2} = 2(10) + 10\sqrt{2}$, and $r = 10$. Since r is known, the circumference can be found; SUFFICIENT.

(2) The length of arc XYZ is the measurement of angle XOZ divided by 360 and multiplied by the circumference. Since angle XOZ equals 90, the length of arc XYZ is thus $\frac{90}{360} = \frac{1}{4}$ of the circumference. Since $\frac{1}{4}$ of the circumference is given as equal to 5π, the circumference can be determined; SUFFICIENT.

The correct answer is D;
each statement alone is sufficient.

137. What is the value of $a^4 - b^4$?

(1) $a^2 - b^2 = 16$
(2) $a + b = 8$

Arithmetic + Algebra Arithmetic operations + Simultaneous equations

The expression $a^4 - b^4$ can be factored as $(a^2 + b^2)(a^2 - b^2)$ and factored further as $(a^2 + b^2)(a + b)(a - b)$.

(1) While this gives the value of $a^2 - b^2$, without the value of $a^2 + b^2$, it is not enough to determine the value of $a^4 - b^4$; NOT sufficient.

(2) While this gives the value of $a + b$, without values for $a^2 + b^2$ and $a - b$, once again there is not enough information to determine $a^4 - b^4$; NOT sufficient.

Taking (1) and (2) together, it is known that $a^2 - b^2 = 16$ and $a + b = 8$. Since $a^2 - b^2 = (a + b)(a - b)$, by substitution $16 = 8(a - b)$, and dividing both sides by 8 gives $2 = a - b$. From this, the two equations $a - b = 2$ and $a + b = 8$ can be solved for a and b simultaneously by first adding the two equations together to get $2a = 10$ and thus $a = 5$. Then, substituting this value of a in $a - b = 2$ yields $5 - b = 2$ and $b = 3$, and thus the value of $a^4 - b^4$ can be determined.

The correct answer is C;
both statements together are sufficient.

138. In a certain business, production index p is directly proportional to efficiency index e, which is in turn directly proportional to investment index i. What is p if $i = 70$?

(1) $e = 0.5$ whenever $i = 60$.
(2) $p = 2.0$ whenever $i = 50$.

Arithmetic Proportions

(1) This gives only values for e and i, and, while p is directly proportional to e, the nature of this proportion is unknown. Therefore, p cannot be determined; NOT sufficient.

(2) Since p is directly proportional to e, which is directly proportional to i, then p is directly proportional to i. Therefore, the following proportion can be set up: $\frac{p}{i} = \frac{2.0}{50}$.
If $i = 70$, then $\frac{p}{70} = \frac{2.0}{50}$. Through cross-multiplying, this equation yields $50p = 140$, or $p = 2.8$; SUFFICIENT.

The correct answer is B;
statement 2 alone is sufficient.

139. If $x \neq -y$, is $\frac{x - y}{x + y} > 1$?

(1) $x > 0$
(2) $y < 0$

Algebra Inequalities

(1) Given that $x > 0$, if $x = 4$ and $y = -3$ then $\frac{x - y}{x + y} = \frac{4 - (-3)}{4 - 3} = \frac{4 + 3}{1} = 7$, which is greater than 1. However, if $x = 4$ and $y = 0$, then

$\frac{x-y}{x+y} = \frac{4-0}{4+0} = 1$, which is not greater than 1; NOT sufficient.

(2) Given that $y < 0$, if $x = 4$ and $y = -3$, then as above, $\frac{x-y}{x+y}$ would be greater than 1. However, if $x = 0$ and $y = -3$, then

$\frac{x-y}{x+y} = \frac{0-(-3)}{0+(-3)} = \frac{3}{-3} = -1$, which is not greater than 1; NOT sufficient.

Both (1) and (2) together are not sufficient. As before, if $x = 4$ and $y = -3$, then $\frac{x-y}{x+y}$ is greater than 1. However, if $x = 2$ and $y = -3$, which also satisfies both (1) and (2), then

$\frac{x-y}{x+y} = \frac{2-(-3)}{2+(-3)} = \frac{5}{-1} = -5$, which is not greater than 1.

The correct answer is E;
both statements together are still not sufficient.

140. In the rectangular coordinate system, are the points (r, s) and (u, v) equidistant from the origin?

(1) $r + s = 1$
(2) $u = 1 - r$ and $v = 1 - s$.

Geometry Coordinate geometry

The distance from (r, s) to $(0, 0)$ is $\sqrt{(r-0)^2+(s-0)^2}$ or $\sqrt{r^2+s^2}$. Similarly, the distance from (u, v) to $(0, 0)$ is $\sqrt{u^2+v^2}$. Therefore, if $r^2 + s^2 = u^2 + v^2$, the two points would be equidistant from the origin.

(1) This says nothing about coordinates u and v; NOT sufficient.

(2) Using this information, $u^2 = (1 - r)^2$ or $1 - 2r + r^2$, and $v^2 = (1 - s)^2$ or $1 - 2s + s^2$. Thus, $u^2 + v^2 = 1 - 2r + r^2 + 1 - 2s + s^2$, or $u^2 + v^2 = 2 - 2(r + s) + r^2 + s^2$, but there is no information about the value of $r + s$; NOT sufficient.

From (1) and (2) together, since $r + s = 1$, it follows by substitution that $u^2 + v^2 = 2 - 2(1) + r^2 + s^2$, or $u^2 + v^2 = r^2 + s^2$.

The correct answer is C;
both statements together are sufficient.

141. On Jane's credit card account, the average daily balance for a 30-day billing cycle is the average (arithmetic mean) of the daily balances at the end of each of the 30 days. At the beginning of a certain 30-day billing cycle, Jane's credit card account had a balance of $600. Jane made a payment of $300 on the account during the billing cycle. If no other amounts were added to or subtracted from the account during the billing cycle, what was the average daily balance on Jane's account for the billing cycle?

(1) Jane's payment was credited on the 21st day of the billing cycle.
(2) The average daily balance through the 25th day of the billing cycle was $540.

Algebra Applied problem

In this situation, the value of the average daily balance for the 30 days depends on the number of days (x) that the balance was $600 and the number of days ($30 - x$) that the balance was $300. The average of the daily balances would be: $\frac{x(600)+(30-x)(300)}{30}$.

(1) If the payment was credited on the 21st day, Jane's balance was $600 for 20 days and $300 for 10 days. Therefore, her average daily balance, which equals $\frac{20(600)+10(300)}{30}$, can be determined; SUFFICIENT.

(2) If x represents the number of days for which the daily balance stayed $600, then the value of x can be determined by solving the equation $\frac{x(600)+(25-x)(300)}{25} = 540$, where the left side represents the average daily balance for the first 25 days. Solving this equation gives a value of 20 for x. The value of the average daily balance for the 30 days, which equals $\frac{x(600)+(30-x)(300)}{30}$, can then be determined as above using $x = 20$; SUFFICIENT.

The correct answer is D;
each statement alone is sufficient.

142. If x is an integer, is $9^x + 9^{-x} = b$?

(1) $3^x + 3^{-x} = \sqrt{b+2}$
(2) $x > 0$

Arithmetic Arithmetic operations

When solving this problem it is helpful to note that $(x^r)(x^{-s}) = x^{r-s}$ and that $(x^r)^2 = x^{2r}$. Note also that $x^0 = 1$.

(1) From this, $3^x + 3^{-x} = \sqrt{b+2}$. Squaring both sides gives:

$$(3^x + 3^{-x})^2 = b + 2$$

$$3^{2x} + 2(3^x \times 3^{-x}) + 3^{-2x} = b + 2$$

$$9^x + 2(3^0) + 9^{-x} = b + 2 \quad \text{property of exponents}$$

$$9^x + 2 + 9^{-x} = b + 2 \quad \text{property of exponents}$$

$$9^x + 9^{-x} = b \quad \text{subtract 2 from both sides;}$$

SUFFICIENT.

(2) This gives no information about the relationship between x and b; NOT sufficient.

The correct answer is A;
statement 1 alone is sufficient.

143. If $m > 0$ and $n > 0$, is $\frac{m+x}{n+x} > \frac{m}{n}$?

(1) $m < n$
(2) $x > 0$

Arithmetic + Algebra Arithmetic operations + Inequalities

Note that $\frac{m+x}{n+x} > \frac{m}{n}$ implies that:

$$\frac{m+x}{n+x} - \frac{m}{n} > 0$$

$$\frac{n(m+x)}{n(n+x)} - \frac{(n+x)m}{n(n+x)} > 0$$

$$\frac{nm+nx-nm-mx}{n(n+x)} > 0$$

$$\frac{(n-m)x}{(n+x)n} > 0$$

(1) From this, it follows that $0 < m < n$ and thus $n - m > 0$. It cannot be determined whether $\frac{(n-m)x}{(n+x)n}$ is positive unless it is known whether $(n-m)x$ and $(n+x)n$ are both positive or both negative; NOT sufficient.

(2) If $n > 0$ and $x > 0$, it follows that $(n + x)n > 0$, but it cannot be determined whether $(n - m)x$ is positive; NOT sufficient.

Using both (1) and (2) together, it can be concluded that $(n - m)x > 0$ and $(n + x)n > 0$, and so $\frac{(n-m)x}{(n+m)n} > 0$, which establishes that $\frac{m+x}{n+x} > \frac{m}{n}$.

The correct answer is C;
both statements together are sufficient.

144. If n is a positive integer, is $\left(\frac{1}{10}\right)^n < 0.01$?

(1) $n > 2$
(2) $\left(\frac{1}{10}\right)^{n-1} < 0.1$

Arithmetic + Algebra Properties of numbers + Inequalities

(1) If n were 1, then $\left(\frac{1}{10}\right)^n = \frac{1}{10}$, which is equivalent to 0.1. So if $n = 1$, $\left(\frac{1}{10}\right)^n > 0.01$. If n were 2, then $\left(\frac{1}{10}\right)^n = \frac{1}{100}$, which is equivalent to 0.01. So if $n = 2$,

$\left(\frac{1}{10}\right)^n = 0.01$. If n were 3, then

$\left(\frac{1}{10}\right)^n = \frac{1}{1000}$, which is equivalent to 0.001 and

$\left(\frac{1}{10}\right)^n < 0.01$. This would hold true for any other positive integer > 2; SUFFICIENT.

(2) If $n = 1$, then $\left(\frac{1}{10}\right)^{n-1}$ would be equal to $\left(\frac{1}{10}\right)^0$ or 1, and $\left(\frac{1}{10}\right)^{n-1} < 0.1$ would yield $1 < 0.1$, which is not true, so n cannot be 1. If $n = 2$, then $\left(\frac{1}{10}\right)^{n-1}$ would be equal to $\left(\frac{1}{10}\right)^1$, and $\left(\frac{1}{10}\right)^{n-1} < 0.1$ would yield $0.1 < 0.1$, which also is not true. Thus, n cannot be 2. It is only when n is equal to 3 or more that the relationship $\left(\frac{1}{10}\right)^{n-1} < 0.1$ holds true; SUFFICIENT.

The correct answer is D;
each statement alone is sufficient.

145. Is $\frac{1}{p} > \frac{r}{r^2+2}$?

(1) $p = r$
(2) $r > 0$

Algebra Inequalities

(1) It is known that $p = r$, so, by substitution, it must be determined whether $\frac{1}{r} > \frac{r}{r^2+2}$. If $r > 0$, then multiplying both sides by r gives $1 > \frac{r^2}{r^2+2}$, which is always true because r^2 is always less than $r^2 + 2$, and this term will always be a fraction. But, if $r < 0$, then multiplying both sides by r, a negative number, reverses the inequality sign and gives $1 < \frac{r^2}{r^2+2}$, which by the same reasoning is not true; NOT sufficient.

(2) This does not mention p or the relationship between r and p; NOT sufficient.

However, if both (1) and (2) are considered together, as discussed above, $p = r$ and $r > 0$ would be sufficient to answer the problem.

The correct answer is C;
both statements together are sufficient.

146. Is n an integer?

(1) n^2 is an integer.
(2) $\sqrt{n}$ is an integer.

Arithmetic Properties of numbers

If n is an integer, then n^2 must also be an integer, since it is the product of 2 integers.

(1) While n^2 is an integer, since $n^2 = n \times n$, then n^2 is an integer if n is an integer; it is unclear whether n is an integer here; NOT sufficient.

(2) Since $\sqrt{n}$ is an integer, it follows that n must be the square of an integer, i, with $i \times i = n$. Since n is the product of two integers, it is also an integer; SUFFICIENT.

The correct answer is B;
statement 2 alone is sufficient.

147. If n is a positive integer, is $n^3 - n$ divisible by 4?

(1) $n = 2k + 1$, where k is an integer.
(2) $n^2 + n$ is divisible by 6.

Arithmetic Arithmetic operations + Properties of numbers

Since n is a positive integer and $n^3 - n = n(n^2 - 1)$ or $n(n-1)(n+1)$, it follows that $n^3 - n$ is the product of the three consecutive integers $n - 1$, n, and $n + 1$.

(1) Since $2k$ is an even integer, then $n = 2k + 1$ must be an odd integer. Therefore, the consecutive integers, $n - 1$, n, and $n + 1$ would have to be even, odd, and even, respectively. Two of the three numbers are therefore divisible by 2. When the product is broken down into factors, there are at least two factors of 2 in the product ($2 \times 2 = 4$) so the product of the three numbers must be divisible by 4; SUFFICIENT.

(2) The expression $n^2 + n$ can be factored as $n(n + 1)$, which represents the product of two consecutive integers. The fact that $n(n + 1)$ is

divisible by 6 does not ensure that $n(n-1)(n+1)$ is divisible by 4. For example, (6)(7) = 42 is divisible by 6, but (5)(6)(7) is not divisible by 4. However, (5)(6) is divisible by 6, and (4)(5)(6) is divisible by 4. Since the exact value of n cannot be determined, it cannot be known whether $n^3 - n$ is divisible by 4; NOT sufficient.

The correct answer is A; statement 1 alone is sufficient.

148. What is the tens digit of positive integer x?

(1) x divided by 100 has a remainder of 30.
(2) x divided by 110 has a remainder of 30.

Arithmetic Properties of numbers

(1) Having a remainder of 30 when x is divided by 100 can only happen if x has a tens digit of 3 and a ones digit of 0, as in 130, 230, 630, and so forth; SUFFICIENT.

(2) When 140 is divided by 110, the quotient is 1 R30. However, 250 divided by 110 yields a quotient of 2 R30, and 360 divided by 110 gives a quotient of 3 R30. Since there is no consistency in the tens digit, more information is needed; NOT sufficient.

The correct answer is A; statement 1 alone is sufficient.

149. If x, y, and z are positive integers, is $x - y$ odd?

(1) $x = z^2$
(2) $y = (z-1)^2$

Arithmetic Arithmetic operations; properties of numbers

(1) This reveals the relationship between two of the variables but does not mention the relationship either one has with y. Therefore the question cannot be answered; NOT sufficient.

(2) If $(z-1)^2$ is simplified, the result is $z^2 - 2z + 1$. Since $y = z^2 - 2z + 1$, a substitution for y can be made in the expression $x - y$. It becomes $x - (z^2 - 2z + 1)$. However, without further information, it cannot be determined whether $x - y$ is odd; NOT sufficient.

When (1) and (2) are taken together, z^2, from (1), can be substituted for x in the expression $x - (z^2 - 2z + 1)$ from (2). It then yields $z^2 - z^2 + 2z - 1$, or simply $2z - 1$. No matter what the positive integer, the product of that integer and 2 will always yield an even number. When 1 is subtracted from any even number, the result is always an odd number. So $x - y$ is odd.

The correct answer is C; both statements together are sufficient.

150. Henry purchased 3 items during a sale. He received a 20 percent discount off the regular price of the most expensive item and a 10 percent discount off the regular price of each of the other 2 items. Was the total amount of the 3 discounts greater than 15 percent of the sum of the regular prices of the 3 items?

(1) The regular price of the most expensive item was \$50, and the regular price of the next most expensive item was \$20.
(2) The regular price of the least expensive item was \$15.

Arithmetic + Algebra Percents + Inequalities + Applied problem

(1) Henry received a 20 percent discount off the \$50 item, so the discount was 0.2(50) = \$10. Additionally, he received a 10 percent discount off the \$20 item, so that discount was 0.1(10) = \$2. He also received a 10 percent discount off the least expensive item.

Letting x represent the price of the least expensive item, the question is thus equivalent to asking whether x satisfies the inequality $\frac{12+(0.1)x}{70+x} > \frac{15}{100}$. By cross-multiplying and solving this inequality for x, $1200 + 10x > 1050 + 15x$, or $150 + 10x > 15x$, or $150 > 5x$, or $30 > x$. So the question can be simplified to "is $x < 30$?"

Since the most expensive item cost \$50 and the next most expensive item cost \$20, this statement implies that the least expensive items cost less than \$20. Thus, $x < 20$, and x does satisfy the inequality; SUFFICIENT.

(2) This reveals only the price of the third item, which is not enough information to determine whether the total amount of the three discounts was greater than 15 percent of the sum of the regular prices of the three items; NOT sufficient.

The correct answer is A; statement 1 alone is sufficient.

151. If x and y are positive, is the ratio of x to y greater than 3?

(1) x is 2 more than 3 times y.
(2) The ratio of $2x$ to $3y$ is greater than 2.

Arithmetic + Algebra Ratios + Inequalities

This question can be rephrased: Is $\frac{x}{y} > 3$?

(1) This is equivalent to $x = 2 + 3y$. Since $2 + 3y > 3y$, it can be said that $x > 3y$. If both sides of this inequality are divided by y, then $\frac{x}{y} > 3$; SUFFICIENT.

(2) This is equivalent to $\frac{2x}{3y} > 2$. When both sides of this inequality are multiplied by $\frac{3}{2}$, the inequality becomes $\frac{x}{y} > 3$; SUFFICIENT.

The correct answer is D; each statement alone is sufficient.

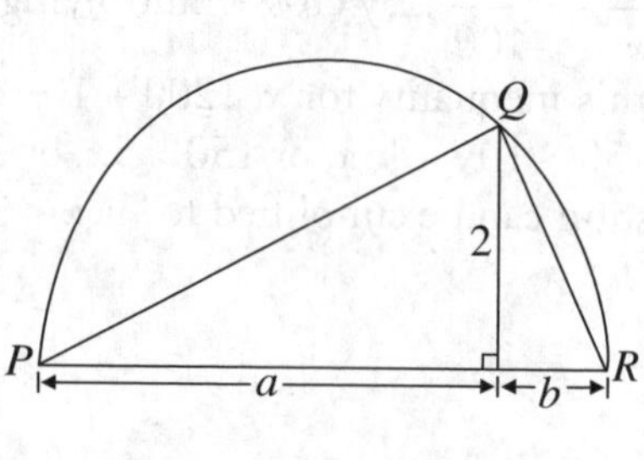

152. If arc PQR above is a semicircle, what is the length of diameter PR?

(1) $a = 4$
(2) $b = 1$

Geometry Circles

Since angle PQR is inscribed in a semicircle, it is a right angle, and ΔPQR is a right triangle. ΔPQR is divided into two right triangles by the vertical line from Q to side PR. Let $x = PQ$ and $y = QR$. The larger right triangle has hypotenuse x, so $x^2 = 4 + a^2$; the smaller right triangle has hypotenuse y, so $y^2 = 4 + b^2$. From ΔPQR, $(a + b)^2 = x^2 + y^2$, so by substitution, $(a + b)^2 = (4 + a^2) + (4 + b^2)$, and by simplification, $a^2 + 2ab + b^2 = 8 + a^2 + b^2$ or $2ab = 8$ or $ab = 4$.

(1) If $a = 4$ is substituted in $ab = 4$, then b must be 1 and diameter PR is 5; SUFFICIENT.

(2) If $b = 1$ is substituted in $ab = 4$, then a must be 4 and diameter PR is 5; SUFFICIENT.

The correct answer is D; each statement alone is sufficient.

153. Does the integer k have a factor p such that $1 < p < k$?

(1) $k > 4!$
(2) $13! + 2 \leq k \leq 13! + 13$

Arithmetic + Algebra Properties of numbers + Inequalities

Note that, if n is any integer greater than 1, then $n!$ (that is, "n factorial") is defined as the product of all the integers from 1 to n, that is, $(1)(2)(3)(4)...(n)$. Also note that k will have a factor p between 1 and k if and only if k is NOT a prime number.

(1) Since $k > 4!$, then $k > 24$, because $4! = (1)(2)(3)(4) = 24$. However, k may or may not be a prime number. For example, if $k = 27$, then the factor p could be 3 or 9, but if $k = 29$, which is a prime number, then k would not have any factors between 1 and 29; NOT sufficient.

(2) From this it can be concluded that k could be any of twelve integers: $13! + 2, 13! + 3, 13! + 4 \ldots 13! + 13$, where $13!$ is the product of the integers from 1 to 13.

Note that 2 is a factor of $13! + 2$, since it is a factor of both $13!$ and 2. Similarly, 3 is a factor of $13! + 3$; 4 is a factor of $13! + 4$; and so on for all the values of k. Thus, for each number k from $13! + 2$ to $13! + 13$, there is a factor p such that $1 < p < k$; SUFFICIENT.

The correct answer is B; statement 2 alone is sufficient.

154. Is x negative?

(1) $x^3(1 - x^2) < 0$
(2) $x^2 - 1 < 0$

Arithmetic + Algebra Arithmetic operations + Inequalities

(1) From this, x could be a negative number between –1 and 0, or it could be a positive number greater than 1. The reasoning behind this conclusion can seem a bit complex. If $x = 0$, $x = 1$, or $x = -1$, then $x^3(1 - x^2) < 0$ is not true. If x is a negative number and less than –1, then the term x^3 is negative, and the term $(1 - x^2)$ is negative; since negative × negative = positive, then $x^3(1 - x^2) < 0$ is not true. However, if $-1 < x < 0$, then x^3 is negative, the term $(1 - x^2)$ is positive, and $x^3(1 - x^2) < 0$ is true. Then, if x is a positive number and greater than 1, then the term x^3 is positive, the term $(1 - x^2)$ is negative, and $x^3(1 - x^2) < 0$ is true. However, if $0 < x < 1$, then x^3 is positive, the term $(1 - x^2)$ is also positive, and $x^3(1 - x^2) < 0$ is not true. So to recap, x could be a negative number between –1 and 0, or it could be a positive number greater than 1, but there is no further information to determine which is the case; NOT sufficient.

(2) If x is a fraction or a decimal less than 1 but greater than –1, then $x^2 - 1 < 0$ is true. For example, if x is $\frac{1}{2}$, then $\left(\frac{1}{2}\right)^2 - 1 < 0$ is equal to $\frac{1}{4} - 1 < 0$, which is true. If $x = -0.25$, then $(-0.25)^2 - 1 < 0$ is equal to $0.0625 - 1 < 0$, which is true, too. Also, if $x = 0$, then $x^2 - 1 < 0$ is true. However, if x is equal to 1 or greater than 1, then $x^2 - 1 < 0$ is not true. If x is equal to –1 or less than –1, then $x^2 - 1 < 0$ again is not true. Thus, it is known that $-1 < x < 1$. Within this range, there is no way to determine whether x is a positive or negative fraction or decimal or whether $x = 0$; NOT sufficient.

From (1), x could either have a value between –1 and 0 or have a value greater than 1. From (2), the value of x is known to be $-1 < x < 1$. From (1) and (2) taken together, x is a negative number.

The correct answer is C;
both statements together are sufficient.

155. Marcia's bucket can hold a maximum of how many liters of water?

(1) The bucket currently contains 9 liters of water.
(2) If 3 liters of water are added to the bucket when it is half full of water, the amount of water in the bucket will increase by $\frac{1}{3}$.

Geometry Volume

(1) This statement only implies that the bucket will hold *at least* 9 liters, but the *maximum capacity* is still unknown; NOT sufficient.

(2) Letting c represent the maximum capacity of Marcia's bucket, the volume of water in the bucket when at half capacity can be expressed as $\frac{1}{2}c$, and if 3 liters are then added, the present volume of water in the bucket can be expressed as $\frac{1}{2}c + 3$.
It is given that, when the 3 liters are added, the volume of water will increase by $\frac{1}{3}$, which is equivalent to multiplying the present volume by $\frac{4}{3}$. This becomes the expression $\frac{4}{3}\left(\frac{1}{2}c\right)$. Therefore, it is known that $\frac{1}{2}c + 3 = \frac{4}{3}\left(\frac{1}{2}c\right)$. This equation can be solved for c, through simplifying to $\frac{1}{2}c + 3 = \frac{2}{3}c$, then subtracting $\frac{1}{2}c$ from each side for $3 = \frac{2}{3}c - \frac{1}{2}c$, and then simplifying to $3 = \frac{1}{6}c$ or $18 = c$.
Thus the equation can be solved to determine the maximum capacity of the bucket; SUFFICIENT.

The correct answer is B;
statement 2 alone is sufficient.

7.0 Reading Comprehension

7.0 Reading Comprehension

Reading comprehension questions appear in the Verbal section of the GMAT® exam. The Verbal section uses multiple-choice questions to measure your ability to read and comprehend written material, to reason and evaluate arguments, and to correct written material to conform to standard written English. Because the Verbal section includes content from a variety of topics, you may be generally familiar with some of the material; however, neither the passages nor the questions assume knowledge of the topics discussed. Reading comprehension questions are intermingled with critical reasoning and sentence correction questions throughout the Verbal section of the exam.

You will have 75 minutes to complete the Verbal section, or an average of about 1¾ minutes to answer each question. Keep in mind, however, that you will need time to read the written passages—and that time is not factored into the 1¾ minute average. You should therefore plan to proceed more quickly through the reading comprehension questions in order to give yourself enough time to read the passages thoroughly.

Reading comprehension questions begin with written passages up to 350 words long. The passages discuss topics from the social sciences, humanities, the physical or biological sciences, and such business-related fields as marketing, economics, and human resource management. The passages are accompanied by questions that will ask you to interpret the passage, apply the information you gather from the reading, and make inferences (or informed assumptions) based on the reading. For these questions, you will see a split computer screen. The written passage will remain visible on the left side as each question associated with that passage appears in turn on the right side. You will see only one question at a time, however. The number of questions associated with each passage may vary.

As you move through the reading comprehension practice questions, try to determine a process that works best for you. You might begin by reading a passage carefully and thoroughly, though some test takers prefer to skim the passages the first time through, or even to read the first question before reading the passage. You may want to reread any sentences that present complicated ideas or introduce terms that are new to you. Read each question and series of answers carefully. Make sure you understand exactly what the question is asking and what the answer choices are.

If you need to, you may go back to the passage and read any parts that are relevant to answering the question. Specific portions of the passages may be highlighted in the related questions.

The following pages describe what reading comprehension questions are designed to measure; present the directions that will precede questions of this type; and describe the various question types. This chapter also provides test-taking strategies, sample questions, and detailed explanations of all the questions. The explanations further illustrate the ways in which reading comprehension questions evaluate basic reading skills.

7.1 What Is Measured

Reading comprehension questions measure your ability to understand, analyze, and apply information and concepts presented in written form. All questions are to be answered on the basis of what is stated or implied in the reading material, and no specific prior knowledge of the material is required.

The GMAT® reading comprehension questions evaluate your ability to do the following:

- **Understand words and statements.**
  Although the questions do not test your vocabulary (they will not ask you to define terms), they do test your ability to interpret special meanings of terms as they are used in the reading passages. The questions will also test your understanding of the English language. These questions may ask about the overall meaning of a passage.
- **Understand logical relationships between points and concepts.**
  This type of question may ask you to determine the strong and weak points of an argument or evaluate the relative importance of arguments and ideas in a passage.
- **Draw inferences from facts and statements.**
  The inference questions will ask you to consider factual statements or information presented in a reading passage and, on the basis of that information, reach conclusions.
- **Understand and follow the development of quantitative concepts as they are presented in written material.**
  This may involve the interpretation of numerical data or the use of simple arithmetic to reach conclusions about material in a passage.

There are six kinds of reading comprehension questions, each of which tests a different skill. The reading comprehension questions ask about the following areas.

Main idea

Each passage is a unified whole—that is, the individual sentences and paragraphs support and develop one main idea or central point. Sometimes you will be told the central point in the passage itself, and sometimes it will be necessary for you to determine the central point from the overall organization or development of the passage. You may be asked in this kind of question to—

- recognize a correct restatement, or paraphrasing, of the main idea of a passage;
- identify the author's primary purpose or objective in writing the passage; or
- assign a title that summarizes, briefly and pointedly, the main idea developed in the passage.

Supporting ideas

These questions measure your ability to comprehend the supporting ideas in a passage and differentiate them from the main idea. The questions also measure your ability to differentiate ideas that are *explicitly stated* in a passage from ideas that are *implied* by the author but that are not explicitly stated. You may be asked about —

- facts cited in a passage;
- the specific content of arguments presented by the author in support of his or her views; or
- descriptive details used to support or elaborate on the main idea.

Whereas questions about the main idea ask you to determine the meaning of a passage *as a whole*, questions about supporting ideas ask you to determine the meanings of individual sentences and paragraphs that *contribute* to the meaning of the passage as a whole. In other words, these questions ask for the main point of *one small part* of the passage.

Inferences

These questions ask about ideas that are not explicitly stated in a passage but are *implied* by the author. Unlike questions about supporting details, which ask about information that is directly stated in a passage, inference questions ask about ideas or meanings that must be inferred from information that is directly stated. Authors can make their points in indirect ways, suggesting ideas without actually stating them. Inference questions measure your ability to understand an author's intended meaning in parts of a passage where the meaning is only suggested. These questions do not ask about meanings or implications that are remote from the passage; rather, they ask about meanings that are developed indirectly or implications that are specifically suggested by the author.

To answer these questions, you may have to—

- logically take statements made by the author one step beyond their literal meanings;
- recognize an alternative interpretation of a statement made by the author; or
- identify the intended meaning of a word used figuratively in a passage.

If a passage explicitly states an effect, for example, you may be asked to infer its cause. If the author compares two phenomena, you may be asked to infer the basis for the comparison. You may be asked to infer the characteristics of an old policy from an explicit description of a new one. When you read a passage, therefore, you should concentrate not only on the explicit meaning of the author's words, but also on the more subtle meaning implied by those words.

Applying information to a context outside the passage itself

These questions measure your ability to discern the relationships between situations or ideas presented by the author and other situations or ideas that might parallel those in the passage. In this kind of question, you may be asked to—

- identify a hypothetical situation that is comparable to a situation presented in the passage;
- select an example that is similar to an example provided in the passage;
- apply ideas given in the passage to a situation not mentioned by the author; or
- recognize ideas that the author would probably agree or disagree with on the basis of statements made in the passage.

Unlike inference questions, application questions use ideas or situations *not* taken from the passage. Ideas and situations given in a question are *like* those given in the passage, and they parallel ideas and situations in the passage; therefore, to answer the question, you must do more than recall what you read. You must recognize the essential attributes of ideas and situations presented in the passage when they appear in different words and in an entirely new context.

Logical structure

These questions require you to analyze and evaluate the organization and logic of a passage. They may ask you—

- how a passage is constructed—for instance, does it define, compare or contrast, present a new idea, or refute an idea?
- how the author persuades readers to accept his or her assertions;
- the reason behind the author's use of any particular supporting detail;
- to identify assumptions that the author is making;
- to assess the strengths and weaknesses of the author's arguments; or
- to recognize appropriate counterarguments.

These questions measure your ability not only to comprehend a passage but also to evaluate it critically. However, it is important for you to realize that logical structure questions do not rely on any kind of formal logic, nor do they require you to be familiar with specific terms of logic or argumentation. You can answer these questions using only the information in the passage and careful reasoning.

About the style and tone

Style and tone questions ask about the expression of a passage and about the ideas in a passage that may be expressed through its diction—the author's choice of words. You may be asked to deduce the author's attitude to an idea, a fact, or a situation from the words that he or she uses to describe it. You may also be asked to select a word that accurately describes the tone of a passage—for instance, "critical," "questioning," "objective," or "enthusiastic."

To answer this type of question, you will have to consider the language of the passage as a whole: It takes more than one pointed, critical word to make the tone of an entire passage "critical." Sometimes, style and tone questions ask what audience the passage was probably intended for or what type of publication it probably appeared in. Style and tone questions may apply to one small part of the passage or to the passage as a whole. To answer them, you must ask yourself what meanings are contained in the words of a passage beyond the literal meanings. Did the author use certain words because of their emotional content, or because a particular audience would expect to hear them? Remember, these questions measure your ability to discern meaning expressed by the author through his or her choice of words.

7.2 Test-Taking Strategies for Reading Comprehension Questions

1. **Do not expect to be completely familiar with any of the material presented in reading comprehension passages.**
   You may find some passages easier to understand than others, but all passages are designed to present a challenge. If you have some familiarity with the material presented in a passage, do not let this knowledge influence your choice of answers to the questions. Answer all questions on the basis of what is *stated or implied* in the passage itself.

2. **Analyze each passage carefully, because the questions require you to have a specific and detailed understanding of the material.**
   You may find it easier to do the analysis first, before moving to the questions. Or, you may find that you prefer to skim the passage the first time and read more carefully once you understand what a question asks. You may even want to read the question before reading the passage. You should choose the method most suitable for you.

3. **Focus on key words and phrases, and make every effort to avoid losing the sense of what is discussed in the passage.**
   Keep the following in mind:
   - Note how each fact relates to an idea or an argument.
   - Note where the passage moves from one idea to the next.
   - Separate main ideas from supporting ideas.
   - Determine what conclusions are reached and why.

4. **Read the questions carefully, making certain that you understand what is asked.**
   An answer choice that accurately restates information in the passage may be incorrect if it does not answer the question. If you need to, refer back to the passage for clarification.

5. **Read all the choices carefully.**
   Never assume that you have selected the best answer without first reading all the choices.

6. **Select the choice that answers the question best in terms of the information given in the passage.**
   Do not rely on outside knowledge of the material to help you answer the questions.

7. **Remember that comprehension—not speed—is the critical success factor when it comes to reading comprehension questions.**

7.3 The Directions

These are the directions that you will see for reading comprehension questions when you take the GMAT® test. If you read them carefully and understand them clearly before going to sit for the exam, you will not need to spend too much time reviewing them once you are at the test center and the exam is under way.

The questions in this group are based on the content of a passage. After reading the passage, choose the best answer to each question. Answer all questions following the passage on the basis of what is *stated or implied in the passage*.

7.4 Reading Comprehension Sample Questions

The questions in this group are based on the content of a passage. After reading the passage, choose the best answer to each question. Answer all questions following the passage on the basis of what is stated or implied in the passage.

Until recently, scientists did not know of a close vertebrate analogue to the extreme form of altruism observed in eusocial insects like ants and bees, whereby individuals cooperate, sometimes even sacrificing their own opportunities to survive and reproduce, for the good of others. However, such a vertebrate society may exist among underground colonies of the highly social rodent *Heterocephalus glaber*, the naked mole rat.

A naked mole rat colony, like a beehive, wasp's nest, or termite mound, is ruled by its queen, or reproducing female. Other adult female mole rats neither ovulate nor breed. The queen is the largest member of the colony, and she maintains her breeding status through a mixture of behavioral and, presumably, chemical control. Queens have been long-lived in captivity, and when they die or are removed from a colony one sees violent fighting for breeding status among the larger remaining females, leading to a takeover by a new queen.

Eusocial insect societies have rigid caste systems, each insect's role being defined by its behavior, body shape, and physiology. In naked mole rat societies, on the other hand, differences in behavior are related primarily to reproductive status (reproduction being limited to the queen and a few males), body size, and perhaps age. Smaller nonbreeding members, both male and female, seem to participate primarily in gathering food, transporting nest material, and tunneling. Larger nonbreeders are active in defending the colony and perhaps in removing dirt from the tunnels. Jarvis's work has suggested that differences in growth rates may influence the length of time that an individual performs a task, regardless of its age.

Cooperative breeding has evolved many times in vertebrates, but unlike naked mole rats, most cooperatively breeding vertebrates (except the wild dog, *Lycaon pictus*) are dominated by a pair of breeders rather than by a single breeding female. The division of labor within social groups is less pronounced among other vertebrates than among naked mole rats, colony size is much smaller, and mating by subordinate females may not be totally suppressed, whereas in naked mole rat colonies subordinate females are not sexually active, and many never breed.

Questions 1–7 refer to the passage above.

1. Which of the following most accurately states the main idea of the passage?

(A) Naked mole rat colonies are the only known examples of cooperatively breeding vertebrate societies.
(B) Naked mole rat colonies exhibit social organization based on a rigid caste system.
(C) Behavior in naked mole rat colonies may well be a close vertebrate analogue to behavior in eusocial insect societies.
(D) The mating habits of naked mole rats differ from those of any other vertebrate species.
(E) The basis for the division of labor among naked mole rats is the same as that among eusocial insects.

2. The passage suggests that Jarvis's work has called into question which of the following explanatory variables for naked mole rat behavior?

(A) Size
(B) Age
(C) Reproductive status
(D) Rate of growth
(E) Previously exhibited behavior

3. It can be inferred from the passage that the performance of tasks in naked mole rat colonies differs from task performance in eusocial insect societies in which of the following ways?
   (A) In naked mole rat colonies, all tasks are performed cooperatively.
   (B) In naked mole rat colonies, the performance of tasks is less rigidly determined by body shape.
   (C) In naked mole rat colonies, breeding is limited to the largest animals.
   (D) In eusocial insect societies, reproduction is limited to a single female.
   (E) In eusocial insect societies, the distribution of tasks is based on body size.

4. According to the passage, which of the following is a supposition rather than a fact concerning the queen in a naked mole rat colony?
   (A) She is the largest member of the colony.
   (B) She exerts chemical control over the colony.
   (C) She mates with more than one male.
   (D) She attains her status through aggression.
   (E) She is the only breeding female.

5. The passage supports which of the following inferences about breeding among *Lycaon pictus*?
   (A) The largest female in the social group does not maintain reproductive status by means of behavioral control.
   (B) An individual's ability to breed is related primarily to its rate of growth.
   (C) Breeding is the only task performed by the breeding female.
   (D) Breeding in the social group is not cooperative.
   (E) Breeding is not dominated by a single pair of dogs.

6. According to the passage, naked mole rat colonies may differ from all other known vertebrate groups in which of the following ways?
   (A) Naked mole rats exhibit an extreme form of altruism.
   (B) Naked mole rats are cooperative breeders.
   (C) Among naked mole rats, many males are permitted to breed with a single dominant female.
   (D) Among naked mole rats, different tasks are performed at different times in an individual's life.
   (E) Among naked mole rats, fighting results in the selection of a breeding female.

7. One function of the third paragraph of the passage is to
   (A) state a conclusion about facts presented in an earlier paragraph
   (B) introduce information that is contradicted by information in the fourth paragraph
   (C) qualify the extent to which two previously mentioned groups might be similar
   (D) show the chain of reasoning that led to the conclusions of a specific study
   (E) demonstrate that, of three explanatory factors offered, two may be of equal significance

A recent study has provided clues to predator-prey dynamics in the late Pleistocene era. Researchers compared the number of tooth fractures in present-day carnivores with tooth fractures in carnivores that lived 36,000 to 10,000 years ago and that were preserved in the Rancho La Brea tar pits in Los Angeles. The breakage frequencies in the extinct species were strikingly higher than those in the present-day species.

In considering possible explanations for this finding, the researchers dismissed demographic bias because older individuals were not overrepresented in the fossil samples. They rejected preservational bias because a total absence of breakage in two extinct species demonstrated that the fractures were not the result of abrasion within the pits. They ruled out local bias because breakage data obtained from other Pleistocene sites were similar to the La Brea data. The explanation they consider most plausible is behavioral differences between extinct and present-day carnivores—in particular, more contact between the teeth of predators and the bones of prey due to more thorough consumption of carcasses by the extinct species. Such thorough carcass consumption implies to the researchers either that prey availability was low, at least seasonally, or that there was intense competition over kills and a high rate of carcass theft due to relatively high predator densities.

Questions 8–12 refer to the passage above.

8. The primary purpose of the passage is to

(A) present several explanations for a well-known fact
(B) suggest alternative methods for resolving a debate
(C) argue in favor of a controversial theory
(D) question the methodology used in a study
(E) discuss the implications of a research finding

9. According to the passage, compared with Pleistocene carnivores in other areas, Pleistocene carnivores in the La Brea area

(A) included the same species, in approximately the same proportions
(B) had a similar frequency of tooth fractures
(C) populated the La Brea area more densely
(D) consumed their prey more thoroughly
(E) found it harder to obtain sufficient prey

10. According to the passage, the researchers believe that the high frequency of tooth breakage in carnivores found at La Brea was caused primarily by

(A) the aging process in individual carnivores
(B) contact between the fossils in the pits
(C) poor preservation of the fossils after they were removed from the pits
(D) the impact of carnivores' teeth against the bones of their prey
(E) the impact of carnivores' teeth against the bones of other carnivores during fights over kills

11. The researchers' conclusion concerning the absence of demographic bias would be most seriously undermined if it were found that

(A) the older an individual carnivore is, the more likely it is to have a large number of tooth fractures

(B) the average age at death of a present-day carnivore is greater than was the average age at death of a Pleistocene carnivore

(C) in Pleistocene carnivore species, older individuals consumed carcasses as thoroughly as did younger individuals

(D) the methods used to determine animals' ages in fossil samples tend to misidentify many older individuals as younger individuals

(E) data concerning the ages of fossil samples cannot provide reliable information about behavioral differences between extinct carnivores and present-day carnivores

12. According to the passage, if the researchers had NOT found that two extinct carnivore species were free of tooth breakage, the researchers would have concluded that

(A) the difference in breakage frequencies could have been the result of damage to the fossil remains in the La Brea pits

(B) the fossils in other Pleistocene sites could have higher breakage frequencies than do the fossils in the La Brea pits

(C) Pleistocene carnivore species probably behaved very similarly to one another with respect to consumption of carcasses

(D) all Pleistocene carnivore species differed behaviorally from present-day carnivore species

(E) predator densities during the Pleistocene era were extremely high

Archaeology as a profession faces two major problems. First, it is the poorest of the poor. Only paltry sums are available for excavating and even less is available for publishing the results and preserving the sites once excavated. Yet archaeologists deal with priceless objects every day. Second, there is the problem of illegal excavation, resulting in museum-quality pieces being sold to the highest bidder.

I would like to make an outrageous suggestion that would at one stroke provide funds for archaeology and reduce the amount of illegal digging. I would propose that scientific archaeological expeditions and governmental authorities sell excavated artifacts on the open market. Such sales would provide substantial funds for the excavation and preservation of archaeological sites and the publication of results. At the same time, they would break the illegal excavator's grip on the market, thereby decreasing the inducement to engage in illegal activities.

You might object that professionals excavate to acquire knowledge, not money. Moreover, ancient artifacts are part of our global cultural heritage, which should be available for all to appreciate, not sold to the highest bidder. I agree. Sell nothing that has unique artistic merit or scientific value. But, you might reply, everything that comes out of the ground has scientific value. Here we part company. Theoretically, you may be correct in claiming that every artifact has potential scientific value. Practically, you are wrong.

I refer to the thousands of pottery vessels and ancient lamps that are essentially duplicates of one another. In one small excavation in Cyprus, archaeologists recently uncovered 2,000 virtually indistinguishable small jugs in a single courtyard. Even precious royal seal impressions known as l'melekh handles have been found in abundance —more than 4,000 examples so far.

The basements of museums are simply not large enough to store the artifacts that are likely to be discovered in the future. There is not enough money even to catalog the finds; as a result, they cannot be found again and become as inaccessible as if they had never been discovered. Indeed, with the help of a computer, sold artifacts could be more accessible than are the pieces stored in bulging museum basements. Prior to sale, each could be photographed and the list of the purchasers could be maintained on the computer. A purchaser could even be required to agree to return the piece if it should become needed for scientific purposes.

It would be unrealistic to suggest that illegal digging would stop if artifacts were sold on the open market. But the demand for the clandestine product would be substantially reduced. Who would want an unmarked pot when another was available whose provenance was known, and that was dated stratigraphically by the professional archaeologist who excavated it?

Questions 13–15 refer to the passage above.

13. The primary purpose of the passage is to propose

(A) an alternative to museum display of artifacts
(B) a way to curb illegal digging while benefiting the archaeological profession
(C) a way to distinguish artifacts with scientific value from those that have no such value
(D) the governmental regulation of archaeological sites
(E) a new system for cataloging duplicate artifacts

14. The author implies that all of the following statements about duplicate artifacts are true EXCEPT

(A) a market for such artifacts already exists
(B) such artifacts seldom have scientific value
(C) there is likely to be a continuing supply of such artifacts
(D) museums are well supplied with examples of such artifacts
(E) such artifacts frequently exceed in quality those already cataloged in museum collections

15. Which of the following is mentioned in the passage as a disadvantage of storing artifacts in museum basements?

(A) Museum officials rarely allow scholars access to such artifacts.
(B) Space that could be better used for display is taken up for storage.
(C) Artifacts discovered in one excavation often become separated from each other.
(D) Such artifacts are often damaged by variations in temperature and humidity.
(E) Such artifacts often remain uncataloged and thus cannot be located once they are put in storage.

Line

During the nineteenth century, occupational information about women that was provided by the United States census—a population count conducted each decade—became more detailed and precise in response to social changes. Through 1840, simple enumeration by household mirrored a home-based agricultural economy and hierarchical social order: the head of the household (presumed male or absent) was specified by name, whereas other household members were only indicated by the total number of persons counted in various categories, including occupational categories. Like farms, most enterprises were family-run, so that the census measured economic activity as an attribute of the entire household, rather than of individuals.

The 1850 census, partly responding to antislavery and women's rights movements, initiated the collection of specific information about each individual in a household. Not until 1870 was occupational information analyzed by gender: the census superintendent reported 1.8 million women employed outside the home in "gainful and reputable occupations." In addition, he arbitrarily attributed to each family one woman "keeping house." Overlap between the two groups was not calculated until 1890, when the rapid entry of women into the paid labor force and social issues arising from industrialization were causing women's advocates and women statisticians to press for more thorough and accurate accounting of women's occupations and wages.

Questions 16–20 refer to the passage above.

16. The primary purpose of the passage is to

(A) explain and critique the methods used by early statisticians
(B) compare and contrast a historical situation with a current-day one
(C) describe and explain a historical change
(D) discuss historical opposition to an established institution
(E) trace the origin of a contemporary controversy

17. Each of the following aspects of nineteenth-century United States censuses is mentioned in the passage EXCEPT the

(A) year in which data on occupations began to be analyzed by gender
(B) year in which specific information began to be collected on individuals in addition to the head of the household
(C) year in which overlap between women employed outside the home and women keeping house was first calculated
(D) way in which the 1890 census measured women's income levels and educational backgrounds
(E) way in which household members were counted in the 1840 census

18. It can be inferred from the passage that the 1840 United States census provided a count of which of the following?

(A) Women who worked exclusively in the home
(B) People engaged in nonfarming occupations
(C) People engaged in social movements
(D) Women engaged in family-run enterprises
(E) Men engaged in agriculture

19. The author uses the adjective "simple" in line 6 most probably to emphasize that the

(A) collection of census information became progressively more difficult throughout the nineteenth century
(B) technology for tabulating census information was rudimentary during the first half of the nineteenth century
(C) home-based agricultural economy of the early nineteenth century was easier to analyze than the later industrial economy
(D) economic role of women was better defined in the early nineteenth century than in the late nineteenth century
(E) information collected by early nineteenth-century censuses was limited in its amount of detail

20. The passage suggests which of the following about the "women's advocates and women statisticians" mentioned in lines 28–29?

(A) They wanted to call attention to the lack of pay for women who worked in the home.
(B) They believed that previous census information was inadequate and did not reflect certain economic changes in the United States.
(C) They had begun to press for changes in census-taking methods as part of their participation in the antislavery movement.
(D) They thought that census statistics about women would be more accurate if more women were employed as census officials.
(E) They had conducted independent studies that disputed the official statistics provided by previous United States censuses.

Traditionally, the first firm to commercialize a new technology has benefited from the unique opportunity to shape product definitions, forcing followers to adapt to a standard or invest in an unproven alternative. Today, however, the largest payoffs may go to companies that lead in developing integrated approaches for successful mass production and distribution.

Producers of the Beta format for videocassette recorders (VCRs), for example, were first to develop the VCR commercially in 1975, but producers of the rival VHS (Video Home System) format proved to be more successful at forming strategic alliances with other producers and distributors to manufacture and market their VCR format. Seeking to maintain exclusive control over VCR distribution, Beta producers were reluctant to form such alliances and eventually lost ground to VHS in the competition for the global VCR market.

Despite Beta's substantial technological head start and the fact that VHS was neither technically better nor cheaper than Beta, developers of VHS quickly turned a slight early lead in sales into a dominant position. Strategic alignments with producers of prerecorded tapes reinforced the VHS advantage. The perception among consumers that prerecorded tapes were more available in VHS format further expanded VHS's share of the market. By the end of the 1980's, Beta was no longer in production.

Questions 21–26 refer to the passage above.

21. The passage is primarily concerned with which of the following?

(A) Evaluating two competing technologies
(B) Tracing the impact of a new technology by narrating a sequence of events
(C) Reinterpreting an event from contemporary business history
(D) Illustrating a business strategy by means of a case history
(E) Proposing an innovative approach to business planning

22. According to the passage, today's successful firms, unlike successful firms in the past, may earn the greatest profits by

(A) investing in research to produce cheaper versions of existing technology
(B) being the first to market a competing technology
(C) adapting rapidly to a technological standard previously set by a competing firm
(D) establishing technological leadership in order to shape product definitions in advance of competing firms
(E) emphasizing the development of methods for the mass production and distribution of a new technology

23. According to the passage, consumers began to develop a preference for VCRs in the VHS format because they believed which of the following?

(A) VCRs in the VHS format were technically better than competing format VCRs.
(B) VCRs in the VHS format were less expensive than competing format VCRs.
(C) VHS was the first standard format for VCRs.
(D) VHS prerecorded videotapes were more available than Beta format tapes.
(E) VCRs in the Beta format would soon cease to be produced.

24. The author implies that one way that VHS producers won control over the VCR market was by

(A) carefully restricting access to VCR technology
(B) giving up a slight early lead in VCR sales in order to improve long-term prospects
(C) retaining a strict monopoly on the production of prerecorded videotapes
(D) sharing control of the marketing of VHS format VCRs
(E) sacrificing technological superiority over Beta format VCRs in order to remain competitive in price

25. The alignment of producers of VHS format VCRs with producers of prerecorded videotapes is most similar to which of the following?

(A) The alignment of an automobile manufacturer with another automobile manufacturer to adopt a standard design for automobile engines
(B) The alignment of an automobile manufacturer with an automotive glass company whereby the manufacturer agrees to purchase automobile windshields only from that one glass company
(C) The alignment of an automobile manufacturer with a petroleum company to ensure the widespread availability of the fuel required by a new type of engine developed by the manufacturer
(D) The alignment of an automobile manufacturer with its dealers to adopt a plan to improve automobile design
(E) The alignment of an automobile dealer with an automobile rental chain to adopt a strategy for an advertising campaign to promote a new type of automobile

26. Which of the following best describes the relation of the first paragraph to the passage as a whole?

(A) It makes a general observation to be exemplified.
(B) It outlines a process to be analyzed.
(C) It poses a question to be answered.
(D) It advances an argument to be disputed.
(E) It introduces conflicting arguments to be reconciled.

During the 1960's and 1970's, the primary economic development strategy of local governments in the United States was to attract manufacturing industries. Unfortunately, this strategy was usually implemented at another community's expense: many manufacturing facilities were lured away from their moorings elsewhere through tax incentives and slick promotional efforts. Through the transfer of jobs and related revenues that resulted from this practice, one town's triumph could become another town's tragedy.

In the 1980's the strategy shifted from this zero-sum game to one called "high-technology development," in which local governments competed to attract newly formed high-technology manufacturing firms. Although this approach was preferable to victimizing other geographical areas by taking their jobs, it also had its shortcomings: high-tech manufacturing firms employ only a specially trained fraction of the manufacturing workforce, and there simply are not enough high-tech firms to satisfy all geographic areas.

Recently, local governments have increasingly come to recognize the advantages of yet a third strategy: the promotion of homegrown small businesses. Small indigenous businesses are created by a nearly ubiquitous resource, local entrepreneurs. With roots in their communities, these individuals are less likely to be enticed away by incentives offered by another community. Indigenous industry and talent are kept at home, creating an environment that both provides jobs and fosters further entrepreneurship.

Questions 27–31 refer to the passage above.

27. The primary purpose of the passage is to

(A) advocate more effective strategies for encouraging the development of high-technology enterprises in the United States
(B) contrast the incentives for economic development offered by local governments with those offered by the private sector
(C) acknowledge and counter adverse criticism of programs being used to stimulate local economic development
(D) define and explore promotional efforts used by local governments to attract new industry
(E) review and evaluate strategies and programs that have been used to stimulate economic development

28. The passage suggests which of the following about the majority of United States manufacturing industries before the high-technology development era of the 1980's?

(A) They lost many of their most innovative personnel to small entrepreneurial enterprises.
(B) They experienced a major decline in profits during the 1960's and 1970's.
(C) They could provide real economic benefits to the areas in which they were located.
(D) They employed workers who had no specialized skills.
(E) They actively interfered with local entrepreneurial ventures.

29. The tone of the passage suggests that the author is most optimistic about the economic development potential of which of the following groups?

(A) Local governments
(B) High-technology promoters
(C) Local entrepreneurs
(D) Manufacturing industry managers
(E) Economic development strategists

30. The passage does NOT state which of the following about local entrepreneurs?

(A) They are found nearly everywhere.
(B) They encourage further entrepreneurship.
(C) They attract out-of-town investors.
(D) They employ local workers.
(E) They are established in their communities.

31. The author of the passage mentions which of the following as an advantage of high-technology development?

(A) It encourages the modernization of existing manufacturing facilities.
(B) It promotes healthy competition between rival industries.
(C) It encourages the growth of related industries.
(D) It takes full advantage of the existing workforce.
(E) It does not advantage one local workforce at the expense of another.

In 1988 services moved ahead of manufacturing as the main product of the United States economy. But what is meant by "services"? Some economists define a service as something that is produced and consumed simultaneously: for example, a haircut. The broader, classical definition is that a service is an intangible something that cannot be touched or stored. Yet electric utilities can store energy, and computer programmers save information electronically. Thus, the classical definition is hard to sustain.

The United States government's definition is more practical: services are the residual category that includes everything that is not agriculture or industry. Under this definition, "services" includes activities as diverse as engineering and driving a bus. However, besides lacking a strong conceptual framework, this definition fails to recognize the distinction between service industries and service occupations. It categorizes workers based on their company's final product rather than on the actual work the employees perform. Thus, the many service workers employed by manufacturers—bookkeepers or janitors, for example—would fall under the industrial rather than the services category. Such ambiguities reveal the arbitrariness of this definition and suggest that, although practical for government purposes, it does not accurately reflect the composition of the current United States economy.

Questions 32–36 refer to the passage above.

32. The author of the passage is primarily concerned with

(A) discussing research data underlying several definitions
(B) arguing for the adoption of a particular definition
(C) exploring definitions of a concept
(D) comparing the advantages of several definitions
(E) clarifying some ambiguous definitions

33. In comparing the United States government's definition of services with the classical definition, the author suggests that the classical definition is

(A) more pragmatic
(B) more difficult to apply
(C) less ambiguous
(D) more widely used
(E) more arbitrary

34. The passage suggests which of the following about service workers in the United States?

(A) The number of service workers may be underestimated by the definition of services used by the government.
(B) There were fewer service workers than agricultural workers before 1988.
(C) The number of service workers was almost equal to the number of workers employed in manufacturing until 1988.
(D) Most service workers are employed in service occupations rather than in service industries.
(E) Most service workers are employed in occupations where they provide services that do not fall under the classical definition of services.

35. The author of the passage mentions which of the following as one disadvantage of the United States government's definition of services?

(A) It is less useful than the other definitions mentioned in the passage.
(B) It is narrower in scope than the other definitions mentioned in the passage.
(C) It is based on the final product produced rather than on the type of work performed.
(D) It does not recognize the diversity of occupations within the service industries.
(E) It misclassifies many workers who are employed in service industries.

36. The author refers to "service workers employed by manufacturers" (lines 23–24) primarily in order to point out

(A) a type of worker not covered by the United States government's system of classifying occupations
(B) a flaw in the United States government's definition of services
(C) a factor that has influenced the growth of the service economy in the United States
(D) a type of worker who is classified on the basis of work performed rather than on the basis of the company's final product
(E) the diversity of the workers who are referred to as service workers

Although numbers of animals in a given region may fluctuate from year to year, the fluctuations are often temporary and, over long periods, trivial. Scientists have advanced three theories of population control to account for this relative constancy.

The first theory attributes a relatively constant population to periodic climatic catastrophes that decimate populations with such frequency as to prevent them from exceeding some particular limit. In the case of small organisms with short life cycles, climatic changes need not be catastrophic: normal seasonal changes in photoperiod (daily amount of sunlight), for example, can govern population growth. This theory — the density-independent view — asserts that climatic factors exert the same regulatory effect on population regardless of the number of individuals in a region.

A second theory argues that population growth is primarily density-dependent — that is, the rate of growth of a population in a region decreases as the number of animals increases. The mechanisms that manage regulation may vary. For example, as numbers increase, the food supply would probably diminish, which would increase mortality. In addition, as Lotka and Volterra have shown, predators can find prey more easily in high-density populations. Other regulators include physiological control mechanisms: for example, Christian and Davis have demonstrated how the crowding that results from a rise in numbers may bring about hormonal changes in the pituitary and adrenal glands that in turn may regulate population by lowering sexual activity and inhibiting sexual maturation. There is evidence that these effects may persist for three generations in the absence of the original provocation. One challenge for density-dependent theorists is to develop models that would allow the precise prediction of the effects of crowding.

A third theory, proposed by Wynne-Edwards and termed "epideictic," argues that organisms have evolved a "code" in the form of social or epideictic behavior displays, such as winter-roosting aggregations or group vocalizing; such codes provide organisms with information on population size in a region so that they can, if necessary, exercise reproductive restraint. However, Wynne-Edwards's theory, linking animal social behavior and population control, has been challenged, with some justification, by several studies.

Questions 37–42 refer to the passage above.

37. The primary purpose of the passage is to

(A) argue against those scientists who maintain that animal populations tend to fluctuate
(B) compare and contrast the density-dependent and epideictic theories of population control
(C) provide examples of some of the ways in which animals exercise reproductive restraint to control their own numbers
(D) suggest that theories of population control that concentrate on the social behavior of animals are more open to debate than are theories that do not
(E) summarize a number of scientific theories that attempt to explain why animal populations do not exceed certain limits

38. It can be inferred from the passage that proponents of the density-dependent theory of population control have not yet been able to

(A) use their theory to explain the population growth of organisms with short life cycles
(B) reproduce the results of the study of Christian and Davis
(C) explain adequately why the numbers of a population can increase as the population's rate of growth decreases
(D) make sufficiently accurate predictions about the effects of crowding
(E) demonstrate how predator populations are themselves regulated

39. Which of the following, if true, would best support the density-dependent theory of population control as it is described in the passage?

(A) As the number of foxes in Minnesota decreases, the growth rate of this population of foxes begins to increase.
(B) As the number of woodpeckers in Vermont decreases, the growth rate of this population of woodpeckers also begins to decrease.
(C) As the number of prairie dogs in Oklahoma increases, the growth rate of this population of prairie dogs also begins to increase.
(D) After the number of beavers in Tennessee decreases, the number of predators of these beavers begins to increase.
(E) After the number of eagles in Montana decreases, the food supply of this population of eagles also begins to decrease.

40. According to the Wynne-Edwards theory as it is described in the passage, epideictic behavior displays serve the function of

(A) determining roosting aggregations
(B) locating food
(C) attracting predators
(D) regulating sexual activity
(E) triggering hormonal changes

41. The challenge posed to the Wynne-Edwards theory by several studies is regarded by the author with

(A) complete indifference
(B) qualified acceptance
(C) skeptical amusement
(D) perplexed astonishment
(E) agitated dismay

42. Which of the following statements would provide the most logical continuation of the final paragraph of the passage?

(A) Thus Wynne-Edwards's theory raises serious questions about the constancy of animal population in a region.
(B) Because Wynne-Edwards's theory is able to explain more kinds of animal behavior than is the density-dependent theory, epideictic explanations of population regulation are now widely accepted.
(C) The results of one study, for instance, have suggested that group vocalizing is more often used to defend territory than to provide information about population density.
(D) Some of these studies have, in fact, worked out a systematic and complex code of social behavior that can regulate population size.
(E) One study, for example, has demonstrated that birds are more likely to use winter-roosting aggregations than group vocalizing in order to provide information on population size.

In recent years, teachers of introductory courses in Asian American studies have been facing a dilemma nonexistent a few decades ago, when hardly any texts in that field were available. Today, excellent anthologies and other introductory texts exist, and books on individual Asian American nationality groups and on general issues important for Asian Americans are published almost weekly. Even professors who are experts in the field find it difficult to decide which of these to assign to students; nonexperts who teach in related areas and are looking for writings for and by Asian Americans to include in survey courses are in an even worse position.

A complicating factor has been the continuing lack of specialized one-volume reference works on Asian Americans, such as biographical dictionaries or desktop encyclopedias. Such works would enable students taking Asian American studies courses (and professors in related fields) to look up basic information on Asian American individuals, institutions, history, and culture without having to wade through mountains of primary source material. In addition, given such works, Asian American studies professors might feel more free to include more challenging Asian American material in their introductory reading lists, since good reference works allow students to acquire on their own the background information necessary to interpret difficult or unfamiliar material.

Questions 43–47 refer to the passage above.

43. The author of the passage is primarily concerned with doing which of the following?

(A) Recommending a methodology
(B) Describing a course of study
(C) Discussing a problem
(D) Evaluating a past course of action
(E) Responding to a criticism

44. The "dilemma" mentioned in line 3 can best be characterized as being caused by the necessity to make a choice when faced with a

(A) lack of acceptable alternatives
(B) lack of strict standards for evaluating alternatives
(C) preponderance of bad alternatives as compared to good
(D) multitude of different alternatives
(E) large number of alternatives that are nearly identical in content

45. The passage suggests that the factor mentioned in lines 15–18 complicates professors' attempts to construct introductory reading lists for courses in Asian American studies in which of the following ways?

    (A) By making it difficult for professors to identify primary source material and to obtain standard information on Asian American history and culture
    (B) By preventing professors from identifying excellent anthologies and introductory texts in the field that are both recent and understandable to students
    (C) By preventing professors from adequately evaluating the quality of the numerous texts currently being published in the field
    (D) By making it more necessary for professors to select readings for their courses that are not too challenging for students unfamiliar with Asian American history and culture
    (E) By making it more likely that the readings professors assign to students in their courses will be drawn solely from primary sources

46. The passage implies that which of the following was true of introductory courses in Asian American studies a few decades ago?

    (A) The range of different textbooks that could be assigned for such courses was extremely limited.
    (B) The texts assigned as readings in such courses were often not very challenging for students.
    (C) Students often complained about the texts assigned to them in such courses.
    (D) Such courses were offered only at schools whose libraries were rich in primary sources.
    (E) Such courses were the only means then available by which people in the United States could acquire knowledge of the field.

47. According to the passage, the existence of good one-volume reference works about Asian Americans could result in

    (A) increased agreement among professors of Asian American studies regarding the quality of the sources available in their field
    (B) an increase in the number of students signing up for introductory courses in Asian American studies
    (C) increased accuracy in writings that concern Asian American history and culture
    (D) the use of introductory texts about Asian American history and culture in courses outside the field of Asian American studies
    (E) the inclusion of a wider range of Asian American material in introductory reading lists in Asian American studies

In the seventeenth-century Florentine textile industry, women were employed primarily in low-paying, low-skill jobs. To explain this segregation of labor by gender, economists have relied on the useful theory of human capital. According to this theory, investment in human capital—the acquisition of difficult job-related skills—generally benefits individuals by making them eligible to engage in well-paid occupations. Women's role as child bearers, however, results in interruptions in their participation in the job market (as compared with men's) and thus reduces their opportunities to acquire training for highly skilled work. In addition, the human capital theory explains why there was a high concentration of women workers in certain low-skill jobs, such as weaving, but not in others, such as combing or carding, by positing that because of their primary responsibility in child rearing women took occupations that could be carried out in the home.

There were, however, differences in pay scales that cannot be explained by the human capital theory. For example, male construction workers were paid significantly higher wages than female taffeta weavers. The wage difference between these two low-skill occupations stems from the segregation of labor by gender: because a limited number of occupations were open to women, there was a large supply of workers in their fields, and this "overcrowding" resulted in women receiving lower wages and men receiving higher wages.

Questions 48–50 refer to the passage above.

48. The passage suggests that combing and carding differ from weaving in that combing and carding are

(A) low-skill jobs performed primarily by women employees
(B) low-skill jobs that were not performed in the home
(C) low-skill jobs performed by both male and female employees
(D) high-skill jobs performed outside the home
(E) high-skill jobs performed by both male and female employees

49. Which of the following, if true, would most weaken the explanation provided by the human capital theory for women's concentration in certain occupations in seventeenth-century Florence?

(A) Women were unlikely to work outside the home even in occupations whose hours were flexible enough to allow women to accommodate domestic tasks as well as paid labor.
(B) Parents were less likely to teach occupational skills to their daughters than they were to their sons.
(C) Women's participation in the Florentine paid labor force grew steadily throughout the sixteenth and seventeenth centuries.
(D) The vast majority of female weavers in the Florentine wool industry had children.
(E) Few women worked as weavers in the Florentine silk industry, which was devoted to making cloths that required a high degree of skill to produce.

50. The author of the passage would be most likely to describe the explanation provided by the human capital theory for the high concentration of women in certain occupations in the seventeenth-century Florentine textile industry as

(A) well founded though incomplete
(B) difficult to articulate
(C) plausible but poorly substantiated
(D) seriously flawed
(E) contrary to recent research

(This passage was adapted from an article written in 1992.)

Some observers have attributed the dramatic growth in temporary employment that occurred in the United States during the 1980's to increased participation in the workforce by certain groups, such as first-time or reentering workers, who supposedly prefer such arrangements. However, statistical analyses reveal that demographic changes in the workforce did not correlate with variations in the total number of temporary workers. Instead, these analyses suggest that factors affecting employers account for the rise in temporary employment. One factor is product demand: temporary employment is favored by employers who are adapting to fluctuating demand for products while at the same time seeking to reduce overall labor costs. Another factor is labor's reduced bargaining strength, which allows employers more control over the terms of employment. Given the analyses, which reveal that growth in temporary employment now far exceeds the level explainable by recent workforce entry rates of groups said to prefer temporary jobs, firms should be discouraged from creating excessive numbers of temporary positions. Government policymakers should consider mandating benefit coverage for temporary employees, promoting pay equity between temporary and permanent workers, assisting labor unions in organizing temporary workers, and encouraging firms to assign temporary jobs primarily to employees who explicitly indicate that preference.

Questions 51–57 refer to the passage above.

51. The primary purpose of the passage is to

(A) present the results of statistical analyses and propose further studies
(B) explain a recent development and predict its eventual consequences
(C) identify the reasons for a trend and recommend measures to address it
(D) outline several theories about a phenomenon and advocate one of them
(E) describe the potential consequences of implementing a new policy and argue in favor of that policy

52. According to the passage, which of the following is true of the "factors affecting employers" that are mentioned in lines 9–10?

(A) Most experts cite them as having initiated the growth in temporary employment that occurred during the 1980's.
(B) They may account for the increase in the total number of temporary workers during the 1980's.
(C) They were less important than demographic change in accounting for the increase of temporary employment during the 1980's.
(D) They included a sharp increase in the cost of labor during the 1980's.
(E) They are more difficult to account for than are other factors involved in the growth of temporary employment during the 1980's.

53. The passage suggests which of the following about the use of temporary employment by firms during the 1980's?

(A) It enabled firms to deal with fluctuating product demand far more efficiently than they did before the 1980's.
(B) It increased as a result of increased participation in the workforce by certain demographic groups.
(C) It was discouraged by government-mandated policies.
(D) It was a response to preferences indicated by certain employees for more flexible working arrangements.
(E) It increased partly as a result of workers' reduced ability to control the terms of their employment.

54. The passage suggests which of the following about the workers who took temporary jobs during the 1980's?

(A) Their jobs frequently led to permanent positions within firms.
(B) They constituted a less demographically diverse group than has been suggested.
(C) They were occasionally involved in actions organized by labor unions.
(D) Their pay declined during the decade in comparison with the pay of permanent employees.
(E) They did not necessarily prefer temporary employment to permanent employment.

55. The first sentence in the passage suggests that the observers mentioned in line 1 would be most likely to predict which of the following?

(A) That the number of new temporary positions would decline as fewer workers who preferred temporary employment entered the workforce
(B) That the total number of temporary positions would increase as fewer workers were able to find permanent positions
(C) That employers would have less control over the terms of workers' employment as workers increased their bargaining strength
(D) That more workers would be hired for temporary positions as product demand increased
(E) That the number of workers taking temporary positions would increase as more workers in any given demographic group entered the workforce

56. In the context of the passage, the word "excessive" (line 23) most closely corresponds to which of the following phrases?

(A) Far more than can be justified by worker preferences
(B) Far more than can be explained by fluctuations in product demand
(C) Far more than can be beneficial to the success of the firms themselves
(D) Far more than can be accounted for by an expanding national economy
(E) Far more than can be attributed to increases in the total number of people in the workforce

57. The passage mentions each of the following as an appropriate kind of governmental action EXCEPT

(A) getting firms to offer temporary employment primarily to a certain group of people
(B) encouraging equitable pay for temporary and permanent employees
(C) facilitating the organization of temporary workers by labor unions
(D) establishing guidelines on the proportion of temporary workers that firms should employ
(E) ensuring that temporary workers obtain benefits from their employers

Many United States companies have, unfortunately, made the search for legal protection from import competition into a major line of work. Since 1980 the United States International Trade Commission (ITC) has received about 280 complaints alleging damage from imports that benefit from subsidies by foreign governments. Another 340 charge that foreign companies "dumped" their products in the United States at "less than fair value." Even when no unfair practices are alleged, the simple claim that an industry has been injured by imports is sufficient grounds to seek relief.

Contrary to the general impression, this quest for import relief has hurt more companies than it has helped. As corporations begin to function globally, they develop an intricate web of marketing, production, and research relationships. The complexity of these relationships makes it unlikely that a system of import relief laws will meet the strategic needs of all the units under the same parent company.

Internationalization increases the danger that foreign companies will use import relief laws against the very companies the laws were designed to protect. Suppose a United States–owned company establishes an overseas plant to manufacture a product while its competitor makes the same product in the United States. If the competitor can prove injury from the imports—and that the United States company received a subsidy from a foreign government to build its plant abroad—the United States company's products will be uncompetitive in the United States, since they would be subject to duties.

Perhaps the most brazen case occurred when the ITC investigated allegations that Canadian companies were injuring the United States salt industry by dumping rock salt, used to de-ice roads. The bizarre aspect of the complaint was that a foreign conglomerate with United States operations was crying for help against a United States company with foreign operations. The "United States" company claiming injury was a subsidiary of a Dutch conglomerate, while the "Canadian" companies included a subsidiary of a Chicago firm that was the second-largest domestic producer of rock salt.

Questions 58–63 refer to the passage above.

58. The passage is chiefly concerned with

(A) arguing against the increased internationalization of United States corporations

(B) warning that the application of laws affecting trade frequently has unintended consequences

(C) demonstrating that foreign-based firms receive more subsidies from their governments than United States firms receive from the United States government

(D) advocating the use of trade restrictions for "dumped" products but not for other imports

(E) recommending a uniform method for handling claims of unfair trade practices

59. It can be inferred from the passage that the minimal basis for a complaint to the International Trade Commission is which of the following?

(A) A foreign competitor has received a subsidy from a foreign government.

(B) A foreign competitor has substantially increased the volume of products shipped to the United States.

(C) A foreign competitor is selling products in the United States at less than fair market value.

(D) The company requesting import relief has been injured by the sale of imports in the United States.

(E) The company requesting import relief has been barred from exporting products to the country of its foreign competitor.

60. The last paragraph performs which of the following functions in the passage?

(A) It summarizes the discussion thus far and suggests additional areas for research.
(B) It presents a recommendation based on the evidence presented earlier.
(C) It discusses an exceptional case in which the results expected by the author of the passage were not obtained.
(D) It introduces an additional area of concern not mentioned earlier.
(E) It cites a specific case that illustrates a problem presented more generally in the previous paragraph.

61. The passage warns of which of the following dangers?

(A) Companies in the United States may receive no protection from imports unless they actively seek protection from import competition.
(B) Companies that seek legal protection from import competition may incur legal costs that far exceed any possible gain.
(C) Companies that are United States owned but operate internationally may not be eligible for protection from import competition under the laws of the countries in which their plants operate.
(D) Companies that are not United States owned may seek legal protection from import competition under United States import relief laws.
(E) Companies in the United States that import raw materials may have to pay duties on those materials.

62. The passage suggests that which of the following is most likely to be true of United States trade laws?

(A) They will eliminate the practice of "dumping" products in the United States.
(B) They will enable manufacturers in the United States to compete more profitably outside the United States.
(C) They will affect United States trade with Canada more negatively than trade with other nations.
(D) Those that help one unit within a parent company will not necessarily help other units in the company.
(E) Those that are applied to international companies will accomplish their intended result.

63. It can be inferred from the passage that the author believes which of the following about the complaint mentioned in the last paragraph?

(A) The ITC acted unfairly toward the complainant in its investigation.
(B) The complaint violated the intent of import relief laws.
(C) The response of the ITC to the complaint provided suitable relief from unfair trade practices to the complainant.
(D) The ITC did not have access to appropriate information concerning the case.
(E) Each of the companies involved in the complaint acted in its own best interest.

Australian researchers have discovered electroreceptors (sensory organs designed to respond to electrical fields) clustered at the tip of the spiny anteater's snout. The researchers made this discovery by exposing small areas of the snout to extremely weak electrical fields and recording the transmission of resulting nervous activity to the brain. While it is true that tactile receptors, another kind of sensory organ on the anteater's snout, can also respond to electrical stimuli, such receptors do so only in response to electrical field strengths about 1,000 times greater than those known to excite electroreceptors.

Having discovered the electroreceptors, researchers are now investigating how anteaters utilize such a sophisticated sensory system. In one behavioral experiment, researchers successfully trained an anteater to distinguish between two troughs of water, one with a weak electrical field and the other with none. Such evidence is consistent with researchers' hypothesis that anteaters use electroreceptors to detect electrical signals given off by prey; however, researchers as yet have been unable to detect electrical signals emanating from termite mounds, where the favorite food of anteaters live. Still, researchers have observed anteaters breaking into a nest of ants at an oblique angle and quickly locating nesting chambers. This ability to quickly locate unseen prey suggests, according to the researchers, that the anteaters were using their electroreceptors to locate the nesting chambers.

Questions 64–69 refer to the passage above.

64. According to the passage, which of the following is a characteristic that distinguishes electroreceptors from tactile receptors?

(A) The manner in which electroreceptors respond to electrical stimuli

(B) The tendency of electroreceptors to be found in clusters

(C) The unusual locations in which electroreceptors are found in most species

(D) The amount of electrical stimulation required to excite electroreceptors

(E) The amount of nervous activity transmitted to the brain by electroreceptors when they are excited

65. Which of the following can be inferred about the experiment described in the first paragraph?

(A) Researchers had difficulty verifying the existence of electroreceptors in the anteater because electroreceptors respond to such a narrow range of electrical field strengths.

(B) Researchers found that the level of nervous activity in the anteater's brain increased dramatically as the strength of the electrical stimulus was increased.

(C) Researchers found that some areas of the anteater's snout were not sensitive to a weak electrical stimulus.

(D) Researchers found that the anteater's tactile receptors were more easily excited by a strong electrical stimulus than were the electroreceptors.

(E) Researchers tested small areas of the anteater's snout in order to ensure that only electroreceptors were responding to the stimulus.

66. The author of the passage most probably discusses the function of tactile receptors (lines 8–13) in order to

(A) eliminate an alternative explanation of anteaters' response to electrical stimuli
(B) highlight a type of sensory organ that has a function identical to that of electroreceptors
(C) point out a serious complication in the research on electroreceptors in anteaters
(D) suggest that tactile receptors assist electroreceptors in the detection of electrical signals
(E) introduce a factor that was not addressed in the research on electroreceptors in anteaters

67. Which of the following can be inferred about anteaters from the behavioral experiment mentioned in the second paragraph?

(A) They are unable to distinguish between stimuli detected by their electroreceptors and stimuli detected by their tactile receptors.
(B) They are unable to distinguish between the electrical signals emanating from termite mounds and those emanating from ant nests.
(C) They can be trained to recognize consistently the presence of a particular stimulus.
(D) They react more readily to strong than to weak stimuli.
(E) They are more efficient at detecting stimuli in a controlled environment than in a natural environment.

68. The passage suggests that the researchers mentioned in the second paragraph who observed anteaters break into a nest of ants would most likely agree with which of the following statements?

(A) The event they observed provides conclusive evidence that anteaters use their electroreceptors to locate unseen prey.
(B) The event they observed was atypical and may not reflect the usual hunting practices of anteaters.
(C) It is likely that the anteaters located the ants' nesting chambers without the assistance of electroreceptors.
(D) Anteaters possess a very simple sensory system for use in locating prey.
(E) The speed with which the anteaters located their prey is greater than what might be expected on the basis of chance alone.

69. Which of the following, if true, would most strengthen the hypothesis mentioned in lines 21–23?

(A) Researchers are able to train anteaters to break into an underground chamber that is emitting a strong electrical signal.
(B) Researchers are able to detect a weak electrical signal emanating from the nesting chamber of an ant colony.
(C) Anteaters are observed taking increasingly longer amounts of time to locate the nesting chambers of ants.
(D) Anteaters are observed using various angles to break into nests of ants.
(E) Anteaters are observed using the same angle used with nests of ants to break into the nests of other types of prey.

Milankovitch proposed in the early twentieth century that the ice ages were caused by variations in the Earth's orbit around the Sun. For some time this theory was considered untestable, largely because there was no sufficiently precise chronology of the ice ages with which the orbital variations could be matched.

To establish such a chronology it is necessary to determine the relative amounts of land ice that existed at various times in the Earth's past. A recent discovery makes such a determination possible: relative land-ice volume for a given period can be deduced from the ratio of two oxygen isotopes, 16 and 18, found in ocean sediments. Almost all the oxygen in water is oxygen 16, but a few molecules out of every thousand incorporate the heavier isotope 18. When an ice age begins, the continental ice sheets grow, steadily reducing the amount of water evaporated from the ocean that will eventually return to it. Because heavier isotopes tend to be left behind when water evaporates from the ocean surfaces, the remaining ocean water becomes progressively enriched in oxygen 18. The degree of enrichment can be determined by analyzing ocean sediments of the period, because these sediments are composed of calcium carbonate shells of marine organisms, shells that were constructed with oxygen atoms drawn from the surrounding ocean. The higher the ratio of oxygen 18 to oxygen 16 in a sedimentary specimen, the more land ice there was when the sediment was laid down.

As an indicator of shifts in the Earth's climate, the isotope record has two advantages. First, it is a global record: there is remarkably little variation in isotope ratios in sedimentary specimens taken from different continental locations. Second, it is a more continuous record than that taken from rocks on land. Because of these advantages, sedimentary evidence can be dated with sufficient accuracy by radiometric methods to establish a precise chronology of the ice ages. The dated isotope record shows that the fluctuations in global ice volume over the past several hundred thousand years have a pattern: an ice age occurs roughly once every 100,000 years. These data have established a strong connection between variations in the Earth's orbit and the periodicity of the ice ages.

However, it is important to note that other factors, such as volcanic particulates or variations in the amount of sunlight received by the Earth, could potentially have affected the climate. The advantage of the Milankovitch theory is that it is testable; changes in the Earth's orbit can be calculated and dated by applying Newton's laws of gravity to progressively earlier configurations of the bodies in the solar system. Yet the lack of information about other possible factors affecting global climate does not make them unimportant.

Questions 70–75 refer to the passage above.

70. In the passage, the author is primarily interested in

(A) suggesting an alternative to an outdated research method

(B) introducing a new research method that calls an accepted theory into question

(C) emphasizing the instability of data gathered from the application of a new scientific method

(D) presenting a theory and describing a new method to test that theory

(E) initiating a debate about a widely accepted theory

71. The author of the passage would be most likely to agree with which of the following statements about the Milankovitch theory?

(A) It is the only possible explanation for the ice ages.

(B) It is too limited to provide a plausible explanation for the ice ages, despite recent research findings.

(C) It cannot be tested and confirmed until further research on volcanic activity is done.

(D) It is one plausible explanation, though not the only one, for the ice ages.

(E) It is not a plausible explanation for the ice ages, although it has opened up promising possibilities for future research.

72. It can be inferred from the passage that the isotope record taken from ocean sediments would be less useful to researchers if which of the following were true?

(A) It indicated that lighter isotopes of oxygen predominated at certain times.
(B) It had far more gaps in its sequence than the record taken from rocks on land.
(C) It indicated that climate shifts did not occur every 100,000 years.
(D) It indicated that the ratios of oxygen 16 and oxygen 18 in ocean water were not consistent with those found in fresh water.
(E) It stretched back for only a million years.

73. According to the passage, which of the following is true of the ratios of oxygen isotopes in ocean sediments?

(A) They indicate that sediments found during an ice age contain more calcium carbonate than sediments formed at other times.
(B) They are less reliable than the evidence from rocks on land in determining the volume of land ice.
(C) They can be used to deduce the relative volume of land ice that was present when the sediment was laid down.
(D) They are more unpredictable during an ice age than in other climatic conditions.
(E) They can be used to determine atmospheric conditions at various times in the past.

74. It can be inferred from the passage that precipitation formed from evaporated ocean water has

(A) the same isotopic ratio as ocean water
(B) less oxygen 18 than does ocean water
(C) less oxygen 18 than has the ice contained in continental ice sheets
(D) a different isotopic composition than has precipitation formed from water on land
(E) more oxygen 16 than has precipitation formed from fresh water

75. It can be inferred from the passage that calcium carbonate shells

(A) are not as susceptible to deterioration as rocks
(B) are less common in sediments formed during an ice age
(C) are found only in areas that were once covered by land ice
(D) contain radioactive material that can be used to determine a sediment's isotopic composition
(E) reflect the isotopic composition of the water at the time the shells were formed

It was once believed that the brain was independent of metabolic processes occurring elsewhere in the body. In recent studies, however, we have discovered that the production and release in brain neurons of the neurotransmitter serotonin (neurotransmitters are compounds that neurons use to transmit signals to other cells) depend directly on the food that the body processes.

Our first studies sought to determine whether the increase in serotonin observed in rats given a large injection of the amino acid tryptophan might also occur after rats ate meals that change tryptophan levels in the blood. We found that, immediately after the rats began to eat, parallel elevations occurred in blood tryptophan, brain tryptophan, and brain serotonin levels. These findings suggested that the production and release of serotonin in brain neurons were normally coupled with blood-tryptophan increases. In later studies we found that injecting insulin into a rat's bloodstream also caused parallel elevations in blood and brain tryptophan levels and in serotonin levels. We then decided to see whether the secretion of the animal's own insulin similarly affected serotonin production. We gave the rats a carbohydrate-containing meal that we knew would elicit insulin secretion. As we had hypothesized, the blood tryptophan level and the concentrations of tryptophan and of serotonin in the brain increased after the meal.

Surprisingly, however, when we added a large amount of protein to the meal, brain tryptophan and serotonin levels fell. Since protein contains tryptophan, why should it depress brain tryptophan levels? The answer lies in the mechanism that provides blood tryptophan to the brain cells. This same mechanism also provides the brain cells with other amino acids found in protein, such as tyrosine and leucine. The consumption of protein increases blood concentration of the other amino acids much more, proportionately, than it does that of tryptophan. The more protein is in a meal, the lower is the ratio of the resulting blood-tryptophan concentration to the concentration of competing amino acids, and the more slowly is tryptophan provided to the brain. Thus the more protein in a meal, the less serotonin subsequently produced and released.

Questions 76–84 refer to the passage above.

76. Which of the following titles best summarizes the contents of the passage?

(A) Neurotransmitters: Their Crucial Function in Cellular Communication
(B) Diet and Survival: An Old Relationship Reexamined
(C) The Blood Supply and the Brain: A Reciprocal Dependence
(D) Amino Acids and Neurotransmitters: The Connection between Serotonin Levels and Tyrosine
(E) The Effects of Food Intake on the Production and Release of Serotonin: Some Recent Findings

77. According to the passage, the speed with which tryptophan is provided to the brain cells of a rat varies with the

(A) amount of protein present in a meal
(B) concentration of serotonin in the brain before a meal
(C) concentration of leucine in the blood rather than on the concentration of tyrosine in the blood after a meal
(D) concentration of tryptophan in the brain before a meal
(E) number of serotonin-containing neurons

78. According to the passage, when the authors began their first studies, they were aware that

(A) they would eventually need to design experiments that involved feeding rats high concentrations of protein
(B) tryptophan levels in the blood were difficult to monitor with accuracy
(C) serotonin levels increased after rats were fed meals rich in tryptophan
(D) there were many neurotransmitters whose production was dependent on metabolic processes elsewhere in the body
(E) serotonin levels increased after rats were injected with a large amount of tryptophan

79. According to the passage, one reason that the authors gave rats carbohydrates was to

(A) depress the rats' tryptophan levels
(B) prevent the rats from contracting diseases
(C) cause the rats to produce insulin
(D) demonstrate that insulin is the most important substance secreted by the body
(E) compare the effect of carbohydrates with the effect of proteins

80. According to the passage, the more protein a rat consumes, the lower will be the

(A) ratio of the rat's blood-tryptophan concentration to the amount of serotonin produced and released in the rat's brain
(B) ratio of the rat's blood-tryptophan concentration to the concentration in its blood of the other amino acids contained in the protein
(C) ratio of the rat's blood-tyrosine concentration to its blood-leucine concentration
(D) number of neurotransmitters of any kind that the rat will produce and release
(E) number of amino acids the rat's blood will contain

81. The authors' discussion of the "mechanism that provides blood tryptophan to the brain cells" (lines 34–35) is meant to

(A) stimulate further research studies
(B) summarize an area of scientific investigation
(C) help explain why a particular research finding was obtained
(D) provide supporting evidence for a controversial scientific theory
(E) refute the conclusions of a previously mentioned research study

82. According to the passage, an injection of insulin was most similar in its effect on rats to an injection of

(A) tyrosine
(B) leucine
(C) blood
(D) tryptophan
(E) protein

83. It can be inferred from the passage that which of the following would be LEAST likely to be a potential source of aid to a patient who was not adequately producing and releasing serotonin?

(A) Meals consisting almost exclusively of protein
(B) Meals consisting almost exclusively of carbohydrates
(C) Meals that would elicit insulin secretion
(D) Meals that had very low concentrations of tyrosine
(E) Meals that had very low concentrations of leucine

84. It can be inferred from the passage that the authors initially held which of the following hypotheses about what would happen when they fed large amounts of protein to rats?

(A) The rats' brain serotonin levels would not decrease.
(B) The rats' brain tryptophan levels would decrease.
(C) The rats' tyrosine levels would increase less quickly than would their leucine levels.
(D) The rats would produce more insulin.
(E) The rats would produce neurotransmitters other than serotonin.

In 1955 Maurice Duverger published *The Political Role of Women*, the first behavioralist, multinational comparison of women's electoral participation ever to use election data and survey data together. His study analyzed women's patterns of voting, political candidacy, and political activism in four European countries during the first half of the twentieth century. Duverger's research findings were that women voted somewhat less frequently than men (the difference narrowing the longer women had the vote) and were slightly more conservative.

Duverger's work set an early standard for the sensitive analysis of women's electoral activities. Moreover, to Duverger's credit, he placed his findings in the context of many of the historical processes that had shaped these activities. However, since these contexts have changed over time, Duverger's approach has proved more durable than his actual findings. In addition, Duverger's discussion of his findings was hampered by his failure to consider certain specific factors important to women's electoral participation at the time he collected his data: the influence of political regimes, the effects of economic factors, and the ramifications of political and social relations between women and men. Given this failure, Duverger's study foreshadowed the enduring limitations of the behavioralist approach to the multinational study of women's political participation.

Questions 85–90 refer to the passage above.

85. The primary purpose of the passage is to

(A) evaluate a research study
(B) summarize the history of a research area
(C) report new research findings
(D) reinterpret old research findings
(E) reconcile conflicting research findings

86. According to the passage, Duverger's study was unique in 1955 in that it

(A) included both election data and survey data
(B) gathered data from sources never before used in political studies
(C) included an analysis of historical processes
(D) examined the influence on voting behavior of the relationships between women and men
(E) analyzed not only voting and political candidacy but also other political activities

87. Which of the following characteristics of a country is most clearly an example of a factor that Duverger, as described in the passage, failed to consider in his study?

(A) A large population
(B) A predominantly Protestant population
(C) A predominantly urban population
(D) A one-party government
(E) Location in the heart of Europe

88. The author implies that Duverger's actual findings are

(A) limited because they focus on only four countries
(B) inaccurate in their description of the four countries in the early 1950's
(C) out-of-date in that they are inapplicable in the four countries today
(D) flawed because they are based on unsound data
(E) biased by Duverger's political beliefs

89. The passage implies that, in comparing four European countries, Duverger found that the voting rates of women and men were most different in the country in which women

(A) were most politically active
(B) ran for office most often
(C) held the most conservative political views
(D) had the most egalitarian relations with men
(E) had possessed the right to vote for the shortest time

90. The author implies that some behavioralist research involving the multinational study of women's political participation that followed Duverger's study did which of the following?

(A) Ignored Duverger's approach
(B) Suffered from faults similar to those in Duverger's study
(C) Focused on political activism
(D) Focused on the influences of political regimes
(E) Focused on the political and social relations between women and men

In 1896 a Georgia couple suing for damages in the accidental death of their two-year-old was told that since the child had made no real economic contribution to the family, there was no liability for damages. In contrast, less than a century later, in 1979, the parents of a three-year-old sued in New York for accidental-death damages and won an award of $750,000.

The transformation in social values implicit in juxtaposing these two incidents is the subject of Viviana Zelizer's excellent book, *Pricing the Priceless Child*. During the nineteenth century, she argues, the concept of the "useful" child who contributed to the family economy gave way gradually to the present-day notion of the "useless" child who, though producing no income for, and indeed extremely costly to, its parents, is yet considered emotionally "priceless." Well established among segments of the middle and upper classes by the mid-1800's, this new view of childhood spread throughout society in the late nineteenth and early twentieth centuries as reformers introduced child labor regulations and compulsory education laws predicated in part on the assumption that a child's emotional value made child labor taboo.

For Zelizer the origins of this transformation were many and complex. The gradual erosion of children's productive value in a maturing industrial economy, the decline in birth and death rates, especially in child mortality, and the development of the companionate family (a family in which members were united by explicit bonds of love rather than duty) were all factors critical in changing the assessment of children's worth. Yet "expulsion of children from the 'cash nexus,' . . . although clearly shaped by profound changes in the economic, occupational, and family structures," Zelizer maintains, "was also part of a cultural process of 'sacralization' of children's lives." Protecting children from the crass business world became enormously important for late nineteenth-century middle-class Americans, she suggests; this sacralization was a way of resisting what they perceived as the relentless corruption of human values by the marketplace.

In stressing the cultural determinants of a child's worth, Zelizer takes issue with practitioners of the new "sociological economics," who have analyzed such traditionally sociological topics as crime, marriage, education, and health solely in terms of their economic determinants. Allowing only a small role for cultural forces in the form of individual "preferences," these sociologists tend to view all human behavior as directed primarily by the principle of maximizing economic gain. Zelizer is highly critical of this approach, and emphasizes instead the opposite phenomenon: the power of social values to transform price. As children became more valuable in emotional terms, she argues, their "exchange" or "surrender" value on the market, that is, the conversion of their intangible worth into cash terms, became much greater.

Questions 91–96 refer to the passage above.

91. It can be inferred from the passage that accidental-death damage awards in America during the nineteenth century tended to be based principally on the

(A) earnings of the person at time of death
(B) wealth of the party causing the death
(C) degree of culpability of the party causing the death
(D) amount of money that had been spent on the person killed
(E) amount of suffering endured by the family of the person killed

92. It can be inferred from the passage that in the early 1800's children were generally regarded by their families as individuals who

(A) needed enormous amounts of security and affection
(B) required constant supervision while working
(C) were important to the economic well-being of a family
(D) were unsuited to spending long hours in school
(E) were financial burdens assumed for the good of society

93. Which of the following alternative explanations of the change in the cash value of children would be most likely to be put forward by sociological economists as they are described in the passage?

(A) The cash value of children rose during the nineteenth century because parents began to increase their emotional investment in the upbringing of their children.
(B) The cash value of children rose during the nineteenth century because their expected earnings over the course of a lifetime increased greatly.
(C) The cash value of children rose during the nineteenth century because the spread of humanitarian ideals resulted in a wholesale reappraisal of the worth of an individual.
(D) The cash value of children rose during the nineteenth century because compulsory education laws reduced the supply, and thus raised the costs, of available child labor.
(E) The cash value of children rose during the nineteenth century because of changes in the way negligence law assessed damages in accidental-death cases.

94. The primary purpose of the passage is to

(A) review the literature in a new academic subfield
(B) present the central thesis of a recent book
(C) contrast two approaches to analyzing historical change
(D) refute a traditional explanation of a social phenomenon
(E) encourage further work on a neglected historical topic

95. It can be inferred from the passage that which of the following statements was true of American families over the course of the nineteenth century?

(A) The average size of families grew considerably.
(B) The percentage of families involved in industrial work declined dramatically.
(C) Family members became more emotionally bonded to one another.
(D) Family members spent an increasing amount of time working with each other.
(E) Family members became more economically dependent on each other.

96. Zelizer refers to all of the following as important influences in changing the assessment of children's worth EXCEPT changes in

(A) the mortality rate
(B) the nature of industry
(C) the nature of the family
(D) attitudes toward reform movements
(E) attitudes toward the marketplace

The majority of successful senior managers do not closely follow the classical rational model of first clarifying goals, assessing the problem, formulating options, estimating likelihoods of success, making a decision, and only then taking action to implement the decision. Rather, in their day-by-day tactical maneuvers, these senior executives rely on what is vaguely termed "intuition" to manage a network of interrelated problems that require them to deal with ambiguity, inconsistency, novelty, and surprise; and to integrate action into the process of thinking.

Generations of writers on management have recognized that some practicing managers rely heavily on intuition. In general, however, such writers display a poor grasp of what intuition is. Some see it as the opposite of rationality; others view it as an excuse for capriciousness.

Isenberg's recent research on the cognitive processes of senior managers reveals that managers' intuition is neither of these. Rather, senior managers use intuition in at least five distinct ways. First, they intuitively sense when a problem exists. Second, managers rely on intuition to perform well-learned behavior patterns rapidly. This intuition is not arbitrary or irrational, but is based on years of painstaking practice and hands-on experience that build skills. A third function of intuition is to synthesize isolated bits of data and practice into an integrated picture, often in an "Aha!" experience. Fourth, some managers use intuition as a check on the results of more rational analysis. Most senior executives are familiar with the formal decision analysis models and tools, and those who use such systematic methods for reaching decisions are occasionally leery of solutions suggested by these methods which run counter to their sense of the correct course of action. Finally, managers can use intuition to bypass in-depth analysis and move rapidly to engender a plausible solution. Used in this way, intuition is an almost instantaneous cognitive process in which a manager recognizes familiar patterns.

One of the implications of the intuitive style of executive management is that "thinking" is inseparable from acting. Since managers often "know" what is right before they can analyze and explain it, they frequently act first and explain later. Analysis is inextricably tied to action in thinking/acting cycles, in which managers develop thoughts about their companies and organizations not by analyzing a problematic situation and then acting, but by acting and analyzing in close concert. Given the great uncertainty of many of the management issues that they face, senior managers often instigate a course of action simply to learn more about an issue. They then use the results of the action to develop a more complete understanding of the issue. One implication of thinking/acting cycles is that action is often part of defining the problem, not just of implementing the solution.

Questions 97–102 refer to the passage above.

97. According to the passage, senior managers use intuition in all of the following ways EXCEPT to

(A) speed up the creation of a solution to a problem
(B) identify a problem
(C) bring together disparate facts
(D) stipulate clear goals
(E) evaluate possible solutions to a problem

98. The passage suggests which of the following about the "writers on management" mentioned in line 12?

(A) They have criticized managers for not following the classical rational model of decision analysis.
(B) They have not based their analyses on a sufficiently large sample of actual managers.
(C) They have relied in drawing their conclusions on what managers say rather than on what managers do.
(D) They have misunderstood how managers use intuition in making business decisions.
(E) They have not acknowledged the role of intuition in managerial practice.

99. Which of the following best exemplifies "an 'Aha!' experience" (lines 29–30) as it is presented in the passage?

(A) A manager risks taking an action whose outcome is unpredictable to discover whether the action changes the problem at hand.
(B) A manager performs well-learned and familiar behavior patterns in creative and uncharacteristic ways to solve a problem.
(C) A manager suddenly connects seemingly unrelated facts and experiences to create a pattern relevant to the problem at hand.
(D) A manager rapidly identifies the methodology used to compile data yielded by systematic analysis.
(E) A manager swiftly decides which of several sets of tactics to implement in order to deal with the contingencies suggested by a problem.

100. According to the passage, the classical model of decision analysis includes all of the following EXCEPT

(A) evaluation of a problem
(B) creation of possible solutions to a problem
(C) establishment of clear goals to be reached by the decision
(D) action undertaken in order to discover more information about a problem
(E) comparison of the probable effects of different solutions to a problem

101. It can be inferred from the passage that which of the following would most probably be one major difference in behavior between Manager X, who uses intuition to reach decisions, and Manager Y, who uses only formal decision analysis?

(A) Manager X analyzes first and then acts; Manager Y does not.
(B) Manager X checks possible solutions to a problem by systematic analysis; Manager Y does not.
(C) Manager X takes action in order to arrive at the solution to a problem; Manager Y does not.
(D) Manager Y draws on years of hands-on experience in creating a solution to a problem; Manager X does not.
(E) Manager Y depends on day-to-day tactical maneuvering; Manager X does not.

102. The passage provides support for which of the following statements?

(A) Managers who rely on intuition are more successful than those who rely on formal decision analysis.
(B) Managers cannot justify their intuitive decisions.
(C) Managers' intuition works contrary to their rational and analytical skills.
(D) Logical analysis of a problem increases the number of possible solutions.
(E) Intuition enables managers to employ their practical experience more efficiently.

According to a recent theory, Archean-age gold-quartz vein systems were formed more than two billion years ago from magmatic fluids that originated from molten granite-like bodies deep beneath the surface of the Earth. This theory is contrary to the widely held view that the systems were deposited from metamorphic fluids, that is, from fluids that formed during the dehydration of wet sedimentary rocks.

The recently developed theory has considerable practical importance. Most of the gold deposits discovered during the original gold rushes were exposed at the Earth's surface and were found because they had shed trails of alluvial gold that were easily traced by simple prospecting methods. Although these same methods still lead to an occasional discovery, most deposits not yet discovered have gone undetected because they are buried and have no surface expression.

The challenge in exploration is therefore to unravel the subsurface geology of an area and pinpoint the position of buried minerals. Methods widely used today include analysis of aerial images that yield a broad geological overview; geophysical techniques that provide data on the magnetic, electrical, and mineralogical properties of the rocks being investigated; and sensitive chemical tests that are able to detect the subtle chemical halos that often envelop mineralization. However, none of these high-technology methods are of any value if the sites to which they are applied have never mineralized, and to maximize the chances of discovery the explorer must therefore pay particular attention to selecting the ground formations most likely to be mineralized. Such ground selection relies to varying degrees on conceptual models, which take into account theoretical studies of relevant factors.

These models are constructed primarily from empirical observations of known mineral deposits and from theories of ore-forming processes. The explorer uses the models to identify those geological features that are critical to the formation of the mineralization being modeled, and then tries to select areas for exploration that exhibit as many of the critical features as possible.

Questions 103–110 refer to the passage above.

103. The author is primarily concerned with

(A) advocating a return to an older methodology
(B) explaining the importance of a recent theory
(C) enumerating differences between two widely used methods
(D) describing events leading to a discovery
(E) challenging the assumptions on which a theory is based

104. According to the passage, the widely held view of Archean-age gold-quartz vein systems is that such systems

(A) were formed from metamorphic fluids
(B) originated in molten granite-like bodies
(C) were formed from alluvial deposits
(D) generally have surface expression
(E) are not discoverable through chemical tests

105. The passage implies that which of the following steps would be the first performed by explorers who wish to maximize their chances of discovering gold?

(A) Surveying several sites known to have been formed more than two billion years ago
(B) Limiting exploration to sites known to have been formed from metamorphic fluid
(C) Using an appropriate conceptual model to select a site for further exploration
(D) Using geophysical methods to analyze rocks over a broad area
(E) Limiting exploration to sites where alluvial gold has previously been found

106. Which of the following statements about discoveries of gold deposits is supported by information in the passage?

(A) The number of gold discoveries made annually has increased between the time of the original gold rushes and the present.
(B) New discoveries of gold deposits are likely to be the result of exploration techniques designed to locate buried mineralization.

(C) It is unlikely that newly discovered gold deposits will ever yield as much as did those deposits discovered during the original gold rushes.
(D) Modern explorers are divided on the question of the utility of simple prospecting methods as a source of new discoveries of gold deposits.
(E) Models based on the theory that gold originated from magmatic fluids have already led to new discoveries of gold deposits.

107. It can be inferred from the passage that which of the following is easiest to detect?

(A) A gold-quartz vein system originating in magmatic fluids
(B) A gold-quartz vein system originating in metamorphic fluids
(C) A gold deposit that is mixed with granite
(D) A gold deposit that has shed alluvial gold
(E) A gold deposit that exhibits chemical halos

108. The theory mentioned in line 1 relates to the conceptual models discussed in the passage in which of the following ways?

(A) It may furnish a valid account of ore-forming processes, and, hence, can support conceptual models that have great practical significance.
(B) It suggests that certain geological formations, long believed to be mineralized, are in fact mineralized, thus confirming current conceptual models.
(C) It suggests that there may not be enough similarity across Archean-age gold-quartz vein systems to warrant the formulation of conceptual models.
(D) It corrects existing theories about the chemical halos of gold deposits, and thus provides a basis for correcting current conceptual models.
(E) It suggests that simple prospecting methods still have a higher success rate in the discovery of gold deposits than do more modern methods.

109. According to the passage, methods of exploring for gold that are widely used today are based on which of the following facts?

(A) Most of the Earth's remaining gold deposits are still molten.
(B) Most of the Earth's remaining gold deposits are exposed at the surface.
(C) Most of the Earth's remaining gold deposits are buried and have no surface expression.
(D) Only one type of gold deposit warrants exploration, since the other types of gold deposits are found in regions difficult to reach.
(E) Only one type of gold deposit warrants exploration, since the other types of gold deposits are unlikely to yield concentrated quantities of gold.

110. It can be inferred from the passage that the efficiency of model-based gold exploration depends on which of the following?

I. The closeness of the match between the geological features identified by the model as critical and the actual geological features of a given area
II. The degree to which the model chosen relies on empirical observation of known mineral deposits rather than on theories of ore-forming processes
III. The degree to which the model chosen is based on an accurate description of the events leading to mineralization

(A) I only
(B) II only
(C) I and II only
(D) I and III only
(E) I, II, and III

After evidence was obtained in the 1920's that the universe is expanding, it became reasonable to ask: will the universe continue to expand indefinitely, or is there enough mass in it for the mutual attraction of its constituents to bring this expansion to a halt? It can be calculated that the critical density of matter needed to brake the expansion and "close" the universe is equivalent to three hydrogen atoms per cubic meter. But the density of the observable universe–luminous matter in the form of galaxies–comes to only a fraction of this. If the expansion of the universe is to stop, there must be enough invisible matter in the universe to exceed the luminous matter in density by a factor of roughly 70.

Our contribution to the search for this "missing matter" has been to study the rotational velocity of galaxies at various distances from their center of rotation. It has been known for some time that outside the bright nucleus of a typical spiral galaxy luminosity falls off rapidly with distance from the center. If luminosity were a true indicator of mass, most of the mass would be concentrated toward the center. Outside the nucleus the rotational velocity would decrease geometrically with distance from the center, in conformity with Kepler's law. Instead we have found that the rotational velocity in spiral galaxies either remains constant with increasing distance from the center or increases slightly. This unexpected result indicates that the falloff in luminous mass with distance from the center is balanced by an increase in nonluminous mass.

Our findings suggest that as much as 90 percent of the mass of the universe is not radiating at any wavelength with enough intensity to be detected on the Earth. Such dark matter could be in the form of extremely dim stars of low mass, of large planets like Jupiter, or of black holes, either small or massive. While it has not yet been determined whether this mass is sufficient to "close" the universe, some physicists consider it significant that estimates are converging on the critical value.

Questions 111–116 refer to the passage above.

111. The passage is primarily concerned with

(A) defending a controversial approach
(B) criticizing an accepted view
(C) summarizing research findings
(D) contrasting competing theories
(E) describing an innovative technique

112. The authors' study indicates that, in comparison with the outermost regions of a typical spiral galaxy, the region just outside the nucleus can be characterized as having

(A) higher rotational velocity and higher luminosity
(B) lower rotational velocity and higher luminosity
(C) lower rotational velocity and lower luminosity
(D) similar rotational velocity and higher luminosity
(E) similar rotational velocity and similar luminosity

113. The passage suggests that the results of the authors' study have changed their ideas about which of the following characteristics of spiral galaxies?

I. The relative luminosity of different regions
II. The relative rotational velocity of different regions
III. The relative distribution of matter in different regions

(A) I only
(B) II only
(C) III only
(D) II and III only
(E) I, II, and III

114. The authors' suggestion that "as much as 90 percent of the mass of the universe is not radiating at any wavelength with enough intensity to be detected on the Earth" (lines 39–42) would be most weakened if which of the following were discovered to be true?

(A) Spiral galaxies are less common than types of galaxies that contain little nonluminous matter.
(B) Luminous and nonluminous matter are composed of the same basic elements.
(C) The bright nucleus of a typical spiral galaxy also contains some nonluminous matter.
(D) The density of the observable universe is greater than most previous estimates have suggested.
(E) Some galaxies do not rotate or rotate too slowly for their rotational velocity to be measured.

115. It can be inferred from information presented in the passage that if the density of the universe were equivalent to significantly less than three hydrogen atoms per cubic meter, which of the following would be true as a consequence?

(A) Luminosity would be a true indicator of mass.
(B) Different regions in spiral galaxies would rotate at the same velocity.
(C) The universe would continue to expand indefinitely.
(D) The density of the invisible matter in the universe would have to be more than 70 times the density of the luminous matter.
(E) More of the invisible matter in spiral galaxies would have to be located in their nuclei than in their outer regions.

116. The authors propose all of the following as possibly contributing to the "missing matter" in spiral galaxies EXCEPT

(A) massive black holes
(B) small black holes
(C) small, dim stars
(D) massive stars
(E) large planets

Line All the cells in a particular plant start out with the same complement of genes. How then can these cells differentiate and form structures as different as roots, stems, leaves, and fruits? The answer is that only a small subset of the genes in a particular kind of cell are expressed, or turned on, at a given time. This is accomplished by a complex system of chemical messengers that in plants include hormones and other regulatory molecules. Five major hormones have been identified: auxin, abscisic acid, cytokinin, ethylene, and gibberellin. Studies of plants have now identified a new class of regulatory molecules called oligosaccharins.

Unlike the oligosaccharins, the five well-known plant hormones are pleiotropic rather than specific; that is, each has more than one effect on the growth and development of plants. The five have so many simultaneous effects that they are not very useful in artificially controlling the growth of crops. Auxin, for instance, stimulates the rate of cell elongation, causes shoots to grow up and roots to grow down, and inhibits the growth of lateral shoots. Auxin also causes the plant to develop a vascular system, to form lateral roots, and to produce ethylene.

The pleiotropy of the five well-studied plant hormones is somewhat analogous to that of certain hormones in animals. For example, hormones from the hypothalamus in the brain stimulate the anterior lobe of the pituitary gland to synthesize and release many different hormones, one of which stimulates the release of hormones from the adrenal cortex. These hormones have specific effects on target organs all over the body. One hormone stimulates the thyroid gland, for example, another the ovarian follicle cells, and so forth. In other words, there is a hierarchy of hormones.

Such a hierarchy may also exist in plants. Oligosaccharins are fragments of the cell wall released by enzymes: different enzymes release different oligosaccharins. There are indications that pleiotropic plant hormones may actually function by activating the enzymes that release these other, more specific chemical messengers from the cell wall.

Questions 117–122 refer to the passage above.

117. According to the passage, the five well-known plant hormones are not useful in controlling the growth of crops because

(A) it is not known exactly what functions the hormones perform
(B) each hormone has various effects on plants
(C) none of the hormones can function without the others
(D) each hormone has different effects on different kinds of plants
(E) each hormone works on only a small subset of a cell's genes at any particular time

118. The passage suggests that the place of hypothalamic hormones in the hormonal hierarchies of animals is similar to the place of which of the following in plants?

(A) Plant cell walls
(B) The complement of genes in each plant cell
(C) A subset of a plant cell's gene complement
(D) The five major hormones
(E) The oligosaccharins

119. The passage suggests that which of the following is a function likely to be performed by an oligosaccharin?

(A) To stimulate a particular plant cell to become part of a plant's root system
(B) To stimulate the walls of a particular cell to produce other oligosaccharins
(C) To activate enzymes that release specific chemical messengers from plant cell walls
(D) To duplicate the gene complement in a particular plant cell
(E) To produce multiple effects on a particular subsystem of plant cells

120. The author mentions specific effects that auxin has on plant development in order to illustrate the

(A) point that some of the effects of plant hormones can be harmful
(B) way in which hormones are produced by plants
(C) hierarchical nature of the functioning of plant hormones
(D) differences among the best-known plant hormones
(E) concept of pleiotropy as it is exhibited by plant hormones

121. According to the passage, which of the following best describes a function performed by oligosaccharins?

(A) Regulating the daily functioning of a plant's cells
(B) Interacting with one another to produce different chemicals
(C) Releasing specific chemical messengers from a plant's cell walls
(D) Producing the hormones that cause plant cells to differentiate to perform different functions
(E) Influencing the development of a plant's cells by controlling the expression of the cells' genes

122. The passage suggests that, unlike the pleiotropic hormones, oligosaccharins could be used effectively to

(A) trace the passage of chemicals through the walls of cells
(B) pinpoint functions of other plant hormones
(C) artificially control specific aspects of the development of crops
(D) alter the complement of genes in the cells of plants
(E) alter the effects of the five major hormones on plant development

In the two decades between 1910 and 1930, more than ten percent of the black population of the United States left the South, where the preponderance of the black population had been located, and migrated to northern states, with the largest number moving, it is claimed, between 1916 and 1918. It has been frequently assumed, but not proved, that the majority of the migrants in what has come to be called the Great Migration came from rural areas and were motivated by two concurrent factors: the collapse of the cotton industry following the boll weevil infestation, which began in 1898, and increased demand in the North for labor following the cessation of European immigration caused by the outbreak of the First World War in 1914. This assumption has led to the conclusion that the migrants' subsequent lack of economic mobility in the North is tied to rural background, a background that implies unfamiliarity with urban living and a lack of industrial skills.

But the question of who actually left the South has never been rigorously investigated. Although numerous investigations document an exodus from rural southern areas to southern cities prior to the Great Migration, no one has considered whether the same migrants then moved on to northern cities. In 1910 more than 600,000 black workers, or ten percent of the black workforce, reported themselves to be engaged in "manufacturing and mechanical pursuits," the federal census category roughly encompassing the entire industrial sector. The Great Migration could easily have been made up entirely of this group and their families. It is perhaps surprising to argue that an employed population could be enticed to move, but an explanation lies in the labor conditions then prevalent in the South.

About thirty-five percent of the urban black population in the South was engaged in skilled trades. Some were from the old artisan class of slavery—blacksmiths, masons, carpenters—which had had a monopoly of certain trades, but they were gradually being pushed out by competition, mechanization, and obsolescence. The remaining 65 percent, more recently urbanized, worked in newly developed industries—tobacco, lumber, coal and iron manufacture, and railroads. Wages in the South, however, were low, and black workers were aware, through labor recruiters and the black press, that they could earn more even as unskilled workers in the North than they could as artisans in the South. After the boll weevil infestation, urban black workers faced competition from the continuing influx of both black and white rural workers, who were driven to undercut the wages formerly paid for industrial jobs. Thus, a move north would be seen as advantageous to a group that was already urbanized and steadily employed, and the easy conclusion tying their subsequent economic problems in the North to their rural background comes into question.

Questions 123–128 refer to the passage above.

123. The author indicates explicitly that which of the following records has been a source of information in her investigation?

(A) United States Immigration Service reports from 1914 to 1930
(B) Payrolls of southern manufacturing firms between 1910 and 1930
(C) The volume of cotton exports between 1898 and 1910
(D) The federal census of 1910
(E) Advertisements of labor recruiters appearing in southern newspapers after 1910

124. In the passage, the author anticipates which of the following as a possible objection to her argument?

(A) It is uncertain how many people actually migrated during the Great Migration.
(B) The eventual economic status of the Great Migration migrants has not been adequately traced.
(C) It is not likely that people with steady jobs would have reason to move to another area of the country.
(D) It is not true that the term "manufacturing and mechanical pursuits" actually encompasses the entire industrial sector.
(E) Of the African American workers living in southern cities, only those in a small number of trades were threatened by obsolescence.

125. According to the passage, which of the following is true of wages in southern cities in 1910?

(A) They were being pushed lower as a result of increased competition.
(B) They had begun to rise so that southern industry could attract rural workers.
(C) They had increased for skilled workers but decreased for unskilled workers.
(D) They had increased in large southern cities but decreased in small southern cities.
(E) They had increased in newly developed industries but decreased in the older trades.

126. The author cites each of the following as possible influences in an African American worker's decision to migrate north in the Great Migration EXCEPT

(A) wage levels in northern cities
(B) labor recruiters
(C) competition from rural workers
(D) voting rights in northern states
(E) the African American press

127. It can be inferred from the passage that the "easy conclusion" mentioned in line 58 is based on which of the following assumptions?

(A) People who migrate from rural areas to large cities usually do so for economic reasons.
(B) Most people who leave rural areas to take jobs in cities return to rural areas as soon as it is financially possible for them to do so.
(C) People with rural backgrounds are less likely to succeed economically in cities than are those with urban backgrounds.
(D) Most people who were once skilled workers are not willing to work as unskilled workers.
(E) People who migrate from their birthplaces to other regions of a country seldom undertake a second migration.

128. The primary purpose of the passage is to

(A) support an alternative to an accepted methodology
(B) present evidence that resolves a contradiction
(C) introduce a recently discovered source of information
(D) challenge a widely accepted explanation
(E) argue that a discarded theory deserves new attention

Historians sometimes forget that history is continually being made and experienced before it is studied, interpreted, and read. These latter activities have their own history, of course, which may impinge in unexpected ways on public events. It is difficult to predict when "new pasts" will overturn established historical interpretations and change the course of history.

In the fall of 1954, for example, C. Vann Woodward delivered a lecture series at the University of Virginia that challenged the prevailing dogma concerning the history, continuity, and uniformity of racial segregation in the South. He argued that the Jim Crow laws of the late nineteenth and early twentieth centuries not only codified traditional practice but also were a determined effort to erase the considerable progress made by black people during and after Reconstruction in the 1870's. This revisionist view of Jim Crow legislation grew in part from the research that Woodward had done for the NAACP legal campaign during its preparation for *Brown v. Board of Education*. The Supreme Court had issued its ruling in this epochal desegregation case a few months before Woodward's lectures.

The lectures were soon published as a book, *The Strange Career of Jim Crow*. Ten years later, in a preface to the second revised edition, Woodward confessed with ironic modesty that the first edition "had begun to suffer under some of the handicaps that might be expected in a history of the American Revolution published in 1776." That was a bit like hearing Thomas Paine apologize for the timing of his pamphlet *Common Sense*, which had a comparable impact. Although *Common Sense* also had a mass readership, Paine had intended to reach and inspire: he was not a historian, and thus not concerned with accuracy or the dangers of historical anachronism. Yet, like Paine, Woodward had an unerring sense of the revolutionary moment, and of how historical evidence could undermine the mythological tradition that was crushing the dreams of new social possibilities. Martin Luther King Jr. testified to the profound effect of *The Strange Career of Jim Crow* on the civil rights movement by praising the book and quoting it frequently.

Questions 129–134 refer to the passage above.

129. The "new pasts" mentioned in line 6 can best be described as the

(A) occurrence of events extremely similar to past events
(B) history of the activities of studying, interpreting, and reading new historical writing
(C) change in people's understanding of the past due to more recent historical writing
(D) overturning of established historical interpretations by politically motivated politicians
(E) difficulty of predicting when a given historical interpretation will be overturned

130. It can be inferred from the passage that the "prevailing dogma" (lines 11–12) held that

(A) Jim Crow laws were passed to give legal status to well-established discriminatory practices in the South
(B) Jim Crow laws were passed to establish order and uniformity in the discriminatory practices of different southern states
(C) Jim Crow laws were passed to erase the social gains that black people had achieved since Reconstruction
(D) the continuity of racial segregation in the South was disrupted by passage of Jim Crow laws
(E) the Jim Crow laws of the late nineteenth and early twentieth centuries were passed to reverse the effect of earlier Jim Crow laws

131. Which of the following is the best example of writing that is likely to be subject to the kinds of "handicaps" referred to in line 31?
    (A) A history of an auto manufacturing plant written by an employee during an auto buying boom
    (B) A critique of a statewide school-desegregation plan written by an elementary school teacher in that state
    (C) A newspaper article assessing the historical importance of a United States president written shortly after the president has taken office
    (D) A scientific paper describing the benefits of a certain surgical technique written by the surgeon who developed the technique
    (E) Diary entries narrating the events of a battle written by a soldier who participated in the battle

132. The passage suggests that C. Vann Woodward and Thomas Paine were similar in all of the following ways EXCEPT
    (A) both had works published in the midst of important historical events
    (B) both wrote works that enjoyed widespread popularity
    (C) both exhibited an understanding of the relevance of historical evidence to contemporary issues
    (D) the works of both had a significant effect on events following their publication
    (E) both were able to set aside worries about historical anachronism in order to reach and inspire

133. The attitude of the author of the passage toward the work of C. Vann Woodward is best described as one of
    (A) respectful regard
    (B) qualified approbation
    (C) implied skepticism
    (D) pointed criticism
    (E) fervent advocacy

134. Which of the following best describes the new idea expressed by C. Vann Woodward in his University of Virginia lectures in 1954?
    (A) Southern racial segregation was continuous and uniform.
    (B) Black people made considerable progress only after Reconstruction.
    (C) Jim Crow legislation was conventional in nature.
    (D) Jim Crow laws did not go as far in codifying traditional practice as they might have.
    (E) Jim Crow laws did much more than merely reinforce a tradition of segregation.

The function of capital markets is to facilitate an exchange of funds among all participants, and yet in practice we find that certain participants are not on a par with others. Members of society have varying degrees of market strength in terms of information they bring to a transaction, as well as of purchasing power and creditworthiness, as defined by lenders.

For example, within minority communities, capital markets do not properly fulfill their functions; they do not provide access to the aggregate flow of funds in the United States. The financial system does not generate the credit or investment vehicles needed for underwriting economic development in minority areas. The problem underlying this dysfunction is found in a rationing mechanism affecting both the available alternatives for investment and the amount of financial resources. This creates a distributive mechanism penalizing members of minority groups because of their socioeconomic differences from others. The existing system expresses definite socially based investment preferences that result from the previous allocation of income and that influence the allocation of resources for the present and future. The system tends to increase the inequality of income distribution. And, in the United States economy, a greater inequality of income distribution leads to a greater concentration of capital in certain types of investments.

Most traditional financial-market analysis studies ignore financial markets' deficiencies in allocation because of analysts' inherent preferences for the simple model of perfect competition. Conventional financial analysis pays limited attention to issues of market structure and dynamics, relative costs of information, and problems of income distribution. Market participants are viewed as acting as entirely independent and homogeneous individuals with perfect foresight about capital-market behavior. Also, it is assumed that each individual in the community at large has the same access to the market and the same opportunity to transact and to express the preference appropriate to his or her individual interest. Moreover, it is assumed that transaction costs for various types of financial instruments (stocks, bonds, etc.) are equally known and equally divided among all community members.

Questions 135–141 refer to the passage above.

135. The main point made by the passage is that

(A) financial markets provide for an optimum allocation of resources among all competing participants by balancing supply and demand
(B) the allocation of financial resources takes place among separate individual participants, each of whom has access to the market
(C) the existence of certain factors adversely affecting members of minority groups shows that financial markets do not function as conventional theory says they function
(D) investments in minority communities can be made by the use of various alternative financial instruments, such as stocks and bonds
(E) since transaction costs for stocks, bonds, and other financial instruments are not equally apportioned among all minority-group members, the financial market is subject to criticism

136. The passage states that traditional studies of the financial market overlook imbalances in the allocation of financial resources because

(A) an optimum allocation of resources is the final result of competition among participants
(B) those performing the studies choose an oversimplified description of the influences on competition
(C) such imbalances do not appear in the statistics usually compiled to measure the market's behavior
(D) the analysts who study the market are unwilling to accept criticism of their methods as biased
(E) socioeconomic differences form the basis of a rationing mechanism that puts minority groups at a disadvantage

137. The author's main point is argued by

(A) giving examples that support a conventional generalization
(B) showing that the view opposite to the author's is self-contradictory
(C) criticizing the presuppositions of a proposed plan
(D) showing that omissions in a theoretical description make it inapplicable in certain cases
(E) demonstrating that an alternative hypothesis more closely fits the data

138. A difference in which of the following would be an example of inequality in transaction costs as alluded to in lines 44–48?

(A) Maximum amounts of loans extended by a bank to businesses in different areas
(B) Fees charged to large and small investors for purchasing stocks
(C) Prices of similar goods offered in large and small stores in an area
(D) Stipends paid to different attorneys for preparing legal suits for damages
(E) Exchange rates in dollars for currencies of different countries

139. Which of the following can be inferred about minority communities on the basis of the passage?

(A) They provide a significant portion of the funds that become available for investment in the financial market.
(B) They are penalized by the tax system, which increases the inequality of the distribution of income between investors and wage earners.
(C) They do not receive the share of the amount of funds available for investment that would be expected according to traditional financial-market analysis.
(D) They are not granted governmental subsidies to assist in underwriting the cost of economic development.
(E) They provide the same access to alternative sources of credit to finance businesses as do majority communities.

140. According to the passage, a questionable assumption of the conventional theory about the operation of financial markets is that

(A) creditworthiness as determined by lenders is a factor determining market access
(B) market structure and market dynamics depend on income distribution
(C) a scarcity of alternative sources of funds would result from taking socioeconomic factors into consideration
(D) those who engage in financial-market transactions are perfectly well informed about the market
(E) inequalities in income distribution are increased by the functioning of the financial market

141. According to the passage, analysts have conventionally tended to view those who participate in financial markets as

(A) judging investment preferences in terms of the good of society as a whole
(B) influencing the allocation of funds through prior ownership of certain kinds of assets
(C) varying in market power with respect to one another
(D) basing judgments about future events mainly on chance
(E) having equal opportunities to engage in transactions

7.5 Reading Comprehension Answer Key

1. C
2. B
3. B
4. B
5. E
6. A
7. C
8. E
9. B
10. D
11. D
12. A
13. B
14. E
15. E
16. C
17. D
18. B
19. E
20. B
21. D
22. E
23. D
24. D
25. C
26. A
27. E
28. C
29. C
30. C
31. E
32. C
33. B
34. A
35. C
36. B
37. E
38. D
39. A
40. D
41. B
42. C
43. C
44. D
45. D
46. A
47. E
48. B
49. A
50. A
51. C
52. B
53. E
54. E
55. A
56. A
57. D
58. B
59. D
60. E
61. D
62. D
63. B
64. D
65. C
66. A
67. C
68. E
69. B
70. D
71. D
72. B
73. C
74. B
75. E
76. E
77. A
78. E
79. C
80. B
81. C
82. D
83. A
84. A
85. A
86. A
87. D
88. C
89. E
90. B
91. A
92. C
93. B
94. B
95. C
96. D
97. D
98. D
99. C
100. D
101. C
102. E
103. B
104. A
105. C
106. B
107. D
108. A
109. C
110. D
111. C
112. D
113. D
114. A
115. C
116. D
117. B
118. D
119. A
120. E
121. E
122. C
123. D
124. C
125. A
126. D
127. C
128. D
129. C
130. A
131. C
132. E
133. A
134. E
135. C
136. B
137. D
138. B
139. C
140. D
141. E

7.6 Reading Comprehension Answer Explanations

The following discussion of reading comprehension is intended to familiarize you with the most efficient and effective aproaches to the kinds of problems common to reading comprehension. The particular questions in this chapter are generally representative of the kinds of reading comprehension questions you will encounter on the GMAT®. Remember that it is the problem solving strategy that is important, not the specific details of a particular question.

Questions 1–7 refer to the passage on page 346.

1. Which of the following most accurately states the main idea of the passage?

(A) Naked mole rat colonies are the only known examples of cooperatively breeding vertebrate societies.
(B) Naked mole rat colonies exhibit social organization based on a rigid caste system.
(C) Behavior in naked mole rat colonies may well be a close vertebrate analogue to behavior in eusocial insect societies.
(D) The mating habits of naked mole rats differ from those of any other vertebrate species.
(E) The basis for the division of labor among naked mole rats is the same as that among eusocial insects.

Main idea

Main idea questions require a true statement about the major focus of the passage. From its opening sentence, this passage depends on a comparison between eusocial insect societies and naked mole rat colonies. Thus, the statement of the main idea must include both those species. The answer to a main idea question should never contain incorrect statements of fact.

A Insects and mole rats are not compared; incorrect statement contradicts lines 36–37.
B Species are not compared; incorrect statement contradicts lines 23–27.
C Correct. This statement of the main idea does include both species, and it is consistent with the facts presented in the passage.
D Mole rats are compared to other vertebrate species rather than to insect societies; incorrect statement contradicts lines 33–36.
E While mole rats are compared to insect societies, the comparison is done incorrectly, contradicting the third paragraph.

The correct answer is C.

2. The passage suggests that Jarvis's work has called into question which of the following explanatory variables for naked mole rat behavior?

(A) Size
(B) Age
(C) Reproductive status
(D) Rate of growth
(E) Previously exhibited behavior

Inference

The fact that an inference must be made is indicated by the word *suggests* in the question. What does the passage say about Jarvis's work? It is mentioned in just one sentence in the passage (lines 33–35); Jarvis posits that growth rate may affect how long any individual rat performs a task, *regardless of its age.* Thus, it can be inferred that the variable that Jarvis's work calls into question is age.

A Jarvis's work discusses rate of growth rather than size.
B Correct. Jarvis's work tends to discount age as a determining factor in rat behavior.
C Reproductive status is not mentioned in connection to Jarvis's work.
D Rate of growth is the factor that determines what tasks the rats do and for how long.
E Previously exhibited behavior is not discussed in the context of Jarvis's work.

The correct answer is B.

3. It can be inferred from the passage that the performance of tasks in naked mole rat colonies differs from task performance in eusocial insect societies in which of the following ways?

(A) In naked mole rat colonies, all tasks are performed cooperatively.
(B) In naked mole rat colonies, the performance of tasks is less rigidly determined by body shape.
(C) In naked mole rat colonies, breeding is limited to the largest animals.
(D) In eusocial insect societies, reproduction is limited to a single female.
(E) In eusocial insect societies, the distribution of tasks is based on body size.

Inference

An inference is drawn from stated information. To answer this question, compare what the passage says about task-performance roles in eusocial insect societies and in naked mole rat colonies. These roles are described in the third paragraph. The insects have *rigid caste systems*, and an individual's role is defined by *its behavior, body shape, and physiology* (lines 22–23). In contrast, roles in naked mole rat colonies are related to *reproductive status... body size, and perhaps age* (lines 25–27); body shape is not mentioned. Thus it is logical to infer that body shape is less critical for the definition of the role of the naked mole rat, if it does indeed have any bearing on its role.

A The passage does not indicate that all tasks are performed cooperatively.
B Correct. While body shape is one of the factors that determine roles in eusocial insect societies, the same is not true of naked mole rat colonies.
C Since no information is given about the breeders' size in insect societies, no comparison may be made.
D No difference is found because reproduction is limited to a single female in both insect and naked mole rat societies.
E *Behavior, body shape, and physiology* determine tasks in the insect societies, not body size.

The correct answer is B.

4. According to the passage, which of the following is a supposition rather than a fact concerning the queen in a naked mole rat colony?

(A) She is the largest member of the colony.
(B) She exerts chemical control over the colony.
(C) She mates with more than one male.
(D) She attains her status through aggression.
(E) She is the only breeding female.

Supporting ideas

This question's wording indicates that the answer involves information that is explicitly stated in the passage. The second paragraph describes the naked mole rat queen as the largest member of the colony, maintaining her breeding status *through a mixture of behavioral and, presumably, chemical control* (lines 15–16). The word *presumably* indicates that the queen's chemical control is a supposition rather than a fact.

A Lines 13–14 indicates her size as a fact.
B Correct. The queen's chemical control of the society is presumed rather than documented.
C Lines 26–27 state her mating habits as a fact.
D Lines 16–20 cite the *violent fighting* that leads to a new queen's takeover as a fact.
E Lines 10–13 state her unique reproductive status as a fact.

The correct answer is B.

5. The passage supports which of the following inferences about breeding among *Lycaon pictus*?

(A) The largest female in the social group does not maintain reproductive status by means of behavioral control.
(B) An individual's ability to breed is related primarily to its rate of growth.
(C) Breeding is the only task performed by the breeding female.
(D) Breeding in the social group is not cooperative.
(E) Breeding is not dominated by a single pair of dogs.

Inference

Since this question asks about an inference, the answer is not directly stated in the passage; it must instead be derived from the information given. Examine what the passage says about *Lycaon pictus* and then look at each of the suggested inferences. The wild dog is mentioned as an exception to the rule that *most cooperatively breeding vertebrates… are dominated by a pair of breeders rather than by a single breeding female* (lines 37–40). It is reasonable to infer that breeding among these wild dogs is not dominated by a pair of breeders.

A The naked mole rat queen does maintain her status through behavioral control; however, this has no bearing on the behavior of these wild dogs.

B Rate of growth is discussed in the context of task distribution in naked mole rat colonies; the passage indicates no connection to breeding among wild dogs.

C The passage offers no evidence that breeding is the female wild dog's only task.

D *Lycaon pictus* is included in the group of *cooperatively breeding vertebrates*.

E **Correct.** This wild dog is an exception to the rule that *most cooperatively breeding vertebrates … are dominated by a pair of breeders.*

The correct answer is E.

6. According to the passage, naked mole rat colonies may differ from all other known vertebrate groups in which of the following ways?

(A) Naked mole rats exhibit an extreme form of altruism.
(B) Naked mole rats are cooperative breeders.
(C) Among naked mole rats, many males are permitted to breed with a single dominant female.
(D) Among naked mole rats, different tasks are performed at different times in an individual's life.
(E) Among naked mole rats, fighting results in the selection of a breeding female.

Supporting ideas

The use of the phrase *according to the passage* indicates that the answer to this question is explicitly stated. Look at the introduction of the passage (lines 1–8), where the subject is first raised. Scientists were unaware of any vertebrate species that acted in the altruistic pattern typical of eusocial insect species, but recently they have determined that the naked mole rat may behave with the same *extreme form of altruism.*

A **Correct.** Unlike any other group of vertebrates, naked mole rats demonstrate altruistic behavior, sacrificing individual opportunities to survive and reproduce for the good of the group.

B Lines 36–37 assert that other vertebrates are cooperative breeders.

C Lines 26–27 say *a few males*, not many, breed with the queen; the passage does not say that naked mole rats are the only vertebrates that have a single breeding female.

D Tasks performed by other vertebrates are not discussed, so it is not possible to know whether naked mole rat behavior is unique.

E The passage does not indicate that this fighting is characteristic of mole rats alone.

The correct answer is A.

7. One function of the third paragraph of the passage is to

(A) state a conclusion about facts presented in an earlier paragraph
(B) introduce information that is contradicted by information in the fourth paragraph
(C) qualify the extent to which two previously mentioned groups might be similar
(D) show the chain of reasoning that led to the conclusions of a specific study
(E) demonstrate that, of three explanatory factors offered, two may be of equal significance

Logical structure

For this question, it is necessary to consider the third paragraph in the context of the whole passage, not in isolation from it. The first two paragraphs draw the similarities between eusocial insect societies and naked mole rat colonies. The third paragraph focuses on the differences between the two groups and describes the rat behavior in more detail.

A The third paragraph presents facts rather than conclusions.
B The fourth paragraph describes other vertebrates; it does not contradict the information provided in the third paragraph.
C **Correct.** After emphasizing their similarities previously in the passage, the author turns to examine the differences between the two groups in the third paragraph.
D The only specific study mentioned is Jarvis's work, which provides new information for the passage, not a conclusion.
E The third paragraph provides information about behavior, not explanations of varying significance.

The correct answer is C.

Questions 8–12 refer to the passage on page 348.

8. The primary purpose of the passage is to

(A) present several explanations for a well-known fact
(B) suggest alternative methods for resolving a debate
(C) argue in favor of a controversial theory
(D) question the methodology used in a study
(E) discuss the implications of a research finding

Main idea

This question depends on understanding the passage as a whole. The first paragraph reports the findings of a recent study. The second paragraph examines possible explanations for the findings, ruling out all but one of them.

A Several explanations are entertained, but only to be dismissed; the number of tooth fractures is not presented as a well-known fact.
B The passage does not mention alternative methods or a debate.
C The likely explanation for the tooth fractures is not shown to be controversial.
D The passage does not question the methodology of the study.
E **Correct.** The passage explores possible explanations for a recent research finding.

The correct answer is E.

9. According to the passage, compared with Pleistocene carnivores in other areas, Pleistocene carnivores in the La Brea area

(A) included the same species, in approximately the same proportions
(B) had a similar frequency of tooth fractures
(C) populated the La Brea area more densely
(D) consumed their prey more thoroughly
(E) found it harder to obtain sufficient prey

Supporting ideas

Skim the passage to find a comparison of La Brea area carnivores with those from other areas. In lines 15–17, the numbers of tooth fractures, or *breakage data*, of Pleistocene carnivores at the La Brea site are compared with those at other sites. The carnivores at the La Brea site had about the same frequency of tooth fractures as the carnivores at other sites.

A Particular species are not compared in the passage.
B **Correct.** Tooth-fracture evidence at the La Brea site and other sites is similar.
C Population density at different sites is not compared.
D Thorough consumption is the most likely explanation of tooth fractures, but there is no evidence of any difference between La Brea and other Pleistocene sites.
E Difficulty of finding prey is implicated in the final sentence, but the La Brea site is not distinguished from other Pleistocene sites.

The correct answer is B.

10. According to the passage, the researchers believe that the high frequency of tooth breakage in carnivores found at La Brea was caused primarily by

(A) the aging process in individual carnivores
(B) contact between the fossils in the pits
(C) poor preservation of the fossils after they were removed from the pits
(D) the impact of carnivores' teeth against the bones of their prey
(E) the impact of carnivores' teeth against the bones of other carnivores during fights over kills

Supporting ideas

As indicated by the phrase *according to the passage*, this question asks about information explicitly stated in the passage. After dismissing three possible causes of the tooth fractures, the author turns to the explanation researchers find *most plausible*: *more contact between the teeth of predators and the bones of prey due to more thorough consumption of carcasses* (lines 22–24).

A Lines 10–12 dismiss aging as the cause.
B Lines 12–15 rule out poor preservation within the pits.
C Preservation after removal from the pits is not discussed.
D **Correct.** Carnivores' tooth fractures were most likely caused by contact with the bones of their prey.
E Line 28 mentions *competition over kills*, but does not link it to tooth fractures.

The correct answer is D.

11. The researchers' conclusion concerning the absence of demographic bias would be most seriously undermined if it were found that

(A) the older an individual carnivore is, the more likely it is to have a large number of tooth fractures
(B) the average age at death of a present-day carnivore is greater than was the average age at death of a Pleistocene carnivore
(C) in Pleistocene carnivore species, older individuals consumed carcasses as thoroughly as did younger individuals
(D) the methods used to determine animals' ages in fossil samples tend to misidentify many older individuals as younger individuals
(E) data concerning the ages of fossil samples cannot provide reliable information about behavioral differences between extinct carnivores and present-day carnivores

Logical structure

Begin by looking at the section on demographic bias. Lines 11–13 state that demographic bias has been ruled out as an explanation because *older individuals were not overrepresented in the fossil samples*. This implies that older carnivores would be expected to have more tooth fractures than younger ones. To answer this question, read each answer choice to find the one statement that undermines the researchers' conclusion. If the method to determine age in the fossil samples is faulty and older carnivores are misidentified as younger ones, then demographic bias cannot be dismissed.

A This statement supports rather than undermines the researchers' conclusion.
B This comparison between present-day and Pleistocene carnivores has no bearing on whether older Pleistocene individuals were overrepresented or not.
C The comparison between older and younger individuals is irrelevant to the researchers' conclusion.
D **Correct.** If older individuals have been misidentified as younger ones, then a higher proportion of older individuals undermines the researchers' conclusion.
E Neither the differences nor the data are relevant to the researchers' conclusion about the proportion of older Pleistocene carnivores.

The correct answer is D.

12. According to the passage, if the researchers had NOT found that two extinct carnivore species were free of tooth breakage, the researchers would have concluded that

(A) the difference in breakage frequencies could have been the result of damage to the fossil remains in the La Brea pits
(B) the fossils in other Pleistocene sites could have higher breakage frequencies than do the fossils in the La Brea pits
(C) Pleistocene carnivore species probably behaved very similarly to one another with respect to consumption of carcasses
(D) all Pleistocene carnivore species differed behaviorally from present-day carnivore species
(E) predator densities during the Pleistocene era were extremely high

Logical structure

This question refers to the preservational bias explanation that the researchers reject (lines 12–15). Two extinct species had no tooth fractures. Thus, the breakage was almost certainly NOT caused by abrasion in the pits because the teeth of those two species would have showed fractures as well. If the researchers had not discovered the exception of the two species, then they could not have ruled out the possibility that the tooth breakage was caused by damage within the pits.

A **Correct.** If all species showed tooth fractures, then the breakage might have been caused by abrasion in the pits.
B The extinct species evidence was relevant to the issue of preservational bias, not local bias.
C Without the extinct species evidence, preservational bias is a strong explanation, and there is little need for the behavioral explanation.
D The passage does not say that all Pleistocene carnivore species were found in the La Brea pits; consequently no universal conclusion about all species can be made.
E The researchers cannot make a conclusion about the whole era based on one site.

The correct answer is A.

Questions 13–15 refer to the passage on page 350.

13. The primary purpose of the passage is to propose

(A) an alternative to museum display of artifacts
(B) a way to curb illegal digging while benefiting the archaeological profession
(C) a way to distinguish artifacts with scientific value from those that have no such value
(D) the governmental regulation of archaeological sites
(E) a new system for cataloging duplicate artifacts

Main Idea

After identifying in the first paragraph two problems that the field of archaeology faces, the author begins the second paragraph by explicitly stating the purpose of the essay: *I would propose that scientific archaeological expeditions and governmental authorities sell excavated artifacts on the open market.* According to the author, this proposal would benefit the field of archaeology (lines 14–16) at the same time that it would reduce illegal digging for antiquities (lines 16–21).

A While explaining in paragraph 5 that museums often store countless artifacts unseen in their basements, the author proposes no alternative for museum display of those artifacts.
B **Correct.** The author argues that selling some antiquities would help archaeology and reduce illegal digging.
C No proposal for the grading of the artifacts is made in the passage.
D The author does not discuss governmental regulation of the sites.
E While the author supports one part of the proposal for selling antiquities by noting that sold artifacts could be cataloged on a computer, this is a detail rather than the main purpose of the passage.

The correct answer is B.

14. The author implies that all of the following statements about duplicate artifacts are true EXCEPT

(A) A market for such artifacts already exists
(B) Such artifacts seldom have scientific value
(C) There is likely to be a continuing supply of such artifacts
(D) Museums are well supplied with examples of such artifacts
(E) Such artifacts frequently exceed in quality those already cataloged in museum collections

Inference

Duplicate artifacts are discussed throughout the passage. Because this question asks the reader to find the one statement that is NOT stated or implied in the passage, the best approach is to eliminate the four statements that are supported by the passage.

A In the closing sentence of the passage, the author implies the market already exists.
B In lines 25–36, the author denies the scientific value of every artifact.
C The author says museum basements are not big enough for artifacts *likely to be discovered in the future* (lines 41–43).
D The fifth paragraph shows that museum basements are *bulging* with artifacts.
E **Correct.** The passage does not support the assertion that the quality of duplicate objects is higher than that of museum pieces.

The correct answer is E.

15. Which of the following is mentioned in the passage as a disadvantage of storing artifacts in museum basements?

(A) Museum officials rarely allow scholars access to such artifacts.
(B) Space that could be better used for display is taken up for storage.
(C) Artifacts discovered in one excavation often become separated from each other.
(D) Such artifacts are often damaged by variations in temperature and humidity.
(E) Such artifacts often remain uncataloged and thus cannot be located once they are put in storage.

Supporting ideas

This question asks for specific information stated in the passage, so begin by finding the discussion of museum storage in the fifth paragraph. There, the author exposes the problems museums face: too little room and too little money. Not enough funding exists to catalog artifacts, so the artifacts *become as inaccessible as if they had never been discovered* (lines 45–46).

A Restrictions on scholars' access to the museums' artifacts are not mentioned in the passage.
B The author does not argue that museums should use space differently.
C No mention is made of the separation of objects from the same excavation.
D The author does not discuss the conditions of storage.
E **Correct.** The author contends that many artifacts are left uncataloged and so, once shelved in the basements, *they cannot be found again.*

The correct answer is E.

Questions 16–20 refer to the passage on page 352.

16. The primary purpose of the passage is to

(A) explain and critique the methods used by early statisticians
(B) compare and contrast a historical situation with a current-day one
(C) describe and explain a historical change
(D) discuss historical opposition to an established institution
(E) trace the origin of a contemporary controversy

Main idea

To determine the primary purpose, consider the passage as a whole. The first sentence explains that during the nineteenth century, occupational information about women in the U.S. census *became more detailed and precise in response to social changes* (lines 1–5). Following a chronological order, the rest of the passage shows how and why the information changed.

A The passage is more concerned with presenting information acquired from the census than with critiquing the methods used to obtain it.
B No comparison to a present-day census is made.
C **Correct.** The passage describes a change from 1840 to 1890 and gives reasons for this change.
D Lines 25–29 show that two groups pressed for greater accuracy, but that cannot be considered *historical opposition* since the groups did not oppose the census itself.
E No contemporary controversy is mentioned.

The correct answer is C.

17. Each of the following aspects of nineteenth-century United States censuses is mentioned in the passage EXCEPT the

(A) year in which data on occupations began to be analyzed by gender
(B) year in which specific information began to be collected on individuals in addition to the head of the household
(C) year in which overlap between women employed outside the home and women keeping house was first calculated
(D) way in which the 1890 census measured women's income levels and educational backgrounds
(E) way in which household members were counted in the 1840 census

Supporting ideas

Use the process of elimination to find the correct answer by checking the possible responses against the information *mentioned in the passage.* Skim the text to locate the necessary information; skimming for specific years is relatively easy because the years stand out visually from the rest of the text. The correct answer is the one piece of information NOT included in the passage.

A Lines 19–20 indicate that it was 1870.
B Lines 16–19 indicate that it was 1850.
C Lines 25–26 indicate that it was 1890.

D **Correct.** The passage does not discuss income levels or educational background.
E Lines 5–12 explain that the 1840 census used *simple enumeration* of all household members.

The correct answer is D.

18. It can be inferred from the passage that the 1840 United States census provided a count of which of the following?

(A) Women who worked exclusively in the home
(B) People engaged in nonfarming occupations
(C) People engaged in social movements
(D) Women engaged in family-run enterprises
(E) Men engaged in agriculture

Inference

Since this question asks for an inference, the answer is not directly stated in the passage; it must instead be derived from the information given. This question depends on a careful review of lines 5–15, which state that the 1840 census counted the head of the household as an individual, and that it counted everyone else in the household by categories, including occupational categories. Thus it is reasonable to infer that the 1840 census provided an overall count of people engaged in occupations, both farming and nonfarming.

A Lines 24–29 reveal that a count of women who worked exclusively at home was not made until 1890.
B Correct. The 1840 census categorized household members by occupation, so it would have provided a count of people working in nonfarming occupations.
C The 1840 census counted households by occupations, not by participation in social movements.
D Lines 19–20 show that occupational categories were not analyzed by gender until 1870.
E Occupations were analyzed by gender only in 1870 (lines 19–20).

The correct answer is B.

19. The author uses the adjective "simple" in line 6 most probably to emphasize that the

(A) collection of census information became progressively more difficult throughout the nineteenth century
(B) technology for tabulating census information was rudimentary during the first half of the nineteenth century
(C) home-based agricultural economy of the early nineteenth century was easier to analyze than the later industrial economy
(D) economic role of women was better defined in the early nineteenth century than in the late nineteenth century
(E) information collected by early nineteenth-century censuses was limited in its amount of detail

Logical structure

Understanding an author's word choice often means examining not just the use of the word itself but the broader context in which it is used. The first sentence says that census information became *more detailed and precise* during the nineteenth century. The next sentence starts with the earliest census described in the passage, which used a method of *simple enumeration*. The author uses *simple* to emphasize the contrast between the general, unspecified information on headcounts recorded in 1840 and the more *detailed and precise* information recorded later.

A The passage does not address the difficulty of collecting census information.
B The passage does not describe the technology for tabulating census information.
C The passage does not compare the ease of analyzing data.
D The use of *simple* does not call attention to the changes in women's status recorded in the census.
E Correct. The author's word choice emphasizes the lack of detail that characterized early nineteenth-century censuses.

The correct answer is E.

20. The passage suggests which of the following about the "women's advocates and women statisticians" mentioned in lines 28–29?

(A) They wanted to call attention to the lack of pay for women who worked in the home.
(B) They believed that previous census information was inadequate and did not reflect certain economic changes in the United States.
(C) They had begun to press for changes in census-taking methods as part of their participation in the antislavery movement.
(D) They thought that census statistics about women would be more accurate if more women were employed as census officials.
(E) They had conducted independent studies that disputed the official statistics provided by previous United States censuses.

Inference

The use of the word *suggests* in the question indicates that the answer involves an inference. Begin by looking at what the text says about the *women's advocates and women statisticians.* Lines 28–29 show that they wanted *more thorough and accurate accounting of women's occupations and wages*, which implies that they must have felt that previous censuses were inadequate in reporting this information. Lines 25–27 show that they were motivated to press for these additions in part because they believed that the economic changes occurring after *the rapid entry of women into the paid labor force* were not reflected in the census.

A Lines 25–29 cite the motives attributed to the two groups; lack of pay for women working at home is not included.

B Correct. They pressed for a more accurate, thorough census because they believed that previously collected information was inadequate and failed to reflect the economic changes wrought by women's rapid entry into the paid labor force.

C The passage does not identify the women's advocates and women statisticians in 1890 as participants in the antislavery movement, which is discussed in the context of the 1850 census.

D The passage does not show that they thought the greater accuracy they sought would be achieved with more women as census officials.

E No independent, statistical studies are mentioned in the passage.

The correct answer is B.

Questions 21–26 refer to the passage on page 354.

21. The passage is primarily concerned with which of the following?

(A) Evaluating two competing technologies
(B) Tracing the impact of a new technology by narrating a sequence of events
(C) Reinterpreting an event from contemporary business history
(D) Illustrating a business strategy by means of a case history
(E) Proposing an innovative approach to business planning

Main idea

To figure out the primary concern of the passage, consider the passage as a whole. The first paragraph draws a contrast between past and present conditions and puts forward a beneficial strategy for businesses, *developing integrated approaches for successful mass production and distribution.* The second and third paragraphs then use a specific case to illustrate the benefits of this strategy.

A The evaluation of VHS and Beta is used only as an example to illustrate the thesis stated in the first paragraph.

B To support the thesis stated in the first paragraph, the author traces the impact of a marketing approach on the business success of a new technology.

C *To reinterpret* an event implies that the author disagrees with an original interpretation, but no evidence indicates such a disagreement.

D Correct. The first paragraph announces the business strategy, and the two subsequent paragraphs illustrate it with a particular case.

E The author is observing, not proposing; no specific plan of action is proposed.

The correct answer is D.

22. According to the passage, today's successful firms, unlike successful firms in the past, may earn the greatest profits by

(A) investing in research to produce cheaper versions of existing technology
(B) being the first to market a competing technology
(C) adapting rapidly to a technological standard previously set by a competing firm
(D) establishing technological leadership in order to shape product definitions in advance of competing firms
(E) emphasizing the development of methods for the mass production and distribution of a new technology

Supporting ideas

The phrase *according to the passage* indicates that the answer is explicitly stated in the passage. The question requires finishing a statement about firms in general; this is a clue to look at the first paragraph, the only place where firms in general are discussed. A contrast is drawn between past (lines 1–4) and present (lines 5–7) conditions. The companies that earn the greatest profits may be those *that lead in developing integrated approaches for successful mass production and distribution.*

A Looking for ways to make cheaper versions is not discussed in the passage.
B Being first was successful in the past, but not now, the author argues.
C The passage does not examine the advantage of rapid adaptation.
D The author believes this method was successful in the past, but not in the present.
E **Correct.** Developing the ways to get a new technology to the greatest number of consumers, through mass production and distribution, may lead to the greatest profits.

The correct answer is E.

23. According to the passage, consumers began to develop a preference for VCRs in the VHS format because they believed which of the following?

(A) VCRs in the VHS format were technically better than competing format VCRs.
(B) VCRs in the VHS format were less expensive than competing format VCRs.
(C) VHS was the first standard format for VCRs.
(D) VHS prerecorded videotapes were more available than Beta format tapes.
(E) VCRs in the Beta format would soon cease to be produced.

Supporting ideas

The question's use of the phrase *according to the passage* means that the answer is stated explicitly in the passage. Consumers' perceptions about the two formats are discussed in lines 26–28; consumers believed *that prerecorded tapes were more available in VHS format*.

A The passage does not suggest that consumers believed in the technical superiority of the VHS format.
B No evidence in the passage indicates that consumers believed the VHS format was less expensive.
C The passage does not support the view that consumers thought that VHS was the first format.
D **Correct.** The passage says that consumers believed prerecorded tapes were more available in the VHS format than in Beta.
E No information in the passage shows that consumers believed the Beta format would stop being produced.

The correct answer is D.

24. The author implies that one way that VHS producers won control over the VCR market was by

(A) carefully restricting access to VCR technology
(B) giving up a slight early lead in VCR sales in order to improve long-term prospects
(C) retaining a strict monopoly on the production of prerecorded videotapes
(D) sharing control of the marketing of VHS format VCRs
(E) sacrificing technological superiority over Beta format VCRs in order to remain competitive in price

Inference

By using the verb *implies*, this question indicates that the answer is not explicitly stated in the passage. The second paragraph contrasts the two approaches to marketing: producers of the VHS format formed *strategic alliances with other producers and distributors to manufacture and market their VCR format*. The producers of Beta, on the other hand, did not form such alliances because they wanted *to maintain exclusive control over VCR distribution*. Taken together, these statements imply that the VHS producers shared control of marketing.

A Restricting access to VCR technology was the unsuccessful strategy of Beta producers.
B Lines 22–24 show that the VHS producers did not yield their *slight early lead in sales* but instead quickly turned it *into a dominant position*.
C Lines 24–26 show just the reverse situation: VHS producers developed *strategic alignments with producers of prerecorded tapes*.
D **Correct.** VHS producers shared control of marketing with other producers and distributors.
E The passage does not suggest that VHS producers sacrificed technological superiority to remain competitive in price.

The correct answer is D.

25. The alignment of producers of VHS format VCRs with producers of prerecorded videotapes is most similar to which of the following?

(A) The alignment of an automobile manufacturer with another automobile manufacturer to adopt a standard design for automobile engines

(B) The alignment of an automobile manufacturer with an automotive glass company whereby the manufacturer agrees to purchase automobile windshields only from that one glass company

(C) The alignment of an automobile manufacturer with a petroleum company to ensure the widespread availability of the fuel required by a new type of engine developed by the manufacturer

(D) The alignment of an automobile manufacturer with its dealers to adopt a plan to improve automobile design

(E) The alignment of an automobile dealer with an automobile rental chain to adopt a strategy for an advertising campaign to promote a new type of automobile

Application

This question tests the reader's understanding of the relationship between the VHS producers and the producers of prerecorded tapes by asking about an analogous relationship. The VHS machines and the tapes are mutually dependent products; a continual and widespread supply of tapes is necessary for a consumer's continuing use and enjoyment of the VHS equipment. In a similar way, a continual and widespread supply of fuel is necessary to a consumer's ongoing use and enjoyment of a car. The best parallel is an alignment of manufacturers to ensure the availability of mutually dependent products.

A The alignment between producers of competing, rather than mutually dependent, products is not analogous.

B This exclusive alignment would instead be analogous to one between a VHS manufacturer and a manufacturer of one of the parts of the VHS machine.

C **Correct.** Prerecorded tapes are clearly analogous to fuel: both are products necessary to the consumer's successful use of the machines that depend on them. The alignment of the auto manufacturer with a petroleum company to ensure the availability of a specific fuel is analogous to the alignment of the VHS producers and the producers of prerecorded tapes to ensure the availability of that entertainment medium.

D This alignment would be analogous to one between VHS manufacturers and distributors, not prerecorded tape producers.

E This alignment between an equipment dealer and an equipment-rental business regarding adoption of an advertising strategy is not analogous.

The correct answer is C.

26. Which of the following best describes the relation of the first paragraph to the passage as a whole?

(A) It makes a general observation to be exemplified.

(B) It outlines a process to be analyzed.

(C) It poses a question to be answered.

(D) It advances an argument to be disputed.

(E) It introduces conflicting arguments to be reconciled.

Logical Structure

To answer this question, look at the structure of the author's argument. The first paragraph takes a position about firms in general. The second and third paragraphs illustrate that position with a specific example.

A **Correct.** The first paragraph offers a general statement about all firms, and the subsequent paragraphs use an extended example to demonstrate that statement.

B The passage does not describe a process or invite further analysis.

C The author is making a declaration (lines 5–7) rather than posing a question.

D The first paragraph advances an argument; however, it is supported, not disputed, by the rest of the passage.

E The first paragraph contrasts past and present conditions, but does not show conflicting arguments.

The correct answer is A.

Questions 27–31 refer to the passage on page 356.

27. The primary purpose of the passage is to

(A) advocate more effective strategies for encouraging the development of high-technology enterprises in the United States
(B) contrast the incentives for economic development offered by local governments with those offered by the private sector
(C) acknowledge and counter adverse criticism of programs being used to stimulate local economic development
(D) define and explore promotional efforts used by local governments to attract new industry
(E) review and evaluate strategies and programs that have been used to stimulate economic development

Main idea

To find the primary purpose, analyze the passage in its entirety. The passage discusses three different strategies or programs that local governments use to stimulate economic development, so the statement of the primary purpose must embrace all three strategies rather than focus on just one. The first paragraph describes how local governments attracted manufacturing industries in the 1960's and 1970's, with the result that one town prospered at another's expense. The second paragraph turns to the growth of high-technology manufacturing firms in the 1980's, which required a specialized workforce. The final paragraph shows the advantages of promoting local entrepreneurship.

A High-technology development is only one of three kinds of economic development the passage discusses.
B The private sector is not mentioned in the passage.
C The passage acknowledges problems but does not counter criticism.
D The passage examines the efforts to attract new industry in the first two paragraphs, but not in the third.
E **Correct.** The passage describes and evaluates strategies and programs used by local governments to stimulate economic growth in their areas.

The correct answer is E.

28. The passage suggests which of the following about the majority of United States manufacturing industries before the high-technology development era of the 1980's?

(A) They lost many of their most innovative personnel to small entrepreneurial enterprises.
(B) They experienced a major decline in profits during the 1960's and 1970's.
(C) They could provide real economic benefits to the areas in which they were located.
(D) They employed workers who had no specialized skills.
(E) They actively interfered with local entrepreneurial ventures.

Inference

This question directs attention to the manufacturing industries discussed in the first paragraph and asks for an inference about these industries. Because of *the transfer of jobs and related revenues*, attracting a manufacturer to a town was a *triumph*; losing such an industry was a *tragedy* (lines 9–11). In order for this conclusion to be true, it is logical to infer that these industries must have had a significant economic impact on the towns in which they were located.

A No information in the passage supports such a loss of personnel.
B The passage does not describe the industries' loss of profits.
C **Correct.** Local governments tried to attract manufacturing industries because they were a significant boon to the local economy.
D The second paragraph mentions the *specially trained fraction of the manufacturing workforce* (lines 20–21) suitable for high-tech jobs, but that does not imply that workers in manufacturing industries were unskilled.
E The passage offers no evidence of this interference.

The correct answer is C.

29. The tone of the passage suggests that the author is most optimistic about the economic development potential of which of the following groups?

(A) Local governments
(B) High-technology promoters
(C) Local entrepreneurs
(D) Manufacturing industry managers
(E) Economic development strategists

Tone

To answer this question about the author's attitude, look at what the author says when evaluating the ways local governments try to stimulate economic growth. In the first two paragraphs, the author points out serious disadvantages in attracting manufacturing (lines 3–10) and high-technology industries (lines 17–20). The final paragraph, however, offers only advantages to promoting local entrepreneurship. The author does not mention any disadvantages here, which implies that the author is most optimistic about this third strategy, which *both provides jobs and fosters further entrepreneurship.*

A The local governments are part of the discussion of all three strategies, not just the one about which the author is most optimistic.
B In lines 17–20, the author points out the *shortcomings* of high-technology development.
C **Correct.** The author has only good things to say about local entrepreneurs.
D The author does not discuss managers of manufacturing industries.
E Other than local governments, the author does not mention economic development strategists.

The correct answer is C.

30. The passage does NOT state which of the following about local entrepreneurs?

(A) They are found nearly everywhere.
(B) They encourage further entrepreneurship.
(C) They attract out-of-town investors.
(D) They employ local workers.
(E) They are established in their communities.

Supporting ideas

Use the process of elimination to discover the only characteristic of local entrepreneurs that is NOT explicitly stated in the passage. To do this, check each answer choice against the description of local entrepreneurs found in lines 23–30 of the passage.

A Lines 26–28 do identify them as *a nearly ubiquitous resource*, meaning that they are found in most places.
B Lines 32–33 say they create an environment that *fosters further entrepreneurship.*
C **Correct.** Out-of-town investors are not mentioned in the passage.
D Lines 31–32 say that *industry and talent are kept at home* and that they create an environment that *provides jobs.*
E Lines 28–29 describe them as having *roots in their communities.*

The correct answer is C.

31. The author of the passage mentions which of the following as an advantage of high-technology development?

(A) It encourages the modernization of existing manufacturing facilities.
(B) It promotes healthy competition between rival industries.
(C) It encourages the growth of related industries.
(D) It takes full advantage of the existing workforce.
(E) It does not advantage one local workforce at the expense of another.

Supporting ideas

To answer this question, look for an advantage of high-technology development that is explicitly mentioned in the passage. In the second paragraph, the efforts of local governments to attract new high-technology firms are judged *preferable* to previous efforts to entice established manufacturing industries from another town to their own. Thus, the introduction of high technology made it possible for local governments to stop *victimizing other geographical areas by taking their jobs* (lines 17–18).

A The passage does not describe modernization of facilities.
B Competition between rival industries is not mentioned in the passage.
C The growth of related industries is not cited as an advantage.
D Lines 19–21 explain that high-tech manufacturing firms employ only a fraction of the workforce.
E **Correct.** Competing for a new industry means that local governments are not trying to attract to their towns an industry established in another town, thus harming that other town's local economy.

The correct answer is E.

Questions 32–36 refer to the passage on page 358.

32. The author of the passage is primarily concerned with

(A) discussing research data underlying several definitions
(B) arguing for the adoption of a particular definition
(C) exploring definitions of a concept
(D) comparing the advantages of several definitions
(E) clarifying some ambiguous definitions

Main idea

The author's primary concern is found by considering the passage as a whole. In the first paragraph, the author raises the central question regarding the meaning of *"services"* and then examines two definitions. The second paragraph analyzes the United States government's definition of *services* in more detail. The author is primarily interested in exploring different definitions of *services.*

A No research data are presented.
B The author points out the weakness of several definitions rather than giving reasons to adopt a particular one.
C **Correct.** The author considers several definitions of *services.*
D The author largely analyzes the disadvantages of the definitions.
E The author points out problems in the definitions rather than providing clarifications of the definitions themselves.

The correct answer is C.

33. In comparing the United States government's definition of services with the classical definition, the author suggests that the classical definition is

(A) more pragmatic
(B) more difficult to apply
(C) less ambiguous
(D) more widely used
(E) more arbitrary

Inference

This question asks the reader to find information that is suggested but not directly stated in the passage. The author discusses the classical definition at the end of the first paragraph, pointing out two examples in which it does not apply and concluding that this definition is *hard to sustain.* By comparison, the government's definition is *more practical* because it is easy to apply; everything that is not agriculture or industry is defined as a service. An examination of the analysis of both definitions reveals that, according to the author, the classical definition is harder to apply.

A The United States government's definition is *more practical* or pragmatic.
B **Correct.** Citing two cases in which the classical definition does not apply, the author implies that this definition is harder to apply than the government's.
C The author calls the classical definition *broader*, citing this definition of a service as *an intangible something*.
D The author does not say that the classical definition is more widely used.
E The author calls the government's definition arbitrary.

The correct answer is B.

34. The passage suggests which of the following about service workers in the United States?

(A) The number of service workers may be underestimated by the definition of services used by the government.
(B) There were fewer service workers than agricultural workers before 1988.
(C) The number of service workers was almost equal to the number of workers employed in manufacturing until 1988.
(D) Most service workers are employed in service occupations rather than in service industries.
(E) Most service workers are employed in occupations where they provide services that do not fall under the classical definition of services.

Inference

The question's use of the word *suggests* means that the answer depends on making an inference. According to the author, one of the failures of the government's definition of services is that *the many service workers employed by manufacturers–bookkeepers or janitors, for example–would fall under the industrial rather than the services category* (lines 22–26). This example shows that the number of service workers is likely to be underestimated.

A **Correct.** Because some service workers are included in the industrial category, it is possible that the total number of service workers may be underestimated.
B The passage does not provide the information to support this statement.
C The author says that services moved ahead of manufacturing as the *main product* in 1988 but does not discuss the number of workers in either area.
D The information in the passage does not support this statement.
E This conclusion cannot be reached on the basis of the information in the passage.

The correct answer is A.

35. The author of the passage mentions which of the following as one disadvantage of the United States government's definition of services?

(A) It is less useful than the other definitions mentioned in the passage.
(B) It is narrower in scope than the other definitions mentioned in the passage.
(C) It is based on the final product produced rather than on the type of work performed.
(D) It does not recognize the diversity of occupations within the service industries.
(E) It misclassifies many workers who are employed in service industries.

Supporting ideas

This question is based on specific information explicitly stated in the passage. According to the author, the government's definition fails because *it categorizes workers based on their company's final product rather than on the actual work the employees perform* (lines 20–22).

A The author calls this definition *practical for government purposes*, so for the government it is more useful than other definitions.
B The definition *includes everything that is not agriculture or industry*, while the classical definition does not include occupations that are clearly services; the government's definition is thus not narrower.
C **Correct.** Workers are categorized by the final product of their company rather than by the type of work they perform at that company.
D Diversity of occupations within the service industries is not discussed.
E The definition misclassifies service workers employed in manufacturing, not service industries.

The correct answer is C.

36. The author refers to "service workers employed by manufacturers" (lines 23–24) primarily in order to point out

(A) a type of worker not covered by the United States government's system of classifying occupations
(B) a flaw in the United States government's definition of services
(C) a factor that has influenced the growth of the service economy in the United States
(D) a type of worker who is classified on the basis of work performed rather than on the basis of the company's final product
(E) the diversity of the workers who are referred to as service workers

Logical structure

The author discusses *the many service workers employed by manufacturers* to illustrate the failure of the government's definition to distinguish between service industries and service occupations. The resulting ambiguities, in the author's view, reveal the *arbitrariness* of the definition and its inaccuracy in reflecting the composition of the economy.

A The worker is covered but misclassified.
B Correct. The author uses this example to point out a serious shortcoming in the government's definition.
C The author mentions the growth of services at the beginning of the passage but does not explore the reasons for it.
D The situation of service workers employed by manufacturers is just the reverse; they are categorized by the company's final product, not by the work they do.
E The author had earlier cited and illustrated the diversity of service activities that are included in the government's residual category of "services."

The correct answer is B.

Questions 37–42 refer to the passage on page 360.

37. The primary purpose of the passage is to

(A) argue against those scientists who maintain that animal populations tend to fluctuate
(B) compare and contrast the density-dependent and epideictic theories of population control
(C) provide examples of some of the ways in which animals exercise reproductive restraint to control their own numbers
(D) suggest that theories of population control that concentrate on the social behavior of animals are more open to debate than are theories that do not
(E) summarize a number of scientific theories that attempt to explain why animal populations do not exceed certain limits

Main idea

A review of the whole passage shows that the author is primarily concerned with presenting three different theories to explain the relative stability of animal populations. After explaining the question in the first paragraph, the author summarizes the density-independent theory in the second paragraph, the density-dependent theory in the third, and the Wynne-Edwards theory in the final paragraph.

A The passage accepts without challenge the premise that animal populations do tend to fluctuate to a *trivial* extent from year to year.
B The author discusses three theories, not two.
C Theories are summarized, but no supporting examples are cited in this passage.
D The author acknowledges the challenges to the theories, but does not indicate that one theory is more open to debate than another.
E Correct. The author examines three theories that account for the *relative constancy* of animal populations.

The correct answer is E.

38. It can be inferred from the passage that proponents of the density-dependent theory of population control have not yet been able to

(A) use their theory to explain the population growth of organisms with short life cycles
(B) reproduce the results of the study of Christian and Davis
(C) explain adequately why the numbers of a population can increase as the population's rate of growth decreases
(D) make sufficiently accurate predictions about the effects of crowding
(E) demonstrate how predator populations are themselves regulated

Inference

The author summarizes the density-dependent theory in the third paragraph, noting at the conclusion of the discussion, *one challenge for density-dependent theorists is to develop models that would allow the precise prediction of crowding.* It is logical to infer from this that these theorists' current predictive models do not offer an optimal, or even satisfactory, degree of precision.

A Organisms with short life cycles are discussed in the context of the density-independent theory.
B No mention is made of attempts to reproduce the study results.
C As the third paragraph illustrates, the theory explains why *the rate of growth of a population in a region decreases as the number of animals increases.*
D **Correct.** The theorists have not yet been able make accurate predictions about the effects of crowding.
E The theory does not specifically address the regulation of predator populations.

The correct answer is D.

39. Which of the following, if true, would best support the density-dependent theory of population control as it is described in the passage?

(A) As the number of foxes in Minnesota decreases, the growth rate of this population of foxes begins to increase.
(B) As the number of woodpeckers in Vermont decreases, the growth rate of this population of woodpeckers also begins to decrease.
(C) As the number of prairie dogs in Oklahoma increases, the growth rate of this population of prairie dogs also begins to increase.
(D) After the number of beavers in Tennessee decreases, the number of predators of these beavers begins to increase.
(E) After the number of eagles in Montana decreases, the food supply of this population of eagles also begins to decrease.

Application

The density-dependent theory argues that *the rate of growth of a population decreases as the number of animals increases.* Regulation of a high-density population is managed by a diminishing food supply, greater opportunities for predators, and physiological control mechanisms that may inhibit sexual activity and sexual maturation.

A **Correct.** The high-density theory holds that an increase in numbers results in a decrease in growth rate (lines 18–21); thus, the inverse shown in this example is equally true: a decrease in numbers results in an increased rate of population growth.
B According to this theory, it is an increase in numbers, rather than a decrease, that results in a decreased rate of population growth.
C The theory would argue that as the number increased, the growth rate would decrease, not increase.
D The theory argues that predators take advantage of high-density populations when a population increases, not decreases.
E A decreased food supply occurs when an increased population competes for it.

The correct answer is A.

40. According to the Wynne-Edwards theory as it is described in the passage, epideictic behavior displays serve the function of

(A) determining roosting aggregations
(B) locating food
(C) attracting predators
(D) regulating sexual activity
(E) triggering hormonal changes

Supporting ideas

This question is based on information specifically stated in the passage. According to the Wynne-Edwards theory, epideictic behavior displays *provide organisms with information on population size in a region so that they can… exercise reproductive restraint* (lines 45–47).

A Roosting aggregations are cited as an example of an epideictic behavior display.
B The function of the display is to *exercise reproductive restraint*, not locate food.
C The function of the display is to *exercise reproductive restraint*, not attract predators.
D Correct. Epideictic behavior displays are said to encourage animals to *exercise reproductive restraint*, thus regulating sexual activity.
E Hormonal changes are proposed by the density-dependent theory, not the Wynne-Edwards theory.

The correct answer is D.

41. The challenge posed to the Wynne-Edwards theory by several studies is regarded by the author with

(A) complete indifference
(B) qualified acceptance
(C) skeptical amusement
(D) perplexed astonishment
(E) agitated dismay

Tone

To determine the author's attitude, it is necessary to examine closely the words the author chooses to convey information. The author says that the theory *has been challenged, with some justification, by several studies*. The inclusion of the parenthetical expression *with some justification* implies that the author agrees with these studies that there are weaknesses in the Wynne-Edwards theory. However, the careful wording of *some* justification suggests that the author does not wholly agree with the challengers, only partially. Thus, the author's attitude can be construed as one of partial or qualified acceptance.

A The author is not indifferent to the challenges, finding instead some basis for them.
B Correct. The author accepts the challenges posed by the studies, finding *some justification* for them, but does not agree fully with those challenges.
C The author takes the challenges to the theory seriously, acknowledging there is *some justification* for them.
D The author betrays no surprise at the challenges to the theory, but rather accepts them.
E The author is not dismayed at the challenges that are offered *with some justification.*

The correct answer is B.

42. Which of the following statements would provide the most logical continuation of the final paragraph of the passage?

(A) Thus Wynne-Edwards's theory raises serious questions about the constancy of animal population in a region.
(B) Because Wynne-Edwards's theory is able to explain more kinds of animal behavior than is the density-dependent theory, epideictic explanations of population regulation are now widely accepted.
(C) The results of one study, for instance, have suggested that group vocalizing is more often used to defend territory than to provide information about population density.
(D) Some of these studies have, in fact, worked out a systematic and complex code of social behavior that can regulate population size.
(E) One study, for example, has demonstrated that birds are more likely to use winter-roosting aggregations than group vocalizing in order to provide information on population size.

Application

This question asks the reader to determine what would logically follow from the last sentence in the paragraph describing the Wynne-Edwards theory. The last sentence mentions studies that challenge the Wynne-Edwards theory, leading the reader to expect specific examples from one or more of those studies. Such examples might attack a weakness of the Wynne-Edwards theory or offer an alternate explanation.

A The Wynne-Edwards theory attempts to explain, not raise questions about, the constancy of animal populations.

B The author has not compared the two theories; rather than being widely accepted, Wynne-Edwards theory has been challenged by several studies.

C **Correct.** The last sentence discusses studies that challenge the theory. This statement follows logically by showing that one such study interprets the epideictic display of group vocalizing as having a different purpose than that proposed by the Wynne-Edwards theory.

D The studies mentioned in the last sentence challenge the Wynne-Edwards theory, leading the reader to expect an explanation of specific points of disagreement, but the studies in this statement instead agree with the theory.

E The studies mentioned in the last sentence challenge the Wynne-Edwards theory, so the reader anticipates an explanation of the specific points of the challenge, but this example supports the theory, simply showing that one population prefers one kind of epideictic display to another.

The correct answer is C.

Questions 43–47 refer to the passage on page 362.

43. The author of the passage is primarily concerned with doing which of the following?

(A) Recommending a methodology
(B) Describing a course of study
(C) Discussing a problem
(D) Evaluating a past course of action
(E) Responding to a criticism

Main idea

This question about the author's intent requires looking at the whole passage. The first paragraph introduces a problem unknown just a short time ago: an overabundance of materials. The second paragraph explains a complicating factor of this problem, the lack of reference works. A consideration of the passage as a whole shows that the author is most interested in discussing a problem.

A A methodology is a system of principles and practices, or methods; no such system is recommended in this passage.

B The author does not describe a particular course in Asian American studies, but rather points out a problem shared by all courses in the field.

C **Correct.** The author discusses the problem created by the existence of too many materials and the nonexistence of easily usable reference works.

D The author discusses a current situation, as the opening, *in recent years*, indicates.

E If the author were responding to a criticism, the passage would have to cite the source of the criticism and discuss the basis of it; no such source is cited here.

The correct answer is C.

44. The "dilemma" mentioned in line 3 can best be characterized as being caused by the necessity to make a choice when faced with a

(A) lack of acceptable alternatives
(B) lack of strict standards for evaluating alternatives
(C) preponderance of bad alternatives as compared to good
(D) multitude of different alternatives
(E) large number of alternatives that are nearly identical in content

Logical structure

This question asks the reader to consider the context in which the author uses the word *dilemma*. The first sentence establishes that this dilemma did not exist previously, *when hardly any texts … were available*. The next sentence introduces the contrast to *today*, when so many excellent choices exist that it is difficult to select from among them.

A As the second sentence makes clear, it is not a lack, but an abundance, of acceptable alternatives that creates the problem.

B The context in which *dilemma* is used, the first two sentences, discusses a relative wealth of materials, not a lack of standards.

C The author calls the anthologies *excellent* and does not describe any of the other materials in a negative light.

D Correct. Teachers face the dilemma of choosing from the wealth of materials listed in the second sentence.

E The second sentence identifies four different kinds of materials, all with varying content: anthologies, introductory texts, books on individual nationality groups, and books on general issues.

The correct answer is D.

45. The passage suggests that the factor mentioned in lines 15–18 complicates professors' attempts to construct introductory reading lists for courses in Asian American studies in which of the following ways?

(A) By making it difficult for professors to identify primary source material and to obtain standard information on Asian American history and culture

(B) By preventing professors from identifying excellent anthologies and introductory texts in the field that are both recent and understandable to students

(C) By preventing professors from adequately evaluating the quality of the numerous texts currently being published in the field

(D) By making it more necessary for professors to select readings for their courses that are not too challenging for students unfamiliar with Asian American history and culture

(E) By making it more likely that the readings professors assign to students in their courses will be drawn solely from primary sources

Inference

When a question asks what a passage *suggests* or *implies*, it is often necessary to look at more than one sentence or at sentences in different parts of the passage. The *complicating factor* cited at the beginning of the second paragraph is the lack of reference works. How this factor affects the way professors construct introductory reading lists is discussed in the final sentence of that paragraph. If students had good reference works to consult for *background information necessary to interpret difficult or unfamiliar material*, then their professors *might feel more free to include more challenging Asian American material in their introductory reading lists*. This sentence suggests that professors currently do not include challenging material on their reading lists because it is too difficult or unfamiliar for their students.

A Identifying primary source material is not a problem; the author notes that there are *mountains* of it.

B The lack of reference works does not prevent professors from identifying the recently published sources available in abundance to them; these sources are listed in the second sentence of the passage.

C The author does not link the lack of reference materials to an inadequate evaluation of texts.

D Correct. Because students cannot easily find basic information that would be available to them in reference works, professors are compelled to select readings that are not too challenging for students unfamiliar with Asian American history and culture.

E If reference works were available, students would not have to consult so many primary sources to find basic information; the passage does not indicate that the professors use solely primary materials.

The correct answer is D.

46. The passage implies that which of the following was true of introductory courses in Asian American studies a few decades ago?

(A) The range of different textbooks that could be assigned for such courses was extremely limited.
(B) The texts assigned as readings in such courses were often not very challenging for students.
(C) Students often complained about the texts assigned to them in such courses.
(D) Such courses were offered only at schools whose libraries were rich in primary sources.
(E) Such courses were the only means then available by which people in the United States could acquire knowledge of the field.

Inference

This question requires information that is implied rather than explicitly stated in the passage. The comparison of introductory courses in Asian American studies taught now with those taught a few decades ago is made in the first sentence, where the author notes that *in recent years*, teachers have faced a *dilemma nonexistent a few decades ago, when hardly any texts … were available.* From this sentence, it is reasonable to infer that a few decades ago, teachers of introductory courses in this field had few texts to choose from.

A **Correct.** Because *hardly any texts were available*, teachers of introductory courses had few choices when they assigned textbooks to students.
B Currently, professors are prevented from assigning challenging works because students do not have reference works to consult for background information, but there is no indication about the difficulty of readings a few decades ago.
C The passage provides no information about student response to the readings.
D The passage does not discuss the primary-source materials available in school libraries.
E The author does not claim that these introductory courses were the sole means of acquiring knowledge in this field.

The correct answer is A.

47. According to the passage, the existence of good one-volume reference works about Asian Americans could result in

(A) increased agreement among professors of Asian American studies regarding the quality of the sources available in their field
(B) an increase in the number of students signing up for introductory courses in Asian American studies
(C) increased accuracy in writings that concern Asian American history and culture
(D) the use of introductory texts about Asian American history and culture in courses outside the field of Asian American studies
(E) the inclusion of a wider range of Asian American material in introductory reading lists in Asian American studies

Supporting ideas

The phrase *according to the passage* indicates that this question concerns information that is explicitly stated in the passage. In the second paragraph, the author identifies two related advantages that would result if good one-volume reference works existed in this field: (1) students would be able to look up basic information easily, and (2) professors would be able to assign more challenging texts because of the students' resulting access to information required to understand those texts. Thus, introductory reading lists could include a wider range of materials than they do presently.

A The author neither indicates that reference works would promote a consensus of opinion on the quality of sources nor calls the quality of sources into question.
B The author does not link the availability of reference works to the popularity of courses.
C The author does not claim that the availability of reference works would increase accuracy in writing about the field.
D The passage mentions that nonexperts, professors who teach in related fields, might also benefit from using reference works, but there is no indication that the existence of a good one-volume work would result in the use of introductory texts in Asian American studies outside the field.

E **Correct.** The existence of a good, easy-to-use reference work would allow professors to include a greater range of materials, including those that are more challenging, in their introductory reading lists.

The correct answer is E.

Questions 48–50 refer to the passage on page 364.

48. The passage suggests that combing and carding differ from weaving in that combing and carding are

(A) low-skill jobs performed primarily by women employees
(B) low-skill jobs that were not performed in the home
(C) low-skill jobs performed by both male and female employees
(D) high-skill jobs performed outside the home
(E) high-skill jobs performed by both male and female employees

Inference

Since the question uses the word *suggests*, the answer is not directly stated in the passage but must be inferred. How was weaving different from carding and combing? Lines 16–17 discuss weaving, combing, and carding; all three activities are characterized as low-skill jobs. There was a concentration of women in low-skill occupations that *could be carried out in the home* (lines 19–20); weaving was one such occupation. Since the passage implies that relatively few women worked in carding and combing, these jobs presumably could *not* be carried out in the home. Thus the passage suggests that carding and combing were low-skill jobs, mostly done by men working outside the home.

A Lines 15–17 imply that women predominated in weaving but that carding and combing were done mainly by men.

B **Correct.** Carding and combing, unlike weaving, could not be done at home.

C The passage suggests that weaving, carding, and combing were all low-skill jobs done by both men and women, although the concentrations of the genders in these jobs were different; this statement does not explain how the passage suggests that *combing and carding differ from weaving.*

D Lines 16–17 characterize all three jobs as low-skill.

E Lines 16–17 characterize all three jobs as low-skill.

The correct answer is B.

49. Which of the following, if true, would most weaken the explanation provided by the human capital theory for women's concentration in certain occupations in seventeenth-century Florence?

(A) Women were unlikely to work outside the home even in occupations whose hours were flexible enough to allow women to accommodate domestic tasks as well as paid labor.
(B) Parents were less likely to teach occupational skills to their daughters than they were to their sons.
(C) Women's participation in the Florentine paid labor force grew steadily throughout the sixteenth and seventeenth centuries.
(D) The vast majority of female weavers in the Florentine wool industry had children.
(E) Few women worked as weavers in the Florentine silk industry, which was devoted to making cloths that required a high degree of skill to produce.

Logical structure

To answer this question, examine the logic of the explanation. How does the human capital theory explain women's concentration in certain occupations? The theory says that women's roles in childbearing made it difficult for them to acquire the skills needed in high-skill jobs. Moreover, their role in child rearing made them choose occupations that could be carried out at home. Evidence against either of these points will weaken the argument.

A **Correct.** If women of that time were generally unlikely to take any jobs outside the home, even those that allowed them to handle their domestic tasks, then these tasks are not the reason that women were in jobs that they could do within the home, as the human capital theory posits.

B Different levels of teaching by parents may help perpetuate job segregation, but this does not weaken the causal explanation provided by human capital theory.

C The growth of women's participation in the paid labor force does not affect the explanation of occupational concentrations provided by the human capital theory.

D The explanation suggests the women chose weaving because they had children to tend at home. The fact that the majority of weavers had children supports the explanation.

E Silk weaving was a high-skill job, exactly the kind of job that women would not have in the human capital explanation. This point supports the explanation.

The correct answer is A.

50. The author of the passage would be most likely to describe the explanation provided by the human capital theory for the high concentration of women in certain occupations in the seventeenth-century Florentine textile industry as

(A) well founded though incomplete
(B) difficult to articulate
(C) plausible but poorly substantiated
(D) seriously flawed
(E) contrary to recent research

Logical structure

This question requires an evaluation of the author's point of view. What does the author think of the human capital explanation of women's occupational concentration in the Florentine textile industry? In line 5, the author characterizes the theory as *useful*, a positive word reflecting a positive evaluation. However, the entire second paragraph is devoted to examining *differences in pay scales that cannot be explained by the human capital theory.* The author's positive view of the theory is qualified by the theory's inability to explain an important point.

A **Correct.** This statement reflects the author's generally positive evaluation, as well as concerns about insufficiencies.

B The author articulates the theory without difficulty and does not criticize it as difficult to articulate.

C To substantiate the theory means to provide evidence that verifies the theory; the author accepts the verification of gender segregation and so would not call the theory *poorly substantiated.*

D The author would not call a theory *useful* if it were seriously flawed.

E The author does not discuss the theory in relation to recent research.

The correct answer is A.

Questions 51–57 refer to the passage on page 366.

51. The primary purpose of the passage is to

(A) present the results of statistical analyses and propose further studies
(B) explain a recent development and predict its eventual consequences
(C) identify the reasons for a trend and recommend measures to address it
(D) outline several theories about a phenomenon and advocate one of them
(E) describe the potential consequences of implementing a new policy and argue in favor of that policy

Main idea

Understanding the author's purpose comes from a careful consideration of the whole passage. The author begins by noting one explanation for the rise in temporary employment, but dismisses it, finding another explanation more likely. The author closes the passage by making specific recommendations to counter the problems caused by temporary employment.

A The author uses statistical analyses as the basis of an explanation, but the analyses act only as support for the larger purpose of explaining a trend; no further studies are proposed.
B The author explores possible reasons for a recent development but recommends ways to curb or change that development; the author does not predict the consequences if the situation is left unchanged or the recommendations unmet.
C **Correct.** The author examines possible reasons for the rise in temporary employment and makes specific recommendations to change the current situation.
D The author discusses possible reasons for a trend, not theories about a phenomenon; no theory is advocated.
E The author makes recommendations but does not describe their consequences.

The correct answer is C.

52. According to the passage, which of the following is true of the "factors affecting employers" that are mentioned in lines 10–13?

(A) Most experts cite them as having initiated the growth in temporary employment that occurred during the 1980's.
(B) They may account for the increase in the total number of temporary workers during the 1980's.
(C) They were less important than demographic change in accounting for the increase of temporary employment during the 1980's.
(D) They included a sharp increase in the cost of labor during the 1980's.
(E) They are more difficult to account for than are other factors involved in the growth of temporary employment during the 1980's.

Supporting ideas

This question is based on information explicitly stated in the lines cited. The statistical analyses *suggest that factors affecting employers account for the rise in temporary employment.*

A *Some observers* attribute the rise to the composition of the workforce; the passage does not identify what most experts believe.
B **Correct.** The factors affecting employers may explain the rise in temporary employment.
C These factors were more important than demographic changes in explaining the rise.
D Such a sharp increase is unlikely because of *labor's reduced bargaining strength* and employers' greater *control over the terms of employment* at this time.
E The author readily explains the two factors as *product demand* and *labor's reduced bargaining strength.*

The correct answer is B.

53. The passage suggests which of the following about the use of temporary employment by firms during the 1980's?

(A) It enabled firms to deal with fluctuating product demand far more efficiently than they did before the 1980's.
(B) It increased as a result of increased participation in the workforce by certain demographic groups.
(C) It was discouraged by government-mandated policies.
(D) It was a response to preferences indicated by certain employees for more flexible working arrangements.
(E) It increased partly as a result of workers' reduced ability to control the terms of their employment.

Inference

This question asks the reader to find information that is suggested but not directly stated in the passage. The author believes that the rise in temporary employment during the 1980's can be explained by two factors affecting employers: *product demand* and *labor's reduced bargaining strength.* Temporary employment allows employers to adapt their workforce to the fluctuating demand for their product. At this time, *labor's reduced bargaining strength* left employers, not workers, in greater control of the terms of employment.

A The passage does not discuss how firms responded to fluctuating product demand before the 1980's, so this conclusion cannot be made.

B The author says that *demographic changes in the workforce did not correlate with variations in the total number of temporary workers,* ruling out this explanation.

C In 1992, the author recommended government-mandated policies because they did not exist.

D The author says that *growth in temporary employment now far exceeds the level explainable by ... groups said to prefer temporary jobs.*

E **Correct.** *Labor's reduced bargaining power* resulted in employers' increased control over the terms of employment as workers experienced correspondingly less control.

The correct answer is E.

54. The passage suggests which of the following about the workers who took temporary jobs during the 1980's?

(A) Their jobs frequently led to permanent positions within firms.

(B) They constituted a less demographically diverse group than has been suggested.

(C) They were occasionally involved in actions organized by labor unions.

(D) Their pay declined during the decade in comparison with the pay of permanent employees.

(E) They did not necessarily prefer temporary employment to permanent employment.

Inference

The question's use of the word *suggests* means that the answer depends on making an inference. The author says that the rise in temporary employment *now far exceeds the level explainable by recent workforce entry rates of groups said to prefer temporary jobs.* Thus, the number of workers employed on a temporary basis is far greater than the number of workers who actually do prefer temporary employment.

A No evidence is presented that temporary jobs led to permanent positions.

B The passage does not support this conclusion.

C The role of temporary workers in labor unions is not discussed.

D The passage does not compare the pay of temporary and permanent workers.

E **Correct.** The number of workers in temporary jobs was higher than the number of workers who stated they preferred temporary work to permanent work.

The correct answer is E.

55. The first sentence in the passage suggests that the observers mentioned in line 1 would be most likely to predict which of the following?

(A) That the number of new temporary positions would decline as fewer workers who preferred temporary employment entered the workforce

(B) That the total number of temporary positions would increase as fewer workers were able to find permanent positions

(C) That employers would have less control over the terms of workers' employment as workers increased their bargaining strength

(D) That more workers would be hired for temporary positions as product demand increased

(E) That the number of workers taking temporary positions would increase as more workers in any given demographic group entered the workforce

Application

These observers specifically attribute the growth of temporary employment to *increased participation in the workforce by certain groups … who supposedly prefer such arrangements.* On the basis of the passage's first sentence, any prediction these observers might make must be about the relation between the number of workers in temporary employment and the preference of these workers for temporary employment. No other issue is discussed. A rise in temporary employment could be explained only by a rise in the number of new workers who prefer temporary jobs, and a decline in temporary employment only by a decline in the number of new workers who prefer temporary work.

A **Correct.** By this rationale, the only reason for a decline in temporary employment would be a corresponding decline in the number of new workers who preferred temporary jobs.

B According to the observers, temporary employment would increase only if a greater number of employers who preferred temporary jobs entered the workforce.

C These observers are not said to consider control over the terms of employment.

D These observers are not said to consider the relationship between product demand and temporary employment.

E The number of workers taking temporary positions would rise only if they were composed of *certain groups, such as first-time or reentering workers*, who, the observers believe, prefer temporary work.

The correct answer is A.

56. In the context of the passage, the word "excessive" (line 23) most closely corresponds to which of the following phrases?

(A) Far more than can be justified by worker preferences

(B) Far more than can be explained by fluctuations in product demand

(C) Far more than can be beneficial to the success of the firms themselves

(D) Far more than can be accounted for by an expanding national economy

(E) Far more than can be attributed to increases in the total number of people in the workforce

Logical structure

A word that indicates judgment, such as *excessive*, must be understood in its context. The author recommends that firms be *discouraged from creating excessive numbers of temporary positions* on the basis of the statistical analyses, which show that the rise in temporary employment *now far exceeds the level explainable by recent workforce entry rates of groups said to prefer temporary jobs.* In this context, *excessive* means far more than is explainable by the number of workers known to prefer temporary work.

A **Correct.** In this context, *excessive* means far more than can be justified by workers' preferences.

B Employers are said to prefer temporary employment because it allows them to respond to fluctuations in product demand; this is unlikely to be characterized as *excessive*.

C The relation of temporary employment to the success of firms is not discussed.

D The relation of temporary employment to an expanding economy is not discussed.

E The author is not judging the number of temporary jobs on the basis of the total workforce, but on the basis of that part of the workforce preferring temporary work.

The correct answer is A.

57. The passage mentions each of the following as an appropriate kind of governmental action EXCEPT

(A) getting firms to offer temporary employment primarily to a certain group of people
(B) encouraging equitable pay for temporary and permanent employees
(C) facilitating the organization of temporary workers by labor unions
(D) establishing guidelines on the proportion of temporary workers that firms should employ
(E) ensuring that temporary workers obtain benefits from their employers

Supporting ideas

The author closes the passage with a list of specific recommendations. Check that list against the possible answers. By the process of elimination, choose the one recommendation the author does not make. The author recommends that government policymakers consider: (1) *mandating benefit coverage for temporary employees,* (2) *promoting pay equity between temporary and permanent workers,* (3) *assisting labor unions in organizing temporary workers,* and (4) *encouraging firms to assign temporary jobs primarily to employees who explicitly indicate that preference.*

A The author does recommend that firms assign temporary jobs to workers who prefer temporary work.
B The author does recommend that pay equity between temporary and permanent workers be encouraged.
C The author does recommend that labor unions be assisted in organizing temporary workers.
D **Correct.** The author does not recommend that such guidelines be established.
E The author does recommend that benefit coverage for temporary workers be mandated.

The correct answer is D.

Questions 58–63 refer to the passage on page 368.

58. The passage is chiefly concerned with

(A) arguing against the increased internationalization of United States corporations
(B) warning that the application of laws affecting trade frequently has unintended consequences
(C) demonstrating that foreign-based firms receive more subsidies from their governments than United States firms receive from the United States government
(D) advocating the use of trade restrictions for "dumped" products but not for other imports
(E) recommending a uniform method for handling claims of unfair trade practices

Main idea

To answer this question, consider the passage as a whole. In the first sentence, the author sets off *unfortunately* in commas, drawing attention to the author's attitude about companies that seek legal protection from imports. In the next paragraph, the author says, *this quest for import relief has hurt more companies than it has helped.* The third paragraph creates a hypothetical situation to show how import relief might hurt American companies, and the last paragraph shows the actual, unintended, and unfortunate consequences of import relief laws.

A Internationalization is accepted as a given (line 22); no argument is made against it.
B **Correct.** The author warns that American companies seeking relief from imports may suffer adverse consequences when the laws are applied to them.
C The author does not make this comparison.
D The author makes neither this distinction nor this recommendation.
E The author issues a warning rather than making a recommendation.

The correct answer is B.

59. It can be inferred from the passage that the minimal basis for a complaint to the International Trade Commission is which of the following?

(A) A foreign competitor has received a subsidy from a foreign government.
(B) A foreign competitor has substantially increased the volume of products shipped to the United States.
(C) A foreign competitor is selling products in the United States at less than fair market value.
(D) The company requesting import relief has been injured by the sale of imports in the United States.
(E) The company requesting import relief has been barred from exporting products to the country of its foreign competitor.

Inference

To make an inference about the minimal basis for a complaint, read what the passage says about complaints. The first paragraph describes two specific kinds of complaints the ITC has received: *damage from imports that benefit from subsidies by foreign governments*; and damage from imports *"dumped"* at *"less than fair value."* The author contends that companies would complain even without any specific basis. In the current climate promoting import relief, *the simple claim that an industry has been injured by imports is sufficient grounds to seek relief.* A *simple claim* provides *sufficient grounds,* which is the *minimal basis* for complaining to the ITC.

A This specific complaint is explicitly stated in lines 3–7, but it is not the minimal basis.
B This possibility is not discussed in the passage.
C This specific complaint is explicitly stated in lines 8–10, but it is not the minimal basis.
D **Correct.** Lines 10–13 show that merely claiming to be injured by imports is enough for a company *to seek relief* and complain to the ITC.
E This possibility is not discussed in the passage.

The correct answer is D.

60. The last paragraph performs which of the following functions in the passage?

(A) It summarizes the discussion thus far and suggests additional areas for research.
(B) It presents a recommendation based on the evidence presented earlier.
(C) It discusses an exceptional case in which the results expected by the author of the passage were not obtained.
(D) It introduces an additional area of concern not mentioned earlier.
(E) It cites a specific case that illustrates a problem presented more generally in the previous paragraph.

Logical structure

The first sentence of the last paragraph identifies its function when it introduces *the most brazen case*; this is a paragraph that will give an example. To discover what this *most brazen case* exemplifies, go back to the previous paragraph, where lines 22–25 provide a general statement about the danger of import laws being used against the companies the laws are supposed to protect. The last paragraph offers a specific example of the problem treated generally and hypothetically in the third paragraph.

A It gives an example; it does not summarize.
B It presents a specific case, not a recommendation.
C It does discuss an exceptional case, but the author is instead using the case because it illustrates the warning established from the beginning of the passage.
D The author has only one area of concern, exemplified in the last paragraph.
E **Correct.** The potential danger of import laws discussed hypothetically in the third paragraph is illustrated by an actual case in the final paragraph.

The correct answer is E.

61. The passage warns of which of the following dangers?

(A) Companies in the United States may receive no protection from imports unless they actively seek protection from import competition.
(B) Companies that seek legal protection from import competition may incur legal costs that far exceed any possible gain.
(C) Companies that are United States owned but operate internationally may not be eligible for protection from import competition under the laws of the countries in which their plants operate.
(D) Companies that are not United States owned may seek legal protection from import competition under United States import relief laws.
(E) Companies in the United States that import raw materials may have to pay duties on those materials.

Supporting ideas

The passage as a whole warns against the potential dangers of import laws. Specifically, it points in lines 22–25 to *the danger that foreign companies will use import relief laws against the very companies the laws were designed to protect.* This specific danger is discussed at length in the third and fourth paragraphs.

A The passage does not discuss this situation.
B The passage does not discuss this situation.
C The passage does not discuss this situation.
D **Correct.** Foreign companies with international operations may use the import relief laws to the detriment of American companies.
E The passage does not discuss this situation.

The correct answer is D.

62. The passage suggests that which of the following is most likely to be true of United States trade laws?

(A) They will eliminate the practice of "dumping" products in the United States.
(B) They will enable manufacturers in the United States to compete more profitably outside the United States.
(C) They will affect United States trade with Canada more negatively than trade with other nations.
(D) Those that help one unit within a parent company will not necessarily help other units in the company.
(E) Those that are applied to international companies will accomplish their intended result.

Inference

An inference is drawn from stated information. The second paragraph explains that global operations increase the complexity of a corporation's relationships, and this *intricate web* of relationships *makes it unlikely that a system of import relief laws will meet the strategic needs of all the units under the same parent company.* This statement leads the reader to infer that the trade laws may help one unit within a parent company, but not necessarily others.

A The passage does not suggest that "dumping" will be eliminated.
B The passage does not discuss this alternative.
C The passage offers no evidence to support this inference.
D **Correct.** The laws cannot meet the needs of all units of a complex parent company.
E Lines 22–24 contend the reverse: internationalization increases the likelihood that invoking import laws will have unintended consequences.

The correct answer is D.

63. It can be inferred from the passage that the author believes which of the following about the complaint mentioned in the last paragraph?

(A) The ITC acted unfairly toward the complainant in its investigation.
(B) The complaint violated the intent of import relief laws.
(C) The response of the ITC to the complaint provided suitable relief from unfair trade practices to the complainant.
(D) The ITC did not have access to appropriate information concerning the case.
(E) Each of the companies involved in the complaint acted in its own best interest.

Inference

An inference requires going beyond the material explicitly stated in the passage to the author's ideas that underlie that material. Reread the last paragraph to see what the author says about that specific complaint. In that case, a foreign competitor with American operations was seeking relief in these laws: *The bizarre aspect of the complaint was that a foreign conglomerate … was crying for help against a United States company.* Import relief laws are supposed to be protecting American companies from foreign competitors instead. The reader can infer that the intent of these laws, that is, the protection of American companies, is violated in this example.

A The passage gives no information about how the ITC acted.
B Correct. The laws are supposed to protect American companies, but the complaint reveals that a foreign company may in fact invoke them against an American company.
C The passage does not reveal the ITC's response to the complaint.
D The passage does not discuss the ITC's access to information.
E The inference is about the complaint itself, not the motivation of the companies.

The correct answer is B.

Questions 64–69 refer to the passage on page 370.

64. According to the passage, which of the following is a characteristic that distinguishes electroreceptors from tactile receptors?

(A) The manner in which electroreceptors respond to electrical stimuli
(B) The tendency of electroreceptors to be found in clusters
(C) The unusual locations in which electroreceptors are found in most species
(D) The amount of electrical stimulation required to excite electroreceptors
(E) The amount of nervous activity transmitted to the brain by electroreceptors when they are excited

Supporting ideas

This question asks for information explicitly stated in the passage, as implied by the phrase *according to the passage.* The first paragraph introduces the recent discovery of electroreceptors, which respond to *extremely weak electrical fields* (line 6), in contrast to tactile receptors, which respond only to *electrical field strengths about 1,000 times greater than those known to excite electroreceptors* (lines 11–13).

A The author contrasts the strength of the electrical fields to which the two kinds of receptors respond, rather than the manner in which the receptors respond.
B No information is given about whether the tactile receptors are clustered; no contrast is shown.
C The passage concerns only one species, anteaters.
D Correct. Electroreceptors and tactile receptors are contrasted on the basis of the electrical stimulation required to excite a response.
E The passage does not discuss the difference in the nervous activity transmitted to the brain, but rather the difference in the strength of electrical fields.

The correct answer is D.

65. Which of the following can be inferred about the experiment described in the first paragraph?

(A) Researchers had difficulty verifying the existence of electroreceptors in the anteater because electroreceptors respond to such a narrow range of electrical field strengths.
(B) Researchers found that the level of nervous activity in the anteater's brain increased dramatically as the strength of the electrical stimulus was increased.
(C) Researchers found that some areas of the anteater's snout were not sensitive to a weak electrical stimulus.
(D) Researchers found that the anteater's tactile receptors were more easily excited by a strong electrical stimulus than were the electroreceptors.
(E) Researchers tested small areas of the anteater's snout in order to ensure that only electroreceptors were responding to the stimulus.

Inference

Since this question asks for an inference, the answer is not directly stated in the passage; it must instead be derived from the information given. The question calls attention to lines 1–6, where the experiment is described. The researchers exposed *small areas of the snout* to electrical stimuli and discovered the electroreceptors *clustered at the tip* of the snout. It is reasonable to infer that some portions of the snout exposed to electrical stimuli—those outside the clusters of electroreceptors—did not respond.

A By showing how sensitive the electroreceptors are, the passage suggests that the range is not narrow.
B The passage does not report a rise in brain activity corresponding to increased electrical stimulation.
C **Correct.** In order to find that electroreceptors were clustered, researchers must have tested areas of the snout outside those clusters.
D The passage discusses the amount of electrical stimulation required to excite the two kinds of receptors rather than the degree of intensity in the response.
E Researchers did not know that electroreceptors existed before the experiment, so they could not have conducted the experiment in this way.

The correct answer is C.

66. The author of the passage most probably discusses the function of tactile receptors (lines 8–13) in order to

(A) eliminate an alternative explanation of anteaters' response to electrical stimuli
(B) highlight a type of sensory organ that has a function identical to that of electroreceptors
(C) point out a serious complication in the research on electroreceptors in anteaters
(D) suggest that tactile receptors assist electroreceptors in the detection of electrical signals
(E) introduce a factor that was not addressed in the research on electroreceptors in anteaters

Logical structure

This question asks for the reason why the author has chosen to include the information about tactile receptors in lines 8–13. Examine the logical structure of the author's discussion. The word *while* typically introduces a contrast or an exception. Tactile receptors are being ruled out as a possible source of the nervous activity in the anteaters' brains during the experiment. If these other sensory organs, which also respond to electrical stimuli, were not ruled out, then the researchers' conclusion about the existence of electroreceptors would not be valid.

A **Correct.** In order to make the case for electroreceptors, the author needs to explain that the less sensitive tactile receptors do not respond to weak electrical fields.
B The passage does not say that the two receptors have identical functions.
C The passage does not suggest that the existence of tactile receptors represents a serious complication for the research on electroreceptors.
D The passage does not indicate that tactile receptors assist electroreceptors.
E The passage does not indicate whether tactile receptors were addressed in the research; the author, however, adds this information to explain that they can be eliminated from consideration in the research rather than to criticize or to point out an omission.

The correct answer is A.

67. Which of the following can be inferred about anteaters from the behavioral experiment mentioned in the second paragraph?

(A) They are unable to distinguish between stimuli detected by their electroreceptors and stimuli detected by their tactile receptors.
(B) They are unable to distinguish between the electrical signals emanating from termite mounds and those emanating from ant nests.
(C) They can be trained to recognize consistently the presence of a particular stimulus.
(D) They react more readily to strong than to weak stimuli.
(E) They are more efficient at detecting stimuli in a controlled environment than in a natural environment.

Inference

An inference is drawn from stated information. This question calls attention to one specific sentence (lines 16–20) where the behavioral experiment is described. Researches *successfully trained* an anteater to tell the difference between a trough of water with a weak electrical field and a trough of water with no electrical field. Thus it is reasonable to infer that anteaters can be trained to recognize an electrical stimulus.

A The experiment was not devised to test the tactile receptors.
B The experiment was conducted only with troughs of water.
C **Correct.** The experiment shows that anteaters can be trained to recognize a particular electrical stimulus.
D The experiment compared only troughs of water.
E The experiment did not compare different environments.

The correct answer is C.

68. The passage suggests that the researchers mentioned in the second paragraph who observed anteaters break into a nest of ants would most likely agree with which of the following statements?

(A) The event they observed provides conclusive evidence that anteaters use their electroreceptors to locate unseen prey.
(B) The event they observed was atypical and may not reflect the usual hunting practices of anteaters.
(C) It is likely that the anteaters located the ants' nesting chambers without the assistance of electroreceptors.
(D) Anteaters possess a very simple sensory system for use in locating prey.
(E) The speed with which the anteaters located their prey is greater than what might be expected on the basis of chance alone.

Application

This question refers to the research activities described in the last two sentences of the passage (lines 26–32). The reader is asked to understand the implications of the information and then to apply them. Observing how quickly anteaters were able to locate unseen prey, the researchers concluded that the anteaters were probably using their electroreceptors to find the ants' nesting chambers. This conclusion implies that the researchers attributed the swiftness of the anteaters' detection of the chambers to something more than simple coincidence.

A The researchers' conclusion is more tentative than this statement, for the ability to locate the unseen ants only *suggests* to them that the anteaters are using electroreceptors.
B The researchers made a tentative conclusion about the use of electroreceptors on the basis of this event, showing they did not believe it to be atypical.
C The last sentence explicitly says that the researchers believe the anteaters were using electroreceptors to discover the ants.
D The passage describes the anteaters' sensory system as *sophisticated*, not simple.
E **Correct.** The rapidity with which anteaters locate unseen prey suggests to the researchers that it is likely the anteaters are relying on their electroreceptors rather than mere chance.

The correct answer is E.

69. Which of the following, if true, would most strengthen the hypothesis mentioned in lines 21–23?

(A) Researchers are able to train anteaters to break into an underground chamber that is emitting a strong electrical signal.
(B) Researchers are able to detect a weak electrical signal emanating from the nesting chamber of an ant colony.
(C) Anteaters are observed taking increasingly longer amounts of time to locate the nesting chambers of ants.
(D) Anteaters are observed using various angles to break into nests of ants.
(E) Anteaters are observed using the same angle used with nests of ants to break into the nests of other types of prey.

Logical structure

As stated in the passage, the researchers believe that anteaters *use electroreceptors to detect electrical signals given off by prey*. This hypothesis would be strengthened if the researchers discovered weak electrical signals, that is, the type of electrical signals to which the anteaters' electroreceptors are known to respond, coming from the sites of insect colonies where the anteaters typically seek their prey.

A To test the use of electroreceptors, a weak electrical field is required; otherwise, the anteaters could be using tactile receptors.
B Correct. The hypothesis is strengthened in this case; a weak electrical signal coming from an ants' nesting chamber and stimulating the anteaters' electroreceptors could be a possible explanation of how the anteaters are drawn to that place.
C If the anteaters were taking longer to find the ants, then the hypothesis would be weakened, not strengthened.
D This observation would neither strengthen nor weaken the hypothesis.
E The angle, even when consistent, is not relevant to the hypothesis about electroreceptors.

The correct answer is B.

Questions 70–75 refer to the passage on page 372.

70. In the passage, the author is primarily interested in

(A) suggesting an alternative to an outdated research method
(B) introducing a new research method that calls an accepted theory into question
(C) emphasizing the instability of data gathered from the application of a new scientific method
(D) presenting a theory and describing a new method to test that theory
(E) initiating a debate about a widely accepted theory

Main idea

This question concerns the main point of the passage. A careful examination of the overall structure of the passage will reveal the main point. In the first paragraph, the author briefly presents Milankovitch's theory and explains why it could not be tested early on. In the second and third paragraphs, the author describes how new methods allow testing of the theory and shows how evidence from the testing supports the theory. While the final paragraph acknowledges that other factors should be considered, the author's primary interest in this passage is in presenting Milankovitch's theory and the recently discovered means of testing it.

A A new research method is described, but no previous method is discussed.
B The new method allows for testing and confirming a theory, rather than casting doubt on it.
C While the last paragraph notes that other factors could have influenced climate, the data from the new method are not challenged, and these factors are not the author's primary interest in this passage.
D Correct. The author presents Milankovitch's theory and describes the oxygen isotope method of testing it.
E The author discusses how a new method of testing supports the theory and, while conceding other factors may be important, does not debate the theory.

The correct answer is D.

71. The author of the passage would be most likely to agree with which of the following statements about the Milankovitch theory?

(A) It is the only possible explanation for the ice ages.
(B) It is too limited to provide a plausible explanation for the ice ages, despite recent research findings.
(C) It cannot be tested and confirmed until further research on volcanic activity is done.
(D) It is one plausible explanation, though not the only one, for the ice ages.
(E) It is not a plausible explanation for the ice ages, although it has opened up promising possibilities for future research.

Application

The author's reaction to the statements about the Milankovitch theory must be based on how the author treats the theory in the passage. The first, second, and third paragraphs describe the theory and the use of a new research method to test the theory. The data from these tests *have established a strong connection between variations in the Earth's orbit and the periodicity of the ice ages*, suggesting that the theory is plausible. In the final paragraph, the author points to other factors that might be involved, suggesting that other theories might also be plausible.

A In the last paragraph, the author suggests that other explanations are possible.
B The third paragraph provides evidence in favor of the theory, suggesting that it is not too limited.
C The author shows how the theory has been tested; volcanic activity is not part of this theory.
D Correct. The author's presentation of the theory and the tests of the theory show that the author finds the theory plausible; the mention of other factors shows the author thinks other theories are also possible.
E The recent work testing the theory shows that it is plausible.

The correct answer is D.

72. It can be inferred from the passage that the isotope record taken from ocean sediments would be less useful to researchers if which of the following were true?

(A) It indicated that lighter isotopes of oxygen predominated at certain times.
(B) It had far more gaps in its sequence than the record taken from rocks on land.
(C) It indicated that climate shifts did not occur every 100,000 years.
(D) It indicated that the ratios of oxygen 16 and oxygen 18 in ocean water were not consistent with those found in fresh water.
(E) It stretched back for only a million years.

Inference

To make an inference about the isotope record from ocean sediments, examine what the passage says about that record. The third paragraph discusses that record and lists its two advantages. First, it is a global record with *remarkably little variation* in samples from varied locations. Second, it is *more continuous* than the record from rocks. If either of these advantages were not true, then it is logical to infer that the record would be less useful.

A According to lines 11–15, the lighter isotope does predominate; this is part of the record and does not affect its usefulness.
B Correct. In lines 37–39, the author states that an advantage of the ocean record is that it is *a more continuous record than that taken from rocks on land*. If this were not true, the ocean record would be less useful.
C If the record were to show that the shifts did not occur every 100,000 years, Milankovitch's theory would be weakened. This impact on the theory does not make the isotope record less useful to researchers. The record is useful precisely because it can offer evidence to confirm or refute such theories.
D This inconsistency would not affect the usefulness of the ocean-water record. Researchers would simply need to accommodate the fresh-water inconsistency.
E The record would still be useful. Lines 42–46 attest to the establishment of a pattern based on data from *the past several hundred thousand years*.

The correct answer is B.

73. According to the passage, which of the following is true of the ratios of oxygen isotopes in ocean sediments?

(A) They indicate that sediments found during an ice age contain more calcium carbonate than sediments formed at other times.
(B) They are less reliable than the evidence from rocks on land in determining the volume of land ice.
(C) They can be used to deduce the relative volume of land ice that was present when the sediment was laid down.
(D) They are more unpredictable during an ice age than in other climatic conditions.
(E) They can be used to determine atmospheric conditions at various times in the past.

Supporting ideas

The phrase *according to the passage* indicates that the answer to the question is stated in the passage. Lines 12–14 state that the relative volume of land ice can be deduced from the ratio of oxygen 18 to oxygen 16 in ocean sediments.

A There is no evidence in the passage about this point.
B The ocean record is described in lines 33–34 as *more continuous*, so it is unlikely to be less reliable. In any case, reliability is not discussed.
C Correct. Lines 13–15 explain that *land-ice volume for a given period can be deduced from the ratio of two oxygen isotopes.*
D There is no evidence in the passage to support this statement.
E The passage does not discuss the use of this record in determining past atmospheric conditions.

The correct answer is C.

74. It can be inferred from the passage that precipitation formed from evaporated ocean water has

(A) the same isotopic ratio as ocean water
(B) less oxygen 18 than does ocean water
(C) less oxygen 18 than has the ice contained in continental ice sheets
(D) a different isotopic composition than has precipitation formed from water on land
(E) more oxygen 16 than has precipitation formed from fresh water

Inference

Any inference about precipitation from evaporated ocean water needs to be based on what the passage says. Lines 20–23 show that *heavier isotopes tend to be left behind when water evaporates from the ocean surfaces.* Therefore, the evaporated water would contain less oxygen 18 and the remaining ocean water would contain more. It is logical to infer that precipitation formed from this evaporated water would also contain less oxygen 18.

A Lines 20–24 explain that the water remaining in the ocean after evaporation has more oxygen 18.
B Correct. Since *the heavier isotopes tend to be left behind*, there will be less oxygen 18 in the evaporated water and in the precipitation that forms from it.
C The passage suggests that the ocean water evaporates and through subsequent precipitation helps form the ice sheets, so the amount of oxygen 18 in the ice sheets should be similar to the amount in the precipitation formed from the evaporated water.
D The passage does not discuss precipitation formed from water on land.
E The passage does not discuss precipitation formed from fresh water.

The correct answer is B.

75. It can be inferred from the passage that calcium carbonate shells

(A) are not as susceptible to deterioration as rocks
(B) are less common in sediments formed during an ice age
(C) are found only in areas that were once covered by land ice
(D) contain radioactive material that can be used to determine a sediment's isotopic composition
(E) reflect the isotopic composition of the water at the time the shells were formed

Inference

Any inference about calcium carbonate shells needs to be based on what the passage says about these shells. Lines 27–29 explain the role of these shells in forming sediments and establishing a chronology for ice ages. The shells *were constructed with oxygen atoms drawn from the surrounding ocean.* Lines 29–32 make it clear that if the sediments reveal a higher ratio of oxygen 18, it is because more oxygen 18 had been left behind when the ocean water evaporated and contributed to the growth of continental ice sheets. It can thus be inferred that the shells that make up those sediments must reflect the proportion of oxygen 18 found in the ocean water at the time they were formed.

A The passage does not make this comparison.
B The passage does not make any reference to the relative abundance of these shells during ice ages; no such inference can be drawn.
C No evidence in the passage supports this inference.
D The passage does not indicate that the shells contained radioactive material.
E **Correct.** The passage explains that oxygen atoms in the surrounding water are one of the building blocks of calcium carbonate shells. The isotopic composition of the surrounding water changes during the ice age cycles, so it is logical that the isotopic composition of the shells will change depending on when they were formed.

The correct answer is E.

Questions 76–84 refer to the passage on page 374.

76. Which of the following titles best summarizes the contents of the passage?

(A) Neurotransmitters: Their Crucial Function in Cellular Communication
(B) Diet and Survival: An Old Relationship Reexamined
(C) The Blood Supply and the Brain: A Reciprocal Dependence
(D) Amino Acids and Neurotransmitters: The Connection between Serotonin Levels and Tyrosine
(E) The Effects of Food Intake on the Production and Release of Serotonin: Some Recent Findings

Main idea

Finding a title that best summarizes a passage requires examining the passage as a whole. This task is made easier by the fact that the second sentence of the first paragraph provides a topic sentence stating the main idea: *In recent studies, however, we have discovered that the production and release in brain neurons of the neurotransmitter serotonin … depend directly on the food that the body processes.* In the second paragraph, the authors cite the results of several studies relating neurotransmitter levels to eating meals and to injections of insulin. In the final paragraph, the authors discuss a study of the effect of a protein-rich meal on serotonin level. Thus, the correct title must show the relationship between food eaten and serotonin produced.

A The function of neurotransmitters is only briefly mentioned.
B The passage does not discuss the relation between diet and survival.
C There is no discussion of blood supply and the brain.
D While tyrosine is briefly mentioned, this was not a main focus of the studies.
E **Correct.** This title offers a summary of the article's contents.

The correct answer is E.

77. According to the passage, the speed with which tryptophan is provided to the brain cells of a rat varies with the

(A) amount of protein present in a meal
(B) concentration of serotonin in the brain before a meal
(C) concentration of leucine in the blood rather than on the concentration of tyrosine in the blood after a meal
(D) concentration of tryptophan in the brain before a meal
(E) number of serotonin-containing neurons

Supporting ideas

The phrase *according to the passage* indicates that the answer is stated in the passage. Look at the third paragraph, which discusses variations in the speed with which tryptophan is provided to the brain. Lines 41–44 state *the more protein is in a meal … the more slowly is tryptophan provided to the brain.*

A **Correct.** The greater the amount of protein, the more slowly tryptophan is provided.
B The relationship is not discussed in the passage, although the concentration of serotonin *after* a meal is measured.
C While leucine and tyrosine are mentioned, their concentrations in the blood are not compared.
D This relationship is not discussed in the passage, although the concentration of tryptophan *after* a meal is measured.
E The researchers do not consider the number of neurons.

The correct answer is A.

78. According to the passage, when the authors began their first studies, they were aware that

(A) they would eventually need to design experiments that involved feeding rats high concentrations of protein
(B) tryptophan levels in the blood were difficult to monitor with accuracy
(C) serotonin levels increased after rats were fed meals rich in tryptophan
(D) there were many neurotransmitters whose production was dependent on metabolic processes elsewhere in the body
(E) serotonin levels increased after rats were injected with a large amount of tryptophan

Supporting ideas

The phrase *according to the passage* indicates that the answer is explicitly stated in the passage. Look at the first sentence of the second paragraph where the focus of the authors' *first studies* is explained. The investigators wanted to see if an increase in serotonin levels would be observed after rats ate meals that changed tryptophan levels in the blood. Earlier research had already established that injecting tryptophan increased serotonin levels.

A The authors' decision to add protein came later in their studies, after they had seen the effects of eating in general.
B The passage does not identify any problems with monitoring tryptophan levels in the blood.
C This was the hypothesis of the first experiment, so the authors could not have known it beforehand.
D This point is irrelevant to the authors' work; only one neurotransmitter, serotonin, is discussed.
E **Correct.** Lines 9–11 show that this increase had already been observed.

The correct answer is E.

79. According to the passage, one reason that the authors gave rats carbohydrates was to

(A) depress the rats' tryptophan levels
(B) prevent the rats from contracting diseases
(C) cause the rats to produce insulin
(D) demonstrate that insulin is the most important substance secreted by the body
(E) compare the effect of carbohydrates with the effect of proteins

Supporting ideas

Since the question says, *according to the passage,* the answer must be explicitly stated in the passage. Look at lines 25–26 which say, *We gave the rats a carbohydrate-containing meal that we knew would elicit insulin secretion.* This sentence shows that the authors gave carbohydrates to the rats to cause the rats to secrete insulin.

A Lines 27–29 show that the carbohydrates increased the blood tryptophan level.
B Preventing disease was not part of the study.
C Correct. The authors had already tried injecting insulin; they then gave the rats carbohydrates to stimulate insulin production.
D The authors make no such claim about insulin.
E The study involving protein came later, so this could not have been the reason for giving the rats carbohydrates.

The correct answer is C.

80. According to the passage, the more protein a rat consumes, the lower will be the

(A) ratio of the rat's blood-tryptophan concentration to the amount of serotonin produced and released in the rat's brain
(B) ratio of the rat's blood-tryptophan concentration to the concentration in its blood of the other amino acids contained in the protein
(C) ratio of the rat's blood-tyrosine concentration to its blood-leucine concentration
(D) number of neurotransmitters of any kind that the rat will produce and release
(E) number of amino acids the rat's blood will contain

Supporting ideas

The phrase *according to the passage* indicates that the answer is stated in the passage. In lines 41–43; the authors state, *The more protein is in a meal, the lower is the ratio of the resulting blood-tryptophan concentration to the concentration of competing amino acids.*

A While lower levels of blood-tryptophan lead to lower serotonin levels, the relationship is not discussed in terms of a ratio.
B Correct. Lines 41–44 show this to be the correct answer choice.
C This relationship is not demonstrated in the passage.
D This point is not made in the passage.
E Lines 38–40 explain that *consumption of protein increases blood concentration of the other amino acids much more* ... Since proteins are made up of amino acids, eating protein would logically increase the number of amino acids.

The correct answer is B.

81. The authors' discussion of the "mechanism that provides blood tryptophan to the brain cells" (lines 34–35) is meant to

(A) stimulate further research studies
(B) summarize an area of scientific investigation
(C) help explain why a particular research finding was obtained
(D) provide supporting evidence for a controversial scientific theory
(E) refute the conclusions of a previously mentioned research study

Logical structure

To find the purpose of this discussion, look at the context in which this reference occurs. At the beginning of the third paragraph, the authors note that, *surprisingly*, adding protein led to lower brain tryptophan and serotonin levels. The question is why were the levels lowered? *The answer lies* in the mechanism cited in lines 34–35. Therefore, the discussion of the mechanism is meant to explain a surprising research finding.

A No further studies are mentioned.
B There are summaries of several studies, but there is no summary of an entire area of scientific investigation.
C **Correct.** The mechanism helps explain the surprising finding about lower brain tryptophan and serotonin levels.
D No theory is advanced, nor is any evidence about it provided.
E There is no attempt to refute any other study.

The correct answer is C.

82. According to the passage, an injection of insulin was most similar in its effect on rats to an injection of

(A) tyrosine
(B) leucine
(C) blood
(D) tryptophan
(E) protein

Supporting ideas

Since the question refers to information given in the passage, the answer can be found by careful reading. In order to find an injection with a similar effect, look first at the effect of injecting insulin. In lines 20–23, the authors state that *injecting insulin caused elevations in blood and brain tryptophan levels and in serotonin levels*. The only other reference to injection occurs earlier in lines 10–13 where rats injected with tryptophan had increased serotonin levels; injecting tryptophan would obviously cause tryptophan levels to increase. Thus the effects of injecting insulin were similar to the effects on injecting tryptophan.

A No evidence suggests that a tyrosine injection would have similar effects.
B The studies did not involve injecting leucine.
C The studies did not involve injecting blood.
D **Correct.** According to the passage, injecting tryptophan raises serotonin and tryptophan levels just as injecting insulin does.
E The studies involved eating protein, not injecting it; eating protein did not raise serotonin levels.

The correct answer is D.

83. It can be inferred from the passage that which of the following would be LEAST likely to be a potential source of aid to a patient who was not adequately producing and releasing serotonin?

(A) Meals consisting almost exclusively of protein
(B) Meals consisting almost exclusively of carbohydrates
(C) Meals that would elicit insulin secretion
(D) Meals that had very low concentrations of tyrosine
(E) Meals that had very low concentrations of leucine

Inference

Since this question asks for an inference, the answer is not directly stated in the passage; it must instead be derived from the information given. What kind of meals would NOT help a patient with low serotonin levels? Meals that increased serotonin would help the patient; meals that lowered serotonin would not. According to the last sentence in the passage, *the more protein in a meal, the less serotonin subsequently produced and released.* Therefore, high-protein meals would be LEAST likely to help the patient.

A **Correct.** Meals with very high levels of protein would tend to lower serotonin and thus to be less beneficial for the patient with inadequate serotonin levels.
B When rats ate a carbohydrate-containing meal, serotonin increased (lines 25–29). Therefore, these meals would tend to raise serotonin levels and so help the patient.

C In the study, meals that elicited insulin secretion raised serotonin levels.
D Since tyrosine is an amino acid found in protein, meals low in tyrosine would be low in protein and so would tend to raise serotonin levels and help the patient.
E Since leucine is an amino acid found in protein, meals low in leucine would be low in protein and so would tend to raise serotonin levels and help the patient.

The correct answer is A.

84. It can be inferred from the passage that the authors initially held which of the following hypotheses about what would happen when they fed large amounts of protein to rats?

(A) The rats' brain serotonin levels would not decrease.
(B) The rats' brain tryptophan levels would decrease.
(C) The rats' tyrosine levels would increase less quickly than would their leucine levels.
(D) The rats would produce more insulin.
(E) The rats would produce neurotransmitters other than serotonin.

Inference

When the authors discuss the results of adding protein to meals, they begin with the word *surprisingly* (line 30). The use of this word indicates that the results differed from the authors' initial hypotheses. The results showed lowered serotonin. It is reasonable to conclude that the researchers initially hypothesized that serotonin levels would not decrease.

A **Correct.** The use of the word *surprisingly* in line 30 suggests that researchers thought serotonin levels would not decrease.
B The researchers had expected that tryptophan levels would not decrease, *since protein contains tryptophan* (lines 32–33).
C Since there is no discussion of the comparative levels of tyrosine and leucine, there was probably no hypothesis about these levels.
D Since the researchers gave a high-carbohydrate meal to increase insulin production, they would not be likely to hypothesize that a high-protein meal would increase insulin production.
E Serotonin is the only neurotransmitter discussed in the research, so it is unlikely that the researchers had an initial hypothesis involving other neurotransmitters.

The correct answer is A.

Questions 85–90 refer to the passage on page 376.

85. The primary purpose of the passage is to

(A) evaluate a research study
(B) summarize the history of a research area
(C) report new research findings
(D) reinterpret old research findings
(E) reconcile conflicting research findings

Main Idea

Determining the primary purpose comes from examining what the author does in the entire passage. In the first paragraph, the author explains Duverger's work on women's electoral participation. In the second paragraph the author points out both the successes and failures of that work. The purpose of this passage, then, is to evaluate Duverger's study.

A **Correct.** The author evaluates Duverger's study of women's electoral activities.
B This passage examines only one research study, not an entire research area.
C Duverger's work was published in 1955; its findings are not new.
D The author explains and evaluates Duverger's findings but does not reinterpret them.
E The author's discussion of Duverger's work does not reveal or attempt to reconcile conflicting findings.

The correct answer is A.

86. According to the passage, Duverger's study was unique in 1955 in that it

(A) included both election data and survey data
(B) gathered data from sources never before used in political studies
(C) included an analysis of historical processes
(D) examined the influence on voting behavior of the relationships between women and men
(E) analyzed not only voting and political candidacy but also other political activities

Supporting ideas

This question is based on information specifically stated in the first sentence of the passage. The author introduces Duverger's work by calling it the first study of *women's electoral participation ever to use election data and survey data together* (lines 3–5).

A **Correct.** Duverger's work was unique because it used election data and survey data together.
B The author does not claim that the data came from sources previously ignored.
C The second paragraph states that Duverger placed his findings in the context of historical processes, but not that he was unique in doing so (lines 15–18).
D Duverger compared the frequency and direction of voting between men and women, not the effect that their relationships had on voting (lines 9–12).
E Duverger's work analyzed political activism, but the author does not claim that it was unique in doing so (lines 5–6).

The correct answer is A.

87. Which of the following characteristics of a country is most clearly an example of a factor that Duverger, as described in the passage, failed to consider in his study?

(A) A large population
(B) A predominantly Protestant population
(C) A predominantly urban population
(D) A one-party government
(E) Location in the heart of Europe

Inference

In the second paragraph, the author notes Duverger's *failure to consider … the influence of political regimes, the effects of economic factors, and the ramifications of political and social relations between women and men* (lines 22–27). This question requires checking this list from the passage against the possible answers; the only point of convergence is the system of government. A *political regime* may be defined as a system of government in which there is only one political party.

A The author does not say that Duverger failed to consider the size of the population.
B No evidence shows that Duverger failed to consider the predominance of a religion.
C The author does not say that Duverger failed to consider the location of the population.
D **Correct.** According to the author of the passage, Duverger failed to consider *the influence of political regimes.*
E Duverger is not faulted for failing to consider the location of the countries that he studied.

The correct answer is D.

88. The author implies that Duverger's actual findings are

(A) limited because they focus on only four countries
(B) inaccurate in their description of the four countries in the early 1950's
(C) out-of-date in that they are inapplicable in the four countries today
(D) flawed because they are based on unsound data
(E) biased by Duverger's political beliefs

Inference

Since the question uses the word *implies*, the answer involves making an inference based on the information in the text. The second paragraph evaluates Duverger's work. The author notes that Duverger *placed his findings in the context … of historical processes.* Because these contexts have changed since 1955, the author believes *Duverger's approach has proved more durable than his actual findings.* The actual findings, then, are out-of-date and irrelevant to the countries today.

A The author does not fault Duverger for studying only four countries.
B The findings are not said to be inaccurate.
C **Correct.** The actual findings, unlike the research method, are out-of-date and inapplicable today.
D The author does not claim that Duverger's data were unsound.
E The author does not criticize Duverger's findings as politically biased.

The correct answer is C.

89. The passage implies that, in comparing four European countries, Duverger found that the voting rates of women and men were most different in the country in which women

(A) were most politically active
(B) ran for office most often
(C) held the most conservative political views
(D) had the most egalitarian relations with men
(E) had possessed the right to vote for the shortest time

Inference

The comparison of voting rates is discussed at the end of the first paragraph and forms the basis for the required inference. Duverger found that *women voted somewhat less frequently than men* but that this difference narrowed *the longer the women had the vote* (lines 10–11). If the rates were most similar where women had been voting the longest, then the rates would be most dissimilar where women had been voting for the shortest time.

A Women's political activism is not suggested as a reason for the difference.
B Women's political candidacy is not suggested as a reason for the difference.
C Women's political views are not suggested as a reason for the difference.
D Women's egalitarian relations with men are not suggested as a reason for the difference.
E **Correct.** Duverger found that the frequency of voting was related to the length of time women had possessed the right to vote. The voting rates between men and women were most different in those countries where women had possessed the right to vote for the shortest time.

The correct answer is E.

90. The author implies that some behavioralist research involving the multinational study of women's political participation that followed Duverger's study did which of the following?

(A) Ignored Duverger's approach
(B) Suffered from faults similar to those in Duverger's study
(C) Focused on political activism
(D) Focused on the influences of political regimes
(E) Focused on the political and social relations between women and men

Inference

The final sentence of the passage links Duverger's study to behavioralist work in general. After noting Duverger's failure to consider several important elements, the author observes, *Duverger's study foreshadowed the enduring limitations of the behavioralist approach to the multinational study of women's political participation* (lines 28–31). Thus, it is reasonable to infer that the author is of the opinion that the behavioralist research that followed Duverger's study suffered from the same limitations.

A The author does not imply that other behavioralists ignored Duverger's approach.
B **Correct.** The author says that Duverger's work revealed the *enduring limitations* also found in later behavioralist research.
C The author does not claim that other behavioralists focused on political activism.
D Later behavioralist work is not said to focus on the influence of political regimes.
E The behavioralists who followed Duverger are not said to have focused on the relations between men and women.

The correct answer is B.

Questions 91–96 refer to the passage on page 378.

91. It can be inferred from the passage that accidental-death damage awards in America during the nineteenth century tended to be based principally on the

(A) earnings of the person at time of death
(B) wealth of the party causing the death
(C) degree of culpability of the party causing the death
(D) amount of money that had been spent on the person killed
(E) amount of suffering endured by the family of the person killed

Inference

An inference is drawn from stated information. The passage begins with one example of an 1896 accidental-death damage award. In the example, no liability for damages was found for a child's death because *the child had made no real economic contribution to the family*. The next paragraph shows that this example is typical of nineteenth-century social values. The logical inference from the information given is that accidental-death damage awards in the nineteenth century tended to be based primarily on a person's earnings at the time of death.

A **Correct.** The example in the first paragraph, establishing the child's *economic contribution to the family* as the basis of finding liability for damages, can be taken to suggest this basis was typical of the times.
B The passage does not discuss the party causing the death, so no inference can be drawn.
C The passage does not discuss degree of culpability.
D The passage offers no support for this alternative.
E The passage does not refer to the family's suffering.

The correct answer is A.

92. It can be inferred from the passage that in the early 1800's children were generally regarded by their families as individuals who

(A) needed enormous amounts of security and affection
(B) required constant supervision while working
(C) were important to the economic well-being of a family
(D) were unsuited to spending long hours in school
(E) were financial burdens assumed for the good of society

Inference

Again, an inference is drawn from stated information. The second paragraph discusses the gradual evolution of a concept across time and suggests that, at the beginning of the nineteenth century, society valued *the "useful" child who contributed to the family economy*. By mid-century, however, among some parts of the population, the modern notion of the *"useless" child* who is *emotionally priceless* began to replace the earlier view. By the late nineteenth and early twentieth centuries, the new view was widespread. Since this question concerns the early 1800's, it is reasonable to infer that children at that time were still generally viewed as useful contributors to the family economy.

A This is closer to the modern view, rather than the view held in the early 1800's.
B The passage does not discuss supervision of children while working.
C **Correct.** Prior to the shift in perspective, that is, in the early 1800's, the *"useful" child* contributed to the family economy.
D The passage does not discuss the hours children spent in school.
E The author describes those children held *"priceless"* in the modern view as *extremely costly* to parents; this is not the view held in the early 1800's.

The correct answer is C.

93. Which of the following alternative explanations of the change in the cash value of children would be most likely to be put forward by sociological economists as they are described in the passage?

(A) The cash value of children rose during the nineteenth century because parents began to increase their emotional investment in the upbringing of their children.
(B) The cash value of children rose during the nineteenth century because their expected earnings over the course of a lifetime increased greatly.
(C) The cash value of children rose during the nineteenth century because the spread of humanitarian ideals resulted in a wholesale reappraisal of the worth of an individual.
(D) The cash value of children rose during the nineteenth century because compulsory education laws reduced the supply, and thus raised the costs, of available child labor.
(E) The cash value of children rose during the nineteenth century because of changes in the way negligence law assessed damages in accidental-death cases.

Application

To see how sociological economists would explain changing views of a child's worth, examine what the passage says about their perspectives. In the final paragraph, the author contrasts Zelizer's culturally based conclusions about a child's worth with the thinking of the sociological economists, who analyze topics *solely in terms of their economic determinants* and who *tend to view all human behavior as directed primarily by the principle of maximizing economic gain.* Therefore, sociological economists would explain the rise in the cash value of children exclusively on the basis of the rise of their economic value.

A Sociological economists would not support a reason based on emotion, only on economics.
B **Correct.** From the perspective of sociological economists, the cash value of children increases as the amount they can be expected to earn over a lifetime increases, a purely economic rationale.
C Sociological economists would not support a reason based on humanitarian ideals rather than economics.
D Since this economic argument is based on the underlying social values about children's education, not simply on economics, sociological economists would not support it.
E Sociological economists would not support a reason based on law rather than economics.

The correct answer is B.

94. The primary purpose of the passage is to
(A) review the literature in a new academic subfield
(B) present the central thesis of a recent book
(C) contrast two approaches to analyzing historical change
(D) refute a traditional explanation of a social phenomenon
(E) encourage further work on a neglected historical topic

Main idea

The author's purpose can be inferred by looking at the structure of the entire passage. In the first paragraph, the author draws the contrast between earlier and modern values in order to introduce the subject of Zelizer's book, the transformation of social values, in the second paragraph. The author discusses the history of this transformation through the middle section of the passage and turns in closing to contrast Zelizer's thesis, which emphasizes the power of social values to transform price, with the economically determined position of the sociological economists.

A The passage focuses on one book only; it is not a broad review of the literature.
B **Correct.** As a structural examination of the entire passage shows, the author presents the thesis of Zelizer's recent book.
C Such a contrast is drawn in the last paragraph only, not throughout the passage.
D A social phenomenon is examined in this passage, but no traditional explanation of the phenomenon needs to be refuted.
E The author of the passage does not call for new studies into this area of research.

The correct answer is B.

95. It can be inferred from the passage that which of the following statements was true of American families over the course of the nineteenth century?

(A) The average size of families grew considerably.
(B) The percentage of families involved in industrial work declined dramatically.
(C) Family members became more emotionally bonded to one another.
(D) Family members spent an increasing amount of time working with each other.
(E) Family members became more economically dependent on each other.

Inference

An inference about American families over the course of the nineteenth century must be based on what Zelizer says about such families. Zelizer believes that the transformation of social values that took place over the course of the nineteenth century can be attributed to a number of causes. Lines 32–34 enumerate those causes, including *the development of the companionate family (a family in which members were united by explicit bonds of love rather than duty)*. Here the passage implies that family members became more emotionally bonded to one another.

A The passage gives no evidence of an increase in average family size.
B The passage does not discuss such a decline.
C Correct. One cause of the change in social values was the development of *the companionate family*, bound more by love than by duty.
D No mention is made of increased time that the families worked together.
E The passage does not establish that there was greater economic dependence within families.

The correct answer is C.

96. Zelizer refers to all of the following as important influences in changing the assessment of children's worth EXCEPT changes in

(A) the mortality rate
(B) the nature of industry
(C) the nature of the family
(D) attitudes toward reform movements
(E) attitudes toward the marketplace

Supporting ideas

This question can be answered by looking at the third paragraph, where the author discusses in detail Zelizer's ideas about the origins of the change. *Factors critical in changing the assessment of children's worth* are listed in lines 28–36, and the "*sacralization*" *of children's lives* is discussed in lines 36–41. Checking the reasons cited in these lines against the possible answers to this question gives, by the process of elimination, the one reason that Zelizer does NOT discuss.

A Zelizer refers to *the decline in birth and death rates, especially in child mortality.*
B Zelizer refers to the decrease in *children's productive value in a maturing industrial economy.*
C Zelizer refers to *the development of the companionate family.*
D Correct. While reformers are mentioned in lines 23–26, attitudes toward reform movements are not discussed in the passage.
E Zelizer refers to "*sacralization*" as a way of protecting children from *the relentless corruption of human values by the marketplace.*

The correct answer is D.

Questions 97–102 refer to the passage on page 380.

97. According to the passage, senior managers use intuition in all of the following ways EXCEPT to

(A) speed up the creation of a solution to a problem
(B) identify a problem
(C) bring together disparate facts
(D) stipulate clear goals
(E) evaluate possible solutions to a problem

Supporting ideas

The use of the phrase *according to the passage* is an indication that the answer is explicitly stated in the passage. Look for this explicit statement. The third paragraph of the passage describes the five ways that managers use intuition. To find the one way that is NOT described, go back to the paragraph and check the possible answers against the list of the ways provided in the paragraph. The list includes all the answer choices except stipulating clear goals.

A Lines 39–41 state that intuition allows managers to *move rapidly to engender a plausible solution.*
B Lines 22–23 explain that managers use intuition to *sense when a problem exists.*
C Lines 28–29 say the third function of intuition is *to synthesize isolated bits of data and practice into an integrated picture.*
D Correct. Stipulating clear goals is not linked with managers' use of intuition.
E Lines 30–32 show that managers use intuition *as a check on the results of more rational analysis*; those results are the solutions reached by formal decision analysis.

The correct answer is D.

98. The passage suggests which of the following about the "writers on management" mentioned in line 12?

(A) They have criticized managers for not following the classical rational model of decision analysis.
(B) They have not based their analyses on a sufficiently large sample of actual managers.
(C) They have relied in drawing their conclusions on what managers say rather than on what managers do.
(D) They have misunderstood how managers use intuition in making business decisions.
(E) They have not acknowledged the role of intuition in managerial practice.

Inference

The question's use of the word *suggests* means that the answer depends on making an inference. The second paragraph dismisses most *writers on management* for displaying *a poor grasp of what intuition is* (line 15). The third paragraph, in contrast, describes Isenberg's work, which shows that *senior managers use intuition in at least five distinct ways* (lines 20–22), and those ways are then discussed in more detail. It can be inferred that Isenberg understands what most *writers on management* do not: how managers use intuition in making business decisions.

A The passage does not link these writers with such a critique of managers.
B No mention is made in the passage of the writers' methods.
C The passage does not indicate that the writers have examined words at the expense of actions.
D Correct. According to the passage, the writers do not understand what intuition is or how managers apply it.
E According to lines 12–15, the writers have acknowledged the application of intuition, but they fail to understand it.

The correct answer is D.

99. Which of the following best exemplifies "an 'Aha!' experience" (line 29–30) as it is presented in the passage?

(A) A manager risks taking an action whose outcome is unpredictable to discover whether the action changes the problem at hand.
(B) A manager performs well-learned and familiar behavior patterns in creative and uncharacteristic ways to solve a problem.
(C) A manager suddenly connects seemingly unrelated facts and experiences to create a pattern relevant to the problem at hand.
(D) A manager rapidly identifies the methodology used to compile data yielded by systematic analysis.
(E) A manager swiftly decides which of several sets of tactics to implement in order to deal with the contingencies suggested by a problem.

Application

Finding an example involves applying the information in the passage to new situations. How do managers reach *an "Aha!" experience*? Lines 28–29 clearly explain that this experience is the result of the managers' ability *to synthesize isolated bits of data and practice into an integrated picture.* Managers connect apparently unrelated pieces of information and elements of their previous experience, and, through these unexpected connections, produce a unified picture or pattern.

A This managerial style is mentioned in the last paragraph, but not as defining the *"Aha!" experience.*

B Lines 23–24 indicate that managers use intuition *to perform well-learned behavior patterns rapidly*, but the result is not an *"Aha!" experience.*

C **Correct.** Through an intuitive appreciation of the subtle interrelationships of disparate facts and experiences, the manager all at once perceives the coherent overarching pattern or picture formed by the interconnections, which lines 28–29 define as the *"Aha!" experience.*

D Lines 31–35 show that managers do possess this ability, but it does not culminate in an *"Aha!" experience.*

E This managerial style is not discussed in the passage.

The correct answer is C.

100. According to the passage, the classical model of decision analysis includes all of the following EXCEPT

(A) evaluation of a problem
(B) creation of possible solutions to a problem
(C) establishment of clear goals to be reached by the decision
(D) action undertaken in order to discover more information about a problem
(E) comparison of the probable effects of different solutions to a problem

Supporting ideas

The use of the phrase *according to the passage* is an indication that the answer is explicitly stated in the passage. What does the passage say about the classical model of decision analysis? The first sentence defines the classical model as *clarifying goals, assessing the problem, formulating options, estimating likelihoods of success, making a decision, and only then taking action to implement the decision.* To solve this process-of-elimination question, check the given list against the possible answers in order to find the one that does not match. Note that the exact wording in the answers may differ from that in the passage; the match is based on underlying meaning.

A Evaluating a problem is identified as *assessing the problem.*

B Creating solutions is identified as *formulating options.*

C Establishing goals is identified as *clarifying goals.*

D Correct. Acting in order to learn more about the problem is not identified in the passage as part of the rational classical model. It does appear as part of the acting/thinking cycle in the last paragraph.

E Comparing probable effects is identified as *estimating likelihoods of success.*

The correct answer is D.

101. It can be inferred from the passage that which of the following would most probably be one major difference in behavior between Manager X, who uses intuition to reach decisions, and Manager Y, who uses only formal decision analysis?

(A) Manager X analyzes first and then acts; Manager Y does not.
(B) Manager X checks possible solutions to a problem by systematic analysis; Manager Y does not.
(C) Manager X takes action in order to arrive at the solution to a problem; Manager Y does not.
(D) Manager Y draws on years of hands-on experience in creating a solution to a problem; Manager X does not.
(E) Manager Y depends on day-to-day tactical maneuvering; Manager X does not.

Application

To answer this question, apply the information in the passage to the specific examples of Manager X, an intuitive decision maker, and Manager Y, who relies exclusively on formal decision analysis. The first paragraph distinguishes between the process of formal decision analysis, in which a decision is made and then action is taken (lines 4–5), and the process of intuition, in which action is integrated into the process of thinking (lines 10–11). The last paragraph reinforces the definition of the intuitive manager as one for whom *"thinking" is inseparable from acting* and *action is often part of defining the problem.* Manager X is likely to act as part of the process of solving a problem, but Manager Y is not.

A Acting only after analysis characterizes the rational model, not intuition.

B Systematic analysis is typical of the rational mode, not the intuitive mode.

C Correct. An intuitive manager acts as a step within the problem-solving process, but a manager who depends on formal decision analysis acts only after making a decision.

D Drawing on experience is linked in the passage with intuition rather than with rational analysis; the passage does not suggest that managers who use formal decision analysis would ignore their experience in so doing.

E *Day-to-day tactical maneuvers* are required of all managers.

The correct answer is C.

102. The passage provides support for which of the following statements?

(A) Managers who rely on intuition are more successful than those who rely on formal decision analysis.

(B) Managers cannot justify their intuitive decisions.

(C) Managers' intuition works contrary to their rational and analytical skills.

(D) Logical analysis of a problem increases the number of possible solutions.

(E) Intuition enables managers to employ their practical experience more efficiently.

Logical structure

This question asks the reader to find what is assumed but never explicitly stated in the passage. The entire passage places value on the use of intuition, so the answer to this question is bound to show a benefit of intuition. Lines 25–27 reveal that intuition is based on *years of painstaking practice and hands-on experience* and lines 38–40 explain that, in contrast to formal decision analysis, intuition allows managers *to move rapidly to engender a plausible solution.* Thus, intuition enables managers to apply their experience quickly and productively, that is, efficiently.

A The first paragraph acknowledges that most successful managers are intuitive, but it does not go so far as to make this comparison.

B The passage as a whole justifies managers' intuitive decisions.

C Intuition does not compete with rational analysis, but complements it; line 25 provides an assurance that intuition is *not arbitrary or irrational.*

D The passage does not support this claim for logical analysis.

E Correct. Managers can reach decisions more efficiently through an intuitive approach based on experience than through time-consuming formal analyses.

The correct answer is E.

Questions 103–110 refer to the passage on page 382.

103. The author is primarily concerned with

(A) advocating a return to an older methodology
(B) explaining the importance of a recent theory
(C) enumerating differences between two widely used methods
(D) describing events leading to a discovery
(E) challenging the assumptions on which a theory is based

Main idea

Examine the entire passage to find the author's primary concern. An analysis of this passage shows that the author introduces a recent theory in the first paragraph, explains the practical importance of the theory in the second, and discusses the methods of exploration the theory makes possible in the third and fourth paragraphs. The author is primarily concerned with presenting a new theory and showing why it is important.

A The only older methodology cited in the passage, *simple prospecting methods,* leads to only an *occasional discovery* (lines 15–17).

B Correct. The author describes a recent theory of ore formation and discusses its importance.

C Three methods of exploration are described in the third paragraph, but differences among them are not discussed.

D The passage describes a theory and the practice derived from it; it does not describe a series of events leading to a discovery.

E The author describes two theories of ore formation in the first paragraph but does not challenge the assumptions on which either one is based.

The correct answer is B.

104. According to the passage, the widely held view of Archean-age gold-quartz vein systems is that such systems

(A) were formed from metamorphic fluids
(B) originated in molten granite-like bodies
(C) were formed from alluvial deposits
(D) generally have surface expression
(E) are not discoverable through chemical tests

Supporting ideas

This question asks for information explicitly stated in the first paragraph where Archean-age gold-quartz vein systems are discussed. The recent theory is *contrary* to the *widely held* theory that Archean-age gold quartz vein systems *were deposited from metamorphic fluids* (lines 6–7).

A Correct. The widely held theory explains that the systems were formed from metamorphic fluids.

B It is the recent theory that holds that the systems were formed *from magmatic fluids that originated from molten granite-like bodies* (lines 3–4); the recent theory is not *the widely held view.*

C Alluvial deposits are mentioned only in the context of *simple prospecting methods* (lines 15–16).

D Lines 18–19 explain that most deposits *have no surface expression.*

E *Sensitive chemical tests* are able to detect deposits where mineralization has occurred (lines 27–28).

The correct answer is A.

105. The passage implies that which of the following steps would be the first performed by explorers who wish to maximize their chances of discovering gold?

(A) Surveying several sites known to have been formed more than two billion years ago
(B) Limiting exploration to sites known to have been formed from metamorphic fluid
(C) Using an appropriate conceptual model to select a site for further exploration
(D) Using geophysical methods to analyze rocks over a broad area
(E) Limiting exploration to sites where alluvial gold has previously been found

Inference

Since the question uses the word *implies*, the answer will be an inference based on what the passage says about exploration. The third and fourth paragraphs describe the process of exploration. The high-technology methods are of no use to the explorer if the sites have not mineralized, *and to maximize the chances of discovery the explorer must therefore pay particular attention to selecting the ground formations most likely to be mineralized* (lines 32–35). Conceptual models based on observation and ore-formation theories allow the explorer to identify the areas most likely to be mineralized (lines 34–35).

A The passage does indicate that age is a factor in selecting a site.
B The earlier theory, rather than the recent theory that is the focus of the passage, argued that gold vein systems were formed from metamorphic fluids. The passage says the recent theory has *considerable practical importance*, suggesting the benefits of applying the newer theory rather than this earlier theory.
C **Correct.** Conceptual models lead the explorer to the sites most likely to have mineralized.
D Geophysical techniques are of no use unless an area has been mineralized (lines 30–33).
E The *simple prospecting methods* that find alluvial gold lead to only an *occasional discovery*; most deposits are buried (lines 15–17).

The correct answer is C.

106. Which of the following statements about discoveries of gold deposits is supported by information in the passage?

(A) The number of gold discoveries made annually has increased between the time of the original gold rushes and the present.
(B) New discoveries of gold deposits are likely to be the result of exploration techniques designed to locate buried mineralization.
(C) It is unlikely that newly discovered gold deposits will ever yield as much as did those deposits discovered during the original gold rushes.
(D) Modern explorers are divided on the question of the utility of simple prospecting methods as a source of new discoveries of gold deposits.
(E) Models based on the theory that gold originated from magmatic fluids have already led to new discoveries of gold deposits.

Supporting ideas

This question requires consideration of explicit information throughout the passage. The second paragraph explains that most deposits are buried (lines 17–19), so the explorer's best means of discovering them is the use of conceptual models to identify the sites most likely to have buried mineralization (lines 35–38). At that point, the explorer may use the high-technology methods possible when buried mineralization is present (lines 22–29).

A The passage does not discuss the number of gold discoveries.
B **Correct.** Since most gold deposits are buried, explorers must find the sites most likely to contain buried mineralization.
C The passage does not discuss the yield of gold discoveries.
D While *simple prospecting methods* lead only to an *occasional discovery*, modern explorers are not said to dispute their utility.
E The passage does not say that gold deposits have already been found by using the models based on this recent theory.

The correct answer is B.

107. It can be inferred from the passage that which of the following is easiest to detect?

(A) A gold-quartz vein system originating in magmatic fluids
(B) A gold-quartz vein system originating in metamorphic fluids
(C) A gold deposit that is mixed with granite
(D) A gold deposit that has shed alluvial gold
(E) A gold deposit that exhibits chemical halos

Application

To answer this question, apply what the passage says about gold deposits to the examples in the answer choices. The second paragraph states that the gold deposits discovered during the gold rushes were *exposed at the Earth's surface*; they were found because *they had shed trails of alluvial gold that were easily traced by simple prospecting methods* (lines 12–16). Most deposits have not been detected because they are buried and have *no surface expression*. Thus the simplest gold to find would be that in a deposit that had shed alluvial gold.

A The recent theory holds that gold-quartz vein systems are formed from magmatic fluids, but does not say that these systems have easily detectable surface expressions.

B The widely held theory contends that gold-quartz vein systems are formed from metamorphic fluids, but does not say whether these have easily detectable surface expressions.

C The passage does not comment on gold deposits mixed with granite, although the recent theory does mention *molten granite-like bodies deep beneath the surface of the Earth* (lines 4–5).

D **Correct.** Finding gold deposits that have shed alluvial gold at the Earth's surface is far easier than finding buried gold deposits.

E One complex, difficult subsurface exploration method involves chemical tests detecting the subtle chemical halos that surround mineralized areas; clearly this is not the *easiest* means of detecting gold deposits.

The correct answer is D.

108. The theory mentioned in line 1 relates to the conceptual models discussed in the passage in which of the following ways?

(A) It may furnish a valid account of ore-forming processes, and, hence, can support conceptual models that have great practical significance.
(B) It suggests that certain geological formations, long believed to be mineralized, are in fact mineralized, thus confirming current conceptual models.
(C) It suggests that there may not be enough similarity across Archean-age gold-quartz vein systems to warrant the formulation of conceptual models.
(D) It corrects existing theories about the chemical halos of gold deposits, and thus provides a basis for correcting current conceptual models.
(E) It suggests that simple prospecting methods still have a higher success rate in the discovery of gold deposits than do more modern methods.

Logical structure

This question requires considering the conceptual models described in lines 35–38 in light of the recent theory (lines 1–4), which the author assures the reader has *considerable practical importance* (lines 10–11). The conceptual models are derived from observation and from *theories of ore-forming processes*. Therefore, the recent theory may explain ore formation in a way that leads to the development of an updated model, and that model may then aid in the discovery of gold deposits.

A **Correct.** The theory provides an explanation of ore formation, which aids in creating a conceptual model that may help explorers find gold deposits.

B The theory does not confirm models, but contributes to forming them.

C The practical value of the theory is that it can help to formulate models.

D The theory does not challenge theories about chemical halos but rather contributes to the development of conceptual models that might allow for their broader application.

E The theory does not compare methods of discovering gold deposits.

The correct answer is A.

109. According to the passage, methods of exploring for gold that are widely used today are based on which of the following facts?

(A) Most of the Earth's remaining gold deposits are still molten.
(B) Most of the Earth's remaining gold deposits are exposed at the surface.
(C) Most of the Earth's remaining gold deposits are buried and have no surface expression.
(D) Only one type of gold deposit warrants exploration, since the other types of gold deposits are found in regions difficult to reach.
(E) Only one type of gold deposit warrants exploration, since the other types of gold deposits are unlikely to yield concentrated quantities of gold.

Supporting ideas

As indicated by the phrase *according to the passage*, this question concerns factual information stated in the passage. In contrast to the gold deposits discovered at the Earth's surface, most *deposits not yet discovered have gone undetected because they are buried and have no surface expression* (lines 17–19). The *methods used widely today* must search for buried minerals rather than minerals on the surface (lines 22–29).

A The passage mentions neither molten gold nor the method to detect it.
B The passage explicitly says that most deposits are buried.
C Correct. The passage explicitly states that most gold deposits are buried, leaving no traces at the Earth's surface.
D The passage neither distinguishes between types of gold nor describes inaccessible regions.
E The passage does not describe types or yields of gold deposits.

The correct answer is C.

110. It can be inferred from the passage that the efficiency of model-based gold exploration depends on which of the following?

I. The closeness of the match between the geological features identified by the model as critical and the actual geological features of a given area
II. The degree to which the model chosen relies on empirical observation of known mineral deposits rather than on theories of ore-forming processes
III. The degree to which the model chosen is based on an accurate description of the events leading to mineralization

(A) I only
(B) II only
(C) I and II only
(D) I and III only
(E) I, II, and III

Inference

The question requires a close reading of the final paragraph to find information that is suggested but not directly stated. The first sentence says that the models are derived from both observation and theories, but observation is not weighed more heavily than the theories, so statement II can be eliminated. The next sentence says that models help explorers *identify those geological features that are critical to the formation of the mineralization being modeled, and then tries to select areas for exploration that exhibit as many of the critical features as possible.* The efficiency of the exploration is affected by the match between the critical features the model identifies and the critical features of the actual site: the closer the match, the greater the efficiency. Thus statement I is true. The more accurate the model is in describing mineralization, the greater the likelihood of selecting an appropriate site, which increases the efficiency of exploration. Statement III must be true as well. Therefore, the correct answer includes statements I and III, while excluding statement II.

A I must be included, but so must III.
B II misstates the information in lines 33–35.
C I is necessary, but II must be excluded.
D Correct. Both I and III give reasons for the greater efficiency of exploration.
E I and III are necessary, but II must be excluded.

The correct answer is D.

Questions 111–116 refer to the passage on page 384.

111. The passage is primarily concerned with

(A) defending a controversial approach
(B) criticizing an accepted view
(C) summarizing research findings
(D) contrasting competing theories
(E) describing an innovative technique

Main idea

Figuring out the authors' primary concern depends on a careful review of the passage as a whole. The first paragraph identifies the larger question that is the context for the researchers' investigation. The second paragraph presents the part of the question the authors researched, concluding with their unexpected results. The third paragraph explains the importance of these findings in relation to the larger question of the universe's possible *"close."* The authors' primary purpose in this passage is to summarize the findings of their research.

A The authors do not discuss approaches to the question they research.
B The authors mention that their findings do not conform to Kepler's law, but they do not criticize other views.
C Correct. This passage presents a summation of the findings of the authors' research.
D The authors do not contrast different theories about the universe's expansion.
E The authors do not discuss new techniques of research.

The correct answer is C.

112. The authors' study indicates that, in comparison with the outermost regions of a typical spiral galaxy, the region just outside the nucleus can be characterized as having

(A) higher rotational velocity and higher luminosity
(B) lower rotational velocity and higher luminosity
(C) lower rotational velocity and lower luminosity
(D) similar rotational velocity and higher luminosity
(E) similar rotational velocity and similar luminosity

Inference

In the second paragraph, the authors observe that *outside the bright nucleus of a typical spiral galaxy luminosity falls off rapidly*; the region just outside the nucleus may thus be characterized as having higher luminosity than the outermost regions of a spiral galaxy. Their research finds that *the rotational velocity in spiral galaxies either remains constant with increasing distance from the center or increases slightly*. The region just outside the nucleus may thus be characterized as sharing with the outermost regions of a spiral galaxy a similar rotational velocity.

A This region was expected to have higher rotational velocity, but the research findings did not corroborate this hypothesis; it is correct that the region has higher luminosity.
B The region does have higher luminosity, but not lower rotational velocity.
C The region has neither lower luminosity nor lower rotational velocity.
D Correct. The region has similar rotational velocity and higher luminosity.
E The region has similar rotational velocity but higher luminosity.

The correct answer is D.

113. The passage suggests that the results of the authors' study have changed their ideas about which of the following characteristics of spiral galaxies?

I. The relative luminosity of different regions
II. The relative rotational velocity of different regions
III. The relative distribution of matter in different regions

(A) I only
(B) II only
(C) III only
(D) II and III only
(E) I, II, and III

Inference

The second sentence of the second paragraph explains that *it has been known for some time* that luminosity is greatest at the center of a spiral galaxy and falls off with distance from the center (lines 19–22). The authors do not change their ideas about luminosity. The authors anticipated that *rotational velocity would decrease geometrically with distance from the center* (lines 24–26) but found instead that rotational velocity is similar throughout the spiral galaxy (lines 27–30). Thus, their findings did change their ideas about rotational velocity. Finally, their unexpected finding suggests that *the falloff in luminous mass with distance from the center is balanced by an increase in nonluminous mass* (lines 30–33). The authors reached this conclusion about invisible matter on the basis of a finding that they did not anticipate, so it is fair to say that their ideas about the distribution of matter changed.

A The authors did not change their ideas about luminosity.
B The authors did change their ideas about rotational velocity, but that was not their only shift.
C The authors changed their ideas about matter, but that was not their only shift.
D Correct. The authors changed their ideas about both rotational velocity and the distribution of matter.
E The authors did not change their ideas about luminosity, although they did change their ideas about rotational velocity and matter.

The correct answer is D.

114. The authors' suggestion that "as much as 90 percent of the mass of the universe is not radiating at any wavelength with enough intensity to be detected on the Earth" (lines 39–42) would be most weakened if which of the following were discovered to be true?

(A) Spiral galaxies are less common than types of galaxies that contain little nonluminous matter.
(B) Luminous and nonluminous matter are composed of the same basic elements.
(C) The bright nucleus of a typical spiral galaxy also contains some nonluminous matter.
(D) The density of the observable universe is greater than most previous estimates have suggested.
(E) Some galaxies do not rotate or rotate too slowly for their rotational velocity to be measured.

Application

The authors' conclusion about nonluminous matter is based on their study of the rotational velocity of spiral galaxies. If spiral galaxies were found to be atypical of galaxies, then it would be possible that, in those other galaxies, nonluminous matter does not increase as luminous matter decreases. If this were the case, the authors' conclusion would be based on a sample of galaxies not representative of the whole, and their argument would be seriously weakened.

A Correct. The authors' conclusion assumes that spiral galaxies are typical of all galaxies; information calling that assumption into question weakens the argument.
B The relation rather than the composition of luminous and nonluminous mass is relevant to the conclusion.
C Nonluminous mass increases as luminous mass decreases: this finding does not rule out that the nucleus contains some nonluminous mass; the argument is not affected.
D The density of the observable universe is only *a fraction* of the density needed to *"close"* the universe, so even if this density were greater, it is not likely to exceed the density of nonluminous matter.
E The authors are concerned only with measurable rotational velocity.

The correct answer is A.

115. It can be inferred from information presented in the passage that if the density of the universe were equivalent to significantly less than three hydrogen atoms per cubic meter, which of the following would be true as a consequence?

(A) Luminosity would be a true indicator of mass.
(B) Different regions in spiral galaxies would rotate at the same velocity.
(C) The universe would continue to expand indefinitely.
(D) The density of the invisible matter in the universe would have to be more than 70 times the density of the luminous matter.
(E) More of the invisible matter in spiral galaxies would have to be located in their nuclei than in their outer regions.

Inference

An inference is drawn from stated information. This question refers to the first paragraph, where the authors explain that *the critical density of matter needed to brake the expansion and "close" the universe is equivalent to three hydrogen atoms per cubic meter* (lines 7–9). If the density is significantly less, then the universe will not "close" but continue to expand indefinitely.

A The authors' finding that luminosity is not a true indicator of mass is not derived from the conclusion that the density is less than three hydrogen atoms per cubic meter.
B The authors' finding that different regions rotate at similar velocities does not come from the hypothesis about the density of the universe.
C Correct. If the critical density needed to "*close*" the universe is equivalent to three hydrogen atoms per cubic meter, then a density of significantly less than this amount means that the universe will continue its expansion.
D This statement would be true of the hypothetical "*close*" of the universe, but if the density is less than three hydrogen atoms per cubic meter, the universe will continue its expansion.
E This statement cannot be inferred from the hypothesis about the density of the universe.

The correct answer is C.

116. The authors propose all of the following as possibly contributing to the "missing matter" in spiral galaxies EXCEPT

(A) massive black holes
(B) small black holes
(C) small, dim stars
(D) massive stars
(E) large planets

Supporting ideas

This question asks the reader to find the list of possible explanations for the "*missing*" or *dark matter* that the authors give in the passage and to check that list against the possible answers. Using the process of elimination will show which answer is not included on the authors' list. In the final paragraph, the authors write, *Such dark matter could be in the form of extremely dim stars of low mass, of large planets like Jupiter, or of black holes, either small or massive* (lines 42–45).

A The authors include massive black holes.
B The authors include small black holes.
C The authors include small, dim stars.
D Correct. The authors do not include massive stars in their list of possible explanations for "*missing matter.*"
E The authors include large planets.

The correct answer is D.

Questions 117–122 refer to the passage on page 386.

117. According to the passage, the five well-known plant hormones are not useful in controlling the growth of crops because

(A) it is not known exactly what functions the hormones perform
(B) each hormone has various effects on plants
(C) none of the hormones can function without the others
(D) each hormone has different effects on different kinds of plants
(E) each hormone works on only a small subset of a cell's genes at any particular time

Supporting ideas

To answer this question, look for information that is explicitly stated in the passage. Lines 16–20 explain that each of the five plant hormones *has more than one effect on the growth and development of plants*; for this reason, they *are not very useful in artificially controlling the growth of crops*.

A Lines 20–25 describe in detail the multiple functions of the hormone auxin.
B Correct. The hormones *have so many simultaneous effects* on plants that they are not useful in controlling the growth of crops.
C The passage provides no evidence to support this reason.
D No information is given in the passage to support this reason.
E The hormones' multiple effects on plant growth, not their specific effect at the cellular level, make them ineffective at artificially controlling crop growth.

The correct answer is B.

118. The passage suggests that the place of hypothalamic hormones in the hormonal hierarchies of animals is similar to the place of which of the following in plants?

(A) Plant cell walls
(B) The complement of genes in each plant cell
(C) A subset of a plant cell's gene complement
(D) The five major hormones
(E) The oligosaccharins

Inference

This question asks the reader to find information that is suggested but not directly stated in the passage and requires examining the analogy between the action of hormones in animals and in plants, which is the subject of the third and fourth paragraphs. In animals, hypothalamic hormones stimulate the pituitary gland to synthesize and release many different hormones; this process causes hormones from the adrenal cortex to be released. A similar *hierarchy of hormones* may exist in plants. The pleiotropic plant hormones may activate the enzymes that, in turn, release oligosaccharins from the cell wall. It is reasonable to infer that, in triggering the action, the plant hormones may act in a way similar to the hypothalamic hormones in animals.

A Plant cell walls do not activate enzymes as the hypothalamic hormones activate the pituitary gland.
B The passage states that all cells of a plant start out with the same complement of genes (lines 1–2), but this statement is not part of the analogy.
C Line 5 refers to the subset of genes, but it is not a part of the analogy.
D Correct. Like hypothalamic hormones in animals, the five major plant hormones may be responsible for releasing the catalysts for growth.
E The oligosaccharins are part of the hierarchy, but they are not equivalent to the hypothalamic hormones in releasing other hormones.

The correct answer is D.

119. The passage suggests that which of the following is a function likely to be performed by an oligosaccharin?

(A) To stimulate a particular plant cell to become part of a plant's root system
(B) To stimulate the walls of a particular cell to produce other oligosaccharins
(C) To activate enzymes that release specific chemical messengers from plant cell walls
(D) To duplicate the gene complement in a particular plant cell
(E) To produce multiple effects on a particular subsystem of plant cells

Inference

Since the question uses the word *suggests*, the answer requires making an inference based on the information in the passage. The analogy between animal and plant hormones describes a process that ends, in animals, with *specific effects on target organs all over the body* (lines 33–34). While the pleiotropic plant hormones have multiple effects, the oligosaccharins are described as *more specific chemical messengers* (lines 43–44). It is reasonable to infer that oligosaccharins affect a specific part of a plant's growth.

A **Correct.** This is the only response that gives an example of an effect on a specific aspect of plant growth and development.
B The last paragraph explains that enzymes release oligosaccharins.
C The pleiotropic plant hormones, not the oligosaccharins, may activate the enzymes (lines 41–43).
D The passage does not discuss such duplication.
E The oligosaccharins, as *more specific chemical messengers*, have a specific effect, not multiple effects, on plant growth.

The correct answer is A.

120. The author mentions specific effects that auxin has on plant development in order to illustrate the

(A) point that some of the effects of plant hormones can be harmful
(B) way in which hormones are produced by plants
(C) hierarchical nature of the functioning of plant hormones
(D) differences among the best-known plant hormones
(E) concept of pleiotropy as it is exhibited by plant hormones

Logical structure

To answer this question, reread the section where auxin is discussed. The second paragraph explains that each of the five major pleiotropic hormones, including auxin, *has more than one effect on the growth and development of plants.* The author then lists auxin's multiple effects as an example of the principle of pleiotropy in plants.

A The passage does not discuss harmful effects.
B The passage discusses the effects of hormones, not their production.
C Auxin is used to exemplify the many different effects of a pleiotropic hormone, not its role in a hierarchy of hormones.
D The differences among the five major hormones are not discussed.
E **Correct.** The author lists auxin's multiple effects to illustrate how pleiotropic hormones affect plant growth.

The correct answer is E.

121. According to the passage, which of the following best describes a function performed by oligosaccharins?

(A) Regulating the daily functioning of a plant's cells
(B) Interacting with one another to produce different chemicals
(C) Releasing specific chemical messengers from a plant's cell walls
(D) Producing the hormones that cause plant cells to differentiate to perform different functions
(E) Influencing the development of a plant's cells by controlling the expression of the cells' genes

Supporting ideas

To answer this question, look for information that is explicitly stated in the passage. Oligosaccharins are *regulatory molecules* (line 13). They form part of the complex system that turns on, or expresses, a small subset of genes in a particular kind of cell. As explained in the first paragraph, this process allows plant cells to differentiate and form different plant structures. Unlike the five major plant hormones, the oligosaccharins affect a specific aspect of the plant's growth (lines 14–15).

A The passage does not discuss the daily functioning of a plant's cells.
B The passage provides no evidence of this interaction.
C The oligosaccharins *are fragments of the cell wall* (line 39) and the *specific chemical messengers from the cell wall* (lines 44–45).
D The oligosaccharins are not said to produce hormones.
E **Correct.** Oligosaccharins are part of the system that turns on, or expresses, the subset of a cell's genes that allows cells to grow into different plant structures.

The correct answer is E.

122. The passage suggests that, unlike the pleiotropic hormones, oligosaccharins could be used effectively to

(A) trace the passage of chemicals through the walls of cells
(B) pinpoint functions of other plant hormones
(C) artificially control specific aspects of the development of crops
(D) alter the complement of genes in the cells of plants
(E) alter the effects of the five major hormones on plant development

Inference

The passage does not explicitly state how oligosaccharins could be used, but a use can be inferred. The second paragraph establishes that the pleiotropic hormones are not useful in artificially controlling crop growth because of their multiple, diverse effects. Oligosaccharins are contrasted with the hormones because they have specific effects. Thus it is reasonable to infer that oligosaccharins might be used to control specific aspects of crop growth.

A Passage of chemicals through cell walls is not discussed.
B The passage does not indicate that oligosaccharins act in this way.
C **Correct.** Because the oligosaccharins have specific rather than multiple effects, they might have the potential to be used to control specific aspects of a crop's growth.
D The oligosaccharins are not said to alter the cells' complement of genes.
E The passage does not show that oligosaccharins alter the hormones' effects.

The correct answer is C.

Questions 123–128 refer to the passage on page 388.

123. The author indicates explicitly that which of the following records has been a source of information in her investigation?

(A) United States Immigration Service reports from 1914 to 1930
(B) Payrolls of southern manufacturing firms between 1910 and 1930
(C) The volume of cotton exports between 1898 and 1910
(D) The federal census of 1910
(E) Advertisements of labor recruiters appearing in southern newspapers after 1910

Supporting ideas

Since the question uses the word *explicitly*, it is clear that the answer can be found in the passage. In lines 29–30, the author refers to the number of African American workers in *manufacturing and mechanical pursuits*, a phrase cited as coming from the federal census and indicating that she was using census data. While she probably used other sources as well, no other source is explicitly mentioned.

A Immigration Service reports are not mentioned in the passage.
B Payroll records are not mentioned in the passage.
C While the decline of the cotton industry is mentioned, records of exports are not.
D **Correct.** The federal census is indicated as a source of information on the employment of African American workers.
E Labor recruiters and the African American press are mentioned, but there is no mention of data being collected from labor recruiting ads.

The correct answer is D.

124. In the passage, the author anticipates which of the following as a possible objection to her argument?

(A) It is uncertain how many people actually migrated during the Great Migration.
(B) The eventual economic status of the Great Migration migrants has not been adequately traced.
(C) It is not likely that people with steady jobs would have reason to move to another area of the country.
(D) It is not true that the term "manufacturing and mechanical pursuits" actually encompasses the entire industrial sector.
(E) Of the African American workers living in southern cities, only those in a small number of trades were threatened by obsolescence.

Logical structure

Answering questions about the author's line of argument requires following the steps in the logical structure of that argument. The author argues that African American migrants to the North had lived and worked in southern urban areas, not rural areas. In lines 33–36, she recognizes that some people may find it *surprising to argue* that African Americans with steady jobs would leave and proceeds to offer *an explanation* based on southern labor conditions. She thus anticipates the objection that workers would not leave steady jobs.

A The actual number of people migrating is not part of the author's argument, which concerns whether the migrants came from urban or rural backgrounds.
B The eventual economic status is outside the scope of the argument.
C **Correct.** The author anticipates this objection and answers it by citing southern labor conditions.
D The exact composition of the industrial sector is not an issue in the argument, so objections about it would not be relevant.

E The number of industrial workers leaving southern cities specifically because of job obsolescence is not at issue and thus not a potential objection. In the final paragraph, the author is simply presenting her case that wage pressures are being experienced by all southern African American urban workers, in both artisan trades and newly developed industries.

The correct answer is C.

125. According to the passage, which of the following is true of wages in southern cities in 1910?

(A) They were being pushed lower as a result of increased competition.
(B) They had begun to rise so that southern industry could attract rural workers.
(C) They had increased for skilled workers but decreased for unskilled workers.
(D) They had increased in large southern cities but decreased in small southern cities.
(E) They had increased in newly developed industries but decreased in the older trades.

Supporting ideas

The phrase *according to the passage* indicates that the answer is stated in the passage and can be found by careful rereading. The last paragraph is about working conditions in the South. Lines 53–55 show that an influx of rural workers had increased competition for the available industrial jobs and driven wages lower.

A **Correct.** Lines 53–55 indicated that wages were going down as more workers arrived and competed for jobs.
B Rural workers arrived in the city because of the boll weevil infestation, not because of the promise of higher wages, and their arrival depressed wages.
C The passage refers to wages for industrial jobs but does not distinguish between the wages of skilled workers and unskilled workers.
D The passage does not discuss wage differences between large and small southern cities.
E The passage provides no information on differences in wages between older trades and new industries.

The correct answer is A.

126. The author cites each of the following as possible influences in an African American worker's decision to migrate north in the Great Migration EXCEPT

(A) wage levels in northern cities
(B) labor recruiters
(C) competition from rural workers
(D) voting rights in northern states
(E) the African American press

Supporting ideas

Use the process of elimination to answer this question regarding what specifically does NOT appear in the passage. Four of the five answers are mentioned as influences on migration, and one is not. Match each answer with its mention in the passage; the choice that does not have a match is the correct answer. In this case, the only answer not mentioned is *voting rights.*

A Northern wage levels are mentioned in lines 49–51.
B Labor recruiters are mentioned in line 48.
C Competition from rural workers is mentioned in lines 52–54.
D Correct. Voting rights in northern states are not mentioned in the passage; the author has not cited them as a possible influence on a migrant's decision.
E The African American press is mentioned in lines 48–49.

The correct answer is D.

127. It can be inferred from the passage that the "easy conclusion" mentioned in line 58 is based on which of the following assumptions?

(A) People who migrate from rural areas to large cities usually do so for economic reasons.
(B) Most people who leave rural areas to take jobs in cities return to rural areas as soon as it is financially possible for them to do so.
(C) People with rural backgrounds are less likely to succeed economically in cities than are those with urban backgrounds.
(D) Most people who were once skilled workers are not willing to work as unskilled workers.
(E) People who migrate from their birthplaces to other regions of a country seldom undertake a second migration.

Inference

An inference requires going beyond the material explicitly stated in the passage to the author's ideas that underlie that material. In this case, the question directs one's attention to line 58 and the phrase *easy conclusion*. In this context, *easy* has the negative connotation of "facile" or "simplistic" and suggests the author's disagreement with the conclusion that the economic problems of the migrants to northern urban areas are linked to their rural backgrounds. The *conclusion* derived from this link is first discussed in lines 17–19, where lack of economic success in the North is tied to a rural background.

A The author does assume economic motives for migration, but this assumption is not linked to the conclusion about difficulties arising from a rural background.

B This point is not discussed in the passage and is not related to the conclusion that a rural background is linked to economic problems.

C Correct. The conclusion referred to in line 58 is based on the assumption that rural backgrounds will hinder economic success in urban settings.

D The conclusion refers to all people from rural backgrounds and does not distinguish between skilled and unskilled workers.

E The conclusion about the economic difficulties of migrants from rural backgrounds makes no assumptions about whether people migrate more than once.

The correct answer is C.

128. The primary purpose of the passage is to

(A) support an alternative to an accepted methodology
(B) present evidence that resolves a contradiction
(C) introduce a recently discovered source of information
(D) challenge a widely accepted explanation
(E) argue that a discarded theory deserves new attention

Logical structure

Answering questions about primary purpose requires thinking about the underlying structure of the passage. In the first paragraph, the author describes the Great Migration and mentions the assumption that most migrants came from rural areas. Some people then concluded that the migrants' economic difficulties were due to their rural background. In the second paragraph, the author speculates that many migrants could have come from urban areas, and in the third paragraph, she offers information that supports her position. Essentially, if the migrants came from urban areas, their subsequent economic difficulties cannot be attributed to their non-existent rural background. An analysis of the structure of the passage thus reveals that the author is presenting a generally accepted view and then challenging it.

A The author is showing the weakness in an explanation; there is no discussion of a methodology or of an alternative methodology.

B The author is introducing a contradiction to prevailing ideas and is seeking to explain and reinforce it rather than to resolve an existing contradiction.

C While census records are briefly mentioned, they are hardly a recently discovered source of information.

D Correct. The author first discusses a widely accepted explanation of the economic difficulties of African American migrants and then challenges that explanation.

E The author argues against an explanation she thinks should be discarded.

The correct answer is D.

Questions 129–134 refer to the passage on page 390.

129. The "new pasts" mentioned in line 6 can best be described as the

(A) occurrence of events extremely similar to past events
(B) history of the activities of studying, interpreting, and reading new historical writing
(C) change in people's understanding of the past due to more recent historical writing
(D) overturning of established historical interpretations by politically motivated politicians
(E) difficulty of predicting when a given historical interpretation will be overturned

Inference

To discover the meaning of the phrase *new pasts*, look at the context in which the phrase occurs. In the first paragraph, the author discusses history and the writing of history. *New pasts* are said to overturn previous interpretations, so *new pasts* must be new interpretations that change the way people understand history. In the second paragraph, the author uses C. Vann Woodward's work as an example of such a change in people's understanding of the past.

A Nothing in the passage supports this interpretation.

B While these activities are mentioned in the previous sentence, they do not constitute *new pasts*.

C **Correct.** The term *new pasts* refers to new perspectives on the past created by more recent historical writing.

D The phrase *new pasts* does refer to the overturning of established historical interpretations, but, as the Woodward example shows, this overturning is carried out by historians, not politicians.

E The problem of prediction does not contribute to the reader's understanding of the term *new pasts*.

The correct answer is C.

130. It can be inferred from the passage that the "prevailing dogma" (lines 11–12) held that

(A) Jim Crow laws were passed to give legal status to well-established discriminatory practices in the South
(B) Jim Crow laws were passed to establish order and uniformity in the discriminatory practices of different southern states
(C) Jim Crow laws were passed to erase the social gains that Black people had achieved since Reconstruction
(D) the continuity of racial segregation in the South was disrupted by passage of Jim Crow laws
(E) the Jim Crow laws of the late nineteenth and early twentieth centuries were passed to reverse the effect of earlier Jim Crow laws

Inference

To determine what it is logical to infer about the "prevailing dogma," look at the context in which this phrase occurs. Woodward challenged the prevailing dogma when he argued that Jim Crow laws *not only codified traditional practice but also were a determined effort to erase the considerable progress made by Black people during and after Reconstruction in the 1870's*. Recognize the logical structure of this sentence. Woodward's argument concedes the prevailing view expressed in the *not only* portion of the sentence: *codified traditional practice*; Woodward's challenge is then expressed in the *but also* portion of the sentence: *determined effort to erase … progress.*

A **Correct.** This correctly states the prevailing view of the Jim Crow laws.

B The passage does not discuss differences in discriminatory practices among the southern states.

C This is Woodward's new viewpoint, not the prevailing dogma.

D The passage implies that the Jim Crow laws continued racial segregation rather than disrupted it.

E The passage does not discuss earlier and later Jim Crow laws.

The correct answer is A.

131. Which of the following is the best example of writing that is likely to be subject to the kinds of "handicaps" referred to in line 31?

(A) A history of an auto manufacturing plant written by an employee during an auto buying boom
(B) A critique of a statewide school-desegregation plan written by an elementary school teacher in that state
(C) A newspaper article assessing the historical importance of a United States president written shortly after the president has taken office
(D) A scientific paper describing the benefits of a certain surgical technique written by the surgeon who developed the technique
(E) Diary entries narrating the events of a battle written by a soldier who participated in the battle

Application

This question involves applying a term from the passage to new situations. Begin by examining the term *handicaps*. Woodward uses the term in reference to an evaluation of the American Revolution that was written in 1776. In 1776, the Revolution had just begun; many very important events were yet to come. One of the answer choices, the article about a U.S. president written shortly after the president takes office, shares this handicap.

A This history does not suffer from the handicap of being too close in time to the events discussed.
B While the school teacher is involved in the issue, the critique does not suffer from the handicap discussed in the passage.
C Correct. A 1776 work on the American Revolution and an article assessing a recently inaugurated president's place in history share the same handicap; the story is far from over.
D The surgeon's scientific paper does not share the handicap of a 1776 history of the American Revolution.
E Such eyewitness accounts may be written close in time to the actual events, but since the event is completed, the entries do not share the handicap of the 1776 history of the American Revolution.

The correct answer is C.

132. The passage suggests that C. Vann Woodward and Thomas Paine were similar in all of the following ways EXCEPT

(A) both had works published in the midst of important historical events
(B) both wrote works that enjoyed widespread popularity
(C) both exhibited an understanding of the relevance of historical evidence to contemporary issues
(D) the works of both had a significant effect on events following their publication
(E) both were able to set aside worries about historical anachronism in order to reach and inspire

Inference

The question's use of the word *suggests* means that the answer depends on making an inference. This question specifically involves comparing what the author says about each man in order to find the one way in which they differ. Lines 32–43 discuss Paine and Woodward in some detail. Both wrote works for a mass readership; both wrote works with great impact on subsequent events.

A Paine's work was published at the start of the American Revolution; Woodward's work was published at the beginning of the Civil Rights movement.
B The passage implies that both works had a *mass readership* (line 36).
C The author states in lines 39–42 that, *like Paine, Woodward had an unerring sense of the revolutionary moment, and of how historical evidence could undermine the mythological tradition.*
D In line 35, the author describes Paine's work as having *a comparable impact* to Woodward's work.

E **Correct.** The author states that Paine *was not a historian, and thus not concerned with accuracy or the dangers of historical anachronism.* Woodward was a historian and so had to be concerned about historical anachronism.

The correct answer is E.

133. The attitude of the author of the passage toward the work of C. Vann Woodward is best described as one of

(A) respectful regard
(B) qualified approbation
(C) implied skepticism
(D) pointed criticism
(E) fervent advocacy

Tone

An author's attitude toward a topic or person is revealed by the structures and language the author uses. What structures and language does the author use about Woodward? The author uses Woodward as an example of a historian who created a *new past*, thereby changing the course of history. The author compares Woodward with Paine, an important historical figure, and notes the impact both men had. By citing Martin Luther King Jr., the author points to the *profound effect* (lines 43–46) of Woodward's work. The author also praises Woodward's *unerring sense of the revolutionary moment.* At no point in the passage does the author criticize Woodward or describe him in negative terms. The author clearly holds Woodward in high regard.

A **Correct.** The author respects Woodward and holds him in high regard.
B The author does not restrict or moderate any approval for Woodward.
C The author does not cast doubt on Woodward's ideas or imply any skepticism about him.
D The passage contains no criticism of Woodward, pointed or otherwise.
E The author writes in a measured way, not a fervent one, and does not speak as an advocate. The author's tone is rational, not the emotional tone of an impassioned advocate.

The correct answer is A.

134. Which of the following best describes the new idea expressed by C. Vann Woodward in his University of Virginia lectures in 1954?

(A) Southern racial segregation was continuous and uniform.
(B) Black people made considerable progress only after Reconstruction.
(C) Jim Crow legislation was conventional in nature.
(D) Jim Crow laws did not go as far in codifying traditional practice as they might have.
(E) Jim Crow laws did much more than merely reinforce a tradition of segregation.

Inference

A description of Woodward's new idea should be based on what the passage says about his revisionist view of Jim Crow legislation. Lines 14–19 of the passage describe the content of Woodward's argument: *He argued that the Jim Crow laws … not only codified traditional practice but also were a determined effort to erase the considerable progress made by Black people during and after Reconstruction.*

A This is a traditional view, not Woodward's *new idea.*
B Woodward argued that Black people had made progress both during and after Reconstruction.
C The passage does not suggest that Woodward viewed Jim Crow legislation as conventional in nature.
D Woodward suggested that the laws did codify traditional practice and also went well beyond such codification.
E **Correct.** Woodward argued that the laws not only reinforced tradition but also attempted to erase the progress that Black people had made.

The correct answer is E.

Questions 135–141 refer to the passage on page 392.

135. The main point made by the passage is that
(A) financial markets provide for an optimum allocation of resources among all competing participants by balancing supply and demand
(B) the allocation of financial resources takes place among separate individual participants, each of whom has access to the market
(C) the existence of certain factors adversely affecting members of minority groups shows that financial markets do not function as conventional theory says they function
(D) investments in minority communities can be made by the use of various alternative financial instruments, such as stocks and bonds
(E) since transaction costs for stocks, bonds, and other financial instruments are not equally apportioned among all minority-group members, the financial market is subject to criticism

Main idea

Look at the passage as a whole to find the main idea. The author begins by stating the function of capital markets and then pointing out that *certain participants are not on a par with others.* In the second paragraph, the author gives examples to support this point and argues that the existing system increases income inequality and the concentration of capital in certain types of investment. In the final paragraph, the author criticizes conventional financial-market analysis.

A Supply and demand are not discussed in the passage.
B This general statement about the market reflects the conventional theory that the author argues against.
C Correct. The author argues that, for members of minority communities, financial markets do not function the way conventional theory says they should.
D While this point is mentioned in the passage, it is not the main point of the passage.
E Transaction costs are mentioned in the final sentence, but the context is the comparison between minority and nonminority groups. This is hardly the main point of the passage.

The correct answer is C.

136. The passage states that traditional studies of the financial market overlook imbalances in the allocation of financial resources because
(A) an optimum allocation of resources is the final result of competition among participants
(B) those performing the studies choose an oversimplified description of the influences on competition
(C) such imbalances do not appear in the statistics usually compiled to measure the market's behavior
(D) the analysts who study the market are unwilling to accept criticism of their methods as biased
(E) socioeconomic differences form the basis of a rationing mechanism that puts minority groups at a disadvantage

Supporting ideas

The use of the word *states* in the question means that the answer is explicitly stated in the passage. To answer the question, find the stated information. Lines 32–33 show that the studies ignore allocation problem*s because of analysts' inherent preferences for the simple model of perfect competition.*

A The passage does not discuss optimum allocation.
B Correct. In lines 32–33, the author attributes the overlooking of imbalances to analysts' preferences for a simplified model.
C The content of market statistics is not discussed in the passage.
D The author does not suggest that the analysts have rejected criticism of their methods or have willfully overlooked imbalances in response to such criticism.
E The author believes that such a rationing mechanism exists, but does not think it is the reason that financial studies ignore allocation problems.

The correct answer is B.

137. The author's main point is argued by

(A) giving examples that support a conventional generalization
(B) showing that the view opposite to the author's is self-contradictory
(C) criticizing the presuppositions of a proposed plan
(D) showing that omissions in a theoretical description make it inapplicable in certain cases
(E) demonstrating that an alternative hypothesis more closely fits the data

Logical structure

To answer a question about structure, look at the entire passage. The first sentence of the passage illustrates this author's approach: The author provides a theoretical description (*The function of capital markets is to facilitate an exchange of funds among all participants)* that is followed by a practical disclaimer (*yet in practice*.) The second paragraph shows why minority communities are a practical exception to the theoretical rule, and the final paragraph explains why this exception is typically omitted from consideration.

A The passage depends on one extended example only (minority communities) rather than depending on multiple examples; the passage argues against the conventional generalization that capital markets are equal.
B Paragraph 3 reveals the flaws of the opposing view, but none of them are self-contradictory.
C The passage reveals a problem; it does not propose a plan.
D Correct. This statement accurately describes the author's approach.
E No alternative hypothesis is offered.

The correct answer is D.

138. A difference in which of the following would be an example of inequality in transaction costs as alluded to in lines 44–48?

(A) Maximum amounts of loans extended by a bank to businesses in different areas
(B) Fees charged to large and small investors for purchasing stocks
(C) Prices of similar goods offered in large and small stores in an area
(D) Stipends paid to different attorneys for preparing legal suits for damages
(E) Exchange rates in dollars for currencies of different countries

Application

To answer this question, begin by looking at the discussion of transaction costs in lines 44–45. Transaction costs are the costs incurred when buying or selling assets; in this case, they are the costs incurred in buying or selling financial instruments such as stocks. Inequality arises if transaction costs are not *equally known and equally divided among all community members*. Look at each answer choice to see whether it is an example of such inequality.

A The maximum amount of a loan is not a transaction cost.
B Correct. Fees for purchasing stocks are transaction costs; different fees for large and small investors are an appropriate example of inequality in transaction costs.
C Prices of goods are not transaction costs.
D Stipends paid to attorneys are not transaction costs for financial instruments.
E Exchange rates are not transaction costs for financial instruments.

The correct answer is B.

139. Which of the following can be inferred about minority communities on the basis of the passage?

(A) They provide a significant portion of the funds that become available for investment in the financial market.
(B) They are penalized by the tax system, which increases the inequality of the distribution of income between investors and wage earners.
(C) They do not receive the share of the amount of funds available for investment that would be expected according to traditional financial-market analysis.
(D) They are not granted governmental subsidies to assist in underwriting the cost of economic development.
(E) They provide the same access to alternative sources of credit to finance businesses as do majority communities.

Inference

An inference involves making a connection between different statements. The passage opens by stating a tenet of conventional theory: capital markets exist *to facilitate an exchange of funds among all participants* (lines 1–2). The second paragraph opens with the statement that for minority communities, capital markets *do not provide access to the aggregate flow of funds.* Specifically, the system does not *generate the credit or investment vehicles needed ... for underwriting economic development in minority areas* (lines 12–14).

Given these statements, it is reasonable to make the connection that minority communities receive a lower level of funds than conventional theory would predict.

A The passage does not discuss the origins of funds available for investment.
B The passage does not discuss the tax system.
C Correct. Traditional analysis suggests that funds are exchanged among all participants, but minority groups do not have the same access or receive the same funds that majority groups do.
D The passage does not discuss governmental subsidies.
E The passage does not suggest that equal access to any sources of credit is provided by minority communities.

The correct answer is C.

140. According to the passage, a questionable assumption of the conventional theory about the operation of financial markets is that

(A) creditworthiness as determined by lenders is a factor determining market access
(B) market structure and market dynamics depend on income distribution
(C) a scarcity of alternative sources of funds would result from taking socioeconomic factors into consideration
(D) those who engage in financial-market transactions are perfectly well informed about the market
(E) inequalities in income distribution are increased by the functioning of the financial market

Supporting ideas

The phrase *according to the passage* indicates that the answer is explicitly stated in the passage. The third paragraph discusses problems with conventional financial analysis. Lines 33–43 outline some of the assumptions involved in the conventional theory; the author considers all these assumptions questionable. Compare this information with the answer choices to find the correct answer.

A The author does not question the definition of creditworthiness by lenders.
B Lines 33–36 indicate that market structure, market dynamics, and income distribution are largely ignored by the conventional theory.
C The passage does not mention any assumption about the consequences of considering socioeconomic factors.
D Correct. Market participants are assumed to have *perfect foresight* (line 39); transaction costs are *equally known* (line 46). The author finds these assumptions questionable; the author points out in lines 4–5 that people *have varying degrees of market strength in terms of information.*
E The conventional theory pays little attention to income distribution (lines 33–36).

The correct answer is D.

141. According to the passage, analysts have conventionally tended to view those who participate in financial markets as

(A) judging investment preferences in terms of the good of society as a whole
(B) influencing the allocation of funds through prior ownership of certain kinds of assets
(C) varying in market power with respect to one another
(D) basing judgments about future events mainly on chance
(E) having equal opportunities to engage in transactions

Supporting ideas

Because the question uses the phrase *according to the passage,* look for an answer that is explicitly stated in the passage. The third paragraph discusses the views of conventional analysts. Lines 41–44 point out that each individual is assumed to have *the same opportunity* to make transactions.

A Criteria for investing are not discussed in the passage.
B Allocation of funds, discussed in the second paragraph, is not linked to analysts' views.
C Market participants are viewed as *homogeneous* (lines 37–38) and having the *same access to the market* (lines 41–42).
D Market participants are assumed to have *perfect foresight* (line 39), so they are acting on the basis of knowledge, not chance.
E **Correct.** Analysts assume that all market participants have the same access to the market and the same opportunity to engage in transactions (lines 41–44).

The correct answer is E.

8.0 Critical Reasoning

8.0 Critical Reasoning

Critical reasoning questions appear in the Verbal section of the GMAT® exam. The Verbal section uses multiple-choice questions to measure your ability to read and comprehend written material, to reason and to evaluate arguments, and to correct written material to conform to standard written English. Because the Verbal section includes content from a variety of topics, you may be generally familiar with some of the material; however, neither the passages nor the questions assume knowledge of the topics discussed. Critical reasoning questions are intermingled with reading comprehension and sentence correction questions throughout the Verbal section of the exam.

You will have 75 minutes to complete the Verbal section, or about 1 3/4 minutes to answer each question. Although critical reasoning questions are based on written passages, these passages are shorter than reading comprehension passages. They tend to be less than 100 words in length and generally are followed by one or two questions. For these questions, you will see a split computer screen. The written passage will remain visible as each question associated with that passage appears in turn on the screen. You will see only one question at a time.

Critical reasoning questions are designed to test the reasoning skills involved in (1) making arguments, (2) evaluating arguments, and (3) formulating or evaluating a plan of action. The materials on which questions are based are drawn from a variety of sources. The GMAT® test does not suppose any familiarity with the subject matter of those materials.

In these questions, you are to analyze the situation on which each question is based, and then select the answer choice that most appropriately answers the question. Begin by reading the passages carefully, then reading the five answer choices. If the correct answer is not immediately obvious to you, see whether you can eliminate some of the wrong answers. Reading the passage a second time may be helpful in illuminating subtleties that were not immediately evident.

Answering critical reasoning questions requires no specialized knowledge of any particular field; you don't have to have knowledge of the terminology and conventions of formal logic. The sample critical reasoning questions in this chapter illustrate the variety of topics the exam may cover, the kinds of questions it may ask, and the level of analysis it requires.

The following pages describe what critical reasoning questions are designed to measure and present the directions that will precede questions of this type. Sample questions and explanations of the correct answers follow.

8.1 What Is Measured

Critical reasoning questions are designed to provide one measure of your ability to reason effectively in the following areas:

- **Argument construction**
  Questions in this category may ask you to recognize such things as the basic structure of an argument, properly drawn conclusions, underlying assumptions, well-supported explanatory hypotheses, and parallels between structurally similar arguments.
- **Argument evaluation**
  These questions may ask you to analyze a given argument and to recognize such things as factors that would strengthen or weaken the given argument; reasoning errors committed in making that argument; and aspects of the method by which the argument proceeds.
- **Formulating and evaluating a plan of action**
  This type of question may ask you to recognize such things as the relative appropriateness, effectiveness, or efficiency of different plans of action; factors that would strengthen or weaken the prospects of success of a proposed plan of action; and assumptions underlying a proposed plan of action.

8.2 Test-Taking Strategies for Critical Reasoning Questions

1. **Read very carefully the set of statements on which a question is based.**

   Pay close attention to—

   - what is put forward as factual information;
   - what is not said but necessarily follows from what is said;
   - what is claimed to follow from facts that have been put forward; and
   - how well substantiated are any claims that a particular conclusion follows from the facts that have been put forward.

   In reading the arguments, it is important to pay attention to the logical reasoning used; the actual truth of statements portrayed as fact is not important.

2. **Identify the conclusion.**
   The conclusion does not necessarily come at the end of the text; it may come somewhere in the middle or even at the beginning. Be alert to clues in the text that an argument follows logically from another statement or statements in the text.

3. **Determine exactly what each question asks.**
   You might find it helpful to read the question first, before reading the material on which it is based; don't assume that you know what you will be asked about an argument. An argument may have obvious flaws, and one question may ask you to detect them. But another question may direct you to select the one answer choice that does NOT describe a flaw in the argument.

4. **Read all the answer choices carefully.**
   Do not assume that a given answer is the best without first reading all the choices.

8.3 The Directions

These are the directions you will see for critical reasoning questions when you take the GMAT® test. If you read them carefully and understand them clearly before going to sit for the exam, you will not need to spend too much time reviewing them when you are at the test center and the exam is underway.

For this question, select the best of the answer choices given.

8.4 Critical Reasoning Sample Questions

For these questions, select the best of the answer choices given.

1. Some economists view the Kennedy–Johnson tax cut of 1964, which radically reduced corporate and individual taxes, as the impetus for the substantial prosperity enjoyed by the United States in the late 1960's and early 1970's.

   Which of the following, if true, would most weaken the claim that the tax cut of 1964 was the impetus for economic prosperity?

   (A) Modernized, more productive factories were built in the late 1960's as a result of the funds made available by the tax cut.
   (B) Improved economic conditions in Western Europe and Japan resulted in substantially increased demand for United States manufactured goods in the late 1960's.
   (C) The tax cut of 1964 contained regulations concerning tax shelters that prompted investors to transfer their savings to more economically productive investments.
   (D) Personal income after taxes rose in the years following 1964.
   (E) In the late 1960's, unemployment was relatively low compared with the early 1960's.

2. In order to increase profits during a prolonged slowdown in sales, the largest manufacturers of automobiles in the United States have instituted record-setting price increases on all their models. The manufacturers believe that this strategy will succeed, even though it is inconsistent with the normal relationship between price and demand.

   The manufacturers' plan to increase profits relies on which of the following assumptions?

   (A) Automobile manufacturers will, of necessity, raise prices whenever they introduce a new model.
   (B) The smaller automobile manufacturers will continue to take away a large percentage of business from the largest manufacturers.
   (C) The increased profit made on cars sold will more than compensate for any decline in sales caused by the price increases.
   (D) New safety restraints that will soon become mandatory for all new cars will not be very costly for manufacturers to install.
   (E) Low financing and extended warranties will attract many price-conscious consumers.

3. "Life expectancy" is the average age at death of the entire live-born population. In the middle of the nineteenth century, life expectancy in North America was 40 years, whereas now it is nearly 80 years. Thus, in those days, people must have been considered old at an age that we now consider the prime of life.

   Which of the following, if true, undermines the argument above?

   (A) In the middle of the nineteenth century, the population of North America was significantly smaller than it is today.
   (B) Most of the gains in life expectancy in the last 150 years have come from reductions in the number of infants who die in their first year of life.
   (C) Many of the people who live to an advanced age today do so only because of medical technology that was unknown in the nineteenth century.
   (D) The proportion of people who die in their seventies is significantly smaller today than is the proportion of people who die in their eighties.
   (E) More people in the middle of the nineteenth century engaged regularly in vigorous physical activity than do so today.

4. From June through August 1987, Premiere Airlines had the best on-time service of 10 United States airlines. From January through March 1988, Premiere Airlines had the worst on-time service of the 10 airlines. The on-time performance ranking of the other nine airlines relative to each other remained unchanged.

Which of the following, if true, would most contribute to an explanation of the facts above?

(A) Although Premiere Airlines only revoked its policy of routinely holding flights for late passengers in the fall of 1987, the other nine airlines never had that policy.

(B) Premiere Airlines reduced its business by 10 percent when it raised its rates in the fall of 1987 to compensate for rising gasoline costs.

(C) Premiere Airlines bought five new planes in the fall of 1987 that proved to have fewer mechanical problems than the ones they replaced.

(D) Premiere Airlines serves New England, which has heavy winter snowfalls, whereas the other airlines do most of their business in warmer regions of the country.

(E) Although all 10 airlines strive to keep their flights on schedule, overcrowded airports increased flight delays for all 10 airlines in January 1988 as compared with June 1987.

5. Homeowners aged 40 to 50 are more likely to purchase ice cream and are more likely to purchase it in large amounts than are members of any other demographic group. The popular belief that teenagers eat more ice cream than adults must, therefore, be false.

The argument is flawed primarily because the author_____.

(A) fails to distinguish between purchasing and consuming

(B) does not supply information about homeowners in age groups other than 40 to 50

(C) depends on popular belief rather than on documented research findings

(D) does not specify the precise amount of ice cream purchased by any demographic group

(E) discusses ice cream rather than more nutritious and healthful foods

6. Not all life depends on energy from sunlight. Microbial life has been found in bedrock more than five kilometers below the surface of the Earth, and bacteria have been found on the deep ocean floor feeding on hydrogen and other gases rising from the interior of the Earth through vents in the ocean floor.

The statements above, if true, best support which of the following as a conclusion?

(A) The location in the bedrock where microbial life was found was not near a system of volcanic vents through which hydrogen and other gases rose from the interior of the Earth.

(B) Bacteria are able to exist at the molten center of the Earth.

(C) A thorough survey of a planet's surface is insufficient to establish beyond a doubt that the planet contains no life.

(D) Life probably exists on Sun-orbiting comets, which are cold agglomerations of space dust and frozen gases.

(E) Finding bacterial remains in coal and oil would establish that the bacteria had been feeding on substances that had not been produced from the energy of sunlight.

7. A company is considering changing its policy concerning daily working hours. Currently, this company requires all employees to arrive at work at 8 a.m. The proposed policy would permit each employee to decide when to arrive—from as early as 6 a.m. to as late as 11 a.m.

The adoption of this policy would be most likely to decrease employees' productivity if the employees' job functions required them to _____.

(A) work without interruption from other employees

(B) consult at least once a day with employees from other companies

(C) submit their work for a supervisor's eventual approval

(D) interact frequently with each other throughout the entire workday

(E) undertake projects that take several days to complete

8. The amount of time it takes for most of a worker's occupational knowledge and skills to become obsolete has been declining because of the introduction of advanced manufacturing technology (AMT). Given the rate at which AMT is currently being introduced in manufacturing, the average worker's old skills become obsolete and new skills are required within as little as five years.

Which of the following plans, if feasible, would allow a company to prepare most effectively for the rapid obsolescence of skills described above?

(A) The company will develop a program to offer selected employees the opportunity to receive training six years after they were originally hired.
(B) The company will increase its investment in AMT every year for a period of at least five years.
(C) The company will periodically survey its employees to determine how the introduction of AMT has affected them.
(D) Before the introduction of AMT, the company will institute an educational program to inform its employees of the probable consequences of the introduction of AMT.
(E) The company will ensure that it can offer its employees any training necessary for meeting their job requirements.

9. <u>Mayor</u>: In each of the past five years, the city has cut school funding and each time school officials complained that the cuts would force them to reduce expenditures for essential services. But each time, only expenditures for nonessential services were actually reduced. So school officials can implement further cuts without reducing any expenditures for essential services.

Which of the following, if true, most strongly supports the mayor's conclusion?

(A) The city's schools have always provided essential services as efficiently as they have provided nonessential services.
(B) Sufficient funds are currently available to allow the city's schools to provide some nonessential services.
(C) Price estimates quoted to the city's schools for the provision of nonessential services have not increased substantially since the most recent school-funding cut.
(D) Few influential city administrators support the funding of costly nonessential services in the city's schools.
(E) The city's school officials rarely exaggerate the potential impact of threatened funding cuts.

10. <u>Advertisement</u>: For sinus pain, three out of four hospitals give their patients Novex. So when you want the most effective painkiller for sinus pain, Novex is the one to choose.

Which of the following, if true, most seriously undermines the advertisement's argument?

(A) Some competing brands of painkillers are intended to reduce other kinds of pain in addition to sinus pain.
(B) Many hospitals that do not usually use Novex will do so for those patients who cannot tolerate the drug the hospitals usually use.
(C) Many drug manufacturers increase sales of their products to hospitals by selling these products to the hospitals at the lowest price the manufacturers can afford.
(D) Unlike some competing brands of painkillers, Novex is available from pharmacies without a doctor's prescription.
(E) In clinical trials Novex has been found to be more effective than competing brands of painkillers that have been on the market longer than Novex.

11. A report that many apples contain a cancer-causing preservative called Alar apparently had little effect on consumers. Few consumers planned to change their apple-buying habits as a result of the report. Nonetheless, sales of apples in grocery stores fell sharply in March, a month after the report was issued.

Which of the following, if true, best explains the reason for the apparent discrepancy described above?

(A) In March, many grocers removed apples from their shelves in order to demonstrate concern about their customers' health.
(B) Because of a growing number of food-safety warnings, consumers in March were indifferent to such warnings.
(C) The report was delivered on television and also appeared in newspapers.
(D) The report did not mention that any other fruit contains Alar, although the preservative is used on other fruit.
(E) Public health officials did not believe that apples posed a health threat because only minute traces of Alar were present in affected apples.

12. Cable-television spokesperson: Subscriptions to cable television are a bargain in comparison to "free" television. Remember that "free" television is not really free. It is consumers, in the end, who pay for the costly advertising that supports "free" television.

Which of the following, if true, is most damaging to the position of the cable-television spokesperson?

(A) Consumers who do not own television sets are less likely to be influenced in their purchasing decisions by television advertising than are consumers who own television sets.
(B) Subscriptions to cable television include access to some public-television channels, which do not accept advertising.
(C) For locations with poor television reception, cable television provides picture quality superior to that provided by free television.
(D) There is as much advertising on many cable-television channels as there is on "free" television channels.
(E) Cable-television subscribers can choose which channels they wish to receive, and the fees.

13. Wood smoke contains dangerous toxins that cause changes in human cells. Because wood smoke presents such a high health risk, legislation is needed to regulate the use of open-air fires and wood-burning stoves.

Which of the following, if true, provides the most support for the argument above?

(A) The amount of dangerous toxins contained in wood smoke is much less than the amount contained in an equal volume of automobile exhaust.
(B) Within the jurisdiction covered by the proposed legislation, most heating and cooking is done with oil or natural gas.
(C) Smoke produced by coal-burning stoves is significantly more toxic than smoke from wood-burning stoves.
(D) No significant beneficial effect on air quality would result if open-air fires were banned within the jurisdiction covered by the proposed legislation.
(E) In valleys where wood is used as the primary heating fuel, the concentration of smoke results in poor air quality.

14. Within 20 years it will probably be possible to identify the genetic susceptibility an individual may have toward any particular disease. Eventually, effective strategies will be discovered to counteract each such susceptibility. Once these effective strategies are found, therefore, the people who follow them will never get sick.

The argument above is based on which of the following assumptions?

(A) For every disease there is only one strategy that can prevent its occurrence.
(B) In the future, genetics will be the only medical specialty of any importance.
(C) All human sicknesses are in part the result of individuals' genetic susceptibilities.
(D) All humans are genetically susceptible to some diseases.
(E) People will follow medical advice when they are convinced that it is effective.

15. A researcher studying drug addicts found that, on average, they tend to manipulate other people a great deal more than nonaddicts do. The researcher concluded that people who frequently manipulate other people are likely to become addicts.

Which of the following, if true, most seriously weakens the researcher's conclusion?

(A) After becoming addicted to drugs, drug addicts learn to manipulate other people as a way of obtaining drugs.
(B) When they are imprisoned, drug addicts often use their ability to manipulate other people to obtain better living conditions.
(C) Some nonaddicts manipulate other people more than some addicts do.
(D) People who are likely to become addicts exhibit unusual behavior patterns other than frequent manipulation of other people.
(E) The addicts that the researcher studied were often unsuccessful in obtaining what they wanted when they manipulated other people.

16. In Swartkans territory, archaeologists discovered charred bone fragments dating back one million years. Analysis of the fragments, which came from a variety of animals, showed that they had been heated to temperatures no higher than those produced in experimental campfires made from branches of white stinkwood, the most common tree around Swartkans.

Which of the following, if true, would, together with the information above, provide the best basis for the claim that the charred bone fragments are evidence of the use of fire by early hominids?

(A) The white stinkwood tree is used for building material by the present-day inhabitants of Swartkans.
(B) Forest fires can heat wood to a range of temperatures that occur in campfires.
(C) The bone fragments were fitted together by the archaeologists to form the complete skeletons of several animals.
(D) Apart from the Swartkans discovery, there is reliable evidence that early hominids used fire as many as 500,000 years ago.
(E) The bone fragments were found in several distinct layers of limestone that contained primitive cutting tools known to have been used by early hominids.

17. A conservation group in the United States is trying to change the long-standing image of bats as frightening creatures. The group contends that bats are feared and persecuted solely because they are shy animals that are active only at night.

Which of the following, if true, would cast the most serious doubt on the accuracy of the group's contention?

(A) Bats are steadily losing natural roosting places such as caves and hollow trees and are thus turning to more developed areas for roosting.
(B) Bats are the chief consumers of nocturnal insects and thus can help make their hunting territory more pleasant for humans.
(C) Bats are regarded as frightening creatures not only in the United States but also in Europe, Africa, and South America.
(D) Raccoons and owls are shy and active only at night, yet they are not generally feared and persecuted.
(E) People know more about the behavior of other greatly feared animal species, such as lions, alligators, and snakes, than they do about the behavior of bats.

18. Opponents of laws that require automobile drivers and passengers to wear seat belts argue that in a free society people have the right to take risks as long as the people do not harm others as a result of taking the risks. As a result, they conclude that it should be each person's decision whether or not to wear a seat belt.

Which of the following, if true, most seriously weakens the conclusion drawn above?

(A) Many new cars are built with seat belts that automatically fasten when someone sits in the front seat.

(B) Automobile insurance rates for all automobile owners are higher because of the need to pay for the increased injuries or deaths of people not wearing seat belts.

(C) Passengers in airplanes are required to wear seat belts during takeoffs and landings.

(D) The rate of automobile fatalities in states that do not have mandatory seat-belt laws is greater than the rate of fatalities in states that do have such laws.

(E) In automobile accidents, a greater number of passengers who do not wear seat belts are injured than are passengers who do wear seat belts.

19. Which of the following best completes the passage below?

People buy prestige when they buy a premium product. They want to be associated with something special. Mass-marketing techniques and price-reduction strategies should not be used because ____.

(A) affluent purchasers currently represent a shrinking portion of the population of all purchasers

(B) continued sales depend directly on the maintenance of an aura of exclusivity

(C) purchasers of premium products are concerned with the quality as well as with the price of the products

(D) expansion of the market niche to include a broader spectrum of consumers will increase profits

(E) manufacturing a premium brand is not necessarily more costly than manufacturing a standard brand of the same product

20. The number of people diagnosed as having a certain intestinal disease has dropped significantly in a rural county this year, as compared to last year. Health officials attribute this decrease entirely to improved sanitary conditions at water-treatment plants, which made for cleaner water this year and thus reduced the incidence of the disease.

Which of the following, if true, would most seriously weaken the health officials' explanation for the lower incidence of the disease?

(A) Many new water-treatment plants have been built in the last five years in the rural county.

(B) Bottled spring water has not been consumed in significantly different quantities by people diagnosed as having the intestinal disease, as compared to people who did not contract the disease.

(C) Because of a new diagnostic technique, many people who until this year would have been diagnosed as having the intestinal disease are now correctly diagnosed as suffering from intestinal ulcers.

(D) Because of medical advances this year, far fewer people who contract the intestinal disease will develop severe cases of the disease.

(E) The water in the rural county was brought up to the sanitary standards of the water in neighboring counties 10 years ago.

21. Rural households have more purchasing power than do urban or suburban households at the same income level, since some of the income urban and suburban households use for food and shelter can be used by rural households for other needs.

Which of the following inferences is best supported by the statement made above?

(A) The average rural household includes more people than does the average urban or suburban household.

(B) Rural households have lower food and housing costs than do either urban or suburban households.

(C) Suburban households generally have more purchasing power than do either rural or urban households.

(D) The median income of urban and suburban households is generally higher than that of rural households.

(E) All three types of households spend more of their income on housing than on all other purchases combined.

22. In Asia, where palm trees are nonnative, the trees' flowers have traditionally been pollinated by hand, which has kept palm fruit productivity unnaturally low. When weevils known to be efficient pollinators of palm flowers were introduced into Asia in 1980, palm fruit productivity increased—by up to 50 percent in some areas—but then decreased sharply in 1984.

    Which of the following statements, if true, would best explain the 1984 decrease in productivity?

    (A) Prices for palm fruit fell between 1980 and 1984 following the rise in production and a concurrent fall in demand.
    (B) Imported trees are often more productive than native trees because the imported ones have left behind their pests and diseases in their native lands.
    (C) Rapid increases in productivity tend to deplete trees of nutrients needed for the development of the fruit-producing female flowers.
    (D) The weevil population in Asia remained at approximately the same level between 1980 and 1984.
    (E) Prior to 1980 another species of insect pollinated the Asian palm trees, but not as efficiently as the species of weevil that was introduced in 1980.

23. With the emergence of biotechnology companies, it was feared that they would impose silence about proprietary results on their in-house researchers and their academic consultants. This constraint, in turn, would slow the development of biological science and engineering.

    Which of the following, if true, would tend to weaken most seriously the prediction of scientific secrecy described above?

    (A) Biotechnological research funded by industry has reached some conclusions that are of major scientific importance.
    (B) When the results of scientific research are kept secret, independent researchers are unable to build on those results.
    (C) Since the research priorities of biotechnology companies are not the same as those of academic institutions, the financial support of research by such companies distorts the research agenda.
    (D) To enhance the companies' standing in the scientific community, the biotechnology companies encourage employees to publish their results, especially results that are important.
    (E) Biotechnology companies devote some of their research resources to problems that are of fundamental scientific importance and that are not expected to produce immediate practical applications.

24. Guitar strings often go "dead"—become less responsive and bright in tone—after a few weeks of intense use. A researcher whose son is a classical guitarist hypothesized that dirt and oil, rather than changes in the material properties of the string, were responsible.

    Which of the following investigations is most likely to yield significant information that would help evaluate the researcher's hypothesis?

    (A) Determining whether a metal alloy is used to make the strings used by classical guitarists
    (B) Determining whether classical guitarists make their strings go dead faster than do folk guitarists
    (C) Determining whether identical lengths of string, of the same gauge, go dead at different rates when strung on various brands of guitars
    (D) Determining whether a dead string and a new string produce different qualities of sound
    (E) Determining whether smearing various substances on new guitar strings causes them to go dead

25. In recent years, many cabinetmakers have been winning acclaim as artists. But since furniture must be useful, cabinetmakers must exercise their craft with an eye to the practical utility of their product. For this reason, cabinetmaking is not art.

Which of the following is an assumption that supports drawing the conclusion above from the reason given for that conclusion?

(A) Some furniture is made to be placed in museums, where it will not be used by anyone.
(B) Some cabinetmakers are more concerned than others with the practical utility of the products they produce.
(C) Cabinetmakers should be more concerned with the practical utility of their products than they currently are.
(D) An object is not an art object if its maker pays attention to the object's practical utility.
(E) Artists are not concerned with the monetary value of their products.

26. Male bowerbirds construct elaborately decorated nests, or bowers. Basing their judgment on the fact that different local populations of bowerbirds of the same species build bowers that exhibit different building and decorative styles, researchers have concluded that the bowerbirds' building styles are a culturally acquired, rather than a genetically transmitted, trait.

Which of the following, if true, would most strengthen the conclusion drawn by the researchers?

(A) There are more common characteristics than there are differences among the bower-building styles of the local bowerbird population that has been studied most extensively.
(B) Young male bowerbirds are inept at bower-building and apparently spend years watching their elders before becoming accomplished in the local bower style.
(C) The bowers of one species of bowerbird lack the towers and ornamentation characteristic of the bowers of most other species of bowerbird.
(D) Bowerbirds are found only in New Guinea and Australia, where local populations of the birds apparently seldom have contact with one another.
(E) It is well known that the song dialects of some songbirds are learned rather than transmitted genetically.

27. A drug that is highly effective in treating many types of infection can, at present, be obtained only from the bark of the ibora, a tree that is quite rare in the wild. It takes the bark of 5,000 trees to make one kilogram of the drug. It follows, therefore, that continued production of the drug must inevitably lead to the ibora's extinction.

Which of the following, if true, most seriously weakens the argument above?

(A) The drug made from ibora bark is dispensed to doctors from a central authority.
(B) The drug made from ibora bark is expensive to produce.
(C) The leaves of the ibora are used in a number of medical products.
(D) The ibora can be propagated from cuttings and grown under cultivation.
(E) The ibora generally grows in largely inaccessible places.

28. Many breakfast cereals are fortified with vitamin supplements. Some of these cereals provide 100 percent of the recommended daily requirement of vitamins. Nevertheless, a well-balanced breakfast, including a variety of foods, is a better source of those vitamins than are such fortified breakfast cereals alone.

Which of the following, if true, would most strongly support the position above?

(A) In many foods, the natural combination of vitamins with other nutrients makes those vitamins more usable by the body than are vitamins added in vitamin supplements.
(B) People who regularly eat cereals fortified with vitamin supplements sometimes neglect to eat the foods in which the vitamins occur naturally.
(C) Foods often must be fortified with vitamin supplements because naturally occurring vitamins are removed during processing.
(D) Unprocessed cereals are naturally high in several of the vitamins that are usually added to fortified breakfast cereals.
(E) Cereals containing vitamin supplements are no harder to digest than similar cereals without added vitamins.

Questions 29–30 are based on the following:

In many corporations, employees are being replaced by automated equipment in order to save money. However, many workers who lose their jobs to automation will need government assistance to survive, and the same corporations that are laying people off will eventually pay for that assistance through increased taxes and unemployment insurance payments.

29. The author is arguing that _____.

(A) higher taxes and unemployment insurance payments will discourage corporations from automating
(B) replacing people through automation to reduce production costs will result in increases of other costs to corporations
(C) many workers who lose their jobs to automation will have to be retrained for new jobs
(D) corporations that are laying people off will eventually rehire many of them
(E) corporations will not save money by automating because people will be needed to run the new machines

30. Which of the following, if true, most strengthens the author's argument?

(A) Many workers who have already lost their jobs to automation have been unable to find new jobs.
(B) Many corporations that have failed to automate have seen their profits decline.
(C) Taxes and unemployment insurance are also paid by corporations that are not automating.
(D) Most of the new jobs created by automation pay less than the jobs eliminated by automation did.
(E) The initial investment in machinery for automation is often greater than the short-term savings in labor costs.

31. When a polygraph test is judged inconclusive, this is no reflection on the examinee. Rather, such a judgment means that the test has failed to show whether the examinee was truthful or untruthful. Nevertheless, employers will sometimes refuse to hire a job applicant because of an inconclusive polygraph test result.

Which of the following conclusions can most properly be drawn from the information above?

(A) Most examinees with inconclusive polygraph test results are in fact untruthful.
(B) Polygraph tests should not be used by employers in the consideration of job applicants.
(C) An inconclusive polygraph test result is sometimes unfairly held against the examinee.
(D) A polygraph test indicating that an examinee is untruthful can sometimes be mistaken.
(E) Some employers have refused to consider the results of polygraph tests when evaluating job applicants.

32. The technological conservatism of bicycle manufacturers is a reflection of the kinds of demand they are trying to meet. The only cyclists seriously interested in innovation and willing to pay for it are bicycle racers. Therefore, innovation in bicycle technology is limited by what authorities will accept as standard for purposes of competition in bicycle races.

Which of the following is an assumption made in drawing the conclusion above?

(A) The market for cheap, traditional bicycles cannot expand unless the market for high-performance competition bicycles expands.
(B) High-performance bicycles are likely to be improved more as a result of technological innovations developed in small workshops than as a result of technological innovations developed in major manufacturing concerns.

(C) Bicycle racers do not generate a strong demand for innovations that fall outside what is officially recognized as standard for purposes of competition.
(D) The technological conservatism of bicycle manufacturers results primarily from their desire to manufacture a product that can be sold without being altered to suit different national markets.
(E) The authorities who set standards for high-performance bicycle racing do not keep informed about innovative bicycle design.

33. Robot satellites relay important communications and identify weather patterns. Because the satellites can be repaired only in orbit, astronauts are needed to repair them. Without repairs, the satellites would eventually malfunction. Therefore, space flights carrying astronauts must continue.

Which of the following, if true, would most seriously weaken the argument above?

(A) Satellites falling from orbit because of malfunctions burn up in the atmosphere.
(B) Although satellites are indispensable in the identification of weather patterns, weather forecasters also make some use of computer projections to identify weather patterns.
(C) The government, responding to public pressure, has decided to cut the budget for space flights and put more money into social welfare programs.
(D) Repair of satellites requires heavy equipment, which adds to the amount of fuel needed to lift a spaceship carrying astronauts into orbit.
(E) Technical obsolescence of robot satellites makes repairing them more costly and less practical than sending new, improved satellites into orbit.

34. A company's two divisions performed with remarkable consistency over the past three years: in each of those years, the pharmaceuticals division has accounted for roughly 20 percent of dollar sales and 40 percent of profits, and the chemicals division for the balance.

Regarding the past three years, which of the following can properly be inferred from the statement above?

(A) Total dollar sales for each of the company's divisions have remained roughly constant.
(B) The pharmaceuticals division has faced stiffer competition in its markets than has the chemicals division.
(C) The chemicals division has realized lower profits per dollar of sales than has the pharmaceuticals division.
(D) The product mix offered by each of the company's divisions has remained unchanged.
(E) Highly profitable products accounted for a higher percentage of the chemicals division's sales than of the pharmaceuticals division's.

35. Advertisement: Today's customers expect high quality. Every advance in the quality of manufactured products raises customer expectations. The company that is satisfied with the current quality of its products will soon find that its customers are not. At MegaCorp, meeting or exceeding customer expectations is our goal.

Which of the following must be true on the basis of the statements in the advertisement above?

(A) MegaCorp's competitors will succeed in attracting customers only if those competitors adopt MegaCorp's goal as their own.
(B) A company that does not correctly anticipate the expectations of its customers is certain to fail in advancing the quality of its products.
(C) MegaCorp's goal is possible to meet only if continuing advances in product quality are possible.
(D) If a company becomes satisfied with the quality of its products, then the quality of its products is sure to decline.
(E) MegaCorp's customers are currently satisfied with the quality of its products.

36. Many companies now have employee assistance programs that enable employees, free of charge, to improve their physical fitness, reduce stress, and learn ways to stop smoking. These programs increase worker productivity, reduce absenteeism, and lessen insurance costs for employee health care. Therefore, these programs benefit the company as well as the employee.

Which of the following, if true, most significantly strengthens the conclusion above?

(A) Physical fitness programs are often the most popular services offered to employees.
(B) Studies have shown that training in stress management is not effective for many people.
(C) Regular exercise reduces people's risk of heart disease and provides them with increased energy.
(D) Physical injuries sometimes result from entering a strenuous physical fitness program too quickly.
(E) Employee assistance programs require companies to hire people to supervise the various programs offered.

Questions 37–38 are based on the following:

Companies O and P each have the same number of employees who work the same number of hours per week. According to records maintained by each company, the employees of Company O had fewer job-related accidents last year than did the employees of Company P. Therefore, employees of Company O are less likely to have job-related accidents than are employees of Company P.

37. Which of the following, if true, would most strengthen the conclusion above?

(A) Company P manufactures products that are more hazardous for workers to produce than does Company O.
(B) Company P holds more safety inspections than does Company O.
(C) Company P maintains a more modern infirmary than does Company O.
(D) Company O paid more for new job-related medical claims than did Company P.
(E) Company P provides more types of health-care benefits than does Company O.

38. Which of the following, if true, would most weaken the conclusion above?

(A) The employees of Company P lost more time at work due to job-related accidents than did the employees of Company O.
(B) Company P considered more types of accidents to be job-related than did Company O.
(C) The employees of Company P were sick more often than were the employees of Company O.
(D) Several employees of Company O each had more than one job-related accident.
(E) The majority of job-related accidents at Company O involved a single machine.

39. Last year the rate of inflation was 1.2 percent, but during the current year it has been 4 percent. We can conclude that inflation is on an upward trend and the rate will be still higher next year.

Which of the following, if true, most seriously weakens the conclusion above?

(A) The inflation figures were computed on the basis of a representative sample of economic data rather than all the available data.
(B) Last year a dip in oil prices brought inflation temporarily below its recent stable annual level of 4 percent.
(C) Increases in the pay of some workers are tied to the level of inflation, and at an inflation rate of 4 percent or above, these pay raises constitute a force causing further inflation.
(D) The 1.2 percent rate of inflation last year represented a 10-year low.
(E) Government intervention cannot affect the rate of inflation to any significant degree.

40. Offshore oil-drilling operations entail an unavoidable risk of an oil spill, but importing oil on tankers presently entails an even greater such risk per barrel of oil. Therefore, if we are to reduce the risk of an oil spill without curtailing our use of oil, we must invest more in offshore operations and import less oil on tankers.

Which of the following, if true, most seriously weakens the argument above?

(A) Tankers can easily be redesigned so that their use entails less risk of an oil spill.
(B) Oil spills caused by tankers have generally been more serious than those caused by offshore operations.
(C) The impact of offshore operations on the environment can be controlled by careful management.
(D) Offshore operations usually damage the ocean floor, but tankers rarely cause such damage.
(E) Importing oil on tankers is currently less expensive than drilling for it offshore.

41. Manufacturers of mechanical pencils make most of their profit on pencil leads rather than on the pencils themselves. The Write Company, which cannot sell its leads as cheaply as other manufacturers can, plans to alter the design of its mechanical pencil so that it will accept only a newly designed Write Company lead, which will be sold at the same price as the Write Company's current lead.

Which of the following, if true, most strongly supports the Write Company's projection that its plan will lead to an increase in its sales of pencil leads?

(A) First-time buyers of mechanical pencils tend to buy the least expensive mechanical pencils available.
(B) Annual sales of mechanical pencils are expected to triple over the next five years.
(C) A Write Company executive is studying ways to reduce the cost of manufacturing pencil leads.
(D) A rival manufacturer recently announced similar plans to introduce a mechanical pencil that would accept only the leads produced by that manufacturer.
(E) In extensive test marketing, mechanical-pencil users found the new Write Company pencil markedly superior to other mechanical pencils they had used.

42. <u>Mourdet Winery</u>: Danville Winery's new wine was introduced to compete with our most popular wine, which is sold in a distinctive tall, black bottle. Danville uses a similar bottle. Thus, it is likely that many customers intending to buy our wine will mistakenly buy theirs instead.

<u>Danville Winery</u>: Not so. The two bottles can be readily distinguished: the label on ours, but not on theirs, is gold colored.

Which of the following, if true, most undermines Danville Winery's response?

(A) Gold is the background color on the label of many of the wines produced by Danville Winery.
(B) When the bottles are viewed side by side, Danville Winery's bottle is perceptibly taller than Mourdet Winery's.
(C) Danville Winery, unlike Mourdet Winery, displays its wine's label prominently in advertisements.
(D) It is common for occasional purchasers to buy a bottle of wine on the basis of a general impression of the most obvious feature of the bottle.
(E) Many popular wines are sold in bottles of a standard design.

43. Which of the following best completes the passage below?

The computer industry's estimate that it loses millions of dollars when users illegally copy programs without paying for them is greatly exaggerated. Most of the illegal copying is done by people with no serious interest in the programs. Thus, the loss to the industry is quite small, because _____.

(A) many users who illegally copy programs never find any use for them
(B) most people who illegally copy programs would not purchase them even if purchasing them were the only way to obtain them
(C) even if the computer industry received all the revenue it claims to be losing, it would still be experiencing financial difficulties
(D) the total market value of all illegal copies is low in comparison to the total revenue of the computer industry
(E) the number of programs that are frequently copied illegally is low in comparison to the number of programs available for sale

44. In the last decade there has been a significant decrease in coffee consumption. During this same time, there has been increasing publicity about the caffeine in coffee's adverse long-term effects on health. Therefore, the decrease in coffee consumption must have been caused by consumers' awareness of the harmful effects of caffeine.

Which of the following, if true, most seriously calls into question the explanation above?

(A) On average, people consume 30 percent less coffee today than they did 10 years ago.
(B) Heavy coffee drinkers may have mild withdrawal symptoms, such as headaches, for a day or so after significantly decreasing their coffee consumption.
(C) Sales of specialty types of coffee have held steady as sales of regular brands have declined.
(D) The consumption of fruit juices and caffeine-free herbal teas has increased over the past decade.
(E) Coffee prices increased steadily in the past decade because of unusually severe frosts in coffee-growing nations.

45. Fewer families lose their houses because of major disasters such as fire or flood than because of a wage earner's illness that results in death or disability. Yet, whereas most mortgage companies require borrowers to carry insurance to protect against major disasters, they do not require insurance to protect against the death or disability of a wage earner.

Which of the following, if true, would contribute most to an explanation of the difference in insurance requirements?

(A) Some people are less aware of tragedies caused by major disasters than of those caused by the death or disability of a wage earner.
(B) Many people are made uncomfortable by having to consider the possibility of their own death or disability or that of a family member.
(C) Few wage earners are insured by their employers against a temporary loss of income resulting from disability.
(D) The value of a property to a mortgage company is not affected by the death or disability of a wage earner.
(E) Insuring against major disasters can be more costly than insuring against death or disability.

46. Which of the following best completes the passage below?

When the products of several competing suppliers are perceived by consumers to be essentially the same, classical economics predicts that price competition will reduce prices to the same minimal levels and all suppliers' profits to the same minimal levels. Therefore, if classical economics is true, and given suppliers' desire to make as much profit as possible, it should be expected that ______.

(A) in a crowded market widely differing prices will be charged for products that are essentially the same as each other

(B) as a market becomes less crowded as suppliers leave, the profits of the remaining suppliers will tend to decrease

(C) each supplier in a crowded market will try to convince consumers that its product differs significantly from its competitors' products.

(D) when consumers are unable to distinguish among the products in a crowded market, consumers will judge that the higher-priced products are of higher quality

(E) suppliers in crowded markets will have more incentive to reduce prices and thus increase sales than to introduce innovations that would distinguish their product from their competitors' products

47. Installing scrubbers in smokestacks and switching to cleaner-burning fuel are the two methods available to Northern Power for reducing harmful emissions from its plants. Scrubbers will reduce harmful emissions more than cleaner-burning fuels will. Therefore, by installing scrubbers, Northern Power will be doing the most that can be done to reduce harmful emissions from its plants.

Which of the following is an assumption on which the argument depends?

(A) Switching to cleaner-burning fuel will not be more expensive than installing scrubbers.

(B) Northern Power can choose from among various kinds of scrubbers, some of which are more effective than others.

(C) Northern Power is not necessarily committed to reducing harmful emissions from its plants.

(D) Harmful emissions from Northern Power's plants cannot be reduced more by using both methods together than by the installation of scrubbers alone.

(E) Aside from harmful emissions from the smoke-stacks of its plants, the activities of Northern Power do not cause significant air pollution.

48. Some anthropologists study modern-day societies of foragers in an effort to learn about our ancient ancestors who were also foragers. A flaw in this strategy is that forager societies are extremely varied. Indeed, any forager society with which anthropologists are familiar has had considerable contact with modern, non-forager societies.

Which of the following, if true, would most weaken the criticism made above of the anthropologists' strategy?

(A) All forager societies throughout history have had a number of important features in common that are absent from other types of societies.

(B) Most ancient forager societies either dissolved or made a transition to another way of life.

(C) All anthropologists study one kind or another of modern-day society.

(D) Many anthropologists who study modern-day forager societies do not draw inferences about ancient societies on the basis of their studies.

(E) Even those modern-day forager societies that have not had significant contact with modern societies are importantly different from ancient forager societies.

49. Contrary to earlier predictions, demand for sugarcane has not increased in recent years. Yet, even though prices and production amounts have also been stable during the last three years, sugarcane growers last year increased their profits by more than 10 percent over the previous year's level.

Any of the following statements, if true about last year, helps to explain the rise in profits EXCEPT:

(A) Many countries that are large consumers of sugarcane increased their production of sugarcane-based ethanol, yet their overall consumption of sugarcane decreased.

(B) Sugarcane growers have saved money on wages by switching from paying laborers an hourly wage to paying them by the amount harvested.

(C) The price of oil, the major energy source used by sugarcane growers in harvesting their crops, dropped by more than 20 percent.

(D) Many small sugarcane growers joined together to form an association of sugarcane producers and began to buy supplies at low group rates.

(E) Rainfall in sugarcane-growing regions was higher than it had been during the previous year, allowing the growers to save money on expensive artificial irrigation.

50. If the county continues to collect residential trash at current levels, landfills will soon be overflowing and parkland will need to be used in order to create more space. Charging each household a fee for each pound of trash it puts out for collection will induce residents to reduce the amount of trash they create; this charge will therefore protect the remaining county parkland.

Which of the following is an assumption made in drawing the conclusion above?

(A) Residents will reduce the amount of trash they put out for collection by reducing the number of products they buy.
(B) The collection fee will not significantly affect the purchasing power of most residents, even if their households do not reduce the amount of trash they put out.
(C) The collection fee will not induce residents to dump their trash in the parklands illegally.
(D) The beauty of county parkland is an important issue for most of the county's residents.
(E) Landfills outside the county's borders could be used as dumping sites for the county's trash.

51. Biometric access-control systems—those using fingerprints, voiceprints, and so forth, to regulate admittance to restricted areas—work by degrees of similarity, not by identity. After all, even the same finger will rarely leave exactly identical prints. Such systems can be adjusted to minimize refusals of access to legitimate access-seekers. Such adjustments, however, increase the likelihood of admitting impostors.

Which of the following conclusions is most strongly supported by the information above?

(A) If a biometric access-control system were made to work by identity, it would not produce any correct admittance decisions.
(B) If a biometric access-control system reliably prevents impostors from being admitted, it will sometimes turn away legitimate access-seekers.
(C) Biometric access-control systems are appropriate only in situations in which admittance of impostors is less of a problem than is mistaken refusal of access.
(D) No biometric access-control systems—based, for example, on numerical codes—are less likely than biometric ones to admit impostors.
(E) Anyone choosing an access-control system should base the choice solely on the ratio of false refusals to false admittances.

52. Although computers can enhance people's ability to communicate, computer games are a cause of underdeveloped communication skills in children. After-school hours spent playing computer games are hours not spent talking with people. Therefore, children who spend all their spare time playing these games have less experience in interpersonal communication than other children have.

The argument depends on which of the following assumptions?

(A) Passive activities such as watching television and listening to music do not hinder the development of communication skills in children.
(B) Most children have other opportunities, in addition to after-school hours, in which they can choose whether to play computer games or to interact with other people.
(C) Children who do not spend all their after-school hours playing computer games spend at least some of that time talking with other people.
(D) Formal instruction contributes little or nothing to children's acquisition of communication skills.
(E) The mental skills developed through playing computer games do not contribute significantly to children's intellectual development.

53. One variety of partially biodegradable plastic beverage container is manufactured from small bits of plastic bound together by a degradable bonding agent such as cornstarch. Since only the bonding agent degrades, leaving the small bits of plastic, no less plastic refuse per container is produced when such containers are discarded than when comparable nonbiodegradable containers are discarded.

Which of the following, if true, most strengthens the argument above?

(A) Both partially biodegradable and non-biodegradable plastic beverage containers can be crushed completely flat by refuse compactors.
(B) The partially biodegradable plastic beverage containers are made with more plastic than comparable nonbiodegradable ones in order to compensate for the weakening effect of the bonding agents.
(C) Many consumers are ecology-minded and prefer to buy a product sold in partially biodegradable plastic beverage containers rather than in nonbiodegradable containers, even if the price is higher.
(D) The manufacturing process for partially biodegradable plastic beverage containers results in less plastic waste than the manufacturing process for non-biodegradable plastic beverage containers.
(E) Technological problems with recycling currently prevent the reuse as food or beverage containers of the plastic from either type of plastic beverage container.

54. Most employees in the computer industry move from company to company, changing jobs several times in their careers. However, Summit Computers is known throughout the industry for retaining its employees. Summit credits its success in retaining employees to its informal, nonhierarchical work environment.

Which of the following, if true, most strongly supports Summit's explanation of its success in retaining employees?

(A) Some people employed in the computer industry change jobs if they become bored with their current projects.
(B) A hierarchical work environment hinders the cooperative exchange of ideas that computer industry employees consider necessary for their work.
(C) Many of Summit's senior employees had previously worked at only one other computer company.
(D) In a nonhierarchical work environment, people avoid behavior that might threaten group harmony and thus avoid discussing with their colleagues any dissatisfaction they might have with their jobs.
(E) The cost of living near Summit is relatively low compared to areas in which some other computer companies are located.

55. Low-income families are often unable to afford as much child care as they need. One government program would award low-income families a refund on the income taxes they pay of as much as $1,000 for each child under age four. This program would make it possible for all low-income families with children under age four to obtain more child care than they otherwise would have been able to afford.

Which of the following, if true, most seriously calls into question the claim that the program would make it possible for all low-income families to obtain more child care?

(A) The average family with children under age four spends more than $1,000 a year on child care.
(B) Some low-income families in which one of the parents is usually available to care for children under age four may not want to spend their income tax refund on child care.
(C) The reduction in government revenues stemming from the income tax refund will necessitate cuts in other government programs, such as grants for higher education.
(D) Many low-income families with children under age four do not pay any income taxes because their total income is too low to be subject to such taxes.
(E) Income taxes have increased substantially over the past 20 years, reducing the money that low-income families have available to spend on child care.

56. Social scientists are underrepresented on the advisory councils of the National Institutes of Health (NIH). Since these councils advise NIH directors and recommend policy, the underrepresentation of social scientists results in a relative lack of NIH financial support for research in the social sciences.

If the statements above are correct, they most strongly support which of the following?

(A) A significant increase in the size of NIH advisory councils would be required in order to increase the representation of social scientists on these councils.
(B) A significant increase in the representation of social scientists on NIH advisory councils would result in an increase in NIH funding for social science research.
(C) A significant increase in funding for social science research would result in improved policy recommendations to NIH directors.
(D) A significant increase in funding for the training of social scientists would result in an increase in the number of social scientists on NIH advisory councils.
(E) A significant increase in the representation of social scientists on NIH advisory councils would have to precede any increase in the number of NIH directors who are social scientists.

57. Among the more effective kinds of publicity that publishers can get for a new book is to have excerpts of it published in a high-circulation magazine soon before the book is published. The benefits of such excerption include not only a sure increase in sales but also a fee paid by the magazine to the book's publisher.

Which of the following conclusions is best supported by the information above?

(A) The number of people for whom seeing an excerpt of a book in a magazine provides an adequate substitute for reading the whole book is smaller than the number for whom the excerpt stimulates a desire to read the book.
(B) Because the financial advantage of excerpting a new book in a magazine usually accrues to the book's publisher, magazine editors are unwilling to publish excerpts from new books.
(C) In calculating the total number of copies that a book has sold, publishers include sales of copies of magazines that featured an excerpt of the book.
(D) The effectiveness of having excerpts of a book published in a magazine, measured in terms of increased sales of a book, is proportional to the circulation of the magazine in which the excerpts are published.
(E) Books that are suitable for excerpting in high-circulation magazines sell more copies than books that are not suitable for excerpting.

58. Insurance Company X is considering issuing a new policy to cover services required by elderly people who suffer from diseases that afflict the elderly. Premiums for the policy must be low enough to attract customers. Therefore, Company X is concerned that the income from the policies would not be sufficient to pay for the claims that would be made.

Which of the following strategies would be most likely to minimize Company X's losses on the policies?

(A) Attracting middle-aged customers unlikely to submit claims for benefits for many years
(B) Insuring only those individuals who did not suffer any serious diseases as children
(C) Including a greater number of services in the policy than are included in other policies of lower cost
(D) Insuring only those individuals who were rejected by other companies for similar policies
(E) Insuring only those individuals who are wealthy enough to pay for the medical services

59. To prevent some conflicts of interest, Congress could prohibit high-level government officials from accepting positions as lobbyists for three years after such officials leave government service. One such official concluded, however, that such a prohibition would be unfortunate because it would prevent high-level government officials from earning a livelihood for three years.

The official's conclusion logically depends on which of the following assumptions?

(A) Laws should not restrict the behavior of former government officials.
(B) Lobbyists are typically people who have previously been high-level government officials.
(C) Low-level government officials do not often become lobbyists when they leave government service.
(D) High-level government officials who leave government service are capable of earning a livelihood only as lobbyists.
(E) High-level government officials who leave government service are currently permitted to act as lobbyists for only three years.

Questions 60–61 are based on the following:

The fewer restrictions there are on the advertising of legal services, the more lawyers there are who advertise their services, and the lawyers who advertise a specific service usually charge less for that service than the lawyers who do not advertise. Therefore, if the state removes any of its current restrictions, such as the one against advertisements that do not specify fee arrangements, overall consumer legal costs will be lower than if the state retains its current restrictions.

60. If the statements above are true, which of the following must be true?

(A) Some lawyers who now advertise will charge more for specific services if they do not have to specify fee arrangements in the advertisements.
(B) More consumers will use legal services if there are fewer restrictions on the advertising of legal services.
(C) If the restriction against advertisements that do not specify fee arrangements is removed, more lawyers will advertise their services.
(D) If more lawyers advertise lower prices for specific services, some lawyers who do not advertise will also charge less than they currently charge for those services.
(E) If the only restrictions on the advertising of legal services were those that apply to every type of advertising, most lawyers would advertise their services.

61. Which of the following, if true, would most seriously weaken the argument concerning overall consumer legal costs?

(A) The state has recently removed some other restrictions that had limited the advertising of legal services.
(B) The state is unlikely to remove all the restrictions that apply solely to the advertising of legal services.
(C) Lawyers who do not advertise generally provide legal services of the same quality as those provided by lawyers who do advertise.
(D) Most lawyers who now specify fee arrangements in their advertisements would continue to do so even if the specification were not required.
(E) Most lawyers who advertise specific services do not lower their fees for those services when they begin to advertise.

62. During the Second World War, about 375,000 civilians died in the United States and about 408,000 members of the United States armed forces died overseas. On the basis of those figures, it can be concluded that it was not much more dangerous to be overseas in the armed forces during the Second World War than it was to stay at home as a civilian.

Which of the following would reveal most clearly the absurdity of the conclusion drawn above?

(A) Counting deaths among members of the armed forces who served in the United States in addition to deaths among members of the armed forces serving overseas
(B) Expressing the difference between the numbers of deaths among civilians and members of the armed forces as a percentage of the total number of deaths
(C) Separating deaths caused by accidents during service in the armed forces from deaths caused by combat injuries
(D) Comparing death rates per thousand members of each group rather than comparing total numbers of deaths
(E) Comparing deaths caused by accidents in the United States to deaths caused by combat in the armed forces

63. Even though most universities retain the royalties from faculty members' inventions, the faculty members retain the royalties from books and articles they write. Therefore, faculty members should retain the royalties from the educational computer software they develop.

The conclusion above would be more reasonably drawn if which of the following were inserted into the argument as an additional premise?

(A) Royalties from inventions are higher than royalties from educational software programs.
(B) Faculty members are more likely to produce educational software programs than inventions.
(C) Inventions bring more prestige to universities than do books and articles.
(D) In the experience of most universities, educational software programs are more marketable than are books and articles.
(E) In terms of the criteria used to award royalties, educational software programs are more nearly comparable to books and articles than to inventions.

64. Red blood cells in which the malarial-fever parasite resides are eliminated from a person's body after 120 days. Because the parasite cannot travel to a new generation of red blood cells, any fever that develops in a person more than 120 days after that person has moved to a malaria-free region is not due to the malarial parasite.

Which of the following, if true, most seriously weakens the conclusion above?

(A) The fever caused by the malarial parasite may resemble the fever caused by flu viruses.
(B) The anopheles mosquito, which is the principal insect carrier of the malarial parasite, has been eradicated in many parts of the world.
(C) Many malarial symptoms other than the fever, which can be suppressed with antimalarial medication, can reappear within 120 days after the medication is discontinued.
(D) In some cases, the parasite that causes malarial fever travels to cells of the spleen, which are less frequently eliminated from a person's body than are red blood cells.
(E) In any region infested with malaria-carrying mosquitoes, there are individuals who appear to be immune to malaria.

65. Most consumers do not get much use out of the sports equipment they purchase. For example, 17 percent of the adults in the United States own jogging shoes, but only 45 percent of the owners jog more than once a year, and only 17 percent jog more than once a week.

Which of the following, if true, casts the most doubt on the claim that most consumers get little use out of the sports equipment they purchase?

(A) Joggers are most susceptible to sports injuries during the first six months in which they jog.
(B) In surveys designed to elicit such information, joggers often exaggerate the frequency with which they jog.
(C) Many consumers purchase jogging shoes for use in activities other than jogging.
(D) Consumers who take up jogging often purchase athletic shoes that can be used in other sports.
(E) Joggers who jog more than once a week are often active participants in other sports as well.

66. Neither a rising standard of living nor balanced trade, by itself, establishes a country's ability to compete in the international marketplace. Both are required simultaneously since standards of living can rise because of growing trade deficits and trade can be balanced by means of a decline in a country's standard of living.

If the facts stated in the passage above are true, a proper test of a country's ability to be competitive is its ability to_____.

(A) balance its trade while its standard of living rises
(B) balance its trade while its standard of living falls
(C) increase trade deficits while its standard of living rises
(D) decrease trade deficits while its standard of living falls
(E) keep its standard of living constant while trade deficits rise

67. A greater number of newspapers are sold in Town S than in Town T. Therefore, the citizens of Town S are better informed about major world events than are the citizens of Town T.

Each of the following, if true, weakens the conclusion above EXCEPT:

(A) Town S has a larger population than Town T.
(B) Most citizens of Town T work in Town S and buy their newspapers there.
(C) The average citizen of Town S spends less time reading newspapers than does the average citizen of Town T.
(D) A weekly newspaper restricted to the coverage of local events is published in Town S.
(E) The average newsstand price of newspapers sold in Town S is lower than the average price of newspapers sold in Town T.

68. When hypnotized subjects are told that they are deaf and are then asked whether they can hear the hypnotist, they reply, "No." Some theorists try to explain this result by arguing that the selves of hypnotized subjects are dissociated into separate parts, and that the part that is deaf is dissociated from the part that replies.

Which of the following challenges indicates the most serious weakness in the attempted explanation described above?

(A) Why does the part that replies not answer, "Yes"?
(B) Why are the observed facts in need of any special explanation?
(C) Why do the subjects appear to accept the hypnotist's suggestion that they are deaf?
(D) Why do hypnotized subjects all respond the same way in the situation described?
(E) Why are the separate parts of the self the same for all subjects?

69. Excavation of the ancient city of Kourion on the island of Cyprus revealed a pattern of debris and collapsed buildings typical of towns devastated by earthquakes. Archaeologists have hypothesized that the destruction was due to a major earthquake known to have occurred near the island in AD 365.

Which of the following, if true, most strongly supports the archaeologists' hypothesis?

(A) Bronze ceremonial drinking vessels that are often found in graves dating from years preceding and following AD 365 were also found in several graves near Kourion.
(B) No coins minted after AD 365 were found in Kourion, but coins minted before that year were found in abundance.
(C) Most modern histories of Cyprus mention that an earthquake occurred near the island in AD 365.
(D) Several small statues carved in styles current in Cyprus in the century between AD 300 and 400 were found in Kourion.
(E) Stone inscriptions in a form of the Greek alphabet that was definitely used in Cyprus after AD 365 were found in Kourion.

Questions 70–71 are based on the following:

To protect certain fledgling industries, the government of Country Z banned imports of the types of products those industries were starting to make. As a direct result, the cost of those products to the buyers, several export-dependent industries in Z, went up, sharply limiting the ability of those industries to compete effectively in their export markets.

70. Which of the following can be most properly inferred from the passage about the products whose importation was banned?

(A) Those products had been cheaper to import than they were to make within Country Z's fledgling industries.
(B) Those products were ones that Country Z was hoping to export in its turn, once the fledgling industries matured.
(C) Those products used to be imported from just those countries to which Country Z's exports went.
(D) Those products had become more and more expensive to import, which resulted in a foreign trade deficit just before the ban.
(E) Those products used to be imported in very small quantities, but they were essential to Country Z's economy.

71. Which of the following conclusions about Country Z's adversely affected export-dependent industries is best supported by the passage?

(A) Profit margins in those industries were not high enough to absorb the rise in costs mentioned above.
(B) Those industries had to contend with the fact that other countries banned imports from Country Z.
(C) Those industries succeeded in expanding the domestic market for their products.
(D) Steps to offset rising materials costs by decreasing labor costs were taken in those industries.
(E) Those industries started to move into export markets that they had previously judged unprofitable.

72. Biological functions of many plants and animals vary in cycles that are repeated every 24 hours. It is tempting to suppose that alteration in the intensity of incident light is the stimulus that controls these daily biological rhythms. But there is much evidence to contradict this hypothesis.

Which of the following, if known, is evidence that contradicts the hypothesis stated in lines 2–5 above?

(A) Human body temperature varies throughout the day, with the maximum occurring in the late afternoon and the minimum in the morning.
(B) While some animals, such as the robin, are more active during the day, others, such as mice, show greater activity at night.
(C) When people move from one time zone to another, their daily biological rhythms adjust in a matter of days to the periods of sunlight and darkness in the new zone.

(D) Certain single-cell plants display daily biological rhythms even when the part of the cell containing the nucleus is removed.
(E) Even when exposed to constant light intensity around the clock, some algae display rates of photosynthesis that are much greater during daylight hours than at night.

73. The local board of education found that, because the current physics curriculum has little direct relevance to today's world, physics classes attracted few high school students. So to attract students to physics classes, the board proposed a curriculum that emphasizes principles of physics involved in producing and analyzing visual images.

Which of the following, if true, provides the strongest reason to expect that the proposed curriculum will be successful in attracting students?

(A) Several of the fundamental principles of physics are involved in producing and analyzing visual images.
(B) Knowledge of physics is becoming increasingly important in understanding the technology used in today's world.
(C) Equipment that a large producer of photographic equipment has donated to the high school could be used in the proposed curriculum.
(D) The number of students interested in physics today is much lower than the number of students interested in physics 50 years ago.
(E) In today's world the production and analysis of visual images is of major importance in communications, business, and recreation.

74. Small-business groups are lobbying to defeat proposed federal legislation that would substantially raise the federal minimum wage. This opposition is surprising since the legislation they oppose would, for the first time, exempt all small businesses from paying any minimum wage.

Which of the following, if true, would best explain the opposition of small-business groups to the proposed legislation?

(A) Under the current federal minimum-wage law, most small businesses are required to pay no less than the minimum wage to their employees.
(B) In order to attract workers, small companies must match the wages offered by their larger competitors, and these competitors would not be exempt under the proposed laws.
(C) The exact number of companies that are currently required to pay no less than the minimum wage but that would be exempt under the proposed laws is unknown.
(D) Some states have set their own minimum wages—in some cases, quite a bit above the level of the minimum wage mandated by current federal law—for certain key industries.
(E) Service companies make up the majority of small businesses and they generally employ more employees per dollar of revenues than do retail or manufacturing businesses.

75. Although aspirin has been proven to eliminate moderate fever associated with some illnesses, many doctors no longer routinely recommend its use for this purpose. A moderate fever stimulates the activity of the body's disease-fighting white blood cells and also inhibits the growth of many strains of disease-causing bacteria.

If the statements above are true, which of the following conclusions is most strongly supported by them?

(A) Aspirin, an effective painkiller, alleviates the pain and discomfort of many illnesses.
(B) Aspirin can prolong a patient's illness by eliminating moderate fever helpful in fighting some diseases.
(C) Aspirin inhibits the growth of white blood cells, which are necessary for fighting some illnesses.
(D) The more white blood cells a patient's body produces, the less severe the patient's illness will be.
(E) The focus of modern medicine is on inhibiting the growth of disease-causing bacteria within the body.

Questions 76–77 are based on the following:

Roland: The alarming fact is that 90 percent of the people in this country now report that they know someone who is unemployed.

Sharon: But a normal, moderate level of unemployment is 5 percent, with one out of 20 workers unemployed. So at any given time if a person knows approximately 50 workers, one or more will very likely be unemployed.

76. Sharon's argument is structured to lead to which of the following as a conclusion?

(A) The fact that 90 percent of the people know someone who is unemployed is not an indication that unemployment is abnormally high.
(B) The current level of unemployment is not moderate.
(C) If at least 5 percent of workers are unemployed, the result of questioning a representative group of people cannot be the percentage Roland cites.
(D) It is unlikely that the people whose statements Roland cites are giving accurate reports.
(E) If an unemployment figure is given as a certain percentage, the actual percentage of those without jobs is even higher.

77. Sharon's argument relies on the assumption that ___.

(A) normal levels of unemployment are rarely exceeded
(B) unemployment is not normally concentrated in geographically isolated segments of the population
(C) the number of people who each know someone who is unemployed is always higher than 90 percent of the population
(D) Roland is not consciously distorting the statistics he presents
(E) knowledge that a personal acquaintance is unemployed generates more fear of losing one's job than does knowledge of unemployment statistics

78. In comparison to the standard typewriter keyboard, the EFCO keyboard, which places the most-used keys nearest the typist's strongest fingers, allows faster typing and results in less fatigue. Therefore, replacement of standard keyboards with the EFCO keyboard will result in an immediate reduction of typing costs.

Which of the following, if true, would most weaken the conclusion drawn above?

(A) People who use both standard and EFCO keyboards report greater difficulty in the transition from the EFCO keyboard to the standard keyboard than in the transition from the standard keyboard to the EFCO keyboard.
(B) EFCO keyboards are no more expensive to manufacture than are standard keyboards and require less frequent repair than do standard keyboards.
(C) The number of businesses and government agencies that use EFCO keyboards is increasing each year.
(D) The more training and experience an employee has had with the standard keyboard, the more costly it is to train that employee to use the EFCO keyboard.
(E) Novice typists can learn to use the EFCO keyboard in about the same amount of time that it takes them to learn to use the standard keyboard.

79. An overly centralized economy, not the changes in the climate, is responsible for the poor agricultural production in Country X since its new government came to power. Neighboring Country Y has experienced the same climatic conditions, but while agricultural production has been falling in Country X, it has been rising in Country Y.

Which of the following, if true, would most weaken the argument above?

(A) Industrial production also is declining in Country X.
(B) Whereas Country Y is landlocked, Country X has a major seaport.

(C) Both Country X and Country Y have been experiencing drought conditions.
(D) The crops that have always been grown in Country X are different from those that have always been grown in Country Y.
(E) Country X's new government instituted a centralized economy with the intention of ensuring an equitable distribution of goods.

80. Because no employee wants to be associated with bad news in the eyes of a superior, information about serious problems at lower levels is progressively softened and distorted as it goes up each step in the management hierarchy. The chief executive is, therefore, less well informed about problems at lower levels than are his or her subordinates at those levels.

The conclusion drawn above is based on the assumption that ______.

(A) problems should be solved at the level in the management hierarchy at which they occur
(B) employees should be rewarded for accurately reporting problems to their superiors
(C) problem-solving ability is more important at higher levels than it is at lower levels of the management hierarchy
(D) chief executives obtain information about problems at lower levels from no source other than their subordinates
(E) some employees are more concerned about truth than about the way they are perceived by their superiors

81. A recent report determined that although only 3 percent of drivers on Maryland highways equipped their vehicles with radar detectors, 33 percent of all vehicles ticketed for exceeding the speed limit were equipped with them. Clearly, drivers who equip their vehicles with radar detectors are more likely to exceed the speed limit regularly than are drivers who do not.

The conclusion drawn above depends on which of the following assumptions?

(A) Drivers who equip their vehicles with radar detectors are less likely to be ticketed for exceeding the speed limit than are drivers who do not.
(B) Drivers who are ticketed for exceeding the speed limit are more likely to exceed the speed limit regularly than are drivers who are not ticketed.
(C) The number of vehicles that were ticketed for exceeding the speed limit was greater than the number of vehicles that were equipped with radar detectors.
(D) Many of the vehicles that were ticketed for exceeding the speed limit were ticketed more than once in the time period covered by the report.
(E) Drivers on Maryland highways exceeded the speed limit more often than did drivers on other state highways not covered in the report.

82. Products sold under a brand name used to command premium prices because, in general, they were superior to nonbrand rival products. Technical expertise in product development has become so widespread, however, that special quality advantages are very hard to obtain these days and even harder to maintain. As a consequence, brand-name products generally neither offer higher quality nor sell at higher prices. Paradoxically, brand names are a bigger marketing advantage than ever.

Which of the following, if true, most helps to resolve the paradox outlined above?

(A) Brand names are taken by consumers as a guarantee of getting a product as good as the best rival products.
(B) Consumers recognize that the quality of products sold under invariant brand names can drift over time.
(C) In many acquisitions of one corporation by another, the acquiring corporation is interested more in acquiring the right to use certain brand names than in acquiring existing production facilities.
(D) In the days when special quality advantages were easier to obtain than they are now, it was also easier to get new brand names established.
(E) The advertising of a company's brand-name products is at times transferred to a new advertising agency, especially when sales are declining.

83. Editorial: Regulations recently imposed by the government of Risemia call for unprecedented reductions in the amounts of pollutants manufacturers are allowed to discharge into the environment. It will take costly new pollution control equipment requiring expensive maintenance to comply with these regulations. Resultant price increases for Risemian manufactured goods will lead to the loss of some export markets. Clearly, therefore, annual exports of Risemian manufactured goods will in the future occur at diminished levels.

Which of the following, if true, most seriously weakens the argument in the editorial?

(A) The need to comply with the new regulations will stimulate the development within Risemia of new pollution control equipment for which a strong worldwide demand is likely to emerge.
(B) The proposed regulations include a schedule of fines for noncompliance that escalate steeply in cases of repeated noncompliance.
(C) Savings from utilizing the chemicals captured by the pollution control equipment will remain far below the cost of maintaining the equipment.
(D) By international standards, the levels of pollutants currently emitted by some of Risemia's manufacturing plants are not considered excessive.
(E) The stockholders of most of Risemia's manufacturing corporations exert substantial pressure on the corporations to comply with environmental laws.

84. When demand for a factory's products is high, more money is spent at the factory for safety precautions and machinery maintenance than when demand is low. Thus the average number of on-the-job accidents per employee each month should be lower during periods when demand is high than when demand is low and less money is available for safety precautions and machinery maintenance.

Which of the following, if true about a factory when demand for its products is high, casts the most serious doubt on the conclusion drawn above?

(A) Its employees ask for higher wages than they do at other times.
(B) Its management hires new workers but lacks the time to train them properly.
(C) Its employees are less likely to lose their jobs than they are at other times.
(D) Its management sponsors a monthly safety award for each division in the factory.
(E) Its old machinery is replaced with modern, automated models.

85. An unusually severe winter occurred in Europe after the continent was blanketed by a blue haze resulting from the eruption of the Laki Volcano in the European republic of Iceland in the summer of 1984. Thus, it is evident that major eruptions cause the atmosphere to become cooler than it would be otherwise.

Which of the following statements, if true, most seriously weakens the argument above?

(A) The cooling effect triggered by volcanic eruptions in 1985 was counteracted by an unusual warming of Pacific waters.
(B) There is a strong statistical link between volcanic eruptions and the severity of the rainy season in India.
(C) A few months after El Chichón's large eruption in April 1982, air temperatures throughout the region remained higher than expected, given the long-term weather trends.
(D) The climatic effects of major volcanic eruptions can temporarily mask the general warming trend resulting from an excess of carbon dioxide in the atmosphere.
(E) Three months after an early springtime eruption in South America during the late nineteenth century, sea surface temperatures near the coast began to fall.

86. Journalist: In physics journals, the number of articles reporting the results of experiments involving particle accelerators was lower last year than it had been in previous years. Several of the particle accelerators at major research institutions were out of service the year before last for repairs, so it is likely that the low number of articles was due to the decline in availability of particle accelerators.

Which of the following, if true, most seriously undermines the journalist's argument?

(A) Every article based on experiments with particle accelerators that was submitted for publication last year actually was published.
(B) The average time scientists must wait for access to a particle accelerator has declined over the last several years.
(C) The number of physics journals was the same last year as in previous years.
(D) Particle accelerators can be used for more than one group of experiments in any given year.
(E) Recent changes in the editorial policies of several physics journals have decreased the likelihood that articles concerning particle-accelerator research will be accepted for publication.

Questions 87–89 are based on the following:

Networks of blood vessels in bats' wings serve only to disperse heat generated in flight. This heat is generated only because bats flap their wings. Thus paleontologists' recent discovery that the winged dinosaur Sandactylus had similar networks of blood vessels in the skin of its wings provides evidence for the hypothesis that Sandactylus flew by flapping its wings, not just by gliding.

87. In the passage, the author develops the argument by ______.

(A) forming the hypothesis that best explains several apparently conflicting pieces of evidence
(B) reinterpreting evidence that had been used to support an earlier theory
(C) using an analogy with a known phenomenon to draw a conclusion about an unknown phenomenon
(D) speculating about how structures observed in present-day creatures might have developed from similar structures in creatures now extinct
(E) pointing out differences in the physiological demands that flight makes on large, as opposed to small, creatures

88. Which of the following, if true, most seriously weakens the argument in the passage?

(A) Sandactylus' wings were far more similar to the wings of bats than to the wings of birds.
(B) Paleontologists do not know whether winged dinosaurs other than Sandactylus had similar networks of blood vessels in the skin of their wings.
(C) The mechanism used by bats for dispersing heat in flight could, in principle, work for much larger flying creatures, such as Sandactylus.
(D) Not all the bats that use the mechanism described in the passage for dispersing heat in flight live in climates similar to the climate in which Sandactylus lived.
(E) Other winged dinosaurs that flew only by gliding had networks of blood vessels in the skin of their wings similar to those that Sandactylus had.

89. The argument in the passage relies on which of the following assumptions?

(A) Sandactylus would not have had networks of blood vessels in the skin of its wings if these networks were of no use to Sandactylus.
(B) All creatures that fly by flapping their wings have networks of blood vessels in the skin of their wings.
(C) Winged dinosaurs that flapped their wings in flight would have been able to fly more effectively than winged dinosaurs that could only glide.
(D) If Sandactylus flew by flapping its wings, then paleontologists would certainly be able to find some evidence that it did so.
(E) Heat generated by Sandactylus in flapping its wings in flight could not have been dispersed by anything other than the blood vessels in its wings.

90. Keith: Compliance with new government regulations requiring the installation of smoke alarms and sprinkler systems in all theaters and arenas will cost the entertainment industry $25 billion annually. Consequently, jobs will be lost and profits diminished. Therefore, these regulations will harm the country's economy.

Laura: The $25 billion spent by some businesses will be revenue for others. Jobs and profits will be gained as well as lost.

Laura responds to Keith by _____.

(A) demonstrating that Keith's conclusion is based on evidence that is not relevant to the issue at hand
(B) challenging the plausibility of the evidence that serves as the basis for Keith's argument.
(C) suggesting that Keith's argument overlooks a mitigating consequence
(D) reinforcing Keith's conclusion by supplying a complementary interpretation of the evidence Keith cites
(E) agreeing with the main conclusion of Keith's argument but construing that conclusion as grounds for optimism rather than for pessimism

91. Businesses are suffering because of a lack of money available for development loans. To help businesses, the government plans to modify the income-tax structure in order to induce individual taxpayers to put a larger portion of their incomes into retirement savings accounts, because as more money is deposited in such accounts, more money becomes available to borrowers.

Which of the following, if true, raises the most serious doubt regarding the effectiveness of the government's plan to increase the amount of money available for development loans for businesses?

(A) When levels of personal retirement savings increase, consumer borrowing always increases correspondingly.
(B) The increased tax revenue the government would receive as a result of business expansion would not offset the loss in revenue from personal income taxes during the first year of the plan.
(C) Even with tax incentives, some people will choose not to increase their levels of retirement savings.
(D) Bankers generally will not continue to lend money to businesses whose prospective earnings are insufficient to meet their loan repayment schedules.
(E) The modified tax structure would give all taxpayers, regardless of their incomes, the same tax savings for a given increase in their retirement savings.

92. In order to finance road repairs, the highway commission of a certain state is considering a 50 percent increase in the 10-cents-per-mile toll for vehicles using its toll highway. The highway commissioner claims that the toll increase will increase the annual revenue generated by the toll highway by at least 50 percent per year.

Which of the following is an assumption on which the highway commissioner's claim depends?

(A) The amount of money required annually for road repairs will not increase from its current level.
(B) The total number of trips made on the toll highway per year will not decrease from its current level.
(C) The average length of a trip made on the toll highway will not decrease from its current level.
(D) The number of drivers who consistently avoid the highway tolls by using secondary roads will not increase from its current level.
(E) The total distance traveled by vehicles on the toll highway per year will not decrease from its current level.

93. A new law gives ownership of patents—documents providing exclusive right to make and sell an invention—to universities, not the government, when those patents result from government-sponsored university research. Administrators at Logos University plan to sell any patents they acquire to corporations in order to fund programs to improve undergraduate teaching.

Which of the following, if true, would cast the most doubt on the viability of the college administrators' plan described above?

(A) Profit-making corporations interested in developing products based on patents held by universities are likely to try to serve as exclusive sponsors of ongoing university research projects.
(B) Corporate sponsors of research in university facilities are entitled to tax credits under new federal tax-code guidelines.
(C) Research scientists at Logos University have few or no teaching responsibilities and participate little if at all in the undergraduate programs in their field.
(D) Government-sponsored research conducted at Logos University for the most part duplicates research already completed by several profit-making corporations.
(E) Logos University is unlikely to attract corporate sponsorship of its scientific research.

Questions 94–95 are based on the following:

Environmentalist: The commissioner of the Fish and Game Authority would have the public believe that increases in the number of marine fish caught demonstrate that this resource is no longer endangered. This is a specious argument, as unsound as it would be to assert that the ever-increasing rate at which rain forests are being cut down demonstrates a lack of danger to that resource. The real cause of the increased fish-catch is a greater efficiency in using technologies that deplete resources.

94. Which of the following strategies is used in the presentation of the environmentalist's position?

(A) Questioning the motives of an opponent
(B) Showing that an opposing position is self-contradictory
(C) Attacking an argument through the use of an analogy
(D) Demonstrating the inaccuracy of certain data
(E) Pointing out adverse consequences of a proposal

95. The environmentalist's statements, if true, best support which of the following as a conclusion?

(A) The use of technology is the reason for the increasing encroachment of people on nature.
(B) It is possible to determine how many fish are in the sea by some way other than by catching fish.
(C) The proportion of marine fish that are caught is as high as the proportion of rain forest trees that are cut down each year.
(D) Modern technologies waste resources by catching inedible fish.
(E) Marine fish continue to be an endangered resource.

96. Commentator: The theory of trade retaliation states that countries closed out of any of another country's markets should close some of their own markets to the other country in order to pressure the other country to reopen its markets. If every country acted according to this theory, no country would trade with any other.

The commentator's argument relies on which of the following assumptions?

(A) No country actually acts according to the theory of trade retaliation.
(B) No country should block any of its markets to foreign trade.
(C) Trade disputes should be settled by international tribunal.
(D) For any two countries, at least one has some market closed to the other.
(E) Countries close their markets to foreigners to protect domestic producers.

97. Although parapsychology is often considered a pseudoscience, it is in fact a genuine scientific enterprise, for it uses scientific methods such as controlled experiments and statistical tests of clearly stated hypotheses to examine the questions it raises.

The conclusion above is properly drawn if which of the following is assumed?

(A) If a field of study can conclusively answer the questions it raises, then it is a genuine science.
(B) Since parapsychology uses scientific methods, it will produce credible results.
(C) Any enterprise that does not use controlled experiments and statistical tests is not genuine science.
(D) Any field of study that employs scientific methods is a genuine scientific enterprise.
(E) Since parapsychology raises clearly statable questions, they can be tested in controlled experiments.

98. Hotco oil burners, designed to be used in asphalt plants, are so efficient that Hotco will sell one to the Clifton Asphalt plant for no payment other than the cost savings between the total amount the asphalt plant actually paid for oil using its former burner during the last two years and the total amount it will pay for oil using the Hotco burner during the next two years. On installation, the plant will make an estimated payment, which will be adjusted after two years to equal the actual cost savings.

Which of the following, if it occurred, would constitute a disadvantage for Hotco of the plan described above?

(A) Another manufacturer's introduction to the market of a similarly efficient burner
(B) The Clifton Asphalt plant's need for more than one new burner
(C) Very poor efficiency in the Clifton Asphalt plant's old burner
(D) A decrease in the demand for asphalt
(E) A steady increase in the price of oil beginning soon after the new burner is installed

99. An experiment was done in which human subjects recognize a pattern within a matrix of abstract designs and then select another design that completes that pattern. The results of the experiment were surprising. The lowest expenditure of energy in neurons in the brain was found in those subjects who performed most successfully in the experiments.

Which of the following hypotheses best accounts for the findings of the experiment?

(A) The neurons of the brain react less when a subject is trying to recognize patterns than when the subject is doing other kinds of reasoning.
(B) Those who performed best in the experiment experienced more satisfaction when working with abstract patterns than did those who performed less well.
(C) People who are better at abstract pattern recognition have more energy-efficient neural connections.
(D) The energy expenditure of the subjects' brains increases when a design that completes the initially recognized pattern is determined.
(E) The task of completing a given design is more capably performed by athletes, whose energy expenditure is lower when they are at rest.

100. One way to judge the performance of a company is to compare it with other companies. This technique, commonly called "benchmarking," permits the manager of a company to discover better industrial practices and can provide a justification for the adoption of good practices.

Any of the following, if true, is a valid reason for benchmarking the performance of a company against companies with which it is not in competition rather than against competitors EXCEPT:

(A) Comparisons with competitors are most likely to focus on practices that the manager making the comparisons already employs.
(B) Getting "inside" information about the unique practices of competitors is particularly difficult.

(C) Since companies that compete with each other are likely to have comparable levels of efficiency, only benchmarking against noncompetitors is likely to reveal practices that would aid in beating competitors.

(D) Managers are generally more receptive to new ideas that they find outside their own industry.

(E) Much of the success of good companies is due to their adoption of practices that take advantage of the special circumstances of their products or markets.

101. For a trade embargo against a particular country to succeed, a high degree of both international accord and ability to prevent goods from entering or leaving that country must be sustained. A total blockade of Patria's ports is necessary to an embargo, but such an action would be likely to cause international discord over the embargo.

The claims above, if true, most strongly support which of the following conclusions?

(A) The balance of opinion is likely to favor Patria in the event of a blockade.

(B) As long as international opinion is unanimously against Patria, a trade embargo is likely to succeed.

(C) A naval blockade of Patria's ports would ensure that no goods enter or leave Patria.

(D) Any trade embargo against Patria would be likely to fail at some time.

(E) For a blockade of Patria's ports to be successful, international opinion must be unanimous.

Questions 102–103 are based on the following:

The average life expectancy for the United States population as a whole is 73.9 years, but children born in Hawaii will live an average of 77 years, and those born in Louisiana, 71.7 years. If a newlywed couple from Louisiana were to begin their family in Hawaii, therefore, their children would be expected to live longer than would be the case if the family remained in Louisiana.

102. Which of the following, if true, would most seriously weaken the conclusion drawn in the passage?

(A) Insurance company statisticians do not believe that moving to Hawaii will significantly lengthen the average Louisianan's life.

(B) The governor of Louisiana has falsely alleged that statistics for his state are inaccurate.

(C) The longevity ascribed to Hawaii's current population is attributable mostly to genetically determined factors.

(D) Thirty percent of all Louisianans can expect to live longer than 77 years.

(E) Most of the Hawaiian Islands have levels of air pollution well below the national average for the United States.

103. Which of the following statements, if true, would most significantly strengthen the conclusion drawn in the passage?

(A) As population density increases in Hawaii, life expectancy figures for that state are likely to be revised downward.

(B) Environmental factors tending to favor longevity are abundant in Hawaii and less numerous in Louisiana.

(C) Twenty-five percent of all Louisianans who move to Hawaii live longer than 77 years.

(D) Over the last decade, average life expectancy has risen at a higher rate for Louisianans than for Hawaiians.

(E) Studies show that the average life expectancy for Hawaiians who move permanently to Louisiana is roughly equal to that of Hawaiians who remain in Hawaii.

104. The cost of producing radios in Country Q is 10 percent less than the cost of producing radios in Country Y. Even after transportation fees and tariff charges are added, it is still cheaper for a company to import radios from Country Q to Country Y than to produce radios in Country Y.

The statements above, if true, best support which of the following assertions?

(A) Labor costs in Country Q are 10 percent below those in Country Y.
(B) Importing radios from Country Q to Country Y will eliminate 10 percent of the manufacturing jobs in Country Y.
(C) The tariff on a radio imported from Country Q to Country Y is less than 10 percent of the cost of manufacturing the radio in Country Y.
(D) The fee for transporting a radio from Country Q to Country Y is more than 10 percent of the cost of manufacturing the radio in Country Q.
(E) It takes 10 percent less time to manufacture a radio in Country Q than it does in Country Y.

105. The average normal infant born in the United States weighs between 12 and 14 pounds at the age of three months. Therefore, if a three-month-old child weighs only 10 pounds, its weight gain has been below the United States average.

Which of the following indicates a flaw in the reasoning above?

(A) Weight is only one measure of normal infant development.
(B) Some three-month-old children weigh as much as 17 pounds.
(C) It is possible for a normal child to weigh 10 pounds at birth.
(D) The phrase "below average" does not necessarily mean insufficient.
(E) Average weight gain is not the same as average weight.

106. In the aftermath of a worldwide stock-market crash, Country T claimed that the severity of the stock-market crash it experienced resulted from the accelerated process of denationalization many of its industries underwent shortly before the crash.

Which of the following, if it could be carried out, would be most useful in an evaluation of Country T's assessment of the causes of the severity of its stock-market crash?

(A) Calculating the average loss experienced by individual traders in Country T during the crash
(B) Using economic theory to predict the most likely date of the next crash in Country T
(C) Comparing the total number of shares sold during the worst days of the crash in Country T to the total number of shares sold in Country T just prior to the crash
(D) Comparing the severity of the crash in Country T to the severity of the crash in countries otherwise economically similar to Country T that have not experienced recent denationalization
(E) Comparing the long-term effects of the crash on the purchasing power of the currency of Country T to the immediate, more severe short-term effects of the crash on the purchasing power of the currency of Country T

107. Kale has more nutritional value than spinach. But since collard greens have more nutritional value than lettuce, it follows that kale has more nutritional value than lettuce.

Any of the following, if introduced into the argument as an additional premise, makes the argument above logically correct EXCEPT:

(A) Collard greens have more nutritional value than kale.
(B) Spinach has more nutritional value than lettuce.
(C) Spinach has more nutritional value than collard greens.
(D) Spinach and collard greens have the same nutritional value.
(E) Kale and collard greens have the same nutritional value.

108. Although custom prosthetic bone replacements produced through a new computer-aided design process will cost more than twice as much as ordinary replacements, custom replacements should still be cost-effective. Not only will surgery and recovery time be reduced, but custom replacements should last longer, thereby reducing the need for further hospital stays.

Which of the following must be studied in order to evaluate the argument presented above?

(A) The amount of time a patient spends in surgery versus the amount of time spent recovering from surgery
(B) The amount by which the cost of producing custom replacements has declined with the introduction of the new technique for producing them
(C) The degree to which the use of custom replacements is likely to reduce the need for repeat surgery when compared with the use of ordinary replacements
(D) The degree to which custom replacements produced with the new technique are more carefully manufactured than are ordinary replacements
(E) The amount by which custom replacements produced with the new technique will drop in cost as the production procedures become standardized and applicable on a larger scale

109. Correctly measuring the productivity of service workers is complex. Consider, for example, postal workers: they are often said to be more productive if more letters are delivered per postal worker. But is this really true? What if more letters are lost or delayed per worker at the same time that more are delivered?

The objection implied above to the productivity measure described is based on doubts about the truth of which of the following statements?

(A) Postal workers are representative of service workers in general.
(B) The delivery of letters is the primary activity of the postal service.
(C) Productivity should be ascribed to categories of workers, not to individuals.
(D) The quality of services rendered can appropriately be ignored in computing productivity.
(E) The number of letters delivered is relevant to measuring the productivity of postal workers.

110. "Fast cycle time" is a strategy of designing a manufacturing organization to eliminate bottlenecks and delays in production. Not only does it speed up production, but it also ensures quality. The reason is that the bottlenecks and delays cannot be eliminated unless all work is done right the first time.

The claim about quality made above rests on a questionable presupposition that _____.

(A) any flaw in work on a product would cause a bottleneck or delay and so would be prevented from occurring on a "fast cycle" production line
(B) the strategy of "fast cycle time" would require fundamental rethinking of product design
(C) the primary goal of the organization is to produce a product of unexcelled quality, rather than to generate profits for stockholders
(D) "fast cycle time" could be achieved by shaving time off each of the component processes in a production cycle
(E) "fast cycle time" is a concept in business strategy that has not yet been put into practice in a factory

111. Sales of telephones have increased dramatically over the last year. In order to take advantage of this increase, Mammoth Industries plans to expand production of its own model of telephone, while continuing its already very extensive advertising of this product.

Which of the following, if true, provides most support for the view that Mammoth Industries cannot increase its sales of telephones by adopting the plan outlined above?

(A) Although it sells all the telephones that it produces, Mammoth Industries' share of all telephone sales has declined over the last year.
(B) Mammoth Industries' average inventory of telephones awaiting shipment to retailers has declined slightly over the last year.
(C) Advertising has made the brand name of Mammoth Industries' telephones widely known, but few consumers know that Mammoth Industries owns this brand.
(D) Mammoth Industries' telephone is one of three brands of telephone that have together accounted for the bulk of the last year's increase in sales.
(E) Despite a slight decline in the retail price, sales of Mammoth Industries' telephones have fallen in the last year.

112. In tests for pironoma, a serious disease, a false positive result indicates that people have pironoma when, in fact, they do not; a false negative result indicates that people do not have pironoma when, in fact, they do. To detect pironoma most accurately, physicians should use the laboratory test that has the lowest proportion of false positive results.

Which of the following, if true, gives the most support to the recommendation above?

(A) The accepted treatment for pironoma does not have damaging side effects.
(B) The laboratory test that has the lowest proportion of false positive results causes the same minor side effects as do the other laboratory tests used to detect pironoma.
(C) In treating pironoma patients, it is essential to begin treatment as early as possible, since even a week of delay can result in loss of life.
(D) The proportion of inconclusive test results is equal for all laboratory tests used to detect pironoma.
(E) All laboratory tests to detect pironoma have the same proportion of false negative results.

113. The difficulty with the proposed high-speed train line is that a used plane can be bought for one-third the price of the train line, and the plane, which is just as fast, can fly anywhere. The train would be a fixed linear system, and we live in a world that is spreading out in all directions and in which consumers choose the free-wheel systems (cars, buses, aircraft), which do not have fixed routes. Thus a sufficient market for the train will not exist.

Which of the following, if true, most severely weakens the argument presented above?

(A) Cars, buses, and planes require the efforts of drivers and pilots to guide them, whereas the train will be guided mechanically.
(B) Cars and buses are not nearly as fast as the high-speed train will be.
(C) Planes are not a free-wheel system because they can fly only between airports, which are less convenient for consumers than the high-speed train's stations would be.
(D) The high-speed train line cannot use currently underutilized train stations in large cities.
(E) For long trips, most people prefer to fly rather than to take ground-level transportation.

Questions 114–115 are based on the following:

According to the Tristate Transportation Authority, making certain improvements to the main commuter rail line would increase ridership dramatically. The authority plans to finance these improvements over the course of five years by raising automobile tolls on the two highway bridges along the route the rail line serves. Although the proposed improvements are indeed needed, the authority's plan for securing the necessary funds should be rejected because it would unfairly force drivers to absorb the entire cost of something from which they receive no benefit.

114. Which of the following, if true, would cast the most doubt on the effectiveness of the authority's plan to finance the proposed improvements by increasing bridge tolls?

(A) Before the authority increases tolls on any of the area bridges, it is required by law to hold public hearings at which objections to the proposed increase can be raised.
(B) Whenever bridge tolls are increased, the authority must pay a private contractor to adjust the automated toll-collecting machines.
(C) Between the time a proposed toll increase is announced and the time the increase is actually put into effect, many commuters buy more tokens than usual to postpone the effects of the increase.
(D) When tolls were last increased on the two bridges in question, almost 20 percent of the regular commuter traffic switched to a slightly longer alternative route that has since been improved.
(E) The chairman of the authority is a member of the Tristate Automobile Club, which has registered strong opposition to the proposed toll increase.

115. Which of the following, if true, would provide the authority with the strongest counter to the objection that its plan is unfair?

(A) Even with the proposed toll increase, the average bridge toll in the tristate region would remain less than the tolls charged in neighboring states.
(B) Any attempt to finance the improvements by raising rail fares would result in a decrease in ridership and so would be self-defeating.
(C) Automobile commuters benefit from well-maintained bridges, and in the tristate region bridge maintenance is funded out of general income tax revenues to which both automobile and rail commuters contribute.
(D) The roads along the route served by the rail line are highly congested and drivers benefit when commuters are diverted from congested roadways to mass transit.
(E) The only alternative way of funding the proposed improvements now being considered is through a regional income tax surcharge, which would affect automobile commuters and rail commuters alike.

116. The pharmaceutical industry argues that because new drugs will not be developed unless heavy development costs can be recouped in later sales, the current 20 years of protection provided by patents should be extended in the case of newly developed drugs. However, in other industries new-product development continues despite high development costs, a fact that indicates that the extension is unnecessary.

Which of the following, if true, most strongly supports the pharmaceutical industry's argument against the challenge made above?

(A) No industries other than the pharmaceutical industry have asked for an extension of the 20-year limit on patent protection.
(B) Clinical trials of new drugs, which occur after the patent is granted and before the new drug can be marketed, often now take as long as 10 years to complete.
(C) There are several industries in which the ratio of research and development costs to revenues is higher than it is in the pharmaceutical industry.
(D) An existing patent for a drug does not legally prevent pharmaceutical companies from bringing to market alternative drugs, provided they are sufficiently dissimilar to the patented drug.
(E) Much recent industrial innovation has occurred in products—for example, in the computer and electronics industries—for which patent protection is often very ineffective.

117. Caterpillars of all species produce an identical hormone called "juvenile hormone" that maintains feeding behavior. Only when a caterpillar has grown to the right size for pupation to take place does a special enzyme halt the production of juvenile hormone. This enzyme can be synthesized and will, on being ingested by immature caterpillars, kill them by stopping them from feeding.

Which of the following, if true, most strongly supports the view that it would NOT be advisable to try to eradicate agricultural pests that go through a caterpillar stage by spraying croplands with the enzyme mentioned above?

(A) Most species of caterpillar are subject to some natural predation.
(B) Many agricultural pests do not go through a caterpillar stage.
(C) Many agriculturally beneficial insects go through a caterpillar stage.
(D) Since caterpillars of different species emerge at different times, several sprayings would be necessary.
(E) Although the enzyme has been synthesized in the laboratory, no large-scale production facilities exist as yet.

118. Firms adopting "profit-related-pay" (PRP) contracts pay wages at levels that vary with the firm's profits. In the metalworking industry last year, firms with PRP contracts in place showed productivity per worker on average 13 percent higher than that of their competitors who used more traditional contracts.

If, on the basis of the evidence above, it is argued that PRP contracts increase worker productivity, which of the following, if true, would most seriously weaken that argument?

(A) Results similar to those cited for the metalworking industry have been found in other industries where PRP contracts are used.
(B) Under PRP contracts costs other than labor costs, such as plant, machinery, and energy, make up an increased proportion of the total cost of each unit of output.
(C) Because introducing PRP contracts greatly changes individual workers' relationships to the firm, negotiating the introduction of PRP contracts is complex and time-consuming.
(D) Many firms in the metalworking industry have modernized production equipment in the last five years, and most of these introduced PRP contracts at the same time.
(E) In firms in the metalworking industry where PRP contracts are in place, the average take-home pay is 15 percent higher than it is in those firms where workers have more traditional contracts.

119. Adult female rats who have never before encountered rat pups will start to show maternal behaviors after being confined with a pup for about seven days. This period can be considerably shortened by disabling the female's sense of smell or by removing the scent-producing glands of the pup.

Which of the following hypotheses best explains the contrast described above?

(A) The sense of smell in adult female rats is more acute than that in rat pups.
(B) The amount of scent produced by rat pups increases when they are in the presence of a female rat that did not bear them.
(C) Female rats that have given birth are more affected by olfactory cues than are female rats that have never given birth.
(D) A female rat that has given birth shows maternal behavior toward rat pups that she did not bear more quickly than does a female rat that has never given birth.
(E) The development of a female rat's maternal interest in a rat pup that she did not bear is inhibited by the odor of the pup.

120. The proposal to hire 10 new police officers in Middletown is quite foolish. There is sufficient funding to pay the salaries of the new officers, but not the salaries of additional court and prison employees to process the increased caseload of arrests and convictions that new officers usually generate.

Which of the following, if true, will most seriously weaken the conclusion drawn above?

(A) Studies have shown that an increase in a city's police force does not necessarily reduce crime.
(B) When one major city increased its police force by 19 percent last year, there were 40 percent more arrests and 13 percent more convictions.
(C) If funding for the new police officers' salaries is approved, support for other city services will have to be reduced during the next fiscal year.
(D) In most United States cities, not all arrests result in convictions, and not all convictions result in prison terms.
(E) Middletown's ratio of police officers to citizens has reached a level at which an increase in the number of officers will have a deterrent effect on crime.

121. Northern Air has dozens of flights daily into and out of Belleville Airport, which is highly congested. Northern Air depends for its success on economy and quick turnaround and consequently is planning to replace its large planes with Skybuses, the novel aerodynamic design of which is extremely fuel efficient. The Skybus' fuel efficiency results in both lower fuel costs and reduced time spent refueling.

Which of the following, if true, could present the most serious disadvantage for Northern Air in replacing its large planes with Skybuses?

(A) The Skybus would enable Northern Air to schedule direct flights to destinations that currently require stops for refueling.
(B) Aviation fuel is projected to decline in price over the next several years.
(C) The fuel efficiency of the Skybus would enable Northern Air to eliminate refueling at some of its destinations, but several mechanics would lose their jobs.
(D) None of Northern Air's competitors that use Belleville Airport are considering buying Skybuses.
(E) The aerodynamic design of the Skybus causes turbulence behind it when taking off that forces other planes on the runway to delay their takeoffs.

122. The earliest Mayan pottery found at Colha, in Belize, is about 3,000 years old. Recently, however, 4,500-year-old stone agricultural implements were unearthed at Colha. These implements resemble Mayan stone implements of a much later period, also found at Colha. Moreover, the implements' designs are strikingly different from the designs of stone implements produced by other cultures known to have inhabited the area in prehistoric times. Therefore, there were surely Mayan settlements in Colha 4,500 years ago.

Which of the following, if true, most seriously weakens the argument?

(A) Ceramic ware is not known to have been used by the Mayan people to make agricultural implements.
(B) Carbon dating of corn pollen in Colha indicates that agriculture began there around 4,500 years ago.
(C) Archaeological evidence indicates that some of the oldest stone implements found at Colha were used to cut away vegetation after controlled burning of trees to open areas of swampland for cultivation.
(D) Successor cultures at a given site often adopt the style of agricultural implements used by earlier inhabitants of the same site.
(E) Many religious and social institutions of the Mayan people who inhabited Colha 3,000 years ago relied on a highly developed system of agricultural symbols.

123. Codex Berinensis, a Florentine copy of an ancient Roman medical treatise, is undated but contains clues to when it was produced. Its first 80 pages are by a single copyist, but the remaining 20 pages are by three different copyists, which indicates some significant disruption. Since a letter in handwriting identified as that of the fourth copyist mentions a plague that killed many people in Florence in 1148, Codex Berinensis was probably produced in that year.

Which of the following, if true, most strongly supports the hypothesis that Codex Berinensis was produced in 1148?

(A) Other than Codex Berinensis, there are no known samples of the handwriting of the first three copyists.
(B) According to the account by the fourth copyist, the plague went on for 10 months.
(C) A scribe would be able to copy a page of text the size and style of Codex Berinensis in a day.
(D) There was only one outbreak of plague in Florence in the 1100's.
(E) The number of pages of Codex Berinensis produced by a single scribe becomes smaller with each successive change of copyist.

124. Outsourcing is the practice of obtaining from an independent supplier a product or service that a company has previously provided for itself. Since a company's chief objective is to realize the highest possible year-end profits, any product or service that can be obtained from an independent supplier for less than it would cost the company to provide the product or service on its own should be outsourced.

Which of the following, if true, most seriously weakens the argument?

(A) If a company decides to use independent suppliers for a product, it can generally exploit the vigorous competition arising among several firms that are interested in supplying that product.
(B) Successful outsourcing requires a company to provide its suppliers with information about its products and plans that can fall into the hands of its competitors and give them a business advantage.
(C) Certain tasks, such as processing a company's payroll, are commonly outsourced, whereas others, such as handling the company's core business, are not.
(D) For a company to provide a product or service for itself as efficiently as an independent supplier can provide it, the managers involved need to be as expert in the area of that product or service as the people in charge of that product or service at an independent supplier are.
(E) When a company decides to use an independent supplier for a product or service, the independent supplier sometimes hires members of the company's staff who formerly made the product or provided the service that the independent supplier now supplies.

8.5 Critical Reasoning Answer Key

1. B
2. C
3. B
4. D
5. A
6. C
7. D
8. E
9. B
10. C
11. A
12. D
13. E
14. C
15. A
16. E
17. D
18. B
19. B
20. C
21. B
22. C
23. D
24. E
25. D
26. B
27. D
28. A
29. B
30. A
31. C
32. C
33. E
34. C
35. C
36. C
37. A
38. B
39. B
40. A
41. E
42. D
43. B
44. E
45. D
46. C
47. D
48. A
49. A
50. C
51. B
52. C
53. B
54. B
55. D
56. B
57. A
58. A
59. D
60. C
61. E
62. D
63. E
64. D
65. C
66. A
67. E
68. A
69. B
70. A
71. A
72. E
73. E
74. B
75. B
76. A
77. B
78. D
79. D
80. D
81. B
82. A
83. A
84. B
85. C
86. E
87. C
88. E
89. A
90. C
91. A
92. E
93. D
94. C
95. E
96. D
97. D
98. E
99. C
100. E
101. D
102. C
103. B
104. C
105. E
106. D
107. A
108. C
109. D
110. A
111. E
112. E
113. C
114. D
115. D
116. B
117. C
118. D
119. E
120. E
121. E
122. D
123. D
124. B

8.6 Critical Reasoning Answer Explanations

The following discussion is intended to familiarize you with the most efficient and effective approaches to critical reasoning questions. The particular questions in this chapter are generally representative of the kinds of critical reasoning questions you will encounter on the GMAT®. Remember that it is the problem solving strategy that is important, not the specific details of a particular question.

1. Some economists view the Kennedy–Johnson tax cut of 1964, which radically reduced corporate and individual taxes, as the impetus for the substantial prosperity enjoyed by the United States in the late 1960's and early 1970's.

   Which of the following, if true, would most weaken the claim that the tax cut of 1964 was the impetus for economic prosperity?

   (A) Modernized, more productive factories were built in the late 1960's as a result of the funds made available by the tax cut.

   (B) Improved economic conditions in Western Europe and Japan resulted in substantially increased demand for United States manufactured goods in the late 1960's.

   (C) The tax cut of 1964 contained regulations concerning tax shelters that prompted investors to transfer their savings to more economically productive investments.

   (D) Personal income after taxes rose in the years following 1964.

   (E) In the late 1960's, unemployment was relatively low compared with the early 1960's.

Argument Evaluation

Situation Some economists claim that the Kennedy-Johnson tax cut of 1964 was responsible for the prosperity of the late 1960's and early 1970's.

Reasoning *Which point weakens the conclusion that the 1964 tax cut caused the later prosperity?* When two events occur close together in time, it is possible for one to be mistaken as the cause of the other; this could be the case with the economists' claim. The conclusion of this argument may be weakened by demonstrating another possible cause of the prosperity. If improved economic conditions among the international trading partners of the United States resulted in a significantly increased demand for United States manufactured goods in the late 1960's, the rise in demand would provide an alternative explanation for the prosperity and weaken the argument.

A The modern, more productive factories made possible by the tax cut offer a reason in support of the conclusion, not against it.

B Correct. This statement properly identifies a factor that weakens the argument by providing an alternative explanation.

C The economically productive investments made possible by the tax cut provide an example that supports, rather than weakens, the conclusion.

D The rise in personal income after 1964 suggests that the tax cut of 1964 was responsible for this increase.

E The lower rate of unemployment in the late 1960's could be attributed to the corporate tax cuts of 1964.

The correct answer is B.

2. In order to increase profits during a prolonged slowdown in sales, the largest manufacturers of automobiles in the United States have instituted record-setting price increases on all their models. The manufacturers believe that this strategy will succeed, even though it is inconsistent with the normal relationship between price and demand.

The manufacturers' plan to increase profits relies on which of the following assumptions?

(A) Automobile manufacturers will, of necessity, raise prices whenever they introduce a new model.

(B) The smaller automobile manufacturers will continue to take away a large percentage of business from the largest manufacturers.

(C) The increased profit made on cars sold will more than compensate for any decline in sales caused by the price increases.

(D) New safety restraints that will soon become mandatory for all new cars will not be very costly for manufacturers to install.

(E) Low financing and extended warranties will attract many price-conscious consumers.

Argument Construction

Situation The largest automobile manufacturers plan to increase prices on all models in order to increase profits during a sales slowdown.

Reasoning *What does the manufacturers' plan assume?* The manufacturers' plan reverses expectations: a slowdown in sales more typically results in decreased prices in order to encourage an increased number of sales. What could be the basis of the manufacturers' thinking that they should raise prices instead? The manufacturers have a goal of increased profits. They are not anticipating an increased number of sales from this plan, but rather a greater profit on the sales they do make.

A The manufacturers' plan concerns existing models rather than new ones; price increases when new models are introduced are a different subject.

B The manufacturers' plan does not address the percentage of business taken away from them by smaller manufacturers, so this point cannot be assumed.

C **Correct.** This statement properly identifies the assumption on which the manufacturers' argument is based: the greater profit on the cars that are sold will make up for a lower number of sales.

D New safety restraints are not a part of the manufacturers' plan, so their inexpensive installation is not assumed.

E The manufacturers' plan is concerned only with generating a greater profit, not with attracting price-conscious consumers who are not likely to respond favorably to the price increases.

The correct answer is C.

3. "Life expectancy" is the average age at death of the entire live-born population. In the middle of the nineteenth century, life expectancy in North America was 40 years, whereas now it is nearly 80 years. Thus, in those days, people must have been considered old at an age that we now consider the prime of life.

Which of the following, if true, undermines the argument above?

(A) In the middle of the nineteenth century, the population of North America was significantly smaller than it is today.
(B) Most of the gains in life expectancy in the last 150 years have come from reductions in the number of infants who die in their first year of life.
(C) Many of the people who live to an advanced age today do so only because of medical technology that was unknown in the nineteenth century.
(D) The proportion of people who die in their seventies is significantly smaller today than is the proportion of people who die in their eighties.
(E) More people in the middle of the nineteenth century engaged regularly in vigorous physical activity than do so today.

Argument Evaluation

Situation Life expectancy for mid-nineteenth-century North Americans was 40 years; now it is almost 80. What we think of as the prime of life must have been considered old in that earlier era.

Reasoning *What point weakens this argument?* The argument relies on the logic of having a great many more 80-year-old people in the population now than was the case 150 years ago. What would challenge this logic? The argument is built upon the *average age at death* and uses a definition of life expectancy that embraces the entire population of those born alive. What if, in the nineteenth century, the number of infants born alive but not surviving their first year was far higher than it is today? Then the *average age at time of death* could be significantly reduced by a very large number of infant deaths. On the basis of such information about infant mortality rates, it would not be fair to assume that what today is considered *the prime of life* was in that earlier time considered *old.*

A The size of the population is irrelevant to the argument.

B **Correct.** This statement properly identifies the factor that undermines the argument: it was falsely assumed that age for an entire population was simply extended when actually the average age at time of death was significantly raised when the number of infants dying in their first year was reduced.

C This point supports rather than weakens the argument.

D This point supports the argument.

E The regular exercise of one of the two populations compared does not affect the argument.

The correct answer is B.

4. From June through August 1987, Premiere Airlines had the best on-time service of 10 United States airlines. From January through March 1988, Premiere Airlines had the worst on-time service of the 10 airlines. The on-time performance ranking of the other nine airlines relative to each other remained unchanged.

Which of the following, if true, would most contribute to an explanation of the facts above?

(A) Although Premiere Airlines only revoked its policy of routinely holding flights for late passengers in the fall of 1987, the other nine airlines never had that policy.

(B) Premiere Airlines reduced its business by 10 percent when it raised its rates in the fall of 1987 to compensate for rising gasoline costs.

(C) Premiere Airlines bought five new planes in the fall of 1987 that proved to have fewer mechanical problems than the ones they replaced.

(D) Premiere Airlines serves New England, which has heavy winter snowfalls, whereas the other airlines do most of their business in warmer regions of the country.

(E) Although all 10 airlines strive to keep their flights on schedule, overcrowded airports increased flight delays for all 10 airlines in January 1988 as compared with June 1987.

Argument Construction

Situation Among a group of 10 airlines, one airline experienced the best on-time service in the summer months of one year and the worst on-time service in the winter months of the next year. The ranking of the other nine airlines remained the same during this entire time.

Reasoning *What point explains the change in on-time performance for one airline but not the others?* The two time periods are identified as June–August and January–March. What distinguishes these two periods? It is clear that two seasons are represented and, depending on the routes the airlines cover, two widely varying weather patterns. If Premiere Airlines is the only one of the 10 airlines that flies to parts of the country where heavy winter snowfalls frequently delay flights, then the seasonal change in the weather explains the change in its on-time performance while that of the other airlines remains the same.

A If the airline no longer delayed flights to accommodate its late passengers, the on-time performance would improve rather than decline, and this would contradict the explanation.

B The airline's loss of business is unrelated to its on-time performance.

C Planes with fewer mechanical problems should have helped on-time performance, not hurt it.

D Correct. This statement properly identifies the factor that supports the explanation for the airline's declining on-time performance: the regional weather-related delays specific to the routes it serves.

E The rankings are relative, so factors explaining delays for all 10 airlines do not explain why one airline went from best to worst while the other nine stayed the same.

The correct answer is D.

5. Homeowners aged 40 to 50 are more likely to purchase ice cream and are more likely to purchase it in larger amounts than are members of any other demographic group. The popular belief that teenagers eat more ice cream than adults must, therefore, be false.

The argument is flawed primarily because the author _____.

(A) fails to distinguish between purchasing and consuming
(B) does not supply information about homeowners in age groups other than 40 to 50
(C) depends on popular belief rather than on documented research findings
(D) does not specify the precise amount of ice cream purchased by any demographic group
(E) discusses ice cream rather than more nutritious and healthful foods

Argument Evaluation

Situation Adults must eat more ice cream than teenagers because adults buy more ice cream than teenagers do.

Reasoning *What is the primary flaw in this argument?* This straightforward argument is based on the faulty assumption that the buyers of the ice cream are also the eaters of the ice cream. The demographic group cited in the argument may indeed purchase more ice cream; it cannot be assumed that the members of this group also consume more of it.

A **Correct.** This statement properly recognizes the flaw in the argument.

B The conclusion cannot be reached on the basis of the information in the first sentence; supplying the purchasing habits of other age groups would not change this situation.

C The first sentence appears to be based on documented research findings.

D The conclusion is about who eats more ice cream, not who buys more; precise amounts are not necessary when the argument is based on a simple comparison of more than or less than.

E The subject is ice cream, not nutrition, so this point is irrelevant.

The correct answer is A.

6. Not all life depends on energy from sunlight. Microbial life has been found in bedrock more than five kilometers below the surface of the Earth, and bacteria have been found on the deep ocean floor feeding on hydrogen and other gases rising from the interior of the Earth through vents in the ocean floor.

The statements above, if true, best support which of the following as a conclusion?

(A) The location in the bedrock where microbial life was found was not near a system of volcanic vents through which hydrogen and other gases rose from the interior of the Earth.

(B) Bacteria are able to exist at the molten center of the Earth.

(C) A thorough survey of a planet's surface is insufficient to establish beyond a doubt that the planet contains no life.

(D) Life probably exists on Sun-orbiting comets, which are cold agglomerations of space dust and frozen gases.

(E) Finding bacterial remains in coal and oil would establish that the bacteria had been feeding on substances that had not been produced from the energy of sunlight.

Argument Construction

Situation Microbes found five kilometers below the surface of the Earth and bacteria found on the deep ocean floor are both evidence that not all life depends on sunlight.

Reasoning *What conclusion may be drawn from this statement?* Since the passage includes information about both microbes below Earth's surface and bacteria on the ocean floor, the conclusion must embrace both situations. The conclusion will not be a specific statement about either one or the other, but rather a general statement about both. What is true equally of the microbes and bacteria discussed here? They are both life forms that exist far below the surface of the Earth.

A The conclusion must include both microbes and bacteria, not simply microbes.

B The conclusion must include both microbes and bacteria, not simply bacteria.

C **Correct.** This statement properly uses the existence of the microbes far below the land's surface and of the bacteria far below the ocean's surface to draw a general conclusion about the potential existence of life below the surface of a planet.

D The passage provides no evidence about comets to lead to this conclusion.

E The conclusion must include both microbes and bacteria, not simply bacteria.

The correct answer is C.

7. A company is considering changing its policy concerning daily working hours. Currently, this company requires all employees to arrive at work at 8 a.m. The proposed policy would permit each employee to decide when to arrive—from as early as 6 a.m. to as late as 11 a.m.

The adoption of this policy would be most likely to decrease employees' productivity if the employees' job functions required them to ______.

(A) work without interruption from other employees
(B) consult at least once a day with employees from other companies
(C) submit their work for a supervisor's eventual approval
(D) interact frequently with each other throughout the entire workday
(E) undertake projects that take several days to complete

Evaluation of a Plan

Situation A company considers changing all employees' starting time from 8 a.m. to individually flexible arrival hours, from 6 to 11 a.m.

Reasoning *When could this plan cause employees' productivity to decline?* Consider the job functions defined in the answer choices and determine which entails requirements that would most likely be in conflict with the proposed plan. If employees frequently need to collaborate with each other throughout the workday, then a plan that allows a five-hour range of start times could well decrease productivity. In this case it would be far more difficult for employees to coordinate their schedules so that they could work together as necessary.

A Working without interruption would be likely to mean improved productivity.

B The flexible hours would still leave plenty of time for daily consultations during the regular business hours of the workday.

C *Eventual approval* indicates that the flexibility exists to permit employees' submissions at any time.

D Correct. This statement properly identifies a situation in which the adoption of the policy would be likely to decrease employees' productivity.

E Such projects would be accomplished just as easily on the proposed flexible schedule.

The correct answer is D.

8. The amount of time it takes for most of a worker's occupational knowledge and skills to become obsolete has been declining because of the introduction of advanced manufacturing technology (AMT). Given the rate at which AMT is currently being introduced in manufacturing, the average worker's old skills become obsolete and new skills are required within as little as five years.

Which of the following plans, if feasible, would allow a company to prepare most effectively for the rapid obsolescence of skills described above?

(A) The company will develop a program to offer selected employees the opportunity to receive training six years after they were originally hired.

(B) The company will increase its investment in AMT every year for a period of at least five years.

(C) The company will periodically survey its employees to determine how the introduction of AMT has affected them.

(D) Before the introduction of AMT, the company will institute an educational program to inform its employees of the probable consequences of the introduction of AMT.

(E) The company will ensure that it can offer its employees any training necessary for meeting their job requirements.

Evaluation of a Plan

Situation The introduction of AMT is making workers' occupational skills obsolete within as little as five years.

Reasoning *Which plan will be most effective in the company's preparation for this expected obsolescence?* Consider the ramifications of each of the possible plans, and evaluate that plan's relative effectiveness in managing the negative impacts of having workers' skills go out of date so rapidly. It should be clear that the introduction of AMT must go hand-in-hand with an internal training program that will ensure a workforce that is adequately prepared to meet job requirements.

A Under this plan, training is available only to *selected* employees and only after their skills have already become obsolete and thus problematic.

B This plan only accelerates the problem and does not address the employees' skills.

C Periodic surveys will not prevent employees' skills from becoming obsolete.

D Having a knowledge of the consequences does not prevent those consequences; employees' skills will still become obsolete.

E **Correct.** This statement properly identifies a plan that would effectively address the company's AMT-driven needs for employees trained in the most current occupational knowledge and skills.

The correct answer is E.

9. Mayor: In each of the past five years, the city has cut school funding and each time school officials complained that the cuts would force them to reduce expenditures for essential services. But each time, only expenditures for nonessential services were actually reduced. So school officials can implement further cuts without reducing any expenditures for essential services.

Which of the following, if true, most strongly supports the mayor's conclusion?

(A) The city's schools have always provided essential services as efficiently as they have provided nonessential services.

(B) Sufficient funds are currently available to allow the city's schools to provide some nonessential services.

(C) Price estimates quoted to the city's schools for the provision of nonessential services have not increased substantially since the most recent school-funding cut.

(D) Few influential city administrators support the funding of costly nonessential services in the city's schools.

(E) The city's school officials rarely exaggerate the potential impact of threatened funding cuts.

Argument Evaluation

Situation A mayor contends that schools can absorb more funding cuts without reducing essential services because school officials had previously said that funding cuts would result in reduced expenditures for essential services, but then only expenditures for nonessential services had to be cut.

Reasoning *Which point supports the mayor's conclusion?* The mayor's conclusion seems to be based solely on the belief that history will repeat itself. What fact would substantiate the mayor's position? If funding is currently available for some nonessential services, then further cuts can be made in this kind of expenditure, while leaving expenditures for essential services untouched. The availability of such funds would strengthen the mayor's argument.

A The efficiency of providing services, whether essential or not, is not the issue.

B **Correct.** This statement properly identifies a point that supports the mayor's conclusion.

C These price estimates are irrelevant since the argument is about expenditures for essential services.

D The argument is about possible cuts in essential services, not in nonessential services.

E This point weakens, rather than strengthens, the mayor's conclusion.

The correct answer is B.

10. Advertisement: For sinus pain, three out of four hospitals give their patients Novex. So when you want the most effective painkiller for sinus pain, Novex is the one to choose.

Which of the following, if true, most seriously undermines the advertisement's argument?

(A) Some competing brands of painkillers are intended to reduce other kinds of pain in addition to sinus pain.

(B) Many hospitals that do not usually use Novex will do so for those patients who cannot tolerate the drug the hospitals usually use.

(C) Many drug manufacturers increase sales of their products to hospitals by selling these products to the hospitals at the lowest price the manufacturers can afford.

(D) Unlike some competing brands of painkillers, Novex is available from pharmacies without a doctor's prescription.

(E) In clinical trials Novex has been found to be more effective than competing brands of painkillers that have been on the market longer than Novex.

Argument Evaluation

Situation An advertisement claims that Novex is the most effective painkiller for sinus pain since three out of four hospitals use it for patients.

Reasoning *What point undermines the advertisement's claim?* The argument for Novex's effectiveness as a painkiller is based upon the hospitals' usage. Consider what might be driving the hospitals' choice of medications to administer. Three out of four hospitals might be giving their patients Novex not because it is the most effective painkiller for sinus pain, but because it is inexpensive. If this is the case, the argument is seriously undermined.

A Other kinds of pain are irrelevant to the argument since the claim is only about sinus pain.

B This point does not undermine the advertisement's claim.

C **Correct.** This statement properly identifies a factor that could well undermine the advertisement's claim: the hospitals may be using this medication because it is the most cost effective for them.

D Novex's nonprescription formula is not relevant to the claim.

E This point strengthens, rather than weakens, the claim.

The correct answer is C.

11. A report that many apples contain a cancer-causing preservative called Alar apparently had little effect on consumers. Few consumers planned to change their apple-buying habits as a result of the report. Nonetheless, sales of apples in grocery stores fell sharply in March, a month after the report was issued.

Which of the following, if true, best explains the reason for the apparent discrepancy described above?

(A) In March, many grocers removed apples from their shelves in order to demonstrate concern about their customers' health.

(B) Because of a growing number of food-safety warnings, consumers in March were indifferent to such warnings.

(C) The report was delivered on television and also appeared in newspapers.

(D) The report did not mention that any other fruit contains Alar, although the preservative is used on other fruit.

(E) Public health officials did not believe that apples posed a health threat because only minute traces of Alar were present in affected apples.

Argument Construction

Situation Despite a report on the cancer-causing agent Alar, which is used to preserve many apples, few consumers planned to stop buying apples. However, sales of apples fell sharply a month after the report.

Reasoning *How can this discrepancy be explained?* If consumers did not intentionally change their buying habits, then some other change must responsible for the decline in apple sales. Why could purchases have decreased? If apples were not available to buy, then sales would obviously fall. The decision of many grocers to remove apples from their shelves in the month following the report would explain the discrepancy.

A **Correct.** This statement properly identifies an explanation for the apparent discrepancy.

B This point suggests that there would be no appreciable change in apple sales.

C How consumers may have heard about the report is irrelevant to the discrepancy between their response and the decline in sales.

D Whether or not they contain Alar, other fruits are not a part of the discussion; thus this point cannot explain the discrepancy.

E The health officials' opinion, if indeed known to consumers, would likely lead to stable apple sales.

The correct answer is A.

12. Cable-television spokesperson: Subscriptions to cable television are a bargain in comparison to "free" television. Remember that "free" television is not really free. It is consumers, in the end, who pay for the costly advertising that supports "free" television.

Which of the following, if true, is most damaging to the position of the cable-television spokesperson?

(A) Consumers who do not own television sets are less likely to be influenced in their purchasing decisions by television advertising than are consumers who own television sets.

(B) Subscriptions to cable television include access to some public-television channels, which do not accept advertising.

(C) For locations with poor television reception, cable television provides picture quality superior to that provided by free television.

(D) There is as much advertising on many cable-television channels as there is on "free" television channels.

(E) Cable-television subscribers can choose which channels they wish to receive, and the fees.

Argument Evaluation

Situation A cable-television spokesperson argues that cable fees are a bargain since so-called "free" television is actually paid for by consumers who underwrite the cost of advertising.

Reasoning *Which point weakens the spokesperson's argument?* The spokesperson's argument compares the bargain price of a subscription to cable television with the "price" of the costly advertising on "free" television. Consider what situation would undermine this comparison. What if cable television airs just as much advertising as "free" television in addition to the subscription fee? Then the cable subscriber is paying twice, and the spokesperson's argument that cable television is a bargain in comparison to "free" television is weakened.

A People who do not watch television are irrelevant to the argument.

B The fact that cable television subscriptions include access to advertising-free public-television channels does not weaken the argument that "free" television is not free.

C The picture quality of cable and free television are not at issue in this argument.

D **Correct.** This statement properly identifies a factor that weakens the spokesperson's argument: since the advertising on "free" television acts as a kind of fee, the presence of similar advertising on many cable channels is necessarily the same kind of hidden cost.

E Consumer choice is not an issue in this argument.

The correct answer is D.

13. Wood smoke contains dangerous toxins that cause changes in human cells. Because wood smoke presents such a high health risk, legislation is needed to regulate the use of open-air fires and wood-burning stoves.

Which of the following, if true, provides the most support for the argument above?

(A) The amount of dangerous toxins contained in wood smoke is much less than the amount contained in an equal volume of automobile exhaust.

(B) Within the jurisdiction covered by the proposed legislation, most heating and cooking is done with oil or natural gas.

(C) Smoke produced by coal-burning stoves is significantly more toxic than smoke from wood-burning stoves.

(D) No significant beneficial effect on air quality would result if open-air fires were banned within the jurisdiction covered by the proposed legislation.

(E) In valleys where wood is used as the primary heating fuel, the concentration of smoke results in poor air quality.

Argument Construction

Situation Wood smoke is hazardous, and restrictive legislation is needed.

Reasoning *Which point supports the need for legislation?* The argument for legislation is based on the position that wood smoke is hazardous to people's health. Any evidence of physical harm resulting from wood smoke supports the argument that legislation is needed. Undoubtedly, poor air quality caused by a high concentration of wood smoke presents just such a health risk.

A This argument is about wood smoke, so comparisons with car exhaust are irrelevant.

B This point suggests that wood smoke presents few dangers to people in the area, and so decreases the need for legislation.

C This argument is about wood smoke, so comparisons with coal-burning stoves are irrelevant.

D The lack of benefit from banning open-air fires is a point against the legislation.

E **Correct.** This statement properly identifies a factor that supports the argument in favor of legislation.

The correct answer is E.

14. Within 20 years it will probably be possible to identify the genetic susceptibility an individual may have toward any particular disease. Eventually, effective strategies will be discovered to counteract each such susceptibility. Once these effective strategies are found, therefore, the people who follow them will never get sick.

The argument above is based on which of the following assumptions?

(A) For every disease there is only one strategy that can prevent its occurrence.
(B) In the future, genetics will be the only medical specialty of any importance.
(C) All human sicknesses are in part the result of individuals' genetic susceptibilities.
(D) All humans are genetically susceptible to some diseases.
(E) People will follow medical advice when they are convinced that it is effective.

Argument Construction

Situation Once genetic susceptibilities to diseases are identified and strategies are developed to counteract these susceptibilities, people who follow the strategies will never get sick.

Reasoning *What assumption is this argument based on?* The argument states that people who follow the appropriate strategies for counteracting their genetic susceptibilities to disease will never get sick. How can it be that they would *never* get sick? The argument requires an assumption about the cause of all sickness. Every known disease of humans must correspond to some genetic susceptibilities. The argument thus follows that individuals get sick from those diseases to which they have genetic susceptibilities and that people will not suffer from any illnesses unless they have such susceptibilities.

A The argument refers to *effective strategies*; the argument does not assume that there is only one strategy for each disease.

B The number of medical specialties needed to discover and apply effective strategies is irrelevant to the argument.

C **Correct.** This statement properly identifies the argument's necessary assumption.

D While this statement may be true, it is not necessary to the argument.

E The argument does not concern the circumstances in which people will follow medical advice.

The correct answer is C.

15. A researcher studying drug addicts found that, on average, they tend to manipulate other people a great deal more than nonaddicts do. The researcher concluded that people who frequently manipulate other people are likely to become addicts.

Which of the following, if true, most seriously weakens the researcher's conclusion?

(A) After becoming addicted to drugs, drug addicts learn to manipulate other people as a way of obtaining drugs.

(B) When they are imprisoned, drug addicts often use their ability to manipulate other people to obtain better living conditions.

(C) Some nonaddicts manipulate other people more than some addicts do.

(D) People who are likely to become addicts exhibit unusual behavior patterns other than frequent manipulation of other people.

(E) The addicts that the researcher studied were often unsuccessful in obtaining what they wanted when they manipulated other people.

Argument Evaluation

Situation A researcher finds that drug addicts manipulate other people more than nonaddicts do and concludes that manipulative people are likely to become drug addicts.

Reasoning *What weakens the conclusion?* Consider how the researcher reached the conclusion. The researcher assumed that being manipulative precedes becoming a drug addict. What justification is given for this progression? What if the sequence is reversed and becoming a drug addict instead leads people to become manipulative? If it could be that being an addict makes people manipulative, the researcher's conclusion would be weakened.

A **Correct.** This statement properly identifies information that weakens the researcher's conclusion.

B Drug addicts' behavior in prison is not relevant to the argument.

C The actions of nonaddicts are not relevant to an argument about addicts.

D The argument concerns manipulative behavior, not other or unusual behavior patterns.

E The success or failure of the subjects' manipulative behavior is not relevant to the conclusion.

The correct answer is A.

16. In Swartkans territory, archaeologists discovered charred bone fragments dating back one million years. Analysis of the fragments, which came from a variety of animals, showed that they had been heated to temperatures no higher than those produced in experimental campfires made from branches of white stinkwood, the most common tree around Swartkans.

Which of the following, if true, would, together with the information above, provide the best basis for the claim that the charred bone fragments are evidence of the use of fire by early hominids?

(A) The white stinkwood tree is used for building material by the present-day inhabitants of Swartkans.

(B) Forest fires can heat wood to a range of temperatures that occur in campfires.

(C) The bone fragments were fitted together by the archaeologists to form the complete skeletons of several animals.

(D) Apart from the Swartkans discovery, there is reliable evidence that early hominids used fire as many as 500,000 years ago.

(E) The bone fragments were found in several distinct layers of limestone that contained primitive cutting tools known to have been used by early hominids.

Argument Evaluation

Situation Archaeologists analyzed charred bone fragments dating back to a million years ago and found that the fragments had been heated to the temperature of a campfire fueled by stinkwood. It is claimed that the fragments show that early hominids used fire.

Reasoning *Which additional piece of information would strengthen the argument?* The information that strengthens this argument will be about the subjects of the argument, not about tangential issues. In this case, the argument is about early hominids' use of fire. Any physical evidence that links the early hominids to the charred bone fragments strengthens the argument. If these bone fragments were found in conjunction with some other evidence of the presence of early hominids, then the evidence from the Swartkans location could be used to support the claim that early hominids used fire.

A The present-day use of stinkwood is irrelevant to the argument that early hominids used fire.

B If forest fires could have been responsible for the charring, the argument is weakened, not strengthened.

C The fact that the charred bone fragments form some complete animal skeletons offers no support to the argument that early hominids used fire.

D The fragments date back one million years, so evidence from 500,000 years ago is irrelevant.

E **Correct.** This statement properly identifies evidence that links early hominids to these bone fragments and so strengthens the argument.

The correct answer is E.

17. A conservation group in the United States is trying to change the long-standing image of bats as frightening creatures. The group contends that bats are feared and persecuted solely because they are shy animals that are active only at night.

Which of the following, if true, would cast the most serious doubt on the accuracy of the group's contention?

(A) Bats are steadily losing natural roosting places such as caves and hollow trees and are thus turning to more developed areas for roosting.

(B) Bats are the chief consumers of nocturnal insects and thus can help make their hunting territory more pleasant for humans.

(C) Bats are regarded as frightening creatures not only in the United States but also in Europe, Africa, and South America.

(D) Raccoons and owls are shy and active only at night, yet they are not generally feared and persecuted.

(E) People know more about the behavior of other greatly feared animal species, such as lions, alligators, and snakes, than they do about the behavior of bats.

Argument Evaluation

Situation A conservation group claims that bats are feared and persecuted only because they are shy, nocturnal animals.

Reasoning *What casts doubt on this claim?* If people fear bats only because these animals are shy and active at night, then other species that share those same attributes should be equally feared. Yet raccoons and owls, similarly shy and nocturnal, do not suffer from the same reputation.

A The location of the bats' nests does not explain the cause of the fear.

B The insect-eating habits of bats might be used in their defense, but this activity does not explain the fear of them.

C Including other parts of the world increases the arena of fear; it does not cast doubt on the cause of it.

D Correct. This statement properly identifies the fact that people do not fear shy, nocturnal raccoons and owls and shows that these attributes are not the reason people fear bats.

E The knowledge of other species is irrelevant to the discussion of bats.

The correct answer is D.

18. Opponents of laws that require automobile drivers and passengers to wear seat belts argue that in a free society people have the right to take risks as long as the people do not harm others as a result of taking the risks. As a result, they conclude that it should be each person's decision whether or not to wear a seat belt.

Which of the following, if true, most seriously weakens the conclusion drawn above?

(A) Many new cars are built with seat belts that automatically fasten when someone sits in the front seat.

(B) Automobile insurance rates for all automobile owners are higher because of the need to pay for the increased injuries or deaths of people not wearing seat belts.

(C) Passengers in airplanes are required to wear seat belts during takeoffs and landings.

(D) The rate of automobile fatalities in states that do not have mandatory seat-belt laws is greater than the rate of fatalities in states that do have such laws.

(E) In automobile accidents, a greater number of passengers who do not wear seat belts are injured than are passengers who do wear seat belts.

Argument Evaluation

Situation Opponents of automobile seat-belt laws contend that all citizens of a free society should be able to take risks as long as their behavior does not harm others.

Reasoning *How would refusing to wear a seat belt harm anyone other than the person who does not use it?* Consider what detriments to others might be associated with drivers and passengers who take the risk of not wearing seat belts. If injuries and deaths increase when people do not wear seat belts, the automobile insurance rates for all car owners rise in order to pay for the costs incurred by those who do not wear seat belts.

A The existence of automatic seat belts in some seats of some cars is coincidental; it is not relevant to the opponents' claim of their right to take risks.

B **Correct.** This statement properly identifies a point that weakens the conclusion. All car owners must pay higher insurance premiums because some people refuse to wear seat belts. Thus, this refusal does in fact harm others.

C The argument is about cars, not airplanes.

D The higher number of fatalities does not weaken the conclusion.

E The higher number of injuries does not weaken the conclusion.

The correct answer is B.

19. Which of the following best completes the passage below?

People buy prestige when they buy a premium product. They want to be associated with something special. Mass-marketing techniques and price-reduction strategies should not be used because _____.

(A) affluent purchasers currently represent a shrinking portion of the population of all purchasers
(B) continued sales depend directly on the maintenance of an aura of exclusivity
(C) purchasers of premium products are concerned with the quality as well as with the price of the products
(D) expansion of the market niche to include a broader spectrum of consumers will increase profits
(E) manufacturing a premium brand is not necessarily more costly than manufacturing a standard brand of the same product

Argument Construction

Situation Consumers seek prestige when they buy premium products, that is to say, expensive, top-quality products. Mass-marketing techniques and price-reduction strategies are not appropriate tools to sell these products to consumers seeking to be associated with something special.

Reasoning *Why are these tools NOT appropriate for selling these products to this group of consumers?* Consider that these consumers want to feel that the premium product they are buying is out of the ordinary. Any strategy that makes the premium product seem more common or easier to own reduces that product's appeal to this group. By definition, mass-marketing techniques appeal to a huge number of people, rather than to a small, select group. Further, reducing prices lowers any associated prestige as well because the product becomes more broadly obtainable. These two techniques would not be appropriate because these consumers would lose the feeling that the product is special.

A Mass-marketing strategies are not an appropriate match for a small, and currently dwindling, group of buyers; price reductions are not an appropriate match for consumers attracted to products by their high prices.

B Correct. This statement properly identifies the point that continued sales depend on making the product seem special and difficult to obtain; mass-marketing techniques and price-reduction strategies would make the product seem quite ordinary and thus hurt sales.

C It has not been established that these strategies would lower the products' quality, and so this offers no reason for avoiding the strategies.

D This statement provides a reason why broader marketing should be employed, rather than supporting an argument that it should be avoided.

E Manufacturing costs are not discussed and so are irrelevant.

The correct answer is B.

20. The number of people diagnosed as having a certain intestinal disease has dropped significantly in a rural county this year, as compared to last year. Health officials attribute this decrease entirely to improved sanitary conditions at water-treatment plants, which made for cleaner water this year and thus reduced the incidence of the disease.

Which of the following, if true, would most seriously weaken the health officials' explanation for the lower incidence of the disease?

(A) Many new water-treatment plants have been built in the last five years in the rural county.

(B) Bottled spring water has not been consumed in significantly different quantities by people diagnosed as having the intestinal disease, as compared to people who did not contract the disease.

(C) Because of a new diagnostic technique, many people who until this year would have been diagnosed as having the intestinal disease are now correctly diagnosed as suffering from intestinal ulcers.

(D) Because of medical advances this year, far fewer people who contract the intestinal disease will develop severe cases of the disease.

(E) The water in the rural county was brought up to the sanitary standards of the water in neighboring counties 10 years ago.

Argument Evaluation

Situation Health officials claim that improved sanitary conditions at water-treatment plants have reduced the number of diagnosed cases of a specific intestinal disease.

Reasoning *What weakens the health officials' claim?* Any alternate explanation of the reduction in such diagnoses weakens their claim. It is possible that other, perhaps similar, problems had been mistakenly diagnosed, and the misdiagnoses contributed to the number of cases reported during the previous year. If a new diagnostic technique permits doctors to distinguish between two health conditions not recognized previously as distinct problems, then the reduction of cases may be due to more precise diagnoses rather than to better sanitary conditions. If the people with the other condition are now correctly diagnosed, the number mistakenly diagnosed with the intestinal disease goes down.

A The number of plants built within the last five years is irrelevant to the question of the impact of improved sanitary conditions during the most recent one-year period.

B Bottled water is here ruled out as an alternative explanation since almost equal quantities were consumed by those who caught the disease and those who did not.

C **Correct.** This statement properly identifies a factor that weakens the officials' argument.

D The number of cases of the disease is the issue, not the severity of the illness.

E The neighboring counties may have had inadequate sanitary conditions as well, and, if so, the health officials' claim is not refuted.

The correct answer is C.

21. Rural households have more purchasing power than do urban or suburban households at the same income level, since some of the income urban and suburban households use for food and shelter can be used by rural households for other needs.

Which of the following inferences is best supported by the statement made above?

(A) The average rural household includes more people than does the average urban or suburban household.

(B) Rural households have lower food and housing costs than do either urban or suburban households.

(C) Suburban households generally have more purchasing power than do either rural or urban households.

(D) The median income of urban and suburban households is generally higher than that of rural households.

(E) All three types of households spend more of their income on housing than on all other purchases combined.

Argument Construction

Situation Rural households have more purchasing power than urban and suburban households with the same income level. This is because they can put to other uses some of the money that urban and suburban households must spend on food and shelter.

Reasoning *What can be inferred from this information?* The passage attributes the higher purchasing power of rural households to their ability to spend some of the income that those other households must use for food and shelter. Therefore, rural households must have relatively lower food and shelter costs.

A The passage gives no information about the number of people in the household, and so no inference about those numbers can be made.

B **Correct.** This statement properly identifies an inference supported by the given information. Since rural households have more money left over after paying for food and shelter, their costs for these necessities must be less.

C This statement contradicts the first two lines of the passage.

D The passage discusses the three types of households only *at the same income level.*

E No information is given about how expenditures are divided, so no inference can be drawn.

The correct answer is B.

22. In Asia, where palm trees are nonnative, the trees' flowers have traditionally been pollinated by hand, which has kept palm fruit productivity unnaturally low. When weevils known to be efficient pollinators of palm flowers were introduced into Asia in 1980, palm fruit productivity increased—by up to 50 percent in some areas—but then decreased sharply in 1984.

Which of the following statements, if true, would best explain the 1984 decrease in productivity?

(A) Prices for palm fruit fell between 1980 and 1984 following the rise in production and a concurrent fall in demand.

(B) Imported trees are often more productive than native trees because the imported ones have left behind their pests and diseases in their native lands.

(C) Rapid increases in productivity tend to deplete trees of nutrients needed for the development of the fruit-producing female flowers.

(D) The weevil population in Asia remained at approximately the same level between 1980 and 1984.

(E) Prior to 1980 another species of insect pollinated the Asian palm trees, but not as efficiently as the species of weevil that was introduced in 1980.

Argument Construction

Situation In 1980, the introduction of weevils to pollinate palm trees in Asia resulted in increased palm fruit productivity. This productivity decreased sharply in 1984.

Reasoning *What explains the sudden decrease in 1984?* The palm trees had experienced a sudden burst of productivity beginning in 1980. What if an after-effect of that spurt was the cause? If that burst of productivity had used up the trees' nutrients, then the trees would be unable to produce the flowers that are pollinated in order to produce fruit. This sudden exhaustion of the trees' resources is the best explanation for the sudden decrease in productivity.

A Falling prices and falling demand do not explain the falling productivity of the trees.

B The lack of pests and diseases among imported trees does not explain the sharply decreased productivity.

C **Correct.** This statement properly identifies a reason for sharply decreased productivity.

D If the weevil population pollinating the trees remained the same, it is reasonable to think that productivity remained the same, so this does not explain the decrease.

E A change that occurred before 1980 does not explain a change that occurred in 1984.

The correct answer is C.

23. With the emergence of biotechnology companies, it was feared that they would impose silence about proprietary results on their in-house researchers and their academic consultants. This constraint, in turn, would slow the development of biological science and engineering.

Which of the following, if true, would tend to weaken most seriously the prediction of scientific secrecy described above?

(A) Biotechnological research funded by industry has reached some conclusions that are of major scientific importance.

(B) When the results of scientific research are kept secret, independent researchers are unable to build on those results.

(C) Since the research priorities of biotechnology companies are not the same as those of academic institutions, the financial support of research by such companies distorts the research agenda.

(D) To enhance the companies' standing in the scientific community, the biotechnology companies encourage employees to publish their results, especially results that are important.

(E) Biotechnology companies devote some of their research resources to problems that are of fundamental scientific importance and that are not expected to produce immediate practical applications.

Argument Evaluation

Situation Biotechnology companies may slow the development of biological science and engineering by imposing restrictions on what their scientists can say and share with others.

Reasoning *What point weakens the prediction?* If the biotechnology companies do not demand silence of their scientists, then the development of biological science and engineering could proceed as freely as it did before the emergence of the companies. By encouraging their employees to publish their results, the companies are promoting, not impeding, the development of biological science and engineering.

A The importance of the findings does not affect the prediction.

B The loss to independent researchers does not weaken the prediction.

C The companies' priorities for research do not affect the prediction.

D Correct. This statement properly identifies a situation that is the reverse of the predicted one.

E The companies' typical policy of conducting some research without a practical application does not weaken the prediction.

The correct answer is D.

24. Guitar strings often go "dead"—become less responsive and bright in tone—after a few weeks of intense use. A researcher whose son is a classical guitarist hypothesized that dirt and oil, rather than changes in the material properties of the string, were responsible.

Which of the following investigations is most likely to yield significant information that would help evaluate the researcher's hypothesis?

(A) Determining whether a metal alloy is used to make the strings used by classical guitarists
(B) Determining whether classical guitarists make their strings go dead faster than do folk guitarists
(C) Determining whether identical lengths of string, of the same gauge, go dead at different rates when strung on various brands of guitars
(D) Determining whether a dead string and a new string produce different qualities of sound
(E) Determining whether smearing various substances on new guitar strings causes them to go dead

Evaluation of a Plan

Situation Dirt and oil are hypothesized to be the cause of lost tone and brightness in guitar strings, rather than changes in the material itself.

Reasoning *Which investigation helps evaluate the hypothesis?* The researcher needs to test the hypothesis directly. Smearing substances (such as dirt and oil) onto new strings and seeing whether they go dead is a direct test. If the strings do not lose their tone, the hypothesis is false. If they do go dead, the hypothesis is a likely explanation of the problem, although not necessarily the only explanation.

A Not enough information is given about the metal alloy to evaluate its effect on the composition of the strings and their loss of tone after intense play.
B The difference in the style of play is outside the scope of the hypothesis.
C The difference in the brands of guitars is outside the scope of the hypothesis.
D The difference between a new string and a dead string has already been established.
E **Correct.** This statement properly identifies a procedure that is a direct test of the hypothesis.

The correct answer is E.

25. In recent years, many cabinetmakers have been winning acclaim as artists. But since furniture must be useful, cabinetmakers must exercise their craft with an eye to the practical utility of their product. For this reason, cabinetmaking is not art.

Which of the following is an assumption that supports drawing the conclusion above from the reason given for that conclusion?

(A) Some furniture is made to be placed in museums, where it will not be used by anyone.

(B) Some cabinetmakers are more concerned than others with the practical utility of the products they produce.

(C) Cabinetmakers should be more concerned with the practical utility of their products than they currently are.

(D) An object is not an art object if its maker pays attention to the object's practical utility.

(E) Artists are not concerned with the monetary value of their products.

Argument Construction

Situation Cabinetmaking cannot be considered an art because furniture is made with an eye to its usefulness.

Reasoning *What assumption is made in the argument?* The argument makes a general statement about all cabinetmakers and all their furniture. The assumption must also be a general statement because it is not logical to reason from a particular statement about *some furniture* or *some cabinetmakers* to a general statement about all cabinetmaking. What excludes pieces of furniture from being considered works of art? The argument states only that their usefulness must be taken into account during their creation. Therefore, the operative assumption must be that an object created with its practical use in mind cannot be a work of art.

A The destination of the object after its creation is not the issue.

B The degree of consideration is not relevant; only the fact of any consideration is relevant.

C The degree of consideration is not relevant; given the conclusion, any consideration of utility means the piece is not a work of art.

D **Correct.** This statement properly identifies the underlying assumption that an object created with any consideration of usefulness is not a work of art.

E Artists' interest or disinterest in the monetary value of their works has nothing to do with what objects are considered works of art.

The correct answer is D.

26. Male bowerbirds construct elaborately decorated nests, or bowers. Basing their judgment on the fact that different local populations of bowerbirds of the same species build bowers that exhibit different building and decorative styles, researchers have concluded that the bowerbirds' building styles are a culturally acquired, rather than a genetically transmitted, trait.

Which of the following, if true, would most strengthen the conclusion drawn by the researchers?

(A) There are more common characteristics than there are differences among the bower-building styles of the local bowerbird population that has been studied most extensively.

(B) Young male bowerbirds are inept at bower building and apparently spend years watching their elders before becoming accomplished in the local bower style.

(C) The bowers of one species of bowerbird lack the towers and ornamentation characteristic of the bowers of most other species of bowerbird.

(D) Bowerbirds are found only in New Guinea and Australia, where local populations of the birds apparently seldom have contact with one another.

(E) It is well known that the song dialects of some songbirds are learned rather than transmitted genetically.

Argument Evaluation

Situation Male bowerbirds that are of the same species but living in different habitats build nests of widely varying styles. Researchers conclude that this nest-building behavior is culturally acquired rather than genetically transmitted.

Reasoning *What evidence strengthens the researchers' conclusion?* The researchers base their conclusion upon the different styles of nests, reasoning that the nests would all be similar if the bower-building behavior was only transmitted through the genes of the species. What would lend support to this reasoning? If young male bowerbirds have no inherent aptitude for nest building and must learn it over a period of years by watching older male bowerbirds, then the argument that bowerbirds acquire their nest-building preferences culturally rather than genetically is strengthened.

A The greater number of similarities than differences in style in one population could be attributed to either cultural acquisition or genetic transmission, so the conclusion is not strengthened.

B **Correct.** This statement properly identifies evidence that supports the researchers' conclusion that nest-building styles are culturally acquired.

C The cited differences are among populations of the same species; differences among species are outside the scope of the conclusion.

D Since no information is given about the nest-building styles of these populations (whether or not they are of the same species), the fact that they have little contact neither strengthens nor weakens the conclusion.

E While this statement does offer an example of learned bird behavior, it does not strengthen the conclusion; the argument is about nest building, not about song dialects.

The correct answer is B.

27. A drug that is highly effective in treating many types of infection can, at present, be obtained only from the bark of the ibora, a tree that is quite rare in the wild. It takes the bark of 5,000 trees to make one kilogram of the drug. It follows, therefore, that continued production of the drug must inevitably lead to the ibora's extinction.

Which of the following, if true, most seriously weakens the argument above?

(A) The drug made from ibora bark is dispensed to doctors from a central authority.

(B) The drug made from ibora bark is expensive to produce.

(C) The leaves of the ibora are used in a number of medical products.

(D) The ibora can be propagated from cuttings and grown under cultivation.

(E) The ibora generally grows in largely inaccessible places.

Argument Evaluation

Situation The extinction of the rare ibora tree is inevitable if production of an effective infection-fighting drug continues.

Reasoning *Which point weakens the argument?* The production of the drug requires such an enormous amount of bark that the continuing existence of the rare tree is in jeopardy. Why is this? The argument assumes that killing the trees in the wild is the only way to obtain the needed bark. Consider from what other sources this tree bark could be harvested. If cuttings from the wild trees could be used to breed and grow the trees as a renewable crop, then the cultivated trees could be used to manufacture the drug, and the majority of the trees in the wild could be left to flourish.

A The method of drug's distribution does not affect the likely extinction of the tree because the bark has already been stripped from the tree for the drug's production.

B The price of the drug does not affect the outcome for the tree because the production of the drug has already taken place.

C Uses for other parts of the tree make its extinction more likely and strengthens the argument.

D Correct. This statement properly identifies a factor that weakens the argument.

E The argument assumes that production of the drug will continue, no matter how inaccessible the tree is.

The correct answer is D.

28. Many breakfast cereals are fortified with vitamin supplements. Some of these cereals provide 100 percent of the recommended daily requirement of vitamins. Nevertheless, a well-balanced breakfast, including a variety of foods, is a better source of those vitamins than are such fortified breakfast cereals alone.

Which of the following, if true, would most strongly support the position above?

(A) In many foods, the natural combination of vitamins with other nutrients makes those vitamins more usable by the body than are vitamins added in vitamin supplements.

(B) People who regularly eat cereals fortified with vitamin supplements sometimes neglect to eat the foods in which the vitamins occur naturally.

(C) Foods often must be fortified with vitamin supplements because naturally occurring vitamins are removed during processing.

(D) Unprocessed cereals are naturally high in several of the vitamins that are usually added to fortified breakfast cereals.

(E) Cereals containing vitamin supplements are no harder to digest than similar cereals without added vitamins.

Argument Evaluation

Situation A well-balanced breakfast with a variety of foods is a better source of vitamins than a breakfast of cereal fortified with vitamin supplements.

Reasoning *What strengthens the argument in favor of a balanced breakfast as a better source of vitamins?* The argument compares the vitamins naturally occurring in foods with those added to cereal. What would make the vitamins in foods superior in nutritional value to the vitamin supplements in fortified cereals? If the combination of vitamins with other nutrients in many foods allowed the body to better use those vitamins, a balanced breakfast would be the preferred source of the vitamins.

A **Correct.** This statement properly identifies a factor that strengthens the argument.

B This statement explains who might benefit from a well-balanced breakfast, but it does not support the conclusion in favor eating a variety of foods.

C This statement shows why foods need to be fortified, but it does not support the conclusion that naturally occurring vitamins in foods are better.

D This statement provides some information about unprocessed cereals, but it does not explain why the vitamins found in a balanced breakfast are superior to the vitamins in fortified cereals.

E The ability of the body to digest fortified or unfortified cereals is outside the scope of the question.

The correct answer is A.

Questions 29–30 are based on the following:

In many corporations, employees are being replaced by automated equipment in order to save money. However, many workers who lose their jobs to automation will need government assistance to survive, and the same corporations that are laying people off will eventually pay for that assistance through increased taxes and unemployment insurance payments.

29. The author is arguing that _____.

(A) higher taxes and unemployment insurance payments will discourage corporations from automating

(B) replacing people through automation to reduce production costs will result in increases of other costs to corporations

(C) many workers who lose their jobs to automation will have to be retrained for new jobs

(D) corporations that are laying people off will eventually rehire many of them

(E) corporations will not save money by automating because people will be needed to run the new machines

Argument Construction

Situation Corporations replace employees with automated equipment to save money, but, through increased taxes and unemployment insurance, those corporations must pay for the government-assistance programs the laid-off employees then need to survive.

Reasoning *What is the author's argument?* To restate the argument, look at the information in the passage. The first sentence says that corporations replace workers with automated equipment in order to save money. The author then states that these same corporations will have other new costs in the form of increased taxes and unemployment insurance payments because the laid-off workers will require government assistance.

A The author says there will be costs to the corporations but does not go so far as to say these costs will discourage the corporations from automating.

B **Correct.** This statement properly identifies the author's argument that, in their efforts to lower costs through automation, corporations will incur increases in other costs.

C The author does not discuss the retraining of employees.

D The author does not discuss the rehiring of employees.

E The corporations would have anticipated the number of employees necessary to run the automated equipment when they initially determined that automation would save money.

The correct answer is B.

30. Which of the following, if true, most strengthens the author's argument?

(A) Many workers who have already lost their jobs to automation have been unable to find new jobs.
(B) Many corporations that have failed to automate have seen their profits decline.
(C) Taxes and unemployment insurance are paid also by corporations that are not automating.
(D) Most of the new jobs created by automation pay less than the jobs eliminated by automation did.
(E) The initial investment in machinery for automation is often greater than the short-term savings in labor costs.

Argument Evaluation

Situation Corporations replace employees with automated equipment to save money, but, through increased taxes and unemployment insurance, those corporations must pay for the government assistance programs the laid-off employees then need to survive. (The same as the previous item.)

Reasoning *What information strengthens the author's argument?* By stating that the need for government-assistance programs will rise, the author clearly assumes that the laid-off employees will not find work and will have to rely on such programs. If other workers who have lost jobs to automation have been unable to find work, then the argument is strengthened because it shows that the author's assumption has proven to be true.

A **Correct.** This statement properly identifies a factor that strengthens the author's argument.

B The argument is about the corporations that do automate, not about those that do not, and thus this statement is irrelevant.

C The fact that such costs are paid and will be paid by all corporations, whether or not they automate, weakens the author's argument by suggesting that the increased costs resulting from automation will be spread over a wider group.

D This statement repeats that the corporations will initially experience lowered costs for employee wages; it does not strengthen the argument.

E The equipment costs that are incurred immediately upon automating are not relevant to the argument. In the passage, the author maintains that corporations *will eventually pay* for the costs of increased government assistance, and it is those long-term costs on which the argument is based.

The correct answer is A.

31. When a polygraph test is judged inconclusive, this is no reflection on the examinee. Rather, such a judgment means that the test has failed to show whether the examinee was truthful or untruthful. Nevertheless, employers will sometimes refuse to hire a job applicant because of an inconclusive polygraph test result.

Which of the following conclusions can most properly be drawn from the information above?

(A) Most examinees with inconclusive polygraph test results are in fact untruthful.

(B) Polygraph tests should not be used by employers in the consideration of job applicants.

(C) An inconclusive polygraph test result is sometimes unfairly held against the examinee.

(D) A polygraph test indicating that an examinee is untruthful can sometimes be mistaken.

(E) Some employers have refused to consider the results of polygraph tests when evaluating job applicants.

Argument Construction

Situation Employers sometimes refuse to hire job applicants because of inconclusive polygraph tests, even though inconclusive tests reveal only the failure of the test itself to determine the truthfulness or untruthfulness of the person tested.

Reasoning *What conclusion can be drawn from this information?* Inconclusive tests do not reveal anything about the person tested; inconclusive tests reveal only the failure of the test. Nevertheless, employers may choose not to hire an applicant whose polygraph test has had an inconclusive result. It is reasonable to conclude that these employers unfairly treat the lack of firm test results as evidence of a flaw—not in the test, but in the applicant.

A This statement makes a judgment that is explicitly contradicted in the passage, which states that an inconclusive test *is no reflection on the examinee.*

B The argument does not support this sweeping conclusion about all uses of polygraph tests; the passage discusses only inconclusive polygraph test results.

C **Correct.** This statement properly identifies a conclusion that can reasonably be drawn from the given information.

D The argument is concerned only with inconclusive tests, not cases when the polygraph test is mistaken.

E Employers who do not consider polygraph tests are irrelevant to the discussion.

The correct answer is C.

32. The technological conservatism of bicycle manufacturers is a reflection of the kinds of demand they are trying to meet. The only cyclists seriously interested in innovation and willing to pay for it are bicycle racers. Therefore, innovation in bicycle technology is limited by what authorities will accept as standard for purposes of competition in bicycle races.

Which of the following is an assumption made in drawing the conclusion on the previous page?

(A) The market for cheap, traditional bicycles cannot expand unless the market for high-performance competition bicycles expands.

(B) High-performance bicycles are likely to be improved more as a result of technological innovations developed in small workshops than as a result of technological innovations developed in major manufacturing concerns.

(C) Bicycle racers do not generate a strong demand for innovations that fall outside what is officially recognized as standard for purposes of competition.

(D) The technological conservatism of bicycle manufacturers results primarily from their desire to manufacture a product that can be sold without being altered to suit different national markets.

(E) The authorities who set standards for high-performance bicycle racing do not keep informed about innovative bicycle design.

Argument Construction

Situation Bicycle racers are the only consumers willing to pay for innovations in bicycle technology. Manufacturers therefore limit innovation to the standards established for competitive bicycle racing.

Reasoning *What is being assumed in this argument?* This argument implies a connection between what bicycle racers want and what bicycle manufacturers make. The passage states that only racers are interested in innovation and willing to pay for it. Bicycle manufacturers have determined it is not worthwhile to produce innovative bicycles that do not meet official standards. What is the implied interaction? It is reasonable to assume that racers must not be interested in buying models that, while innovative, do not meet official standards for racing; they will pay only for those innovations that are acceptable in competition.

A The argument concerns innovation in bicycle technology. It is not about the entire market for all bicycles, so no assumption is made about traditional bicycles.

B The passage does not discuss where the best innovations are likely to be created, so no assumption about small workshops versus large manufacturers is made.

C Correct. This statement properly identifies the conclusion's underlying assumption that bicycle racers do not buy bicycles they cannot use for racing.

D The passage does not discuss different national markets; no assumption can be made about them.

E The passage does not indicate what the authorities do or do not know; this statement is extraneous to the passage and cannot be assumed.

The correct answer is C.

33. Robot satellites relay important communications and identify weather patterns. Because the satellites can be repaired only in orbit, astronauts are needed to repair them. Without repairs, the satellites would eventually malfunction. Therefore, space flights carrying astronauts must continue.

Which of the following, if true, would most seriously weaken the argument above?

(A) Satellites falling from orbit because of malfunctions burn up in the atmosphere.

(B) Although satellites are indispensable in the identification of weather patterns, weather forecasters also make some use of computer projections to identify weather patterns.

(C) The government, responding to public pressure, has decided to cut the budget for space flights and put more money into social welfare programs.

(D) Repair of satellites requires heavy equipment, which adds to the amount of fuel needed to lift a spaceship carrying astronauts into orbit.

(E) Technical obsolescence of robot satellites makes repairing them more costly and less practical than sending new, improved satellites into orbit.

Argument Evaluation

Situation Space flights carrying astronauts must continue so that the astronauts can repair robot satellites in orbit.

Reasoning *What information would most weaken the argument?* It is argued that satellite repairs are needed to avoid potential malfunctions and that astronauts are needed to perform the repairs. Information that challenges either of these needs weakens the argument. High-technology equipment may quickly become obsolescent. A less expensive and more practical solution to the problem of repairing obsolescent satellites is to launch new, improved satellites. This suggestion of a better alternative weakens the argument considerably.

A Malfunction can destroy the satellite; this statement lends some support to the argument to continue space flights to avoid satellite malfunctions.

B Since satellites are judged to be *indispensable*, this statement suggests that their repair continues to be necessary.

C While budget cuts for space flights provide a context for the argument in favor of continuing flights, this statement does not weaken the argument.

D Increased fuel costs do not weaken the argument that space flights are needed to maintain the satellites.

E **Correct.** This statement properly identifies a factor that weakens the argument.

The correct answer is E.

34. A company's two divisions performed with remarkable consistency over the past three years: in each of those years, the pharmaceuticals division has accounted for roughly 20 percent of dollar sales and 40 percent of profits, and the chemicals division for the balance.

Regarding the past three years, which of the following can properly be inferred from the statement above?

(A) Total dollar sales for each of the company's divisions have remained roughly constant.

(B) The pharmaceuticals division has faced stiffer competition in its markets than has the chemicals division.

(C) The chemicals division has realized lower profits per dollar of sales than has the pharmaceuticals division.

(D) The product mix offered by each of the company's divisions has remained unchanged.

(E) Highly profitable products accounted for a higher percentage of the chemicals division's sales than of the pharmaceuticals division's.

Argument Construction

Situation For three years, the pharmaceutical division of a company has accounted for 20 percent of the dollar sales and 40 percent of the profits, and the chemicals division for the balance.

Reasoning *What can be inferred from these numbers?* If the pharmaceuticals division made 40 percent of the company's profits on 20 percent of the company's dollar sales, then the chemicals division made 60 percent of the profits on 80 percent of the sales. Comparing these percentages makes it clear that the pharmaceuticals division makes more profit per dollar of sales than the chemicals division does.

A The information is about percentages, not total dollars.

B There is no information about the competition faced by either division; the higher profit margin for the pharmaceuticals division would suggest, if anything, less intense competition in its markets.

C **Correct.** This statement properly identifies an inference that can be drawn from the given information.

D Since there is no information about the product mix, no inference about it is possible.

E The passage does not distinguish between highly profitable products and other products, so this inference cannot be drawn from the information.

The correct answer is C.

35. Advertisement: Today's customers expect high quality. Every advance in the quality of manufactured products raises customer expectations. The company that is satisfied with the current quality of its products will soon find that its customers are not. At MegaCorp, meeting or exceeding customer expectations is our goal.

Which of the following must be true on the basis of the statements in the advertisement above?

(A) MegaCorp's competitors will succeed in attracting customers only if those competitors adopt MegaCorp's goal as their own.

(B) A company that does not correctly anticipate the expectations of its customers is certain to fail in advancing the quality of its products.

(C) MegaCorp's goal is possible to meet only if continuing advances in product quality are possible.

(D) If a company becomes satisfied with the quality of its products, then the quality of its products is sure to decline.

(E) MegaCorp's customers are currently satisfied with the quality of its products.

Argument Construction

Situation An advertisement for MegaCorp observes that every advance in quality raises customer expectations; it is not enough for a company to be satisfied with current quality.

Reasoning *What conclusion can be based on the assertions in the advertisement?* Meeting or exceeding customer expectations is MegaCorp's goal. Since advances in quality are said to increase expectations, those advances must continue. Therefore, the advertisement assumes there exists a continually increasing level of product quality to which the company can aspire.

A The ad provides no information about MegaCorp's competitors so no conclusion about them is possible.

B The ad says that customers' expectations come from the quality of the product itself, not from how MegaCorp anticipates those expectations.

C **Correct.** This statement properly identifies a conclusion that can be drawn from the advertisement's argument.

D While the ad implies that a company should not be satisfied with current quality, it does not go so far as to say that such an attitude causes quality to decline.

E MegaCorp states its goal, but there is no evidence that it currently meets that goal.

The correct answer is C.

36. Many companies now have employee assistance programs that enable employees, free of charge, to improve their physical fitness, reduce stress, and learn ways to stop smoking. These programs increase worker productivity, reduce absenteeism, and lessen insurance costs for employee health care. Therefore, these programs benefit the company as well as the employee.

Which of the following, if true, most significantly strengthens the conclusion above?

(A) Physical fitness programs are often the most popular services offered to employees.

(B) Studies have shown that training in stress management is not effective for many people.

(C) Regular exercise reduces people's risk of heart disease and provides them with increased energy.

(D) Physical injuries sometimes result from entering a strenuous physical fitness program too quickly.

(E) Employee assistance programs require companies to hire people to supervise the various programs offered.

Argument Evaluation

Situation Employee assistance programs benefit the company as well as the employees.

Reasoning *What evidence shows that the programs do benefit both the company and the employees?* The argument already points out several benefits for the company, but the conclusion maintains that there are positive results for the employees as well. The existence of such benefits to employees needs to be substantiated. If regular exercise lowers their risk for some serious diseases, employees can indeed benefit from their participation in these programs. Furthermore, increased employee energy benefits the employees as well as the company.

A The popularity of physical fitness programs does not explain how employee assistance programs benefit both company and employee.

B Evidence that the stress management program is ineffective weakens the argument rather than strengthens it.

C **Correct.** This statement properly identifies evidence that strengthens the conclusion.

D Injuries benefit neither the company nor the employees.

E The need to hire supervisors is an increased cost for the company, not a benefit.

The correct answer is C.

Questions 37–38 are based on the following:

Companies O and P each have the same number of employees who work the same number of hours per week. According to records maintained by each company, the employees of Company O had fewer job-related accidents last year than did the employees of Company P. Therefore, employees of Company O are less likely to have job-related accidents than are employees of Company P.

37. Which of the following, if true, would most strengthen the conclusion above?

(A) Company P manufactures products that are more hazardous for workers to produce than does Company O.

(B) Company P holds more safety inspections than does Company O.

(C) Company P maintains a more modern infirmary than does Company O.

(D) Company O paid more for new job-related medical claims than did Company P.

(E) Company P provides more types of health-care benefits than does Company O.

Argument Evaluation

Situation Two companies have the same number of employees working the same number of hours a week, but one company's employees reportedly had fewer job-related accidents last year and so are likely to have fewer job-related accidents in general.

Reasoning *What point would most strengthen this argument?* The argument generalizes from the number of last year's job-related accidents at the two companies to a continuing reduced likelihood of such accidents at the one company. Specific information that suggests that the one company is inherently a safer place than the other would support the generalized argument. If one company's employees must work on a product that is more hazardous to make, then it is reasonable to conclude that they will continue to suffer more job-related accidents than the employees at the other company. Since the product is not going to change, it is likely that the proportion of accidents will not either.

A **Correct.** This statement properly identifies specific information that strengthens the conclusion.

B A greater attention to safety does not lead to the conclusion that there will be a greater number of accidents.

C Having a modern infirmary does not cause more or fewer accidents; it simply provides a place for accident victims to receive care.

D The greater amount paid for job-related medical claims may indicate that, although the accidents were fewer, they were more serious, but it does not strengthen the argument about the occurrence of the accidents.

E One company's superior health-care benefits are irrelevant to the likelihood of accidents.

The correct answer is A.

38. Which of the following, if true, would most weaken the conclusion above?

(A) The employees of Company P lost more time at work due to job-related accidents than did the employees of Company O.

(B) Company P considered more types of accidents to be job-related than did Company O.

(C) The employees of Company P were sick more often than were the employees of Company O.

(D) Several employees of Company O each had more than one job-related accident.

(E) The majority of job-related accidents at Company O involved a single machine.

Argument Evaluation

Situation Two companies have the same number of employees working the same number of hours a week, but one company's employees reportedly had fewer job-related accidents last year and so are likely to have fewer job-related accidents in general. (The same as the previous item.)

Reasoning *What point would most weaken the argument?* The passage concludes that one company is safer than the other because it reported fewer job-related accidents than the other did. Since the argument relies on the comparison of one company's reported accidents to the other company's reported accidents, any information that suggests their reporting was done differently would undermine both the argument's comparison and the conclusion. Differences in the way the companies reported the accidents would make the accident rates difficult to compare directly. Since the company reporting the greater number of job-related accidents also considers more types of accidents to be job-related, the basis of the comparison is weakened and so is the argument.

A The greater amount of time lost at work by the employees of the company with the greater number of job-related accidents is to be expected; the argument is not affected.

B **Correct.** This statement properly identifies the fact that the company reporting the greater number of accidents used a broader definition. Thus, the basis of the comparison is faulty, and the conclusion is weakened.

C Illness is not the same as a job-related accident, so more reports of illness are irrelevant to a comparison of accidents.

D This statement is consistent with Company O's reporting that fewer of its employees had job-related accidents; it does not undermine the conclusion.

E Identifying one major cause of job-related accidents at Company O does not weaken the conclusion that the company is likely to have fewer accidents than Company P.

The correct answer is B.

39. Last year the rate of inflation was 1.2 percent, but during the current year it has been 4 percent. We can conclude that inflation is on an upward trend and the rate will be still higher next year.

Which of the following, if true, most seriously weakens the conclusion above?

(A) The inflation figures were computed on the basis of a representative sample of economic data rather than all of the available data.

(B) Last year a dip in oil prices brought inflation temporarily below its recent stable annual level of 4 percent.

(C) Increases in the pay of some workers are tied to the level of inflation, and at an inflation rate of 4 percent or above, these pay raises constitute a force causing further inflation.

(D) The 1.2 percent rate of inflation last year represented a 10-year low.

(E) Government intervention cannot affect the rate of inflation to any significant degree.

Argument Evaluation

Situation The rate of inflation was 1.2 percent last year but is 4 percent in the current year. It is therefore expected to rise above 4 percent next year.

Reasoning *What point weakens this conclusion?* The conclusion is based on an *upward trend* that is derived from data for two years. Data from only two years provide rather weak evidence of a *trend.* Additional evidence that provides a context for the annual inflation rates during the most recent two-year period will promote a more solid evaluation of this prediction of next year's inflation rate. If inflation has recently been *stable* at 4 percent, and the temporary drop the previous year is accounted for by lower oil prices, then the basis for the prediction seems quite weak.

A As long as the sample was representative, the figures should be accurate. This point does not weaken the conclusion.

B **Correct.** This statement properly identifies a point that weakens the conclusion.

C This statement explains one process by which inflation increases and tends to support the conclusion that inflation will continue to rise.

D Learning that last year's figure was the lowest rate of inflation in 10 years does not provide enough information to conclude whether the rate of inflation will rise next year.

E The failure of government intervention to affect the rate of inflation could be seen to support, not weaken, the conclusion.

The correct answer is B.

40. Offshore oil-drilling operations entail an unavoidable risk of an oil spill, but importing oil on tankers presently entails an even greater such risk per barrel of oil. Therefore, if we are to reduce the risk of an oil spill without curtailing our use of oil, we must invest more in offshore operations and import less oil on tankers.

Which of the following, if true, most seriously weakens the argument above?

(A) Tankers can easily be redesigned so that their use entails less risk of an oil spill.

(B) Oil spills caused by tankers have generally been more serious than those caused by offshore operations.

(C) The impact of offshore operations on the environment can be controlled by careful management.

(D) Offshore operations usually damage the ocean floor, but tankers rarely cause such damage.

(E) Importing oil on tankers is currently less expensive than drilling for it offshore.

Argument Evaluation

Situation Currently, the risk of an oil spill is greater from oil tankers than it is from offshore oil drilling. In order to reduce the risk of an oil spill, we should expand offshore operations and import less oil on tankers.

Reasoning *What point weakens this argument?* The argument is based on the current situation, but present conditions need not continue in the future if they can be improved. What if oil tankers can be redesigned so that they pose less risk of an oil spill? In that case, the argument is weakened because the lowered risk of oil spills resulting from improved oil tanker design could actually make tankers less problematic than offshore operations.

A **Correct.** This statement properly identifies a weakness in the argument.

B The more serious nature of the oil spills caused by tankers strengthens the argument.

C Careful management controlling the environmental impact of offshore operations supports the argument rather than weakens it.

D While offshore operations may cause other environmental damage, this point does not weaken the argument about oil spills.

E Importing oil on tankers may be an attractive economic alternative, but because this point is unrelated to oil spills, it does not weaken the argument.

The correct answer is A.

41. Manufacturers of mechanical pencils make most of their profit on pencil leads rather than on the pencils themselves. The Write Company, which cannot sell its leads as cheaply as other manufacturers can, plans to alter the design of its mechanical pencil so that it will accept only a newly designed Write Company lead, which will be sold at the same price as the Write Company's current lead.

Which of the following, if true, most strongly supports the Write Company's projection that its plan will lead to an increase in its sales of pencil leads?

(A) First-time buyers of mechanical pencils tend to buy the least expensive mechanical pencils available.
(B) Annual sales of mechanical pencils are expected to triple over the next five years.
(C) A Write Company executive is studying ways to reduce the cost of manufacturing pencil leads.
(D) A rival manufacturer recently announced similar plans to introduce a mechanical pencil that would accept only the leads produced by that manufacturer.
(E) In extensive test marketing, mechanical-pencil users found the new Write Company pencil markedly superior to other mechanical pencils they had used.

Evaluation of a Plan

Situation A manufacturer of mechanical pencils plans to produce a new pencil that accepts only the redesigned pencil leads that the company also intends to make and sell. Despite the fact that its leads are sold for a higher price than competitors' leads, the company anticipates that this approach will generate increased lead sales.

Reasoning *What point supports the plan's success?* It is clear that increased lead sales are directly tied to the sales and ongoing use of the new pencil that can use only that type of lead. If the new pencils sell well and then get used frequently, the buyers will need to purchase leads regularly. If thorough test marketing has shown that potential buyers find the new pencil greatly superior to use, then the pencil buyers will have to purchase the only available leads that fit their pencils, no matter whether the leads are more expensive, and the projection that sales of these pencil leads will increase is strengthened.

A It is not known whether the Write Company's pencil is the least expensive, nor are the lead-buying habits of first-time buyers known. This information thus does not strengthen the projection.

B This expectation applies for all manufacturers and does not show that the Write Company's plan will cause increased sales of its pencil leads.

C Reducing the cost of manufacturing the leads could lead to greater profits but not to greater sales, since the passage states that the price will remain the same.

D A rival manufacturer's announcement to follow the same plan does not affect whether the plan will be successful for the Write Company.

E **Correct.** This statement properly identifies a point that supports the plan's success.

The correct answer is E.

42. Mourdet Winery: Danville Winery's new wine was introduced to compete with our most popular wine, which is sold in a distinctive tall, black bottle. Danville uses a similar bottle. Thus, it is likely that many customers intending to buy our wine will mistakenly buy theirs instead.

Danville Winery: Not so. The two bottles can be readily distinguished: the label on ours, but not on theirs, is gold colored.

Which of the following, if true, most undermines Danville Winery's response?

(A) Gold is the background color on the label of many of the wines produced by Danville Winery.

(B) When the bottles are viewed side by side, Danville Winery's bottle is perceptibly taller than Mourdet Winery's.

(C) Danville Winery, unlike Mourdet Winery, displays its wine's label prominently in advertisements.

(D) It is common for occasional purchasers to buy a bottle of wine on the basis of a general impression of the most obvious feature of the bottle.

(E) Many popular wines are sold in bottles of a standard design.

Argument Evaluation

Situation Mourdet Winery sells its most popular wine in a tall, distinctive black bottle. It complains that its customers may be confused by the similarity of the bottle being used for Danville Winery's new wine and thus may mistakenly buy the competing Danville product. Danville Winery rejects this claim, pointing to Danville's unique gold label.

Reasoning *What point undermines Danville Winery's response?* At issue is the degree of difference between the two wineries' packaging of their products. Danville Winery claims that its use of the gold label distinguishes its bottles. What if some purchasers do not look closely enough to see that difference? If occasional purchasers make their purchases based on a general impression of the most obvious features of the bottle, they might easily confuse the two tall, black bottles. Danville Winery's gold label may make little difference to such purchasers, who could overlook the label as they select the bottle by its seemingly distinctive form.

A If Danville Winery uses gold labels frequently, then consumers probably associate gold with Danville; this supports the response rather than undermining it.

B The difference in the height of the bottles gives consumers another way to distinguish between the wineries' products, so this does not undermine the response.

C The prominent display of the uniquely gold label in advertising should help associate the label with Danville Winery, which supports the response.

D **Correct.** This statement properly identifies a point that undermines Danville Winery's response.

E Other wines in standard bottles are irrelevant to the argument.

The correct answer is D.

43. Which of the following best completes the passage below?

The computer industry's estimate that it loses millions of dollars when users illegally copy programs without paying for them is greatly exaggerated. Most of the illegal copying is done by people with no serious interest in the programs. Thus, the loss to the industry is quite small, because ____.

(A) many users who illegally copy programs never find any use for them

(B) most people who illegally copy programs would not purchase them even if purchasing them were the only way to obtain them

(C) even if the computer industry received all the revenue it claims to be losing, it would still be experiencing financial difficulties

(D) the total market value of all illegal copies is low in comparison to the total revenue of the computer industry

(E) the number of programs that are frequently copied illegally is low in comparison to the number of programs available for sale

Argument Construction

Situation The computer industry's estimate of its losses due to illegally copied programs is exaggerated because most of the illegal copying is done by people who are not greatly interested in the programs.

Reasoning *Why would the loss to the industry be said to be small?* The industry's loss due to illegal copying of programs must be evaluated in terms of the sales lost; the actual loss to the industry is directly related to the legitimate sales opportunities that have been lost. Would the people illegally copying the programs buy them if they could not otherwise obtain them? If it were true that most of them have *no serious interest in the programs*, they would be unlikely to purchase them. In this case, few sales would be lost and the loss to the industry could be considered small.

A What users do (or do not do) with programs once they have them does not explain why the loss to the industry is small.

B Correct. This statement properly identifies the fact that if the illegal copiers were unlikely to purchase the same programs, then the industry has not lost potential sales.

C The greater financial difficulties of the industry do not explain why the loss incurred because of the illegally copied programs is small.

D This comparison is faulty: the loss is not being considered in the context of total industry revenues but in the context of total sales of programs.

E This comparison is faulty: the low number of illegal copies would have to be compared with the number of copies sold, not the number *available for sale.*

The correct answer is B.

44. In the last decade there has been a significant decrease in coffee consumption. During this same time, there has been increasing publicity about the caffeine in coffee's adverse long-term effects on health. Therefore, the decrease in coffee consumption must have been caused by consumers' awareness of the harmful effects of caffeine.

Which of the following, if true, most seriously calls into question the explanation above?

(A) On average, people consume 30 percent less coffee today than they did 10 years ago.

(B) Heavy coffee drinkers may have mild withdrawal symptoms, such as headaches, for a day or so after significantly decreasing their coffee consumption.

(C) Sales of specialty types of coffee have held steady as sales of regular brands have declined.

(D) The consumption of fruit juices and caffeine-free herbal teas has increased over the past decade.

(E) Coffee prices increased steadily in the past decade because of unusually severe frosts in coffee-growing nations.

Argument Evaluation

Situation The decrease in coffee consumption in the last decade can be explained by consumers' increased awareness of the detrimental effects of the caffeine in coffee.

Reasoning *What point weakens this explanation?* A conclusion may be weakened when another explanation at least as compelling as the original is offered. Coffee consumption may have decreased over the decade for some reason other than consumers' awareness of the adverse health effects of caffeine. If the price of coffee has increased in the same period that consumption has decreased, then the decrease may well be the result of consumers' attention to price rather than their attention to health. Higher prices would offer a good alternative explanation that would weaken the original explanation.

A This point supports the explanation.

B Withdrawal symptoms would occur only after decreased consumption has occurred.

C This point about differing types of coffee does not weaken the explanation.

D This point could support the explanation if it were the proven result of a switch by former coffee drinkers; it does not weaken the explanation in any event.

E **Correct.** This statement properly identifies an alternative rationale and undermines the given explanation.

The correct answer is E.

45. Fewer families lose their houses because of major disasters such as fire or flood than because of a wage earner's illness that results in death or disability. Yet, whereas most mortgage companies require borrowers to carry insurance to protect against major disasters, they do not require insurance to protect against the death or disability of a wage earner.

Which of the following, if true, would contribute most to an explanation of the difference in insurance requirements?

(A) Some people are less aware of tragedies caused by major disasters than of those caused by the death or disability of a wage earner.

(B) Many people are made uncomfortable by having to consider the possibility of their own death or disability or that of a family member.

(C) Few wage earners are insured by their employers against a temporary loss of income resulting from disability.

(D) The value of a property to a mortgage company is not affected by the death or disability of a wage earner.

(E) Insuring against major disasters can be more costly than insuring against death or disability.

Argument Evaluation

Situation Most mortgage companies require borrowers to carry insurance to protect their homes against major disasters, though not against the death or disability of a wage earner; however, more families lose their homes because of the death or disability of a wage earner than because of a major disaster.

Reasoning *Why do mortgage companies not require homeowners to carry insurance to protect against losing their homes due to lost income?* Consider what is being insured and by whom. The mortgage companies protect their investment in the collateral property when they require homeowners to carry insurance against major disasters. Their investment is not in the people who live in the house, but in the property. Mortgage companies do not require insurance protecting against the death and disability of wage earners because the value of the property is not affected by the death or disability of the people who live there.

A Some people's awareness of tragedies is not relevant to the policies of mortgage companies.

B The uncomfortable feelings many people have about death and disability do not influence of the policies of mortgage companies.

C The lack of disability insurance supplied by employers does not affect the policies of mortgage companies.

D Correct. This statement properly identifies the factor that explains the difference in insurance requirements: mortgage companies invest in property, not people, and a wage earner's loss of income does not affect the value of the property.

E The greater cost of insuring against major disasters does not affect the policies of mortgage companies.

The correct answer is D.

46. Which of the following best completes the passage below?

When the products of several competing suppliers are perceived by consumers to be essentially the same, classical economics predicts that price competition will reduce prices to the same minimal levels and all suppliers' profits to the same minimal levels. Therefore, if classical economics is true, and given suppliers' desire to make as much profit as possible, it should be expected that _____.

(A) in a crowded market widely differing prices will be charged for products that are essentially the same as each other

(B) as a market becomes less crowded as suppliers leave, the profits of the remaining suppliers will tend to decrease

(C) each supplier in a crowded market will try to convince consumers that its product differs significantly from its competitors' products

(D) when consumers are unable to distinguish among the products in a crowded market, consumers will judge that the higher-priced products are of higher quality

(E) suppliers in crowded markets will have more incentive to reduce prices and thus increase sales than to introduce innovations that would distinguish their product from their competitors' products

Argument Construction

Situation Classical economics holds that prices and profits are minimal when consumers perceive the products of competing suppliers to be the same.

Reasoning *According to classical economics, what strategy are suppliers most likely to use to maximize profits in such a situation?* The given information states that the force driving prices and profits down in this case is the consumers' perception that the competing products are *essentially the same*. It is reasonable to assume that, with prices already at *minimal levels*, it is not possible to lower them any more. What can be done? The suppliers' most likely strategy would then be to change the consumers' perception of their products. It can be expected that an individual supplier would try to convince consumers that its product greatly differs from (and is certainly preferable to) the products of its competitors.

A *Prices* will be reduced by competition *to the same minimal levels*; they will not differ widely.

B The passage discusses the conditions of a crowded market, not a market that is becoming less crowded.

C **Correct.** This statement properly suggests that the most likely strategy for any one supplier in a crowded market is convincing consumers that its product is very different from those of its competitors.

D Since *prices* will be reduced to *the same minimal levels*, it would be difficult, if not impossible, to distinguish between higher- and lower-priced products.

E Since *prices* will be reduced to *the same minimal levels*, it would be impossible to reduce them even more.

The correct answer is C.

47. Installing scrubbers in smokestacks and switching to cleaner-burning fuel are the two methods available to Northern Power for reducing harmful emissions from its plants. Scrubbers will reduce harmful emissions more than cleaner-burning fuels will. Therefore, by installing scrubbers, Northern Power will be doing the most that can be done to reduce harmful emissions from its plants.

Which of the following is an assumption on which the argument depends?

(A) Switching to cleaner-burning fuel will not be more expensive than installing scrubbers.

(B) Northern Power can choose from among various kinds of scrubbers, some of which are more effective than others.

(C) Northern Power is not necessarily committed to reducing harmful emissions from its plants.

(D) Harmful emissions from Northern Power's plants cannot be reduced more by using both methods together than by the installation of scrubbers alone.

(E) Aside from harmful emissions from the smokestacks of its plants, the activities of Northern Power do not cause significant air pollution.

Argument Construction

Situation A power plant can reduce emissions by installing scrubbers and by switching to cleaner-burning fuel; installing scrubbers reduces emissions more than switching fuels. By installing scrubbers, the company is doing the most that it can do.

Reasoning *What assumption is this argument based on?* The assumption must come from what is stated in the argument; it cannot be about material not discussed in the argument at all. Here, the conclusion that the company is doing the most that it can do is based on choosing between the two options rather than choosing both options together. This argument assumes, then, that installing the scrubbers alone is just as effective as both installing scrubbers *and* switching to cleaner-burning fuel.

A Since cost is not discussed in the argument, this statement cannot be assumed.

B Different kinds of scrubbers are not mentioned, so this point may not be assumed.

C Nothing in the argument reflects the company's lack of commitment.

D **Correct.** This statement properly identifies the argument's necessary assumption.

E The company's other activities are not a part of the argument.

The correct answer is D.

48. Some anthropologists study modern-day societies of foragers in an effort to learn about our ancient ancestors who were also foragers. A flaw in this strategy is that forager societies are extremely varied. Indeed, any forager society with which anthropologists are familiar has had considerable contact with modern, non-forager societies.

Which of the following, if true, would most weaken the criticism made above of the anthropologists' strategy?

(A) All forager societies throughout history have had a number of important features in common that are absent from other types of societies.

(B) Most ancient forager societies either dissolved or made a transition to another way of life.

(C) All anthropologists study one kind or another of modern-day society.

(D) Many anthropologists who study modern-day forager societies do not draw inferences about ancient societies on the basis of their studies.

(E) Even those modern-day forager societies that have not had significant contact with modern societies are importantly different from ancient forager societies.

Argument Evaluation

Situation Studying contemporary foraging societies in order to understand ancient foragers is flawed because forager societies are so widely varied and also because the contemporary foragers have had so much contact with modern societies.

Reasoning *Which point weakens this argument?* The argument rejects the comparison of modern-day foraging societies to ancient ones because of the variety of existing forager societies and because the modern-day foragers have been in contact with other modern cultures. What situation would support making this comparison? What if modern-day foragers remain similar to ancient foragers because of non-changing features of foraging societies throughout history? If these are features that are not shared with other cultures, then the argument that anthropologists cannot learn about ancient foragers by studying their modern counterparts is weakened.

A **Correct.** This statement properly identifies the factor that weakens the argument: a comparison could well be a valuable source of understanding if all foraging societies are shown to share common features not found in other societies.

B This point is irrelevant to the comparison and thus does not weaken the argument.

C This point does not address the issue of comparing a modern society to an ancient one.

D That some anthropologists do not compare ancient and modern societies does not weaken the argument that such comparisons should not be made.

E This point strengthens, rather than weakens, the argument.

The correct answer is A.

49. Contrary to earlier predictions, demand for sugarcane has not increased in recent years. Yet, even though prices and production amounts have also been stable during the last three years, sugarcane growers last year increased their profits by more than 10 percent over the previous year's level.

Any of the following statements, if true about last year, helps to explain the rise in profits EXCEPT:

(A) Many countries that are large consumers of sugarcane increased their production of sugarcane-based ethanol, yet their overall consumption of sugarcane decreased.

(B) Sugarcane growers have saved money on wages by switching from paying laborers an hourly wage to paying them by the amount harvested.

(C) The price of oil, the major energy source used by sugarcane growers in harvesting their crops, dropped by more than 20 percent.

(D) Many small sugarcane growers joined together to form an association of sugarcane producers and began to buy supplies at low group rates.

(E) Rainfall in sugarcane-growing regions was higher than it had been during the previous year, allowing the growers to save money on expensive artificial irrigation.

Argument Construction

Situation Even though demand for sugarcane has not increased, and although prices and production amounts have been stable, sugarcane growers experienced a 10 percent rise in profits last year.

Reasoning *Which piece of information does NOT help explain the rise in profits?* All the answer choices will show a reason that profits rose except one. Consider each one to determine which situation would NOT be likely to contribute to increased profits. Any changes that lowered costs for the sugarcane growers WOULD be able to contribute to a rise in their profits. On the other hand, if it is true that many historically large consumers of sugarcane reduced their overall consumption last year, then the lower demand for sugarcane would be unlikely to drive increases in profits. Such a decrease in total consumption would be more likely to drive prices and profits down than up.

A **Correct.** This statement properly identifies a factor that does not explain a rise in profits.

B Saving money on wages would contribute to a rise in profits.

C Saving money on oil would contribute to a rise in profits.

D Saving money on supplies bought at a lower rate would contribute to a rise in profits.

E Saving money on irrigation would contribute to a rise in profits.

The correct answer is A.

50. If the county continues to collect residential trash at current levels, landfills will soon be overflowing and parkland will need to be used in order to create more space. Charging each household a fee for each pound of trash it puts out for collection will induce residents to reduce the amount of trash they create; this charge will therefore protect the remaining county parkland.

Which of the following is an assumption made in drawing the conclusion above?

(A) Residents will reduce the amount of trash they put out for collection by reducing the number of products they buy.

(B) The collection fee will not significantly affect the purchasing power of most residents, even if their households do not reduce the amount of trash they put out.

(C) The collection fee will not induce residents to dump their trash in the parklands illegally.

(D) The beauty of county parkland is an important issue for most of the county's residents.

(E) Landfills outside the county's borders could be used as dumping sites for the county's trash.

Argument Construction

Situation Landfills will overflow and parkland will have to be used instead if current trash collection levels continue. Charging fees per pound of trash collected will inhibit trash growth and protect parkland.

Reasoning *What assumption underlies the conclusion?* The assumption that underlies an argument is always about the specific subjects discussed in the argument; it cannot be about extraneous material. Here, the assumption is about the plan, the parkland, and the fee, all mentioned in the argument. To reach the conclusion that the plan will protect the parkland, the argument must assume that county residents will comply with the new fee, reducing both the trash they generate and the need to convert parkland to landfills. It is assumed that residents will not resort to some illegal means of avoiding the new fee, and it is certainly assumed that they will not contribute to the destruction of parklands by dumping trash in them illegally.

A No mention is made of a change in buying habits in the argument.

B The relation of the fee to residents' purchasing power is not discussed.

C Correct. This statement properly identifies the fact that the argument rests on the assumption that the fee will not create illegal dumping.

D The beauty of the parkland and its importance to residents are not discussed.

E Landfills outside the county are not discussed.

The correct answer is C.

51. Biometric access-control systems—those using fingerprints, voiceprints, and so forth, to regulate admittance to restricted areas—work by degrees of similarity, not by identity. After all, even the same finger will rarely leave exactly identical prints. Such systems can be adjusted to minimize refusals of access to legitimate access-seekers. Such adjustments, however, increase the likelihood of admitting impostors.

Which of the following conclusions is most strongly supported by the information above?

(A) If a biometric access-control system were made to work by identity, it would not produce any correct admittance decisions.

(B) If a biometric access-control system reliably prevents impostors from being admitted, it will sometimes turn away legitimate access-seekers.

(C) Biometric access-control systems are appropriate only in situations in which admittance of impostors is less of a problem than is mistaken refusal of access.

(D) No biometric access-control systems—based, for example, on numerical codes—are less likely than biometric ones to admit impostors.

(E) Anyone choosing an access-control system should base the choice solely on the ratio of false refusals to false admittances.

Argument Construction

Situation Biometric access-control systems work by degrees of similarity, not by identity. Adjusting the system to minimize refusals of access to legitimate access-seekers increases the likelihood that impostors will gain access.

Reasoning *What conclusion do these statements support?* A conclusion may be drawn only from what is stated or implied. Here, a conclusion may be drawn by stating the inverse of what has previously been said: just as impostors will gain access if the system is adjusted to lessen the chance of refusal to legitimate access-seekers, so legitimate access-seeker will occasionally be denied access if the system is adjusted to keep out impostors.

A Not enough evidence is given about identity recognition to reach such a conclusion.

B Correct. This statement is the inverse of a given statement and so properly identifies a reasonable conclusion.

C The statements do not discuss the appropriate situations for the systems.

D No comparison is made, so no comparative conclusion may be drawn.

E The statements do not indicate the basis on which to choose the system.

The correct answer is B.

52. Although computers can enhance people's ability to communicate, computer games are a cause of underdeveloped communication skills in children. After-school hours spent playing computer games are hours not spent talking with people. Therefore, children who spend all their spare time playing these games have less experience in interpersonal communication than other children have.

The argument depends on which of the following assumptions?

(A) Passive activities such as watching television and listening to music do not hinder the development of communication skills in children.

(B) Most children have other opportunities, in addition to after-school hours, in which they can choose whether to play computer games or to interact with other people.

(C) Children who do not spend all their after-school hours playing computer games spend at least some of that time talking with other people.

(D) Formal instruction contributes little or nothing to children's acquisition of communication skills.

(E) The mental skills developed through playing computer games do not contribute significantly to children's intellectual development.

Argument Construction

Situation Spending after-school hours playing computer games does not enhance communication skills because children are not talking with other people during this time. Children who spend all their spare time playing computer games do not have as much interpersonal communication as other children do.

Reasoning *What assumption does this argument depend on?* The unstated assumption in an argument must be about the subjects discussed in the argument; it cannot be about a subject that is not mentioned. Here, playing computer games is said to replace talking with people. Thus the argument assumes that children who do not spend all their spare time playing computer games instead spend at least some of that time talking with people.

A Other activities, such as watching television, are not discussed in the argument.

B The argument is limited to after-school hours or spare time.

C **Correct.** This statement properly identifies the assumption on which the argument is based.

D Formal instruction is not discussed in the argument.

E Only the underdevelopment of communication skills is blamed on the games.

The correct answer is C.

53. One variety of partially biodegradable plastic beverage container is manufactured from small bits of plastic bound together by a degradable bonding agent such as cornstarch. Since only the bonding agent degrades, leaving the small bits of plastic, no less plastic refuse per container is produced when such containers are discarded than when comparable nonbiodegradable containers are discarded.

Which of the following, if true, most strengthens the argument above?

(A) Both partially biodegradable and nonbiodegradable plastic beverage containers can be crushed completely flat by refuse compactors.

(B) The partially biodegradable plastic beverage containers are made with more plastic than comparable non-biodegradable ones in order to compensate for the weakening effect of the bonding agents.

(C) Many consumers are ecology-minded and prefer to buy a product sold in partially biodegradable plastic beverage containers rather than in nonbiodegradable containers, even if the price is higher.

(D) The manufacturing process for partially biodegradable plastic beverage containers results in less plastic waste than the manufacturing process for nonbiodegradable plastic beverage containers.

(E) Technological problems with recycling currently prevent the reuse as food or beverage containers of the plastic from either type of plastic beverage container.

Argument Evaluation

Situation One kind of partially biodegradable beverage container produces as much plastic refuse per container as a nonbiodegradable container does because only the bonding agent, not the plastic, degrades once the container is discarded.

Reasoning *Which point strengthens the argument?* The information that strengthens the argument will be about the subjects of the argument, not about tangential issues. In this case, discovering that the partially biodegradable containers actually use more plastic than comparable non-biodegradable ones in order to compensate for the weakness of the biodegradable bonding agent would strengthen the argument.

A The container's ability to be crushed flat is irrelevant to the argument.

B **Correct.** This statement properly identifies a point that strengthens the argument by saying that the container actually produces more plastic refuse.

C Consumers' preferences are not relevant to the argument about residual plastic.

D The argument is not concerned with waste from manufacturing processes, but only with the product itself.

E The reuse of the containers is not a part of the argument.

The correct answer is B.

54. Most employees in the computer industry move from company to company, changing jobs several times in their careers. However, Summit Computers is known throughout the industry for retaining its employees. Summit credits its success in retaining employees to its informal, nonhierarchical work environment.

Which of the following, if true, most strongly supports Summit's explanation of its success in retaining employees?

(A) Some people employed in the computer industry change jobs if they become bored with their current projects.

(B) A hierarchical work environment hinders the cooperative exchange of ideas that computer industry employees consider necessary for their work.

(C) Many of Summit's senior employees had previously worked at only one other computer company.

(D) In a non-hierarchical work environment, people avoid behavior that might threaten group harmony and thus avoid discussing with their colleagues any dissatisfaction they might have with their jobs.

(E) The cost of living near Summit is relatively low compared to areas in which some other computer companies are located.

Argument Evaluation

Situation A computer company attributes its success in retaining employees to its informal, non-hierarchical work environment.

Reasoning *Which point strengthens the company's argument?* The company says that employees stay at the company for one reason: its work environment. The argument can therefore be strengthened only by a point that relates to the specific work environment. If employees feel that a more formal, hierarchical structure would interfere with their ability to do their jobs, the argument is strengthened.

A This point is irrelevant since it does not concern the structure of the work environment.

B Correct. This statement properly identifies a point that strengthens the company's argument, relating the work environment to job satisfaction and therefore to employees' remaining at the company.

C The previous work experience of senior employees is irrelevant.

D While this point shows how the work environment might affect employee behavior on the job, it does not show how it would affect whether employees remain at the company.

E This point presents an alternate explanation—employees stay due to low cost of living—and so tends to weaken the company's argument.

The correct answer is B.

55. Low-income families are often unable to afford as much child care as they need. One government program would award low-income families a refund on the income taxes they pay of as much as $1,000 for each child under age four. This program would make it possible for all low-income families with children under age four to obtain more child care than they otherwise would have been able to afford.

Which of the following, if true, most seriously calls into question the claim that the program would make it possible for all low-income families to obtain more child care?

(A) The average family with children under age four spends more than $1,000 a year on child care.

(B) Some low-income families in which one of the parents is usually available to care for children under age four may not want to spend their income tax refund on child care.

(C) The reduction in government revenues stemming from the income tax refund will necessitate cuts in other government programs, such as grants for higher education.

(D) Many low-income families with children under age four do not pay any income taxes because their total income is too low to be subject to such taxes.

(E) Income taxes have increased substantially over the past 20 years, reducing the money that low-income families have available to spend on child care.

Evaluation of a Plan

Situation To help low-income families pay for child care, a government project would provide these families with tax refunds for each young child. The claim is made that the program will allow all low-income families to obtain more child care.

Reasoning *What point undermines the claim?* The claim is that *all* low-income families would receive money to buy more care; the money would be in the form of income tax refunds. The program thus assumes that issuing refunds through the income tax system is an effective mechanism for providing funding to all these families. Does the income tax system indeed provide a satisfactory distribution channel? What if some low-income families have such low incomes that they do not pay income taxes? If they don't pay such taxes, then they cannot receive tax refunds, and the planned process for delivering funding will be unsuccessful.

A The amount that families spend is irrelevant to the claim that they would have more money to buy care.

B Although the money is to be in the form of a refund that could be spent however the family wished, it is the availability of additional money that is the point of the claim.

C The effect of the refund program on other programs is irrelevant to the claim.

D **Correct.** This statement properly identifies a situation that undermines the program's claim.

E If an increased tax burden has left less money for child care, the need for the program is great; this does not undermine the claim.

The correct answer is D.

56. Social scientists are underrepresented on the advisory councils of the National Institutes of Health (NIH). Since these councils advise NIH directors and recommend policy, the underrepresentation of social scientists results in a relative lack of NIH financial support for research in the social sciences.

If the statements above are correct, they most strongly support which of the following?

(A) A significant increase in the size of NIH advisory councils would be required in order to increase the representation of social scientists on these councils.

(B) A significant increase in the representation of social scientists on NIH advisory councils would result in an increase in NIH funding for social science research.

(C) A significant increase in funding for social science research would result in improved policy recommendations to NIH directors.

(D) A significant increase in funding for the training of social scientists would result in an increase in the number of social scientists on NIH advisory councils.

(E) A significant increase in the representation of social scientists on NIH advisory councils would have to precede any increase in the number of NIH directors who are social scientists.

Argument Construction

Situation There are few social scientists on NIH advisory councils, so there is little NIH financial support for social-science research.

Reasoning *What conclusion can be drawn from these statements?* If the relative lack of social scientists on NIH advisory panels leads to relative lack of funding for social science research, then increasing the representation should increase the funding.

A It does not follow from the given information that the advisory councils would have to be significantly enlarged to increase the representation.

B **Correct.** This statement properly identifies a conclusion that can reasonably be drawn from the given information: since lack of representation leads to lack of money, more representation should lead to more money.

C Since the given statements do not discuss the quality of policy recommendations, no conclusion on this point can be drawn.

D The discussion concerns funds for research, not for training, so this conclusion cannot be drawn.

E Since the statements do not discuss how people become NIH directors, this conclusion is not justified.

The correct answer is B.

57. Among the more effective kinds of publicity that publishers can get for a new book is to have excerpts of it published in a high-circulation magazine soon before the book is published. The benefits of such excerption include not only a sure increase in sales but also a fee paid by the magazine to the book's publisher.

Which of the following conclusions is best supported by the information above?

(A) The number of people for whom seeing an excerpt of a book in a magazine provides an adequate substitute for reading the whole book is smaller than the number for whom the excerpt stimulates a desire to read the book.

(B) Because the financial advantage of excerpting a new book in a magazine usually accrues to the book's publisher, magazine editors are unwilling to publish excerpts from new books.

(C) In calculating the total number of copies that a book has sold, publishers include sales of copies of magazines that featured an excerpt of the book.

(D) The effectiveness of having excerpts of a book published in a magazine, measured in terms of increased sales of a book, is proportional to the circulation of the magazine in which the excerpts are published.

(E) Books that are suitable for excerpting in high-circulation magazines sell more copies than books that are not suitable for excerpting.

Argument Construction

Situation Having an excerpt from a new book published in a high-circulation magazine leads to increased book sales; the magazine also pays a fee to the book's publisher.

Reasoning *What conclusion does this information support?* A conclusion must be based only on the information provided. Since the given information discusses the effect of excerpting on the sale of books, the conclusion should be about book sales. One reasonable conclusion is that reading an excerpt prompts an increased number of people to buy a book instead of merely reading the excerpt.

A **Correct.** This statement properly identifies the conclusion best supported by the given information; if excerpting leads to more book sales, then more people must decide to buy the book than decide to read only the excerpt.

B This conclusion contradicts a statement in the argument; magazine editors do buy excerpts, so this conclusion is not justified.

C Information about how publishers calculate sales is not part of the information provided, so this conclusion is not justified.

D The argument is limited to high-circulation magazines, so a conclusion related to circulation in general is unwarranted.

E The argument is only concerned with books that are suitable for excerpting, so there is no basis for this conclusion.

The correct answer is A.

58. Insurance Company X is considering issuing a new policy to cover services required by elderly people who suffer from diseases that afflict the elderly. Premiums for the policy must be low enough to attract customers. Therefore, Company X is concerned that the income from the policies would not be sufficient to pay for the claims that would be made.

Which of the following strategies would be most likely to minimize Company X's losses on the policies?

(A) Attracting middle-aged customers unlikely to submit claims for benefits for many years

(B) Insuring only those individuals who did not suffer any serious diseases as children

(C) Including a greater number of services in the policy than are included in other policies of lower cost

(D) Insuring only those individuals who were rejected by other companies for similar policies

(E) Insuring only those individuals who are wealthy enough to pay for the medical services

Evaluation of a Plan

Situation An insurance company considers an affordable policy for the elderly but the company's income from the policies must exceed expenditures on claims.

Reasoning *What strategy will minimize the company's losses?* The insurance company's proposed plan would include a high-risk group, the elderly, who are likely to submit claims immediately. By expanding the customer base to include those who are less likely to submit claims for many years, the company will increase its income and thus minimize its losses.

A **Correct.** This statement properly identifies a strategy that minimizes policy losses.

B No connection is made between childhood diseases and geriatric diseases, so this point is irrelevant.

C Offering more services would tend to increase costs, and thus losses.

D Individuals rejected by other companies are more likely to make claims that would increase losses.

E Wealthy people would only buy insurance if they planned to make claims; this point is irrelevant.

The correct answer is A.

59. To prevent some conflicts of interest, Congress could prohibit high-level government officials from accepting positions as lobbyists for three years after such officials leave government service. One such official concluded, however, that such a prohibition would be unfortunate because it would prevent high-level government officials from earning a livelihood for three years.

The official's conclusion logically depends on which of the following assumptions?

(A) Laws should not restrict the behavior of former government officials.

(B) Lobbyists are typically people who have previously been high-level government officials.

(C) Low-level government officials do not often become lobbyists when they leave government service.

(D) High-level government officials who leave government service are capable of earning a livelihood only as lobbyists.

(E) High-level government officials who leave government service are currently permitted to act as lobbyists for only three years.

Argument Construction

Situation Congress might make former officials wait three years before working as lobbyists. An official argues that this rule would keep these people from working.

Reasoning *What assumption must be true for this argument to hold together?* The argument is logical only if it is assumed that the sole possible job opportunity for the ex-officials is lobbying.

A This broad assumption is not needed.

B This statement may be true, but it is not needed as an assumption.

C Low-level officials are irrelevant to the argument.

D **Correct.** This statement properly identifies the argument's necessary assumption.

E The current situation is not relevant to the argument.

The correct answer is D.

Questions 60–61 are based on the following:

The fewer restrictions there are on the advertising of legal services, the more lawyers there are who advertise their services, and the lawyers who advertise a specific service usually charge less for that service than the lawyers who do not advertise. Therefore, if the state removes any of its current restrictions, such as the one against advertisements that do not specify fee arrangements, overall consumer legal costs will be lower than if the state retains its current restrictions.

60. If the statements above are true, which of the following must be true?

(A) Some lawyers who now advertise will charge more for specific services if they do not have to specify fee arrangements in the advertisements.

(B) More consumers will use legal services if there are fewer restrictions on the advertising of legal services.

(C) If the restriction against advertisements that do not specify fee arrangements is removed, more lawyers will advertise their services.

(D) If more lawyers advertise lower prices for specific services, some lawyers who do not advertise will also charge less than they currently charge for those services.

(E) If the only restrictions on the advertising of legal services were those that apply to every type of advertising, most lawyers would advertise their services.

Argument Construction

Situation Consumer legal costs will be reduced if the state removes even one restriction on lawyers' advertisements because the fewer the restrictions, the greater the number of lawyers who advertise, and lawyers who advertise charge less than lawyers who do not advertise.

Reasoning *What conclusion can logically be drawn?* The argument sets up an inverse proportion: the fewer the number of restrictions on ads, the greater the number of lawyers who advertise. This is true of all restrictions and all lawyers. Therefore, removing any one restriction necessarily increases the number of lawyers who advertise.

A The lawyers may charge more, but it is equally possible that no lawyer will charge more.

B No evidence in the passage supports an increased use of legal services.

C **Correct.** This statement properly identifies the conclusion that logically follows, because reducing any restriction will increase the number of lawyers who advertise.

D Lawyers who continue not to advertise are not compelled to lower their fees.

E The argument concerns numbers of advertisers rather than types; it remains possible that few lawyers would advertise.

The correct answer is C.

61. Which of the following, if true, would most seriously weaken the argument concerning overall consumer legal costs?

(A) The state has recently removed some other restrictions that had limited the advertising of legal services.

(B) The state is unlikely to remove all the restrictions that apply solely to the advertising of legal services.

(C) Lawyers who do not advertise generally provide legal services of the same quality as those provided by lawyers who do advertise.

(D) Most lawyers who now specify fee arrangements in their advertisements would continue to do so even if the specification were not required.

(E) Most lawyers who advertise specific services do not lower their fees for those services when they begin to advertise.

Argument Evaluation

Situation Consumer legal costs will be reduced if the state removes even one restriction on lawyers' advertisements because the fewer the restrictions, the greater the number of lawyers who advertise, and lawyers who advertise charge less than lawyers who do not advertise. (The same as the previous item.)

Reasoning *What point weakens the conclusion about lower consumer costs?* The conclusion relies upon the supposition that lawyers who currently advertise charge the consumer less than other lawyers for the same legal services. What if this does not continue to hold true? If more lawyers begin to advertise, they may not charge any less for their services than they did previously, and they are, given the supposition, likely to be more expensive than those who currently advertise. In this case, increasing the number of lawyers who advertise would not lower overall consumer legal costs.

A The removal of other restrictions does not affect consumer legal costs.

B The argument is about lowering consumer costs through increasing the number of lawyers who advertise, not about the likelihood of the state's removing restrictions on such advertising.

C The quality of the legal services is irrelevant to the cost of these services.

D The content of the ad is irrelevant.

E **Correct.** This statement properly identifies a point that weakens the conclusion that less-restricted advertising will result in lower costs. While it may be true that more lawyers will advertise if there are fewer restrictions, the cost paid by consumers will not decrease if most of the newly advertising lawyers do not charge lower fees.

The correct answer is E.

62. During the Second World War, about 375,000 civilians died in the United States and about 408,000 members of the United States armed forces died overseas. On the basis of those figures, it can be concluded that it was not much more dangerous to be overseas in the armed forces during the Second World War than it was to stay at home as a civilian.

Which of the following would reveal most clearly the absurdity of the conclusion drawn above?

(A) Counting deaths among members of the armed forces who served in the United States in addition to deaths among members of the armed forces serving overseas

(B) Expressing the difference between the numbers of deaths among civilians and members of the armed forces as a percentage of the total number of deaths

(C) Separating deaths caused by accidents during service in the armed forces from deaths caused by combat injuries

(D) Comparing death rates per thousand members of each group rather than comparing total numbers of deaths

(E) Comparing deaths caused by accidents in the United States to deaths caused by combat in the armed forces

Argument Evaluation

Situation The relatively small difference in the number of deaths at home and overseas during the war years shows that it was only slightly more dangerous to be a member of the armed forces overseas than a civilian at home.

Reasoning *What point casts the most serious doubt on the conclusion?* This comparison of two different populations treats them as though they are essentially the same, so consider what dissimilarity between the populations might account for the similarity in the number of deaths. One population, the members of the armed forces stationed abroad, is much smaller than the other population, the civilians in the United States. A similar number of total deaths in a far smaller population actually reveals just how dangerous it was to be in the armed forces overseas. Moreover, the military draws its members from a young and fit population while the general American population includes people of all ages and health conditions. Using the death rate per thousand for each population allows for a more accurate comparison; this comparison will show the significantly higher rate for the smaller population.

A Including the members of the military who died in the United States together with those who died overseas increases only slightly the smaller population being compared. The two populations are still enormously different in size.

B Expressing the difference as a percentage of the total number of deaths is beside the point; what matters is the difference in the size of the populations.

C Separating the kinds of deaths within the smaller population does not affect the comparison between two different populations.

D **Correct.** This statement correctly identifies the point that gravely weakens the conclusion.

E Comparing kinds of deaths in the two populations does not lead to a conclusion comparing the numbers of deaths in those populations.

The correct answer is D.

63. Even though most universities retain the royalties from faculty members' inventions, the faculty members retain the royalties from books and articles they write. Therefore, faculty members should retain the royalties from the educational computer software they develop.

The conclusion above would be more reasonably drawn if which of the following were inserted into the argument as an additional premise?

(A) Royalties from inventions are higher than royalties from educational software programs.
(B) Faculty members are more likely to produce educational software programs than inventions.
(C) Inventions bring more prestige to universities than do books and articles.
(D) In the experience of most universities, educational software programs are more marketable than are books and articles.
(E) In terms of the criteria used to award royalties, educational software programs are more nearly comparable to books and articles than to inventions.

Argument Construction

Situation Faculty members get the royalties from their books, but universities get the royalties from faculty inventions. Faculty members should get the royalties from their educational computer software.

Reasoning *What premise should be added to the argument?* This argument needs to state as a premise its underlying assumption regarding the nature of computer programs. If they are like inventions, then universities should retain the royalties. If they are like books and articles, then faculty members should retain the royalties. The conclusion states that faculty members should receive royalties for educational software without stating that software is comparable to books. The missing premise must show the relationship between educational software and either inventions or books and articles.

A The amount of the royalties is not at issue.
B The number of computer programs produced by faculty members is not relevant.
C The prestige of inventions is irrelevant.
D The marketability of educational software is not being compared.
E **Correct.** This statement properly identifies a premise that establishes the relationship required to complete the argument.

The correct answer is E.

64. Red blood cells in which the malarial-fever parasite resides are eliminated from a person's body after 120 days. Because the parasite cannot travel to a new generation of red blood cells, any fever that develops in a person more than 120 days after that person has moved to a malaria-free region is not due to the malarial parasite.

Which of the following, if true, most seriously weakens the conclusion above?

(A) The fever caused by the malarial parasite may resemble the fever caused by flu viruses.

(B) The anopheles mosquito, which is the principal insect carrier of the malarial parasite, has been eradicated in many parts of the world.

(C) Many malarial symptoms other than the fever, which can be suppressed with antimalarial medication, can reappear within 120 days after the medication is discontinued.

(D) In some cases, the parasite that causes malarial fever travels to cells of the spleen, which are less frequently eliminated from a person's body than are red blood cells.

(E) In any region infested with malaria-carrying mosquitoes, there are individuals who appear to be immune to malaria.

Argument Evaluation

Situation The malarial-fever parasite lives in red blood cells, but these cells are eliminated after 120 days. If the infected person moves to a malaria-free region, any new fever that occurs after 120 days cannot be due to the malarial-fever parasite.

Reasoning *What weakens the conclusion?* The passage says that the malarial parasites that reside in red blood cells are eliminated after 120 days. What if malarial parasites can also reside in other places in a person's body? If the parasites can reside in the spleen, from which they are not eliminated as frequently, as well as in red blood cells, they may not be eliminated within 120 days. Therefore, they could cause malarial fever after the 120-day period. In that case, the conclusion ruling out a new generation of malarial parasites as the cause of new fever is unfounded.

A The issue is not about a similarity of symptoms but about where the parasites reside.

B The existence of malaria-free regions is not in question.

C Other malarial symptoms are not discussed; they are irrelevant.

D **Correct.** This statement properly identifies a point that weakens the conclusion.

E Immunity to malaria is irrelevant to a discussion of the reappearance of the disease.

The correct answer is D.

65. Most consumers do not get much use out of the sports equipment they purchase. For example, 17 percent of the adults in the United States own jogging shoes, but only 45 percent of the owners jog more than once a year, and only 17 percent jog more than once a week.

Which of the following, if true, casts the most doubt on the claim that most consumers get little use out of the sports equipment they purchase?

(A) Joggers are most susceptible to sports injuries during the first six months in which they jog.

(B) In surveys designed to elicit such information, joggers often exaggerate the frequency with which they jog.

(C) Many consumers purchase jogging shoes for use in activities other than jogging.

(D) Consumers who take up jogging often purchase athletic shoes that can be used in other sports.

(E) Joggers who jog more than once a week are often active participants in other sports as well.

Argument Evaluation

Situation To demonstrate that sports equipment gets little use after purchase, the example is given that fewer than half the jogging shoes sold are used for jogging more than once a year.

Reasoning *What point weakens the conclusion?* The conclusion concerns the broad category of "use" while the evidence is related to a specific activity. Jogging shoes are used for jogging, but they may be used for other activities as well. A consumer among the 45 percent of owners jogging only once a year may indeed wear jogging shoes every day, as might the consumer among the 55 percent wearing jogging shoes to jog even less frequently.

A The existence of joggers who are not jogging due to injury only contributes to the original conclusion; it does not cast doubt on it.

B If the frequency of jogging is even less than that cited, the conclusion is strengthened rather than weakened.

C **Correct.** This statement properly identifies a factor that weakens the conclusion that sports equipment purchases get little use.

D These consumers could be among the 45 percent who are conceded by the argument to jog more frequently than once a year.

E The argument concedes that a minority of joggers, the 17 percent who jog more than once a week, do use their jogging shoes regularly.

The correct answer is C.

66. Neither a rising standard of living nor balanced trade, by itself, establishes a country's ability to compete in the international marketplace. Both are required simultaneously since standards of living can rise because of growing trade deficits and trade can be balanced by means of a decline in a country's standard of living.

If the facts stated in the passage above are true, a proper test of a country's ability to be competitive is its ability to _____.

(A) balance its trade while its standard of living rises.
(B) balance its trade while its standard of living falls
(C) increase trade deficits while its standard of living rises.
(D) decrease trade deficits while its standard of living falls
(E) keep its standard of living constant while trade deficits rise

Argument Evaluation

Situation A country's ability to compete in the international marketplace depends on both a rising standard of living and balanced trade.

Reasoning *What must a country do to be considered competitive?* The passage states that there are two conditions that must be met simultaneously. The standard of living must rise, and trade must be balanced. While it is possible for the standard of living to rise when trade is not balanced and for trade to be balanced while the standard of living is falling, neither of these situations allows the country to be considered competitive internationally. The country must both balance trade and have a rising standard of living.

A **Correct.** This statement properly identifies the two requirements the country must meet at the same time.

B One of the two conditions is not met; the standard of living must be rising, not falling.

C One of the two conditions is not met; trade must be balanced.

D Neither of the conditions is met; trade must be balanced, and the standard of living must be rising.

E Neither of the conditions is met; the standard of living must be rising, not constant, and trade must be balanced.

The correct answer is A.

67. A greater number of newspapers are sold in Town S than in Town T. Therefore, the citizens of Town S are better informed about major world events than are the citizens of Town T.

Each of the following, if true, weakens the conclusion above EXCEPT:

(A) Town S has a larger population than Town T.

(B) Most citizens of Town T work in Town S and buy their newspapers there.

(C) The average citizen of Town S spends less time reading newspapers than does the average citizen of Town T.

(D) A weekly newspaper restricted to the coverage of local events is published in Town S.

(E) The average newsstand price of newspapers sold in Town S is lower than the average price of newspapers sold in Town T.

Argument Evaluation

Situation Because more newspapers are sold in Town S than Town T, the citizens of Town S are assumed to be better informed about major world events than the citizens of Town T.

Reasoning *Which statement does NOT weaken the conclusion?* The conclusion is clearly faulty; the degree to which citizens are informed, a qualitative measure, cannot be based merely on the number of newspapers sold locally. All the statements will necessarily expose the weakness of this faulty conclusion, with the exception of one that does NOT. While the lower price of newspapers in Town S may explain why more newspapers are sold there, this fact does not weaken the conclusion that the citizens of Town S are better informed simply because more newspapers are sold there.

A If the population of Town S is larger, the percentage of newspaper buyers in Town S may be no greater than in Town T, and the conclusion is weakened.

B If most citizens of Town T buy their newspapers in Town S, Town S may misleadingly show evidence of an apparently higher per-resident rate of newspaper sales. Since the higher sales in Town S can be attributed to purchases by nonresidents, the conclusion about the citizens of Town S is weakened.

C The amount of time spent reading the newspaper is relevant to being well informed. If Town S's citizens spend less time reading the newspaper than Town T's citizens, then they are likely to be less well informed, and the conclusion is weakened.

D If the citizens of Town S are buying and reading newspapers about local events, rather than world events, they may be less informed about world events than citizens in Town T, and the conclusion is weakened.

E Correct. This statement properly identifies a statement that does NOT weaken the conclusion.

The correct answer is E.

68. When hypnotized subjects are told that they are deaf and are then asked whether they can hear the hypnotist, they reply, "No." Some theorists try to explain this result by arguing that the selves of hypnotized subjects are dissociated into separate parts, and that the part that is deaf is dissociated from the part that replies.

Which of the following challenges indicates the most serious weakness in the attempted explanation described above?

(A) Why does the part that replies not answer, "Yes"?

(B) Why are the observed facts in need of any special explanation?

(C) Why do the subjects appear to accept the hypnotist's suggestion that they are deaf?

(D) Why do hypnotized subjects all respond the same way in the situation described?

(E) Why are the separate parts of the self the same for all subjects?

Argument Evaluation

Situation People under hypnosis are told they are deaf. When asked by the hypnotist whether they can hear, they hear the question and respond, "No." A theory explains this puzzling result by stating that the hypnotized subjects dissociate the part of themselves that is deaf from the part that replies to the question.

Reasoning *Which question points to a weakness in the theory?* According to the theory, hypnotized people dissociate themselves into separate parts: the hearing part and the deaf part. Then, they must be using the hearing part of themselves when they respond to the hypnotist's question; obviously, if they were using the deaf part of themselves at that point, they would not hear or thus respond at all. So, if they are using the hearing part of themselves, as the theorists maintain, why would they respond, "No," to the question, "Can you hear me?" The hearing part would more logically answer, "Yes."

A **Correct.** This statement properly identifies a challenge that demonstrates the weakness in the theory.

B This question does not address the weakness in the explanation; instead it asks why there needs to be an explanation at all.

C The fact that the subjects accept the hypnotic suggestion that they are deaf is assumed as part of the argument.

D The theorists do not attempt to explain why all subjects behave similarly, so this question is irrelevant to pinpointing the weakness of the theorists' explanation.

E The theorists' explanation does not address why the parts of the self are the same for all subjects, so this question does not get to the center—and the weakness—of their argument.

The correct answer is A.

69. Excavation of the ancient city of Kourion on the island of Cyprus revealed a pattern of debris and collapsed buildings typical of towns devastated by earthquakes. Archaeologists have hypothesized that the destruction was due to a major earthquake known to have occurred near the island in AD 365.

Which of the following, if true, most strongly supports the archaeologists' hypothesis?

(A) Bronze ceremonial drinking vessels that are often found in graves dating from years preceding and following AD 365 were also found in several graves near Kourion.

(B) No coins minted after AD 365 were found in Kourion, but coins minted before that year were found in abundance.

(C) Most modern histories of Cyprus mention that an earthquake occurred near the island in AD 365.

(D) Several small statues carved in styles current in Cyprus in the century between AD 300 and 400 were found in Kourion.

(E) Stone inscriptions in a form of the Greek alphabet that was definitely used in Cyprus after AD 365 were found in Kourion.

Argument Evaluation

Situation The excavation of Kourion reveals a pattern of destruction typical in towns destroyed by earthquakes. Archaeologists suggest Kourion was destroyed when an earthquake hit nearby in AD 365.

Reasoning *Which statement best supports the archaeologists' hypothesis?* An earthquake struck near Cyprus in AD 365; this fact is not disputed. If this earthquake is the one responsible for the devastation of Kourion, then there should be evidence of active occupation before AD 365, but no evidence of activity after that date. The dates on the coins found on the site suggest that life in Kourion was flourishing before AD 365; the total lack of coins after the year of the earthquake supports the idea that the city had been destroyed.

A The existence of vessels made both before and after AD 365 suggests that Kourion was not destroyed by the earthquake.

B Correct. This statement properly identifies evidence that supports the archaeologists' hypothesis.

C The occurrence of the earthquake is not in question; this statement simply confirms a fact already assumed in the argument.

D The existence of statues carved in styles current after the date of the earthquake (AD 365–AD 400) argues against the town's destruction in AD 365.

E The existence of inscriptions using an alphabet common only after the earthquake argues against the theory that the earthquake destroyed Kourion.

The correct answer is B.

Questions 70–71 are based on the following:

To protect certain fledgling industries, the government of Country Z banned imports of the types of products those industries were starting to make. As a direct result, the cost of those products to the buyers, several export-dependent industries in Z, went up, sharply limiting the ability of those industries to compete effectively in their export markets.

70. Which of the following can be most properly inferred from the passage about the products whose importation was banned?

(A) Those products had been cheaper to import than they were to make within Country Z's fledgling industries.

(B) Those products were ones that Country Z was hoping to export in its turn, once the fledgling industries matured.

(C) Those products used to be imported from just those countries to which Country Z's exports went.

(D) Those products had become more and more expensive to import, which resulted in a foreign trade deficit just before the ban.

(E) Those products used to be imported in very small quantities, but they were essential to Country Z's economy.

Argument Construction

Situation Country Z bans the importation of products that would compete with those that some of its new industries are beginning to make. Consequently, the export-dependent local industries that buy these products must pay more for them, and these exporters are now less competitive in their markets.

Reasoning *What inference can be made about the banned imports?* A proper inference requires careful analysis of the information given. Export-dependent industries must now buy the products they need from the fledgling industries. The fact that these domestically produced products are more expensive is *a direct result* of the ban. It is reasonable to infer that the imported products were less expensive than the same products made by Country Z's fledgling industries.

A **Correct.** This statement properly identifies the reasonable inference that these products were less expensive as imports.

B No information in the passage indicates future plans, so no inference about the future can be drawn.

C The passage provides no information to support the inference that the import markets and export markets are the same.

D The passage provides no information to support an inference about the rising price of the imported products and consequent trade deficit.

E The necessity of the imported products to Country Z's economy cannot be inferred from the information given.

The correct answer is A.

71. Which of the following conclusions about Country Z's adversely affected export-dependent industries is best supported by the passage?

(A) Profit margins in those industries were not high enough to absorb the rise in costs mentioned above.
(B) Those industries had to contend with the fact that other countries banned imports from Country Z.
(C) Those industries succeeded in expanding the domestic market for their products.
(D) Steps to offset rising materials costs by decreasing labor costs were taken in those industries.
(E) Those industries started to move into export markets that they had previously judged unprofitable.

Argument Construction

Situation Country Z bans the importation of products that would compete with those that some of its new industries are beginning to make. Consequently, the export-dependent local industries that buy these products must pay more for them, and these exporters are now less competitive in their markets. (The same as the previous item.)

Reasoning *What conclusion can be drawn about the export-dependent industries?* Any conclusion must be supported by the facts in the passage. The export-dependent industries could no longer compete effectively when they had to purchase necessary products at greater expense from local industries. The export-dependent industries' inability to adjust successfully to the rise in costs suggests that staying competitive in their markets required tight cost control to maintain their profit margins. It is reasonable to conclude then that their profit margins were not high enough for them to be able to absorb the increased costs caused by their new need to purchase domestically made products.

A **Correct.** This statement properly identifies the conclusion that the export-dependent industries were low-margin businesses that could not successfully accommodate the higher prices of the domestically made products.

B The passage provides no information about other countries' ban of imports from Country Z, so no conclusion may be drawn.

C Not enough information is given in the passage to support this conclusion, nor is it likely that *export-dependent* industries could successfully expand their domestic markets.

D No information about cutting labor costs is given in the passage, so no conclusion may be drawn.

E The passage has no information to support the conclusion that the industries moved into different markets.

The correct answer is A.

72. Biological functions of many plants and animals vary in cycles that are repeated every 24 hours. It is tempting to suppose that alteration in the intensity of incident light is the stimulus that controls these daily biological rhythms. But there is much evidence to contradict this hypothesis.

Which of the following, if known, is evidence that contradicts the hypothesis stated in the lines above?

(A) Human body temperature varies throughout the day, with the maximum occurring in the late afternoon and the minimum in the morning.

(B) While some animals, such as the robin, are more active during the day, others, such as mice, show greater activity at night.

(C) When people move from one time zone to another, their daily biological rhythms adjust in a matter of days to the periods of sunlight and darkness in the new zone.

(D) Certain single-cell plants display daily biological rhythms even when the part of the cell containing the nucleus is removed.

(E) Even when exposed to constant light intensity around the clock, some algae display rates of photosynthesis that are much greater during daylight hours than at night.

Argument Evaluation

Situation Biological rhythms of many plants and animals work in 24-hour cycles. The alteration of the intensity of light is thought to control these cycles.

Reasoning *What evidence contradicts the hypothesis that light is the controlling stimulus?* Look for an example demonstrating that intensity of light cannot be the controlling stimulus of the 24-hour cycle. Algae exposed to a constant intensity of light throughout the 24-hour cycle nevertheless exhibit a far greater activity of biological functions during daylight hours than at night. The example of the algae thus contradicts the hypothesis.

A No reason is given to explain the variation of human body temperature throughout the day; this statement is irrelevant to the hypothesis.

B No cause is given for the varied activity cycles of different animals; this statement is irrelevant to the hypothesis.

C The ability to adapt to daylight and darkness in a different time zone lends support to the hypothesis.

D The ability of single-cell plants to continue functioning in the 24-hour cycle despite lacking a nucleus is irrelevant to the hypothesis.

E **Correct.** This statement properly identifies evidence that contradicts the hypothesis.

The correct answer is E.

73. The local board of education found that, because the current physics curriculum has little direct relevance to today's world, physics classes attracted few high school students. So to attract students to physics classes, the board proposed a curriculum that emphasizes principles of physics involved in producing and analyzing visual images.

Which of the following, if true, provides the strongest reason to expect that the proposed curriculum will be successful in attracting students?

(A) Several of the fundamental principles of physics are involved in producing and analyzing visual images.

(B) Knowledge of physics is becoming increasingly important in understanding the technology used in today's world.

(C) Equipment that a large producer of photographic equipment has donated to the high school could be used in the proposed curriculum.

(D) The number of students interested in physics today is much lower than the number of students interested in physics 50 years ago.

(E) In today's world the production and analysis of visual images is of major importance in communications, business, and recreation.

Evaluation of a Plan

Situation Low enrollment in physics classes is blamed on the lack of relevance of the current curriculum to the current world. To attract more students, the board proposes a new curriculum emphasizing the principles of physics involved in producing and analyzing visual images.

Reasoning *What is the best reason for the success of this plan?* To attract more students, the class must be relevant to today's world. Evidence that the proposed content of the curriculum is indeed relevant would provide strong support for the plan. If producing and analyzing visual images is of major importance in communications, business, and recreation, the curriculum has clear relevance to today's world and should therefore attract students.

A This statement does not explain why students would be attracted to the class.

B This statement explains why students should take physics, but not why they would be attracted to the class.

C The availability of appropriate equipment is important once students are registered for the class, but it does not explain why they would be attracted to the class in the first place.

D The downward trend in enrollment does not suggest much success for the new class.

E **Correct.** This statement properly identifies a factor that contributes to the success of the proposed plan to increase enrollment.

The correct answer is E.

74. Small-business groups are lobbying to defeat proposed federal legislation that would substantially raise the federal minimum wage. This opposition is surprising since the legislation they oppose would, for the first time, exempt all small businesses from paying any minimum wage.

Which of the following, if true, would best explain the opposition of small-business groups to the proposed legislation?

(A) Under the current federal minimum-wage law, most small businesses are required to pay no less than the minimum wage to their employees.

(B) In order to attract workers, small companies must match the wages offered by their larger competitors, and these competitors would not be exempt under the proposed laws.

(C) The exact number of companies that are currently required to pay no less than the minimum wage but that would be exempt under the proposed laws is unknown.

(D) Some states have set their own minimum wages—in some cases, quite a bit above the level of the minimum wage mandated by current federal law—for certain key industries.

(E) Service companies make up the majority of small businesses and they generally employ more employees per dollar of revenues than do retail or manufacturing businesses.

Evaluation of a Plan

Situation Small businesses oppose proposed legislation raising the federal minimum wage, even though they would be exempt from paying the minimum wage.

Reasoning *Why would small businesses oppose legislation that apparently favors them?* The argument finds it *surprising* that the small businesses oppose a plan that exempts them. The perspective of the small businesses must be that there is little value in the exemption. What could be their reasoning? Even though they are exempt, small businesses must compete for workers by offering wages similar to those offered by larger businesses. The larger businesses, not being exempt, would have to increase wages to the federal minimum, forcing the small businesses to do the same in order to attract workers.

A The current law does not exempt small businesses; this does not explain why small businesses are opposed to a new law under which they would be exempt from paying the federal minimum wage.

B Correct. This statement properly identifies a factor that explains small businesses' opposition to the legislation.

C The unknown number of exempt companies is irrelevant to why the small businesses oppose the legislation.

D This statement about state minimum wage levels does not explain why small businesses are opposed to the proposed law.

E The relative importance of payroll costs for small businesses suggests that they would be in favor of the law; it does not explain their opposition to it.

The correct answer is B.

75. Although aspirin has been proven to eliminate moderate fever associated with some illnesses, many doctors no longer routinely recommend its use for this purpose. A moderate fever stimulates the activity of the body's disease-fighting white blood cells and also inhibits the growth of many strains of disease-causing bacteria.

If the statements above are true, which of the following conclusions is most strongly supported by them?

(A) Aspirin, an effective painkiller, alleviates the pain and discomfort of many illnesses.
(B) Aspirin can prolong a patient's illness by eliminating moderate fever helpful in fighting some diseases.
(C) Aspirin inhibits the growth of white blood cells, which are necessary for fighting some illnesses.
(D) The more white blood cells a patient's body produces, the less severe the patient's illness will be.
(E) The focus of modern medicine is on inhibiting the growth of disease-causing bacteria within the body.

Argument Construction

Situation Many doctors do not recommend taking aspirin for moderate fever associated with illness because moderate fever activates the immune system and hinders the growth of disease-carrying bacteria.

Reasoning *What is the best conclusion from this information?* This passage maintains that moderate fever can help fight some diseases by activating the immune system and inhibiting the growth of some bacteria that cause disease. Aspirin suppresses moderate fever. By doing so, aspirin can be viewed as hindering a beneficial process and prolonging an illness.

A The passage says nothing about aspirin's role as a painkiller, so no conclusion can be drawn about aspirin's painkilling properties.

B Correct. This statement properly identifies the conclusion that can be drawn from the information.

C Since moderate fever promotes the *activity* of the white blood cells, it is fair to conclude that suppressing the fever with aspirin affects the *activity* of the white blood cells. Since nothing is said about the effect of aspirin on the *growth* of white blood cells, no conclusion can be made about such growth.

D The passage does not provide enough information to conclude that the greater the number of white blood cells, the less severe the illness.

E The passage is about aspirin and moderate fever, not about the focus of modern medicine, so this statement is irrelevant to the material in the passage.

The correct answer is B.

Questions 76–77 are based on the following:

Roland: The alarming fact is that 90 percent of the people in this country now report that they know someone who is unemployed.

Sharon: But a normal, moderate level of unemployment is 5 percent, with one out of 20 workers unemployed. So at any given time if a person knows approximately 50 workers, one or more will very likely be unemployed.

76. Sharon's argument is structured to lead to which of the following as a conclusion?

(A) The fact that 90 percent of the people know someone who is unemployed is not an indication that unemployment is abnormally high.

(B) The current level of unemployment is not moderate.

(C) If at least 5 percent of workers are unemployed, the result of questioning a representative group of people cannot be the percentage Roland cites.

(D) It is unlikely that the people whose statements Roland cites are giving accurate reports.

(E) If an unemployment figure is given as a certain percentage, the actual percentage of those without jobs is even higher.

Argument Construction

Situation Roland is alarmed that 90 percent of the population knows someone who is out of work. Sharon replies that a normal level of unemployment is 5 percent, illustrating her point by saying that if a person knows 50 workers, at least one of them is likely to be unemployed.

Reasoning *Sharon's reply leads to what conclusion about unemployment?* Sharon begins her reply with "but," indicating that she is about to counter either Roland's statistic or his alarm; she accepts the statistic and addresses the alarm. If the normal unemployment rate is 5 percent and if the average person knows 50 workers, then knowing one person out of work is within the normal and expected range, not a cause for alarm. Sharon shows that it is possible for 90 percent of the population to know someone unemployed and for unemployment to be a normal rate of 5 percent at the same time.

A **Correct.** This statement properly identifies the conclusion to which the argument is leading.

B Sharon's argument is made in the abstract. No information is provided about the current level of unemployment.

C Sharon does not challenge Roland's statistics, and her argument is designed to make a conclusion not about their accuracy, but only about their interpretation.

D There is no information about the accuracy of Roland's reports, so no conclusion can be made about how likely or unlikely they are to be accurate.

E No information in Sharon's argument supports this conclusion.

The correct answer is A.

77. Sharon's argument relies on the assumption that _____.

(A) normal levels of unemployment are rarely exceeded
(B) unemployment is not normally concentrated in geographically isolated segments of the population
(C) the number of people who each know someone who is unemployed is always higher than 90 percent of the population
(D) Roland is not consciously distorting the statistics he presents
(E) knowledge that a personal acquaintance is unemployed generates more fear of losing one's job than does knowledge of unemployment statistics

Argument Construction

Situation Roland is alarmed that 90 percent of the population knows someone who is out of work. Sharon replies that a normal level of unemployment is 5 percent, illustrating her point by saying that if a person knows 50 workers, at least one of them is likely to be unemployed. (The same as the previous item.)

Reasoning *What assumption does Sharon make in putting together her argument?* Sharon makes an equalizing statement about people and their acquaintance when she posits that, if an average person knows 50 workers, at least one of them is likely to be unemployed. Sharon's generalization must assume that this is the case equally throughout the country and that unemployment is not concentrated in some geographically isolated areas.

A Sharon's argument is about a normal level of unemployment; how rarely or frequently that level is exceeded is outside the scope of her argument.

B Correct. This statement properly identifies an assumption that underlies Sharon's argument about the average person and how many unemployed people that average person knows.

C Sharon's argument is based on a given normal rate of unemployment and a given normal circle of acquaintance, not on this assumption.

D Sharon's argument is not based on the figure Roland cites and does not assume its accuracy or inaccuracy; her argument merely points out that his figure is not inconsistent with a normal rate of unemployment.

E The fear of losing a job is not part of Sharon's argument; this statement is irrelevant.

The correct answer is B.

78. In comparison to the standard typewriter keyboard, the EFCO keyboard, which places the most-used keys nearest the typist's strongest fingers, allows faster typing and results in less fatigue. Therefore, replacement of standard keyboards with the EFCO keyboard will result in an immediate reduction of typing costs.

Which of the following, if true, would most weaken the conclusion drawn above?

(A) People who use both standard and EFCO keyboards report greater difficulty in the transition from the EFCO keyboard to the standard keyboard than in the transition from the standard keyboard to the EFCO keyboard.

(B) EFCO keyboards are no more expensive to manufacture than are standard keyboards and require less frequent repair than do standard keyboards.

(C) The number of businesses and government agencies that use EFCO keyboards is increasing each year.

(D) The more training and experience an employee has had with the standard keyboard, the more costly it is to train that employee to use the EFCO keyboard.

(E) Novice typists can learn to use the EFCO keyboard in about the same amount of time that it takes them to learn to use the standard keyboard.

Argument Evaluation

Situation Compared to the standard typewriter keyboard, the EFCO keyboard promotes faster typing while producing less fatigue. Replacing standard keyboards with EFCO keyboards promises immediate reduction of typing costs.

Reasoning *What point would weaken the conclusion about reduced typing costs?* Whenever a word such as *immediate* is part of an argument, it is wise to be alert. Given the comparison with the standard keyboard, it is logical that over the longer term the EFCO keyboard will save money. What problems might there be initially that would counteract the possibility of *immediate* savings? Personnel must first be retrained on the new EFCO keyboard, and it is possible that the costs of the training could offset any short-term savings. If the more experience employees have had with the standard keyboard, the more costly the initial training, then adopting the new keyboard could have high short-term costs that preclude *immediate* savings.

A The greater ease of changing from the standard keyboard to the EFCO keyboard for typists experienced in both would support, not weaken, the conclusion.

B The fewer repairs required by EFCO keyboards should save money in the long run; immediate costs will not go up since the price of both keyboards is the same. The conclusion is not weakened.

C The increasing use of EFCO keyboards supports the conclusion, suggesting that other offices have found the switch advantageous.

D **Correct.** This statement properly identifies information that weakens the conclusion that savings will be immediate.

E For new typists, training time is the same for both keyboards; this statement does not weaken the conclusion.

The correct answer is D.

79. An overly centralized economy, not the changes in the climate, is responsible for the poor agricultural production in Country X since its new government came to power. Neighboring Country Y has experienced the same climatic conditions, but while agricultural production has been falling in Country X, it has been rising in Country Y.

Which of the following, if true, would most weaken the argument above?

(A) Industrial production also is declining in Country X.
(B) Whereas Country Y is landlocked, Country X has a major seaport.
(C) Both Country X and Country Y have been experiencing drought conditions.
(D) The crops that have always been grown in Country X are different from those that have always been grown in Country Y.
(E) Country X's new government instituted a centralized economy with the intention of ensuring an equitable distribution of goods.

Argument Evaluation

Situation Two countries sharing similar climatic conditions differ widely in agricultural production, one experiencing a rise and the other a decline. The decline is blamed on an overly centralized economy.

Reasoning *What point most weakens the argument that the economy is to blame?* If a factor other than the economy could account for the differences in agricultural production, then the argument is weakened. If the two countries grow different kinds of crops that may react differently to the same climatic conditions, then the types of crops, rather than the economy, could be responsible for the differences in production.

A The economy might indeed be to blame for declining industrial production, which would strengthen the argument, but not enough information is given about the country's industry to allow that evaluation of blame to be made.

B The availability of a seaport does not explain the differences in agricultural production.

C Similar climatic conditions have already been established in the argument.

D Correct. This statement properly identifies a factor that weakens the argument.

E The government's intention when instituting the economy does not have any bearing on whether the economy is responsible for the decline or not.

The correct answer is D.

80. Because no employee wants to be associated with bad news in the eyes of a superior, information about serious problems at lower levels is progressively softened and distorted as it goes up each step in the management hierarchy. The chief executive is, therefore, less well informed about problems at lower levels than are his or her subordinates at those levels.

The conclusion drawn above is based on the assumption that _____.

(A) problems should be solved at the level in the management hierarchy at which they occur

(B) employees should be rewarded for accurately reporting problems to their superiors

(C) problem-solving ability is more important at higher levels than it is at lower levels of the management hierarchy

(D) chief executives obtain information about problems at lower levels from no source other than their subordinates

(E) some employees are more concerned about truth than about the way they are perceived by their superiors

Argument Construction

Situation No employee wants to report bad news to a superior, so information about problems is softened and distorted as it goes up the ranks of management. As a result, chief executives know less about problems at lower levels than their subordinates do.

Reasoning *What assumption is being made in this argument?* This passage contends that information travels step by step upward through an organization, and that information becomes increasingly distorted along the route with each additional individual's reluctance to be candid with a superior about problems. What must be true about this information flow to support the conclusion? In order to conclude that chief executives are *less well informed* about problems than their subordinates, the argument must logically assume that they have no source of information except their subordinates.

A This argument is not about how problems should be solved, only about how chief executives learn of them.

B No recommendation for solving the problem is assumed; only the method of discovering the problem is assumed.

C The passage does not discuss problem solving ability and where it is best served, so this statement cannot be assumed.

D Correct. This statement properly identifies an assumption that underlies the argument.

E This statement contradicts the first sentence of the passage and so cannot possibly be assumed.

The correct answer is D.

81. A recent report determined that although only 3 percent of drivers on Maryland highways equipped their vehicles with radar detectors, 33 percent of all vehicles ticketed for exceeding the speed limit were equipped with them. Clearly, drivers who equip their vehicles with radar detectors are more likely to exceed the speed limit regularly than are drivers who do not.

The conclusion drawn above depends on which of the following assumptions?

(A) Drivers who equip their vehicles with radar detectors are less likely to be ticketed for exceeding the speed limit than are drivers who do not.

(B) Drivers who are ticketed for exceeding the speed limit are more likely to exceed the speed limit regularly than are drivers who are not ticketed.

(C) The number of vehicles that were ticketed for exceeding the speed limit was greater than the number of vehicles that were equipped with radar detectors.

(D) Many of the vehicles that were ticketed for exceeding the speed limit were ticketed more than once in the time period covered by the report.

(E) Drivers on Maryland highways exceeded the speed limit more often than did drivers on other state highways not covered in the report.

Argument Construction

Situation Although only 3 percent of drivers on Maryland's highways have radar detectors in their vehicles, 33 percent of vehicles recently ticketed for driving over the speed limit on Maryland highways have had radar detectors. Drivers who have radar detectors are thus more likely to exceed the speed limit regularly than drivers who do not.

Reasoning *What assumption must be true for the conclusion to be drawn?* The argument moves from a particular sample, that is, the percentage of vehicles ticketed for exceeding the speed limit that were equipped with radar detectors, to a generalization about the regular driving behaviors of all drivers who have radar detectors in their vehicles. Between the example and the generalization must stand an assumption. What can the assumption be? Only if the drivers ticketed in this instance are assumed to make a regular habit of exceeding the speed limit can the conclusion be drawn that drivers with radar detectors are more likely to do so *regularly* than drivers who are not ticketed.

A While this statement about being ticketed may be true, the conclusion pertains to the recurrent exceeding of the speed limit, so this statement is not relevant.

B **Correct.** This statement properly identifies the conclusion's necessary assumption about ticketed drivers' being more likely to drive in excess of the speed limit than nonticketed drivers.

C From the original passage it is already known that 67 percent of all ticketed vehicles did not have radar detectors. This statement is about the number of vehicles ticketed, not about the regular habits of drivers, so it is not assumed for the conclusion.

D While this additional information could help support the conclusion, it is not a necessary assumption in the conclusion because it is about the particular example of the drivers in Maryland, not about drivers' habits in general.

E Learning that Maryland drivers are not representative of other drivers undermines the conclusion about all drivers, so it is clearly not assumed.

The correct answer is B.

82. Products sold under a brand name used to command premium prices because, in general, they were superior to nonbrand rival products. Technical expertise in product development has become so widespread, however, that special quality advantages are very hard to obtain these days and even harder to maintain. As a consequence, brand-name products generally neither offer higher quality nor sell at higher prices. Paradoxically, brand names are a bigger marketing advantage than ever.

Which of the following, if true, most helps to resolve the paradox outlined above?

(A) Brand names are taken by consumers as a guarantee of getting a product as good as the best rival products.

(B) Consumers recognize that the quality of products sold under invariant brand names can drift over time.

(C) In many acquisitions of one corporation by another, the acquiring corporation is interested more in acquiring the right to use certain brand names than in acquiring existing production facilities.

(D) In the days when special quality advantages were easier to obtain than they are now, it was also easier to get new brand names established.

(E) The advertising of a company's brand-name products is at times transferred to a new advertising agency, especially when sales are declining.

Argument Evaluation

Situation In both quality and price, brand-name and nonbrand products have now become similar. Yet brand names offer a bigger marketing advantage than ever.

Reasoning *How can this paradox be explained?* It is given that a brand-name product's only distinction from its rival products is a recognizable name. What must be true to give brand-name products a bigger marketing advantage? Could consumers be relying on their outdated knowledge and believing that brand names continue to guarantee that a product's quality is at least as good as, and possibly higher than, that of the rival products at the same price? If so, they would choose to purchase the brand-name product trusting they would, at a minimum, get comparable quality for the same price.

A **Correct.** This statement correctly identifies the consumer behavior that explains the marketing advantage of brand names.

B Consumers would be less likely to buy brand-name products if they were unsure of their quality, so this statement does not resolve the paradox.

C Corporations value brand names, but this statement does not say why, nor does it explain the marketing advantage of brand names.

D The relative ease or difficulty of establishing brand names does not explain why they are a marketing advantage.

E The shift from one advertising agency to another to counteract falling sales does not account for the general marketing advantage brand names enjoy.

The correct answer is A.

83. Editorial: Regulations recently imposed by the government of Risemia call for unprecedented reductions in the amounts of pollutants manufacturers are allowed to discharge into the environment. It will take costly new pollution control equipment requiring expensive maintenance to comply with these regulations. Resultant price increases for Risemian manufactured goods will lead to the loss of some export markets. Clearly, therefore, annual exports of Risemian manufactured goods will in the future occur at diminished levels.

Which of the following, if true, most seriously weakens the argument in the editorial?

(A) The need to comply with the new regulations will stimulate the development within Risemia of new pollution control equipment for which a strong worldwide demand is likely to emerge.

(B) The proposed regulations include a schedule of fines for noncompliance that escalate steeply in cases of repeated noncompliance.

(C) Savings from utilizing the chemicals captured by the pollution control equipment will remain far below the cost of maintaining the equipment.

(D) By international standards, the levels of pollutants currently emitted by some of Risemia's manufacturing plants are not considered excessive.

(E) The stockholders of most of Risemia's manufacturing corporations exert substantial pressure on the corporations to comply with environmental laws.

Argument Evaluation

Situation An editorial states that manufacturers in Risemia must pay for expensive new pollution control equipment in order to comply with recent regulations. Increased costs will lead to increased prices and consequently to the loss of some export markets. Exports will thus go down.

Reasoning *What point weakens the argument?* First, recognize the underlying assumptions regarding the exports of manufactured goods. While the kinds of goods previously exported may be priced out of their markets and experience a loss, it is apparently assumed that the existing goods are the only ones that Risemia is able to manufacture for export. What if new products were exported in their place? If so, the total annual exports would not necessarily fall. The new regulations call for new, expensive pollution control equipment. If this equipment were manufactured in Risemia, it would be likely to find an international market anywhere similar environmental restrictions were applied.

A **Correct.** This statement properly identifies a weakness in the editorial's argument since it is possible that the potential loss of some exports will be compensated for by the addition of a new export, the pollution control equipment, for which there could be strong international demand.

B Fines for noncompliance increase the cost to manufacturers and thus their prices, so this statement tends to support the argument.

C Since the new equipment will cost more to maintain than it will save, the manufacturers' costs will again go up. This statement supports the argument.

D The comparative level of pollutants is irrelevant because manufacturers must comply with the new regulations in Risemia and pay the resultant costs, no matter how their level of pollutant emission compares with that of other countries.

E The stockholders' determination that manufacturers comply with the new regulations supports the argument rather than weakening it.

The correct answer is A.

84. When demand for a factory's products is high, more money is spent at the factory for safety precautions and machinery maintenance than when demand is low. Thus the average number of on-the-job accidents per employee each month should be lower during periods when demand is high than when demand is low and less money is available for safety precautions and machinery maintenance.

Which of the following, if true about a factory when demand for its products is high, casts the most serious doubt on the conclusion drawn above?

(A) Its employees ask for higher wages than they do at other times.

(B) Its management hires new workers but lacks the time to train them properly.

(C) Its employees are less likely to lose their jobs than they are at other times.

(D) Its management sponsors a monthly safety award for each division in the factory.

(E) Its old machinery is replaced with modern, automated models.

Argument Evaluation

Situation Because more money is spent on safety precautions and machinery maintenance at a factory when demand for its product is high, the average number of job-related accidents per employee at the factory should be lower when demand is high.

Reasoning *What point casts doubt on the conclusion?* Consider what other conditions can result from high demand for a factory's products. What if, when demand is high, more employees are hired to meet the demand? If, in the effort to increase production, there is not enough time for proper training, then it is likely that the new, poorly trained employees will have more job-related accidents than experienced, well-trained workers.

A The conclusion is about safety rather than wages, so the employees' demand for higher wages is irrelevant.

B **Correct.** This statement properly identifies a point that undermines the conclusion.

C The conclusion is about safety, not about job security, so this point is irrelevant.

D Actively promoting safety with an award would tend to support the argument, not weaken it.

E Replacing outdated machinery with more modern machinery should result in a safer workplace; this point strengthens the conclusion.

The correct answer is B.

85. An unusually severe winter occurred in Europe after the continent was blanketed by a blue haze resulting from the eruption of the Laki Volcano in the European republic of Iceland in the summer of 1984. Thus, it is evident that major eruptions cause the atmosphere to become cooler than it would be otherwise.

Which of the following statements, if true, most seriously weakens the argument above?

(A) The cooling effect triggered by volcanic eruptions in 1985 was counteracted by an unusual warming of Pacific waters.

(B) There is a strong statistical link between volcanic eruptions and the severity of the rainy season in India.

(C) A few months after El Chichón's large eruption in April 1982, air temperatures throughout the region remained higher than expected, given the long-term weather trends.

(D) The climatic effects of major volcanic eruptions can temporarily mask the general warming trend resulting from an excess of carbon dioxide in the atmosphere.

(E) Three months after an early springtime eruption in South America during the late nineteenth century, sea surface temperatures near the coast began to fall.

Argument Evaluation

Situation Europe experienced an exceptionally cold winter after a volcanic eruption in the summer of 1984 covered the continent in a blue haze. Major eruptions must cause the atmosphere to become cooler.

Reasoning *Which statement weakens this argument?* The argument is weak because it makes a generalization on the basis of only one example. Any example of a volcanic eruption that was not followed by a cooling of the atmosphere weakens this argument. The example of the eruption of El Chichón in 1982, which resulted in higher than normal air temperatures, contradicts the generalization of cooler temperatures following volcanic eruptions.

A This statement supports the argument by establishing that other volcanic eruptions triggered a cooling effect, even though another event counteracted it.

B The argument is about the relationship between volcanic eruption and a cooler atmosphere, not between volcanic eruption and increased rain.

C **Correct.** This statement properly identifies a weakness in the argument.

D This statement supports the argument because it implies that volcanic eruptions cool the atmosphere, given that their effects *mask the general warming trend.*

E The argument is about a cooling in the atmosphere, which could in turn lower sea surface temperatures, so this example tends to support the argument.

The correct answer is C.

86. Journalist: In physics journals, the number of articles reporting the results of experiments involving particle accelerators was lower last year than it had been in previous years. Several of the particle accelerators at major research institutions were out of service the year before last for repairs, so it is likely that the low number of articles was due to the decline in availability of particle accelerators.

Which of the following, if true, most seriously undermines the journalist's argument?

(A) Every article based on experiments with particle accelerators that was submitted for publication last year actually was published.

(B) The average time scientists must wait for access to a particle accelerator has declined over the last several years.

(C) The number of physics journals was the same last year as in previous years.

(D) Particle accelerators can be used for more than one group of experiments in any given year.

(E) Recent changes in the editorial policies of several physics journals have decreased the likelihood that articles concerning particle-accelerator research will be accepted for publication.

Argument Evaluation

Situation A journalist attributes the low number of articles about particle accelerators in physics journals to the fact that several accelerators at major research institutions had been out of service the previous year.

Reasoning *What point undermines the journalist's argument?* The journalist assumes that the researchers' lack of access to the accelerators is responsible for the decline in the number of articles. What else could explain fewer articles? What if the decline is due, not to the availability of the accelerators for experiments, but to policies regarding publishing articles related to such experiments? An alternate explanation is that changes in the editorial policies of physics journals, rather than the effect of the out-of-service accelerators, could well be responsible for the lower number of published articles about particle-accelerator research.

A This statement rules out the possibility that submitted articles were not published, and eliminating this alternate explanation tends to support the argument.

B A decline in waiting time would seem to promote more articles about accelerator research being written and published, not fewer.

C While the decline in articles could be explained by a decline in the number of journals, this statement eliminates that alternate explanation.

D If the accelerators can be used for multiple experiments, then it is reasonable to expect more articles related to them, not fewer.

E **Correct.** This statement properly identifies a point that undermines the journalist's reasoning.

The correct answer is E.

Questions 87–89 are based on the following:

Networks of blood vessels in bats' wings serve only to disperse heat generated in flight. This heat is generated only because bats flap their wings. Thus paleontologists' recent discovery that the winged dinosaur Sandactylus had similar networks of blood vessels in the skin of its wings provides evidence for the hypothesis that Sandactylus flew by flapping its wings, not just by gliding.

87. In the passage, the author develops the argument by _____.

(A) forming the hypothesis that best explains several apparently conflicting pieces of evidence
(B) reinterpreting evidence that had been used to support an earlier theory
(C) using an analogy with a known phenomenon to draw a conclusion about an unknown phenomenon
(D) speculating about how structures observed in present-day creatures might have developed from similar structures in creatures now extinct
(E) pointing out differences in the physiological demands that flight makes on large, as opposed to small, creatures

Argument Evaluation

Situation The network of blood vessels in bats' wings is compared with a similar structure in the wings of the dinosaur Sandactylus to explain how the dinosaur flew.

Reasoning *How is this argument developed?* The author first shows that a physical characteristic of bats' wings is directly related to their style of flight. The author then argues that the similar structure found in the wings of Sandactylus is evidence that the dinosaur had a style of flight similar to that of bats. The structure of this argument is a comparison, or analogy, between a known phenomenon (bats) and an unknown one (Sandactylus).

A The evidence of the blood vessels in the wings does not conflict with other evidence.
B Only one theory—that Sandactylus flew by flapping its wings as well as by gliding—is proposed; no earlier theory is discussed.
C **Correct.** This statement properly identifies how the argument compares the wings of bats and of Sandactylus in order to draw a conclusion about how the dinosaur flew.
D The theory is not about how the structures in the bats developed from the structures in the dinosaurs, but rather about how Sandactylus flew.
E The comparison between bats and Sandactylus points out similarities, not differences.

The correct answer is C.

88. Which of the following, if true, most seriously weakens the argument in the passage?

(A) Sandactylus' wings were far more similar to the wings of bats than to the wings of birds.
(B) Paleontologists do not know whether winged dinosaurs other than Sandactylus had similar networks of blood vessels in the skin of their wings.
(C) The mechanism used by bats for dispersing heat in flight could, in principle, work for much larger flying creatures, such as Sandactylus.
(D) Not all the bats that use the mechanism described in the passage for dispersing heat in flight live in climates similar to the climate in which Sandactylus lived.
(E) Other winged dinosaurs that flew only by gliding had networks of blood vessels in the skin of their wings similar to those that Sandactylus had.

Argument Evaluation

Situation The network of blood vessels in bats' wings is compared with a similar structure in the wings of the dinosaur Sandactylus to explain how the dinosaur flew. (The same as the previous item.)

Reasoning *Which point weakens the argument?* Based on the evidence of similar structures found in the wings of bats and of Sandactylus, the conclusion suggests that Sandactylus flew not only by gliding, but also by flapping its wings as bats do. What if the wing structures shared by bats and Sandactylus are also found in other dinosaurs that are known to have flown only by gliding? The author's argument would be weakened by evidence that other dinosaurs that did not flap their wings in flight nonetheless had similar blood-vessel networks in their wings.

A This point supports the argument.
B Since the argument concerns only Sandactylus, lack of knowledge about other dinosaurs does not affect the hypothesis about flight.
C This point supports the argument.
D Some of the bats do live in climates similar to the one in which Sandactylus lived; not enough information is provided to determine whether climate is relevant to the argument.
E **Correct.** This statement properly identifies a factor that weakens the argument: having similar wing structures does not necessitate similar wing-flapping flight styles.

The correct answer is E.

89. The argument in the passage relies on which of the following assumptions?

(A) Sandactylus would not have had networks of blood vessels in the skin of its wings if these networks were of no use to Sandactylus.

(B) All creatures that fly by flapping their wings have networks of blood vessels in the skin of their wings.

(C) Winged dinosaurs that flapped their wings in flight would have been able to fly more effectively than winged dinosaurs that could only glide.

(D) If Sandactylus flew by flapping its wings, then paleontologists would certainly be able to find some evidence that it did so.

(E) Heat generated by Sandactylus in flapping its wings in flight could not have been dispersed by anything other than the blood vessels in its wings.

Argument Construction

Situation The network of blood vessels in bats' wings is compared with a similar structure in the wings of the dinosaur Sandactylus to explain how the dinosaur flew. (The same as the previous item.)

Reasoning *What assumption does this argument make?* The networks of blood vessels in the wings of bats are shown to have a purpose: to disperse the heat generated by wing-flapping flight. In proposing that a similar structure had a similar purpose in Sandactylus, the argument assumes that the network of blood vessels found in the dinosaur wings had a purpose.

A **Correct.** This statement properly identifies the assumption that underlies the argument: there was a purpose for the network of blood vessels found in the wings of Sandactylus.

B This statement is too broad to be assumed; the comparison between bats and Sandactylus cannot be extended to all flying creatures.

C No conclusion is drawn about the efficiency of flight, so this point is not assumed.

D The argument does not assume that evidence is certain to be found.

E Since this point is not addressed in the argument, it cannot be assumed.

The correct answer is A.

90. Keith: Compliance with new government regulations requiring the installation of smoke alarms and sprinkler systems in all theaters and arenas will cost the entertainment industry $25 billion annually. Consequently, jobs will be lost and profits diminished. Therefore, these regulations will harm the country's economy.

Laura: The $25 billion spent by some businesses will be revenue for others. Jobs and profits will be gained as well as lost.

Laura responds to Keith by _____.

(A) demonstrating that Keith's conclusion is based on evidence that is not relevant to the issue at hand
(B) challenging the plausibility of the evidence that serves as the basis for Keith's argument
(C) suggesting that Keith's argument overlooks a mitigating consequence
(D) reinforcing Keith's conclusion by supplying a complementary interpretation of the evidence Keith cites
(E) agreeing with the main conclusion of Keith's argument but construing that conclusion as grounds for optimism rather than for pessimism

Argument Construction

Situation Keith argues that the cost of new regulations will result in a loss of jobs and profits, hurting the national economy. Laura points out that while one industry will suffer, others will gain by supplying the goods and services required by the regulations.

Reasoning *What is the strategy Laura uses in the counterargument?* Laura uses the same evidence, the $25 billion spent on meeting new regulations, but comes to a different conclusion. While Keith focuses on the losses to one industry, Laura looks at the gains to other industries. By suggesting a consequence that Keith did not mention, she places the outcome in a more positive light.

A Laura accepts the relevance of Keith's evidence and uses it herself when she replies that *the $25 billion spent by some businesses will be revenue for others.*

B Laura does not challenge Keith's evidence; she uses the same evidence as the basis of her own argument.

C **Correct.** This statement properly identifies the strategy Laura employs in her counterargument. Laura points out that Keith did not consider that, in this case, losses for one industry mean gains for others.

D Laura rejects rather than reinforces Keith's conclusion; while he notes the losses in jobs and profits that will harm the economy, she points out that *jobs and profits will be gained as well as lost.*

E Laura does not agree with Keith that the regulations will harm the national economy; she argues instead that gains in other industries will compensate for the losses in one industry.

The correct answer is C.

91. Businesses are suffering because of a lack of money available for development loans. To help businesses, the government plans to modify the income-tax structure in order to induce individual taxpayers to put a larger portion of their incomes into retirement savings accounts, because as more money is deposited in such accounts, more money becomes available to borrowers.

Which of the following, if true, raises the most serious doubt regarding the effectiveness of the government's plan to increase the amount of money available for development loans for businesses?

(A) When levels of personal retirement savings increase, consumer borrowing always increases correspondingly.

(B) The increased tax revenue the government would receive as a result of business expansion would not offset the loss in revenue from personal income taxes during the first year of the plan.

(C) Even with tax incentives, some people will choose not to increase their levels of retirement savings.

(D) Bankers generally will not continue to lend money to businesses whose prospective earnings are insufficient to meet their loan repayment schedules.

(E) The modified tax structure would give all taxpayers, regardless of their incomes, the same tax savings for a given increase in their retirement savings.

Evaluation of a Plan

Situation Because the lack of available money for development loans is harming businesses, the government plans to modify the income-tax structure, encouraging taxpayers to put more money into retirement accounts. This plan is intended to ensure that with more money put into these accounts, more money will in turn be available to business borrowers.

Reasoning *What potential flaw in this plan might prevent it from being effective?* What is the expectation behind the plan? The government's plan supposes that the money invested in retirement accounts will be readily available to business borrowers in the form of development loans. Consider what circumstances might hinder that availability. What if consumer borrowers compete with businesses? If it is known that, historically, increased savings in personal retirement accounts results in increased consumer borrowing, then the government's effort to target businesses as the sole beneficiaries of this plan could well fail.

A **Correct.** This statement properly identifies a reason that the government's plan could be less effective in meeting its goal.

B The goal of the plan is to increase the amount of money available as development loans for businesses, so this point is irrelevant to the effectiveness of the plan.

C The effectiveness of the plan would be determined not by what *some people* do, but by what most people do.

D The plan would increase the money available specifically for development loans, not existing loans.

E The universal tax savings does not affect the effectiveness of the plan.

The correct answer is A.

92. In order to finance road repairs, the highway commission of a certain state is considering a 50 percent increase in the 10-cents-per-mile toll for vehicles using its toll highway. The highway commissioner claims that the toll increase will increase the annual revenue generated by the toll highway by at least 50 percent per year.

Which of the following is an assumption on which the highway commissioner's claim depends?

(A) The amount of money required annually for road repairs will not increase from its current level.

(B) The total number of trips made on the toll highway per year will not decrease from its current level.

(C) The average length of a trip made on the toll highway will not decrease from its current level.

(D) The number of drivers who consistently avoid the highway tolls by using secondary roads will not increase from its current level.

(E) The total distance traveled by vehicles on the toll highway per year will not decrease from its current level.

Argument Construction

Situation A state highway commission considers a 50 percent increase in the 10-cents-a-mile toll on its toll highway; this increase promises at least a 50 percent increase in the revenue generated by the toll highway.

Reasoning *On what assumption does this argument depend?* The toll is charged on a per-mile basis. A 50 percent increase in the toll will bring a 50 percent increase in revenue only if the total number of miles traveled on the toll highway per year does not decrease.

A Road repairs are not included in the argument about the increase in the annual *revenue*, so this assumption is not made.

B The toll highway generates revenue based on the number of miles traveled, not the number of trips, so this assumption is not part of the argument.

C The average length of a trip does not determine the annual revenue that the toll highway brings in; since the toll is charged per mile, it is the total distance per year that determines the amount of annual revenue.

D The revenue is determined by the number of miles traveled on the toll highway, not the number of drivers who either take it or avoid it.

E **Correct.** This statement properly recognizes the assumption underlying the commissioner's claim: with the revenue generated on a per-mile basis, a 50 percent increase in the toll will result in a 50 percent increase in the revenue as long as the total number of miles traveled on the toll highway remains the same.

The correct answer is E.

93. A new law gives ownership of patents—documents providing exclusive right to make and sell an invention—to universities, not the government, when those patents result from government-sponsored university research. Administrators at Logos University plan to sell any patents they acquire to corporations in order to fund programs to improve undergraduate teaching.

Which of the following, if true, would cast the most doubt on the viability of the college administrators' plan described above?

(A) Profit-making corporations interested in developing products based on patents held by universities are likely to try to serve as exclusive sponsors of ongoing university research projects.

(B) Corporate sponsors of research in university facilities are entitled to tax credits under new federal tax-code guidelines.

(C) Research scientists at Logos University have few or no teaching responsibilities and participate little if at all in the undergraduate programs in their field.

(D) Government-sponsored research conducted at Logos University for the most part duplicates research already completed by several profit-making corporations.

(E) Logos University is unlikely to attract corporate sponsorship of its scientific research.

Evaluation of a Plan

Situation Universities own the patents resulting from government-sponsored research at their institutions. One university plans to sell its patents to corporations to fund a program to improve teaching.

Reasoning *Which point casts doubt on the university's plan?* The university's plan assumes there will be a market for its patents, and that the corporations will want to buy them. What might make this untrue? If some of the corporations have already done the same or similar research, they will not be prospective buyers of the university's patents.

A This point is irrelevant to the plan to sell patents in order to fund a program.

B The university plans to sell the patents to the corporations, not to invite the corporations to sponsor research.

C This point is irrelevant to the university's plan to sell off patents.

D Correct. This statement properly identifies a factor that casts doubt on the university's plan to sell its patents to corporations.

E The plan concerns selling patents, not attracting corporate sponsorship for research.

The correct answer is D.

Questions 94–95 are based on the following:

Environmentalist: The commissioner of the Fish and Game Authority would have the public believe that increases in the number of marine fish caught demonstrate that this resource is no longer endangered. This is a specious argument, as unsound as it would be to assert that the ever-increasing rate at which rain forests are being cut down demonstrates a lack of danger to that resource. The real cause of the increased fish-catch is a greater efficiency in using technologies that deplete resources.

94. Which of the following strategies is used in the presentation of the environmentalist's position?

(A) Questioning the motives of an opponent
(B) Showing that an opposing position is self-contradictory
(C) Attacking an argument through the use of an analogy
(D) Demonstrating the inaccuracy of certain data
(E) Pointing out adverse consequences of a proposal

Argument Construction

Situation A public official argues that increased catches show that marine fish are no longer endangered. An environmentalist attacks the position and cites technology as the cause of the increased catch.

Reasoning *What strategy does the environmentalist use to state a position?* Consider how the environmentalist structures the argument. The environmentalist describes the commissioner's argument as *specious*, or deceptive, and then uses an analogy to rain forests to demonstrate that the commissioner's argument is built on false premises.

A The position, but not the motives, of the commissioner is questioned.

B The environmentalist says that the official's position is *specious* but does not claim that is self-contradictory.

C **Correct.** This statement properly identifies the strategy used in the argument: the environmentalist attacks the commissioner's position by comparing it to an absurd argument about the rain forests.

D The environmentalist does not use any data.

E No proposal is offered; thus no adverse consequences are examined.

The correct answer is C.

95. The environmentalist's statements, if true, best support which of the following as a conclusion?

(A) The use of technology is the reason for the increasing encroachment of people on nature.

(B) It is possible to determine how many fish are in the sea by some way other than by catching fish.

(C) The proportion of marine fish that are caught is as high as the proportion of rain forest trees that are cut down each year.

(D) Modern technologies waste resources by catching inedible fish.

(E) Marine fish continue to be an endangered resource.

Argument Construction

Situation A public official argues that increased catches show that marine fish are no longer endangered. An environmentalist attacks the position and cites technology as the cause of the increased catch. (The same as the previous item.)

Reasoning *What conclusion do the environmentalist's statements support?* The environmentalist casts doubt by saying the commissioner *would have the public believe* that the increased catch shows that the fish are no longer endangered; the phrasing indicates that environmentalist believes just the reverse. The environmentalist does believe the marine fish are endangered, and, after attacking the commissioner's argument as *specious*, or false, and offering an analogy to make that argument look ridiculous, the environmentalist gives an alternate explanation for the increased catch that is consistent with that belief.

A *The encroachment of people on nature* is not examined.

B No methods to determine the number are discussed in the statements.

C The environmentalist compares the two arguments, not the two proportions.

D The fish are not said to be inedible.

E **Correct.** This statement properly identifies a conclusion supported by the environmentalist's statements: the marine fish are endangered.

The correct answer is E.

96. Commentator: The theory of trade retaliation states that countries closed out of any of another country's markets should close some of their own markets to the other country in order to pressure the other country to reopen its markets. If every country acted according to this theory, no country would trade with any other.

The commentator's argument relies on which of the following assumptions?

(A) No country actually acts according to the theory of trade retaliation.

(B) No country should block any of its markets to foreign trade.

(C) Trade disputes should be settled by international tribunal.

(D) For any two countries, at least one has some market closed to the other.

(E) Countries close their markets to foreigners to protect domestic producers.

Argument Construction

Situation The theory of trade retaliation is explained as the action and reaction of closing markets between trading nations; no country would ever trade with another, the observation is offered, if every country acted according to the theory.

Reasoning *What assumption underlies this argument?* What makes the commentator conclude that no country would be trading if the theory were operative? The commentator must perceive of some condition as a given here. The argument assumes an initial action, a country's closing of a market to a trading partner, that is followed by a reaction, the retaliatory closing of a market by that partner. In this unending pattern of action-reaction, at least one of the two countries must have a market closed to the other.

A Any one country may act according to the theory, but not *every* country.

B The argument assumes that countries do block markets to foreign trade.

C An international tribunal is not mentioned in the argument.

D Correct. This statement properly identifies the assumption required to create the never-ending action-reaction pattern.

E The argument does not discuss the protection of domestic trade.

The correct answer is D.

97. Although parapsychology is often considered a pseudoscience, it is in fact a genuine scientific enterprise, for it uses scientific methods such as controlled experiments and statistical tests of clearly stated hypotheses to examine the questions it raises.

The conclusion above is properly drawn if which of the following is assumed?

(A) If a field of study can conclusively answer the questions it raises, then it is a genuine science.

(B) Since parapsychology uses scientific methods, it will produce credible results.

(C) Any enterprise that does not use controlled experiments and statistical tests is not genuine science.

(D) Any field of study that employs scientific methods is a genuine scientific enterprise.

(E) Since parapsychology raises clearly statable questions, they can be tested in controlled experiments.

Argument construction

Situation The argument states that parapsychology is a genuine science because it uses scientific methods.

Reasoning *What assumption does the argument make?* The argument asserts that parapsychology is a science *for it uses scientific methods*. The argument thus assumes that the use of scientific methods proves that a field of study is a genuine science.

A The argument is based on an assumption about how the questions are investigated rather than on how well they are answered.

B The argument is not about whether the results are credible, so this assumption is irrelevant.

C The argument does not concern what is *not* genuine science, so there is no need for this assumption.

D Correct. This statement properly identifies the argument's assumption that the use of scientific methods is sufficient to make an enterprise genuine science.

E This assumption about the relation between statable hypotheses and controlled experiments is not necessary to the argument.

The correct answer is D.

98. Hotco oil burners, designed to be used in asphalt plants, are so efficient that Hotco will sell one to the Clifton Asphalt plant for no payment other than the cost savings between the total amount the asphalt plant actually paid for oil using its former burner during the last two years and the total amount it will pay for oil using the Hotco burner during the next two years. On installation, the plant will make an estimated payment, which will be adjusted after two years to equal the actual cost savings.

Which of the following, if it occurred, would constitute a disadvantage for Hotco of the plan described above?

(A) Another manufacturer's introduction to the market of a similarly efficient burner

(B) The Clifton Asphalt plant's need for more than one new burner

(C) Very poor efficiency in the Clifton Asphalt plant's old burner

(D) A decrease in the demand for asphalt

(E) A steady increase in the price of oil beginning soon after the new burner is installed

Evaluation of a Plan

Situation Hotco produces a very efficient oil burner. It sells a burner to an asphalt plant, stating that the price of the burner is how much money the plant saves on oil using the new burner.

Reasoning *Hotco will be at a disadvantage if which of the following occurs?* Hotco is to be paid based on how much money the plant saves on oil over a two-year period. There is an assumption that a number of factors will remain relatively stable from the previous two years to the next two years. What is a factor that could cause a disadvantage for Hotco? If the price of oil goes up, then the plant will experience smaller savings than Hotco anticipated, despite the plant's using less oil than previously because of its new, more efficient burners. If the plant's savings go down, Hotco will not get the payment it is expecting.

A The burner is already installed, so a competitor is not a problem.

B The plant's need for multiple burners should be an opportunity for Hotco, not a disadvantage.

C If the old burner was very inefficient, the new burner should save a great deal of money that would ultimately go to Hotco.

D If demand decreases, less oil would need to be purchased, and Hotco would get more money.

E **Correct.** This statement properly identifies a factor that would constitute a disadvantage for the plan: since the payment for the burner is based on savings in oil purchases, any increases in the price of oil will decrease savings and thus decrease payments to Hotco.

The correct answer is E.

99. An experiment was done in which human subjects recognize a pattern within a matrix of abstract designs and then select another design that completes that pattern. The results of the experiment were surprising. The lowest expenditure of energy in neurons in the brain was found in those subjects who performed most successfully in the experiments.

Which of the following hypotheses best accounts for the findings of the experiment?

(A) The neurons of the brain react less when a subject is trying to recognize patterns than when the subject is doing other kinds of reasoning.

(B) Those who performed best in the experiment experienced more satisfaction when working with abstract patterns than did those who performed less well.

(C) People who are better at abstract pattern recognition have more energy-efficient neural connections.

(D) The energy expenditure of the subjects' brains increases when a design that completes the initially recognized pattern is determined.

(E) The task of completing a given design is more capably performed by athletes, whose energy expenditure is lower when they are at rest.

Argument Construction

Situation Experimental subjects worked with pattern recognition and completion. The subjects who performed best showed the lowest expenditure of energy in neurons in the brain.

Reasoning *Which hypothesis best accounts for the findings?* In order to account for the findings, the hypothesis must suggest a plausible link between successful performance and the energy expenditure of neurons in the brain. Consider each answer choice, and evaluate its plausibility and logic. Where is there a reasonably direct relationship between the given factors and the conclusion that is drawn? Understand that hypotheses based on factors not included in the experiment cannot be used to account for the findings.

A The experiment did not compare types of reasoning so this hypothesis does not account for the results.

B Subjects' satisfaction is not in question in this experiment.

C Correct. This statement properly identifies a hypothesis that connects subjects' performance with their energy expenditure and so could account for the experiment's results.

D The experiment did not compare energy expenditure in different phases of the experiment.

E No information is offered on the subjects, so no hypothesis about athletes is warranted.

The correct answer is C.

100. One way to judge the performance of a company is to compare it with other companies. This technique, commonly called "benchmarking," permits the manager of a company to discover better industrial practices and can provide a justification for the adoption of good practices.

Any of the following, if true, is a valid reason for benchmarking the performance of a company against companies with which it is not in competition rather than against competitors EXCEPT:

(A) Comparisons with competitors are most likely to focus on practices that the manager making the comparisons already employs.
(B) Getting "inside" information about the unique practices of competitors is particularly difficult.
(C) Since companies that compete with each other are likely to have comparable levels of efficiency, only benchmarking against noncompetitors is likely to reveal practices that would aid in beating competitors.
(D) Managers are generally more receptive to new ideas that they find outside their own industry.
(E) Much of the success of good companies is due to their adoption of practices that take advantage of the special circumstances of their products or markets.

Argument Construction

Situation "Benchmarking" is a technique for judging the performance of a company by comparing it with other companies. The goal is to find and adopt better industrial practices.

Reasoning *Which one condition does NOT recommend benchmarking against noncompetitors? Which one condition IS a well-founded reason to benchmark against competitors?* First, sort through the given information and the answer choices for the question to gain an understanding of the potential advantages or disadvantages of comparing a company to its competitors or to noncompetitors. What are the reasons in favor of benchmarking against noncompetitors? Information about noncompeting companies is easier to obtain; it can offer new insights; and it may be easier to put into practice. Why then might a manager choose to benchmark against competitors? Competing companies do share special circumstances involving products and markets. If companies are often successful because of practices related to these special circumstances within their industry, then benchmarking against competitors will reveal these practices and so be more fruitful than benchmarking against noncompetitors.

A Since benchmarking against competitors would yield few new practices, it would be better to benchmark against noncompetitors.

B If information about competitors is hard to obtain, benchmarking against noncompetitors is preferable.

C Since benchmarking against noncompetitors would yield practices useful in beating competitors, benchmarking against noncompetitors is preferable.

D If managers are more likely to adopt new practices learned from benchmarking against noncompetitors, then this technique is preferable.

E **Correct.** This statement properly identifies the rationale that supports a company's benchmarking against its competitors.

The correct answer is E.

101. For a trade embargo against a particular country to succeed, a high degree of both international accord and ability to prevent goods from entering or leaving that country must be sustained. A total blockade of Patria's ports is necessary to an embargo, but such an action would be likely to cause international discord over the embargo.

The claims above, if true, most strongly support which of the following conclusions?

(A) The balance of opinion is likely to favor Patria in the event of a blockade.
(B) As long as international opinion is unanimously against Patria, a trade embargo is likely to succeed.
(C) A naval blockade of Patria's ports would ensure that no goods enter or leave Patria.
(D) Any trade embargo against Patria would be likely to fail at some time.
(E) For a blockade of Patria's ports to be successful, international opinion must be unanimous.

Argument Construction

Situation The success of a trade embargo requires both international accord and the ability to enforce the embargo. In the case of Patria, an embargo would require a total blockade of the ports, but the blockade itself would likely lead to international discord.

Reasoning *What conclusion can be drawn from this information?* A conclusion must be based only on the information provided. Since the given information discusses the general conditions for a successful trade embargo and the conditions specific to the possible embargo in Patria, the conclusion should be about the likelihood of success for a trade embargo against Patria. Since international accord is necessary for the success of an embargo but the blockade required in this case would create international discord, the contradictions of this paradoxical situation make any embargo unlikely to succeed.

A Since no information is given about the balance of opinion, no conclusion about it is justified.
B This conclusion contradicts the given information, and so it is not justified.
C This statement simply defines the purpose of a blockade; it is not a conclusion from the information given.
D **Correct.** This statement properly identifies a conclusion supported by the claims.
E This statement contradicts the given information and cannot be a justifiable conclusion.

The correct answer is D.

Questions 102–103 are based on the following:

The average life expectancy for the United States population as a whole is 73.9 years, but children born in Hawaii will live an average of 77 years, and those born in Louisiana, 71.7 years. If a newlywed couple from Louisiana were to begin their family in Hawaii, therefore, their children would be expected to live longer than would be the case if the family remained in Louisiana.

102. Which of the following, if true, would most seriously weaken the conclusion drawn in the passage?

(A) Insurance company statisticians do not believe that moving to Hawaii will significantly lengthen the average Louisianan's life.

(B) The governor of Louisiana has falsely alleged that statistics for his state are inaccurate.

(C) The longevity ascribed to Hawaii's current population is attributable mostly to genetically determined factors.

(D) Thirty percent of all Louisianans can expect to live longer than 77 years.

(E) Most of the Hawaiian Islands have levels of air pollution well below the national average for the United States.

Argument Evaluation

Situation Because average life expectancy is greater in Hawaii than in Louisiana, it is said that the prospective children of a newlywed Louisiana couple who moved to Hawaii would live longer.

Reasoning *What point weakens the conclusion?* The passage says that people in Hawaii live longer but does not say why they do. If the cause lies largely in the genetic endowment of native Hawaiians, then the couple's hopes for their children are unfounded because their children will inherit their parents' genetic makeup.

A The argument concerns only people born in Hawaii, not people like the newlywed couple who move there.

B Since the governor's statement is false, the statistics showing Louisiana's shorter life span remain true; the conclusion is not weakened.

C Correct. This statement properly identifies a point that would weaken the conclusion.

D The conclusion concerns the average life span of all Louisianans, not 30 percent of them. This 30 percent would be included in the statistical average.

E The lower levels of pollution may contribute to the longer life span Hawaiians enjoy; thus, this strengthens rather than weakens the conclusion.

The correct answer is C.

103. Which of the following statements, if true, would most significantly strengthen the conclusion drawn in the passage?

(A) As population density increases in Hawaii, life expectancy figures for that state are likely to be revised downward.

(B) Environmental factors tending to favor longevity are abundant in Hawaii and less numerous in Louisiana.

(C) Twenty-five percent of all Louisianans who move to Hawaii live longer than 77 years.

(D) Over the last decade, average life expectancy has risen at a higher rate for Louisianans than for Hawaiians.

(E) Studies show that the average life expectancy for Hawaiians who move permanently to Louisiana is roughly equal to that of Hawaiians who remain in Hawaii.

Argument Evaluation

Situation Because average life expectancy is greater in Hawaii than in Louisiana, it is said that the prospective children of a newlywed Louisiana couple who moved to Hawaii would live longer. (The same as the previous item.)

Reasoning *What point strengthens the conclusion?* If the reason that people born in Hawaii live longer may be explained by favorable environmental factors that are absent or infrequent in Louisiana, then the couple's hopes for their children are well founded. All children born in Hawaii benefit from environmental factors that favor longevity, so the children of the Louisiana couple would have a longer life expectancy.

A The downward trend of life expectancy weakens the conclusion.

B Correct. This statement properly identifies a factor that strengthens the conclusion.

C The argument is about the average life span; the 25 percent of Louisianans who live longer are irrelevant. This percentage would be included in the statistical average.

D The rise in life expectancy would be included in the statistics, so that rise still brings the average to 71.7 years.

E The reverse move—of Hawaiians to Louisiana—is irrelevant to the conclusion.

The correct answer is B.

104. The cost of producing radios in Country Q is 10 percent less than the cost of producing radios in Country Y. Even after transportation fees and tariff charges are added, it is still cheaper for a company to import radios from Country Q to Country Y than to produce radios in Country Y.

The statements above, if true, best support which of the following assertions?

(A) Labor costs in Country Q are 10 percent below those in Country Y.

(B) Importing radios from Country Q to Country Y will eliminate 10 percent of the manufacturing jobs in Country Y.

(C) The tariff on a radio imported from Country Q to Country Y is less than 10 percent of the cost of manufacturing the radio in Country Y.

(D) The fee for transporting a radio from Country Q to Country Y is more than 10 percent of the cost of manufacturing the radio in Country Q.

(E) It takes 10 percent less time to manufacture a radio in Country Q than it does in Country Y.

Argument Construction

Situation One country's manufacturing costs for a product are 10 percent higher than another country's. Even with tariffs and transportation costs, importing is a less expensive option than local production.

Reasoning *What conclusion can be drawn from this information?* Because production costs are 10 percent higher in Country Y than in Country Q, importing radios is less expensive only if the combined costs of tariffs and transportation are less than 10 percent of the manufacturing costs.

A Lower labor costs may explain the lower production costs in Country Q, but there may be a variety of other reasons as well.

B It is possible that manufacturing jobs would be decreased, but no evidence in the passage leads to that conclusion.

C **Correct.** This statement properly identifies the point that, for importing to be less expensive, tariffs and transportation costs together must be less than 10 percent of manufacturing costs. Therefore, tariffs alone must be less than 10 percent

D If transportation costs were more than 10 percent, importing would be more expensive, not less.

E Less production time may explain the lower costs in Country Q, but there may be a variety of other reasons as well.

The correct answer is C.

105. The average normal infant born in the United States weighs between 12 and 14 pounds at the age of three months. Therefore, if a three-month-old child weighs only 10 pounds, its weight gain has been below the United States average.

Which of the following indicates a flaw in the reasoning above?

(A) Weight is only one measure of normal infant development.

(B) Some three-month-old children weigh as much as 17 pounds.

(C) It is possible for a normal child to weigh 10 pounds at birth.

(D) The phrase "below average" does not necessarily mean insufficient.

(E) Average weight gain is not the same as average weight.

Argument Evaluation

Situation An infant's low weight at three months, compared with the national average, shows that the child's weight gain has not been average.

Reasoning *How is this reasoning flawed?* The conclusion relies on a direct connection between average weight and average weight gain. While the infant's weight is known to be below average for a three-month-old child, no conclusion can be drawn about this infant's weight gain. No information is given about average birth weights or average weight gains.

A The passage does not say that weight is the sole measure of development; this statement fails to point out any error in the reasoning.

B The greater weight of some infants would be calculated in reaching the average.

C This birth weight may be consistent with the weight range at three months; not enough information is provided to make a judgment.

D The passage does not claim that *below average* is the same as *insufficient*, so pointing out the distinction does not show an error in the reasoning.

E **Correct.** This statement properly identifies the logical flaw in the reasoning, which takes evidence about average weight to draw a conclusion about average weight gain. The two measures are not the same.

The correct answer is E.

106. In the aftermath of a worldwide stock-market crash, Country T claimed that the severity of the stock-market crash it experienced resulted from the accelerated process of denationalization many of its industries underwent shortly before the crash.

Which of the following, if it could be carried out, would be most useful in an evaluation of Country T's assessment of the causes of the severity of its stock-market crash?

(A) Calculating the average loss experienced by individual traders in Country T during the crash

(B) Using economic theory to predict the most likely date of the next crash in Country T

(C) Comparing the total number of shares sold during the worst days of the crash in Country T to the total number of shares sold in Country T just prior to the crash

(D) Comparing the severity of the crash in Country T to the severity of the crash in countries otherwise economically similar to Country T that have not experienced recent denationalization

(E) Comparing the long-term effects of the crash on the purchasing power of the currency of Country T to the immediate, more severe short-term effects of the crash on the purchasing power of the currency of Country T

Argument Evaluation

Situation A country attributes the severity of its stock-market crash to the denationalization of its industries shortly before the crash.

Reasoning *How could the country determine whether denationalization caused the severity of the crash?* Country T concludes that there is one reason for the severity of its crash, denationalization. If Country T can find countries similar economically to itself that also suffered a stock market crash, but that had not denationalized, then it has the basis for a sound comparison. If these countries' crashes were not as severe, then the conclusion is justified. If the countries had crashes as severe or more severe, then the conclusion is not justified. The comparison with economically similar countries that have experienced crashes but had not denationalized should thus provide evidence showing whether denationalization was to blame or not.

A This method shows only the severity of the loss in Country T; it does nothing to show the cause of the loss.

B Predicting the date of the next crash does not explain the cause of the current one.

C Comparing the number of shares sold before and during the crash may show how bad the crash was, but it does not reveal its cause.

D Correct. This statement properly identifies an action that would help assess the cause of the crash.

E Comparing long- and short-term effects will reveal the severity of the crash rather than the cause of that severity.

The correct answer is D.

107. Kale has more nutritional value than spinach. But since collard greens have more nutritional value than lettuce, it follows that kale has more nutritional value than lettuce.

Any of the following, if introduced into the argument as an additional premise, makes the argument above logically correct EXCEPT:

(A) Collard greens have more nutritional value than kale.
(B) Spinach has more nutritional value than lettuce.
(C) Spinach has more nutritional value than collard greens.
(D) Spinach and collard greens have the same nutritional value.
(E) Kale and collard greens have the same nutritional value.

Argument Construction

Situation Using the symbol > to mean "has (or have) more nutritional value than," this statement can be expressed as kale > spinach, and collard greens > lettuce. The conclusion that kale > lettuce remains valid if all but one of the premises is added.

Reasoning *Which premise makes the conclusion incorrect?* The information given in the passage is that kale > spinach and that collard greens > lettuce. This is not enough to conclude that kale > lettuce; another premise is needed to establish the relative nutritional value of kale and lettuce. Look at each premise offered in the answers to see whether the conclusion kale > lettuce remains valid. The ranking of vegetables may change with the additional premises; the conclusion, kale > lettuce, must not change. Find the one answer that does NOT support the conclusion.

A **Correct.** This statement properly identifies an additional premise that would invalidate the argument. If collard greens > kale, then it is possible that lettuce > kale, because the ranking could be collard greens > lettuce > kale > spinach.

B If spinach > lettuce, then kale > lettuce because kale > spinach.

C If spinach > collard greens, then kale > lettuce because the ranking would then be kale > spinach > collard greens > lettuce.

D If spinach = collard greens, then kale > lettuce because the ranking would be kale > spinach = collard greens > lettuce.

E If kale = collard greens, then kale > lettuce because kale = collard greens > lettuce.

The correct answer is A.

108. Although custom prosthetic bone replacements produced through a new computer-aided design process will cost more than twice as much as ordinary replacements, custom replacements should still be cost-effective. Not only will surgery and recovery time be reduced, but custom replacements should last longer, thereby reducing the need for further hospital stays.

Which of the following must be studied in order to evaluate the argument presented above?

(A) The amount of time a patient spends in surgery *versus* the amount of time spent recovering from surgery
(B) The amount by which the cost of producing custom replacements has declined with the introduction of the new technique for producing them
(C) The degree to which the use of custom replacements is likely to reduce the need for repeat surgery when compared with the use of ordinary replacements
(D) The degree to which custom replacements produced with the new technique are more carefully manufactured than are ordinary replacements
(E) The amount by which custom replacements produced with the new technique will drop in cost as the production procedures become standardized and applicable on a larger scale

Argument Evaluation

Situation Custom prosthetic bone replacements, although twice as expensive as ordinary replacements, should be cost effective because they reduce the time of surgery, recovery, and potential future hospitalizations.

Reasoning *What research study would help in evaluating this argument?* The custom replacements must be compared with the ordinary replacements on the basis of the costs of surgery, recovery, and potential repeat hospitalizations. Repeat surgery involves all three kinds of costs; the extent to which such repeat surgery can be avoided is a sound measure of the cost effectiveness of the two types of replacements.

A Comparing time in surgery with time in recovery does not lead to a conclusion about the two kinds of replacements and their cost effectiveness.

B The cost effectiveness of the custom replacements is being projected in the current moment; a previous decline in production costs would already have been taken into account.

C **Correct.** This statement properly identifies evidence of cost effectiveness that would assist in evaluating the argument.

D The analysis is about cost effectiveness; it is not about the level of care taken in manufacture.

E Anticipating a future drop in production costs is outside the scope of the analysis, which should be based on current conditions.

The correct answer is C.

109. Correctly measuring the productivity of service workers is complex. Consider, for example, postal workers: they are often said to be more productive if more letters are delivered per postal worker. But is this really true? What if more letters are lost or delayed per worker at the same time that more are delivered?

The objection implied above to the productivity measure described is based on doubts about the truth of which of the following statements?

(A) Postal workers are representative of service workers in general.
(B) The delivery of letters is the primary activity of the postal service.
(C) Productivity should be ascribed to categories of workers, not to individuals.
(D) The quality of services rendered can appropriately be ignored in computing productivity.
(E) The number of letters delivered is relevant to measuring the productivity of postal workers.

Argument Evaluation

Situation In considering how best to measure productivity, the assumption is made that the more letters postal workers deliver, the more productive they are. This assumption is then challenged: What if the number of delayed and lost letters increases proportionately with the number of letters delivered?

Reasoning *Which statement would NOT be accepted by those objecting to the measure?* The point of the objection is that the number of letters delivered is, by itself, an inadequate measure of postal workers' productivity. The challenge introduces the issue of the quality of the work being performed by suggesting that the number of misdirected letters should also be taken into account. The challenge is based on rejecting the idea that quality can be ignored when measuring productivity.

A The argument uses postal workers as an example; the challenge does not question the fairness of the example.

B Letter delivery is assumed to be the primary activity of postal workers because their productivity is measured on that basis; the challenge does not reject this point.

C The argument does discuss a category of workers, postal workers, rather than individuals; the challenge does not reject this point.

D **Correct.** This statement properly identifies the point that is the basis of the challenge to the measure; the objection does NOT accept the position that quality can be ignored in evaluating productivity.

E There is no doubt that counting letters delivered is part of measuring productivity; the challenge is to its being the only measure.

The correct answer is D.

110. "Fast cycle time" is a strategy of designing a manufacturing organization to eliminate bottlenecks and delays in production. Not only does it speed up production, but it also ensures quality. The reason is that the bottlenecks and delays cannot be eliminated unless all work is done right the first time.

The claim about quality made above rests on a questionable presupposition that _____.

(A) any flaw in work on a product would cause a bottleneck or delay and so would be prevented from occurring on a "fast cycle" production line

(B) the strategy of "fast cycle time" would require fundamental rethinking of product design

(C) the primary goal of the organization is to produce a product of unexcelled quality, rather than to generate profits for stockholders

(D) "fast cycle time" could be achieved by shaving time off each of the component processes in a production cycle

(E) "fast cycle time" is a concept in business strategy that has not yet been put into practice in a factory

Argument Construction

Situation Eliminating production bottlenecks and delays is a strategy that ensures higher quality because all work must be done right the first time.

Reasoning *What questionable assumption is the basis for the claim about ensured quality?* The argument assumes that any problem with a product would cause a bottleneck or a delay in production. It is entirely possible that there might be flaws that might not cause such problems; thus, the assumption is questionable.

A **Correct.** This statement properly identifies the questionable assumption that all flaws must cause bottlenecks or delays. The assumption is questionable since flaws might well exist without causing such problems.

B The claim is about the quality of the product, so the assumption must relate to the production of the product; rethinking product design is an unrelated issue.

C The primary goal of the organization is outside the scope of the claim.

D The assumption is about the product that is the result of "fast cycle time"; it is not about a specific method for implementing "fast cycle time."

E The assumption is about the product; it is not concerned with whether the method has previously been put into practice.

The correct answer is A.

111. Sales of telephones have increased dramatically over the last year. In order to take advantage of this increase, Mammoth Industries plans to expand production of its own model of telephone, while continuing its already very extensive advertising of this product.

Which of the following, if true, provides most support for the view that Mammoth Industries *cannot* increase its sales of telephones by adopting the plan outlined above?

(A) Although it sells all the telephones that it produces, Mammoth Industries' share of all telephone sales has declined over the last year.

(B) Mammoth Industries' average inventory of telephones awaiting shipment to retailers has declined slightly over the last year.

(C) Advertising has made the brand name of Mammoth Industries' telephones widely known, but few consumers know that Mammoth Industries owns this brand.

(D) Mammoth Industries' telephone is one of three brands of telephone that have together accounted for the bulk of the last year's increase in sales.

(E) Despite a slight decline in the retail price, sales of Mammoth Industries' telephones have fallen in the last year.

Evaluation of a Plan

Situation A company wants to take advantage of the rising sales of telephones to produce more of its current telephone model and to continue its extensive advertising of the product.

Reasoning *What point suggests that the plan will fail?* The company plans to increase production of its current model. If that product has been successful so far, then expanded production and continued advertising should lead to continued success. Any evidence that the company's product has been failing—at a time when overall product sales are generally increasing—would undermine the anticipated success of a plan to increase sales. Expanding the production of an unsuccessful product will not lead to more of its being sold.

A If the company is successfully selling all its phones, then a plan to produce more is likely to increase sales. This statement argues for rather than against the plan.

B The decline in inventory suggests that demand is outpacing production, so producing more telephones is again likely to increase sales.

C It is irrelevant to the argument that consumers do not know the owner of the brand name.

D If the sales of its telephone have been successful, then the company's plan to produce more is likely to increase sales. This statement argues for rather than against the plan.

E **Correct.** This statement properly identifies evidence supporting the view that the plan will NOT succeed.

The correct answer is E.

112. In tests for pironoma, a serious disease, a false positive result indicates that people have pironoma when, in fact, they do not; a false negative result indicates that people do not have pironoma when, in fact, they do. To detect pironoma most accurately, physicians should use the laboratory test that has the lowest proportion of false positive results.

Which of the following, if true, gives the most support to the recommendation above?

(A) The accepted treatment for pironoma does not have damaging side effects.

(B) The laboratory test that has the lowest proportion of false positive results causes the same minor side effects as do the other laboratory tests used to detect pironoma.

(C) In treating pironoma patients, it is essential to begin treatment as early as possible, since even a week of delay can result in loss of life.

(D) The proportion of inconclusive test results is equal for all laboratory tests used to detect pironoma.

(E) All laboratory tests to detect pironoma have the same proportion of false negative results.

Argument Construction

Situation Laboratory tests for a serious disease may give false results: either a false positive, which wrongly indicates the presence of the disease when it is absent, or a false negative, which wrongly indicates the absence of the disease when it is present. Accurate testing for the disease should use the one test (of all the laboratory tests) that has the lowest proportion of false positives.

Reasoning *What is the most accurate way to detect the disease?* The given recommendation is to use the test that least often indicates a false positive. What therefore needs to be true about the accuracy of all the laboratory tests? If the proportion of false positives is the determining variable in the choice of the most accurate test, then the different tests for the disease must have the same proportion of false negative results. Thus, the test that leads to the lowest proportion of false positive results must have the fewest false results overall and must give the most accurate results of all the tests.

A The treatment of the disease is outside the scope of this question about accurate testing.

B Possible side effects are irrelevant to determining which test is most accurate.

C The treatment plan is irrelevant to an evaluation of the diagnostic tests.

D The existence of an equal number of inconclusive results for all tests leaves unanswered the question of which test is most accurate, that is, which test has the fewest false results.

E **Correct.** This statement properly identifies the fact supporting the recommendation.

The correct answer is E.

113. The difficulty with the proposed high-speed train line is that a used plane can be bought for one-third the price of the train line, and the plane, which is just as fast, can fly anywhere. The train would be a fixed linear system, and we live in a world that is spreading out in all directions and in which consumers choose the free-wheel systems (cars, buses, aircraft), which do not have fixed routes. Thus a sufficient market for the train will not exist.

Which of the following, if true, most severely weakens the argument presented above?

(A) Cars, buses, and planes require the efforts of drivers and pilots to guide them, whereas the train will be guided mechanically.

(B) Cars and buses are not nearly as fast as the high-speed train will be.

(C) Planes are not a free-wheel system because they can fly only between airports, which are less convenient for consumers than the high-speed train's stations would be.

(D) The high-speed train line cannot use currently underutilized train stations in large cities.

(E) For long trips, most people prefer to fly rather than to take ground-level transportation.

Argument Evaluation

Situation A free-wheel system of transportation, the airplane, is as fast as a fixed linear system, the high-speed train. Because people prefer free-wheel systems that do not have fixed routes, the high-speed train will never find a sufficient market.

Reasoning *What is the potential weakness in this argument?* The passage argues that consumers will choose to fly rather than use the high-speed train. The argument is based upon a consumer preference for free-wheel systems over fixed linear systems. The definition of a free-wheel system is one that does *not have fixed routes.* The argument is weakened by any challenge to the definition of flying as a free-wheel transportation system. It is true that airplanes may be able to go almost anywhere, but commercial airlines do establish fixed routes and necessarily must travel to and from airports. Furthermore, if airports are less conveniently located for consumers than are train terminals, consumers might well prefer the more convenient of the two fixed-route alternatives.

A The method of guidance is irrelevant to the argument.

B The passage compares the speed and system models of airplanes and high-speed trains. The argument does not incorporate buses and cars, which are included only to give examples of free-wheel systems, and so this statement is irrelevant.

C **Correct.** This statement properly identifies the weakness in the argument: airplanes are not truly a free-wheel system because they are restricted to traveling between airports. Additionally, airports tend to be less conveniently located than are train terminals, which has further potential to weaken the argument in favor of airplanes.

D The inability of high-speed trains to use some convenient train stations strengthens, rather than weakens, the argument in favor of airplanes.

E Consumer preference for air travel over ground travel on long trips strengthens, rather than weakens, the argument in favor of airplanes.

The correct answer is C.

Questions 114–115 are based on the following:

114. According to the Tristate Transportation Authority, making certain improvements to the main commuter rail line would increase ridership dramatically. The authority plans to finance these improvements over the course of five years by raising automobile tolls on the two highway bridges along the route the rail line serves. Although the proposed improvements are indeed needed, the authority's plan for securing the necessary funds should be rejected because it would unfairly force drivers to absorb the entire cost of something from which they receive no benefit.

Which of the following, if true, would cast the most doubt on the effectiveness of the authority's plan to finance the proposed improvements by increasing bridge tolls?

(A) Before the authority increases tolls on any of the area bridges, it is required by law to hold public hearings at which objections to the proposed increase can be raised.

(B) Whenever bridge tolls are increased, the authority must pay a private contractor to adjust the automated toll-collecting machines.

(C) Between the time a proposed toll increase is announced and the time the increase is actually put into effect, many commuters buy more tokens than usual to postpone the effects of the increase.

(D) When tolls were last increased on the two bridges in question, almost 20 percent of the regular commuter traffic switched to a slightly longer alternative route that has since been improved.

(E) The chairman of the authority is a member of the Tristate Automobile Club, which has registered strong opposition to the proposed toll increase.

Evaluation of a Plan

Situation A transportation authority plans to pay for improvements to a commuter rail line by raising automobile tolls on the two highway bridges along the route the rail line serves. One objection to this plan is that drivers will have to pay for something from which they will not benefit.

Reasoning *What casts doubt on how well the financing plan would work?* Any financing plan is based on estimates of costs and revenues, and any factor that significantly increases costs or lowers revenues threatens the effectiveness of that plan. The authority's plan makes a revenue projection based on the current number of drivers who use the bridges and thus will pay the increased tolls. If there is a precedent that a significant percentage of regular commuters had previously used an alternate route in order to avoid the increased tolls on these specific bridges, then the revenue basis for the financing plan is considerably undermined. If that substitute route has since become an even more appealing alternative, the effectiveness of the plan is further threatened.

A Objections to the plan at public hearings do not affect how well the financing plan will work.

B The one-time costs of changing the automatic toll-collectors would not be significant given the five years of revenue from the increased tolls.

C Revenue lost to token hoarding is insignificant compared to the revenue gained from five years of increased tolls.

D **Correct.** This statement properly identifies a factor that weakens the authority's financing plan.

E Opposition to the increased toll can be expected; it does not mean that the plan will be less effective.

The correct answer is D.

115. Which of the following, if true, would provide the authority with the strongest counter to the objection that its plan is unfair?

(A) Even with the proposed toll increase, the average bridge toll in the tristate region would remain less than the tolls charged in neighboring states.

(B) Any attempt to finance the improvements by raising rail fares would result in a decrease in ridership and so would be self-defeating.

(C) Automobile commuters benefit from well-maintained bridges, and in the tristate region bridge maintenance is funded out of general income tax revenues to which both automobile and rail commuters contribute.

(D) The roads along the route served by the rail line are highly congested and drivers benefit when commuters are diverted from congested roadways to mass transit.

(E) The only alternative way of funding the proposed improvements now being considered is through a regional income tax surcharge, which would affect automobile commuters and rail commuters alike.

Evaluation of a Plan

Situation A transportation authority plans to pay for improvements to a commuter rail line by raising automobile tolls on the two highway bridges along the route the rail line serves. One objection to this plan is that drivers will have to pay for something from which they will not benefit. (The same as the previous item.)

Reasoning *What is the best rebuttal to the charge of unfairness?* It is objected that the drivers pay the increased toll but receive no benefit. The best way for the authority to answer this objection is to point out a way that drivers do benefit. Because some people will choose the train instead of the car, traffic congestion will decrease.

A The relatively low toll shows merely that these drivers are not paying as much as their counterparts in neighboring states.

B Showing that this particular alternative approach would not work does not counter the argument that the drivers receive no benefit.

C This alternate plan does not show that the bridge toll is fair.

D Correct. This statement properly identifies the rebuttal to the allegations of unfairness: improving traffic congestion is a significant benefit for drivers.

E This alternative plan distributes the cost among a wider group of people, but it does not answer the objection that the bridge toll is unfair to drivers.

The correct answer is D.

116. The pharmaceutical industry argues that because new drugs will not be developed unless heavy development costs can be recouped in later sales, the current 20 years of protection provided by patents should be extended in the case of newly developed drugs. However, in other industries new-product development continues despite high development costs, a fact that indicates that the extension is unnecessary.

Which of the following, if true, most strongly supports the pharmaceutical industry's argument against the challenge made above?

(A) No industries other than the pharmaceutical industry have asked for an extension of the 20-year limit on patent protection.

(B) Clinical trials of new drugs, which occur after the patent is granted and before the new drug can be marketed, often now take as long as 10 years to complete.

(C) There are several industries in which the ratio of research and development costs to revenues is higher than it is in the pharmaceutical industry.

(D) An existing patent for a drug does not legally prevent pharmaceutical companies from bringing to market alternative drugs, provided they are sufficiently dissimilar to the patented drug.

(E) Much recent industrial innovation has occurred in products—for example, in the computer and electronics industries—for which patent protection is often very ineffective.

Argument Evaluation

Situation The pharmaceutical industry argues for longer patents for new drugs to offset high development costs, claiming that no new drugs can be developed profitably otherwise. Its critics argue that the patent extension is unnecessary because other industries with high development costs keep developing new products.

Reasoning *How can the pharmaceutical industry best answer the challenge concerning other industries?* The pharmaceutical industry must explain how it differs from other industries. Unlike other industries, it must wait for clinical trials of new drugs before those drugs can be marketed. The clinical trials may take half the patent period, so the pharmaceutical industry may have only half the time allowed to other industries to market new products and recover development costs.

A Other industries' failure to ask for the same extension does not justify the pharmaceutical industry request.

B Correct. This statement properly identifies evidence that supports the pharmaceutical industry's argument.

C Pointing out that other industries may have even higher ratios of costs to revenues weakens the pharmaceutical industry's argument.

D If alternative drugs can rival a patented drug, then the extended patent protection the pharmaceutical industry seeks would appear to be useless.

E Innovation's effects on patent protection in other industries do not explain why the pharmaceutical industry needs longer patent protection.

The correct answer is B.

117. Caterpillars of all species produce an identical hormone called "juvenile hormone" that maintains feeding behavior. Only when a caterpillar has grown to the right size for pupation to take place does a special enzyme halt the production of juvenile hormone. This enzyme can be synthesized and will, on being ingested by immature caterpillars, kill them by stopping them from feeding.

Which of the following, if true, most strongly supports the view that it would NOT be advisable to try to eradicate agricultural pests that go through a caterpillar stage by spraying croplands with the enzyme mentioned above?

(A) Most species of caterpillar are subject to some natural predation.
(B) Many agricultural pests do not go through a caterpillar stage.
(C) Many agriculturally beneficial insects go through a caterpillar stage.
(D) Since caterpillars of different species emerge at different times, several sprayings would be necessary.
(E) Although the enzyme has been synthesized in the laboratory, no large-scale production facilities exist as yet.

Argument Evaluation

Situation The feeding behavior of immature caterpillars of all species is regulated by the "juvenile hormone"; an enzyme stops the production of this hormone when the caterpillars have reached an appropriate level of growth. At any earlier stage, ingesting this enzyme, which can be produced synthetically, kills the immature caterpillars because they stop feeding. It can then be argued that it is unwise to spray croplands with this enzyme to eradicate agricultural pests that undergo a caterpillar stage.

Reasoning *What evidence strengthens the argument that the synthetic enzyme should NOT be sprayed on croplands?* Spraying the enzyme will kill all insects that go through a caterpillar stage. If the goal is to eradicate insect pests by killing them at the caterpillar stage, why is this spraying inadvisable? The relationship between crops and insects is complicated; while some insects harm crops, others benefit them. If the spraying kills all susceptible insects, regardless of whether they harm or help the crops, it can also destroy agriculturally beneficial insects. This is a good reason to conclude that spraying is not advisable.

A Spraying would eradicate all pests that go through a caterpillar stage and so is more effective than natural predators would be. This statement provides no reason not to spray.

B Spraying affects only those agricultural pests that do go through a caterpillar stage, so this statement is irrelevant.

C **Correct.** This statement properly identifies evidence that strengthens the argument against doing such spraying.

D The need to spray repeatedly does not mean that spraying is inadvisable, but simply that the process will be more complicated.

E The lack of production facilities for the synthetic hormone does not mean that the spraying is inadvisable.

The correct answer is C.

118. Firms adopting "profit-related-pay" (PRP) contracts pay wages at levels that vary with the firm's profits. In the metalworking industry last year, firms with PRP contracts in place showed productivity per worker on average 13 percent higher than that of their competitors who used more traditional contracts.

If, on the basis of the evidence above, it is argued that PRP contracts increase worker productivity, which of the following, if true, would most seriously weaken that argument?

(A) Results similar to those cited for the metalworking industry have been found in other industries where PRP contracts are used.

(B) Under PRP contracts costs other than labor costs, such as plant, machinery, and energy, make up an increased proportion of the total cost of each unit of output.

(C) Because introducing PRP contracts greatly changes individual workers' relationships to the firm, negotiating the introduction of PRP contracts is complex and time-consuming.

(D) Many firms in the metalworking industry have modernized production equipment in the last five years, and most of these introduced PRP contracts at the same time.

(E) In firms in the metalworking industry where PRP contracts are in place, the average take-home pay is 15 percent higher than it is in those firms where workers have more traditional contracts.

Argument Evaluation

Situation Last year, firms using profit-related-pay (PRP) contracts found that productivity per worker increased significantly as compared to firms that used traditional wage contracts.

Reasoning *What point weakens the argument that PRP contracts increase productivity?* The argument directly attributes increased productivity to the existence of PRP contracts. Any information that other factors might have contributed to the increase in productivity would weaken the argument. If production equipment was modernized during the same period that the new contracts took effect, then it is possible that the modernized equipment was responsible for the higher level of productivity.

A Similar findings in other industries strengthen rather than weaken the argument.

B If workers are more productive, labor costs are a smaller proportion of total costs and nonlabor costs are a greater proportion. This point does not weaken the argument.

C The difficulty of negotiating the contracts is irrelevant to a conclusion about what happens once the contracts are in place.

D **Correct.** This statement properly identifies information that weakens the argument.

E The higher pay of workers on PRP contracts is consistent with their higher productivity. This statement does not weaken the argument.

The correct answer is D.

119. Adult female rats who have never before encountered rat pups will start to show maternal behaviors after being confined with a pup for about seven days. This period can be considerably shortened by disabling the female's sense of smell or by removing the scent-producing glands of the pup.

Which of the following hypotheses best explains the contrast described above?

(A) The sense of smell in adult female rats is more acute than that in rat pups.

(B) The amount of scent produced by rat pups increases when they are in the presence of a female rat that did not bear them.

(C) Female rats that have given birth are more affected by olfactory cues than are female rats that have never given birth.

(D) A female rat that has given birth shows maternal behavior toward rat pups that she did not bear more quickly than does a female rat that has never given birth.

(E) The development of a female rat's maternal interest in a rat pup that she did not bear is inhibited by the odor of the pup.

Argument Construction

Situation Adult female rats having no previous familiarity with rat pups, that is, those that have never given birth to pups, display maternal behavior after seven days. Disabling the female's sense of smell or removing the scent-producing glands of the pups shortens this time period considerably.

Reasoning *What might explain the shorter time period after this intervention?* The scent of the pups is clearly the issue. When this scent is absent from the interaction, either by making the females unable to smell it or making the pups unable to produce it, the females display maternal behavior more quickly.

A Pointing to the difference between the sense of smell in the adult females and in the pups does not explain why the females without a sense of smell accept pups more quickly.

B The greater amount of scent the pups produce does not reveal why removing the scent glands allows the females to display maternal behaviors more quickly.

C The experiment concerns only those females that have not given birth, so the contrast with those that have is irrelevant.

D The speed with which adult females that have given birth accept pups that are not their own is irrelevant to an experiment involving only females that have not given birth.

E **Correct.** This statement properly identifies a hypothesis that explains the shorter time period for the female's acceptance of the pup.

The correct answer is E.

120. The proposal to hire 10 new police officers in Middletown is quite foolish. There is sufficient funding to pay the salaries of the new officers, but not the salaries of additional court and prison employees to process the increased caseload of arrests and convictions that new officers usually generate.

Which of the following, if true, will most seriously weaken the conclusion drawn above?

(A) Studies have shown that an increase in a city's police force does not necessarily reduce crime.

(B) When one major city increased its police force by 19 percent last year, there were 40 percent more arrests and 13 percent more convictions.

(C) If funding for the new police officers' salaries is approved, support for other city services will have to be reduced during the next fiscal year.

(D) In most United States cities, not all arrests result in convictions, and not all convictions result in prison terms.

(E) Middletown's ratio of police officers to citizens has reached a level at which an increase in the number of officers will have a deterrent effect on crime.

Evaluation of a Plan

Situation A proposal to hire new police officers is dismissed as foolish because there is not enough funding to cover the salaries of the increased support staff necessary when arrests and convictions go up.

Reasoning *What evidence weakens the conclusion that hiring new officers will increase costs for support staff?* The conclusion is based on the argument that hiring new officers usually increases the caseload, which in turn increases the need for court and prison support staff. Under what circumstances might this not be true? What if an increase in the number of officers will bring the ratio of police officers to citizens to the level known to *deter* crime from occurring in the first place? Less crime means fewer arrests and convictions overall, and so no additional funding for court and prison support staff should be necessary.

A If crime is not reduced, then arrests and convictions will remain the same or possibly go up; this statement does not weaken the conclusion.

B The example supports the argument rather than weakening its conclusion.

C Tight funding supports the argument's claim that it will be difficult or impossible to fund salaries of support staff.

D This generalization is as true of Middletown as it is of any other American city, but it only states the obvious and does not weaken the conclusion about increased caseloads for the courts.

E **Correct.** This statement properly identifies a point that weakens the conclusion.

The correct answer is E.

121. Northern Air has dozens of flights daily into and out of Belleville Airport, which is highly congested. Northern Air depends for its success on economy and quick turnaround and consequently is planning to replace its large planes with Skybuses, the novel aerodynamic design of which is extremely fuel efficient. The Skybus' fuel efficiency results in both lower fuel costs and reduced time spent refueling.

Which of the following, if true, could present the most serious disadvantage for Northern Air in replacing their large planes with Skybuses?

(A) The Skybus would enable Northern Air to schedule direct flights to destinations that currently require stops for refueling.

(B) Aviation fuel is projected to decline in price over the next several years.

(C) The fuel efficiency of the Skybus would enable Northern Air to eliminate refueling at some of its destinations, but several mechanics would lose their jobs.

(D) None of Northern Air's competitors that use Belleville Airport are considering buying Skybuses.

(E) The aerodynamic design of the Skybus causes turbulence behind it when taking off that forces other planes on the runway to delay their takeoffs.

Evaluation of a Plan

Situation An airline flies in and out of a highly congested airport many times a day. Because the airline's success depends on low costs and quick turnaround, it plans to replace its current planes with Skybuses, the more fuel-efficient design of which will reduce both fuel costs and the time spent refueling.

Reasoning *What could be the plan's most serious disadvantage?* Since it is given that the Skybuses provide fuel economy and quicker refueling, what could be a disadvantage of the proposed plan? What if the use of the particular aircraft somehow contributed to the congestion at the busy airport or caused slower turnaround? While the Skybus' design promotes fuel economy, if it also creates turbulence on takeoff, the turbulence would then delay the takeoffs of any other planes. Since the airport is congested and the airline flies through it many times a day, such takeoff delays would ultimately impede Northern Air's turnaround time, as well as its success.

A The ability to schedule direct flights would be an advantage, not a disadvantage.

B The decline in aviation fuel might make the plan seem less pressing, but lower fuel costs would not diminish the advantage of fuel-efficient planes.

C The ability to eliminate refueling is an advantage to the airline, and the loss of jobs is a disadvantage to the mechanics rather than to the airline.

D The decisions made by other airlines are irrelevant to the plan.

E **Correct.** This statement properly identifies a potentially serious disadvantage to the plan.

The correct answer is E.

122. The earliest Mayan pottery found at Colha, in Belize, is about 3,000 years old. Recently, however, 4,500-year-old stone agricultural implements were unearthed at Colha. These implements resemble Mayan stone implements of a much later period, also found at Colha. Moreover, the implements' designs are strikingly different from the designs of stone implements produced by other cultures known to have inhabited the area in prehistoric times. Therefore, there were surely Mayan settlements in Colha 4,500 years ago.

Which of the following, if true, most seriously weakens the argument?

(A) Ceramic ware is not known to have been used by the Mayan people to make agricultural implements.

(B) Carbon dating of corn pollen in Colha indicates that agriculture began there around 4,500 years ago.

(C) Archaeological evidence indicates that some of the oldest stone implements found at Colha were used to cut away vegetation after controlled burning of trees to open areas of swampland for cultivation.

(D) Successor cultures at a given site often adopt the style of agricultural implements used by earlier inhabitants of the same site.

(E) Many religious and social institutions of the Mayan people who inhabited Colha 3,000 years ago relied on a highly developed system of agricultural symbols.

Argument Evaluation

Situation Recently, 4,500-year-old stone agricultural implements have been found in Colha, a location where 3,000-year old Mayan pottery had previously been found. The implements resemble other Mayan implements of a much later time that were also found in Colha, and they are unlike the implements used by other local cultures in prehistoric times. These recently discovered implements thus prove that Mayan culture was established in Colha 4,500 years ago.

Reasoning *Which point weakens the argument?* First, identify the underlying assumption. The argument assumes the distinctive 4,500-year-old implements must be Mayan because they are similar to implements the Mayans are known to have used there much later. What if there is another reason for the similarity? What if a culture that comes to an occupied site tends to adapt its implements to the style of the resident culture's implements? In that case, the Mayans could have come to the occupied community of Colha at some later point, and the later Mayan agricultural tools could be copies of the earlier culture's tools.

A The argument does not suggest that the Mayans used ceramics for implements, so this point does not weaken the argument; it is irrelevant to it.

B Since the point of the argument is who, specifically, established a settlement in Colha 4,500 years ago, merely pointing out the settlement's existence does not weaken or strengthen the argument.

C Discovering how the implements were used does not explain who was using them, so this information is not relevant to the conclusion and thus does not weaken the argument.

D Correct. This statement properly identifies the weakness in the argument that the similarity between the 4,500-year-old implements and the later Mayan implements may be attributed to the Mayans' adopting the style of implements used earlier by another culture.

E The Mayans' *highly developed* system of agricultural symbols 3,000 years ago suggests the culture is even older, which tends to support, rather than weaken, the argument.

The correct answer is D.

123. Codex Berinensis, a Florentine copy of an ancient Roman medical treatise, is undated but contains clues to when it was produced. Its first 80 pages are by a single copyist, but the remaining 20 pages are by three different copyists, which indicates some significant disruption. Since a letter in handwriting identified as that of the fourth copyist mentions a plague that killed many people in Florence in 1148, Codex Berinensis was probably produced in that year.

Which of the following, if true, most strongly supports the hypothesis that Codex Berinensis was produced in 1148?

(A) Other than Codex Berinensis, there are no known samples of the handwriting of the first three copyists.

(B) According to the account by the fourth copyist, the plague went on for 10 months.

(C) A scribe would be able to copy a page of text the size and style of Codex Berinensis in a day.

(D) There was only one outbreak of plague in Florence in the 1100's.

(E) The number of pages of Codex Berinensis produced by a single scribe becomes smaller with each successive change of copyist.

Argument Evaluation

Situation The Florentine copy of an ancient Roman work is undated but provides clues as to the time it was produced. The first 80 pages of Codex Berinenis are the work of one copyist. The fact that the last 20 pages are the work of a succession of three different copyists is an indication of serious turmoil at the time the copying was done. Since a letter in the fourth copyist's handwriting reveals that a plague killed many people there in 1148, Codex Berinenis was probably produced in that year.

Reasoning *Which information supports the hypothesis dating the Codex to 1148?* Consider the basis of the hypothesis: the succession of copyists indicating the work was significantly disrupted, and the fourth copyist's letter indicating the plague of 1148 caused serious loss of life. From this it is argued that the plague of 1148 was the reason for the multiple copyists and that the work can thus be dated to that year. What if there were multiple plagues? In that case, Codex Berinensis could have been produced at another time. If instead only one plague occurred in the 1100's, the elimination of that possibility supports the hypothesis that the work was done in 1148.

A Examples of the copyists' handwriting might help date Codex Berinensis; the absence of handwriting samples does not help support 1148 as the date.

B The length of the plague, while it may account for the succession of copyists, does not help support the particular year the work was done.

C The amount of work a copyist could achieve each day does not provide any information about the year the work appeared.

D **Correct.** This statement properly identifies a circumstance that supports the hypothesis.

E The productivity or tenure of the various copyists is irrelevant to establishing the date.

The correct answer is D.

124. Outsourcing is the practice of obtaining from an independent supplier a product or service that a company has previously provided for itself. Since a company's chief objective is to realize the highest possible year-end profits, any product or service that can be obtained from an independent supplier for less than it would cost the company to provide the product or service on its own should be outsourced.

Which of the following, if true, most seriously weakens the argument?

(A) If a company decides to use independent suppliers for a product, it can generally exploit the vigorous competition arising among several firms that are interested in supplying that product.

(B) Successful outsourcing requires a company to provide its suppliers with information about its products and plans that can fall into the hands of its competitors and give them a business advantage.

(C) Certain tasks, such as processing a company's payroll, are commonly outsourced, whereas others, such as handling the company's core business, are not.

(D) For a company to provide a product or service for itself as efficiently as an independent supplier can provide it, the managers involved need to be as expert in the area of that product or service as the people in charge of that product or service at an independent supplier are.

(E) When a company decides to use an independent supplier for a product or service, the independent supplier sometimes hires members of the company's staff who formerly made the product or provided the service that the independent supplier now supplies.

Argument Evaluation

Situation In order to realize the highest year-end profits, a company should outsource any service or product that can be obtained from an independent supplier for less than it would cost the company to provide that service or product itself.

Reasoning *What weakens this argument?* When could outsourcing a service or product result in a business disadvantage or lower profits? It is clear that the company must give independent suppliers enough information to enable them to provide the contracted products and services, but this means that the company can lose control over who has possession of such critical information. If the information becomes known to the company's competitors and gives them a business advantage, the company's profitability may be harmed rather than helped by outsourcing. This possibility weakens the argument.

A This would strengthen the argument since the pricing competition among independent suppliers is an advantage for the company.

B Correct. This statement properly identifies one disadvantage of outsourcing: the company no longer controls access to its information and plans. With the increased possibility of competitors' gaining access to its proprietary information, the company's business is put at risk.

C Providing examples of the tasks typically outsourced or handled internally does not affect the argument.

D Expertise in a particular area is an advantage of outsourcing and thus a strength of the argument.

E The supplier's hiring of members of the company's staff to handle work no longer performed within the company is not shown to be a disadvantage.

The correct answer is B.

9.0 Sentence Correction

9.0 Sentence Correction

Sentence correction questions appear in the Verbal section of the GMAT® exam. The Verbal section uses multiple-choice questions to measure your ability to read and comprehend written material, to reason and evaluate arguments, and to correct written material to conform to standard written English. Because the Verbal section includes passages from several different content areas, you may be generally familiar with some of the material; however, neither the passages nor the questions assume detailed knowledge of the topics discussed. Sentence correction questions are intermingled with critical reasoning and reading comprehension questions throughout the Verbal section of the exam. You will have 75 minutes to complete the Verbal section, or about 1 3/4 minutes to answer each question.

Sentence correction questions present a statement in which words are underlined. The questions ask you to select from the answer options the best expression of the idea or relationship described in the underlined section. The first answer choice always repeats the original phrasing, whereas the other four provide alternatives. In some cases, the original phrasing is the best choice. In other cases, the underlined section has obvious or subtle errors that require correction. These questions require you to be familiar with the stylistic conventions and grammatical rules of standard written English and to demonstrate your ability to improve incorrect or ineffective expressions.

You should begin these questions by reading the sentence carefully. Note whether there are any obvious grammatical errors as you read the underlined section. Then read the five answer choices carefully. If there was a subtle error you did not recognize the first time you read the sentence, it may become apparent after you have read the answer choices. If the error is still unclear, see whether you can eliminate some of the answers as being incorrect. Remember that in some cases, the original selection may be the best answer.

9.1 Basic English Grammar Rules

Sentence correction questions ask you to recognize and potentially correct at least one of the following grammar rules. However, these rules are not exhaustive. If you are interested in learning more about English grammar as a way to prepare for the GMAT® exam, there are several resources available on the Web.

Agreement

Standard English requires elements within a sentence to be consistent. There are two types of agreement: noun-verb and pronoun.

Noun-verb agreement: Singular subjects take singular verbs, whereas plural subjects take plural verbs.
Examples:
Correct: "I walk to the store." Incorrect: "I walks to the store."
Correct: "We go to school." Incorrect: "We goes to school."
Correct: "The number of residents has grown." Incorrect: "The number of residents have grown."
Correct: "The masses have spoken." Incorrect: "The masses has spoken."
Pronoun agreement: A pronoun must agree with the noun or pronoun it refers to in person, number, and gender.
Examples:
Correct: "When you dream, you are usually asleep." Incorrect: "When one dreams, you are usually asleep."

Correct: "When the kids went to sleep, they slept like logs." Incorrect: "When the kids went to sleep, he slept like a log."

Diction

Words should be chosen to correctly and effectively reflect the appropriate part of speech. There are several words that are commonly used incorrectly. When answering sentence correction questions, pay attention to the following conventions.

Among/between: Among is used to refer to relationships involving more than two objects. *Between* is used to refer to relationships involving only two objects.
Examples:
Correct: "We divided our winnings among the three of us." Incorrect: "We divided our winnings between the three of us."
Correct: "She and I divided the cake between us." Incorrect: "She and I divided the cake among us."

As/like: As can be a preposition meaning "in the capacity of," but more often is a conjunction of manner and is followed by a verb. *Like* is generally used as a preposition, and therefore is followed by a noun, an object pronoun, or a verb ending in "ing."
Examples:
Correct: "I work as a librarian." Incorrect: "I work like a librarian."
Correct: "Do as I say, not as I do." Incorrect: "Do like I say, not like I do."
Correct: "It felt like a dream." Incorrect: "It felt as a dream."
Correct: "People like you inspire me." Incorrect: "People as you inspire me."
Correct: "There's nothing like biking on a warm, autumn day." Incorrect: "There's nothing as biking on a warm fall day."

Mass and count words: Mass words are nouns quantified by an amount rather than by a number. *Count* nouns can be quantified by a number.
Examples:
Correct: "We bought a loaf of bread." Incorrect: "We bought one bread."
Correct: "He wished me much happiness." Incorrect: "He wished me many happinesses."
Correct: "We passed many buildings." Incorrect: "We passed much buildings."

Pronouns: Myself should not be used as a substitute for *I* or *me.*
Examples:
Correct: "Mom and I had to go to the store." Incorrect: "Mom and myself had to go to the store."
Correct: "He gave the present to Dad and me." Incorrect: "He gave the present to Dad and myself."

Grammatical Construction

Good grammar requires complete sentences. Be on the lookout for improperly formed constructions.

Fragments: Parts of a sentence that are disconnected from the main clause are called fragments.
Example:
Correct: "We saw the doctor and his nurse at the party." Incorrect: "We saw the doctor at the party. And his nurse."

Run-on sentences: A run-on sentence is two independent clauses that run together without proper punctuation.
Examples:
Correct: "Jose Canseco is still a feared batter; most pitchers don't want to face him."
Incorrect: "Jose Canseco is still a feared batter most pitchers don't want to face him."

Constructions: Avoid wordy, redundant constructions.
Example:
Correct: "We could not come to the meeting because of a conflict." Incorrect: "The reason we could not come to the meeting is because of a conflict."

Idiom

It is important to avoid nonstandard expressions, though English idioms sometimes do not follow conventional grammatical rules. Be careful to use the correct idiom when using the constructions and parts of speech.

Prepositions: Specific prepositions have specific purposes.
Examples:
Correct: "She likes to jog in the morning." Incorrect: "She likes to jog on the morning."
Correct: "They ranged in age from 10 to 15." Incorrect: "They ranged in age from 10 up to 15."

Correlatives: Word combinations such as "not only . . . but also" should be followed by an element of the same grammatical type.
Examples:
Correct: "I have called not only to thank her but also to tell her about the next meeting."
Incorrect: "I have called not only to thank her but also I told her about the next meeting."

Forms of comparison: Many forms follow precise constructions. *Fewer* refers to a specific number, whereas *less than* refers to a continuous quantity. *Between . . . and* is the correct form to designate a choice. *Farther* refers to distance, whereas *further* refers to degree.
Examples:
Correct: "There were fewer children in my class this year." Incorrect: "There were less children in my class this year."
Correct: "There was less devastation than I was told." Incorrect: "There was fewer devastation than I was told."
Correct: "We had to choose between chocolate and vanilla." Incorrect: "We had to choose between chocolate or vanilla." (It is also correct to say, "We had to choose chocolate or vanilla.")
Correct: "I ran farther than John, but he took his weight training further than I did." Incorrect: "I ran further than John, but he took his weight training farther than I did."

Logical Predication

Watch out for phrases that detract from the logical argument.

Modification problems: Modifiers should be positioned so it is clear what word or words they are meant to modify. If modifiers are not positioned clearly, they can cause illogical references or comparisons, or distort the meaning of the statement.
Examples:
Correct: "I put the cake that I baked by the door." Incorrect: "I put the cake by the door that I baked."

Correct: "Reading my mind, she gave me the delicious cookie." Incorrect: "Reading my mind, the cookie she gave me was delicious."
Correct: "In the Middle Ages, the world was believed to be flat." Incorrect: "In the Middle Ages, the world was flat."

Parallelism

Constructing a sentence that is parallel in structure depends on making sure that the different elements in the sentence balance each other; this is a little bit like making sure that the two sides of a mathematical equation are balanced. To make sure that a sentence is grammatically correct, check to see that phrases, clauses, verbs, and other sentence elements parallel each other.
Examples:
Correct: "I took a bath, went to sleep, and woke up refreshed." Incorrect: "I took a bath, sleeping, and waking up refreshed."
Correct: "The only way to know is to take the plunge." Incorrect: "The only way to know is taking the plunge."

Rhetorical Construction

Good sentence structure avoids constructions that are awkward, wordy, redundant, imprecise, or unclear, even when they are free of grammatical errors.
Example:
Correct: "Before we left on vacation, we watered the plants, checked to see that the stove was off, and set the burglar alarm." Incorrect: "Before we left to go on our vacation, we watered, checked to be sure that the stove had been turned off, and set it."

Verb Form

In addition to watching for problems of agreement or parallelism, make sure that verbs are used in the correct tense. Be alert to whether a verb should reflect past, present, or future tense.
Example:
Correct: "I went to school yesterday." "I go to school every weekday." "I will go to school tomorrow."

Each tense also has a perfect form (used with the past participle—i.e., walked, ran), a progressive form (used with the present participle—i.e., walking, running), and a perfect progressive form (also used with the present participle—i.e., walking, running).

Present perfect: Used with *has* or *have,* the present perfect tense describes an action that occurred at an indefinite time in the past or that began in the past and continues into the present.
Examples:
Correct: "I have traveled all over the world." (at an indefinite time)
Correct: "He has gone to school since he was five years old." (continues into the present)

Past perfect: This verb form is used with *had* to show the order of two events that took place in the past.
Example:
Correct: "By the time I left for school, the cake had been baked."

Future perfect: Used with *will have,* this verb form describes an event in the future that will precede another event.
Example:
Correct: "By the end of the day, I will have studied for all my tests."

Present progressive: Used with *am, is,* or *are,* this verb form describes an ongoing action that is happening now.

Example:
Correct: "I am studying for exams." "The student is studying for exams." "We are studying for exams."

Past progressive: Used with *was* or *were,* this verb form describes something that was happening when another action occurred.
Example:
Correct: "The student was studying when the fire alarm rang." "They were studying when the fire broke out."

Future progressive: Used with *will be* or *shall be,* this verb tense describes an ongoing action that will continue into the future.
Example:
Correct: "The students will be studying for exams throughout the month of December."

Present perfect progressive: Used with *have been* or *has been,* this verb tense describes something that began in the past, continues into the present, and may continue into the future.
Example:
Correct: "The student has been studying hard in the hope of acing the test."

Past perfect progressive: Used with *had been,* this verb form describes an action of some duration that was completed before another past action occurred.
Example:
Correct: "Before the fire alarm rang, the student had been studying."

Future perfect progressive: Used with *will have been*, this verb form describes a future, ongoing action that will occur before a specified time.
Example:
Correct: "By the end of next year, the students will have been studying math for five years."

9.2 Study Suggestions

There are two basic ways you can study for sentence correction questions:

- **Read material that reflects standard usage.**
  One way to gain familiarity with the basic conventions of standard written English is simply to read. Suitable material will usually be found in good magazines and nonfiction books, editorials in outstanding newspapers, and the collections of essays used by many college and university writing courses.

- **Review basic rules of grammar and practice with writing exercises.**
  Begin by reviewing the grammar rules laid out in this chapter. Then, if you have school assignments (such as essays and research papers) that have been carefully evaluated for grammatical errors, it may be helpful to review the comments and corrections.

9.3 What Is Measured

Sentence correction questions test three broad aspects of language proficiency:

- **Correct expression.**
  A correct sentence is grammatically and structurally sound. It conforms to all the rules of standard written English, including noun-verb agreement, noun-pronoun agreement, pronoun consistency, pronoun case, and verb tense sequence. A correct sentence will not have dangling, misplaced, or improperly formed modifiers; unidiomatic or inconsistent expressions; or faults in parallel construction.
- **Effective expression.**
  An effective sentence expresses an idea or relationship clearly and concisely as well as grammatically. This does not mean that the choice with the fewest and simplest words is necessarily the best answer. It means that there are no superfluous words or needlessly complicated expressions in the best choice.
- **Proper diction.**
  An effective sentence also uses proper diction. (Diction refers to the standard dictionary meanings of words and the appropriateness of words in context.) In evaluating the diction of a sentence, you must be able to recognize whether the words are well chosen, accurate, and suitable for the context.

9.4 Test-Taking Strategies for Sentence Correction Questions

1. **Read the entire sentence carefully.**
   Try to understand the specific idea or relationship that the sentence should express.
2. **Evaluate the underlined passage for errors and possible corrections before reading the answer choices.**
   This strategy will help you discriminate among the answer choices. Remember, in some cases the underlined passage is correct.
3. **Read each answer choice carefully.**
   The first answer choice always repeats the underlined portion of the original sentence. Choose this answer if you think that the sentence is best as originally written, but do so *only after* examining all the other choices.
4. **Try to determine how to correct what you consider to be wrong with the original sentence.**
   Some of the answer choices may change things that are not wrong, whereas others may not change everything that is wrong.
5. **Make sure that you evaluate the sentence and the choices thoroughly.**
   Pay attention to general clarity, grammatical and idiomatic usage, economy and precision of language, and appropriateness of diction.
6. **Read the whole sentence, substituting the choice that you prefer for the underlined passage.**
   A choice may be wrong because it does not fit grammatically or structurally with the rest of the sentence. Remember that some sentences will require no correction. When the given sentence requires no correction, choose the first answer.

9.5 The Directions

These are the directions that you will see for sentence correction questions when you take the GMAT® test. If you read them carefully and understand them clearly before going to sit for the exam, you will not need to spend too much time reviewing them once you are at the test center and the exam is under way.

Sentence correction questions present a sentence, part or all of which is underlined. Beneath the sentence, you will find five ways of phrasing the underlined passage. The first answer choice repeats the original underlined passage; the other four are different. If you think the original phrasing is best, choose the first answer; otherwise choose one of the others.

This type of question tests your ability to recognize the correctness and effectiveness of expression in standard written English. In choosing your answer, follow the requirements of standard written English; that is, pay attention to grammar, choice of words, and sentence construction. Choose the answer that produces the most effective sentence; this answer should be clear and exact, without awkwardness, ambiguity, redundancy, or grammatical error.

9.6 Sentence Correction Sample Questions

Sentence correction questions present a sentence, part or all of which is underlined. Beneath the sentence, you will find five ways of phrasing the underlined passage. The first answer choice repeats the original; the other four are different. If you think the original phrasing is best, choose the first answer; otherwise choose one of the others.

This type of question tests your ability to recognize the correctness and effectiveness of expression in standard written English. In choosing your answer, follow the requirements of standard written English; that is, pay attention to grammar, choice of words, and sentence construction. Choose the answer that produces the most effective sentence; this answer should be clear and exact, without awkwardness, ambiguity, redundancy, or grammatical error.

1. Although a surge in retail sales have raised hopes that there is a recovery finally underway, many economists say that without a large amount of spending the recovery might not last.

(A) have raised hopes that there is a recovery finally
(B) raised hopes for there being a recovery finally
(C) had raised hopes for a recovery finally being
(D) has raised hopes that a recovery is finally
(E) raised hopes for a recovery finally

2. Of all the vast tides of migration that have swept through history, maybe none is more concentrated as the wave that brought 12 million immigrants onto American shores in little more than three decades.

(A) maybe none is more concentrated as
(B) it may be that none is more concentrated as
(C) perhaps it is none that is more concentrated than
(D) maybe it is none that was more concentrated than
(E) perhaps none was more concentrated than

3. Diabetes, together with its serious complications, ranks as the nation's third leading cause of death, surpassed only by heart disease and cancer.

(A) ranks as the nation's third leading cause of death, surpassed only
(B) rank as the nation's third leading cause of death, only surpassed
(C) has the rank of the nation's third leading cause of death, only surpassed
(D) are the nation's third leading causes of death, surpassed only
(E) have been ranked as the nation's third leading causes of death, only surpassed

4. A survey by the National Council of Churches showed that in 1986 there were 20,736 female ministers, almost 9 percent of the nation's clergy, twice as much as 1977.

(A) twice as much as 1977
(B) twice as many as 1977
(C) double what it was in 1977
(D) double the figure for 1977
(E) a number double that of 1977's

5. As its sales of computer products have surpassed those of measuring instruments, the company has become increasingly willing to compete for the mass market sales they would in the past have conceded to rivals.

(A) they would in the past have conceded to rivals
(B) they would have conceded previously to their rivals
(C) that in the past would have been conceded previously to rivals
(D) it previously would have conceded to rivals in the past
(E) it would in the past have conceded to rivals

6. Like the idolization accorded the Brontës and Brownings, James Joyce and Virginia Woolf are often subjected to the kind of veneration that blurs the distinction between the artist and the human being.

(A) Like the idolization accorded the Brontës and Brownings
(B) As the Brontës' and Brownings' idolization
(C) Like that accorded to the Brontës and Brownings
(D) As it is of the Brontës and Brownings
(E) Like the Brontës and Brownings

7. Carnivorous mammals can endure what would otherwise be lethal levels of body heat because they have a heat-exchange network which kept the brain from getting too hot.

(A) which kept
(B) that keeps
(C) which has kept
(D) that has been keeping
(E) having kept

8. Rising inventories, when unaccompanied correspondingly by increases in sales, can lead to production cutbacks that would hamper economic growth.

(A) when unaccompanied correspondingly by increases in sales, can lead
(B) when not accompanied by corresponding increases in sales, possibly leads
(C) when they were unaccompanied by corresponding sales increases, can lead
(D) if not accompanied by correspondingly increased sales, possibly leads
(E) if not accompanied by corresponding increases in sales, can lead

9. Sunspots, vortices of gas associated with strong electromagnetic activity, are visible as dark spots on the surface of the Sun but have never been sighted on the Sun's poles or equator.

(A) are visible as dark spots on the surface of the Sun but have never been sighted on
(B) are visible as dark spots that never have been sighted on the surface of the Sun
(C) appear on the surface of the Sun as dark spots although never sighted at
(D) appear as dark spots on the surface of the Sun, although never having been sighted at
(E) appear as dark spots on the Sun's surface, which have never been sighted on

10. Unlike the United States, Japanese unions appear, reluctant to organize lower-paid workers.

(A) Unlike the United States, Japanese unions appear, reluctant to organize
(B) Unlike those in the United States, Japanese unions appear reluctant to organize
(C) In Japan, unlike the United States, unions appear reluctant about organizing
(D) Japanese unions, unlike the United States, appear reluctant to organize
(E) Japanese unions, unlike those in the United States, appear reluctant about organizing

11. Warning that computers in the United States are not secure, the National Academy of Sciences has urged the nation to revamp computer security procedures, institute new emergency response teams, creating a special nongovernment organization to take charge of computer security planning.

(A) creating a special nongovernment organization to take
(B) creating a special nongovernment organization that takes
(C) creating a special nongovernment organization for taking
(D) and create a special nongovernment organization for taking
(E) and create a special nongovernment organization to take

12. After gradual declension down to about 39 hours in 1970, the workweek in the United States has steadily increased to the point that the average worker now puts in an estimated 164 extra hours of paid labor a year.

(A) After gradual declension down
(B) Following a gradual declension down
(C) After gradual declining down
(D) After gradually declining
(E) Following gradually declining

13. As Hurricane Hugo approached the Atlantic coast, it increased dramatically in strength, becoming the tenth most intense hurricane to hit the United States mainland in the twentieth century and most intense since Camille in 1969.

(A) most intense since Camille in 1969
(B) most intense after Camille in 1969
(C) the most intense since Camille in 1969
(D) the most intense after 1969, which had Camille
(E) since 1969 and Camille, the most intense

14. The commission has directed advertisers to restrict the use of the word "natural" to foods that do not contain color or flavor additives, chemical preservatives, or nothing that has been synthesized.

(A) or nothing that has been
(B) or that has been
(C) and nothing that is
(D) or anything that has been
(E) and anything

15. The Iroquois were primarily planters, but supplementing their cultivation of maize, squash, and beans with fishing and hunting.

(A) but supplementing
(B) and had supplemented
(C) and even though they supplemented
(D) although they supplemented
(E) but with supplementing

16. As contrasted with the honeybee, the yellow jacket can sting repeatedly without dying and carries a potent venom that can cause intense pain.

(A) As contrasted with the honeybee
(B) In contrast to the honeybee's
(C) Unlike the sting of the honeybee
(D) Unlike that of the honeybee
(E) Unlike the honeybee

17. None of the attempts to specify the causes of crime explains why most of the people exposed to the alleged causes do not commit crimes and, conversely, why so many of those not so exposed have.

(A) have
(B) has
(C) shall
(D) do
(E) could

18. Computers are becoming faster, more powerful, and more reliable, and so too are modems, they are the devices to allow two or more computers to share information over regular telephone lines.

(A) so too are modems, they are the devices to allow
(B) so too are modems, the devices that allow
(C) so too modems, the devices allowing
(D) also modems, they are the devices that allow
(E) also modems, which are the devices to allow

19. In virtually all types of tissue in every animal species, dioxin induces the production of enzymes that are the organism's trying to metabolize, or render harmless, the chemical that is irritating it.

(A) trying to metabolize, or render harmless, the chemical that is irritating it
(B) trying that it metabolize, or render harmless, the chemical irritant
(C) attempt to try to metabolize, or render harmless, such a chemical irritant
(D) attempt to try and metabolize, or render harmless, the chemical irritating it
(E) attempt to metabolize, or render harmless, the chemical irritant

20. Based on accounts of various ancient writers, scholars have painted a sketchy picture of the activities of an all-female cult that, perhaps as early as the sixth century BC, worshipped a goddess known in Latin as Bona Dea, "the good goddess."

(A) Based on accounts of various ancient writers
(B) Basing it on various ancient writers' accounts
(C) With accounts of various ancient writers used for a basis
(D) By the accounts of various ancient writers they used
(E) Using accounts of various ancient writers

21. Paleontologists believe that fragments of a primate jawbone unearthed in Burma and estimated at 40 to 44 million years old provide evidence of a crucial step along the evolutionary path that led to human beings.

(A) at 40 to 44 million years old provide evidence of
(B) as being 40 to 44 million years old provides evidence of
(C) that it is 40 to 44 million years old provides evidence of what was
(D) to be 40 to 44 million years old provide evidence of
(E) as 40 to 44 million years old provides evidence of what was

22. The end of the eighteenth century saw the emergence of prize-stock breeding, with individual bulls and cows receiving awards, fetching unprecedented prices, and excited enormous interest whenever they were put on show.

(A) excited
(B) it excited
(C) exciting
(D) would excite
(E) it had excited

23. Of all the possible disasters that threaten American agriculture, the possibility of an adverse change in climate is maybe the more difficult for analysis.

(A) is maybe the more difficult for analysis
(B) is probably the most difficult to analyze
(C) is maybe the most difficult for analysis
(D) is probably the more difficult to analyze
(E) is, it may be, the analysis that is most difficult

24. For members of the seventeenth-century Ashanti nation in Africa, animal-hide shields with wooden frames were essential items of military equipment, a method to protect warriors against enemy arrows and spears.

(A) a method to protect
(B) as a method protecting
(C) protecting
(D) as a protection of
(E) to protect

25. The golden crab of the Gulf of Mexico has not been fished commercially in great numbers, primarily on account of living at great depths—2,500 to 3,000 feet down.

(A) on account of living
(B) on account of their living
(C) because it lives
(D) because of living
(E) being they live

26. Galileo was convinced that natural phenomena, as manifestations of the laws of physics, would appear the same to someone on the deck of a ship moving smoothly and uniformly through the water as a person standing on land.

(A) water as a
(B) water as to a
(C) water; just as it would to a
(D) water, as it would to the
(E) water; just as to the

27. Health officials estimate that 35 million Africans are in danger of contracting trypanosomiasis, or "African sleeping sickness," a parasitic disease spread by the bites of tsetse flies.

(A) are in danger of contracting
(B) are in danger to contract
(C) have a danger of contracting
(D) are endangered by contraction
(E) have a danger that they will contract

28. Beyond the immediate cash flow crisis that the museum faces, its survival depends on if it can broaden its membership and leave its cramped quarters for a site where it can store and exhibit its more than 12,000 artifacts.

(A) if it can broaden its membership and leave
(B) whether it can broaden its membership and leave
(C) whether or not it has the capability to broaden its membership and can leave
(D) its ability for broadening its membership and leaving
(E) the ability for it to broaden its membership and leave

29. Along with the drop in producer prices announced yesterday, the strong retail sales figures released today seem like it is indicative that the economy, although growing slowly, is not nearing a recession.

(A) like it is indicative that
(B) as if to indicate
(C) to indicate that
(D) indicative of
(E) like an indication of

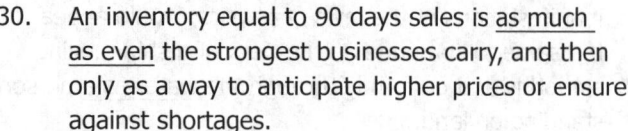

30. An inventory equal to 90 days sales is as much as even the strongest businesses carry, and then only as a way to anticipate higher prices or ensure against shortages.

(A) as much as even
(B) so much as even
(C) even so much as
(D) even as much that
(E) even so much that

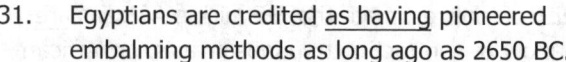

31. Egyptians are credited as having pioneered embalming methods as long ago as 2650 BC.

(A) as having
(B) with having
(C) to have
(D) as the ones who
(E) for being the ones who

32. The Commerce Department announced that the economy grew during the second quarter at a 7.5 percent annual rate, while inflation eased when it might have been expected for it to rise.

(A) it might have been expected for it to rise
(B) it might have been expected to rise
(C) it might have been expected that it should rise
(D) its rise might have been expected
(E) there might have been an expectation it would rise

33. Although schistosomiasis is not often fatal, it is so debilitating that it has become an economic drain on many developing countries.

(A) it is so debilitating that it has become an economic
(B) it is of such debilitation, it has become an economical
(C) so debilitating is it as to become an economic
(D) such is its debilitation, it becomes an economical
(E) there is so much debilitation that it has become an economical

34. Efforts to equalize the funds available to school districts, a major goal of education reformers and many states in the 1970's, has not significantly reduced the gaps existing between the richest and poorest districts.

(A) has not significantly reduced the gaps existing
(B) has not been significant in reducing the gap that exists
(C) has not made a significant reduction in the gap that exists
(D) have not significantly reduced the gap that exists
(E) have not been significant in a reduction of the gaps existing

35. Federal authorities involved in the investigation have found the local witnesses are difficult to locate, reticent, and are suspicious of strangers.

(A) the local witnesses are difficult to locate, reticent, and are
(B) local witnesses to be difficult to locate, reticent, and are
(C) that local witnesses are difficult to locate, reticent, and
(D) local witnesses are difficult to locate and reticent, and they are
(E) that local witnesses are difficult to locate and reticent, and they are

36. In 1527 King Henry VIII sought to have his marriage to Queen Catherine annulled so as to marry Anne Boleyn.

(A) so as to marry
(B) and so could be married to
(C) to be married to
(D) so that he could marry
(E) in order that he would marry

37. In one of the bloodiest battles of the Civil War, fought at Sharpsburg, Maryland, on September 17, 1862, four times as many Americans were killed as would later be killed on the beaches of Normandy during D-Day.

(A) Americans were killed as
(B) Americans were killed than
(C) Americans were killed than those who
(D) more Americans were killed as there
(E) more Americans were killed as those who

38. Dr. Tonegawa won the Nobel Prize for discovering how the body can constantly change its genes to fashion a seeming unlimited number of antibodies, each specifically targeted at an invading microbe or foreign substance.

(A) seeming unlimited number of antibodies, each specifically targeted at
(B) seeming unlimited number of antibodies, each targeted specifically to
(C) seeming unlimited number of antibodies, all specifically targeted at
(D) seemingly unlimited number of antibodies, all of them targeted specifically to
(E) seemingly unlimited number of antibodies, each targeted specifically at

39. Scientists have recently discovered what could be the largest and oldest living organism on Earth, a giant fungus that is an interwoven filigree of mushrooms and rootlike tentacles spawned by a single fertilized spore some 10,000 years ago and extending for more than 30 acres in the soil of a Michigan forest.

(A) extending
(B) extends
(C) extended
(D) it extended
(E) is extending

40. The plot of *The Bostonians* centers on the rivalry between Olive Chancellor, an active feminist, with her charming and cynical cousin, Basil Ransom, when they find themselves drawn to the same radiant young woman whose talent for public speaking has won her an ardent following.

(A) rivalry between Olive Chancellor, an active feminist, with her charming and cynical cousin, Basil Ransom
(B) rivals Olive Chancellor, an active feminist, against her charming and cynical cousin, Basil Ransom
(C) rivalry that develops between Olive Chancellor, an active feminist, and Basil Ransom, her charming and cynical cousin
(D) developing rivalry between Olive Chancellor, an active feminist, with Basil Ransom, her charming and cynical cousin
(E) active feminist, Olive Chancellor, and the rivalry with her charming and cynical cousin Basil Ransom

41. While larger banks can afford to maintain their own data-processing operations, many smaller regional and community banks are finding that the cost associated with upgrading data-processing equipment and with the development and maintenance of new products and technical staff are prohibitive.

(A) cost associated with
(B) costs associated with
(C) costs arising from
(D) cost of
(E) costs of

42. Quasars, at billions of light-years from Earth the most distant observable objects in the universe, believed to be the cores of galaxies in an early stage of development.

(A) believed to be
(B) are believed to be
(C) some believe them to be
(D) some believe they are
(E) it is believed that they are

43. Five fledgling sea eagles left their nests in western Scotland this summer, bringing to 34 the number of wild birds successfully raised since transplants from Norway began in 1975.

(A) bringing
(B) and brings
(C) and it brings
(D) and it brought
(E) and brought

44. The automotive conveyor-belt system, which Henry Ford modeled after an assembly-line technique introduced by Ransom Olds, reduced from a day and a half to 93 minutes the required time of assembling a Model T.

(A) from a day and a half to 93 minutes the required time of assembling a Model T
(B) the time being required to assemble a Model T, from a day and a half down to 93 minutes
(C) the time being required to assemble a Model T, a day and a half to 93 minutes
(D) the time required to assemble a Model T from a day and a half to 93 minutes
(E) from a day and a half to 93 minutes, the time required for the assembling of a Model T

45. According to some analysts, the gains in the stock market reflect growing confidence that the economy will avoid the recession that many had feared earlier in the year and instead come in for a "soft landing," followed by a gradual increase in business activity.

(A) that the economy will avoid the recession that many had feared earlier in the year and instead come
(B) in the economy to avoid the recession, what many feared earlier in the year, rather to come
(C) in the economy's ability to avoid the recession, something earlier in the year many had feared, and instead to come
(D) in the economy to avoid the recession many were fearing earlier in the year, and rather to come
(E) that the economy will avoid the recession that was feared earlier this year by many, with it instead coming

46. To Josephine Baker, Paris was her home long before it was fashionable to be an expatriate, and she remained in France during the Second World War as a performer and an intelligence agent for the Resistance.

(A) To Josephine Baker, Paris was her home long before it was fashionable to be an expatriate
(B) For Josephine Baker, long before it was fashionable to be an expatriate, Paris was her home
(C) Josephine Baker made Paris her home long before to be an expatriate was fashionable
(D) Long before it was fashionable to be an expatriate, Josephine Baker made Paris her home
(E) Long before it was fashionable being an expatriate, Paris was home to Josephine Baker

47. By providing such services as mortgages, home improvement loans, automobile loans, financial advice, and staying within the metropolitan areas, Acme Bank has become one of the most profitable savings banks in the nation.

(A) financial advice, and staying
(B) financial advice, and by staying
(C) and financial advice, staying
(D) and financial advice, and staying
(E) and financial advice, and by staying

48. The report recommended that the hospital should eliminate unneeded beds, expensive services should be consolidated, and use space in other hospitals.

(A) should eliminate unneeded beds, expensive services should be consolidated, and use space in other hospitals
(B) should eliminate unneeded beds, expensive services should be consolidated, and other hospitals' space be used
(C) should eliminate unneeded beds, expensive services should be consolidated, and to use space in other hospitals
(D) eliminate unneeded beds, consolidate expensive services, and other hospitals' space used
(E) eliminate unneeded beds, consolidate expensive services, and use space in other hospitals

49. Many house builders offer rent-to-buy programs that enable a family with insufficient savings for a conventional down payment to be able to move into new housing and to apply part of the rent to a purchase later.

(A) programs that enable a family with insufficient savings for a conventional down payment to be able to move into new housing and to apply
(B) programs that enable a family with insufficient savings for a conventional down payment to move into new housing and to apply
(C) programs; that enables a family with insufficient savings for a conventional down payment to move into new housing, to apply
(D) programs, which enables a family with insufficient savings for a conventional down payment to move into new housing, applying
(E) programs, which enable a family with insufficient savings for a conventional down payment to be able to move into new housing, applying

50. That educators have not anticipated the impact of microcomputer technology can hardly be said that it is their fault: Alvin Toffler, one of the most prominent students of the future, did not even mention microcomputers in *Future Shock*, published in 1970.

(A) That educators have not anticipated the impact of microcomputer technology can hardly be said that it is their fault
(B) That educators have not anticipated the impact of microcomputer technology can hardly be said to be at fault
(C) It can hardly be said that it is the fault of educators who have not anticipated the impact of microcomputer technology
(D) It can hardly be said that educators are at fault for not anticipating the impact of microcomputer technology
(E) The fact that educators are at fault for not anticipating the impact of microcomputer technology can hardly be said

51. The Olympic Games helped to keep peace among the pugnacious states of the Greek world in that a sacred truce was proclaimed during the festival's month.

(A) world in that a sacred truce was proclaimed during the festival's month
(B) world, proclaiming a sacred truce during the festival's month
(C) world when they proclaimed a sacred truce for the festival month
(D) world, for a sacred truce was proclaimed during the month of the festival
(E) world by proclamation of a sacred truce that was for the month of the festival

52. While all states face similar industrial waste problems, the predominating industries and the regulatory environment of the states obviously determines the types and amounts of waste produced, as well as the cost of disposal.

(A) all states face similar industrial waste problems, the predominating industries and the regulatory environment of the states obviously determines
(B) each state faces a similar industrial waste problem, their predominant industries and regulatory environment obviously determine
(C) all states face a similar industrial waste problem; their predominating industries and regulatory environment obviously determines
(D) each state faces similar industrial waste problems, the predominant industries and the regulatory environment of each state obviously determines
(E) all states face similar industrial waste problems, the predominant industries and the regulatory environment of each state obviously determine

53. Section 13(d) of the Securities Exchange Act of 1934 requires anyone who buys more than 5 percent of a company's stock make a public disclosure of the purchase.

(A) make
(B) will also make
(C) to make
(D) must make
(E) must then make

54. When Congress reconvenes, some newly elected members from rural states will try and establish tighter restrictions for the amount of grain farmers are to be allowed to grow and to encourage more aggressive sales of United States farm products overseas.

(A) and establish tighter restrictions for the amount of grain farmers are to be allowed to grow and to encourage
(B) and establish tighter restrictions on the amount of grain able to be grown by farmers and encouraging
(C) establishing tighter restrictions for the amount of grain farmers are allowed to grow and to encourage
(D) to establish tighter restrictions on the amount of grain capable of being grown by farmers and encouraging
(E) to establish tighter restrictions on the amount of grain farmers will be allowed to grow and to encourage

55. Doctors generally agree that such factors as cigarette smoking, eating rich foods high in fats, and alcohol consumption not only do damage by themselves but also aggravate genetic predispositions toward certain diseases.

(A) not only do damage by themselves but also aggravate
(B) do damage by themselves but also are aggravating to
(C) are damaging by themselves but also are aggravating
(D) not only do damage by themselves, they are also aggravating to
(E) are doing damage by themselves, and they are also aggravating

56. In a plan to stop the erosion of East Coast beaches, the Army Corps of Engineers proposed building parallel to shore a breakwater of rocks that would rise six feet above the waterline and act as a buffer, so that it absorbs the energy of crashing waves and protecting the beaches.

(A) act as a buffer, so that it absorbs
(B) act like a buffer so as to absorb
(C) act as a buffer, absorbing
(D) acting as a buffer, absorbing
(E) acting like a buffer, absorb

57. Affording strategic proximity to the Strait of Gibraltar, Morocco was also of interest to the French throughout the first half of the twentieth century because they assumed that if they did not hold it, their grip on Algeria was always insecure.

(A) if they did not hold it, their grip on Algeria was always insecure
(B) without it their grip on Algeria would never be secure
(C) their grip on Algeria was not ever secure if they did not hold it
(D) without that, they could never be secure about their grip on Algeria
(E) never would their grip on Algeria be secure if they did not hold it

58. Once they had seen the report from the medical examiner, the investigators did not doubt whether the body recovered from the river was the man who had attempted to escape from the state prison.

(A) did not doubt whether the body recovered from the river was
(B) have no doubt whether the body recovered from the river was
(C) had not doubted that the body recovered from the river was
(D) have no doubt whether the body recovered from the river was that of
(E) had no doubt that the body recovered from the river was that of

59. His studies of ice-polished rocks in his Alpine homeland, far outside the range of present-day glaciers, led Louis Agassiz in 1837 to propose the concept of an age in which great ice sheets had existed in now currently temperate areas.

(A) in which great ice sheets had existed in now currently temperate areas
(B) in which great ice sheets existed in what are now temperate areas
(C) when great ice sheets existed where there were areas now temperate
(D) when great ice sheets had existed in current temperate areas
(E) when great ice sheets existed in areas now that are temperate

60. More and more in recent years, cities are stressing the arts as a means to greater economic development and investing millions of dollars in cultural activities, despite strained municipal budgets and fading federal support.

(A) to greater economic development and investing
(B) to greater development economically and investing
(C) of greater economic development and invest
(D) of greater development economically and invest
(E) for greater economic development and the investment of

61. Since 1986 enrollments of African Americans, American Indians, and Hispanic Americans in full-time engineering programs in the United States has steadily increased, while the number of other students who enter the field has fallen.

(A) has steadily increased, while the number of other students who enter the field has fallen
(B) has steadily increased, while other students entering the field have declined in number
(C) increased steadily, while there was a decline in the number of other students entering the field
(D) have steadily increased, while the number of other students entering the field has fallen
(E) have steadily increased, while that of other students who enter the field fell

62. A 1972 agreement between Canada and the United States reduced the amount of phosphates that municipalities had been allowed to dump into the Great Lakes.

(A) reduced the amount of phosphates that municipalities had been allowed to dump
(B) reduced the phosphate amount that municipalities had been dumping
(C) reduces the phosphate amount municipalities have been allowed to dump
(D) reduced the amount of phosphates that municipalities are allowed to dump
(E) reduces the amount of phosphates allowed for dumping by municipalities

63. A proposal has been made to trim the horns from rhinoceroses to discourage poachers; the question is whether tourists will continue to visit game parks and see rhinoceroses after their horns are trimmed.

(A) whether tourists will continue to visit game parks and see rhinoceroses after their horns are
(B) whether tourists will continue to visit game parks to see one once their horns are
(C) whether tourists will continue to visit game parks to see rhinoceroses once the animals' horns have been
(D) if tourists will continue to visit game parks and see rhinoceroses once the animals' horns are
(E) if tourists will continue to visit game parks to see one after the animals' horns have been

64. The technical term "pagination" is a process that leaves editors, instead of printers, assemble the page images that become the metal or plastic plates used in printing.

(A) is a process that leaves editors, instead of printers, assemble
(B) refers to a process that allows editors, rather than printers, to assemble
(C) is a process leaving the editors, rather than printers, to assemble
(D) refers to a process which allows editors, but not to printers, the assembly of
(E) has reference to the process leaving to editors, instead of the printer, assembling

65. The only way for growers to salvage frozen citrus is to process them quickly into juice concentrate before they rot when warmer weather returns.

(A) to process them quickly into juice concentrate before they rot when warmer weather returns
(B) if they are quickly processed into juice concentrate before warmer weather returns to rot them
(C) for them to be processed quickly into juice concentrate before the fruit rots when warmer weather returns
(D) if the fruit is quickly processed into juice concentrate before they rot when warmer weather returns
(E) to have it quickly processed into juice concentrate before warmer weather returns and rots the fruit

66. Unlike a typical automobile loan, which requires a 15 to 20 percent down payment, the lease-loan buyer is not required to make an initial deposit on the new vehicle.

(A) the lease-loan buyer is not required to make
(B) with lease-loan buying there is no requirement of
(C) lease-loan buyers are not required to make
(D) for the lease-loan buyer there is no requirement of
(E) a lease-loan does not require the buyer to make

67. Defense attorneys have occasionally argued that their clients' misconduct stemmed from a reaction to something ingested, but in attributing criminal or delinquent behavior to some food allergy, the perpetrators are in effect told that they are not responsible for their actions.

(A) in attributing criminal or delinquent behavior to some food allergy
(B) if criminal or delinquent behavior is attributed to an allergy to some food
(C) in attributing behavior that is criminal or delinquent to an allergy to some food
(D) if some food allergy is attributed as the cause of criminal or delinquent behavior
(E) in attributing a food allergy as the cause of criminal or delinquent behavior

68. Unlike computer skills or other technical skills, there is a disinclination on the part of many people to recognize the degree to which their analytical skills are weak.

(A) Unlike computer skills or other technical skills, there is a disinclination on the part of many people to recognize the degree to which their analytical skills are weak.
(B) Unlike computer skills or other technical skills, which they admit they lack, many people are disinclined to recognize that their analytical skills are weak.
(C) Unlike computer skills or other technical skills, analytical skills bring out a disinclination in many people to recognize that they are weak to a degree.
(D) Many people, willing to admit that they lack computer skills or other technical skills, are disinclined to recognize that their analytical skills are weak.
(E) Many people have a disinclination to recognize the weakness of their analytical skills while willing to admit their lack of computer skills or other technical skills.

69. A report by the American Academy for the Advancement of Science has concluded that much of the currently uncontrolled dioxins to which North Americans are exposed comes from the incineration of wastes.

(A) much of the currently uncontrolled dioxins to which North Americans are exposed comes
(B) much of the currently uncontrolled dioxins that North Americans are exposed to come
(C) much of the dioxins that are currently uncontrolled and that North Americans are exposed to comes
(D) many of the dioxins that are currently uncontrolled and North Americans are exposed to come
(E) many of the currently uncontrolled dioxins to which North Americans are exposed come

70. Displays of the aurora borealis, or "northern lights," can heat the atmosphere over the Arctic enough to affect the trajectories of ballistic missiles, induce electric currents that can cause blackouts in some areas and corrosion in north-south pipelines.

(A) to affect the trajectories of ballistic missiles, induce
(B) that the trajectories of ballistic missiles are affected, induce
(C) that it affects the trajectories of ballistic missiles, induces
(D) that the trajectories of ballistic missiles are affected and induces
(E) to affect the trajectories of ballistic missiles and induce

71. The cameras of the *Voyager II* spacecraft detected six small, previously unseen moons circling Uranus, which doubles to 12 the number of satellites now known as orbiting the distant planet.

(A) which doubles to 12 the number of satellites now known as orbiting
(B) doubling to 12 the number of satellites now known to orbit
(C) which doubles to 12 the number of satellites now known in orbit around
(D) doubling to 12 the number of satellites now known as orbiting
(E) which doubles to 12 the number of satellites now known that orbit

72. Architects and stonemasons, huge palace and temple clusters were built by the Maya without benefit of the wheel or animal transport.

(A) huge palace and temple clusters were built by the Maya without benefit of the wheel or animal transport
(B) without the benefits of animal transport or the wheel, huge palace and temple clusters were built by the Maya
(C) the Maya built huge palace and temple clusters without the benefit of animal transport or the wheel
(D) there were built, without the benefit of the wheel or animal transport, huge palace and temple clusters by the Maya
(E) were the Maya who, without the benefit of the wheel or animal transport, built huge palace and temple clusters

73. According to a recent poll, owning and living in a freestanding house on its own land is still a goal of a majority of young adults, like that of earlier generations.

(A) like that of earlier generations
(B) as that for earlier generations
(C) just as earlier generations did
(D) as have earlier generations
(E) as it was of earlier generations

74. Often visible as smog, ozone is formed in the atmosphere from hydrocarbons and nitrogen oxides, two major pollutants emitted by automobiles, react with sunlight.

(A) ozone is formed in the atmosphere from
(B) ozone is formed in the atmosphere when
(C) ozone is formed in the atmosphere, and when
(D) ozone, formed in the atmosphere when
(E) ozone, formed in the atmosphere from

75. Salt deposits and moisture threaten to destroy the Mohenjo-Daro excavation in Pakistan, the site of an ancient civilization that flourished at the same time as the civilizations in the Nile delta and the river valleys of the Tigris and Euphrates.

(A) that flourished at the same time as the civilizations
(B) that had flourished at the same time as had the civilizations
(C) that flourished at the same time those had
(D) flourishing at the same time as those did
(E) flourishing at the same time as those were

76. Never before had taxpayers confronted so many changes at once as they had in the Tax Reform Act of 1986.

(A) so many changes at once as they had in
(B) at once as many changes as
(C) at once as many changes that there were with
(D) as many changes at once as they confronted in
(E) so many changes at once that confronted them in

77. Even though the direct costs of malpractice disputes amounts to a sum lower than 1 percent of the $541 billion the nation spent on health care last year, doctors say fear of lawsuits plays a major role in health-care inflation.

(A) amounts to a sum lower
(B) amounts to less
(C) amounted to less
(D) amounted to lower
(E) amounted to a lower sum

78. Visitors to the park have often looked up into the leafy canopy and saw monkeys sleeping on the branches, whose arms and legs hang like socks on a clothesline.

(A) saw monkeys sleeping on the branches, whose arms and legs hang
(B) saw monkeys sleeping on the branches, whose arms and legs were hanging
(C) saw monkeys sleeping on the branches, with arms and legs hanging
(D) seen monkeys sleeping on the branches, with arms and legs hanging
(E) seen monkeys sleeping on the branches, whose arms and legs have hung

79. The Parthenon was a church from 1204 until 1456, when Athens was taken by General Mohammed the Conqueror, the Turkish sultan, who established a mosque in the building and used the Acropolis as a fortress.

(A) who established a mosque in the building and used the Acropolis as
(B) who, establishing a mosque in the building, used the Acropolis like
(C) who, when he had established a mosque in the building, used the Acropolis like
(D) who had established a mosque in the building, using the Acropolis to be
(E) establishing a mosque in the building and using the Acropolis as

80. New hardy varieties of rice show promise of producing high yields without the costly requirements of irrigation and application of commercial fertilizer by earlier high-yielding varieties.

(A) requirements of irrigation and application of commercial fertilizer by earlier high-yielding varieties
(B) requirements by earlier high-yielding varieties of application of commercial fertilizer and irrigation
(C) requirements for application of commercial fertilizer and irrigation of earlier high-yielding varieties
(D) application of commercial fertilizer and irrigation that was required by earlier high-yielding varieties
(E) irrigation and application of commercial fertilizer that were required by earlier high-yielding varieties

81. In an effort to reduce their inventories, Italian vintners have cut prices; their wines have been priced to sell, and they are.

(A) have been priced to sell, and they are
(B) are priced to sell, and they have
(C) are priced to sell, and they do
(D) are being priced to sell, and have
(E) had been priced to sell, and they have

82. Senator Lasker has proposed legislation requiring that employers should retain all older workers indefinitely or show just cause for dismissal.

(A) that employers should retain all older workers
(B) that all older workers be retained by employers
(C) the retaining by employers of all older workers
(D) employers' retention of all older workers
(E) employers to retain all older workers

83. Most state constitutions now mandate that the state budget be balanced each year.

(A) mandate that the state budget be balanced
(B) mandate the state budget to be balanced
(C) mandate that the state budget will be balanced
(D) have a mandate for a balanced state budget
(E) have a mandate to balance the state budget

84. Under the Safe Drinking Water Act, the Environmental Protection Agency is required either to approve individual state plans for controlling the discharge of wastes into underground water or that they enforce their own plan for states without adequate regulations.

(A) that they enforce their
(B) for enforcing their
(C) they should enforce their
(D) it should enforce its
(E) to enforce its

85. Dirt roads may evoke the bucolic simplicity of another century, but financially strained townships point out that dirt roads cost twice as much as maintaining paved roads.

(A) dirt roads cost twice as much as maintaining paved roads
(B) dirt roads cost twice as much to maintain as paved roads do
(C) maintaining dirt roads costs twice as much as paved roads do
(D) maintaining dirt roads costs twice as much as it does for paved roads
(E) to maintain dirt roads costs twice as much as for paved roads

86. Although early soap operas were first aired on evening radio in the 1920's, they had moved to the daytime hours of the 1930's when the evening schedule became crowded with comedians and variety shows.

(A) were first aired on evening radio in the 1920's, they had moved to the daytime hours of the 1930's
(B) were first aired on evening radio in the 1920's, they were moved to the daytime hours in the 1930's
(C) were aired first on evening radio in the 1920's, moving to the daytime hours in the 1930's
(D) were aired first in the evening on 1920's radio, they moved to the daytime hours of the 1930's
(E) aired on evening radio first in the 1920's, they were moved to the 1930's in the daytime hours

87. The energy source on *Voyager 2* is not a nuclear reactor, in which atoms are actively broken apart; rather a kind of nuclear battery that uses natural radioactive decay to produce power.

(A) apart; rather
(B) apart, but rather
(C) apart, but rather that of
(D) apart, but that of
(E) apart; it is that of

88. The recent surge in the number of airplane flights has clogged the nation's air-traffic control system, to lead to 55 percent more delays at airports, and prompts fears among some officials that safety is being compromised.

(A) to lead to 55 percent more delays at airports, and prompts
(B) leading to 55 percent more delay at airports and prompting
(C) to lead to a 55 percent increase in delay at airports and prompt
(D) to lead to an increase of 55 percent in delays at airports, and prompted
(E) leading to a 55 percent increase in delays at airports and prompting

89. Presenters at the seminar, one who is blind, will demonstrate adaptive equipment that allows visually impaired people to use computers.

(A) one who
(B) one of them who
(C) and one of them who
(D) one of whom
(E) one of which

90. The peaks of a mountain range, acting like rocks in a streambed, produce ripples in the air flowing over them; the resulting flow pattern, with crests and troughs that remain stationary although the air that forms them is moving rapidly, are known as "standing waves."

(A) crests and troughs that remain stationary although the air that forms them is moving rapidly, are
(B) crests and troughs that remain stationary although they are formed by rapidly moving air, are
(C) crests and troughs that remain stationary although the air that forms them is moving rapidly, is
(D) stationary crests and troughs although the air that forms them is moving rapidly, are
(E) stationary crests and troughs although they are formed by rapidly moving air, is

91. The Senate approved immigration legislation that would grant permanent residency to millions of aliens currently residing here and if employers hired illegal aliens they would be penalized.

(A) if employers hired illegal aliens they would be penalized
(B) hiring illegal aliens would be a penalty for employers
(C) penalize employers who hire illegal aliens
(D) penalizing employers hiring illegal aliens
(E) employers to be penalized for hiring illegal aliens

92. Despite protests from some waste-disposal companies, state health officials have ordered the levels of bacteria in seawater at popular beaches to be measured and that the results be published.

(A) the levels of bacteria in seawater at popular beaches to be measured and that the results be
(B) that seawater at popular beaches should be measured for their levels of bacteria, with the results being
(C) the measure of levels of bacteria in seawater at popular beaches and the results to be
(D) seawater measured at popular beaches for levels of bacteria, with their results
(E) that the levels of bacteria in seawater at popular beaches be measured and the results

93. By a vote of 9 to 0, the Supreme Court awarded the Central Intelligence Agency broad discretionary powers enabling it to withhold from the public the identities of its sources of intelligence information.

(A) enabling it to withhold from the public
(B) for it to withhold from the public
(C) for withholding disclosure to the public of
(D) that enable them to withhold from public disclosure
(E) that they can withhold public disclosure of

94. The Coast Guard is conducting tests to see whether pigeons can be trained to help find survivors of wrecks at sea.

(A) to see whether pigeons can be trained to help find
(B) to see whether pigeons can be trained as help to find
(C) to see if pigeons can be trained for helping to find
(D) that see if pigeons are able to be trained in helping to find
(E) that see whether pigeons are able to be trained for help in finding

95. Unlike Schoenberg's 12-tone system that dominated the music of the postwar period, Bartók founded no school and left behind only a handful of disciples.

(A) Schoenberg's 12-tone system that dominated
(B) Schoenberg and his 12-tone system which dominated
(C) Schoenberg, whose 12-tone system dominated
(D) the 12-tone system of Schoenberg that has dominated
(E) Schoenberg and the 12-tone system, dominating

96. Ranked as one of the most important of Europe's young playwrights, Franz Xaver Kroetz has written 40 plays; his works—translated into more than 30 languages—are produced more often than any contemporary German dramatist.

(A) than any
(B) than any other
(C) than are any
(D) than those of any other
(E) as are those of any

97. The stars, some of them at tremendous speeds, are in motion just as the planets are, yet being so far away from Earth that their apparent positions in the sky do not change enough for their movement to be observed during a single human lifetime.

(A) The stars, some of them at tremendous speeds, are in motion just as the planets are, yet being
(B) Like the planets, the stars are in motion, some of them at tremendous speeds, but they are
(C) Although like the planets the stars are in motion, some of them at tremendous speeds, yet
(D) As the planets, the stars are in motion, some of them at tremendous speeds, but they are
(E) The stars are in motion like the planets, some of which at tremendous speeds are in motion but

98. As rainfall began to decrease in the Southwest about the middle of the twelfth century, most of the Monument Valley Anasazi abandoned their homes to join other clans whose access to water was less limited.

(A) whose access to water was less limited
(B) where there was access to water that was less limited
(C) where they had less limited water access
(D) with less limitations on water access
(E) having less limitations to water access

99. Just as reading Samuel Pepys's diary gives a student a sense of the seventeenth century—of its texture and psyche—so Jane Freed's guileless child narrator takes the operagoer inside turn-of-the-century Vienna.

(A) so Jane Freed's guileless child narrator takes the operagoer
(B) so listening to Jane Freed's guileless child narrator takes the operagoer
(C) so the guileless child narrator of Jane Freed takes the operagoer
(D) listening to Jane Freed's guileless child narrator takes the operagoer
(E) Jane Freed's guileless child narrator takes the operagoer to her opera

100. Bihar is India's poorest state, with an annual per capita income of $111, lower than in the most impoverished countries of the world.

(A) lower than in
(B) lower than that of
(C) and lower than that of
(D) which is lower than in
(E) which is lower than it is in

101. El Niño, the periodic abnormal warming of the sea surface off Peru, a phenomenon in which changes in the ocean and atmosphere combine allowing the warm water that has accumulated in the western Pacific to flow back to the east.

(A) a phenomenon in which changes in the ocean and atmosphere combine allowing the warm water that has accumulated
(B) a phenomenon where changes in the ocean and atmosphere are combining to allow the warm water that is accumulating
(C) a phenomenon in which ocean and atmosphere changes combine and which allows the warm water that is accumulated
(D) is a phenomenon in which changes in the ocean and atmosphere combine to allow the warm water that has accumulated
(E) is a phenomenon where ocean and atmosphere changes are combining and allow the warm water accumulating

102. Beatrix Potter, in her book illustrations, carefully coordinating them with her narratives, capitalized on her keen observation and love of the natural world.

(A) Beatrix Potter, in her book illustrations, carefully coordinating them with her narratives,
(B) In her book illustrations, carefully coordinating them with her narratives, Beatrix Potter
(C) In her book illustrations, which she carefully coordinated with her narratives, Beatrix Potter
(D) Carefully coordinated with her narratives, Beatrix Potter, in her book illustrations
(E) Beatrix Potter, in her book illustrations, carefully coordinated them with her narratives and

103. The development of a new jumbo rocket that is expected to carry the United States into its next phase of space exploration will be able to deliver a heavier load of instruments into orbit than the space shuttle and at a lower cost.

(A) The development of a new jumbo rocket that is expected to carry the United States into its next phase of space exploration will be able to deliver a heavier load of instruments into orbit than the space shuttle and at a lower cost.
(B) The development of a new jumbo rocket is expected to carry the United States into its next phase of space exploration and be able to deliver a heavier load of instruments into orbit at a lower cost than the space shuttle.
(C) The new development of a jumbo rocket, which is expected to carry the United States into its next phase of space exploration, will be able to deliver a heavier load of instruments into orbit at a lower cost than the space shuttle.
(D) A newly developed jumbo rocket, which is expected to carry the United States into its next phase of space exploration, will be able to deliver a heavier load of instruments into orbit than the space shuttle can, and at a lower cost.
(E) A newly developed jumbo rocket, which is expected to carry the United States into its next phase of space exploration, will be able to deliver a heavier load of instruments into orbit than the space shuttle and to cost less.

104. Nuclear fusion is the force that powers the Sun, the stars, and hydrogen bombs, merging the nuclei of atoms and not splitting them apart, as in nuclear reactors.

(A) merging the nuclei of atoms and not splitting them apart, as in nuclear reactors
(B) merging the nuclei of atoms instead of splitting them apart, like nuclear reactors
(C) merging the nuclei of atoms rather than splitting them apart, as nuclear reactors do
(D) and merges the nuclei of atoms but does not split them apart, as is done in nuclear reactors
(E) and merges the nuclei of atoms, unlike atomic reactors that split them apart

105. Originally developed for detecting air pollutants, a technique called proton-induced X-ray emission, which can quickly analyze the chemical elements in almost any substance without destroying it, is finding uses in medicine, archaeology, and criminology.

(A) Originally developed for detecting air pollutants, a technique called proton-induced X-ray emission, which can quickly analyze the chemical elements in almost any substance without destroying it,
(B) Originally developed for detecting air pollutants, having the ability to analyze the chemical elements in almost any substance without destroying it, a technique called proton-induced X-ray emission
(C) A technique originally developed for detecting air pollutants, called proton-induced X-ray emission, which can quickly analyze the chemical elements in almost any substance without destroying it,
(D) A technique originally developed for detecting air pollutants, called proton-induced X-ray emission, which has the ability to analyze the chemical elements in almost any substance quickly and without destroying it,
(E) A technique that was originally developed for detecting air pollutants and has the ability to analyze the chemical elements in almost any substance quickly and without destroying the substance, called proton-induced X-ray emission,

106. Among the objects found in the excavated temple were small terra-cotta effigies left by supplicants who were either asking the goddess Bona Dea's aid in healing physical and mental ills or thanking her for such help.

(A) in healing physical and mental ills or thanking her for such help
(B) in healing physical and mental ills and to thank her for helping
(C) in healing physical and mental ills, and thanking her for helping
(D) to heal physical and mental ills or to thank her for such help
(E) to heal physical and mental ills or thanking her for such help

107. In his research paper, Dr. Frosh, medical director of the Payne Whitney Clinic, distinguishes mood swings, which may be violent without their being grounded in mental disease, from genuine manic-depressive psychosis.

(A) mood swings, which may be violent without their being grounded in mental disease, from genuine manic-depressive psychosis
(B) mood swings, perhaps violent without being grounded in mental disease, and genuine manic-depressive psychosis
(C) between mood swings, which may be violent without being grounded in mental disease, and genuine manic-depressive psychosis
(D) between mood swings, perhaps violent without being grounded in mental disease, from genuine manic-depressive psychosis
(E) genuine manic-depressive psychosis and mood swings, which may be violent without being grounded in mental disease

108. The first decision for most tenants living in a building undergoing being converted to cooperative ownership is if to sign a no-buy pledge with the other tenants.

(A) being converted to cooperative ownership is if to sign
(B) being converted to cooperative ownership is whether they should be signing
(C) being converted to cooperative ownership is whether or not they sign
(D) conversion to cooperative ownership is if to sign
(E) conversion to cooperative ownership is whether to sign

109. Published in Harlem, the owner and editor of the *Messenger* were two young journalists, Chandler Owen and A. Philip Randolph, who would later make his reputation as a labor leader.

(A) Published in Harlem, the owner and editor of the *Messenger* were two young journalists, Chandler Owen and A. Philip Randolph, who would later make his reputation as a labor leader.
(B) Published in Harlem, two young journalists, Chandler Owen and A. Philip Randolph, who would later make his reputation as a labor leader, were the owner and editor of the *Messenger*.
(C) Published in Harlem, the *Messenger* was owned and edited by two young journalists, A. Philip Randolph, who would later make his reputation as a labor leader, and Chandler Owen.
(D) The *Messenger* was owned and edited by two young journalists, Chandler Owen and A. Philip Randolph, who would later make his reputation as a labor leader, and published in Harlem.
(E) The owner and editor being two young journalists, Chandler Owen and A. Philip Randolph, who would later make his reputation as a labor leader, the *Messenger* was published in Harlem.

110. In June of 1987, *The Bridge of Trinquetaille*, Vincent van Gogh's view of an iron bridge over the Rhone sold for $20.2 million and it was the second highest price ever paid for a painting at auction.

(A) Rhone sold for $20.2 million and it was
(B) Rhone, which sold for $20.2 million, was
(C) Rhone, was sold for $20.2 million,
(D) Rhone was sold for $20.2 million, being
(E) Rhone, sold for $20.2 million, and was

111. As a baby emerges from the darkness of the womb with a rudimentary sense of vision, it would be rated about 20/500, or legally blind if it were an adult with such vision.

(A) As a baby emerges from the darkness of the womb with a rudimentary sense of vision, it would be rated about 20/500, or legally blind if it were an adult with such vision.
(B) A baby emerges from the darkness of the womb with a rudimentary sense of vision that would be rated about 20/500, or legally blind as an adult.
(C) As a baby emerges from the darkness of the womb, its rudimentary sense of vision would be rated about 20/500; qualifying it to be legally blind if an adult.
(D) A baby emerges from the darkness of the womb with a rudimentary sense of vision that would be rated about 20/500; an adult with such vision would be deemed legally blind.
(E) As a baby emerges from the darkness of the womb, its rudimentary sense of vision, which would deemed legally blind for an adult, would be rated about 20/500.

112. The Federal Reserve Board's reduction of interest rates on loans to financial institutions is both an acknowledgment of past economic trends and an effort to influence their future direction.

(A) reduction of interest rates on loans to financial institutions is both an acknowledgment of past economic trends and an effort
(B) reduction of interest rates on loans to financial institutions is an acknowledgment both of past economic trends as well as an effort
(C) reduction of interest rates on loans to financial institutions both acknowledge past economic trends and attempt
(D) reducing interest rates on loans to financial institutions is an acknowledgment both of past economic trends and an effort
(E) reducing interest rates on loans to financial institutions both acknowledge past economic trends as well as attempt

113. The original building and loan associations were organized as limited life funds, whose members made monthly payments on their share subscriptions, then taking turns drawing on the funds for home mortgages.

(A) subscriptions, then taking turns drawing
(B) subscriptions, and then taking turns drawing
(C) subscriptions and then took turns drawing
(D) subscriptions and then took turns, they drew
(E) subscriptions and then drew, taking turns

114. Gall's hypothesis of there being different mental functions localized in different parts of the brain is widely accepted today.

(A) of there being different mental functions localized in different parts of the brain is widely accepted today
(B) of different mental functions that are localized in different parts of the brain is widely accepted today
(C) that different mental functions are localized in different parts of the brain is widely accepted today
(D) which is that there are different mental functions localized in different parts of the brain is widely accepted today
(E) which is widely accepted today is that there are different mental functions localized in different parts of the brain

115. George Sand (Aurore Lucile Dupin) was one of the first European writers to consider the rural poor to be legitimate subjects for literature and portray these with sympathy and respect in her novels.

(A) to be legitimate subjects for literature and portray these
(B) should be legitimate subjects for literature and portray these
(C) as being legitimate subjects for literature and portraying them
(D) as if they were legitimate subjects for literature and portray them
(E) legitimate subjects for literature and to portray them

116. Out of America's fascination with all things antique have grown a market for bygone styles of furniture and fixtures that are bringing back the chaise lounge, the overstuffed sofa, and the claw-footed bathtub.

(A) things antique have grown a market for bygone styles of furniture and fixtures that are bringing
(B) things antique has grown a market for bygone styles of furniture and fixtures that is bringing
(C) things that are antiques has grown a market for bygone styles of furniture and fixtures that bring
(D) antique things have grown a market for bygone styles of furniture and fixtures that are bringing
(E) antique things has grown a market for bygone styles of furniture and fixtures that bring

117. New theories propose that catastrophic impacts of asteroids and comets may have caused reversals in the Earth's magnetic field, the onset of ice ages, splitting apart continents 80 million years ago, and great volcanic eruptions.

(A) splitting apart continents
(B) the splitting apart of continents
(C) split apart continents
(D) continents split apart
(E) continents that were split apart

118. Students in the metropolitan school district lack math skills to such a large degree as to make it difficult to absorb them into a city economy becoming ever more dependent on information-based industries.

(A) lack math skills to such a large degree as to make it difficult to absorb them into a city economy becoming
(B) lack math skills to a large enough degree that they will be difficult to absorb into a city's economy that becomes
(C) lack of math skills is so large as to be difficult to absorb them into a city's economy that becomes
(D) are lacking so much in math skills as to be difficult to absorb into a city's economy becoming
(E) are so lacking in math skills that it will be difficult to absorb them into a city economy becoming

119. The decision by one of the nation's largest banks to admit to $3 billion in potential losses on foreign loans could mean less lending by commercial banks to developing countries and increasing the pressure on multigovernment lenders to supply the funds.

(A) increasing the pressure
(B) the increasing pressure
(C) increased pressure
(D) the pressure increased
(E) the pressure increasing

120. It has been estimated that the annual cost to the United States of illiteracy in lost industrial output and tax revenues is at least $20 billion a year.

(A) the annual cost to the United States of illiteracy in lost industrial output and tax revenues is at least $20 billion a year
(B) the annual cost of illiteracy to the United States is at least $20 billion a year because of lost industrial output and tax revenues
(C) illiteracy costs the United States at least $20 billion a year in lost industrial output and tax revenues
(D) $20 billion a year in lost industrial output and tax revenues is the annual cost to the United States of illiteracy
(E) lost industrial output and tax revenues cost the United States at least $20 billion a year because of illiteracy

121. A firm that specializes in the analysis of handwriting claims from a one-page writing sample that it can assess more than 300 personality traits, including enthusiasm, imagination, and ambition.

(A) from a one-page writing sample that it can assess
(B) from a one-page writing sample it has the ability of assessing
(C) the ability, from a one-page writing sample, of assessing
(D) to be able, from a one-page writing sample, to assess
(E) being able to assess, from a one-page writing sample

122. More than 30 years ago Dr. Barbara McClintock, the Nobel Prize winner, reported that genes can "jump," as pearls moving mysteriously from one necklace to another.

(A) as pearls moving mysteriously from one necklace to another
(B) like pearls moving mysteriously from one necklace to another
(C) as pearls do that move mysteriously from one necklace to others
(D) like pearls do that move mysteriously from one necklace to others
(E) as do pearls that move mysteriously from one necklace to some other one

123. In Holland, a larger percentage of the gross national product is spent on defense of their coasts from rising seas than is spent on military defense in the United States.

(A) In Holland, a larger percentage of the gross national product is spent on defense of their coasts from rising seas than is spent on military defense in the United States.
(B) In Holland they spend a larger percentage of their gross national product on defending their coasts from rising seas than the United States does on military defense.
(C) A larger percentage of Holland's gross national product is spent on defending their coasts from rising seas than the United States spends on military defense.
(D) Holland spends a larger percentage of its gross national product defending its coasts from rising seas than the military defense spending of the United States.
(E) Holland spends a larger percentage of its gross national product on defending its coasts from rising seas than the United States does on military defense.

124. Canadian scientists have calculated that one human being should be struck every nine years by a meteorite, while each year 16 buildings can be expected to sustain damage from such objects.

(A) one human being should be struck every nine years by a meteorite
(B) a human being should be struck by a meteorite once in every nine years
(C) a meteorite will strike one human being once in every nine years
(D) every nine years a human being will be struck by a meteorite
(E) every nine years a human being should be struck by a meteorite

125. Samuel Sewall viewed marriage, as other seventeenth-century colonists, like a property arrangement rather than an emotional bond based on romantic love.

(A) Samuel Sewall viewed marriage, as other seventeenth-century colonists, like a property arrangement rather than
(B) As did other seventeenth-century colonists, Samuel Sewall viewed marriage to be a property arrangement rather than viewing it as
(C) Samuel Sewall viewed marriage to be a property arrangement, like other seventeenth-century colonists, rather than viewing it as
(D) Marriage to Samuel Sewall, like other seventeenth-century colonists, was viewed as a property arrangement rather than
(E) Samuel Sewall, like other seventeenth-century colonists, viewed marriage as a property arrangement rather than

126. A wildlife expert predicts that the reintroduction of the caribou into northern Minnesota would fail if the density of the timber wolf population in that region is more numerous than one wolf for every 39 square miles.

(A) would fail if the density of the timber wolf population in that region is more numerous than
(B) would fail provided the density of the timber wolf population in that region is more than
(C) should fail if the timber wolf density in that region was greater than
(D) will fail if the density of the timber wolf population in that region is greater than
(E) will fail if the timber wolf density in that region were more numerous than

127. Found throughout Central and South America, sloths hang from trees by long rubbery limbs and sleep 15 hours a day, moving infrequently enough that two species of algae grow on its coat and between its toes.

(A) sloths hang from trees by long rubbery limbs and sleep 15 hours a day, moving infrequently enough
(B) sloths hang from trees by long rubbery limbs, they sleep 15 hours a day, and with such infrequent movements
(C) sloths use their long rubbery limbs to hang from trees, sleep 15 hours a day, and move so infrequently
(D) the sloth hangs from trees by its long rubbery limbs, sleeping 15 hours a day and moving so infrequently
(E) the sloth hangs from trees by its long rubbery limbs, sleeps 15 hours a day, and it moves infrequently enough

128. Today, because of improvements in agricultural technology, the same amount of acreage produces double the apples that it has in 1910.

(A) double the apples that it has
(B) twice as many apples as it did
(C) as much as twice the apples it has
(D) two times as many apples as there were
(E) a doubling of the apples that it did

129. Joan of Arc, a young Frenchwoman who claimed to be divinely inspired, turned the tide of English victories in her country by liberating the city of Orléans and she persuaded Charles VII of France to claim his throne.

(A) she persuaded Charles VII of France to claim his throne
(B) persuaded Charles VII of France in claiming his throne
(C) persuading that the throne be claimed by Charles VII of France
(D) persuaded Charles VII of France to claim his throne
(E) persuading that Charles VII of France should claim the throne

130. As a result of medical advances, many people that might at one time have died as children of such infections as diphtheria, pneumonia, or rheumatic fever now live well into old age.

(A) that might at one time have died as children
(B) who might once have died in childhood
(C) that as children might once have died
(D) who in childhood might have at one time died
(E) who, when they were children, might at one time have died

131. Cajuns speak a dialect brought to southern Louisiana by the 4000 Acadians who migrated there in 1755; their language is basically seventeenth-century French to which has been added English, Spanish, and Italian words.

(A) to which has been added English, Spanish, and Italian words
(B) added to which is English, Spanish, and Italian words
(C) to which English, Spanish, and Italian words have been added
(D) with English, Spanish, and Italian words having been added to it
(E) and, in addition, English, Spanish, and Italian words are added

132. One view of the economy contends that a large drop in oil prices should eventually lead to lowering interest rates, as well as lowering fears about inflation, a rally in stocks and bonds, and a weakening of the dollar.

(A) lowering interest rates, as well as lowering fears about inflation,
(B) a lowering of interest rates and of fears about inflation,
(C) a lowering of interest rates, along with fears about inflation,
(D) interest rates being lowered, along with fears about inflation,
(E) interest rates and fears about inflation being lowered, with

133. Although the term "psychopath" is popularly applied to an especially brutal criminal, in psychology it is someone who is apparently incapable of feeling compassion or the pangs of conscience.

(A) it is someone who is
(B) it is a person
(C) they are people who are
(D) it refers to someone who is
(E) it is in reference to people

134. Recently implemented "shift-work equations" based on studies of the human sleep cycle have reduced sickness, sleeping on the job, fatigue among shift workers, and have raised production efficiency in various industries.

(A) fatigue among shift workers, and have raised
(B) fatigue among shift workers, and raised
(C) and fatigue among shift workers while raising
(D) lowered fatigue among shift workers, and raised
(E) and fatigue among shift workers was lowered while raising

135. Spanning more than 50 years, Friedrich Müller began his career in an unpromising apprenticeship as a Sanskrit scholar and culminated in virtually every honor that European governments and learned societies could bestow.

(A) Müller began his career in an unpromising apprenticeship as
(B) Müller's career began in an unpromising apprenticeship as
(C) Müller's career began with the unpromising apprenticeship of being
(D) Müller had begun his career with the unpromising apprenticeship of being
(E) the career of Müller has begun with an unpromising apprenticeship of

136. Joachim Raff and Giacomo Meyerbeer are examples of the kind of composer who receives popular acclaim while living, often goes into decline after death, and never regains popularity again.

(A) often goes into decline after death, and never regains popularity again
(B) whose reputation declines after death and never regains its status again
(C) but whose reputation declines after death and never regains its former status
(D) who declines in reputation after death and who never regained popularity again
(E) then has declined in reputation after death and never regained popularity

137. The company announced that its profits declined much less in the second quarter than analysts had expected it to and its business will improve in the second half of the year.

(A) had expected it to and its business will improve
(B) had expected and that its business would improve
(C) expected it would and that it will improve its business
(D) expected them to and its business would improve
(E) expected and that it will have improved its business

138. The direction in which the Earth and the other solid planets—Mercury, Venus, and Mars—spins were determined from collisions with giant celestial bodies in the early history of the solar system.

(A) spins were determined from
(B) spins were determined because of
(C) spins was determined through
(D) spin was determined by
(E) spin was determined as a result of

9.7 Sentence Correction Answer Key

1. D	32. B	63. C	94. A	125. E
2. E	33. A	64. B	95. C	126. D
3. A	34. D	65. E	96. D	127. D
4. D	35. C	66. E	97. B	128. B
5. E	36. D	67. B	98. A	129. D
6. E	37. A	68. D	99. B	130. B
7. B	38. E	69. E	100. B	131. C
8. E	39. A	70. E	101. D	132. B
9. A	40. C	71. B	102. C	133. D
10. B	41. B	72. C	103. D	134. C
11. E	42. B	73. E	104. C	135. B
12. D	43. A	74. B	105. A	136. C
13. C	44. D	75. A	106. A	137. B
14. D	45. A	76. D	107. C	138. D
15. D	46. D	77. C	108. E	
16. E	47. E	78. D	109. C	
17. D	48. E	79. A	110. C	
18. B	49. B	80. E	111. D	
19. E	50. D	81. C	112. A	
20. E	51. D	82. E	113. C	
21. D	52. E	83. A	114. C	
22. C	53. C	84. E	115. E	
23. B	54. E	85. B	116. B	
24. C	55. A	86. B	117. B	
25. C	56. C	87. B	118. E	
26. B	57. B	88. E	119. C	
27. A	58. E	89. D	120. C	
28. B	59. B	90. C	121. D	
29. C	60. A	91. C	122. B	
30. A	61. D	92. E	123. E	
31. B	62. D	93. A	124. D	

9.8 Sentence Correction Answer Explanations

The following discussion of sentence correction is intended to familiarize you with the most efficient and effective approaches to these kinds of questions. The particular questions in this chapter are generally representative of the kinds of sentence correction questions you will encounter on the GMAT®.

1. Although a surge in retail sales have raised hopes that there is a recovery finally underway, many economists say that without a large amount of spending the recovery might not last.

(A) have raised hopes that there is a recovery finally
(B) raised hopes for there being a recovery finally
(C) had raised hopes for a recovery finally being
(D) has raised hopes that a recovery is finally
(E) raised hopes for a recovery finally

Agreement + Rhetorical construction

The subject of the first clause, the singular noun *surge*, must take the singular verb *has raised* rather than the plural *have raised*; the context of the sentence demonstrates that the verb tense must show action continuing into the present, as the use of the present perfect does here. *There is* may frequently be omitted to create a more concise sentence, and that is the case here: *a recovery is finally* ... is a better construction.

A Subject and verb do not agree; *there is* is wordy
B *Raised* is the wrong verb tense; *for there being* is awkward and wordy
C *Had raised* is the wrong verb tense; *for ... being* is awkward and wordy
D Correct. In this sentence, the subject and verb agree, and the verb is in the appropriate tense; *a recovery is finally* is clear and concise.
E *Raised*, indicating completed action, is the wrong verb tense; *for a recovery finally* is awkward and ungrammatical

The correct answer is D.

2. Of all the vast tides of migration that have swept through history, maybe none is more concentrated as the wave that brought 12 million immigrants onto American shores in little more than three decades.

(A) maybe none is more concentrated as
(B) it may be that none is more concentrated as
(C) perhaps it is none that is more concentrated than
(D) maybe it is none that was more concentrated than
(E) perhaps none was more concentrated than

Idiom + Verb form

This sentence depends on the comparative structure *x is more than y*. Here, an idiomatically incorrect construction *x* (*none*) *is more as y* (*the wave*) is used. In addition, the second part of the sentence uses the past tense verb *brought*, indicating that the event is over. The verb used in the comparative construction must also be past tense, *x* (*none*) *was more concentrated than y* (*the wave*). *Maybe* and *perhaps* are interchangeable; *perhaps* is slightly more formal.

A Incorrect idiom is used for comparison; *is concentrated* is the wrong tense
B Incorrect idiom is used for comparison; *it may be that* is wordy
C *It is none that is more* ... is a wordy and ungrammatical construction
D *It is none that was more* ... is a wordy and ungrammatical construction
E Correct. The correct comparative construction is used in this sentence; the verb is past tense.

The correct answer is E.

3. Diabetes, together with its serious complications, ranks as the nation's third leading cause of death, surpassed only by heart disease and cancer.

(A) ranks as the nation's third leading cause of death, surpassed only
(B) rank as the nation's third leading cause of death, only surpassed
(C) has the rank of the nation's third leading cause of death, only surpassed
(D) are the nation's third leading causes of death, surpassed only
(E) have been ranked as the nation's third leading causes of death, only surpassed

Agreement + Logical predication

This sentence correctly matches the singular verb, *ranks*, with the singular subject, *diabetes*, and uses the present tense to indicate a current situation. The phrase following *diabetes* is set off by a pair of commas, indicating that it is descriptive information that may be dropped from the sentence; it is not a part of the subject. *Only* is placed with precision next to the group of words it actually limits, *by heart disease and cancer*. Placed before *surpassed*, *only* would more ambiguously limit *surpassed*.

A **Correct.** In the original sentence, the subject and verb agree, and the proper tense is used; *only* is correctly placed next to the phrase it limits.
B *Rank* does not agree with *diabetes*; *only* limits *surpassed* rather than *by heart disease and cancer*
C *Has the rank of* is wordy and unidiomatic; *only* limits *surpassed* rather than *by heart disease and cancer*
D Construction *are … causes* does not agree with *diabetes*
E Construction *have been ranked … causes* does not agree with *diabetes* and uses the wrong verb tense; *only* limits *surpassed* rather than *by heart disease and cancer*

The correct answer is A.

4. A survey by the National Council of Churches showed that in 1986 there were 20,736 female ministers, almost 9 percent of the nation's clergy, twice as much as 1977.

(A) twice as much as 1977
(B) twice as many as 1977
(C) double what it was in 1977
(D) double the figure for 1977
(E) a number double that of 1977's

Diction

Some quantities, such as people, can be counted; other quantities, such as respect, cannot. It can be said that a person earned *much* respect, or that *many* people attended an event. Here, *much* is incorrectly applied to ministers. *As 1977* incorrectly completes the comparison; it would have to be *as many as in 1977*, which is not one of the possible answers. Another way to make the comparison emphasizes the number, 20,736; a number can be doubled. *Double the figure for 1977* places the focus on the number and correctly completes the comparison.

A *Much* incorrectly refers to *ministers*; *as* should be *as in*
B *As 1977* does not correctly complete this comparison; it should be *as in 1977*
C *What it was* is awkward, wordy, and unclear
D **Correct.** *Double the figure* places the emphasis of the sentence on the number of ministers; *for 1977* correctly completes the comparison.
E Wordy and awkward construction

The correct answer is D.

5. As its sales of computer products have surpassed those of measuring instruments, the company has become increasingly willing to compete for the mass market sales <u>they would in the past have conceded to rivals</u>.

(A) they would in the past have conceded to rivals
(B) they would have conceded previously to their rivals
(C) that in the past would have been conceded previously to rivals
(D) it previously would have conceded to rivals in the past
(E) it would in the past have conceded to rivals

Agreement + Rhetorical construction

When a number of words intervene between a pronoun and its referent, an error such as the one in this sentence is easy to make. The subject of the main clause is the singular noun *company*, which must be followed by the singular pronoun *it*.

A Plural pronoun *they* does not agree with singular *the company*
B Plural pronouns *they* and *their* do not agree with *the company*
C *Previously* repeats the idea of *in the past*; the passive voice construction is weak and ambiguous
D Use of both *previously* and *in the past* is redundant
E **Correct.** In this concise sentence, the singular pronoun *it* agrees with the singular referent *the company*.

The correct answer is E.

6. <u>Like the idolization accorded the Brontës and Brownings</u>, James Joyce and Virginia Woolf are often subjected to the kind of veneration that blurs the distinction between the artist and the human being.

(A) Like the idolization accorded the Brontës and Brownings
(B) As the Brontës' and Brownings' idolization
(C) Like that accorded to the Brontës and Brownings
(D) As it is of the Brontës and Brownings
(E) Like the Brontës and Brownings

Logical predication

This sentence intends to compare nineteenth- and twentieth-century writers. Instead the comparison becomes ambiguous and illogical. *Like* must be used to compare similar elements: *Joyce* and *Woolf* are *like* the *Brontës* and the *Brownings*; they are not *like* the *idolization*.

A *The idolization accorded* is not comparable to Joyce and Woolf
B The conjunction *as* may introduce a clause but not a phrase; Joyce and Woolf are compared to *idolization* rather than to the writers
C *That* is ambiguous, and Joyce and Woolf are compared to *that* rather than to the writers
D *It* is ambiguous; *as it is of* is awkward and wordy; the twentieth-century writers are compared to *it* rather than to the nineteenth-century writers
E **Correct.** In this sentence, *like* introduces a clear and concise comparison that correctly links the nineteenth- and twentieth-century writers.

The correct answer is E.

7. Carnivorous mammals can endure what would otherwise be lethal levels of body heat because they have a heat-exchange network <u>which kept</u> the brain from getting too hot.

(A) which kept
(B) that keeps
(C) which has kept
(D) that has been keeping
(E) having kept

Idiom + Verb form

The two underlined words contain two separate errors. The pronoun *which* introduces nonrestrictive clauses, which include information relevant but not critical to an understanding of the sentence. The pronoun *that* introduces a restrictive clause, which is critical to understanding the sentence because the clause defines its antecedent. Here, the clause following *which* defines *heat-exchange network*, so *that* must be used in place of *which*. The use of the past tense (*kept*) is incorrect because a current situation is discussed; the present tense (*keeps*) is consistent with the other verbs in the sentence.

A *Which* is incorrectly used for a clause that defines; *kept* is the wrong tense
B Correct. *That* introduces a restrictive clause; *keeps* indicates a current situation and is consistent with the other verbs in the sentence.
C *Which* incorrectly introduces a restrictive clause; *has kept* is the wrong tense
D The complete sentence is written in the present tense; there is no reason to switch tenses in the restrictive clause
E *Having* is awkward and imprecise; *kept* is the incorrect tense

The correct answer is B.

8. Rising inventories, <u>when unaccompanied correspondingly by increases in sales, can lead</u> to production cutbacks that would hamper economic growth.

(A) when unaccompanied correspondingly by increases in sales, can lead
(B) when not accompanied by corresponding increases in sales, possibly leads
(C) when they were unaccompanied by corresponding sales increases, can lead
(D) if not accompanied by correspondingly increased sales, possibly leads
(E) if not accompanied by corresponding increases in sales, can lead

Diction + Logical predication

The modifying phrase *when … sales* is needlessly difficult to understand. The adverb *correspondingly* is incorrectly and ambiguously used; using the adjective *corresponding* to modify *increases in sales* makes the intended meaning more clear. *Unaccompanied* is not wrong but *not accompanied* puts greater emphasis on the negative. *When* indicates a period of time; *if* indicates a condition. *If* is preferable here.

A *Correspondingly* is awkward and ambiguous; *when* is used to refer to a condition
B Plural subject *inventories* does not agree with the singular verb *leads*; *when* is used to refer to a condition
C Past tense *were* indicates a completed event, but *can lead* indicates a possibility that continues; *when* is used to refer to a condition
D *Correspondingly increased sales* is awkward and unclear; verb (*leads*) does not agree with the subject (*inventories*)
E Correct. *If* properly introduces a condition in this sentence; *not accompanied* emphasizes the negative; *corresponding* modifies *increases in sales*; the modifier is clear and comprehensible.

The correct answer is E.

9. Sunspots, vortices of gas associated with strong electromagnetic activity, are visible as dark spots on the surface of the Sun but have never been sighted on the Sun's poles or equator.

(A) are visible as dark spots on the surface of the Sun but have never been sighted on
(B) are visible as dark spots that never have been sighted on the surface of the Sun
(C) appear on the surface of the Sun as dark spots although never sighted at
(D) appear as dark spots on the surface of the Sun, although never having been sighted at
(E) appear as dark spots on the Sun's surface, which have never been sighted on

Logical predication + Parallelism

The correct parallel structure in the original sentence emphasizes the contrast between where sunspots are found (*are visible … Sun*) and where they are not (*have never been sighted … equator*). *Sunspots* is the subject of the sentence, *are* is the verb of the first part of the contrast and *have been sighted* is the verb of the second. (The adjective *visible* is a complement and is parallel to the past participle *sighted*.) Both parts of the sentence conclude with phrases indicating location. The contrast itself is indicated by the conjunction *but*.

A **Correct.** This sentence clearly and correctly draws a contrast between where sunspots are found and where they are not.
B Changing the modifying clause so that *that never … Sun* distorts the meaning of the sentence; the contrast is lost
C *Although* typically introduces a subordinate clause, which has a subject and a verb, but here there is no subject and *sighted* is not a complete verb
D *Although* usually introduces a subordinate clause, but there is no subject of the clause and *having been sighted* is not a complete verb phrase
E The relative pronoun *which* should immediately follow its referent; here *which* illogically follows *surface*, and its intended referent, either *sunspots* or *dark spots*, becomes unclear

The correct answer is A.

10. Unlike the United States, Japanese unions appear, reluctant to organize lower-paid workers.

(A) Unlike the United States, Japanese unions appear reluctant to organize
(B) Unlike those in the United States, Japanese unions appear reluctant to organize
(C) In Japan, unlike the United States, unions appear reluctant about organizing
(D) Japanese unions, unlike the United States, appear reluctant to organize
(E) Japanese unions, unlike those in the United States, appear reluctant about organizing

Idiom

The intention of this sentence is to contrast American unions with Japanese unions. However, it mistakenly contrasts *the United States* with *Japanese unions*. This error is easily corrected by using the pronoun *those* to represent *unions* in the United States. The most effective structure is to begin the sentence, *Unlike those in the United States*, allowing the main clause to be about the Japanese unions.

A The *United States*, rather than *unions* in the United States, is contrasted with *Japanese unions*
B **Correct.** The contrasting element placed at the beginning of the sentence emphasizes difference; the correct contrast is drawn between *Japanese unions* and *those* (referring to *unions*) *in the United States*.
C *In Japan* would have to be balanced by *in the United States*, but the preposition *in* cannot follow the preposition *unlike*; this construction is awkward and imprecise
D *Japanese unions* are contrasted with *the United States* rather than with *unions in the United States*.
E A more effective sentence begins with the contrasting element (*unlike …*) and then places the subject and verb of the main clause together; *reluctant* must be followed by an infinitive (*to organize*)

The correct answer is B.

11. Warning that computers in the United States are not secure, the National Academy of Sciences has urged the nation to revamp computer security procedures, institute new emergency response teams, creating a special nongovernment organization to take charge of computer security planning.

(A) creating a special nongovernment organization to take
(B) creating a special nongovernment organization that takes
(C) creating a special nongovernment organization for taking
(D) and create a special nongovernment organization for taking
(E) and create a special nongovernment organization to take

Parallelism + Grammatical construction

This sentence contains a list of three elements, all of which should be parallel. The last element should be preceded by the conjunction *and.* In this sentence, the last element must be made parallel to the previous two: (1) *to revamp computer security procedures,* (2) *institute new emergency response teams, and* (3) *create a special nongovernment organization to take charge of computer security planning.* Omitting *and* causes the reader to anticipate still another element in the series when there is none. Using the participle *creating* not only violates parallelism but also causes misreading since the participial phrase could modify the first part of the sentence. *To* does not need to be repeated with *institute* and *create* because it is understood.

A *Creating* is not parallel to *to revamp* and (*to* understood) *institute*; *and* is needed in this series
B *Creating* violates the parallelism of the previous two elements; *and* is needed in this series; since the organization does not yet exist, *that takes* is illogical
C *Creating* is not parallel to *to revamp* and (*to* understood) *institute*; *and* is needed in this series; *to* has the sense of *in order to*, but *for taking* is neither precise nor idiomatic
D In the construction *create ... to take*, the sense of *to* is *in order to*; *for taking* is not idiomatically correct
E **Correct.** The three elements in the series are parallel in this sentence, and the last is preceded by *and.*

The correct answer is E.

12. After gradual declension down to about 39 hours in 1970, the workweek in the United States has steadily increased to the point that the average worker now puts in an estimated 164 extra hours of paid labor a year.

(A) After gradual declension down
(B) Following a gradual declension down
(C) After gradual declining down
(D) After gradually declining
(E) Following gradually declining

Diction + Rhetorical construction

One of the meanings of *declension* is a *decline*, but *declension* is rarely, if ever, used in this sense in the modern era. Replacing *declension* with *decline* would be acceptable, but it is preferable to use the participle *declining* with the adverb *gradually*: *after gradually declining. Declining* shows movement in only one direction, so the redundant adverb *down* must be omitted.

A Wordy, redundant, and stilted construction uses the rare *declension* in place of the familiar *decline*
B Construction is wordy and redundant; *declension* in the sense of *decline* is not a familiar or contemporary usage
C *Declining* must be modified by the adverb *gradually*, not the adjective *gradual*; *down* is redundant
D **Correct.** In this sentence, *after gradually declining* is clear, correct, concise, and idiomatic.
E Phrase must be introduced by a preposition (*after*), not a participle (*following*)

The correct answer is D.

13. As Hurricane Hugo approached the Atlantic coast, it increased dramatically in strength, becoming the tenth most intense hurricane to hit the United States mainland in the twentieth century and most intense since Camille in 1969.

(A) most intense since Camille in 1969
(B) most intense after Camille in 1969
(C) the most intense since Camille in 1969
(D) the most intense after 1969, which had Camille
(E) since 1969 and Camille, the most intense

Idiom

The superlative form is used for comparisons involving more than two elements, and it should be used here because the comparison involves all hurricanes to hit the United States mainland in the twentieth century. Because *tenth* appears between *the* and *most intense* in the first phrase, *the* must be repeated in the second phrase: *the most intense*. While in some constructions, such as *the most frightening and most intense*, *the* would be understood and so would not need to be repeated, the definite article *the* is required in this superlative form construction. *Since* is preferable to *after* in this sentence because *since* emphasizes the continuity of the action.

A Correct idiom here is *the most intense*
B Construction requires the repetition of *the*; *since* is preferable to *after*
C Correct. In this sentence, the correct superlative construction is used.
D *Since* is preferable to *after*; *which had Camille* is wordy and awkward
E Inverted word order is awkward and confusing

The correct answer is C.

14. The commission has directed advertisers to restrict the use of the word "natural" to foods that do not contain color or flavor additives, chemical preservatives, or nothing that has been synthesized.

(A) or nothing that has been
(B) or that has been
(C) and nothing that is
(D) or anything that has been
(E) and anything

Idiom + logical predication

The use of *do not* and *nothing* in the same sentence creates a double negative and reverses the intended meaning. *Anything* should be used instead of *nothing*. Logically, a "natural" food cannot contain any prohibited ingredient, so the list of prohibited ingredients must be connected by *or*.

A The use of *nothing* creates a double negative
B *That has been synthesized* distorts the meaning by referring to foods, rather than to something added to a food
C The use of *nothing* creates a double negative; *and* should be *or*
D Correct. This sentence correctly avoids a double negative and uses parallel elements.
E *And* distorts the meaning of the sentence

The correct answer is D.

15. The Iroquois were primarily planters, but supplementing their cultivation of maize, squash, and beans with fishing and hunting.

(A) but supplementing
(B) and had supplemented
(C) and even though they supplemented
(D) although they supplemented
(E) but with supplementing

Grammatical construction + Verb form

The participle *supplementing* would normally be expected to modify the first clause, describing or extending its meaning, but the logic of this sentence demands a contrast, not an extension. Consequently, the second part of the sentence must be revised to emphasize the contrast properly. The logic of the sentence also argues against a construction that would set the two clauses and the importance of their content equal when they clearly should not be. The best solution is to have the main clause describe the primary activity, and a subordinate clause, *although they supplemented*, describe the supplementary activity.

A The construction using *supplementing* fails to support the intended meaning of the sentence

B *And* does not convey contrast; *had supplemented* is the past perfect tense but the simple past is required to match *were*

C *And* does not convey contrast and should be omitted; *and even though* creates a sentence fragment

D Correct. Using *although* creates a subordinate clause in this sentence and logically links that clause with the main clause; the simple past *supplemented* parallels the simple past *were.*

E *But with* is awkward and unclear; *supplementing* is a modifier when a contrasting clause is needed

The correct answer is D.

16. As contrasted with the honeybee, the yellow jacket can sting repeatedly without dying and carries a potent venom that can cause intense pain.

(A) As contrasted with the honeybee
(B) In contrast to the honeybee's
(C) Unlike the sting of the honeybee
(D) Unlike that of the honeybee
(E) Unlike the honeybee

Idiom + Logical predication

The intent of the sentence is to contrast the honeybee and the yellow jacket. Correct idioms for such a contrast include *in contrast with x, y*; *in contrast to x, y*; and *unlike x, y*. In all these idioms, *x* and *y* must be grammatically and logically parallel. *As contrasted with* is not a correct idiom.

A *As contrasted with* is not a correct idiom

B Because of its apostrophe, *the honeybee's* is not parallel to *the yellow jacket*

C *The sting of the honeybee* is not parallel to *the yellow jacket*

D *That of the honeybee* is not parallel to *the yellow jacket*

E Correct. This sentence uses a correct idiom, and *the honeybee* is properly parallel to *the yellow jacket.*

The correct answer is E.

17. None of the attempts to specify the causes of crime explains why most of the people exposed to the alleged causes do not commit crimes and, conversely, why so many of those not so exposed have.

(A) have
(B) has
(C) shall
(D) do
(E) could

Grammatical construction + Parallelism

The sentence compares one group of people, *most of the people exposed to the alleged causes*, with another group of people, *so many of those not so exposed.* To maintain the comparison, the verb in the second part should match the verb in the first part. Since the first verb is *do not commit*, the second verb should be the parallel *do.* There is no need to repeat *commit crimes* since it is understood in this construction.

A Verb should be *do*, not *have*

B Verb should be *do*, not *has*

C Verb should be *do*, not *shall*

D Correct. This sentence correctly uses the verb *do* to complete the comparison and maintain the parallelism with *do not commit.*

E Verb should be *do*, not *could*

The correct answer is D.

18. Computers are becoming faster, more powerful, and more reliable, and so too are modems, they are the devices to allow two or more computers to share information over regular telephone lines.

(A) so too are modems, they are the devices to allow
(B) so too are modems, the devices that allow
(C) so too modems, the devices allowing
(D) also modems, they are the devices that allow
(E) also modems, which are the devices to allow

Grammatical construction + Rhetorical construction

The structure of the first main clause and the comma following *reliable* lead the reader to expect a second main clause. The clause *so too are modems* correctly fulfills this expectation. However, the clause introduced by *they are* is another main clause, and its inclusion creates a run-on sentence. *To allow* is not an idiomatic way to modify *devices*; either *that allow* or *allowing* would be correct.

A *They are* creates a run-on sentence; *to allow* is not an appropriate way to modify *the devices*
B Correct. This sentence provides a correct main clause; *that allow* is an appropriate way to modify *the devices.*
C Verb *are* is necessary to make this a main clause
D Use of *also* is awkward, ungrammatical, and confusing; the reader is initially led to think that computers are also becoming modems, but this is clearly not the intended meaning of the sentence
E *Also* should again be replaced by a clause; *to allow* does not correctly modify *devices*

The correct answer is B.

19. In virtually all types of tissue in every animal species, dioxin induces the production of enzymes that are the organism's trying to metabolize, or render harmless, the chemical that is irritating it.

(A) trying to metabolize, or render harmless, the chemical that is irritating it
(B) trying that it metabolize, or render harmless, the chemical irritant
(C) attempt to try to metabolize, or render harmless, such a chemical irritant
(D) attempt to try and metabolize, or render harmless, the chemical irritating it
(E) attempt to metabolize, or render harmless, the chemical irritant

Diction

The *–ing* form of a verb can be used as a noun (e.g., *Running* is her favorite sport.), but it is often awkward, particularly when used with a possessive, as in this case. Substituting the noun *attempt* for the gerund *trying* eliminates the problem. While *chemical that is irritating it* and *chemical irritating it* are both grammatically correct, they are excessively wordy.

A *Trying* is awkward, especially as the object of *organism's*
B *Trying that it metabolize* is ungrammatical
C *Attempt to try* is redundant
D *Attempt to try and* is redundant
E Correct. In this sentence, the noun *attempt* replaces the gerund *trying* as the object of *organism's.*

The correct answer is E.

20. Based on accounts of various ancient writers, scholars have painted a sketchy picture of the activities of an all-female cult that, perhaps as early as the sixth century BC, worshipped a goddess known in Latin as Bona Dea, "the good goddess."

(A) Based on accounts of various ancient writers
(B) Basing it on various ancient writers' accounts
(C) With accounts of various ancient writers used for a basis
(D) By the accounts of various ancient writers they used
(E) Using accounts of various ancient writers

Logical predication

The underlined phrase is a modifier; it is used as an adjective to describe the noun that immediately follows it. In this case, the phrase incorrectly modifies *scholars*, which does not make any sense. What are the scholars doing? When the modifier begins with *using*, it correctly links the scholars with the modifier that describes their activity.

A *Based on* ... incorrectly modifies *scholars*
B The pronoun *it* does not have a clear reference
C This choice is wordy and awkward
D This choice is wordy and awkward
E **Correct.** In this sentence, *using accounts of various writers* correctly modifies *scholars* in a clear and concise expression of their activity.

The correct answer is E.

21. Paleontologists believe that fragments of a primate jawbone unearthed in Burma and estimated <u>at 40 to 44 million years old provide evidence of</u> a crucial step along the evolutionary path that led to human beings.

(A) at 40 to 44 million years old provide evidence of
(B) as being 40 to 44 million years old provides evidence of
(C) that it is 40 to 44 million years old provides evidence of what was
(D) to be 40 to 44 million years old provide evidence of
(E) as 40 to 44 million years old provides evidence of what was

Idiom + Agreement

The verb *estimated* must be followed by the infinitive *to be*, not the preposition *at*. The fragments *were estimated to be* a certain age. The plural subject *fragments* requires the plural verb *provide*.

A *Estimated* is incorrectly followed by *at*
B *Estimated* should be followed by *to be*, not *as being*; the singular verb *provides* incorrectly follows the plural subject *fragments*
C Introducing a clause, *that it is* ..., creates an ungrammatical sentence; the singular verb *provides* does not agree with the plural subject *fragments*
D **Correct.** In this sentence, the verb *estimated* is correctly followed by the infinitive *to be*.
E *Estimated* is incorrectly followed by *as*; the singular verb *provides* does not match the plural subject *fragments*

The correct answer is D.

22. The end of the eighteenth century saw the emergence of prize-stock breeding, with individual bulls and cows receiving awards, fetching unprecedented prices, and <u>excited</u> enormous interest whenever they were put on show.

(A) excited
(B) it excited
(C) exciting
(D) would excite
(E) it had excited

Parallelism

The bulls and cows are described in a series of participial phrases. Items in a series should be parallel: *receiving awards* is parallel to *fetching unprecedented prices*, but *excited* must be changed to *exciting* to make the third phrase, *exciting enormous interest*, parallel to the first two.

A *Excited* is not parallel to *receiving* and *fetching*
B Unclear referent for *it*; sentence construction relying on the introduction of a new independent clause is awkward and creates new errors in the first sentence; *it excited* is not parallel to *receiving* and *fetching*
C **Correct.** In this sentence, *exciting* is parallel to *receiving* and *fetching*.
D *Would excite* is not parallel to *receiving* and *fetching*
E Unclear referent for *it*; sentence construction relying on the introduction of a new independent clause is awkward and creates new errors in the first sentence; *it had excited* is not parallel to *receiving* and *fetching*

The correct answer is C.

23. Of all the possible disasters that threaten American agriculture, the possibility of an adverse change in climate is maybe the more difficult for analysis.

(A) is maybe the more difficult for analysis
(B) is probably the most difficult to analyze
(C) is maybe the most difficult for analysis
(D) is probably the more difficult to analyze
(E) is, it may be, the analysis that is most difficult

Idiom

This sentence compares *an adverse change in climate* to *all* possible disasters, so the superlative form *most difficult* must be used in place of the comparative form *more difficult.* The sentence also uses two incorrect idioms: *maybe* should be replaced by *probably*, and the adjective *difficult* should be followed by the infinitive *to analyze* rather than the phrase *for analysis.*

A *Maybe* must be replaced by *probably, more* by *most*, and *for analysis* by *to analyze*
B Correct. All three idioms are used correctly, clarifying the meaning of the sentence.
C *Maybe* must be replaced by *probably* and *for analysis* by *to analyze*
D *More* must be replaced by the superlative form *most*
E *It may be* is wordy and must be replaced by *probably*; *the analysis that is the most difficult* is wordy, awkward, and unclear

The correct answer is B.

24. For members of the seventeenth-century Ashanti nation in Africa, animal-hide shields with wooden frames were essential items of military equipment, a method to protect warriors against enemy arrows and spears.

(A) a method to protect
(B) as a method protecting
(C) protecting
(D) as a protection of
(E) to protect

Logical predication + rhetorical construction

The underlined part of the sentence begins a phrase describing *items of military equipment.* It is awkward and inaccurate to describe *items* as *a method.* Replacing the underlined phrase with the participle *protecting* creates a modifying phrase that clearly explains the purpose of the *items of military equipment.*

A *A method to protect* is an awkward reference to *items*
B The singular *a method* should not refer to the plural *items*; *as a method protecting* is not idiomatic
C Correct. In this sentence, *protecting* properly introduces a modifying phrase revealing the purpose of the *items.*
D Beginning the phrase with *as* is incorrect; using the noun form *protection* creates wordiness
E The infinitive *to protect* cannot act as an adjective modifying *items*; the participial form of the verb, *protecting*, is required

The correct answer is C.

25. The golden crab of the Gulf of Mexico has not been fished commercially in great numbers, primarily on account of living at great depths—2,500 to 3,000 feet down.

(A) on account of living
(B) on account of their living
(C) because it lives
(D) because of living
(E) being they live

Diction

The second part of the sentence explains the first: the crab is not fished *because* it lives at great depths. The clearest and most direct way of showing the relationship between the two parts of the sentence is to use *because* to introduce a subordinate clause.

A *On account of living* is awkward and wordy
B *On account of* is awkward and wordy; *their* does not agree with *crab*

C **Correct.** Using *because* to introduce a subordinate clause is the best way to show the effect-cause relation of the two parts of this sentence.
D *Because of living* is not the correct idiom
E *Being* is neither logical nor idiomatic; *they* does not agree with *crab*

The correct sentence is C.

26. Galileo was convinced that natural phenomena, as manifestations of the laws of physics, would appear the same to someone on the deck of a ship moving smoothly and uniformly through the water as a person standing on land.

(A) water as a
(B) water as to a
(C) water; just as it would to a
(D) water, as it would to the
(E) water; just as to the

Idiom + Parallelism

The second part of this sentence is a comparison. The correct, parallel, and idiomatic structure makes the comparison clear. In this case, a phenomenon appears *the same to x as to y*, or *the same to someone… as to a person.* The two parts of the comparison must be parallel.

A The omission of the preposition *to* violates both the idiom and the parallelism
B **Correct.** The sentence uses the correct idiom … *the same to someone … as to a person.* The two parts of the comparison are parallel.
C The use of a semicolon creates a sentence fragment
D The idiom is *the same to x as to y*, but this change would make it incorrect: *the same to x, as it would be to y*
E The use of a semicolon introduces a sentence fragment

The correct answer is B.

27. Health officials estimate that 35 million Africans are in danger of contracting trypanosomiasis, or "African sleeping sickness," a parasitic disease spread by the bites of tsetse flies.

(A) are in danger of contracting
(B) are in danger to contract
(C) have a danger of contracting
(D) are endangered by contraction
(E) have a danger that they will contract

Idiom

This sentence depends on the correct idiomatic expression: *are in danger* is always followed by *of.*

A **Correct.** In this sentence, the correct idiom is used in the expression *are in danger of contracting.*
B *Are in danger* must be followed by *of*, not the infinitive
C *Have a danger* is not the correct idiom
D This wordy passive voice construction cannot be followed by *trypanosomiasis*
E *Have a danger* is not the correct idiom; the structure is wordy and ungrammatical

The correct answer is A.

28. Beyond the immediate cash flow crisis that the museum faces, its survival depends on if it can broaden its membership and leave its cramped quarters for a site where it can store and exhibit its more than 12,000 artifacts.

(A) if it can broaden its membership and leave
(B) whether it can broaden its membership and leave
(C) whether or not it has the capability to broaden its membership and can leave
(D) its ability for broadening its membership and leaving
(E) the ability for it to broaden its membership and leave

Idiom

This sentence requires the correct use of an idiom; *depends on* must be followed by *whether*, not *if.*

A *Depends on if* is not a correct idiomatic expression
B **Correct.** *Depends on whether* is the correct idiom to use in this sentence.
C Adding *it has the capability to* creates an unnecessarily wordy construction
D *Its ability* should be followed by *to broaden*, not *for broadening*
E *The ability for it to broaden* is wordy, awkward, and ungrammatical

The correct answer is B.

29. Along with the drop in producer prices announced yesterday, the strong retail sales figures released today seem like it is indicative that the economy, although growing slowly, is not nearing a recession.

(A) like it is indicative that
(B) as if to indicate
(C) to indicate that
(D) indicative of
(E) like an indication of

Idiom

This sentence depends on the correct use of an idiom. The verb *seem* should be followed by an infinitive, *to indicate*; the relative pronoun *that* introduces a clause. Subordinate clauses, such as the one that completes this sentence, can be introduced by a relative pronoun (*who, which, that*) or by a conjunction, but never by a preposition (*like*).

A The preposition *like* cannot introduce a clause
B The verb *seem* may be followed by *as if* in some contexts, but here the result is an ungrammatical and illogical construction
C **Correct.** In this sentence, the verb *seem* is correctly followed by the infinitive *to indicate*, and the pronoun *that* correctly introduces a clause.
D The adjective *indicative of* cannot introduce a clause
E The preposition *like* cannot introduce a clause; *an indication of* is wordy

The correct answer is C.

30. An inventory equal to 90 days sales is as much as even the strongest businesses carry, and then only as a way to anticipate higher prices or ensure against shortages.

(A) as much as even
(B) so much as even
(C) even so much as
(D) even as much that
(E) even so much that

Idiom

The sentence depends on the correct use of the idiom *as much as* to indicate comparison: *they like x as much as y*. *Not so much as* is another idiom used only in the negative: *not so much as a whisper was heard from the crowd*. In this sentence, the adverb *even* modifies *the strongest businesses* and must come just before it.

A **Correct.** This sentence uses the correct idiom, *as much as*, and maintains the proper placement of the modifier *even*.
B *So much as* is not the correct idiom
C *Even* must be next to *the strongest businesses*; *so much as* is an incorrect idiom
D *Even* must be next to *the strongest businesses*; *as much that* is an incorrect idiom
E *Even* must be next to *the strongest businesses*; *so much that* is an incorrect idiom

The correct answer is A.

31. Egyptians are credited as having pioneered embalming methods as long ago as 2650 BC.

(A) as having
(B) with having
(C) to have
(D) as the ones who
(E) for being the ones who

Idiom

The verb *to credit* can be used in a number of ways. This sentence depends on the correct use of the idiom *to credit x with*.

A *The Egyptians are regarded as having* would be correct, but *credit* requires *with*
B **Correct.** *The Egyptians are credited with having* is the correct idiom for this sentence.
C *The Egyptians are believed to have* would be correct, but *credit* requires *with*
D This alternative is unnecessarily wordy; *credit* requires *with*
E This alternative is awkward and wordy; *credit* requires *with*

The correct answer is B.

32. The Commerce Department announced that the economy grew during the second quarter at a 7.5 percent annual rate, while inflation eased when it might have been expected for it to rise.

(A) it might have been expected for it to rise
(B) it might have been expected to rise
(C) it might have been expected that it should rise
(D) its rise might have been expected
(E) there might have been an expectation it would rise

Idiom

The correct idiomatic expression is *x is expected to y*. In this sentence, the construction must remain idiomatic even when a different tense is used: *might have been expected to rise.*

A *For it to rise* does not complete the idiomatic expression correctly
B Correct. In this sentence, *to rise* completes the idiom correctly.
C *That it should rise* does not complete the idiomatic expression correctly
D *Its rise* is not parallel to *inflation* and introduces an awkward clause
E This construction is unnecessarily wordy

The correct answer is B.

33. Although schistosomiasis is not often fatal, it is so debilitating that it has become an economic drain on many developing countries.

(A) it is so debilitating that it has become an economic
(B) it is of such debilitation, it has become an economical
(C) so debilitating is it as to become an economic
(D) such is its debilitation, it becomes an economical
(E) there is so much debilitation that it has become an economical

Idiom

This sentence correctly uses the idiomatic construction *so x that y* where *y* is a subordinate clause that explains or describes *x*: *so debilitating that it has become … It* clearly refers to *schistosomiasis*, which is correctly modified by the adjective *debilitating.*

A Correct. In this sentence, the pronoun reference is clear, and the *so x that y* construction is concise.
B The noun *debilitation* creates an awkward, wordy alternative; the subordinate clause is not introduced by *that*; *economical* does not have the same meaning as *economic*
C The construction *so x as to y* is not a correct idiom
D The construction introduced by *such* is awkward and wordy; *that* is omitted; *economical* does not have the same meaning as *economic*
E The noun *debilitation* creates an awkward, wordy alternative; *economical* does not have the same meaning as *economic*

The correct answer is A.

34. Efforts to equalize the funds available to school districts, a major goal of education reformers and many states in the 1970's, has not significantly reduced the gaps existing between the richest and poorest districts.

(A) has not significantly reduced the gaps existing
(B) has not been significant in reducing the gap that exists
(C) has not made a significant reduction in the gap that exists
(D) have not significantly reduced the gap that exists
(E) have not been significant in a reduction of the gaps existing

Agreement

The plural subject of this sentence, *efforts*, does not agree with the singular verb *has … reduced. Efforts* requires the plural verb *have reduced.*

A *Has reduced* does not agree with *efforts*
B Subject and verb do not agree; changes make the construction wordy
C *Efforts* does not agree with *has reduced*; *made a significant reduction in* is wordy
D Correct. In this clear, concise sentence, *efforts* agrees with the plural verb *have … reduced.*
E This alternative is wordy and awkward

The correct answer is D.

35. Federal authorities involved in the investigation have found the local witnesses are difficult to locate, reticent, and are suspicious of strangers.

(A) the local witnesses are difficult to locate, reticent, and are
(B) local witnesses to be difficult to locate, reticent, and are
(C) that local witnesses are difficult to locate, reticent, and
(D) local witnesses are difficult to locate and reticent, and they are
(E) that local witnesses are difficult to locate and reticent, and they are

Grammatical construction + Parallelism

The underlined part of the sentence is a clause that must be introduced by the conjunction *that.* The witnesses are described in a series of three adjectives, or complements, each of which must be parallel; the witnesses are *difficult to locate, reticent,* and *suspicious of strangers.*

A *That* is omitted; the three elements in the series are not parallel
B The clause requires *that*; the three complements in the series are not parallel
C **Correct.** *That* introduces the clause in this sentence; the series of complements is parallel.
D *That* is incorrectly omitted; the three complements in the series are not parallel
E A parallel series should be *x, y, and z,* not *x and y and they are z*

The correct answer is C.

36. In 1527 King Henry VIII sought to have his marriage to Queen Catherine annulled so as to marry Anne Boleyn.

(A) so as to marry
(B) and so could be married to
(C) to be married to
(D) so that he could marry
(E) in order that he would marry

Grammatical construction

This sentence uses the construction *x happened so that y could happen*; *so* introduces a clause of purpose or result, explaining the reason for the action in the main clause. *Henry … sought to have his marriage … annulled so that he could marry Anne Boleyn.* The relationship between the two clauses is clear.

A *So as to marry* is not idiomatically correct; it does not identify who will marry
B This alternative is ungrammatical and illogical: Henry could not marry simply on the basis of seeking an annulment
C The infinitive must be preceded by a conjunction (*in order*); *to marry* is preferable to the wordier *to be married to*
D **Correct.** This sentence's construction clearly shows the reason that Henry sought an annulment.
E *In order that* is followed by *may* or *might*; the conditional *would marry* is incorrect

The correct answer is D.

37. In one of the bloodiest battles of the Civil War, fought at Sharpsburg, Maryland, on September 17, 1862, four times as many Americans were killed as would later be killed on the beaches of Normandy during D-Day.

(A) Americans were killed as
(B) Americans were killed than
(C) Americans were killed than those who
(D) more Americans were killed as there
(E) more Americans were killed as those who

Idiom

This sentence correctly compares the number of Americans killed in two battles. The comparison is expressed using the idiom *as many … as.*

A **Correct.** The sentence correctly uses the idiom *as many … as* to compare the number of Americans killed on September 17, 1862, and on D-Day. The correct idiom for comparison showing equality is *as many … as.*
B *As many … than* is incorrect
C *As many … than* is incorrect; *those who* is wordy

D *More* is redundant; *there* is unnecessary
E *More* is redundant; *those who* is wordy

The correct answer is A.

38. Dr. Tonegawa won the Nobel Prize for discovering how the body can constantly change its genes to fashion a seeming unlimited number of antibodies, each specifically targeted at an invading microbe or foreign substance.

(A) seeming unlimited number of antibodies, each specifically targeted at
(B) seeming unlimited number of antibodies, each targeted specifically to
(C) seeming unlimited number of antibodies, all specifically targeted at
(D) seemingly unlimited number of antibodies, all of them targeted specifically to
(E) seemingly unlimited number of antibodies, each targeted specifically at

Diction

Adjectives modify nouns and pronouns. Adverbs modify adjectives, verbs, and other adverbs. The adverb *seemingly*, not the adjective *seeming*, should be used to modify the adjective *unlimited*. The idiomatic form to be used here is *targeted … at* rather than *targeted … to*. Logic requires that *each* antibody is meant to deal individually with *an invading microbe or foreign substance*.

A The adjective *seeming* should instead be the adverb *seemingly*
B The adjective *seeming* should be the adverb *seemingly*; the preposition following *targeted* must be *at*, not *to*
C The adjective *seeming* should instead be the adverb *seemingly*; the use of *all* instead of *each* does not make sense
D Preposition following *targeted* must be *at*, not *to*; the use of *all* instead of *each* does not make sense
E **Correct.** This sentence correctly uses *seemingly* instead of *seeming*, *at* instead of *to*, and *each* instead of *all*.

The correct answer is E.

39. Scientists have recently discovered what could be the largest and oldest living organism on Earth, a giant fungus that is an interwoven filigree of mushrooms and rootlike tentacles spawned by a single fertilized spore some 10,000 years ago and extending for more than 30 acres in the soil of a Michigan forest.

(A) extending
(B) extends
(C) extended
(D) it extended
(E) is extending

Parallelism + Verb form

The original sentence is correctly written. The giant fungus is described as an *interwoven filigree spawned … some 10,000 years ago and extending for more than 30 acres*. The present participle *extending* parallels the past participle *spawned*.

A **Correct.** This sentence has the participles *spawned* and *extending* in a correct parallel construction. *Spawned* refers to something that happened in the past, while *extending* refers to something that continues into the present.
B *Extends* is a present tense verb, not the participle needed for parallel structure; the ostensible parallel between *extends* and the distant verb *is* is superficial and would result in an awkward and unclear sentence
C *Extended* looks parallel to *spawned*, but this phrase would mean that the fungus extended only in the past when the fungus clearly lives on in the present
D *It extended* is not parallel to *spawned* and indicates an event completed in the past
E *Is extending* is the progressive form of the present tense verb, not the participle required for parallelism

The correct answer is A.

40. The plot of *The Bostonians* centers on the rivalry between Olive Chancellor, an active feminist, with her charming and cynical cousin, Basil Ransom, when they find themselves drawn to the same radiant young woman whose talent for public speaking has won her an ardent following.

(A) rivalry between Olive Chancellor, an active feminist, with her charming and cynical cousin, Basil Ransom
(B) rivals Olive Chancellor, an active feminist, against her charming and cynical cousin, Basil Ransom
(C) rivalry that develops between Olive Chancellor, an active feminist, and Basil Ransom, her charming and cynical cousin
(D) developing rivalry between Olive Chancellor, an active feminist, with Basil Ransom, her charming and cynical cousin
(E) active feminist, Olive Chancellor, and the rivalry with her charming and cynical cousin Basil Ransom

Idiom

Olive Chancellor and Basil Ransom are rivals. The situation can be expressed with the construction *the rivalry between x and y* or the construction *the rivals x and y*. The construction *rivalry between ... with* is incorrect.

A *With* is incorrect in the construction *the rivalry between x and y*
B *Against* is incorrect in the construction *the rivals x and y*
C Correct. This sentence uses the construction *the rivalry between x and y* correctly; it also clearly identifies both parties in the rivalry.
D *With* is incorrect in the construction *the rivalry between x and y*
E This sentence does not make it clear that *Olive* is a party to the rivalry

The correct answer is C.

41. While larger banks can afford to maintain their own data-processing operations, many smaller regional and community banks are finding that the cost associated with upgrading data-processing equipment and with the development and maintenance of new products and technical staff are prohibitive.

(A) cost associated with
(B) costs associated with
(C) costs arising from
(D) cost of
(E) costs of

Agreement + Parallelism

What *are prohibitive*? For the sake of subject-verb agreement, the plural noun *costs* must be used rather than the singular *cost*: *the costs ... are prohibitive*. The phrase *associated with* is required to complete the parallel construction *costs associated with upgrading ... and with the development of....*

A The singular *cost* does not agree with the plural verb *are*
B Correct. The plural noun *costs* agrees with the plural verb *are*; using *costs associated with* means that *with upgrading* is parallel to *with the development*.
C *From upgrading* is not parallel to *with the development of*
D The singular *cost* does not agree with the plural verb *are*; *of upgrading* is not parallel to *with the development of*
E *Of upgrading* is not parallel to *with the development of*

The correct answer is B.

42. Quasars, at billions of light-years from Earth the most distant observable objects in the universe, believed to be the cores of galaxies in an early stage of development.

(A) believed to be
(B) are believed to be
(C) some believe them to be
(D) some believe they are
(E) it is believed that they are

Grammatical construction

The original sentence is not actually a sentence; it is a sentence fragment because it lacks a verb. The verb *are* must be placed before *believed to be* to create a complete sentence.

A This sentence fragment lacks a verb
B Correct. The verb *are believed to be* grammatically completes the sentence and connects *quasars* to *cores*.
C The clause *some believe them to be* does not supply a verb to complete the sentence
D The clause *some believe they are* does not supply a verb to complete the sentence
E The clause *it is believed that they are* does not supply a verb to complete the sentence

The correct answer is B.

43. Five fledgling sea eagles left their nests in western Scotland this summer, <u>bringing</u> to 34 the number of wild birds successfully raised since transplants from Norway began in 1975.

(A) bringing
(B) and brings
(C) and it brings
(D) and it brought
(E) and brought

Verb form + Grammatical construction

Bringing is the present participle of the verb *to bring*. As used here, it correctly describes an action that happens at the same time as the action in the main clause; *bringing* indicates that the number of wild birds became 34 when the five eagles left their nests.

A Correct. The participle *bringing* correctly links the two ideas in the sentence.
B In this construction, the subject of the second verb must be the same as the subject of the first verb, but *five eagles* cannot grammatically or logically be the subject of *brings*
C There is no referent for *it*
D There is no referent for *it*
E *Five eagles* can be the grammatical subject of *brought*, but not the logical one; it was not the eagles themselves but rather the entire action of their leaving their nests that brought the number to 34

The correct answer is A.

44. The automotive conveyor-belt system, which Henry Ford modeled after an assembly-line technique introduced by Ransom Olds, reduced <u>from a day and a half to 93 minutes the required time of assembling a Model T</u>.

(A) from a day and a half to 93 minutes the required time of assembling a Model T
(B) the time being required to assemble a Model T, from a day and a half down to 93 minutes
(C) the time being required to assemble a Model T, a day and a half to 93 minutes
(D) the time required to assemble a Model T from a day and a half to 93 minutes
(E) from a day and a half to 93 minutes, the time required for the assembling of a Model T

Rhetorical construction + Idiom

The underlined portion of the original sentence is awkward because the verb *reduced* is followed by a prepositional phrase rather than the direct object *time*. Changing this structure so that the object immediately follows the verb, *reduced the time*, also allows an idiomatic error to be corrected. *Required* should be followed by an infinitive, *to assemble*, rather than a prepositional phrase, *of assembling*. The phrase indicating time should be used to complete the sentence: *reduced the time required to assemble a Model T from a day and a half to 93 minutes.*

A Placement of phrases creates an awkward construction; *required … of assembling* is not idiomatic
B *Being required* and *down to* are wordy constructions; the comma is unnecessary
C *Being required* is wordy; the construction *from … to* indicates time, not *to* alone
D Correct. This sentence has a clear, concise, and idiomatic construction.
E Beginning with the prepositional phrase is awkward; the comma is unnecessary; *required for the assembling of* is wordy and awkward

The correct answer is D.

45. According to some analysts, the gains in the stock market reflect growing confidence that the economy will avoid the recession that many had feared earlier in the year and instead come in for a "soft landing," followed by a gradual increase in business activity.

(A) that the economy will avoid the recession that many had feared earlier in the year and instead come
(B) in the economy to avoid the recession, what many feared earlier in the year, rather to come
(C) in the economy's ability to avoid the recession, something earlier in the year many had feared, and instead to come
(D) in the economy to avoid the recession many were fearing earlier in the year, and rather to come
(E) that the economy will avoid the recession that was feared earlier this year by many, with it instead coming

Grammatical construction + Rhetorical construction

The original sentence successfully avoids the problems that may occur in a long sentence with multiple modifiers. Two subordinate clauses begin with *that*, and one of them is contained within another. *That many had feared earlier in the year* clearly defines *the recession. That the economy will avoid… and instead* (*will* understood) *come…* is the subordinate clause that follows the main clause; its subject, *economy*, is followed by two parallel verbs, *will avoid* and (*will* understood) *come. Instead* before the second verb properly indicates contrast.

A Correct. This sentence contains two correct subordinate clauses introduced by *that.*

B *What* cannot replace *that*; *the economy to avoid the recession* is awkward and unclear; *rather to come* does not complete the second part of the sentence idiomatically

C *Earlier in the year* should follow *many had feared*, rather than preceding it; *instead to come* does not complete the second part of the sentence idiomatically

D *The recession* must be followed by *that*; *were fearing* is the wrong tense; *rather to come* does not complete the second part of the sentence idiomatically

E The passive voice construction *that was feared…* is weak and wordy; *with it instead coming* is awkward, wordy, and ungrammatical

The correct answer is A.

46. To Josephine Baker, Paris was her home long before it was fashionable to be an expatriate, and she remained in France during the Second World War as a performer and an intelligence agent for the Resistance.

(A) To Josephine Baker, Paris was her home long before it was fashionable to be an expatriate
(B) For Josephine Baker, long before it was fashionable to be an expatriate, Paris was her home
(C) Josephine Baker made Paris her home long before to be an expatriate was fashionable
(D) Long before it was fashionable to be an expatriate, Josephine Baker made Paris her home
(E) Long before it was fashionable being an expatriate, Paris was home to Josephine Baker

Rhetorical construction

This compound sentence (consisting of two independent clauses joined by the coordinating conjunction *and*) would be most clearly expressed if Josephine Baker were the subject of the first clause since *she* is the subject of the second clause: *Josephine Baker made Paris her home* would clearly parallel *she remained in France.* The adverb clause *long… expatriate* is best placed before the main clause.

A *To Josephine Baker… her* is redundant and awkward; the subject of the first main clause is *Paris* rather than *Baker*

B *For Josephine Baker… her* is redundant and awkward; putting two introductory elements together before the main clause is awkward

C Inversion of the expected word order in *to be an expatriate was unfashionable* is awkward

D Correct. The clearest, most economical order for this sentence is to put the adverb clause first, and make *Baker* the subject of the first main clause, parallel to *she* in the second.

E *Being* is awkward; *Baker* should be the subject of the first main clause, parallel to *she* in the second main clause

The correct answer is D.

47. By providing such services as mortgages, home improvement loans, automobile loans, financial advice, and staying within the metropolitan areas, Acme Bank has become one of the most profitable savings banks in the nation.

(A) financial advice, and staying
(B) financial advice, and by staying
(C) and financial advice, staying
(D) and financial advice, and staying
(E) and financial advice, and by staying

Grammatical construction + Parallelism

The first part of the sentence describes the two reasons for Acme Bank's success; those reasons should be written in two parallel phrases: *by providing such services as … advice* and *by staying within metropolitan areas.* When *by* is dropped, *staying* seems to be part of the list of services. *Staying* also appears to be the final element in a series because four elements have preceded it, each correctly separated with a comma, followed by the conjunction *and*, which makes the reader anticipate a final element. The list should read: *mortgages, home improvement loans, automobile loans, and financial advice.*

A *Staying* is not parallel to *by providing*; the final element in a series should be preceded by *and*

B Final element in a series should be preceded by *and*

C *Staying* is not parallel to *by providing*; a second *and* is needed to join the two phrases *by providing* … and *by staying* …

D *Staying* is not parallel to *by providing*

E **Correct.** In this sentence, the final element in the series is properly preceded by *and*; the two phrases *by providing* … and *by staying* … are parallel and correctly joined by *and*.

The correct answer is E.

48. The report recommended that the hospital should eliminate unneeded beds, expensive services should be consolidated, and use space in other hospitals.

(A) should eliminate unneeded beds, expensive services should be consolidated, and use space in other hospitals
(B) should eliminate unneeded beds, expensive services should be consolidated, and other hospitals' space be used
(C) should eliminate unneeded beds, expensive services should be consolidated, and to use space in other hospitals
(D) eliminate unneeded beds, consolidate expensive services, and other hospitals' space used
(E) eliminate unneeded beds, consolidate expensive services, and use space in other hospitals

Grammatical construction + Parallelism

The underlined portion of the sentence is incoherent and runs together two sentences (*the hospital should eliminate unneeded beds*; *expensive services should be consolidated*). Making the report's three recommendations into a series of three grammatically parallel elements corrects this problem. Since the report *recommended*, it is redundant to use *should*. Each of the three parallel elements may consist of a verb and an object: (1) *eliminate unneeded beds*, (2) *consolidate expensive services*, and (3) *use space in other hospitals.*

A Incoherent construction includes a run-on sentence; following *recommended*, *should* is redundant

B Following *recommended*, *should* is redundant; the three elements in the series are not parallel

C Following *recommended*, *should* is redundant; the second and third elements are not parallel to the first

D *Other hospitals' space used* is awkward and not parallel to the other two elements

E **Correct.** In this concise sentence, each of the three parallel elements in the series consists of a verb and an object.

The correct answer is E.

49. Many house builders offer rent-to-buy programs that enable a family with insufficient savings for a conventional down payment to be able to move into new housing and to apply part of the rent to a purchase later.

(A) programs that enable a family with insufficient savings for a conventional down payment to be able to move into new housing and to apply
(B) programs that enable a family with insufficient savings for a conventional down payment to move into new housing and to apply
(C) programs; that enables a family with insufficient savings for a conventional down payment to move into new housing, to apply
(D) programs, which enables a family with insufficient savings for a conventional down payment to move into new housing, applying
(E) programs, which enable a family with insufficient savings for a conventional down payment to be able to move into new housing, applying

Rhetorical construction

In a lengthy sentence consisting of many phrases, it is essential to determine which phrases and words are necessary to the sentence and which words may be eliminated because they are unnecessary. The relative pronoun *that* correctly refers to *programs* and introduces the subordinate clause; *family* is followed by two phrases that are clear and correct. *To be able to move*, however, is needlessly wordy, repeating the meaning of *enable*, and can be reduced to *to move*. This creates a parallel construction in which *programs* ... *enable a family* ... *to move* ... *and to apply*.

A *To be able to move* is wordy; *to apply* is not logically parallel to the infinitive phrase *(able) to move*

B **Correct.** In this sentence, eliminating the wordy construction *to be able* allows *to move* to be parallel to *to apply*.

C Using a semicolon here causes *that* to refer too broadly to the entire previous clause rather than specifically to *programs*; the two infinitives should be joined by the conjunction *and*, not separated by a comma

D The restrictive clause following *programs* defines *programs* and must be followed by *that*; *which* incorrectly introduces a nonrestrictive clause, set off in a pair of commas, containing relevant but not critical information; *enables* does not agree with the plural subject

E *That* introduces a restrictive clause that defines *programs*; *which* introduces a nonrestrictive clause, set off by a pair of commas, that may be dropped from the sentence; *that* is required here because the clause defines *programs*

The correct answer is B.

50. That educators have not anticipated the impact of microcomputer technology can hardly be said that it is their fault: Alvin Toffler, one of the most prominent students of the future, did not even mention microcomputers in *Future Shock*, published in 1970.

(A) That educators have not anticipated the impact of microcomputer technology can hardly be said that it is their fault
(B) That educators have not anticipated the impact of microcomputer technology can hardly be said to be at fault
(C) It can hardly be said that it is the fault of educators who have not anticipated the impact of microcomputer technology
(D) It can hardly be said that educators are at fault for not anticipating the impact of microcomputer technology
(E) The fact that educators are at fault for not anticipating the impact of microcomputer technology can hardly be said

Grammatical construction

Although it is possible to begin a sentence with a subordinate clause beginning with *that*, this inverted construction often results in errors such as those found here. In the original sentence, the subordinate clause *that … technology* is followed by the main verb, *can … be said*, but then the verb is followed by yet another subordinate clause, *that it is their fault*. The best way to solve this problem is by putting the sentence in the expected order, with the main clause (*It can hardly be said*) preceding the subordinate clause (*that …*). For greater clarity and concision, the two subordinate clauses should be condensed into one: *educators are at fault for not anticipating the impact of microcomputer technology*.

A Inverting the usual order results in an ungrammatical construction in which the main verb is both preceded and followed by a subordinate clause
B *Can hardly be said to be at fault* does not grammatically complete the subordinate clause
C Construction *that it is … who have not* is wordy and awkward; it also distorts meaning and lacks completion
D Correct. This sentence has the main clause followed by one subordinate clause correctly introduced by *that*.
E *The fact* is wordy; the inverted construction does not successfully convey the meaning of the sentence

The correct answer is D.

51. The Olympic Games helped to keep peace among the pugnacious states of the Greek <u>world in that a sacred truce was proclaimed during the festival's month</u>.

(A) world in that a sacred truce was proclaimed during the festival's month
(B) world, proclaiming a sacred truce during the festival's month
(C) world when they proclaimed a sacred truce for the festival month
(D) world, for a sacred truce was proclaimed during the month of the festival
(E) world by proclamation of a sacred truce that was for the month of the festival

Idiom + Rhetorical construction

This sentence depends on using the correct conjunction to join two independent clauses. *In that* is a conjunction that means inasmuch as; because *in that* has largely gone out of use, it is considered stilted and overly formal. It also uses two words when one would do. In this sentence, the second clause explains the first one, so the conjunction *for*, meaning because, is the most appropriate choice for joining the two independent clauses of the compound sentence.

A *In that* is stilted and overly formal
B It is not clear who would be doing the *proclaiming*; a clause is preferable to a phrase here
C *They* is ambiguous, possibly referring to either the *states* or the *Games*
D Correct. In this sentence, the conjunction *for* joins the two clauses correctly and economically.
E Wordy and awkward construction

The correct answer is D.

52. While all states face similar industrial waste problems, the predominating industries and the regulatory environment of the states obviously determines the types and amounts of waste produced, as well as the cost of disposal.

(A) all states face similar industrial waste problems, the predominating industries and the regulatory environment of the states obviously determines
(B) each state faces a similar industrial waste problem, their predominant industries and regulatory environment obviously determine
(C) all states face a similar industrial waste problem; their predominating industries and regulatory environment obviously determines
(D) each state faces similar industrial waste problems, the predominant industries and the regulatory environment of each state obviously determines
(E) all states face similar industrial waste problems, the predominant industries and the regulatory environment of each state obviously determine

Agreement + Idiom

This sentence requires careful attention to number and agreement. The main clause has a compound subject, *the predominating industries and the regulatory environment*, which must take a plural verb, *determine*, rather than the singular verb shown in the original sentence. The sentence begins with the conjunction *while*, here used to mean *although*, and contrasts the similar situation of *all states* with the varying conditions of *each state*. *The regulatory environment* is singular and must logically be completed by *of each state* rather than *of the states*; the point of the main clause is that all *states* do not share the same *predominating industries* and *regulatory environment*.

A The compound subject does not agree with the singular verb *determines*; main clause should call attention to the conditions of *each state*, not *the states*
B *Each state* must be compared to all other states; *their* does not agree with *each*
C Using a semicolon results in a sentence fragment; subject and verb do not agree
D *Each state* must be compared to all other states; subject and verb do not agree
E **Correct.** This sentence makes the clear distinction between the problem *all states* share and the conditions *each state* faces; subject and verb agree.

The correct answer is E.

53. Section 13(d) of the Securities Exchange Act of 1934 requires anyone who buys more than 5 percent of a company's stock make a public disclosure of the purchase.

(A) make
(B) will also make
(C) to make
(D) must make
(E) must then make

Idiom

The verb *require* may be followed by an object (*it required more time*), a relative pronoun (*the summons required that he appear*), an infinitive (*I am required to go*), or an adverb (*they are required now*). This sentence uses the idiomatic construction *require x to do y*. *Require* is used transitively, taking a direct object, *anyone*, which must be followed by the infinitive *to make*. No other verb form is acceptable.

A *Requires* must be followed by the infinitive *to make*, not the verb *make*
B *Requires* must be completed by the infinitive, not a future tense verb
C **Correct.** *Requires* is correctly completed in this sentence by the infinitive *to make.*
D *Requires* must be followed by the infinitive *to make*, not the verb *must make*
E *Requires* must be completed by *to make*, not *must then make*

The correct answer is C.

54. When Congress reconvenes, some newly elected members from rural states will try and establish tighter restrictions for the amount of grain farmers are to be allowed to grow and to encourage more aggressive sales of United States farm products overseas.

(A) and establish tighter restrictions for the amount of grain farmers are to be allowed to grow and to encourage
(B) and establish tighter restrictions on the amount of grain able to be grown by farmers and encouraging
(C) establishing tighter restrictions for the amount of grain farmers are allowed to grow and to encourage
(D) to establish tighter restrictions on the amount of grain capable of being grown by farmers and encouraging
(E) to establish tighter restrictions on the amount of grain farmers will be allowed to grow and to encourage

Idiom

This sentence requires attention to the small, linking words so often overlooked. When *will try* is used with another verb to show purpose or intent, the correct expression is *will try to*, not *will try and*. The correct preposition following *restrictions* is not *for* but *on*. *Are to be allowed to grow* is wordy; the infinitive *to be* should be omitted for a tighter and clearer expression.

A *To*, indicating purpose, should replace *and* before *establish*; *restrictions* is incorrectly followed by *for* rather than *on*; *to be* is wordy and should be omitted
B *And* before *establish* does not show purpose; the passive voice *able to be grown by* is weak and wordy; the constructions *and establish* … and *encouraging* … are not parallel
C *Will try establishing* does not show intent or purpose; *restrictions* must be followed by *on*, not *for*; parallelism is lost
D Passive voice construction *capable of being grown by* is weak and wordy; *encouraging* and *to establish* are not parallel
E **Correct.** *To establish* indicates purpose and parallels *to encourage*; *restrictions* is correctly followed by *on*; the wordiness of the verb phrase has been eliminated.

The correct answer is E.

55. Doctors generally agree that such factors as cigarette smoking, eating rich foods high in fats, and alcohol consumption <u>not only do damage by themselves but also aggravate</u> genetic predispositions toward certain diseases.

(A) not only do damage by themselves but also aggravate
(B) do damage by themselves but also are aggravating to
(C) are damaging by themselves but also are aggravating
(D) not only do damage by themselves, they are also aggravating to
(E) are doing damage by themselves, and they are also aggravating

Idiom + Logical predication

This correctly written sentence uses the construction *not only (x) … but also (y)*; *x* is the simple present verb *do damage* and *y* is the parallel verb *aggravate*. The simple present tense should be used for a general statement such as this one. When used as a verb, *aggravate* clearly means to make worse; the adjective *aggravating* is instead widely interpreted to mean *annoying*.

A **Correct.** This sentence correctly uses the *not only … but also* construction to explain the parallel effects of the factors.
B *Are aggravating to* is not parallel to *do damage; aggravating* suggests a different meaning than does *aggravate*; using *but also* without using *not only* is incorrect
C The form *are aggravating* distorts the meaning of the sentence; using *but also* without using *not only* is incorrect
D Using *not only* without using *but also* is incorrect; *are aggravating to* is not parallel to *do damage; aggravating* suggests a different meaning
E The simple present tense, rather than the present progressive, should be used to present a general statement; *aggravating* distorts meaning

The correct answer is A.

56. In a plan to stop the erosion of East Coast beaches, the Army Corps of Engineers proposed building parallel to shore a breakwater of rocks that would rise six feet above the waterline and act as a buffer, so that it absorbs the energy of crashing waves and protecting the beaches.

(A) act as a buffer, so that it absorbs
(B) act like a buffer so as to absorb
(C) act as a buffer, absorbing
(D) acting as a buffer, absorbing
(E) acting like a buffer, absorb

Parallelism + Idiom

The last part of the sentence describes the breakwater and should consist of two grammatically parallel phrases, *absorbing … and protecting*, in order to show two equal functions. *Act* is followed by *like* to mean *to behave or comport oneself* and describes the action of a person: *He acted like a fool.* Here, *act as* describes the function of a thing; *the breakwater … acts as a buffer*. As an inanimate object, a breakwater cannot "behave" itself; it must be performing some function.

A *So that it absorbs* should be *absorbing* to parallel *protecting*
B *Act as* is the proper idiom to describe things; *so as to absorb* is awkward and should be changed to *absorbing* to be parallel to *protecting*
C Correct. The idiom *act as* is used correctly in this sentence; *absorbing* is properly parallel to *protecting*.
D Modifying clause is *that would rise … and* (*would* understood) *act; acting* cannot be used instead of *act*
E Modifying clause is *that would rise … and* (*would* understood) *act; acting* cannot be used instead of *act*; *absorb* is not parallel to *protecting*

The correct answer is C.

57. Affording strategic proximity to the Strait of Gibraltar, Morocco was also of interest to the French throughout the first half of the twentieth century because they assumed that if they did not hold it, their grip on Algeria was always insecure.

(A) if they did not hold it, their grip on Algeria was always insecure
(B) without it their grip on Algeria would never be secure
(C) their grip on Algeria was not ever secure if they did not hold it
(D) without that, they could never be secure about their grip on Algeria
(E) never would their grip on Algeria be secure if they did not hold it

Grammatical construction + Verb form

Conditional constructions require specific verb tenses. For a past condition, the subordinate clause introduced by *if* uses the past indicative, and the main clause uses the conditional *if x happened, then y would happen.*

A The verb *was* should be the conditional *would be*; wordy and imprecise
B Correct. This clear, concise sentence correctly uses the conditional *would never be*.
C The verb *was* should be the conditional *would be;* pronoun *it* is ambiguous and could refer to either *Morocco* or *Algeria*
D *It*, not *that*, should be used to refer back to Morocco; *could never be secure about their grip* is awkward
E Inverted word order is awkward and confusing; *it* could refer to either *Morocco* or *Algeria*

The correct answer is B.

58. Once they had seen the report from the medical examiner, the investigators did not doubt whether the body recovered from the river was the man who had attempted to escape from the state prison.

(A) did not doubt whether the body recovered from the river was
(B) have no doubt whether the body recovered from the river was
(C) had not doubted that the body recovered from the river was
(D) have no doubt whether the body recovered from the river was that of
(E) had no doubt that the body recovered from the river was that of

Diction

When *doubt* is used in a negative context such as *there is no doubt* or *he does not doubt*, it should be followed by *that*. *That* also introduces a clause following *doubt* in questions. In other contexts, *whether* or *if* should be used to introduce a clause following doubt: *I doubt whether he will come.*

The investigators saw the report and then drew a conclusion; to maintain the proper sequence of verbs, the simple past tense should be used for the main verb of this sentence. A dead *body* cannot be a *man*; *the body* is *that of* a *man*.

A *Whether* should be *that*; the body is *that of* a man
B Incorrect use of present verb *have* instead of *had*; *whether* should be *that*; the body is *that of* a man
C Incorrect use of past perfect verb *had not doubted* instead of *did not doubt*; the body is *that of* a man
D Incorrect use of present verb *have* instead of *had*; *whether* should be *that*
E **Correct.** In this sentence, *had no doubt* is the proper tense and is correctly followed by *that*; *that of* is used to refer to the body of a man.

The correct answer is E.

59. His studies of ice-polished rocks in his Alpine homeland, far outside the range of present-day glaciers, led Louis Agassiz in 1837 to propose the concept of an age in which great ice sheets had existed in now currently temperate areas.

(A) in which great ice sheets had existed in now currently temperate areas
(B) in which great ice sheets existed in what are now temperate areas
(C) when great ice sheets existed where there were areas now temperate
(D) when great ice sheets had existed in current temperate areas
(E) when great ice sheets existed in areas now that are temperate

Verb form

In which or *when* can be used interchangeably in this sentence. The verb form here should be the simple past *existed* rather than the past perfect *had existed*. *Now currently* is redundant because both adverbs express the same idea.

A *Had existed* should be *existed*; *now currently* is redundant
B **Correct.** The simple past verb tense is correctly used in this sentence; *now* is placed and used correctly.
C *Where there were areas now temperate* is wordy and confusing
D *Had existed* should be *existed*; *current* should be *currently*; *in current temperate areas* is unclear
E *Now* is an adverb and should be placed just after the verb *are*

The correct answer is B.

60. More and more in recent years, cities are stressing the arts as a means to greater economic development and investing millions of dollars in cultural activities, despite strained municipal budgets and fading federal support.

(A) to greater economic development and investing
(B) to greater development economically and investing
(C) of greater economic development and invest
(D) of greater development economically and invest
(E) for greater economic development and the investment of

Diction + Parallelism

In this correct sentence, the idiom *as a means to* is properly used; the adjective *economic* appropriately modifies the noun *development*; and *investing* is parallel to *stressing*.

A **Correct.** The idiom *as a means to* is correct in this sentence; *stressing* and *investing* are parallel.
B Adverb *economically* is the wrong part of speech and conveys the incorrect meaning
C *As a means of* is not the correct idiom; *invest* should be *investing* to parallel *stressing*
D *Of* should be *to* because the correct idiom is *as a means to*; adverb *economically* is the wrong part of speech and conveys the incorrect meaning; *invest* should be *investing* to parallel *stressing*
E *As a means for* is not a correct idiom; *the investment of* is awkward and is not parallel to *stressing*

The correct answer is A.

61. Since 1986 enrollments of African Americans, American Indians, and Hispanic Americans in full-time engineering programs in the United States has steadily increased, while the number of other students who enter the field has fallen.

(A) has steadily increased, while the number of other students who enter the field has fallen
(B) has steadily increased, while other students entering the field have declined in number
(C) increased steadily, while there was a decline in the number of other students entering the field
(D) have steadily increased, while the number of other students entering the field has fallen
(E) have steadily increased, while that of other students who enter the field fell

Agreement + Verb form

The subject *enrollments* is plural so the verb must also be plural. When *since* refers to time, it should generally be followed by the present perfect tense, which describes action that began in the past and continues into the present.

A *Has … increased* should be *have … increased* to agree with *enrollments*
B Verb *has … increased* should be *have … increased* to agree with *enrollments; have declined in number* is awkward and unclear
C Verb *increased* is simple past tense and should be *have increased*; *was* should be *has been*
D **Correct.** This sentence correctly uses *have increased*, which agrees with the plural *enrollments* and is the appropriate present perfect tense.
E *That* should be the plural *those* to correctly refer to the plural *enrollments; fell* should be *have fallen* to parallel *have increased*

The correct answer is D.

62. A 1972 agreement between Canada and the United States reduced the amount of phosphates that municipalities had been allowed to dump into the Great Lakes.

(A) reduced the amount of phosphates that municipalities had been allowed to dump
(B) reduced the phosphate amount that municipalities had been dumping
(C) reduces the phosphate amount municipalities have been allowed to dump
(D) reduced the amount of phosphates that municipalities are allowed to dump
(E) reduces the amount of phosphates allowed for dumping by municipalities

Verb form + Idiom

An agreement that occurred in 1972 is correctly described with the past tense verb *reduced.* Since the dumping continues into the present, the past perfect verb *had been allowed* should instead be the present *are allowed.*

A *Had been allowed* should be *are allowed*
B *The phosphate amount* should be *the amount of phosphates*; the meaning of the sentence is changed by the omission of any form of *allow*
C The present tense *reduces* should be the past tense *reduced*; *the phosphate amount* should be *the amount of phosphates*; *have been allowed* should be *are allowed*
D Correct. The past tense *reduced* is correctly used in this sentence to describe a past action, and the present tense *are allowed* is used to describe the present situation.
E The present tense *reduces* should be the past tense *reduced*; *allowed for dumping* is an incorrect idiom; *allowed for dumping by municipalities* is awkward

The correct answer is D.

63. A proposal has been made to trim the horns from rhinoceroses to discourage poachers; the question is whether tourists will continue to visit game parks and see rhinoceroses after their horns are trimmed.

(A) whether tourists will continue to visit game parks and see rhinoceroses after their horns are
(B) whether tourists will continue to visit game parks to see one once their horns are
(C) whether tourists will continue to visit game parks to see rhinoceroses once the animals' horns have been
(D) if tourists will continue to visit game parks and see rhinoceroses once the animals' horns are
(E) if tourists will continue to visit game parks to see one after the animals' horns have been

Logical predication + Diction + Verb form

The tourists are visiting for the purpose of seeing the rhinoceroses; purpose is expressed by using *to,* not by *and.* Since *their* could refer to either tourists or to rhinoceroses, it is inappropriately ambiguous whose horns are being trimmed. The verb following *after* should be the present perfect *have been trimmed* to reflect that the trimming must occur before the tourists arrive. When only two alternatives are possible, to *continue to visit* or *not to continue to visit, whether* (or *whether or not*) is properly used rather than *if.*

A *And see* should be *to see*; *their* is ambiguous; *are* should be *have been*
B Omitting *rhinoceroses* changes the meaning of the sentence; *one* has no referent; *their* absurdly and unambiguously refers to tourists; *are* should be *have been*
C Correct. In this sentence, *to* correctly precedes *see*; it is clear that the horns belong to the animals; *have been* is the correct tense following *once.*
D *Whether* is preferred to *if*; *and see* should be *to see*; *are* should be *have been*
E *Whether* is preferred to *if*; *one* has no referent

The correct answer is C.

64. The technical term "pagination" is a process that leaves editors, instead of printers, assemble the page images that become the metal or plastic plates used in printing.

(A) is a process that leaves editors, instead of printers, assemble
(B) refers to a process that allows editors, rather than printers, to assemble
(C) is a process leaving the editors, rather than printers, to assemble
(D) refers to a process which allows editors, but not to printers, the assembly of
(E) has reference to the process leaving to editors, instead of the printer, assembling

Logical predication + Diction

The original sentence suffers from the imprecise use of words. The subject of this sentence is *the technical term "pagination."* A *term* is not a process but rather a means of referring to a process, and thus the verb *is* should be replaced by *refers to.* While *let* and *leave* can be used interchangeably in some contexts, *leave* is not an acceptable substitute for *let* when *let* means *to permit or allow.*

A *Is* should be *refers to*; *leaves* should be *lets*
B Correct. In this sentence, *refers to* and *allows* are appropriate verbs; the infinitive *to assemble* correctly follows *allow*. The relative pronoun *that* is properly used to introduce a restrictive clause.
C *Is* should be *refers to; leaving* is incorrect; *the* should be omitted before *editors*
D *But not to* should be *rather than* or *instead of*; *the assembly of* should be *to assemble*; *which* should be *that*
E *Has reference to* is wordy; *leaving* is incorrect; *printer* should be plural to match *editors*

The correct answer is B.

65. The only way for growers to salvage frozen citrus is to process them quickly into juice concentrate before they rot when warmer weather returns.

(A) to process them quickly into juice concentrate before they rot when warmer weather returns
(B) if they are quickly processed into juice concentrate before warmer weather returns to rot them
(C) for them to be processed quickly into juice concentrate before the fruit rots when warmer weather returns
(D) if the fruit is quickly processed into juice concentrate before they rot when warmer weather returns
(E) to have it quickly processed into juice concentrate before warmer weather returns and rots the fruit

Parallelism + Agreement

Parallelism requires that the same word forms perform the same functions in the sentence. Here, the linking verb *is* requires two infinitives: *to salvage … to process* (or *to have … processed).* A pronoun must match the noun it refers to. *Citrus* is singular and requires the singular pronoun *it*, not the plural pronouns *them* and *they.*

A *Citrus* does not agree with *them* and *they*
B *If they are quickly processed* is not parallel to the infinitive *to salvage*; *they* does not agree with *citrus*
C *For them to be processed quickly* is not parallel to the infinitive *to salvage*; *them* does not agree with its reference
D *If the fruit is quickly processed* is not parallel to the infinitive *to salvage; they* does not agree with *fruit*
E Correct. This sentence has correct parallel infinitives and uses the words *it* and *fruit* to refer unambiguously to *citrus.* The use of *before* rather than *when* also clearly establishes the cause-and-effect relationship between weather and rotting.

The correct answer is E.

66. Unlike a typical automobile loan, which requires a 15 to 20 percent down payment, the lease-loan buyer is not required to make an initial deposit on the new vehicle.

(A) the lease-loan buyer is not required to make
(B) with lease-loan buying there is no requirement of
(C) lease-loan buyers are not required to make
(D) for the lease-loan buyer there is no requirement of
(E) a lease-loan does not require the buyer to make

Logical predication + Parallelism

A comparison or contrast evaluates two parallel elements. The point of this sentence is to contrast two kinds of loans, but the sentence has been written so that *a typical automobile loan* is contrasted with *the lease-loan buyer*. The correct contrast is between *a typical automobile loan* and *a lease-loan*. This change makes the two verbs active voice (*requires … does not require*) and parallel.

A *Loan* is incorrectly contrasted with *lease-loan buyer*
B *Loan* is contrasted with *lease-loan buying* instead of *lease-loan*; prepositional phrase (*with …*) begins an awkward and wordy construction
C *Loan* is contrasted with *lease-loan buyers* instead of *lease-loan*
D *Loan* is contrasted with *lease-loan buyer* instead of *lease-loan*; prepositional phrase (*for…*) begins an awkward and wordy construction
E Correct. In this sentence, *loan* is properly contrasted with *lease-loan*, and, in place of the passive voice *is required*, the active voice *does … require* parallels *requires*.

The correct answer is E.

67. Defense attorneys have occasionally argued that their clients' misconduct stemmed from a reaction to something ingested, but in attributing criminal or delinquent behavior to some food allergy, the perpetrators are in effect told that they are not responsible for their actions.

(A) in attributing criminal or delinquent behavior to some food allergy
(B) if criminal or delinquent behavior is attributed to an allergy to some food
(C) in attributing behavior that is criminal or delinquent to an allergy to some food
(D) if some food allergy is attributed as the cause of criminal or delinquent behavior
(E) in attributing a food allergy as the cause of criminal or delinquent behavior

Logical predication + Idiom

The original sentence contains an incorrect idiom and a misplaced modifier. The correct idiom in the active voice is one *attributes x* (an effect) *to y* (a cause). In the passive voice, *x* (the effect) *is attributed to y* (the cause). The modifying phrase (*in attributing…*) incorrectly describes *perpetrators* when it should describe *defense attorneys.* The best way to correct the sentence is to transform the modifying phrase into a subordinate clause that uses the idiom correctly: *criminal or delinquent behavior* (x) *is attributed to* (verb phrase) *an allergy to some food* (y).

A Misplaced modifier; incorrect idiom
B Correct. In this sentence, the modification error has been eliminated with the use of the correct idiom, *is attributed to.*
C Modifier describes *perpetrators*, not *attorneys*; wordy and imprecise
D *X is attributed as the cause of y* is not the correct idiom
E Modifier incorrectly describes *perpetrators*; idiom is misused

The correct answer is B.

68. Unlike computer skills or other technical skills, there is a disinclination on the part of many people to recognize the degree to which their analytical skills are weak.

(A) Unlike computer skills or other technical skills, there is a disinclination on the part of many people to recognize the degree to which their analytical skills are weak.
(B) Unlike computer skills or other technical skills, which they admit they lack, many people are disinclined to recognize that their analytical skills are weak.
(C) Unlike computer skills or other technical skills, analytical skills bring out a disinclination in many people to recognize that they are weak to a degree.
(D) Many people, willing to admit that they lack computer skills or other technical skills, are disinclined to recognize that their analytical skills are weak.
(E) Many people have a disinclination to recognize the weakness of their analytical skills while willing to admit their lack of computer skills or other technical skills.

Logical predication + Rhetorical construction

The point of this sentence is to contrast how people feel about their *computer skills or other technical skills* with how they feel about their *analytical skills.* However, the awkward, wordy construction that begins with *there is* confuses this comparison, so that *computer skills*… are illogically contrasted with *disinclination.* Making the sentence more concise allows the contrast to be clear.

A An awkward, wordy construction prevents clarity of meaning; the comparison of *computer skills* … to *disinclination* is illogical
B *Computer skills or other technical skills* are illogically compared to *many people*
C The construction *skills bring out a disinclination in many people* is wordy, awkward, and idiomatically incorrect
D Correct. Making *people* the subject of the sentence allows a construction that clearly contrasts how they feel about the two sets of skills.
E *Have a disinclination* is wordy (the verb *disinclined* is preferred) and, when followed by *while willing*, creates an incomplete construction

The correct answer is D.

69. A report by the American Academy for the Advancement of Science has concluded that much of the currently uncontrolled dioxins to which North Americans are exposed comes from the incineration of wastes.

(A) much of the currently uncontrolled dioxins to which North Americans are exposed comes
(B) much of the currently uncontrolled dioxins that North Americans are exposed to come
(C) much of the dioxins that are currently uncontrolled and that North Americans are exposed to comes
(D) many of the dioxins that are currently uncontrolled and North Americans are exposed to come
(E) many of the currently uncontrolled dioxins to which North Americans are exposed come

Diction + Agreement

Much is used for an uncountable quantity such as effort or rain; *many* must be used for a countable quantity such as people or *dioxins.* As the subject of the subordinate clause, *many* must then be followed by the plural verb *come* rather than the singular *comes.*

A *Much* is used instead of *many*
B *Much* is used instead of *many*
C *Much* is used instead of *many*; *that are* is wordy
D *That are* is wordy and awkward, and if this construction were to be used, to maintain the parallel, *that* would have to be repeated in the clause *that North Americans are exposed to*
E Correct. In this concise sentence, *many* is correctly used with *dioxins*, and the subject and verb agree.

The correct answer is E.

70. Displays of the aurora borealis, or "northern lights," can heat the atmosphere over the Arctic enough to affect the trajectories of ballistic missiles, induce electric currents that can cause blackouts in some areas and corrosion in north-south pipelines.

(A) to affect the trajectories of ballistic missiles, induce
(B) that the trajectories of ballistic missiles are affected, induce
(C) that it affects the trajectories of ballistic missiles, induces
(D) that the trajectories of ballistic missiles are affected and induces
(E) to affect the trajectories of ballistic missiles and induce

Grammatical construction + Logical predication

This sentence describes two effects of the aurora borealis. It heats the atmosphere enough *to affect* x and *(to) induce y*; the preposition *to* does not need to be repeated because it is understood. The conjunction *and* is necessary to show that the two effects are equal and separate. When they are separated only by a comma, the second effect appears to be part of the first one, which is not true.

A *To affect* and (*to* understood) *induce* should be joined by the conjunction *and* rather than separated by a comma
B The correct idiom is *can heat … enough to affect*; *that* violates the idiom and introduces an illogical sequence of verbs (*are affected, induce*)
C The correct idiom is *can heat … enough to affect*; *that* violates the idiom; the verbs should be joined by a conjunction rather than separated by a comma
D *That* violates the correct idiom *can heat … enough to affect*; the verbs illogically change tenses
E **Correct.** In this sentence, the two effects are shown to be equal and separate in a grammatical construction that correctly joins *to affect* and (*to* understood) *induce*.

The correct answer is E.

71. The cameras of the *Voyager II* spacecraft detected six small, previously unseen moons circling Uranus, which doubles to 12 the number of satellites now known as orbiting the distant planet.

(A) which doubles to 12 the number of satellites now known as orbiting
(B) doubling to 12 the number of satellites now known to orbit
(C) which doubles to 12 the number of satellites now known in orbit around
(D) doubling to 12 the number of satellites now known as orbiting
(E) which doubles to 12 the number of satellites now known that orbit

Modification + Grammatical construction + Idiom

In the second part of this sentence, *which* appears to refer vaguely back to everything that has preceded it instead of referring to a specific noun. Using a participle (*doubling*) rather than a pronoun (*which*) allows the phrase to modify properly the entire clause that precedes it. *Known as orbiting* is an awkward and unlikely expression, which should be replaced by the more idiomatic *known to orbit.*

A *Which* has no clear referent; *known as orbiting* is not idiomatic
B **Correct.** In this sentence, the phrase beginning with *doubling* correctly modifies the preceding clause; *known to orbit* is the correct idiom.
C *Which* has no clear referent; *in orbit around* is wordy and awkward
D *Known as orbiting* is not idiomatic
E *Which* has no clear referent; *that orbit* is not grammatically correct

The correct answer is B.

72. Architects and stonemasons, huge palace and temple clusters were built by the Maya without benefit of the wheel or animal transport.

(A) huge palace and temple clusters were built by the Maya without benefit of the wheel or animal transport
(B) without the benefits of animal transport or the wheel, huge palace and temple clusters were built by the Maya
(C) the Maya built huge palace and temple clusters without the benefit of animal transport or the wheel
(D) there were built, without the benefit of the wheel or animal transport, huge palace and temple clusters by the Maya
(E) were the Maya who, without the benefit of the wheel or animal transport, built huge palace and temple clusters

Logical predication + Verb form

Architects and stonemasons are people, not things. This introductory element cannot logically modify *huge palace and temple clusters*. Revising the sentence so that *the Maya* immediately follows *architects and stonemasons* not only corrects the error in modification, it also transforms the sentence from the passive voice (*were built*) to the preferred active voice (*built*).

A *Architects and stonemasons* illogically modifies *huge palace and temple clusters*
B Moving the prepositional phrase (*without* ...) does not correct the modification error
C Correct. In this sentence, *architects and stonemasons* describes *the Maya*, and the active voice *built* replaces the passive voice *were built*.
D The introduction of *there were* does not correct the modification error; wordy and awkward passive construction
E *Architects and masons, were the Maya* is not a grammatical construction

The correct answer is C.

73. According to a recent poll, owning and living in a freestanding house on its own land is still a goal of a majority of young adults, like that of earlier generations.

(A) like that of earlier generations
(B) as that for earlier generations
(C) just as earlier generations did
(D) as have earlier generations
(E) as it was of earlier generations

Logical predication + Parallelism

This sentence compares a single goal shared by generations. The second part of the sentence must have the same structure as the first part: a clause with a subject and a verb. *Like* is used to introduce a phrase, but *as* must be used to introduce a clause. The phrase *owning* ... *land* is the subject of the first clause; in the correct sentence, the pronoun *it* refers back to the phrase and is the subject of the second clause. The first verb *is* also parallels the second verb *was*. *A goal* does not need to be repeated in the second clause because it is understood. The prepositional phrases *of a majority of young adults* and *of earlier generations* are parallel and correct.

A *Like* introduces a phrase, but a clause, introduced by *as*, is required to make the comparison parallel
B The phrase is not parallel to the main clause
C Subject and verb of the second clause must correspond to those of the first
D The clause is illogical and not parallel to the main clause
E Correct. In this sentence *as* shows comparison and introduces a subordinate clause in which all grammatical elements correspond to those in the main clause.

The correct answer is E.

74. Often visible as smog, ozone is formed in the atmosphere from hydrocarbons and nitrogen oxides, two major pollutants emitted by automobiles, react with sunlight.

(A) ozone is formed in the atmosphere from
(B) ozone is formed in the atmosphere when
(C) ozone is formed in the atmosphere, and when
(D) ozone, formed in the atmosphere when
(E) ozone, formed in the atmosphere from

Grammatical construction + Idiom

The preposition *from* is incorrect; *ozone is formed from x and y react* is not a grammatical structure. Replacing *from* with the conjunction *when* makes the sentence complete: *ozone is formed when x and y react.* A main clause is followed by a subordinate clause.

A The preposition *from* introduces an incoherent and ungrammatical construction
B Correct. The conjunction *when* introduces a subordinate clause, which completes the sentence correctly and coherently.
C *And when* distorts the meaning, suggesting that ozone is formed in two ways
D Omitting the main verb, *is*, results in a sentence fragment
E These changes result in a sentence fragment

The correct answer is B.

75. Salt deposits and moisture threaten to destroy the Mohenjo-Daro excavation in Pakistan, the site of an ancient civilization that flourished at the same time as the civilizations in the Nile delta and the river valleys of the Tigris and Euphrates.

(A) that flourished at the same time as the civilizations
(B) that had flourished at the same time as had the civilizations
(C) that flourished at the same time those had
(D) flourishing at the same time as those did
(E) flourishing at the same time as those were

Verb form + Agreement

The underlined portion of the sentence is a relative clause that describes *an ancient civilization*; the clause correctly uses the simple past tense, *flourished*, to describe civilizations that existed simultaneously.

A Correct. In this sentence, the relative clause correctly uses the simple past tense.
B Use of the past perfect, *had flourished*, is incorrect because it indicates a time prior to another action; the second *had* is redundant and unnecessary
C The plural pronoun *those* cannot refer to the singular *civilization* and thus lacks a referent; *as* is missing but necessary; *had* is the wrong verb tense
D The plural pronoun *those* cannot refer to the singular *civilization* and thus lacks a referent; *did* is awkward and unnecessary
E The plural pronoun *those* cannot refer to the singular *civilization* and thus lacks a referent; *were* is awkward and unnecessary

The correct answer is A.

76. Never before had taxpayers confronted so many changes at once as they had in the Tax Reform Act of 1986.

(A) so many changes at once as they had in
(B) at once as many changes as
(C) at once as many changes that there were with
(D) as many changes at once as they confronted in
(E) so many changes at once that confronted them in

Verb form + Idiom

This sentence compares changes before and after 1986. The correct idiom for the kind of comparison shown here is *as many … as.* Two periods in time are compared, and the verbs must reflect the difference. The period before 1986 requires the past perfect, *had confronted*, because it is the earlier of the two; the period beginning in 1986 requires the simple past, *confronted*, because it is the later.

A *So many … as* is not the correct idiom; *had* is the wrong verb tense
B *At once* is awkwardly placed; a clause must follow *as* to complete the sentence
C *At once* is awkwardly placed; *as many … that* is not the correct idiom; *there were with* is awkward and wordy
D Correct. This sentence uses the correct idiom *as many … as*, and *confronted* is the appropriate verb tense.
E *So many … that* is not the correct idiom; the subject of the verb should be *they*

The correct answer is D.

77. Even though the direct costs of malpractice disputes amounts to a sum lower than 1 percent of the $541 billion the nation spent on health care last year, doctors say fear of lawsuits plays a major role in health-care inflation.

(A) amounts to a sum lower
(B) amounts to less
(C) amounted to less
(D) amounted to lower
(E) amounted to a lower sum

Agreement + Verb form

In this sentence, the verb *amounts* is wrong for two distinct reasons: first, it does not agree with the subject *costs*; second, it should be in the past tense, *amounted*, since it shows action completed *last year*. *Sum* is redundant when used with the verb *amount*. The sentence does require a noun (*less*), not an adjective (*lower*), as the object of the preposition *to*.

A *Amounts* does not agree with *costs*; sentence requires past, not present, tense; *sum* is redundant
B Past tense verb is needed for action completed *last year*
C Correct. In this sentence, the past tense verb, *amounted*, properly indicates action completed *last year*, and the noun *less* is used as the object of the preposition *to*.
D A noun (*less*), not an adjective (*lower*), is needed as the object of the preposition *to*
E *A lower sum* is wordy and redundant because *sum* repeats the idea in *amounted*

The correct answer is C.

78. Visitors to the park have often looked up into the leafy canopy and saw monkeys sleeping on the branches, whose arms and legs hang like socks on a clothesline.

(A) saw monkeys sleeping on the branches, whose arms and legs hang
(B) saw monkeys sleeping on the branches, whose arms and legs were hanging
(C) saw monkeys sleeping on the branches, with arms and legs hanging
(D) seen monkeys sleeping on the branches, with arms and legs hanging
(E) seen monkeys sleeping on the branches, whose arms and legs have hung

Verb form + Logical predication

The subject of the main clause is *visitors*, which should be followed by two verbs using the same tense: *have looked* and *have seen*. *Have* does not need to be repeated in the second verb; it is entirely correct simply to let it be understood. The modifying clause *whose arms and legs* illogically refers to *branches*, which immediately precedes it, rather than to *monkeys*. Replacing the clause with the phrase *with arms and legs hanging* corrects this error.

A *Saw* is the wrong verb tense; the clause incorrectly modifies *branches*
B *Saw* is the wrong verb tense; the clause does not modify *monkeys*
C *Saw* is the wrong verb tense
D Correct. The verb tense is correct in this sentence, and the phrase correctly modifies *monkeys*.
E The clause modifies *branches* rather than *monkeys*; *have hung* is the wrong tense

The correct answer is D.

79. The Parthenon was a church from 1204 until 1456, when Athens was taken by General Mohammed the Conqueror, the Turkish sultan, who established a mosque in the building and used the Acropolis as a fortress.

(A) who established a mosque in the building and used the Acropolis as
(B) who, establishing a mosque in the building, used the Acropolis like
(C) who, when he had established a mosque in the building, used the Acropolis like
(D) who had established a mosque in the building, using the Acropolis to be
(E) establishing a mosque in the building and using the Acropolis as

Verb form + Idiom

In the original sentence, the two verbs, *established* and *used*, correctly use the simple past tense for actions completed at the same time. The correct idiomatic construction *used x as y* appears at the close of the sentence: *used the Acropolis as a fortress.*

A **Correct.** This sentence properly has simple past verbs to show action completed at the same time; the correct idiom is used.
B Idiomatic construction calls for *as*, not *like*
C Past perfect verb *had established* incorrectly indicates the two actions were not carried out simultaneously; idiomatic construction calls for *as*, not *like*
D Verb *had established* is the incorrect tense; *using x to be y* is an incorrect idiomatic construction
E *Establishing* and *using* illogically modify *Athens*

The correct answer is A.

80. New hardy varieties of rice show promise of producing high yields without the costly requirements of irrigation and application of commercial fertilizer by earlier high-yielding varieties.

(A) requirements of irrigation and application of commercial fertilizer by earlier high-yielding varieties
(B) requirements by earlier high-yielding varieties of application of commercial fertilizer and irrigation
(C) requirements for application of commercial fertilizer and irrigation of earlier high-yielding varieties
(D) application of commercial fertilizer and irrigation that was required by earlier high-yielding varieties
(E) irrigation and application of commercial fertilizer that were required by earlier high-yielding varieties

Logical predication + Idiom

This sentence confuses two constructions: *requirements of x* and *required by y. The requirements of x by y* is incorrect. *Requirements* is also an obstacle between *costly* and the two procedures that are *costly.* Thus, a more direct expression would be *costly irrigation and application* … The two procedures can then be modified by the clause *that were required by* as the best way to show their relationship to the earlier rice varieties.

A *Requirements* … *by* is not a correct idiomatic construction
B *Requirements by* is not a correct idiomatic construction; following *application of fertilizer*, *irrigation* can be misread as *application of irrigation*
C In this construction, *earlier high-yielding varieties* applies to *irrigation* alone
D *Irrigation* may be misread as *application of irrigation*; *was required* appears to refer to *irrigation* alone
E **Correct.** This sentence's construction clearly shows that two separate procedures *were required by* the earlier rice varieties.

The correct answer is E.

81. In an effort to reduce their inventories, Italian vintners have cut prices; their wines have been priced to sell, and they are.

(A) have been priced to sell, and they are
(B) are priced to sell, and they have
(C) are priced to sell, and they do
(D) are being priced to sell, and have
(E) had been priced to sell, and they have

Verb form

The first complete verb phrase is *have been priced to sell.* The second verb does not need to repeat the word *sell* because it is understood from the first use. However, the second verb must be correctly conjugated with the understood *sell. They are sell* is not correct; *they do sell* is correct.

A *They are* would require *selling* to complete it, not *sell*
B *They have* would require *sold* to complete it, not *sell*
C **Correct.** This sentence properly uses *they do* in place of *they do sell*, a grammatically correct verb.
D *Have* would require *sold* to complete it, not *sell*; omitting the subject *they* means that the comma should be omitted as well
E *They have* would require *sold* to complete it, not *sell*; the use of the past perfect *had been priced* distorts meaning

The correct answer is C.

82. Senator Lasker has proposed legislation requiring that employers should retain all older workers indefinitely or show just cause for dismissal.

(A) that employers should retain all older workers
(B) that all older workers be retained by employers
(C) the retaining by employers of all older workers
(D) employers' retention of all older workers
(E) employers to retain all older workers

Idiom

In this sentence *requiring* could be used in two possible constructions, the first a clause and the second a phrase: *requiring that employers retain* or *requiring employers to retain.* Both these alternatives are correct. However, introducing *should* into the clause is not correct.

A *Requiring that employers should retain* is not a correct construction
B The passive voice construction illogically makes *workers* the subject of *show*
C *Requiring the retaining* is awkward, and it leads to an ungrammatical construction with *or show ...*
D Using the noun *retention* produces an ungrammatical construction with *or show*
E **Correct.** This phrase uses an idiomatically correct construction after *requiring.*

The correct answer is E.

83. Most state constitutions now mandate that the state budget be balanced each year.

(A) mandate that the state budget be balanced
(B) mandate the state budget to be balanced
(C) mandate that the state budget will be balanced
(D) have a mandate for a balanced state budget
(E) have a mandate to balance the state budget

Verb form + Rhetorical construction

The subjunctive mood is required when a subordinate clause beginning with *that* follows a verb such as *request, require, ask*, or *mandate.* The subjunctive uses the base form of the verb (*be*); this form does not change. This sentence demonstrates the correct use of the subjunctive: *mandate that* is followed by the subjunctive *be balanced.*

A **Correct.** The subjunctive *be balanced* correctly follows *mandates that* in this sentence.
B *To be balanced* is an infinitive, not a subjunctive
C *Will be balanced* is a future indicative verb, not a subjunctive
D *Have a mandate for* is not as clear and concise as *mandate that*
E *Have a mandate to* is not as clear and concise as *mandate that*

The correct answer is A.

84. Under the Safe Drinking Water Act, the Environmental Protection Agency is required either to approve individual state plans for controlling the discharge of wastes into underground water or that they enforce their own plan for states without adequate regulations.

(A) that they enforce their
(B) for enforcing their
(C) they should enforce their
(D) it should enforce its
(E) to enforce its

Idiom + Parallelism + Agreement

Correlative conjunctions are pairs of words used together: *either/or, neither/nor, not only/but also.* The word, phrase, or clause that follows one half of the pair must be parallel to that which follows the other half. In this sentence, *either* is followed by the infinitive *to approve*, which means that *or* must also be followed by an infinitive, *to enforce.* The plural pronoun *their* does not agree with the singular subject, *Environmental Protection Agency.*

A *That they enforce* is not parallel to *to approve*; *they* and *their* do not agree with the singular subject
B *For enforcing* is not parallel to *to approve*; *their* does not agree with the singular subject
C *They should enforce* is not parallel to *to approve*; *they* does not agree with the singular subject
D *It should enforce* is not parallel to *to approve*
E **Correct.** In this sentence, *to enforce* is parallel to *to approve*, and *its* agrees with the singular subject.

The correct answer is E.

85. Dirt roads may evoke the bucolic simplicity of another century, but financially strained townships point out that dirt roads cost twice as much as maintaining paved roads.

(A) dirt roads cost twice as much as maintaining paved roads
(B) dirt roads cost twice as much to maintain as paved roads do
(C) maintaining dirt roads costs twice as much as paved roads do
(D) maintaining dirt roads costs twice as much as it does for paved roads
(E) to maintain dirt roads costs twice as much as for paved roads

Logical predication + Parallelism

This sentence intends to compare the costs necessary *to maintain* two kinds of roads, but it compares *dirt roads* generally with *maintaining paved roads*. For the correct focus, the comparison must be formulated *x costs twice as much to maintain as y* rather than *x costs twice as much as maintaining y*. *X* (*dirt roads*) and *y* (*paved roads*) must appear in grammatically parallel constructions.

A *Dirt roads* are compared to *maintaining paved roads*
B Correct. The costs *to maintain* the roads are emphasized in this sentence construction; *dirt roads cost* and *paved roads do* (*cost* understood) are parallel.
C *Maintaining dirt roads* is compared to *paved roads* in general
D *It* has no referent; the elements being compared are not parallel
E *To maintain dirt roads* is not parallel to *for paved roads*

The correct answer is B.

86. Although early soap operas were first aired on evening radio in the 1920's, they had moved to the daytime hours of the 1930's when the evening schedule became crowded with comedians and variety shows.

(A) were first aired on evening radio in the 1920's, they had moved to the daytime hours of the 1930's
(B) were first aired on evening radio in the 1920's, they were moved to the daytime hours in the 1930's
(C) were aired first on evening radio in the 1920's, moving to the daytime hours in the 1930's
(D) were aired first in the evening on 1920's radio, they moved to the daytime hours of the 1930's
(E) aired on evening radio first in the 1920's, they were moved to the 1930's in the daytime hours

Verb form + Parallelism

The two clauses about soap operas should be parallel. The first verb *were … aired* should be balanced by another passive voice verb in the simple past tense, *were moved*. The past perfect *had moved* indicates action completed before the action in the simple past *were aired*, suggesting that the 1930's were finished sometime during the 1920's. The prepositional phrase *in the 1920's* should be balanced by *in the 1930's*.

A *Had moved* is neither parallel to *were aired* nor correct in tense; *in* is preferable to *of* in the prepositional phrase
B Correct. In this sentence, the two verbs are parallel, as are the two prepositional phrases.
C This construction results in a sentence fragment
D *Moved* is not parallel to *were aired*; the prepositional phrases are not parallel
E *Aired* is not parallel to *were moved*; the prepositional phrases are not parallel

The correct answer is B.

87. The energy source on *Voyager 2* is not a nuclear reactor, in which atoms are actively broken apart; rather a kind of nuclear battery that uses natural radioactive decay to produce power.

(A) apart; rather
(B) apart, but rather
(C) apart, but rather that of
(D) apart, but that of
(E) apart; it is that of

Grammatical construction

This sentence focuses on a contrast by using the construction *not x, but rather y*; *x* and *y* are parallel. In this sentence *not x* (*a nuclear reactor*), should be followed by *but rather y* (*a kind of nuclear battery*). A comma, not a semicolon, should separate the two parallel parts of the contrast; using a semicolon results in a sentence fragment unless a subject and verb are provided in the construction.

A Using a semicolon results in a sentence fragment; *not x* should be balanced by *but rather y*
B Correct. In this sentence, the contrast is clearly drawn in the correct construction *not a nuclear reactor…, but rather a kind of nuclear battery*.
C *That of* has no referent and results in an illogical, ungrammatical construction
D *Rather* should be included to emphasize contrast; *that of* has no referent
E No word is used to indicate contrast; *that of* has no referent

The correct answer is B.

88. The recent surge in the number of airplane flights has clogged the nation's air-traffic control system, to lead to 55 percent more delays at airports, and prompts fears among some officials that safety is being compromised.

(A) to lead to 55 percent more delays at airports, and prompts
(B) leading to 55 percent more delay at airports and prompting
(C) to lead to a 55 percent increase in delay at airports and prompt
(D) to lead to an increase of 55 percent in delays at airports, and prompted
(E) leading to a 55 percent increase in delays at airports and prompting

Parallelism + Diction

The intent of the sentence is to show two effects of the surge in flights. These effects should be stated in parallel ways, instead of the construction *to lead* ... and *prompts* ... used in the original sentence. Using participial phrases introduced by *leading* and *prompting* solves this problem. The phrase *55 percent more delays* is not as clear as the phrase *a 55 percent increase in delays.*

A *To lead* and *prompts* are not parallel; *55 percent more delays* is not clear
B *55 percent more delay* is unclear
C *To lead* and *prompt* are not parallel; the meaning of *increase in delay* is not clear
D A participial phrase introduced by *leading* is preferable to the unclear infinitive phrase *to lead to*; *an increase of 55 percent in delays* is awkward and wordy
E Correct. *Leading* and *prompting* are parallel in this sentence; the phrase *a 55 percent increase in delays* is clear

The correct answer is E.

89. Presenters at the seminar, one who is blind, will demonstrate adaptive equipment that allows visually impaired people to use computers.

(A) one who
(B) one of them who
(C) and one of them who
(D) one of whom
(E) one of which

Idiom

The writer is trying to include information regarding *one* of the *presenters* at the seminar; the phrase must correctly refer back to *presenters*. The pronouns *who* or *whom* should be used to refer to people. In this situation, the correct pronoun is *whom* because an objective case pronoun must be used following the preposition *of*.

A *One who* could only be used after an introductory word such as *including*
B *One of them who* is awkward and ungrammatical
C *And* creates the impression that the blind presenter is not part of the group; *one of them who* is awkward and ungrammatical
D Correct. This sentence uses the proper objective pronoun *whom*; the phrase clearly conveys the idea of one person out of a larger group.
E The pronoun *which* can only refer to objects, events, or unnamed animals; it cannot be used to refer to people

The correct answer is D.

90. The peaks of a mountain range, acting like rocks in a streambed, produce ripples in the air flowing over them; the resulting flow pattern, with crests and troughs that remain stationary although the air that forms them is moving rapidly, are known as "standing waves."

(A) crests and troughs that remain stationary although the air that forms them is moving rapidly, are
(B) crests and troughs that remain stationary although they are formed by rapidly moving air, are
(C) crests and troughs that remain stationary although the air that forms them is moving rapidly, is
(D) stationary crests and troughs although the air that forms them is moving rapidly, are
(E) stationary crests and troughs although they are formed by rapidly moving air, is

Agreement

The subject of the second independent clause is *the resulting flow pattern*; this singular subject requires the singular verb *is known*, not the plural verb *are known*. While the long descriptive construction between the subject and verb may make it difficult to see this relationship, notice that the modifying phrase is set off with commas. The use of the active voice in the verbs of the subordinate clauses provides greater clarity of meaning.

A The plural verb does not agree with the singular subject
B The plural verb does not agree with the singular subject; the subordinate clause in the passive voice following *although* is awkward and unclear
C Correct. In this sentence, the singular verb *is known* agrees with the subject *the resulting flow pattern*.
D The plural verb does not agree with the singular subject; awkward and confusing construction
E The clause following *although* is awkward and unclear

The correct answer is C.

91. The Senate approved immigration legislation that would grant permanent residency to millions of aliens currently residing here and if employers hired illegal aliens they would be penalized.

(A) if employers hired illegal aliens they would be penalized
(B) hiring illegal aliens would be a penalty for employers
(C) penalize employers who hire illegal aliens
(D) penalizing employers hiring illegal aliens
(E) employers to be penalized for hiring illegal aliens

Parallelism + Logical predication

The intent of the sentence is to state the two provisions of a new law: it *would grant x* and (would) *penalize y*. The use of parallel verb forms would clarify the meaning of the sentence. While it is correct to repeat the auxiliary verb *would*, it is equally correct to omit it. In the original sentence, the word *they* is unclear; it could refer to *employers* or to *illegal aliens*.

A The provisions are not stated in parallel ways; it is unclear whether employers or illegal aliens would be penalized
B The provisions are not stated in parallel ways; apparent parallel of *residing … and hiring* is illogical and misleading; using the noun form *penalty* creates an awkward construction
C Correct. In this sentence, the verb *penalize* is parallel to the verb *grant*; it is clear from the relative clause who would be penalized.
D The participle *penalizing* is not parallel with the verb *grant* and is confusing with the participle *residing*
E The passive infinitive *to be penalized* is not parallel with the verb *grant*; the entire construction is awkward and difficult to understand

The correct answer is C.

92. Despite protests from some waste-disposal companies, state health officials have ordered the levels of bacteria in seawater at popular beaches to be measured and that the results be published.

(A) the levels of bacteria in seawater at popular beaches to be measured and that the results be
(B) that seawater at popular beaches should be measured for their levels of bacteria, with the results being
(C) the measure of levels of bacteria in seawater at popular beaches and the results to be
(D) seawater measured at popular beaches for levels of bacteria, with their results
(E) that the levels of bacteria in seawater at popular beaches be measured and the results

Idiom + Parallelism

The state's orders can be expressed using either of two idioms: *order x to be y* or *order that x be y*. The orders should be expressed consistently, and they should be expressed in grammatically parallel forms. The statements *ordered the levels … to be measured and the results to be published* and *ordered that the levels … be measured and (that* understood*) the results be published* are equally correct. In the second example, it is not necessary to repeat *that* or *be*.

A *The levels … be measured* and *that the results be published* are not parallel
B *Should* is not part of either correct idiom; plural pronoun *their* does not agree with singular *seawater*
C Neither correct idiom is used
D Neither correct idiom is used; no clear or logical referent for *their*
E Correct. The sentence correctly uses the idiom *order that x be y*; the correct statement reads, ordered *that the levels … be measured and* (that) *the results* (be) *published.* For the sake of conciseness, *that* and *be* are not repeated.

The correct answer is E.

93. By a vote of 9 to 0, the Supreme Court awarded the Central Intelligence Agency broad discretionary powers enabling it to withhold from the public the identities of its sources of intelligence information.

(A) enabling it to withhold from the public
(B) for it to withhold from the public
(C) for withholding disclosure to the public of
(D) that enable them to withhold from public disclosure
(E) that they can withhold public disclosure of

Logical predication + Agreement

In this correct sentence, the underlined phrase clearly modifies *powers*; *it* refers to *the Central Intelligence Agency. To withhold from the public* is concise, idiomatic, and clear.

A **Correct.** The sentence clearly and grammatically explains that the Court granted powers that enable the Central Intelligence Agency to withhold certain information from the public.
B An *–ing* modifier should begin the phrase describing powers; *for it to* … is not idiomatic
C *For withholding* is not the correct idiom; *withholding disclosure* is inaccurate since it is actually *the identities* that are to be withheld; *disclosure to the public of* is awkward
D *Them* does not agree with *the Central Intelligence Agency*; *withhold … disclosure* is wordy and imprecise since it is in fact *the identities* that are withheld
E *They* does not agree with *the Central Intelligence Agency*; *withhold … disclosure* is inaccurate since it is *the identities* that are withheld

The correct answer is A.

94. The Coast Guard is conducting tests to see whether pigeons can be trained to help find survivors of wrecks at sea.

(A) to see whether pigeons can be trained to help find
(B) to see whether pigeons can be trained as help to find
(C) to see if pigeons can be trained for helping to find
(D) that see if pigeons are able to be trained in helping to find
(E) that see whether pigeons are able to be trained for help in finding

Idiom + Rhetorical construction

This correct sentence clearly states the purpose of the test, *to see whether pigeons can be trained*, and the purpose of the training, *to help find survivors.* The sentence is concise and idiomatically correct.

A **Correct.** This sentence concisely states both the purpose of the test and the purpose of the training.
B *As help to find* is not the correct idiom
C *For helping to find* is not the correct idiom; *whether* is preferred to *if* when there are only two alternatives
D *That see* is ungrammatical; *whether* is preferred to *if* when there are only two alternatives; *are able to be* should be replaced by the concise *can*; *in helping to find* should be *to help find*
E *For helping in finding* is not the correct idiom; *are able to be* should be replaced by the concise *can*

The correct answer is A.

95. Unlike Schoenberg's 12-tone system that dominated the music of the postwar period, Bartók founded no school and left behind only a handful of disciples.

(A) Schoenberg's 12-tone system that dominated
(B) Schoenberg and his 12-tone system which dominated
(C) Schoenberg, whose 12-tone system dominated
(D) the 12-tone system of Schoenberg that has dominated
(E) Schoenberg and the 12-tone system, dominating

Comparison + Modification

The original sentence makes the logical error of comparing *Bartók* to the *12-tone system.* The lack of clarity results in the implication that the *system* might have founded a school or left behind disciples. The sentence must clearly indicate that it is the individuals, *Bartók* and *Schoenberg*, who are being compared. It must also make it plain that it was the *system* that dominated the music of the postwar period.

A Illogically compares *Bartók* to the *12-tone system*, rather than to *Schoenberg*
B Incorrect use of *and* illogically compares *Bartók* to the *system*; incorrect pronoun use
C Correct. This sentence makes the logical comparison between the individuals, and the relative clause clarifies that it is the *system* that dominated the music of the postwar period.
D Illogically compares *Bartók* to the *system*, rather than to *Schoenberg*; perfect verb form *has dominated* distorts the meaning by indicating that the system continues to dominate music today
E Incorrect use of *and* illogically compares *Bartók* to the *system* as well as *Schoenberg;* introduces confusion about what *dominating* modifies

The correct answer is C.

96. Ranked as one of the most important of Europe's young playwrights, Franz Xaver Kroetz has written 40 plays; his works—translated into more than 30 languages—are produced more often than any contemporary German dramatist.

(A) than any
(B) than any other
(C) than are any
(D) than those of any other
(E) as are those of any

Logical predication + Parallelism

The two elements compared in this sentence should be parallel. However, the sentence says Kroetz's *works … are produced more often than any … dramatist.* A *dramatist* cannot be *produced* and cannot be compared to *works.* Kroetz's *works* must be compared to *works* of other dramatists: *Kroetz's works … are produced more often than those* (*works* understood) *of any other dramatist.*

A Illogical comparison is between *works* and *dramatist*
B Illogical comparison is between *works* and *any other dramatist*
C This alternative illogically compares *works* and *dramatist*
D Correct. In this sentence, Kroetz's *works* are compared to *those* (the pronoun referring to *works*) of other dramatists.
E *More often* must be completed by *than*, not *as*; the phrase *those of any* illogically includes Kroetz's works; the correct *those of any other* excludes Kroetz's works

The correct answer is D.

97. The stars, some of them at tremendous speeds, are in motion just as the planets are, yet being so far away from Earth that their apparent positions in the sky do not change enough for their movement to be observed during a single human lifetime.

(A) The stars, some of them at tremendous speeds, are in motion just as the planets are, yet being
(B) Like the planets, the stars are in motion, some of them at tremendous speeds, but they are
(C) Although like the planets the stars are in motion, some of them at tremendous speeds, yet
(D) As the planets, the stars are in motion, some of them at tremendous speeds, but they are
(E) The stars are in motion like the planets, some of which at tremendous speeds are in motion but

Grammatical construction + Rhetorical construction

The first part of the original sentence intends to compare stars and planets; the comparison would be more effective at the beginning of the sentence: *Like the planets, the stars.* This alternative construction would lead the reader to expect the verb immediately following the subject, *are*, and then the completion of the clause, *in motion.* The modifying phrase, *some of them at tremendous speeds*, is best placed after *motion.* This whole construction, *Like the planets, the stars are in motion, some of them at tremendous speeds*, is a main clause and must be followed by a comma before a coordinating conjunction (such as *yet* or *but*) introduces a second main clause. The second clause must have a subject and a verb; *being* is neither and must be replaced by *they are.*

A Placements of the modifying phrase and the comparison are awkward and ineffective; *being* provides neither a subject nor a verb for the second main clause

B Correct. The comparison is clear and effective in this sentence; the second clause includes a subject and a verb.

C Both *although* and *yet* indicate contrast, so only one of them may be used; wordy, awkward phrasing leads to an ungrammatical construction

D Conjunction *as* may introduce a clause; the preposition *like* must be used for a comparison of two nouns

E Placement of *like the planets* is awkward; *some of which* is awkward and ambiguous; *are in motion* is said twice; subject and verb of the second clause are omitted

The correct answer is B.

98. As rainfall began to decrease in the Southwest about the middle of the twelfth century, most of the Monument Valley Anasazi abandoned their homes to join other clans whose access to water was less limited.

(A) whose access to water was less limited
(B) where there was access to water that was less limited
(C) where they had less limited water access
(D) with less limitations on water access
(E) having less limitations to water access

Diction + Logical predication

In the original sentence, the underlined clause provides a clear, correct, and succinct comparison, explaining the reason for the migration. The possessive pronoun *whose* correctly refers to its immediate antecedent, *clans*, and modifies *access.* For those other clans, access to water was *less limited* than it was for the Anasazi.

A Correct. This sentence uses a clear, concise clause that correctly connects *access to water* with *clans* by using the possessive pronoun *whose.*

B *Where there was … that was* is awkward, wordy, and redundant

C *They* is ambiguous and might refer to either the *Anasazi* or *other clans*; *less limited water access* is awkward

D *Limitations* is a countable quantity, so it must be modified by *fewer*, not *less*

E As a countable quantity, *limitations* should be modified by *fewer*, not *less*; *having* is ambiguous because it is unclear whether it refers to the *Anasazi* or *other clans*

The correct answer is A.

99. Just as reading Samuel Pepys's diary gives a student a sense of the seventeenth century—of its texture and psyche—so Jane Freed's guileless child-narrator takes the operagoer inside turn-of-the-century Vienna.

(A) so Jane Freed's guileless child narrator takes the operagoer
(B) so listening to Jane Freed's guileless child narrator takes the operagoer
(C) so the guileless child narrator of Jane Freed takes the operagoer
(D) listening to Jane Freed's guileless child narrator takes the operagoer
(E) Jane Freed's guileless child narrator takes the operagoer to her opera

Idiom + Parallelism

This sentence is based on the comparative construction *just as x, so y*; *x* and *y* must be grammatically parallel elements. The underlined portion of the sentence makes up most of the *y* element, which must be revised to make it parallel to the *x* element. The first part of the comparison is about reading a diary, and the second part is about listening to a narrator. *Reading Samuel Pepys's diary gives a student* … is parallel to *listening to Jane Freed's … narrator takes the operagoer* …

A When *listening to* is omitted, the second element is not parallel to the first
B Correct. In this sentence, all the elements of the comparison are parallel.
C Omission of *listening to* and replacement of the possessive *Jane Freed's* with *of Jane Freed* prevent the second element from being parallel to the first
D *So* completes the comparison and must be included
E *Jane Freed's guileless child* … is not parallel to *reading Samuel Pepys's diary*

The correct answer is B.

100. Bihar is India's poorest state, with an annual per capita income of $111, lower than in the most impoverished countries of the world.

(A) lower than in
(B) lower than that of
(C) and lower than that of
(D) which is lower than in
(E) which is lower than it is in

Idiom

This sentence depends on the comparative structure *x is lower* (or any other comparative adjective) *than y*; *x* and *y* are parallel elements. The intention of the sentence is to compare *x* (*the annual per capita income* of Bihar) with *y* (*the annual per capita income of the most impoverished countries of the world*), but it fails to complete the comparison because *y* (*in the most … world*) is not equal to *x*. In order to compare two equal elements while avoiding the laborious repetition of *the annual per capita income*, the pronoun *that* may be used in the second element.

A Incomplete comparison of annual incomes because the second element omits the pronoun *that*
B Correct. In this sentence, the *annual per capita income* of Bihar is compared with *that of* other countries.
C Conjunction *and* has no grammatical function when placed before *lower*
D Comparison is not between equal and like elements
E Use of the relative clause and the pronoun *it* allow the correct comparison to be made, but the construction is needlessly wordy

The correct answer is B.

101. El Niño, the periodic abnormal warming of the sea surface off Peru, a phenomenon in which changes in the ocean and atmosphere combine allowing the warm water that has accumulated in the western Pacific to flow back to the east.

(A) a phenomenon in which changes in the ocean and atmosphere combine allowing the warm water that has accumulated

(B) a phenomenon where changes in the ocean and atmosphere are combining to allow the warm water that is accumulating
(C) a phenomenon in which ocean and atmosphere changes combine and which allows the warm water that is accumulated
(D) is a phenomenon in which changes in the ocean and atmosphere combine to allow the warm water that has accumulated
(E) is a phenomenon where ocean and atmosphere changes are combining and allow the warm water accumulating

Grammatical construction + Logical predication

This accumulation of phrases and clauses results in a sentence fragment; there is no main verb. This problem is easily solved by inserting the verb to be: *El Niño ... is a phenomenon ...* The clause defining *phenomenon* (*in which changes in the ocean and atmosphere combine*) is clear and correct, but the subsequent phrase, *allowing ...* is not. If the participial phrase were to modify the previous clause, a comma would have to be inserted between *combine* and *allowing*. A better choice would be to follow *combine* with *to allow*, showing purpose. In this sense, the environmental changes combine in order to allow the water to flow back east.

A Lacking a main verb, this construction is a sentence fragment; *allowing* should be replaced by *to allow*
B Construction is a sentence fragment; present progressive verb tense (*are combining, is accumulating*) indicates action in progress, which is inappropriate here
C Construction is a sentence fragment; making a separate clause *and which allows ...* prevents the relationships from being easily understood
D Correct. The addition of *is* completes the sentence; *combine to allow* shows the purpose of the changes.
E *Where* cannot correctly refer to *phenomenon*; *are combining* is the wrong tense; the relationships among the parts of the sentence are unclear and the phrasing is awkward

The correct answer is D.

102. Beatrix Potter, in her book illustrations, carefully coordinating them with her narratives, capitalized on her keen observation and love of the natural world.

(A) Beatrix Potter, in her book illustrations, carefully coordinating them with her narratives,
(B) In her book illustrations, carefully coordinating them with her narratives, Beatrix Potter
(C) In her book illustrations, which she carefully coordinated with her narratives, Beatrix Potter
(D) Carefully coordinated with her narratives, Beatrix Potter, in her book illustrations
(E) Beatrix Potter, in her book illustrations, carefully coordinated them with her narratives and

Logical predication + Rhetorical construction

This sentence awkwardly presents two phrases intended to modify *Beatrix Potter* and loses the clarity and logic of the meaning. In the original sentence, these modifiers sound choppy and create too much separation between the subject, *Beatrix Potter*, and the verb *capitalized.* Beginning the sentence with *in her book illustrations* and following that phrase with the relative clause *which she carefully coordinated with her narratives* allows the subject, *Beatrix Potter*, to be united with the verb, *capitalized*, for a stronger main clause.

A The modifying elements are poorly placed and leave the subject too far from the verb
B Phrase *carefully coordinating ...* illogically modifies the noun that immediately precedes it (*book illustrations*); Potter, not the illustrations, did the coordinating; awkward and unclear
C Correct. The correct placement of the modifying elements makes this sentence easier to understand; the use of *which* clearly links the two elements.
D *Carefully coordinated ...* absurdly modifies *Beatrix Potter* rather than *her illustrations*
E *Them* cannot refer to *book illustrations* because the plural noun is the object of the preposition *in*; the relationships among the parts of the sentence are unclear

The correct answer is C.

103. The development of a new jumbo rocket that is expected to carry the United States into its next phase of space exploration will be able to deliver a heavier load of instruments into orbit than the space shuttle and at a lower cost.

(A) The development of a new jumbo rocket that is expected to carry the United States into its next phase of space exploration will be able to deliver a heavier load of instruments into orbit than the space shuttle and at a lower cost.

(B) The development of a new jumbo rocket is expected to carry the United States into its next phase of space exploration and be able to deliver a heavier load of instruments into orbit at a lower cost than the space shuttle.

(C) The new development of a jumbo rocket, which is expected to carry the United States into its next phase of space exploration, will be able to deliver a heavier load of instruments into orbit at a lower cost than the space shuttle.

(D) A newly developed jumbo rocket, which is expected to carry the United States into its next phase of space exploration, will be able to deliver a heavier load of instruments into orbit than the space shuttle can, and at a lower cost.

(E) A newly developed jumbo rocket, which is expected to carry the United States into its next phase of space exploration, will be able to deliver a heavier load of instruments into orbit than the space shuttle and to cost less.

Logical predication

The challenge here is to revise the sentence and present a complex idea as simply as possible. What will deliver the instruments into orbit? They will be delivered not by the development of a rocket but rather by the rocket itself; the *jumbo rocket*, not its development, must be the subject of the sentence. The phrase *a heavier load of instruments than the space shuttle* suggests a comparison between the *load of instruments* and the *shuttle*, whereas it is actually the different capabilities of the *rocket* and the *shuttle* that are being compared. The comparison should be written: the *jumbo rocket will be able to deliver a heavier load … than the space shuttle can. That* is used to introduce restrictive clauses; such clauses are essential to the meaning of a sentence. The *that is expected … exploration* clause is not essential; it should be introduced by *which* and set off with commas.

A The subject should be the *rocket*, not its *development*; verb *can* is needed after *space shuttle* to create a correct comparison; *that* should be replaced by *which* and the clause should be set off with commas

B The subject should be the *rocket*, not its *development*; verb *can* is needed after *space shuttle* to create a correct comparison

C The subject should be the *rocket*, not its *development*; verb *can* is needed after *space shuttle* to create a correct comparison

D Correct. The *rocket* is the subject of this sentence; the comparison between the *rocket* and the *shuttle* is clear; the nonrestrictive clause is correctly introduced and punctuated.

E Verb *can* is needed after *space shuttle* to create a correct comparison; *to cost less* is confusing because it seems to parallel *to deliver*

The correct answer is D.

104. Nuclear fusion is the force that powers the Sun, the stars, and hydrogen bombs, merging the nuclei of atoms and not splitting them apart, as in nuclear reactors.

(A) merging the nuclei of atoms and not splitting them apart, as in nuclear reactors
(B) merging the nuclei of atoms instead of splitting them apart, like nuclear reactors
(C) merging the nuclei of atoms rather than splitting them apart, as nuclear reactors do
(D) and merges the nuclei of atoms but does not split them apart, as is done in nuclear reactors
(E) and merges the nuclei of atoms, unlike atomic reactors that split them apart

Idiom + Logical predication

And not is an awkward way to establish a contrast; *instead of*, *rather than*, or *unlike* are more appropriate idioms to express a contrast. The comma following *bombs* is paired with the comma following *apart*, and this comma pair sets off the participial phrase introduced by *merging*. *As* introduces a clause; since a clause requires a subject and a verb, *as* cannot be followed by the prepositional phrase *in nuclear reactors*.

A *And not* is not a correct idiom; *as* should be followed by a clause

B Although *like* can grammatically be followed by a noun phrase such as *nuclear reactors*, here the basis of comparison is unclear, and the usage is incorrect

C **Correct.** *Rather than* is a correct idiom for comparison in this sentence; *as* is followed by a clause with a subject, *nuclear reactors*, and a verb, *do*; the comparison is clear and complete.

D Illogical and awkward construction attempts to make *merges* the second verb of the restrictive clause parallel to *powers* and *does not split*; punctuation makes clear this separate action cannot be the case; *as is done* is awkward and wordy

E Illogical and awkward construction incorrectly makes *merges* the second verb of the restrictive clause and a separate action parallel to *powers*; comparison is awkwardly drawn; switch from nuclear to atomic is unexplained and unsupported

The correct answer is C.

105. Originally developed for detecting air pollutants, a technique called proton-induced X-ray emission, which can quickly analyze the chemical elements in almost any substance without destroying it, is finding uses in medicine, archaeology, and criminology.

(A) Originally developed for detecting air pollutants, a technique called proton-induced X-ray emission, which can quickly analyze the chemical elements in almost any substance without destroying it,

(B) Originally developed for detecting air pollutants, having the ability to analyze the chemical elements in almost any substance without destroying it, a technique called proton-induced X-ray emission

(C) A technique originally developed for detecting air pollutants, called proton-induced X-ray emission, which can quickly analyze the chemical elements in almost any substance without destroying it,

(D) A technique originally developed for detecting air pollutants, called proton-induced X-ray emission, which has the ability to analyze the chemical elements in almost any substance quickly and without destroying it,

(E) A technique that was originally developed for detecting air pollutants and has the ability to analyze the chemical elements in almost any substance quickly and without destroying the substance, called proton-induced X-ray emission,

Rhetorical construction

The original sentence successfully avoids the problems that may occur in a long sentence with multiple modifiers. The sentence opens with the modifier *originally developed for detecting air pollutants*. This participial phrase is immediately followed by the word *technique* that it modifies; *technique* is in turn followed by the phrase *called proton-induced X-ray emission*. Finally, the nonrestrictive clause *which … destroying it* is correctly placed next to *emission* and set off from the rest of the sentence by a pair of commas.

A **Correct.** The modifiers are all correctly placed and punctuated; the meaning is clear.

B Placement of two long modifiers at the beginning of the sentence is awkward and makes it difficult to locate the subject; second modifier (*having…*) actually modifies the first modifier

C *Called proton-induced X-ray emission* should be placed next to *a technique* and should not be set off by commas; relative clause introduced by *which* incorrectly and illogically modifies *emission*

D *Called proton-induced X-ray emission* should be placed next to *a technique* and should not be set off by commas; relative clause introduced by *which* incorrectly and illogically modifies *emission*; *has the ability to* is wordy

E *Called proton-induced X-ray emission* should be placed next to *a technique* and should not be set off by commas; *has the ability to* is wordy

The correct answer is A.

106. Among the objects found in the excavated temple were small terra-cotta effigies left by supplicants who were either asking the goddess Bona Dea's aid in healing physical and mental ills or thanking her for such help.

(A) in healing physical and mental ills or thanking her for such help

(B) in healing physical and mental ills and to thank her for helping

(C) in healing physical and mental ills, and thanking her for helping

(D) to heal physical and mental ills or to thank her for such help

(E) to heal physical and mental ills or thanking her for such help

Parallelism + Idiom

This correct sentence uses parallel structure to explain that *supplicants were either asking … or thanking*. The correlative pair *either/or* is correctly used since each element is followed by the same part of speech: *either asking … or thanking*. The pair of correlative conjunctions *either … or* always work together; *either* may only be followed by *or*. The noun *aid* is correctly followed by *in healing* rather than by the infinitive *to heal*.

A **Correct.** The original sentence uses parallel structure to make its point; the idioms are correctly used.

B *And* is incorrect following *either*, and its use changes the meaning of the sentence; *to thank* is not parallel to *asking*; *for helping* is awkward

C No comma should be used following *ills*; *and* is incorrect following *either*, and its use changes the meaning of the sentence; *for helping* is awkward

D *To heal* is incorrect following *aid; to thank* is not parallel to *asking*

E *To heal* is incorrect following *aid*

The correct answer is A.

107. In his research paper, Dr. Frosh, medical director of the Payne Whitney Clinic, distinguishes mood swings, which may be violent without their being grounded in mental disease, from genuine manic-depressive psychosis.

(A) mood swings, which may be violent without their being grounded in mental disease, from genuine manic-depressive psychosis
(B) mood swings, perhaps violent without being grounded in mental disease, and genuine manic-depressive psychosis
(C) between mood swings, which may be violent without being grounded in mental disease, and genuine manic-depressive psychosis
(D) between mood swings, perhaps violent without being grounded in mental disease, from genuine manic-depressive psychosis
(E) genuine manic-depressive psychosis and mood swings, which may be violent without being grounded in mental disease

Idiom + Rhetorical construction

This sentence contrasts two problems, and it must use the correct idiomatic expression to do so clearly and effectively: Dr. Frosh *distinguishes between x* (mood swings) *and y* (psychosis). The clause that describes mood swings (*which may*...) should be as clear and concise as possible; the possessive pronoun *their* is awkward and should be omitted.

A Fails to use the correct idiomatic expression; *their* should be omitted

B Incorrect idiomatic expression; the phrase *perhaps violent* ... is awkward and unclear

C **Correct.** In this sentence, the correct idiomatic expression makes the contrast clear, and the unnecessary possessive *their* is omitted.

D Idiom incorrectly formulated as *distinguishes between x from y*; the phrase *perhaps violent* ... is awkward and unclear

E The preposition *between* has been omitted from the idiom

The correct answer is C.

108. The first decision for most tenants living in a building undergoing being converted to cooperative ownership is if to sign a no-buy pledge with the other tenants.

(A) being converted to cooperative ownership is if to sign
(B) being converted to cooperative ownership is whether they should be signing
(C) being converted to cooperative ownership is whether or not they sign
(D) conversion to cooperative ownership is if to sign
(E) conversion to cooperative ownership is whether to sign

Diction + Idiom

This sentence fails because of poor word choice: *undergoing being converted* is as redundant as it is awkward. The process of *being converted* does not need to be shown since *undergoing* already contains the idea of process. To complete the sentence grammatically, *undergoing* should be followed by the noun *conversion* rather than the phrase *being converted*. When only two alternatives are possible, to sign or not to sign, *whether* (or *whether or not*) is properly used rather than *if*.

A *Being converted* is redundant and awkward; *if* is incorrectly substituted for *whether*

B *Being converted* must be replaced by the noun *conversion*; *whether* must be followed by the concise infinitive *to sign*

C *Being converted* must be replaced by the noun *conversion*; *whether* must be followed by the concise infinitive *to sign*

D *Whether* should be used in place of *if*

E **Correct.** In this sentence, the noun *conversion* grammatically completes the phrase begun by *undergoing*, and *whether* is correctly followed by *to sign.*

The correct answer is E.

109. Published in Harlem, the owner and editor of the *Messenger* were two young journalists, Chandler Owen and A. Philip Randolph, who would later make his reputation as a labor leader.

(A) Published in Harlem, the owner and editor of the *Messenger* were two young journalists, Chandler Owen and A. Philip Randolph, who would later make his reputation as a labor leader.
(B) Published in Harlem, two young journalists, Chandler Owen and A. Philip Randolph, who would later make his reputation as a labor leader, were the owner and editor of the *Messenger*.
(C) Published in Harlem, the *Messenger* was owned and edited by two young journalists, A. Philip Randolph, who would later make his reputation as a labor leader, and Chandler Owen.
(D) The *Messenger* was owned and edited by two young journalists, Chandler Owen and A. Philip Randolph, who would later make his reputation as a labor leader, and published in Harlem.
(E) The owner and editor being two young journalists, Chandler Owen and A. Philip Randolph, who would later make his reputation as a labor leader, the *Messenger* was published in Harlem.

Logical predication + Agreement

A modifying phrase must be placed near the word it modifies. Here, the incorrect placement of the modifying phrase *published in Harlem* makes the phrase describe *the owner and editor* when it should describe *the Messenger*. The use of the singular *owner and editor* is puzzling: did one journalist own and the other edit? Or did they jointly own and edit? It is also unclear which of the two journalists is described in the clause beginning *who.*

A *Published in Harlem* incorrectly modifies *the owner and editor*; references are unclear
B *Published in Harlem* incorrectly modifies *two young journalists*; references are unclear
C Correct. In this sentence, the modifier correctly describes its object, *the Messenger*; the verbs indicate that both journalists played both roles; and the relative clause clearly shows Randolph, not Owen, as the owner of the reputation.
D The relative clause (*who ... leader*) lacks a clear referent; placement of *published in Harlem* is awkward and unclear
E *Being* introduces an awkward construction; the relative clause (*who ... leader*) does not have a clear referent

The correct answer is C.

110. In June of 1987, *The Bridge of Trinquetaille*, Vincent van Gogh's view of an iron bridge over the Rhone sold for $20.2 million and it was the second highest price ever paid for a painting at auction.

(A) Rhone sold for $20.2 million and it was
(B) Rhone, which sold for $20.2 million, was
(C) Rhone, was sold for $20.2 million,
(D) Rhone was sold for $20.2 million, being
(E) Rhone, sold for $20.2 million, and was

Grammatical construction + Verb form

This sentence requires the addition of commas to prevent misreading. The modifying phrase *Vincent van Gogh's view of an iron bridge over the Rhone* must be set off in a pair of commas because it describes the subject of the sentence, *The Bridge of Trinquetaille.* Modifiers that interrupt a sentence are always set off in a pair of commas. Without a comma after *Rhone,* it is easy to mistake the modifying phrase for the subject of the sentence because the verb immediately follows it. Another comma is needed after *million* once the unnecessary *and it was* is omitted. Once again, the comma sets off a long modifying phrase. Finally, to be idiomatic, the verb should be in the passive voice, not the active voice: the painting *was sold* for a certain amount.

A Commas after *Rhone* and *million* are required; unnecessary words should be omitted; the sentence requires the passive voice
B This construction says illogically that the painting was *the second highest price*
C Correct. In this sentence, necessary commas set off modifying phrases, and the verb is in the passive voice.
D A comma after *Rhone* is required; *being* is awkward and unnecessary
E This construction says illogically that the painting was *the second highest price*

The correct answer is C.

111. As a baby emerges from the darkness of the womb with a rudimentary sense of vision, it would be rated about 20/500, or legally blind if it were an adult with such vision.

(A) As a baby emerges from the darkness of the womb with a rudimentary sense of vision, it would be rated about 20/500, or legally blind if it were an adult with such vision.
(B) A baby emerges from the darkness of the womb with a rudimentary sense of vision that would be rated about 20/500, or legally blind as an adult.
(C) As a baby emerges from the darkness of the womb, its rudimentary sense of vision would be rated about 20/500; qualifying it to be legally blind if an adult.
(D) A baby emerges from the darkness of the womb with a rudimentary sense of vision that would be rated about 20/500; an adult with such vision would be deemed legally blind.
(E) As a baby emerges from the darkness of the womb, its rudimentary sense of vision, which would deemed legally blind for an adult, would be rated about 20/500.

Grammatical construction

This sentence fails to convey its meaning because its construction is faulty. It begins with a subordinate clause, whose subject is *a baby*; the subject of the main clause, *it* appears to refer back to *baby*. However, reading the main clause reveals that *it* is intended to refer to the *sense of vision* the first time it is used and to the *baby* the second time. The whole sentence must be revised, and the relationships between the two parts of the sentence must be clarified.

A Repeated use of *it* creates confusion because the referent is not clear
B The final phrase is awkwardly and ambiguously attached to the sentence
C The use of a semicolon instead of a comma creates a sentence fragment
D Correct. One independent clause describes a baby's vision, the other an adult's; the two independent but linked main clauses are correctly separated with a semicolon in this version of the sentence.
E Subordinate clause beginning with *which* is awkward and ambiguous

The correct answer is D.

112. The Federal Reserve Board's reduction of interest rates on loans to financial institutions is both an acknowledgment of past economic trends and an effort to influence their future direction.

(A) reduction of interest rates on loans to financial institutions is both an acknowledgment of past economic trends and an effort
(B) reduction of interest rates on loans to financial institutions is an acknowledgment both of past economic trends as well as an effort
(C) reduction of interest rates on loans to financial institutions both acknowledge past economic trends and attempt
(D) reducing interest rates on loans to financial institutions is an acknowledgment both of past economic trends and an effort
(E) reducing interest rates on loans to financial institutions both acknowledge past economic trends as well as attempt

Diction + Agreement

This sentence joins two parallel elements with the construction *both x and y*: *both an acknowledgement … and an effort.* Just as *both* is followed by an article and a noun, *and* is followed by an article and a noun. The parallelism makes the sentence easier to understand, which is particularly helpful in a sentence as long and full of phrases as this one is.

A Correct. Correct parallel structure is maintained in the *both x and y* construction of this sentence.
B *Both* must precede *an acknowledgment*; *both … as well as* is not the correct construction
C The plural verbs *acknowledge* and *attempt* do not agree with the singular noun *reduction*
D *Reducing* is awkward; *both* must precede *an acknowledgment*
E *Reducing* is awkward; *both … as well as* is a redundant, incorrect construction; the subject and verb do not agree

The correct answer is A.

113. The original building and loan associations were organized as limited life funds, whose members made monthly payments on their share subscriptions, then taking turns drawing on the funds for home mortgages.

(A) subscriptions, then taking turns drawing
(B) subscriptions, and then taking turns drawing
(C) subscriptions and then took turns drawing
(D) subscriptions and then took turns, they drew
(E) subscriptions and then drew, taking turns

Verb form + Parallelism

The *members* performed a sequence of two actions: first they *made monthly payments* … and then *took turns drawing* … The two actions must be expressed by the parallel past tense verbs *made* and *took*. The substitution of *taking* for *took* disrupts the parallelism and makes the sentence hard to understand.

A The participle *taking* is not parallel to the verb *made*
B Adding *and* does not solve the lack of parallelism
C Correct. In this sentence, the second verb, *took*, is parallel to the first verb, *made*; the two verbs are correctly joined by *and* as compound verbs with the same subject, *members*.
D Illogical construction creates a run-on sentence
E Construction is illogical, failing to show what the members *drew*; the final phrase makes no sense

The correct answer is C.

114. Gall's hypothesis of there being different mental functions localized in different parts of the brain is widely accepted today.

(A) of there being different mental functions localized in different parts of the brain is widely accepted today
(B) of different mental functions that are localized in different parts of the brain is widely accepted today
(C) that different mental functions are localized in different parts of the brain is widely accepted today
(D) which is that there are different mental functions localized in different parts of the brain is widely accepted today
(E) which is widely accepted today is that there are different mental functions localized in different parts of the brain

Grammatical construction

A lengthy description such as this one (*there … brain*) requires a relative clause: *Gall's hypothesis that* … With its subject-verb structure, a clause clearly and correctly identifies *Gall's hypothesis.* A series of phrases provides neither the same clarity nor grammatical correctness.

A A clause is required; this series of phrases is unclear and ungrammatical
B This construction distorts meaning by separating parts of the description
C Correct. This sentence uses a relative clause that identifies *Gall's hypothesis* clearly and correctly.
D *Which is* and *there are* introduce a wordy and awkward construction
E *Which is widely accepted today* implies that *Gall's* other theories are not accepted today, distorting the meaning of the sentence

The correct answer is C.

115. George Sand (Aurore Lucile Dupin) was one of the first European writers to consider the rural poor to be legitimate subjects for literature and portray these with sympathy and respect in her novels.

(A) to be legitimate subjects for literature and portray these
(B) should be legitimate subjects for literature and portray these
(C) as being legitimate subjects for literature and portraying them
(D) as if they were legitimate subjects for literature and portray them
(E) legitimate subjects for literature and to portray them

Idiom + Diction + Parallelism

When *consider* means *think* or *believe after careful deliberation*, it does not require *as* or any other expression before the object. The most concise phrase is thus *to consider the rural poor legitimate subjects for literature*. This phrase should have a parallel in *to portray them with sympathy and respect*. While it is not essential to repeat *to*, the repetition elegantly reinforces the parallelism. The correct pronoun must follow *portray*: Sand portrayed *them*. The pronoun *them* refers to the rural poor and is the direct object. *These* cannot act as a direct object.

A *To be* is unnecessary; *these* must be replaced by *them*
B *Should be* is wordy and requires *that* following *consider*; *these* should be *them*
C *As being* is awkward and unnecessary; *portraying* and *to consider* are not parallel
D *As if they were* distorts the meaning
E Correct. In this sentence, the correct idiom is used with the verb *consider*; the correct pronoun, *them*, replaces the incorrect *these*; *to consider* and *to portray* are parallel.

The correct answer is E.

116. Out of America's fascination with all things antique have grown a market for bygone styles of furniture and fixtures that are bringing back the chaise lounge, the overstuffed sofa, and the claw-footed bathtub.

(A) things antique have grown a market for bygone styles of furniture and fixtures that are bringing
(B) things antique has grown a market for bygone styles of furniture and fixtures that is bringing
(C) things that are antiques has grown a market for bygone styles of furniture and fixtures that bring
(D) antique things have grown a market for bygone styles of furniture and fixtures that are bringing
(E) antique things has grown a market for bygone styles of furniture and fixtures that bring

Agreement

This sentence uses an inverted word order that makes it difficult to see at first that *a market* is the subject of the sentence. The plural verb *have grown* does not agree with *market* and so must be replaced with the singular *has grown*. *Market* is also the subject of the second verb, which should be *is bringing*, not *are bringing*. The present progressive verb *is bringing* shows ongoing action, which is more appropriate than *bring* in this context. The plural nouns (*styles, fixtures*) that appear between the subject and the verb are objects of prepositions.

A *Have grown* and *are bringing* do not agree with the subject, *a market*
B Correct. In this sentence, *a market* agrees with *has grown* and *is bringing*.
C *That are antiques* is wordy and awkward; uses *bring* instead of the present progressive verb *is bringing*; *bring* does not agree with *a market*
D *A market* agrees with neither *have grown* nor *are bringing*
E Uses *bring* rather than the more appropriate present progressive *is bringing*; *bring* does not agree with *a market*

The correct answer is B.

117. New theories propose that catastrophic impacts of asteroids and comets may have caused reversals in the Earth's magnetic field, the onset of ice ages, splitting apart continents 80 million years ago, and great volcanic eruptions.

(A) splitting apart continents
(B) the splitting apart of continents
(C) split apart continents
(D) continents split apart
(E) continents that were split apart

Parallelism

This sentence lists four effects of catastrophic impacts; each effect, except the one included in the underlined portion, is given in noun form: *reversals, the onset, eruptions*. *Splitting* is a participle and thus not parallel to the other nouns. *Splitting* may be transformed into a noun by adding the article *the*.

A *Splitting*, as a participle, is not parallel to *reversals, the onset,* and *eruptions*
B Correct. *The splitting* is a gerund, or noun form, and is properly used in this sentence; it is parallel to the other nouns.
C Verb *split* is not parallel to *reversals, the onset,* and *eruptions*
D *Split* could be an adjective or a verb; in either case it is not parallel to the nouns
E The *catastrophic impacts* caused *a splitting* of continents; they did not cause the *continents*

The correct answer is B.

118. Students in the metropolitan school district lack math skills to such a large degree as to make it difficult to absorb them into a city economy becoming ever more dependent on information-based industries.

(A) lack math skills to such a large degree as to make it difficult to absorb them into a city economy becoming
(B) lack math skills to a large enough degree that they will be difficult to absorb into a city's economy that becomes
(C) lack of math skills is so large as to be difficult to absorb them into a city's economy that becomes
(D) are lacking so much in math skills as to be difficult to absorb into a city's economy becoming
(E) are so lacking in math skills that it will be difficult to absorb them into a city economy becoming

Rhetorical construction

The underlined portion is so awkward and wordy that it makes the whole sentence difficult to understand. The sentence reveals an ongoing situation (the economy is *becoming*…), so the use of the present progressive tense (*are lacking in*) in place of the present tense (*lack*) is appropriate. The long, awkward modifier *to such a large degree as to make it difficult* must be simplified and condensed. The idiomatic construction *so x … that* can be joined with the progressive verb for greater clarity and economy: *Students … are so lacking in math skills that it will be difficult …*

A *Lack* should be *are lacking in*; the awkward modifier should be condensed by using the *so x … that* construction
B *Lack* should be *are lacking in*; *to a large enough degree that* is not a correct idiom; *that becomes* should be *becoming*
C The use of the noun *lack* results in an ungrammatical construction
D *So much … as to be difficult* is not a correct idiomatic expression
E Correct. In this sentence, the present progressive verb *are lacking* reveals an ongoing situation; the construction *so … that* is clear, concise, and correct.

The correct answer is E.

119. The decision by one of the nation's largest banks to admit to \$3 billion in potential losses on foreign loans could mean less lending by commercial banks to developing countries and increasing the pressure on multigovernment lenders to supply the funds.

(A) increasing the pressure
(B) the increasing pressure
(C) increased pressure
(D) the pressure increased
(E) the pressure increasing

Parallelism

This sentence shows two results of a decision: the first is *less lending*. The second, *increasing the pressure*, should be parallel to the first but is not. Although *lending* and *increasing* may look similar because they are both formed from verbs and use the *-ing* ending, they do not have the same function. *Lending* is a gerund, or noun, modified by the adjective *less*. *Increasing* is a participle and introduces a phrase. *Increasing the pressure* can be made parallel to the adjective-noun form of *less lending* by revising it to *increased pressure*.

A *Increasing the pressure* is not parallel to *less lending*
B *The increasing pressure* is not parallel to *less lending*
C Correct. In this sentence, *increased pressure* is parallel to *less lending*.
D *The pressure increased* is not parallel to *less lending*
E *The pressure increasing* is not parallel to *less lending*

The correct answer is C.

120. It has been estimated that the annual cost to the United States of illiteracy in lost industrial output and tax revenues is at least \$20 billion a year.

(A) the annual cost to the United States of illiteracy in lost industrial output and tax revenues is at least \$20 billion a year
(B) the annual cost of illiteracy to the United States is at least \$20 billion a year because of lost industrial output and tax revenues
(C) illiteracy costs the United States at least \$20 billion a year in lost industrial output and tax revenues
(D) \$20 billion a year in lost industrial output and tax revenues is the annual cost to the United States of illiteracy
(E) lost industrial output and tax revenues cost the United States at least \$20 billion a year because of illiteracy

Rhetorical construction

The awkward and wordy sequence of phrases in the underlined portion make the sentence very difficult to understand; the best way to make the sentence more direct is to focus on the subject and verb of the clause. As subject and verb, *illiteracy costs* makes the emphasis immediate and clear, and the use of *cost* as a verb rather than a noun eliminates one of the prepositional phrases (*to the United States*) by requiring a direct object instead. *Annual* and *a year* are redundant.

A Stringing a sequence of phrases together obscures the relationship between subject and verb; redundancy and wordiness should be eliminated
B *Because of* is the incorrect idiom and should be replaced by *in*; wordy and redundant
C Correct. In this sentence, the subject and verb immediately identify the focus of the clause.
D The inverted word order only contributes to the incoherence of the phrases; wordy and redundant
E The reversal of phrases is illogical and distorts meaning

The correct answer is C.

121. A firm that specializes in the analysis of handwriting claims from a one-page writing sample that it can assess more than 300 hundred personality traits, including enthusiasm, imagination, and ambition.

(A) from a one-page writing sample that it can assess
(B) from a one-page writing sample it has the ability of assessing
(C) the ability, from a one-page writing sample, of assessing
(D) to be able, from a one-page writing sample, to assess
(E) being able to assess, from a one-page writing sample

Idiom + Rhetorical construction

The meaning of this sentence becomes lost in an awkward and ungrammatical construction. The verb *claims* may be followed by one of two correct constructions: *claims that* + a subordinate clause, or *claims* + the infinitive. When the prepositional phrase *from a one-page writing sample* is placed between *claims* and *that*, the result confuses and distorts the meaning by suggesting that the claim is contained in the writing sample. Instead, the firm claims *to be able … to assess.* The prepositional phrase should be placed between a pair of commas to show clearly that it is additional information not crucial to understanding the sentence.

A The prepositional phrase following the verb distorts the meaning of the sentence
B Placing the phrase after *claims* distorts meaning; *that* is omitted; *the ability of assessing* is wordy and awkward
C *The ability … of assessing* is not a correct idiom
D Correct. The correct idiomatic construction (*claims to be able to assess*) is used in this sentence, and the prepositional phrase is set off in a pair of commas to prevent misreading.
E *Claims … being able* is not a correct idiom

The correct answer is D.

122. More than 30 years ago Dr. Barbara McClintock, the Nobel Prize winner, reported that genes can "jump," as pearls moving mysteriously from one necklace to another.

(A) as pearls moving mysteriously from one necklace to another
(B) like pearls moving mysteriously from one necklace to another
(C) as pearls do that move mysteriously from one necklace to others
(D) like pearls do that move mysteriously from one necklace to others
(E) as do pearls that move mysteriously from one necklace to some other one

Diction

Clauses have subjects and verbs and are introduced by conjunctions or relative pronouns; phrases do not have subjects and verbs and are frequently introduced by prepositions. The preposition *like*, not the conjunction *as*, should introduce the underlined phrase.

A *As* incorrectly introduces a phrase when *like* is required
B Correct. In this sentence, the preposition *like* properly introduces the phrase.
C McClintock's simile creates an image that is not real; the use of the verb *do* indicates the pearls' movement as a reality
D *Like* incorrectly introduces a clause; the verb *do* indicates a reality instead of an image that is only imagined
E *Pearls* do not actually move; McClintock is suggesting an image only. *Some other one* is a wordy replacement for *another*

The correct answer is B.

123. In Holland, a larger percentage of the gross national product is spent on defense of their coasts from rising seas than is spent on military defense in the United States.

(A) In Holland, a larger percentage of the gross national product is spent on defense of their coasts from rising seas than is spent on military defense in the United States.

(B) In Holland they spend a larger percentage of their gross national product on defending their coasts from rising seas than the United States does on military defense.
(C) A larger percentage of Holland's gross national product is spent on defending their coasts from rising seas than the United States spends on military defense.
(D) Holland spends a larger percentage of its gross national product defending its coasts from rising seas than the military defense spending of the United States.
(E) Holland spends a larger percentage of its gross national product on defending its coasts from rising seas than the United States does on military defense.

Logical predication + Parallelism

The comparison between Holland and the United States is not clear because it is not parallel; making the comparison parallel eliminates the other problems in the sentence, such as the use of a plural pronoun (*their*) without a referent. Starting the sentence *Holland spends* makes the emphasis clear. To be parallel, the comparison should be: *Holland spends more x on y than the United States spends on z.* The grammatical structure is the same in each clause: the country is the subject; *spends* and *does* (*spend* understood) are the verbs; (*x*) *the percentage of gross national product* is the point of comparison; (*y*) *on defending* … and (*z*) *on military defense* are parallel phrases completing the sentence.

A A lack of parallelism leads this sentence to say that part of Holland's gross national product is spent *on military defense in the United States*; *their* has no referent
B *In Holland they spend* is not parallel to *the United States spends*; *they* has no referent
C *A … percentage … is spent on* is not parallel to *the United States spends*
D The clause *Holland spends* … is not parallel to the phrase *the military defense spending of the United States*
E **Correct.** This sentence has two parallel clauses that make the comparison clear and easily understood.

The correct answer is E.

124. Canadian scientists have calculated that <u>one human being should be struck every nine years by a meteorite</u>, while each year 16 buildings can be expected to sustain damage from such objects.

(A) one human being should be struck every nine years by a meteorite
(B) a human being should be struck by a meteorite once in every nine years
(C) a meteorite will strike one human being once in every nine years
(D) every nine years a human being will be struck by a meteorite
(E) every nine years a human being should be struck by a meteorite

Verb form

What this sentence says is not what it logically intends. The verb *should* implies obligation; in this sentence, it indicates that one human being *ought* to be struck every nine years, as though that person somehow deserved it. The scientists clearly mean that a human being *will* be struck by a meteorite roughly every nine years.

A The use of *should* illogically suggests that one human being deserves to be struck
B *Should* suggests that a person *ought* to be struck, rather than that a person *will* be
C *Every nine years* is an approximation, but the phrase *one human being once in every nine years* is too precise for the situation, suggesting that a specific individual will be struck
D **Correct.** In this sentence, *will be struck* is free of the unintended connotations of *should be struck.*
E *Should* suggests that a person *ought* to be struck, rather than that a person *will* be

The correct answer is D.

125. Samuel Sewall viewed marriage, as other seventeenth-century colonists, like a property arrangement rather than an emotional bond based on romantic love.

(A) Samuel Sewall viewed marriage, as other seventeenth-century colonists, like a property arrangement rather than
(B) As did other seventeenth-century colonists, Samuel Sewall viewed marriage to be a property arrangement rather than viewing it as
(C) Samuel Sewall viewed marriage to be a property arrangement, like other seventeenth-century colonists, rather than viewing it as
(D) Marriage to Samuel Sewall, like other seventeenth-century colonists, was viewed as a property arrangement rather than
(E) Samuel Sewall, like other seventeenth-century colonists, viewed marriage as a property arrangement rather than

Diction + Idiom

As is a conjunction that may introduce a subordinate clause (a clause always has a subject and a verb); *like* is a preposition that may introduce a phrase (a phrase never has a subject and a verb). The phrase *like other seventeenth-century colonists* modifies Samuel Sewell and should immediately follow his name. The sentence should use the idiomatic construction *view x as y: viewed (x) marriage as (y) a property arrangement.*

A *As* is used with a phrase instead of *like*; *viewed x like y* is not a correct idiom
B *Viewed x to be y* is not a correct idiom; *rather than* requires grammatically parallel elements, but *to be* and *viewing* are not parallel
C *Viewed x to be y* is not a correct idiom; the phrase *like* … illogically modifies *arrangement*; the *rather than* construction is not parallel
D *Marriage to Samuel Sewall* is awkward and, followed by *was viewed*, very unclear
E Correct. In this sentence, the modifying phrase is properly introduced by *like*; *viewed x as y* is the correct idiomatic expression.

The correct answer is E.

126. A wildlife expert predicts that the reintroduction of the caribou into northern Minnesota would fail if the density of the timber wolf population in that region is more numerous than one wolf for every 39 square miles.

(A) would fail if the density of the timber wolf population in that region is more numerous than
(B) would fail provided the density of the timber wolf population in that region is more than
(C) should fail if the timber wolf density in that region was greater than
(D) will fail if the density of the timber wolf population in that region is greater than
(E) will fail if the timber wolf density in that region were more numerous than

Verb form + Diction

The prediction is made using the construction *y will happen if x happens first* (an alternate form is *if x happens, y will happen*). Here, the *if* clause uses the present tense: *x* (the density of the wolf population) *is.* The main clause must use the future tense, *y* (the reintroduction of caribou) *will fail*, not the conditional *would fail. Density* is not a countable quantity, so it cannot be modified by *more numerous*, which is used solely for countable quantities; *greater* is correct.

A *Would fail* is conditional but the future tense is required; *density* should be modified by *greater*
B This construction requires *will fail*, not *would fail*; *if* is preferred to *provided*; *density* should be modified by *greater*
C *Will fail*, not *should fail*, is required; *timber wolf density* does not clearly refer to the population; the tense of the final verb is incorrect
D Correct. The verb *will fail* is in the future tense in this sentence; *density* is appropriately modified by *greater.*
E *Timber wolf density* does not clearly refer to the population; the tense and number of the final verb are incorrect; *density* cannot be modified by *numerous*

The correct answer is D.

127. Found throughout Central and South America, sloths hang from trees by long rubbery limbs and sleep 15 hours a day, moving infrequently enough that two species of algae grow on its coat and between its toes.

(A) sloths hang from trees by long rubbery limbs and sleep 15 hours a day, moving infrequently enough
(B) sloths hang from trees by long rubbery limbs, they sleep 15 hours a day, and with such infrequent movements
(C) sloths use their long rubbery limbs to hang from trees, sleep 15 hours a day, and move so infrequently
(D) the sloth hangs from trees by its long rubbery limbs, sleeping 15 hours a day and moving so infrequently
(E) the sloth hangs from trees by its long rubbery limbs, sleeps 15 hours a day, and it moves infrequently enough

Agreement + Idiom

The plural *sloths* in the underlined section of the sentence does not agree with the singular *its* (*its coat, its toes*) in the given section of the sentence, and so *sloths* must be replaced by *the sloth*. When *its* is then inserted before *long rubbery limbs*, it becomes clear that the limbs belong to the sloth, not the trees. The phrase *moving infrequently enough that* is not idiomatic. The correct construction is *so x that y*: *moving so infrequently that two species*...

A *Sloths* does not agree with *its*; *moving infrequently enough* is not the correct idiom
B *Sloths* does not agree with *its*; *hang* ... *they sleep* ... *with such infrequent movements* introduces a comma splice and is awkward, wordy, and not parallel
C *Sloths* does not agree with *its*; this structure says that sloths use their *long rubbery limbs to* ... *sleep*
D Correct. *The sloth* agrees with *its*; the construction *moving so x that y* is properly used in this sentence.
E *Hangs* ... *sleeps* ... *it moves* is not a parallel construction; *infrequently enough that* is not a correct idiom

The correct answer is D.

128. Today, because of improvements in agricultural technology, the same amount of acreage produces double the apples that it has in 1910.

(A) double the apples that it has
(B) twice as many apples as it did
(C) as much as twice the apples it has
(D) two times as many apples as there were
(E) a doubling of the apples that it did

Logical predication + Diction + Verb form

The adjective *double* cannot modify the verb *produces*; only an adverb (*twice*) can modify a verb. The sentence compares the number of apples produced today and in 1910; because apples are a countable quantity, the comparison should use the construction *as many as*. The two elements being compared must be grammatically parallel. *The same amount* ... *produces* is paralleled by *as it did* (*produce* understood). The subjects *amount* and *it* are parallel, as are the verbs *produces* and *did* (*produce*). Finally, an action that occurred in 1910 requires a verb in the past tense.

A *Double* is used in place of *twice*; the comparative construction *as many as* is needed; the verb tense *has* is incorrect with *in 1910*
B Correct. In this sentence, an adverb modifies the verb; *as many as* is used for a countable quantity; the two elements being compared are parallel; the verb is in the past tense.
C *Much* is used where *many* is required; the verb tense *has* is incorrect with *in 1910*
D *Two times* is wordy; *there were* is vague because it does not refer to *amount of acreage*
E *A doubling of the apples* is awkward and, when joined with *that it did*, illogical

The correct answer is B.

129. Joan of Arc, a young Frenchwoman who claimed to be divinely inspired, turned the tide of English victories in her country by liberating the city of Orléans and she persuaded Charles VII of France to claim his throne.

(A) she persuaded Charles VII of France to claim his throne
(B) persuaded Charles VII of France in claiming his throne
(C) persuading that the throne be claimed by Charles VII of France
(D) persuaded Charles VII of France to claim his throne
(E) persuading that Charles VII of France should claim the throne

Parallelism

Because this sentence consists of many parts, including lengthy modifiers (*a young Frenchwoman* …; *by liberating*…), it is crucial to make the basic structure of it—the subject and verbs of the main clause—as clear and as concisely expressed as possible. *Joan of Arc* is the subject, *turned* is the first verb of the main clause, and *persuaded* is the second verb; so the sentence should be *Joan … turned … and persuaded.* Inserting *she* before the second verb both violates the parallelism and adds an unnecessary word.

A *Persuaded*, not *she persuaded*, is parallel to *turned*
B The idiomatic construction is *persuade x to do y*, not *persuade x in doing y*
C Here *persuading* is linked to *liberating*, but Joan did not *turn the tide of English victories* by *persuading* Charles to claim the throne; *be claimed by* is wordy
D Correct. In this sentence, *persuaded* is parallel to *turned*, and the idiomatic construction *persuade x to do y* is used.
E Parallel form links *persuading* and *liberating* when *persuaded* should be parallel to *turned*; *persuade that x* is not a correct idiom

The correct answer is D.

130. As a result of medical advances, many people that might at one time have died as children of such infections as diphtheria, pneumonia, or rheumatic fever now live well into old age.

(A) that might at one time have died as children
(B) who might once have died in childhood
(C) that as children might once have died
(D) who in childhood might have at one time died
(E) who, when they were children, might at one time have died

Parallelism + Agreement

The sentence has one error in pronoun usage and two errors in parallelism. The pronoun *who*, rather than *that*, should be used to refer to people. *Once*, not the ambiguous and wordy *at one time*, is parallel to the adverb *now*, and *in childhood*, not *as children*, is parallel to *into old age*. Parallel structure involves not only how parallel elements are formed but also where they are placed in the sentence: here adverbs (*once* and *now*) should be placed first, followed by verbs (*have died* and *live*), and then by prepositional phrases (*in childhood* and *into old age*).

A *Who* should replace *that*; *once* should replace *at one time*; *in childhood* should replace *as children*
B Correct. This sentence correctly uses *who* to refer to *people*; parallel structures are maintained by using *once* to parallel *now* and *in childhood* to parallel *into old age*.
C *Who* should replace *that*; *in childhood* should replace *as children* and should be placed after *died* to be parallel in position to *into old age*
D *Once* should replace *at one time*; the parallel elements should appear in parallel positions
E *When they were children* is awkward and not parallel to *into old age* in wording or placement; *once* should replace *at one time*

The correct answer is B.

131. Cajuns speak a dialect brought to southern Louisiana by the 4,000 Acadians who migrated there in 1755; their language is basically seventeenth-century French to which has been added English, Spanish, and Italian words.

(A) to which has been added English, Spanish, and Italian words
(B) added to which is English, Spanish, and Italian words
(C) to which English, Spanish, and Italian words have been added
(D) with English, Spanish, and Italian words having been added to it
(E) and, in addition, English, Spanish, and Italian words are added

Agreement + Logical predication

The sentence describes the Cajun language as *seventeenth-century French* and then modifies that description by noting the addition of words from other languages. Since *words* is a plural noun, a plural verb is required. The inverted word order in the original sentence is awkward.

A The verb must be the plural *have*, not the singular *has*; the inversion of the subject and the verb is awkward
B Verb must be plural; since the action began in the past, the present perfect form *have been added* is required
C Correct. The relative clause in this sentence has the correct verb form, and its placement makes it clear that it modifies the noun *French*. The clause also follows normal subject-verb word order.
D This awkward construction is not an appropriate way to modify the noun *French*
E Verb tense is incorrect; it is not clear that the construction modifies the noun *French*

The correct answer is C.

132. One view of the economy contends that a large drop in oil prices should eventually lead to lowering interest rates, as well as lowering fears about inflation, a rally in stocks and bonds, and a weakening of the dollar.

(A) lowering interest rates, as well as lowering fears about inflation,
(B) a lowering of interest rates and of fears about inflation,
(C) a lowering of interest rates, along with fears about inflation,
(D) interest rates being lowered, along with fears about inflation,
(E) interest rates and fears about inflation being lowered, with

Parallelism + Diction

The sentence uses parallel structure to describe the anticipated effects of a drop in oil prices. Parallel noun phrases list two effects, *a rally … and a weakening*, so the first effect in the series must be written as *a lowering*. *Lowering* is a participle, whereas *a lowering* is a gerund and functions as a noun. For the sake of both clarity and conciseness, the effects on interest rates and fears should be combined into a single noun phrase: *a lowering of interest rates and of fears about inflation*.

A Each noun in the parallel series should be introduced by the indefinite article *a*; rates and fears should be combined
B Correct. The series *a lowering … a rally … and a weakening* uses parallel structure correctly; *a lowering of interest rates and of fears* gracefully combines two effects in this sentence.
C Parallelism is maintained with *a lowering*, but the use of *along with* makes it unclear that *fears* is parallel to *rates*
D Parallelism is not maintained; the phrase *interest rates being lowered* is awkward
E Parallelism is not maintained; the phrase *interest rates and fears about inflation being lowered* is awkward

The correct answer is B.

133. Although the term "psychopath" is popularly applied to an especially brutal criminal, in psychology it is someone who is apparently incapable of feeling compassion or the pangs of conscience.

(A) it is someone who is
(B) it is a person
(C) they are people who are
(D) it refers to someone who is
(E) it is in reference to people

Logical predication + Grammatical construction + Agreement

The intent of the sentence is to define the term "psychopath." In this sentence, the pronoun *it* refers back to *the term* and seems illogically to refer forward to *someone*. Logically, an inanimate *term* cannot be *a person* or *someone*. The sentence needs to be reworded so that it is clear that "psychopath" is a term that is used to define a specific kind of person.

A This construction illogically asserts that *the term* is a person
B This construction illogically asserts that *the term* is a person
C Plural pronoun *they* does not agree with the singular noun *the term*; this construction also asserts that *the term* is a person
D Correct. In this sentence, the verb *refers* clearly links the term to a particular kind of person; the alignment of pronouns and antecedents is both logical and grammatical.
E To be correct, this construction needs a main verb such as *used*; the construction *is used in reference to* is awkward and much wordier than the single word *refers*; the plural *people* should be singular: *a person* or *an individual*

The correct answer is D.

134. Recently implemented "shift-work equations" based on studies of the human sleep cycle have reduced sickness, sleeping on the job, fatigue among shift workers, and have raised production efficiency in various industries.

(A) fatigue among shift workers, and have raised
(B) fatigue among shift workers, and raised
(C) and fatigue among shift workers while raising
(D) lowered fatigue among shift workers, and raised
(E) and fatigue among shift workers was lowered while raising

Grammatical construction

Implementing the equations has reduced *sickness, sleeping on the job*, and *fatigue*; at the same time, it has increased *efficiency*. The three parallel elements *(have reduced x, y, and z)* require *and* before the final element.

A The omission of *and* before *fatigue* creates an unclear sentence
B The omission of *and* before *fatigue* creates an unclear sentence
C Correct. The use of *and* in this sentence unites the three parallel elements; the phrase *while raising* provides a clear contrast with *have reduced.*
D *And* is required to link the parallel elements; the verb *reduced* applies to all three parallel elements, so inserting *lowered* before *fatigue* illogically suggests that fatigue actually increased
E The insertion of *was lowered* destroys the parallel structure, and thus *while raising* has no logical referent here

The correct answer is C.

135. Spanning more than 50 years, Friedrich Müller began his career in an unpromising apprenticeship as a Sanskrit scholar and culminated in virtually every honor that European governments and learned societies could bestow.

(A) Müller began his career in an unpromising apprenticeship as
(B) Müller's career began in an unpromising apprenticeship as
(C) Müller's career began with the unpromising apprenticeship of being
(D) Müller had begun his career with the unpromising apprenticeship of being
(E) the career of Müller has begun with an unpromising apprenticeship of

Logical predication + Idiom

What spanned more than 50 years? It was Müller's career that spanned 50 years and *culminated in virtually every honor*. The correct subject of the sentence must be *Müller's career*.

A *Müller's career*, not *Müller*, should be the subject of the sentence
B Correct. Using *Müller's career* as the subject of the sentence solves the modification problem with *spanning* … and provides a logical subject for *culminated*.
C *Apprenticeship of being* is an incorrect idiom; *apprenticeship as* is correct
D *Müller's career*, not *Müller*, should be the subject of the sentence; past perfect tense is inappropriate; *apprenticeship of being* is an incorrect idiom
E *Müller's career* is preferable to *the career of Müller*; present perfect tense is incorrect; *apprenticeship of* should be *apprenticeship as*

The correct answer is B.

136. Joachim Raff and Giacomo Meyerbeer are examples of the kind of composer who receives popular acclaim while living, often goes into decline after death, and never regains popularity again.

(A) often goes into decline after death, and never regains popularity again
(B) whose reputation declines after death and never regains its status again
(C) but whose reputation declines after death and never regains its former status
(D) who declines in reputation after death and who never regained popularity again
(E) then has declined in reputation after death and never regained popularity

Verb tense + Parallelism

Faulty parallelism in the relative clause *who receives … goes … regains* … makes it unclear who or what is being described. The original clause begins by describing a certain kind of composer. As written, with *who* as the subject of *goes* and *regains*, the last two descriptions illogically continue to refer to the kind of composer. Logically it must be the reputation that declines after the composer's death.

A Illogically suggests the composer goes into decline after death; redundant *again*
B The two clauses are not parallel, lack a coordinating conjunction, and do not describe the same thing; redundant *again*
C Correct. This sentence presents the proper logic while maintaining parallel structure and consistent verb tense.
D The verb tenses are inconsistent with present tense used in the first phrase; redundant *again*
E The verb tenses are inconsistent with present tense used in the first phrase; to maintain parallelism, the verbs must be *receives … declines … regains*

The correct answer is C.

137. The company announced that its profits declined much less in the second quarter than analysts had expected it to and its business will improve in the second half of the year.

(A) had expected it to and its business will improve
(B) had expected and that its business would improve
(C) expected it would and that it will improve its business
(D) expected them to and its business would improve
(E) expected and that it will have improved its business

Parallelism + Verb tense + Antecedent

The original sentence has three problems. First, the sentence must clarify that the analysts held their expectations before the company's announcement. That is, it must use the past perfect tense *had expected* to show action prior to the past tense of *announced.* The sentence must also use the subjunctive *would* rather than *will* for the company's uncertain business improvement in the future. Second, the use of the singular pronoun *it* to refer to plural *profits* is incorrect. Finally, two parallel clauses are needed because the company made two announcements: one about the decline of profits and one about the future of its business.

A Use of *it* to refer to *profits* is incorrect; use of *will* is incorrect; the second announcement is not clear

B **Correct.** Removal of *it to* avoids the error in grammar and eliminates unnecessary words in this sentence. The addition of *that* before *its business would* creates another parallel clause associated with *announced* and clarifies that there is a second announcement. Finally, this sentence properly uses *had expected* and *would.*

C Incorrectly uses *expected;* use of *it* to refer to *profits* is incorrect, and *would* is unnecessary; the overuse of *it* and *its* is confusing and changes the meaning; *will* is incorrectly used instead of *would*

D Incorrectly uses *expected; them to* is both unnecessary and awkward; also, a second announcement is not made clear

E Incorrectly uses *expected*; incorrectly uses the future perfect tense (*will have improved)* that implies the action will be completed rather than ongoing; changes the meaning

The correct answer is B.

138. The direction in which the Earth and the other solid planets—Mercury, Venus, and Mars—spins were determined from collisions with giant celestial bodies in the early history of the solar system.

(A) spins were determined from
(B) spins were determined because of
(C) spins was determined through
(D) spin was determined by
(E) spin was determined as a result of

Agreement + Idiom

Two verbs collide in the underlined section, and both have agreement errors. *Spins* should be plural to agree with its subject *the Earth and the other solid planets*; *were determined* should be singular to agree with its subject *the direction*. The idiom *determined by* is used to express cause; *determined from* is incorrect in this context.

A *Spins* should be *spin*; *were* should be *was*; *from* should be *by*
B *Spins* should be *spin*; *were* should be *was*; *because of* should be *by*
C *Spins* should be *spin*; *through* should be *by*
D Correct. In this sentence, *spin* agrees with the plural subject *the Earth and the other solid planets*; *was determined* agrees with its subject *the direction*; the idiom *determined by* is used to express cause.
E The wordy *as a result of* is not the correct idiom

The correct answer is D.

10.0 Analytical Writing Assessment

10.0 Analytical Writing Assessment

The Analytical Writing Assessment (AWA) consists of two 30-minute writing tasks:

- **Analysis of an Issue.**
  You must analyze a given issue or opinion and then explain your point of view on the subject by citing relevant reasons and/or examples drawn from your experience, observations, or reading.
- **Analysis of an Argument.**
  You must read a brief argument, analyze the reasoning behind it, and then write a critique of the argument. In this task, you are not asked to state your opinion but rather to analyze the one given. You may, for example, consider what questionable assumptions underlie the author's thinking, what alternative explanations or counterexamples might weaken the conclusion, or what sort of evidence could help strengthen or refute the argument.

For both tasks, you will use the computer keyboard to type in your response. You will be able to use typical word-processing functions—that is, you can cut, copy, paste, undo, and redo. These functions can be accessed either by using the keyboard or by using the mouse to click on icons on the screen. You will be able to take notes when planning your response.

It is important that you plan carefully before you begin writing. Read the specific analytical writing task several times to make sure you understand exactly what is expected. Think about how you might present your analysis. You may want to sketch an outline to help you plan and organize. Keep in mind the 30-minute time limit as you plan your response—keep your analysis brief enough to give you plenty of time to write a first draft, read it over carefully, and make any necessary corrections or revisions before you run out of time. As you write, try to keep your language clear, your sentences concise, and the flow of your ideas logical. State your premise clearly at the beginning, and make sure you present a strong conclusion at the end.

10.1 What Is Measured

The Analytical Writing Assessment is designed as a direct measure of your ability to think critically and communicate your ideas. More specifically, the Analysis of an Issue task tests your ability to explore the complexities of an issue or opinion and, if appropriate, to take a position that is informed by your understanding of those complexities. The Analysis of an Argument task tests your ability to formulate an appropriate and constructive critique of a specific conclusion based upon a specific line of thinking.

The issue and argument that you will find on the test concern topics of general interest, some related to business and some pertaining to a variety of other subjects. It is important to note, however, that no AWA question presupposes any specific knowledge of business or other specific content areas. Only your capacity to write analytically is assessed.

College and university faculty members from various subject-matter areas, including but not limited to management education, will evaluate your AWA essays. For information on how readers are qualified, visit www.mba.com. Readers are trained to be sensitive and fair in evaluating the responses of nonnative speakers of English. A computer scoring program will also evaluate your essays. Your responses will be scored on the basis of—

- the overall quality of your ideas;
- your ability to organize, develop, and express those ideas;
- how well you provide relevant supporting reasons and examples; and
- your ability to control the elements of standard written English.

10.2 Test-Taking Strategies for the Analytical Writing Assessment Questions

General

1. **Read the question carefully.**
   Make sure you have taken all parts of a question into account before you begin to respond to it.
2. **Do not start to write immediately.**
   Take a few minutes to think about the question and plan a response before you begin writing. You may find it helpful to write a brief outline or jot down some ideas on the erasable notepad provided. Take care to organize your ideas and develop them fully, but leave time to reread your response and make any revisions that you think would improve it.

Analysis of an Issue

1. **Be careful about taking a position.**
   Although many Analysis of an Issue questions require you to take a position, think carefully before you do so. Readers will assess your ability to think and write critically. Try to show that you recognize and understand the complexities of an issue or an opinion before you take a position on it. Consider the issue from different perspectives, and think about your own experiences and things you have read that relate to the issue. Rather than announce a position, your answer should develop a position logically.
2. **Avoid presenting a "catalog" of examples.**
   It is essential to illustrate and develop your ideas by means of examples drawn from your observations, experiences, and reading, but keep in mind that one or two well-chosen, well-developed examples are much more effective than a long list.

Analysis of an Argument

1. **Focus on the task of analyzing and critiquing a line of thinking or reasoning.**
   Get used to asking yourself questions such as the following: *What questionable assumptions might underlie the thinking? What alternative explanations might be given? What counterexamples might be raised? What additional evidence might prove useful in fully and fairly evaluating the reasoning?*

2. **Develop fully any examples you use.**
   Do not simply list your examples—explain how they illustrate your point.

3. **Discuss alternative explanations or counterexamples.**
   These techniques allow you to introduce illustrations and examples drawn from your observations, experiences, and reading.

4. **Make sure your response reads like a narrative.**
   Your response should not read like an outline. It should use full sentences, a coherent organizational scheme, logical transitions between points, and appropriately introduced and developed examples.These are the directions that you will see for the Analytical Writing Assessment. If you read them carefully and understand them clearly before going to sit for the exam, you will not need to spend too much time reviewing them when you take the GMAT® exam.

10.3 The Directions

The directions for the two writing tasks in the Analytical Writing Assessment read as follows:

ANALYSIS OF AN ISSUE

In this section, you will need to analyze the issue presented and explain your views on it. There is no "correct" answer. Instead, you should consider various perspectives as you develop your own position on the issue.

Writing Your Response: Take a few minutes to think about the issue and plan a response before you begin writing. Be sure to organize your ideas and develop them fully, but leave time to reread your response and make any revisions that you think are necessary.

Evaluation of Your Response: Scores will take into account how well you—

- organize, develop, and express your ideas about the issue presented;
- provide relevant supporting reasons and examples; and
- control the elements of standard written English.

ANALYSIS OF AN ARGUMENT

In this section, you will be asked to write a critique of the argument presented. *You are* not *asked to present your own views on the subject.*

Writing Your Response: Take a few minutes to evaluate the argument and plan a response before you begin writing. Be sure to leave enough time to reread your response and make any revisions that you think are necessary.

Evaluation of Your Response: Scores will reflect how well you—

- organize, develop, and express your ideas about the argument presented;
- provide relevant supporting reasons and examples; and
- control the elements of standard written English.

10.4 GMAT® Scoring Guide: Analysis of an Issue

6 Outstanding

A 6 paper presents a cogent, well-articulated analysis of the complexities of the issue and demonstrates mastery of the elements of effective writing.

A typical paper in this category exhibits the following characteristics:

- explores ideas and develops a position on the issue with insightful reasons and/or persuasive examples
- is clearly well organized
- demonstrates superior control of language, including diction and syntactic variety
- demonstrates superior facility with the conventions (grammar, usage, and mechanics) of standard written English but may have minor flaws

5 Strong

A 5 paper presents a well-developed analysis of the complexities of the issue and demonstrates a strong control of the elements of effective writing.

A typical paper in this category exhibits the following characteristics:

- develops a position on the issue with well-chosen reasons and/or examples
- is generally well organized
- demonstrates clear control of language, including diction and syntactic variety
- demonstrates facility with the conventions of standard written English but may have minor flaws

4 Adequate

A 4 paper presents a competent analysis of the issue and demonstrates adequate control of the elements of writing.

A typical paper in this category exhibits the following characteristics:

- develops a position on the issue with relevant reasons and/or examples
- is adequately organized
- demonstrates adequate control of language, including diction and syntax, but may lack syntactic variety
- displays control of the conventions of standard written English but may have some flaws

3 Limited

A 3 paper demonstrates some competence in its analysis of the issue and in its control of the elements of writing but is clearly flawed.

A typical paper in this category exhibits one or more of the following characteristics:

- is vague or limited in developing a position on the issue
- is poorly organized
- is weak in the use of relevant reasons or examples
- uses language imprecisely and/or lacks sentence variety
- contains occasional major errors or frequent minor errors in grammar, usage, and mechanics

2 Seriously Flawed

A 2 paper demonstrates serious weaknesses in analytical writing skills.

A typical paper in this category exhibits one or more of the following characteristics:

- is unclear or seriously limited in presenting or developing a position on the issue
- is disorganized
- provides few, if any, relevant reasons or examples
- has serious and frequent problems in the use of language and sentence structure
- contains numerous errors in grammar, usage, or mechanics that interfere with meaning

1 Fundamentally Deficient

A 1 paper demonstrates fundamental deficiencies in analytical writing skills.

A typical paper in this category exhibits one or more of the following characteristics:

- provides little evidence of the ability to develop or organize a coherent response to the topic
- has severe and persistent errors in language and sentence structure
- contains a pervasive pattern of errors in grammar, usage, and mechanics that severely interferes with meaning

0 No Score

A paper in this category is off topic, not written in English, is merely attempting to copy the topic, or consists only of keystroke characters.

NR Blank

10.5 Sample: Analysis of an Issue

Read the statement and the instructions that follow it and then make any notes that will help you plan your response.

"People often complain that products are not made to last. They feel that making products that wear out fairly quickly wastes both natural and human resources. What they fail to see, however, is that such manufacturing practices keep costs down for the consumer and stimulate demand."

Which do you find more compelling: the complaint about products that do not last or the response to it? Explain your positions using relevant reasons and/or examples from your own experience, observations, or reading.

Sample Paper 6

Many people feel that products are not made to last, and correspondingly, many natural and human resources are wasted. On the other hand, it can be noted that such manufacturing practices keep costs down and hence stimulate demand. In this discussion, I shall present arguments favoring the former statement and refuting the latter statement.

Products that are not made to last waste a great deal of natural and human resources. The exact amount of wasted natural resources depends on the specific product. For example in the automobile industry, the Yugo is the classic example of an underpriced vehicle that was not made to last. Considering that the average Yugo had (not "has" since they are no longer produced!) a life expectancy of two years and 25,000 miles, it was a terrible waste.

Automobile industry standards today create vehicles that are warrantied for about five years and 50,000 miles. By producing cheap Yugos that last less than half as long as most cars are warrantied, the Yugo producer is wasting valuable natural resources. These same resources could be used by Ford or Toyota to produce an Escort or Tercel that will last twice as long, thereby reducing the usage of natural resources by a factor of two.

Human resources in this example are also wasteful. On the production side, manufacturers of a poor quality automobile, like the Yugo, get no personal or profession satisfaction from the fact that their product is the worst automobile in the United States. This knowledge adversely affects the productivity of the Yugo workers.

Conversely, the workers at the Saturn plants constantly receive positive feedback on their successful products. Saturn prides itself with its reputation for quality and innovation—as is seen in its recent massive recall to fix a defect. This recall was handled so well that Saturn's image was actually bolstered. Had a recall occurred at a Yugo plant, the bad situation would have become even worse.

Another factor in the human resources area is the reaction by the consumer. A great deal of human resources have been wasted by Yugo owners waiting for the dreaded tow truck to show up to haul away the Yugo carcass. Any vehicle owner who is uncertain of his/her vehicle's performance at 7 a.m. as he/she is about to drive to work, senses a great deal of despair. This is a great waste of human resources for the consumer.

While the consumer senses the waste of natural and human resources in a poor quality product, so does the manufacturer. People who argue that low quality manufacturing processes keep costs low for the consumer and hence stimulate demand should look at the Yugo example. In the mid-1980's the Yugo was by far the cheapest car in the United States at $3,995. By 1991, the Yugo was no longer sold here and was synonymous with the word "lemon."

Explanation of Score 6

The response above is ambitious and somewhat unusual in its focusing on just one example, the lesson of the now defunct Yugo. Responses, especially outstanding ones, typically discuss several different examples that build support for the writer's position on the issue. This sample response, then, should not be taken as necessarily endorsing a one-example writing strategy. What it does serve to underscore is how much is to be gained by developing, not just listing, examples. The strength of the response lies in the organized and thorough way in which it explores the related aspects of the example it cites. The clear organizational scheme (two major points, with the second point subdivided) is readily apparent: Yugo's substandard cars (1) waste natural resources and (2) waste human resources by (a) destroying worker morale and productivity and (b) inconveniencing and upsetting customers. The persuasiveness of the writer's thinking is especially evident in the discussion of the second major point, the waste of human resources. Here the writer not only considers customers as well as workers but also introduces the matter of the Saturn recall in order to show, by contrast with the case of Yugo, how a superior product, satisfied workers, and a company image good for marketing are interrelated.

The response complements its outstanding organizational clarity and thorough development with some syntactic variety and an occasional rhetorical flair (e.g., the image of the despairing Yugo owner waiting for "the dreaded tow truck . . . to haul away the Yugo carcass" in paragraph 6). It is important to point out, however, that the writing is not perfect. For one thing, the opening paragraph is essentially a repeat of the question. In addition, the writing is not—and is not expected to be—entirely free from minor flaws (e.g., "profession satisfaction" [paragraph 4] should obviously be "professional satisfaction," and "Saturn prides itself with" [paragraph 5] should be "Saturn prides itself on"). Nevertheless, these occasional flaws are not serious enough to detract from the general impression that this is an excellent response to the question.

Sample Paper 4

I find the response to the complaint more compelling. Although the complaint is valid, it is most often the case the building a product to last forever will indeed cost more than the average consumer is willing to pay. Creating such a product would require more materials and/or more heavy-duty wear resistant materials which inherently are more expensive. Another factor that would drive costs up is the fact that demand for products would decrease. The demand would decrease since people do not have to replace old products with new product as often. With the increased variable costs for materials combined with a reduction in the production volume associated with lower demand, manufacturers must raise prices to break even or maintain the current level of profits.

Although a few producers may make products to last, it is understandable how these companies can be driven out of existence. If a new competitor enters the market with a similar product that has a shorter life but a substantially lower price, then they will probably steal major portions of the other company's market share. The effects depend heavily upon the consumers' perception of quality and what the customers requirements from the product actually are.

For example, consumers may decide between two types of automobiles. One car may be built to last a long time but may not have the performance or be as comfortable as another car that is cheaper. So most consumers would purchase the cheaper car even though it may not last as long as the heavy-duty car. Consumers may not realize that the more expensive car is of higher quality in the sense that it will last longer and will not be willing to pay the extra cost.

Consumer decisions also depend on what consumers are actually looking for in a product. Consumers typically get tired of driving the same car for many years and want to buy new cars fairly often. This tendency forces producers to keep costs low enough to allow low enough prices for people to buy cars often. People don't want cars to last forever.

In conclusion, producers are in the situation that they're in due to external forces from the consumers. Producers must compete and they have found the best way satisfy the majority of the consumers.

Explanation of Score 4

This response presents a competent analysis of the issue. It develops its position by explaining some of the ways in which the factors mentioned in the question—manufacturing costs and consumer demand—are affected by making products that do not last very long. By way of illustration, the response cites the example of consumers choosing automobiles. Although this example is relevant, it lacks specificity: no actual types of cars are described in terms of the key issue, durability, and no contrast between more and less durable types is developed to prove a point.

Although the response is competently organized and therefore generally easy to follow in its main lines, its clarity is marred by an awkward transition from the second paragraph to the third. The main idea of the second paragraph is that many consumers will abandon a made-to-last expensive product in favor of a substantially cheaper version with a shorter life. But the last sentence of this paragraph, a sentence that is signally unclear, marks an ill-prepared-for change in the direction of the entire response. The "effects" (the word, used loosely and unclearly, seems to refer to the consumer's final decisions about what to buy) are seen to depend not only upon the simple choice between cost and quality but also upon a complex of new forces—aspects of consumer psychology and "requirements" (consumer needs?)—that now suddenly and puzzlingly face the reader. Although the third and fourth paragraphs go on to develop the writer's views about these new forces, the reader never quite recovers from the sense that the response has abruptly changed course. What is more, the consideration of consumer psychology and "requirements" can cause the writer to stray into side issues. For example, pointing out that customers may choose a car on the basis of performance and comfort rather than durability has no direct bearing on the complaint that products are not made to last.

The wording of this response is generally appropriate, although the language is occasionally awkward, as in "keep costs low enough to allow low enough prices" (paragraph 4) and "producers are in the situation that they're in" (paragraph 5).

Sample Paper 2

I find the response better than the complaint of people. The response seems to originate without much thought involved. It is more of an emotional complaint than one anchored in logic or thought. Yes, it is a waste of human resources but that is without consideration to the benefits: lower costs and stimulated demand. Thus, the response fails to recognize the benefits.

The strength of the response is that it forces the reader to reconsider the complaint. It adds a new dimension to the argument. It, however, fails to address the issue of wasting human resources. Does this mean the responder agrees with the notion of wasting resources.

In all actuality both the response and complaint as ineffective. The complaint doesn't recognize or address the benefits, like the response doesn't address the issue of wasting resources. The response, however, does bring in a new dimension and thus weakens the argument of the complaint.

Explanation of Score 2

In this piece of writing, the writer's purpose seems to waver between defending "the response" against "the complaint" and weighing the relative strengths and limitations of both. In addition, the writer offers no new reasons or specific examples and so ends up merely repeating assertions made in "the complaint" and "the response."

The writing is marked throughout by vagueness. The writer's decision to adopt the topic's terms "response" and "complaint" as a convenient shorthand for the two positions articulated leads immediately to a confusing lack of specificity, compounded in the first paragraph by the fact that the two terms are mixed up (e.g., "response" in the second and the fifth sentences is meant to refer to "complaint"). The first paragraph is made even more confusing because the pronouns "it" and "that" lack antecedents in the sentence "Yes, it is a waste of human resources but that is without consideration to the benefits."

The general lack of clarity is aggravated by errors in conventional English grammar and usage, most of them concentrated in paragraph 3. The first sentence begins with an unidiomatic phrase ("In all actuality") and lacks a verb ("both the response and complaint as ineffective"). The second sentence incorrectly uses "like" instead of "just as": "The complaint doesn't recognize or address... like the response doesn't address." In short, the writing fits the description of seriously flawed prose in the scoring guide: it displays "serious and frequent problems in the use of language and sentence structure."

10.6 Analysis of an Issue Sample Topics

"In some countries, television and radio programs are carefully censored for offensive language and behavior. In other countries, there is little or no censorship."

In your view, to what extent should government or any other group be able to censor television or radio programs? Explain, giving relevant reasons and/or examples to support your position.

"It is unrealistic to expect individual nations to make, independently, the sacrifices necessary to conserve energy. International leadership and worldwide cooperation are essential if we expect to protect the world's energy resources for future generations."

Discuss the extent to which you agree or disagree with the opinion stated above. Support your views with reasons and/or examples from your own experience, observations, or reading.

"Corporations and other businesses should try to eliminate the many ranks and salary grades that classify employees according to their experience and expertise. A 'flat' organizational structure is more likely to encourage collegiality and cooperation among employees."

Discuss the extent to which you agree or disagree with the opinion stated above. Support your views with reasons and/or examples from your own experience, observations, or reading.

"Of all the manifestations* of power, restraint in the use of that power impresses people most."

*manifestations: apparent signs or indicators

Explain what you think this quotation means and discuss the extent to which you agree or disagree with it. Develop your position with reasons and/or specific examples drawn from history, current events, or your own experience, observations, or reading.

"All groups and organizations should function as teams in which everyone makes decisions and shares responsibilities and duties. Giving one person central authority and responsibility for a project or task is not an effective way to get work done."

To what extent do you agree or disagree with the opinion expressed above? Support your views with reasons and/or specific examples drawn from your own work or school experiences, your observations, or your reading.

"There is only one definition of success—to be able to spend your life in your own way."

To what extent do you agree or disagree with this definition of success? Support your position by using reasons and examples from your reading, your own experience, or your observation of others.

"The best way to give advice to other people is to find out what they want and then advise them how to attain it."

Discuss the extent to which you agree or disagree with the opinion expressed above. Support your point of view with reasons and/or examples from your own experience, observations, or reading.

"For hundreds of years, the monetary system of most countries has been based on the exchange of metal coins and printed pieces of paper. However, because of recent developments in technology, the international community should consider replacing the entire system of coins and paper with a system of electronic accounts of credits and debits."

Discuss the extent to which you agree or disagree with the opinion stated above. Support your views with reasons and/or examples from your own experience, observations, or reading.

"Employees should keep their private lives and personal activities as separate as possible from the workplace."

Discuss the extent to which you agree or disagree with the opinion stated above. Support your views with reasons and/or examples from your own experience, observations, or reading.

"In any enterprise, the process of making or doing something is ultimately more important than the final product."

Discuss the extent to which you agree or disagree with the opinion expressed above. Support your point of view with reasons and/or examples from your own experience, observations, or reading.

"When someone achieves greatness in any field—such as the arts, science, politics, or business—that person's achievements are more important than any of his or her personal faults."

Discuss the extent to which you agree or disagree with the opinion stated above. Support your views with reasons and/or examples from your own experience, observations, or reading.

"Education has become the main provider of individual opportunity in our society. Just as property and money once were the keys to success, education has now become the element that most ensures success in life."

In your opinion, how accurate is the view expressed above? Explain, using reasons and examples based on your own experience, observations, or reading.

"Responsibility for preserving the natural environment ultimately belongs to each individual person, not to government."

Discuss the extent to which you agree or disagree with the opinion stated above. Support your views with reasons and/or examples from your own experience, observations, or reading.

"Organizations should be structured in a clear hierarchy in which the people at each level, from top to bottom, are held accountable for completing a particular component of the work. Any other organizational structure goes against human nature and will ultimately prove fruitless."

Discuss the extent to which you agree or disagree with the opinion expressed above. Support your point of view with reasons and/or examples from your own experience, observations, or reading.

"Nations should cooperate to develop regulations that limit children's access to adult material on the Internet."*

*The Internet is a worldwide computer network.

Discuss the extent to which you agree or disagree with the opinion stated above. Support your views with reasons and/or examples from your own experience, observations, or reading.

"Public buildings reveal much about the attitudes and values of the society that builds them. Today's new schools, courthouses, airports, and libraries, for example, reflect the attitudes and values of today's society."

Discuss the extent to which you agree or disagree with the opinion stated above. Support your views with reasons and/or examples from your own experience, observations, or reading.

"Some people believe that the best approach to effective time management is to make detailed daily and long-term plans and then to adhere to them. However, this highly structured approach to work is counterproductive. Time management needs to be flexible so that employees can respond to unexpected problems as they arise."

Discuss the extent to which you agree or disagree with the opinion expressed above. Support your point of view with reasons and/or examples from your own experience, observations, or reading.

"If the primary duty and concern of a corporation is to make money, then conflict is inevitable when the corporation must also acknowledge a duty to serve society."

From your perspective, how accurate is the above statement? Support your position with reasons and/or examples from your own experience, observations, or reading.

"Some employers who recruit recent college graduates for entry-level jobs evaluate applicants only on their performance in business courses such as accounting, marketing, and economics. However, other employers also expect applicants to have a broad background in such courses as history, literature, and philosophy."

Do you think that, in the application process, employers should emphasize one type of background—either specialization in business courses or a more varied academic preparation—over the other? Why or why not? Develop your position by using reasons and/or examples from your own experience, observations, or reading.

"In this age of automation, many people complain that humans are becoming subservient to machines. But, in fact, machines are continually improving our lives."

Discuss the extent to which you agree or disagree with the opinion expressed above. Support your point of view with reasons and/or examples from your own experience, observations, or reading.

"Job security and salary should be based on employee performance, not on years of service. Rewarding employees primarily for years of service discourages people from maintaining consistently high levels of productivity."

Discuss the extent to which you agree or disagree with the opinion stated above. Support your views with reasons and/or examples from your own experience, observations, or reading.

"Clearly, government has a responsibility to support the arts. However, if that support is going to produce anything of value, government must place no restrictions on the art that is produced."

To what extent do you agree or disagree with the opinion expressed above? Develop your position by giving specific reasons and/or examples from your own experience, observations, or reading.

"Schools should be responsible only for teaching academic skills and not for teaching ethical and social values."

Discuss the extent to which you agree or disagree with the opinion expressed above. Support your point of view with reasons and/or examples from your own experience, observations, or reading.

"A powerful business leader has far more opportunity to influence the course of a community or a nation than does any government official."

Discuss the extent to which you agree or disagree with the opinion stated above. Support your views with reasons and/or examples from your own experience, observations, or reading.

"The best strategy for managing a business, or any enterprise, is to find the most capable people and give them as much authority as possible."

Discuss the extent to which you agree or disagree with the opinion stated above. Support your views with reasons and/or examples from your own experience, observations, or reading.

"Location has traditionally been one of the most important determinants of a business's success. The importance of location is not likely to change, no matter how advanced the development of computer communications and others kinds of technology becomes."

Discuss the extent to which you agree or disagree with the opinion stated above. Support your views with reasons and/or examples from your own experience, observations, or reading.

"A company's long-term success is primarily dependent on the job satisfaction and the job security felt by the company's employees."

Discuss the extent to which you agree or disagree with the opinion stated above. Support your views with reasons and/or examples from your own experience, observations, or reading.

"Because businesses use high-quality advertising to sell low-quality products, schools should give students extensive training in how to make informed decisions before making purchases."

Discuss the extent to which you agree or disagree with the opinion expressed above. Support your point of view with reasons and/or examples from your own experience, observations, or reading.

"Too many people think only about getting results. The key to success, however, is to focus on the specific task at hand and not to worry about results."

What do you think this piece of advice means, and do you think that it is, on the whole, worth following? Support your views with reasons and/or examples drawn from your own experience, observations, or reading.

"Companies benefit when they discourage employees from working extra hours or taking work home. When employees spend their leisure time without 'producing' something for the job, they will be more focused and effective when they return to work."

Discuss the extent to which you agree or disagree with the opinion expressed above. Support your point of view with reasons and/or examples from your own experience, observations, or reading.

"Financial gain should be the most important factor in choosing a career."

Discuss the extent to which you agree or disagree with the opinion stated above. Support your views with reasons and/or examples from your own experience, observations, or reading.

"You can tell the ideas of a nation by its advertisements."

Explain what you think this quotation means and discuss the extent to which you agree or disagree with it. Develop your position with reasons and/or specific examples drawn from history, current events, or your own experience, observations, or reading.

"People are likely to accept as a leader only someone who has demonstrated an ability to perform the same tasks that he or she expects others to perform."

Discuss the extent to which you agree or disagree with the opinion stated above. Support your views with reasons and/or examples from your own experience, observations, or reading.

"All citizens should be required to perform a specified amount of public service. Such service would benefit not only the country as a whole but also the individual participants."

Discuss the extent to which you agree or disagree with the opinion stated above. Support your views with reasons and/or examples from your own experience, observations, or reading.

"Business relations are infected through and through with the disease of short-sighted motives. We are so concerned with immediate results and short-term goals that we fail to look beyond them."

Assuming that the term "business relations" can refer to the decisions and actions of any organization—for instance, a small family business, a community association, or a large international corporation—explain the extent to which you think that this criticism is valid. In your discussion of the issue, use reasons and/or examples from your own experience, your observation of others, or your reading.

"Businesses and other organizations have overemphasized the importance of working as a team. Clearly, in any human group, it is the strong individual, the person with the most commitment and energy, who gets things done."

Discuss the extent to which you agree or disagree with the opinion stated above. Support your views with reasons and/or examples from your own experience, observations, or reading.

"Since science and technology are becoming more and more essential to modern society, schools should devote more time to teaching science and technology and less to teaching the arts and humanities."

Discuss the extent to which you agree or disagree with the opinion stated above. Support your views with reasons and/or examples from your own experience, observations, or reading.

"Courtesy is rapidly disappearing from everyday interactions, and as a result, we are all the poorer for it."

From your perspective, is this an accurate observation? Why or why not? Explain, using reasons and/or examples from your own experience, observations, or reading.

"It is difficult for people to achieve professional success without sacrificing important aspects of a fulfilling personal life."

Discuss the extent to which you agree or disagree with the opinion stated above. Support your views with reasons and/or examples from your own experience, observations, or reading.

"With the increasing emphasis on a global economy and international cooperation, people need to understand that their role as citizens of the world is more important than their role as citizens of a particular country."

Discuss the extent to which you agree or disagree with the opinion stated above. Support your views with reasons and/or examples from your own experience, observations, or reading.

"The best way to preserve the natural environment is to impose penalties—whether fines, imprisonment, or other punishments—on those who are most responsible for polluting or otherwise damaging it."

Discuss the extent to which you agree or disagree with the opinion expressed above. Support your point of view with reasons and/or examples from your own experience, observations, or reading.

"Scientists are continually redefining the standards for what is beneficial or harmful to the environment. Since these standards keep shifting, companies should resist changing their products and processes in response to each new recommendation until those recommendations become government regulations."

Discuss the extent to which you agree or disagree with the opinion stated above. Support your views with reasons and/or examples from your own experience, observations, or reading.

"The most important reason for studying history is not that knowledge of history can make us better people or a better society but that it can provide clues to solving the societal problems that we face today."

Discuss the extent to which you agree or disagree with the opinion expressed above. Support your point of view with reasons and/or examples from your own experience, observations, or reading.

"All companies should invest heavily in advertising because high-quality advertising can sell almost any product or service."

Discuss the extent to which you agree or disagree with the opinion expressed above. Support your point of view with reasons and/or examples from your own experience, observations, or reading.

"The most effective way for a businessperson to maximize profits over a long period of time is to follow the highest standards of ethics."

Discuss the extent to which you agree or disagree with the opinion stated above. Support your views with reasons and/or examples from your own experience, observations, or reading.

"Businesses are as likely as are governments to establish large bureaucracies, but bureaucracy is far more damaging to a business than it is to a government."

Discuss the extent to which you agree or disagree with the opinion expressed above. Support your point of view with reasons and/or examples from your own experience, observations, or reading.

"The primary responsibility for preventing environmental damage belongs to government, not to individuals or private industry."

Discuss the extent to which you agree or disagree with the opinion expressed above. Support your point of view with reasons and/or examples from your own experience, observations, or reading.

"In matching job candidates with job openings, managers must consider not only such variables as previous work experience and educational background but also personality traits and work habits, which are more difficult to judge."

What do you consider essential in an employee or colleague? Explain, using reasons and/or examples from your work or work-like experiences, or from your observations of others.

"Ask most older people to identify the key to success, and they are likely to reply 'hard work.' Yet, I would tell people starting off in a career that work in itself is not the key. In fact, you have to approach work cautiously—too much or too little can be self-defeating."

To what extent do you agree or disagree with this view of work? Develop your position by using reasons and/or examples from your reading, experience, or observations.

"How far should a supervisor go in criticizing the performance of a subordinate? Some highly successful managers have been known to rely on verbal abuse and intimidation. Do you think that this is an effective means of communicating expectations? If not, what alternative should a manager use in dealing with someone whose work is less than satisfactory?"

Explain your views on this issue. Be sure to support your position with reasons and/or examples from your own experience, observations, or reading.

"The presence of a competitor is always beneficial to a company. Competition forces a company to change itself in ways that improve its practices."

Discuss the extent to which you agree or disagree with the opinion stated above. Support your views with reasons and/or examples from your own experience, observations, or reading.

"Successful individuals typically set their next goal somewhat—but not too much—above their last achievement. In this way, they steadily raise their level of aspiration."

In your opinion, how accurate is this statement? Explain, using specific reasons and examples from your reading, your own experience, or your observation of others.

"The term 'user friendly' is usually applied to the trouble-free way that computer software moves people from screen to screen, function to function. However, the term can also refer to a government office, a library, public transportation, or anything designed to provide information or services in an easy, friendly way. Just as all societies have many striking examples of user-friendly services, so do they abound in examples of user-unfriendly systems."

Identify a system or service that you have found to be either "user-friendly" or "user-unfriendly." Discuss, from the user's perspective, in what way the system either is or is not easy to use and explain the consequences or effect of such a system.

"Popular entertainment is overly influenced by commercial interests. Superficiality, obscenity, and violence characterize films and television today because those qualities are commercially successful."

Discuss the extent to which you agree or disagree with this opinion. To support your position, use reasons and/or examples from your reading, your observations, or your experiences as a consumer of popular entertainment.

"Never tell people how to do things. Tell them what to do, and they will surprise you with their ingenuity."

To what extent do you agree or disagree with the opinion expressed above?

Explain your point of view by giving reasons and/or examples from your own experience, observations, or reading.

"The secret of business is to know something that nobody else knows."

Explain what you think the above quotation means and discuss the extent to which you agree or disagree with it. Support your position with relevant reasons and/or examples from your own experience, observations, or reading.

"Everywhere, it seems, there are clear and positive signs that people are becoming more respectful of one another's differences."

In your opinion, how accurate is the view expressed above? Use reasons and/or examples from your own experience, observations, or reading to develop your position.

"What is the final objective of business? It is to make the obtaining of a living—the obtaining of food, clothing, shelter, and a minimum of luxuries—so mechanical and so little time-consuming that people shall have time for other things."— A business leader, circa 1930

Explain what you think the quotation above means and discuss the extent to which you agree or disagree with the view of business it expresses. Support your views with reasons and/or examples from your own experience, observations, or reading.

"Juvenile crime is a serious social problem, and businesses must become more involved in helping to prevent it."

Discuss the extent to which you agree or disagree with the opinion expressed above. Support your point of view with reasons and/or examples from your own experience, observations, or reading.

"Employers should have no right to obtain information about their employees' health or other aspects of their personal lives without the employees' permission."

Discuss the extent to which you agree or disagree with the opinion stated above. Support your views with reasons and/or examples from your own experience, observations, or reading.

"Even at its best, a government is a tremendous burden to business, though a necessary one."

Discuss the extent to which you agree or disagree with the opinion expressed above. Support your point of view with reasons and/or examples from your own experience, observations, or reading.

"What education fails to teach us is to see the human community as one. Rather than focus on the unique differences that separate one nation from another, education should focus on the similarities among all people and places on Earth."

What do you think of the view of education expressed above? Explain, using reasons and/or specific examples from your own experience, observations, or reading.

"As government bureaucracy increases, citizens become more and more separated from their government."

Discuss the extent to which you agree or disagree with the opinion expressed above. Support your point of view with reasons and/or examples from your own experience, observations, or reading.

"The goal of business should not be to make as big a profit as possible. Instead, business should also concern itself with the well-being of the public."

Discuss the extent to which you agree or disagree with the opinion expressed above. Support your point of view with reasons and/or examples from your own experience, observations, or reading.

"The rise of multinational corporations is leading to global homogeneity.* Because people everywhere are beginning to want the same products and services, regional differences are rapidly disappearing."

* homogeneity: sameness, similarity

Discuss the extent to which you agree or disagree with the opinion expressed above. Support your point of view with reasons and/or examples from your own experience, observations, or reading.

"Manufacturers are responsible for ensuring that their products are safe. If a product injures someone, for whatever reason, the manufacturer should be held legally and financially accountable for the injury."

Discuss the extent to which you agree or disagree with the opinion expressed above. Support your point of view with reasons and/or examples from your own experience, observations, or reading.

"Work greatly influences people's personal lives—their special interests, their leisure activities, even their appearance away from the workplace."

Discuss the extent to which you agree or disagree with the opinion expressed above. Support your point of view with reasons and/or examples from your own experience, observations, or reading.

"Since the physical work environment affects employee productivity and morale, the employees themselves should have the right to decide how their workplace is designed."

Discuss the extent to which you agree or disagree with the opinion stated above. Support your views with reasons and/or examples from your own experience, observations, or reading.

"The most important quality in an employee is not specific knowledge or technical competence. Instead, it is the ability to work well with other employees."

Discuss the extent to which you agree or disagree with the opinion expressed above. Support your point of view with reasons and/or examples from your own experience, observations, or reading.

"So long as no laws are broken, there is nothing unethical about doing whatever you need to do to promote existing products or to create new products."

Discuss the extent to which you agree or disagree with the opinion expressed above. Support your point of view with reasons and/or examples from your own experience, observations, or reading.

"Commercialism has become too widespread. It has even crept into schools and places of worship. Every nation should place limits on what kinds of products, if any, can be sold at certain events or places."

Discuss the extent to which you agree or disagree with the opinion expressed above. Support your point of view with reasons and/or examples from your own experience, observations, or reading.

"Companies should not try to improve employees' performance by giving incentives—for example, awards or gifts. These incentives encourage negative kinds of behavior instead of encouraging a genuine interest in doing the work well."

Discuss the extent to which you agree or disagree with the opinion stated above. Support your views with reasons and/or examples from your own experience, observations, or reading.

"People often give the following advice: "Be yourself. Follow your instincts and behave in a way that feels natural."

Do you think that, in general, this is good advice? Why or why not? Develop your point of view by giving reasons and/or examples from your own experience, observations, or reading.

"The people we remember best are the ones who broke the rules."

Discuss the extent to which you agree or disagree with the opinion expressed above. Support your point of view with reasons and/or examples from your own experience, observations, or reading.

"There are essentially two forces that motivate people: self-interest and fear."

Discuss the extent to which you agree or disagree with the opinion stated above. Support your position with reasons and/or examples from your own experience, observations, or reading.

"For a leader there is nothing more difficult, and therefore more important, than to be able to make decisions."

Discuss the extent to which you agree or disagree with the opinion expressed above. Support your point of view with reasons and/or examples from your own experience, observations, or reading.

"Although 'genius' is difficult to define, one of the qualities of genius is the ability to transcend traditional modes of thought and create new ones."

Explain what you think the above statement means and discuss the extent to which you agree or disagree with this definition of genius. In your discussion, be sure to include at least one example of someone who, in your opinion, exemplifies genius or a particular characteristic of genius.

"Most people would agree that buildings represent a valuable record of any society's past, but controversy arises when old buildings stand on ground that modern planners feel could be better used for modern purposes."

In your opinion, which is more important—preserving historic buildings or encouraging modern development? Explain your position, using reasons and examples based on your own experiences, observations, or reading.

"The ability to deal with people is as purchasable a commodity as sugar or coffee, and it is worth more than any other commodity under the sun."

Explain what you think the above quotation means and discuss the extent to which you agree or disagree with it. Support your position with relevant reasons and/or examples from your own experience, observations, or reading.

"As individuals, people save too little and borrow too much."

From your perspective, how accurate is the view expressed above? In your discussion, be sure to consider the conditions under which it is appropriate to save money and the conditions under which it is appropriate to borrow. Develop your position using reasons and/or examples from your own experience, observations, or reading.

"No one can possibly achieve any real and lasting success or 'get rich' in business by conforming to conventional practices or ways of thinking."

Discuss the extent to which you agree or disagree with the opinion stated above. Support your views with reasons and/or examples from your own experience, observations, or reading.

"Business and government must do more, much more, to meet the needs and goals of women in the workplace."

What do you think of the opinion expressed above? In your discussion, be sure to use reasons and/or examples from your own experience, observations, or reading.

"We shape our buildings and afterward our buildings shape us."

Explain what you think this statement means and discuss the extent to which you do or do not agree with it. Support your views with reasons and/or specific examples from your experience, observations, or reading.

"A business should not be held responsible for providing customers with complete information about its products or services; customers should have the responsibility of gathering information about the products or services they may want to buy."

Discuss the extent to which you agree or disagree with the opinion stated above. Support your views with reasons and/or examples from your own experience, observations, or reading.

"Advertising is the most influential and therefore the most important artistic achievement of the twentieth century."

Discuss the extent to which you agree or disagree with the opinion expressed above. Support your point of view with reasons and/or examples from your own experience, observations, or reading.

"Whether promoting a product, an event, or a person, an advertising campaign is most effective when it appeals to emotion rather than to reason."

Discuss the extent to which you agree or disagree with the opinion expressed above. Support your point of view with reasons and/or examples from your own experience, observations, or reading.

"As technologies and the demand for certain services change, many workers will lose their jobs. The responsibility for those people to adjust to such change should belong to the individual worker, not to government or to business."

Discuss the extent to which you agree or disagree with the opinion stated above. Support your position with specific reasons and/or examples drawn from your reading, your observations, or your own experience.

"Each generation must accept blame not only for the hateful words and actions of some of its members but also for the failure of other members to speak out against those words and actions."

Discuss the extent to which you agree or disagree with the opinion expressed above. Support your point of view with reasons and/or examples from your own experience, observations, or reading.

"The study of history is largely a waste of time because it prevents us from focusing on the challenges of the present."

Discuss the extent to which you agree or disagree with the opinion expressed above. Support your point of view with reasons and/or examples from your own experience, observations, or reading.

"People often complain that products are not made to last. They feel that making products that wear out fairly quickly wastes both natural and human resources. What they fail to see, however, is that such manufacturing practices keep costs down for the consumer and stimulate demand."

Which do you find more compelling: the complaint about products that do not last or the response to it? Explain your position using relevant reasons and/or examples drawn from your own experience, observations, or reading.

"Government should establish regulations to reduce or eliminate any suspected health hazards in the environment, even when the scientific studies of these health hazards are incomplete or contradictory."

Discuss the extent to which you agree or disagree with the opinion stated above. Support your views with reasons and/or examples from your own experience, observations, or reading.

"Employees should show loyalty to their company by fully supporting the company's managers and policies, even when the employees believe that the managers and policies are misguided."

Discuss the extent to which you agree or disagree with the opinion stated above. Support your views with reasons and/or examples from your own experience, observations, or reading.

"To be successful, companies should trust their workers and give them as much freedom as possible. Any company that tries to control employees' behavior through a strict system of rewards and punishments will soon find that such controls have a negative effect on employee morale and, consequently, on the company's success."

Discuss the extent to which you agree or disagree with the opinion stated above. Support your views with reasons and/or examples from your own experience, observations, or reading.

"If parents want to prepare their children to succeed in life, teaching the children self-discipline is more important than teaching them self-esteem."

Discuss the extent to which you agree or disagree with the opinion stated above. Support your views with reasons and/or examples from your own experience, observations, or reading.

"Companies are never justified in employing young children, even if the child's family would benefit from the income." Discuss the extent to which you agree or disagree with the opinion stated above. Support your views with reasons and/or examples from your own experience, observations, or reading.

"In order to understand a society, we must examine the contents of its museums and the subjects of its memorials. What a society chooses to preserve, display, and commemorate is the truest indicator of what the society values."

Discuss the extent to which you agree or disagree with the opinion stated above. Support your views with reasons and/or examples from your own experience, observations, or reading.

"In business, more than in any other social arena, men and women have learned how to share power effectively."

Discuss the extent to which you agree or disagree with the opinion stated above. Support your views with reasons and/or examples from your own experience, observations, or reading.

"In order to accommodate the increasing number of undergraduate students, colleges and universities should offer most courses through distance learning, such as videotaped instruction that can be accessed through the Internet or cable television. Requiring students to appear at a designated time and place is no longer an effective or efficient way of teaching most undergraduate courses."

Discuss the extent to which you agree or disagree with the opinion stated above. Support your views with reasons and/or examples from your own experience, observations, or reading.

"If a nation is to ensure its own economic success, it must maintain a highly competitive educational system in which students compete among themselves and against students from other countries."

Discuss the extent to which you agree or disagree with the opinion stated above. Support your views with reasons and/or examples from your own experience, observations, or reading.

"In order to force companies to improve policies and practices considered unethical or harmful, society should rely primarily on consumer action—such as refusal to buy product—rather than legislative action."

Discuss the extent to which you agree or disagree with the opinion stated above. Support your views with reasons and/or examples from your own experience, observations, or reading.

"The automobile has caused more problems than it has solved. Most societies would probably be much better off if the automobile had never been invented."

Discuss the extent to which you agree or disagree with the opinion stated above. Support your views with reasons and/or examples from your own experience, observations, or reading.

"An advanced degree may help someone get a particular job. Once a person begins working, however, the advanced degree and the formal education it represents are rarely relevant to success on the job."

Discuss the extent to which you agree or disagree with the opinion stated above. Support your views with reasons and/or examples from your own experience, observations, or reading.

"Most people today place too much emphasis on satisfying their immediate desires. The overall quality of life would be greatly improved if we all focused instead on meeting our long-term needs."

Discuss the extent to which you agree or disagree with the opinion stated above. Support your views with reasons and/or examples from your own experience, observations, or reading.

"The value of any nation should be measured more by its scientific and artistic achievements than by its business successes."

Discuss the extent to which you agree or disagree with the opinion stated above. Support your views with reasons and/or examples from your own experience, observations, or reading.

"All archaeological treasures should remain in the country in which they were originally discovered. These works should not be exported, even if museums in other parts of the world are better able to preserve and display them."

Discuss the extent to which you agree or disagree with the opinion stated above. Support your views with reasons and/or examples from your own experience, observations, or reading.

"The most effective way for managers to assign work is to divide complex tasks into their simpler component parts. This way, each worker completes a small portion of the task but contributes to the whole."

Discuss the extent to which you agree or disagree with the opinion stated above. Support your views with reasons and/or examples from your own experience, observations, or reading.

"People are overwhelmed by the increasing amount of information available on the computer. Therefore, the immediate goal of the information technology industry should be to help people learn how to obtain the information they need efficiently and wisely."

Discuss the extent to which you agree or disagree with the opinion stated above. Support your views with reasons and/or examples from your own experience, observations, or reading.

"Employees should not have full access to their own personnel files. If, for example, employees were allowed to see certain confidential materials, the people supplying that information would not be likely to express their opinions candidly."

Discuss the extent to which you agree or disagree with the opinion stated above. Support your views with reasons and/or examples from your own experience, observations, or reading.

"All personnel evaluations at a company should be multidirectional—that is, people at every level of the organization should review not only those working 'under' them but also those working 'over' them."

Discuss the extent to which you agree or disagree with the opinion stated above. Support your views with reasons and/or examples from your own experience, observations, or reading.

"The most effective business leaders are those who maintain the highest ethical standards."

Discuss the extent to which you agree or disagree with the opinion stated above. Support your views with reasons and/or examples from your own experience, observations, or reading.

"Because of recent advancements in business and technology, the overall quality of life in most societies has never been better than at the present time."

Discuss the extent to which you agree or disagree with the opinion stated above. Support your views with reasons and/or examples from your own experience, observations, or reading.

"In most fields—including education, politics, and business—the prevailing philosophy never stays in place very long. This pattern of constantly shifting from one theoretical position to another is an inevitable reflection of human nature: people soon tire of the status quo."

Discuss the extent to which you agree or disagree with the opinion stated above. Support your views with reasons and/or examples from your own experience, observations, or reading.

"It is essential that the nations of the world increase spending on the building of space stations and on the exploration of other planets, even if that means spending less on other government programs."

Discuss the extent to which you agree or disagree with the opinion stated above. Support your views with reasons and/or examples from your own experience, observations, or reading.

"Technology ultimately separates and alienates people more than it serves to bring them together."

Discuss the extent to which you agree or disagree with the opinion stated above. Support your views with reasons and/or examples from your own experience, observations, or reading.

"All employees should help decide how the profits of their company or business should be used."

Discuss the extent to which you agree or disagree with the opinion stated above. Support your views with reasons and/or examples from your own experience, observations, or reading.

"A government should provide funding for the arts, but only for those artistic works that reflect the values and attitudes of the majority of the population."

Discuss the extent to which you agree or disagree with the opinion stated above. Support your views with reasons and/or examples from your own experience, observations, or reading.

"The well-being of a society depends more on the success of small businesses than on the success of a few large, high-profile corporations."

Discuss the extent to which you agree or disagree with the opinion stated above. Support your views with reasons and/or examples from your own experience, observations, or reading.

"People's loyalty to political parties and political leaders significantly hinders their ability to form their own opinions about an issue."

Discuss the extent to which you agree or disagree with the opinion stated above. Support your views with reasons and/or examples from your own experience, observations, or reading.

"It makes no sense for people with strong technological skills to go to college if they know that they can earn a good salary without a college degree."

Discuss the extent to which you agree or disagree with the opinion stated above. Support your views with reasons and/or examples from your own experience, observations, or reading.

"Companies should not allow the trend toward informality in dress and conduct at the workplace to continue; formality in dress and behavior helps create a more disciplined and productive work environment."

Discuss the extent to which you agree or disagree with the opinion stated above. Support your views with reasons and/or examples from your own experience, observations, or reading.

"Whether people accept or reject an idea depends more on the way it is presented to them than on the merits of the idea itself."

Discuss the extent to which you agree or disagree with the opinion stated above. Support your views with reasons and/or examples from your own experience, observations, or reading.

"Schools should not teach specialized information and techniques, which might soon become outdated. Instead, schools should encourage a more general approach to learning."

Discuss the extent to which you agree or disagree with the opinion stated above. Support your views with reasons and/or examples from your own experience, observations, or reading.

"The current trend of moving frequently from company to company has negative consequences: it causes instability in the workplace and, as a result, instability in society. Therefore, companies should require employees to make a long-term commitment to the organization."

Discuss the extent to which you agree or disagree with the opinion stated above. Support your views with reasons and/or examples from your own experience, observations, or reading.

"The most effective leaders are those who can solve complex problems by finding simple, immediate solutions."

Discuss the extent to which you agree or disagree with the opinion stated above. Support your views with reasons and/or examples from your own experience, observations, or reading.

"Formal education should not come to an end when people graduate from college. Instead, people should frequently enroll in courses throughout their lives."

Discuss the extent to which you agree or disagree with the opinion stated above. Support your views with reasons and/or examples from your own experience, observations, or reading.

"Laws pertaining to relatively minor crimes must be vigorously enforced if a society hopes to stop more serious crimes."

Discuss the extent to which you agree or disagree with the opinion stated above. Support your views with reasons and/or examples from your own experience, observations, or reading.

"In general, a company's most valuable employees are those who are concerned more with efficiency than with quality."

Discuss the extent to which you agree or disagree with the opinion stated above. Support your views with reasons and/or examples from your own experience, observations, or reading.

"Instead of relying on the advice of outside experts, organizations should place greater value on the advice that can come only from their own highly experienced employees."

Discuss the extent to which you agree or disagree with the opinion stated above. Support your views with reasons and/or examples from your own experience, observations, or reading.

"When judging the qualifications of potential employees, business employers should rely solely on objective information, such as a candidate's résumé and education. Personal interviews are much too subjective and are therefore not a valid basis on which to judge a person's qualifications for a job."

Discuss the extent to which you agree or disagree with the opinion stated above. Support your views with reasons and/or examples from your own experience, observations, or reading.

"We can learn more about a society by observing how its people spend their leisure time than by observing them at work."

Discuss the extent to which you agree or disagree with the opinion stated above. Support your views with reasons and/or examples from your own experience, observations, or reading.

"Governments should not be responsible for regulating businesses and other organizations. Instead, society would benefit if the organizations themselves assumed most of the responsibility for establishing and enforcing their own standards and regulations."

Discuss the extent to which you agree or disagree with the opinion stated above. Support your views with reasons and/or examples from your own experience, observations, or reading.

"In any business or other organization, it is better to have managers with strong leadership skills than managers with expertise and work experience in a particular field."

Discuss the extent to which you agree or disagree with the opinion stated above. Support your views with reasons and/or examples from your own experience, observations, or reading.

"Employees should not be asked to provide formal evaluations of their supervisor because they have little basis for judging or even understanding their supervisor's performance."

Discuss the extent to which you agree or disagree with the opinion stated above. Support your views with reasons and/or examples from your own experience, observations, or reading.

"Although many people object to advertisements and solicitations that intrude into their lives through such means as the telephone, the Internet, and television, companies and organizations must have the right to contact potential customers and donors whenever and however they wish."

Discuss the extent to which you agree or disagree with the opinion stated above. Support your views with reasons and/or examples from your own experience, observations, or reading.

"In business courses, professors should teach only factual information and skills, not ethics."

Discuss the extent to which you agree or disagree with the opinion stated above. Support your views with reasons and/or examples from your own experience, observations, or reading.

"In some companies, employees are allowed to express their feelings and opinions about the company by sending electronic messages to everyone in the company. In other companies, this type of communication is strictly prohibited."

What restrictions, if any, do you think companies should place on employees' electronic communications? Support your views with reasons and/or examples from your own experience, observations, or reading.

"Some people claim that in order to protect national parks and historical sites, public access to them should be greatly restricted. Others argue that there should be few restrictions, if any, because such places were intended for everyone to use."

Explain your position on this issue. Support your views with reasons and/or examples from your own experience, observations, or reading.

"Some people claim that the growth of mass media has stifled intellectual curiosity. Others, however, argue that the availability of so much information and entertainment has encouraged individuals to expand their intellect and creativity."

Explain your position on this issue. Support your views with reasons and/or examples from your own experience, observations, or reading.

"Some experts maintain that students learn best in a highly structured environment, one that emphasizes discipline, punctuality, and routine. Others insist that educators, if they are to help students maximize their potential, ought to maintain an atmosphere of relative freedom and spontaneity."

Explain your position on the issue of structure versus freedom in an ideal learning environment. Support your views with reasons and/or examples from your own experience, observations, or reading.

10.7 GMAT® Scoring Guide: Analysis of an Argument

6 Outstanding

A 6 paper presents a cogent, well-articulated critique of the argument and demonstrates mastery of the elements of effective writing.

A typical paper in this category exhibits the following characteristics:

- clearly identifies important features of the argument and analyzes them insightfully
- develops ideas cogently, organizes them logically, and connects them with clear transitions
- effectively supports the main points of the critique
- demonstrates control of language, including diction and syntactic variety
- demonstrates facility with the conventions of standard written English but may have minor flaws

5 Strong

A 5 paper presents a well-developed critique of the argument and demonstrates good control of the elements of effective writing.

A typical paper in this category exhibits the following characteristics:

- clearly identifies important features of the argument and analyzes them in a generally thoughtful way
- develops ideas clearly, organizes them logically, and connects them with appropriate transitions
- sensibly supports the main points of the critique
- demonstrates control of language, including diction and syntactic variety
- demonstrates facility with the conventions of standard written English but may have occasional flaws

4 Adequate

A 4 paper presents a competent critique of the argument and demonstrates adequate control of the elements of writing.

A typical paper in this category exhibits the following characteristics:

- identifies and analyzes important features of the argument
- develops and organizes ideas satisfactorily but may not connect them with transitions
- supports the main points of the critique
- demonstrates sufficient control of language to convey ideas with reasonable clarity
- generally follows the conventions of standard written English but may have some flaws

3 Limited

A 3 paper demonstrates some competence in analytical writing skills and in its control of the elements of writing but is plainly flawed.

A typical paper in this category exhibits one or more of the following characteristics:

- does not identify or analyze most of the important features of the argument, although some analysis of the argument is present
- mainly analyzes tangential or irrelevant matters, or reasons poorly
- is limited in the logical development and organization of ideas
- offers support of little relevance and value for points of the critique
- does not convey meaning clearly
- contains occasional major errors or frequent minor errors in grammar, usage, and mechanics

2 Seriously Flawed

A 2 paper demonstrates serious weaknesses in analytical writing skills.

A typical paper in this category exhibits one or more of the following characteristics:

- does not present a critique based on logical analysis, but may instead present the writer's own views on the subject
- does not develop ideas, or is disorganized and illogical
- provides little, if any, relevant or reasonable support
- has serious and frequent problems in the use of language and in sentence structure
- contains numerous errors in grammar, usage, and mechanics that interfere with meaning

1 Fundamentally Deficient

A 1 paper demonstrates fundamental deficiencies in analytical writing skills.

A typical paper in this category exhibits more than one of the following characteristics:

- provides little evidence of the ability to understand and analyze the argument
- provides little evidence of the ability to develop an organized response
- has severe and persistent errors in language and sentence structure
- contains a pervasive pattern of errors in grammar, usage, and mechanics that results in incoherence

0 No Score

A paper in this category is off topic, not written in English, is merely attempting to copy the topic, or consists only of keystroke characters.

NR Blank

10.8 Sample: Analysis of an Argument

Read the statement and the instructions that follow it, and then make any notes that will help you plan your response.

The following appeared as part of an article in a daily newspaper:

"The computerized on-board warning system that will be installed in commercial airliners will virtually solve the problem of midair plane collisions. One plane's warning system can receive signals from another's transponder—a radio set that signals a plane's course—in order to determine the likelihood of a collision and recommend evasive action."

Discuss how well reasoned you find this argument. In your discussion, be sure to analyze the line of reasoning and the use of evidence in the argument. For example, you may need to consider what questionable assumptions underlie the thinking and what alternative explanations or counterexamples might weaken the conclusion. You can also discuss what sort of evidence would strengthen or refute the argument, what changes in the argument would make it more logically sound, and what, if anything, would help you better evaluate its conclusion.

Sample Paper 6

The argument that this warning system will virtually solve the problem of midair plane collisions omits some important concerns that must be addressed to substantiate the argument. The statement that follows the description of what this warning system will do simply describes the system and how it operates. This alone does not constitute a logical argument in favor of the warning system, and it certainly does not provide support or proof of the main argument.

Most conspicuously, the argument does not address the cause of the problem of midair plane collisions, the use of the system by pilots and flight specialists, or who is involved in the midair plane collisions. First, the argument assumes that the cause of the problem is that the planes' courses, the likelihood of collisions, and actions to avoid collisions are unknown or inaccurate. In a weak attempt to support its claim, the argument describes a system that makes all of these things accurately known. But if the cause of the problem of midair plane collisions is that pilots are not paying attention to their computer systems or flight operations, the warning system will not solve the collision problem. Second, the argument never addresses the interface between individuals and the system and how this will affect the warning system's objective of obliterating the problem of collisions. If the pilot or flight specialist does not conform to what the warning system suggests, midair collisions will not be avoided. Finally, if planes other than commercial airliners are involved in the collisions, the problem of these collisions cannot be solved by a warning system that will not be installed on non-commercial airliners. The argument also does not address what would happen in the event that the warning system collapses, fails, or does not work properly.

Because the argument leaves out several key issues, it is not sound or persuasive. If it included the items discussed above instead of solely explaining what the system supposedly does, the argument would have been more thorough and convincing.

Explanation of Score 6

This response is, as the scoring guide requires of a 6, "cogent" and "well articulated": all the points made not only bear directly on the argument to be analyzed but also contribute to a single, integrated development of the writer's critique. The writer begins by making the controlling point that a mere description of the warning system's mode of operation cannot serve as a true argument proving the system's effectiveness, since the description overlooks several major considerations. The writer then identifies these considerations—what causes midair collisions, how pilots will actually use the commercial airline warning system, what kinds of airplanes are typically involved in midair collisions—and, citing appropriate counterexamples (e.g., what if pilots do not pay attention to their instruments?), explains fully how each oversight undermines the conclusion that the warning system will virtually eliminate midair plane collisions.

Throughout, the writer complements the logically organized development of this critique with good, clear prose that demonstrates the ability not only to control language and vary sentence structure but also to express ideas forcibly (e.g., "the argument never addresses the interface between individuals and the system"). Of course, as in any response written under time constraints, occasional minor flaws can be found. For example, "the argument assumes that the cause of the problem is that the planes' courses, the likelihood of collisions, and actions to avoid collisions are unknown or inaccurate" is wordy and imprecise: how can a course, a likelihood, or actions be inaccurate? But flaws such as these, minor and infrequent, do not interfere with the overall clarity and forcefulness of this outstanding response.

Sample Paper 4

The argument is not logically convincing. It does not state whether all planes can receive signals from each other. It does not state whether planes constantly receive signals. If they only receive signals once every certain time interval, collisions will not definitely be prevented. Further if they receive a signal right before they are about to crash, they cannot avoid each other.

The main flaw in the argument is that it assumes that the two planes, upon receiving each other's signals, will know which evasive action to take. For example, the two planes could be going towards each other and then receive the signals. If one turns at an angle to the left and the other turns at an angle to the right, the two planes will still crash. Even if they receive an updated signal, they will not have time to avoid each other.

The following argument would be more sound and persuasive. The new warning system will solve the problem of midair plane collisions. Each plane will receive constant, continual signals from each other. If the two planes are headed in a direction where they will crash, the system will coordinate the signals, and tell one plane to go one way, and the other plane to go another way. The new system will ensure that the two planes will turn in different directions so they don't crash by trying to prevent the original crash. In addition, the two planes will be able to see themselves and the other on a computer screen, to aid in the evasive action.

Explanation of Score 4

This response competently cites a number of deficiencies in the argument presented: the information given about the nature of the signals sent and received and the evasive action recommended does not warrant the conclusion that the onboard warning system "will virtually solve the problem of midair plane collisions." However, in discussing these insufficiencies in the argument, the response reveals an unevenness in the quality of its reasoning. For example, while it is perfectly legitimate to point out that the argument assumes too much and says too little about the evasive action that will be recommended by the warning system, it is farfetched to suggest that the system might be so poorly designed as to route two approaching airplanes to the same spot. Likewise, while it is fair to question the effectiveness of a warning signal about which the argument says so little, it is not reasonable to assume that the system would be designed to space signals so far apart that they would prove useless. Rather than invent implausibly bad versions of the warning system to prove that it might be ineffective, a stronger response would analyze unexplored possibilities inherent in the information that is given—for example, the possibility that pilots might not be able to respond quickly and effectively to the radio signals the argument says they will receive when the new system is installed. The "more sound and persuasive argument" in the last paragraph, while an improvement on the original, continues to overlook this possibility and also assumes that other types of aircraft without transponders will pose no problems.

The organization of ideas, while generally sound, is sometimes weakened by needless repetition of the same points, as in sentences 4 and 5 of the last paragraph. The writing contains minor instances of awkwardness (e.g., "Each plane will receive constant, continual signals from each other" in paragraph 3), but is free of flaws that make understanding difficult. However, though the writing is generally clean and clear, the syntax does not show much variety. A few sentences begin with "if" clauses, but almost all the rest, even those that begin with a transitional phrase such as "for example" or "in addition," conform to a "subject, verb, complement" pattern. The first paragraph, in which the second and third sentences begin the same way ("It does not state"), is particularly repetitious.

Sample Paper 2

This argument has no information about air collisions. I think most cases happen in new airports because the air traffic I heavy. In this case sound airport control could solve the problem.

I think this argument is logically reasonable. Its assumption is that plane collisions are caused by planes that don't know each others positions. So pilots can do nothing, if they know each others position through the system it will solve the problem.

If it can provide evidence the problem is lack of knowledge of each others positions, it will be more sound and persuasive.

More information about air collisions is helpful, (the reason for air collisions).

Explanation of Score 2

This response is seriously flawed in several ways. First of all, it has very little substance. The writer appears to make only one point—that while it seems reasonable to assume that midair collisions would be less likely if pilots were sure of each other's positions, readers cannot adequately judge this assumption without more information about where, why, and how such collisions occur. This point, furthermore, is neither explained by a single reason beyond what is given in the topic nor supported by a single example. Legitimate though it is, it cannot, alone and undeveloped, serve as an adequate response to the argument.

Aside from being undeveloped, the response is confusing. At the outset, it seems to be critical of the argument. The writer begins by pointing to the inadequacy of the information given; then speculates, without evidence, that "most cases happen in new airports"; and then suggests that the problem should be addressed by improving "airport control," not (it is implied) by installing onboard warning systems. After criticizing the argument in the first paragraph, the writer confusingly seems to endorse it in the second. Then, in the remainder of the response, the writer returns to a critical stance.

The general lack of coherence is reflected in the serious and frequent writing problems that make meaning hard to determine—for example, the elliptical and ungrammatical "So pilots can do nothing, if they know each others position through the system it will solve the problem" (paragraph 2) or "If it can provide evidence the problem is lack of knowledge of each others positions, it will be more sound and persuasive" (paragraph 3). The prose suffers from a variety of basic errors in grammar, usage, and mechanics.

10.9 Analysis of an Argument Sample Topics

The following appeared as part of an annual report sent to stockholders by Olympic Foods, a processor of frozen foods:

"Over time, the costs of processing go down because as organizations learn how to do things better, they become more efficient. In color film processing, for example, the cost of a 3-by-5-inch print fell from 50 cents for five-day service in 1970 to 20 cents for one-day service in 1984. The same principle applies to the processing of food. And since Olympic Foods will soon celebrate its 25th birthday, we can expect that our long experience will enable us to minimize costs and thus maximize profits."

Discuss how well reasoned you find this argument. In your discussion be sure to analyze the line of reasoning and the use of evidence in the argument. For example, you may need to consider what questionable assumptions underlie the thinking and what alternative explanations or counterexamples might weaken the conclusion. You can also discuss what sort of evidence would strengthen or refute the argument, what changes in the argument would make it more logically sound, and what, if anything, would help you better evaluate its conclusion.

The following appeared in a memorandum from the business department of the Apogee Company:

"When the Apogee Company had all its operations in one location, it was more profitable than it is today. Therefore, the Apogee Company should close down its field offices and conduct all its operations from a single location. Such centralization would improve profitability by cutting costs and helping the company maintain better supervision of all employees."

Discuss how well reasoned . . . etc.

The following appeared in a memorandum issued by a large city's council on the arts:

"In a recent citywide poll, 15 percent more residents said that they watch television programs about the visual arts than was the case in a poll conducted five years ago. During these past five years, the number of people visiting our city's art museums has increased by a similar percentage. Since the corporate funding that supports public television, where most of the visual arts programs appear, is now being threatened with severe cuts, we can expect that attendance at our city's art museums will also start to decrease. Thus some of the city's funds for supporting the arts should be reallocated to public television."

Discuss how well reasoned . . . etc.

The following appeared in a report presented for discussion at a meeting of the directors of a company that manufactures parts for heavy machinery:

"The falling revenues that the company is experiencing coincide with delays in manufacturing. These delays, in turn, are due in large part to poor planning in purchasing metals. Consider further that the manager of the department that handles purchasing of raw materials has an excellent background in general business, psychology, and sociology, but knows little about the properties of metals. The company should, therefore, move the purchasing manager to the sales department and bring in a scientist from the research division to be manager of the purchasing department."

Discuss how well reasoned . . . etc.

The following appeared in an announcement issued by the publisher of *The Mercury*, a weekly newspaper:

"Since a competing lower-priced newspaper, *The Bugle*, was started five years ago, *The Mercury*'s circulation has declined by 10,000 readers. The best way to get more people to read *The Mercury* is to reduce its price below that of *The Bugle*, at least until circulation increases to former levels. The increased circulation of *The Mercury* will attract more businesses to buy advertising space in the paper."

Discuss how well reasoned . . . etc.

The following appeared as part of an article in a magazine devoted to regional life:

"Corporations should look to the city of Helios when seeking new business opportunities or a new location. Even in the recent recession, Helios's unemployment rate was lower than the regional average. It is the industrial center of the region, and historically it has provided more than its share of the region's manufacturing jobs. In addition, Helios is attempting to expand its economic base by attracting companies that focus on research and development of innovative technologies."

Discuss how well reasoned . . . etc.

The following appeared in the health section of a magazine on trends and lifestyles:

"People who use the artificial sweetener aspartame are better off consuming sugar, since aspartame can actually contribute to weight gain rather than weight loss. For example, high levels of aspartame have been shown to trigger a craving for food by depleting the brain of a chemical that registers satiety, or the sense of being full. Furthermore, studies suggest that sugars, if consumed after at least 45 minutes of continuous exercise, actually enhance the body's ability to burn fat. Consequently, those who drink aspartame-sweetened juices after exercise will also lose this calorie-burning benefit. Thus it appears that people consuming aspartame rather than sugar are unlikely to achieve their dietary goals."

Discuss how well reasoned . . . etc.

The following appeared in the editorial section of a corporate newsletter:

"The common notion that workers are generally apathetic about management issues is false, or at least outdated: a recently published survey indicates that 79 percent of the nearly 1,200 workers who responded to survey questionnaires expressed a high level of interest in the topics of corporate restructuring and redesign of benefits programs."

Discuss how well reasoned . . . etc.

The following appeared in the opinion column of a financial magazine:

"On average, middle-aged consumers devote 39 percent of their retail expenditure to department store products and services, while for younger consumers the average is only 25 percent. Since the number of middle-aged people will increase dramatically within the next decade, department stores can expect retail sales to increase significantly during that period. Furthermore, to take advantage of the trend, these stores should begin to replace some of those products intended to attract the younger consumer with products intended to attract the middle-aged consumer."

Discuss how well reasoned . . . etc.

The following appeared in the editorial section of a local newspaper:

"This past winter, 200 students from Waymarsh State College traveled to the state capitol building to protest against proposed cuts in funding for various state college programs. The other 12,000 Waymarsh students evidently weren't so concerned about their education: they either stayed on campus or left for winter break. Since the group who did not protest is far more numerous, it is more representative of the state's college students than are the protesters. Therefore the state legislature need not heed the appeals of the protesting students."

Discuss how well reasoned . . . etc.

The following appeared in the editorial section of a local newspaper:

"In the first four years that Montoya has served as mayor of the city of San Perdito, the population has decreased and the unemployment rate has increased. Two businesses have closed for each new business that has opened. Under Varro, who served as mayor for four years before Montoya, the unemployment rate decreased and the population increased. Clearly, the residents of San Perdito would be best served if they voted Montoya out of office and reelected Varro."

Discuss how well reasoned . . . etc.

The following appeared as part of a promotional campaign to sell advertising space in the *Daily Gazette* to grocery stores in the Marston area:

"Advertising the reduced price of selected grocery items in the *Daily Gazette* will help you increase your sales. Consider the results of a study conducted last month. Thirty sale items from a store in downtown Marston were advertised in *The Gazette* for four days. Each time one or more of the 30 items was purchased, clerks asked whether the shopper had read the ad. Two-thirds of the 200 shoppers asked answered in the affirmative. Furthermore, more than half the customers who answered in the affirmative spent over $100 at the store."

Discuss how well reasoned . . . etc.

The following appeared as part of a campaign to sell advertising time on a local radio station to local businesses:

"The Cumquat Café began advertising on our local radio station this year and was delighted to see its business increase by 10 percent over last year's totals. Their success shows you how you can use radio advertising to make your business more profitable."

Discuss how well reasoned . . . etc.

The following appeared as part of a newspaper editorial:

"Two years ago Nova High School began to use interactive computer instruction in three academic subjects. The school dropout rate declined immediately, and last year's graduates have reported some impressive achievements in college. In future budgets the school board should use a greater portion of the available funds to buy more computers, and all schools in the district should adopt interactive computer instruction throughout the curriculum."

Discuss how well reasoned . . . etc.

The following appeared as a part of an advertisement for Adams, who is seeking reelection as governor:

"Reelect Adams, and you will be voting for proven leadership in improving the state's economy. Over the past year alone, 70 percent of the state's workers have had increases in their wages, 5,000 new jobs have been created, and six corporations have located their headquarters here. Most of the respondents in a recent poll said they believed that the economy is likely to continue to improve if Adams is reelected. Adams's opponent, Zebulon, would lead our state in the wrong direction, because Zebulon disagrees with many of Adams's economic policies."

Discuss how well reasoned . . . etc.

The following appeared as part of an article in the education section of a Waymarsh city newspaper:

"Throughout the last two decades, those who earned graduate degrees found it very difficult to get jobs teaching their academic specialties at the college level. Those with graduate degrees from Waymarsh University had an especially hard time finding such jobs. But better times are coming in the next decade for all academic job seekers, including those from Waymarsh. Demographic trends indicate that an increasing number of people will be reaching college age over the next 10 years; consequently, we can expect that the job market will improve dramatically for people seeking college-level teaching positions in their fields."

Discuss how well reasoned . . . etc.

The following appeared in an article in a consumer-products magazine:

"Two of today's best-selling brands of full-strength prescription medication for the relief of excess stomach acid, Acid-Ease and Pepticaid, are now available in milder nonprescription forms. Doctors have written 76 million more prescriptions for full-strength Acid-Ease than for full-strength Pepticaid. So people who need an effective but milder nonprescription medication for the relief of excess stomach acid should choose Acid-Ease."

Discuss how well reasoned . . . etc.

The following is an excerpt from a memo written by the head of a governmental department:

"Neither stronger ethics regulations nor stronger enforcement mechanisms are necessary to ensure ethical behavior by companies doing business with this department. We already have a code of ethics that companies doing business with this department are urged to abide by, and virtually all of these companies have agreed to follow it. We also know that the code is relevant to the current business environment because it was approved within the last year, and in direct response to specific violations committed by companies with which we were then working—not in abstract anticipation of potential violations, as so many such codes are."

Discuss how well reasoned . . . etc.

The following appeared as part of an article in the travel section of a newspaper:

"Over the past decade, the restaurant industry in the country of Spiessa has experienced unprecedented growth. This surge can be expected to continue in the coming years, fueled by recent social changes: personal incomes are rising, more leisure time is available, single-person households are more common, and people have a greater interest in gourmet food, as evidenced by a proliferation of publications on the subject."

Discuss how well reasoned . . . etc.

The following appeared in an article in a health–and–fitness magazine:

"Laboratory studies show that Saluda Natural Spring Water contains several of the minerals necessary for good health and that it is completely free of bacteria. Residents of Saluda, the small town where the water is bottled, are hospitalized less frequently than the national average. Even though Saluda Natural Spring Water may seem expensive, drinking it instead of tap water is a wise investment in good health."

Discuss how well reasoned . . . etc.

The following appeared as part of an editorial in an industry newsletter:

"While trucking companies that deliver goods pay only a portion of highway maintenance costs and no property tax on the highways they use, railways spend billions per year maintaining and upgrading their facilities. The government should lower the railroad companies' property taxes, since sending goods by rail is clearly a more appropriate mode of ground transportation than highway shipping. For one thing, trains consume only a third of the fuel a truck would use to carry the same load, making them a more cost-effective and environmentally sound mode of transport. Furthermore, since rail lines already exist, increases in rail traffic would not require building new lines at the expense of taxpaying citizens."

Discuss how well reasoned . . . etc.

The following appeared in the editorial section of a newspaper:

"As public concern over drug abuse has increased, authorities have become more vigilant in their efforts to prevent illegal drugs from entering the country. Many drug traffickers have consequently switched from marijuana, which is bulky, or heroin, which has a market too small to justify the risk of severe punishment, to cocaine. Thus enforcement efforts have ironically resulted in an observed increase in the illegal use of cocaine."

Discuss how well reasoned . . . etc.

The following appeared in a speech delivered by a member of the city council:

"Twenty years ago, only half of the students who graduated from Einstein High School went on to attend a college or university. Today, two–thirds of the students who graduate from Einstein do so. Clearly, Einstein has improved its educational effectiveness over the past two decades. This improvement has occurred despite the fact that the school's funding, when adjusted for inflation, is about the same as it was 20 years ago. Therefore, we do not need to make any substantial increase in the school's funding at this time."

Discuss how well reasoned . . . etc.

The following appeared in a memo from the customer service division to the manager of Mammon Savings and Loan:

"We believe that improved customer service is the best way for us to differentiate ourselves from competitors and attract new customers. We can offer our customers better service by reducing waiting time in teller lines from an average of six minutes to an average of three. By opening for business at 8:30 instead of 9:00, and by remaining open for an additional hour beyond our current closing time, we will be better able to accommodate the busy schedules of our customers. These changes will enhance our bank's image as the most customer-friendly bank in town and give us the edge over our competition."

Discuss how well reasoned . . . etc.

The following appeared as part of an article in a magazine on lifestyles:

"Two years ago, City L was listed 14th in an annual survey that ranks cities according to the quality of life that can be enjoyed by those living in them. This information will enable people who are moving to the state in which City L is located to confidently identify one place, at least, where schools are good, housing is affordable, people are friendly, the environment is safe, and the arts flourish."

Discuss how well reasoned . . . etc.

The following appeared in a memorandum from a member of a financial management and consulting firm:

"We have learned from an employee of Windfall, Ltd., that its accounting department, by checking about 10 percent of the last month's purchasing invoices for errors and inconsistencies, saved the company some $10,000 in overpayments. In order to help our clients increase their net gains, we should advise each of them to institute a policy of checking all purchasing invoices for errors. Such a recommendation could also help us get the Windfall account by demonstrating to Windfall the rigorousness of our methods."

Discuss how well reasoned . . . etc.

The following appeared in a newspaper editorial:

"As violence in movies increases, so do crime rates in our cities. To combat this problem we must establish a board to censor certain movies, or we must limit admission to persons over 21 years of age. Apparently our legislators are not concerned about this issue since a bill calling for such actions recently failed to receive a majority vote."

Discuss how well reasoned . . . etc.

The following appeared in the editorial section of a local newspaper:

"Commuter use of the new subway train is exceeding the transit company's projections. However, commuter use of the shuttle buses that transport people to the subway stations is below the projected volume. If the transit company expects commuters to ride the shuttle buses to the subway rather than drive there, it must either reduce the shuttle bus fares or increase the price of parking at the subway stations."

Discuss how well reasoned . . . etc.

The following was excerpted from the speech of a spokesperson for Synthetic Farm Products, Inc.:

"Many farmers who invested in the equipment needed to make the switch from synthetic to organic fertilizers and pesticides feel that it would be too expensive to resume synthetic farming at this point. But studies of farmers who switched to organic farming last year indicate that their current crop yields are lower. Hence their purchase of organic farming equipment, a relatively minor investment compared to the losses that would result from continued lower crop yields, cannot justify persisting on an unwise course. And the choice to farm organically is financially unwise, given that it was motivated by environmental rather than economic concerns."

Discuss how well reasoned . . . etc

The following appeared in a newspaper story giving advice about investments:

"As overall life expectancy continues to rise, the population of our country is growing increasingly older. For example, more than 20 percent of the residents of one of our more populated regions are now at least 65 years old, and occupancy rates at resort hotels in that region declined significantly during the past six months. Because of these two related trends, a prudent investor would be well advised to sell interest in hotels and invest in hospitals and nursing homes instead."

Discuss how well reasoned . . . etc.

The following appeared as part of the business plan of an investment and financial consulting firm:

"Studies suggest that an average coffee drinker's consumption of coffee increases with age, from age 10 through age 60. Even after age 60, coffee consumption remains high. The average cola drinker's consumption of cola, however, declines with increasing age. Both of these trends have remained stable for the past 40 years. Given that the number of older adults will significantly increase as the population ages over the next 20 years, it follows that the demand for coffee will increase and the demand for cola will decrease during this period. We should, therefore, consider transferring our investments from Cola Loca to Early Bird Coffee."

Discuss how well reasoned . . . etc.

The following appeared in the editorial section of a West Cambria newspaper:

"A recent review of the West Cambria volunteer ambulance service revealed a longer average response time to accidents than was reported by a commercial ambulance squad located in East Cambria. In order to provide better patient care for accident victims and to raise revenue for our town by collecting service fees for ambulance use, we should disband our volunteer service and hire a commercial ambulance service."

Discuss how well reasoned . . . etc.

The following is part of a business plan being discussed at a board meeting of the Perks Company:

"It is no longer cost-effective for the Perks Company to continue offering its employees a generous package of benefits and incentives year after year. In periods when national unemployment rates are low, Perks may need to offer such a package in order to attract and keep good employees, but since national unemployment rates are now high, Perks does not need to offer the same benefits and incentives. The money thus saved could be better used to replace the existing plant machinery with more technologically sophisticated equipment, or even to build an additional plant."

Discuss how well reasoned . . . etc.

The following appeared as part of a plan proposed by an executive of the Easy Credit Company to the president:

"The Easy Credit Company would gain an advantage over competing credit card services if we were to donate a portion of the proceeds from the use of our cards to a well-known environmental organization in exchange for the use of its symbol or logo on our card. Since a recent poll shows that a large percentage of the public is concerned about environmental issues, this policy would attract new customers, increase use among existing customers, and enable us to charge interest rates that are higher than the lowest ones available."

Discuss how well reasoned . . . etc.

The following appeared as part of a recommendation from the financial planning office to the administration of Fern Valley University:

"In the past few years, Fern Valley University has suffered from a decline in both enrollments and admissions applications. The reason can be discovered from our students, who most often cite poor teaching and inadequate library resources as their chief sources of dissatisfaction with Fern Valley. Therefore, in order to increase the number of students attending our university, and hence to regain our position as the most prestigious university in the greater Fern Valley metropolitan area, it is necessary to initiate a fund-raising campaign among the alumni that will enable us to expand the range of subjects we teach and to increase the size of our library facilities."

Discuss how well reasoned . . . etc.

The following appeared in an article in a college departmental newsletter:

"Professor Taylor of Jones University is promoting a model of foreign language instruction in which students receive 10 weeks of intensive training, then go abroad to live with families for 10 weeks. The superiority of the model, Professor Taylor contends, is proved by the results of a study in which foreign language tests given to students at 25 other colleges show that first-year foreign language students at Jones speak more fluently after only 10 to 20 weeks in the program than do nine out of 10 foreign language majors elsewhere at the time of their graduation."

Discuss how well reasoned . . . etc.

The following appeared as part of an article in the business section of a local newspaper:

"Motorcycle X has been manufactured in the United States for more than 70 years. Although one foreign company has copied the motorcycle and is selling it for less, the company has failed to attract motorcycle X customers—some say because its product lacks the exceptionally loud noise made by motorcycle X. But there must be some other explanation. After all, foreign cars tend to be quieter than similar American-made cars, but they sell at least as well. Also, television advertisements for motorcycle X highlight its durability and sleek lines, not its noisiness, and the ads typically have voice-overs or rock music rather than engine-roar on the sound track."

Discuss how well reasoned . . . etc.

The following appeared in the editorial section of a campus newspaper:

"Because occupancy rates for campus housing fell during the last academic year, so did housing revenues. To solve the problem, campus housing officials should reduce the number of available housing units, thereby increasing the occupancy rates. Also, to keep students from choosing to live off-campus, housing officials should lower the rents, thereby increasing demand."

Discuss how well reasoned . . . etc.

The following appeared in an Avia Airlines departmental memorandum:

"On average, 9 out of every 1,000 passengers who traveled on Avia Airlines last year filed a complaint about our baggage-handling procedures. This means that although some 1 percent of our passengers were unhappy with those procedures, the overwhelming majority were quite satisfied with them; thus it would appear that a review of the procedures is not important to our goal of maintaining or increasing the number of Avia's passengers."

Discuss how well reasoned . . . etc.

The following appeared as part of an article in a weekly newsmagazine:

"The country of Sacchar can best solve its current trade deficit problem by lowering the price of sugar, its primary export. Such an action would make Sacchar better able to compete for markets with other sugar-exporting countries. The sale of Sacchar's sugar abroad would increase, and this increase would substantially reduce Sacchar's trade deficit."

Discuss how well reasoned . . . etc.

The following appeared as part of an article in a trade publication:

"Stronger laws are needed to protect new kinds of home-security systems from being copied and sold by imitators. With such protection, manufacturers will naturally invest in the development of new home-security products and production technologies. Without stronger laws, therefore, manufacturers will cut back on investment. From this will follow a corresponding decline not only in product quality and marketability, but also in production efficiency, and thus ultimately a loss of manufacturing jobs in the industry."

Discuss how well reasoned . . . etc.

The following appeared in the opinion section of a national newsmagazine:

"To reverse the deterioration of the postal service, the government should raise the price of postage stamps. This solution will no doubt prove effective, since the price increase will generate larger revenues and will also reduce the volume of mail, thereby eliminating the strain on the existing system and contributing to improved morale."

Discuss how well reasoned . . . etc.

The following appeared in an article in the health section of a newspaper:

"There is a common misconception that university hospitals are better than community or private hospitals. This notion is unfounded, however: the university hospitals in our region employ 15 percent fewer doctors, have a 20 percent lower success rate in treating patients, make far less overall profit, and pay their medical staff considerably less than do private hospitals. Furthermore, many doctors at university hospitals typically divide their time among teaching, conducting research, and treating patients. From this it seems clear that the quality of care at university hospitals is lower than that at other kinds of hospitals."

Discuss how well reasoned . . . etc.

The following is part of a business plan created by the management of the Megamart grocery store:

"Our total sales have increased this year by 20 percent since we added a pharmacy section to our grocery store. Clearly, the customer's main concern is the convenience afforded by one-stop shopping. The surest way to increase our profits over the next couple of years, therefore, is to add a clothing department along with an automotive supplies and repair shop. We should also plan to continue adding new departments and services, such as a restaurant and a garden shop, in subsequent years. Being the only store in the area that offers such a range of services will give us a competitive advantage over other local stores."

Discuss how well reasoned . . . etc.

The following appeared as part of a column in a popular entertainment magazine:

"The producers of the forthcoming movie *3003* will be most likely to maximize their profits if they are willing to pay Robin Good several million dollars to star in it—even though that amount is far more than any other person involved with the movie will make. After all, Robin has in the past been paid a similar amount to work in several films that were very financially successful."

Discuss how well reasoned . . . etc.

The following appeared in a memorandum from the directors of a security and safety consulting service:

"Our research indicates that over the past six years no incidents of employee theft have been reported within 10 of the companies that have been our clients. In analyzing the security practices of these 10 companies, we have further learned that each of them requires its employees to wear photo identification badges while at work. In the future, therefore, we should recommend the use of such identification badges to all of our clients."

Discuss how well reasoned . . . etc.

The following appeared as part of an article in the business section of a local newspaper:

"The owners of the Cumquat Café evidently made a good business decision in moving to a new location, as can be seen from the fact that the Café will soon celebrate its second anniversary there. Moreover, it appears that businesses are not likely to succeed at the old location: since the Café's move, three different businesses—a tanning salon, an antique emporium, and a pet-grooming shop—have occupied its former spot."

Discuss how well reasoned . . . etc.

The following appeared in the editorial section of a local newspaper:

"The profitability of Croesus Company, recently restored to private ownership, is a clear indication that businesses fare better under private ownership than under public ownership."

Discuss how well reasoned . . . etc.

The following appeared in the editorial section of a local newspaper:

"If the paper from every morning edition of the nation's largest newspaper were collected and rendered into paper pulp that the newspaper could reuse, about 5 million trees would be saved each year. This kind of recycling is unnecessary, however, since the newspaper maintains its own forests to ensure an uninterrupted supply of paper."

Discuss how well reasoned . . . etc.

The following appeared as part of a business plan recommended by the new manager of a musical rock group called Zapped:

"To succeed financially, Zapped needs greater name recognition. It should therefore diversify its commercial enterprises. The rock group Zonked plays the same type of music that Zapped plays, but it is much better known than Zapped because, in addition to its concert tours and four albums, Zonked has a series of posters, a line of clothing and accessories, and a contract with a major advertising agency to endorse a number of different products."

Discuss how well reasoned . . . etc.

The following appeared in a magazine article on trends and lifestyles:

"In general, people are not as concerned as they were a decade ago about regulating their intake of red meat and fatty cheeses. Walk into the Heart's Delight, a store that started selling organic fruits and vegetables and whole-grain flours in the 1960's, and you will also find a wide selection of cheeses made with high butterfat content. Next door, the owners of the Good Earth Café, an old vegetarian restaurant, are still making a modest living, but the owners of the new House of Beef across the street are millionaires."

Discuss how well reasoned . . . etc.

The following editorial appeared in the Elm City paper:

"The construction last year of a shopping mall in downtown Oak City was a mistake. Since the mall has opened, a number of local businesses have closed, and the downtown area suffers from an acute parking shortage, and arrests for crime and vagrancy have increased in the nearby Oak City Park. Elm City should pay attention to the example of the Oak City mall and deny the application to build a shopping mall in Elm City."

Discuss how well reasoned . . . etc.

The following appeared as part of an editorial in a weekly newsmagazine:

"Historically, most of this country's engineers have come from our universities; recently, however, our university-age population has begun to shrink, and decreasing enrollments in our high schools clearly show that this drop in numbers will continue throughout the remainder of the decade. Consequently, our nation will soon be facing a shortage of trained engineers. If we are to remain economically competitive in the world marketplace, then we must increase funding for education—and quickly."

Discuss how well reasoned . . . etc.

The following appeared in an Excelsior Company memorandum:

"The Excelsior Company plans to introduce its own brand of coffee. Since coffee is an expensive food item, and since there are already many established brands of coffee, the best way to gain customers for the Excelsior brand is to do what Superior, the leading coffee company, did when it introduced the newest brand in its line of coffees: conduct a temporary sales promotion that offers free samples, price reductions, and discount coupons for the new brand."

Discuss how well reasoned . . . etc.

The following appeared as part of an article in a health club trade publication:

"After experiencing a decline in usage by its members, Healthy Heart fitness center built an indoor pool. Since usage did not increase significantly, it appears that health club managers should adopt another approach—lowering membership fees rather than installing expensive new features."

Discuss how well reasoned . . . etc.

The following appeared as part of an article in a popular arts-and-leisure magazine:

"The safety codes governing the construction of public buildings are becoming far too strict. The surest way for architects and builders to prove that they have met the minimum requirements established by these codes is to construct buildings by using the same materials and methods that are currently allowed. But doing so means that there will be very little significant technological innovation within the industry, and hence little evolution of architectural styles and design—merely because of the strictness of these safety codes."

Discuss how well reasoned . . . etc.

The following is from a campaign by Big Boards Inc. to convince companies in River City that their sales will increase if they use Big Boards billboards for advertising their locally manufactured products:

"The potential of Big Boards to increase sales of your products can be seen from an experiment we conducted last year. We increased public awareness of the name of the current national women's marathon champion by publishing her picture and her name on billboards in River City for a period of three months. Before this time, although the champion had just won her title and was receiving extensive national publicity, only five percent of 15,000 randomly surveyed residents of River City could correctly name the champion when shown her picture; after the three-month advertising experiment, 35 percent of respondents from a second survey could supply her name."

Discuss how well reasoned . . . etc.

The following appeared as part of an article on government funding of environmental regulatory agencies:

"When scientists finally learn how to create large amounts of copper from other chemical elements, the regulation of copper mining will become unnecessary. For one thing, since the amount of potentially available copper will no longer be limited by the quantity of actual copper deposits, the problem of over-mining will quickly be eliminated altogether. For another, manufacturers will not need to use synthetic copper substitutes, the production of which creates pollutants. Thus, since two problems will be settled—over-mining and pollution—it makes good sense to reduce funding for mining regulation and either save the money or reallocate it where it is needed more."

Discuss how well reasoned . . . etc.

The following appeared as part of an article in a popular science magazine:

"Scientists must typically work 60 to 80 hours a week if they hope to further their careers; consequently, good and affordable all-day child care must be made available to both male and female scientists if they are to advance in their fields. Moreover, requirements for career advancement must be made more flexible so that preschool-age children can spend a significant portion of each day with a parent."

Discuss how well reasoned . . . etc.

The following appeared as part of a recommendation by one of the directors of the Beta Company:

"The Alpha Company has just reduced its workforce by laying off 15 percent of its employees in all divisions and at all levels, and it is encouraging early retirement for other employees. As you know, the Beta Company manufactures some products similar to Alpha's, but our profits have fallen over the last few years. To improve Beta's competitive position, we should try to hire a significant number of Alpha's former workers, since these experienced workers can provide valuable information about Alpha's successful methods, will require little training, and will be particularly motivated to compete against Alpha."

Discuss how well reasoned . . . etc.

The following appeared in the letters-to-the-editor section of a local newspaper:

"*Muscle Monthly*, a fitness magazine that regularly features pictures of bodybuilders using state-of-the-art exercise machines, frequently sells out, according to the owner of Skyview Newsstand. To help maximize fitness levels in our town's residents, we should, therefore, equip our new community fitness center with such machines."

Discuss how well reasoned . . . etc.

The following appeared as part of an article in the business section of a local newspaper:

"The Cumquat Café made a mistake in moving to a new location. After one year at the new spot, it is doing about the same volume of business as before, but the owners of the RoboWrench plumbing supply wholesale outlet that took over its old location are apparently doing better: RoboWrench is planning to open a store in a neighboring city."

Discuss how well reasoned . . . etc.

The following appeared in a memorandum from the director of human resources to the executive officers of Company X:

"Last year, we surveyed our employees on improvements needed at Company X by having them rank, in order of importance, the issues presented in a list of possible improvements. Improved communications between employees and management was consistently ranked as the issue of highest importance by the employees who responded to the survey. As you know, we have since instituted regular communications sessions conducted by high-level management, which the employees can attend on a voluntary basis. Therefore, it is likely that most employees at Company X now feel that the improvement most needed at the company has been made."

Discuss how well reasoned . . . etc.

The following appeared in a memorandum from the vice president of Road Food, an international chain of fast-food restaurants:

"This past year, we spent almost as much on advertising as did our main competitor, Street Eats, which has fewer restaurants than we do. Although it appeared at first that our advertising agency had created a campaign along the lines we suggested, in fact our total profits were lower than those of Street Eats. In order to motivate our advertising agency to perform better, we should start basing the amount that we pay it on how much total profit we make each year."

Discuss how well reasoned . . . etc.

The following appeared in the promotional literature for Cerberus dog food:

"Obesity is a great problem among pet dogs, just as it is among their human owners. Obesity in humans is typically caused by consuming more calories than the body needs. For humans, a proper diet for losing weight is a reduced-calorie diet that is high in fiber and carbohydrates but low in fat. Therefore, the best way for dog owners to help their dogs lose weight in a healthy way is to restrict the dog's diet to Cerberus reduced calorie dog food, which is high in fiber and carbohydrates but low in fat."

Discuss how well reasoned . . . etc.

The following appeared in an article in a travel magazine:

"After the airline industry began requiring airlines to report their on-time rates, Speedee Airlines achieved the number one on-time rate, with more than 89 percent of its flights arriving on time each month. And now Speedee is offering more flights to more destinations than ever before. Clearly, Speedee is the best choice for today's business traveler."

Discuss how well reasoned . . . etc.

The following appeared in a memorandum to the planning department of an investment firm:

"Costs have begun dropping for several types of equipment currently used to convert solar energy into electricity. Moreover, some exciting new technologies for converting solar energy are now being researched and developed. Hence we can expect that solar energy will soon become more cost efficient and attractive than coal or oil as a source of electrical power. We should, therefore, encourage investment in Solario, a new manufacturer of solar-powered products. After all, Solario's chief executive was once on the financial planning team for Ready-to-Ware, a software engineering firm that has shown remarkable growth since its recent incorporation."

Discuss how well reasoned . . . etc.

The following appeared in a memorandum from a company's marketing department:

"Since our company started manufacturing and marketing a deluxe air filter six months ago, sales of our economy filter—and company profits—have decreased significantly. The deluxe air filter sells for 50 percent more than the economy filter, but the economy filter lasts for only one month while the deluxe filter can be used for two months before it must be replaced. To increase repeat sales of our economy filter and maximize profits, we should discontinue the deluxe air filter and concentrate all our advertising efforts on the economy filter."

Discuss how well reasoned . . . etc.

The following appeared in a memorandum from the president of a company that makes shampoo:

"A widely publicized study claims that HR2, a chemical compound in our shampoo, can contribute to hair loss after prolonged use. This study, however, involved only 500 subjects. Furthermore, we have received no complaints from our customers during the past year, and some of our competitors actually use more HR2 per bottle of shampoo than we do. Therefore, we do not need to consider replacing the HR2 in our shampoo with a more expensive alternative."

Discuss how well reasoned . . . etc.

The following appeared in the editorial section of a local newspaper:

"The tragic crash of a medical helicopter last week points up a situation that needs to be addressed. The medical-helicopter industry supposedly has more stringent guidelines for training pilots and maintaining equipment than do most other airline industries, but these guidelines do not appear to be working: statistics reveal that the rate of medical-helicopter accidents is much higher than the rate of accidents for nonmedical helicopters or commercial airliners."

Discuss how well reasoned . . . etc.

The following appeared as part of a recommendation from the business manager of a department store:

"Local clothing stores reported that their profits decreased, on average, for the three-month period between August 1 and October 31. Stores that sell products for the home reported that, on average, their profits increased during this same period. Clearly, consumers are choosing to buy products for their homes instead of clothing. To take advantage of this trend, we should reduce the size of our clothing departments and enlarge our home furnishings and household products departments."

Discuss how well reasoned . . . etc.

The following appeared in a letter to the editor of a regional newspaper:

"In response to petitions from the many farmers and rural landowners throughout our region, the legislature has spent valuable time and effort enacting severe laws to deter motorists from picking fruit off the trees, trampling through the fields, and stealing samples of foliage. But how can our local lawmakers occupy themselves with such petty vandalism when crime and violence plague the nation's cities? The fate of apples and leaves is simply too trivial to merit their attention."

Discuss how well reasoned . . . etc.

The following appeared as part of an editorial in a campus newspaper:

"With an increasing demand for highly skilled workers, this nation will soon face a serious labor shortage. New positions in technical and professional occupations are increasing rapidly, while at the same time the total labor force is growing slowly. Moreover, the government is proposing to cut funds for aid to education in the near future."

Discuss how well reasoned . . . etc.

The following appeared as part of a memorandum from a government agency:

"Given the limited funding available for the building and repair of roads and bridges, the government should not spend any money this year on fixing the bridge that crosses the Styx River. This bridge is located near a city with a weakening economy, so it is not as important as other bridges; moreover, the city population is small and thus unlikely to contribute a significant enough tax revenue to justify the effort of fixing the bridge."

Discuss how well reasoned . . . etc.

The following appeared as part of an article in an entertainment magazine:

"A series of books based on the characters from a popular movie are consistently best sellers in local bookstores. Seeking to capitalize on the books' success, Vista Studios is planning to produce a movie sequel based on the books. Due to the success of the books and the original movie, the sequel will undoubtedly be profitable."

Discuss how well reasoned . . . etc.

The following appeared in a letter to the editor of a popular science and technology magazine:

"It is a popular myth that consumers are really benefiting from advances in agricultural technology. Granted, consumers are, on the average, spending a decreasing proportion of their income on food. But consider that the demand for food does not rise in proportion with real income. As real income rises, therefore, consumers can be expected to spend a decreasing proportion of their income on food. Yet agricultural technology is credited with having made our lives better."

Discuss how well reasoned . . . etc.

The following appeared in the editorial section of a local newspaper:

"This city should be able to improve existing services and provide new ones without periodically raising the taxes of the residents. Instead, the city should require that the costs of services be paid for by developers who seek approval for their large new building projects. After all, these projects can be highly profitable to the developers, but they can also raise a city's expenses and increase the demand for its services."

Discuss how well reasoned . . . etc.

The following appeared in the editorial section of a local newspaper:

"In order to avoid the serious health threats associated with many landfills, our municipality should build a plant for burning trash. An incinerator could offer economic as well as ecological advantages over the typical old-fashioned type of landfill: incinerators can be adapted to generate moderate amounts of electricity, and ash residue from some types of trash can be used to condition garden soil."

Discuss how well reasoned . . . etc.

The following appeared in the editorial section of a monthly business newsmagazine:

"Most companies would agree that as the risk of physical injury occurring on the job increases, the wages paid to employees should also increase. Hence it makes financial sense for employers to make the workplace safer: they could thus reduce their payroll expenses and save money."

Discuss how well reasoned . . . etc.

The following appeared as part of a company memorandum:

"Adopting an official code of ethics regarding business practices may in the long run do our company more harm than good in the public eye. When one of our competitors received unfavorable publicity for violating its own code of ethics, it got more attention from the media than it would have if it had had no such code. Rather than adopt an official code of ethics, therefore, we should instead conduct a publicity campaign that stresses the importance of protecting the environment and assisting charitable organizations."

Discuss how well reasoned . . . etc.

The following appeared in the editorial section of a daily newspaper:

"Although forecasts of presidential elections based on opinion polls measure current voter preference, many voters keep changing their minds about whom they prefer until the last few days before the balloting. Some do not even make a final decision until they enter the voting booth. Forecasts based on opinion polls are therefore little better at predicting election outcomes than a random guess would be."

Discuss how well reasoned . . . etc.

The following appeared in the editorial section of a newspaper in the country of West Cambria:

"The practice of officially changing speed limits on the highways—whether by increasing or decreasing them—is a dangerous one. Consider what happened over the past decade whenever neighboring East Cambria changed its speed limits: an average of 3 percent more automobile accidents occurred during the week following the change than had occurred during the week preceding it—even when the speed limit was lowered. This statistic shows that the change in speed limit adversely affected the alertness of drivers."

Discuss how well reasoned . . . etc.

The following appeared as part of a memorandum from the vice president of Nostrum, a large pharmaceutical corporation:

"The proposal to increase the health and retirement benefits that our employees receive should not be implemented at this time. An increase in these benefits is not only financially unjustified, since our last year's profits were lower than those of the preceding year, but also unnecessary, since our chief competitor, Panacea, offers its employees lower health and retirement benefits than we currently offer. We can assume that our employees are reasonably satisfied with the health and retirement benefits that they now have since a recent survey indicated that two-thirds of the respondents viewed them favorably."

Discuss how well reasoned . . . etc.

The following appeared as part of an article on trends in television:

"A recent study of viewers' attitudes toward prime-time television programs shows that many of the programs that were judged by their viewers to be of high quality appeared on (noncommercial) television networks, and that, on commercial television, the most popular shows are typically sponsored by the best-selling products. Thus, it follows that businesses who use commercial television to promote their products will achieve the greatest advertising success by sponsoring only highly rated programs—and, ideally, programs resembling the highly rated noncommercial programs on public channels as much as possible."

Discuss how well reasoned . . . etc.

The following appeared as part of an article in the business section of a daily newspaper:

"Company A has a large share of the international market in video-game hardware and software. Company B, the pioneer in these products, was once a $12 billion-a-year giant but collapsed when children became bored with its line of products. Thus Company A can also be expected to fail, especially given the fact that its games are now in so many American homes that the demand for them is nearly exhausted."

Discuss how well reasoned . . . etc.

The following appeared as part of an article in a photography magazine:

"When choosing whether to work in color or in black-and-white, the photographer who wishes to be successful should keep in mind that because color photographs are more true to life, magazines use more color photographs than black-and-white ones, and many newspapers are also starting to use color photographs. The realism of color also accounts for the fact that most portrait studios use more color film than black-and-white film. Furthermore, there are more types of color film than black-and-white film available today. Clearly, photographers who work in color have an advantage over those who work in black-and-white."

Discuss how well reasoned . . . etc.

The following appeared as part of a letter to the editor of a local newspaper:

"It makes no sense that in most places 15-year-olds are not eligible for their driver's license while people who are far older can retain all of their driving privileges by simply renewing their license. If older drivers can get these renewals, often without having to pass another driving test, then 15-year-olds should be eligible to get a license. Fifteen-year-olds typically have much better eyesight, especially at night; much better hand-eye coordination; and much quicker reflexes. They are also less likely to feel confused by unexpected developments or disoriented in unfamiliar surroundings, and they recover from injuries more quickly."

Discuss how well reasoned . . . etc.

The following appeared in an ad for a book titled *How to Write a Screenplay for a Movie*:

"Writers who want to succeed should try to write film screenplays rather than books, since the average film tends to make greater profits than does even a best-selling book. It is true that some books are also made into films. However, our nation's film producers are more likely to produce movies based on original screenplays than to produce films based on books, because in recent years the films that have sold the most tickets have usually been based on original screenplays."

Discuss how well reasoned . . . etc.

The following appeared as part of an article in a daily newspaper:

"The computerized onboard warning system that will be installed in commercial airliners will virtually solve the problem of midair plane collisions. One plane's warning system can receive signals from another's transponder—a radio set that signals a plane's course—in order to determine the likelihood of a collision and recommend evasive action."

Discuss how well reasoned . . . etc.

The following appeared in a memorandum from the ElectroWares company's marketing department:

"Since our company started manufacturing and marketing a deluxe light bulb six months ago, sales of our economy light bulb—and company profits—have decreased significantly. Although the deluxe light bulb sells for 50 percent more than the economy bulb, it lasts twice as long. Therefore, to increase repeat sales and maximize profits, we should discontinue the deluxe light bulb."

Discuss how well reasoned . . . etc.

The following is taken from an editorial in a local newspaper:

"Over the past decade, the price per pound of citrus fruit has increased substantially. Eleven years ago, Megamart charged 15 cents a pound for lemons, but today it commonly charges over a dollar a pound. In only one of these last 11 years was the weather unfavorable for growing citrus crops. Evidently, then, citrus growers have been responsible for the excessive increase in the price of citrus fruit, and strict pricing regulations are needed to prevent them from continuing to inflate prices."

Discuss how well reasoned . . . etc.

The following appeared as part of an article in a local newspaper:

"Over the past three years the tartfish industry has changed markedly: fishing technology has improved significantly, and the demand for tartfish has grown in both domestic and foreign markets. As this trend continues, the tartfish industry on Shrimp Island can expect to experience the same overfishing problems that are already occurring with mainland fishing industries: without restrictions on fishing, fishers see no reason to limit their individual catches. As the catches get bigger, the tartfish population will be dangerously depleted while the surplus of tartfish will devalue the catch for fishers. Government regulation is the only answer: tartfish-fishing should be allowed only during the three-month summer season, when tartfish reproduce and thus are most numerous, rather than throughout the year."

Discuss how well reasoned . . . etc.

The following appeared in a proposal from the development office at Platonic University:

"Because Platonic University has had difficulty in meeting its expenses over the past three years, we need to find new ways to increase revenues. We should consider following the example of Greene University, which recently renamed itself after a donor who gave it $100 million. If Platonic University were to advertise to its alumni and other wealthy people that it will rename either individual buildings or the entire university itself after the donors who give the most money, the amount of donations would undoubtedly increase."

Discuss how well reasoned . . . etc.

The following appeared as part of an article in the business section of a local newspaper:

"Hippocrene Plumbing Supply recently opened a wholesale outlet in the location once occupied by the Cumquat Café. Hippocrene has apparently been quite successful there because it is planning to open a large outlet in a nearby city. But the Cumquat Café, one year after moving to its new location, has seen its volume of business drop somewhat from the previous year's. Clearly, the former site was the better business location, and the Cumquat Café has made a mistake in moving to its new address."

Discuss how well reasoned . . . etc.

The following appeared in the editorial section of a local paper:

"Applications for advertising spots on KMTV, our local cable television channel, decreased last year. Meanwhile a neighboring town's local channel, KOOP, changed its focus to farming issues and reported an increase in advertising applications for the year. To increase applications for its advertisement spots, KMTV should focus its programming on farming issues as well."

Discuss how well reasoned . . . etc.

The following appeared as part of an article in a computer magazine:

"A year ago Apex Manufacturing bought its managers computers for their homes and paid for telephone connections so that they could access Apex computers and data files from home after normal business hours. Since last year, productivity at Apex has increased by 15 percent. Other companies can learn from the success at Apex: given home computers and access to company resources, employees will work additional hours at home and thereby increase company profits."

Discuss how well reasoned . . . etc.

The following was excerpted from an article in a farming trade publication:

"Farmers who switched from synthetic to organic farming last year have seen their crop yields decline. Many of these farmers feel that it would be too expensive to resume synthetic farming at this point, given the money that they invested in organic farming supplies and equipment. But their investments will be relatively minor compared to the losses from continued lower crop yields. Organic farmers should switch to synthetic farming rather than persist in an unwise course. And the choice to farm organically is financially unwise, given that it was motivated by environmental rather than economic concerns."

Discuss how well reasoned . . . etc.

The following appeared in a letter to prospective students from the admissions office at Plateau College:

"Every person who earned an advanced degree in science or engineering from Olympus University last year received numerous offers of excellent jobs. Typically, many graduates of Plateau College have gone on to pursue advanced degrees at Olympus. Therefore, enrolling as an undergraduate at Plateau College is a wise choice for students who wish to ensure success in their careers."

Discuss how well reasoned . . . etc.

The following appeared in a memorandum sent by a vice-president of the Nadir Company to the company's human resources department:

"Nadir does not need to adopt the costly 'family-friendly' programs that have been proposed, such as part-time work, work at home, and jobsharing. When these programs were made available at the Summit Company, the leader in its industry, only a small percentage of employees participated in them. Rather than adversely affecting our profitability by offering these programs, we should concentrate on offering extensive training that will enable employees to increase their productivity."

Discuss how well reasoned . . . etc.

The following appeared as part of an article in a trade magazine for breweries:

"Magic Hat Brewery recently released the results of a survey of visitors to its tasting room last year. Magic Hat reports that the majority of visitors asked to taste its low-calorie beers. To boost sales, other small breweries should brew low-calorie beers as well."

Discuss how well reasoned . . . etc.

The following appeared in an editorial from a newspaper serving the town of Saluda:

"The Saluda Consolidated High School offers more than 200 different courses from which its students can choose. A much smaller private school down the street offers a basic curriculum of only 80 different courses, but it consistently sends a higher proportion of its graduating seniors on to college than Consolidated does. By eliminating at least half of the courses offered there and focusing on a basic curriculum, we could improve student performance at Consolidated and also save many tax dollars."

Discuss how well reasoned . . . etc.

The following appeared as part of an article in the book section of a newspaper:

"Currently more and more books are becoming available in electronic form—either free-of-charge on the Internet or for a very low price-per-book on compact disc.* Thus literary classics are likely to be read more widely than ever before. People who couldn't have purchased these works at bookstore prices will now be able to read them for little or no money; similarly, people who find it inconvenient to visit libraries and wait for books to be returned by other patrons will now have access to whatever classic they choose from their home or work computers. This increase in access to literary classics will radically affect the public taste in reading, creating a far more sophisticated and learned reading audience than has ever existed before."

*A compact disc is a small portable disc capable of storing relatively large amounts of data that can be read by a computer.

Discuss how well reasoned . . . etc.

The following appeared as an editorial in a magazine concerned with educational issues:

"In our country, the real earnings of men who have only a high-school degree have decreased significantly over the past 15 years, but those of male college graduates have remained about the same. Therefore, the key to improving the earnings of the next generation of workers is to send all students to college. Our country's most important educational goal, then, should be to establish enough colleges and universities to accommodate all high school graduates."

Discuss how well reasoned . . . etc.

The following appeared as part of a business plan created by the management of the Take Heart Fitness Center:

"After opening the new swimming pool early last summer, Take Heart saw a 12 percent increase in the use of the center by its members. Therefore, in order to increase membership in Take Heart, we should continue to add new recreational facilities in subsequent years: for example, a multipurpose game room, a tennis court, and a miniature golf course. Being the only center in the area offering this range of activities would give us a competitive advantage in the health and recreation market."

Discuss how well reasoned . . . etc.

The following appeared in a letter from a staff member in the office of admissions at Argent University:

"The most recent nationwide surveys show that undergraduates choose their major field primarily based on their perception of job prospects in that field. At our university, economics is now the most popular major, so students must perceive this field as having the best job prospects. Therefore, we can increase our enrollment if we focus our advertising and recruiting on publicizing the accomplishments of our best-known economics professors and the success of our economics graduates in finding employment."

Discuss how well reasoned . . . etc.

The following appeared as part of a memorandum from the loan department of the Frostbite National Bank:

"We should not approve the business loan application of the local group that wants to open a franchise outlet for the Kool Kone chain of ice cream parlors. Frostbite is known for its cold winters, and cold weather can mean slow ice cream sales. For example, even though Frostbite is a town of 10,000 people, it has only one ice cream spot—the Frigid Cow. Despite the lack of competition, the Frigid Cow's net revenues fell by 10 percent last winter."

Discuss how well reasoned . . . etc.

The following appeared as part of a letter to the editor of a local newspaper:

"Bayview High School is considering whether to require all of its students to wear uniforms while at school. Students attending Acorn Valley Academy, a private school in town, earn higher grades on average and are more likely to go on to college. Moreover, Acorn Valley reports few instances of tardiness, absenteeism, or discipline problems. Since Acorn Valley requires its students to wear uniforms, Bayview High School would do well to follow suit and require its students to wear uniforms as well."

Discuss how well reasoned . . . etc.

The following appeared in a memo to the Saluda town council from the town's business manager:

"Research indicates that those who exercise regularly are hospitalized less than half as often as those who don't exercise. By providing a well-equipped gym for Saluda's municipal employees, we should be able to reduce the cost of our group health insurance coverage by approximately 50 percent and thereby achieve a balanced town budget."

Discuss how well reasoned . . . etc.

The following appeared in a memorandum written by the assistant manager of a store that sells gourmet food items from various countries:

"A local wine store made an interesting discovery last month: it sold more French than Italian wine on days when it played recordings of French accordion music, but it sold more Italian than French wine on days when Italian songs were played. Therefore, I recommend that we put food specialties from one particular country on sale for a week at a time and play only music from that country while the sale is going on. By this means we will increase our profits in the same way that the wine store did, and we will be able to predict more precisely what items we should stock at any given time."

Discuss how well reasoned . . . etc.

The following appeared in a memorandum from the director of research and development at Ready-to-Ware, a software engineering firm:

"The package of benefits and incentives that Ready-to-Ware offers to professional staff is too costly. Our quarterly profits have declined since the package was introduced two years ago, at the time of our incorporation. Moreover, the package had little positive effect, as we have had only marginal success in recruiting and training high-quality professional staff. To become more profitable again, Ready-to-Ware should, therefore, offer the reduced benefits package that was in place two years ago and use the savings to fund our current research and development initiatives."

Discuss how well reasoned . . . etc.

The following appeared as a memorandum from the vice-president of the Dolci candy company:

"Given the success of our premium and most expensive line of chocolate candies in a recent taste test and the consequent increase in sales, we should shift our business focus to producing additional lines of premium candy rather than our lower-priced, ordinary candies. When the current economic boom ends and consumers can no longer buy major luxury items, such as cars, they will still want to indulge in small luxuries, such as expensive candies."

Discuss how well reasoned . . . etc.

The following appeared in a memorandum from the business office of the Lovin' Cupful, a national restaurant chain:

"The Lovin' Cupful franchises in our northeast region have begun serving customers Almost, a brand new powdered instant tea, in place of brewed tea. Waiters report that only about 2 percent of the customers have complained, and that customers who want refills typically ask for 'more tea.' It appears, then, that 98 percent of the customers are perfectly happy with the switch, or else they cannot tell powdered instant from brewed tea. Therefore, in order to take advantage of the lower price per pound of Almost, all of our restaurants should begin substituting it for brewed tea."

Discuss how well reasoned . . . etc.

The following appeared in a memorandum from the director of marketing for a pharmaceutical company:

"According to a survey of 5,000 urban residents, the prevalence of stress headaches increases with educational level, so that stress headaches occur most often among people with graduate-school degrees. It is well established that, nationally, higher educational levels usually correspond with higher levels of income. Therefore, in marketing our new pain remedy, Omnilixir, we should send free samples primarily to graduate students and to people with graduate degrees, and we should concentrate on advertising in professional journals rather than in general interest magazines."

Discuss how well reasoned . . . etc.

The following appeared as part of an editorial in the Waymarsh city newspaper:

"Last year the parents of first graders in our school district expressed satisfaction with the reading skills their children developed but complained strongly about their children's math skills. To remedy this serious problem and improve our district's elementary education, everyone in the teacher-training program at Waymarsh University should be required to take more courses in mathematics."

Discuss how well reasoned . . . etc.

The following appeared in a letter to the editor of a River City newspaper:

"The Clio Development Group should not be permitted to build a multilevel parking garage on Dock Street since most of the buildings on the block would have to be demolished. Because these buildings were erected decades ago, they have historic significance and must therefore be preserved as economic assets in the effort to revitalize a restored riverfront area. Recall how Lakesburg has benefited from business increases in its historic downtown center. Moreover, there is plenty of vacant land for a parking lot elsewhere in River City."

Discuss how well reasoned . . . etc.

The following appeared in a corporate planning memorandum for a company that develops amusement parks:

"Because travel from our country to foreign countries has increased dramatically in recent years, our next project should be a 'World Tour' theme park with replicas of famous foreign buildings, rides that have international themes, and refreshment stands serving only foods from the country represented by the nearest ride. The best location would be near our capital city, which has large percentages of international residents and of children under the age of 16. Given the advantages of this site and the growing interest in foreign countries, the 'World Tour' theme park should be as successful as our space-travel theme park, where attendance has increased tenfold over the past decade."

Discuss how well reasoned . . . etc.

The following appeared in a memorandum from the publisher to the staff of *The Clarion*, a large metropolitan newspaper:

"During the recent campaign for mayor, a clear majority of city readers who responded to our survey indicated a desire for more news about city government. To increase circulation, and thus our profits, we should therefore consistently devote a greater proportion of space in all editions of *The Clarion* to coverage of local news."

Discuss how well reasoned . . . etc.

The following appeared in a memorandum from the assistant manager of Pageturner Books:

"Over the past two years, Pageturner's profits have decreased by 5 percent, even though we have added a popular café as well as a music section selling CDs and tapes. At the same time, we have experienced an increase in the theft of merchandise. We should therefore follow the example of Thoreau Books, which increased its profits after putting copies of its most frequently stolen books on a high shelf behind the payment counter. By doing likewise with copies of the titles that our staff reported stolen last year, we too can increase profitability."

Discuss how well reasoned . . . etc.

The following appeared in a letter to the editor of a River City newspaper:

"The Clio Development Group's plan for a multilevel parking garage on Dock Street should be approved in order to strengthen the economy of the surrounding area. Although most of the buildings on the block would have to be demolished, they are among the oldest in the city and thus of little current economic value. Those who oppose the project should realize that historic preservation cannot be the only consideration: even Athens or Jerusalem will knock down old buildings to put up new ones that improve the local economy."

Discuss how well reasoned . . . etc.

The following appeared in a memorandum from the owner of Carlo's Clothing to the staff:

"Since Disc Depot, the music store on the next block, began a new radio advertising campaign last year, its business has grown dramatically, as evidenced by the large increase in foot traffic into the store. While the Disc Depot's owners have apparently become wealthy enough to retire, profits at Carlo's Clothing have remained stagnant for the past three years. In order to boost our sales and profits, we should therefore switch from newspaper advertising to frequent radio advertisements like those for Disc Depot."

Discuss how well reasoned . . . etc.

The following appeared as part of the business plan of the Capital Idea investment firm:

"Across town in the Park Hill district, the Thespian Theater, Pizzazz Pizza, and the Niblick Golf Club have all had business increases over the past two years. Capital Idea should therefore invest in the Roxy Playhouse, the Slice-o'-Pizza, and the Divot Golf Club, three new businesses in the Irongate district. As a condition, we should require them to participate in a special program: Any customer who patronizes two of the businesses will receive a substantial discount at the third. By motivating customers to patronize all three, we will thus contribute to the profitability of each and maximize our return."

Discuss how well reasoned . . . etc.

The following appeared as part of an article in a newsletter for farmers:

"Users of Solacium, a medicinal herb now grown mainly in Asia, report that it relieves tension and promotes deep sleep. A recent study indicates that a large number of college students who took pills containing one of the ingredients in Solacium suffered less anxiety. To satisfy the anticipated demands for this very promising therapeutic herb and to reap the financial benefits, farmers in this country should begin growing it."

Discuss how well reasoned . . . etc.

The following appeared in a memorandum from the president of Aurora, a company that sells organic milk (milk produced without the use of chemical additives):

"Sales of organic food products in this country have tripled over the past five years. If Aurora is to profit from this continuing trend, we must diversify and start selling products such as organic orange juice and organic eggs in addition to our regular product line. With the recent increase of articles in health magazines questioning the safety of milk and other food products, customers are even more likely to buy our line of organic products. And to help ensure our successful expansion, we should hire the founder of a chain of health-food stores to serve as our vice president of marketing."

Discuss how well reasoned . . . etc.

The following appeared in a memorandum from the human resources department of Diversified Manufacturing:

"Managers at our central office report that their employees tend to be most productive in the days immediately preceding a vacation. To help counteract our declining market share, we could increase the productivity of our professional staff members, who currently receive four weeks paid vacation a year, by limiting them to a maximum of one week's continuous vacation time. They will thus take more vacation breaks during a year and give us more days of maximum productivity."

Discuss how well reasoned . . . etc.

The following appeared in a memorandum from a regional supervisor of post office operations:

"During a two-week study of postal operations, the Presto City post office handled about twice as many items as the Lento City post office, even though the cities are about the same size. Moreover, customer satisfaction appears to be higher in Presto City, since the study found fewer complaints regarding the Presto City post office. Therefore, the postmasters at these two offices should exchange assignments: the Presto City postmaster will solve the problems of inefficiency and customer dissatisfaction at the Lento City office while the Lento City postmaster learns firsthand the superior methods of Presto City."

Discuss how well reasoned . . . etc.

The following appeared in a memorandum written by the managing director of the Exeunt Theater Company:

"Now that we have moved to a larger theater, we can expect to increase our revenues from ticket sales. To further increase profits, we should start producing the plays that have been most successful when they were performed in our nation's largest cities. In addition, we should hire the Adlib Theater Company's director of fund-raising, since corporate contributions to Adlib have increased significantly over the three years that she has worked for Adlib."

Discuss how well reasoned . . . etc.

The following appeared in a memorandum from the human resources department of HomeStyle, a house remodeling business:

"This year, despite HomeStyle's move to new office space, we have seen a decline in both company morale and productivity, and a corresponding increase in administrative costs. To rectify these problems, we should begin using a newly developed software package for performance appraisal and feedback. Managers will save time by simply choosing comments from a preexisting list; then the software will automatically generate feedback for the employee. The human resources department at CounterBalance, the manufacturer of the countertops we install, reports satisfaction with the package."

Discuss how well reasoned . . . etc.

The following appeared as part of an article in a weekly newsmagazine:

"The country of Oleum can best solve the problem of its balance of trade deficit by further increasing the tax on its major import, crude oil. After Oleum increased the tax on imported crude oil four months ago, consumption of gasoline declined by 20 percent. Therefore, by imposing a second and significantly higher tax increase next year, Oleum will dramatically decrease its balance of trade deficit."

Discuss how well reasoned . . . etc.

The following appeared as part of a business plan by the Capital Idea investment firm:

"In recent years the worldwide demand for fish has grown, and improvements in fishing technology have made larger catches and thus increased supply possible: for example, last year's tuna catch was 9 percent greater than the previous year's. To capitalize on these trends, we should therefore invest in the new tartfish processing plant on Tartfish Island, where increasing revenues from tourism indicate a strong local economy."

Discuss how well reasoned . . . etc.

The following appeared in a speech by a stockholder of Consolidated Industries at the company's annual stockholders' meeting:

"In the computer hardware division last year, profits fell significantly below projections, the product line decreased from 20 to only 5 items, and expenditures for employee benefits increased by 15 percent. Nevertheless, Consolidated's board of directors has approved an annual salary of more than $1 million for our company's chief executive officer. The present board members should be replaced because they are unconcerned about the increasing costs of employee benefits and salaries, in spite of the company's problems generating income."

Discuss how well reasoned . . . etc.

The following appeared in a memorandum from the business planning department of Avia Airlines:

"Of all the cities in their region, Beaumont and Fletcher are showing the fastest growth in the number of new businesses. Therefore, Avia should establish a commuter route between them as a means of countering recent losses on its main passenger routes. And to make the commuter route more profitable from the outset, Avia should offer a 1/3 discount on tickets purchased within two days of the flight. Unlike tickets bought earlier, discount tickets will be nonrefundable, and so gain from their sale will be greater."

Discuss how well reasoned . . . etc.

The following appeared in a memorandum from the vice president of Gigantis, a development company that builds and leases retail store facilities:

"Nationwide over the past five years, sales have increased significantly at outlet stores that deal exclusively in reduced-price merchandise. Therefore, we should publicize the new mall that we are building at Pleasantville as a central location for outlet shopping and rent store space only to outlet companies. By taking advantage of the success of outlet stores, this plan should help ensure full occupancy of the mall and enable us to recover quickly the costs of building the mall."

Discuss how well reasoned . . . etc.

The following appeared in a memorandum written by the chair of the music department to the president of Omega University:

"Mental health experts have observed that symptoms of mental illness are less pronounced in many patients after group music-therapy sessions, and job openings in the music-therapy field have increased during the past year. Consequently, graduates from our degree program for music therapists should have no trouble finding good positions. To help improve the financial status of Omega University, we should therefore expand our music-therapy degree program by increasing its enrollment targets."

Discuss how well reasoned . . . etc.

The following appeared in a memorandum to the work-group supervisors of the GBS Company:

"The CoffeeCart beverage and food service located in the lobby of our main office building is not earning enough in sales to cover its costs, and so the cart may discontinue operating at GBS. Given the low staff morale, as evidenced by the increase in the number of employees leaving the company, the loss of this service could present a problem, especially since the staff morale questionnaire showed widespread dissatisfaction with the snack machines. Therefore, supervisors should remind the employees in their group to patronize the cart—after all, it was leased for their convenience so that they would not have to walk over to the cafeteria on breaks."

Discuss how well reasoned . . . etc.

The following appeared as part of an article in a trade magazine:

"During a recent trial period in which government inspections at selected meat-processing plants were more frequent, the amount of bacteria in samples of processed chicken decreased by 50 percent on average from the previous year's level. If the government were to institute more frequent inspections, the incidence of stomach and intestinal infections throughout the country could thus be cut in half. In the meantime, consumers of Excel Meats should be safe from infection because Excel's main processing plant has shown more improvement in eliminating bacterial contamination than any other plant cited in the government report."

Discuss how well reasoned . . . etc.

Appendix A Percentile Ranking Tables

Table 1
Percentages of Examinees Tested from January 2003 through December 2005 (including Repeaters) Who Scored Below Specified Verbal Scores

Verbal Scaled Score	Percentage Below	Verbal Scaled Score	Percentage Below
46–60	99	26	43
45	98	25	38
43-44	97	24	36
42	95	23	31
41	93	22	29
40	90	21	25
39	88	20	21
38	85	19	17
37	83	18	16
36	80	17	13
35	76	16	10
34	71	15	8
33	69	14	7
32	66	13	5
31	61	12	4
30	59	11	3
29	56	10	2
28	51	7–9	1
27	45	0–6	0

Number of Candidates = 622,975
Mean = 27.3
Standard deviation = 9.0

Table 2
Percentages of Examinees Tested from January 2003 through December 2005 (including Repeaters) Who Scored Below Specified Quantitative Scores

Quantitative Scaled Score	Percentage Below	Quantitative Scaled Score	Percentage Below
51–60	99	30	31
50	95	29	27
49	90	28	25
48	86	27	21
47	82	26	20
46	80	25	17
45	78	24	15
44	73	23	13
43	71	22	11
42	67	21	10
41	64	20	8
40	62	19	7
39	58	18	6
38	56	17	5
37	53	16	4
36	49	15	4
35	45	14	3
34	43	13	2
33	41	11-12	2
32	37	7–10	1
31	33	0–6	0

Number of Candidates = 622,975
Mean = 35
Standard deviation = 10.5

Table 3
Percentages of Examinees Tested from January 2003 through December 2005 (including Repeaters) Who Scored Below Specified Total Scores

Total Scaled Score	Percentage Below	Total Scaled Score	Percentage Below
760–800	99	500	39
750	98	490	36
740	98	480	33
730	97	470	31
720	96	460	27
710	94	450	24
700	92	440	22
690	91	430	20
680	89	420	18
670	88	410	16
660	86	400	14
650	83	390	12
640	80	380	11
630	78	370	10
620	76	360	8
610	73	350	7
600	70	340	6
590	67	330	5
580	64	320	4
570	61	300-310	3
560	58	290	2
550	54	280	2
540	51	270	2
530	47	260	2
520	45	230-250	1
510	42	200–220	0

Number of Candidates = 622,975
Mean = 526.6
Standard deviation = 117

Table 4
Percentages of Examinees Tested from January 2002 through December 2004 (including Repeaters) Who Scored Below Specified AWA Scores

AWA Scaled Score	Percentage Below
6.0	95
5.5	87
5.0	73
4.5	55
4.1	34
3.5	18
3.0	8
2.5	4
2.0	3
1.5	3
1.0	3
0.5	2
0.0	0

Number of Candidates = 622,975
Mean = 4.1
Standard deviation = 1.1

Appendix B Extra Answer Sheets

Diagnostic Answer Sheet - Quantitative

1.	27.
2.	28.
3.	29.
4.	30.
5.	31.
6.	32.
7.	33.
8.	34.
9.	35.
10.	36.
11.	37.
12.	38.
13.	39.
14.	40.
15.	41.
16.	42.
17.	43.
18.	44.
19.	45.
20.	46.
21.	47.
22.	48.
23.	
24.	
25.	
26.	

Diagnostic Answer Sheet - Verbal

1.	27.
2.	28.
3.	29.
4.	30.
5.	31.
6.	32.
7.	33.
8.	34.
9.	35.
10.	36.
11.	37.
12.	38.
13.	39.
14.	40.
15.	41.
16.	42.
17.	43.
18.	44.
19.	45.
20.	46.
21.	47.
22.	48.
23.	49.
24.	50.
25.	51.
26.	52.

Diagnostic Answer Sheet - Quantitative

1.	27.
2.	28.
3.	29.
4.	30.
5.	31.
6.	32.
7.	33.
8.	34.
9.	35.
10.	36.
11.	37.
12.	38.
13.	39.
14.	40.
15.	41.
16.	42.
17.	43.
18.	44.
19.	45.
20.	46.
21.	47.
22.	48.
23.	
24.	
25.	
26.	

Diagnostic Answer Sheet - Verbal

1.	27.
2.	28.
3.	29.
4.	30.
5.	31.
6.	32.
7.	33.
8.	34.
9.	35.
10.	36.
11.	37.
12.	38.
13.	39.
14.	40.
15.	41.
16.	42.
17.	43.
18.	44.
19.	45.
20.	46.
21.	47.
22.	48.
23.	49.
24.	50.
25.	51.
26.	52.

Diagnostic Answer Sheet - Quantitative

1.
2.
3.
4.
5.
6.
7.
8.
9.
10.
11.
12.
13.
14.
15.
16.
17.
18.
19.
20.
21.
22.
23.
24.
25.
26.
27.
28.
29.
30.
31.
32.
33.
34.
35.
36.
37.
38.
39.
40.
41.
42.
43.
44.
45.
46.
47.
48.

Diagnostic Answer Sheet - Verbal

1.
2.
3.
4.
5.
6.
7.
8.
9.
10.
11.
12.
13.
14.
15.
16.
17.
18.
19.
20.
21.
22.
23.
24.
25.
26.
27.
28.
29.
30.
31.
32.
33.
34.
35.
36.
37.
38.
39.
40.
41.
42.
43.
44.
45.
46.
47.
48.
49.
50.
51.
52.

Problem Solving Answer Sheet

1.
2.
3.
4.
5.
6.
7.
8.
9.
10.
11.
12.
13.
14.
15.
16.
17.
18.
19.
20.
21.
22.
23.
24.
25.
26.
27.
28.
29.
30.
31.
32.
33.
34.
35.
36.
37.
38.
39.
40.
41.
42.
43.
44.
45.
46.
47.
48.
49.
50.
51.
52.
53.
54.
55.
56.
57.
58.
59.
60.
61.
62.
63.
64.
65.
66.
67.
68.
69.
70.
71.
72.
73.
74.
75.
76.
77.
78.
79.
80.
81.
82.
83.
84.
85.
86.
87.
88.
89.
90.
91.
92.
93.
94.
95.
96.
97.
98.
99.
100.
101.
102.
103.
104.
105.
106.
107.
108.
109.
110.
111.
112.
113.
114.
115.
116.
117.
118.
119.
120.
121.
122.
123.
124.

Problem Solving Answer Sheet (continued)

125.
126.
127.
128.
129.
130.
131.
132.
133.
134.
135.
136.
137.
138.
139.
140.
141.
142.
143.
144.
145.
146.
147.
148.
149.
150.
151.
152.
153.
154.
155.
156.
157.
158.
159.
160.
161.
162.
163.
164.
165.
166.
167.
168.
169.
170.
171.
172.
173.
174.
175.
176.
177.
178.
179.
180.
181.
182.
183.
184.
185.
186.
187.
188.
189.
190.
191.
192.
193.
194.
195.
196.
197.
198.
199.
200.
201.
202.
203.
204.
205.
206.
207.
208.
209.
210.
211.
212.
213.
214.
215.
216.
217.
218.
219.
220.
221.
222.
223.
224.
225.
226.
227.
228.
229.
230.
231.
232.
233.
234.
235.
236.
237.
238.
239.
240.
241.
242.
243.
244.
245.
246.
247.
248.
249.

Problem Solving Answer Sheet

1.
2.
3.
4.
5.
6.
7.
8.
9.
10.
11.
12.
13.
14.
15.
16.
17.
18.
19.
20.
21.
22.
23.
24.
25.
26.
27.
28.
29.
30.
31.
32.
33.
34.
35.
36.
37.
38.
39.
40.
41.
42.
43.
44.
45.
46.
47.
48.
49.
50.
51.
52.
53.
54.
55.
56.
57.
58.
59.
60.
61.
62.
63.
64.
65.
66.
67.
68.
69.
70.
71.
72.
73.
74.
75.
76.
77.
78.
79.
80.
81.
82.
83.
84.
85.
86.
87.
88.
89.
90.
91.
92.
93.
94.
95.
96.
97.
98.
99.
100.
101.
102.
103.
104.
105.
106.
107.
108.
109.
110.
111.
112.
113.
114.
115.
116.
117.
118.
119.
120.
121.
122.
123.
124.

Problem Solving Answer Sheet (continued)

125.
126.
127.
128.
129.
130.
131.
132.
133.
134.
135.
136.
137.
138.
139.
140.
141.
142.
143.
144.
145.
146.
147.
148.
149.
150.
151.
152.
153.
154.
155.
156.
157.
158.
159.
160.
161.
162.
163.
164.
165.
166.
167.
168.
169.
170.
171.
172.
173.
174.
175.
176.
177.
178.
179.
180.
181.
182.
183.
184.
185.
186.
187.
188.
189.
190.
191.
192.
193.
194.
195.
196.
197.
198.
199.
200.
201.
202.
203.
204.
205.
206.
207.
208.
209.
210.
211.
212.
213.
214.
215.
216.
217.
218.
219.
220.
221.
222.
223.
224.
225.
226.
227.
228.
229.
230.
231.
232.
233.
234.
235.
236.
237.
238.
239.
240.
241.
242.
243.
244.
245.
246.
247.
248.
249.

Problem Solving Answer Sheet

1.
2.
3.
4.
5.
6.
7.
8.
9.
10.
11.
12.
13.
14.
15.
16.
17.
18.
19.
20.
21.
22.
23.
24.
25.
26.
27.
28.
29.
30.
31.
32.
33.
34.
35.
36.
37.
38.
39.
40.
41.
42.
43.
44.
45.
46.
47.
48.
49.
50.
51.
52.
53.
54.
55.
56.
57.
58.
59.
60.
61.
62.
63.
64.
65.
66.
67.
68.
69.
70.
71.
72.
73.
74.
75.
76.
77.
78.
79.
80.
81.
82.
83.
84.
85.
86.
87.
88.
89.
90.
91.
92.
93.
94.
95.
96.
97.
98.
99.
100.
101.
102.
103.
104.
105.
106.
107.
108.
109.
110.
111.
112.
113.
114.
115.
116.
117.
118.
119.
120.
121.
122.
123.
124.

Problem Solving Answer Sheet (continued)

125.
126.
127.
128.
129.
130.
131.
132.
133.
134.
135.
136.
137.
138.
139.
140.
141.
142.
143.
144.
145.
146.
147.
148.
149.
150.
151.
152.
153.
154.
155.
156.
157.
158.
159.
160.
161.
162.
163.
164.
165.
166.
167.
168.
169.
170.
171.
172.
173.
174.
175.
176.
177.
178.
179.
180.
181.
182.
183.
184.
185.
186.
187.
188.
189.
190.
191.
192.
193.
194.
195.
196.
197.
198.
199.
200.
201.
202.
203.
204.
205.
206.
207.
208.
209.
210.
211.
212.
213.
214.
215.
216.
217.
218.
219.
220.
221.
222.
223.
224.
225.
226.
227.
228.
229.
230.
231.
232.
233.
234.
235.
236.
237.
238.
239.
240.
241.
242.
243.
244.
245.
246.
247.
248.
249.

Problem Solving Answer Sheet

1.
2.
3.
4.
5.
6.
7.
8.
9.
10.
11.
12.
13.
14.
15.
16.
17.
18.
19.
20.
21.
22.
23.
24.
25.
26.
27.
28.
29.
30.
31.
32.
33.
34.
35.
36.
37.
38.
39.
40.
41.
42.
43.
44.
45.
46.
47.
48.
49.
50.
51.
52.
53.
54.
55.
56.
57.
58.
59.
60.
61.
62.
63.
64.
65.
66.
67.
68.
69.
70.
71.
72.
73.
74.
75.
76.
77.
78.
79.
80.
81.
82.
83.
84.
85.
86.
87.
88.
89.
90.
91.
92.
93.
94.
95.
96.
97.
98.
99.
100.
101.
102.
103.
104.
105.
106.
107.
108.
109.
110.
111.
112.
113.
114.
115.
116.
117.
118.
119.
120.
121.
122.
123.
124.

Problem Solving Answer Sheet (continued)

125.
126.
127.
128.
129.
130.
131.
132.
133.
134.
135.
136.
137.
138.
139.
140.
141.
142.
143.
144.
145.
146.
147.
148.
149.
150.
151.
152.
153.
154.
155.
156.
157.
158.
159.
160.
161.
162.
163.
164.
165.
166.
167.
168.
169.
170.
171.
172.
173.
174.
175.
176.
177.
178.
179.
180.
181.
182.
183.
184.
185.
186.
187.
188.
189.
190.
191.
192.
193.
194.
195.
196.
197.
198.
199.
200.
201.
202.
203.
204.
205.
206.
207.
208.
209.
210.
211.
212.
213.
214.
215.
216.
217.
218.
219.
220.
221.
222.
223.
224.
225.
226.
227.
228.
229.
230.
231.
232.
233.
234.
235.
236.
237.
238.
239.
240.
241.
242.
243.
244.
245.
246.
247.
248.
249.

Data Sufficiency Answer Sheet

1.	32.	63.	94.	125.
2.	33.	64.	95.	126.
3.	34.	65.	96.	127.
4.	35.	66.	97.	128.
5.	36.	67.	98.	129.
6.	37.	68.	99.	130.
7.	38.	69.	100.	131.
8.	39.	70.	101.	132.
9.	40.	71.	102.	133.
10.	41.	72.	103.	134.
11.	42.	73.	104.	135.
12.	43.	74.	105.	136.
13.	44.	75.	106.	137.
14.	45.	76.	107.	138.
15.	46.	77.	108.	139.
16.	47.	78.	109.	140.
17.	48.	79.	110.	141.
18.	49.	80.	111.	142.
19.	50.	81.	112.	143.
20.	51.	82.	113.	144.
21.	52	83.	114.	145.
22.	53.	84.	115.	146.
23.	54.	85.	116.	147.
24.	55.	86.	117.	148.
25.	56.	87.	118.	149.
26.	57.	88.	119.	150.
27.	58.	89.	120.	151.
28.	59.	90.	121.	152.
29.	60.	91.	122.	153.
30.	61.	92.	123.	154.
31.	62.	93.	124.	155.

Data Sufficiency Answer Sheet

1.
2.
3.
4.
5.
6.
7.
8.
9.
10.
11.
12.
13.
14.
15.
16.
17.
18.
19.
20.
21.
22.
23.
24.
25.
26.
27.
28.
29.
30.
31.
32.
33.
34.
35.
36.
37.
38.
39.
40.
41.
42.
43.
44.
45.
46.
47.
48.
49.
50.
51.
52
53.
54.
55.
56.
57.
58.
59.
60.
61.
62.
63.
64.
65.
66.
67.
68.
69.
70.
71.
72.
73.
74.
75.
76.
77.
78.
79.
80.
81.
82.
83.
84.
85.
86.
87.
88.
89.
90.
91.
92.
93.
94.
95.
96.
97.
98.
99.
100.
101.
102.
103.
104.
105.
106.
107.
108.
109.
110.
111.
112.
113.
114.
115.
116.
117.
118.
119.
120.
121.
122.
123.
124.
125.
126.
127.
128.
129.
130.
131.
132.
133.
134.
135.
136.
137.
138.
139.
140.
141.
142.
143.
144.
145.
146.
147.
148.
149.
150.
151.
152.
153.
154.
155.

Data Sufficiency Answer Sheet

1.
2.
3.
4.
5.
6.
7.
8.
9.
10.
11.
12.
13.
14.
15.
16.
17.
18.
19.
20.
21.
22.
23.
24.
25.
26.
27.
28.
29.
30.
31.
32.
33.
34.
35.
36.
37.
38.
39.
40.
41.
42.
43.
44.
45.
46.
47.
48.
49.
50.
51.
52
53.
54.
55.
56.
57.
58.
59.
60.
61.
62.
63.
64.
65.
66.
67.
68.
69.
70.
71.
72.
73.
74.
75.
76.
77.
78.
79.
80.
81.
82.
83.
84.
85.
86.
87.
88.
89.
90.
91.
92.
93.
94.
95.
96.
97.
98.
99.
100.
101.
102.
103.
104.
105.
106.
107.
108.
109.
110.
111.
112.
113.
114.
115.
116.
117.
118.
119.
120.
121.
122.
123.
124.
125.
126.
127.
128.
129.
130.
131.
132.
133.
134.
135.
136.
137.
138.
139.
140.
141.
142.
143.
144.
145.
146.
147.
148.
149.
150.
151.
152.
153.
154.
155.

Reading Comprehension Answer Sheet

1.
2.
3.
4.
5.
6.
7.
8.
9.
10.
11.
12.
13.
14.
15.
16.
17.
18.
19.
20.
21.
22.
23.
24.
25.
26.
27.
28.
29.
30.
31.
32.
33.
34.
35.
36.
37.
38.
39.
40.
41.
42.
43.
44.
45.
46.
47.
48
49.
50.
51.
52.
53.
54.
55.
56.
57.
58.
59.
60.
61.
62.
63.
64.
65.
66.
67.
68.
69.
70.
71.
72.
73.
74.
75.
76.
77.
78.
79.
80.
81.
82.
83.
84.
85.
86.
87.
88.
89.
90.
91.
92.
93.
94.
95.
96.
97.
98.
99.
100.
101.
102.
103.
104.
105.
106.
107.
108.
109.
110.
111.
112.
113.
114.
115.
116.
117.
118.
119.
120.
121.
122.
123.
124.
125.
126.
127.
128.
129.
130.
131.
132.
133.
134.
135.
136.
137.
138.
139.
140.
141.

Reading Comprehension Answer Sheet

1.
2.
3.
4.
5.
6.
7.
8.
9.
10.
11.
12.
13.
14.
15.
16.
17.
18.
19.
20.
21.
22.
23.
24.
25.
26.
27.
28.
29.
30.
31.
32.
33.
34.
35.
36.
37.
38.
39.
40.
41.
42.
43.
44.
45.
46.
47.
48
49.
50.
51.
52.
53.
54.
55.
56.
57.
58.
59.
60.
61.
62.
63.
64.
65.
66.
67.
68.
69.
70.
71.
72.
73.
74.
75.
76.
77.
78.
79.
80.
81.
82.
83.
84.
85.
86.
87.
88.
89.
90.
91.
92.
93.
94.
95.
96.
97.
98.
99.
100.
101.
102.
103.
104.
105.
106.
107.
108.
109.
110.
111.
112.
113.
114.
115.
116.
117.
118.
119.
120.
121.
122.
123.
124.
125.
126.
127.
128.
129.
130.
131.
132.
133.
134.
135.
136.
137.
138.
139.
140.
141.

Reading Comprehension Answer Sheet

1.
2.
3.
4.
5.
6.
7.
8.
9.
10.
11.
12.
13.
14.
15.
16.
17.
18.
19.
20.
21.
22.
23.
24.
25.
26.
27.
28.
29.
30.
31.
32.
33.
34.
35.
36.
37.
38.
39.
40.
41.
42.
43.
44.
45.
46.
47.
48
49.
50.
51.
52.
53.
54.
55.
56.
57.
58.
59.
60.
61.
62.
63.
64.
65.
66.
67.
68.
69.
70.
71.
72.
73.
74.
75.
76.
77.
78.
79.
80.
81.
82.
83.
84.
85.
86.
87.
88.
89.
90.
91.
92.
93.
94.
95.
96.
97.
98.
99.
100.
101.
102.
103.
104.
105.
106.
107.
108.
109.
110.
111.
112.
113.
114.
115.
116.
117.
118.
119.
120.
121.
122.
123.
124.
125.
126.
127.
128.
129.
130.
131.
132.
133.
134.
135.
136.
137.
138.
139.
140.
141.

Critical Reasoning Answer Sheet

1.
2.
3.
4.
5.
6.
7.
8.
9.
10.
11.
12.
13.
14.
15.
16.
17.
18.
19.
20.
21.
22.
23.
24.
25.
26
27.
28.
29.
30.
31.
32.
33.
34.
35.
36.
37.
38.
39.
40.
41.
42.
43.
44.
45.
46.
47.
48.
49.
50.
51.
52.
53.
54.
55.
56.
57.
58.
59.
60.
61.
62
63.
64.
65.
66.
67.
68.
69.
70.
71.
72.
73.
74.
75.
76.
77.
78.
79.
80.
81.
82.
83.
84.
85.
86.
87.
88.
89.
90.
91.
92.
93.
94.
95.
96.
97.
98.
99.
100.
101.
102.
103.
104.
105.
106.
107.
108.
109.
110.
111.
112.
113.
114.
115.
116.
117.
118.
119.
120.
121.
122.
123.
124.

Critical Reasoning Answer Sheet

1.
2.
3.
4.
5.
6.
7.
8.
9.
10.
11.
12.
13.
14.
15.
16.
17.
18.
19.
20.
21.
22.
23.
24.
25.
26
27.
28.
29.
30.
31.
32.
33.
34.
35.
36.
37.
38.
39.
40.
41.
42.
43.
44.
45.
46.
47.
48.
49.
50.
51.
52.
53.
54.
55.
56.
57.
58.
59.
60.
61.
62
63.
64.
65.
66.
67.
68.
69.
70.
71.
72.
73.
74.
75.
76.
77.
78.
79.
80.
81.
82.
83.
84.
85.
86.
87.
88.
89.
90.
91.
92.
93.
94.
95.
96.
97.
98.
99.
100.
101.
102.
103.
104.
105.
106.
107.
108.
109.
110.
111.
112.
113.
114.
115.
116.
117.
118.
119.
120.
121.
122.
123.
124.

Critical Reasoning Answer Sheet

1.
2.
3.
4.
5.
6.
7.
8.
9.
10.
11.
12.
13.
14.
15.
16.
17.
18.
19.
20.
21.
22.
23.
24.
25.
26
27.
28.
29.
30.
31.
32.
33.
34.
35.
36.
37.
38.
39.
40.
41.
42.
43.
44.
45.
46.
47.
48.
49.
50.
51.
52.
53.
54.
55.
56.
57.
58.
59.
60.
61.
62
63.
64.
65.
66.
67.
68.
69.
70.
71.
72.
73.
74.
75.
76.
77.
78.
79.
80.
81.
82.
83.
84.
85.
86.
87.
88.
89.
90.
91.
92.
93.
94.
95.
96.
97.
98.
99.
100.
101.
102.
103.
104.
105.
106.
107.
108.
109.
110.
111.
112.
113.
114.
115.
116.
117.
118.
119.
120.
121.
122.
123.
124.

Sentence Correction Answer Sheet

1.
2.
3.
4.
5.
6.
7.
8.
9.
10.
11.
12.
13.
14.
15.
16.
17.
18.
19.
20.
21.
22.
23.
24.
25.
26.
27.
28.
29.
30.
31.
32.
33.
34.
35.
36.
37.
38.
39.
40.
41.
42.
43.
44.
45.
46.
47.
48
49.
50.
51.
52.
53.
54.
55.
56.
57.
58.
59.
60.
61.
62.
63.
64.
65.
66.
67.
68.
69.
70.
71.
72.
73.
74.
75.
76.
77.
78.
79.
80.
81.
82.
83.
84.
85.
86.
87.
88.
89.
90.
91.
92.
93.
94.
95.
96.
97.
98.
99.
100.
101.
102.
103.
104.
105.
106.
107.
108.
109.
110.
111.
112.
113.
114.
115.
116.
117.
118.
119.
120.
121.
122.
123.
124.
125.
126.
127.
128.
129.
130.
131.
132.
133.
134.
135.
136.
137.
138.

Sentence Correction Answer Sheet

1.
2.
3.
4.
5.
6.
7.
8.
9.
10.
11.
12.
13.
14.
15.
16.
17.
18.
19.
20.
21.
22.
23.
24.
25.
26.
27.
28.
29.
30.
31.
32.
33.
34.
35.
36.
37.
38.
39.
40.
41.
42.
43.
44.
45.
46.
47.
48
49.
50.
51.
52.
53.
54.
55.
56.
57.
58.
59.
60.
61.
62.
63.
64.
65.
66.
67.
68.
69.
70.
71.
72.
73.
74.
75.
76.
77.
78.
79.
80.
81.
82.
83.
84.
85.
86.
87.
88.
89.
90.
91.
92.
93.
94.
95.
96.
97.
98.
99.
100.
101.
102.
103.
104.
105.
106.
107.
108.
109.
110.
111.
112.
113.
114.
115.
116.
117.
118.
119.
120.
121.
122.
123.
124.
125.
126.
127.
128.
129.
130.
131.
132.
133.
134.
135.
136.
137.
138.

Sentence Correction Answer Sheet

1.
2.
3.
4.
5.
6.
7.
8.
9.
10.
11.
12.
13.
14.
15.
16.
17.
18.
19.
20.
21.
22.
23.
24.
25.
26.
27.
28.
29.
30.
31.
32.
33.
34.
35.
36.
37.
38.
39.
40.
41.
42.
43.
44.
45.
46.
47.
48
49.
50.
51.
52.
53.
54.
55.
56.
57.
58.
59.
60.
61.
62.
63.
64.
65.
66.
67.
68.
69.
70.
71.
72.
73.
74.
75.
76.
77.
78.
79.
80.
81.
82.
83.
84.
85.
86.
87.
88.
89.
90.
91.
92.
93.
94.
95.
96.
97.
98.
99.
100.
101.
102.
103.
104.
105.
106.
107.
108.
109.
110.
111.
112.
113.
114.
115.
116.
117.
118.
119.
120.
121.
122.
123.
124.
125.
126.
127.
128.
129.
130.
131.
132.
133.
134.
135.
136.
137.
138.